ROTHMANS RUGBY UNION YEARBOOK 1992-93

Editor: Stephen Jones
Statistician: John Griffiths

ROTHMANS

HEADLINE

First published in 1992
by HEADLINE BOOK PUBLISHING PLC

Cover photographs: Two international captains in action in the 1992 Five Nations
Championship. *Front:* Will Carling of England in the match against Wales at
Twickenham, which England won 24-0 to achieve the Grand Slam for the second year in
succession. *Back:* Scotland's David Sole, who retired at the end of the 1991-92 season, in
their 18-10 victory over Ireland in Dublin.

All photographs by Colorsport unless otherwise credited.

10 9 8 7 6 5 4 3 2 1

ISBN 0-7472-7907-1

Photoset by Cylinder Typesetting Limited, London

Printed and bound in Great Britain by
Richard Clay Ltd, Bungay, Suffolk

HEADLINE BOOK PUBLISHING PLC
Headline House
79 Great Titchfield Street
London W1P 7FN

CONTENTS

EDITORIAL PREFACE

There was no question of the Yearbook reverting to its old size this time. The number of pages was increased last year to include a special section on the World Cup, yet such is the proliferation of major rugby around the world that the extra space has been consolidated in this edition, the 21st. As ever, there are many new features and improvements. The Results of International Matches section has been expanded to reflect the rise of the non-traditional rugby nations, and a special Sevens section is included to take into account the revival of interest in the shortened version of the game – a revival touched off, beyond doubt, by the Cathay Pacific-Hong Kong Bank Sevens in Hong Kong, and one which will reach a climax with the World Cup Sevens at Murrayfield in 1993.

Our Five Players of the Year, chosen by a panel of our contributors from all the major rugby-playing countries, nevertheless reflect the excellence of Australia and of England in the period of rugby which ended in May 1992. Two players from the English Grand Slam team, Peter Winterbottom and Jon Webb, are included; also David Campese, the unpredictable but 24-carat genius, and Simon Poidevin, the warrior flanker, are chosen, along with Marc Cecillon, France's brilliant forward.

As usual, we would like to offer our warmest thanks to our team of contributors from all over the world, with a special mention for the guardian of our tours section, Chris Rhys, and also for Colin Elsey and his colleagues at Colorsport, who provide the photographs.

We are also pleased to welcome as our new South African correspondent John Robbie, the former Irish scrum-half turned South African journalist. It is appropriate to pay tribute to John's predecessor. Reg Sweet has been our man in South Africa since the Yearbook started more than 20 years ago. From his base in Durban he has been a meticulous and sympathetic recorder of the South African scene, and this in an era when the playing of the game itself was only rarely the main story. Reg stands down to concentrate on his other interests, with our sincere thanks.

Finally, our special thanks to our long-suffering house editor, Caroline North. She has held the post for a decade and her ability to guide the book through the often tortuous processes of production mean that we and the rugby world as a whole are in her debt.

Stephen Jones *Editor*
John Griffiths *Statistician*

PLEASE NOTE: The main statistical sections of the Yearbook are complete up to 30 April 1992. Full coverage of the tours which took place in summer 1992 will be contained in the next issue.

The winner of our World Cup competition in the 1991-92 Yearbook was Paul Bolton, of Stirchley, Birmingham, who won two tickets and a full VIP hospitality package at Twickenham for the England v USA World Cup match.

4

AUSTRALIA RULE THE WORLD, ENGLAND CONQUER EUROPE, THE GAME STORMS ON

REVIEW OF THE 1991-92 SEASON
The Editor

Such is the pace of the action and the number of mega-events in rugby these days that by the end of the Northern Hemisphere season 1991-92 the World Cup already seemed a distant memory. The early excitement caused by the possible return to international competition of South Africa, the high-profile exploits of the dominant England team in Europe and the controversial batch of law changes announced by the IRB in March soon took the spotlight.

However, even the passage of time could not diminish the impact of the World Cup. There were some years of controversy as the organisers, Rugby World Cup, tried to set in place the playing framework in all its aspects and also the commercial programme. The organisers attracted heavy criticism before and after the tournament, especially when it was revealed that the profit was considerably less than the organisers themselves had predicted. Although not all the criticism was deserved, they must now step up considerably their public relations image and structure to keep the wider world of rugby more fully informed. The 1995 event, to be held in South Africa, is of such potential that no one, RWC, administrators or players, has any excuse for poor performance. At least the principle of playing the tournament in one country is established. Who knows, the French might now get off their backsides and claim the 1999 event for themselves.

The 1991 tournament itself, when the players took over, was another matter. It was superb. Not only that, but the spectacle and the wall-to-wall press coverage ensured that in the hearts and minds of both rugby people and non-rugby people, it took off in spectacular fashion.Everywhere, people were discussing the tournament, whether the exploits of Australia, the winners and a credit to themselves and to their coaches and country for their marvellous skills and power and also their demeanour; of England, who ploughed on with magnificent courage to the final; of Wales, who failed to qualify for the knock-out stage after a history-tearing defeat by the Samoans; of Western Samoa, who played ferociously and who richly deserved their place in the quarter-final; of Canada, who bore comparison in the forwards with any team.

Indeed, it is not fanciful to say that every team in the tournament added something and that the whole affair, with the vast pressure and vast interest, was almost scrupulously clean and trouble-free; the roughing of David Bishop, the New Zealand referee, by Daniel Dubroca, the French coach, at the end of the France-England quarter-

The England team which beat Wales at Twickenham in the International Championship to win a back-to-back Grand Slam for the first time since 1924. L-R, back row: R J Hill (replacement), N Heslop (replacement), T A K Rodber (replacement), J M Webb, D Richards, M C Bayfield, W A Dooley, M G Skinner, P J Winterbottom, J A Probyn, J Leonard, M Hynes (replacement); front row: R Underwood, J C Guscott, C R Andrew, W D C Carling (capt), B C Moore, C D Morris, S J Halliday, D Pears (replacement), C J Olver (replacement).

final was an isolated incident. From the quarter-final onwards, the tournament provided high-octane and high-level rugby, not to mention controversy. It was the perfect launching pad for rugby's next step in the remarkable advance of the game – geographical and technical – of the last few years. That advance will quicken when South Africa begin the touring round and when the British Lions as a concept is given further sustenance.

As far as the European scene was concerned there was almost an air of resignation pervading the other countries at the excellence of England. No one could claim that England were up against vintage opposition or even, in some cases, any worthwhile opposition at all. But their second successive Grand Slam was regal: the team played proudly, expansively and with utter commitment. They sacrificed for their sport and they were rewarded. Time will tell how quickly the team will break up, and the likes of Wade Dooley and Peter Winterbottom will not easily be replaced.

At the other end of the scale were the Irish. Many people believed they would come through and their dizzy moments of impending glory, when they led Australia inside the last few minutes of normal time in the World Cup quarter-final, were apparently further fuel for optimism. Gordon Hamilton's charge for the try which took them ahead in that match was probably the most uproariously-cheered moment the sport has seen; Australia's recovery was clinical. Ireland never approached those heights in the rest of the season. Their campaign came dramatically off the rails: they were whitewashed in the Five Nations, torn to pieces by England and then on tour in New Zealand they were humiliated – they held on well in the first Test but against a miserably poor All Black team. Otherwise, they were savaged and anyone with the good of the game at heart will be avidly following the progress of their recovery. There were even signs during the season that the old pride and morale were drifting away.

At least Wales began to move in the right direction. The old self-confidence is conspicuously absent in most of Welsh rugby, but at least the WRU are now giving a strong lead from Cardiff in the technical, marketing and administrative fields – their last lead depending on the WRU committee's desire to reform itself. Robert Norster and Alan Davies, the manager and coach of the national team, won the full-scale respect of their players and by the last game of the season, which brought victory over Scotland, the first red shoots of revival were showing above the surface. As yet they were not established, and the fitness revolution has yet to hit the country and cause the same profound changes in shape and endurance as it did in England.

England retained the lead in rugby administration – RFU president Peter Yarranton became Sir Peter – and Twickenham, packed to the rafters almost weekly, it seemed, staged memorable spectaculars, especially on Pilkington Cup final day when Bath, a club of unquenchable appetite, added the Cup to their League title but only in the last second of extra time. Stuart Barnes dropped a remarkable goal to send Bath's legions into paroxysms but of relief as much as triumph. Harlequins, who were missing some leading players, put up a staggering performance of wisdom and commitment. Paul Ackford came storming out of retirement to rule the line-out, Bath's weak area. It took all of Bath's legendary spirit to win a match which typified English rugby for the whole season – two teams of high technical accomplishment and fitness playing highly-disciplined rugby before a capacity audience. However, on the subject of discipline, too many English commentators were too keen to criticise other nations while whitewashing their own players at all levels.

As ever, there was the sadness associated with the death of leading figures all over the rugby world, not least that of two marvellous club servants in Terry Tandy of Gloucester, the long-serving secretary, and Eric Smith, the heart of the remarkable Orrell club. Orrell had another memorable season, a tribute to to Eric and to their own excellence, and it was only a last-second drop kick by Huw Davies of Wasps which robbed Orrell of a victory which would, as it turned out, have deprived Bath of the League title and taken it to the thriving Northern outpost. The passing of young men such as Kerry Fitzgerald, the superb Australian referee and of John Howe, the West Hartlepool lock popular throughout the first-class game, helped put even the most colourful, busy and high-profile season ever played into perspective.

The most sensational drop-kick that British rugby has seen has soared over. Bath have won the Pilkington Cup with the last kick of extra time and Jeremy Guscott and Gareth Chilcott share Stuart Barnes' joy.

ROTHMANS FIVE PLAYERS OF THE YEAR

The basis for selection for the Rothmans Five Players of the Year was the European season 1991-92. Perhaps not surprisingly, the choices of our panel of contributors reflect the two major events of that season – the World Cup, won by Australia, and the Grand Slam won by England. The Five Players are: **Peter Winterbottom,** the England flanker, who had a storming season towards the end of a career of absolute commitment; **Jonathan Webb,** playing at full-back in the Grand Slam team, who broke records for points-scoring but played beautifully as well; **David Campese,** who won so many awards after the World Cup, partly for his impish personality and entertainment value but also for his lethal finishing; **Simon Poidevin,** the flanker, who rounded off a superb career by driving Australia towards the World Cup from the back row; **Marc Cecillon,** who did not enjoy so satisfying a season, being shunted around the French pack. But he was the heart of the team, and will be the heart of the French recovery.

NB: No player can be nominated more than once. Career details given are correct up to 30 April. 1992.

Previous nominations
1989-90: **Will Carling, Patrice Lagisquet, Steve McDowell, David Sole, Paul Ackford**
1990-91: **Dean Richards, Gary Armstrong, Wade Dooley, Serge Blanco, Rory Underwood**

PETER WINTERBOTTOM

Peter Winterbottom arrived in international rugby in 1982 as an explosive and destructive flanker. Since then, with the vastly increasing demands on players and especially those in his position on the openside flank, he has probably given as much to his country's cause as any player in history. He has been selfless, committed and practically indestructible and has prevailed as England's No 7 even though many other fine English flankers, such as Andy Robinson, David Cooke and Gary Rees, have pushed him throughout his career.

In 1991-92, just when the rigours of his sporting life might have been expected to tell, Winterbottom had his finest season. England were involved in a fierce programme of preparation and playing and they asked much of him: to be on the ball when England were in possession, to range far and wide when they were not; and also, they asked him to hammer on round the fringes to draw in the opposition. This was the reason why he briefly compared unfavourably with Michael Jones, the panther-like All Black, when the two teams met to open the World Cup. Jones was allowed to roam and was free from close-driving duties.

For the rest of the season he was simply outstanding. Alongside two from Dean Richards, Tim Rodber, Mike Teague or Mick Skinner, he was never bettered. He and the back row were major figures in the semi-final win over Scotland, in the two victories in Paris – one in the World Cup, one in the Championship – and in the World Cup final itself. His tackling was always deadly.

Perhaps more significantly, his all-round expertise was remarkable. In the early days, his hands let him down. He was a fine player without the ball, when driving into the tackle and on to the loose ball. He was, in some respects, a player who stood out more in a poor side, such as the 1983 British Lions and some of the England teams of the period. But he lacked the constructive talents. By last season he had become the complete player. He had become clinical as well as heroic. On a brief return to South Africa for a festival match, he astonished onlookers with his all-round excellence.

He duly reached the half-century of caps during the season, and pocketed the second English Grand Slam. Right at the very end, after a gruelling season and a fraught build-up, he appeared to lead Harlequins in the Pilkington final, the longest match at the end of the longest season. Again, he was tireless and outstanding. His team did not win the trophy so the final accolade, the final flourish of a trophy, was denied him. Otherwise, Winterbottom met all targets.

Peter Winterbottom *Born Leeds, Yorkshire, 31 May 1960; flanker; plays for Harlequins; 52 caps for England since first cap against Australia in 1982; 4 Test appearances for the British Lions.*

DAVID CAMPESE

David Campese, to the joy of all who watch and promote the game, has gone back on his decision to retire after the 1991 World Cup and, on the evidence of the recent Scotland tour of Australia, seems to be on his sharpest form. There seemed every chance as the Yearbook went to press that he could reach the remarkable figure of 50 tries for Australia. He was standing on 48 after the Scottish tour (to be reported in full in next year's Yearbook).

The astonishing thing about Campese is that some people still think of him as purely an entertainer, a gaudy player whose profile is always heightened by the risks he takes, by the impish humour he displays off the pitch. However, his grand total of tries, when he finally retires, will see him recognised for what he unquestionably is – the greatest finisher and the greatest match-winner rugby has seen.

Campese was in the forefront of those players who helped the World Cup burst out into wider consciousness. He became as famous as any British rugby player, or even any British sportsman, as Australia blazed their trail through the World Cup. He played beautifully throughout, scoring twice in the Pool 3 opener against Argentina at Stradey Park

Jonathan Webb.

David Campese.

Peter Winterbottom.

and again in the heavy defeat of hapless Wales. He showed to greatest effect, however, in the latter stages of the tournament. Inside eight days, he inspired Australia to final victory in the epic quarter-final at Lansdowne Road against the furious, fighting Irish; then, with a lacerating try scored by Campese himself, and another set up for Tim Horan with a superb pass, he saw off the All Blacks in an emotional semi-final and took Australia to Twickenham and the final itself.

As ever, he grafted on all the usual talents to that of finishing. His kicking was extraordinary, his defence not nearly so poor as some would have you believe – he is one of the greatest shadowers and tacklers in the game. He was well used by Bob Dwyer, the Australian coach, to make the initial cut and thrust as well as to pop up for the final burst. Throughout the tournament, whether entertaining or scoring on the pitch, or moving into outspoken mode off the field, he was always in the spotlight, and yet still, despite everything, maintained his reputation as something of a loner, certainly that of a singular man. He was a regular visitor to Britain from his winter base in Milan long after the tournament had ended – he had to accept a succession of prestigious awards for the impact he made on the consciousness of British sport.

Barry John, the legendary former Welsh fly-half, had this to say of Campese after the tournament. 'Like Pele, he is associated with the very best and historic moments in sport; he has special genius which shows that an individual can still paint his own portrait and leave an indelible mark for all to treasure. The ingredients are the same; stature, presence, personality, style and an immense belief in the God-given talents.'

David Campese *Born Queanbeyan, Australian Capital Territory, 21 October 1962; wing or full-back; plays for Randwick, Milan, New South Wales; 64 caps since first cap against New Zealand in 1982.*

JONATHAN WEBB

Jon Webb's career at club level with Bristol and at Test level with England was always something of a frustrating affair, not least to himself. Webb came into the England team during the 1987 World Cup as a full-back of obvious talent but eventually, after a short run in domestic matches as England's full-back, his run of caps dried and his form became sporadic. His rising medical career was quite obviously a handicap, with its long hours and onerous responsibilities. The pale-faced Webb, plagued by inconsistency, occasionally looked a haunted figure in club and country colours, and in England's 1990 and 1991 Five Nations teams he was supplanted by the high-scoring Simon Hodgkinson.

By the start of the 1990-91 season, Webb decided on a move from Bristol to Bath, a club famous for providing an environment in which players can discover, or re-discover, themselves. This way guaranteed no success, because Bath already had the likes of Jon Callard and Audley Lumsden on their books. Gradually, form and confidence returned. By the time England toured Australia and Fiji in the summer of 1991, Webb was back in contention and the selectors eventually left Hodgkinson out of the Tests in favour of Webb's more incisive talents as a runner from the back.

Webb kept on coming. In the World Cup he was impressive; in the Five Nations Championship of 1992 he was simply regal. His goal-kicking had lost most of the old fallibility. He scored 67 points in the four games of the England Grand Slam, a record. Significantly, that total included three tries, evidence of the fact that Webb moved with purpose and skill as an attacker, hitting the line with timing and pace and perception; and that his all-round game had blossomed to new heights. In defence, he was rock solid, too. It is hard to remember, during the whole season, a time when Webb was in bother under the high ball.

And not only in the white jersey. Webb had a brilliant season with Bath, tiding them through the week-in week-out round of pressure club matches as they advanced on the double of Cup and League titles. For much of the season, he was playing as well and probably better than any other full-back in the world. This was a marvellous feat because his medical career was still demanding (he became a Fellow of the Royal College of Surgeons) and it remained to be seen if he could continue to juggle the demands well enough to play the game at Test level. At least he has the consolation that, at the back of the Bath and England teams in 1991-92, the real Jon Webb stood up.

Jonathan Webb *Born London, 24 August 1963; full-back; plays for Bath; 27 caps since first cap against Australia (as replacement) in 1987 World Cup.*

MARC CECILLON

French selectors and coaches have never been too kind to their forwards, especially in the back five of the scrum. Recent history shows such a catalogue of shunting that the likes of Eric Champ, Laurent Rodriguez, Dominique Erbani and others could never really work out if they were regarded as locks, No 8s or flankers. Marc Cecillon was of the opinion that he was a flanker for much of his early career in the French side. He came into the team in the Five Nations Championship of 1988, even though that was nearly ten seasons after he first appeared in the France B team, at Bourg-en-Bresse against Wales B in 1979.

By season 1991-92, French coach Pierre Berbizier had started to shunt Cecillon around, too. At least Cecillon bridged the gap between the eras of Daniel Dubroca and Berbizier, because Berbizier axed other forwards. But Cecillon was suddenly on a round of the lock, No 8 and flanking positions as well. He was at No 8 against England in the World Cup as the Dubroca and Blanco eras ended but, oddly, at lock when

England returned to Paris in the Championship. He would hardly qualify as a line-out force to threaten the likes of Wade Dooley.

Given all that switching, his performances during the season were remarkable. He was the rock of France, one of the few constant factors in a team which was trying desperately to find itself. He was probably the best French forward in the quarter-final defeat by England in Paris in October; he was most certainly the most effective Frenchman in the Five Nations matches, where France won two from four and ended in mid-table. He was the focal point of the whole French forward effort.

Cecillon revealed footballing ability and versatility and the capability to concentrate his energies on the game itself; but more than anything, he showed massive power. He was always able to hold the drive long enough for his mates to group round – indeed, he became the key to Berbizier's plan for a pack of mighty driving maulers and it was by no means the fault of Cecillon that the plan did not really succeed. Certainly, France and Cecillon could have done with better, taller jumpers in the line-out and Cecillon stationed permanently in the back row to use the power to best effect from good first-phase possession.

Perhaps the match against Wales at Cardiff showed Cecillon in the best light. Neither side played well. There were too many mistakes, too many nerves and too little true Test play. France could easily have lost. But Cecillon gave France the one constant factor. With his power on the burst and in the loose, he simply dragged France onwards, wrapping up the ball and ensuring the next scrum, giving France a refuge as other parts of their game failed. Wales, graphically, lacked anyone of this stature and experience.

Marc Cecillon *Born Bourgoin, 3 July 1959; plays for Bourgoin-Jallieu; flanker, No 8 or lock; 22 caps for France since first cap against Ireland in 1988.*

SIMON POIDEVIN

When Simon Poidevin came out of one of his occasional periods of semi-retirement to join Australia's squad for the 1991 Test matches against England and New Zealand, and thereafter for the World Cup, he had nothing left to prove. He had been outstandingly successful, whether with Randwick at club level, with the New South Wales state team or with Australia. He had done it all. He had already passed a half-century of caps for his country, and a major proportion of them were gained, as he pointed out with a kind of rueful pride, in one of the hardest schools of all – the Test clashes between Australia and New Zealand. Furthermore, he had been a member of the 1984 Grand Slam tour in the UK and Ireland and had already earned his place in history as one of his country's most influential forwards – not to mention the longest-serving,

Marc Cecillon.

Simon Poidevin.

since he had first appeared in an Australian Test jersey against Fiji in 1980.

He came back into a successful team in 1991, as Australia hammered England at the Sydney Football Stadium and went on to share a two-match series with New Zealand, which Australia really should have won 2-0. New Zealand players admitted that of all the Australians they have met over the years, it was Poidevin whom they respected above all others.

Yet if the legend was established well beforehand, then in the 1991 World Cup, it was extended. Poidevin was no runaway favourite to play in Australia's first-choice line-up when the tournament began, even though he appeared against Argentina in the opening match. There was always the outstanding Jeff Miller also competing for the openside place. Yet when the tournament became white-hot, Poidevin and Australia were drawn irresistibly together. Coach Bob Dwyer opted for Poidevin, and it was a highly significant move. He appeared in the final group match, against Wales at Cardiff, and remained, alongside Miller and with Willie Ofahengaue at No 8, for the dramatic quarter-final against Ireland, for the semi-final against New Zealand, also in Dublin, and for the final itself at Twickenham.

That run of matches probably saw Poidevin at the peak of his effectiveness. He was outstanding, not only with his strength and competitive edge at close quarters, but also in support around the pitch and in defence. He was indestructible and also constructive, and alongside Troy Coker and Ofahengaue, he gave the mighty English back row a memorable battle in the final, with honours finishing even. In the final he played opposite a kindred spirit: Peter Winterbottom, England's openside flanker, had been through the same sort of gruelling career and yet had come through as a complete player. Poidevin was able to add the final shine of a winners' medal.

Simon Poidevin *Born Goulburn, New South Wales, 31 October 1958; flanker; plays for Randwick and New South Wales; 59 caps since first cap against Fiji in 1980.*

AUSTRALIA TRIUMPH AND
THE WORLD STOPS FOR RUGBY

REVIEW OF THE 1991 WORLD CUP
SECOND TOURNAMENT IN BRITAIN,
IRELAND AND FRANCE

There is always a long period of anxiety prior to a tournament such as the 1991 Rugby World Cup. Would the long period of intensive commercial activity actually end in profit for the tournament and therefore in funds for the impecunious smaller rugby countries? Would the whole thing take off in the eyes of the sport-saturated British rugby public? Would it all be a scrummage-dominated damp squib, appealing only to a few rugby aficionados around Britain and leaving the wider world of sport as cold as ice?

The answer was a revelation. The tournament was an outstanding success, a thrill for everyone inside the game but, more importantly, for a few weeks in the autumn of 1991, everyone was talking rugby, whether on Radio 1 programmes or in clubs or pubs or bars or wherever sporting people gathered. And they did not discuss only the brilliance of Australia, the eventual winners, or of England, who powered through the tournament to a richly-deserved place as the runners-up. People spoke also of the wonderful Western Samoans, the surprise package who beat Wales at Cardiff and progressed, to the joy of all their compatriots in the Islands, to the quarter-finals; of Canada, who measured up to any team in the forwards; of New Zealand, conspicuously fading after years of dominance; of Scotland and Ireland and all the others who performed so well and so graphically; even of Italy, who held the All Blacks to a ten-point margin in a pool match. It is no exaggeration to say that none of the 16 teams failed to add their own stamp of excellence or colour to a wonderful month of rugby.

Apart from the teams, there were the glorious individuals: David Campese, of course – 'Campo' extended his lead as the heaviest scorer rugby has ever seen at Test level – Willie Ofahengaue, the Australians' massive flanker, won almost as much publicity, as did their peerless half-backs, Michael Lynagh and Nick Farr-Jones, and the lock, John Eales. Will Carling, Wade Dooley and Brian Moore entered the hearts of Englishmen. There were so many striking individual successes, and not all from the supposedly upper echelons. The likes of Norm Hadley, Gord MacKinnon and Dan Jackart of Canada were outstanding forwards, as was Massimo Cuttitta, the Italian prop. Italy had superb half-backs in Ivan Francescato and Diego Dominguez and Kevin Swords, the giant American forward, was among the foremost locks.

Japan played some brilliant close-passing rugby and Yoshida, their electric left wing, would have been a contender for any team of the tour-

Nick Farr-Jones, the vastly influential Australian captain, celebrates as the Wallabies take the trophy Down Under.

nament. Adrian Garvey, the Zimbabwe prop, was a striking figure with his pace in the loose – he scored two tries against Scotland at Murrayfield. Argentina, ultimately disappointing, had a magnificent prop in the still-youthful Frederico Mendez, and their promising young pack gained from the experience. Samoa had excellence throughout their team, notably in Frank Bunce in the centre and Pat Lam in the back row; Fiji under-achieved, yet both they and Romania, the two non-qualifiers from Pool 4, showed potential. Romania demonstrated a competitive spirit when, for the last few years, their morale has been wayward. Fiji never really settled, were never happy under floodlights or in the dull French weather.

The news on the commercial front was ultimately disappointing, with the profits a good deal lower than expected. There was the effect of the recession, of course; but the costs of the tournament soared way beyond estimates in several areas and the commercial programme as a whole appeared, to the outsider at least, to be unwieldy. Nor was the public relations operation on behalf of the organisers themselves good enough. There really must be a shake-up and general improvement of the whole operation for the 1995 event in South Africa. It is not the object of the tournament to drag in every last penny of profit but, on the other hand, the worldwide development of the game will be helped beyond measure if funds from the central source of Rugby World Cup and the IRB can be handed on.

The next step for the organisers was to announce the qualifying format for the 1995 event, and it appeared that only four countries would go straight through to South Africa, plus the host country. To join those five, the likes of France, Ireland and Wales would, it seemed, have to join the hordes of other hopefuls in worldwide qualifying events. Not a pleasant prospect, perhaps, for the old guard, but one which fairness and democracy demand.

All in all, the impact of the 1991 Rugby World Cup was immense. It showed the game in an excellent light, because there was very little foul play to detract from the spectacle. Off the field, as ever in rugby and in contrast the situation in other sports, there was only harmony – thousands of followers having a ball in rugby's most high-profile month.

FINAL

AUSTRALIA 12, ENGLAND 6

In many ways, this was the perfect finale. The match was a strikingly vivid affair before a packed house and a massive television audience in many countries around the globe. England, who had been criticised in

Wade Dooley gained a clear edge for England in the battle for possession in the World Cup final.

many quarters for their lack of back play in the tournament and especially in an attritional semi-final win over the Scots at Murrayfield, suddenly tried to break out. The ball went spinning across the line with ambition and pace. The spectacle gained immeasurably.

However, there was something of an unreal air about it all. England were praised for their approach, and it won them and the game at large many new admirers. But they ran into a magnificent Australian defence wall in which the centres, Tim Horan and Jason Little, played wonderfully well. Australia were calm and competent and they never allowed England through, despite all their efforts.

Indeed, England's tactics departed too far from their established style. They were lacking the fine touches because the all-running game was not familiar to them. They also missed the chance to proceed on a narrow front, a chance handed to them by a marvellous effort from their forwards. Wade Dooley in the line-out and the heroic Mike Teague and his back row gained a clear edge in the battle for possession.

So England will have to live with the fact that a little more caution and tactical nous might have won them the trophy. It is probable that they themselves did not expect to win more possession and were therefore not quite ready to react and depart from their plans. On the other hand, the England management denied that the pre-match instructions were to run the ball so frequently. Perhaps England were slightly carried away by the heady atmosphere of the occasion and were unable to change plans on the hoof.

Australia deserved their victory. They scored one try and that from short range, when Daly was driven over after a line-out. They celebrated victory with all the good humour and grace they had shown throughout the tournament. Rugby people all over the world, including Englishmen, rejoiced for the likes of Bob Dwyer and Bob Templeton, the coaches whose abilities and character had done so much to shape the team, and for the statesmanlike Nick Farr-Jones, the captain who richly deserved the triumphant moment when he lifted the Webb Ellis trophy, handed to him by the Queen. It was truly a regal occasion, one which England graced, but which left them a little short of final fulfilment.

Australia departed for a ticker-tape parade in Sydney. They were quick to take advantage of the new-found following in Australia, too. They took the trophy itself on a grand tour of outposts and centres of Australian sport, allowing the country to share fully in a superb victory by one of history's best and most attractive teams.

Willie Ofahengaue blasts away for Australia, harassed by Richard Hill, in the World Cup final.

FINAL 2 November, Twickenham
AUSTRALIA 12 (1G 2PG)   **ENGLAND** 6 (2PG)

AUSTRALIA: Roebuck; Campese, Little, Horan, Egerton; Lynagh, Farr-Jones (*capt*);
Daly, Kearns, McKenzie, McCall, Eales, Poidevin, Coker, Ofahengaue
Scorers *Try:* Daly   *Conversion:* Lynagh   *Penalty Goals:* Lynagh (2)
ENGLAND: Webb; Halliday, Carling (*capt*), Guscott, Underwood; Andrew, Hill;
Leonard, Moore, Probyn, Ackford, Dooley, Skinner, Teague, Winterbottom
Scorer *Penalty Goals:* Webb (2)
Referee W D Bevan (Wales)

SEMI-FINALS

ENGLAND 9, SCOTLAND 6
AUSTRALIA 16, NEW ZEALAND 6

These were two high-octane games, battles for the supremacy of the two hemispheres and fuelled also by the rivalry of long history. They were very different matches: the Scotland-England game was a titanic battle but one fought on a narrow front. The Australia-New Zealand match, especially in the first half, contained electric movement, not to mention the remarkable David Campese.

England were on top in the forward battle at Murrayfield and were criticised not only by those who preferred a little passing and flow simply for the sake of it. They did not cash in on their supremacy with points on the board and so were always susceptible to a late Scots rally. A little more adventure and they could have killed off the Scots much earlier. As it was, they had to wait for a late drop-kick from Rob Andrew to take them to the final.

Having said that, England's forward effort and commitment were outstanding. The quality of their possession was substantially higher than that enjoyed by the Scots. Dooley had another big match and Jon Webb and Simon Halliday defended calmly. For the Scots, John Jeffrey marked his last Murrayfield Test before retirement with a typically spritely effort, and Gary Armstrong stood firm against the English tide. Yet Scotland were beaten more convincingly than the score suggested.

In Dublin it seemed for a time that the score would reach amazing proportions. Australia led 13-0 at half-time, playing brilliantly. Campese cut through diagonally for the first try and handed on beautifully to Horan for the second. Lynagh added a conversion and a penalty.

New Zealand fought back well just when it seemed that the margin would be embarrassing. Yet Grant Fox could inspire nothing from the New Zealand backs and the Australians held on in some comfort for a richly-satisfying victory, one which caused them considerably fewer palpitations than the match they had endured against the Irish in the same Lansdowne Road stadium a week before.

SEMI-FINAL 26 October, Murrayfield
ENGLAND 9 (2PG 1DG)   **SCOTLAND 6** (2PG)

ENGLAND: Webb; Halliday, Carling (*capt*), Guscott, Underwood; Andrew, Hill; Leonard, Moore, Probyn, Ackford, Dooley, Skinner, Teague, Winterbottom
Scorers *Penalty Goals:* Webb (2)   *Dropped Goal:* Andrew
SCOTLAND: A G Hastings; Stanger, S Hastings, Lineen, Tukalo; Chalmers, Armstrong; Sole (*capt*), Allan, Burnell, Gray, Weir, Jeffrey, White, Calder
Scorer *Penalty Goals:* A G Hastings (2)
Referee K V J Fitzgerald (Australia)

SEMI-FINAL 27 October, Lansdowne Road
AUSTRALIA 16 (1G 2PG 1T)   **NEW ZEALAND 6** (2PG)

AUSTRALIA: Roebuck; Campese, Little, Horan, Egerton; Lynagh, Farr-Jones (*capt*); Daly, Kearns, McKenzie, McCall, Eales, Poidevin, Coker, Ofahengaue
Scorers *Tries:* Campese, Horan   *Conversion:* Lynagh   *Penalty Goals:* Lynagh (2)
NEW ZEALAND: Crowley; Kirwan, Innes, McCahill, Timu; Fox, Bachop; McDowell, Fitzpatrick, Loe, I D Jones, G W Whetton (*capt*), A J Whetton, Brooke, Carter
Scorer *Penalty Goals:* Fox (2)
Referee J M Fleming (Scotland)

THIRD-FOURTH PLAY-OFF 30 October, Cardiff Arms Park
NEW ZEALAND 13 (3PG 1T)   **SCOTLAND 6** (2PG)

NEW ZEALAND: Wright; Kirwan, Innes, Little, Tuigamala; Preston, Bachop; McDowell, Fitzpatrick, Loe, I D Jones, G W Whetton (*capt*), Earl, Brooke, M N Jones
Replacement Philpott for Tuigamala (40 mins)
Scorers *Try:* Little   *Penalty Goals:* Preston (3)
SCOTLAND: A G Hastings; Stanger, S Hastings, Lineen, Tukalo; Chalmers, Armstrong; Sole (*capt*), Allan, Burnell, Gray, Weir, Jeffrey, White, Calder
Replacement Dods for Stanger (47 mins)
Scorer *Penalty Goals:* A G Hastings (2)
Referee S R Hilditch (Ireland)

KNOCK-OUT STAGES

QUARTER-FINALS

ENGLAND 19, FRANCE 10
SCOTLAND 28, WESTERN SAMOA 6
AUSTRALIA 19, IRELAND 18
NEW ZEALAND 29, CANADA 13

The four quarter-finals, two staged on Saturday and two on Sunday, ensured that the tournament would have a massive impact no matter what was to follow. All four matches were remarkable in their way, and they provided brilliance, bitter controversy and drama, not to mention rugby of genuine world class. Not far short of 200,000 people watched the four games.

In Paris, England ruthlessly exposed the failings of the French pack with a typically selfless, driving performance, helped significantly by remarkable levels of support from Englishmen in what is supposed to be a hostile arena favouring the home country. Tries by Underwood, after lovely approach work from Guscott, and, late in the match, by Carling, sent England through in decisive fashion, and the way in which England rallied after France came back at them in the second half showed massive depths of courage and character.

The drama was not over with the final whistle. Daniel Dubroca, the French coach, manhandled and abused David Bishop, the New Zealand referee, in the tunnel immediately after the match. Initially, the French Federation and Rugby World Cup tried to draw a veil over the incident, but they soon realised the serious error of their ways. The incident was condemned on all sides and Dubroca decided to resign – a sad end to the coaching career of a decent man who suffered an aberration in the pressure of the occasion.

Just before the teams took the field in Paris, the Scots were polishing off the Western Samoans at Murrayfield. However, it took an outstanding performance, and despite the relative security of the Scottish lead, the Samoans were never subdued.

The Scots took them on at close quarters, sending the back row and even Gavin Hastings, the full-back, on charging runs around the fringes. It was a masterly plan, and well executed. Samoa showed ambition and endless morale, and they delighted the crowd with some sweeping movements and, after the final whistle, by a loudly-acclaimed lap of honour which marked the departure of a team that made the tournament what it was.

Drama piled on drama in Dublin the next day as Ireland came storming back. Campese glided over for two tries but Ireland, playing with vast passion, came back to 12-15 with five minutes remaining. Then, in a movement etched in memory, Ireland launched Gordon Hamilton towards the line. He was chased by Campese but managed to scrape over the line for a try which was acclaimed almost with hysteria. Australia, therefore, trailed inside the last five minutes of normal time.

Yet two Irish defensive mistakes allowed Australia a final attacking platform and, from the next ball they won, Australia worked Lynagh over in the right-hand corner for the saving try, a tribute to their confidence and coolness but no reward for Ireland. Australian coach Dwyer revealed that his knees were still knocking an hour after the match had ended.

Canada did not really threaten an upset against New Zealand in the fourth quarter-final, played in heavy conditions in Lille. Yet their pack played superbly and they scored excellent tries through Chris Tynan and Al Charron. There were times when Canada's verve and close driving had New Zealand on the back foot, and it was only the fact that New Zealand started confidently and established a lead that saved them considerable embarrassment. Samoa and Canada proved, in the quarter-finals and before, that the old guard of established nations was no more.

QUARTER-FINAL 19 October, Parc des Princes
ENGLAND 19 (1G 3PG 1T)   **FRANCE 10** (2PG 1T)

ENGLAND: Webb; Heslop, Carling (*capt*), Guscott, Underwood; Andrew, Hill; Leonard, Moore, Probyn, Ackford, Dooley, Skinner, Teague, Winterbottom
Scorers *Tries:* Underwood, Carling   *Conversion:* Webb   *Penalty Goals:* Webb (3)
FRANCE: Blanco (*capt*); Saint-André, Sella, Mesnel, Lafond; Lacroix, Galthié; Lascubé, Marocco, Ondarts, Cadieu, Roumat, Champ, Cecillon, Cabannes
Scorers *Try:* Lafond   *Penalty Goals:* Lacroix (2)
Referee D J Bishop (New Zealand)

QUARTER-FINAL 19 October, Murrayfield
SCOTLAND 28 (2G 4PG 1T)   **WESTERN SAMOA 6** (1PG 1DG)

SCOTLAND: A G Hastings; Stanger, S Hastings, Shiel, Tukalo; Chalmers, Armstrong; Sole (*capt*), Allan, Burnell, Gray, Weir, Jeffrey, White, Calder
Scorers *Tries:* Jeffrey (2), Stanger   *Conversions:* A G Hastings (2)
Penalty Goals: A G Hastings (4)
WESTERN SAMOA: Aiolupo; Lima, Vaega, Bunce, Tagaloa; Bachop, Vaea; Fatialofa (*capt*), Toomalatai, Alalatoa, Birtwistle, Ioane, Vaifale, Lam, Perelini
Scorers *Penalty Goal:* Vaea   *Dropped Goal:* Bachop
Referee W D Bevan (Wales)

QUARTER-FINAL 20 October, Lansdowne Road
AUSTRALIA 19 (2G 1PG 1T)   **IRELAND 18** (1G 3PG 1DG)

AUSTRALIA: Roebuck; Campese, Little, Horan, Egerton; Lynagh, Farr-Jones (*capt*); Daly, Kearns, McKenzie, McCall, Eales, Poidevin, Ofahengaue, Miller
Replacement Slattery for Farr-Jones (18 mins)
Scorers *Tries:* Campese (2), Lynagh   *Conversions:* Lynagh (2)   *Penalty Goal:* Lynagh
IRELAND: Staples; Geoghegan, Mullin, Curtis, Clarke; Keyes, Saunders; Popplewell, Smith, D C Fitzgerald, Lenihan, Francis, Matthews (*capt*), Robinson, Hamilton
Scorers *Try:* Hamilton   *Conversion:* Keyes   *Penalty Goals:* Keyes (3)
Dropped Goal: Keyes
Referee J M Fleming (Scotland)

QUARTER-FINAL 20 October, Lille
NEW ZEALAND 29 (3G 1PG 2T)   **CANADA 13** (1G 1PG 1T)

NEW ZEALAND: Timu; Kirwan, Innes, McCahill, Tuigamala; Fox, Bachop; McDowell, Fitzpatrick, Loe, I D Jones, G W Whetton (*capt*), A J Whetton, Brooke, Henderson

Scorers *Tries:* Timu (2), Kirwan, Brooke, McCahill   *Conversions:* Fox (3)
Penalty Goal: Fox
CANADA: Wyatt (*capt*); D S Stewart, C Stewart, Woods, Gray; Rees, Tynan; Evans,
Speirs, Szabo, van den Brink, Hadley, Charron, Ennis, MacKinnon
Scorers *Tries:* Tynan, Charron   *Conversion:* Rees   *Penalty Goal:* Wyatt
Referee F A Howard (England)

POOL 1

The pool and the tournament began disappointingly when New Zealand beat England in a match which was low on excitement and in
which England fought a losing battle with their own nerves. As it
turned out, it was the best New Zealand effort of the tournament, but
no showpiece with which to follow the opening ceremony.

Italy's sparkling win over the USA in a splendid match at Otley was
much easier on the eye, and Italy reached another peak by scoring two
tries and delighting the crowd in defeat against New Zealand at Leicester.
However, both the big teams came through strongly.

A major feature of the pool was the fact that Twickenham was full or
almost full for the two lesser matches. For the stadium to be sold out for
the USA match on a weekday was the perfect illustration of the impact
of the whole tournament. The USA celebrated with a try by Ray Nelson,
the full-back, after a break in the centre by Mark Williams.

POOL 1	P	W	D	L	F	A	Pts
New Zealand	3	3	0	0	95	39	9
England	3	2	0	1	85	33	7
Italy	3	1	0	2	57	76	5
USA	3	0	0	3	24	113	3

3 October, Twickenham
NEW ZEALAND 18 (1G 4PG)   **ENGLAND 12** (3PG 1DG)

NEW ZEALAND: Wright; Kirwan, Innes, McCahill, Timu; Fox, Bachop; McDowell,
Fitzpatrick, Loe, I D Jones, G W Whetton (*capt*), A J Whetton, Brooke, M N Jones
Replacement Earl for Brooke (70 mins)
Scorers *Try:* M N Jones   *Conversion:* Fox   *Penalty Goals:* Fox (4)
ENGLAND: Webb; Underwood, Carling (*capt*), Guscott, Oti; Andrew, Hill; Leonard,
Moore, Probyn, Ackford, Dooley, Teague, Richards, Winterbottom
Scorers *Penalty Goals:* Webb (3)   *Dropped Goal:* Andrew
Referee J M Fleming (Scotland)

5 October, Otley
ITALY 30 (4G 2PG)   **USA 9** (1G 1PG)

ITALY: Troiani; Vaccari, Gaetaniello, Barba, Marcello Cuttitta; Dominguez,
Francescato; Massimo Cuttitta, Pivetta, Properzi-Curti, Favaro, Croci, Saetti,
Checchinato, Zanon (*capt*)

John Kirwan takes a hold of Jeremy Guscott in New Zealand's convincing win over England. The match was a thoroughly disappointing World Cup opener, and as the event itself grew in pace and spectacle, the All Blacks inexorably faded.

Scorers *Tries:* Barba, Francescato, Vaccari, Gaetaniello   *Conversions:* Dominguez (4)
Penalty Goals: Dominguez (2)
USA: Nelson; Hein, Williams, Higgins, Whitaker; De Jong, Daily; Lippert, Flay, Paoli,
Swords, Leversee, Vizard (*capt*), Ridnell, Farley *Replacement* Lipman for Vizard (57 mins)
Scorers *Try:* Swords   *Conversion:* Williams   *Penalty Goal:* Williams
Referee O E Doyle (Ireland)

8 October, Gloucester
NEW ZEALAND 46 (4G 2PG 4T)   **USA 6** (2PG)

NEW ZEALAND: Wright; Timu, Innes, McCahill, Tuigamala; Preston, Bachop;
McDowell, Fitzpatrick, Purvis, I D Jones, G W Whetton (*capt*), A J Whetton, Earl,
M N Jones
Scorers *Tries:* Wright (3), Earl, Purvis, Timu, Innes, Tuigamala
Conversions: Preston (4)   *Penalty Goals:* Preston (2)
USA: Sheehy; Hein, Williams, Burke, Whitaker; O'Brien, Pidcock; Lippert, Johnson,
Mottram, Swords (*capt*), Tunnacliffe, Sawicki, Ridnell, Lipman *Replacement* Manga for
Lippert (51 mins)
Scorers *Penalty Goals:* Williams (2)
Referee E Sklar (Argentina)

8 October, Twickenham
ENGLAND 36 (4G 4PG)   **ITALY 6** (1G)

ENGLAND: Webb; Oti, Carling (*capt*), Guscott, Underwood; Andrew, Hill; Leonard,
Moore, Probyn, Ackford, Redman, Teague, Richards, Winterbottom
Replacement Rendall for Probyn (53 mins)
Scorers *Tries:* Underwood, Guscott (2), Webb   *Conversions:* Webb (4)
Penalty Goals: Webb (4)
ITALY: Troiani; Vaccari, Gaetaniello, Barba, Marcello Cuttitta; Dominguez,
Francescato; Massimo Cuttitta, Pivetta, Properzi-Curti, Favaro, Croci, Saetti, Zanon
(*capt*), Giovanelli *Replacement* Bonomi for Troiani (48 mins)
Scorers *Try:* Marcello Cuttitta   *Conversion:* Dominguez
Referee J B Anderson (Scotland)

11 October, Twickenham
ENGLAND 37 (4G 3PG 1T)   **USA 9** (1G 1PG)

ENGLAND: Hodgkinson; Heslop, Carling (*capt*), Halliday, Underwood; Andrew,
Hill; Leonard, Olver, Pearce, Dooley, Redman, Skinner, Richards, Rees
Scorers *Tries:* Underwood (2), Carling, Skinner, Heslop   *Conversions:* Hodgkinson (4)
Penalty Goals: Hodgkinson (3)
USA: Nelson; Hein, Williams, Higgins, Sheehy; O'Brien, Pidcock; Manga, Flay,
Mottram, Tunnacliffe, Swords (*capt*), Lipman, Ridnell, Farley *Replacements* de Jong for
Higgins (40 mins); Wilkerson for Farley (70 mins)
Scorers *Try:* Nelson   *Conversion:* Williams   *Penalty Goal:* Williams
Referee L J Peard (Wales)

13 October, Leicester
NEW ZEALAND 31 (3G 3PG 1T)   **ITALY 21** (2G 3PG)

NEW ZEALAND: Wright; Kirwan, Innes, Little, Tuigamala; Fox, Hewett;
McDowell, Fitzpatrick, Loe, I D Jones, G W Whetton (*capt*), A J Whetton, Brooke,
Carter *Replacement* Philpott for Wright (73 mins)

A memorable moment for Italy's Massimo Bonomi – a try against the All Blacks. Philpott (left) and Innes of New Zealand are in pursuit.

Scorers *Tries:* Innes, Brooke, Tuigamala, Hewett   *Conversions:* Fox (3)
Penalty Goals: Fox (3)
ITALY: Vaccari; Venturi, Gaetaniello, Dominguez, Marcello Cuttitta; Bonomi,
Francescato; Massimo Cuttitta, Pivetta (*capt*), Properzi-Curti, Favaro, Croci,
Bottacchiari, Checchinato, Giovanelli *Replacement* Grespan for Properzi-Curti (44 mins)
Scorers *Tries:* Marcello Cuttitta, Bonomi   *Conversions:* Dominguez (2)
Penalty Goals: Dominguez (3)
Referee K V J Fitzgerald (Australia)

POOL 2

Scotland were expected to dominate this group and they duly came
through, comfortably disposing of Japan and Zimbabwe. However,
they trailed for a long time in the face of a riotous Irish performance at
Murrayfield, and it was only very late in the match that the Irish wilted
slightly and Scotland were rehabilitated.

Zimbabwe were generally outclassed even though they scored some
excellent tries. Japan were well beaten for possession against Scotland
and Ireland, but they showed some breathtaking talent in the backs and
brilliant support play. On the day when they achieved parity of
possession, against Zimbabwe at Ravenhill, Belfast, they played
superbly, reaching the 50 mark with nine tries, some of which came
after movements launched from deep in Japanese territory. Zimbabwe
therefore conceded more than 50 points in each game, but their future
may be brighter than their past since large numbers of the black population are now turning to the game in Zimbabwe.

POOL 2	P	W	D	L	F	A	Pts
Scotland	3	3	0	0	122	36	9
Ireland	3	2	0	1	102	51	7
Japan	3	1	0	2	77	87	5
Zimbabwe	3	0	0	3	31	158	3

5 October, Murrayfield
SCOTLAND 47 (5G 3PG 2T)   **JAPAN 9** (1G 1DG)

SCOTLAND: A G Hastings; Stanger, S Hastings, Lineen, Tukalo; Chalmers,
Armstrong; Sole (*capt*), Allan, Burnell, Gray, Weir, Jeffrey, White, Calder
Replacements Wyllie for Chalmers (70 mins); D Milne for Sole (75 mins)
Scorers *Tries:* penalty try, White, Tukalo, G Hastings, S Hastings, Stanger, Chalmers
Conversions: G Hastings (5)   *Penalty Goals:* G Hastings (2), Chalmers
JAPAN: Hosokawa; Masuho, Kutsuki, Hirao (*capt*), Yoshida; Matsuo, Murata; Ota,
Kunda, Takura, Hayashi, Tifaga, Kajihara, Latu, Nakashima
Scorer *Try:* Hosokawa   *Conversion:* Hosokawa   *Dropped Goal:* Hosokawa
Referee E Morrison (England)

6 October, Lansdowne Road
IRELAND 55 (4G 5PG 4T)   **ZIMBABWE 11** (1PG 2T)

IRELAND: Staples; Geoghegan, Cunningham, Curtis, Crossan; Keyes, Saunders; Popplewell, Smith, D C Fitzgerald, Lenihan, Francis, Matthews (*capt*), Robinson, Hamilton
Scorers *Tries:* Robinson (4), Popplewell (2), Curtis, Geoghegan   *Conversions:* Keyes (4)
Penalty Goals: Keyes (5)
ZIMBABWE: Currin (*capt*); Brown, Letcher, Tsimba, Walters; Kuhn, Ferreira; Hunter, Beattie, Garvey, Martin, Demblon, Botha, Catterall, Dawson
Replacement Schultz for Kuhn (29 mins)
Scorers *Tries:* Dawson, Schultz   *Penalty Goal:* Ferreira
Referee K H Lawrence (New Zealand)

9 October, Lansdowne Road
IRELAND 32 (2G 4PG 2T)   **JAPAN 16** (2G 1T)

IRELAND: Staples; Clarke, Mullin, Curtis, Crossan; Keyes, Saunders; J J Fitzgerald, Kingston (*capt*), Halpin, Galwey, Francis, O'Hara, Mannion, Hamilton
Replacement Cunningham for Crossan (60 mins)
Scorers *Tries:* Staples, O'Hara, Mannion (2)   *Conversions:* Keyes (2)
Penalty Goals: Keyes (4)
JAPAN: Hosokawa; Masuho, Kutsuki, Hirao (*capt*), Yoshida; Matsuo, Horikoshi; Ota, Fujita, Takura, Hayashi, Oyagi, Tifaga, Latu, Kajihara *Replacements* Kunda for Fujita (52 mins); Miyamato for Tifaga (73 mins)
Scorers *Tries:* Yoshida, Hayashi, Kajihara   *Conversions:* Hosokawa (2)
Referee L Colati (Fiji)

9 October, Murrayfield
SCOTLAND 51 (5G 2PG 1DG 3T)   **ZIMBABWE 12** (2G)

SCOTLAND: Dods (*capt*); Stanger, S Hastings, Lineen, Tukalo; Wyllie, Oliver; Burnell, K S Milne, Watt, Cronin, Weir, Turnbull, White, Marshall
Replacement Chalmers for Stanger (78 mins)
Scorers *Tries:* Tukalo (3), Stanger, Turnbull, Hastings, Weir, White
Conversions: Dods (5)   *Penalty Goals:* Dods (2)   *Dropped Goal:* Wyllie
ZIMBABWE: Currin (*capt*); Schultz, Tsimba, Letcher, Walters; Brown, MacMillan; Nicholls, Beattie, Garvey, Martin, Nguruve, Muirhead, Catterall, Dawson
Replacements Hunter for Garvey (46 mins); Chimbima for Walters (56 mins); Roberts for Hunter (78 mins)
Scorers *Tries:* Garvey (2)   *Conversions:* Currin (2)
Referee D Reordan (USA)

12 October, Murrayfield
SCOTLAND 24 (2G 3PG 1DG)   **IRELAND 15** (4PG 1DG)

SCOTLAND: A G Hastings; Stanger, S Hastings, Lineen, Tukalo; Chalmers, Armstrong; Sole (*capt*), Allan, Burnell, Gray, Weir, Jeffrey, White, Calder
Replacement Shiel for Chalmers (43 mins)
Scorers *Tries:* Shiel, Armstrong   *Conversions:* G Hastings (2)
Penalty Goals: G Hastings (3)   *Dropped Goal:* Chalmers
IRELAND: Staples; Geoghegan, Curtis, Mullin, Crossan; Keyes, Saunders; Popplewell, Smith, D C Fitzgerald, Lenihan, Francis, Matthews (*capt*), Robinson, Hamilton
Scorer *Penalty Goals:* Keyes (4)   *Dropped Goal:* Keyes
Referee F A Howard (England)

Brian Robinson tackles Scotland's Derek White in Ireland's spirited performance at Murrayfield in Pool 2.

14 October, Belfast
JAPAN 52 (5G 2PG 4T)   **ZIMBABWE 8** (2T)

JAPAN: Hosokawa; Masuho, Kutsuki, Hirao (*capt*), Yoshida; Matsuo, Horikoshi; Ota, Kunda, Takura, Hayashi, Oyagi, Tifaga, Latu, Kajihara
Scorers *Tries:* Yoshida (2), Masuho (2), Kutsuki (2), Horikoshi, Tifaga, Matsuo
Conversions: Hosokawa (5)   *Penalty Goals:* Hosokawa (2)
ZIMBABWE: Currin (*capt*); Schultz, Tsimba, Letcher, Walters; Brown, MacMillan; Nicholls, Beattie, Garvey, Martin, Botha, Nguruve, Catterall, Dawson
Replacement Snyder for Garvey (70 mins)
Scorers *Tries:* Tsimba, Nguruve
Referee R Hourquet (France)

POOL 3

This was easily the most difficult group from which to emerge and easily the most newsworthy pool. Australia had to work hard to subdue Argentina at Llanelli, but that was as nothing compared to the experience of Wales, the other pool favourites, against the Samoans. Wales began well enough, but Western Samoa were inspired. They played straightforward, hard-nosed rugby. They accepted a modicum of good fortune when Vaega was awarded a try after Robert Jones apparently reached the ball first, but their sensational win turned previous history upside-down, and condemned Wales to miss out on the quarter-finals.

Wales did beat Argentina, who did not build on the promise of their first effort against Australia. There was no way that Wales could challenge Australia, and they duly subsided by 38-3, overwhelmed in the line-out and in most other phases, too.

For many people, the best match in the group was a rumbustious 9-3 win for Australia over the Samoans on a wet day at Pontypool, when the ferocious nature of exchanges and high standards created a fine impression. Western Samoa duly beat the Pumas at Pontypridd and took a well-deserved place in the knock-out stages. The reaction at home in Samoa, where huge crowds gathered to watch a television transmission beamed on to a screen at the national sports stadium, was reportedly ecstatic.

POOL 3	P	W	D	L	F	A	Pts
Australia	3	3	0	0	79	25	9
Western Samoa	3	2	0	1	54	34	7
Wales	3	1	0	2	32	61	5
Argentina	3	0	0	3	38	83	3

4 October, Llanelli
AUSTRALIA 32 (3G 2PG 2T)   **ARGENTINA 19** (1G 1PG 2DG 1T)

AUSTRALIA: Roebuck; Campese, Little, Horan, Egerton; Lynagh, Farr-Jones (*capt*);

Daly, Kearns, McKenzie, Coker, McCall, Poidevin, Eales, Ofahengaue
Replacement Nucifora for Kearns (50 mins)
Scorers *Tries:* Campese (2), Horan (2), Kearns *Conversions:* Lynagh (3)
Penalty Goals: Lynagh (2)
ARGENTINA: del Castillo; Teran, Laborde, Garcia Simon, Cuesta Silva; Arbizu,
Camardon; Mendez, Le Fort, Cash, Sporleder, Llanes, Garreton (*capt*), Carreras,
Santamarina *Replacement* Bosch for Le Fort (40 mins)
Scorers *Tries:* Teran (2) *Conversion:* del Castillo *Penalty Goal:* del Castillo
Dropped Goals: Arbizu (2)
Referee D J Bishop (New Zealand)

6 October, Cardiff Arms Park
WESTERN SAMOA 16 (1G 2PG 1T) **WALES 13** (1G 1PG 1T)

WESTERN SAMOA: Aiolupo; Lima, Vaega, Bunce, Tagaloa; Bachop, Vaea; Fatialofa
(*capt*), Toomalaiti, Alalatoa, Birtwistle, Keenan, Vaifale, Lam, Perelini
Scorers *Tries:* Vaega, Vaifale *Conversion:* Vaea *Penalty Goals:* Vaea (2)
WALES: Clement; I C Evans (*capt*), Gibbs, Hall, Emyr; Ring, Jones; Griffiths, Waters,
Delaney, May, Moseley, Lewis, Davies, Collins *Replacements* Morris for May (29 mins);
Rayer for Clement (48 mins); Jenkins for Collins (52 mins)
Scorers *Tries:* Emyr, Evans *Conversion:* Ring *Penalty Goal:* Ring
Referee P Robin (France)

9 October, Pontypool
AUSTRALIA 9 (3PG) **WESTERN SAMOA 3** (1PG)

AUSTRALIA: Roebuck; Campese, Herbert, Horan, Flett; Lynagh, Farr-Jones (*capt*);
Lillicrap, Kearns, Crowley, Coker, Cutler, Miller, Eales, Nasser *Replacement* Slattery
for Farr-Jones (10 mins)
Scorer *Penalty Goals:* Lynagh (3)
WESTERN SAMOA: Aiolupo; Lima, Vaega, Bunce, Faamasino; Bachop, Vaea;
Fatialofa (*capt*), Toomalatai, Alalatoa, Birtwistle, Keenan, Paramore, Perelini, Kaleopa
Replacement Tagaloa for Lima (52 mins)
Scorer *Penalty Goal:* Vaea
Referee E Morrison (England)

9 October, Cardiff Arms Park
WALES 16 (4PG 1T) **ARGENTINA 7** (1PG 1T)

WALES: Rayer; I C Evans (*capt*), Hall, Gibbs, Emyr; Ring, Jones; Griffiths, Jenkins,
Delaney, Arnold, Moseley, Lewis, P T Davies, Webster
Scorers *Try:* Arnold *Penalty Goals:* Ring (3), Rayer
ARGENTINA: del Castillo; Teran, Laborde, Garcia Simon, Cuesta Silva; Arbizu,
Camardon; Mendez, Le Fort, Molina, Sporleder, Llanes, Garreton (*capt*), Carreras,
Santamarina
Scorers *Try:* Garcia Simon *Penalty Goal:* del Castillo
Referee R Hourquet (France)

12 October, Cardiff Arms Park
AUSTRALIA 38 (4G 2PG 2T) **WALES 3** (1PG)

AUSTRALIA: Roebuck; Campese, Horan, Little, Egerton; Lynagh, Slattery; Daly,
Kearns, McKenzie, McCall, Eales, Poidevin, Ofahengaue, Miller

Scorers *Tries:* Roebuck (2), Slattery, Campese, Lynagh, Horan   *Conversions:* Lynagh (4)
Penalty Goals: Lynagh (2)
WALES: Clement; I C Evans (*capt*), Hall, Gibbs, Emyr; Ring, Jones; Griffiths, Jenkins, Delaney, Arnold, Moseley, Lewis, P T Davies, Webster *Replacements* D W Evans for Emyr (75 mins); Rayer for Gibbs (79 mins)
Scorer *Penalty Goal:* Ring
Referee K H Lawrence (New Zealand)

13 October, Pontypridd
WESTERN SAMOA 35 (4G 1PG 2T)   **ARGENTINA 12** (1G 2PG)

WESTERN SAMOA: Aiolupo; Lima, Vaega, Bunce, Tagaloa; Bachop, Vaea; Fatialofa (*capt*), Toomalatai, Alalatoa, Birtwistle, Keenan, Vaifale, Lam, Perelini
Scorers *Tries:* Tagaloa (2), Lima (2), Bunce, Bachop   *Conversions:* Vaea (4)
Penalty Goal: Vaea
ARGENTINA: Angaut; Teran, Laborde, Garcia Simon, Cuesta Silva; Arbizu, Camardon; Aguirre, Bosch, Cash, Buabse, Sporleder, Irarrazabal, Santamarina, Garreton (*capt*) *Replacements* Meson for Angaut (53 mins); Carreras for Irarrazabal (60 mins)
Scorers *Try:* Teran   *Conversion:* Arbizu   *Penalty Goals:* Laborde, Arbizu
Referee B Anderson (Scotland) *Replacement* J M Fleming (40 mins)

POOL 4

This was the most difficult pool to predict beforehand. France were strong favourites to come through, and they did so, although they rarely found high gears. But what of the 'undercard'? Would Fiji be able to subdue their natural homesickness and build on the promising performance, especially in the forwards, they gave against England at Suva in the summer? Would Romania find themselves now that there were greater freedoms and, here and there, better facilities available to them? Would Canada fulfil their own predictions that they would shake the old order?

As it turned out, Fiji played disappointingly. They never looked happy. Romania revealed that they were competitive and improving, but they were not improving quickly enough. It was Canada who powered through with France, disposing of Romania in Toulouse and of Fiji in Bayonne. Their forwards averaged around 230 pounds per man, and were based on the fine British Columbia team.

France beat Canada only by 19-13, and there was a period when the result was in the balance. France's lack of dominating forward play in the pool matches gave early notice that they would struggle against the England pack in Paris.

The drawback in this pool, in the opinion of some Canadians and Fijians, was that they felt isolated from the mainstream World Cup activities, another reminder, if one was needed, that the tournament needs to be concentrated within one country or, in the Northern Hemisphere, into the four home unions alone, or France alone.

POOL 4	P	W	D	L	F	A	Pts
France	3	3	0	0	82	25	9
Canada	3	2	0	1	45	33	7
Romania	3	1	0	2	31	64	5
Fiji	3	0	0	3	27	63	3

4 October, Béziers
FRANCE 30 (1G 4PG 3T)   **ROMANIA 3** (1PG)

FRANCE: Blanco (*capt*); Saint-André, Lacroix, Mesnel, Lagisquet; Camberabero, Galthié; Lascubé, Marocco, Ondarts, Cadieu, Roumat, Champ, Benazzi, Cabannes *Replacement* Lafond for Lagisquet (70 mins)
Scorers *Tries:* penalty try, Saint-André, Roumat, Lafond   *Conversion:* Camberabero *Penalty Goals:* Camberabero (4)
ROMANIA: Dumitru; Sasu, Lungu, Sava, Racean; Nichitean, Neaga; Leonte, Ion, Stan, Ciorascu, Cojocariu, Dinu, Dumitras (*capt*), Guranescu
Scorer *Penalty Goal:* Nichitean
Referee L J Peard (Wales)

5 October, Bayonne
CANADA 13 (3PG 1T)   **FIJI 3** (1DG)

CANADA: D S Stewart; Palmer, C Stewart, Lecky, Gray; Rees, Tynan; Evans, Speirs, Jackart, Robertsen, Hadley, Charron, Ennis (*capt*), MacKinnon
Scorers *Try:* D S Stewart   *Penalty Goals:* Rees (3)
FIJI: Koroduadua; Seru, Aria, Nadruku, Lovo; Serevi, Tabulutu; Taga (*capt*), Naivilawasa, Naituivau, Savai, Domoni, Kato, Tawake, Dere *Replacement* Baleiwai for Naivilawasa (76 mins)
Scorer *Dropped Goal:* Serevi
Referee K V J Fitzgerald (Australia)

8 October, Grenoble
FRANCE 33 (3G 1PG 3T)   **FIJI 9** (1G 1PG)

FRANCE: Blanco (*capt*); Lafond, Sella, Mesnel, Saint-André; Camberabero, Galthié; Lascubé, Marocco, Ondarts, Cadieu, Roumat, Champ, Benazzi, Cabannes
Scorers *Tries:* Lafond (3), Sella (2), Camberabero   *Conversions:* Camberabero (3) *Penalty Goal:* Camberabero
FIJI: Koroduadua; Seru, Aria, Naisoro, Lovo; Serevi, Vosanibole; Taga (*capt*), Baleiwai, Vuli, Savai, Domoni, Naruma, Tawake, Dere *Replacements* Tabulutu for Vosanibole; Volavola for Taga; Kato for Domoni
Scorers *Try:* Naruma   *Conversion:* Koroduadua   *Penalty Goal:* Koroduadua
Referee W D Bevan (Wales)

9 October, Toulouse
CANADA 19 (1G 2PG 1DG 1T)   **ROMANIA 11** (1PG 2T)

CANADA: Wyatt (*capt*); Palmer, C Stewart, Lecky, D S Stewart; Rees, Graf; Evans, Svoboda, Jackart, van den Brink, Hadley, Breen, Ennis, MacKinnon

Scorers *Tries:* MacKinnon, Ennis   *Conversion:* Wyatt   *Penalty Goals:* Wyatt (2)
Dropped Goal: Rees
ROMANIA: Dumitru; Sasu, Lungu, Fulina, Racean; Nichitean, Neaga; Leonte, Ion,
Stan, Ciorascu, Cojacariu, Dinu, Dumitras (*capt*), Doja *Replacements* Brinza for Doja
(15 mins); Sava for Dumitru (33 mins); Vlad for Leonte (70 mins)
Scorers *Tries:* Lungu, Sasu   *Penalty Goal:* Nichitean
Referee A R MacNeill (Australia)

12 October, Brive
ROMANIA 17 (1G 1PG 2T)   FIJI 15 (2PG 3DG)

ROMANIA: Racean; Sasu, Lungu, Fulina, Colceriu; Nichitean, Neaga; Stan, Ion,
Vlad, Ciorascu, Cojocariu, Dinu, Dumitras (*capt*), Marin *Replacement* Ivanciuc for
Nichitean
Scorers *Tries:* Ion, Dumitras, Sasu   *Penalty Goal:* Nichitean   *Conversion:* Racean
FIJI: Turuva; Seru, Nadruku, Naisoro, Vonolagi; Rabaka, Tabulutu; Volavola,
Baleiwai, Vuli, Savai, Nadolo, Tawake, Olsson, Dere (*capt*) *Replacements* Naituivau for
Volavola; Naruma for Olsson
Scorers *Penalty Goals:* Turuva (2)   *Dropped Goals:* Rabaka (2), Turuva
Referee O E Doyle (Ireland)

13 October, Agen
FRANCE 19 (1G 3PG 1T)   CANADA 13 (2PG 1DG 1T)

FRANCE: Blanco (*capt*); Lafond, Sella, Mesnel, Saint-André; Camberabero, Galthié;
Lascubé, Marocco, Ondarts, Cadieu, Roumat, Champ, Benazzi, Cabannes
Replacements Lacroix for Camberabero (40 mins); Sadourny for Sella (50 mins)
Scorers *Tries:* Lafond, Saint-André   *Conversion:* Camberabero
Penalty Goals: Lacroix (2), Camberabero
CANADA: Wyatt (*capt*); Palmer, C Stewart, Woods, Gray; Rees, Tynan; Evans,
Svoboda, Jackart, Robertsen, Hadley, Charron, Ennis, MacKinnon
Replacements van den Brink for Robertsen (25 mins); D S Stewart for Wyatt (45 mins)
Scorers *Try:* Wyatt   *Dropped Goal:* Rees   *Penalty Goals:* Wyatt, Rees
Referee S R Hilditch (Ireland)

WORLD CUP SQUADS

Abbreviations: *E – England, NZ – New Zealand, It – Italy, US – United States, S – Scotland, I – Ireland, J – Japan, Z – Zimbabwe, A – Australia, WS – Western Samoa, W – Wales, Arg – Argentina, F – France, C – Canada, R – Romania, Fj – Fiji,* (R) *– Replacement,* * *– late replacement.*

NEW ZEALAND Captain G W Whetton **Manager** J Sturgeon **Coach** A Wyllie
POOL 1 winners Lost 6-16 to Australia in semi-final; beat Scotland 13-6 in 3rd place play-off

Squad *Full-backs:* T J Wright (Auckland) *E, US, It, S;* S Philpott (Canterbury) *It*(R), *S*(R); K J Crowley* (Taranaki) *A. Threequarters:* J J Kirwan (Auckland) *E, It, C, A, S;* V L Tuigamala (Auckland) *US, It, C, S;* J K R Timu (Otago) *E, US, C, A;* C R Innes (Auckland) *E, US, It, C, A, S;* B J McCahill (Auckland) *E, US, C, A;* W K Little (North Harbour) *It, S. Half-backs:* G J Fox (Auckland) *E, It, C, A;* J P Preston (Canterbury) *US, S;* G T M Bachop (Canterbury) *E, US, C, A, S;* J A Hewett (Auckland) *It. Forwards:* S B T Fitzpatrick (Auckland) *E, US, It, C, A, S;* G W Dowd (North Harbour); G H Purvis (Waikato) *US;* R W Loe (Waikato) *E, It, C, A, S;* S C McDowell (Auckland) *E, US, It, C, A, S;* A T Earl (Canterbury) *E*(R), *US, S;* S B Gordon (Waikato); I D Jones (North Auckland) *E, US, It, C, A, S;* G W Whetton (Auckland) *E, US, It, C, A, S;* P W Henderson (Otago) *C;* M N Jones (Auckland) *E, US, S;* M P Carter (Auckland) *It, A;* A J Whetton (Auckland) *E, US, It, C, A;* Z V Brooke (Auckland) *E, It, C, A, S.*

ENGLAND Captain W D C Carling **Manager** G D Cooke **Coach** R M Uttley
POOL 1 runners-up Lost 6-12 to Australia in final

Squad *Full-backs:* S D Hodgkinson (Nottingham) *US;* J M Webb (Bath) *NZ, It, F, S, A. Threequarters:* R Underwood (Leicester) *NZ, It, US, F, S, A;* N J Heslop (Orrell) *US, F;* C Oti (Wasps) *NZ, It;* W D C Carling (Harlequins) *NZ, It, US, F, S, A;* J C Guscott (Bath) *NZ, It, F, S, A;* S J Halliday (Harlequins) *US, S, A;* C R Andrew (Wasps) *NZ, It, US, F, S, A;* D Pears (Harlequins); R J Hill (Bath) *NZ, It, US, F, S, A;* C D Morris (Orrell). *Forwards:* B C Moore (Harlequins) *NZ, It, F, S, A;* C J Olver (Northampton) *US;* J Leonard (Harlequins) *NZ, It, US, F, S, A;* P A G Rendall (Askeans) *It*(R); J A Probyn (Askeans) *NZ, It, F, S, A;* G S Pearce (Northampton) *US;* P J Ackford (Harlequins) *NZ, It, F, S, A;* W A Dooley (Preston Grasshoppers) *NZ, US, F, S, A;* N C Redman (Bath) *It, US;* M C Teague (Gloucester) *NZ, It, F, S, A;* M G Skinner (Harlequins) *US, F, S, A;* P J Winterbottom (Harlequins) *NZ, It, F, S, A;* G W Rees (Nottingham) *US;* D Richards (Leicester) *NZ, It, US.*

ITALY Captain G Zanon **Manager** G Dondi **Coach** B Fourcade
POOL 1 3rd place

Squad *Full-backs:* L Troiani (Scavolini L'Aquila) *US, E;* D Tebaldi (Officine Savi Noceto). *Threequarters:* Marcello Cuttitta (Amatori Mediolanum) *US, E, NZ;* P Vaccari (Nutrilinea Calvisano) *US, E, NZ;* E Venturi (Cagnoni Rovigo) *NZ;* S Bordon (Cagnoni Rovigo); D Dominguez (Amatori Mediolanum) *US, E, NZ;* S Barba (Amatori Mediolanum) *US, E;* F Gaetaniello (Ecomar Livorno) *US, E, NZ. Half-backs:* M Bonomi (Amatori Mediolanum) *E*(R), *NZ;* I Francescato (Pastajolly Tarvisium) *US, E, NZ;* F Pietrosanti (Scavolini L'Aquila). *Forwards:* C Orlandi (Bilboa Piacenza); G Pivetta (Iranian Loom San Dona) *US, E, NZ;* Massimo Cuttitta (Amatori Mediolanum) *US, E, NZ;* G Grespan (Benetton Treviso) *NZ*(R); F Properzi-Curti (Amatori Mediolanum) *US, E, NZ;* G Rossi (Delicius Parma); A Colella (Scavolini L'Aquila); G Croci (Amatori Mediolanum) *US, E, NZ;* R Favaro (Benetton Treviso) *US, E, NZ;* A Bottacchiari (Scavolini L'Aquila) *NZ;* R Saetti (Petrarca Padova) *US, E;* C Checchinato (Cagnoni Rovigo) *US, NZ;* M Giovanelli (Amatori Mediolanum) *E, NZ;* G Zanon (Benetton Treviso) *US, E.*

Japan's Hiroyuki Kajihara and Katsuhiro Matsuo (No 10) prepare to pounce on a loose ball in the Pool 2 match against Ireland.

USA Captain B G Vizard **Manager** E Schram **Coach** J Perkins
POOL 1 4th place

Squad *Full-backs:* R B Nelson (Belmont Shore) *It, E*; P Sheehy (Washington) *NZ, E. Threequarters:* G M Hein (Old Blues) *It, NZ, E*; E A Whitaker (Old Blues) *It, NZ*; J R Burke (Albany Knicks) *NZ*; K G Higgins (Old Blues) *It, E*; M A Williams (Aspen) *It, NZ, E. Half-backs:* C P O'Brien (Old Blues) *NZ, E*; M G de Jong (Denver Barbarians) *It, E*(R); B Daily (San Jose Seahawks) *It*; M D Pidcock (Pensacola) *NZ, E. Forwards:* A W Flay (Jersey Shore) *It, E*; P W Johnson (Louisville) *NZ*; C Lippert (Old Mission Beach Athletic Club) *It, NZ*; L Manga (South Jersey) *NZ*(R), *E*; N Mottram (Boulder) *NZ, E*; A F Paoli (Denver Barbarians) *It*; W N Leversee (Old Mission Beach Athletic Club) *It*; K R Swords (Beacon Hill) *It, NZ, E*; C E Tunnacliffe (Belmont Shore) *NZ, E*; A M Ridnell (Old Puget Sound) *It, NZ, E*; R Farley (Philadelphia Whitemarsh) *It, E*; S Lipman (Santa Monica) *It*(R), *NZ, E*; M H Sawicki (Chicago Lions) *NZ*; J P Wilkerson (Belmont Shore) *E*(R); B G Vizard (Old Mission Beach Athletic Club) *It*.

SCOTLAND Captain D M B Sole **Manager** D S Paterson **Coach** I R McGeechan
POOL 2 winners Lost 6-9 to England in semi-final; lost 6-13 to New Zealand in 3rd place play-off

Squad *Full-backs:* P W Dods (Gala) *Z, NZ*(R); A G Hastings (Watsonians) *J, I WS, E, NZ. Threequarters:* M Moncrieff (Gala) *Z, I, WS, E, NZ*; A G Stanger (Hawick) *J, Z, I, WS, E, NZ*; I Tukalo (Selkirk) *J, Z, I, WS, E, NZ*; S Hastings (Watsonians) *J, Z, I, WS, E, NZ*; S R P Lineen (Boroughmuir) *J, Z, I, E, NZ*; A G Shiel (Melrose) *I*(R), *WS. Half-backs:* D S Wyllie (Stewart's-Melville FP) *J*(R), *Z*; C M Chalmers (Melrose) *J, Z*(R), *I, WS, E, NZ*; G Armstrong (Jedforest) *J, I, WS, E, NZ*; G H Oliver (Hawick) *Z. Forwards:* J Allan (Edinburgh Academicals) *J, I, WS, E, NZ*; K S Milne (Heriot's FP) *Z*; D M B Sole (Edinburgh Academicals) *J, I, WS, E, NZ*; A P Burnell (London Scottish) *J, Z, I, WS, E, NZ*; D F Milne (Heriot's FP) *J*(R); A G J Watt (Glasgow High-Kelvinside) *Z*; D F Cronin (Bath) *Z*; C A Gray (Nottingham) *J, I, WS, E, NZ*; G W Weir (Melrose) *J, Z, I, WS, E, NZ*; F Calder (Stewart's-Melville FP) *J, I, WS, E, NZ*; G R Marshall (Selkirk) *Z*; D J Turnbull (Hawick) *Z*; D B White (London Scottish) *J, Z, I, WS, E, NZ*; J Jeffrey (Kelso) *J, I, WS, E, NZ*.

IRELAND Captain P M Matthews **Manager** K Reid **Coach** C F Fitzgerald
POOL 2 runners-up Lost 18-19 to Australia in quarter-final

Squad *Full-backs:* K J Murphy (Cork Constitution); J E Staples (London Irish) *Z, J, S, A. Threequarters:* D J Clarke (Dolphin) *J, A*; K D Crossan (Instonians) *Z, J, S*; S P Geoghegan (London Irish) *Z, S, A*; D M Curtis (London Irish) *Z, J, S, A*; P P A Danaher (Garryowen); B J Mullin (Blackrock College) *J, S, A. Half-backs:* V J G Cunningham (St Mary's College) *Z, J*(R); R P Keyes (Cork Constitution) *Z, J, S, A*; L F P Aherne (Lansdowne); R Saunders (London Irish) *Z, J, S, A. Forwards:* D C Fitzgerald (De La Salle-Palmerston) *Z, S, A*; J J Fitzgerald (Young Munster) *J*; G F Halpin (London Irish) *J*; N J Popplewell (Greystones) *Z, S, A*; T J Kingston (Dolphin) *J*; S J Smith (Ballymena) *Z, S, A*; N P J Francis (Blackrock College) *Z, J, S, A*; M J Galwey (Shannon) *J*; D G Lenihan (Cork Constitution) *Z, S, A*; P M Matthews (Wanderers) *Z, S, A*; G F Hamilton (Ballymena) *Z, J, S, A*; P T J O'Hara (Cork Constitution) *J*; N P Mannion (Lansdowne) *J*; B F Robinson (Ballymena) *Z, S, A*.

JAPAN Captain S Hirao **Manager** S Konno **Coach** H Shukuzawa
POOL 2 3rd place

Squad *Full-backs:* T Hosokawa (Kobe Steel) *S, I, Z*; T Maeda (NTT Kansai). *Threequarters:* T Masuho (Waseda U) *S, I, Z*; T Matsuda (Kanto Gakuen U); Y Yoshida (Isetan) *S, I, Z*; S Hirao (Kobe Steel)

Tony Ridnell, who played in all three Pool 1 matches for the USA in the World Cup.

S, I, Z; E Kutsuki (Toyota) *S, I, Z*; Y Motoki (Meiji U). *Half-backs:* K Matsuo (World) *S, I, Z*; S Aoki (Ricoh); M Horikoshi (Kobe Steel) *I, Z*; W Murata (Toshiba Fuchu) *S*. *Forwards:* M Kunda (Toshiba Fuchu) *S, I*(R), *Z*; T Fujita (IBM) *I*; O Ota (Nihon Denki) *S, I, Z*; K Kimura (Toyota); M Takura (Mitsubishi Jiko Kyoto) *S, I, Z*; K Takahashi (Toyota); T Hayashi (Kobe Steel) *S, I, Z*; E Tifaga (Niko Niko Do) *S, I, Z*; A Oyagi (Kobe Steel) *I, Z*; H Kajihara (Toshiba Fuchu) *S, I, Z*; K Miyamato (Sanyo) *I*(R); S Nakashima (Nihon Denki) *S*; H Ouchi (Ryukoku U); S T Latu (Sanyo) *S, I, Z*.

ZIMBABWE Captain B S Currin **Manager** A Woldemar **Coach** I Buchanan
POOL 2 4th place

Squad *Full-back:* B S Currin (Old Hararians) *I, S, J*. *Threequarters:* E Chimbima (Old Hararians) *S*(R); W H Schultz (Karoi) *I*(R), *S, J*; I E Noble (Old Miltonians); M S Letcher (Karoi) *I, S, J*; R U Tsimba (Old Hararians) *I, S, J*. *Half-backs:* C Brown (Harare Sports Club) *I, S, J*; D A Walters (Karoi) *I, S, J*; R F Kuhn (Old Hararians) *I*; A M Ferreira (Old Georgians) *I*; E A MacMillan (Old Hararians) *S, J*. *Forwards:* B A Beattie (Old Miltonians) *I, S, J*; C P Roberts (Harare Sports Club) *S*(R); R N Hunter (Old Miltonians) *I, S*(R); A H Nicholls (Old Hararians) *S, J*; G M Snyder (Harare Sports Club) *J*(R); A C Garvey (Old Miltonians) *I, S, J*; H Nguruve (Old Georgians) *S, J*; B W Marais (Old Hararians); C J Botha (Old Hararians) *I, J*; B N Dawson (Old Miltonians) *I, S, J*; C R Demblon (Old Hararians) *I*; D G Muirhead (Old Miltonians) *S*; M Nyala (Old Hararians); B W Catterall (Old Hararians) *I, S, J*; M L Martin (Harare Sports Club) *I, S, J*.

AUSTRALIA Captain N C Farr-Jones **Manager** J Breen **Coach** R S F Dwyer
POOL 3 winners Winners World Cup

Squad *Full-back:* M C Roebuck (NSW) *Arg, WS, W, I, NZ, E*. *Threequarters:* D I Campese (NSW) *Arg, WS, W, I, NZ, E*; R H Egerton (NSW) *Arg, W, I, NZ, E*; J A Flett (NSW) *WS*; A G Herbert (Queensland) *WS*; T J Horan (Queensland) *Arg, WS, W, I, NZ, E*; J S Little (Queensland) *Arg, W, I, NZ, E*; R C Tombs (NSW). *Half-backs:* D J Knox (NSW); M P Lynagh (Queensland) *Arg, WS, W, I, NZ, E*; P J Slattery (Queensland) *WS*(R), *W, I*(R); N C Farr-Jones (NSW) *Arg, WS, I, NZ, E*. *Forwards:* P N Kearns (NSW) *Arg, WS, W, I, NZ, E*; D V Nucifora (Queensland) *Arg*(R); A J Daly (NSW) *Arg, W, I, NZ, E*; E J A McKenzie (NSW) *Arg, W, I, NZ, E*; D J Crowley (Queensland) *WS*; C P Lillicrap (Queensland) *WS*; J A Eales (Queensland) *Arg, WS, W, I, NZ, E*; R J McCall (Queensland) *Arg, W, I, NZ, E*; S A G Cutler (NSW) *WS*; B P Nasser (Queensland) *WS*; V Ofahengaue (NSW) *Arg, W, I, NZ, E*; S P Poidevin (NSW) *Arg, W, I, NZ, E*; J S Miller (Queensland) *WS, W, I*; T Coker (Queensland) *Arg, WS, NZ, E*.

WESTERN SAMOA Captain P Fatialofa **Manager** T Simi **Coach** S L P Schuster
POOL 3 runners-up Lost 6-28 to Scotland in quarter-final

Squad *Full-back:* A A Aiolupo (Moata'a) *W, A, Arg, S*. *Threequarters:* T D L Tagaloa (Wellington) *W, A*(R), *Arg, S*; B Lima (Wellington) *W, A, Arg, S*; T Faamasino (Rongotai) *A*; T Vaega (Suburbs) *W, A, Arg, S*; F Tuilagi (Marist St Joseph); F Bunce (Helensville) *W, A, Arg, S*; K Sio (Scopa); P D Saena (Moata'a). *Half-backs:* S J Bachop (Canterbury) *W, A, Arg, S*; M M Vaea (Marist St Joseph) *W, A, Arg, S*; T Nu'uali'itia (Counties). *Forwards:* S Toomalatui (Wellington) *W, A, Arg, S*; S Fanolua (Southern); P Fatialofa (Auckland) *W, A, Arg, S*; V Alalatoa (Manly) *W, A, Arg, S*; T Sio (Northern Suburbs); M L Birtwistle (Wellington) *W, A, Arg, S*; E Ioane (Auckland) *S*; M G Keenan (Auckland) *W, A, Arg*; S Lemamea (Lefaga); S Vaifale (Marist St Joseph) *W, Arg, S*; J Paramore (Counties) *A*; A Perelini (Auckland) *W, A, Arg, S*; P R Lam (Auckland) *W, A, Arg, S*; D Kaleopa (Marist) *A*.

WALES Captain I C Evans   **Manager** R L Norster   **Coach** A B C Davies
POOL 3 3rd place

Squad *Full-backs:* A Clement (Swansea) *WS, A;* M A Rayer (Cardiff) *WS*(R), *Arg, A*(R).
Threequarters: I C Evans (Llanelli) *WS, Arg, A;* S P Ford (Cardiff); A Emyr (Cardiff) *WS, Arg, A;*
M R Hall (Cardiff) *WS, Arg, A;* I S Gibbs (Neath) *WS, Arg, A;* D W Evans (Cardiff) *A*(R).
Half-backs: M G Ring (Cardiff) *WS, Arg, A;* A Davies (Neath); A H Booth (Cardiff); R N Jones
(Swansea) *WS, Arg, A. Forwards:* K Waters (Newbridge) *WS;* G R Jenkins (Pontypool)
WS(R), *Arg, A;* M Davis (Newport); H Williams-Jones (S Wales Police); M Griffiths (Cardiff)
WS, Arg, A; L Delaney (Llanelli) *WS, Arg, A;* P S May (Llanelli) *WS;* S Williams★ (Neath);
K Moseley (Newport) *WS, Arg, A;* P Arnold (Swansea) *Arg, A;* R G Collins (Cardiff) *WS;* M S Morris
(Neath) *WS*(R); R E Webster (Swansea) *Arg, A;* E W Lewis (Llanelli) *WS, Arg, A;* P T Davies
(Llanelli) *WS, Arg, A.*

ARGENTINA Captain P A Garreton   **Manager** F M Alvarez   **Coach** L Grardin
POOL 3 4th place

Squad *Full-backs:* G J del Castillo (Jockey Club Rosario) *A, W;* G P Angaut (La Plata) *WS.*
Threequarters: D Cuesta Silva (San Isidro) *A, W, WS;* G M Jorge (Pucara); M J Teran (Tucuman)
A, W, WS; S E Meson (Tucuman) *WS*(R); M Allen (San Isidro); H M Garcia Simon (Pueyrredon)
A, W, WS; E H Laborde (Pucara) *A, W, WS. Half-backs:* L Arbizu (Belgrano) *A, W, WS;*
G F Camardon (Alumni) *A, W, WS;* L A Zanoni (Pueyrredon). *Forwards:* R A Le Fort (Tucuman)
A, W; M A Bosch (Olivos) *A*(R), *WS;* F E Mendez (Mendoza) *A, W;* M E Aguirre (Alumni) *WS;*
D M Cash (San Isidro) *A, WS;* L E Molina (Tucuman) *W;* G A Llanes (La Plata) *A, W;* P L Sporleder
(Curupayti) *A, W, WS;* P M Buabse (Los Tarcos) *WS;* P A Garreton (Tucuman U) *A, W, WS;*
J M Santamarina (Tucuman) *A, W, WS;* F J Irarrazabal (Newman) *WS;* M G Lombardi (Alumni);
M Carreras (Olivos) *A, W, WS*(R).

FRANCE Captain S Blanco   **Manager** H Foures   **Coach** D Dubroca
POOL 4 winners   Lost 10-19 to England in quarter-final

Squad *Full-backs:* S Blanco (Biarritz) *R, Fj, C, E;* J-L Sadourny (Colomiers) *C*(R).
Threequarters: J-B Lafond (Racing Club de France) *R*(R), *Fj, C, E;* P Lagisquet (Bayonne) *R;*
P Saint-André (Montferrand) *R, Fj, C, E;* P Hontas (Biarritz); P Sella (Agen) *Fj, C, E;* F Mesnel
(Racing Club de France) *R, Fj, C, E. Half-backs:* D Camberabero (Béziers) *R, Fj, C;* T Lacroix (Dax)
R, C(R), *E;* H Sanz (Narbonne); F Galthié (Colomiers) *R, Fj, C, E. Forwards:* G Lascubé (Agen)
R, Fj, C, E; P Ondarts (Biarritz) *R, Fj, C, E;* P Gimbert (Bègles); P Marocco (Montferrand)
R, Fj, C, E; L Armary (Lourdes); O Roumat (Dax) *R, Fj, C, E;* J-M Cadieu (Toulouse) *R, Fj, C, E;*
A Benazzi (Agen) *R, Fj, C;* T Devergie (Nîmes); L Cabannes (Racing Club de France) *R, Fj, C, E;*
E Champ (Toulon) *R, Fj, C, E;* M Courtiols (Bègles); P Benetton (Agen); M Cecillon (Bourgoin) *E.*

CANADA Captain M A Wyatt   **Manager** M Luke   **Coach** I Birtwell
POOL 4 runners-up   Lost 13-29 to New Zealand in quarter-final

Squad *Full-backs:* M A Wyatt (Velox Valhallians) *R, F, NZ;* D S Stewart (UBC) *Fj, R, F*(R), *NZ.*
Threequarters: S D Gray (Kats) *Fj, F, NZ;* P Palmer (UBC Old Boys) *Fj, R, F;* T A Woods (James Bay)
F, NZ; J L Lecky (Meralomas) *Fj, R;* D C Lougheed (Toronto Welsh); C Stewart (Meralomas)
Fj, R, F, NZ. Half-backs: G L Rees (Oak Bay Castaways) *Fj, R, F, NZ;* J D Graf (UBC Old Boys) *R;*
C J Tynan (Meralomas) *Fj, F, NZ. Forwards:* D A Speirs (Meralomas) *Fj, NZ;* K F Svoboda
(Ajax Wanderers) *R, F;* G Dukelow (Cowichan); E A Evans (UBC Old Boys) *Fj, R, F, NZ;*
D C Jackart (UBC Old Boys) *Fj, R, F;* P Szabo (Ex-Britannia Lions) *NZ;* A J Charron (Ottawa Irish)

Fj, F, NZ; N Hadley (UBC Old Boys) *Fj, R, F, NZ*; J Knauer (Meralomas); J R Robertsen (UBC Old Boys) *Fj, F*; R van den Brink (Kats) *R, F*(R), *NZ*; B Breen (Meralomas) *R*; G I MacKinnon (Ex-Britannia Lions) *Fj, R, F, NZ*; R E Radu (James Bay); G D Ennis (Kats) *Fj, R, F, NZ*.

ROMANIA Captain H Dumitras **Manager** A Bojinescu **Coach** P Ianusevici
POOL 4 3rd place

Squad *Full-backs:* M Dumitru (Rapid Metrou) *F, C*; S Tofan (Dinamo). *Threequarters:* L Colceriu (Steua) *Fj*; C Sasu (Farul) *F, C, Fj*; N Racean (University) *F, C, Fj*; N Fulina (Farul) *C, Fj*; G Sava (Stinta Cemin) *F, C*(R); A Lungu (Dinamo) *F, C, Fj*. *Half-backs:* N Nichitean (Stinta Cemin) *F, C, Fj*; I Ivanciuc (Suceava) *Fj*(R); M Foca (Farul Constanta); D Neaga (Dinamo) *F, C, Fj*. *Forwards:* G Ion (Dinamo) *F, C, Fj*; C Gheorghe (Grivita); G Leonte (Mielan) *F, C*; G Vlad (Grivita) *C*(R), *Fj*; C Stan (Contactoare) *F, C, Fj*; V Ionescu (Rapid Metrou); H Dumitras (Pau) *F, C, Fj*; C Cojocariu (Dinamo) *F, C, Fj*; S Ciorascu (Angoulême) *F, C, Fj*; G Dinu (Grivita) *F, C, Fj*; A Guranescu (Dinamo) *F*; I Doja (Dinamo) *C*; T Brinza (Grivita) *C*(R); N Marin (Farul) *Fj*.

FIJI Captain M Taga **Manager** Dr J Taka **Coach** S Viriviri
POOL 4 4th place

Squad *Full-backs:* S Koroduadua (Police) *C, F*; O Turuva (Yavusania) *R*. *Threequarters:* F Seru (Nabua) *C, F, R*; T Vonolagi (Army) *R*; T Lovo (Queen Victoria School OB) *C, F*; S Aria (Regent) *C, F*; K Naisoro (FSC) *F, R*; N Nadruku (Hyatt) *C, R*. *Half-backs:* W Serevi (Nabua) *C, F*; T Rabaka (Mount St Mary's) *R*; M Vosanibole (Army) *F*; P Tabulutu (Nabua) *C, F*(R), *R*. *Forwards:* D Baleiwai (Duavata) *C*(R), *F, R*; S Naivilawasa (Police) *C*; N Vuli (PWD) *F, R*; M Taga (Queen Victoria School OB) *C, F*; E Naituivau (Army) *C, R*(R); P Volavola (Brothers) *F*(R), *R*; I Savai (Regent) *C, F, R*; A Nadolo (Queen Victoria School OB) *R*; S Domoni (Waimanu) *C, F*; P Naruma (Police) *F, R*(R); A Dere (Army) *C, F, R*; L Kato (Saunaka) *C, F*(R); M Olsson (St John's Marist) *R*; I Tawake (Yalovata) *C, F, R*.

WORLD CUP RECORDS
(final stages only)

LEADING SCORERS
Most points in the competition

126	G J Fox	New Zealand	1987
82	M P Lynagh	Australia	1987
68	R P Keyes	Ireland	1991
66	M P Lynagh	Australia	1991
62	A G Hastings	Scotland	1987

Most tries in the competition

6	C I Green	New Zealand	1987
6	J J Kirwan	New Zealand	1987
6	D I Campese	Australia	1991
6	J-B Lafond	France	1991

Most conversions in the competition

30	G J Fox	New Zealand	1987
20	M P Lynagh	Australia	1987
16	A G Hastings	Scotland	1987

Most penalty goals in the competition

21	G J Fox	New Zealand	1987
16	R P Keyes	Ireland	1991
14	J M Webb	England	1991
13	A G Hastings	Scotland	1991

Most dropped goals in the competition

3	J Davies	Wales	1987
2	by several players		

MOST POINTS IN A MATCH
By a team

74	New Zealand v Fiji	1987
70	New Zealand v Italy	1987
70	France v Zimbabwe	1987
60	England v Japan	1987
60	Scotland v Zimbabwe	1987

By a player

30	D Camberabero	France v Zimbabwe	1987
27	A G Hastings	Scotland v Romania	1987
26	G J Fox	New Zealand v Fiji	1987
24	J M Webb	England v Italy	1991
23	G Laporte	France v Romania	1987
23	R P Keyes	Ireland v Zimbabwe	1991
22	G J Fox	New Zealand v Italy	1987
22	G J Fox	New Zealand v Argentina	1987
22	G J Fox	New Zealand v Scotland	1987

MOST TRIES IN A MATCH

By a team

13	France v Zimbabwe	1987
12	New Zealand v Italy	1987
12	New Zealand v Fiji	1987
11	Scotland v Zimbabwe	1987

By a player

4	I C Evans	Wales v Canada	1987
4	C I Green	New Zealand v Fiji	1987
4	J A Gallagher	New Zealand v Fiji	1987

MOST CONVERSIONS IN A MATCH

By a team

10	New Zealand v Fiji	1987
9	France v Zimbabwe	1987
8	New Zealand v Italy	1987
8	France v Romania	1987
8	Scotland v Zimbabwe	1987
8	Scotland v Romania	1987

By a player

10	G J Fox	New Zealand v Fiji	1987
9	D Camberabero	France v Zimbabwe	1987
8	G J Fox	New Zealand v Italy	1987
8	G Laporte	France v Romania	1987
8	A G Hastings	Scotland v Zimbabwe	1987
8	A G Hastings	Scotland v Romania	1987

MOST PENALTY GOALS IN A MATCH

By a team

6	New Zealand v Scotland	1987
6	New Zealand v Argentina	1987
5	Argentina v Italy	1987
5	Zimbabwe v Scotland	1987
5	Ireland v Zimbabwe	1991

By a player

6	G J Fox	New Zealand v Scotland	1987
6	G J Fox	New Zealand v Argentina	1987
5	H Porta	Argentina v Italy	1987
5	M Grobler	Zimbabwe v Scotland	1987
5	R P Keyes	Ireland v Zimbabwe	1991

MOST DROPPED GOALS IN A MATCH

By a team

3	Fiji v Romania	1991
2	Wales v Ireland	1987
2	Ireland v Canada	1987
2	Argentina v Australia	1991

By a player

2	J Davies	Wales v Ireland	1987
2	L Arbizu	Argentina v Australia	1991
2	T Rabaka	Fiji v Romania	1991

WORLD CUP QUALIFYING TOURNAMENTS

AMERICAS GROUP

23 Sep	1989	Canada	21-3	United States	(Toronto)
8 Nov	1989	Argentina	23-6	United States	(Buenos Aires)
30 Mar	1990	Canada	15-6	Argentina	(Vancouver)
7 Apr	1990	United States	6-13	Argentina	(Santa Barbara)
9 Jun	1990	United States	14-12	Canada	(Seattle)
16 Jun	1990	Argentina	15-19	Canada	(Buenos Aires)

Final Table

	P	W	D	L	F	A	Pts
Canada	4	3	0	1	67	38	6
Argentina	4	2	0	2	57	46	4
United States	4	1	0	3	29	69	2

Argentinian Appearances
Full-backs: A A Scolni *US*1, *C*1, *US*2; P Garzon *C*2
Threequarters: F Schacht *US*1, *C*1; D Halle *US*2; D Cuesta Silva *C*2; M H Loffreda *US*1, *C*1, *US*2; S Salvat *C*1, *US*2, *C*2; M Allen *C*2; C I Mendy *US*1, *C*2; R Zanero *C*1; S Meson *US*1,2
Halves: D Halle *US*1; H Vidou *C*1, *US*2; S Meson *C*2; F Silvestre *US*1, *C*1, *US*2; E F Gomez *C*2
Forwards: D M Cash *US*1, *C*1, *US*2, *C*2; A S Rocca *US*1, *C*1, *US*2, *C*2; J J Angelillo *US*1, *C*1, *US*2; L E Molina *C*2; M Valesani *US*1, *C*1, *US*2, *C*2; P Buabse *US*1; J Grondona *C*1; J Simes *C*2(R), *US*2; A Iachetti *C*2; P A Garreton *US*1, *C*2; P di Nisio *C*1, *US*2; S Bunader *US*1, *C*2; P Camerlinckx *C*1, *US*2(R); M Baeck *US*2; J G Allen *US*1, M J S Bertranou *C*1, *US*2, *C*2

Captains: J G Allen *US*1; M H Loffreda *C*1, *US*2; A Iachetti *C*2
Leading Scorer: S Meson – 18

To Pool 3 of the Finals

Canadian Appearances
Full-backs: D S Stewart *US*1, *Arg*2(R); M A Wyatt *Arg*1, *US*2, *Arg*2
Threequarters: M A Wyatt *US*1; P Palmer *Arg*1, *US*2, *Arg*2; I C Stuart *US*1, *Arg*1, *US*2, *Arg*2; D C Lougheed *Arg*2; S T T Brown *US*1; S D Gray *Arg*1, *US*2; J D Graf *Arg*2; T A Woods *US*1, *Arg*1, *US*2
Halves: G L Rees *US*1, *Arg*1,2; J D Graf *US*1; R P Ross *US*1(R), 2; C J Tynan *Arg*1, *US*2, *Arg*2
Forwards: E A Evans *US*1, *Arg*1,2; K F Svoboda *Arg*1, *US*2, *Arg*2; D A Spiers *US*1; P Szabo *US*1, *Arg*1, *US*2, *Arg*2; G A Dukelow *US*2; J R Robertsen *US*1, *Arg*1, *US*2, *Arg*2; N Hadley *US*1, *Arg*2; R E Hindson *Arg*1; C H Fowler *US*2; A J Charron *Arg*1, *US*2, *Arg*2; B Breen *US*2; R E Radu *US*1, *Arg*1(R),2; G D Ennis *US*1, *Arg*1, *US*2, *Arg*2(R); G I MacKinnon *US*1, *Arg*1,2

Captains: G D Ennis *US*1; M A Wyatt *Arg*1, *US*2, *Arg*2
Leading Scorer: M A Wyatt – 33

To Pool 4 of the Finals

United States Appearances
Full-backs: A Montgomery *C*1; R Nelson *Arg*1,2, *C*2
Threequarters: B Williams *C*1; M Williams *Arg*1,2, *C*2; K Higgins *C*1, *Arg*1,2;
B Corcoran *Arg*1,2; C O'Brien *C*1; J Burke *C*2; G Hein *C*1, *Arg*1,2; C Williams *C*2;
C Lewis *C*2; S LaPorta *Arg* 1(R)
Halves: M Caulder *C*1; C O'Brien *Arg*1,2; M Saunders *C*1; B Daily *Arg*1,2, *C*2;
M de Jong *C*2
Forwards: C Lippert *C*1, *Arg*1,2 *C*2; F Paoli *C*1, *Arg*1; P Johnson *C*1, *Arg*1(R);
N Mottram *Arg*2; T McCormack *Arg*1,2, *C*2; D James *C*2; R Isaac *C*1, *Arg*1; K Swords
*C*1, *Arg*1,2, *C*2; W Leversee *Arg*2, *C*2; M Sawicki *Arg*2; M Siano *C*1, *Arg*1; B Vizard *C*1,2;
G Lambert *C*1, *Arg*1,2; R Farley *Arg*1,2, *C*2; S Lipman *C*2; A Manga *Arg*1(R)

Captain: M Saunders *C*1; K Higgins *Arg*1,2; B Vizard *C*2
Leading Scorer: C O'Brien – 11

To Pool 1 of the Finals

AFRICAN GROUP

5 May 1990	Morocco	12-16	Tunisia	(Harare)
5 May 1990	Zimbabwe	22-9	Ivory Coast	(Harare)
8 May 1990	Tunisia	12-7	Ivory Coast	(Harare)
8 May 1990	Zimbabwe	16-0	Morocco	(Harare)
12 May 1990	Tunisia	13-24	Zimbabwe	(Harare)
12 May 1990	Morocco	11-4	Ivory Coast	(Harare)

Final Table

	P	W	D	L	F	A	Pts
Zimbabwe	3	3	0	0	62	22	6
Tunisia	3	2	0	1	41	43	4
Morocco	3	1	0	2	23	36	2
Ivory Coast	3	0	0	3	20	45	0

Zimbabwean Appearances
Full-backs: M Cremer *Iv*; A Rex *M*, *T*
Threequarters: Z Dzinomurumbi *Iv*, *M*, *T*; M Letcher *Iv*, *M*, *T*; D Walters *Iv*;
M Cremer *M*, *T*; E Chimbima *Iv*, *M*, *T*
Halves: R Kuhn *Iv*; D Walters *M*, *T*; A Ferreira *Iv*, *M*, *T*
Forwards: R Moore *Iv*, *M*, *T*; P Albasini *Iv*, *M*, *T*; A Garvey *Iv*, *M*; G Davidson *M*(R);
W Cornish *T*; B Matthewman *Iv*, *T*, *M*; A Horton *Iv*, *M*, *T*; N Bushell *Iv*, *M*, *T*;
H Nguruve *Iv*, *M*, *T*; B Dawson *Iv*, *M*, *T*

Captain: A Ferreira *Iv*, *M*, *T*
Leading Scorer: A Ferreira – 43

To Pool 2 of the Finals

ASIAN-PACIFIC GROUP

| 8 Apr 1990 | South Korea | 7-74 | Western Samoa | (Tokyo) |
| 8 Apr 1990 | Japan | 28-16 | Tonga | (Tokyo) |

11 Apr 1990	Tonga	3-12	Western Samoa	(Tokyo)
11 Apr 1990	Japan	26-10	South Korea	(Tokyo)
15 Apr 1990	Tonga	45-22	South Korea	(Tokyo)
15 Apr 1990	Japan	11-37	Western Samoa	(Tokyo)

Final Table

	P	W	D	L	F	A	Pts
Western Samoa	3	3	0	0	123	21	6
Japan	3	2	0	1	65	63	4
Tonga	3	1	0	2	64	62	2
South Korea	3	0	0	3	39	145	0

Japanese Appearances
Full-back: T Hosokawa *Tg, SK, WS*
Threequarters: T Goda *Tg, SK, WS*; E Kutsuki *Tg, SK, WS*; K Yoshinaga *WS*; S Hirao *Tg, SK*; Y Yoshida *Tg, SK, WS*
Halves: K Matsuo *Tg, SK, WS*; M Horikoshi *Tg, SK*; H Watanabe *WS*
Forwards: O Ota *Tg, SK, WS*; T Fujita *Tg, SK, WS*; M Takura *Tg, SK, WS*; K Takahashi *WS*(R); M Kunda *WS*(R); T Hayashi *Tg, WS*; A Oyagi *Tg, SK, WS*; E Luaiufa *SK*; H Kajihara *Tg, SK, WS*; S T Latu *Tg, SK, WS*; S Nakashima *Tg, SK, WS*

Captains: S Hirao *Tg, SK*; T Fujita *WS*
Leading Scorer: T Hosokawa – 41

To Pool 2 of the Finals

Western Samoan Appearances
Full-back: A Aiolupo *SK, Tg, J*
Threequarters: T Tagaloa *SK, Tg, J*; J Ah Kuoi *SK, Tg*; T Manoo *SK, Tg, J*; K Sio *J*; T Faamasino *SK, Tg, J*
Halves: P D Saena *SK, Tg, J*; M Moke *SK, Tg, J*
Forwards: P Fatialofa *SK, Tg, J*; S Toomalati *SK, Tg, J*; A Leuu *SK, J*; T Sio *Tg*; P Fuatai *SK, Tg, J*; S P Ching *SK, Tg*; P Leavai *J*; S Vaifale *SK, Tg, J*; H Schuster *SK, Tg, J*; D Kaleope *SK, Tg, J*; S Lemamea *J*(R)

Captain: P Fatialofa *SK, Tg, J*
Leading Scorer: A Aiolupo – 44

To Pool 3 of the Finals

EUROPEAN GROUP

30 Sep	1990	Italy	30-6	Spain	(Rovigo)
30 Sep	1990	Romania	45-7	Holland	(Treviso)
3 Oct	1990	Italy	24-11	Holland	(Treviso)
3 Oct	1990	Romania	19-6	Spain	(Padua)
7 Oct	1990	Spain	22-12	Holland	(Rovigo)
7 Oct	1990	Italy	29-21	Romania	(Padua)

Final Table

	P	W	D	L	F	A	Pts
Italy	3	3	0	0	83	38	6
Romania	3	2	0	1	85	42	4
Spain	3	1	0	2	34	61	2
Holland	3	0	0	3	30	91	0

Italian Appearances
Full-back: L Troiani *Sp, H, R*
Threequarters: E Venturi *Sp, H, R*; S Barba *Sp, H, R*; S Bordon *R*; F Gaetaniello *Sp, H*; M Brunello *Sp, H, R*
Halves: M Bonomi *Sp, H, R*; U Casellato *Sp*; F Pietrosanti *H*; I Francescato *R*
Forwards: M Cuttitta *Sp, H, R*; G Pivetta *Sp, R*; M Goti *H*; F Properzi-Curti *Sp, H, R*; G Grespan *R*(R); G Croci *Sp, H, R*; C Checchinato *Sp*; R Favaro *H, R*; R Saetti *Sp, H, R*; G Zanon *Sp, H, R*; M Giovanelli *Sp, H, R*

Captain: G Zanon *Sp, H, R*
Leading Scorer: L Troiani – 44

To Pool 1 of the Finals

Romanian Appearances:
Full-back: M Dumitru *H, Sp, It*
Threequarters: S Chirila *H, Sp, It*; N Fulina *H, Sp*; A Lungu *It*; G Sava *H, Sp, It*; N Racean *H, Sp, It*; M Toader *It*(R)
Halves: G Ignat *H, Sp*; N Nichitean *Sp*(R), *It*; D Neaga *H, Sp*; S Seceleanu *It*
Forwards: G Dumitrescu *H, Sp, It*; G Ion *H, Sp, It*; G Leonte *H, Sp, It*; V Tufa *It*(R); C Cojocariu *H, Sp, It*; S Ciorascu *H, Sp*; T Oroian *It*; G Dinu *H, Sp, It*; T Brinza *It*; H Dumitras *H, Sp*; I Doja *It*; C Stan *H*(R); A Radulescu *H, Sp, It*(R)

Captains: H Dumitras *H, Sp*; G Ion *It*
Leading Scorers: G Ignat and N Nichitean – 25

To Pool 4 of the Finals

TOURS 1991-92

ENGLAND TO AUSTRALIA AND FIJI 1991

The tour caused a good deal of controversy before it even began. There were those who felt that it was an unnecessary exercise and that the hard-worked England squad should have stayed at home and rested for the rigours of the World Cup to come. Others, including the England team management, insisted that it was a valuable exercise.

As it turned out, it had something of a negative value since England struggled through most of the trip and were heavily defeated in the Test match in Sydney against Australia. For the first time, too, it was obvious that Australia were powerful contenders for the World Cup – they proved fast and fit and clever. It also became obvious that Australia now lead the world in rugby thinking and preparation.

The bonus for England was the emergence of the giant lock Martin Bayfield, who toured well and played in the Australian Test in the absence of the injured Dooley. The rehabilitation of Jon Webb at full-back continued and he ousted Simon Hodgkinson, the hero of the 1991 Grand Slam campaign.

THE TOURING PARTY

Manager G D Cooke   **Coach** R M Uttley   **Assistant Coach** R Best
Captain W D C Carling

FULL-BACKS

S D Hodgkinson (Nottingham)
J M Webb (Bath)

THREEQUARTERS

R Underwood (Leicester and RAF)
I Hunter (Northampton)
N J Heslop (Orrell)
C Oti (Wasps)
W D C Carling (Harlequins)
J C Guscott (Bath)
S J Halliday (Harlequins)
D P Hopley (Wasps)

HALF-BACKS

C R Andrew (Wasps)
D Pears (Harlequins)
R J Hill (Bath)
C D Morris (Orrell)

FORWARDS

J Leonard (Saracens)
G S Pearce (Northampton)
P A G Rendall (Wasps)
J A Probyn (Wasps)
B C Moore (Harlequins)
C J Olver (Northampton)
P J Ackford (Harlequins)
W A Dooley (Preston Grasshoppers)
M C Bayfield (Northampton)
N C Redman (Bath)
J P Hall (Bath)
G W Rees (Nottingham)
M G Skinner (Harlequins)
M C Teague (Gloucester)
P J Winterbottom (Harlequins)
D Richards (Leicester)

TOUR RECORD

All matches   Played 7   Won 3   Lost 4   Points for 151   Against 132
International matches   Played 2   Won 1   Lost 1   Points for 43   Against 52

SCORING DETAILS

All Matches						International matches					
For:	22T	12C	10PG	3DG	151 Pts	For:	4T	3C	5PG	2DG	43 Pts
Against:	15T	12C	13PG	3DG	132 Pts	Against:	6T	5C	5PG	1PG	52 Pts

MATCH DETAILS

1991	OPPONENTS	VENUE	RESULT
7 July	New South Wales	Sydney	L 19-21
10 July	Victoria President's XV	Melbourne	W 26- 9
14 July	Queensland	Brisbane	L 14-20
16 July	Fiji B	Lautoka	L 13-27
20 July	FIJI	Suva	W 28-12
23 July	Emerging Australians	Gosford	W 36- 3
27 July	AUSTRALIA	Sydney	W 40-15

Scorers: 41 – Webb (1T 9PG 5C); 17 – Hodgkinson (1PG 7C); 10 – Andrew (1T 2DG); 8 – Guscott, Heslop, Hopley, Hunter, Morris, Underwood (2T each); 7 – Pears (1T 1DG); 4 – Hill, Oti, Probyn, Rees, Richards, Skinner, Teague (1T each)
Appearances: 5 – Skinner (inc 1 as replacement, and 1 as 'temporary' replacement), Guscott (inc 1 as replacement), Teague; 4 – Ackford, Redman, Hodgkinson (inc 1 as replacement), Probyn, Winterbottom, Webb, Underwood, Oti, Carling, Andrew, Hill, Leonard, Moore, Bayfield, Richards; 3 – Rees, Heslop, Hunter, Halliday, Hopley, Pears, Morris, Rendall, Pearce, Olver; 2 – Dooley, Hall

MATCH 1   7 July, Waratah Rugby Park, Sydney

New South Wales 21 (2G 3PG)   **England XV 19** (2G 1PG 1T)
New South Wales: M C Roebuck (Eastwood); D I Campese (Randwick), C Wells (Drummoyne), R G Tombs (Norths), R H Egerton (Sydney U); J Allen (Norths), N C Farr-Jones (Sydney U) *(capt)*; A J Daly (Easts), P N Kearns (Randwick), E J A McKenzie (Randwick), W Waugh (Randwick), S A G Cutler (Gordon), S P Poidevin (Randwick), B T Gavin (Easts), V Ofahengaue (Manly)
Scorers *Tries:* Tombs, Farr-Jones   *Conversions:* Roebuck (2)   *Penalty Goals:* Roebuck (3)
England XV: Webb; Heslop, Carling *(capt)*, Guscott, Underwood; Andrew, Hill; Leonard, Moore, Probyn, Ackford, Dooley, Hall, Teague, Winterbottom *Temporary replacement:* Skinner for Teague (27 to 37 mins)
Scorers *Tries:* Heslop, Webb, Underwood   *Conversions:* Webb (2)
Penalty Goal: Webb
Referee K V J Fitzgerald (Queensland)

MATCH 2   10 July, Olympic Park, Melbourne

Victoria President's XV 9 (1G 1PG)   **England XV 26** (3G 2T)
President's XV: T Kelaher (Randwick & NSW); C Smith (Moorabbin), P Gascoigne (Moorabbin), R Sanders (Moorabbin), D I Campese (Randwick & NSW); D J Knox (Randwick & NSW), A Fraser (Melbourne Harlequins); E E Rodriguez (Warringah & NSW), M Alp (Powerhouse), N Raikuna (Moorabbin), S Hughes (Melbourne Harlequins), T Kava (Randwick & NSW), D Williams (Easts) *(capt)*, T Coker (Wests & Queensland), K Stout (Kiwi-Hawthorn) *Replacement* P Cullinan (Powerhouse) for Stout (68 mins)
Scorers *Try:* Sanders   *Conversion:* Knox   *Penalty Goal:* Knox
England XV: Hodgkinson; Hunter, Hopley, Halliday, Oti; Pears, Morris; Rendall, Olver *(capt)*, Pearce, Bayfield, Redman, Skinner, Richards, Rees
Scorers *Tries:* Hunter, Rees, Richards, Hopley, Pears   *Conversions:* Hodgkinson (3)
Referee M Keogh (ACT)

MATCH 3   14 July, Ballymore, Brisbane

Queensland 20 (1G 1PG 1DG 2T)   **England XV 14** (1G 2T)
Queensland: G J Martin (Queensland U); I M Williams (Souths), T J Horan (Souths),
J S Little (Souths), P V Carozza (Wests); M P Lynagh (Queensland U) (*capt*),
P J Slattery (Queensland U); C P Lillicrap (Queensland U), D V Nucifora
(Queensland U), D J Crowley (Souths), R J McCall (Brothers), J A Eales (Brothers),
J S Miller (Queensland U), S J N Scott-Young (Souths), B P Nasser (Queensland U)
Replacement R Moroney (Queensland U) for Crowley (18 mins)
Scorers *Tries:* Carozza, Nasser, Scott-Young   *Conversion:* Lynagh
Penalty Goal: Lynagh   *Dropped Goal:* Lynagh
England XV: Hodgkinson; Underwood, Carling (*capt*), Guscott, Oti; Andrew, Hill;
Leonard, Moore, Pearce, Ackford, Dooley, Teague, Richards, Winterbottom
Scorers *Tries:* Guscott, Hill, Oti   *Conversion:* Hodgkinson
Referee A R MacNeill (NSW)

MATCH 4   16 July, Lautoka

Fiji B 27 (3G 2PG 1DG)   **England XV 13** (3PG 1T)
Fiji B: M Natuilagilagi (Suva); T Lovo (Suva), J Taqaiwai (Rewa), V Koroibulileka
(Suva), S Aria (Nadi); W Serevi (Suva), M Vosanibole (Suva); N Vuli (Lautoka),
D Balewai (Rewa), S Sadria (Suva), A Nadolo (Suva), M Rasari (Suva), P Naruma
(Suva), I Tawake (Nadroga) (*capt*), P Kubuwai (Suva) *Replacements* V Rauluni (Suva) for
Taqaiwai (60 mins); A Koroitamana (Rewa) for Vosanibole (70 mins)
Scorers *Tries:* Serevi, Vosanibole, Tawake   *Conversions:* Serevi (3)
Penalty Goals: Serevi (2)   *Dropped Goal:* Serevi
England XV: Webb; Hunter, Hopley, Halliday, Heslop; Pears, Morris; Rendall, Olver
(*capt*), Pearce, Redman, Bayfield, Hall, Skinner, Rees *Replacements* Guscott for Heslop
(42 mins); Hodgkinson for Pears (50 mins)
Scorers *Try:* Skinner   *Penalty Goals:* Webb (3)
Referee L Colati (Fiji RU)

MATCH 5   20 July, National Stadium, Suva   Test Match
FIJI 12 (1G 1PG 1DG)   ENGLAND 28 (2G 2PG 2DG 1T)

Although the final margin was convincing and deserved, England were
occasionally in such disarray that, had Fiji sorted out their tactics, a
major shock could certainly have been on the cards. But instead of
sticking to their traditional open game, Fiji opted for a succession of ill-
directed drop kicks. With the impetus lost, England – thanks to two
lucky bounces and a splendid try created by a break from Andrew –
cleared the danger.

Fiji had levelled the match at 12-12 in the second half, and Serevi
(who had played brilliantly in Fiji B's midweek defeat of the tourists)
was in excellent form. But England, helped by a fine line-out display
from the new cap, Bayfield, scored a further 16 points in the last 14
minutes to avert a further tour disaster. The late points included tries
for Underwood, from Andrew's incisive break, and for Andrew – his
first in 37 internationals – after a cruel bounce had eluded four players.

FIJI: O Turuva (Saunaka & Nadi); T Vonolagi (Army & Suva), J Taqaiwai
(Duavata & Rewa), V Rauluni (Nabua & Suva), F Seru (Nabua & Suva); W Serevi

(Nabua & Suva), P Tabulutu (Nabua & Suva); E Naituvau (Army & Suva), S Naiviliwasa (Police & Suva), M Taga (QVS OB & Suva) (*capt*), S Domoni (Waimanu & Suva), I Savai (Regent & Nadi), A Dere (Army & Suva), M G Olsson (St John Marist & Suva), I Tawake (Yalovata & Nadroga)
Scorers *Try:* Seru   *Conversion:* Serevi   *Penalty Goal:* Serevi   *Dropped Goal:* Serevi
ENGLAND: Webb; Underwood, Guscott, Carling (*capt*), Oti; Andrew, Hill; Leonard, Moore, Probyn, Redman, Bayfield, Teague, Richards, Rees *Replacement* Skinner for Teague (40 mins)
Scorers *Tries:* Probyn, Underwood, Andrew   *Conversions:* Webb (2)
Penalty Goals: Webb (2)   *Dropped Goals:* Andrew (2)
Referee B Kinsey (Australia)

MATCH 6   23 July, Gosford

Emerging Australians 3 (1PG)   **England XV 36** (3G 1PG 1DG 3T)
Emerging Australians: D J Knox (Randwick & NSW); D K Junee (Eastwood & NSW), C Wells (Drummoyne & NSW), D Maguire (Brothers & Queensland), C Newman (Royals & ACT); J Allen (Norths & NSW), A Macdonald (Randwick & NSW); M Murray (Randwick & NSW) (*capt*), P Palmer (Woollongong & NSW), G Didier (Royals & ACT), T Coker (Wests & Queensland), G Morgan (Souths & Queensland), S J N Scott-Young (Souths & Queensland), S N Tuynman (Eastwood & NSW), D J Wilson (Easts & Queensland) *Replacements* A Blades (Gordon & NSW) for Murray (60 mins); J Fenwick (Sydney U & NSW) for Coker (69 mins)
England XV: Hodgkinson; Hunter, Halliday, Hopley, Heslop; Pears, Morris; Rendall, Olver (*capt*), Pearce, Redman, Ackford, Skinner, Teague, Winterbottom
Scorers *Tries:* Morris (2), Heslop, Hopley, Hunter, Teague   *Conversions:* Hodgkinson (3)   *Penalty Goal:* Hodgkinson   *Dropped Goal:* Pears
Referee M Powell (Queensland)

MATCH 7   27 July, Sydney Football Stadium   Test Match
AUSTRALIA 40 (4G 4PG 1T)   ENGLAND 15 (1G 3PG)

Five tries by Australia left the 1991 Grand Slam winners still searching for their first victory in an international in Australia after seven attempts. Australia followed their previous week's thrashing of Wales with another superb display, recording their biggest ever win over England. The victory was based around a magnificent performance from the Australian pack and on sheer pace and dexterity.

The Man of the Match was the No 8, Gavin, who dominated Richards in the back row. But the performances of Ofahengaue on the flank and the athletic young lock, Eales, were not far behind. The 18-stone Ofahengaue scored two tries, crashing past the English cover. Lynagh became the first player to pass 600 points in international rugby with his match haul of 20, while Campese extended his world try-scoring record to 40. Australia could even afford to allow their captain, Farr-Jones, to rest a niggling hamstring injury. He departed just before the hour.

AUSTRALIA: M C Roebuck (NSW); D I Campese (NSW), T J Horan (Queensland), J S Little (Queensland), R H Egerton (NSW); M P Lynagh (Queensland),

John Eales, already on his way to becoming one of the most influential forwards around, takes a clean catch in front of England's Martin Bayfield during Australia's Test win at the Sydney Football Stadium in 1991.

N C Farr-Jones (NSW) (*capt*); A J Daly (NSW), P N Kearns (NSW), E J A McKenzie (NSW), R J McCall (Queensland), J A Eales (Queensland), S P Poidevin (NSW), B T Gavin (NSW), V Ofahengaue (NSW) *Replacement* P J Slattery (Queensland) for Farr-Jones (56 mins)
Scorers *Tries:* Campese (2), Ofahengaue (2), Roebuck   *Conversions:* Lynagh (4)
Penalty Goals: Lynagh (4)
ENGLAND: Webb; Underwood, Guscott, Carling (*capt*), Oti; Andrew, Hill; Leonard, Moore, Probyn, Ackford, Bayfield, Teague, Richards, Winterbottom
Scorers *Try:* Guscott   *Conversion:* Webb   *Penalty Goals:* Webb (3)
Referee K H Lawrence (New Zealand)

WALES TO AUSTRALIA 1991

With hindsight this was hailed as the tour that should never have taken place. The same sentiments had been expressed after the equally disastrous tour to New Zealand in 1988. In short, Paul Thorburn's team proved once again that Wales don't travel well.

The build-up to the trip had not gone smoothly. Wales had struggled to achieve a draw against Ireland in the Five Nations Championship, had gone down to the Barbarians earlier in the season and travelled with a record 36-3 defeat against the French still very much in mind. If the results on the field were humiliating, some of the incidents off the field merely heaped further shame on the tour party. A post-international fracas between fellow players at Ballymore hit the headlines and led to an official inquest by the Welsh Rugby Union secretary Denis Evans. In his report Evans said he was 'appalled by some of the findings' and set up a code of conduct for all Welsh players to follow. 'The honour of representing Wales carries with it off-the-field responsibilities. Players unable to bear those responsibilities will not be selected to play for Wales. The honour of representing Wales also demands a high level of commitment relevant to the demands of international rugby. I am less than satisfied with that which was displayed in Australia and that again will no longer be tolerated.'

Ron Waldron, the national coach and team manager, resigned from his post shortly after the tour on health grounds and was replaced by Alan Davies, as coach, and Robert Norster, as team manager. The tour captain, and Welsh record points-scorer, Paul Thorburn, also stepped down from the international arena prior to the World Cup.

As far as the tour was concerned, the writing was on the wall after the first match at Perth in which the tourists struggled to overcome Western Australia 22-6. There was a brave fightback against Queensland, where Wales recovered from a 23-6 half-time deficit to 23-20 and then 26-24 in the second half, but they still conceded five tries to four. More alarmingly, they lost the line-out count 22-8 to John Eales and Rod McCall. There was a victory over ACT in ankle-deep mud in Canberra before New South Wales provided a taste of what was to come in the Test with the biggest defeat ever handed out to a Welsh representative side. New South Wales' 71-8 triumph included 13 tries, another record, five of them by David Campese.

THE TOURING PARTY

Captain D C T Rowlands
Coach R Waldron   **Captain** P H Thorburn

FULL-BACKS	THREEQUARTERS
P H Thorburn (Neath)	**I C Evans** (Llanelli)
A Clement (Swansea)	**I Jones** (Llanelli)
L Evans (Llanelli)	**S P Ford** (Cardiff)

I S Gibbs (Neath)
D W Evans (Cardiff)
M R Hall (Cardiff)
S L Lewis (Pontypridd)

HALF-BACKS

N R Jenkins (Pontypridd)
A Davies (Neath)
C Bridges (Neath)
R N Jones (Swansea)

FORWARDS

K Waters (Newbridge)
K H Phillips (Neath)
M Griffiths (Cardiff)

H Williams-Jones (South Wales Police)
P Knight (Pontypridd)
M Davis (Newport)
Glyn D Llewellyn (Neath)
Gareth O Llewellyn (Neath)
P Arnold (Swansea)
R Goodey (Pontypool)
R E Webster (Swansea)
E W Lewis (Llanelli)
R G Collins (Cardiff)
M Morris (Neath)
P T Davies (Llanelli)
*S Legge (Glamorgan Wanderers)

*Replacement for I Hembrow (Cardiff) who withdrew
after selection

TOUR RECORD

All matches Played 6 Won 3 Lost 3 Points for 102 Against 185
International matches Played 1 Lost 1 Points for 6 Against 63

SCORING DETAILS

All Matches					International matches				
For:	17T	5C	3PG	5DG	102 Pts	For:	–	–	1PG	1DG	6 Pts
Against:	31T	17C	9PG	–	185 Pts	Against:	12T	6C	1PG	–	63 Pts

MATCH DETAILS

1991	OPPONENTS	VENUE	RESULT
30 June	Western Australia	Perth	W 22- 6
7 July	Queensland	Brisbane	L 24-35
10 July	Australian Capital Territory	Canberra	W 7- 3
14 July	New South Wales	Sydney	L 8-71
17 July	Queensland Country	Rockhampton	W 35- 7
21 July	AUSTRALIA	Brisbane	L 6-63

*Scorers: 19 – A Davies (5DG 1T); 15 – D W Evans (1PG 4C 1T); 12 – Hall (3T); 8 – R N Jones (2T), L Evans (2T),
Webster (2T); 5 – Thorburn (1PG 1C); 4 – E W Lewis (1T), Clement (1T), Legge (1T), Ford (1T), G O Llewellyn (1T),
penalty try (1T); 3 – Jenkins (1PG)*
*Appearances: 5 – I C Evans, Gibbs, Collins, Arnold (inc 1 as replacement); 4 – Thorburn, Hall, A Davies, Williams-Jones,
G O Llewellyn (inc 1 as replacement), P T Davies, R N Jones (inc 1 as replacement); 3 – Clement (inc 1 as replacement), Ford,
D Evans (inc 1 as replacement), Bridges, Waters, Phillips, Griffiths, M Davis, G D Llewellyn, E W Lewis, Legge; 2 – I
Jones, S L Lewis, Jenkins, Knight, Goodey, Webster, Morris; 1 – L Evans*

MATCH 1 30 June, Perth

Western Australia 6 (2PG) **Wales XV 22** (1PG 1DG 4T)
Western Australia: T M Fearn; J Austin, B Ellison, W B Kini, M Skiffington;
W B Johns, M F Ryburn; R M Walters, A M Box, M Te Paa, J P Welborn, P H Roberts
(*capt*), R W Edwards, T Tamanivalu, R J Smith *Replacement* T Thomas for Roberts
Scorer *Penalty Goals* Johns (2)

Wales XV: Thorburn (*capt*); I C Evans, D W Evans, Gibbs, I Jones; A Davies,
R N Jones; Griffiths, Waters, Williams-Jones, Goodey, G O Llewellyn, E W Lewis,
P T Davies, Collins *Replacement* Legge for P T Davies
Scorers *Tries:* D W Evans, A Davies, E W Lewis, R N Jones *Penalty Goal:* D W Evans
Dropped Goal: A Davies
Referee F Westhuizen (New South Wales)

MATCH 2   7 July, Brisbane

Queensland 35 (3G 3PG 2T)   **Wales XV 24** (1G 2DG 3T)
Queensland: A G Herbert; I M Williams, J Little, T J Horan, P V Carozza; M P Lynagh
(*capt*), P J Slattery; C A Lillicrap, D V Nucifora, R Moroney, R J McCall, J A Eales,
J S Miller, S J N Scott-Young, B P Nasser
Scorers *Tries:* Little, Scott-Young, Slattery, Lillicrap, Lynagh *Conversions:* Lynagh (3)
Penalty Goals: Lynagh (3)
Wales XV: Thorburn (*capt*); I C Evans, Gibbs, Hall, Ford; A Davies, Bridges; Griffiths,
Phillips, Knight, G O Llewellyn, Arnold, Morris, P T Davies, Webster
Replacement R N Jones for Bridges
Scorers *Tries:* Webster (2), Ford, G O Llewellyn *Conversion:* Thorburn
Dropped Goals: A Davies (2)
Referee B M Kinsey (New South Wales)

MATCH 3   10 July, Canberra

Australian Capital Territory 3 (1PG)   **Wales XV 7** (1PG 1T)
Australian Capital Territory: A Apps; C Newman, A Fulivai, B Girvan (*capt*),
A Goodwin; P W Cornish, T Louden; L Donnellan, J Taylor, G L Didier, M McInnes,
C Sweeny, J Ross, P Stejskal, D Carline *Replacement* J Pead for Carline
Scorer *Penalty Goal:* Apps
Wales XV: Clement; I C Evans, Gibbs, S L Lewis, I Jones; Jenkins, R N Jones (*capt*);
M Davis, Waters, Knight, G D Llewellyn, Arnold, E W Lewis, Legge, Collins
Scorers *Try:* Legge *Penalty Goal:* Jenkins
Referee P Thomas (New South Wales)

MATCH 4   14 July, Sydney

New South Wales 71 (8G 1PG 5T)   **Wales XV 8** (2T)
New South Wales: M Roebuck; D I Campese, R Tombs, C Wells, R Egerton; J Allen,
N C Farr-Jones (*capt*); A J Daly, P N Kearns, E J A McKenzie, S A G Cutler, W Waugh,
V Ofahengaue, B T Gavin, S P Poidevin *Replacements* A Ekert for Farr-Jones; M Foldi
for Ofahengaue; D Junee for Wells
Scorers *Tries:* Campese (5), Gavin, Waugh, McKenzie, Egerton, Roebuck, Ekert,
Farr-Jones, penalty try *Conversions:* Roebuck (8) *Penalty Goal:* Roebuck
Wales XV: Thorburn (*capt*); I C Evans, Gibbs, Hall, Ford; Jenkins, R N Jones;
M Davis, Waters, Williams-Jones, G D Llewellyn, Arnold, Webster, P T Davies, Collins
Scorers *Tries:* Hall, R N Jones
Referee B Leask (Queensland)

MATCH 5   17 July, Rockhampton

Queensland Country 7 (1PG 1T)   **Wales XV 35** (4G 1DG 2T)
Queensland Country: P Sprecher; R Leeson, R Constable, D O'Sullivan, D Garnett;
M Busby, M Catchpole; W Kettle, W Shaw, R Moroney, S Thorn, G Morgan, F Perrin,
B Curran (*capt*), A Maneche-Jones *Replacement* M De Rooy for Maneche-Jones
Scorers *Try:* Perrin   *Penalty Goal:* Sprecher
Wales XV: L Evans; Hall, D W Evans, S L Lewis, Clement; A Davies (*capt*), Bridges;
Griffiths, Phillips, Williams-Jones, Goodey, G O Llewellyn, Morris, Legge, Collins
Replacement Arnold for G O Llewellyn
Scorers *Tries:* Hall (2), L Evans (2), Clement, penalty try   *Conversions:* D W Evans (4)
Dropped Goal: A Davies
Referee P Marshall

MATCH 6   22 July, Ballymore Oval, Brisbane   **Test**

AUSTRALIA 63 (6G 1PG 6T)   **WALES 6** (1PG 1DG)

The comments of Wallaby coach Bob Dwyer and captain Nick Farr-Jones in the wake of Wales' heaviest international defeat were both damning and exact in their prediction. 'Wales could struggle to be competitive by the World Cup. If we don't beat them at the Arms Park, and beat them well, I will be disappointed', said Farr-Jones. Having reached a low ebb in Australia, Wales slipped even further from grace when they failed to qualify for the quarter-finals of the World Cup three months later. Australia beat Wales in their group 38-3.

Dwyer's view of his side's 12-try victory, a record number against Wales in an international, was that they were allowed more freedom than when they notched up their previous highest international score, against the USA at the same venue in 1990. The Eagles had been beaten 67-9, while South Korea had perished 65-18 at Ballymore in 1987. Those scores put the Welsh performance into its proper perspective.

It took only two minutes for Tim Horan to bag the first try, and there were 19 points in 18 minutes at the start. It was 23-6 at half-time and 40 points flowed in the second half as Wales slumped to an even worse defeat than they had suffered in the two Tests in New Zealand in 1988. Michael Lynagh added to the 19 points he scored against the tourists for Queensland, coming within one point of his Test best, and one point short of Fergie McCormick's record against Wales, as he scored 23 points. He also missed with eight kicks.

It was a rather inauspicious first cap for the 20-year-old Newport prop Mark Davis, although Marty Roebuck and Rob Egerton enjoyed their debuts on the other side by scoring a try apiece. The other Wallaby newcomer was John Eales. The referee, Fred Howard, surpassed Roger Quittenton's English record of 18 internationals as he took charge of his 19th Test.

AUSTRALIA: M Roebuck (New South Wales); R Egerton (New South Wales),
J S Little (Queensland), T J Horan (Queensland), D I Campese (New South Wales);

M P Lynagh (Queensland), N C Farr-Jones (New South Wales) (*capt*); A J Daly
(New South Wales), P N Kearns (New South Wales), E J A McKenzie
(New South Wales), R J McCall (Queensland), J A Eales (Queensland), V Ofahengaue
(New South Wales), B T Gavin (New South Wales), J S Miller (Queensland)
Replacement P J Slattery (Queensland) for Farr-Jones
Scorers *Tries:* Lynagh (2), Kearns (2), Gavin (2), Roebuck, Campese, Egerton, Horan,
Little, Ofahengaue   *Conversions:* Lynagh (6)   *Penalty Goal:* Lynagh
WALES: Thorburn (*capt*); I C Evans, Hall, Gibbs, Ford; A Davies, Bridges; M Davis,
Phillips, Williams-Jones, G D Llewellyn, Arnold, E W Lewis, P T Davies, Collins
Replacements Clement for Thorburn; D W Evans for Ford; G O Llewellyn for P T Davies
Scorers *Penalty Goal:* Thorburn   *Dropped Goal:* A Davies
Referee F Howard (England)

NEW ZEALAND TO ARGENTINA 1991

New Zealand emerged from a potentially difficult tour with a 100 per cent record from the nine games. In recent seasons England, France and Australia have all been beaten in international meetings with the Pumas, while the All Blacks had been held 21-21 in 1985 at Buenos Aires.

Although the team generally performed below expectations, the management pronounced themselves satisfied with the tour. Coach Alex Wyllie stressed that the trip was experimental, and one in which evidence of the strength in depth of the squad would be an important factor for the forthcoming World Cup.

But well though Fox, Michael Jones (when injury-free), Kirwan Innes, Henderson and Gary Whetton performed, problems did arise. Brewer's injury was to prove important and long-term – he eventually missed the World Cup. Mannix at fly-half and Philpott at full-back did not match up to Fox and Crowley in their general play, and there appeared to be a lack of motivation in the first choice front row. Critics had a field day with the continuing non-selection of Wayne Shelford. Although Tucumán, the champions, and the Pumas B XV gave the tourists hard games, the All Black deficiencies at the very top level were not to be exploited by Argentina. They became apparent later.

THE TOURING PARTY

Manager J A Sturgeon   **Coach** A J Wyllie
Captain G W Whetton

FULL-BACKS

K J Crowley (Taranaki)
S Philpott (Canterbury)

THREEQUARTERS

J J Kirwan (Auckland)
J K R Timu (Otago)
T J Wright (Auckland)
C R Innes (Auckland)
W K Little (North Harbour)
B J McCahill (Auckland)
J T Stanley (Auckland)

HALF-BACKS

G J Fox (Auckland)
S J Mannix (Wellington)
G T M Bachop (Canterbury)
P W McGahan (North Harbour)

FORWARDS

W D Gatland (Waikato)
S B T Fitzpatrick (Auckland)
L C Hullena (Wellington)
S C McDowell (Auckland)
G H Purvis (Waikato)
R W Loe (Waikato)
C D Tregaskis (Wellington)
I D Jones (North Auckland)
S B Gordon (Waikato)
G W Whetton (Auckland)
P W Henderson (Otago)
M N Jones (Auckland)
A T Earl (Canterbury)
A J Whetton (Auckland)
Z V Brooke (Auckland)
M R Brewer (Otago)

TOUR RECORD

All matches   Played 9   Won 9   Points for 358   Against 80
International matches   Played 2   Won 2   Points for 64   Against 20

SCORING DETAILS

All Matches					International matches				
For:	53T 34C 24PG 2DG	358 Pts			For:	6T 5C 9PG 1DG	64 Pts		
Against:	5T 3C 15PG 3DG	80 Pts			Against: 2T	– 4PG –	20 Pts		

MATCH DETAILS

1991	OPPONENTS	VENUE	RESULT
16 June	Rosario Selection	Rosario	W 81- 9
19 June	Cordoba Selection	Cordoba	W 38- 9
22 June	Buenos Aires Selection	Buenos Aires	W 37- 9
25 June	Tucumán Selection	Tucumán	W 21- 9
29 June	Argentina B	Buenos Aires	W 22- 6
2 July	Cuyo Selection	Mendoza	W 47-12
6 July	ARGENTINA	Buenos Aires	W 28-14
9 July	Mar del Plata Selection	Mar del Plata	W 48- 6
13 July	ARGENTINA	Buenos Aires	W 36- 6

Scorers: 74 – Fox (16PG 13C); 52 – Mannix (2T 4PG 16C); 36 – Wright (9T), Timu (9T); 34 – Crowley (2T 4PG 2DG 4C); 32 – Kirwan (8T); 14 – Philpott (3T 1C); 12 – Innes, Brooke, Henderson (3T each); 8 – M N Jones, Fitzpatrick, G W Whetton (2T each); 4 – Bachop, Earl, McCahill, McGahan, A J Whetton (1T each)

MATCH 1   16 June, Rosario

Rosario Selection 9 (1PG 2DG)   **New Zealand XV 81** (9G 1PG 6T)
Rosario Selection: *Penalty Goal:* Crexell   *Dropped Goals:* Bouza, del Castillo
New Zealand XV: *Tries:* Wright (5), Timu (3), GW Whetton (2), Innes, Henderson, Brooke, Mannix, Philpott   *Conversions:* Mannix (8), Philpott
Penalty Goal: Mannix

MATCH 2   19 June, Cordoba

Cordoba Selection 9 (1G 1PG)   **New Zealand XV 38** (4G 2PG 2T)
Cordoba Selection: *Try:* Garzon   *Conversion:* Menendez   *Penalty Goal:* Menendez
New Zealand XV: *Tries:* Timu (2), Crowley (2), Kirwan, Innes   *Conversions:* Fox (4)
Penalty Goals: Fox (2)

MATCH 3   22 June, Buenos Aires

Buenos Aires Selection 9 (1G 1PG)   **New Zealand XV 37** (2G 3PG 4T)
Buenos Aires Selection: *Try:* Lombardi   *Conversion:* Mendez   *Penalty Goal:* Lanfranco
New Zealand XV: *Tries:* Kirwan (3), Wright (2), Bachop   *Conversions:* Mannix (2)
Penalty Goals: Mannix (3)

MATCH 4   25 June, Tucumán

Tucumán Selection 9 (3PG)   **New Zealand XV 21** (2G 3PG)
Tucumán Selection: *Penalty Goals:* Meson (3)
New Zealand XV: *Tries:* A J Whetton, Kirwan   *Conversions:* Fox (2)
Penalty Goals: Fox (3)

MATCH 5   29 June, Buenos Aires

Argentina B 6 (1PG 1DG)   **New Zealand XV 22** (2G 2PG 1T)
Argentina B: *Penalty Goal:* Laborde   *Dropped Goal:* Laborde
New Zealand XV: *Tries:* Kirwan (2), M N Jones   *Conversions:* Fox (2)
Penalty Goals: Fox (2)

MATCH 6   2 July, Mendoza

Cuyo XV 12 (1G 2PG)   **New Zealand XV 47** (4G 4PG 1DG 2T)
Cuyo XV: *Try:* Gomez   *Conversion:* Gioeni   *Penalty Goals:* Gioeni (2)
New Zealand XV: *Tries:* Timu (2), Fitzpatrick (2), Mannix, Philpott
Conversions: Crowley (4)   *Penalty Goals:* Crowley (4)   *Dropped Goal:* Crowley

MATCH 7   6 July, Velez Sarsfield Stadium, Buenos Aires   1st Test

ARGENTINA 14 (2PG 2T)   NEW ZEALAND 28 (1G 5PG 1DG 1T)

New Zealand won the first international thanks to the prolific kicking of Grant Fox, and also through domination of the line-outs, which the tourists won 22-12. But New Zealand had to wait until the 63rd minute to score their first try, and they were pushed all the way by a youthful home team who were anxious to impress after heavy defeats in England and Scotland in 1990, and in New Zealand a year earlier.

The All Blacks led 12-6 at half-time by four Fox penalties to two from the Pumas scrum-half, Vidou. Fox added another penalty goal two minutes into the second half. The Pumas' new captain, Garreton, narrowed the gap with a try in the corner after confusion in the New Zealand defence. New Zealand worries were eased by a spectacular 48-metre dropped goal from full-back Crowley and a try by Earl. Carreras of Argentina and Wright of New Zealand crossed for tries in the closing minutes. Fox's 17 points took his tally in All Blacks matches to a record 791 points, beating Don Clarke's record of 781, which had stood since 1964.

ARGENTINA: G del Castillo (Rosario Jockey Club); M Teran (Tucumán RFC), H M Garcia Simon (Pueyrredon), S Meson (Tucumán RFC), D Cuesta Silva (San Isidro Club); L Arbizu (Belgrano), H Vidou (Buenos Aires Cricket & RFC); F E Mendez (Mendoza RFC), R A Le Fort (Tucumán RFC), D M Cash (San Isidro Club), P Sporleder (Curupayti), G Llanes (La Plata), P A Garreton (University of Tucumán) (*capt*), M Carreras (Olivos), J Santamarina (Tucumán RFC) *Replacement* G Angaut (La Plata) for del Castillo (31 mins)
Scorers *Tries:* Garreton, Carreras   *Penalty Goals:* Vidou (2)
NEW ZEALAND: Crowley; Timu, Innes, Little, Wright; Fox, Bachop; McDowell, Fitzpatrick, Loe, G W Whetton (*capt*), I D Jones, A J Whetton, Henderson, M N Jones *Replacement* Earl for A J Whetton (28 mins)
Scorers *Tries:* Earl, Wright   *Conversion:* Fox   *Penalty Goals:* Fox (5)
Dropped Goal: Crowley
Referee B W Stirling (Ireland)

MATCH 8   9 July, Mar del Plata

Mar del Plata Selection 6 (2PG)   **New Zealand XV 48** (6G 3T)
Mar del Plata: *Penalty Goals:* Gilardi, Cassagna
New Zealand XV: *Tries:* Timu (2), Henderson (2), McGahan, Brooke, McCahill, Innes, Philpott   *Conversions:* Mannix (6)

MATCH 9   13 July, Velez Sarsfield Stadium, Buenos Aires   2nd Test

ARGENTINA 6 (2PG)   NEW ZEALAND 36 (4G 4PG)

New Zealand gave a much-improved display and controlled the second international, which was attended by an Argentinian record crowd of over 47,000 at the Velez Sarsfield Stadium. The tourists scored four tries to add to a 20-point haul from Grant Fox; the Argentinian reply was limited to two penalties by del Castillo.

Stung by criticism of their earlier performances, New Zealand rallied to score their first try through Brooke after 14 minutes, and were ahead 15-3 at the break. Tries followed at regular intervals in the second period, from Michael Jones, Kirwan and Wright. Fox missed just one of nine goal attempts.

New Zealand again dominated the line-outs (25-10) and took the scrums (16-12). Gary Whetton won his 50th cap (the second New Zealander to do so, after Colin Meads with 55), while the performance encouraged coach Wyllie to view the forthcoming Bledisloe Cup games with more confidence in his post-tour comments.

ARGENTINA: G del Castillo (Rosario Jockey Club); M Teran (Tucumán RFC), H M Garcia Simon (Pueyrredon), M Allen (Club Atletico San Isidro), D Cuesta Silva (San Isidro Club); L Arbizu (Belgrano), G Camardon (Alumni); F E Mendez (Mendoza RFC), R A Le Fort (Tucumán RFC), D M Cash (San Isidro Club), P Sporleder (Curupayti), G Llanes (La Plata); P A Garreton (University of Tucumán) (*capt*), M Carreras (Olivos), J Santamarina (Tucumán RFC) *Replacements* S Meson (Tucumán RFC) for Teran (50 mins); G Angaut (La Plata) for Meson (77 mins)
Scorer *Penalty Goals:* del Castillo (2)
NEW ZEALAND: Crowley; Kirwan, Innes, Little, Wright; Fox, Bachop; McDowell, Fitzpatrick, Loe, G W Whetton (*capt*), I D Jones, Earl, Brooke, M N Jones
Scorers *Tries:* Brooke, M N Jones, Kirwan, Wright   *Conversions:* Fox (4)   *Penalty Goals:* Fox (4)
Referee B W Stirling (Ireland)

SCOTLAND TO NORTH AMERICA 1991

Bill McMurtrie

Twice within two months in 1991 Scotland were on the receiving end of Canadian aspirations. Canada beat Scotland 24-4 in the Hong Kong Sevens quarter-finals and followed up with a 24-19 win over the Scottish touring team in the May international in Saint John, New Brunswick. It was the Scots' only defeat after five wins on a tour that took them from coast to coast in Canada as well as across the border for two matches in the United States.

Canada's points in the Saint John match were all from Mark Wyatt's boot whereas Scotland scored two tries. The home captain set a record for international rugby with his eight penalty goals in the match, and his 24 points followed 21 scored in Canada's victory over Japan two weeks earlier. Yet Canada's first victory against one of the world's major rugby nations was thoroughly deserved. The Scots made no excuse that they were well short of full strength and did not award caps for the tour's two Tests, although they treated both matches as internationals.

Douglas Morgan, the former Scotland and Lions scrum-half who was coach on the tour, did not allow the defeat to detract from the value of the overall venture. Bonuses were to be found in the continuing development of players such as Mark Moncrieff, Graham Shiel, Andy Nicol, Stuart Reid, Ronnie Kirkpatrick, Doddie Weir, Andy Macdonald and Alan Watt.

Despite the result of the final match, the Scots had a proud defensive record. They conceded only two tries: Scott Stewart, the British Columbia full-back, scored one in the final minute of the opening match, and Merv Popadynec touched down the other immediately before the interval of the Edmonton match in which the Scots beat Alberta 76-7. Thereafter the tourists played 360 minutes of rugby without giving away a try. In response to those two tries conceded the Scots scored 36, including 14 against Alberta.

THE TOURING PARTY

Captain D S Wyllie   **Manager** D S Paterson
Coach D W Morgan   **Assistant Coach** J R Dixon

FULL-BACK

P W **Dods** (Gala)

THREEQUARTERS

M **Dods** (Gala)
M **Moncrieff** (Gala)
W L **Renwick** (London Scottish)
A G **Stanger** (Hawick)
I C **Jardine** (Stirling County)
R J S **Shepherd** (Edinburgh Academicals)

A G **Shiel** (Melrose)
D S **Wyllie** (Stewart's-Melville FP)

HALF-BACKS

C M **Chalmers** (Melrose)
A D **Nicol** (Dundee HSFP)
G H **Oliver** (Hawick)

FORWARDS

D F **Milne** (Heriot's FP)
G B **Smith** (Moseley)

A G J Watt (Glasgow High/Kelvinside)   **G W Weir** (Melrose)
G D Wilson (Boroughmuir)   **J P Amos** (Gala)
J Allan (Edinburgh Academicals)   **R M Kirkpatrick** (Jedforest)
K S Milne (Heriot's FP)   **G R Marshall** (Selkirk)
A E D Macdonald (Heriot's FP)   **D J Turnbull** (Hawick)
B J Richardson (Edinburgh Academicals)   **S J Reid** (Boroughmuir)

TOUR RECORD
All matches   Played 6   Won 5   Lost 1   Points for 232   Against 67
International matches   Played 2   Won 1   Lost 1   Points for 60   Against 36

SCORING DETAILS
All Matches

For:	36T	23C	14PG	–	232 Pts
Against:	2T	1C	19PG	–	67 Pts

International matches

For:	7T	4C	8PG	60 Pts
Against:	–	–	12PG	36 Pts

MATCH DETAILS

1991	OPPONENTS	VENUE	RESULT
8 May	British Columbia XV	Vancouver	W 29- 9
11 May	Alberta	Edmonton	W 76- 7
15 May	Rugby East (USA)	New York	W 24-12
18 May	UNITED STATES	Hartford, Ct	W 41-12
22 May	Ontario	Toronto	W 43- 3
25 May	CANADA	Saint John, New Brunswick	L 19-24

Points scorers: 56 – P W Dods (10C 12PG); 44 – M Dods (3T 2PG 13C); 20 – Stanger (5T); 16 – Moncrieff (4T), Reid (4T); 12 – Kirkpatrick (3T), Nicol (3T), Watt (3T); 8 – Renwick (2T), Shiel (2T), Wyllie (2T); 4 – Amos (1T), Macdonald (1T), Turnbull (1T), Smith (1T), Wilson (1T)
Appearances: 6 – Weir (inc 1 as replacement), Wyllie; 5 – Reid (inc 1 as replacement), Shiel, Turnbull (inc 1 as replacement); 4 – P W Dods, Kirkpatrick, Macdonald, Moncrieff, Stanger, Watt; 3 – Allan, Amos, Chalmers, M Dods, Marshall, D F Milne, K S Milne, Nicol, Oliver, Renwick, Richardson, Smith; 2 – Jardine, Shepherd, Wilson

MATCH 1   8 May, Thunderbird Stadium, Vancouver

British Columbia XV 9 (1G 1PG)   **Scotland XV 29** (1G 1PG 5T)
British Columbia XV: S Stewart (UBC); J Hurford (James Bay), C Stewart (Meralomas), M Doyle (Kats), S Robinson (Oak Bay Castaways); I Mackay (Kats) (*capt*), J Graf (UBCOB); G Dukelow (Cowinchan), M Cardinal (James Bay), T Knight (Kats), J Knauer (Meralomas), N Hadley (UBCOB), R Frame (Meralomas), M Tupper (UBC), C McKenzie (UBCOB)
Scorers *Try:* S Stewart   *Conversion:* Graf   *Penalty Goal:* Graf
Scotland XV: P W Dods; Stanger, Wyllie (*capt*), Shiel, Moncrieff; Chalmers, Oliver; Wilson, Allan, Smith, Weir, Macdonald, Turnbull, Amos, Marshall *Replacement* Reid for Marshall
Scorers *Tries:* Shiel (2), Moncrieff, Smith, Stanger, Turnbull   *Conversion:* P W Dods
Penalty Goal: P W Dods
Referee D Reordan (USA)

MATCH 2   11 May, Ellerslie Rugby Park, Edmonton

Alberta 7 (1PG 1T)   **Scotland XV 76** (10G 4T)
Alberta: O Davies (Leprechauns); B Bowd (Red Deer Titans), M Walton

(Edmonton Tigers), L Kerr (Calgary Irish), M Popadynec (Calgary Irish); L Williams (Calgary Saints), J Loveday (Calgary Irish) (*capt*); R Washburn (Nor'Westers), G Scott (Tigers), S Barry (CCIAC), K Whitley (Calgary Irish), F Konopaki (CCIAC), G S Falconer (Calgary Hornets), P White (Druids), I Cathery (Calgary Saints)
Replacement T Koch for Barry
Scorers *Try:* Popadynec   *Penalty Goal:* Williams
Scotland XV: M Dods; Moncrieff, Jardine, Wyllie (*capt*), Renwick; Shepherd, Nicol; D F Milne, K S Milne, Watt, Macdonald, Richardson, Turnbull, Kirkpatrick, Reid
Replacement Weir for Richardson
Scorers *Tries:* Moncrieff (3), M Dods (2), Kirkpatrick (2), Renwick (2), Watt (2), Nicol, Reid, Wyllie   *Conversions:* M Dods (10)
Referee A Biddlecombe (Vancouver)

MATCH 3   15 May, Gaelic Park, New York

Rugby East 12 (4PG)   **Scotland XV 24** (3G 2PG)
Rugby East: P Sheehy (Washington); T Ford (Fort Lauderdale), J Walier (Old Blue), T Sullivan (Washington), R Lewis (Washington); G Judge (Hartford), M Pidcock (Boca Raton); L Manga (Philadelphia-Whitemarsh), J Robbins (Washington), S Gootkind (Life Chiropractic), J Keller (Winged Foot), J Duffy (Washington), M Siano (Philadelphia-Whitemarsh), G Lambert (Whiteplains), B Clark (Boston) (*capt*)
Scorer *Penalty Goals:* Judge (4)
Scotland XV: M Dods; Stanger, Wyllie (*capt*), Shiel, Renwick; Shepherd, Nicol; Smith, K S Milne, Watt, Richardson, Weir, Kirkpatrick, Amos, Reid
Scorers *Tries:* Nicol, Stanger, Watt   *Conversions:* M Dods (3)
Penalty Goals: M Dods (2)
Referee M Binning (Potomac)

MATCH 4   18 May, Dillon Stadium, Hartford, Connecticut   Test

UNITED STATES 12 (4PG)   SCOTLAND 41 (3G 5PG 2T)

For the third time in four games the Scots conceded the opening penalty goal when they played the United States at Dillon Stadium beside the old Colt revolver factory in Hartford, Connecticut. The tourists also had to contend with subtle and unsubtle off-the-ball obstruction, and the match was still hanging in the balance, with the Scots leading 15-12, when Marshall's scrummage pick-up let Macdonald in for a try after 55 minutes. The tourists' game stepped up a gear, and four more tries followed, three in the last ten minutes, two each by Reid and Stanger.

First, Chalmers was the pivot for Reid to put Oliver away, and although Williams denied the scrum-half only inches from the goal-line, Reid followed up to score. It was then that the USA made their strongest assault, but when the Scots raised the siege they immediately scored again, Chalmers chipping through for Stanger's first try. Shiel's short pass gave the wing his second, and Reid's other try followed a mazy run by Chalmers.

UNITED STATES: R Nelson (Belmont Shore); R Lewis (Washington), Kevin Higgins (Old Blues), J Burke (Albany Knicks), C Williams (Old Blues); M De Jong

(Denver Barbarians), B Daily (San Jose Seahawks); C Lippert (OMBAC), T Flay (Old Puget Sound), N J Mottram (Boulder), K Swords (Beacon Hill), W Liversee (OMBAC), T Ridnell (Old Puget Sound), R Farley (Philadelphia-Whitemarsh), B Vizard (OMBAC) (*capt*)
Scorer *Penalty Goals:* De Jong (4)
SCOTLAND: P W Dods; Stanger, Wyllie (*capt*), Shiel, Moncrieff; Chalmers, Oliver; D F Milne, Allan, Watt, Macdonald, Weir, Turnbull, Marshall, Reid
Scorers *Tries:* Reid (2), Stanger (2), Macdonald   *Conversions:* P W Dods (3)
Penalty Goals: P W Dods (5)
Referee G Gadjovich (Canada)

MATCH 5   22 May, Fletchers Fields, Toronto

Ontario 3 (1PG)   **Scotland XV 43** (5G 3PG 1T)
Ontario: S MacKinnon (Ajax Wanderers); S Jamieson (Kingston Panthers), C Wilson (Balmy Beach), R Castel (Ottawa Irish), W Lyttleton (Balmy Beach); B Wood (Irish Canadians) (*capt*), A Kirkpatrick (Brampton); M Allison (Brampton), S Valice (Ottawa Irish), S Fitzgerald (Crusaders), G B Rabarts (Irish Canadians), I Middleton (Crusaders), J Tomlinson (Balmy Beach), J Hutchinson (Toronto Barbarians), B Dixon (Brampton) *Replacement* T McGann for Kirkpatrick
Scorer *Penalty Goal:* MacKinnon
Scotland XV: P W Dods; M Dods, Wyllie (*capt*), Jardine, Renwick; Shiel, Nicol; Wilson, K S Milne, Smith, Weir, Richardson, Kirkpatrick, Amos, Marshall
Replacement Turnbull for Marshall
Scorers *Tries:* Amos, M Dods, Kirkpatrick, Nicol, Wilson, Wyllie
Conversions: P W Dods (5)   *Penalty Goals:* P W Dods (3)
Referee M Binning (United States)

MATCH 6   25 May, Canada Games Stadium, Saint John, New Brunswick   Test

CANADA 24 (8PG)   SCOTLAND 19 (1G 3PG 1T)

Scotland, experimenting on tour as well as preparing for the World Cup, went into the Canadian international with only seven capped players, just two in the pack, and the home team knew how to beat the tourists. The Canadian forwards, stronger in upper body, took on the Scots in head-to-head, physical combat and monopolised the second phase until, too late, Scotland found their rucking game and staged a brave comeback that could have turned the match but for their own indiscipline.

MacKinnon and Ennis were big, strong, fast, athletic forwards in the mould of Scottish rugby's ideal, as was Al Charron, the Ontario lock whose tackles on Turnbull and Shiel typified the fury of the Canadian commitment in defence. Time after time the Scots took the ball in to set up mauls only to lose it to the Canadians' ripping expertise, which also did much to counter the Scottish line-out gains by Andy Macdonald and Doddie Weir.

Scotland's scrummage also creaked, and the tourists found that they had nothing by which to exploit the first-half advantage from the stiff, mild wind that breezed in off Kennebecasis Bay. The interval score was

6-6 – two penalty goals by Peter Dods against two kicked for Canada by Wyatt. Three more by Wyatt set Canada up with a 15-6 lead seven minutes after the restart, and Gareth Rees also turned the screws with huge kicks sailing downfield on the wind.

Wyatt scored another penalty goal for Canada before Scotland at last found their feet. Dods initiated the recovery with his fifth penalty goal, and after Shiel's precise kick into the right corner, Reid and Kirkpatrick combined off the base of the five-metre scrum for the former to score, as he had done in the Test against the United States the previous week. Dods converted for 15-18, and Scotland were back in the game. Cool heads were needed, but Watt and Turnbull lost theirs. Watt swung a punch at Evans, Turnbull tackled Rees late, and Wyatt kicked goals from both penalties awarded as a result.

Time was still left for a defiant Scottish response. Oliver revived the flow from a tackle on Shiel, Kirkpatrick released a commendably accurate, long pass to Moncrieff, who was intruding off his own flank, and the Gala wing's inside feed sent Stanger in to score.

CANADA (*British Columbia unless stated*): M Wyatt (*capt*); S Gray, C Stewart, J Lecky, T Woods; G Rees, J Graf; E Evans, M Cardinal, D Jackart, A Charron (Ontario), N Hadley, G MacKinnon, B Breen, G Ennis *Replacement* I Gordon for Charron
Scorer *Penalty Goals:* Wyatt (8)
SCOTLAND: P W Dods; Stanger, Wyllie (*capt*), Shiel, Moncrieff; Chalmers, Oliver; D F Milne, Allan, Watt, Macdonald, Weir, Turnbull, Kirkpatrick, Reid
Scorers *Tries:* Reid, Stanger *Conversion:* P W Dods *Penalty Goals:* P W Dods (3)
Referee S W Griffiths (England)

IRELAND TO NAMIBIA 1991

Ireland's World Cup warm-up tour ended in disaster with defeats in both internationals against Namibia, who were not functioning as a rugby country when the World Cup draw was made and so did not take part. There were mitigating factors for the Irish. There were a number of injuries, including a serious knee ligament problem for Rigney; the tour was out of season and intended as an experiment; and Windhoek, the capital, is over 5,500 feet above sea-level.

Furthermore, Namibia were at the very top of the South African Currie Cup table when they played as South West Africa, and they had already beaten other World Cup qualifiers Italy (17-7 and 33-19), and Zimbabwe (34-15 and 53-9). Only Italy, 4-3 winners on the try count in the second Test, had come close to defeating them.

Ireland were impressed by the Namibian full-back, Stoop, by the wing and captain, Mans, and by the flanker Maritz, all of whom would make many other national XVs. It would not be untruthful to suggest that no Irishman enhanced his reputation. Ralph Keyes, left at home injured, was probably better off there. It seemed that Africa's youngest rugby nation had sent Ireland back to the drawing-board.

THE TOURING PARTY

Manager K Reid   **Coach** C Fitzgerald   **Assistant Coach** J Moloney
Captain P M Matthews

FULL-BACKS

J E Staples (London Irish)
K J Murphy (Cork Constitution)

THREEQUARTERS

S P Geoghegan (London Irish)
B J Mullin (Blackrock College)
D M Curtis (London Irish)
K D Crossan (Instonians)
R W Wallace (Garryowen)
D J Clarke (Dolphin)

HALF-BACKS

V J G Cunningham (St Mary's)
N M P Barry (Garryowen)
R Saunders (London Irish)
L F P Aherne (Lansdowne)

FORWARDS

J J Fitzgerald (Young Munster)
N J Popplewell (Greystones)
D C Fitzgerald (Lansdowne)
G F Halpin (Wanderers)
S J Smith (Ballymena)
T J Kingston (Dolphin)
B J Rigney (Greystones)
N P J Francis (London Irish)
M J Galwey (Shannon)
*D G Lenihan (Cork Constitution)
P M Matthews (Wanderers)
G F Hamilton (NIFC)
P T J O'Hara (Sunday's Well)
B F Robinson (Ballymena)
N P Mannion (Lansdowne)

Replacement during tour

TOUR RECORD

All matches   Played 4   Won 2   Lost 2   Points for 101   Against 61
International matches   Played 2   Lost 2   Points for 21   Against 41

SCORING DETAILS

All Matches

For:	14T 9C	7PG	2DG	101 Pts
Against:	9T 5C	4PG	1DG	61 Pts

International matches

For:	3T 3C	1PG	–	21 Pts
Against:	6T 4C	2PG	1DG	41 Pts

MATCH DETAILS

1991	OPPONENTS	VENUE	RESULT
17 July	Namibia B	Windhoek	W 45-16
20 July	NAMIBIA	Windhoek	L 6-15
23 July	Namibia South Sub-Union	Keetmanschoop	W 35- 4
27 July	NAMIBIA	Windhoek	L 15-26

Scorers: 20 – Wallace (5T); 17 – Mullin (2PG 1DG 4C); 14 – Aherne (1T 2PG 2C); 8 – Barry (2PG 1C), Staples (1T 2C); 4 – Crossan, Galwey, D C Fitzgerald, Cunningham, Smith, Popplewell (1T each), penalty try; 3 – Curtis (1DG), Murphy (1PG)

MATCH 1   17 July, Windhoek

Namibia B 16 (1G 2PG 1T)   **Ireland XV 45** (3G 4PG 1DG 3T)
Namibia B: T Steenkamp; A Greef, W Lotter, G Vermeulen, W Wentzel; M Oliver, J Cermook; R Mostert, S Smith, J Turner, K Goosen, B Malgas, H Brink, A Skinner, A van Rooyen
Scorers *Tries:* Wentzel (2)   *Conversion:* Steenkamp   *Penalty Goals:* Steenkamp (2)
Ireland XV: Murphy; Wallace, Mullin, Clarke, Crossan; Cunningham, Aherne; Popplewell, Smith, D C Fitzgerald, Galwey, Francis, Matthews, *(capt)*, Robinson, O'Hara
Scorers *Tries:* Wallace (2), Crossan, Popplewell, Smith, D C Fitzgerald
Conversions: Mullin (3)   *Penalty Goals:* Mullin (2), Aherne (2)   *Dropped Goal:* Mullin
Referee M Theunissen (Namibia)

MATCH 2   20 July, Windhoek   1st Test

NAMIBIA 15 (1G 2PG 1DG)   **IRELAND 6** (1G)

Ireland slumped to defeat in the first international, and suffered a further blow when lock Brian Rigney was ruled out of the tour and of the World Cup with a cruciate knee ligament injury. Mullin and Geoghegan also finished with injuries, but irrespective of these setbacks the Irish gave a poor display and were deservedly beaten.

An early dropped goal by Coetzee and a converted try from Stoop, who took advantage of indecision in the Irish defence, gave Namibia a 9-0 lead within 20 minutes. Ireland narrowed the gap after 43 minutes with a penalty try after referee Norling penalised a Namibian scrummage collapse. But two penalties by Coetzee snuffed out any hopes of an Irish recovery, and guided his side to their first win over one of the major rugby nations.

NAMIBIA: A Stoop (Wanderers); G Mans (Wanderers) *(capt)*, H Snyman (Wanderers), J Deysel (Trans Namib), E Meyer (United); J Coetzee (Police), B Buitendag (Trans Namb); C Derks (Trans Namb), W Alberts (Waltersbaai), M Grobler (United), A Kotze (Otjivarango), A van der Merwe (Grootfontein), J Barnard (Wanderers), S Losper (United), W Maritz (Police)
Scorers *Try:* Stoop   *Conversion:* Coetzee   *Penalty Goals:* Coetzee (2)
Dropped Goal: Coetzee
IRELAND: Staples; Geoghegan, Mullin, Curtis, Clarke; Cunningham, Saunders; Popplewell, Smith, D C Fitzgerald, Rigney, Francis, Matthews *(capt)*, Robinson, O'Hara *Replacements* Mannion for Rigney (22 mins); Wallace for Geoghegan (74 mins)
Scorers *Try:* penalty try   *Conversion:* Mullin
Referee C Norling (Wales)

MATCH 3   23 July, Keetmanschoop

Namibia South Sub-Union 4 (1T)   **Ireland XV 35** (3G 3PG 2T)
Namibia South Sub-Union: G Bester; K Adriaanse, B Nieuwoudt, A Etsebeth,
B Swartz; H von Wyk, D Karsten; P von Wiedlligh, D O'Callaghan, W Schroer,
K Goosen, E van der Merwe, R Thompson, L Labuschagne, L Descande
Scorer *Try:* von Wiedlligh
Ireland XV: Murphy; Wallace, Curtis, Clarke, Crossan; Barry, Aherne; J J Fitzgerald,
Kingston, Halpin, Lenihan, Galwey, Hamilton, Mannion, O'Hara
Scorers *Tries:* Wallace (3), Aherne, Galwey   *Conversions:* Aherne (2), Barry
Penalty Goals: Barry (2), Murphy
Referee P Coetzer (Windhoek Central)

MATCH 4   27 July, Windhoek   2nd Test
NAMIBIA 26 (3G 2T)   IRELAND 15 (2G 1DG)

Namibia won the series 2-0 when they comfortably defeated Ireland
26-15 in the second international, and by an imposing 5-1 on tries.
Ireland were without their captain, Matthews, who had a stomach
upset. They took an early lead, and were ahead 12-10 at the interval,
but in the second half they were overrun and the tour subsided tamely.

Staples gave Ireland the lead ten minutes into the match with a try
which he converted himself, only for Stoop to touch down seven
minutes later. A try by Coetzee, which he also converted himself, gave
Namibia the lead, but the fourth try of the opening 30 minutes, scored
by Cunningham of Ireland and converted by Staples, gave Ireland the
lead at the break.

The second half was one-way traffic. A procession of tries from Mans
(46 mins), Maritz (on the hour) and Barnard (ten minutes before the
end) – the last two converted by Coetzee – was interrupted only by a
dropped goal for Ireland by Curtis. Namibia will look forward to
challenging as one of Africa's representatives at the 1995 World Cup.

NAMIBIA: A Stoop (Wanderers); G Mans (Wanderers) (*capt*), H Snyman (Wanderers),
J Deysel (Trans Namib), E Meyer (United); J Coetzee (Police), B Buitendag
(Trans Namib); C Derks (Trans Namib), W Alberts (Waltersbaai), M Grobler (United),
A Kotze (Otjivarango), A van der Merwe (Grootfontein), J Barnard (Wanderers),
S Losper (United), W Maritz (Police) *Replacement* A van Rooyen (Wanderers) for Losper
(40 mins)
Scorers *Tries:* Stoop, Coetzee, Mans, Maritz, Barnard   *Conversions:* Coetzee (3)
IRELAND: Staples; Clarke, Mullin, Curtis, Crossan; Cunningham, Saunders (*capt*);
Popplewell, Smith, D C Fitzgerald, Lenihan, Francis, Mannion, Robinson, Hamilton
Replacements Barry for Crossan (40 mins); Galwey for Francis (54 mins)
Scorers *Tries* Staples, Cunningham   *Conversions:* Staples (2)   *Dropped Goal:* Curtis
Referee C Norling (Wales)

FRANCE TO USA 1991

Following the cancellation of a scheduled tour to South Africa, France took their entire World Cup preliminary squad of 36 players to the USA for a mixture of match practice and altitude training at Vail, Denver and Colorado Springs. After some deliberation, France awarded full caps for the two international matches, but many critics suggested that the tourists might have been better advised to have honed their World Cup squad against more competitive nations. The USA also used the tour to finalise their own World Cup plans.

On the credit side, France paraded what American observers considered to be the finest set of threequarters seen in the USA, but were often let down by over-aggressive performances – especially from the Bègles front row – in matches where France were in total command. All told, the French points tally was 154 to 33, with 27 tries scored and none conceded. Their play left happy memories but indiscipline and even brutality did not make them popular tourists. Even in their own training sessions there were clashes. Such ill-temper indicated problems ahead.

THE TOURING PARTY

Manager H Foures   **Coach** D Dubroca   **Assistant Coach** J Trillo
Captain S Blanco

FULL-BACKS

S **Blanco** (Biarritz)
J-L Sadourny (US Colomiers)

THREEQUARTERS

P **Lagisquet** (Bayonne)
P **Saint-André** (Montferrand)
J-P Bullich (Narbonne)
J-B Lafond (Racing Club de France)
P **Hontas** (Biarritz)
S **Viars** (Brive)
P **Sella** (Agen)
F **Mesnel** (Racing Club de France)
R **Frentzel** (Bègles-Bordeaux)
M **Marfaing** (Stade Toulousain)

HALF-BACKS

D **Camberabero** (Béziers)
T **Lacroix** (Dax)
F **Galthié** (US Colomiers)
H **Sanz** (Narbonne)

FORWARDS

G **Lascubé** (Agen)
S **Simon** (Bègles-Bordeaux)
P **Ondarts** (Biarritz)
P **Gimbert** (Bègles-Bordeaux)
P **Gallart** (Béziers)
P **Marocco** (Montferrand)
V **Moscato** (Bègles-Bordeaux)
J-F Tordo (Nice)
O **Roumat** (Dax)
T **Devergie** (Nîmes)
J **Condom** (Biarritz)
J-M Cadieu (Stade Toulousain)
E **Melville** (Toulon)
M **Cecillon** (Bourgoin)
A **Benazzi** (Agen)
E **Champ** (Toulon)
M **Courtiols** (Bègles-Bordeaux)
X **Blond** (Racing Club de France)
L **Cabannes** (Racing Club de France)
P **Benetton** (Agen)

TOUR RECORD

All matches   Played 4   Won 4   Points for 154   Against 33
International matches   Played 2   Won 2   Points for 51   Against 12

SCORING DETAILS

All Matches					International matches				
For:	27T 17C 4PG	–	154 Pts		For:	10T 4C 1PG	–	51 Pts
Against: –	– 10PG 1DG		33 Pts		Against: –	– 4PG	–	12 Pts

MATCH DETAILS

1991	OPPONENTS	VENUE	RESULT
10 July	Western RFU	Vail	W 42-15
13 July	USA	Denver	W 41- 9
17 July	USA B	Colorado Springs	W 61- 6
20 July	USA	Colorado Springs	W 10- 3*

* *Abandoned after 42 minutes due to electrical storm*

Scorers: 43 – Lacroix (2T 3PG 13C); 16 – Viars (4T); 15 – Camberabero (1T 1PG 4C); 12 – Blanco (3T), Sadourny (3T); 8 – Mesnel (2T), Marfaing (2T); 4 – Cecillon, Champ, Courtiols, Cabannes, Hueber, Saint-André, Bullich, Lafond, Hontas (1T each), penalty try

MATCH 1   10 July, Vail

Western RFU 15 (4PG 1DG)   **French XV 42** (6G 2PG)
Western RFU *Penalty Goals:* Hayward (4)   *Dropped Goal:* Hayward
French XV: *Tries:* Viars (2), Marfaing, Hueber, Cabannes, penalty try   *Conversions:* Lacroix (6)   *Penalty Goals:* Lacroix (2)
Referee D Head

MATCH 2   13 July, Denver   1st Test
USA 9 (3PG)   FRANCE 41 (3G 1PG 5T)

This was an exasperating match, full of French flair but ruined by totally unnecessary aggression from their front row. The Bègles trio, notably Simon, seemed more intent on winning physical battles than on concentrating on the game. This was particularly regrettable as their superb threequarters were intent on entertaining a section of American society which expected rugby education as well as a Test match. The need to provide an exhibition of skills was paramount.

However, the French backs did provide scintillating rugby, running in six of the eight tries before 3,500 people at the Denver Barbarians ground. The local side stuck at their task, although three players were replaced after injury and three others carried serious knocks. The half-time score was 21-3, all the American points coming via the boot of O'Brien.

USA: R Nelson (Belmont Shore); K Higgins (Old Blues), M Williams (Aspen), C O'Brien (Old Blues), G Hein (Old Blues); M De Jong (Denver Barbarians), B Daily (San Jose Seahawks); C Lippert (OMBAC), T Flay (Jersey Shore), N Mottram (Boulder), K Swords (Beacon Hill, Boston), W Liversee (OMBAC), B Vizard (OMBAC) *(capt)*, T Ridnell (Old Puget Sound), S Lipman (Santa Monica) *Replacements* E Whitaker (Old Blues) for Higgins (8 mins); P Johnson (Louisville) for Flay (35 mins); R Farley (Philadelphia-Whitemarsh) for Leversee (54 mins)
Scorer *Penalty Goals:* O'Brien (3)
FRANCE: Blanco *(capt)*; Lafond, Sella, Mesnel, Saint-André; Camberabero, Galthié; Simon, Moscato, Gimbert, Cadieu, Roumat, Champ, Cecillon, Courtiols
Replacements Benazzi for Cadieu (62 mins); Tordo for Courtiols (72 mins)

Mark Leech

Olivier Roumat gains possession as the USA's Brian Vizard goes over the top in the first Test in Denver.

Scorers *Tries:* Blanco (2), Lafond, Saint-André, Champ, Courtiols, Cecillon, Mesnel
Conversions: Camberabero (3) *Penalty Goal:* Camberabero
Referee A Adams (South Africa)

MATCH 3   17 July, Colorado Springs

USA B 6 (2PG)   **French XV 61** (7G 1PG 4T)
USA B *Penalty Goals:* O'Brien (2)
French XV *Tries:* Sadourny (3), Hontas (2), Viars (2), Bullich, Lacroix, Marfaing,
Camberabero   *Conversions:* Lacroix (7)   *Penalty Goal:* Lacroix
Referee D Reordan

MATCH 4   20 July, Colorado Springs   2nd Test

USA 3 (1PG)   **FRANCE 10** (1G 1T) *(match abandoned after 42 mins)*

A violent storm caused one of those rare events, an abandoned international. There was torrential rain, with thunder and lightning. When
the scoreboard received a direct hit from lightning, referee Albert
Adams called off the match – the French remembered the death of
Jean-François Phliponeau after he was struck by lightning during a
match in the 1970s. Incidentally, the second French touch-down, by
Blanco, was to be his 38th and last in international rugby.

USA: R Nelson (Belmont Shore); G Hein (Old Blues), M Williams (Aspen), C O'Brien
(Old Blues), E Whitaker (Old Blues); M De Jong (Denver Barbarians), B Daily
(San Jose Seahawks); C Lippert (OMBAC), P Johnson (Louisville), F Paoli
(Denver Barbarians), C Tunnacliffe (Belmont Shore), K Swords (Beacon Hill, Boston),
M Sawicki (Chicago Lions), T Ridnell (Old Puget Sound), R Farley
(Philadelphia-Whitemarsh) *(capt)* *Replacement* J Burke (Albany Knicks) for De Jong
(27 mins)
Scorer *Penalty Goal:* O'Brien
FRANCE: Blanco *(capt)*; Saint-André, Sella, Mesnel, Lagisquet; Camberabero,
Hueber; Lascubé, Marocco, Ondarts, Benazzi, Devergie, Benetton, Melville, Cabannes
Scorers *Tries:* Mesnel, Blanco   *Conversion:* Camberabero
Referee A Adams (South Africa)

AUSTRALIA v NEW ZEALAND 1991

MATCH 1   6 August, Ballymore, Brisbane   1st Test

Australia B 15 (1G 3PG)   **New Zealand B** 21 (1G 5PG)
Australia B *Try:* Herbert   *Conversion:* Knox   *Penalty Goals:* Knox (3)
New Zealand B *Try:* Crossan   *Conversion:* Crossan   *Penalty Goals:* Crossan (5)

MATCH 2   10 August, Sydney Football Stadium

AUSTRALIA 21 (2G 3PG)   NEW ZEALAND 12 (1G 2PG)

Australia, who had already scored 103 points to 21 (and 17 tries to one) in beating Wales and England, consolidated their status as World Cup favourites with another impressive home win.

New Zealand had led 6-0 after a 16th-minute converted try from Ian Jones, but Australia immediately hit back with a try from Tim Gavin, who dived on a loose ball over the New Zealand line.

Australia were held 9-9 by New Zealand at half-time, but they controlled the second half and should have won by a greater margin after dominating in the mauls and in loose play. An impressive Australian defence allowed New Zealand only one late penalty goal in the second half, and the Wallabies secured their second successive win over their great rivals with a Rob Egerton try in the 66th minute, when he poached the ball from John Kirwan's grasp.

AUSTRALIA: M C Roebuck (New South Wales); D I Campese (New South Wales), T J Horan (Queensland), J S Little (Queensland), R H Egerton (New South Wales); M P Lynagh (Queensland), N C Farr-Jones (New South Wales) (*capt*); A J Daly (New South Wales), P N Kearns (New South Wales), E J A McKenzie (New South Wales), R J McCall (Queensland), J A Eales (Queensland), V Ofahengaue (New South Wales), B T Gavin (New South Wales), S P Poidevin (New South Wales)
Scorers *Tries:* Gavin, Egerton   *Conversions:* Lynagh (2)   *Penalty Goals:* Lynagh (3)
NEW ZEALAND: T J Wright (Auckland); J J Kirwan (Auckland), C R Innes (Auckland), W K Little (North Harbour), J K R Timu (Otago); G J Fox (Auckland), G T M Bachop (Canterbury); S C McDowell (Auckland), S B T Fitzpatrick (Auckland), R W Loe (Waikato), I D Jones (North Auckland), G W Whetton (Auckland) (*capt*), M N Jones (Auckland), Z V Brooke (Auckland), A T Earl (Canterbury)
Scorers *Try:* I D Jones   *Conversion:* Fox   *Penalty Goals:* Fox (2)
Referee R J Megson (Scotland)

MATCH 3   20 August, Pukekohe

Counties 12 (1G 2PG)   **Australian XV** 17 (3PG 2T)
Counties *Try:* Adams   *Conversion:* Lloyd   *Penalty Goals:* Lloyd (2)
Australian XV *Tries:* Slattery, Martin   *Penalty Goals:* Knox (3)

MATCH 4   34 August, Eden Park, Auckland   2nd Test

NEW ZEALAND 6 (2PG)   AUSTRALIA 3 (1PG)

New Zealand retained the Bledisloe Cup with a narrow and deserved win against Australia in a match highlighted by a greater commitment from the New Zealand forwards than they had displayed a fortnight earlier in Sydney. The match turned into a kicking duel between Fox and Lynagh, the leading points-scorers in international rugby. Fox converted two of his five penalty attempts, while Lynagh had to be content with a solitary success from seven kicks. Both players had difficulty with a new-design ball, Lynagh failing near the end with two straightforward kicks which, had they been successful, would have taken the match and the Cup.

Although Scottish referee Ken McCartney awarded 32 penalties during the match, the game never threatened to get out of control. New Zealand were well served by Mark Carter, their new cap, who was often first to the breakdown, while Australia missed the services of Gavin, who had been injured in a club game a week earlier.

NEW ZEALAND: T J Wright (Auckland); J J Kirwan (Auckland), C R Innes (Auckland), B J McCahill (Auckland), J K R Timu (Otago); G J Fox (Auckland), G T M Bachop (Canterbury); S C McDowell (Auckland), S B T Fitzpatrick (Auckland), R W Loe (Waikato), I D Jones (North Auckland), G W Whetton (Auckland) (*capt*), M P Carter (Auckland), Z V Brooke (Auckland), M N Jones (Auckland)
Scorer *Penalty Goals:* Fox (2)
AUSTRALIA: M C Roebuck (New South Wales); D I Campese (New South Wales), T J Horan (Queensland), J S Little (Queensland), R H Egerton (New South Wales); M P Lynagh (Queensland), N C Farr-Jones (New South Wales) (*capt*); A J Daly (New South Wales), P N Kearns (New South Wales), E J A McKenzie (New South Wales), R J McCall (Queensland), J A Eales (Queensland), V Ofahengaue (New South Wales), T Coker (Queensland), S P Poidevin (New South Wales)
Scorer *Penalty Goal:* Lynagh
Referee K W McCartney (Scotland)

Peter Bush

Phil Kearns tries to evade the attentions of All Black Steve McDowell in the second Test, which New Zealand won 6-3 to retain the Bledisloe Cup.

WORLD XV IN NEW ZEALAND 1992
(NZRU Centenary celebrations)

Manager B J Lochore (New Zealand) **Coach** I R McGeechan (Scotland)
Assistant coach R Templeton (Australia)

FULL-BACKS

A G Hastings (Watsonians & Scotland)
A J Joubert (OFS & South Africa)

THREEQUARTERS

P Hendriks (Transvaal)
Y Yoshida (Meiji University & Japan)
J C Guscott (Bath & England)
T J Horan (Queensland & Australia)
J S Little (Queensland & Australia)
J P Claassens (Transvaal)
M J Knoetze (Transvaal)

HALF-BACKS

H E Botha (Northern Transvaal, Rovigo
 & South Africa)
D Camberabero (Béziers & France)
N C Farr-Jones (New South Wales &
 Australia)
A D Nicol (Dundee HSFP & Scotland)

FORWARDS

P Fatialofa (Auckland & Western Samoa)

E J A McKenzie (New South Wales &
 Australia)
F E Mendez (Mendoza & Argentina)
D M B Sole (Edinburgh Acads &
 Scotland)
P N Kearns (New South Wales &
 Australia)
U L Schmidt (Northern Transvaal &
 South Africa)
J A Eales (Queensland & Australia)
O Roumat (Dax & France)
P FitzSimons (New South Wales &
 Australia)
G J Whetton (Auckland & New Zealand)
T Coker (Harlequins, Queensland &
 Australia)
G MacKinnon (British Columbia &
 Canada)
W Ofahengaue (New South Wales &
 Australia)
M Cecillon (Bourgoin & France)
A Perelini (Auckland & Western Samoa)
B Nasser (Queensland & Australia)
D B White (London Scottish & Scotland)

TOUR RECORD
All matches   Played 4   Won 2   Lost 2   Points for 143   Against 97

SCORING DETAILS
All Matches
For: 22T 17C 5PG   2DG 143 Pts
Against: 16T   9C 5PG   –   97 Pts

MATCH DETAILS

1992	OPPONENTS	VENUE	RESULT
15 April	Hanan Shield XV	South Canterbury	W 74- 3
18 April	NEW ZEALAND	Christchurch	W 28-14
22 April	NEW ZEALAND	Wellington	L 26-54
25 April	NEW ZEALAND	Auckland	L 15-26

MATCH 1   15 April, Timaru, South Canterbury

Hanan Shield XV 3 (1PG)   **World XV 74** (11G 2T)
Hanan Shield XV: T Bool; S Todd, I Howden, C Gard, C Dorgan; B Fairweather,

B Matthews; R Morgan, S Curie, D McRae, M O'Grady, G Stanley, J Smitheram, D Hinds, J Simpson
Scorer *Penalty Goal:* Fairweather
World XV: Joubert; Hendriks, Claassens, Guscott, Yoshida; Camberabero, Nicol; Sole (*capt*), Schmidt, Mendez, Roumat, Cecillon, Nasser, MacKinnon, White
Replacements Hastings for Joubert; Knoetze for Yoshida; Horan for Claassens; Fatialofa for Sole; Kearns for Schmidt; Ofahengaue for Nasser; Perelini for MacKinnon (all 40 mins)
Scorers *Tries:* Joubert (3), Guscott (2), White (2), Hendriks (2), Ofahengaue, Cecillon, Horan, Nicol *Conversions:* Camberabero (11)
Referee W D Bevan (Wales)

MATCH 2   18 April, Lancaster Park, Christchurch
NEW ZEALAND 14 (2PG 2T)   **WORLD XV 28** (2G 2PG 2DG 1T)
NEW ZEALAND: G J L Cooper (Otago); J J Kirwan (Auckland), W K Little (North Harbour), F Bunce (North Harbour), V L Tuigamala (Auckland); G J Fox (Auckland), G T M Bachop (Canterbury); S C McDowell (Auckland), S B T Fitzpatrick (Auckland) (*capt*), R W Loe (Waikato), I D Jones (North Auckland), M S B Cooksley (Counties), M N Jones (Auckland), P W Henderson (Otago), R S Turner (North Harbour) *Replacement* A R Pene (Otago) for M N Jones (35 mins)
Scorers *Tries:* Turner, Tuigamala *Penalty Goals:* Fox (2)
WORLD XV: Hastings, Knoetze, Horan, Guscott, Hendriks; Camberabero, Nicol; Sole (*capt*), Kearns, Fatialofa, Cecillon, Roumat, MacKinnon, Ofahengaue, White
Replacement Mendez for Fatialofa (49 mins)
Scorers *Tries:* Hendriks (2), Knoetze *Conversions:* Camberabero (2)
Penalty Goals: Hastings, Camberabero *Dropped Goals:* Camberabero (2)
Referee W D Bevan (Wales)

MATCH 3   22 April, Athletic Park, Wellington
NEW ZEALAND 54 (7G 3T)   **WORLD XV 26** (3G 2T)
NEW ZEALAND: G J L Cooper (Otago); J K R Timu (Otago), E Clarke (Auckland), F Bunce (North Harbour), V L Tuigamala (Auckland); W K Little (North Harbour), A D Strachan (Auckland); S C McDowell (Auckland), S B T Fitzpatrick (Auckland) (*capt*), R W Loe (Waikato), B P Larsen (North Harbour), I D Jones (North Auckland), J W Joseph (Otago), P W Henderson (Southland), A R Pene (Otago)
Replacements R S Turner (North Harbour) for Henderson (32 mins); G J Fox (Auckland) for Little (67 mins); J J Kirwan (Auckland) for Cooper (70 mins)
Scorers *Tries:* Cooper (2), Loe (2), Clarke (2), Pene, Tuigamala, Larsen, Strachan *Conversions:* Cooper (6), Fox
WORLD XV: Joubert; Yoshida, Claassens, Guscott, Hendriks; Botha, Farr-Jones (*capt*); McKenzie, Schmidt, Mendez, Roumat, Eales, Perelini, Nasser, Cecillon
Replacements Knoetze for Guscott (40 mins); Coker for Eales (59 mins); Hastings for Joubert (66 mins)
Scorers *Tries:* Yoshida, Eales, Cecillon, Hendriks, Hastings *Conversions:* Botha (3)
Referee D J Bishop (New Zealand)

MATCH 4   25 April, Eden Park, Auckland
NEW ZEALAND 26 (2G 2PG 2T)   **WORLD XV 15** (1G 3PG)
NEW ZEALAND: G J L Cooper (Otago); J J Kirwan (Auckland), F Bunce (North Harbour), E Clarke (Auckland), V L Tuigamala (Auckland); W K Little (North Harbour), A D Strachan (Auckland); S C McDowell (Auckland),

S B T Fitzpatrick (Auckland) *(capt)*, R W Loe (Waikato), I D Jones (North Auckland),
B P Larsen (North Harbour), M N Jones (Auckland), P W Henderson (Southland),
A R Pene (Otago) *Replacement* J W Joseph (Otago) for Henderson (19 mins)
Scorers *Tries:* Pene, Kirwan, Loe, Clarke   *Conversions:* Cooper (2)
Penalty Goals: Cooper (2)
WORLD XV: Hastings; Knoetze, Horan, Claassens, Hendriks; Botha, Farr-Jones
(capt); Sole, Kearns, Fatialofa, Coker, G Whetton, Ofahengaue, MacKinnon, White
Replacements Nicol for Farr-Jones (64 mins); Little for Claassens (65 mins); FitzSimons
for Ofahengaue (76 mins)
Scorers *Try:* Fatialofa   *Conversion:* Botha   *Penalty Goals:* Botha (3)
Referee W D Bevan (Wales)

OTHER TOURS

Italy to Namibia

8 June: Namibia B 15, Italy XV 18 (Windhoek) **11 June:** Welwitschia 6, Italy XV 67 (Walvis Bay) **15 June:** NAMIBIA 17, ITALY 7 (Windhoek) **18 June:** Northern Union 6, Italy XV 48 (Tsumeb) **22 June:** NAMIBIA 33, ITALY 19 (Windhoek)

Japan to USA and Canada

27 April: USA 20, JAPAN 9 (Blaine) **1 May:** Midwest 0, Japan XV 58 (Blaine) **4 May:** USA 27, JAPAN 15 (Chicago) **8 May:** Rugby Canada 23, Japan XV 29 (Edmonton) **11 May:** CANADA 49, JAPAN 26 (Vancouver)

Western Samoa XV to New Zealand

17 April: Waikato 7, Western Samoa XV 16 (Hamilton) **20 April:** Taranaki 15, Western Samoa XV 28 (New Plymouth) **25 April:** Bay of Plenty 22, Western Samoa XV 21 (Rotorua) **28 April:** Auckland 42, Western Samoa XV 3 (Auckland) **1 May:** King Country 12, Western Samoa XV 21 (Te Kuiti)

Fijian XV to New Zealand and Australia

May: Bay of Plenty 31, Fiji XV 42 (Rotorua) **12 May:** Auckland 36, Fiji XV 6 (Auckland) **15 May:** Canterbury 24, Fiji XV 47 (Christchurch) **19 May:** Queensland 40, Fiji XV 13 (Brisbane)

Romania to New Zealand

15 May: Wanganui 18, Romania XV 26 (Wanganui) **18 May:** Horowhenua 12, Romania XV 48 (Levin) **22 May:** Wairarapa Bush 32, Romania XV 25 (Masterton) **25 May:** Hawke's Bay 24, Romania XV 17 (Napier) **29 May:** King Country 6, Romania XV 28 (Taumarunui) **2 June:** Counties 17, Romania XV 30 (Pukekohe) **5 June:** Thames Valley 17, Romania XV 20 (Paeroa) **9 June:** NEW ZEALAND XV 60, ROMANIA 30 (Auckland)

Soviet Union to New Zealand

25 May: Nelson Bays 24, Soviet Union XV 25 (Nelson) **29 May:** Marlborough 16, Soviet Union XV 23 (Blenheim) **1 June:** Canterbury 73, Soviet Union XV 15 (Christchurch) **5 June:** Mid Canterbury 10, Soviet Union XV 33 (Ashburton) **8 June:** Otago 37, Soviet Union XV 11 (Dunedin) **12 June:** Taranaki 38, Soviet Union XV 16 (New Plymouth) **16 June:** NEW ZEALAND XV 56, SOVIET UNION 6 (Hamilton) **18 June:** King Country 15, Soviet Union XV 22 (Te Kuiti)

ENGLAND'S DOMINANT MEN REPEAT THEIR MOMENTOUS SLAM

THE INTERNATIONAL CHAMPIONSHIP 1992
David Llewellyn *Sunday Express*

To win one Grand Slam is impressive; to win a second without pause is momentous. If consistency is the hallmark of greatness there can be little doubt that England's magnificent back-to-back achievement leaves them perched high above their rivals in the Northern Hemisphere.

The gallery of carping and criticism which seems to dog every successful England team in every sport was left like so much flotsam in the wake of some fine all-round performances. Throughout the Championship, England revealed an ability to adapt their game to the prevailing conditions. Unlike in the first Grand Slam of their pair, they did not limit their options. They looked to their pack to win possession and to their goal-kicker to capitalise on every opportunity, but they spread the ball whenever they could and whenever the opposition allowed.

The critics said that the opposition was inferior, but the fact is that England were so much better than the rest. Their preparation, squad strength, coaching and finishing are light years ahead of everyone else's.

If there was some storming rugby during the Championship then there was also some thundering good refereeing – notably in Mr Hilditch's sending off of two Frenchmen in the brutish finish to what had been one of the finest displays of controlled play by England. When will players learn that violence does not equate with virility? The code of French machismo appears to embrace acts of cowardice – kicking an unprotected head, swinging a punch anonymously into a maul – not exactly the stuff of which heroes are made. Mr Hilditch became officially *persona non grata* in one French village. Just how welcome would Moscato and Lascubé, the two dismissed men, be if rural England stooped to such pettiness? Mr Burger of South Africa also made an impression on the French, but while Mr Hilditch needed a police escort to leave the Parc des Princes pitch, Mr Burger was applauded on to the ground when he officiated at the match between France and Ireland.

Much has been done since the Championship ended to repair relations between France and England, yet more could be done if refereeing standards could be unified. To that end, Mr Hilditch subsequently arbitrated in a French championship match and gave a series of talks on what British referees look for in a match. Perhaps there will be less confusion next time round as to the consequences of a player throwing his toys out of his pram when things are not going well.

Elsewhere in the Championship, Ireland were as bad as England were good. It was not easy to see where they would go from their

Jon Webb, one of the Rothmans Five Players of the Year, scores a try for England in Paris. Webb contributed 19 points in the match, and became England's most-capped full-back with 26 appearances.

whitewash – except to New Zealand in the summer. It is rather more difficult to predict whether they can recover soon.

Wales have been there. After the World Cup they were labelled third-rate; now, coach Alan Davies and team manager Bob Norster have been retained after achieving a victory in Cardiff against Scotland as well as an uplifting win in Dublin. They have a long way to go, but they have come a long way, too. Pride was restored; the spirit is there and the players are willing.

Scotland lost a couple of games and most of their legends, but unearthed a handful of new industrial gems in Smith, McIvor and Edwards as well as finding a more than adequate stand-in for the injured Gary Armstrong in scrum-half Nicol.

For the second season running an England player reached 60 points in the Championship. Full-back Jon Webb surpassed his predecessor, Simon Hodgkinson, with a record 67. He numbered three tries among that haul as England set a Championship record of 118 points, including 15 tries. He also played beautifully.

France rediscovered their self-control and, too late to mount a title challenge, their flamboyance and flair. Of the new men, Viars is a veritable points machine and Tordo's speed is startling. If they can put their tempers on the back burner they may get back to where they once belonged.

If there was a player of the Championship it had to be Webb, but not merely for his scoring. He had other good points, not least his incursions into the line, his coolness and courage under the high ball and his catching, tackling and kicking from hand. He also displayed humour, apologising to his breathless team-mates after scoring a try against Ireland just 23 seconds into the match. Will Carling underlined his class; Emyr Lewis of Wales was often awesome; Ian Smith wrote his own tale in Scotland's back row chronicles. Guscott showed that he can give much in the way of strategy and power as well as take chances when they are offered.

Yet the Five Nations was as memorable for its farewells as for England's 'Double Slammy'. Underwood, the deadliest of finishers, finished. Calder and Jeffrey went before the start, as did Ackford and Blanco. Scotland's admirable captain, Sole, waited until the end; not so Mullin, who jumped ship mid-Championship. White has retired, and Lenihan has also gone. A new generation of legends is in the making.

FINAL TABLE

	P	W	D	L	F	A	Pts
England	4	4	0	0	118	29	8
France	4	2	0	2	75	62	4
Scotland	4	2	0	2	47	56	4
Wales	4	2	0	2	40	63	4
Ireland	4	0	0	4	46	116	0

18 January, Lansdowne Road
IRELAND 15 (1G 3PG)   **WALES 16** (3PG 1DG 1T)

This was the day the *hwyl* replaced the howl in Wales. No one was carried away by the slender victory over another struggling side, but the character shown in achieving the win was a small step for British rugby and a giant step for Wales. Yet it took long enough for the Dragons – as the Welsh Rugby Union wish the team to be known – to catch their breath, let alone breathe fire. Ireland had the early passion, possession and position but, fortunately for Wales, little luck. That all went Wales' way for the first 50 minutes, until they got their act together. In retrospect, it was the failure of the Irish to capitalise that shattered their whole season. If they could only have beaten Wales, the optimism of 1991 may have carried through.

Wales should have been down to 14 men after a quarter of an hour when lock Copsey took exception to his opposite number in the line-out and punched the bejasus out of Francis, leaving one of Ireland's key ball-winners groggy. As luck would have it, referee Howard – the last man to send off a Welshman in the Championship when he dismissed Kevin Moseley two years ago – missed the Copsey caper and simply warned the player after a linesman had drawn his attention to the offence. Ireland's Keyes kicked the resultant penalty, his second of the match, and added a third after Stephens (dropped goal) and Jenkins (penalty) had levelled matters for Wales and the Dragon was looking a trifle toothless. When Irish wing Wallace rounded off a rare move by the backs shortly after the restart, Keyes' touchline conversion appeared to be the *coup de grâce*. The recent history of Welsh rugby had shown an almost complete lack of fighting spirit in adversity, and the true test of the supposed new Welsh spirit now arrived.

Character and commitment spearheaded a remarkable turnaround. As the back row asserted themselves and Clement had his best game in a Wales shirt, fortunes swung. Two more Jenkins penalties were crowned by a try for Davies, the debutant at No 8, and Wales had recorded their first Championship win since beating England in 1989.

IRELAND: J E Staples (London Irish); R M Wallace (Garryowen), B J Mullin (Blackrock Coll), D M Curtis (London Irish), K D Crossan (Instonians); R P Keyes (Constitution), R Saunders (London Irish); N J Popplewell (Greystones), S J Smith (Ballymena), D C Fitzgerald (De La Salle/Palmerston), D G Lenihan (Constitution), N P T Francis (Blackrock Coll), P M Matthews (Wanderers) (*capt*), B F Robinson (Ballymena), M J Fitzgibbon (Shannon)
Scorers *Try:* Wallace   *Conversion:* Keyes   *Penalty Goals:* Keyes (3)
WALES: A Clement (Swansea); I C Evans (Llanelli) (*capt*), I S Gibbs (Swansea), N R Jenkins (Pontypridd), M R Hall (Cardiff); C J Stephens (Llanelli), R N Jones (Swansea); M Griffiths (Cardiff), G R Jenkins (Swansea), L Delaney (Llanelli), G O Llewellyn (Neath), A H Copsey (Llanelli), E W Lewis (Llanelli), S Davies (Swansea), R E Webster (Swansea)
Scorers *Try:* Davies   *Penalty Goals:* N R Jenkins (3)   *Dropped Goal:* Stephens
Referee F A Howard (England)

Scott Gibbs on the burst in the welcome win for Wales in Dublin.

18 January, Murrayfield
SCOTLAND 7 (1PG 1T)   ENGLAND 25 (1G 4PG 1DG 1T)

As results go the match looked like a pushover, but it was never that. Scotland shoved the England pack and their reputation all over the place in a first half which was morally a tartan triumph. But it was the Scots' own fault that possession was not transformed into points.

England took the field in their traditional all-white strip after an 11th-hour agreement was reached with Cotton Traders over the redesigned World Cup kit, which was discarded to the joy of traditionalists. Scotland started with two new flankers as Calder and Jeffrey stepped out of the game and into legend. Their replacements, Smith and McIvor, did not let the side down. Gloucester's Smith, trawled up in the Anglo-Scots net after England had let him drift through a qualification loophole, was fast and dangerous in the loose.

Harlequins lock Edwards, who also arrived via the Anglos, competed fiercely and successfully at the line-out. There was no Armstrong, either, but in Nicol Scotland had discovered an able deputy. England were without Ackford (retired), Hill and Richards (both relegated to the bench), as new coach Dick Best and the management followed the form book. Morris was back at scrum-half after a three-year absence while Second Lieutenant Rodber marched into Richards' No 8 jersey.

By the time Rodber was helped from the field with spinal concussion, England's pack had suffered the indignity of conceding a pushover try. Enter Richards on the hour and the England forwards were back to their best, streaming after him like so many iron filings to a magnet. The backs then did their bit. Underwood scored his first try at Murrayfield and Halliday's brilliant, diagonal break scattered Scotland's midfield defence and produced a try for Morris. Webb, having already landed four penalties, converted and Guscott treated the crowd to a marvellous dropped goal. England were home.

SCOTLAND: A G Hastings (Watsonians); A G Stanger (Hawick), S Hastings (Watsonians), S R P Lineen (Boroughmuir), I Tukalo (Selkirk); C M Chalmers (Melrose), A D Nicol (Dundee HSFP); D M B Sole (Edinburgh Acads) (*capt*), K S Milne (Heriot's FP), A P Burnell (London Scottish), N G B Edwards (Harlequins), G W Weir (Melrose), D J McIvor (Edinburgh Acads), D B White (London Scottish), I R Smith (Gloucester)
Scorers *Try:* White   *Penalty Goal:* A G Hastings
ENGLAND: J M Webb (Bath); S J Halliday (Harlequins), W D C Carling (Harlequins) (*capt*), J C Guscott (Bath), R Underwood (RAF & Leicester); C R Andrew (Stade Toulousain), C D Morris (Orrell); J Leonard (Harlequins), B C Moore (Harlequins), J A Probyn (Wasps), M C Bayfield (Northampton), W A Dooley (Preston Grasshoppers), M G Skinner (Harlequins), T A K Rodber (Army & Northampton), P J Winterbottom (Harlequins) *Replacement* D Richards (Leicester) for Rodber
Scorers *Tries:* Underwood, Morris   *Conversion:* Webb   *Penalty Goals:* Webb (4)   *Dropped Goal:* Guscott
Referee W D Bevan (Wales)

1 February, Twickenham
ENGLAND 38 (4G 2PG 2T)   IRELAND 9 (1G 1PG)

Records were smashed, Ireland were crushed, but more importantly, rumours that England could not turn it on were hushed. A virtuoso performance at full-back from Webb, whose 22 points equalled Lambert's 81-year-old Championship record for an England player, was just one of the highlights. There was a satisfying symmetry to Webb's achievement. He opened the scoring with one of the fastest tries in the history of the Championship after 23 seconds and wrapped it all up with his second of the match – which, naturally, he converted – in the last minute. The fact that this was England's highest score against Ireland was irrelevant in the end. More remarkable was the fact that possession was divided 50-50 between the two sides. England were vastly more proficient in using it, whether in the forwards or in the backs. This was perfectly illustrated when hooker Moore and Morris combined beautifully with the interval approaching and the scrum-half touched down for the try.

All this time, Ireland looked to be there or thereabouts. Keyes opened up England's defence with a classic dummy and his conversion levelled matters. Midway through the first half a penalty from the fly-half took the score to Webb 9, Keyes 9 – but that was as far as Ireland's scoring went.

Thereafter, energies were focused on keeping out the marauding English. By the time Underwood had scored his 34th try for England and Halliday had touched down for his first in the Championship, the shattered Irish were reeling to an English tune.

Afterwards captain Carling admitted it had been the hardest and most tiring match he had played in since Australia in 1988. But if the pursuit of excellence is exhausting, at least England had victory to savour. All Ireland coach Fitzgerald and skipper Matthews had in their defence was that this was the finest England performance they had witnessed.

ENGLAND: J M Webb (Bath); S J Halliday (Harlequins), W D C Carling (Harlequins) (*capt*), J C Guscott (Bath), R Underwood (RAF & Leicester); C R Andrew (Stade Toulousain), C D Morris (Orrell); J Leonard (Harlequins), B C Moore (Harlequins), J A Probyn (Wasps), M C Bayfield (Northampton), W A Dooley (Preston Grasshoppers), M G Skinner (Harlequins), T A K Rodber (Army & Northampton), P J Winterbottom (Harlequins)
Scorers *Tries:* Webb (2), Morris, Guscott, Underwood, Halliday   *Conversions:* Webb (4)   *Penalty Goals:* Webb (2)
IRELAND: J E Staples (London Irish); R M Wallace (Garryowen), B J Mullin (Blackrock Coll), D M Curtis (London Irish), S P Geoghegan (London Irish); R P Keyes (Constitution), L F P Aherne (Lansdowne); N J Popplewell (Greystones), S J Smith (Ballymena), G F Halpin (London Irish), M J Galwey (Shannon), N P T Francis (Blackrock Coll), P M Matthews (Wanderers) (*capt*), B F Robinson (Ballymena), M J Fitzgibbon (Shannon)
Scorers *Try:* Keyes   *Conversion:* Keyes   *Penalty Goal:* Keyes
Referee W D Bevan (Wales)

1 February, Cardiff Arms Park
WALES 9 (3PG) FRANCE 12 (1G 1PG 1DG)

The spirit of Dublin was not carried over to this match, another home defeat for Wales. It was a close thing, and Wales could have won because France were poor. Still, it was an historic match, with a first for the Five Nations Championship when French lock Mougeot, clearly more of a sweater than a jumper at the line-out, trotted off just as the match was about to restart after the interval. He was replaced by the more accomplished Roumat, a vastly better line-out man. The official French line was that Mougeot went off suffering from a calf injury. But his unaided and apparently untroubled departure appealed to cynics throughout the Principality: had rugby just experienced its first tactical substitution?

Roumat, who had been warming up for some minutes before Mougeot pulled up lame, certainly made a massive difference to the share of line-out ball, but he added little else to what was unquestionably a mediocre French performance. Wales, who had an abundance of second-half possession but lacked midfield penetration, came back into the game more and more. Sadly, they had to rely on the boot of Jenkins to do this but it was a fightback at least.

Jenkins' three penalties raised hopes of a repeat of the Dublin finish, but Wales did not have quite the composure to steal it. There was no sign of a try as stirring as the one scored by Saint-André for France in the first half, which illustrated French attacking flair and speed of pass at its best. It was a rare enough moment for France, and something beyond Wales on the day.

Afterwards, France added insult to Mougeot's injury by criticising the tactics of the Welsh front row. Referee Doyle penalised France on several occasions for collapsing the scrum, but props Lascubé and Gimbert claimed Griffiths was the culprit. The front row friction sparked off a couple of scuffles during the match and the Frenchmen concluded by saying they preferred playing against England, who, they asserted, had a much stronger set of forwards.

WALES: A Clement (Swansea); I C Evans (Llanelli) (*capt*), I S Gibbs (Swansea), N R Jenkins (Pontypridd), M R Hall (Cardiff); C J Stephens (Llanelli), R N Jones (Swansea); M Griffiths (Cardiff), G R Jenkins (Swansea), L Delaney (Llanelli), G O Llewellyn (Neath), A H Copsey (Llanelli), E W Lewis (Llanelli), S Davies (Swansea), R E Webster (Swansea)
Scorers *Penalty Goals:* N R Jenkins (3)
FRANCE: J-B Lafond (Racing Club de France); P Saint-André (Montferrand), P Sella (Agen) (*capt*), F Mesnel (Racing Club de France), S Viars (Brive); A Penaud (Brive), F Galthié (Colomiers); G Lascubé (Agen), V Moscato (Bègles), P Gimbert (Bègles), J-M Cadieu (Toulouse), C Mougeot (Bègles), J-F Tordo (Nice), M Cecillon (Bourgoin), L Cabannes (Racing Club de France) *Replacement* O Roumat (Dax) for Mougeot
Scorers *Try:* Saint-André *Conversion:* Lafond *Penalty Goal:* Viars
Dropped Goal: Penaud
Referee O E Doyle (Ireland)

15 February, Parc des Princes
FRANCE 13 (1G 1PG 1T)   ENGLAND 31 (3G 3PG 1T)

The evil that players do lives after them; the good is often buried under the wrong sort of headlines. So it was in Paris. England gave a clinical performance: a fine try by Webb which set him on the path to 19 points in the match; dominance in most phases of the game; rock steady defence and self-control throughout. All this and England's all-round excellence will probably be forgotten thanks to ten minutes of madness and mayhem.

What will be remembered is the sight of referee Hilditch being escorted off the pitch by a phalanx of security men, having sent off two French players towards the end of the match. Another, Tordo, should have followed Lascubé and Moscato as the French approach degenerated.

Gimbert flattened Moore, who had already suffered an attempt at eye-gouging by a French forward within the first two minutes as the match erupted in ugly fashion. The authorities acted swiftly, and 90 minutes after the final whistle Lascubé and Moscato had been banned from all rugby until 1 September. Moscato promptly told the world he was going to take up boxing and Lascubé refereeing. The debate raged long after the match. Many Frenchmen felt that their players were being victimised in an Anglo-Saxon conspiracy, although later FFR president Lapasset ordered the team, and also French rugby as a whole, to put its house in order.

France had earlier lost their captain, Philippe Sella, with a gashed scalp. Shortly after his departure the rest of the team lost their heads. It detracted from a magnificent England victory. They were far from boring: an exhilarating performance helped them to beat their own Championship record of 90 points with one match remaining and a second successive Grand Slam a distinct possibility.

On the way Webb became England's most capped full-back on his 26th appearance and Richards their most-capped No 8 with 32. France used all three replacements, a Five Nations first.

FRANCE: J-B Lafond (Racing Club de France); P Saint-André (Montferrand), P Sella (Agen) (*capt*), F Mesnel (Racing Club de France), S Viars (Brive); A Penaud (Brive), F Galthié (Colomiers); G Lascubé (Agen), V Moscato (Bègles), P Gimbert (Bègles), M Cecillon (Bourgoin), C Mougeot (Bègles), J-F Tordo (Nice), A van Heerden (Tarbes), L Cabannes (Racing Club de France) *Replacements* J-L Sadourny (Colomiers) for Sella; O Roumat (Dax) for Mougeot; P Montlaur (Agen) for Sadourny
Scorers *Tries:* Viars, Penaud   *Conversion:* Viars   *Penalty Goal:* Viars
ENGLAND: J M Webb (Bath); S J Halliday (Harlequins), W D C Carling (Harlequins) (*capt*), J C Guscott (Bath), R Underwood (RAF & Leicester); C R Andrew (Stade Toulousain), C D Morris (Orrell); J Leonard (Harlequins), B C Moore (Harlequins), J A Probyn (Wasps), M C Bayfield (Northampton), W A Dooley (Preston Grasshoppers), M G Skinner (Harlequins), D Richards (Leicester), P J Winterbottom (Harlequins) *Replacement* D Pears (Harlequins) for Andrew
Scorers *Tries:* Webb, Underwood, Morris, penalty try   *Conversions:* Webb (3)
Penalty Goals: Webb (3)
Referee S R Hilditch (Ireland)

The drama is only beginning as Steve Hilditch of Ireland sends off Gregoire Lascubé of France. He was later to dismiss Vincent Moscato as England thundered to victory.

15 February, Lansdowne Road
IRELAND 10 (2PG 1T)   SCOTLAND 18 (2G 2PG)

Everything went wrong for Ireland. Dublin became the unfair city, the city of boos, as fly-half Keyes suffered the humiliation of home crowd jeers every time he touched, or more correctly, kicked, the ball. The unfortunate Keyes began well, as did Ireland. The forwards won possession from Keyes' kick-off. He received the ball again and followed up with a perfectly-judged grub kick. Left wing Geoghegan pounced on to the ball and raced over the Scotland line. That was the end of the good news for Ireland. Referee Spreadbury adjudged Geoghegan to have been offside at Keyes' kick and the score was disallowed.

From that point on, Keyes could not put a foot right. His kicking was not just inept, it was abysmal. If he didn't go directly to touch then the ball unerringly found the welcoming arms of Gavin Hastings, and when Keyes did hoof it over the goal-line invariably there was not an Irish threequarter in sight. It is little wonder the crowd was frustrated, but surely the voicing of that frustration could and should have been more muted. It couldn't have helped Keyes.

It didn't help Ireland much, either – not that they had much answer to any aspect of Scotland's play. The Scottish back row of White, Smith and McIvor was outstanding, while Weir had a comfortable afternoon in the line-out against Francis. Scrum-half Nicol once again made life without Armstrong bearable for Scotland and capped an admirable performance with a try. Gavin Hastings converted that and Stanger's 14th try in 22 games, which rounded off a superb 26th-minute move in which White featured prominently.

Needless to say, Keyes failed to convert Wallace's try ten minutes from the final whistle, but it would have been a travesty if the Irish had got any closer to the Scots. Certainly, this second home defeat condemned them to a whitewash as they were hardly in the form or frame of mind to win in Paris, as it proved.

IRELAND: K J Murphy (Constitution); R M Wallace (Garryowen), B J Mullin (Blackrock Coll), P P A Danaher (Garryowen), S P Geoghegan (London Irish); R P Keyes (Constitution), L F P Aherne (Lansdowne); N J Popplewell (Greystones), S J Smith (Ballymena), G F Halpin (London Irish), M J Galwey (Shannon), N P T Francis (Blackrock Coll), P M Matthews (Wanderers) (*capt*), B F Robinson (Ballymena), M J Fitzgibbon (Shannon) *Replacements* D C Fitzgerald (De La Salle/Palmerston) for Halpin; D M Curtis (London Irish) for Geoghegan
Scorers *Try:* Wallace   *Penalty Goals:* Keyes (2)
SCOTLAND: A G Hastings (Watsonians); A G Stanger (Hawick), S Hastings (Watsonians), S R P Lineen (Boroughmuir), I Tukalo (Selkirk); C M Chalmers (Melrose), A D Nicol (Dundee HSFP); D M B Sole (Edinburgh Acads) (*capt*), K S Milne (Heriot's FP), A P Burnell (London Scottish), N G B Edwards (Harlequins), G W Weir (Melrose), D J McIvor (Edinburgh Acads), D B White (London Scottish), I R Smith (Gloucester) *Replacement* R I Wainwright (Edinburgh Acads) for Edwards
Scorers *Tries:* Stanger, Nicol   *Conversions:* A G Hastings (2)
Penalty Goals: A G Hastings (2)
Referee A Spreadbury (England)

7 March, Twickenham
ENGLAND 24 (3G 2PG)   WALES 0

This match was a piece of history. England won a back-to-back Grand Slam for the first time since 1924, when Wavell Wakefield's team achieved the feat. But if it was England's season, then it was Dooley's day. It was the giant lock's 50th cap. Carling invited Dooley to lead out the side and the Preston Grasshopper rounded off a superb occasion by scoring a try near the end.

More records toppled. England's 118 points surpassed the 102 amassed in the 1976 Championship by Wales. Full-back Webb, surely the player of the tournament, finished with 67 points in the four matches, beating the previous individual mark of 60 set by the admirable Hodgkinson in 1991. Webb's fine all-round display against Wales also helped him to become England's leading points-scorer with 246 from 27 matches, eclipsing the 240 in 25 of Dusty Hare.

If the match lacked some pace and panache it was due more to the fact that Wales, although they failed to score at Twickenham for the first time since the scoreless draw of 1962, harried and hassled throughout. It was a spirited, rather than a negative, performance by Wales, who had to recover from yet another tyre-squealing start by England when Carling barged past Clement to touch down after 61 seconds. England were 15 points up within half an hour.

Wales' response was to sit on defence. They did it better than many. With little to offer in attack they concentrated their efforts on keeping England out, and managed to do so for fully three quarters of an hour. Admittedly, the Welsh cause was helped by some poor handling and disappointing finishing by England as they showed the signs of a long, hard 15 months of high-pressure, high-profile international rugby. But at least Carling and his men were invariably able to rectify their mistakes.

Dooley's final flourish, when he took a short pass from Andrew and crashed over for his third international try, was an heroic end to an historic season – the stuff of which legends are made.

ENGLAND: J M Webb (Bath); S J Halliday (Harlequins), W D C Carling (Harlequins) (*capt*), J C Guscott (Bath), R Underwood (RAF & Leicester); C R Andrew (Stade Toulousain), C D Morris (Orrell); J Leonard (Harlequins), B C Moore (Harlequins), J A Probyn (Wasps), M C Bayfield (Northampton), W A Dooley (Preston Grasshoppers), M G Skinner (Harlequins), D Richards (Leicester), P J Winterbottom (Harlequins) *Replacement* N Heslop (Orrell) for Carling
Scorers *Tries:* Carling, Skinner, Dooley   *Conversions:* Webb (3)
Penalty Goals: Webb (2)
WALES: A Clement (Swansea); I C Evans (Llanelli) (*capt*), N R Jenkins (Pontypridd), I S Gibbs (Swansea), M R Hall (Cardiff); C J Stephens (Llanelli), R N Jones (Swansea); M Griffiths (Cardiff), G R Jenkins (Swansea), L Delaney (Llanelli), G O Llewellyn (Neath), A H Copsey (Llanelli), M S Morris (Neath), S Davies (Swansea), R W Webster (Swansea) *Replacement* M Rayer (Cardiff) for Clement
Referee R J Megson (Scotland)

7 March, Murrayfield
SCOTLAND 10 (2PG 1T)   FRANCE 6 (2PG)

France did not win the match but they won the battle against themselves as they put the memory of the double sending-off and general indiscipline against England in Paris behind them. It could be argued that concentrating on self-control lost the French some of their flair as well as their sense of direction – Weir's superb tackle on Lafond was less significant on closer inspection since the French wing was running laterally across his 22.

Scotland found plenty to be pleased about, though, despite a paucity of points. Firstly, there was victory – appropriately enough on captain Sole's final home appearance before his retirement. It was also White's last Murrayfield match, as he too had decided to quit international rugby at the end of the season. White treated the crowd to some stirring stuff as he set a record for a Scottish No 8 in winning his 28th cap and pulled off the tackle of the match to prevent Mesnel scoring what looked to be a certain try.

White's performance highlighted a second plus for the Scots, their defence. It is now 14 years since France last won at Murrayfield, and coach Berbizier acknowledged that the Scottish defence was first-class, although he did add that he felt the French backs showed little inventiveness when they had the ball, which was frequently. One or two of the older French backs seemed lacking in ideas and appetite.

Scotland opened the scoring after just four minutes. Full-back Gavin Hastings found touch with a clever kick just a couple of yards from the French line. Weir was made the target man by the French and that gave Edwards, the Harlequins lock, an untroubled catch. Sole and Burnell drove the delighted Anglo over for his first international try. Edwards' try was cause for a double celebration: he had been backed at 40-1 by his brother Philip to score the first try of the match. One other winner was South African referee Freek Burger, who earned praise for his handling throughout. He appeared to have the sympathy of both sets of players.

SCOTLAND: A G Hastings (Watsonians); A G Stanger (Hawick), S Hastings (Watsonians), S R P Lineen (Boroughmuir), I Tukalo (Selkirk); C M Chalmers (Melrose), A D Nicol (Dundee HSFP); D M B Sole (Edinburgh Acads) *(capt)*, K S Milne (Heriot's FP), A P Burnell (London Scottish), N G B Edwards (Harlequins), G W Weir (Melrose), D J McIvor (Edinburgh Acads), D B White (London Scottish), R I Wainwright (Edinburgh Acads)
Scorers *Try:* Edwards   *Penalty Goals:* A G Hastings (2)
FRANCE: J-L Sadourny (Colomiers); J-B Lafond (Racing Club de France), P Sella (Agen) *(capt)*, F Mesnel (Racing Club de France), P Saint-André (Montferrand); A Penaud (Brive), F Galthié (Colomiers); L Armary (Lourdes), J-P Genet (Racing Club de France), P Gallart (Béziers), M Cecillon (Bourgoin), O Roumat (Dax), J-F Tordo (Nice), A van Heerden (Tarbes), L Cabannes (Racing Club de France)
Scorer *Penalty Goals:* Lafond (2)
Referee F Burger (South Africa)

21 March, Cardiff
WALES 15 (1G 3PG)   **SCOTLAND 12** (3PG 1DG)

Even if the standard of play was not of the highest, there was every reason for Wales to celebrate their first Championship win at home for three seasons. It proved that the new coaching regime of Davies and Norster had salvaged something from the wreckage of the previous couple of years. Scotland were left kicking themselves, having missed a hatful of goals as well as having failed to capitalise on a ten-minute period of intense pressure when the ultimately admirable Welsh defence creaked a touch.

Wales survived, and deservedly so. Webster's decisive try, scored after a powerful burst by Wales prop Williams-Jones at the end of a messy, tense first quarter, was just what they needed. It put their noses in front and Scotland's out of joint, for two minutes earlier the Scots had pulled level thanks to a Chalmers dropped goal.

Scotland did appear to have scored a try midway through the second half when wing Tukalo charged down a kick and dived on the ball over the line, but he was adjudged to have knocked on and the score was disallowed.

It was not a happy half for the Scots. They lost prop Paul Burnell with a knee injury after an hour. He was replaced by Gloucester's Peter Jones, who won his first cap. As usual, his club colleague Smith on the flank had a fine game, but for all his efforts, and those of the rest of the pack, they lacked something behind the scrum. So did Wales, particularly at fly-half where Neil Jenkins had a wretched time, wasting drop-outs and opportunities in a nervy-looking performance. His goal-kicking, however, was once again thoroughly accurate, as three penalties and a conversion demonstrated. The arrival of the steely Bidgood in the centre certainly seemed to give them a midfield heart.

Self-respect is back in Wales. Two wins in the Championship was an unthinkable scenario before the start of the tournament: now here they were, complete with the right spirit and having relinquished their grip on the wooden spoon. That transformation was worthy of celebration.

WALES: A Clement (Swansea); I C Evans (Llanelli) (*capt*), R A Bidgood (Newport), I S Gibbs (Swansea), M R Hall (Cardiff); N R Jenkins (Pontypridd), R N Jones (Swansea); M Griffiths (Cardiff), G R Jenkins (Swansea), H Williams-Jones (South Wales Police), G O Llewellyn (Neath), A H Copsey (Llanelli), E W Lewis (Llanelli), S Davies (Swansea), R E Webster (Swansea)
Scorers *Try:* Webster   *Conversion:* N R Jenkins   *Penalty Goals:* N R Jenkins (3)
SCOTLAND: A G Hastings (Watsonians); A G Stanger (Hawick), S Hastings (Watsonians), S R P Lineen (Boroughmuir), I Tukalo (Selkirk); C M Chalmers (Melrose), A D Nicol (Dundee HSFP); D M B Sole (Edinburgh Acads) (*capt*), K S Milne (Heriot's FP), A P Burnell (London Scottish), N G B Edwards (Harlequins), G W Weir (Melrose), D J McIvor (Edinburgh Acads), D B White (London Scottish), I R Smith (Gloucester) *Replacement* P M Jones (Gloucester) for Burnell
Scorers *Penalty Goals:* Chalmers (2), A G Hastings   *Dropped Goal:* Chalmers
Referee M Desclaux (France)

21 March, Parc des Princes
FRANCE 44 (5G 2PG 2T)   **IRELAND 12** (4PG)

Brendan Mullin must have known something. After 45 international appearances and a record 15 tries for his country, he must have had a premonition that Ireland's last match in the Five Nations Championship would produce their heaviest defeat ever. Mullin retired three weeks before the match, leaving Ireland in disarray.

At least he volunteered – Keyes, top scorer and hero of the World Cup for Ireland was demoted to the bench and replaced by McAleese. Phil Matthews' injury meant not only a new flanker, Hogan, but also a new captain. Danaher was handed that burden, and it was unfortunate for him that France chose the occasion to return to what they do best – playing fast and glorious rugby.

If bursts of French flair were fitful, at least they were there. Seven tries is an impressive haul, and when a player such as Viars picks up 24 points – a record for one player – teams like Ireland have no way back. They were not so much lambs to the slaughter as tethered goats. It seemed a far cry from the start of the season and from Ireland's marvellous performance against Australia in the World Cup quarter-final.

Penaud ran in two tries and Viars also scored a couple in addition to his five conversions and two penalties. All Ireland could manage were four penalty goals from the boot of McAleese. And while the absence of Blanco is still lamented in France the French could take heart from Sadourny, whose try echoed some of the best efforts of his illustrious predecessor at full-back.

Coach Berbizier declared himself satisfied with his team who, he felt, had sorted out not only their problems of self-discipline but also how to use the ball effectively. For Ireland the future was black, literally so since their tour of New Zealand and the waiting All Blacks loomed. Coach Fitzgerald claimed he was not bothered by the huge margin, but even he, the optimist, was downcast. The subsequent tour of New Zealand proved that he had every reason to be.

FRANCE: J-L Sadourny (Colomiers); P Saint-André (Montferrand), P Sella (Agen) (*capt*), F Mesnel (Racing Club de France), S Viars (Brive); A Penaud (Brive), A Hueber (Toulon); L Armary (Lourdes), J-P Genet (Racing Club de France), P Gallart (Béziers), J-M Cadieu (Toulouse), O Roumat (Dax), J-F Tordo (Nice), M Cecillon (Bourgoin), L Cabannes (Racing Club de France) *Replacement* J-B Lafond (Racing Club de France) for Saint-André
Scorers *Tries:* Viars (2), Penaud (2), Cecillon, Cabannes, Sadourny
Conversions: Viars (5)   *Penalty Goals:* Viars (2)
IRELAND: K J Murphy (Constitution); R M Wallace (Garryowen), D M Curtis (London Irish), P P A Danaher (Garryowen) (*capt*), S P Geoghegan (London Irish); D R McAleese (Ballymena), L F P Aherne (Lansdowne); N J Popplewell (Greystones), S J Smith (Ballymena), G F Halpin (London Irish), B J Rigney (Greystones), M J Galwey (Shannon), P Hogan (Garryowen), B F Robinson (Ballymena), M J Fitzgibbon (Shannon)
Scorers *Penalty Goals:* McAleese (4)
Referee F Burger (South Africa)

RESULTS OF INTERNATIONAL MATCHES (*up to 31 March 1992*)

Cap matches only
Years for Five Nations' matches are for the second half of the season: eg 1972 means season 1971-72. Years for matches against touring teams from the Southern Hemisphere refer to the actual year of the match.

Points-scoring was first introduced in 1886, when an International Board was formed by Scotland, Ireland and Wales. Points values varied between countries until 1890, when England agreed to join the Board, and uniform values were adopted.
WC indicates a fixture played during the Rugby World Cup.

Northern Hemisphere seasons	Try	Conversion	Penalty goal	Dropped goal	Goal from mark
1890-91	1	2	2	3	3
1891-92 to 1892-93	2	3	3	4	4
1893-94 to 1904-05	3	2	3	4	4
1905-06 to 1947-48	3	2	3	4	3
1948-49 to 1970-71	3	2	3	3	3
1971-72 onwards	4	2	3	3	3*

*The goal from mark ceased to exist when free kick clause was introduced, 1977-78.

ENGLAND v SCOTLAND
Played 109   England won 53, Scotland won 39, Drawn 17

1871 Raeburn Place (Edinburgh) **Scotland** 1G 1T to 1T
1872 The Oval (London) **England** 1G 1DG 2T to 1DG
1873 Glasgow **Drawn** no score
1874 The Oval **England** 1DG to 1T
1875 Raeburn Place **Drawn** no score
1876 The Oval **England** 1G 1T to 0
1877 Raeburn Place **Scotland** 1 DG to 0
1878 The Oval **Drawn** no score
1879 Raeburn Place **Drawn** Scotland 1DG England 1G
1880 Manchester **England** 2G 3T to 1G
1881 Raeburn Place **Drawn** Scotland 1G 1T England 1DG 1T
1882 Manchester **Scotland** 2T to 0
1883 Raeburn Place **England** 2T to 1T
1884 Blackheath (London) **England** 1G to 1T
1885 No Match
1886 Raeburn Place **Drawn** no score
1887 Manchester **Drawn** 1T each
1888 No Match
1889 No Match
1890 Raeburn Place **England** 1G 1T to 0
1891 Richmond (London) **Scotland** 9-3
1892 Raeburn Place **England** 5-0
1893 Leeds **Scotland** 8-0
1894 Raeburn Place **Scotland** 6-0
1895 Richmond **Scotland** 6-3
1896 Glasgow **Scotland** 11-0
1897 Manchester **England** 12-3

1898 Powderhall (Edinburgh) **Drawn** 3-3
1899 Blackheath **Scotland** 5-0
1900 Inverleith (Edinburgh) **Drawn** 0-0
1901 Blackheath **Scotland** 18-3
1902 Inverleith **England** 6-3
1903 Richmond **Scotland** 10-6
1904 Inverleith **Scotland** 6-3
1905 Richmond **Scotland** 8-0
1906 Inverleith **England** 9-3
1907 Blackheath **Scotland** 8-3
1908 Inverleith **Scotland** 16-10
1909 Richmond **Scotland** 18-8
1910 Inverleith **England** 14-5
1911 Twickenham **England** 13-8
1912 Inverleith **Scotland** 8-3
1913 Twickenham **England** 3-0
1914 Inverleith **England** 16-15
1920 Twickenham **England** 13-4
1921 Inverleith **England** 18-0
1922 Twickenham **England** 11-5
1923 Inverleith **England** 8-6
1924 Twickenham **England** 19-0
1925 Murrayfield **Scotland** 14-11
1926 Twickenham **Scotland** 17-9
1927 Murrayfield **Scotland** 21-13
1928 Twickenham **England** 6-0
1929 Murrayfield **Scotland** 12-6
1930 Twickenham **Drawn** 0-0
1931 Murrayfield **Scotland** 28-19
1932 Twickenham **England** 16-3
1933 Murrayfield **Scotland** 3-0
1934 Twickenham **England** 6-3

1935 Murrayfield **Scotland** 10-7
1936 Twickenham **England** 9-8
1937 Murrayfield **England** 6-3
1938 Twickenham **Scotland** 21-16
1939 Murrayfield **England** 9-6
1947 Twickenham **England** 24-5
1948 Murrayfield **Scotland** 6-3
1949 Twickenham **England** 19-3
1950 Murrayfield **Scotland** 13-11
1951 Twickenham **England** 5-3
1952 Murrayfield **England** 19-3
1953 Twickenham **England** 26-8
1954 Murrayfield **England** 13-3
1955 Twickenham **England** 9-6
1956 Murrayfield **England** 11-6
1957 Twickenham **England** 16-3
1958 Murrayfield **Drawn** 3-3
1959 Twickenham **Drawn** 3-3
1960 Murrayfield **England** 21-12
1961 Twickenham **England** 6-0
1962 Murrayfield **Drawn** 3-3
1963 Twickenham **England** 10-8
1964 Murrayfield **Scotland** 15-6
1965 Twickenham **Drawn** 3-3
1966 Murrayfield **Scotland** 6-3
1967 Twickenham **England** 27-14
1968 Murrayfield **England** 8-6

1969 Twickenham **England** 8-3
1970 Murrayfield **Scotland** 14-5
1971 Twickenham **Scotland** 16-15
1971 Murrayfield **Scotland** 26-6
Special Centenary match – non-championship
1972 Murrayfield **Scotland** 23-9
1973 Twickenham **England** 20-13
1974 Murrayfield **Scotland** 16-14
1975 Twickenham **England** 7-6
1976 Murrayfield **Scotland** 22-12
1977 Twickenham **England** 26-6
1978 Murrayfield **England** 15-0
1979 Twickenham **Drawn** 7-7
1980 Murrayfield **England** 30-18
1981 Twickenham **England** 23-17
1982 Murrayfield **Drawn** 9-9
1983 Twickenham **Scotland** 22-12
1984 Murrayfield **Scotland** 18-6
1985 Twickenham **England** 10-7
1986 Murrayfield **Scotland** 33-6
1987 Twickenham **England** 21-12
1988 Murrayfield **England** 9-6
1989 Twickenham **Drawn** 12-12
1990 Murrayfield **Scotland** 13-7
1991 Twickenham **England** 21-12
1991 Murrayfield *WC* **England** 9-6
1992 Murrayfield **England** 25-7

ENGLAND v IRELAND
Played 105   England won 61, Ireland won 36, Drawn 8

1875 The Oval (London) **England** 1G
  1DG 1T to 0
1876 Dublin **England** 1G 1T to 0
1877 The Oval **England** 2G 2T to 0
1878 Dublin **England** 2G 1T to 0
1879 The Oval **England** 2G 1DG 2T to 0
1880 Dublin **England** 1G 1T to 1T
1881 Manchester **England** 2G 2T to 0
1882 Dublin **Drawn** 2T each
1883 Manchester **England** 1G 3T to 1T
1884 Dublin **England** 1G to 0
1885 Manchester **England** 2T to 1T
1886 Dublin **England** 1T to 0
1887 Dublin **Ireland** 2G to 0
1888 No Match
1889 No Match
1890 Blackheath (London) **England** 3T
  to 0
1891 Dublin **England** 9-0
1892 Manchester **England** 7-0
1893 Dublin **England** 4-0
1894 Blackheath **Ireland** 7-5
1895 Dublin **England** 6-3
1896 Leeds **Ireland** 10-4
1897 Dublin **Ireland** 13-9
1898 Richmond (London) **Ireland** 9-6
1899 Dublin **Ireland** 6-0
1900 Richmond **England** 15-4
1901 Dublin **Ireland** 10-6
1902 Leicester **England** 6-3

1903 Dublin **Ireland** 6-0
1904 Blackheath **England** 19-0
1905 Cork **Ireland** 17-3
1906 Leicester **Ireland** 16-6
1907 Dublin **Ireland** 17-9
1908 Richmond **England** 13-3
1909 Dublin **England** 11-5
1910 Twickenham **Drawn** 0-0
1911 Dublin **Ireland** 3-0
1912 Twickenham **England** 15-0
1913 Dublin **England** 15-4
1914 Twickenham **England** 17-12
1920 Dublin **England** 14-11
1921 Twickenham **England** 15-0
1922 Dublin **England** 12-3
1923 Leicester **England** 23-5
1924 Belfast **England** 14-3
1925 Twickenham **Drawn** 6-6
1926 Dublin **Ireland** 19-15
1927 Twickenham **England** 8-6
1928 Dublin **England** 7-6
1929 Twickenham **Ireland** 6-5
1930 Dublin **Ireland** 4-3
1931 Twickenham **Ireland** 6-5
1932 Dublin **England** 11-8
1933 Twickenham **England** 17-6
1934 Dublin **England** 13-3
1935 Twickenham **England** 14-3
1936 Dublin **Ireland** 6-3
1937 Twickenham **England** 9-8

1938 Dublin **England** 36-14
1939 Twickenham **Ireland** 5-0
1947 Dublin **Ireland** 22-0
1948 Twickenham **Ireland** 11-10
1949 Dublin **Ireland** 14-5
1950 Twickenham **England** 3-0
1951 Dublin **Ireland** 3-0
1952 Twickenham **England** 3-0
1953 Dublin **Drawn** 9-9
1954 Twickenham **England** 14-3
1955 Dublin **Drawn** 6-6
1956 Twickenham **England** 20-0
1957 Dublin **England** 6-0
1958 Twickenham **England** 6-0
1959 Dublin **England** 3-0
1960 Twickenham **England** 8-5
1961 Dublin **Ireland** 11-8
1962 Twickenham **England** 16-0
1963 Dublin **Drawn** 0-0
1964 Twickenham **Ireland** 18-5
1965 Dublin **Ireland** 5-0
1966 Twickenham **Drawn** 6-6
1967 Dublin **England** 8-3
1968 Twickenham **Drawn** 9-9
1969 Dublin **Ireland** 17-15

1970 Twickenham **England** 9-3
1971 Dublin **England** 9-6
1972 Twickenham **Ireland** 16-12
1973 Dublin **Ireland** 18-9
1974 Twickenham **Ireland** 26-21
1975 Dublin **Ireland** 12-9
1976 Twickenham **Ireland** 13-12
1977 Dublin **England** 4-0
1978 Twickenham **England** 15-9
1979 Dublin **Ireland** 12-7
1980 Twickenham **England** 24-9
1981 Dublin **England** 10-6
1982 Twickenham **Ireland** 16-15
1983 Dublin **Ireland** 25-15
1984 Twickenham **England** 12-9
1985 Dublin **Ireland** 13-10
1986 Twickenham **England** 25-20
1987 Dublin **Ireland** 17-0
1988 Twickenham **England** 35-3
1988 Dublin **England** 21-10
Non-championship match
1989 Dublin **England** 16-3
1990 Twickenham **England** 23-0
1991 Dublin **England** 16-7
1992 Twickenham **England** 38-9

ENGLAND v WALES
Played 98   England won 39, Wales won 47, Drawn 12

1881 Blackheath (London) **England** 7G 1DG 6T to 0
1882 No Match
1883 Swansea **England** 2G 4T to 0
1884 Leeds **England** 1G 2T to 1G
1885 Swansea **England** 1G 4T to 1G 1T
1886 Blackheath **England** 1GM 2T to 1G
1887 Llanelli **Drawn** no score
1888 No Match
1889 No Match
1890 Dewsbury **Wales** 1T to 0
1891 Newport **England** 7-3
1892 Blackheath **England** 17-0
1893 Cardiff **Wales** 12-11
1894 Birkenhead **England** 24-3
1895 Swansea **England** 14-6
1896 Blackheath **England** 25-0
1897 Newport **Wales** 11-0
1898 Blackheath **England** 14-7
1899 Swansea **Wales** 26-3
1900 Gloucester **Wales** 13-3
1901 Cardiff **Wales** 13-0
1902 Blackheath **Wales** 9-8
1903 Swansea **Wales** 21-5
1904 Leicester **Drawn** 14-14
1905 Cardiff **Wales** 25-0
1906 Richmond (London) **Wales** 16-3
1907 Swansea **Wales** 22-0
1908 Bristol **Wales** 28-18
1909 Cardiff **Wales** 8-0
1910 Twickenham **England** 11-6
1911 Swansea **Wales** 15-11
1912 Twickenham **England** 8-0

1913 Cardiff **England** 12-0
1914 Twickenham **England** 10-9
1920 Swansea **Wales** 19-5
1921 Twickenham **England** 18-3
1922 Cardiff **Wales** 28-6
1923 Twickenham **England** 7-3
1924 Swansea **England** 17-9
1925 Twickenham **England** 12-6
1926 Cardiff **Drawn** 3-3
1927 Twickenham **England** 11-9
1928 Swansea **England** 10-8
1929 Twickenham **England** 8-3
1930 Cardiff **England** 11-3
1931 Twickenham **Drawn** 11-11
1932 Swansea **Wales** 12-5
1933 Twickenham **Wales** 7-3
1934 Cardiff **England** 9-0
1935 Twickenham **Drawn** 3-3
1936 Swansea **Drawn** 0-0
1937 Twickenham **England** 4-3
1938 Cardiff **Wales** 14-8
1939 Twickenham **England** 3-0
1947 Cardiff **England** 9-6
1948 Twickenham **Drawn** 3-3
1949 Cardiff **Wales** 9-3
1950 Twickenham **Wales** 11-5
1951 Swansea **Wales** 23-5
1952 Twickenham **Wales** 8-6
1953 Cardiff **England** 8-3
1954 Twickenham **England** 9-6
1955 Cardiff **Wales** 3-0
1956 Twickenham **Wales** 8-3
1957 Cardiff **England** 3-0

1958 Twickenham **Drawn** 3-3
1959 Cardiff **Wales** 5-0
1960 Twickenham **England** 14-6
1961 Cardiff **Wales** 6-3
1962 Twickenham **Drawn** 0-0
1963 Cardiff **England** 13-6
1964 Twickenham **Drawn** 6-6
1965 Cardiff **Wales** 14-3
1966 Twickenham **Wales** 11-6
1967 Cardiff **Wales** 34-21
1968 Twickenham **Drawn** 11-11
1969 Cardiff **Wales** 30-9
1970 Twickenham **Wales** 17-13
1971 Cardiff **Wales** 22-6
1972 Twickenham **Wales** 12-3
1973 Cardiff **Wales** 25-9
1974 Twickenham **England** 16-12
1975 Cardiff **Wales** 20-4

1976 Twickenham **Wales** 21-9
1977 Cardiff **Wales** 14-9
1978 Twickenham **Wales** 9-6
1979 Cardiff **Wales** 27-3
1980 Twickenham **England** 9-8
1981 Cardiff **Wales** 21-19
1982 Twickenham **England** 17-7
1983 Cardiff **Drawn** 13-13
1984 Twickenham **Wales** 24-15
1985 Cardiff **Wales** 24-15
1986 Twickenham **England** 21-18
1987 Cardiff **Wales** 19-12
1987 Brisbane *WC* **Wales** 16-3
1988 Twickenham **Wales** 11-3
1989 Cardiff **Wales** 12-9
1990 Twickenham **England** 34-6
1991 Cardiff **England** 25-6
1992 Twickenham **England** 24-0

ENGLAND v FRANCE

Played 68   England won 37, France won 24, Drawn 7

1906 Paris **England** 35-8
1907 Richmond (London) **England** 41-13
1908 Paris **England** 19-0
1909 Leicester **England** 22-0
1910 Paris **England** 11-3
1911 Twickenham **England** 37-0
1912 Paris **England** 18-8
1913 Twickenham **England** 20-0
1914 Paris **England** 39-13
1920 Twickenham **England** 8-3
1921 Paris **England** 10-6
1922 Twickenham **Drawn** 11-11
1923 Paris **England** 12-3
1924 Twickenham **England** 19-7
1925 Paris **England** 13-11
1926 Twickenham **England** 11-0
1927 Paris **France** 3-0
1928 Twickenham **England** 18-8
1929 Paris **England** 16-6
1930 Twickenham **England** 11-5
1931 Paris **France** 14-13
1947 Twickenham **England** 6-3
1948 Paris **France** 15-0
1949 Twickenham **England** 8-3
1950 Paris **France** 6-3
1951 Twickenham **France** 11-3
1952 Paris **England** 6-3
1953 Twickenham **England** 11-0
1954 Paris **France** 11-3
1955 Twickenham **France** 16-9
1956 Paris **France** 14-9
1957 Twickenham **England** 9-5
1958 Paris **England** 14-0
1959 Twickenham **Drawn** 3-3

1960 Paris **Drawn** 3-3
1961 Twickenham **Drawn** 5-5
1962 Paris **France** 13-0
1963 Twickenham **England** 6-5
1964 Paris **England** 6-3
1965 Twickenham **England** 9-6
1966 Paris **France** 13-0
1967 Twickenham **France** 16-12
1968 Paris **France** 14-9
1969 Twickenham **England** 22-8
1970 Paris **France** 35-13
1971 Twickenham **Drawn** 14-14
1972 Paris **France** 37-12
1973 Twickenham **England** 14-6
1974 Paris **Drawn** 12-12
1975 Twickenham **France** 27-20
1976 Paris **France** 30-9
1977 Twickenham **France** 4-3
1978 Paris **France** 15-6
1979 Twickenham **England** 7-6
1980 Paris **England** 17-13
1981 Twickenham **France** 16-12
1982 Paris **England** 27-15
1983 Twickenham **France** 19-15
1984 Paris **France** 32-18
1985 Twickenham **Drawn** 9-9
1986 Paris **France** 29-10
1987 Twickenham **France** 19-15
1988 Paris **France** 10-9
1989 Twickenham **England** 11-0
1990 Paris **England** 26-7
1991 Twickenham **England** 21-19
1991 Paris *WC* **England** 19-10
1992 Paris **England** 31-13

ENGLAND v NEW ZEALAND

Played 16   England won 3, New Zealand won 13, Drawn 0

1905 Crystal Palace (London) **New Zealand** 15-0
1925 Twickenham **New Zealand** 17-11

1925 Twickenham **New Zealand** 17-11
1936 Twickenham **England** 13-0
1954 Twickenham **New Zealand** 5-0

1963 *1* Auckland **New Zealand** 21-11
    2 Christchurch **New Zealand** 9- 6
    New Zealand won series 2-0
1964 Twickenham **New Zealand** 14-0
1967 Twickenham **New Zealand** 23-11
1973 Twickenham **New Zealand** 9-0
1973 Auckland **England** 16-10
1978 Twickenham **New Zealand** 16-6

1979 Twickenham **New Zealand** 10-9
1983 Twickenham **England** 15-9
1985 *1* Christchurch **New Zealand** 18-13
    2 Wellington **New Zealand** 42- 15
    New Zealand won series 2-0
1991 Twickenham *WC* **New Zealand** 18-12

ENGLAND v SOUTH AFRICA
Played 9   England won 2, South Africa won 6, Drawn 1

1906 Crystal Palace (London) **Drawn** 3-3
1913 Twickenham **South Africa** 9-3
1932 Twickenham **South Africa** 7-0
1952 Twickenham **South Africa** 8-3
1961 Twickenham **South Africa** 5-0

1969 Twickenham **England** 11-8
1972 Johannesburg **England** 18-9
1984 *1* Port Elizabeth **South Africa** 33-15
    2 Johannesburg **South Africa** 35-9
    South Africa won series 2-0

ENGLAND v AUSTRALIA
Played 18   England won 6, Australia won 12, Drawn 0

1909 Blackheath (London) **Australia** 9-3
1928 Twickenham **England** 18-11
1948 Twickenham **Australia** 11-0
1958 Twickenham **England** 9-6
1963 Sydney **Australia** 18-9
1967 Twickenham **Australia** 23-11
1973 Twickenham **England** 20-3
1975 *1* Sydney **Australia** 16-9
    2 Brisbane **Australia** 30-21
    Australia won series 2-0

1976 Twickenham **England** 23-6
1982 Twickenham **England** 15-11
1984 Twickenham **Australia** 19-3
1987 Sydney *WC* **Australia** 19-6
1988 *1* Brisbane **Australia** 22-16
    2 Sydney **Australia** 28-8
    Australia won series 2-0
1988 Twickenham **England** 28-19
1991 Sydney **Australia** 40-15
1991 Twickenham *WC* **Australia** 12-6

ENGLAND v NEW ZEALAND NATIVES
Played 1   England won 1

1889 Blackheath **England** 1G 4T to 0

ENGLAND v RFU PRESIDENT'S XV
Played 1   President's XV won 1

1971 Twickenham **President's XV** 28-11

ENGLAND v ARGENTINA
Played 5   England won 3, Argentina won 1, Drawn 1

1981 *1* Buenos Aires **Drawn** 19-19
    2 Buenos Aires **England** 12-6
    England won series 1-0 with 1 draw

1990 *1* Buenos Aires **England** 25-12
    2 Buenos Aires **Argentina** 15-13
    Series drawn 1-1
1990 Twickenham **England** 51-0

ENGLAND v ROMANIA
Played 2   England won 2

1985 Twickenham **England** 22-15

1989 Bucharest **England** 58-3

ENGLAND v JAPAN
Played 1   England won 1

1987 Sydney *WC* **England** 60-7

ENGLAND v UNITED STATES
Played 2   England won 2

1987 Sydney *WC* **England** 34-6	1991 Twickenham *WC* **England** 37-9

ENGLAND v FIJI
Played 3   England won 3

1988 Suva **England** 25-12	1991 Suva **England** 28-12
1989 Twickenham **England** 58-23	

ENGLAND v ITALY
Played 1   England won 1

1991 Twickenham *WC* **England** 36-6

SCOTLAND v IRELAND
Played 104   Scotland won 54, Ireland won 45, Drawn 4, Abandoned 1

1877 Belfast **Scotland** 4G 2DG 2T to 0	1914 Dublin **Ireland** 6-0
1878 No Match	1920 Inverleith **Scotland** 19-0
1879 Belfast **Scotland** 1G 1DG 1T to 0	1921 Dublin **Ireland** 9-8
1880 Glasgow **Scotland** 1G 2DG 2T to 0	1922 Inverleith **Scotland** 6-3
1881 Belfast **Ireland** 1DG to 1T	1923 Dublin **Scotland** 13-3
1882 Glasgow **Scotland** 2T to 0	1924 Inverleith **Scotland** 13-8
1883 Belfast **Scotland** 1G 1T to 0	1925 Dublin **Scotland** 14-8
1884 Raeburn Place (Edinburgh) **Scotland** 2G 2T to 1T	1926 Murrayfield **Ireland** 3-0
	1927 Dublin **Ireland** 6-0
1885 Belfast **Abandoned** Ireland 0 Scotland 1T	1928 Murrayfield **Ireland** 13-5
	1929 Dublin **Scotland** 16-7
1885 Raeburn Place **Scotland** 1G 2T to 0	1930 Murrayfield **Ireland** 14-11
1886 Raeburn Place **Scotland** 3G 1DG 2T to 0	1931 Dublin **Ireland** 8-5
	1932 Murrayfield **Ireland** 20-8
1887 Belfast **Scotland** 1G 1GM 2T to 0	1933 Dublin **Scotland** 8-6
1888 Raeburn Place **Scotland** 1G to 0	1934 Murrayfield **Scotland** 16-9
1889 Belfast **Scotland** 1DG to 0	1935 Dublin **Ireland** 12-5
1890 Raeburn Place **Scotland** 1DG 1T to 0	1936 Murrayfield **Ireland** 10-4
1891 Belfast **Scotland** 14-0	1937 Dublin **Ireland** 11-4
1892 Raeburn Place **Scotland** 2-0	1938 Murrayfield **Scotland** 23-14
1893 Belfast **Drawn** 0-0	1939 Dublin **Ireland** 12-3
1894 Dublin **Ireland** 5-0	1947 Murrayfield **Ireland** 3-0
1895 Raeburn Place **Scotland** 6-0	1948 Dublin **Ireland** 6-0
1896 Dublin **Drawn** 0-0	1949 Murrayfield **Ireland** 13-3
1897 Powderhall (Edinburgh) **Scotland** 8-3	1950 Dublin **Ireland** 21-0
	1951 Murrayfield **Ireland** 6-5
1898 Belfast **Scotland** 8-0	1952 Dublin **Ireland** 12-8
1899 Inverleith (Edinburgh) **Ireland** 9-3	1953 Murrayfield **Ireland** 26-8
1900 Dublin **Drawn** 0-0	1954 Belfast **Ireland** 6-0
1901 Inverleith **Scotland** 9-5	1955 Murrayfield **Scotland** 12-3
1902 Belfast **Ireland** 5-0	1956 Dublin **Ireland** 14-10
1903 Inverleith **Scotland** 3-0	1957 Murrayfield **Ireland** 5-3
1904 Dublin **Scotland** 19-3	1958 Dublin **Ireland** 12-6
1905 Inverleith **Ireland** 11-5	1959 Murrayfield **Ireland** 8-3
1906 Dublin **Scotland** 13-6	1960 Dublin **Scotland** 6-5
1907 Inverleith **Scotland** 15-3	1961 Murrayfield **Scotland** 16-8
1908 Dublin **Ireland** 16-11	1962 Dublin **Scotland** 20-6
1909 Inverleith **Scotland** 9-3	1963 Murrayfield **Scotland** 3-0
1910 Belfast **Scotland** 14-0	1964 Dublin **Scotland** 6-3
1911 Inverleith **Ireland** 16-10	1965 Murrayfield **Ireland** 16-6
1912 Dublin **Ireland** 10-8	1966 Dublin **Scotland** 11-3
1913 Inverleith **Scotland** 29-14	1967 Murrayfield **Ireland** 5-3

Scotland's Ian Smith is tackled in the 1992 International Championship match against Ireland. The Scots won 18-10 to record their 54th victory over the Irish.

1968 Dublin **Ireland** 14-6
1969 Murrayfield **Ireland** 16-0
1970 Dublin **Ireland** 16-11
1971 Murrayfield **Ireland** 17-5
1972 No Match
1973 Murrayfield **Scotland** 19-14
1974 Dublin **Ireland** 9-6
1975 Murrayfield **Scotland** 20-13
1976 Dublin **Scotland** 15-6
1977 Murrayfield **Scotland** 21-18
1978 Dublin **Ireland** 12-9
1979 Murrayfield **Drawn** 11-11
1980 Dublin **Ireland** 22-15

1981 Murrayfield **Scotland** 10-9
1982 Dublin **Ireland** 21-12
1983 Murrayfield **Ireland** 15-13
1984 Dublin **Scotland** 32-9
1985 Murrayfield **Ireland** 18-15
1986 Dublin **Scotland** 10-9
1987 Murrayfield **Scotland** 16-12
1988 Dublin **Ireland** 22-18
1989 Murrayfield **Scotland** 37-21
1990 Dublin **Scotland** 13-10
1991 Murrayfield **Scotland** 28-25
1991 Murrayfield *WC* **Scotland** 24-15
1992 Dublin **Scotland** 18-10

SCOTLAND v WALES

Played 96   Scotland won 41, Wales won 53, Drawn 2

1883 Raeburn Place (Edinburgh)
    Scotland 3G to 1G
1884 Newport **Scotland** 1DG 1T to 0
1885 Glasgow **Drawn** no score
1886 Cardiff **Scotland** 2G 1T to 0
1887 Raeburn Place **Scotland** 4G 8T to 0
1888 Newport **Wales** 1T to 0
1889 Raeburn Place **Scotland** 2T to 0
1890 Cardiff **Scotland** 1G 2T to 1T
1891 Raeburn Place **Scotland** 15-0
1892 Swansea **Scotland** 7-2
1893 Raeburn Place **Wales** 9-0
1894 Newport **Wales** 7-0
1895 Raeburn Place **Scotland** 5-4
1896 Cardiff **Wales** 6-0
1897 No Match
1898 No Match
1899 Inverleith (Edinburgh) **Scotland**
    21-10
1900 Swansea **Wales** 12-3
1901 Inverleith **Scotland** 18-8
1902 Cardiff **Wales** 14-5
1903 Inverleith **Scotland** 6-0
1904 Swansea **Wales** 21-3
1905 Inverleith **Wales** 6-3
1906 Cardiff **Wales** 9-3
1907 Inverleith **Scotland** 6-3
1908 Swansea **Wales** 6-5
1909 Inverleith **Wales** 5-3
1910 Cardiff **Wales** 14-0
1911 Inverleith **Wales** 32-10
1912 Swansea **Wales** 21-6
1913 Inverleith **Wales** 8-0
1914 Cardiff **Wales** 24-5
1920 Inverleith **Scotland** 9-5
1921 Swansea **Scotland** 14-8
1922 Inverleith **Drawn** 9-9
1923 Cardiff **Scotland** 11-8
1924 Inverleith **Scotland** 35-10
1925 Swansea **Scotland** 24-14
1926 Murrayfield **Scotland** 8-5
1927 Cardiff **Scotland** 5-0
1928 Murrayfield **Wales** 13-0
1929 Swansea **Wales** 14-7
1930 Murrayfield **Scotland** 12-9

1931 Cardiff **Wales** 13-8
1932 Murrayfield **Wales** 6-0
1933 Swansea **Scotland** 11-3
1934 Murrayfield **Wales** 13-6
1935 Cardiff **Wales** 10-6
1936 Murrayfield **Wales** 13-3
1937 Swansea **Scotland** 13-6
1938 Murrayfield **Scotland** 8-6
1939 Cardiff **Wales** 11-3
1947 Murrayfield **Wales** 22-8
1948 Cardiff **Wales** 14-0
1949 Murrayfield **Scotland** 6-5
1950 Swansea **Wales** 12-0
1951 Murrayfield **Scotland** 19-0
1952 Cardiff **Wales** 11-0
1953 Murrayfield **Wales** 12-0
1954 Swansea **Wales** 15-3
1955 Murrayfield **Scotland** 14-8
1956 Cardiff **Wales** 9-3
1957 Murrayfield **Scotland** 9-6
1958 Cardiff **Wales** 8-3
1959 Murrayfield **Scotland** 6-5
1960 Cardiff **Wales** 8-0
1961 Murrayfield **Scotland** 3-0
1962 Cardiff **Scotland** 8-3
1963 Murrayfield **Wales** 6-0
1964 Cardiff **Wales** 11-3
1965 Murrayfield **Wales** 14-12
1966 Cardiff **Wales** 8-3
1967 Murrayfield **Scotland** 11-5
1968 Cardiff **Wales** 5-0
1969 Murrayfield **Wales** 17-3
1970 Cardiff **Wales** 18-9
1971 Murrayfield **Wales** 19-18
1972 Cardiff **Wales** 35-12
1973 Murrayfield **Scotland** 10-9
1974 Cardiff **Wales** 6-0
1975 Murrayfield **Scotland** 12-10
1976 Cardiff **Wales** 28-6
1977 Murrayfield **Wales** 18-9
1978 Cardiff **Wales** 22-14
1979 Murrayfield **Wales** 19-13
1980 Cardiff **Wales** 17-6
1981 Murrayfield **Scotland** 15-6
1982 Cardiff **Scotland** 34-18

1983 Murrayfield **Wales** 19-15
1984 Cardiff **Scotland** 15-9
1985 Murrayfield **Wales** 25-21
1986 Cardiff **Wales** 22-15
1987 Murrayfield **Scotland** 21-15

1988 Cardiff **Wales** 25-20
1989 Murrayfield **Scotland** 23-7
1990 Cardiff **Scotland** 13-9
1991 Murrayfield **Scotland** 32-12
1992 Cardiff **Wales** 15-12

SCOTLAND v FRANCE
Played 63   Scotland won 30, France won 30, Drawn 3

1910 Inverleith (Edinburgh)
    Scotland 27-0
1911 Paris **France** 16-15
1912 Inverleith **Scotland** 31-3
1913 Paris **Scotland** 21-3
1914 No Match
1920 Paris **Scotland** 5-0
1921 Inverleith **France** 3-0
1922 Paris **Drawn** 3-3
1923 Inverleith **Scotland** 16-3
1924 Paris **France** 12-10
1925 Inverleith **Scotland** 25-4
1926 Paris **Scotland** 20-6
1927 Murrayfield **Scotland** 23-6
1928 Paris **Scotland** 15-6
1929 Murrayfield **Scotland** 6-3
1930 Paris **France** 7-3
1931 Murrayfield **Scotland** 6-4
1947 Paris **France** 8-3
1948 Murrayfield **Scotland** 9-8
1949 Paris **Scotland** 8-0
1950 Murrayfield **Scotland** 8-5
1951 Paris **France** 14-12
1952 Murrayfield **France** 13-11
1953 Paris **France** 11-5
1954 Murrayfield **France** 3-0
1955 Paris **France** 15-0
1956 Murrayfield **Scotland** 12-0
1957 Paris **Scotland** 6-0
1958 Murrayfield **Scotland** 11-9
1959 Paris **France** 9-0
1960 Murrayfield **France** 13-11
1961 Paris **France** 11-0

1962 Murrayfield **France** 11-3
1963 Paris **Scotland** 11-6
1964 Murrayfield **Scotland** 10-0
1965 Paris **France** 16-8
1966 Murrayfield **Drawn** 3-3
1967 Paris **Scotland** 9-8
1968 Murrayfield **France** 8-6
1969 Paris **Scotland** 6-3
1970 Murrayfield **France** 11-9
1971 Paris **France** 13-8
1972 Murrayfield **Scotland** 20-9
1973 Paris **France** 16-13
1974 Murrayfield **Scotland** 19-6
1975 Paris **France** 10-9
1976 Murrayfield **France** 13-6
1977 Paris **France** 23-3
1978 Murrayfield **France** 19-16
1979 Paris **France** 21-17
1980 Murrayfield **Scotland** 22-14
1981 Paris **France** 16-9
1982 Murrayfield **Scotland** 16-7
1983 Paris **France** 19-15
1984 Murrayfield **Scotland** 21-12
1985 Paris **France** 11-3
1986 Murrayfield **Scotland** 18-17
1987 Paris **France** 28-22
1987 Christchurch *WC* **Drawn** 20-20
1988 Murrayfield **Scotland** 23-12
1989 Paris **France** 19-3
1990 Murrayfield **Scotland** 21-0
1991 Paris **France** 15-9
1992 Murrayfield **Scotland** 10-6

SCOTLAND v NEW ZEALAND
Played 16   Scotland won 0, New Zealand won 14, Drawn 2

1905 Inverleith (Edinburgh)
    New Zealand 12-7
1935 Murrayfield **New Zealand** 18-8
1954 Murrayfield **New Zealand** 3-0
1964 Murrayfield **Drawn** 0-0
1967 Murrayfield **New Zealand** 14-3
1972 Murrayfield **New Zealand** 14-9
1975 Auckland **New Zealand** 24-0
1978 Murrayfield **New Zealand** 18-9
1979 Murrayfield **New Zealand** 20-6

1981 *1* Dunedin **New Zealand** 11-4
    2 Auckland **New Zealand** 40-15
    New Zealand won series 2-0
1983 Murrayfield **Drawn** 25-25
1987 Christchurch *WC* **New Zealand** 30-3
1990 *1* Dunedin **New Zealand** 31-16
    2 Auckland **New Zealand** 21-18
    New Zealand won series 2-0
1991 Cardiff *WC* **New Zealand** 13-6

SCOTLAND v SOUTH AFRICA
Played 8   Scotland won 3, South Africa won 5, Drawn 0

1906 Glasgow **Scotland** 6-0

1912 Inverleith **South Africa** 16-0

1932 Murrayfield **South Africa** 6-3
1951 Murrayfield **South Africa** 44-0
1960 Port Elizabeth **South Africa** 18-10

1961 Murrayfield **South Africa** 12-5
1965 Murrayfield **Scotland** 8-5
1969 Murrayfield **Scotland** 6-3

SCOTLAND v AUSTRALIA
Played 12   Scotland won 7, Australia won 5, Drawn 0

1927 Murrayfield **Scotland** 10-8
1947 Murrayfield **Australia** 16-7
1958 Murrayfield **Scotland** 12-8
1966 Murrayfield **Scotland** 11-5
1968 Murrayfield **Scotland** 9-3
1970 Sydney **Australia** 23-3
1975 Murrayfield **Scotland** 10-3

1981 Murrayfield **Scotland** 24-15
1982 *1* Brisbane **Scotland** 12-7
　　 2 Sydney **Australia** 33-9
　　 Series drawn 1-1
1984 Murrayfield **Australia** 37-12
1988 Murrayfield **Australia** 32-13

SCOTLAND v SRU PRESIDENT'S XV
Played 1   Scotland won 1

1973 Murrayfield **Scotland** 27-16

SCOTLAND v ROMANIA
Played 6   Scotland won 4, Romania won 2

1981 Murrayfield **Scotland** 12-6
1984 Bucharest **Romania** 28-22
1986 Bucharest **Scotland** 33-18

1987 Dunedin *WC* **Scotland** 55-28
1989 Murrayfield **Scotland** 32-0
1991 Bucharest **Romania** 18-12

SCOTLAND v ZIMBABWE
Played 2   Scotland won 2

1987 Wellington *WC* **Scotland** 60-21

1991 Murrayfield *WC* **Scotland** 51-12

SCOTLAND v FIJI
Played 1   Scotland won 1

1989 Murrayfield **Scotland** 38-17

SCOTLAND v ARGENTINA
Played 1   Scotland won 1

1990 Murrayfield **Scotland** 49-3

SCOTLAND v JAPAN
Played 1   Scotland won 1

1991 Murrayfield *WC* **Scotland** 47-9

SCOTLAND v WESTERN SAMOA
Played 1   Scotland won 1

1991 Murrayfield *WC* **Scotland** 28-6

IRELAND v WALES
Played 95   Ireland won 32, Wales won 57, Drawn 6

1882 Dublin **Wales** 2G 2T to 0
1883 No Match
1884 Cardiff **Wales** 1DG 2T to 0
1885 No Match

1886 No Match
1887 Birkenhead **Wales** 1DG 1T to 3T
1888 Dublin **Ireland** 1G 1DG 1T to 0
1889 Swansea **Ireland** 2T to 0

1890 Dublin **Drawn** 1G each
1891 Llanelli **Wales** 6-4
1892 Dublin **Ireland** 9-0
1893 Llanelli **Wales** 2-0
1894 Belfast **Ireland** 3-0
1895 Cardiff **Wales** 5-3
1896 Dublin **Ireland** 8-4
1897 No Match
1898 Limerick **Wales** 11-3
1899 Cardiff **Ireland** 3-0
1900 Belfast **Wales** 3-0
1901 Swansea **Wales** 10-9
1902 Dublin **Wales** 15-0
1903 Cardiff **Wales** 18-0
1904 Belfast **Ireland** 14-12
1905 Swansea **Wales** 10-3
1906 Belfast **Ireland** 11-6
1907 Cardiff **Wales** 29-0
1908 Belfast **Wales** 11-5
1909 Swansea **Wales** 18-5
1910 Dublin **Wales** 19-3
1911 Cardiff **Wales** 16-0
1912 Belfast **Ireland** 12-5
1913 Swansea **Wales** 16-13
1914 Belfast **Wales** 11-3
1920 Cardiff **Wales** 28-4
1921 Belfast **Wales** 6-0
1922 Swansea **Wales** 11-5
1923 Dublin **Ireland** 5-4
1924 Cardiff **Ireland** 13-10
1925 Belfast **Ireland** 19-3
1926 Swansea **Wales** 11-8
1927 Dublin **Ireland** 19-9
1928 Cardiff **Ireland** 13-10
1929 Belfast **Drawn** 5-5
1930 Swansea **Wales** 12-7
1931 Belfast **Wales** 15-3
1932 Cardiff **Ireland** 12-10
1933 Belfast **Ireland** 10-5
1934 Swansea **Wales** 13-0
1935 Belfast **Ireland** 9-3
1936 Cardiff **Wales** 3-0
1937 Belfast **Ireland** 5-3
1938 Swansea **Wales** 11-5
1939 Belfast **Wales** 7-0
1947 Swansea **Wales** 6-0

1948 Belfast **Ireland** 6-3
1949 Swansea **Ireland** 5-0
1950 Belfast **Wales** 6-3
1951 Cardiff **Drawn** 3-3
1952 Dublin **Wales** 14-3
1953 Swansea **Wales** 5-3
1954 Dublin **Wales** 12-9
1955 Cardiff **Wales** 21-3
1956 Dublin **Ireland** 11-3
1957 Cardiff **Wales** 6-5
1958 Dublin **Wales** 9-6
1959 Cardiff **Wales** 8-6
1960 Dublin **Wales** 10-9
1961 Cardiff **Wales** 9-0
1962 Dublin **Drawn** 3-3
1963 Cardiff **Ireland** 14-6
1964 Dublin **Wales** 15-6
1965 Cardiff **Wales** 14-8
1966 Dublin **Ireland** 9-6
1967 Cardiff **Ireland** 3-0
1968 Dublin **Ireland** 9-6
1969 Cardiff **Wales** 24-11
1970 Dublin **Ireland** 14-0
1971 Cardiff **Wales** 23-9
1972 No Match
1973 Cardiff **Wales** 16-12
1974 Dublin **Drawn** 9-9
1975 Cardiff **Wales** 32-4
1976 Dublin **Wales** 34-9
1977 Cardiff **Wales** 25-9
1978 Dublin **Wales** 20-16
1979 Cardiff **Wales** 24-21
1980 Dublin **Ireland** 21-7
1981 Cardiff **Wales** 9-8
1982 Dublin **Ireland** 20-12
1983 Cardiff **Wales** 23-9
1984 Dublin **Wales** 18-9
1985 Cardiff **Ireland** 21-9
1986 Dublin **Wales** 19-12
1987 Cardiff **Ireland** 15-11
1987 Wellington *WC* **Wales** 13-6
1988 Dublin **Wales** 12-9
1989 Cardiff **Ireland** 19-13
1990 Dublin **Ireland** 14-8
1991 Cardiff **Drawn** 21-21
1992 Dublin **Wales** 16-15

IRELAND v FRANCE
Played 65   Ireland won 25, France won 35, Drawn 5

1909 Dublin **Ireland** 19-8
1910 Paris **Ireland** 8-3
1911 Cork **Ireland** 25-5
1912 Paris **Ireland** 11-6
1913 Cork **Ireland** 24-0
1914 Paris **Ireland** 8-6
1920 Dublin **France** 15-7
1921 Paris **France** 20-10
1922 Dublin **Ireland** 8-3
1923 Paris **France** 14-8
1924 Dublin **Ireland** 6-0
1925 Paris **Ireland** 9-3

1926 Belfast **Ireland** 11-0
1927 Paris **Ireland** 8-3
1928 Belfast **Ireland** 12-8
1929 Paris **Ireland** 6-0
1930 Belfast **France** 5-0
1931 Paris **France** 3-0
1947 Paris **France** 12-8
1948 Paris **Ireland** 13-6
1949 Dublin **France** 16-9
1950 Paris **Drawn** 3-3
1951 Dublin **Ireland** 9-8
1952 Paris **Ireland** 11-8

1953 Belfast **Ireland** 16-3
1954 Paris **France** 8-0
1955 Dublin **France** 5-3
1956 Paris **France** 14-8
1957 Dublin **Ireland** 11-6
1958 Paris **France** 11-6
1959 Dublin **Ireland** 9-5
1960 Paris **France** 23-6
1961 Dublin **France** 15-3
1962 Paris **France** 11-0
1963 Dublin **France** 24-5
1964 Paris **France** 27-6
1965 Dublin **Drawn** 3-3
1966 Paris **France** 11-6
1967 Dublin **France** 11-6
1968 Paris **France** 16-6
1969 Dublin **Ireland** 17-9
1970 Paris **France** 8-0
1971 Dublin **Drawn** 9-9
1972 Paris **Ireland** 14-9
1972 Dublin **Ireland** 24-14
Non-championship match

1973 Dublin **Ireland** 6-4
1974 Paris **France** 9-6
1975 Dublin **Ireland** 25-6
1976 Paris **France** 26-3
1977 Dublin **France** 15-6
1978 Paris **France** 10-9
1979 Dublin **Drawn** 9-9
1980 Paris **France** 19-18
1981 Dublin **France** 19-13
1982 Paris **France** 22-9
1983 Dublin **Ireland** 22-16
1984 Paris **France** 25-12
1985 Dublin **Drawn** 15-15
1986 Paris **France** 29-9
1987 Dublin **France** 19-13
1988 Paris **France** 25-6
1989 Dublin **France** 26-21
1990 Paris **France** 31-12
1991 Dublin **France** 21-13
1992 Paris **France** 44-12

IRELAND v NEW ZEALAND
Played 10   Ireland won 0, New Zealand won 9, Drawn 1

1905 Dublin **New Zealand** 15-0
1924 Dublin **New Zealand** 6-0
1935 Dublin **New Zealand** 17-9
1954 Dublin **New Zealand** 14-3
1963 Dublin **New Zealand** 6-5

1973 Dublin **Drawn** 10-10
1974 Dublin **New Zealand** 15-6
1976 Wellington **New Zealand** 11-3
1978 Dublin **New Zealand** 10-6
1989 Dublin **New Zealand** 23-6

IRELAND v SOUTH AFRICA
Played 10   Ireland won 1, South Africa won 8, Drawn 1

1906 Belfast **South Africa** 15-12
1912 Dublin **South Africa** 38-0
1931 Dublin **South Africa** 8-3
1951 Dublin **South Africa** 17-5
1960 Dublin **South Africa** 8-3
1961 Cape Town **South Africa** 24-8

1965 Dublin **Ireland** 9-6
1970 Dublin **Drawn** 8-8
1981 *1* Cape Town **South Africa** 23-15
     2 Durban **South Africa** 12-10
     South Africa won series 2-0

IRELAND v AUSTRALIA
Played 13   Ireland won 6, Australia won 7, Drawn 0

1927 Dublin **Australia** 5-3
1947 Dublin **Australia** 16-3
1958 Dublin **Ireland** 9-6
1967 Dublin **Ireland** 15-8
1967 Sydney **Ireland** 11-5
1968 Dublin **Ireland** 10-3
1976 Dublin **Australia** 20-10

1979 *1* Brisbane **Ireland** 27-12
     2 Sydney **Ireland** 9-3
     Ireland won series 2-0
1981 Dublin **Australia** 16-12
1984 Dublin **Australia** 16-9
1987 Sydney *WC* **Australia** 33-15
1991 Dublin *WC* **Australia** 19-18

IRELAND v NEW ZEALAND NATIVES
Played 1   New Zealand Natives won 1

1888 Dublin **New Zealand Natives**
    4G 1T to 1G 1T

IRELAND v IRU PRESIDENT'S XV
Played 1   Drawn 1

1974 Dublin **Drawn** 18-18

IRELAND v ROMANIA
Played 1   Ireland won 1

1986 Dublin **Ireland** 60-0

IRELAND v CANADA
Played 1   Ireland won 1

1987 Dunedin *WC* **Ireland** 46-19

IRELAND v TONGA
Played 1   Ireland won 1

1987 Brisbane *WC* **Ireland** 32-9

IRELAND v WESTERN SAMOA
Played 1   Ireland won 1

1988 Dublin **Ireland** 49-22

IRELAND v ITALY
Played 1   Ireland won 1

1988 Dublin **Ireland** 31-15

IRELAND v ARGENTINA
Played 1   Ireland won 1

1990 Dublin **Ireland** 20-18

IRELAND v NAMIBIA
Played 2   Namibia won 2

1991 *1* Windhoek **Namibia** 15-6   *2* Windhoek **Namibia** 26-15
Namibia won series 2-0

IRELAND v ZIMBABWE
Played 1   Ireland won 1

1991 Dublin *WC* **Ireland** 55-11

IRELAND v JAPAN
Played 1   Ireland won 1

1991 Dublin *WC* **Ireland** 32-16

WALES v FRANCE
Played 66   Wales won 36, France won 27, Drawn 3

1908 Cardiff **Wales** 36-4	1921 Cardiff **Wales** 12-4
1909 Paris **Wales** 47-5	1922 Paris **Wales** 11-3
1910 Swansea **Wales** 49-14	1923 Swansea **Wales** 16-8
1911 Paris **Wales** 15-0	1924 Paris **Wales** 10-6
1912 Newport **Wales** 14-8	1925 Cardiff **Wales** 11-5
1913 Paris **Wales** 11-8	1926 Paris **Wales** 7-5
1914 Swansea **Wales** 31-0	1927 Swansea **Wales** 25-7
1920 Paris **Wales** 6-5	1928 Paris **France** 8-3

1929 Cardiff **Wales** 8-3
1930 Paris **Wales** 11-0
1931 Swansea **Wales** 35-3
1947 Paris **Wales** 3-0
1948 Swansea **France** 11-3
1949 Paris **France** 5-3
1950 Cardiff **Wales** 21-0
1951 Paris **France** 8-3
1952 Swansea **Wales** 9-5
1953 Paris **Wales** 6-3
1954 Cardiff **Wales** 19-13
1955 Paris **Wales** 16-11
1956 Cardiff **Wales** 5-3
1957 Paris **Wales** 19-13
1958 Cardiff **France** 16-6
1959 Paris **France** 11-3
1960 Cardiff **France** 16-8
1961 Paris **France** 8-6
1962 Cardiff **Wales** 3-0
1963 Paris **France** 5-3
1964 Cardiff **Drawn** 11-11
1965 Paris **France** 22-13
1966 Cardiff **Wales** 9-8
1967 Paris **France** 20-14
1968 Cardiff **France** 14-9
1969 Paris **Drawn** 8-8

1970 Cardiff **Wales** 11-6
1971 Paris **Wales** 9-5
1972 Cardiff **Wales** 20-6
1973 Paris **France** 12-3
1974 Cardiff **Drawn** 16-16
1975 Paris **Wales** 25-10
1976 Cardiff **Wales** 19-13
1977 Paris **France** 16-9
1978 Cardiff **Wales** 16-7
1979 Paris **France** 14-13
1980 Cardiff **Wales** 18-9
1981 Paris **France** 19-15
1982 Cardiff **Wales** 22-12
1983 Paris **France** 16-9
1984 Cardiff **France** 21-16
1985 Paris **France** 14-3
1986 Cardiff **France** 23-15
1987 Paris **France** 16-9
1988 Cardiff **France** 10-9
1989 Paris **France** 31-12
1990 Cardiff **France** 29-19
1991 Paris **France** 36-3
1991 Cardiff **France** 22-9
Non-championship match
1992 Cardiff **France** 12-9

WALES v NEW ZEALAND
Played 15   Wales won 3, New Zealand won 12, Drawn 0

1905 Cardiff **Wales** 3-0
1924 Swansea **New Zealand** 19-0
1935 Cardiff **Wales** 13-12
1953 Cardiff **Wales** 13-8
1963 Cardiff **New Zealand** 6-0
1967 Cardiff **New Zealand** 13-6
1969 *1* Christchurch **New Zealand** 19-0
    2 Auckland **New Zealand** 33-12
    New Zealand won series 2-0

1972 Cardiff **New Zealand** 19-16
1978 Cardiff **New Zealand** 13-12
1980 Cardiff **New Zealand** 23-3
1987 Brisbane *WC* **New Zealand** 49-6
1988 *1* Christchurch **New Zealand** 52-3
    2 Auckland **New Zealand** 54-9
    New Zealand won series 2-0
1989 Cardiff **New Zealand** 34-9

WALES v SOUTH AFRICA
Played 7   Wales won 0, South Africa won 6, Drawn 1

1906 Swansea **South Africa** 11-0
1912 Cardiff **South Africa** 3-0
1931 Swansea **South Africa** 8-3
1951 Cardiff **South Africa** 6-3

1960 Cardiff **South Africa** 3-0
1964 Durban **South Africa** 24-3
1970 Cardiff **Drawn** 6-6

WALES v AUSTRALIA
Played 15   Wales won 8, Australia won 7, Drawn 0

1908 Cardiff **Wales** 9-6
1927 Cardiff **Australia** 18-8
1947 Cardiff **Wales** 6-0
1958 Cardiff **Wales** 9-3
1966 Cardiff **Australia** 14-11
1969 Sydney **Wales** 19-16
1973 Cardiff **Wales** 24-0
1975 Cardiff **Wales** 28-3

1978 *1* Brisbane **Australia** 18-8
    2 Sydney **Australia** 19-17
    Australia won series 2-0
1981 Cardiff **Wales** 18-13
1984 Cardiff **Australia** 28-9
1987 Rotorua *WC* **Wales** 22-21
1991 Brisbane **Australia** 63-6
1992 Cardiff *WC* **Australia** 38-3

Kenny Waters of Wales gets to grips with Western Samoa's Matthew Vaea in the Pool 3 match in the 1991 World Cup. Western Samoa beat Wales 16-13, and went on to the quarter-final stage of the tournament.

WALES v NEW ZEALAND NATIVES
Played 1   Wales won 1

1888 Swansea **Wales** 1G 2T to 0

WALES v NEW ZEALAND ARMY
Played 1   New Zealand Army won 1

1919 Swansea **New Zealand Army** 6-3

WALES v ROMANIA
Played 2   Romania won 2

1983 Bucharest **Romania** 24-6   1988 Cardiff **Romania** 15-9

WALES v FIJI
Played 2   Wales won 2

1985 Cardiff **Wales** 40-3   1986 Suva **Wales** 22-15

WALES v TONGA
Played 2   Wales won 2

1986 Nuku'Alofa **Wales** 15-7   1987 Palmerston North *WC* **Wales** 29-16

WALES v WESTERN SAMOA
Played 3   Wales won 2, Western Samoa won 1

1986 Apia **Wales** 32-14   1991 Cardiff *WC* **Western Samoa** 16-13
1988 Cardiff **Wales** 28-6

WALES v CANADA
Played 1   Wales won 1

1987 Invercargill *WC* **Wales** 40-9

WALES v UNITED STATES
Played 1   Wales won 1

1987 Cardiff **Wales** 46-0

WALES v NAMIBIA
Played 2   Wales won 2

1990 *1* Windhoek **Wales** 18-9   *2* Windhoek **Wales** 34-30
                                                   Wales won series 2-0

WALES v BARBARIANS
Played 1   Barbarians won 1

1990 Cardiff **Barbarians** 31-24

WALES v ARGENTINA
Played 1   Wales won 1

1991 Cardiff *WC* **Wales** 16-7

FRANCE v NEW ZEALAND
Played 28   France won 5, New Zealand won 23, Drawn 0

1906 Paris **New Zealand** 38-8
1925 Toulouse **New Zealand** 30-6
1954 Paris **France** 3-0
1961 *1* Auckland **New Zealand** 13-6
    2 Wellington **New Zealand** 5-3
    3 Christchurch **New Zealand** 32- 3
    New Zealand won series 3-0
1964 Paris **New Zealand** 12-3
1967 Paris **New Zealand** 21-15
1968 *1* Christchurch **New Zealand** 12-9
    2 Wellington **New Zealand** 9-3
    3 Auckland **New Zealand** 19-12
    New Zealand won series 3-0
1973 Paris **France** 13-6
1977 *1* Toulouse **France** 18-13
    2 Paris **New Zealand** 15-3
    Series drawn 1-1
1979 *1* Christchurch **New Zealand** 23-9
    2 Auckland **France** 24-19
    Series drawn 1-1

1981 *1* Toulouse **New Zealand** 13-9
    2 Paris **New Zealand** 18-6
    New Zealand won series 2-0
1984 *1* Christchurch **New Zealand** 10-9
    2 Auckland **New Zealand** 31-18
    New Zealand won series 2-0
1986 Christchurch **New Zealand** 18-9
1986 *1* Toulouse **New Zealand** 19-7
    2 Nantes **France** 16-3
    Series drawn 1-1
1987 Auckland *WC* **New Zealand** 29-9
1989 *1* Christchurch **New Zealand** 25-17
    2 Auckland **New Zealand** 34-20
    New Zealand won series 2-0
1990 *1* Nantes **New Zealand** 24-3
    2 Paris **New Zealand** 30-12
    New Zealand won series 2-0

FRANCE v SOUTH AFRICA
Played 19   France won 3, South Africa won 12, Drawn 4

1913 Bordeaux **South Africa** 38-5
1952 Paris **South Africa** 25-3
1958 *1* Cape Town **Drawn** 3-3
    2 Johannesburg **France** 9-5
    France won series 1-0, with 1 draw
1961 Paris **Drawn** 0-0
1964 Springs (SA) **France** 8-6
1967 *1* Durban **South Africa** 26-3
    2 Bloemfontein **South Africa** 16-3
    3 Johannesburg **France** 19-14
    4 Cape Town **Drawn** 6-6
    South Africa won series 2-1, with 1 draw
1968 *1* Bordeaux **South Africa** 12-9
    2 Paris **South Africa** 16-11
    South Africa won series 2-0

1971 *1* Bloemfontein **South Africa** 22-9
    2 Durban **Drawn** 8-8
    South Africa won series 1-0, with 1 draw
1974 *1* Toulouse **South Africa** 13-4
    2 Paris **South Africa** 10-8
    South Africa won series 2-0
1975 *1* Bloemfontein **South Africa** 38-25
    2 Pretoria **South Africa** 33-18
    South Africa won series 2-0
1980 Pretoria **South Africa** 37-15

FRANCE v AUSTRALIA
Played 23   France won 12, Australia won 9, Drawn 2

1928 Paris **Australia** 11-8
1948 Paris **France** 13-6
1958 Paris **France** 19-0
1961 Sydney **France** 15-8
1967 Paris **France** 20-14
1968 Sydney **Australia** 11-10
1971 *1* Toulouse **Australia** 13-11
    2 Paris **France** 18-9
    Series drawn 1-1
1972 *1* Sydney **Drawn** 14-14
    2 Brisbane **France** 16-15
    France won series 1-0, with 1 draw
1976 *1* Bordeaux **France** 18-15
    2 Paris **France** 34-6
    France won series 2-0

1981 *1* Brisbane **Australia** 17-15
    2 Sydney **Australia** 24-14
    Australia won series 2-0
1983 *1* Clermont-Ferrand **Drawn** 15-15
    2 Paris **France** 15-6
    France won series 1-0, with 1 draw
1986 Sydney **Australia** 27-14
1987 Sydney *WC* **France** 30-24
1989 *1* Strasbourg **Australia** 32-15
    2 Lille **France** 25-19
    Series drawn 1-1
1990 *1* Sydney **Australia** 21-9
    2 Brisbane **Australia** 48-31
    3 Sydney **France** 28-19
    Australia won series 2-1

117

FRANCE v UNITED STATES
Played 5   France won 4, United States won 1

1920 Paris **France** 14-5	1991 *1* Denver **France** 41-9
1924 Paris **United States** 17-3	2 Colorado Springs **France** 10-3★
1976 Chicago **France** 33-14	*★Abandoned after 43 mins*
	France won series 2-0

FRANCE v ROMANIA
Played 37   France won 27, Romania won 8, Drawn 2

1924 Paris **France** 59-3	1975 Bordeaux **France** 36-12
1938 Bucharest **France** 11-8	1976 Bucharest **Romania** 15-12
1957 Bucharest **France** 18-15	1977 Clermont-Ferrand **France** 9-6
1957 Bordeaux **France** 39-0	1978 Bucharest **France** 9-6
1960 Bucharest **Romania** 11-5	1979 Montauban **France** 30-12
1961 Bayonne **Drawn** 5-5	1980 Bucharest **Romania** 15-0
1962 Bucharest **Romania** 3-0	1981 Narbonne **France** 17-9
1963 Toulouse **Drawn** 6-6	1982 Bucharest **Romania** 13-9
1964 Bucharest **France** 9-6	1983 Toulouse **France** 26-15
1965 Lyons **France** 8-3	1984 Bucharest **France** 18-3
1966 Bucharest **France** 9-3	1986 Lille **France** 25-13
1967 Nantes **France** 11-3	1986 Bucharest **France** 20-3
1968 Bucharest **Romania** 15-14	1987 Wellington *WC* **France** 55-12
1969 Tarbes **France** 14-9	1987 Agen **France** 49-3
1970 Bucharest **France** 14-3	1988 Bucharest **France** 16-12
1971 Béziers **France** 31-12	1990 Auch **Romania** 12-6
1972 Constanza **France** 15-6	1991 Bucharest **France** 33-21
1973 Valence **France** 7-6	1991 Béziers *WC* **France** 30-3
1974 Bucharest **Romania** 15-10	

FRANCE v NEW ZEALAND MAORIS
Played 1   New Zealand Maoris won 1

1926 Paris **New Zealand Maoris** 12-3

FRANCE v GERMANY
Played 15   France won 13, Germany won 2

1927 Paris **France** 30-5	1934 Hanover **France** 13-9
1927 Frankfurt **Germany** 17-16	1935 Paris **France** 18-3
1928 Hanover **France** 14-3	1936 *1* Berlin **France** 19-14
1929 Paris **France** 24-0	2 Hanover **France** 6-3
1930 Berlin **France** 31-0	*France won series 2-0*
1931 Paris **France** 34-0	1937 Paris **France** 27-6
1932 Frankfurt **France** 20-4	1938 Frankfurt **Germany** 3-0
1933 Paris **France** 38-17	1938 Bucharest **France** 8-5

FRANCE v ITALY
Played 17   France won 17

1937 Paris **France** 43-5	1960 Treviso **France** 26-0
1952 Milan **France** 17-8	1961 Chambéry **France** 17-0
1953 Lyons **France** 22-8	1962 Brescia **France** 6-3
1954 Rome **France** 39-12	1963 Grenoble **France** 14-12
1955 Grenoble **France** 24-0	1964 Parma **France** 12-3
1956 Padua **France** 16-3	1965 Pau **France** 21-0
1957 Agen **France** 38-6	1966 Naples **France** 21-0
1958 Naples **France** 11-3	1967 Toulon **France** 60-13
1959 Nantes **France** 22-0	

FRANCE v BRITISH XVs
Played 5   France won 2, British XVs won 3

1940 Paris **British XV** 36-3	1946 Paris **France** 10-0
1945 Paris **France** 21-9	1989 Paris **British XV** 29-27
1945 Richmond **British XV** 27-6	

FRANCE v NEW ZEALAND ARMY
Played 1   New Zealand Army won 1

1946 Paris **New Zealand Army** 14-9

FRANCE v ARGENTINA
Played 23   France won 19, Argentina won 3, Drawn 1

1949 *1* Buenos Aires **France** 5-0
    2 Buenos Aires **France** 12-3
    France won series 2-0
1954 *1* Buenos Aires **France** 22-8
    2 Buenos Aires **France** 30-3
    France won series 2-0
1960 *1* Buenos Aires **France** 37-3
    2 Buenos Aires **France** 12-3
    3 Buenos Aires **France** 29-6
    France won series 3-0
1974 *1* Buenos Aires **France** 20-15
    2 Buenos Aires **France** 31-27
    France won series 2-0
1975 *1* Lyons **France** 29-6
    2 Paris **France** 36-21
    France won series 2-0
1977 *1* Buenos Aires **France** 26-3
    2 Buenos Aires **Drawn** 18-18
    France won series 1-0, with 1 draw

1982 *1* Toulouse **France** 25-12
    2 Paris **France** 13-6
    France won series 2-0
1985 *1* Buenos Aires **Argentina** 24-16
    2 Buenos Aires **France** 23-15
    Series drawn 1-1
1986 *1* Buenos Aires **Argentina** 15-13
    2 Buenos Aires **France** 22-9
    Series drawn 1-1
1988 *1* Buenos Aires **France** 18-15
    2 Buenos Aires **Argentina** 18-6
    Series drawn 1-1
1988 *1* Nantes **France** 29-9
    2 Lille **France** 28-18
    France won series 2-0

FRANCE v CZECHOSLOVAKIA
Played 2   France won 2

1956 Toulouse **France** 28-3	1968 Prague **France** 19-6

FRANCE v FIJI
Played 3   France won 3

1964 Paris **France** 21-3	1991 Grenoble *WC* **France** 33-9
1987 Auckland *WC* **France** 31-16	

FRANCE v JAPAN
Played 1   France won 1

1973 Bordeaux **France** 30-18

FRANCE v ZIMBABWE
Played 1   France won 1

1987 Auckland *WC* **France** 70-12

FRANCE v CANADA
Played 1   France won 1

1991 Agen *WC* **France** 19-13

NEW ZEALAND v SOUTH AFRICA
Played 37   New Zealand won 15, South Africa won 20, Drawn 2

1921 *1* Dunedin **New Zealand** 13-5
2 Auckland **South Africa** 9-5
3 Wellington **Drawn** 0-0
Series drawn 1-1, with 1 draw
1928 *1* Durban **South Africa** 17-0
2 Johannesburg **New Zealand** 7-6
3 Port Elizabeth **South Africa** 11-6
4 Cape Town **New Zealand** 13-5
Series drawn 2-2
1937 *1* Wellington **New Zealand** 13-7
2 Christchurch **South Africa** 13-6
3 Auckland **South Africa** 17-6
South Africa won series 2-1
1949 *1* Cape Town **South Africa** 15-11
2 Johannesburg **South Africa** 12-6
3 Durban **South Africa** 9-3
4 Port Elizabeth **South Africa** 11-8
South Africa won series 4-0
1956 *1* Dunedin **New Zealand** 10-6
2 Wellington **South Africa** 8-3
3 Christchurch **New Zealand** 17-10
4 Auckland **New Zealand** 11-5
New Zealand won series 3-1
1960 *1* Johannesburg **South Africa** 13-0

2 Cape Town **New Zealand** 11-3
3 Bloemfontein **Drawn** 11-11
4 Port Elizabeth **South Africa** 8-3
South Africa won series 2-1, with 1 draw
1965 *1* Wellington **New Zealand** 6-3
2 Dunedin **New Zealand** 13-0
3 Christchurch **South Africa** 19-16
4 Auckland **New Zealand** 20-3
New Zealand won series 3-1
1970 *1* Pretoria **South Africa** 17-6
2 Cape Town **New Zealand** 9-8
3 Port Elizabeth **South Africa** 14-3
4 Johannesburg **South Africa** 20-17
South Africa won series 3-1
1976 *1* Durban **South Africa** 16-7
2 Bloemfontein **New Zealand** 15-9
3 Cape Town **South Africa** 15-10
4 Johannesburg **South Africa** 15-14
South Africa won series 3-1
1981 *1* Christchurch **New Zealand** 14-9
2 Wellington **South Africa** 24-12
3 Auckland **New Zealand** 25-22
New Zealand won series 2-1

NEW ZEALAND v AUSTRALIA
Played 93   New Zealand won 64, Australia won 24, Drawn 5

1903 Sydney **New Zealand** 22-3
1905 Dunedin **New Zealand** 14-3
1907 *1* Sydney **New Zealand** 26-6
2 Brisbane **New Zealand** 14-5
3 Sydney **Drawn** 5-5
New Zealand won series 2-0, with 1 draw
1910 *1* Sydney **New Zealand** 6-0
2 Sydney **Australia** 11-0
3 Sydney **New Zealand** 28-13
New Zealand won series 2-1
1913 *1* Wellington **New Zealand** 30-5
2 Dunedin **New Zealand** 25-13
3 Christchurch **Australia** 16-5
New Zealand won series 2-1
1914 *1* Sydney **New Zealand** 5-0
2 Brisbane **New Zealand** 17-0
3 Sydney **New Zealand** 22-7
New Zealand won series 3-0
1929 *1* Sydney **Australia** 9-8
2 Brisbane **Australia** 17-9
3 Sydney **Australia** 15-13
Australia won series 3-0
1931 Auckland **New Zealand** 20-13
1932 *1* Sydney **Australia** 22-17
2 Brisbane **New Zealand** 21-3
3 Sydney **New Zealand** 21-13
New Zealand won series 2-1
1934 *1* Sydney **Australia** 25-11
2 Sydney **Drawn** 3-3
Australia won series 1-0, with 1 draw
1936 *1* Wellington **New Zealand** 11-6

2 Dunedin **New Zealand** 38-13
New Zealand won series 2-0
1938 *1* Sydney **New Zealand** 24-9
2 Brisbane **New Zealand** 20-14
3 Sydney **New Zealand** 14-6
New Zealand won series 3-0
1946 *1* Dunedin **New Zealand** 31-8
2 Auckland **New Zealand** 14-10
New Zealand won series 2-0
1947 *1* Brisbane **New Zealand** 13-5
2 Sydney **New Zealand** 27-14
New Zealand won series 2-0
1949 *1* Wellington **Australia** 11-6
2 Auckland **Australia** 16-9
Australia won series 2-0
1951 *1* Sydney **New Zealand** 8-0
2 Sydney **New Zealand** 17-11
3 Brisbane **New Zealand** 16-6
New Zealand won series 3-0
1952 *1* Christchurch **Australia** 14-9
2 Wellington **New Zealand** 15-8
Series drawn 1-1
1955 *1* Wellington **New Zealand** 16-8
2 Dunedin **New Zealand** 8-0
3 Auckland **Australia** 8-3
New Zealand won series 2-1
1957 *1* Sydney **New Zealand** 25-11
2 Brisbane **New Zealand** 22-9
New Zealand won series 2-0
1958 *1* Wellington **New Zealand** 25-3
2 Christchurch **Australia** 6-3

3 Auckland **New Zealand** 17-8
New Zealand won series 2-1
1962 *1* Brisbane **New Zealand** 20-6
2 Sydney **New Zealand** 14-5
New Zealand won series 2-0
1962 *1* Wellington **Drawn** 9-9
2 Dunedin **New Zealand** 3-0
3 Auckland **New Zealand** 16-8
New Zealand won series 2-0, with 1 draw
1964 *1* Dunedin **New Zealand** 14-9
2 Christchurch **New Zealand** 18- 3
3 Wellington **Australia** 20-5
New Zealand won series 2-1
1967 Wellington **New Zealand** 29-9
1968 *1* Sydney **New Zealand** 27-11
2 Brisbane **New Zealand** 19-18
New Zealand won series 2-0
1972 *1* Wellington **New Zealand** 29-6
2 Christchurch **New Zealand** 30-17
3 Auckland **New Zealand** 38-3
New Zealand won series 3-0
1974 *1* Sydney **New Zealand** 11-6
2 Brisbane **Drawn** 16-16
3 Sydney **New Zealand** 16-6
New Zealand won series 2-0, with 1 draw
1978 *1* Wellington **New Zealand** 13-12
2 Christchurch **New Zealand** 22-6
3 Auckland **Australia** 30-16
New Zealand won series 2-1
1979 Sydney **Australia** 12-6
1980 *1* Sydney **Australia** 13-9

2 Brisbane **New Zealand** 12-9
3 Sydney **Australia** 26-10
Australia won series 2-1
1982 *1* Christchurch **New Zealand** 23-16
2 Wellington **Australia** 19-16
3 Auckland **New Zealand** 33-18
New Zealand won series 2-1
1983 Sydney **New Zealand** 18-8
1984 *1* Sydney **Australia** 16-9
2 Brisbane **New Zealand** 19-15
3 Sydney **New Zealand** 25-24
New Zealand won series 2-1
1985 Auckland **New Zealand** 10-9
1986 *1* Wellington **Australia** 13-12
2 Dunedin **New Zealand** 13-12
3 Auckland **Australia** 22-9
Australia won series 2-1
1987 Sydney **New Zealand** 30-16
1988 *1* Sydney **New Zealand** 32-7
2 Brisbane **Drawn** 19-19
3 Sydney **New Zealand** 30-9
New Zealand won series 2-0, with 1 draw
1989 Auckland **New Zealand** 24-12
1990 *1* Christchurch **New Zealand** 21-6
2 Auckland **New Zealand** 27-17
3 Wellington **Australia** 21-9
New Zealand won series 2-1
1991 *1* Sydney **Australia** 21-12
2 Auckland **New Zealand** 6-3
1991 Dublin *WC* **Australia** 16-6

NEW ZEALAND v UNITED STATES
Played 2   New Zealand won 2

1913 Berkeley **New Zealand** 51-3

1991 Gloucester *WC* **New Zealand** 46-6

NEW ZEALAND v ROMANIA
Played 1   New Zealand won 1

1981 Bucharest **New Zealand** 14-6

NEW ZEALAND v ARGENTINA
Played 7   New Zealand won 6, Drawn 1

1985 *1* Buenos Aires **New Zealand** 33-20
2 Buenos Aires **Drawn** 21-21
New Zealand won series 1-0, with 1 draw
1987 Wellington *WC* **New Zealand**
46-15
1989 *1* Dunedin **New Zealand** 60-9

2 Wellington **New Zealand** 49-12
New Zealand won series 2-0
1991 *1* Buenos Aires **New Zealand** 28-14
2 Buenos Aires **New Zealand** 36-6
New Zealand won series 2-0

NEW ZEALAND v ITALY
Played 2   New Zealand won 2

1987 Auckland *WC* **New Zealand** 70-6

1991 Leicester *WC* **New Zealand** 31-21

NEW ZEALAND v FIJI
Played 1   New Zealand won 1

1987 Christchurch *WC* **New Zealand** 74-13

NEW ZEALAND v CANADA
Played 1   New Zealand won 1

1991 Lille *WC* **New Zealand** 29-13

SOUTH AFRICA v AUSTRALIA
Played 28   South Africa won 21, Australia won 7, Drawn 0

1933 *1* Cape Town **South Africa** 17-3
    2 Durban **Australia** 21-6
    3 Johannesburg **South Africa** 12-3
    4 Port Elizabeth **South Africa** 11-0
    5 Bloemfontein **Australia** 15-4
    South Africa won series 3-2
1937 *1* Sydney **South Africa** 9-5
    2 Sydney **South Africa** 26-17
    South Africa won series 2-0
1953 *1* Johannesburg **South Africa** 25-3
    2 Cape Town **Australia** 18-14
    3 Durban **South Africa** 18-8
    4 Port Elizabeth **South Africa** 22-9
    South Africa won series 3-1
1956 *1* Sydney **South Africa** 9-0
    2 Brisbane **South Africa** 9-0
    South Africa won series 2-0
1961 *1* Johannesburg **South Africa** 28-3
    2 Port Elizabeth **South Africa** 23-11
    South Africa won series 2-0

1963 *1* Pretoria **South Africa** 14-3
    2 Cape Town **Australia** 9-5
    3 Johannesburg **Australia** 11-9
    4 Port Elizabeth **South Africa** 22-6
    Series drawn 2-2
1965 *1* Sydney **Australia** 18-11
    2 Brisbane **Australia** 12-8
    Australia won series 2-0
1969 *1* Johannesburg **South Africa** 30-11
    2 Durban **South Africa** 16-9
    3 Cape Town **South Africa** 11-3
    4 Bloemfontein **South Africa** 19-8
    South Africa won series 4-0
1971 *1* Sydney **South Africa** 19-11
    2 Brisbane **South Africa** 14-6
    3 Sydney **South Africa** 18-6
    South Africa won series 3-0

SOUTH AFRICA v WORLD XVs
Played 3   South Africa won 3

1977 Pretoria **South Africa** 45-24
1989 *1* Cape Town **South Africa** 20-19

    2 Johannesburg **South Africa** 22-16
    South Africa won series 2-0

SOUTH AFRICA v SOUTH AMERICA
Played 8   South Africa won 7, South America won 1

1980 *1* Johannesburg **South Africa** 24-9
    2 Durban **South Africa** 18-9
    South Africa won series 2-0
1980 *1* Montevideo **South Africa** 22-13
    2 Santiago **South Africa** 30-16
    South Africa won series 2-0

1982 *1* Pretoria **South Africa** 50-18
    2 Bloemfontein **South America** 21-12
    Series drawn 1-1
1984 *1* Pretoria **South Africa** 32-15
    2 Cape Town **South Africa** 22-13
    South Africa won series 2-0

SOUTH AFRICA v UNITED STATES
Played 1   South Africa won 1

1981 Glenville **South Africa** 38-7

SOUTH AFRICA v NEW ZEALAND CAVALIERS
Played 4   South Africa won 3, New Zealand Cavaliers won 1

1986 *1* Cape Town **South Africa** 21-15
    2 Durban **New Zealand Cavaliers**
      19-18

    3 Pretoria **South Africa** 33-18
    4 Johannesburg **South Africa** 24-10
    South Africa won series 3-1

Eddie Evans of Canada takes possession as All Black Alan Whetton moves in to tackle him in the 1991 World Cup quarter-final in Lille. New Zealand won 29-13, but were severely tested by the valiant Canadians.

AUSTRALIA v UNITED STATES
Played 5   Australia won 5

1912 Berkeley **Australia** 12-8	1987 Brisbane *WC* **Australia** 47-12
1976 Los Angeles **Australia** 24-12	1990 Brisbane **Australia** 67-9
1983 Sydney **Australia** 49-3	

AUSTRALIA v NEW ZEALAND MAORIS
Played 10   Australia won 4, New Zealand Maoris won 4, Drawn 2

1928 Wellington **New Zealand Maoris** 9-8
1931 Palmerston North **Australia** 14-3
1936 Palmerston North **Australia** 31-6
1946 Hamilton **New Zealand Maoris** 20-0
1949 *1* Sydney **New Zealand Maoris** 12-3
   2 Brisbane **Drawn** 8-8

   3 Sydney **Australia** 18-3
   Series drawn 1-1, with 1 draw
1958 *1* Brisbane **Australia** 15-14
   2 Sydney **Drawn** 3-3
   3 Melbourne **New Zealand Maoris** 13-6
   Series drawn 1-1, with 1 draw

AUSTRALIA v FIJI
Played 15   Australia won 12, Fiji won 2, Drawn 1

1952 *1* Sydney **Australia** 15-9
   2 Sydney **Fiji** 17-15
   Series drawn 1-1
1954 *1* Brisbane **Australia** 22-19
   2 Sydney **Fiji** 18-16
   Series drawn 1-1
1961 *1* Brisbane **Australia** 24-6
   2 Sydney **Australia** 20-14
   3 Melbourne **Drawn** 3-3
   Australia won series 2-0, with 1 draw

1972 Suva **Australia** 21-19
1976 *1* Sydney **Australia** 22-6
   2 Brisbane **Australia** 21-9
   3 Sydney **Australia** 27-17
   Australia won series 3-0
1980 Suva **Australia** 22-9
1984 Suva **Australia** 16-3
1985 *1* Brisbane **Australia** 52-28
   2 Sydney **Australia** 31-9
   Australia won series 2-0

AUSTRALIA v TONGA
Played 2   Australia won 1, Tonga won 1

1973 *1* Sydney **Australia** 30-12	*2* Brisbane **Tonga** 16-11
	Series drawn 1-1

AUSTRALIA v JAPAN
Played 3   Australia won 3

1975 *1* Sydney **Australia** 37-7	1987 Sydney *WC* **Australia** 42-23
2 Brisbane **Australia** 50-25	
Australia won series 2-0	

AUSTRALIA v ARGENTINA
Played 9   Australia won 5, Argentina won 3, Drawn 1

1979 *1* Buenos Aires **Argentina** 24-13
   2 Buenos Aires **Australia** 17-12
   Series drawn 1-1
1983 *1* Brisbane **Argentina** 18-3
   2 Sydney **Australia** 29-13
   Series drawn 1-1
1986 *1* Brisbane **Australia** 39-19

   2 Sydney **Australia** 26-0
   Australia won series 2-0
1987 *1* Buenos Aires **Drawn** 19-19
   2 Buenos Aires **Argentina** 27-19
   Argentina won series 1-0, with 1 draw
1991 Llanelli *WC* **Australia** 32-19

AUSTRALIA v WESTERN SAMOA
Played 1   Australia won 1

1991 Pontypool *WC* **Australia** 9-3

AUSTRALIA v ITALY
Played 3   Australia won 3

1983 Rovigo **Australia** 29-7   1988 Rome **Australia** 55-6
1986 Brisbane **Australia** 39-18

AUSTRALIA v CANADA
Played 2   Australia won 2

1985 *1* Sydney **Australia** 59-3   *2* Brisbane **Australia** 43-15
                                                    Australia won series 2-0

AUSTRALIA v KOREA
Played 1   Australia won 1

1987 Brisbane **Australia** 65-18

WORLD CUP WINNERS

New Zealand once: 1987
Australia once: 1991

GRAND SLAM WINNERS

England 10 times: 1913, 1914, 1921, 1923, 1924, 1928, 1957, 1980, 1991, 1992.
Wales 8 times: 1908, 1909, 1911, 1950, 1952, 1971, 1976, 1978.
France 4 times: 1968, 1977, 1981, 1987.   **Scotland** 3 times: 1925, 1984, 1990.
Ireland once: 1948.

TRIPLE CROWN WINNERS

Wales 17 times: 1893, 1900, 1902, 1905, 1908, 1909, 1911, 1950, 1952, 1965, 1969, 1971,
1976, 1977, 1978, 1979, 1988.   **England** 17 times: 1883, 1884, 1892, 1913, 1914, 1921,
1923, 1924, 1928, 1934, 1937, 1954, 1957, 1960, 1980, 1991, 1992.   **Scotland** 10 times:
1891, 1895, 1901, 1903, 1907, 1925, 1933, 1938, 1984, 1990.   **Ireland** 6 times: 1894,
1899, 1948, 1949, 1982, 1985.

INTERNATIONAL CHAMPIONSHIP WINNERS

Year	Winner	Year	Winner	Year	Winner	Year	Winner
1883	England	1911	Wales	1939	England / Wales / Ireland	1968	France
1884	England	1912	England / Ireland			1969	Wales
1885*	——			1947	Wales / England	1970	France / Wales
1886	England / Scotland	1913	England			1971	Wales
1887	Scotland	1914	England	1948	Ireland	1972*	——
1888*	——	1920	England / Scotland / Wales	1949	Ireland	1973	Quintuple tie
1889*	——			1950	Wales		
1890	England / Scotland	1921	England	1951	Ireland	1974	Ireland
1891	Scotland	1922	Wales	1952	Wales	1975	Wales
1892	England	1923	England	1953	England	1976	Wales
1893	Wales	1924	England	1954	England / France / Wales	1977	France
1894	Ireland	1925	Scotland			1978	Wales
1895	Scotland	1926	Scotland / Ireland	1955	France / Wales	1979	Wales
1896	Ireland	1927	Scotland / Ireland			1980	England
1897*	——			1956	Wales	1981	France
1898*	——	1928	England	1957	England	1982	Ireland
1899	Ireland	1929	Scotland	1958	England	1983	France / Ireland
1900	Wales	1930	England	1959	France	1984	Scotland
1901	Scotland	1931	Wales	1960	France / England	1985	Ireland
1902	Wales	1932	England / Wales / Ireland	1961	France	1986	France / Scotland
1903	Scotland			1962	France	1987	France
1904	Scotland			1963	England	1988	Wales / France
1905	Wales	1933	Scotland	1964	Scotland / Wales		
1906	Ireland / Wales	1934	England			1989	France
		1935	Ireland	1965	Wales	1990	Scotland
1907	Scotland	1936	Wales	1966	Wales	1991	England
1908	Wales	1937	England	1967	France	1992	England
1909	Wales	1938	Scotland				
1910	England						

Matches not completed, for various reasons

Wales have won the title outright most times, 21; England have won it 20 times,
Scotland 13, Ireland 10, and France 9.

B INTERNATIONALS 1991-92

28 December 1991, Murrayfield
Scotland B 19 (1G 3PG 1T)   Ireland B 29 (2G 3PG 2T)

Scotland B: M Appleson (London Scottish); D A Stark (Ayr), F J Harrold (London Scottish), I C Jardine (Stirling County), M Moncrieff (Gala); G P J Townsend (Gala), A D Nicol (Dundee HSFP); G D Wilson (Boroughmuir), M W Scott (Dunfermline), G B Robertson (Stirling County), N G B Edwards (Harlequins), R Scott (London Scottish), D J McIvor (Edinburgh Acads), I R Smith (Gloucester) (capt), D L M McIntosh (Pontypridd) *Replacement* M J de G Allingham (Heriot's FP) for Nicol
Scorers *Tries:* Stark, Nicol   *Conversion:* Appleson   *Penalty Goals:* Appleson, Townsend (2)
Ireland B: C R Wilkinson (Malone); N Furlong (UC Galway), M Ridge (Blackrock Coll), M McCall (Bangor), R M Wallace (Garryowen); D R McAleese (Ballymena), A Blair (Dungannon); P J Soden (Cork Const), J Murphy (Greystones) (capt), P D McCarthy (Cork Const), K Potts (St Mary's Coll), G M Fulcher (UC Dublin), D McCartney (Ballymena), M J Fitzgibbon (Shannon), B G O'Mahony (UC Cork)
Scorers *Tries:* Ridge, McCarthy, Potts, Fitzgibbon   *Conversions:* McAleese (2) *Penalty Goals:* McAleese (3)
Referee C Thomas (Wales)

19 January 1992, Madrid
Spain 3 (1PG)   England B 34 (2G 1PG 1DG 4T)

Spain: F Puerto; P Gutierrez, J Azkargarta, A Mino, C Moreno; M Sanchez, J Macariego; J Alvarez, A Alvarez, J Moral, A Gonzalez, H Massani, J Etxevarria, J Gutierrez, A Malo (capt)
Scorer *Penalty Goal:* Moreno
England B: I Hunter (Northampton); J Fallon (Bath), P de Glanville (Bath), J Buckton (Saracens), A Underwood (Cambridge U); S Barnes (Bath) (capt), S Douglas (Newcastle Gosforth); G Baldwin (Northampton), G Dawe (Bath), A Mullins (Harlequins), M Haag (Bath), D Sims (Gloucester), M Greenwood (Nottingham), B Clarke (Bath), N Back (Leicester)
Scorers *Tries:* Hunter (2), Douglas, Clarke, Underwood, Back   *Conversions:* Barnes (2) *Penalty Goal:* Barnes   *Dropped Goal:* Barnes
Referee M Desclaux (France)

31 January 1992, Richmond, London
England B 47 (4G 1PG 5T)   Ireland B 15 (2G 1PG)

England B: I Hunter (Northampton); J Fallon (Bath), P de Glanville (Bath), J Buckton (Saracens), A Underwood (Leicester); S Barnes (Bath) (capt), S Bates (Wasps); G Baldwin (Northampton), G Dawe (Bath), A Mullins (Harlequins), M Haag (Bath), D Sims (Gloucester), M Greenwood (Nottingham), B Clarke (Bath), N Back (Leicester)
Scorers *Tries:* Hunter, Underwood (3), Haag, Fallon (2), Back, Clarke
Conversions: Barnes (4)   *Penalty Goal:* Barnes
Ireland B: C Wilkinson (Malone); R Carey (Dungannon), M Ridge (Blackrock Coll), M McCall (Bangor), N Furlong (UC Galway); P Hennebry (Terenure Coll), A Rolland (Blackrock Coll); J Fitzgerald (Young Munster) (capt), A Adair (Instonians), P Millar (Ballymena), B Rigney (Greystones), T Coughlin (Old Belvedere), K Leahy (Wanderers), P Johns (Dublin U), D McCartney (Ballymena)
Scorers *Tries:* Wilkinson, Ridge   *Conversions:* Hennebry (2)   *Penalty Goal:* Hennebry
Referee G Gadjovich (Canada)

2 February 1992, Albi
France B 27 (2G 5PG)   Scotland B 18 (2G 2PG)

France B: S Ougier (Toulouse); P Bernat Salles (Pau), M Marfaing (Toulouse), H Couffignal (Colomiers), B Lorenzin (Albi); D Pouyau (Bayonne), J Cazalbou (Toulouse); L Armary (Lourdes) (*capt*), J-P Genet (Racing Club de France), R Crespy (Brive), H Miorin (Toulouse), J-F Gourragne (Béziers), P Chamayou (Narbonne), M Courtiols (Bègles), C Deslandes (Racing Club de France) *Replacement* F Seguier (Castres) for Cazalbou
Scorers *Tries:* Couffignal, Cazalbou   *Conversions:* Pouyau (2)   *Penalty Goals:* Pouyau (5)
Scotland B: M Appleson (London Scottish); D A Stark (Ayr), D W Caskie (Gloucester), I C Jardine (Stirling County), M Moncrieff (Gala); G P J Townsend (Gala), D Patterson (Edinburgh Acads); P M Jones (Gloucester), M W Scott (Dunfermline), G B Robertson (Stirling County), R Scott (London Scottish), A E D Macdonald (Heriot's FP), S J Reid (Boroughmuir), R I Wainwright (Edinburgh Acads) (*capt*), D L M McIntosh (Pontypridd)
Scorers *Tries:* Jardine, Wainwright   *Conversions:* Appleson, Townsend
Penalty Goals: Townsend (2)
Referee S W Piercy (England)

15 February 1992, Stade Jean Bouin, Paris
France B 18 (1G 4PG)   England B 22 (1G 4PG 1T)

France B: J-C Langlade (Nîmes); D Berty (Toulouse), E Bonneval (Toulouse), E Blanc (Racing Club de France), S Weller (Grenoble); F Velo (Grenoble), G Accoceberry (Tyrosse) (*capt*); P Tapie (Grenoble), F Landreau (Narbonne), E Michaud (Bordeaux University), G Bourguignon (Narbonne), J-P Revallier (Graulhet), B Dalla Riva (Toulouse), P Benetton (Agen), N Hallinger (Mazamet)
Replacements L van der Linden (Brive) for Dalla Riva; S Marty (Montpellier) for Weller; T Devergie (Nîmes) for Revallier
Scorers *Try:* Bonneval   *Conversion:* Velo   *Penalty Goals:* Velo (4)
England B: I Hunter (Northampton); J Fallon (Bath), J Buckton (Saracens), P de Glanville (Bath), A Underwood (Leicester); S Barnes (Bath)(*capt*), S Bates (Wasps); G Baldwin (Northampton), G Dawe (Bath), A Mullins (Harlequins), M Johnson (Leicester), D Sims (Gloucester), M Greenwood (Nottingham), B Clarke (Bath), J Cassell (Saracens)
Scorers *Tries:* Underwood, Fallon   *Conversion:* Barnes   *Penalty Goals:* Barnes (4)
Referee R McDowell (Ireland)

7 March 1992, Rome
Italy B 10 (1PG 1DG 1T)   England B 16 (1G 2PG 1T)

Italy B: L Troiani, P Vaccari, S Barba, S Bordon, Marcello Cuttitta; D Dominguez, A Ghini; Massimo Cuttitta, G Pivetta (*capt*), A Piazza, R Favoro, D Sasenna, A Bottacchiari, D Beratta, M Giovanelli *Replacement* G Croci for Sasenna
Scorers *Try:* Croci   *Penalty Goal:* Dominguez   *Dropped Goal:* Dominguez
England B: I Hunter (Northampton); J Fallon (Bath), J Buckton (Saracens) P de Glanville (Bath), A Underwood (Leicester); S Barnes (Bath) (*capt*), S Bates (Wasps); G Baldwin (Northampton), G Dawe (Bath), A Mullins (Harlequins), D Sims (Gloucester), M Johnson (Leicester), N Back (Leicester), B Clarke (Bath), M Greenwood (Nottingham) *Replacement* D Scully (Wakefield) for Bates
Scorers *Tries:* Hunter, Scully   *Conversion:* Barnes   *Penalty Goals:* Barnes (2)
Referee R Yeman (Wales)

Tony Underwood, who had such a fine season for England B, streaks away from the Irish defence in the crushing England B victory at Richmond.

OTHER INTERNATIONAL MATCHES 1991-92

8 June 1991, Calgary
CANADA 34 (3G 4PG 1T)   USA 15 (1G 3PG)

CANADA: M Wyatt (Velox Vahallians & British Columbia) *(capt)*; P Palmer (UBC Old Boys & British Columbia), C Stewart (Meralomas & British Columbia), D Lougheed (Toronto Welsh & Ontario), S Stewart (UBC & British Columbia); G Rees (Oak Bay Castaways & British Columbia), C Tynan (Meralomas & British Columbia); E Evans (UBC Old Boys & British Columbia), K Svoboda (Ajax Wanderers & Ontario), D Jackart (UBC Old Boys & British Columbia), N Hadley (UBC Old Boys & British Columbia), R van den Brink (Kats, Vancouver & British Columbia), R Radu (James Bay & British Columbia), B Breen (Meralomas & British Columbia), G Ennis (Kats, Vancouver & British Columbia)

Scorers *Tries:* Ennis (2), Palmer (2)   *Conversions:* Wyatt (3)   *Penalty Goals:* Wyatt (4)

USA: B Hayward (Albuquerque); K Higgins (Old Blues), J Burke (Albany Kicks), C O'Brien (Old Blues), C Williams (Old Blues); G Judge (Hartford Wanderers), M Pidcock (Pensacola); C Lippert (OMBAC, San Diego), J Schraml (Milwaukee), N Mottram (Boulder), K Swords (Beacon Hill, Boston), A Ridnell (Old Puget Sound), B Hough (OMBAC, San Diego), R Farley (Philadelphia/Whitemarsh), B Vizard (OMBAC, San Diego) *(capt) Replacements* R Nelson (Belmont Shore) for Higgins (5 mins); L Manga (South Jersey) for Lippert (70 mins); M DeJong (Denver Barbarians) for Judge (70 mins)

Scorers *Try:* Nelson   *Conversion:* O'Brien   *Penalty Goals:* Judge (3)

Referee S Griffiths (England)

31 August, National Stadium, Bucharest
Romania 18 (2G 2PG)   Scotland 12 (1G 2PG)

Romania: D Piti (Farul Constanta); C Sasu (Farul Constanta), G Sava (Stiinta Baia Mare), A Lungu (Dinamo Bucharest), L Colceriu (Steaua Bucharest); F Ion (Dinamo Bucharest), D Naega (Dinamo Bucharest); G Leonte (Mielan), G Ion (Dinamo Bucharest), C Stan (Contactoare Buzau), C Cojocariu (Dinamo Bucharest), S Ciorascu (Angoulême), G Dinu (Grivita Bucharest), A Guranescu (Dinamo Bucharest), H Dumitras (Pau) *(capt)*

Scorers *Tries:* Sasu, Ciorascu   *Conversions:* F Ion (2)   *Penalty Goals:* F Ion (2)

Scotland: P W Dods (Gala); A G Stanger (Hawick), S R P Lineen (Boroughmuir), D S Wyllie (Stewart's-Melville FP), I Tukalo (Selkirk); C M Chalmers (Melrose), G Armstrong (Jedforest); D M B Sole (Edinburgh Acads) *(capt)*, J Allan (Edinburgh Acads), A P Burnell (London Scottish), D F Cronin (Bath), G W Weir (Melrose), D J Turnbull (Hawick), F Calder (Stewart's-Melville FP), D B White (London Scottish)

Scorers *Try:* Tukalo   *Conversion:* Dods   *Penalty Goals:* Dods (2)

Referee A Ceccon (France)

7 September, Twickenham
ENGLAND 53 (7G 1PG 2T)   USSR 0

England: S D Hodgkinson (Nottingham); R Underwood (Leicester & RAF), J C Guscott (Bath), W D C Carling (Harlequins) *(capt)*, C Oti (Wasps); C R Andrew (Wasps), R J Hill (Bath); J Leonard (Harlequins), B C Moore (Harlequins), J A Probyn (Askeans); P J Ackford (Harlequins), W A Dooley (Preston Grasshoppers), M G Skinner (Harlequins), M C Teague (Gloucester), G W Rees (Nottingham) *Replacements* D Pears (Harlequins) for Hodgkinson (47 mins); S J Halliday (Harlequins) for Guscott (56 mins)

Scorers *Tries:* Oti (2), Guscott (2), Underwood (2), Skinner (2), Andrew   *Conversions:* Andrew (4), Hodgkinson (3)   *Penalty Goal:* Hodgkinson

USSR: V Voropaev (Monino); I Kuperman (Krasnoyarsk), V Sorokin (Minono), A Gomozkhin (Krasnoyarsk), I Mironov (Monino); S Boldakov (Alma-Ata), A Bychkov (Alma-Ata); I Khokhlov (Alma-Ata), S Molchanov (Moscow) *(capt)*, E Kabylkin (Krasnoyarsk), S Sergeev (Moscow), E Ganiakhin (Alma-Ata), A Tikhonov (Monino), A Ogryzhkov (Alma-Ata), V Negodin (Krasnoyarsk) *Replacements* A Zakarliuk (Krasnoyarsk) for Kuperman (40 mins); S Romanov (Moscow) for Gomozkhin (55 mins) **Referee** J B Anderson (Scotland)

28 December, Murrayfield
Scotland A 36 (3G 2PG 3T) Spain 16 (1G 1PG 1DG 1T)

Scotland A: P W Dods (Gala) *(capt)*; A G Stanger (Hawick), D W Caskie (Gloucester), D S Wyllie (Stewart's-Melville FP), A Moore (Edinburgh Acads); A G Shiel (Melrose), G H Oliver (Hawick); P M Jones (Gloucester), K S Milne (Heriot's FP), A P Burnell (London Scottish), D F Cronin (London Scottish), A E D Macdonald (Heriot's FP), S J Reid (Boroughmuir), G R Marshall (Selkirk), G W Weir (Melrose)
Scorers *Tries:* Dods (2), Wyllie, Moore, Macdonald, Weir   *Conversions:* Dods (3)
Penalty Goals: Dods (2)
Spain: O Gonzalez (Santaboiana); P Gutierrez (Arquitectura), J Azkargorta (Getxo), A Mino (Ciencas), C Moreno (Salvador); M Sanchez (Ciencas), J Mazariegos (Salvador); J Alvarez (Salvador) *(capt)*, J Alducin (San Juan Luz), J L Moral (Entrepinares), A Malo (Santaboiana), A Gonzalez (Madrid), J Etxebarria (Getxo), J Gutierrez (Arquitectura), E Illaregui (San Juan Luz) *Replacements* F Castro (Getxo) for Moral; J Rodriguez (Arquitectura) for Illaregui
Scorers *Tries:* P Gutierrez, Etxebarria   *Conversion:* Sanchez   *Penalty Goal:* Sanchez
Dropped Goal: Sanchez
Referee G Simmonds (Wales)

UNDER-21 RUGBY 1991-92

1 September, Castlecroft
England U-21s 94 (11G 7T)   **Belgium 0**

England U-21s: R Liley (Wakefield); A Adebayo (Bath), L Boyle (Leicester), P Flood (Bridgend), S Bromley (Liverpool St Helens); N Matthews (Gloucester), S Douglas (Newcastle Gosforth); G Rowntree (Leicester), R Cockerill (Coventry), W Bullock (Coventry), M Johnson (Leicester), D Sims (Gloucester), G Adams (Bath) (*capt*), M Rennell (Bedford), J Pearson (Bristol) *Replacement* S Cassidy (West Hartlepool) for Pearson
Scorers *Tries:* Bromley (3), Douglas (3), Adebayo (2), Matthews (2), Rennell (2), Boyle, Cockerill, Flood, Liley, Pearson, Sims *Conversions:* Liley (11)
Referee F Howard (Liverpool)

16 October, Rodney Parade (Newport)
Wales U-21s 22 (2G 2PG 1T)   **Ireland U-21s 15** (2G 1PG)

Wales U-21s: *Tries:* L Evans, S Williams, R Howley *Conversions:* N Jenkins (2) *Penalty Goals:* N Jenkins (2)
Ireland U-21s: *Tries:* N Woods, G Longwell *Conversions:* N Woods (2) *Penalty Goal:* N Woods

23 October, Donnybrook (Dublin)
Ireland U-21s 19 (1G 2PG 1DG 1T)   **England U-21s 10** (2PG 1T)

Ireland U-21s: C O'Shea (Lansdowne); B O'Shea (Shannon), R Hunter (Loughborough U), M Ridge (Blackrock), N Woods (Blackrock); N Malone (Loughborough U), N Hogan (Terenure); L Murphy (UCC), M McDermott (Blackrock), P Wallace (UCC), G Longwell (Queen's U), S Rooney (UCD), L Toland (Old Crescent), R Wilson (Instonians), V Costello (Blackrock) *Replacement* M Kernahan (Glasgow U) for McDermott
Scorers *Tries:* C O'Shea, Costello *Conversion:* Woods *Penalty Goals:* Woods (2) *Dropped Goal:* Woods
England U-21s: S Wills (Leicester); J Sleightholme (Wakefield), P Flood (Bridgend), S Ravenscroft (Saracens), M Lloyd (Bristol); D Willett (Bath), S Douglas (Newcastle Gosforth); G Clark (Swansea U), R Cockerill (Coventry), G Rowntree (Leicester), R Bramley (Wakefield), R West (Gloucester), M Rennell (Bedford), G Adams (Bath) (*capt*), C Wilkins (Wasps) *Replacement* M Mapletoft (Rugby) for Wills
Scorers *Try:* Flood *Penalty Goals:* Wills (2)
Referee D Davies (Wales)

18 April 1992, Bridgehaugh, Stirling
Scotland U-21s 19 (5PG 1T)   **Wales U-21s 28** (1G 2PG 4T)

Scotland U-21s: M M Thomson (Stewart's-Melville FP); K R Milligan (Stewart's-Melville FP), W M Tonkin (Currie), R J S Shepherd (Edinburgh Acads), J R Newton (Dundee HSFP); G P J Townsend (Gala), B W Redpath (Melrose); R B McNulty (Stewart's-Melville FP), C J Cowan (Dundee HSFP), R K Hastings (West of Scotland), M J McVie (Edinburgh Acads), J M Clinkenbeard (Currie), A G Ness (Glasgow High/Kelvinside) (*capt*), G N Flockhart (Stirling County), S J Campbell (Dundee HSFP)
Scorers *Try:* Campbell *Penalty Goals:* Newton (5)
Wales U-21s: J Westwood (Newport); W T Proctor (Llanelli), J Redrup (Bristol), N Boobyer (Llanelli), P Harries (Pontypridd); M McCarthy (Neath), R Howley (Bridgend); M Davis (Newport), A Phillips (Bridgend Ath), K W Allen (Aberavon), D Jones (Llanelli), A Gibbs (Newbridge), O Lloyd (Bridgend), S Quinnell (Llanelli), S Williams (Neath) (*capt*) *Replacement* J Lewis (Pontypridd) for Boobyer
Scorers *Tries:* Boobyer, Harries, Quinnell (2), Westwood *Conversion:* Westwood *Penalty Goals:* McCarthy, Westwood
Referee D Lamont (Ireland)

2 May, Twickenham
England U-21s 21 (1G 3PG 2DG)   **French Armed Forces 21** (3G 1PG)

England U-21s: M Mapletoft (Rugby); R Bryce (Sale), M Dawson (Northampton), S Ravenscroft (Saracens), J Sleightholme (Wakefield); P Grayson (Preston Grasshoppers), K Bracken (Bristol); C Clark (Swansea U), R Cockerill (Coventry), G Rowntree (Leicester), R West (Gloucester), I Desmond (Harlequins), G Adams (Bath) (*capt*), M Rennell (Bedford), R Bramley (Wakefield)
Scorers *Try:* Dawson *Conversion:* Grayson *Penalty Goals:* Grayson (3) *Dropped Goals:* Grayson (2)
French Armed Forces *Tries:* Soubira, Bertrand, Marfaing *Conversions:* Marfaing (3) *Penalty Goal:* Marfaing
Referee C Thomas (Wales)

3 May, Leiden
Netherlands 12 (2G)   **England U-21s 48** (5G 2PG 3T)

Netherlands *Tries:* Michelsen, Nagtegaal *Conversions:* Bos (2)
England U-21s: C Thompson (Sheffield U); S Wills (Leicester), J Alexander (Harlequins), P Flood (Bridgend) (*capt*), M Griffiths (Blackheath); A Handley (De La Salle), I Sanders (Bath); D Molloy (Wasps), R Kellam (Newbury), D Crompton (Exeter), A Meadows (Newcastle Gosforth), D Blyth (Waterloo), C Millhouse (Bristol), L Dallaglio

(Wasps), A Diprose (Loughborough U) *Replacements* C Lee (West Hartlepool) for Alexander; P Urwin (Blaydon) for Blyth
Scorers *Tries:* Wills (3), Thompson, Griffiths, Sanders, Meadows, penalty try   *Conversions:* Thompson (5)
Penalty Goals: Thompson (2)
Referee B Smith (Ireland)

Other representative matches: Scotland U-21s 28, Scotland Students 23 (Murrayfield); England Students U-21s 16, Scotland U-21s 19 (Newcastle)

30 April 1992, Saracens: Vauxhall National Under-21 Sevens: Semi-finals: Moseley 6, Wasps 4; Harlequins 22, Northampton 0 **Final:** Harlequins 22, Moseley 20 **18-19 April, Sunbury: 12th London Irish Under-21 15-a-side tournament** *for the Beamish Trophy:* **Semi-finals:** Sale 3, Saracens 0; Loughborough University 9, West Hartlepool 3 **Final:** Sale 12, Loughborough University 3 *Beamish Player of the Tournament:* Grant (West Hartlepool)

Under-21 Divisional Championship: North 44, South-West 21; Midlands 10, London & South-East 16; London & South-East 13, South-West 17; North 12, Midlands 0; London & South-East 17, North 20; South-West 21, Midlands 19

18 April 1992, Twickenham: ADT County Under-21 Championship: Final Surrey 16 (1G 2PG 1T), Lancashire 16 (1G 2PG 1T) **Divisional Rounds: London & South-East:** Surrey 47, Sussex 9; Kent 28, Hertfordshire 26; Kent 14, Surrey 14; Hertfordshire 37, Sussex 4; Surrey 37, Hertfordshire 7; Sussex 4, Kent 55; Middlesex 10, Army 3; Hampshire 28, Eastern Counties 8; Eastern Counties 18, Middlesex 3; Hampshire 52, Army 3; Middlesex 9, Hampshire 36; Army 7, Eastern Counties 38 **London & South-East play-off:** Surrey 14, Hampshire 9 **Midlands:** North Midlands 6, East Midlands 15; East Midlands 28, Notts, Lincs & Derbys 0; Notts, Lincs & Derbys 4, North Midlands 6; Leicestershire 32, Staffordshire 0; Staffordshire 6, Warwickshire 22; Warwickshire 31, Leicestershire 7 **Midlands play-off semi-finals:** East Midlands 15, Leicestershire 6; Warwickshire 28, North Midlands 12 **Midlands play-off final:** East Midlands 16, Warwickshire 12 **North:** Cheshire 9, Lancashire 15; Yorkshire 13, Cheshire 14; Lancashire 22, Yorkshire 12; Durham 8, Northumberland 13; Cumbria 3, Northumberland 31; Cumbria 6, Durham 15 **North play-off:** Lancashire 12, Northumberland 0 **South & South-West:** Dorset & Wilts 3, Berkshire 21; RAF 12, Berkshire 17; Dorset & Wilts 19, Oxfordshire 15; Oxfordshire 11, RAF 12; Oxfordshire 3, Buckinghamshire 62; Berkshire 22, Oxfordshire 4; Berkshire 0, Buckinghamshire 19; Buckinghamshire 41, Dorset & Wilts 0; Buckinghamshire 61, RAF 0; Cornwall 22, Gloucestershire 9; Devon 45, Royal Navy 6; Devon 12, Cornwall 9; Cornwall 37, Royal Navy 10; Gloucestershire 30, Somerset 12; Somerset 3, Devon 38; Somerset 3, Cornwall 39; Gloucestershire 50, Devon 7; Royal Navy 9, Somerset 6; Royal Navy 22, Gloucestershire 18 **South & South-West play-off:** Cornwall 11, Buckinghamshire 9 **Semi-finals:** Lancashire 18, Cornwall 9 (Waterloo); East Midlands 10, Surrey 35 (Northampton)

ITALY CHALLENGE FRENCH SUPREMACY

THE FIRA CHAMPIONSHIP 1990-92
Chris Rhys

France again emerged as winners of the FIRA Championship, which is nowadays held over a two-year period of home and away matches with the reverse fixtures played in the second season. The CIS, with their political difficulties, did well to complete their allocated fixtures.

While France maintained control of the Championship, the significant move was made by Italy, who maintained the considerable improvement they showed at the World Cup to finish comfortably clear of Romania and the CIS in second place. Italy have never beaten France at full international level, but their loss at Tarbes by 21-18 was probably their best performance against the French. In what proved to be the deciding match of the Championship, France won with a 78th-minute penalty from full-back Ougier after the Italians had fought back from a 15-6 deficit. Both teams scored two tries.

Both France and Italy won their other three matches in 1991-92. France dominated Spain at Perpignan, scoring ten tries; later, on the same afternoon that their first XV beat Romania in a full international at Le Havre, the 'reserve' XV scored seven tries in Moscow to defeat the CIS. Three Toulouse youngsters were given their first caps against Romania: Ougier at full-back and the centres Deylaud and Marfaing. The try-scorers were Saint-André, Cadieu and Galthié, and there was a penalty try.

Italy, meanwhile, put significant daylight between themselves and Romania with a 39-13 win at Rovigo, to which Diego Dominguez contributed 23 points. Their season was completed by wins in Moscow and Madrid.

Romania warmed up for the French match with a 34-6 win against the CIS to take third place. There were tries from Racean (2), Dumitras and David, and Ignat contributed 16 points. Spain lost seven of their eight games at the foot of Group A, but the sole victory was their first against one of the top competitors in European rugby, a momentous 6-0 win against Romania. Spain's points came from penalties by Moreno and Nunez.

RESULTS

Date	Venue	Result			
1990					
30 Sep	Treviso	Italy	30	Spain	6
3 Oct	Padova	Romania	19	Spain	6
21 Oct	Moscow	Soviet Union	3	Romania	10
24 Nov	Rovigo	Italy	34	Soviet Union	12

1991

Date	Venue	Result			
2 Mar	Rome	Italy	6	France	15
17 Mar	Lorient	France	38	Soviet Union	12
21 Apr	Bucharest	Romania	18	Italy	21
28 Apr	Madrid	Spain	6	France	24
11 May	Moscow	Soviet Union	30	Spain	3
22 Jun	Bucharest	Romania	21	France	33
3 Nov	Moscow	CIS	3	Italy	21
17 Nov	Seville	Spain	16	CIS	19

1992

Date	Venue	Result			
9 Feb	Madrid	Spain	21	Italy	22
16 Feb	Tarbes	France	21	Italy	18
22 Mar	Perpignan	France	53	Spain	4
4 Apr	Madrid	Spain	6	Romania	0
18 Apr	Rovigo	Italy	39	Romania	13
10 May	Bucharest	Romania	34	CIS	6
28 May	Le Havre	France	25	Romania	6
28 May	Moscow	CIS	15	France	36

FINAL TABLE

	P	W	D	L	F	A	Pts
France	8	8	0	0	245	85	24
Italy	8	6	0	2	194	109	20
Romania	8	3	0	5	121	139	14
CIS	8	2	0	6	94	192	12
Spain	8	1	0	7	68	197	10

Season	Winners	Runners-Up	Third
1973-74	**France**	Romania	Spain
1974-75	**Romania**	France	Italy
1975-76	**France**	Italy	Romania
1976-77	**Romania**	France	Italy
1977-78	**France**	Romania	Spain
1978-79	**France**	Romania	Soviet Union
1979-80	**France**	Romania	Italy
1980-81	**Romania**	France	Soviet Union
1981-82	**France**	Italy	Romania
1982-83	**Romania**	Italy	Soviet Union
1983-84	**France**	Romania	Italy
1984-85	**France**	Romania	Soviet Union
1985-86	**France**	Soviet Union	Italy
1986-87	**France**	Soviet Union	Romania
1987-88	**France**	Soviet Union	Romania
1988-89	**France**	Soviet Union	Romania
1989-90	**France** / **Romania** / **Soviet Union**		
1990-92	**France**	Italy	Romania

Philippe Saint-André of France, pictured here on his way to a try against Wales in the Five Nations Championship, was a member of the dominant French side in the FIRA Championship. He was one of ten try-scorers against Spain at Perpignan in March.

SEVENS TOURNAMENTS 1991-92
THE 1992 CATHAY PACIFIC-HONG KONG BANK SEVENS
Nick Cain   *Rugby World & Post*

Fiji may blow hot and cold in the 15-a-side game, but when it comes to sevens, they sizzle. Given the monsoon-like deluge which swamped Hong Kong over the Sevens weekend, leaving the pretenders to Fiji's crown aquaplaning across a pitch ankle-deep in water and mud, this was some feat. In fact Fiji were in such sizzling form they could have put a hot platter of Szechuan-style king prawns to shame.

They defied the elements to claim a record third successive title and left a good New Zealand side wallowing in their wake after a demonstration of athleticism and wet-weather rugby skills that stunned the 30,000 rain-sodden spectators at So Kun Po. Indeed, the conditions were so bad on the Sunday that the HKRFU organising committee, having received a unanimous 'no' vote after asking team managers whether they wished to abandon the event, decided to dispense with scrummages and instead award a tapped penalty to the side putting in. It proved to be a sound decision, not only because it kept the ball from being buried at every set-piece but also because it afforded us the privilege of seeing the Fijian mastery of handling in the wet. We will be lucky to see such skills again – unless, of course, we rush off to Fiji at the first peal of thunder.

Rain may be a great leveller where most teams are concerned, but when the Fijians heard about the storm headed for the Crown Colony they couldn't have cared a jot: 'We frequently play in worse conditions than this in Fiji – we're used to it', said Waisale Serevi, their brilliant play-maker, after masterminding the 22-6 victory over New Zealand. In 20 minutes' play on a pitch that resembled a rice paddy they had dropped the ball just once.

While Serevi's bag of tricks created the openings, Fiji's main strike weapon was the 6 feet 4 inch lock Mesake Rasari. Against France in the quarter-finals and Australia in the semis – the likes of Philippe Sella, Tim Horan, Jason Little and Willie Ofahengaue notwithstanding – Rasari was unstoppable. He was not only one of the biggest men on show, he was also one of the fastest, and he rammed the point home with a hat-trick of tries in the final against the Kiwis. Suffice it to say that coach Ratu Kitione Tuibua's insistence that Rasari be flown back to Fiji for sevens trials from his soldiering duties as a member of the United Nations Peace-keeping Force in the Lebanon paid off handsomely.

What makes this an oddity is that Fiji would have been unlikely to have flown a player halfway around the world if the mission had been 15-a-side rugby rather than sevens. Success in sevens – and in Hong Kong in particular – has become the Holy Grail of Fijian rugby. The crowd at So Kun Po would yield a 'Who's Who' of Fijian government notables, so it is not surprising that victory in Hong Kong is rewarded with a public holiday or that the players are fêted like conquering heroes back in their island republic. Serevi's comment that 'the difference between the World Cup and the Hong Kong Sevens was that we trained harder for Hong Kong' puts the Fijian love affair with the abbreviated code in perspective.

Ironically, sevens excellence, and the six months a year the Fijians devote to it, does very little to develop their expertise in the 15-a-side game, and that, ultimately, is the yardstick by which all rugby nations are judged. The tragedy of this is that a player like Serevi, described by their Kiwi World Cup coach George Simpkin as 'the most gifted player I have ever seen', might not fulfil his potential to become one of the world's great fly-halves due to his, and his countrymens', lack of exposure to the full code.

It is, paradoxically, a lack of exposure and commitment to the Hong Kong Sevens over the past decade that has led to a decline in British sevens standards. This year's representatives, in the guise of the Barbarians and the Irish Wolfhounds, were once again relegated to the ranks of the also-rans. While the Gavin Hastings-led Barbarians were run out of the quarter-finals by the speedy Koreans, the Wolfhounds were down-graded to the Plate, where they lost to the powerful Tongans in the semis. It was left to Hong Kong, a polyglot of expatriate servicemen, policemen and businessmen, to salvage British pride by shading Tonga in a humdinger Plate final.

The refusal of the likes of the RFU and IRFU to send representative sides to Hong Kong is sorely mistaken. They should bear in mind that the benefits of exposure to the best sevens tournament in the world far outweigh the short-term expedient of trying to ensure that your team isn't embarrassed. Come the inaugural World Cup Sevens at Murrayfield, the Northern Hemisphere, with England and Ireland in the vanguard, will probably pay the price for this indifference. The cannibal caricature on the T-shirts sported by the Fijian contingent in Hong Kong offered an early warning: 'We'll eat 'em'.

Rest assured, they weren't talking about sizzling king prawns.

RESULTS
Pool A: Fiji 34, Sri Lanka 0; Japan 18, Sri Lanka 0; Fiji 38, Japan 0 **Pool B:** France 22, Papua New Guinea 0; Irish Wolfhounds 28, Papua New Guinea 0; France 22, Irish Wolfhounds 6 **Pool C:** Argentina 10, Germany 4; American Eagles 22, Germany 0; Argentina 12, American Eagles 0 **Pool D:** Australia 42, Singapore 0; Tonga 20, Singapore 4; Australia 18, Tonga 0 **Pool E:** Barbarians 36, Taiwan 0; Taiwan 24, Romania 0; Barbarians 22, Romania 0 **Pool F:** Canada 50, Thailand 0; South Korea 30, Thailand 4; South Korea 16, Canada 12 **Pool G:** Western Samoa 54, Arabian Gulf 0; Namibia 34, Arabian Gulf 0; Western Samoa 8, Namibia 0 **Pool H:** New Zealand 54, Malaysia 0; Hong Kong 22, Malaysia 0; New Zealand 38, Hong Kong 0

BOWL: Quarter-finals: Papua New Guinea 14, Sri Lanka 10; Germany 20, Singapore 10; Romania 32, Thailand 0; Malaysia 8, Arabian Gulf 4 **Semi-finals:** Papua New Guinea 10, Germany 4; Romania 30, Malaysia 6 **Final:** Romania 18, Papua New Guinea 12

Even the electric Tim Horan of Australia is unable to catch Mesake Rasari, the extraordinary Fijian, as he strides away to score in the quarter-final of the Hong Kong Sevens.

PLATE: Quarter-finals: Irish Wolfhounds 12, Japan 0; Tonga 20, US Eagles 6; Taipei 20, Canada 10; Hong Kong 16, Namibia 4 **Semi-finals:** Tonga 22, Irish Wolfhounds 16; Hong Kong 16, Taipei 12 **Final:** Hong Kong 12, Tonga 8 (*aet*)

CUP: Quarter-finals: Fiji 22, France 6; Australia 28, Argentina 0; South Korea 16, Barbarians 10; New Zealand 18, Western Samoa 12 **Semi-finals:** Fiji 28, Australia 4; New Zealand 14, South Korea 0 **Final:** Fiji 22, New Zealand 6

Teams in the final
Fiji: F Seru, Vili Rauluni, W Serevi, S Rabaka; M Rasari, Vesito Rauluni (*capt*), R Sakeasi *Replacement* E Nadura for Rasari
Scorers *Tries:* Rasari (3), Seru   *Conversions:* Serevi (3)
New Zealand: T Wright (*capt*), G Osborne, G Bachop, S Pierce; E Rush, P Lam, D Seymour *Replacements* G Alley for Seymour; P Bale for Wright
Scorers *Try:* Pierce   *Conversion:* Osborne
Referee L Peard (Wales)

SICILY SEVENS 1992

Rugby World Cup Sevens qualifying tournament, 29-31 May, Club Amatori Sport, Catania.

After the first two days and three stages, the leading 8 nations went through to the Sicily Trophy and the remainder to the Etna Cup, where Sicily Select VII joined the event. The last four in the Sicily Trophy qualify for the Murrayfield World Cup Sevens finals, 16-18 April 1993.

STAGE 1
Pool A: Namibia 18, Poland 0; Portugal 12, Sweden 16; Gulf 6, Poland 13; Portugal 6, Namibia 24; Sweden 16, Gulf 10; Poland 6, Portugal 9; Sweden 0, Namibia 38; Gulf 6, Portugal 18; Poland 0, Sweden 22; Namibia 42, Gulf 0 **Pool B:** Zimbabwe 10, Hong Kong 10; Belgium 10, Morocco 0; Sri Lanka 10, Czechoslovakia 17; Belgium 0, Zimbabwe 38; Sri Lanka 4, Hong Kong 30; Morocco 12, Czechoslovakia 12; Sri Lanka 6, Belgium 28; Morocco 6, Zimbabwe 16; Hong Kong 20, Czechoslovakia 8; Morocco 6, Sri Lanka 16; Hong Kong 28, Belgium 0; Zimbabwe 24, Czechoslovakia 12; Hong Kong 32, Morocco 16; Zimbabwe 22, Sri Lanka 4; Belgium 22, Czechoslovakia 6 **Pool C:** Spain 10, Tunisia 8; Taiwan 12, Germany 6; Malaysia 12, Kenya 12; Taiwan 22, Spain 12; Malaysia 0, Tunisia 22; Germany 20, Kenya 6; Malaysia 4, Taiwan 32; Germany 0, Spain 14; Tunisia 22, Kenya 0; Germany 14, Malaysia 12; Tunisia 12, Taiwan 12; Spain 22, Kenya 6; Tunisia 16, Germany 14; Spain 20, Malaysia 10; Taiwan 34 Kenya 0

STAGE 2
Pool D: Namibia 24, Taiwan 10; Namibia 28, Hong Kong 4; Hong Kong 12, Taiwan 12
Pool E: Sweden 0, Spain 24; Sweden 4, Zimbabwe 20; Zimbabwe 18, Spain 16 **Pool F:** Portugal 8, Tunisia 18; Portugal 18, Belgium 6; Belgium 10, Tunisia 18 **Pool G:** Poland 0, Germany 12; Poland 12, Czechoslovakia 12; Czechoslovakia 16, Germany 30

STAGE 3
Pool H: Namibia 22, Poland 0; Portugal 12, Poland 6; Namibia 24, Portugal 6 **Pool I:** Taiwan 30, Czechoslovakia 10; Tunisia 10, Czechoslovakia 12; Taiwan 19, Tunisia 6 **Pool M:** Zimbabwe 18, Belgium 4; Spain 24, Belgium 0; Zimbabwe 12, Spain 16

ETNA CUP
Pool J: Gulf 12, Malaysia 20; Morocco 24, Malaysia 12; Gulf 18, Morocco 6 **Pool K:** Sicily 12, Kenya 12; Sri Lanka 0, Kenya 24; Sicily 32, Sri Lanka 0 **Pool L:** Hong Kong 24, Germany 0; Sweden 14, Germany 0; Hong Kong 32, Sweden 0
Quarter-finals: Poland 10, Kenya 18; Tunisia 22, Morocco 0; Germany 6, Sicily 22; Belgium 10, Malaysia 14 **Semi-finals:** Kenya 12, Sicily 15; Tunisia 14, Malaysia 10
Final: Sicily 10, Tunisia 8

SICILY TROPHY
Quarter-finals: Namibia 16, Zimbabwe 10; Spain 10, Portugal 6; Taiwan 20, Sweden 12; Hong Kong 26, Czechoslovakia 6 **Semi-finals:** Namibia 24, Taiwan 6; Spain 12, Hong Kong 14 **Final:** Namibia 26, Hong Kong 12

Qualifiers for Murrayfield: NAMIBIA, HONG KONG, TAIWAN, SPAIN
The qualifiers join Argentina, Australia, England, Scotland, Ireland, Wales, France, New Zealand, Fiji, Western Samoa, Tonga, Italy, Romania, Netherlands, USA, Canada, South Africa and South Korea

Namibia, winners of the Sicily Trophy, qualified for the Rugby World Cup Sevens finals, to take place at Murrayfield in 1993, along with Hong Kong, Taiwan and Spain.

THE MIDDLESEX SEVENS 1992
(sponsored by Save & Prosper)

The portents for the Middlesex Sevens were not good, for the day dawned grey and stormy and the early ties were not exactly blessed with excitement and class. The Western Samoans, fielding a team composed entirely of players from the Islands and with none of the New Zealand-based players, struggled in their opening match against London Welsh and pulled through only late in the game. However, early appearances were somewhat deceptive. Apart from the odd shower the weather improved, and so did the Samoans. By the end they were playing brilliant sevens, hard-running and even harder tackling. They picked up speed and surged through the competition, hammering the hitherto impressive London Scottish in the final by five tries to one.

The Samoans had come to Twickenham as part of a sevens tour to publicise and raise funds for recovery after the cyclone which hit the Islands earlier in the year. The events were squeezed out of the news in Europe but the devastation to livestock, crops, homes and facilities was almost total. A collection at the Sevens and allied events kicked off a fund for Western Samoa and the part the rugby players played could not be over-praised.

The feature of the final was the complete refusal of the Samoans to allow London Scottish to find their stride and to unleash their moves. The Samoans came up so quickly and tackled with such a thump that London Scottish momentum was destroyed. Vaisuai scored two tries, and Faogali and Meleisea one each. There was also a penalty try awarded for obstruction. The alien conditions and the surroundings made no difference to the young champions.

The experiment to scale down the involvement of Middlesex-based teams to include the top teams from Division 1 of the Courage Leagues was not a success. Hardly any of the invitees brought a full squad and some had obviously been unable to prepare. Boroughmuir, the other guest side, were easily beaten by London Scottish in the semi-final, and Harlequins were dumped by the Samoans in the other semi – although not before they had given the visitors something of a fright. However, the likes of Gloucester, Orrell and Leicester were disappointing and the smaller clubs, traditionally the heroes of the crowd, made little impression. Eton Manor subsided by 46-0 to Wasps and Camberley could not force their way past Orrell in the first round proper. It was a good job that the crowd, made smaller and muted by the weather, were roused by the Samoans. They saved the day and the spectacle.

RESULTS
Sixth round: Harlequins 26, Gloucester 4; Askeans 6, Rosslyn Park 10; Camberley 12, Orrell 18; London Welsh 4, Western Samoa 18; Boroughmuir 18, Richmond 12; Saracens 0, Bath 14; Eton Manor 0, Wasps 46; Leicester 34, London Scottish 0

Seventh round: Harlequins 16, Rosslyn Park 12; Orrell 6, Western Samoa 26; Boroughmuir 22, Bath 16; Wasps 6, London Scottish 12 **Semi-finals:** Harlequins 12, Western Samoa 18; Boroughmuir 6, London Scottish 12 **Final:** Western Samoa 30, London Scottish 6

Teams in the final
London Scottish: K Troup, F Harrold, M Appleson, C Russell; A Walker, A Withers-Green, I Morrison (*capt*)
Scorers *Try:* Harrold   *Conversion:* Appleson
Western Samoa: T Meleisea, L Malasia, P Faogali, V Vitale; M Iupeli (*capt*), K Toleafoa, A Vaisuai
Scorers *Tries:* Faogali, Vaisuai (2), Meleisea, penalty try   *Conversions:* Faogali (5)
Referee C Rees (London Society)

WINNERS

1926	**Harlequins**	1959	**Loughborough Colleges**
1927	**Harlequins**	1960	**London Scottish**
1928	**Harlequins**	1961	**London Scottish**
1929	**Harlequins**	1962	**London Scottish**
1930	**London Welsh**	1963	**London Scottish**
1931	**London Welsh**	1964	**Loughborough Colleges**
1932	**Blackheath**	1965	**London Scottish**
1933	**Harlequins**	1966	**Loughborough Colleges**
1934	**Barbarians**	1967	**Harlequins**
1935	**Harlequins**	1968	**London Welsh**
1936	**Sale**	1969	**St Luke's College**
1937	**London Scottish**	1970	**Loughborough Colleges**
1938	**Metropolitan Police**	1971	**London Welsh**
1939	**Cardiff**	1972	**London Welsh**
1940	**St Mary's Hospital**	1973	**London Welsh**
1941	**Cambridge University**	1974	**Richmond**
1942	**St Mary's Hospital**	1975	**Richmond**
1943	**St Mary's Hospital**	1976	**Loughborough Colleges**
1944	**St Mary's Hospital**	1977	**Richmond**
1945	**Notts**	1978	**Harlequins**
1946	**St Mary's Hospital**	1979	**Richmond**
1947	**Rosslyn Park**	1980	**Richmond**
1948	**Wasps**	1981	**Rosslyn Park**
1949	**Heriot's FP**	1982	**Stewart's-Melville FP**
1950	**Rosslyn Park**	1983	**Richmond**
1951	**Richmond II**	1984	**London Welsh**
1952	**Wasps**	1985	**Wasps**
1953	**Richmond**	1986	**Harlequins**
1954	**Rosslyn Park**	1987	**Harlequins**
1955	**Richmond**	1988	**Harlequins**
1956	**London Welsh**	1989	**Harlequins**
1957	**St Luke's College**	1990	**Harlequins**
1958	**Blackheath**	1991	**London Scottish**
		1992	**Western Samoa**

Harlequins have won the title 13 times, Richmond 9 (including one by their second VII), London Welsh 8, London Scottish 7, St Mary's Hospital and Loughborough Colleges 5 each, Rosslyn Park 4, Wasps 3, Blackheath and St Luke's College (now Exeter University) twice, Barbarians, Sale, Met Police, Cardiff, Cambridge University, Notts (now Nottingham), Heriot's FP, Stewart's-Melville FP and Western Samoa once each

THE WORTHINGTON NATIONAL SEVENS 1992

QUALIFIERS
From South-West qualifying (Exeter RFC, 5 April 1992): Bristol, Exeter **From North qualifying** (Orrell RFC, 5 April 1992): Orrell; (Morley RFC, 5 April 1992): Wakefield, Morley **From London qualifying** (Stoop Memorial Ground, 12 April 1992): London Scottish, Harlequins, Saracens **From Midlands qualifying** (Northampton RFC, 14 April 1992): Rugby, Leicester, Bedford
Bath qualified as host club

FINALS DAY
26 April, Recreation Ground, Bath
Pool A finishing order: Bath, Wakefield, Bedford **Pool B finishing order:** London Scottish, Rugby, Orrell **Pool C finishing order:** Bristol, Harlequins, Morley **Pool D finishing order:** Leicester, Saracens, Exeter
Semi-finals: Bath 0, London Scottish 34; Bristol 14, Leicester 18 **Final:** London Scottish 28, Leicester 0

Previous winners: Harlequins (1989), Northampton (1990), Bath (1991)

ENGLAND'S GREATEST SLAM AND THEIR FINEST HOURS?

THE 1991-92 SEASON IN ENGLAND
David Hands *The Times*

Recession? In economic terms perhaps, but, as Harold Macmillan might have said: 'You never had it so good' when it came to English rugby in World Cup year. That, of course, is the rub: England's national side recorded many achievements in 1991-92 but they could not win the World Cup. The reasons why are advanced elsewhere but, to this observer at least, England seemed happy just to be on stage at Twickenham that day. It was a reflection of a mood of tranquility – contrasting with the grimmer attitude of 1990-91 – which was apparent throughout the Five Nations Championship and which may have communicated itself to the many thousands of youngsters who watched the World Cup on television. They watched England win the first back-to-back Grand Slam for 68 years and were inspired to take up the game and to find new heroes who were not footballers or cricketers or athletes.

For that was England's triumph in 1991-92. The game advanced far nearer the great mass of the population than ever before, and the trick for those who administrate it during the 1990s is how best to ride the dragon of popularity without allowing Rugby Union's traditions to be consumed in the dragon's breath. The Rugby Football Union's technical administrators and youth development officers up and down the country reported a wave of enthusiasm in the wake of the World Cup; of schools returning to the game, of new teams springing up, many of them involving youngsters whose knowledge of rugby's history is nil but who want to play a fast contact sport and emulate the Carlings, the Underwoods, the Richards and the Moores.

The RFU has a better understanding of this watershed season than many are prepared to give them credit for, but there is a difference between recognising your Rubicon and building the appropriate bridge. The England squad, building on their precocious schemes of late 1990-91, finally won approval from the International Rugby Football Board for their promotional 'Run with the Ball' campaign and are now seeking ways of expanding their sporting fame within the amateur regulations. They, too, would be wise to heed the warning issued by Geoff Cooke, the team manager since 1987, who was reappointed in April 1992 to continue until the 1995 World Cup. In his report for the season, Cooke stressed that 'the reality is that we are still no better than third in world terms, behind Australia and New Zealand, and with the reappearance of South Africa, we could easily slip to fourth place. The challenge for the future is clear. England must work hard to retain its status, for all the other northern [hemisphere] countries will be even more determined than ever to knock us off our pedestal'.

In other words, sporting fame is ephemeral. That was underlined by the retirement from international rugby of Paul Ackford, after the World Cup final, and Rory Underwood, England's most-capped player. Other key elements of England's success of the last three years, Mike Teague, Simon Halliday and Mickey Skinner, are unlikely to be seen again, but they have written their names large in the history of the English game, particularly Underwood who, after eight years, called a halt as England's leading try-scorer with 35 from his 55 appearances. There was pressure from below on all of them, for in 1991-92 – unlike in the previous season – it was notable that England's other representative sides also attained a striking success rate. The B team completed their own Grand Slam of four victories out of four before embarking on their most ambitious project yet, an eight-match tour of New Zealand; the Under-21s had a hiccup against the Irish during the World Cup but ended the season strongly; the Students, preparing for their own World Cup in Italy, lost only to the French – as did the Colts – while the Schools too enjoyed a Grand Slam, albeit one of less than definitive proportions. A competitive edge, physique and fitness abounded throughout, although the skills of the game were sometimes less evident.

The appeal to the public was unparalleled. On six occasions Twickenham was sold out – including the World Cup pool game against the USA, the Varsity Match and the Pilkington Cup final – and major matches at headquarters produced aggregate crowds of 606,400 and record receipts of £7,369,000. Such heady popularity convinced the RFU that the time was ripe to proceed apace with the rebuilding programme at Twickenham. Competitive rates in the building industry encouraged the hope that the new East Stand, costing in the region of £25 million in all, would be completed at the same rapid rate as the North Stand, and it is hoped that the bottom tier of the new structure will be ready when England resume relationships with South Africa on 14 November 1992.

In terms of performance England oscillated during the World Cup; on tour in Australia and Fiji three months earlier they had tried to broaden the style that won the 1991 Grand Slam and had come unstuck against Australia to the tune of a record 40-15 defeat. Against the best the world could offer they did not satisfactorily solve their stylistic problems, although their strength and resolve were enough to carry them into the final, where a more judicious tactical blend might, on the day, have won the Webb Ellis Cup. It did not, and England said farewell to Roger Uttley, their coach of four years' standing, who helped restore self-belief and purpose to the English game. He was replaced by Richard Best, the Harlequins coach, who encouraged a more liberal approach in the short time at his disposal, although the opposition in the Five Nations Championship was not to be compared with that of the World Cup.

For various reasons not one of the other four countries was anything near full strength. It then becomes the task of the perceived champion country to live up to overblown expectations, and England came close to doing so as they tramped to their second Slam. They scored more points in the Championship than any previous side and played some exceptional rugby against Ireland and, away from home, France, although their joy at the fifth successive defeat of the French was over-shadowed by the descent of that game into shame when two French forwards were sent off for foul play. What they could not do was finish in the grand manner at Twickenham against Wales, who defended so stoutly that England, while never in danger of defeat, had to work for their three tries, the last of which was scored by Wade Dooley in his 50th game for England.

From a long international season two players stood out: Peter Winterbottom and Jonathan Webb. The tireless Winterbottom, another to join the exclusive 50 games club after ten seasons, can hardly have played more consistent rugby at flank forward either for his country or his club, Harlequins. To his iron tackling he has grafted handling skills and a sense of positional play, which have enabled him to resist the challenges of such good players as Gary Rees, Andy Robinson and the emerging Neil Back and Martin Pepper. Webb, relaxed and efficient, underpinned the whole by his goal-kicking, which brought him a record Championship tally, and by the penetration of his offence and the solidity of his defence.

Both players featured in the Pilkington Cup final, Winterbottom as captain of Harlequins and Webb at full-back for Bath who, a week earlier, had won the Courage Clubs Championship on points difference from Orrell. In winning the double for the second time – they also took League and Cup in 1989 – Bath set a marvellous example to other aspiring clubs. Theirs was not the most formidable set-piece pack in the country and at times, notably in the early part of a League season deferred until November because of the World Cup, they appeared to struggle, but they have an indomitable spirit which seldom admits defeat. Their only League loss was at Orrell, who did not have the all-round strength to cast off their bridesmaid tag yet could point to a last-gasp dropped goal by Huw Davies of Wasps as the reason for the League title slipping from their grasp.

Since Stuart Barnes did exactly the same in the Cup final to win the match for Bath, one might argue that dropped goals were back in fashion at a time when the International Board debated whether or not to downgrade their value. In the end the Board did not, although they did admit many other Law changes in a bid to speed up the game – whether those who watched a fascinating Cup final felt the Laws needed so much tinkering is open to debate. Whatever else it was during 1991-92, Rugby Union in England was a game of endless contrasts, and that remains its fascination.

ENGLISH INTERNATIONAL PLAYERS
(up to 31 March 1992)

ABBREVIATIONS

A – Australia; *Arg* – Argentina; *F* – France; *Fj* – Fiji; *I* – Ireland; *It* – Italy; *J* – Japan; *M* – Maoris; *NZ* – New Zealand; *R* – Romania; *S* – Scotland; *SA* – South Africa; *US* – United States; *W* – Wales; (C) – Centenary match v Scotland at Murrayfield, 1971 (non-championship); *P* – England v President's Overseas XV at Twickenham in RFU's Centenary season, 1970-71; (R) – Replacement. Entries in square brackets [ ] indicate appearances in the World Cup.

Note: Years given for Five Nations' matches are for second half of season; eg 1972 means season 1971-72. Years for all other matches refer to the actual year of the match. When a series has taken place, figures have been used to denote the particular matches in which players have featured. Thus 1984 *SA* 2 indicates that a player appeared in the second Test of the series.

Aarvold, C D (Cambridge U, W Hartlepool, Headingley, Blackheath) 1928 *A, W, I, F, S,* 1929 *W, I, F,* 1931 *W, S, F,* 1932 *SA, W, I, S,* 1933 *W*
Ackford, P J (Harlequins) 1988 *A,* 1989 *S, I, F, W, R, Fj,* 1990 *I, F, W, S, Arg* 3, 1991 *W, S, I, F, A,* [*NZ, It, F, S, A*]
Adams, A A (London Hospital) 1910 *F*
Adams, F R (Richmond) 1875 *I, S,* 1876 *S,* 1877 *I,* 1878 *S,* 1879 *S, I*
Adey, G J (Leicester) 1976 *I, F*
Adkins, S J (Coventry) 1950 *I, F, S,* 1953 *W, I, F, S*
Agar, A E (Harlequins) 1952 *SA, W, S, I, F,* 1953 *W, I*
Alcock, A (Guy's Hospital) 1906 *SA*
Alderson, F H R (Hartlepool R) 1891 *W, I, S,* 1892 *W, S,* 1893 *W*
Alexander, H (Richmond) 1900 *I, S,* 1901 *W, I, S,* 1902 *W, I*
Alexander, W (Northern) 1927 *F*
Allison, D F (Coventry) 1956 *W, I, S, F,* 1957 *W,* 1958 *W, S*
Allport, A (Blackheath) 1892 *W,* 1893 *I,* 1894 *W, I, S*
Anderson, S (Rockcliff) 1899 *I*
Anderson, W F (Orrell) 1973 *NZ* 1
Anderton, C (Manchester FW) 1889 *M*
Andrew, C R (Cambridge U, Nottingham, Wasps, Toulouse) 1985 *R, F, S, I, W,* 1986 *W, S, I, F,* 1987 *I, F, W,* [*J* (R), *US*], 1988 *S, I* 1,2, *A* 1,2, *Fj, A,* 1989 *S, I, F, W, R, Fj,* 1990 *I, F, W, S, Arg* 3, 1991 *W, S, I, F, Fj, A,* [*NZ, It, US, F, S, A*], 1992 *S, I, F, W*
Archer, H (Bridgwater A) 1909 *W, F, I*
Armstrong, R (Northern) 1925 *W*
Arthur, T G (Wasps) 1966 *W, I*
Ashby, R C (Wasps) 1966 *I, F,* 1967 *A*
Ashcroft, A (Waterloo) 1956 *W, I, S, F,* 1957 *W, I, F, S,* 1958 *W, A, I, F, S,* 1959 *I, F, S*
Ashcroft, A H (Birkenhead Park) 1909 *A*
Ashford, W (Richmond) 1897 *W, I,* 1898 *S, W*
Ashworth, A (Oldham) 1892 *I*
Askew, J G (Cambridge U) 1930 *W, I, F*
Aslett, A R (Richmond) 1926 *W, I, F, S,* 1929 *S, F*
Assinder, E W (O Edwardians) 1909 *A, W*
Aston, R L (Blackheath) 1890 *S, I*
Auty, J R (Headingley) 1935 *S*

Bailey, M D (Cambridge U, Wasps) 1984 *SA* 1,2, 1987 [*US*], 1989 *Fj,* 1990 *I, F, S* (R)
Bainbridge, S (Gosforth, Fylde) 1982 *F, W,* 1983 *F, W, S, I, NZ,* 1984 *S, I, F, W,* 1985 *NZ* 1,2, 1987 *F, W, S,* [*J, US*]
Baker, D G S (OMTs) 1955 *W, I, F, S*
Baker, E M (Moseley) 1895 *W, I, S,* 1896 *W, I, S,* 1897 *W*
Baker, H C (Clifton) 1887 *W*
Bance, J F (Bedford) 1954 *S*
Barley, B (Wakefield) 1984 *I, F, W, A,* 1988 *A* 1,2, *Fj*
Barnes, S (Bristol, Bath) 1984 *A,* 1985 *R* (R), *NZ* 1,2, 1986 *S* (R), *F* (R), 1987 *I* (R), 1988 *Fj*
Barr, R J (Leicester) 1932 *SA, W, I*
Barrett, E I M (Lennox) 1903 *S*
Barrington, T J M (Bristol) 1931 *W, I*
Barrington-Ward, L E (Edinburgh U) 1910 *W, I, F, S*
Barron, J H (Bingley) 1896 *S,* 1897 *W, I*
Bartlett, J T (Waterloo) 1951 *W*
Bartlett, R M (Harlequins) 1957 *W, I, F, S,* 1958 *I, F, S*

Barton, J (Coventry) 1967 *I, F, W,* 1972 *F*
Batchelor, T B (Oxford U) 1907 *F*
Bates, S M (Wasps) 1989 *R*
Bateson, A H (Otley) 1930 *W, I, F, S*
Bateson, H D (Liverpool) 1879 *I*
Batson, T (Blackheath) 1872 *S,* 1874 *S,* 1875 *I*
Batten, J M (Cambridge U) 1874 *S*
Baume, J L (Northern) 1950 *S*
Baxter, J (Birkenhead Park) 1900 *W, I, S*
Bayfield, M C (Northampton) 1991 *Fj, A,* 1992 *S, I, F, W*
Bazley, R C (Waterloo) 1952 *I, F,* 1953 *W, I, F, S,* 1955 *W, I, F, S*
Beaumont, W B (Fylde) 1975 *I, A* 1(R),2, 1976 *A, W, S, I, F,* 1977 *S, I, F, W,* 1978 *F, W, S, I, NZ,* 1979 *S, I, F, W, NZ,* 1980 *I, F, W, S,* 1981 *W, S, I, F, Arg* 1,2, 1982 *A, S*
Bedford, H (Morley) 1889 *M,* 1890 *S, I*
Bedford, L L (Headingley) 1931 *W, I*
Beer, I D S (Harlequins) 1955 *F, S*
Beese, M C (Liverpool) 1972 *W, I, F*
Bell, F J (Northern) 1900 *W*
Bell, H (New Brighton) 1884 *I*
Bell, J L (Darlington) 1878 *I*
Bell, P J (Blackheath) 1968 *W, I, F, S*
Bell, R W (Northern) 1900 *W, I, S*
Bendon, G J (Wasps) 1959 *W, I, F, S*
Bennett, N O (St Mary's Hospital, Waterloo) 1947 *W, S, F,* 1948 *A, W, I, S*
Bennett, W N (Bedford, London Welsh) 1975 *A* 1, 1976 *S* (R), 1979 *S, I, F, W*
Bennetts, B B (Penzance) 1909 *A, W*
Bentley, J (Sale) 1988 *I* 2, *A* 1
Bentley, J E (Gipsies) 1871 *S,* 1872 *S*
Berridge, M J (Northampton) 1949 *W, I*
Berry, H (Gloucester) 1910 *W, I, F, S*
Berry, J (Tyldesley) 1891 *W, I, S*
Berry, J T W (Leicester) 1939 *W, I, S*
Beswick, E (Swinton) 1882 *I, S*
Biggs, J M (UCH) 1878 *S,* 1879 *I*
Birkett, J G G (Harlequins) 1906 *S, F, SA,* 1907 *F, W, S,* 1908 *F, W, I, S,* 1910 *W, I, S,* 1911 *W, F, I, S,* 1912 *W, I, S, F*
Birkett, L (Clapham R) 1875 *S,* 1877 *I, S*
Birkett, R H (Clapham R) 1871 *S,* 1875 *S,* 1876 *S,* 1877 *I*
Bishop, C C (Blackheath) 1927 *F*
Black, B H (Blackheath) 1930 *W, I, F, S,* 1931 *W, I, S, F,* 1932 *S,* 1933 *W*
Blacklock, J H (Aspatria) 1898 *I,* 1899 *I*
Blakeway, P J (Gloucester) 1980 *I, F, W, S,* 1981 *W, S, I, F,* 1982 *F, W,* 1984 *I, F, W, SA* 1, 1985 *R, F, S, I*
Blakiston, A F (Northampton) 1920 *S,* 1921 *W, I, S, F,* 1922 *W,* 1923 *S, F,* 1924 *W, I, F, S,* 1925 *NZ, W, I, S, F*
Blatherwick, T (Manchester) 1878 *I*
Body, J A (Gipsies) 1872 *S,* 1873 *S*
Bolton, C A (United Services) 1909 *F*
Bolton, R (Harlequins) 1933 *W,* 1936 *S,* 1937 *S,* 1938 *W, I*
Bolton, W N (Blackheath) 1882 *I, S,* 1883 *W, I, S,* 1884 *W, I, S,* 1885 *I,* 1887 *I, S*
Bonaventura, M S (Blackheath) 1931 *W*
Bond, A M (Sale) 1978 *NZ,* 1979 *S, I, NZ,* 1980 *I,* 1982 *I*
Bonham-Carter, E (Oxford U) 1891 *S*
Bonsor, F (Bradford) 1886 *W, I, S,* 1887 *W, S,* 1889 *M*
Boobbyer, B (Rosslyn Park) 1950 *W, I, F, S,* 1951 *W,*

F, 1952 *S, I, F*
Booth, L A (Headingley) 1933 *W, I, S,* 1934 *S,* 1935 *W, I, S*
Botting, I J (Oxford U) 1950 *W, I*
Boughton, H J (Gloucester) 1935 *W, I, S*
Boyle, C W (Oxford U) 1873 *S*
Boyle, S B (Gloucester) 1983 *W, S, I*
Boylen, F (Hartlepool R) 1908 *F, W, I, S*
Bradby, M S (United Services) 1922 *I, F*
Bradley, R (W Hartlepool) 1903 *W*
Bradshaw, H (Bramley) 1892 *S,* 1893 *W, I, S,* 1894 *W, I, S*
Brain, S E (Coventry) 1984 *SA* 2, *A* (R), 1985 *R, F, S, I, W, NZ* 1,2, 1986 *W, S, I, F*
Braithwaite, J (Leicester) 1905 *NZ*
Braithwaite-Exley, B (Headingley) 1949 *W*
Brettargh, A T (Liverpool OB) 1900 *W,* 1903 *I, S,* 1904 *W, I, S,* 1905 *I, S*
Brewer, J (Gipsies) 1876 *I*
Briggs, A (Bradford) 1892 *W, I, S*
Brinn, A (Gloucester) 1972 *W, I, S*
Broadley, T (Bingley) 1893 *W, S,* 1894 *W, I, S,* 1896 *S*
Bromet, W E (Richmond) 1891 *W, I,* 1892 *W, I, S,* 1893 *W, I, S,* 1895 *W, I, S,* 1896 *I*
Brook, P W P (Harlequins) 1930 *S,* 1931 *F,* 1936 *S*
Brooke, T J (Richmond) 1968 *F, S*
Brooks, F G (Bedford) 1906 *SA*
Brooks, M J (Oxford U) 1874 *S*
Brophy, T J (Liverpool) 1964 *I, F, S,* 1965 *W, I,* 1966 *W, I, F*
Brough, J W (Silloth) 1925 *NZ, W*
Brougham, H (Harlequins) 1912 *W, I, S, F*
Brown, A A (Exeter) 1938 *S*
Brown, L G (Oxford U, Blackheath) 1911 *W, F, I, S,* 1913 *SA, W, F, I, S,* 1914 *W, I, S, F,* 1921 *W, I, S, F,* 1922 *W*
Brown, T W (Bristol) 1928 *S,* 1929 *W, I, S, F,* 1932 *S,* 1933 *W, I, S*
Brunton, J (N Durham) 1914 *W, I, S*
Brutton, E B (Cambridge U) 1886 *S*
Bryden, C C (Clapham R) 1876 *I,* 1877 *S*
Bryden, H A (Clapham R) 1874 *S*
Buckingham, R A (Leicester) 1927 *F*
Bucknall, A L (Richmond) 1969 *SA,* 1970 *I, W, S, F,* 1971 *W, I, F, S* (2[1C])
Buckton, J R D (Saracens) 1988 *A* (R), 1990 *Arg* 1,2
Budd, A (Blackheath) 1878 *I,* 1879 *S, I,* 1881 *W, S*
Budworth, R T D (Blackheath) 1890 *W,* 1891 *W, S*
Bull, A G (Northampton) 1914 *W*
Bullough, E (Wigan) 1892 *W, I, S*
Bulpitt, M P (Blackheath) 1970 *S*
Bulteel, A J (Manchester) 1876 *I*
Bunting, W L (Moseley) 1897 *I, S,* 1898 *I, S, W,* 1899 *S,* 1900 *S,* 1901 *I, S*
Burland, D W (Bristol) 1931 *W, I, F,* 1932 *I, S,* 1933 *W, I, S*
Burns, B H (Blackheath) 1871 *S*
Burton, G W (Blackheath) 1879 *S, I,* 1880 *S,* 1881 *I, W, S*
Burton, H C (Richmond) 1926 *W*
Burton, M A (Gloucester) 1972 *W, I, F, S, SA,* 1974 *F, W,* 1975 *S, A* 1,2, 1976 *A, W, S, I, F,* 1978 *F, W*
Bush, J A (Clifton) 1872 *S,* 1873 *S,* 1875 *S,* 1876 *I, S*
Butcher, C J S (Harlequins) 1984 *SA* 1,2, *A*
Butcher, W V (Streatham) 1903 *S,* 1904 *W, I, S,* 1905 *W, I, S*
Butler, A G (Harlequins) 1937 *W, I*
Butler, P E (Gloucester) 1975 *A* 1, 1976 *F*
Butterfield, J (Northampton) 1953 *F, S,* 1954 *W, NZ, I, S, F,* 1955 *W, I, F, S,* 1956 *W, I, S, F,* 1957 *W, I, F, S,* 1958 *W, A, I, F, S,* 1959 *W, I, F, S*
Byrne, F A (Moseley) 1897 *W*
Byrne, J F (Moseley) 1894 *W, I, S,* 1895 *I, S,* 1896 *I,* 1897 *W, I, S,* 1898 *I, S, W,* 1899 *I*

Cain, J J (Waterloo) 1950 *W*
Campbell, D A (Cambridge U) 1937 *W, I*
Candler, P L (St Bart's Hospital) 1935 *W,* 1936 *NZ, W, I, S,* 1937 *W, I, S,* 1938 *W, S*
Cannell, L B (Oxford U, St Mary's Hospital) 1948 *F, 1949 W, I, F, S,* 1950 *W, I, F, S,* 1952 *SA, W,* 1953 *W, I, F,* 1956 *I, S, F,* 1957 *W, I*
Caplan, D W N (Headingley) 1978 *S, I*
Cardus, R M (Roundhay) 1979 *F, W*

Carey, G M (Blackheath) 1895 *W, I, S,* 1896 *W, I*
Carleton, J (Orrell) 1979 *NZ,* 1980 *I, F, W, S,* 1981 *W, S, I, F, Arg* 1,2, 1982 *A, S, I, F, W,* 1983 *F, W, S, I, NZ,* 1984 *S, I, F, W, A*
Carling, W D C (Durham U, Harlequins) 1988 *F, W, S, I* 1,2, *A*2, *Fj, A,* 1989 *S, I, F, W, Fj,* 1990 *I, F, W, S, Arg* 1,2,3, 1991 *W, S, I, F, Fj, A,* [*NZ, It, US, F, S, A*], 1992 *S, I, F, W*
Carpenter, A D (Gloucester) 1932 *SA*
Carr, R S L (Manchester) 1939 *W, I, S*
Cartwright, V H (Nottingham) 1903 *W, I, S,* 1904 *W, S,* 1905 *W, I, S, NZ,* 1906 *W, I, S, F, SA*
Catcheside, H C (Percy Park) 1924 *W, I, F, S,* 1926 *W, I,* 1927 *I, S*
Cattell, R H B (Blackheath) 1895 *W, I, S,* 1896 *W, I, S,* 1900 *W*
Cave, J W (Richmond) 1889 *M*
Cave, W T C (Blackheath) 1905 *W*
Challis, R (Bristol) 1957 *I, F, S*
Chambers, E L (Bedford) 1908 *F,* 1910 *W, I*
Chantrill, B S (Bristol) 1924 *W, I, F, S*
Chapman, C E (Cambridge U) 1884 *W*
Chapman, F E (Hartlepool) 1910 *W, I, F, S,* 1912 *W,* 1914 *W, I*
Cheesman, W I (OMTs) 1913 *SA, W, F, I*
Cheston, E C (Richmond) 1873 *S,* 1874 *S,* 1875 *I, S,* 1876 *S*
Chilcott, G J (Bath) 1984 *A,* 1986 *I, F,* 1987 *F* (R), *W,* [*J, US, W*(R)], 1988 *I* 2 (R), *Fj,* 1989 *I* (R), *F, W, R*
Christopherson, P (Blackheath) 1891 *W, S*
Clark, C W H (Liverpool) 1876 *I*
Clarke, A J (Coventry) 1935 *W, I, S,* 1936 *NZ, W, I*
Clarke, S J S (Cambridge U, Blackheath) 1963 *W, I, F, S, NZ* 1,2, *A,* 1964 *NZ, W, I,* 1965 *I, F, S*
Clayton, J H (Liverpool) 1871 *S*
Clements, J W (O Cranleighans) 1959 *I, F, S*
Cleveland, C R (Blackheath) 1887 *W, S*
Clibborn, W G (Richmond) 1886 *W, I, S,* 1887 *W, I, S*
Clough, F J (Cambridge U, Orrell) 1986 *I, F,* 1987 [*J*(R), *US*]
Coates, C H (Yorkshire W) 1880 *S,* 1881 *S,* 1882 *S*
Coates, V H M (Bath) 1913 *SA, W, F, I, S*
Cobby, W (Hull) 1900 *W*
Cockerham, A (Bradford Olicana) 1900 *W*
Colclough, M J (Angoulême, Wasps, Swansea) 1978 *S, I,* 1979 *NZ,* 1980 *F, W, S,* 1981 *W, S, I, F,* 1982 *A, S, I, F, W,* 1983 *F, NZ,* 1984 *S, I, F, W,* 1986 *W, S, I, F*
Coley, E (Northampton) 1929 *F,* 1932 *W*
Collins, P J (Camborne) 1952 *S, I, F*
Collins, W E (O Cheltonians) 1874 *S,* 1875 *I, S,* 1876 *I, S*
Considine, S G U (Bath) 1925 *F*
Conway, G S (Cambridge U, Rugby, Manchester) 1920 *F, I, S,* 1921 *F,* 1922 *W, I, F, S,* 1923 *W, I, S, F,* 1924 *W, I, F, S,* 1925 *NZ,* 1927 *W*
Cook, J G (Bedford) 1937 *S*
Cook, P W (Richmond) 1965 *I, F*
Cooke, D A (Harlequins) 1976 *W, S, I, F*
Cooke, D H (Harlequins) 1981 *W, S, I, F,* 1984 *I,* 1985 *R, F, S, I, W, NZ* 1,2
Cooke, P (Richmond) 1939 *W, I*
Coop, T (Leigh) 1892 *S*
Cooper, J G (Moseley) 1909 *A, W*
Cooper, M J (Moseley) 1973 *F, S, NZ* 2 (R), 1975 *F, W,* 1976 *A, W,* 1977 *S, I, F, W*
Coopper, S F (Blackheath) 1900 *W,* 1902 *W, I,* 1905 *W, I, S,* 1907 *W*
Corbett, L J (Bristol) 1921 *F,* 1923 *W, I,* 1924 *W, I, F, S,* 1925 *NZ, W, I, S, F,* 1927 *W, I, S, F*
Corless, B J (Coventry, Moseley) 1976 *A, I* (R), 1977 *S, I, F, W,* 1978 *F, W, S, I*
Cotton, F E (Loughborough Colls, Coventry, Sale) 1971 *S* (2[1C]), *P,* 1973 *W, I, F, S, NZ* 2, *A,* 1974 *S, I,* 1975 *I, F, W,* 1976 *A, W, S, I, F,* 1977 *S, I, F, W,* 1978 *S, I,* 1979 *NZ,* 1980 *I, F, W, S,* 1981 *W*
Coulman, M J (Moseley) 1967 *A, I, F, S, W,* 1968 *W, I, F, S*
Coulson, T J (Coventry) 1927 *W,* 1928 *A, W*
Court, E D (Blackheath) 1885 *W*
Coverdale, H (Blackheath) 1910 *F,* 1912 *I, F,* 1920 *W*
Cove-Smith, R (OMTs) 1921 *S, F,* 1922 *I, F, S,* 1923 *W, I, S, F,* 1924 *W, I, S, F,* 1925 *NZ, W, I, S, F,* 1927 *W, I, S, F,* 1928 *A, W, I, F, S,* 1929 *W, I*
Cowling, R J (Leicester) 1977 *S, I, F, W,* 1978 *F, NZ,*

1979 *S*, *I*
Cowman, A R (Loughborough Colls, Coventry) 1971 *S* (2[1C]), *P*, 1973 *W*, *I*
Cox, N S (Sunderland) 1901 *S*
Cranmer, P (Richmond, Moseley) 1934 *W*, *I*, *S*, 1935 *W*, *I*, *S*, 1936 *NZ*, *W*, *I*, *S*, 1937 *W*, *I*, *S*, 1938 *W*, *I*, *S*
Creed, R N (Coventry) 1971 *P*
Cridlan, A G (Blackheath) 1935 *W*, *I*, *S*
Crompton, C A (Blackheath) 1871 *S*
Crosse, C W (Oxford U) 1874 *S*, 1875 *I*
Cumberlege, B S (Blackheath) 1920 *W*, *I*, *S*, 1921 *W*, *I*, *S*, *F*, 1922 *W*
Cumming, D C (Blackheath) 1925 *S*, *F*
Cunliffe, F L (RMA) 1874 *S*
Currey, F I (Marlborough N) 1872 *S*
Currie, J D (Oxford U, Harlequins, Bristol) 1956 *W*, *I*, *S*, *F*, 1957 *W*, *I*, *F*, *S*, 1958 *W*, *A*, *I*, *F*, *S*, 1959 *W*, *I*, *F*, *S*, 1960 *W*, *I*, *F*, *S*, 1961 *SA*, 1962 *W*, *I*, *F*
Cusani, D A (Orrell) 1987 *I*
Cusworth, L (Leicester) 1979 *NZ*, 1982 *F*, *W*, 1983 *F*, *W*, *NZ*, 1984 *S*, *I*, *F*, *W*, 1988 *F*, *W*

D'Aguilar, F B G (Royal Engineers) 1872 *S*
Dalton, T J (Coventry) 1969 *S* (R)
Danby, T (Harlequins) 1949 *W*
Daniell, J (Richmond) 1899 *W*, 1900 *I*, *S*, 1902 *I*, *S*, 1904 *I*, *S*
Darby, A J L (Birkenhead Park) 1899 *I*
Davenport, A (Ravenscourt Park) 1871 *S*
Davey, J (Redruth) 1908 *S*, 1909 *W*
Davey, R F (Teignmouth) 1931 *W*
Davidson, Jas (Aspatria) 1897 *S*, 1898 *S*, *W*, 1899 *I*, *S*
Davidson, Jos (Aspatria) 1899 *W*, *S*
Davies, G H (Cambridge U, Coventry, Wasps) 1981 *S*, *I*, *F*, *Arg* 1,2, 1982 *A*, *S*, *I*, 1983 *F*, *W*, *S*, 1984 *S*, *SA* 1,2, 1985 *R* (R), *NZ* 1,2, 1986 *W*, *S*, *I*, *F*
Davies, P H (Sale) 1927 *I*
Davies, V G (Harlequins) 1922 *W*, 1925 *NZ*
Davies, W J A (United Services, RN) 1913 *SA*, *W*, *F*, *I*, *S*, 1914 *I*, *S*, *F*, 1920 *F*, *I*, *S*, 1921 *W*, *I*, *S*, *F*, 1922 *I*, *F*, *S*, 1923 *W*, *I*, *S*, *F*
Davies, W P C (Harlequins) 1953 *S*, 1954 *NZ*, *I*, 1955 *W*, *I*, *F*, *S*, 1956 *W*, 1957 *F*, *S*, 1958 *W*
Davis, A M (Harlequins) 1963 *W*, *I*, *S*, *NZ* 1,2, 1964 *NZ*, *W*, *I*, *F*, *S*, 1966 *W*, 1967 *A*, 1969 *SA*, 1970 *I*, *W*, *S*
Dawe, R G R (Bath) 1987 *I*, *F*, *W*, [*US*]
Dawson, E F (RIEC) 1878 *I*
Day, H L V (Leicester) 1920 *W*, 1922 *W*, *F*, 1926 *S*
Dean, G J (Harlequins) 1931 *I*
Dee, J M (Hartlepool R) 1962 *S*, 1963 *NZ* 1
Devitt, Sir T G (Blackheath) 1926 *I*, *F*, 1928 *A*, *W*
Dewhurst, J H (Richmond) 1887 *W*, *I*, *S*, 1890 *W*
De Winton, R F C (Marlborough N) 1893 *W*
Dibble, R (Bridgwater A) 1906 *S*, *F*, *SA*, 1908 *F*, *W*, *I*, *S*, 1909 *A*, *W*, *F*, *I*, *S*, 1910 *S*, 1911 *W*, *F*, 1912 *W*, *I*, *S*
Dicks, J (Northampton) 1934 *W*, *I*, *S*, 1935 *W*, *I*, *S*, 1936 *S*, 1937 *I*
Dillon, E W (Blackheath) 1904 *W*, *I*, *S*, 1905 *W*
Dingle, A J (Hartlepool R) 1913 *I*, 1914 *S*, *F*
Dixon, P J (Harlequins, Gosforth) 1971 *P*, 1972 *W*, *I*, *F*, *S*, 1973 *I*, *F*, *S*, 1974 *S*, *I*, *F*, *W*, 1975 *I*, 1976 *F*, 1977 *S*, *I*, *F*, *W*, 1978 *F*, *S*, *I*, *NZ*
Dobbs, G E B (Devonport A) 1906 *W*, *I*
Doble, S A (Moseley) 1972 *SA*, 1973 *NZ* 1, *W*
Dobson, D D (Newton Abbot) 1902 *W*, *I*, *S*, 1903 *W*, *I*, *S*
Dobson, T H (Bradford) 1895 *S*
Dodge, P W (Leicester) 1978 *W*, *S*, *I*, *NZ*, 1979 *S*, *I*, *F*, *W*, 1980 *W*, *S*, 1981 *W*, *S*, *I*, *F*, *Arg* 1,2, 1982 *A*, *S*, *F*, *W*, 1983 *F*, *W*, *S*, *I*, *NZ*, 1985 *R*, *F*, *S*, *I*, *W*, *NZ* 1,2
Donnelly, M P (Oxford U) 1947 *I*
Dooley, W A (Preston Grasshoppers, Fylde) 1985 *R*, *F*, *S*, *I*, *W*, *NZ* 2 (R), 1986 *W*, *S*, *I*, *F*, 1987 *F*, *W*, [*A*, *US*, *W*], 1988 *F*, *W*, *S*, *I* 1,2, *A* 1,2, *Fj*, *A*, 1989 *S*, *I*, *F*, *W*, *R*, *Fj*, 1990 *I*, *F*, *W*, *S*, *Arg* 1,2,3, 1991 *W*, *S*, *I*, *F*, [*NZ*, *US*, *F*, *S*, *A*], 1992 *S*, *I*, *F*, *W*
Dovey, B A (Rosslyn Park) 1963 *W*, *I*
Down, P J (Bristol) 1909 *A*
Dowson, A O (Moseley) 1899 *S*
Drake-Lee, N J (Cambridge U, Leicester) 1963 *W*, *I*, *F*, *S*, 1964 *NZ*, *W*, *I*, 1965 *W*
Duckett, H (Bradford) 1893 *I*, *S*
Duckham, D J (Coventry) 1969 *I*, *F*, *S*, *W*, *SA*, 1970 *I*,

W, *S*, *F*, 1971 *W*, *I*, *F*, *S* (2[1C]), *P*, 1972 *W*, *I*, *F*, *S*, 1973 *NZ* 1, *W*, *I*, *F*, *S*, *NZ* 2, *A*, 1974 *S*, *I*, *F*, *W*, 1975 *I*, *F*, *W*, 1976 *A*, *W*, *S*
Dudgeon, H W (Richmond) 1897 *S*, 1898 *I*, *S*, *W*, 1899 *W*, *I*, *S*
Dugdale, J M (Ravenscourt Park) 1871 *S*
Dun, A F (Wasps) 1984 *W*
Duncan, R F H (Guy's Hospital) 1922 *I*, *F*, *S*
Dunkley, P E (Harlequins) 1931 *I*, *S*, 1936 *NZ*, *W*, *I*, *S*
Duthie, J (W Hartlepool) 1903 *W*
Dyson, J W (Huddersfield) 1890 *S*, 1892 *S*, 1893 *I*, *S*

Ebdon, P J (Wellington) 1897 *W*, *I*
Eddison, J H (Headingley) 1912 *W*, *I*, *S*, *F*
Edgar, C S (Birkenhead Park) 1901 *S*
Edwards, R (Newport) 1921 *W*, *I*, *S*, *F*, 1922 *W*, *F*, 1923 *W*, 1924 *W*, *F*, *S*, 1925 *NZ*
Egerton, D W (Bath) 1988 *I* 2, *A* 1, *Fj* (R), *A*, 1989 *Fj*, 1990 *I*, *Arg* 2 (R)
Elliot, C H (Sunderland) 1886 *W*
Elliot, E W (Sunderland) 1901 *W*, *I*, *S*, 1904 *W*
Elliot, W (United Services, RN) 1932 *I*, *S*, 1933 *W*, *I*, *S*, 1934 *W*, *I*
Elliott, A E (St Thomas's Hospital) 1894 *S*
Ellis, J (Wakefield) 1939 *S*
Ellis, S S (Queen's House) 1880 *I*
Emmott, C (Bradford) 1892 *W*
Enthoven, H J (Richmond) 1878 *I*
Estcourt, N S D (Blackheath) 1955 *S*
Evans, B J (Leicester) 1988 *A* 2, *Fj*
Evans, E (Sale) 1948 *A*, 1950 *W*, 1951 *I*, *F*, *S*, 1952 *SA*, *W*, *S*, *I*, *F*, 1953 *I*, *F*, *S*, 1954 *W*, *NZ*, *I*, *F*, 1956 *W*, *I*, *S*, *F*, 1957 *W*, *I*, *F*, *S*, 1958 *W*, *A*, *I*, *F*, *S*
Evans, G W (Coventry) 1972 *S*, 1973 *W* (R), *F*, *S*, *NZ* 2, 1974 *S*, *I*, *F*, *W*
Evans, N L (RNEC) 1932 *W*, *I*, *S*, 1933 *W*, *I*
Evanson, A M (Richmond) 1883 *W*, *I*, *S*, 1884 *S*
Evanson, W A D (Richmond) 1875 *S*, 1877 *S*, 1878 *S*, 1879 *S*, *I*
Evershed, F (Blackheath) 1889 *M*, 1890 *W*, *S*, *I*, 1892 *W*, *I*, *S*, 1893 *W*, *I*, *S*
Eyres, W C T (Richmond) 1927 *I*

Fagan, A R St L (Richmond) 1887 *I*
Fairbrother, K E (Coventry) 1969 *I*, *F*, *S*, *W*, *SA*, 1970 *I*, *W*, *S*, *F*, 1971 *W*, *I*, *F*
Faithfull, C K T (Harlequins) 1924 *I*, 1926 *F*, *S*
Fallas, H (Wakefield T) 1884 *I*
Fegan, J H C (Blackheath) 1895 *W*, *I*, *S*
Fernandes, C W L (Leeds) 1881 *I*, *W*, *S*
Fidler, J H (Gloucester) 1981 *Arg* 1,2, 1984 *SA* 1,2
Field, E (Middlesex W) 1893 *W*, *I*
Fielding, K J (Moseley, Loughborough Colls) 1969 *I*, *F*, *S*, *SA*, 1970 *I*, *F*, 1972 *W*, *I*, *F*, *S*
Finch, R T (Cambridge U) 1880 *S*
Finlan, J F (Moseley) 1967 *I*, *F*, *S*, *W*, *NZ*, 1968 *W*, *I*, 1969 *I*, *F*, *S*, *W*, 1970 *F*, 1973 *NZ* 1
Finlinson, H W (Blackheath) 1895 *W*, *I*, *S*
Finney, S (RIE Coll) 1872 *S*, 1873 *S*
Firth, F (Halifax) 1894 *W*, *I*, *S*
Fletcher, N C (OMTs) 1901 *W*, *I*, *S*, 1903 *S*
Fletcher, T (Seaton) 1897 *W*
Fletcher, W R B (Marlborough N) 1873 *S*, 1875 *S*
Fookes, E F (Sowerby Bridge) 1896 *W*, *I*, *S*, 1897 *W*, *I*, *S*, 1898 *I*, *W*, 1899 *I*, *S*
Ford, P J (Gloucester) 1964 *W*, *I*, *F*, *S*
Forrest, J W (United Services, RN) 1930 *W*, *I*, *F*, *S*, 1931 *W*, *I*, *S*, *F*, 1934 *I*, *S*
Forrest, R (Wellington) 1899 *W*, 1900 *S*, 1902 *I*, *S*, 1903 *I*, *S*
Foulds, R T (Waterloo) 1929 *W*, *I*
Fowler, F D (Manchester) 1878 *S*, 1879 *S*
Fowler, H (Oxford U) 1878 *S*, 1881 *W*, *S*
Fowler, R H (Leeds) 1877 *I*
Fox, F H (Wellington) 1890 *W*, *S*
Francis, T E S (Cambridge U) 1926 *W*, *I*, *F*, *S*
Frankcom, G P (Cambridge U, Bedford) 1965 *W*, *I*, *F*, *S*
Fraser, E C (Blackheath) 1875 *I*
Fraser, G (Richmond) 1902 *W*, *I*, *S*, 1903 *W*, *I*
Freakes, H D (Oxford U) 1938 *W*, 1939 *W*, *I*
Freeman, H (Marlborough N) 1872 *S*, 1873 *S*, 1874 *S*
French, R J (St Helens) 1961 *W*, *I*, *F*, *S*
Fry, H A (Liverpool) 1934 *W*, *I*, *S*

Fry, T W (Queen's House) 1880 *I, S*, 1881 *W*
Fuller, H G (Bath) 1882 *I, S*, 1883 *W, I, S*, 1884 W

Gadney, B C (Leicester, Headingley) 1932 *I, S*, 1933 *I, S*, 1934 *W, I, S*, 1935 *S*, 1936 *NZ, W, I, S*, 1937 *S*, 1938 *W*
Gamlin, H T (Blackheath) 1899 *W, S*, 1900 *W, I, S*, 1901 *S*, 1902 *W, I, S*, 1903 *W, I, S*, 1904 *W, I, S*
Gardner, E R (Devonport Services) 1921 *W, I, S*, 1922 *W, I, F*, 1923 *W, I, S, F*
Gardner, H P (Richmond) 1878 *I*
Garnett, H W T (Bradford) 1877 *S*
Gavins, M N (Leicester) 1961 *W*
Gay, D J (Bath) 1968 *W, I, F, S*
Gent, D R (Gloucester) 1905 *NZ*, 1906 *W, I*, 1910 *W, I*
Genth, J S M (Manchester) 1874 *S*, 1875 *S*
George, J T (Falmouth) 1947 *S, F*, 1949 *I*
Gerrard, R A (Bath) 1932 *SA*, *W, I, S*, 1933 *W, I, S*, 1934 *W, I, S*, 1936 *NZ, W, I, S*
Gibbs, G A (Bristol) 1947 *F*, 1948 *I*
Gibbs, J C (Harlequins) 1925 *NZ, W*, 1926 *F*, 1927 *W, I, S, F*
Gibbs, N (Harlequins) 1954 *S, F*
Giblin, L F (Blackheath) 1896 *W, I*, 1897 *S*
Gibson, A S (Manchester) 1871 *S*
Gibson, C O P (Northern) 1901 *W*
Gibson, G R (Northern) 1899 *W*, 1901 *S*
Gibson, T A (Northern) 1905 *W, S*
Gilbert, F G (Devonport Services) 1923 *W, I*
Gilbert, R (Devonport A) 1908 *W, I, S*
Giles, J L (Coventry) 1935 *W, I*, 1937 *W, I*, 1938 *I, S*
Gittings, W J (Coventry) 1967 *NZ*
Glover, P B (Bath) 1967 *A*, 1971 *F, P*
Godfray, R E (Richmond) 1905 *NZ*
Godwin, H O (Coventry) 1959 *F, S*, 1963 *S*, *NZ* 1,2, *A*, 1964 *NZ, I, F, S*, 1967 *NZ*
Gordon-Smith, G W (Blackheath) 1900 *W, I, S*
Gotley, A L H (Oxford U) 1910 *F, S*, 1911 *W, F, I, S*
Graham, D (Aspatria) 1901 *W*
Graham, H J (Wimbledon H) 1875 *I, S*, 1876 *I, S*
Graham, J D G (Wimbledon H) 1876 *I*
Gray, A (Otley) 1947 *W, I, S*
Green, J (Skipton) 1905 *I*, 1906 *S, F, SA*, 1907 *F, W, I, S*
Green, J F (West Kent) 1871 *S*
Greenwell, J H (Rockcliff) 1893 *W, I*
Greenwood, J E (Cambridge U, Leicester) 1912 *F*, 1913 *SA, W, F, I, S*, 1914 *W, S, F*, 1920 *W, F, I, S*
Greenwood, J R H (Waterloo) 1966 *I, F, S*, 1967 *A*, 1969 *I*
Greg, W (Manchester) 1876 *I, S*
Gregory, G G (Bristol) 1931 *I, S, F*, 1932 *SA, W, I, S*, 1933 *W, I, S*, 1934 *W, I, S*
Gregory, J A (Blackheath) 1949 *W*
Grylls, W M (Redruth) 1905 *I*
Guest, R H (Waterloo) 1939 *W, I, S*, 1947 *W, I, S, F*, 1948 *A, W, I, S*, 1949 *F, S*
Guillemard, A G (West Kent) 1871 *S*, 1872 *S*
Gummer, C H A (Plymouth A) 1929 *F*
Gunner, C R (Marlborough N) 1876 *I*
Gurdon, C (Richmond) 1880 *I, S*, 1881 *I, W, S*, 1882 *I, S*, 1883 *S*, 1884 *W, S*, 1885 *I*, 1886 *W, I, S*
Gurdon, E T (Richmond) 1878 *S*, 1879 *I*, 1880 *S*, 1881 *I, W, S*, 1882 *S*, 1883 *W, I, S*, 1884 *W, I, S*, 1885 *W, I*, 1886 *S*
Guscott, J C (Bath) 1989 *R, Fj*, 1990 *I, F, W, S, Arg* 3, 1991 *W, S, I, F, Fj, A*, *[NZ, It, F, S, A]*, 1992 *S, I, F, W*

Haigh, L (Manchester) 1910 *W, I, S*, 1911 *W, F, I, S*
Hale, P M (Moseley) 1969 *SA*, 1970 *I, W*
Hall, C (Gloucester) 1901 *I, S*
Hall, J (N Durham) 1894 *W, I, S*
Hall, J P (Bath) 1984 *S* (R), *I, F, SA* 1,2, *A*, 1985 *R, F, S, I, W, NZ* 1,2, 1986 *W, S*, 1987 *I, F, W, S*, 1990 *Arg* 3
Hall, N M (Richmond) 1947 *W, I, S, F*, 1949 *W, I*, 1952 *SA, W, S, I, F*, 1953 *W, I, F, S*, 1955 *W, I*
Halliday, S J (Bath, Harlequins) 1986 *W, S*, 1987 *S*, 1988 *S, I* 1,2, *A* 1, *A*, 1989 *S, I, F, W, R, Fj* (R), 1990 *W, S*, 1991 *[US, S, A]*, 1992 *S, I, F, W*
Hamersley, A St G (Marlborough N) 1871 *S*, 1872 *S*, 1873 *S*, 1874 *S*
Hamilton-Hill, E A (Harlequins) 1936 *NZ, W, I*
Hamilton-Wickes, R H (Cambridge U) 1924 *I*, 1925

NZ, W, I, S, F, 1926 *W, I, S*, 1927 *W*
Hammett, E D G (Newport) 1920 *W, F, S*, 1921 *W, I, S, F*, 1922 *W*
Hammond, C E L (Harlequins) 1905 *S, NZ*, 1906 *W, I, S, F*, 1908 *W, I*
Hancock, A W (Northampton) 1965 *F, S*, 1966 *F*
Hancock, G E (Birkenhead Park) 1939 *W, I, S*
Hancock, J H (Newport) 1955 *W, I*
Hancock, P F (Blackheath) 1886 *W, I*, 1890 *W*
Hancock, P S (Richmond) 1904 *W, I, S*
Hands, R H M (Blackheath) 1910 *F, S*
Handford, F G (Manchester) 1909 *W, F, I, S*
Hanley, J (Plymouth A) 1927 *W, S, F*, 1928 *W, I, F, S*
Hannaford, R C (Bristol) 1971 *W, I, F*
Hanvey, R J (Aspatria) 1926 *W, I, F, S*
Harding, E H (Devonport Services) 1931 *I*
Harding, R M (Bristol) 1985 *R, F, S*, 1987 *S*, *[A, J, W]*, 1988 *I* 1(R),2, *A* 1,2, *Fj*
Harding, V S J (Saracens) 1961 *F, S*, 1962 *W, I, F, S*
Hardwick, P F (Percy Park) 1902 *I, S*, 1903 *W, I, S*, 1904 *W, I, S*
Hardy, E M P (Blackheath) 1951 *I, F, S*
Hare, W H (Nottingham, Leicester) 1974 *W*, 1978 *F, NZ*, 1979 *NZ*, 1980 *I, F, W, S*, 1981 *W, S, Arg* 1,2, 1982 *F, W*, 1983 *F, W, S, I, NZ*, 1984 *S, I, F, W, SA* 1,2
Harper, C H (Exeter) 1899 *W*
Harriman, A T (Harlequins) 1988 *A*
Harris, S W (Blackheath) 1920 *I, S*
Harris, T W (Northampton) 1929 *S*, 1932 *I*
Harrison, A C (Hartlepool R) 1931 *I, S*
Harrison, A L (United Services, RN) 1914 *I, F*
Harrison, G (Hull) 1877 *I, S*, 1879 *S, I*, 1880 *S*, 1885 *W, I*
Harrison, H C (United Services, RN) 1909 *S*, 1914 *I, S, F*
Harrison, M E (Wakefield) 1985 *NZ* 1,2, 1986 *S, I, F*, 1987 *I, F, W, S*, *[A, J, US, W]*, 1988 *F, W*
Hartley, B C (Blackheath) 1901 *S*, 1902 *S*
Haslett, L W (Birkenhead Park) 1926 *I, F*
Hastings, G W D (Gloucester) 1955 *W, I, F, S*, 1957 *W, I, F, S*, 1958 *W, A, I, F, S*
Havelock, H (Hartlepool R) 1908 *F, W, I*
Hawcridge, J J (Bradford) 1885 *W, I*
Hayward, L W (Cheltenham) 1910 *I*
Hazell, D St G (Leicester) 1955 *W, I, F, S*
Hearn, R D (Bedford) 1966 *F, S*, 1967 *I, F, S, W*
Heath, A H (Oxford U) 1876 *S*
Heaton, J (Waterloo) 1935 *W, I, S*, 1939 *W, I, S*, 1947 *I, S, F*
Henderson, A P (Edinburgh Wands) 1947 *W, I, S, F*, 1948 *I, S, F*, 1949 *W, I*
Henderson, R S F (Blackheath) 1883 *W, S*, 1884 *W, S*, 1885 *W*
Heppell, W G (Devonport A) 1903 *I*
Herbert, A J (Wasps) 1958 *F, S*, 1959 *W, I, F, S*
Hesford, R (Bristol) 1981 *S* (R), 1982 *A, S, F* (R), 1983 *F* (R), 1985 *R, F, S, I, W*
Heslop, N J (Orrell) 1990 *Arg* 1,2,3, 1991 *W, S, I, F*, *[US, F]*, 1992 *W*(R)
Hetherington, J G G (Northampton) 1958 *A, I*, 1959 *W, I, F, S*
Hewitt, E N (Coventry) 1951 *W, I, F*
Hewitt, W W (Queen's House) 1881 *I, W, S*, 1882 *I*
Hickson, J L (Bradford) 1887 *W, I, S*, 1890 *W, S, I*
Higgins, R (Liverpool) 1954 *W, NZ, I, S*, 1955 *W, I, F, S*, 1957 *W, I, F, S*, 1959 *W*
Hignell, A J (Cambridge U, Bristol) 1975 *A* 2, 1976 *A, W, S, I*, 1977 *S, I, F, W*, 1978 *W*, 1979 *S, I, F, W*
Hill, B A (Blackheath) 1903 *I, S*, 1904 *W, I*, 1905 *W, NZ*, 1906 *SA*, 1907 *F, W*
Hill, R J (Bath) 1984 *SA* 1,2, 1985 *I* (R), *NZ* 2 (R), 1986 *F* (R), 1987 *I, F, W*, *[US]*, 1989 *Fj*, 1990 *I, F, W, S, Arg* 1,2,3, 1991 *W, S, I, F, Fj, A*, *[NZ, It, US, F, S, A]*
Hillard, R J (Oxford U) 1925 *NZ*
Hiller, R (Harlequins) 1968 *W, I, F, S*, 1969 *I, F, S, W, SA*, 1970 *I, W, S*, 1971 *I, F, S* (2[1C]), *P*, 1972 *W, I*
Hind, A E (Leicester) 1905 *NZ*, 1906 *W*
Hind, G R (Blackheath) 1910 *S*, 1911 *I*
Hobbs, R F A (Blackheath) 1899 *S*, 1903 *W*
Hobbs, R G S (Richmond) 1932 *SA, W, I, S*
Hodges, H A (Nottingham) 1906 *W, I*
Hodgkinson, S D (Nottingham) 1989 *R, Fj*, 1990 *I, F, W, S, Arg* 1,2,3, 1991 *W, S, I, F*, *[US]*

Hodgson, J McD (Northern) 1932 *SA, W, I, S,* 1934 *W, I,* 1936 *I*
Hodgson, S A M (Durham City) 1960 *W, I, F, S,* 1961 *SA, W,* 1962 *W, I, F, S,* 1964 *W*
Hofmeyr, M B (Oxford U) 1950 *W, F, S*
Hogarth, T B (Hartlepool R) 1906 *F*
Holford, G (Gloucester) 1920 *W, F*
Holland, D (Devonport A) 1912 *W, I, S*
Holliday, T E (Aspatria) 1923 *S, F,* 1925 *I, S, F,* 1926 *F, S*
Holmes, C B (Manchester) 1947 *S,* 1948 *I, F*
Holmes, E (Manningham) 1890 *S, I*
Holmes, W A (Nuneaton) 1950 *W, I, F, S,* 1951 *W, I, F, S,* 1952 *SA, S, I, F,* 1953 *W, I, F, S*
Holmes, W B (Cambridge U) 1949 *W, I, F, S*
Hook, W G (Gloucester) 1951 *S,* 1952 *SA, W*
Hooper, C A (Middlesex W) 1894 *W, I, S*
Hopley, F J V (Blackheath) 1907 *F, W,* 1908 *I*
Hordern, P C (Gloucester) 1931 *I, S, F,* 1934 *W*
Horley, C H (Swinton) 1885 *I*
Hornby, A N (Manchester) 1877 *I, S,* 1878 *S, I,* 1880 *I,* 1881 *I, S,* 1882 *I, S*
Horrocks-Taylor, J P (Cambridge U, Leicester, Middlesbrough) 1958 *W, A,* 1961 *S,* 1962 *S,* 1963 *NZ 1,2, A,* 1964 *NZ, W*
Horsfall, E L (Harlequins) 1949 *W*
Horton, A L (Blackheath) 1965 *W, I, F, S,* 1966 *F, S,* 1967 *NZ*
Horton, J P (Bath) 1978 *W, S, I, NZ,* 1980 *I, F, W, S,* 1981 *W,* 1983 *S, I,* 1984 *SA 1,2*
Horton, N E (Moseley, Toulouse) 1969 *I, F, S, W,* 1971 *I, F, S,* 1974 *S,* 1975 *W,* 1977 *S, I, F, W,* 1978 *F, W,* 1979 *S, I, F, W,* 1980 *I*
Hosen, R W (Bristol, Northampton) 1963 *NZ 1,2, A,* 1964 *F, S,* 1967 *A, I, F, S, W*
Hosking, G R d'A (Devonport Services) 1949 *W, I, F, S,* 1950 *W*
Houghton, S (Runcorn) 1892 *I,* 1896 *W*
Howard, P D (O Millhillians) 1930 *W, I, F, S,* 1931 *W, I, S, F*
Hubbard, G C (Blackheath) 1892 *W, I*
Hubbard, J C (Harlequins) 1930 *S*
Hudson, A (Gloucester) 1906 *W, I, F,* 1908 *F, W, I, S,* 1910 *F*
Hughes, G E (Barrow) 1896 *S*
Hulme, F C (Birkenhead Park) 1903 *W, I,* 1905 *W, I*
Hunt, J T (Manchester) 1882 *I, S,* 1884 *W*
Hunt, R (Manchester) 1880 *I,* 1881 *W, S,* 1882 *I*
Hunt, W H (Manchester) 1876 *S,* 1877 *I, S,* 1878 *I*
Huntsman, R P (Headingley) 1985 *NZ 1,2*
Hurst, A C B (Wasps) 1962 *S*
Huskisson, T F (OMTs) 1937 *W, I, S,* 1938 *W, I,* 1939 *W, I, S*
Hutchinson, F (Headingley) 1909 *F, I, S*
Hutchinson, J E (Durham City) 1906 *I*
Hutchinson, W C (RIE Coll) 1876 *S* 1877 *I*
Hutchinson, W H H (Hull) 1875 *I,* 1876 *I*
Huth, H (Huddersfield) 1879 *S*
Hyde, J P (Northampton) 1950 *F, S*
Hynes, W B (United Services, RN) 1912 *F*

Ibbitson, E D (Headingley) 1909 *W, F, I, S*
Imrie, H M (Durham City) 1906 *NZ,* 1907 *I*
Inglis, R E (Blackheath) 1886 *W, I, S*
Irvin, S H (Devonport A) 1905 *W*
Isherwood, F W (Ravenscourt Park) 1872 *S*

Jackett, E J (Leicester, Falmouth) 1905 *NZ,* 1906 *W, I, S, F, SA,* 1907 *W, I, S,* 1909 *W, F, I, S*
Jackson, A H (Blackheath) 1878 *I,* 1880 *I*
Jackson, B S (Broughton Park) 1970 *S* (R), *F*
Jackson, P B (Coventry) 1956 *W, I, F,* 1957 *W, I, F, S,* 1958 *W, A, F, S,* 1959 *W, I, F, S,* 1961 *S,* 1963 *W, I, F, S*
Jackson, W J (Halifax) 1894 *S*
Jacob, F (Cambridge U) 1897 *W, I, S,* 1898 *I, S, W,* 1899 *W, I*
Jacob, H P (Blackheath) 1924 *W, I, F, S,* 1930 *F*
Jacob, P G (Blackheath) 1898 *I*
Jacobs, C R (Northampton) 1956 *W, I, S, F,* 1957 *I, F, S,* 1958 *W, A, F, S,* 1960 *W, I, F, S,* 1961 *SA, W, I, F, S,* 1963 *NZ 1,2, A,* 1964 *W, I, F, S*
Jago, R A (Devonport A) 1906 *W, I, SA,* 1907 *W, I*
Janion, J P A G (Bedford) 1971 *W, I, F, S* (2[1C]), *P,*

1972 *W, S, SA,* 1973 *A,* 1975 *A 1,2*
Jarman, J W (Bristol) 1900 *W*
Jeavons, N C (Moseley) 1981 *S, I, F, Arg* 1,2, 1982 *A, S, I, F, W,* 1983 *F, W, S, I*
Jeeps, R E G (Northampton) 1956 *W,* 1957 *W, I, F, S,* 1958 *W, A, I, F, S,* 1959 *I,* 1960 *W, I, F, S,* 1961 *SA, W, I, F, S,* 1962 *W, I, F, S*
Jeffery, G L (Blackheath) 1886 *W, I, S,* 1887 *W, I, S*
Jennins, C R (Waterloo) 1967 *A, I, F*
Jewitt, J (Hartlepool R) 1902 *W*
Johns, W A (Gloucester) 1909 *W, F, I, S,* 1910 *W, I, F*
Johnston, W R (Bristol) 1910 *W, I, S,* 1912 *W, I, S, F,* 1913 *SA, W, F, I, S,* 1914 *W, I, S, F*
Jones, F P (N Brighton) 1893 *S*
Jones, H A (Barnstaple) 1950 *W, I, F*
Jorden, A M (Cambridge U, Blackheath, Bedford) 1970 *F,* 1973 *I, F, S,* 1974 *F,* 1975 *W, S*
Jowett, D (Heckmondwike) 1889 *M,* 1890 *S, I,* 1891 *W, I, S*
Judd, P E (Coventry) 1962 *W, I, F, S,* 1963 *S, NZ* 1,2, *A,* 1964 *NZ,* 1965 *I, F, S,* 1966 *W, I, F, S,* 1967 *A, I, F, S, W, NZ*

Kayll, H E (Sunderland) 1878 *S*
Keeling, J H (Guy's Hospital) 1948 *A, W*
Keen, B W (Newcastle U) 1968 *W, I, F, S*
Keeton, G H (Leicester) 1904 *W, I, S*
Kelly, G A (Bedford) 1947 *W, I, S,* 1948 *W*
Kelly, T S (London Devonians) 1906 *W, I, S, F, SA,* 1907 *F, W, I, S,* 1908 *F, I, S*
Kemble, A T (Liverpool) 1885 *W, I,* 1887 *I*
Kemp, D T (Blackheath) 1935 *W*
Kemp, T A (Richmond) 1937 *W, I,* 1939 *S,* 1948 *A, W*
Kendall, P D (Birkenhead Park) 1901 *S,* 1902 *W,* 1903 *S*
Kendall-Carpenter, J MacG K (Oxford U, Bath) 1949 *I, F, S,* 1950 *W, I, F, S,* 1951 *I, F, S,* 1952 *SA, S, I, F,* 1953 *W, I, F, S,* 1954 *W, NZ, I, F*
Kendrew, D A (Leicester) 1930 *W, I,* 1933 *I, S,* 1934 *S,* 1935 *W, I,* 1936 *NZ, W, I*
Kennedy, R D (Camborne S of M) 1949 *I, F, S*
Kent, C P (Rosslyn Park) 1977 *S, I, F, W,* 1978 *F* (R)
Kent, T (Salford) 1891 *W, I, S,* 1892 *W, I, S*
Kershaw, A C A (United Services, RN) 1920 *W, F, I, S,* 1921 *W, I, S, F,* 1922 *W, I, F, S,* 1923 *W, I, S, F*
Kewley, E (Liverpool) 1874 *S,* 1875 *S,* 1876 *I, S,* 1877 *I, S,* 1878 *S*
Kewney, A L (Leicester) 1906 *W, I, S, F,* 1909 *A, W, F, I, S,* 1911 *W, F, I, S,* 1912 *I, S,* 1913 *SA*
Key, A (O Cranleighans) 1930 *I,* 1933 *W*
Keyworth, M (Swansea) 1976 *A, W, S, I*
Kilner, B (Wakefield T) 1880 *I*
Kindersley, R S (Exeter) 1883 *W,* 1884 *S,* 1885 *W*
King, I (Harrogate) 1954 *W, NZ, I*
King, J A (Headingley) 1911 *W, F, I, S,* 1912 *W, I, S,* 1913 *SA, W, F, I, S*
King, Q E M A (Army) 1921 *S*
Kingston, P (Gloucester) 1975 *A,* 1,2, 1979 *I, F, W*
Kitching, A E (Blackheath) 1913 *I*
Kittermaster, H J (Harlequins) 1925 *NZ, W, I,* 1926 *W, I, F, S*
Knight, F (Plymouth) 1909 *A*
Knight, P M (Bristol) 1972 *F, S, SA*
Knowles, E (Millom) 1896 *S,* 1897 *S*
Knowles, T C (Birkenhead Park) 1931 *S*
Krige, J A (Guy's Hospital) 1920 *W*

Labuschagne, N A (Harlequins, Guy's Hospital) 1953 *W,* 1955 *W, I, F, S*
Lagden, R O (Richmond) 1911 *S*
Laird, H C C (Harlequins) 1927 *W, I, S,* 1928 *A, W, I, F, S,* 1929 *W, I*
Lambert, D (Harlequins) 1907 *F,* 1908 *F, W, S,* 1911 *W, F, I*
Lampkowski, M S (Headingley) 1976 *A, W, S, I*
Lapage, W N (United Services, RN) 1908 *F, W, I, S*
Larter, P J (Northampton, RAF) 1967 *A, NZ,* 1968 *W, I, F, S,* 1969 *I, F, S, W, SA,* 1970 *I, W, F, S,* 1971 *W, I, F, S* (2[1C]), *P,* 1972 *SA,* 1973 *NZ* 1, *W*
Law, A F (Richmond) 1877 *S*
Law, D E (Birkenhead Park) 1927 *I*
Lawrence, Hon H A (Richmond) 1873 *S,* 1874 *S,* 1875 *I, S*
Lawrie, P W (Leicester) 1910 *S,* 1911 *S*
Lawson, R G (Workington) 1925 *I*

Lawson, T M (Workington) 1928 *A, W*
Leadbetter, M M (Broughton Park) 1970 *F*
Leadbetter, V H (Edinburgh Wands) 1954 *S, F*
Leake, W R M (Harlequins) 1891 *W, I, S*
Leather, G (Liverpool) 1907 *I*
Lee, F H (Marlborough N) 1876 *S*, 1877 *I*
Lee, H (Blackheath) 1907 *F*
Le Fleming, J (Blackheath) 1887 *W*
Leonard, J (Saracens, Harlequins) 1990 *Arg* 1,2,3, 1991 *W, S, I, F, Fj, A*, [*NZ, It, US, F, S, A*], 1992 *S, I, F, W*
Leslie-Jones, F A (Richmond) 1895 *W, I*
Lewis, A O (Bath) 1952 *SA, W, S, I, F*, 1953 *W, I, F, S*, 1954 *F*
Leyland, R (Waterloo) 1935 *W, I, S*
Linnett, M S (Moseley) 1989 *Fj*
Livesay, R O'H (Blackheath) 1898 *W*, 1899 *W*
Lloyd, R H (Harlequins) 1967 *NZ*, 1968 *W, I, F, S*
Locke, H M (Birkenhead Park) 1923 *S, F*, 1924 *W, F, S*, 1925 *W, I, S, F*, 1927 *W, I, S*
Lockwood, R E (Heckmondwike) 1887 *W, I, S*, 1889 *M*, 1891 *W, I, S*, 1892 *W, I, S*, 1893 *W, I*, 1894 *W, I*
Login, S H M (RN Coll) 1876 *I*
Lohden, F C (Blackheath) 1893 *W*
Longland, R J (Northampton) 1932 *S*, 1933 *W, S*, 1934 *W, I, S*, 1935 *W, I, S*, 1936 *NZ, W, I, S*, 1937 *W, I, S*, 1938 *W, I, S*
Lowe, C N (Cambridge U, Blackheath) 1913 *SA, W, F, I, S*, 1914 *W, I, S, F*, 1920 *W, F, I, S*, 1921 *W, I, S, F*, 1922 *W, I, F, S*, 1923 *W, I, S, F*
Lowrie, F (Wakefield T) 1889 *M*, 1890 *W*
Lowry, W M (Birkenhead Park) 1920 *F*
Lozowski, R A P (Wasps) 1984 *A*
Luddington, W G E (Devonport Services) 1923 *W, I, S, F*, 1924 *W, I, F, S*, 1925 *W, I, S, F*, 1926 *W*
Luscombe, F (Gipsies) 1872 *S*, 1873 *S*, 1875 *I, S*, 1876 *I, S*
Luscombe, J H (Gipsies) 1871 *S*
Luxmoore, A F C C (Richmond) 1900 *S*, 1901 *W*
Luya, H F (Waterloo, Headingley) 1948 *W, I, S, F*, 1949 *W*
Lyon, A (Liverpool) 1871 *S*
Lyon, G H d'O (United Services, RN) 1908 *S*, 1909 *A*

McCanlis, M A (Gloucester) 1931 *W, I*
McFadyean, C W (Moseley) 1966 *I, F, S*, 1967 *A, I, F, S, W, NZ*, 1968 *W, I*
MacIlwaine, A H (United Services, Hull & E Riding) 1912 *W, I, S, F*, 1920 *I*
Mackie, O G (Wakefield T, Cambridge U) 1897 *S*, 1898 *I*
Mackinlay, J E H (St George's Hospital) 1872 *S*, 1873 *S*, 1875 *I*
MacLaren, W (Manchester) 1871 *S*
MacLennan, R R F (OMTs) 1925 *I, S, F*
McLeod, N F (RIE Coll) 1879 *S, I*
Madge, R J P (Exeter) 1948 *A, W, I, S*
Malir, F W S (Otley) 1930 *W, I, S*
Mangles, R H (Richmond) 1897 *W, I*
Manley, D C (Exeter) 1963 *W, I, F, S*
Mann, W E (United Services, Army) 1911 *W, F, I*
Mantell, N D (Rosslyn Park) 1975 *A* 1
Markendale, E T (Manchester R) 1880 *I*
Marques, R W D (Cambridge U, Harlequins) 1956 *W, I, S, F*, 1957 *W, I, F, S*, 1958 *W, A, I, F, S*, 1959 *W, I, F, S*, 1960 *W, I, F, S*, 1961 *SA, W*
Marquis, J C (Birkenhead Park) 1900 *I, S*
Marriott, C J B (Blackheath) 1884 *W, I, S*, 1886 *W, I, S*, 1887 *I*
Marriott, E E (Manchester) 1876 *I*
Marriott, V R (Harlequins) 1963 *NZ* 1,2, *A*, 1964 *NZ*
Marsden, G H (Morley) 1900 *W, I, S*
Marsh, H (RIE Coll) 1873 *S*
Marsh, J (Swinton) 1892 *I*
Marshall, H (Blackheath) 1893 *W*
Marshall, M W (Blackheath) 1873 *S*, 1874 *S*, 1875 *I, S*, 1876 *I, S*, 1877 *I, S*, 1878 *S, I*
Marshall, R M (Oxford U) 1938 *I, S*, 1939 *W, I, S*
Martin, C R (Bath) 1985 *F, S, I, W*
Martin, N O (Harlequins) 1972 *F* (R)
Martindale, S A (Kendal) 1929 *F*
Massey, E J (Leicester) 1925 *W, I, S*
Mathias, J L (Bristol) 1905 *W, I, S, NZ*
Matters, J C (RNE Coll) 1899 *S*

Matthews, J R C (Harlequins) 1949 *F, S*, 1950 *I, F, S*, 1952 *SA, W, S, I, F*
Maud, P (Blackheath) 1893 *W, I*
Maxwell, A W (New Brighton, Headingley) 1975 *A* 1, 1976 *A, W, S, I, F*, 1978 *F*
Maxwell-Hyslop, J E (Oxford U) 1922 *I, F, S*
Maynard, A F (Cambridge U) 1914 *W, I, S*
Meikle, G W C (Waterloo) 1934 *W, I, S*
Meikle, S S C (Waterloo) 1929 *S*
Mellish, F W (Blackheath) 1920 *W, F, I, S*, 1921 *W, I*
Melville, N D (Wasps) 1984 *A*, 1985 *I, W, NZ* 1,2, 1986 *W, S, I, F*, 1988 *F, W, S, I* 1
Merriam, L P B (Blackheath) 1920 *W, F*
Michell, A T (Oxford U) 1875 *I, S*, 1876 *I*
Middleton, B B (Birkenhead Park) 1882 *I*, 1883 *I*
Middleton, J A (Richmond) 1922 *S*
Miles, J H (Leicester) 1903 *W*
Millett, H (Richmond) 1920 *F*
Mills, F W (Marlborough N) 1872 *S*, 1873 *S*
Mills, S G F (Gloucester) 1981 *Arg* 1,2, 1983 *W*, 1984 *SA* 1, *A*
Mills, W A (Devonport A) 1906 *W, I, S, F, SA*, 1907 *F, W, I, S*, 1908 *F, W*
Milman, D L K (Bedford) 1937 *W*, 1938 *W, I, S*
Milton, C H (Camborne S of M) 1906 *I*
Milton, J G (Camborne S of M) 1904 *W, I, S*, 1905 *S*, 1907 *I*
Milton, W H (Marlborough N) 1874 *S*, 1875 *I*
Mitchell, F (Blackheath) 1895 *W, I, S*, 1896 *W, I, S*
Mitchell, W G (Richmond) 1890 *W, S, I*, 1891 *W, I, S*, 1893 *S*
Mobbs, E R (Northampton) 1909 *A, W, F, I, S*, 1910 *I, F*
Moberly, W O (Ravenscourt Park) 1872 *S*
Moore, B C (Nottingham, Harlequins) 1987 *S*, [*A, J, W*], 1988 *F, W, S, I* 1,2, *A* 1,2, *Fj, A*, 1989 *S, I, F, W, R, Fj*, 1990 *I, F, W, S, Arg* 1,2, 1991 *W, S, I, F, Fj, A*, [*NZ, It, F, S, A*], 1992 *S, I, F, W*
Moore, E J (Blackheath) 1883 *I, S*
Moore, N J N H (Bristol) 1904 *W, I, S*
Moore, P B C (Blackheath) 1951 *W*
Moore, W K T (Leicester) 1947 *W, I*, 1949 *F, S*, 1950 *I, F, S*
Mordell, R J (Rosslyn Park) 1978 *W*
Morfitt, S (W Hartlepool) 1894 *W, I, S*, 1896 *W, I, S*
Morgan, J R (Hawick) 1920 *W*
Morgan, W G D (Medicals, Newcastle) 1960 *W, I, F, S*, 1961 *SA, W, I, F, S*
Morley, A J (Bristol) 1972 *SA*, 1973 *NZ* 1, *W, I*, 1975 *S, A* 1,2
Morris, A D W (United Services, RN) 1909 *A, W, F*
Morris, C D (Liverpool St Helens, Orrell) 1988 *A*, 1989 *S, I, F, W*, 1992 *S, I, F, W*
Morrison, P H (Cambridge U) 1890 *W, S, I*, 1891 *I*
Morse, S (Marlborough N) 1873 *S*, 1874 *S*, 1875 *S*
Mortimer, W (Marlborough N) 1899 *W*
Morton, H J S (Blackheath) 1909 *I, S*, 1910 *W, I*
Moss, F (Broughton) 1885 *W, I*, 1886 *W*
Mullins, A R (Harlequins) 1989 *Fj*
Mycock, J (Sale) 1947 *W, I, S, F*, 1948 *A*
Myers, E (Bradford) 1920 *I, S*, 1921 *W, I*, 1922 *W, I, F, S*, 1923 *W, I, S, F*, 1924 *W, I, F, S*, 1925 *S, F*
Myers, H (Keighley) 1898 *I*

Nanson, W M B (Carlisle) 1907 *F, W*
Nash, E H (Richmond) 1875 *I*
Neale, B A (Rosslyn Park) 1951 *I, F, S*
Neale, M E (Blackheath) 1912 *F*
Neame, S (O Cheltonians) 1879 *S, I*, 1880 *I, S*
Neary, A (Broughton Park) 1971 *W, I, F, S* (2[1C]), *P*, 1972 *W, I, F, S, SA*, 1973 *NZ* 1, *W, I, F, S, NZ* 2, *A*, 1974 *S, I, F, W*, 1975 *I, F, W, S, A* 1, 1976 *A, W, S, I, F*, 1977 *I*, 1978 *F* (R), 1979 *S, I, F, W, NZ*, 1980 *I, F, W, S*
Nelmes, B G (Cardiff) 1975 *A* 1,2, 1978 *W, S, I, NZ*
Newbold, C J (Blackheath) 1904 *W, I, S*, 1905 *W, I, S*
Newman, S C (Oxford U) 1947 *F*, 1948 *A, W*
Newton, A W (Blackheath) 1907 *S*
Newton, P A (Blackheath) 1882 *S, I, W*
Newton-Thompson, J O (Oxford U) 1947 *S, F*
Nichol, W (Brighouse R) 1892 *W, S*
Nicholas, P L (Exeter) 1902 *W*
Nicholson, B E (Harlequins) 1938 *W, I*
Nicholson, E S (Leicester) 1935 *W, I, S*, 1936 *NZ, W*

Nicholson, E T (Birkenhead Park) 1900 *W, I*
Nicholson, T (Rockcliff) 1893 *I*
Ninnes, B F (Coventry) 1971 *W*
Norman, D J (Leicester) 1932 *SA, W*
North, E H G (Blackheath) 1891 *W, I, S*
Northmore, S (Millom) 1897 *I*
Novak, M J (Harlequins) 1970 *W, S, F*
Novis, A L (Blackheath) 1929 *S, F*, 1930 *W, I, F*, 1933 *I, S*

Oakeley, F E (United Services, RN) 1913 *S*, 1914 *I, S, F*
Oakes, R F (Hartlepool R) 1897 *W, I, S*, 1898 *I, S, W*, 1899 *W, S*
Oakley, L F L (Bedford) 1951 *W*
Obolensky, A (Oxford U) 1936 *NZ, W, I, S*
Old, A G B (Middlesbrough, Leicester, Sheffield) 1972 *W, I, F, S, SA*, 1973 *NZ 2, A*, 1974 *S, I, F, W*, 1975 *I, A 2*, 1976 *S, I*, 1978 *F*
Oldham, W L (Coventry) 1908 *S*, 1909 *A*
Olver, C J (Northampton) 1990 *Arg 3*, 1991 [*US*]
O'Neill, A (Teignmouth, Torquay A) 1901 *W, I, S*
Openshaw, W E (Manchester) 1879 *I*
Orwin, J (Gloucester, RAF, Bedford) 1985 *R, F, S, I, W, NZ* 1,2, 1988 *F, W, S, I* 1,2, *A* 1,2
Osborne, R R (Manchester) 1871 *S*
Osborne, S H (Oxford U) 1905 *S*
Oti, C (Cambridge U, Nottingham, Wasps) 1988 *S, I* 1, 1989 *S, I, F, W, R*, 1990 *Arg* 1,2, 1991 *Fj, A*, [*NZ, It,*]
Oughtred, B (Hartlepool R) 1901 *S*, 1902 *W, I, S*, 1903 *W, I*
Owen, J E (Coventry) 1963 *W, I, F, S, A*, 1964 *NZ, 1965 W, I, F, S*, 1966 *I, F, S*, 1967 *NZ*
Owen-Smith, H G O (St Mary's Hospital) 1934 *W, I, S*, 1936 *NZ, W, I, S*, 1937 *W, I, S*

Page, J J (Bedford, Northampton) 1971 *W, I, F, S*, 1975 *S*
Palliant, J N (Notts) 1967 *I, F, S*
Palmer, A C (London Hospital) 1909 *I, S*
Palmer, F H (Richmond) 1905 *W*
Palmer, G V (Richmond) 1928 *I, F, S*
Palmer, J A (Bath) 1984 *SA* 1,2, 1986 *I* (R)
Pargetter, T A (Coventry) 1962 *S*, 1963 *F, NZ* 1
Parker, G W (Gloucester) 1938 *I, S*
Parker, Hon S (Liverpool) 1874 *S*, 1875 *S*
Parsons, E I (RAF) 1939 *S*
Parsons, M J (Northampton) 1968 *W, I, F, S*
Patterson, W M (Sale) 1961 *SA, S*
Pattisson, R M (Blackheath) 1883 *I, S*
Paul, J E (RIE Coll) 1875 *S*
Payne, A T (Bristol) 1935 *I, S*
Payne, C M (Harlequins) 1964 *I, F, S*, 1965 *I, F, S*, 1966 *W, I, F, S*
Payne, J H (Broughton) 1882 *S*, 1883 *W, I, S*, 1884 *I*, 1885 *W, I*
Pearce, G S (Northampton) 1979 *S, I, F, W*, 1981 *Arg* 1,2, 1982 *A, S*, 1983 *F, W, S, I, NZ*, 1984 *SA* 2, *A*, 1985 *R, F, S, I, W, NZ* 1,2, 1986 *W, S, I, F*, 1987 *I, F, W, S*, [*A, US, W*], 1988 *Fj*, 1991 [*US*]
Pears, D (Harlequins) 1990 *Arg* 1,2, 1992 *F*(R)
Pearson, A W (Blackheath) 1875 *I, S*, 1876 *I, S*, 1877 *S*, 1878 *S, I*
Peart, T G A H (Hartlepool R) 1964 *F, S*
Pease, F E (Hartlepool R) 1887 *I*
Penny, S H (Leicester) 1909 *A*
Penny, W J (United Hospitals) 1878 *I*, 1879 *S, I*
Percival, L J (Rugby) 1891 *I*, 1892 *I*, 1893 *S*
Periton, H G (Waterloo) 1925 *W*, 1926 *W, I, F, S*, 1927 *W, I, S, F*, 1928 *A, I, F, S*, 1929 *W, I, S, F*, 1930 *W, I, F, S*
Perrott, E S (O Cheltonians) 1875 *I*
Perry, D G (Bedford) 1963 *F, S, NZ* 1,2, *A* 1964 *NZ, W, I*, 1965 *W, I, F, S*, 1966 *W, I, F*
Perry, S V (Cambridge U, Waterloo) 1947 *W, I*, 1948 *A, W, I, S, F*
Peters, J (Plymouth) 1906 *S, F*, 1907 *I, S*, 1908 *W*
Phillips, C (Birkenhead Park) 1880 *S*, 1881 *I, S*
Phillips, M S (Fylde) 1958 *A, I, F, S*, 1959 *W, I, F, S*, 1960 *W, I, F, S*, 1961 *W, I*, 1963 *W, I, F, S, NZ* 1,2, *A*, 1964 *NZ, W, I, F, S*
Pickering, A S (Harrogate) 1907 *I*
Pickering, R D A (Bradford) 1967 *I, F, S, W*, 1968 *F, S*
Pickles, R C W (Bristol) 1922 *I, F*

Pierce, R (Liverpool) 1898 *I*, 1903 *S*
Pilkington, W N (Cambridge U) 1898 *S*
Pillman, C H (Blackheath) 1910 *W, I, F, S*, 1911 *W, F, I, S*, 1912 *W, F*, 1913 *SA, W, F, I, S*, 1914 *W, I, S*
Pillman, R L (Blackheath) 1914 *F*
Pinch, J (Lancaster) 1896 *W, I*, 1897 *S*
Pinching, W W (Guy's Hospital) 1872 *S*
Pitman, I J (Oxford U) 1922 *S*
Plummer, K C (Bristol) 1969 *W*, 1976 *S, I, F*
Poole, F O (Oxford U) 1895 *W, I, S*
Poole, R W (Hartlepool R) 1896 *S*
Pope, E B (Blackheath) 1931 *W, S, F*
Portus, G V (Blackheath) 1908 *F, I*
Poulton, R W (later **Poulton Palmer**) (Oxford U, Harlequins, Liverpool) 1909 *F, I, S*, 1910 *W*, 1911 *S*, 1912 *W, I, S*, 1913 *SA, W, F, I, S*, 1914 *W, I, S, F*
Powell, D L (Northampton) 1966 *W, I*, 1969 *I, F, S, W*, 1971 *W, I, F, S* (2[1C])
Pratten, W E (Blackheath) 1927 *S, F*
Preece, I (Coventry) 1948 *I, S, F*, 1949 *F, S*, 1950 *W, I, F, S*, 1951 *W, I, F*
Preece, P S (Coventry) 1972 *SA*, 1973 *NZ* 1, *W, I, F, S, NZ* 2, 1975 *I, F, W, A* 2, 1976 *W* (R)
Preedy, M (Gloucester) 1984 *SA* 1
Prentice, F D (Leicester) 1928 *I, F, S*
Prescott, R E (Harlequins) 1937 *W, I*, 1938 *I*, 1939 *W, I, S*
Preston, N J (Richmond) 1979 *NZ*, 1980 *I, F*
Price, H L (Harlequins) 1922 *I, S*, 1923 *W, I*
Price, J (Coventry) 1961 *I*
Price, P L A (RIE Coll) 1877 *I, S*, 1878 *S*
Price, T W (Cheltenham) 1948 *S, F*, 1949 *W, I, F, S*
Probyn, J A (Wasps, Askeans) 1988 *F, W, S, I* 1,2, *A* 1,2, *A*, 1989 *S, I, R* (R), 1990 *I, F, W, S, Arg* 1,2,3, 1991 *W, S, I, F, Fj, A*, [*NZ, It, F, S, A*], 1992 *S, I, F, W*
Prout, D H (Northampton) 1968 *W, I*
Pullin, J V (Bristol) 1966 *W*, 1968 *W, I, F, S*, 1969 *I, F, S, W, SA*, 1970 *I, W, S, F*, 1971 *W, I, F, S* (2[1C]), *P*, 1972 *W, I, F, S, SA*, 1973 *NZ* 1, *W, I, F, S, NZ* 2, *A*, 1974 *S, I, F, W*, 1975 *I, W*(R), *S, A* 1,2, 1976 *F*
Purdy, S J (Rugby) 1962 *S*
Pyke, J (St Helens Recreation) 1892 *W*
Pym, J A (Blackheath) 1912 *W, I, S, F*

Quinn, J P (New Brighton) 1954 *W, NZ, I, S, F*

Rafter, M (Bristol) 1977 *S, F, W*, 1978 *F, W, S, I, NZ*, 1979 *S, I, F, W, NZ*, 1980 *W*(R), 1981 *W, Arg* 1,2
Ralston, C W (Richmond) 1971 *S* (C), *P*, 1972 *W, I, F, S, SA*, 1973 *NZ* 1, *W, I, F, S, NZ* 2, *A*, 1974 *S, I, F, W*, 1975 *I, F, W, S*
Ramsden, H E (Bingley) 1898 *W, S*
Ranson, J M (Rosslyn Park) 1963 *NZ* 1,2, *A*, 1964 *W, I, F, S*
Raphael, J E (OMTs) 1902 *W, I, S*, 1905 *W, S, NZ*, 1906 *W, S, F*
Ravenscroft, J (Birkenhead Park) 1881 *I*
Rawlinson, W C W (Blackheath) 1876 *S*
Redfern, S (Leicester) 1984 *I* (R)
Redman, N C (Bath) 1984 *A*, 1986 *S* (R), 1987 *I, S*, [*A, J, W*], 1988 *Fj*, 1990 *Arg* 1,2, 1991 *Fj*, [*It, US*]
Redmond, G F (Cambridge U) 1970 *F*
Redwood, B W (Bristol) 1968 *W, I*
Rees, G W (Nottingham) 1984 *SA* 2 (R), *A*, 1986 *I, F*, 1987 *F, W, S*, [*A, J, US, W*], 1988 *S* (R), *I* 1,2 *A* 1,2, *Fj*, 1989 *W* (R), *R* (R), *Fj* (R), 1990 *Arg* 3 (R), 1991 *Fj*, [*US*]
Reeve, J S R (Harlequins) 1929 *F*, 1930 *W, I, F, S*, 1931 *W, I, S*
Regan, M (Liverpool) 1953 *W, I, F, S*, 1954 *W, NZ, I, S, F*, 1956 *I, S, F*
Rendall, P A G (Wasps, Askeans) 1984 *W, SA* 2, 1986 *W, S*, 1987 *I, F, S*, [*A, J, W*], 1988 *F, W, S, I* 1,2, *A* 1,2, *A*, 1989 *S, I, F, W, R*, 1990 *I, F, W, S*, 1991 [*It* (R)]
Rew, H (Blackheath) 1929 *S, F*, 1930 *F, S*, 1931 *W, S, F*, 1934 *W, I, S*
Reynolds, F J (O Cranleighans) 1937 *S*, 1938 *I, S*
Reynolds, S (Richmond) 1900 *W, I, S*, 1901 *I*
Rhodes, J (Castleford) 1896 *W, I, S*
Richards, D (Leicester) 1986 *I, F*, 1987 *S*, [*A, J, US, W*], 1988 *F, W, S, I* 1, *A* 1,2, *Fj, A*, 1989 *S, I, F, W, R*, 1990 *Arg* 3, 1991 *W, S, I, F, Fj, A*, [*NZ, It, US*], 1992 *S*(R), *F, W*

155

Richards, E E (Plymouth A) 1929 *S, F*
Richards, J (Bradford) 1891 *W, I, S*
Richards, S B (Richmond) 1965 *W, I, F, S,* 1967 *A, I, F, S, W*
Richardson, J V (Birkenhead Park) 1928 *A, W, I, F, S*
Richardson, W R (Manchester) 1881 *I*
Rickards, C H (Gipsies) 1873 *S*
Rimmer, G (Waterloo) 1949 *W, I,* 1950 *W,* 1951 *W, I, F,* 1952 *SA, W,* 1954 *W, NZ, I, S*
Rimmer, L I (Bath) 1961 *SA, W, I, F, S*
Ripley, A G (Rosslyn Park) 1972 *W, I, F, S, SA,* 1973 *NZ* 1, *W, I, F, S, NZ* 2, *A,* 1974 *S, I, F, W,* 1975 *I, F, S, A* 1,2, 1976 *A, W, S*
Risman, A B W (Loughborough Coll) 1959 *W, I, F, S,* 1961 *SA, W, I, F*
Ritson, J A S (Northern) 1910 *F, S,* 1912 *F,* 1913 *SA, W, F, I, S*
Rittson-Thomas, G C (Oxford U) 1951 *W, I, F*
Robbins, G L (Coventry) 1986 *W, S*
Robbins, P G D (Oxford U, Moseley, Coventry) 1956 *W, I, S, F,* 1957 *W, I, F, S,* 1958 *W, A, I, S,* 1960 *W, I, F, S,* 1961 *SA, W,* 1962 *S*
Roberts, A D (Northern) 1911 *W, F, I, S,* 1912 *I, S, F,* 1914 *I*
Roberts, E W (RNE Coll) 1901 *W, I,* 1905 *NZ,* 1906 *W, I,* 1907 *S*
Roberts, G D (Harlequins) 1907 *S,* 1908 *F, W*
Roberts, J (Sale) 1960 *W, I, F, S,* 1961 *SA, W, I, F, S,* 1962 *W, I, F, S,* 1963 *W, I, F, S,* 1964 *NZ*
Roberts, R S (Coventry) 1932 *I*
Roberts, S (Swinton) 1887 *W, I*
Roberts, V G (Penryn, Harlequins) 1947 *F,* 1949 *W, I, F, S,* 1950 *I, F, S,* 1951 *W, I, F, S,* 1956 *W, I, S, F*
Robertshaw, A R (Bradford) 1886 *W, I, S,* 1887 *W, S*
Robinson, A (Blackheath) 1889 *M,* 1890 *W, S, I*
Robinson, E F (Coventry) 1954 *S,* 1961 *I, F, S*
Robinson, G C (Percy Park) 1897 *I, S,* 1898 *I,* 1899 *W,* 1900 *I, S,* 1901 *I, S*
Robinson, J J (Headingley) 1893 *S,* 1902 *W, I, S*
Robinson, R A (Bath) 1988 *A* 2, *Fj, A,* 1989 *S, I, F, W*
Robson, A (Northern) 1924 *W, I, F, S,* 1926 *W*
Robson, M (Oxford U) 1930 *W, I, F, S*
Rodber, T A K (Army, Northampton) 1992 *S, I*
Rogers, D P (Bedford) 1961 *I, F, S,* 1962 *W, I, F,* 1963 *W, I, F, S, NZ* 1,2, *A,* 1964 *NZ, W, I, F, S,* 1965 *W, I, F, S,* 1966 *W, I, F, S,* 1967 *A, S, W, NZ,* 1969 *I, F, S, W*
Rogers, J H (Moseley) 1890 *W, S, I,* 1891 *S*
Rogers, W L Y (Bristol) 1905 *W, I*
Rollitt, D M (Bristol) 1967 *I, F, S, W,* 1969 *I, F, S, W,* 1975 *S, A* 1,2
Roncoroni, A D S (West Herts, Richmond) 1933 *W, I, S*
Rose, W M H (Cambridge U, Coventry, Harlequins) 1981 *I, F,* 1982 *A, S, I,* 1987 *I, F, W, S, [A]*
Rossborough, P A (Coventry) 1971 *W,* 1973 *NZ* 2, *A,* 1974 *S, I,* 1975 *I, F*
Rosser, D W A (Wasps) 1965 *W, I, F, S,* 1966 *W*
Rotherham, Alan (Richmond) 1883 *W, S,* 1884 *W, S,* 1885 *W, I,* 1886 *W, I, S,* 1887 *W, I, S*
Rotherham, Arthur (Richmond) 1898 *S, W,* 1899 *W, I, S*
Roughley, D (Liverpool) 1973 *A,* 1974 *S, I*
Rowell, R E (Leicester) 1964 *W,* 1965 *W*
Rowley, A J (Coventry) 1932 *SA*
Rowley, H C (Manchester) 1879 *S, I,* 1880 *I, S,* 1881 *I, W, S,* 1882 *I, S*
Royds, P M R (Blackheath) 1898 *S, W,* 1899 *W*
Royle, A V (Broughton R) 1889 *M*
Rudd, E L (Liverpool) 1965 *W, I, S,* 1966 *W, I, S*
Russell, R F (Leicester) 1905 *NZ*
Rutherford, D (Percy Park, Gloucester) 1960 *W, I, F, S,* 1961 *SA,* 1965 *W, I, F, S,* 1966 *W, I, F, S,* 1967 *NZ*
Ryalls, H J (N Brighton) 1885 *W, I*
Ryan, D (Wasps) 1990 *Arg* 1,2
Ryan, P H (Richmond) 1955 *W, I*

Sadler, E H (Army) 1933 *I, S*
Sagar, J W (Cambridge U) 1901 *W, I*
Salmon, J L B (Harlequins) 1985 *NZ* 1,2, 1986 *W, S,* 1987 *I, F, W, S, [A, J, US, W]*
Sample, C H (Cambridge U) 1884 *I,* 1885 *I,* 1886 *S*
Sanders, D L (Harlequins) 1954 *W, NZ, I, S, F,* 1956 *W, I, S, F*

Sanders, F W (Plymouth A) 1923 *I, S, F*
Sandford, J R P (Marlborough N) 1906 *I*
Sangwin, R D (Hull and E Riding) 1964 *NZ, W*
Sargent, G A F (Gloucester) 1981 *I* (R)
Savage, K F (Northampton) 1966 *W, I, F, S,* 1967 *A, I, F, S, W, NZ,* 1968 *W, F, S*
Sawyer, C M (Broughton) 1880 *S,* 1881 *I*
Saxby, L E (Gloucester) 1932 *SA, W*
Schofield, J W (Manchester) 1880 *I*
Scholfield, J A (Preston Grasshoppers) 1911 *W*
Schwarz, R O (Richmond) 1899 *S,* 1901 *W, I*
Scorfield, E S (Percy Park) 1910 *F*
Scott, C T (Blackheath) 1900 *W, I,* 1901 *I, W*
Scott, E K (St Mary's Hospital, Redruth) 1947 *W,* 1948 *A, W, I, S*
Scott, F S (Bristol) 1907 *W*
Scott, H (Manchester) 1955 *F*
Scott, J P (Rosslyn Park, Cardiff) 1978 *F, W, S, I, NZ,* 1979 *S* (R), *I, F, W, NZ,* 1980 *I, F, W, S,* 1981 *W, S, I, F, Arg* 1,2, 1982 *I, F, W,* 1983 *F, W, S, I, NZ,* 1984 *S, I, F, W, SA* 1,2
Scott, J S M (Oxford U) 1958 *F*
Scott, M T (Cambridge U) 1887 *I,* 1890 *S, I*
Scott, W M (Cambridge U) 1889 *M*
Seddon, R L (Broughton R) 1887 *W, I, S*
Sellar, K A (United Services, RN) 1927 *W, I, S,* 1928 *A, W, I, F*
Sever, H S (Sale) 1936 *NZ, W, I, S,* 1937 *W, I, S,* 1938 *W, I, S*
Shackleton, I R (Cambridge U) 1969 *SA,* 1970 *I, W, S*
Sharp, R A W (Oxford U, Wasps, Redruth) 1960 *W, I, F, S,* 1961 *I, F,* 1962 *W, I, F,* 1963 *W, I, F, S,* 1967 *A*
Shaw, C H (Moseley) 1906 *S, SA,* 1907 *F, W, I, S*
Shaw, F (Cleckheaton) 1898 *I*
Shaw, J F (RNE Coll) 1898 *S, W*
Sheppard, A (Bristol) 1981 *W* (R), 1985 *W*
Sherrard, C W (Blackheath) 1871 *S,* 1872 *S*
Sherriff, G A (Saracens) 1966 *S,* 1967 *A, NZ*
Shewring, H E (Bristol) 1905 *I, NZ,* 1906 *W, S, F, SA,* 1907 *F, W, I, S*
Shooter, J H (Morley) 1899 *I, S,* 1900 *I, S*
Shuttleworth, D W (Headingley) 1951 *S,* 1953 *S*
Sibree, H J H (Harlequins) 1908 *F,* 1909 *I, S*
Silk, N (Harlequins) 1965 *W, I, F, S*
Simms, K G (Cambridge U, Liverpool, Wasps) 1985 *R, F, S, I, W,* 1986 *I, F,* 1987 *I, F, W, [A, J, W],* 1988 *F, W*
Simpson, C P (Harlequins) 1965 *W*
Simpson, P D (Bath) 1983 *NZ,* 1984 *S,* 1987 *I*
Simpson, T (Rockcliff) 1902 *S,* 1903 *W, I, S,* 1904 *I, S,* 1905 *I, S,* 1906 *S, SA,* 1909 *F*
Skinner, M G (Harlequins) 1988 *F, W, S, I* 1,2, 1989 *Fj,* 1990 *I, F, W, S, Arg* 1,2, 1991 *Fj* (R), *[US, F, S, A],* 1992 *S, I, F, W*
Sladen, G M (United Services, RN) 1929 *W, I, S*
Slemen, M A C (Liverpool) 1976 *I, F,* 1977 *S, I, F, W,* 1978 *F, W, S, I, NZ,* 1979 *S, I, F, W, NZ,* 1980 *I, F, W, S,* 1981 *W, S, I, F,* 1982 *A, S, I, F, W,* 1983 *NZ,* 1984 *S*
Slocock, L A N (Liverpool) 1907 *F, W, I, S,* 1908 *F, W, I, S*
Slow, C F (Leicester) 1934 *S*
Small, H D (Oxford U) 1950 *W, I, F, S*
Smallwood, A M (Leicester) 1920 *F, I,* 1921 *W, I, S, F,* 1922 *I, S,* 1923 *W, I, S, F,* 1925 *I, S*
Smart, C E (Newport) 1979 *F, W, NZ,* 1981 *S, I, F, Arg* 1,2, 1982 *A, S, I, F, W,* 1983 *F, W, S, I*
Smart, S E J (Gloucester) 1913 *SA, W, F, I, S,* 1914 *W, I, S, F,* 1920 *W, I, S*
Smeddle, R W (Cambridge U) 1929 *W, I, S,* 1931 *F*
Smith, C C (Gloucester) 1901 *W*
Smith, D F (Richmond) 1910 *W, I*
Smith, J V (Cambridge U, Rosslyn Park) 1950 *W, I, F, S*
Smith, K (Roundhay) 1974 *F, W,* 1975 *W, S*
Smith, M J K (Oxford U) 1956 *W*
Smith, S J (Sale) 1973 *I, F, S, A,* 1974 *I, F,* 1975 *W* (R), 1976 *F,* 1977 *F* (R), 1979 *NZ,* 1980 *I, F, W, S,* 1981 *W, S, I, F, Arg* 1,2, 1982 *A, S, I, F, W,* 1983 *F, W, S*
Smith, S R (Richmond) 1959 *W, F, S,* 1964 *F, S*
Smith, S T (Wasps) 1985 *R, F, S, I, W, NZ* 1,2, 1986 *W, S*
Smith, T A (Northampton) 1951 *W*
Soane, F (Bath) 1893 *S,* 1894 *W, I, S*

Sobey, W H (O Millhillians) 1930 *W*, *F*, *S*, 1932 *SA*, *W*
Solomon, B (Redruth) 1910 *W*
Sparks, R H W (Plymouth A) 1928 *I*, *F*, *S*, 1929 *W*, *I*, *S*, 1931 *I*, *S*, *F*
Speed, H (Castleford) 1894 *W*, *I*, *S*, 1896 *S*
Spence, F W (Birkenhead Park) 1890 *I*
Spencer, J (Harlequins) 1966 *W*
Spencer, J S (Cambridge U, Headingley) 1969 *I*, *F*, *S*, *W*, *SA*, 1970 *I*, *W*, *S*, *F*, 1971 *W*, *I*, *S* (2[1C]), *P*
Spong, R S (O Millhillians) 1929 *F*, 1930 *W*, *I*, *F*, *S*, 1931 *F*, 1932 *SA*, *W*
Spooner, R H (Liverpool) 1903 *W*
Springman, H H (Liverpool) 1879 *S*, 1887 *S*
Spurling, A (Blackheath) 1882 *I*
Spurling, N (Blackheath) 1886 *I*, *S*, 1887 *W*
Squires, P J (Harrogate) 1973 *F*, *S*, *NZ* 2, *A*, 1974 *S*, *I*, *F*, *W*, 1975 *I*, *F*, *W*, *S*, *A* 1,2, 1976 *A*, *W*, 1977 *S*, *I*, *F*, *W*, 1978 *F*, *W*, *S*, *I*, *NZ*, 1979 *S*, *I*, *F*, *W*
Stafford, R C (Bedford) 1912 *W*, *I*, *S*, *F*
Stafford, W F H (RE) 1874 *S*
Stanbury, E (Plymouth A) 1926 *W*, *I*, *S*, 1927 *W*, *I*, *S*, *F*, 1928 *A*, *W*, *I*, *F*, *S*, 1929 *W*, *I*, *S*, *F*
Standing, G (Blackheath) 1883 *W*, *I*
Stanger-Leathes, C F (Northern) 1905 *I*
Stark, K J (O Alleynians) 1927 *W*, *I*, *S*, *F*, 1928 *A*, *W*, *I*, *F*, *S*
Starks, A (Castleford) 1896 *W*, *I*
Starmer-Smith, N C (Harlequins) 1969 *SA*, 1970 *I*, *W*, *S*, *F*, 1971 *S* (C), *P*
Start, S P (United Services, RN) 1907 *S*
Steeds, J H (Saracens) 1949 *F*, *S*, 1950 *I*, *F*, *S*
Steele-Bodger, M R (Cambridge U) 1947 *W*, *I*, *S*, *F*, 1948 *A*, *W*, *I*, *S*, *F*
Steinthal, F E (Ilkley) 1913 *W*, *F*
Stevens, C B (Penzance-Newlyn, Harlequins) 1969 *SA*, 1970 *I*, *W*, *S*, 1971 *P*, 1972 *W*, *I*, *F*, *S*, *SA*, 1973 *NZ* 1, *W*, *I*, *F*, *S*, *NZ* 2, *A*, 1974 *S*, *I*, *F*, *W*, 1975 *I*, *F*, *W*, *S*
Still, E R (Oxford U, Ravenscourt P) 1873 *S*
Stirling, R V (Leicester, RAF, Wasps) 1951 *W*, *I*, *F*, *S*, 1952 *SA*, *W*, *S*, *I*, *F*, 1953 *W*, *I*, *F*, *S*, 1954 *W*, *NZ*, *I*, *S*, *F*
Stoddart, A E (Blackheath) 1885 *W*, *I*, 1886 *W*, *I*, *S*, 1889 *M*, 1890 *W*, *I*, 1893 *W*, *S*
Stoddart, W B (Liverpool) 1897 *W*, *I*, *S*
Stokes, F (Blackheath) 1871 *S*, 1872 *S*, 1873 *S*
Stokes, L (Blackheath) 1875 *I*, 1876 *S*, 1877 *I*, *S*, 1878 *S*, 1879 *S*, *I*, 1880 *I*, *S*, 1881 *I*, *W*, *S*
Stone, F le S (Blackheath) 1914 *F*
Stoop, A D (Harlequins) 1905 *S*, 1906 *S*, *F*, *SA*, 1907 *F*, *W*, 1910 *W*, *I*, *S*, 1911 *W*, *F*, *I*, *S*, 1912 *W*, *S*
Stoop, F M (Harlequins) 1910 *S*, 1911 *F*, *I*, 1913 *SA*
Stout, F M (Richmond) 1897 *W*, *I*, 1898 *I*, *S*, *W*, 1899 *I*, *S*, 1903 *S*, 1904 *W*, *I*, *S*, 1905 *W*, *I*, *S*
Stout, P W (Richmond) 1898 *S*, *W*, 1899 *W*, *I*, *S*
Stringer, N C (Wasps) 1982 *A* (R), 1983 *NZ* (R), 1984 *SA* 1 (R), *A*, 1985 *R*
Strong, E L (Oxford U) 1884 *W*, *I*, *S*
Summerscales, G E (Durham City) 1905 *NZ*
Sutcliffe, J W (Heckmondwike) 1889 *M*
Swarbrick, D W (Oxford U) 1947 *W*, *I*, *F*, 1948 *A*, *W*, 1949 *I*
Swayne, D H (Oxford U) 1931 *W*
Swayne, J W R (Bridgwater) 1929 *W*
Swift, A H (Swansea) 1981 *Arg* 1,2, 1983 *F*, *W*, *S*, 1984 *SA* 2
Syddall, J P (Waterloo) 1982 *I*, 1984 *A*
Sykes, A R V (Blackheath) 1914 *F*
Sykes, F D (Northampton) 1955 *F*, *S*, 1963 *NZ* 2, *A*
Sykes, P W (Wasps) 1948 *F*, 1952 *S*, *I*, *F*, 1953 *W*, *I*, *F*
Syrett, R E (Wasps) 1958 *W*, *A*, *I*, *F*, 1960 *W*, *I*, *F*, *S*, 1962 *W*, *I*, *F*

Tallent, J A (Cambridge U, Blackheath) 1931 *S*, *F*, 1932 *SA*, *W*, 1935 *I*
Tanner, C C (Cambridge U, Gloucester) 1930 *S*, 1932 *SA*, *W*, *I*, *S*
Tarr, F N (Leicester) 1909 *A*, *W*, *F*, 1913 *S*
Tatham, W M M (Oxford U) 1882 *S*, 1883 *W*, *I*, *S*, 1884 *W*, *I*, *S*
Taylor, A S (Blackheath) 1883 *W*, *I*, 1886 *W*, *I*
Taylor, E W (Rockcliff) 1892 *I*, 1893 *I*, 1894 *W*, *I*, *S*, 1895 *W*, *I*, *S*, 1896 *W*, *I*, 1897 *W*, *I*, *S*, 1899 *I*
Taylor, F (Leicester) 1920 *F*, *I*

Taylor, F M (Leicester) 1914 *W*
Taylor, H H (Blackheath) 1879 *S*, 1880 *S*, 1881 *I*, *W*, 1882 *S*
Taylor, J T (W Hartlepool) 1897 *I*, 1899 *I*, 1900 *I*, 1901 *W*, *I*, 1902 *W*, *I*, *S*, 1903 *W*, *I*, 1905 *S*
Taylor, P J (Northampton) 1955 *W*, *I*, 1962 *W*, *I*, *F*, *S*
Taylor, R B (Northampton) 1966 *W*, 1967 *I*, *F*, *S*, *W*, *NZ*, 1969 *F*, *S*, *W*, *SA*, 1970 *I*, *W*, *S*, *F*, 1971 *S* (2[1C])
Taylor, W J (Blackheath) 1928 *A*, *W*, *I*, *F*, *S*
Teague, M C (Gloucester) 1985 *F* (R), *NZ* 1,2, 1989 *S*, *I*, *F*, *W*, *R*, 1990 *F*, *W*, *S*, 1991 *W*, *S*, *I*, *F*, *Fj*, *A*, [*NZ*, *It*, *F*, *S*, *A*]
Teden, D E (Richmond) 1939 *W*, *I*, *S*
Teggin, A (Broughton R) 1884 *I*, 1885 *W*, 1886 *I*, *S*, 1887 *I*, *S*
Tetley, T S (Bradford) 1876 *S*
Thomas, C (Barnstaple) 1895 *W*, *I*, *S*, 1899 *I*
Thompson, P H (Headingley, Waterloo) 1956 *W*, *I*, *S*, *F*, 1957 *W*, *I*, *F*, *S*, 1958 *W*, *A*, *I*, *F*, *S*, 1959 *W*, *I*, *F*, *S*
Thomson, G T (Halifax) 1878 *S*, 1882 *I*, *S*, 1883 *W*, *I*, *S*, 1884 *I*, *S*, 1885 *I*
Thomson, W B (Blackheath) 1892 *W*, 1895 *W*, *I*, *S*
Thorne, J D (Bristol) 1963 *W*, *I*, *F*
Tindall, V R (Liverpool U) 1951 *W*, *I*, *F*, *S*
Tobin, F (Liverpool) 1871 *S*
Todd, A F (Blackheath) 1900 *I*, *S*
Todd, R (Manchester) 1877 *S*
Toft, H B (Waterloo) 1936 *S*, 1937 *W*, *I*, *S*, 1938 *W*, *I*, *S*, 1939 *W*, *I*, *S*
Toothill, J T (Bradford) 1890 *S*, *I*, 1891 *W*, *I*, 1892 *W*, *I*, *S*, 1893 *W*, *I*, *S*, 1894 *W*, *I*
Tosswill, L R (Exeter) 1902 *W*, *I*, *S*
Touzel, C J C (Liverpool) 1877 *I*, *S*
Towell, A C (Bedford) 1948 *F*, 1951 *S*
Travers, B H (Harlequins) 1947 *W*, *I*, 1948 *A*, *W*, 1949 *F*, *S*
Treadwell, W T (Wasps) 1966 *I*, *F*, *S*
Trick, D M (Bath) 1983 *I*, 1984 *SA* 1
Tristram, H B (Oxford U) 1883 *S*, 1884 *W*, *S*, 1885 *W*, 1887 *S*
Troop, C L (Aldershot S) 1933 *I*, *S*
Tucker, J S (Bristol) 1922 *W*, 1925 *NZ*, *W*, *I*, *S*, *F*, 1926 *W*, *I*, *S*, 1927 *W*, *I*, *S*, *F*, 1928 *A*, *W*, *I*, *F*, *S*, 1929 *W*, *I*, *F*, 1930 *W*, *I*, *F*, *S*, 1931 *W*
Tucker, W E (Blackheath) 1894 *W*, *I*, 1895 *W*, *I*, *S*
Tucker, W E (Blackheath) 1926 *I*, 1930 *W*, *I*
Turner, D P (Richmond) 1871 *S*, 1872 *S*, 1873 *S*, 1874 *S*, 1875 *I*, *S*
Turner, E B (St George's Hospital) 1876 *I*, 1877 *I*, 1878 *I*
Turner, G R (St George's Hospital) 1876 *S*
Turner, H J C (Manchester) 1871 *S*
Turner, M F (Blackheath) 1948 *S*, *F*
Turquand-Young, D (Richmond) 1928 *A*, *W*, 1929 *I*, *S*, *F*
Twynam, H T (Richmond) 1879 *I*, 1880 *I*, 1881 *W*, 1882 *I*, 1883 *I*, 1884 *W*, *I*, *S*

Underwood, A M (Exeter) 1962 *W*, *I*, *F*, *S*, 1964 *I*
Underwood, R (Leicester, RAF) 1984 *I*, *F*, *W*, *A*, 1985 *R*, *F*, *S*, *I*, *W*, 1986 *W*, *I*, *F*, 1987 *I*, *F*, *W*, *S*, [*A*, *J*, *W*], 1988 *F*, *W*, *S*, *I* 1,2, *A* 1,2, *Fj*, *A*, 1989 *S*, *I*, *F*, *W*, *R*, *Fj*, 1990 *I*, *F*, *W*, *S*, *Arg* 3, 1991 *W*, *S*, *I*, *F*, *Fj*, *A*, [*NZ*, *It*, *US*, *F*, *S*, *A*], 1992 *S*, *I*, *F*, *W*
Unwin, E J (Rosslyn Park, Army) 1937 *S*, 1938 *W*, *I*, *S*
Unwin, G T (Blackheath) 1898 *S*
Uren, R (Waterloo) 1948 *I*, *S*, *F*, 1950 *I*
Uttley, R M (Gosforth) 1973 *I*, *F*, *S*, *NZ* 2, *A*, 1974 *I*, *F*, *W*, 1975 *F*, *W*, *S*, *A* 1,2, 1977 *S*, *I*, *F*, *W*, 1978 *NZ*, 1979 *S*, 1980 *I*, *F*, *W*, *S*

Valentine, J (Swinton) 1890 *W*, 1896 *W*, *I*, *S*
Vanderspar, C H R (Richmond) 1873 *S*
Van Ryneveld, C B (Oxford U) 1949 *W*, *I*, *F*, *S*
Varley, H (Liversedge) 1892 *S*
Vassall, H (Blackheath) 1881 *W*, *S*, 1882 *I*, *S*, 1883 *W*
Vassall, H H (Blackheath) 1908 *I*
Vaughan, D B (Headingley) 1948 *A*, *W*, *I*, *S*, 1949 *I*, *F*, *S*, 1950 *W*
Vaughan-Jones, A (Army) 1932 *I*, *S*, 1933 *W*
Verelst, C L (Liverpool) 1876 *I*, 1878 *I*
Vernon, G F (Blackheath) 1878 *S*, *I*, 1880 *I*, *S*, 1881 *I*
Vickery, G (Aberavon) 1905 *I*
Vivyan, E J (Devonport A) 1901 *W*, 1904 *W*, *I*, *S*
Voyce, A T (Gloucester) 1920 *I*, *S*, 1921 *W*, *I*, *S*, *F*,

ENGLISH INTERNATIONAL RECORDS

Both team and individual records are for official England international matches up to 31 March 1992.

TEAM RECORDS

Highest score
60 v Japan (60-7) 1987 Sydney
v individual countries
51 v Argentina (51-0) 1990 Twickenham
28 v Australia (28-19) 1988 Twickenham
58 v Fiji (58-23) 1989 Twickenham
41 v France (41-13) 1907 Richmond
38 v Ireland (38-9) 1992 Twickenham
36 v Italy (36-6) 1991 Twickenham
60 v Japan (60-7) 1987 Sydney
16 v N Zealand (16-10) 1973 Auckland
58 v Romania (58-3) 1989 Bucharest
30 v Scotland (30-18) 1980 Murrayfield
18 v S Africa (18-9) 1972 Johannesburg
37 v US (37-9) 1991 Twickenham
34 v Wales (34-6) 1990 Twickenham

Biggest winning points margin
55 v Romania (58-3) 1989 Bucharest
v individual countries
51 v Argentina (51-0) 1990 Twickenham
17 v Australia { (20-3) 1973 Twickenham
             { (23-6) 1976 Twickenham
35 v Fiji (58-23) 1989 Twickenham
37 v France (37-0) 1911 Twickenham
32 v Ireland (35-3) 1988 Twickenham
30 v Italy (36-6) 1991 Twickenham
53 v Japan (60-7) 1987 Sydney
13 v N Zealand (13-0) 1936 Twickenham
55 v Romania (58-3) 1989 Bucharest
20 v Scotland (26-6) 1977 Twickenham
9 v S Africa (18-9) 1972 Johannesburg
28 v US { (34-6) 1987 Sydney
       { (37-9) 1991 Twickenham
28 v Wales (34-6) 1990 Twickenham

Highest score by opposing team
42 N Zealand (15-42) 1985 Wellington
by individual countries
19 Argentina (19-19) 1981 Buenos Aires
40 Australia (15-40) 1991 Sydney
23 Fiji (58-23) 1989 Twickenham
37 France (12-37) 1972 Colombes
26 Ireland (21-26) 1974 Twickenham
6 Italy (36-6) 1991 Twickenham
7 Japan (60-7) 1987 Sydney
42 N Zealand (15-42) 1985 Wellington
15 Romania (22-15) 1985 Twickenham
33 Scotland (6-33) 1986 Murrayfield
35 S Africa (9-35) 1984 Johannesburg
9 United States (37-9) 1991 Twickenham
34 Wales (21-34) 1967 Cardiff

Biggest losing points margin
27 v N Zealand (15-42) 1985 Wellington
27 v Scotland (6-33) 1986 Murrayfield
v individual countries
2 v Argentina (13-15) 1990 Buenos Aires
25 v Australia (15-40) 1991 Sydney
25 v France (12-37) 1972 Colombes
22 v Ireland (0-22) 1947 Dublin
27 v N Zealand (15-42) 1985 Wellington
27 v Scotland (6-33) 1986 Murrayfield
26 v S Africa (9-35) 1984 Johannesburg
25 v Wales (0-25) 1905 Cardiff

No defeats v Fiji, Italy, Japan, Romania or United States

Most tries by England in an international
13 v Wales 1881 Blackheath

Most tries against England in an international
8 by Wales (6-28) 1922 Cardiff

Most points by England in International Championship in a season – 118
in season 1991-92

Most tries by England in International Championship in a season – 20
in season 1913-14

INDIVIDUAL RECORDS

Most capped player
R Underwood   55   1984-92
in individual positions
Full-back
J M Webb   27   1987-92
Wing
R Underwood   55   1984-92
Centre
W D C Carling   36[1]   1988-92
Fly-half
C R Andrew   47(48)[2]   1985-92
Scrum-half
R J Hill   29   1984-91
Prop
G S Pearce   36   1979-91
Hooker
J V Pullin   42   1966-76
Lock
W A Dooley   50   1985-92
Flanker
P J Winterbottom   52   1982-92
No 8
D Richards   33   1986-92

[1]*David Duckham, 36 caps, played 14 times at centre and 22 times on the wing*
[2]*Andrew has also played once as a full-back*

Longest international career
J Heaton 13 seasons 1935-47

Most consecutive internationals – 36
J V Pullin 1968-75

Most internationals as captain
W D C Carling 29 1988-92

Most points in internationals – 246
J M Webb (27 matches) 1987-92

Most points in International Championship in a season – 67
J M Webb (4 matches) 1991-92

Most points in an international – 24
J M Webb v Italy 1991 Twickenham

Most tries in internationals – 35
R Underwood (55 matches) 1984-92

Most tries in International Championship in a season – 8
C N Lowe (4 matches) 1913-14

Most tries in an international – 5
D Lambert v France 1907 Richmond
R Underwood v Fiji 1989 Twickenham

Most conversions in internationals – 37
J M Webb (27 matches) 1987-92

Most conversions in International Championship in a season – 11
J M Webb (4 matches) 1991-92

Most conversions in an international – 8
S D Hodgkinson v Romania 1989 Bucharest

Most dropped goals in internationals – 14
C R Andrew (48 matches) 1985-92

Most penalty goals in internationals – 67
W H Hare (25 matches) 1974-84

Most penalty goals in International Championship in a season – 18
S D Hodgkinson (4 matches) 1990-91

Most points on major tour – 56
S D Hodgkinson (4 matches) Argentina 1990
W H Hare scored 79 points on the N American tour of 1982, but this was not a major tour

Most points in a tour match – 36
W N Bennett v Western Australia 1975 Perth

Most tries in a tour match – 4
A J Morley v Western Australia 1975 Perth
P S Preece v New South Wales 1975 Sydney

R E Webb scored 4 tries v Canada in 1967, and J Carleton scored 4 against Mid-West at Cleveland in 1982, but these were not on major tours

OPPORTUNIST MIDLANDS STEAL IN

ADT DIVISIONAL CHAMPIONSHIP 1991
Michael Austin

The Championship ran concurrently with the World Cup, which enabled the opportunists from the Midlands to steal in and exploit the depletion of London, winners for the three previous years, to take the title for the first time since 1985. London lost eight players to the England squad, compared with the Midlands' five, but the absence of automatic choices offered a back-handed benefit to the selectors because players from the lower strata were given otherwise unforseeable opportunities.

A succinct appraisal was that the Midlands played to their potential under the inspiring influence of Rupert Moon, later to commit himself to Wales. The North, the runners-up, were rebuilding, the young London squad looked disappointing despite a summer tour to Australia and the South and South-West were outgunned once more.

The Midlands, coached by Peter Rossborough, the former Coventry and England full-back, provided three of the most impressive players in Moon, Rodber (capped by England later in the season) and Back, a flanker of immense potential, as they won all three matches. An opening victory of 15-9, in which Rodber scored the game's only try, was their first success against the North for six years. The result was distinctly ironic in that a key figure, Liley, the Midlands full-back with Wakefield origins, had been passed over by the North earlier in the season. His availability was doubly appreciated by the Midlands as Hodgkinson was on England duty. Liley scored 11 points against the North, 24 against the South-West and 16 against London to become the Championship's leading scorer for a season with 51, exceeding Andrew's total of 44 for London the previous year.

While the Midlands rose above the loss of Richards, Rees, Pearce, Olver and Hodgkinson to England's cause, for various reasons the North were able to field only two Orrell players compared with ten in the previous Championship. Only four players – Greenwood, Ashurst, Hunter and Ainscough – were available from First Division clubs. Inevitably, skill levels and performances suffered, despite the emergence of two promising newcomers: Bromley, a powerful wing from Liverpool St Helens, and Frankland, the Newcastle Gosforth hooker.

The North won one match, eminently predictably, by 34-9 against the South-West, who have not beaten them in seven meetings since 1980. Ainscough scored 18 points for the North and the margin of defeat equalled the South-West's biggest since the competition's inception in 1977. Their disappointing record shows 15 losses in the past 20 games. The protracted failure of Bath, Bristol and Gloucester to combine efficiently as a team representing the Division has become one of the mysteries of the English game. Robinson, the South-West captain, summed up the plight: 'We just seem to be locked into a cycle of defeat'.

The South-West, with Robinson as their solitary international player, held London, with six caps, to 8-0 in their opening game, a result which barely filled the holders or their coach, Dick Best, with confidence. London had a new identity but a flawed one as England's demands on Carling, Andrew, Leonard, Moore, Probyn, Ackford, Skinner and Winterbottom forced too many players to be replaced simultaneously.

London salvaged a draw with the North through a try and conversion from Thresher with six minutes remaining, and could have won the title by beating the Midlands at Northampton as the competition reached a natural climax. Instead, the pre-tournament favourites lost 24-15, having led through an interception try from Harriman. The Midlands were without Rupert Moon, who had scored two excellent tries against the South-West the previous week before suffering a shoulder injury in a high tackle by Sims, the opposing No 8. The scrum-half role passed to Richard Moon, his elder brother, and the captaincy to Wells, who formed the competition's outstanding unit, the Midlands back row, with Back and Rodber.

A Championship drawing poor crowds had its detractors and supporters in almost equal numbers. Lancashire put forward a motion, later withdrawn, at the Rugby Football Union annual meeting the previous July that 'in 1991-92, the Divisional Championship will not take place'. However, Geoff Cooke, the England team manager, appreciated the value of the tournament. He called for more fixtures for the divisions against touring teams and for them to spend more time abroad. He also emphasised the increasing need to identify young talent and to nurture it beneath the divisional and national umbrella. To that end, an Under-21 Divisional Championship was inaugurated and won by the North. Both Divisional competitions, together with the County Championship at full and Under-21 level, were encompassed in the second of a three-year agreement, worth half a million pounds, between sponsors ADT and the Rugby Football Union.

Final Table	P	W	D	L	F	A	Pts
Midlands	3	3	0	0	75	34	6
North	3	1	1	1	55	36	3
London	3	1	1	1	35	36	3
South & South-West	3	0	0	3	19	78	0

The North have won the Championship 4 times, London 3 times and the Midlands once.

5 October, Metropolitan Police RFC

London Division 8 (2T) **South & South-West Division 0**
London Division: A Buzza (Wasps); A T Harriman (Harlequins), J Buckton (Saracens), F J Clough (Wasps) (*capt*), D Hopley (Wasps); P Challinor (Harlequins), S Bates

(Wasps); G Holmes (Wasps), D Barnett (Rosslyn Park), A Mullins (Harlequins), R Kinsey (Wasps), R Langhorn (Harlequins), M Russell (Harlequins), D Ryan (Wasps), M Rigby (Wasps) *Replacement* G Thompson (Harlequins) for Buckton
Scorers *Tries:* Hopley, Buzza
South & South-West Division: J Callard (Bath); J Fallon (Bath), S Morris (Gloucester), P de Glanville (Bath), P Hull (Bristol); N Matthews (Gloucester), S Knight (Bath); C Hocking (Plymouth Albion), J Hawker (Gloucester), R Lee (Bath), J Etheridge (Northampton), M Haag (Bath), P Ashmead (Gloucester), C Barrow (Bristol), A Robinson (Bath) *(capt)* *Replacements* D Willett (Bath) for Morris; I Sanders (Bath) for de Glanville
Referee C J Harrison (East Midlands Society)

5 October, Moseley RFC

Midlands Division 15 (1G 3PG)   **Northern Division 9** (2PG 1DG)
Midlands Division: J Liley (Leicester); E Saunders (Rugby), I Bates (Leicester), S Potter (Nottingham), S Hackney (Leicester); R Angell (Coventry), Rupert Moon (Llanelli) *(capt)*; G Baldwin (Northampton), R Cockerill (Coventry), T Revan (Rugby), M Johnson (Leicester), M C Bayfield (Northampton), J Wells (Leicester), T A K Rodber (Northampton), N Back (Leicester)
Scorers *Try:* Rodber   *Conversion:* Liley   *Penalty Goals:* Liley (3)
Northern Division: I Hunter (Northampton); S Bromley (Liverpool St Helens), B Barley (Wakefield), K G Simms (Liverpool St Helens) *(capt)*, D Cooke (West Hartlepool); G Ainscough (Orrell), D Scully (Wakefield); M Whitcombe (Sale), N Frankland (Newcastle Gosforth), S Peters (Waterloo), D Baldwin (Sale), J Howe (West Hartlepool), M Greenwood (Nottingham), A Macfarlane (Sale), N Ashurst (Orrell)
Scorer *Penalty Goals:* Ainscough (2)   *Dropped Goal:* Ainscough
Referee A Spreadbury (Somerset Society)

12 October, Bristol RFC

South & South West Division 10 (2PG 1T)   **Midlands Division 36** (3G 6PG)
South & South-West Division: J Callard (Bath); J Fallon (Bath), R Knibbs (Bristol), J Redrup (Bristol), P Hull (Bristol); N Matthews (Gloucester), S Knight (Bath); C Hocking (Plymouth Albion), J Hawker (Gloucester), R Lee (Bath), M Haag (Bath), J Etheridge (Northampton), P Ashmead (Gloucester), D Sims (Gloucester), R A Robinson (Bath) *(capt)* *Replacement* D Willett (Bath) for Callard
Scorers *Try:* Knight   *Penalty Goals:* Callard (2)
Midlands Division: J Liley (Leicester); E Saunders (Rugby), I Bates (Leicester), S Potter (Nottingham), S Hackney (Leicester); R Angell (Coventry), Rupert Moon (Llanelli) *(capt)*; M Linnett (Moseley), R Cockerill (Coventry), T Revan (Rugby), M Johnson (Leicester), M C Bayfield (Northampton), J Wells (Leicester), T A K Rodber (Northampton), N Back (Leicester) *Replacements* S Lloyd (Moseley) for Bayfield; A Kardooni (Leicester) for Moon
Scorers *Tries:* Moon (2), Back   *Conversions:* Liley (3)   *Penalty Goals:* Liley (6)
Referee R C Rees (London Society)

12 October, West Hartlepool RFC

Northern Division 12 (1G 2PG)   **London Division 12** (2G)
Northern Division: I Hunter (Northampton); S Bromley (Liverpool St Helens), B Barley (Wakefield), K G Simms (Liverpool St Helens) *(capt)*, D Cooke (West Hartlepool); G Ainscough (Orrell), D Scully (Wakefield); M Whitcombe (Sale), N Frankland (Newcastle Gosforth), S Peters (Waterloo), D Baldwin (Sale), J Howe (West Hartlepool), M Greenwood (Nottingham), A Macfarlane (Sale), N Ashurst (Orrell)
Scorers *Try:* Hunter   *Conversion:* Ainscough   *Penalty Goals:* Ainscough (2)
London Division: A Buzza (Wasps); A T Harriman (Harlequins), F J Clough (Wasps)

(*capt*), J Buckton (Saracens), S Thresher (Harlequins); P Challinor (Harlequins), S Bates (Wasps); G Holmes (Wasps), D Barnett (Rosslyn Park), A Mullins (Harlequins), R Langhorn (Harlequins), R Kinsey (Wasps), M Russell (Harlequins), D Ryan (Wasps), M Rigby (Wasps)

Scorers *Tries:* Russell, Thresher   *Conversions:* Thresher (2)

Referee A Savage (North Midlands Society)

19 October, Northampton RFC

Midlands Division 24 (2G 4PG)   **London Division 15** (2G 1PG)

Midlands Division: J Liley (Leicester); E Saunders (Rugby), I Bates (Leicester), S Potter (Nottingham), S Hackney (Leicester); R Angell (Coventry), Richard Moon (Rosslyn Park); M Linnett (Moseley), R Cockerill (Coventry), T Revan (Rugby), M Johnson (Leicester), M C Bayfield (Northampton), J Wells (Leicester) (*capt*), T A K Rodber (Northampton) N Back (Leicester) *Replacement* W Kilford (Nottingham) for Hackney

Scorers *Tries:* Back, Revan   *Conversions:* Liley (2)   *Penalty Goals:* Liley (4)

London Division: A Buzza (Wasps); A T Harriman (Harlequins), F J Clough (Wasps) (*capt*), J Buckton (Saracens), S Thresher (Harlequins); P Challinor (Harlequins), S Bates (Wasps); G Holmes (Wasps), D Barnett (Rosslyn Park), A Mullins (Harlequins), R Kinsey (Wasps), S Dear (Rosslyn Park), M Russell (Harlequins), D Ryan (Wasps), M Rigby (Wasps) *Replacement* R Glenister (Harlequins) for Challinor

Scorers *Tries:* Harriman, Buckton   *Conversions:* Thresher (2)   *Penalty Goal:* Thresher

Referee L Prideaux (Cornwall Society)

19 October, Gloucester RFC

South & South-West Division 9 (1G 1PG)   **Northern Division 34** (3G 4PG 1T)

South & South-West Division: A Lumsden (Bath); J Fallon (Bath), R Knibbs (Bristol), J Redrup (Bristol), P Hull (Bristol); N Matthews (Gloucester), S Knight (Bath); R Phillips (Gloucester), J Hawker (Gloucester), M Crane (Bath), M Haag (Bath), J Etheridge (Northampton), N Maslen (Bath), D Sims (Gloucester), R A Robinson (Bath) (*capt*)

Scorers *Try:* Fallon   *Conversion:* Hull   *Penalty Goal:* Hull

Northern Division: I Hunter (Northampton); S Bromley (Liverpool St Helens), B Barley (Wakefield), K G Simms (Liverpool St Helens) (*capt*), D Cooke (West Hartlepool); G Ainscough (Orrell), D Scully (Wakefield); M Whitcombe (Sale), N Frankland (Newcastle Gosforth), S Peters (Waterloo), D Baldwin (Sale), K Westgarth (Newcastle Gosforth), M Greenwood (Nottingham), A Macfarlane (Sale), N Ashurst (Orrell)

Scorers *Tries:* Bromley (2), Cooke, Scully   *Conversions:* Ainscough (3)
Penalty Goals: Ainscough (4)

Referee S V Griffiths (North Midlands Society)

BATH AT THE LAST ON THE LONGEST DAY OF ALL

PILKINGTON CUP 1991-92
Michael Austin

2 May, Twickenham
Harlequins 12 (1G 2PG)   **Bath 15** (1G 2PG 1DG) *(after extra time)*

Multiple attributes have carried Bath to success in all their seven Cup final appearances, none more so than a stubborn refusal to be denied victory. This was typified in 1991-92 by Stuart Barnes, who linked inspiration with desperation to drop a goal to beat Harlequins, the holders, in the last of 20 minutes of extra time. No one in England exploits the dropped goal better than Barnes, and his crucial kick contrasted with the efforts of Challinor and Pears, who missed two attempts each for Harlequins in the agonising closing minutes.

Barnes, whose late try beat Leicester in the final three years earlier, this time landed the decisive kick right-footed from 40 yards to reward Redman's catch at the last line-out, on Bath's throw. It was deeply ironic because Harlequins' jumpers, notably Ackford, who produced a towering performance, had monopolised possession by a count of 35-17. With Edwards at the front and Ackford in the middle, Harlequins won the ball on 14 of Bath's 30 throws, which provided the most remarkable and unexpected statistic of a tense and exhausting match.

A crowd of 60,500, a world record for a club match, saw Harlequins surprise Bath just as Northampton had shocked them, albeit with an extra-time defeat, in the previous final. Bath, the favourites, were confounded, first by a 12-3 deficit at half-time, and overall by the single-minded determination of a disrupted Harlequins' pack. Ackford, who had retired after the World Cup final six months earlier, and Russell, an England B flanker, both responded to Harlequins' call at a few days' notice. Russell had been absent for more than two months through ankle trouble. They helped to repair the injury, suspension and unavailability crises, which included the loss of Skinner and Langhorn, both sent off in a League match against Gloucester the previous week. The match marked the end of an era: Dick Best was coaching Harlequins for the final time and Halliday, the former Bath centre, played for Harlequins in his record-breaking seventh, and probably last, final.

It was dubbed 'the longest game in the longest season', the last final of a season of intense demands on leading players over eight months packed with major matches. Both teams were still ablaze with commitment and passion, which compensated for a lack of finesse, especially disappointing in view of the high-class backs on show. Bath were off-colour in more than one sense. Barnes had relied on a home cure for influenza during the week and Fallon, Guscott and de Glanville, their try-scorer, had also been suffering similarly. Mistakes were also prompted by fatigue, long after Pears landed a penalty goal in the third minute following offside at a maul. This gave notice of the forward pressure Harlequins were soon to exert with their solid scrummage complementing line-out ball, from which Carling launched raking diagonal kicks.

Winterbottom's try, after 31 minutes, grew from a rolling maul built from a line-out. Pears' conversion, from 15 yards inside the touchline, brought Harlequins a lead beyond their expectations of nine points. Webb kicked two penalty goals for Bath, awarded following a stray elbow at a line-out and for going over the top of a ruck, and Pears scored his second penalty for Quins in between.

As Harlequins led 12-6 with eight minutes remaining, the authentic drama began to unfold as Ojomoh, Ubogu and Hill drove upfield and de Glanville scored in the north-east corner. The try was partly the product of advantage being played by Fred Howard, refereeing his sixth Cup final to equal the record held by Roger Quittenton of the London Society. Webb landed the conversion and the final went into extra time for the second successive year, and the third time since 1982, when Moseley and Gloucester shared the trophy. Ultimately, the match was not the running classic that Harlequins helped to fashion in 1988 and Bath in 1990, but for sheer effort, tension and drama, it has been bettered by none.

Harlequins: D Pears; M A Wedderburn, S J Halliday, W D C Carling, E G Davis; A P Challinor, T C Luxton; M J Hobley, B C Moore, A R Mullins, N G B Edwards, P J Ackford, M P Russell, C M A Sheasby, P J Winterbottom (*capt*)
Scorers *Try:* Winterbottom   *Conversion:* Pears   *Penalty Goals:* Pears (2)
Bath: J M Webb; A H Swift, P R de Glanville, J C Guscott, J A Fallon; S Barnes, R J Hill; G J Chilcott, R G R Dawe, V E Ubogu, M Haag, N C Redman, R A Robinson (*capt*), B B Clarke, S Ojomoh
Scorers *Try:* de Glanville   *Conversion:* Webb   *Penalty Goals:* Webb (2)
Dropped Goal: Barnes
Referee F A Howard (Liverpool Society)

Bath had survived two tantalising matches at Northampton and Gloucester, both of which extended into extra time, on the way to their seventh final in nine years. They beat Gloucester 27-18 in the semi-finals, Swift, the former England wing, scoring one of two tries in the second period of extra time to equal the competition record of 18 held by Carr, the former Bristol wing. Gloucester were level at 15-15 after 80 minutes. Tim Smith, who had scored three penalty goals and a dropped goal, edged them ahead with a fourth penalty. Bath, who scored three tries to none, finished with a flourish as Fallon added his second try to Swift's. Barnes converted the last two in brisk succession from the touchline to match Smith's 15 points for Gloucester.

The 13-9 win at Franklins Gardens was equally fraught. Before extra time was needed, Bath were on terms at 9-9 only because Olver, the Northampton captain and England reserve hooker, suggested forcefully to referee Fred Howard that Barnes had 'pinched' a yard or two when taking a quick and successful penalty kick at goal. Howard ordered the game to be restarted with another penalty on halfway, and Barnes again landed a kick. Fallon scored the winning try as Northampton, the previous year's beaten finalists, rued their indiscipline.

Bath, who secured their eighth successive League and Cup win over Bristol in the quarter-finals, had inflicted Nottingham's heaviest Cup defeat. Harlequins needed to travel, but not far, in three of the four rounds leading to Twickenham. They overpowered Bedford 33-3 and defeated Rosslyn Park after beating Wasps at Sudbury following the controversial postponement of the original match. Wasps asked the Rugby Football Union to investigate, believing that their pitch, thawing after a heavy frost, was playable. Harlequins took the opposite view, giving rise to suggestions that they did not want to risk injury to their eight international players due to appear in Five Nations Championship games the following week. Harlequins had invested £1,500 in hotel accommodation on the eve of the game, a fact offered as proof that they wanted the match to go ahead. Pears, re-converted to fly-half, scored all Harlequins' 15 points in the semi-final win over Leicester, who had already lost a League match at Stoop the previous week. Harlequins led 12-3 with wind assistance before half-time, Pears sprinting through a gap for a try. Rory Underwood created one in reply for Liley.

The eventual climax to the competition typified its earlier mood, although not everything went smoothly. The RFU had to redraw the second round after the sponsors pointed out that the first draw involved a beaten club, Broughton Park, and that another, Barkers' Butts, from Coventry, had been erroneously placed in the South and South-West section, rather than the North and Midlands. So Moseley v Coventry, Richmond v Barkers' Butts and Broughton Park v Harrogate became void and the administrative error was rectified.

Orrell and the re-emerging Newcastle Gosforth led the northern challenge before losing in the quarter-finals while Manchester, founded in 1860 but four divisions lower in the Courage Leagues, knocked out Broughton Park, one of an unusual number of such surprises. Winnington Park, who won at Otley, High Wycombe, who beat Redruth and Askeans, and Harrogate, 61-4 winners over Nuneaton, all eliminated higher-placed clubs. Zoing, of Harrogate, equalled Cusworth's competition record of four dropped goals in a second-round match against West Hartlepool. Tynedale had the distinction of knocking out Wakefield at the same stage, Loughborough Students accounted for Headingley and Clifton, fielding 11 former Bristol players and coached by Alan Morley, beat Plymouth Albion.

The prime achievement belonged to Thurrock, of London 1, who bridged four divisions to despatch London Irish, a National League 1 club, by 16-10 on the flatlands of Essex, with 20 electricity pylons as a backdrop. Thurrock, who lost money on erecting a temporary stand, fielded 11 former colts. They went out bravely to Rosslyn Park in the fourth round.

Four clubs qualified for the first time, increasing the total participants to 209 in 21 seasons. They were Manchester, Moderns, from Nottingham, Stockton and Towcestrians, who were among many to appreciate Pilkington's sponsorship in the first year of a second three-year term, providing £1 million over that period.

RESULTS

First Round
Askeans 19, Havant 10; Barkers' Butts 6, Sudbury 3; Barnstaple 6, Richmond 26; Berry Hill 15, Matson 16; Camborne 17, Henley 13; Combe Down 25, Old Mid-Whitgiftians 9; Fylde 17, Hereford 10; Halifax 17, Stourbridge 8; Harrogate 61, Nuneaton 4; Headingley 16, Paviors 3; High Wycombe 16, Redruth 12; Lichfield 12, Tynedale 16; Lydney 29, Old Colfeians 15; Manchester 7, Broughton Park 3; Metropolitan Police 6, Exeter 14; Otley 11, Winnington Park 12; Reading 24, Sutton & Epsom 23; Roundhay 18, Loughborough Students 30; Ruislip 35, Lewes 7; Salisbury 16, Clifton 27; Sidcup 10, Thurrock 38; Stockton 17, Towcestrians 10; Torquay Athletic 10, Cheshunt 19; Widnes 16, Sheffield 19; Wigton 9, Moderns 3

Second Round
Camborne 23, Reading 13; Cheshunt 9, Ruislip 23; Clifton 21, Plymouth Albion 0; Combe Down 6, Thurrock 16; Coventry 20, Stockton 6; Exeter 6, London Scottish 21; Fylde 16, Winnington Park 12; Harrogate 18, West Hartlepool 21; High Wycombe 22, Askeans 16; Loughborough Students 17, Headingley 15; Manchester 22, Barkers' Butts 9; Matson 12, Lydney 15; Newcastle Gosforth 10, Morley 9; Richmond 22, Blackheath 12; Sale 18, Moseley 12; Sheffield 13, Bedford 30; Tynedale 21, Wakefield 20; Waterloo 21, Liverpool St Helens 10; Wigton 30, Halifax 3

Third Round
Bath 52, Nottingham 0; Bedford 3, Harlequins 33; Bristol 30, Clifton 4; Coventry 7, Northampton 31; Fylde 6, Leicester 34; London Scottish 20, Tynedale 3; Loughborough Students 16, Rosslyn Park 26; Lydney 7, Sale 13; Manchester 18, Wigton 12; Newcastle Gosforth 52, Ruislip 0; Orrell 50, Camborne 0; Rugby 3, Gloucester 23; Saracens 33, Richmond 9; Thurrock 16, London Irish 10; Wasps 32, High Wycombe 3; West Hartlepool 16, Waterloo 18

Fourth Round
Bristol 13, Saracens 6; Gloucester 20, London Scottish 7; Manchester 9, Newcastle Gosforth 21; Northampton 9, Bath 13 (aet); Rosslyn Park 44, Thurrock 15; Sale 0, Orrell 36; Wasps 9, Harlequins 20; Waterloo 12, Leicester 20

Quarter-finals
Bristol 6, Bath 15; Newcastle Gosforth 0, Leicester 10; Orrell 16, Gloucester 25; Rosslyn Park 12, Harlequins 34

Semi-finals
Gloucester 18, Bath 27 (aet); Harlequins 15, Leicester 9

Previous finals (all at Twickenham)
1972 Gloucester 17 Moseley 6
1973 Coventry 27 Bristol 15
1974 Coventry 26 London Scottish 6
1975 Bedford 28 Rosslyn Park 12
1976 Gosforth 23 Rosslyn Park 14

1977 Gosforth 27 Waterloo 11
1978 Gloucester 6 Leicester 3
1979 Leicester 15 Moseley 12
1980 Leicester 21 London Irish 9
1981 Leicester 22 Gosforth 15
1982 Gloucester 12 Moseley 12
      (*title shared*)
1983 Bristol 28 Leicester 22
1984 Bath 10 Bristol 9
1985 Bath 24 London Welsh 15
1986 Bath 25 Wasps 17
1987 Bath 19 Wasps 12
1988 Harlequins 28 Bristol 22
1989 Bath 10 Leicester 6
1990 Bath 48 Gloucester 6
1991 Harlequins 25, Northampton 13
      (*after extra time*);

COUNTY CUP WINNERS 1991-92

Berkshire	**Newbury**
Buckinghamshire	**High Wycombe**
Cheshire	**Macclesfield**
Cornwall	**Launceston**
Cumbria	**Aspatria**
Dorset/Wilts	**Salisbury**
Devon	**Exeter**
Durham	**Hartlepool Rovers**
Eastern Counties	**Sudbury**
East Midlands	**Towcestrians**
Gloucestershire	**Lydney**
Hampshire	**Basingstoke**
Hertfordshire	**Tabard**
Kent	**Old Colfeians**
Lancashire	**Vale of Lune**
Leicestershire	**Vipers**
Middlesex	**Ruislip**
North Midlands	**Hereford**
Northumberland	**Tynedale**
Notts, Lincs & Derbys	**Amber Valley**
Oxfordshire	**Henley**
Somerset	**Bridgwater & Albion**
Staffordshire	**Lichfield**
Surrey	**Old Alleynians**
Sussex	**Horsham**
Warwickshire	**Leamington**
Yorkshire	**Harrogate**

Harlequin Will Carling, who played so brilliantly in a losing cause in the Pilkington Cup final, makes a typically powerful run at the heart of Bath.

BATH REFUSE TO FALTER, ORRELL A KICK FROM GLORY

THE COURAGE LEAGUES 1991-92

There is simply no question that this was the most exciting season in the history of the Courage Leagues programme. Especially at the top of Division 1 and also down through the Leagues, the high-octane nature of activity since titles and promotion and relegation were introduced was plain to see.

Bath, for all their excellence as a team and as an institution, had problems throughout the season. They were docked a point for a simple secretarial error when they did not register a fourth-choice full-back, Heatherley, for a match against London Irish. An informer – who lacked the backbone to reveal his identity – pointed out that the player was unregistered. Bath later lost to Orrell on a famous day for the Lancastrians and also trailed by a huge margin at Harlequins.

Was the machine faltering? Perhaps the forwards were not as strong as they had been, especially in the line-out. But the will to win and the pride was stronger than ever. Bath came surging back to draw at Harlequins, and they thundered through the remainder of their programme under the pressure of the knowledge that one more slip would condemn them. Admittedly, they were helped on one vivid day of action as the climax approached when Nottingham dumped Northampton's powerful challenge and Wasps beat Orrell, but Bath came through to beat Saracens on the last League Saturday and the title was theirs.

The Wasps victory over Orrell saw sport at its most cruel. Orrell had a marvellous season, marshalling brilliantly their limited resources. They know better than anyone that they have often failed narrowly to bridge the gap between top three and top. This time, coming down the home stretch and in the knowledge that the destiny of the title was in their hands, they were leading Wasps in injury time, only to have Huw Davies of Wasps drop-kick the match away from them in the last second. That kick took away the title, because Orrell duly beat Harlequins and Nottingham in their final games and so lost the title only on points difference. To compare so favourably with mighty Bath was a massive achievement and a tribute to coach Des Seabrook and everyone at the club. Northampton's rise to the status of genuine contender was similarly praiseworthy.

Saracens rather blotted their copybook by showing almost nothing of their true selves in the showpiece final match at Bath, but they finished as London's top club. Considering that they have lost major players to other London clubs this was particularly satisfying. It illustrated that there is no reason on earth why players should feel the need to leave Southgate for apparently greener pastures. Saracens are as good a base as any to launch a bid for a representative career.

There are clear signs, too, that Division 2 is awakening. Standards have been low in the Division but that has changed, not least because two clubs as nominally strong as Rosslyn Park and Nottingham were relegated and join the second flight for season 1992-93. Nottingham found their form too late, they were too good to sink. The revival of Newcastle Gosforth and Waterloo promises to make Division 2 strongly competitive.

The two co-residents of Richmond Athletic Ground, Richmond and London Scottish, both won promotion. The Scottish will test themselves in Division 1 in the new season and Richmond climbed back to Division 2. Two highly-committed junior clubs from both ends of England – Aspatria from Cumbria and Havant from the deep south – proudly ascend to the National 3 Division for the new season.

West Hartlepool, meanwhile, take their place in Division 1, a wonderful achievement and one which brooks no argument. They were six points clear in second place of Waterloo in third. They will find it tough in the top division, partly because they will be without John Howe, a club hero who died after collapsing in the League match against Morley; and partly because, with the restructuring of the League to allow for home and away fixtures, it appears that at least four clubs will be relegated from Division 1 at the end of the season. Still, at worst they can savour their time in the top flight, and could easily maintain status and do wonders for the game in the north-east.

The roll of honour of teams who enjoyed 'perfect' seasons in the League was long. In the North Division: Rotherham, Wharfedale, Horden, Driffield, Wath, Mosborough, Manchester, Thornton Cleveley, Ormskirk and Birchfield; in the South & South West Division: Plymouthians, Old Sulians, Chard, Aldermaston and Bicester; in London Division: Cambridge, Wymondham, Ongar, New Milton, Thames Poly, Orpington, Wimbledonians, Old Caterhamians, Kew Occasionals, Brighton, Seaford and Sunallon and in Midlands Division: Long Buckby, Westwood, Oakham, Stamford College and Alcester.

The advent of home and away play and the extended nature of League action for 1992-93 obviously reflects the status of the League programme. But it also reflects the complete failure of the leading clubs to make non-league fixtures worthwhile. There were ways and means of maintaining old fixtures with Welsh and other clubs. Instead, the English clubs simply ran away from the fixtures. The main impetus for the increase in the League programme is that the treasurer needs more League games and fewer meaningless Saturdays. The upshot is twofold. First, there will be a time of farce as huge chunks of the Divisions are relegated away to allow for the smaller ten-club set-up. Secondly, the commitments for players, yet again, are increased. Already, the goose which laid the golden egg of Leagues may be on the point of being throttled.

NATIONAL DIVISION

National 1

	P	W	D	L	F	A	Pts
Bath*	12	10	1	1	277	126	20
Orrell	12	10	0	2	204	95	20
Northampton	12	9	1	2	209	136	19
Gloucester	12	7	1	4	193	168	15
Saracens	12	7	1	4	176	165	15
Leicester	12	6	1	5	262	216	13
Wasps	12	6	0	6	177	180	12
Harlequins	12	5	1	6	213	207	11
London Irish	12	3	3	6	147	237	9
Bristol	12	4	0	8	192	174	8
Rugby	12	2	3	7	124	252	7
Nottingham	12	2	1	9	133	204	5
Rosslyn Park	12	0	1	11	111	258	1

*One point deducted for fielding an unregistered player

National 2

	P	W	D	L	F	A	Pts
L Scottish	12	11	0	1	304	130	22
W Hartlepool	12	11	0	1	244	89	22
Waterloo	12	8	0	4	206	184	16
Newcastle Gos	12	7	0	5	371	140	14
Wakefield	12	7	0	5	187	194	14

A wonderful League effort by Bath comes to an end. Gareth Chilcott and Stuart Barnes acclaim the return of the Division 1 trophy after the win over Saracens.

	P	W	D	L	F	A	Pts
Coventry	12	7	0	5	187	196	14
Moseley	12	6	0	6	215	196	12
Sale	12	6	0	6	204	209	12
Morley	12	4	0	8	171	202	8
Bedford	12	4	0	8	168	204	8
Blackheath	12	4	0	8	140	266	8
Plymouth	12	3	0	9	153	209	6
Liverpool SH	12	0	0	12	87	418	0

National 3

	P	W	D	L	F	A	Pts
Richmond	12	10	1	1	296	124	21
Fylde	12	9	1	2	198	109	19
Clifton	12	9	0	3	298	132	18
Exeter	12	8	2	2	203	138	18
Redruth	12	6	1	5	155	123	13
Broughton Pk	12	5	1	6	196	157	11
Askeans	12	5	1	6	149	203	11
Sheffield	12	5	1	6	146	228	11
Otley	12	5	0	7	177	190	10
Roundhay	12	3	2	7	161	240	8
Headingley	12	4	0	8	139	220	8
Nuneaton	12	1	2	9	153	237	4
Lydney	12	2	0	10	91	261	4

National 4 North

	P	W	D	L	F	A	Pts
Aspatria	12	11	0	1	253	100	22
Hereford	12	10	1	1	223	133	21
Kendal	12	8	1	3	157	123	17
Preston Grass	12	8	0	4	195	123	16
Lichfield	12	6	1	5	174	177	13
Stourbridge	12	6	0	6	163	137	12
Harrogate	12	6	0	6	170	175	12
Winnington Pk	12	4	1	7	159	173	9
Towcestrians	12	4	0	8	123	153	8
Durham City	12	4	0	8	133	215	8
Walsall	12	3	1	8	139	187	7
Vale of Lune	12	3	1	8	119	185	7
Northern	12	2	0	10	105	232	4

National 4 South

	P	W	D	L	F	A	Pts
Havant	12	11	0	1	301	91	22
Basingstoke	12	11	0	1	218	88	22
London Welsh	12	9	0	3	292	160	18
Sudbury	12	8	0	4	235	150	16
High Wycombe	12	8	0	4	196	139	16
Camborne	12	7	0	5	166	195	14
North Walsham	12	5	0	7	153	152	10
Maidstone	12	5	0	7	147	180	10
Weston SM	12	4	0	8	175	215	8
Met Police	12	3	0	9	149	195	6
Southend	12	3	0	9	134	240	6
Sidcup	12	3	0	9	103	290	6
Ealing	12	1	0	11	112	286	2

NORTH DIVISION

North 1

	P	W	D	L	F	A	Pts
Rotherham	10	10	0	0	245	68	20
Tynedale	10	9	0	1	274	107	18
Bradford & B	10	7	0	3	200	119	14
Sandal	10	5	0	5	140	115	10
Middlesbrough	10	5	0	5	120	131	10
Hartlepool R	10	5	1	4	92	105	9
Hull Ionians	10	4	0	6	121	186	8
Stockton	10	3	1	6	79	241	7
Widnes	10	3	0	7	152	147	6
Wigton	10	3	0	7	106	161	6
Birkenhead Pk	10	0	0	10	74	223	0

North 2

	P	W	D	L	F	A	Pts
Wharfedale	10	10	0	0	254	55	20
Lymm	10	9	0	1	192	89	18
O Crossleyans	10	7	0	3	175	84	14
Huddersfield	10	6	0	4	145	91	12
West Park St H	10	6	0	4	180	166	12
Halifax	10	4	0	6	147	159	8
Northwich	10	3	2	5	120	164	8
Alnwick	10	4	1	5	118	99	7
Sandbach	10	2	1	7	88	189	5
Wigan	10	1	1	8	66	172	3
Carlisle	10	0	1	9	51	268	1

North-East 1

	P	W	D	L	F	A	Pts
York	10	9	0	1	187	70	18
West Park Bram	10	9	0	1	139	53	18
Blaydon	10	7	0	3	189	106	14
Roundhegians	10	6	1	3	136	93	13
Morpeth	10	6	0	4	134	139	12
O Brodleians	10	5	0	5	121	149	10
Keighley	10	4	1	5	146	194	9
Gateshead Fell	10	3	0	7	117	149	6
Pontefract	10	2	0	8	108	191	4
Novocastrians	10	2	0	8	86	172	4
Bramley	10	1	0	9	115	162	2

North-East 2

	P	W	D	L	F	A	Pts
Bridlington	10	8	2	0	173	63	18
Selby	10	8	0	2	153	82	16
Thornensians	10	7	1	2	123	55	15
Redcar	10	6	1	3	146	101	13
Blyth	10	5	0	5	107	128	10
Ripon	10	3	2	5	103	154	8
O Hymerians	10	3	1	6	146	126	7
Westoe	10	3	1	6	96	92	7
Beverley	10	3	1	6	130	175	7
Rockcliff	10	3	0	7	89	103	6
Ashington	10	1	1	8	65	252	3

Durham & Northumberland 1

	P	W	D	L	F	A	Pts
Horden	10	10	0	0	290	62	20
Acklam	10	8	0	2	206	76	16
Bishop Auck	10	7	0	3	210	92	14
Mowden Pk	10	7	0	3	140	72	14
Ryton	10	5	0	5	94	106	10
Seghill	10	4	0	6	99	180	8
Darlington RA	10	4	0	6	71	163	8
Darlington*	10	4	0	6	82	179	8
Consett	10	3	0	7	115	188	6
Sunderland	10	3	0	7	90	185	6
Hartlepool*	10	0	0	10	61	164	0

Points deducted for fielding ineligible players

Durham & Northumberland 2

	P	W	D	L	F	A	Pts
Percy Pk	10	9	0	1	147	71	18
Guisborough	10	8	0	2	135	42	16
Whitby	10	8	0	2	146	64	16
Seaham	10	7	1	2	88	60	15
W Hart TDSOB	10	5	0	5	78	83	10
Winlaton Vul	10	4	1	5	95	113	9
N Durham	10	4	0	6	99	133	8
Ponteland	10	3	0	7	63	110	6
Medicals	10	3	0	7	105	153	6
Seaton Carew	10	2	0	8	50	117	4
Barnard Castle	10	1	0	9	73	160	0

Durham & Northumberland 3

	P	W	D	L	F	A	Pts
Chester-le-S	10	9	0	1	152	66	18
Wallsend	10	8	1	1	233	62	17
N Shields	10	7	2	1	175	65	16
Houghton	10	7	2	1	238	56	15
Billingham	10	6	0	4	151	106	12
S Tyneside Coll	10	4	0	6	151	179	8
Wensleydale	10	4	1	5	100	142	7
Wearside	10	3	0	7	77	190	6
Richmondshire	10	2	0	8	87	134	2
Newton Aycliffe	10	1	1	8	83	279	2
Hartlepool BBOB	10	0	1	9	83	251	1

Durham & Northumberland 4

	P	W	D	L	F	A	Pts
Jarrovians	7	6	0	1	174	51	12
Sedgefield	7	6	0	1	134	48	10
Durham CS	7	6	0	1	115	59	10
Knaresborough	7	4	0	3	121	59	8
Prudhoe	7	3	0	4	67	104	4
Washington	7	2	0	5	36	129	4
Shildon	7	1	0	6	50	148	2
Hartlepool Ath	7	0	0	7	36	151	0

Yorkshire 1

	P	W	D	L	F	A	Pts
Driffield	10	10	0	0	231	24	20
Doncaster	10	8	0	2	163	100	16
Cleckheaton	10	7	0	3	161	58	14
Pocklington	10	7	0	3	137	109	14
O Otliensians	10	6	0	4	143	92	12
Hemsworth	10	4	1	5	78	123	9
N Ribblesdale	10	4	0	6	177	146	8
Malton & Nor	10	4	0	6	85	138	8
York RI	10	2	0	8	94	213	4
Leodiensians	10	1	1	8	60	196	3
Castleford	10	1	0	9	72	202	2

Yorkshire 2

	P	W	D	L	F	A	Pts
Bradford Salem	10	8	1	1	192	52	17
Goole	10	8	1	1	140	67	17
Wheatley Hills	10	6	1	3	162	95	13
Yarnbury	10	6	1	3	125	89	13
Sheffield Oaks	10	6	1	3	114	101	13
Ilkley	10	5	0	5	96	120	10
Barnsley	10	4	1	5	134	123	9
Knottingley	10	3	0	7	86	135	6
Huddersfield YM	10	1	2	7	62	138	4
Scarborough	10	1	2	7	59	149	4
Moortown	10	2	0	8	64	171	4

Yorkshire 3

	P	W	D	L	F	A	Pts
Wath	10	10	0	0	248	46	20
O Modernians	10	8	0	2	139	84	16
Dinnington	10	7	0	3	144	83	14
W Leeds	10	6	0	4	148	92	12
Northallerton	10	6	0	4	102	120	12
Leeds CSSA	10	4	0	6	108	185	8
Sheffield Tigers	10	3	1	6	84	120	7
Wibsey	10	3	0	7	113	148	6
Marist	10	3	0	7	94	171	6
Hessle	10	2	1	7	89	130	5
Stanley Rod	10	2	0	8	95	185	4

Yorkshire 4

	P	W	D	L	F	A	Pts
Hullensians	10	9	1	0	131	46	19
Halifax Vans	10	8	0	2	153	48	16
Airebronians	10	7	1	2	157	99	15
Wetherby	10	6	0	4	93	96	12
Baildon	10	6	0	4	80	94	12
O Rishworthians	10	5	1	4	132	89	11
Leeds Corinths	10	4	2	4	118	91	10
Burley	10	3	0	7	74	106	6
Heath	10	2	1	7	69	138	5
Ossett	10	1	0	9	68	154	2
Leeds YMCA	10	1	0	9	31	145	0

Yorkshire 5

	P	W	D	L	F	A	Pts
Skipton	10	9	0	1	202	45	18
Danum Phoenix	10	9	0	1	201	78	18
Hornsea	10	7	0	3	146	75	14

	P	W	D	L	F	A	Pts
De La Salle	10	6	1	3	211	57	13
Hull & ER	10	6	1	3	204	71	13
Withernsea	10	4	1	5	77	131	9
Phoenix Pk	10	3	2	5	93	136	8
BP Chemicals	10	3	1	6	98	163	7
Yorks Main	10	1	2	7	57	234	4
Yorks CW	10	1	0	9	34	265	2
Castle Coll	10	2	0	8	46	114	2

Yorkshire 6

	P	W	D	L	F	A	Pts
Mosborough	5	5	0	0	99	24	10
Rowntrees	5	3	1	1	58	37	7
Adwick-le-St	5	3	0	2	112	75	6
Stockbridge	5	2	0	3	68	74	4
Rawmarsh	5	1	1	3	59	64	3
New Earswick	5	0	0	5	23	145	0

North-West 1

	P	W	D	L	F	A	Pts
Manchester	10	10	0	0	242	47	20
Macclesfield	10	8	1	1	217	47	17
Chester	10	6	2	2	234	105	14
Wirral	10	6	1	3	146	126	13
New Brighton	10	6	0	4	184	96	12
Sedgley Pk	10	5	1	4	119	145	11
Davenport	10	4	0	6	107	158	8
St Edwards OB	10	2	1	7	99	133	5
Caldy	10	2	0	8	67	281	4
Egremont	10	1	1	8	60	191	3
Cockermouth	10	1	1	8	76	222	3

North-West 2

	P	W	D	L	F	A	Pts
Ashton on M	10	8	1	1	202	47	17
Blackburn	10	7	2	1	198	64	16
Merseyside Pol	10	7	1	2	232	62	15
Wilmslow	10	6	1	3	118	133	13
O Aldwinians	10	5	0	5	115	124	10
Kirkby Lonsdale	10	5	0	5	125	148	10
Rochdale	10	5	0	5	98	125	10
Warrington	10	3	0	7	97	153	6
S Liverpool	10	2	1	7	99	162	5
Netherhall	10	2	0	8	59	170	4
Workington	10	2	0	8	80	235	4

NW East North

	P	W	D	L	F	A	Pts
O Salians	10	8	1	1	175	59	17
Rossendale	10	7	1	2	98	61	15
Furness	10	6	2	2	135	97	14
Crewe & Nant	10	6	0	4	111	101	12
Penrith	10	5	0	5	130	94	10
Oldham	10	4	1	5	107	105	9
Moresby	10	4	1	5	96	137	9
Vickers	10	4	0	6	93	147	8
Windermere	10	3	1	6	116	116	7

	P	W	D	L	F	A	Pts
Keswick	10	2	1	7	77	153	5
De La Salle	10	1	2	7	64	132	4

NW East 1

	P	W	D	L	F	A	Pts
Altringham Ker	10	9	0	1	281	68	18
Metrovick	10	8	0	2	201	58	16
Calder Vale	10	7	0	3	152	60	14
Tyldesley	10	7	0	3	194	117	14
Burnage	10	7	0	3	156	123	14
Bury	10	3	2	5	80	222	8
Eccles	10	3	0	7	89	117	6
Manchester YMCA	10	2	1	7	66	161	5
Fleetwood	10	3	1	6	95	159	5
Broughton	10	2	0	8	106	188	4
O Bedians	10	2	0	8	71	218	4

NW East 2

	P	W	D	L	F	A	Pts
Marple	10	8	0	2	252	46	16
Littleborough	10	8	0	2	176	53	16
Bolton	10	8	0	2	101	73	16
Congleton	10	7	0	3	122	72	14
Bowdon	10	6	0	4	114	96	12
Aston-U-Lyne	10	5	0	5	86	84	10
Colne & Nelson	10	5	0	5	109	166	10
Chorley	10	4	0	6	114	101	8
Heaton Moor	10	2	1	7	124	170	5
Didsbury Toc H	10	1	1	8	66	151	3
Wigan Tech	10	0	0	10	30	282	0

NW East 3

	P	W	D	L	F	A	Pts
Thornton Clev	10	10	0	0	421	57	20
Blackpool	10	9	0	1	268	33	18
Holmes Chapel	10	8	0	2	337	84	16
Dukinfield	10	7	0	3	115	95	14
Burtonwood	10	4	0	6	122	130	8
Lostock	10	4	0	6	122	158	8
Shell Carr	10	4	0	6	64	214	8
N Manchester	10	3	1	6	92	123	7
Clitheroe	10	3	1	6	112	156	7
Atherton	10	2	0	8	58	364	4
Agecroft	10	0	0	10	37	334	0

NW North

	P	W	D	L	F	A	Pts
U Eden	9	8	0	1	293	73	16
St Benedicts	9	8	0	1	228	70	16
Smith Bros	9	7	0	2	191	94	14
Carnforth	9	5	1	3	125	111	11
British Steel	9	5	0	4	117	113	10
Millom	9	3	1	5	122	135	7
Creighton	9	3	1	5	93	122	7
Silloth	9	3	0	6	111	169	6
Whitehaven	9	1	1	7	88	156	3
Ambleside	9	0	0	9	32	357	0

NW West 1

	P	W	D	L	F	A	Pts
Ormskirk	10	10	0	0	330	48	20
Oldershaw	10	9	0	1	205	62	18
Vagabonds	10	7	0	3	131	60	14
Aspull	10	5	0	5	115	127	10
Southport	10	5	0	5	85	134	10
Ruskin Pk	10	4	0	6	101	113	8
Liverpool Coll	10	4	0	6	99	153	8
Douglas (IOM)	10	4	0	6	97	197	8
Newton-le-W	10	3	0	7	112	110	6
Leigh	10	2	0	8	76	193	4
O Instonians	10	2	0	8	58	212	4

NW West 2

	P	W	D	L	F	A	Pts
St Mary's OB	10	9	0	1	156	41	18
O Parkonians	10	8	0	2	204	54	16
Eagle	10	8	0	2	162	89	16
O Anselmians	10	6	1	3	133	99	13
Hoylake	10	6	0	4	151	78	12
Shell Stanlow	10	4	0	6	110	102	8
PT Sunlight	10	4	0	6	125	104	8
Sefton	10	3	1	6	88	135	7
Mossley Hill	10	3	1	6	49	183	7
Vulcan	10	1	1	8	58	157	3
Rockferrians	10	1	0	9	64	258	2

NW West 3

	P	W	D	L	F	A	Pts
Birchfield	7	7	0	0	160	50	14
Wallasey	7	6	0	1	120	64	12
Halton	7	5	0	2	117	69	10
Hightown	7	4	0	3	79	75	8
Moore	7	3	0	4	112	90	6
Helsby	7	2	0	5	82	87	4
Whitehouse Pk	7	1	0	6	54	172	2
Lucas	7	0	0	7	59	176	0

SOUTH & SOUTH-WEST DIVISION

South-West 1

	P	W	D	L	F	A	Pts
Berry Hill	10	8	0	2	262	99	16
Cinderford	10	8	0	2	180	87	16
Torquay	10	6	2	2	140	114	14
Cheltenham	10	6	0	4	164	142	12
Brixham	10	6	0	4	129	150	12
Newbury	10	5	0	5	142	145	10
Reading	10	4	0	6	123	163	8
St Ives	10	4	0	6	109	162	8
Maidenhead	10	3	1	6	205	166	7
Gordon League	10	3	0	7	102	175	6
Salisbury	10	1	1	9	70	223	1

South-West 2

	P	W	D	L	F	A	Pts
Henley	10	8	1	1	283	103	17

Sherborne	10	8	0	2	208	88	16
Penryn	10	7	1	2	188	104	15
Marlow	10	6	0	4	140	224	12
Matson	10	5	0	5	132	120	10
Combe Down	10	4	1	5	122	156	9
Stroud	10	4	0	6	185	142	8
Oxford	10	3	0	7	135	193	6
Tauton	10	3	0	7	119	184	6
Barnstaple	10	3	0	7	92	190	6
Abbey	10	2	1	7	95	195	5

Southern Counties

	P	W	D	L	F	A	Pts
Banbury	10	9	0	1	262	91	18
Aylesbury	10	8	1	1	141	73	17
Windsor	10	7	2	1	169	59	16
Swanage & W	10	6	0	4	140	110	12
Wimborne	10	5	0	5	94	97	10
Bournemouth	10	4	1	5	152	128	9
Olney	10	4	1	5	130	118	9
Dorchester	10	3	1	6	112	162	7
Bletchley	10	2	1	7	92	149	5
Redingensians	10	2	1	7	96	212	5
Grove	10	1	0	9	65	254	2

Western Counties

	P	W	D	L	F	A	Pts
Clevedon	10	9	0	1	224	64	18
Bridgwater & A	10	8	0	2	266	74	16
Culverhaysians	10	8	0	2	122	44	16
Okehampton	10	7	1	2	135	89	15
Penzance-New	10	6	0	4	116	96	12
Spartans	10	5	0	5	130	117	10
Launceston	10	4	1	5	148	133	9
Avonmouth	10	4	0	6	137	111	8
Devon & C Con	10	2	0	8	89	194	4
Tiverton	10	1	0	9	83	210	2
Newquay H	10	0	0	10	13	331	0

Cornwall & Devon

	P	W	D	L	F	A	Pts
Bideford	10	8	0	2	191	85	16
Plymouth CS	10	8	0	2	156	103	16
Crediton	10	7	1	2	201	85	15
Truro	10	6	0	4	130	89	12
Sidmouth	10	5	1	4	94	107	11
Saltash	10	4	2	4	113	120	10
Hayle	10	4	1	5	98	151	9
Exmouth	10	4	0	6	153	150	8
Teignmouth	10	3	0	7	104	158	6
South Molton	10	2	1	7	130	150	5
Exeter Sara	10	1	0	9	52	224	2

Glos & Somerset

	P	W	D	L	F	A	Pts
Gloucester OB	10	9	0	1	254	76	18
Drybrook	10	8	0	2	235	87	16

Wiveliscombe	10	7	0	3	205	124	14
Keynsham	10	7	0	3	163	89	14
Oldfield OB	10	7	0	3	142	116	14
Dings Crusaders	10	6	0	4	163	142	12
Whitehall	10	4	0	6	145	159	8
Frome	10	3	0	7	92	219	6
Coney Hill	10	2	0	8	88	110	4
Cirencester	10	2	0	8	72	272	4
Cleve	10	0	0	10	60	225	0

Cornwall 1

	P	W	D	L	F	A	Pts
Liskeard-Looe	10	8	0	2	158	56	16
Bude	10	7	1	2	143	85	15
St Austell	10	7	0	3	122	50	14
Veor	10	7	0	3	139	97	14
Bodmin	10	6	1	3	115	105	13
Stithians	10	6	0	4	107	109	12
Falmouth	10	4	0	6	108	119	8
Redruth Alb	10	4	0	6	100	117	8
Illogan Park	10	3	0	7	104	175	6
Helston	10	1	0	9	80	131	2
Wadebridge Cam	10	1	0	9	59	191	2

Cornwall 2

	P	W	D	L	F	A	Pts
St Just	10	9	0	1	137	63	18
Camborne SoM	10	7	0	3	242	82	14
St Day	10	7	0	3	122	97	14
St Agnes	10	5	0	5	125	111	10
Roseland	10	2	0	8	108	178	4
Lankelly Fowey	10	0	0	10	56	259	0

Devon 1

	P	W	D	L	F	A	Pts
Devonport S	10	9	0	1	232	69	18
Ivybridge	10	7	1	2	209	100	15
Paignton	10	7	0	3	131	59	14
Ilfracombe	10	6	1	3	103	69	13
Honiton	10	6	0	4	133	109	12
Technicians	10	5	1	4	77	94	11
Topsham	10	5	0	5	119	115	10
O Public Oaks	10	4	1	5	63	105	9
Newton Abbot	10	2	0	8	72	166	4
Jesters	10	1	0	9	55	154	2
Cullompton	10	1	0	9	76	230	2

Devon 2A

	P	W	D	L	F	A	Pts
Plymothians	9	9	0	0	240	44	18
Plymouth Arg	9	7	1	1	195	86	15
Prince Rock	9	6	1	2	130	61	13
Plymstock	9	5	0	4	94	94	10
Tamar Sara	9	4	0	5	62	69	8
Victoria	9	3	2	4	69	84	8
Plympton	9	4	0	5	83	112	8

Devonport HSOB	9	3	0	6	69	111	6
Plymouth YMCA	9	2	0	7	51	186	4
St Columba	9	0	0	9	17	163	0

Devon 2B

	P	W	D	L	F	A	Pts
Tavistock	12	11	0	1	362	94	22
Kingsbridge	12	10	0	2	250	111	20
Totnes	12	8	0	4	268	181	16
Dartmouth	12	4	1	7	87	231	9
Withycombe	12	3	1	8	128	176	7
Salcombe	12	3	0	9	107	217	6
North Tawton	12	2	0	10	71	263	4

Gloucester 1

	P	W	D	L	F	A	Pts
O Patesians	10	7	1	2	180	104	15
North Bristol	10	7	0	3	172	74	14
Thornbury	10	6	1	3	178	84	13
Frampton Cott	10	6	1	3	135	102	13
St Mary's OB	10	6	0	4	155	87	12
Cheltenham N	10	6	0	4	123	95	12
Saintbridge	10	5	0	5	111	112	10
Longlevens	10	4	0	6	118	153	8
Bream	10	3	1	6	107	187	7
Brockworth	10	3	0	7	87	120	6
Widden OB	10	0	0	10	47	295	0

Gloucester 2

	P	W	D	L	F	A	Pts
Ashley Down OB	10	9	0	1	221	72	18
Bristol Sara	10	6	1	3	142	87	13
Old Richians	10	6	1	3	141	98	13
Old Cryptians	10	6	1	3	154	125	13
Cotham Park	10	6	0	4	157	115	12
Barton Hill	10	6	0	4	99	122	12
Chipping S	10	4	1	5	81	102	9
Bristol Tele	10	4	1	5	83	124	9
Hucclecote	10	3	1	6	93	130	7
Tredworth	10	1	1	8	51	182	3
Chelt Saracens	10	1	0	9	84	149	2

Gloucester 3

	P	W	D	L	F	A	Pts
Painswick	12	10	1	1	271	66	21
Stow-on-the-W	12	10	0	2	290	80	20
Cheltenham CS	12	10	0	2	220	96	20
Bristolians	12	8	1	3	219	128	17
Chosen Hill FP	12	6	1	5	118	134	13
Cainscross	12	6	0	6	182	163	12
Colstonians	12	5	0	7	100	180	10
Southmead	12	5	0	7	114	215	10
Dursley	12	5	0	7	138	247	10
Bishopston	12	4	0	8	156	150	8
Tewkesbury	12	3	0	9	178	257	6
Kingswood	12	2	1	9	93	190	5
O Elizabethans	12	2	0	10	113	286	4

Gloucester 4

	P	W	D	L	F	A	Pts
Tetbury	10	8	2	0	201	57	18
Gloucester AB	10	7	0	3	153	57	14
Bristol Aero	10	7	0	3	146	69	14
Westbury on S	10	6	2	2	106	73	14
Broad Plain	10	5	2	3	162	111	12
Gloucester CS	10	5	1	4	155	142	11
Aretians	10	5	1	4	114	114	11
Newent	10	4	1	5	125	111	9
Smiths	10	2	1	7	99	148	5
Minchinhampton	10	1	0	9	62	285	2
Dowty	10	0	0	10	61	217	0

Somerset 1

	P	W	D	L	F	A	Pts
O Sulians	10	10	0	0	208	59	20
Redcliffians	10	8	0	2	256	72	16
Bristol Harl	10	7	1	2	155	89	15
Midsomer Nor	10	6	1	3	138	98	13
Hornets	10	5	1	4	121	95	11
Minehead Bar	10	5	1	4	116	123	11
Walcot OB	10	4	0	6	98	132	8
St Bernadettes	10	3	1	6	82	124	7
Stothert & P	10	2	1	7	100	246	5
Wellington	10	1	0	9	94	178	2
Yatton	10	1	0	9	78	230	2

Somerset 2

	P	W	D	L	F	A	Pts
Wells	12	10	0	2	195	84	20
Imperial	12	10	0	2	199	99	20
Yeovil	12	7	1	4	198	129	15
Westland	12	7	1	4	132	89	15
Gordano	12	7	0	5	226	129	14
Crewkerne	12	7	0	5	158	92	14
Tor	12	7	0	5	128	142	14
N Petherton	12	6	0	6	152	139	12
Avonvale	12	4	2	6	103	160	10
Winscombe	12	4	0	8	120	174	8
Blagdon	12	4	0	8	116	195	8
Backwell	12	3	0	9	137	183	6
Burnham on S	12	0	0	12	46	295	0

Somerset 3

	P	W	D	L	F	A	Pts
Chard	11	11	0	0	335	57	22
Bath CS	11	10	0	1	258	92	20
Avon	11	9	0	2	268	97	18
Bath OE	11	8	0	3	184	83	16
Castle Cary	11	7	0	4	205	101	14
Cheddar Valley	11	5	0	6	138	142	10
Chew Valley	11	5	0	6	124	166	10
O Ashtonians	11	4	0	7	132	152	8
Aller	11	4	0	7	111	144	8
South West Gas	11	2	0	9	50	389	4
St Brendans OB	11	1	0	10	59	261	2
Morganians	11	0	0	11	49	229	0

Berks/Dorset/Wilts 1

	P	W	D	L	F	A	Pts
Bracknell	10	9	1	0	222	50	19
Chippenham	10	9	0	1	237	64	18
Devizes	10	6	0	4	159	103	12
Swindon	10	6	0	4	129	132	12
Corsham	10	5	0	5	131	128	10
North Dorset	10	4	0	6	158	166	8
Bournemouth P	10	4	0	6	121	208	8
Wootton Bass	10	3	1	6	120	150	7
Melksham	10	3	1	6	113	166	7
Swindon Coll	10	3	0	7	80	155	6
Weymouth	10	1	1	8	81	229	3

Berks/Dorset/Wilts 2

	P	W	D	L	F	A	Pts
Aldermaston	10	10	0	0	267	51	20
Lychett Min	10	8	0	2	142	93	16
Bradford on A	10	6	0	4	124	86	12
Puddletown	10	6	0	4	109	131	12
Tadley	10	5	0	5	143	126	10
Warminster	10	4	0	6	145	144	8
Marlborough	10	4	0	6	126	141	8
Hungerford	10	4	0	6	100	115	8
Supermarine	10	4	0	6	102	143	8
Minety	10	4	0	6	83	149	8
Oakmedians	10	0	0	10	55	217	0

Berks/Dorset/Wilts 3E

	P	W	D	L	F	A	Pts
Calne	8	7	0	1	142	61	14
Thatcham	8	6	0	2	166	32	12
Berkshire SH	8	5	0	3	129	97	10
Amesbury	8	2	0	6	79	205	4
Colerne	8	0	0	8	54	175	0

Berks/Dorset/Wilts 3W

	P	W	D	L	F	A	Pts
Blandford	12	10	0	2	268	79	20
Trowbridge	12	9	0	3	303	117	18
Bridport	12	8	0	4	275	115	16
Westbury	12	8	0	4	197	99	16
Poole	12	4	1	7	107	211	9
Plessey Christ	12	1	1	10	89	417	3
Portcastrians	12	1	0	11	90	291	2

Bucks & Oxon 1

	P	W	D	L	F	A	Pts
Bicester	10	10	0	0	194	37	20
Slough	10	9	0	1	192	77	18
Chinnor	10	8	0	2	167	51	16
Chiltern	10	6	1	3	178	101	13
Oxford Mara	10	5	1	4	160	89	11
Oxford OB	10	5	0	5	140	136	10
Witney	10	4	0	6	88	124	8
Beaconsfield	10	3	0	7	101	155	6
Milton Keynes	10	2	0	8	71	200	4

	P	W	D	L	F	A	Pts
Wheatley	10	2	0	8	37	184	4
Pennanians	10	0	0	10	40	214	0

Bucks & Oxon 2

	P	W	D	L	F	A	Pts
Drifters	11	9	2	0	214	73	20
Chesham	11	8	0	3	148	91	16
Abingdon	11	7	1	3	183	111	15
Buckingham	11	6	1	4	151	153	13
Littlemore	11	6	0	5	179	110	12
Didcot	11	5	2	4	155	152	12
Gosford AB	11	5	1	5	143	126	11
Cholsey	11	5	0	6	178	129	10
Chipping Nor	11	4	0	7	129	139	8
Phoenix	11	4	0	7	92	162	8
Thames Vall Pol	11	3	0	8	150	208	6
Harwell	11	0	1	10	61	329	1

LONDON DIVISION

London 1

	P	W	D	L	F	A	Pts
Thurrock	10	8	0	2	222	89	16
Eton Manor	10	7	0	3	132	107	14
O Mid Whitgift	10	6	0	4	223	147	12
O Alleynian	10	6	0	4	172	107	12
Sutton & Epsom	10	6	0	4	225	180	10
Streatham-Croy	10	5	0	5	123	115	10
Dorking	10	5	0	5	102	181	10
O Gaytonians	10	4	0	6	153	150	8
Cheshunt	10	4	0	6	159	162	8
Ruislip	10	4	0	6	143	206	8
Lewes	10	0	0	10	56	280	0

London 2 North

	P	W	D	L	F	A	Pts
Tabard	10	9	1	0	167	59	19
Barking	10	7	1	2	187	140	15
Chingford	10	6	0	4	159	98	12
Norwich	10	6	1	3	128	133	12
Woodford	10	5	0	5	157	119	10
Bishop's Stort	10	5	0	5	162	144	10
Harlow	10	5	0	5	142	136	10
Finchley	10	4	0	6	149	145	8
Ipswich	10	2	1	7	84	190	5
Letchworth	10	2	0	8	99	153	4
OMT	10	2	0	8	79	196	4

London 2 South

	P	W	D	L	F	A	Pts
O Colfeians	10	8	1	1	226	110	17
Guildford & G	10	8	0	2	186	69	16
Westcombe Pk	10	8	0	2	207	120	16
Worthing	10	7	1	2	214	121	14
Camberley	10	7	0	3	184	102	14
Esher	10	5	0	5	153	146	9
Gravesend	10	3	0	7	150	200	6
O Juddian	10	3	0	7	155	243	6

	P	W	D	L	F	A	Pts
O Blues	10	3	0	7	129	156	4
US Portsmouth	10	2	0	8	110	289	3
Tunbridge W	10	0	0	10	81	239	0

London 3 NE

	P	W	D	L	F	A	Pts
Cambridge	10	10	0	0	264	62	20
O Edwardians	10	8	0	2	182	112	16
Brentwood	10	7	0	3	206	86	14
Chelmsford	10	7	0	3	131	153	14
Basildon	10	6	0	4	173	143	12
Romford & GP	10	5	0	5	180	117	10
Colchester	10	5	0	5	150	126	10
Canvey Island	10	3	1	6	120	198	7
Saffron Walden	10	2	0	8	77	214	4
Cantabrigian	10	1	0	9	79	164	2
Westcliff	10	0	1	9	72	259	1

London 3 NW

	P	W	D	L	F	A	Pts
Upper Clapton	10	9	0	1	157	73	18
Lensbury	10	8	0	2	220	115	16
Grasshoppers	10	8	0	2	187	85	16
O Verulamians	10	7	0	3	234	87	14
Kingsburians	10	6	0	4	159	180	12
Welwyn	10	5	0	5	142	163	10
O Albanians	10	4	0	6	122	154	8
Hertford	10	3	0	7	88	151	6
Fullerians	10	3	0	7	95	184	6
Hemel Hemp	9	0	0	9	56	162	0
St Mary's H	9	1	0	8	90	197	0

London 3 SE

	P	W	D	L	F	A	Pts
Charlton Pk	10	9	0	1	317	83	18
Thanet Wands	10	8	0	2	154	87	16
Horsham	10	7	1	2	176	108	15
Dartfordians	10	6	0	4	154	161	12
Beckenham	10	7	0	3	232	92	11
Chichester	10	4	0	6	105	155	8
Crawley	10	4	0	6	113	176	8
O Brockleians	10	3	1	6	106	172	7
O Beccehamian	10	2	1	7	76	156	5
Hove	10	2	1	7	97	164	3
Hastings & Bex	10	1	0	9	83	291	2

London 3 SW

	P	W	D	L	F	A	Pts
KCS OB	10	9	0	1	149	66	18
O Reigatian	10	9	1	0	136	56	17
O Walcountians	10	7	0	3	169	86	13
Portsmouth	10	4	3	3	124	129	10
Purley	10	4	2	4	118	114	9
Winchester	10	4	1	5	123	185	9
O Emanuel	10	4	0	6	164	131	8
Cranleigh	10	3	1	6	79	138	7
Alton	10	3	1	6	92	155	7

| Guy's Hospital | 10 | 3 | 1 | 6 | 139 | 187 | 6 |
| Eastleigh | 10 | 0 | 0 | 10 | 79 | 167 | 0 |

Eastern Counties 1

	P	W	D	L	F	A	Pts
Rochford	10	8	1	1	185	68	17
Campion	10	8	0	2	216	99	16
Braintree	10	8	0	2	161	105	15
Woodbridge	10	7	0	3	126	94	14
West Norfolk	10	6	0	4	136	134	12
Bury St Ed	10	3	3	4	144	126	9
Ravens	10	4	0	6	133	194	8
Crusaders	10	3	1	6	83	142	7
Ely	10	2	1	7	78	170	5
Shelford	10	1	1	8	86	138	3
Met Pol Chig	10	1	1	8	83	161	2

Eastern Counties 2

	P	W	D	L	F	A	Pts
Maldon	10	7	2	1	168	83	16
Upminster	10	7	1	2	98	59	15
Lowestoft & Y	10	6	1	3	164	104	13
Newmarket	10	5	1	4	137	95	11
Wanstead	10	5	1	4	91	83	11
Bancroft	10	5	0	5	139	96	10
Holt	10	5	0	5	123	115	10
East London	10	4	0	6	109	93	8
Redbridge	10	3	0	7	81	199	6
S Woodham Ferr	10	2	1	7	79	169	5
Diss	10	2	1	7	63	156	5

Eastern Counties 3

	P	W	D	L	F	A	Pts
Wymondham	10	10	0	0	242	67	20
Thames Sports	10	8	0	2	159	91	16
Old Bealonians	10	7	1	2	221	99	15
Thetford	10	6	0	4	135	102	12
Lakenham Hewett	10	5	1	4	142	120	10
Ipswich YMCA	10	5	0	5	142	174	10
O Palmerians	10	4	1	5	95	107	9
Harwich & Dover	10	3	0	7	178	155	6
Beccles	10	2	1	7	103	189	5
London Hosp	10	1	2	7	121	216	3
O Brentwoods	10	1	0	9	67	285	2

Eastern Counties 4

	P	W	D	L	F	A	Pts
Haverhill	9	7	0	2	173	97	14
Loughton	9	7	0	2	148	81	14
Stowmarket	9	6	0	3	108	85	12
O Cooperians	9	5	1	3	159	73	11
Ilford Wands	9	5	0	4	141	72	10
Fakenham	9	4	2	3	81	68	10
Southwold	9	4	0	5	95	142	7
Dereham	9	2	1	6	71	189	5
Clacton	9	2	0	7	118	141	4
Wisbech	9	1	0	8	59	205	2
Mayfield OB	0	0	0	0	0	0	0

Eastern Counties 5

	P	W	D	L	F	A	Pts
Ongar	10	10	0	0	259	39	20
Hadleigh	10	9	0	1	240	106	18
Brightlingsea	10	6	0	4	146	110	12
Felixstowe	10	6	0	4	108	136	12
Essex Police	10	5	1	4	124	92	11
Billericay	10	5	1	4	130	130	11
Swaffham	10	3	2	5	109	147	8
Thurston	10	3	1	6	130	140	7
March	10	2	1	7	83	152	5
Norwich Union	10	2	0	8	78	182	4
Stanford	10	1	0	9	62	235	2

Eastern Counties 6

	P	W	D	L	F	A	Pts
Witham	10	9	0	1	296	67	18
Burnham-on-C	10	9	0	1	275	57	18
Essex U	10	8	1	1	502	72	17
Broadland	10	6	1	3	195	98	13
Sawston	10	5	0	5	100	201	10
Mersea Island	10	4	0	6	102	210	8
Chigwell	10	3	1	6	124	195	7
Watton	10	3	0	7	98	188	6
Leiston	10	3	0	7	123	229	6
Mistley	10	3	0	7	94	310	6
Burwell	10	0	1	9	53	335	1

Hampshire 1

	P	W	D	L	F	A	Pts
Jersey	10	9	0	1	237	94	18
Millbrook	10	7	0	3	123	118	14
Southampton	10	6	1	3	97	75	13
Gosport	10	6	1	3	171	121	12
Tottonians	10	6	0	4	121	71	12
Esso	10	5	1	4	146	110	11
Isle of Wight	10	5	0	5	126	79	10
Petersfield	10	5	0	5	135	115	10
Guernsey	10	2	1	7	113	163	5
Sandown & S	10	1	0	9	61	195	2
Fareham Heaths	10	1	0	9	66	255	2

Hampshire 2

	P	W	D	L	F	A	Pts
New Milton	10	10	0	0	269	60	20
Farnborough	10	9	0	1	302	42	18
Andover	10	7	0	3	195	81	13
Overton	10	6	0	4	173	105	12
Trojans	10	6	0	4	132	105	11
Jersey UB	10	4	0	6	149	140	8
Fordingbridge	10	4	0	6	88	129	8
Nomads	10	3	0	7	67	262	6
Romsey	10	2	0	8	111	169	4
Ellingham	10	2	0	8	81	266	4
Ventnor	10	2	0	8	53	261	2

Hertfordshire 1

	P	W	D	L	F	A	Pts
O Elizabethans	11	10	0	1	338	42	20
Harpenden	11	10	0	1	242	20	20
Stevenage	11	7	2	2	205	82	16
Hitchin	11	8	1	2	185	84	15
Barnet	11	6	1	4	208	110	13
St Albans	11	5	1	5	120	162	11
Ashmoleans	11	5	0	6	155	153	10
Datchworth	11	5	0	6	135	164	10
Royston	11	3	1	7	100	225	7
Watford	11	2	0	9	78	359	4
Bacavians	11	1	0	10	90	267	2
Tring	11	1	0	10	59	266	2

Kent 1

	P	W	D	L	F	A	Pts
Erith	10	8	1	1	183	110	17
Gillingham Anch	10	8	0	2	229	78	16
Sheppey	10	7	0	3	169	91	14
Sevenoaks	10	5	3	2	151	100	13
Park House	10	5	2	3	173	101	12
O Dunstonians	10	5	1	4	140	125	11
Betteshanger	10	5	1	4	144	136	11
Bromley	10	3	0	7	102	164	6
Medway	10	2	1	7	55	165	5
Sittingbourne	10	2	1	7	51	162	5
Tonbridge	10	0	0	10	48	213	0

Kent 2

	P	W	D	L	F	A	Pts
Canterbury	10	8	0	2	221	92	16
Snowdown CW	10	7	1	2	110	76	15
New Ash Green	10	6	1	3	114	103	13
Met Police Hayes	10	5	2	3	108	131	12
Ashford	10	5	1	4	106	103	11
Dover	10	5	1	4	138	160	11
Folkestone	10	5	0	5	183	134	10
Vigo	10	3	1	6	98	95	7
O Elthamians	10	3	0	7	98	116	6
O Shootershillian	10	3	0	7	109	179	6
Midland Bank	10	1	1	8	79	175	3

Kent 3

	P	W	D	L	F	A	Pts
Thames Poly	11	11	0	0	137	39	22
Nat West Bank	11	9	1	1	182	54	19
Deal	11	8	1	2	134	77	17
Bexley	11	8	0	3	118	54	16
Linton	11	7	0	4	125	82	14
Gravesendians	11	5	2	4	121	115	12
Cranbrook	11	4	1	6	67	91	9
Old Olavians	11	4	0	7	87	121	8
Greenwich	11	3	0	8	74	124	6
Williamsonians	11	2	0	9	129	202	4

| Lloyds Bank | 11 | 2 | 0 | 9 | 54 | 161 | 4 |
| Citizens | 11 | 0 | 1 | 10 | 43 | 151 | 1 |

Kent 4

	P	W	D	L	F	A	Pts
Orpington	11	11	0	0	259	69	22
Whitstable	11	9	0	2	209	91	18
Kent Police	11	8	0	3	141	102	16
STC Footscray	11	7	0	4	177	80	14
Darenth Valley	11	7	0	4	146	89	14
Lordswood	11	7	0	4	128	128	14
Centurians	11	5	0	6	72	133	10
Westerham	11	5	0	6	90	160	10
Edenbridge	11	4	0	7	128	107	8
U of Kent	10	1	0	9	60	141	2
East Peckham	11	1	0	10	91	224	2
Hong Kong Bank	10	0	0	10	32	209	0

Middlesex 1

	P	W	D	L	F	A	Pts
Staines	10	9	0	1	281	122	18
O Millhillians	10	9	0	1	212	101	18
Haringey	10	7	0	3	185	79	14
Harrow	10	6	0	4	149	110	12
Centaurs	10	6	0	4	174	139	12
London NZ	10	4	1	5	134	142	9
Uxbridge	10	4	0	6	113	122	8
Hendon	10	4	0	6	143	201	8
Twickenham	10	3	1	6	125	160	7
Hackney	10	2	0	8	68	199	4
Mill Hill	10	0	0	10	82	291	0

Middlesex 2

	P	W	D	L	F	A	Pts
O Meadonians	10	9	0	1	194	59	18
Antlers	10	9	0	1	226	98	18
Hampstead	10	8	1	1	266	87	17
Sudbury Court	10	7	0	3	113	105	14
Civil Service	10	5	1	4	166	139	11
O Abbotstonians	10	4	1	5	153	137	9
O Isleworthians	10	3	1	6	94	129	7
O Haberdashers	10	3	0	7	135	182	6
H'smith & Fulham	10	2	0	8	65	185	4
O Grammarians	10	2	0	8	60	276	4
Orleans FP	10	1	0	9	91	166	2

Middlesex 3

	P	W	D	L	F	A	Pts
Roxeth Manor OB	10	8	1	1	230	127	17
Wembley	10	8	0	2	176	86	16
Thamesians	10	7	0	3	221	128	14
Feltham	10	7	0	3	151	116	14
O Hamptonians	10	4	2	4	156	98	10
O Tottonians	10	5	0	5	141	127	10
Enfield Ignats	10	5	0	5	155	161	10
O Paulines	10	4	0	6	137	176	8
St Bart's Hosp	10	2	0	8	139	246	4

| Osterley | 10 | 2 | 0 | 8 | 72 | 215 | 4 |
| HAC | 10 | 1 | 1 | 8 | 131 | 229 | 2 |

Middlesex 4

	P	W	D	L	F	A	Pts
O Actonians	10	8	1	1	129	49	17
Belsize Pk	10	8	0	2	141	107	16
Barclays Bank	9	6	1	2	243	64	13
London Cornish	10	6	0	4	187	147	12
Northolt	10	5	1	4	160	75	11
London French	10	5	0	5	168	145	10
UCS OB	10	5	0	5	133	187	10
Pinner & Gramm	10	3	2	5	118	99	8
St Nicholas OB	9	3	1	5	100	164	7
Meadhurst	10	1	0	9	68	247	2
Royal Free H	8	0	0	8	38	201	0

Middlesex 5

	P	W	D	L	F	A	Pts
Bank of England	9	8	0	1	259	84	16
Hayes	8	7	0	1	139	42	14
Quintin	8	6	0	2	188	56	12
GWR	9	6	0	3	164	168	12
Kodak	9	4	0	5	91	132	8
University Coll	6	3	0	3	89	100	6
Middlesex Hosp	7	2	1	4	79	109	5
St George's Hosp	6	2	0	4	46	105	4
British Air	9	1	1	7	34	126	3
Southgate	9	0	0	9	51	218	0

Surrey 1

	P	W	D	L	F	A	Pts
Wimbledonians	10	10	0	0	232	56	20
Warlingham	10	9	0	1	215	62	18
Wimbledon	10	8	0	2	224	72	16
Guildfordians	10	6	0	4	105	109	12
John Fisher OB	10	5	1	4	148	97	11
O Whitgiftians	10	5	1	4	119	126	11
O Rutlishians	10	4	0	6	100	217	8
Shirley Wands	10	2	1	7	77	111	5
Effingham	10	2	1	7	79	196	5
Raynes Park	10	1	0	9	67	162	2
Mitcham	10	1	0	9	91	249	2

Surrey 2

	P	W	D	L	F	A	Pts
Kingston	10	9	1	0	174	58	19
O Reedonians	10	8	0	2	274	102	16
University Vand	10	8	0	2	171	83	16
Cobham	10	6	0	4	141	101	12
Merton	10	6	0	4	151	117	12
Farnham	10	4	2	4	138	115	10
Barnes Harrods	10	4	0	6	228	128	8
O Cranleighans	10	3	1	6	117	138	7
Law Society	10	2	1	7	110	213	5
O Tiffinians	10	2	0	8	74	264	4
Charing X/West	10	0	1	9	77	336	0

Surrey 3

	P	W	D	L	F	A	Pts
Bec OB	9	8	0	1	192	48	16
Reigate & Red	9	7	0	2	171	85	14
Haileyburians	9	7	0	2	136	85	14
Chobham	9	6	0	3	150	103	12
Wandsworthians	9	4	0	5	81	78	8
O Bevonians	9	3	0	6	87	139	6
O Pelhamians	9	3	0	6	92	163	6
Battersea Irons	9	3	0	6	68	185	6
London Fire Br	9	2	0	7	68	98	4
O Freemans	9	2	0	7	75	136	4

Surrey 4

	P	W	D	L	F	A	Pts
O Caterhamians	9	9	0	0	270	81	18
Kings Coll Hosp	9	6	0	3	189	98	12
Chipstead	9	5	0	4	122	78	10
Shene OG	9	5	0	4	126	124	10
O Suttonians	9	5	0	4	112	118	10
Royal Holloway C	9	4	1	4	119	130	9
Woking	9	4	0	5	139	110	8
O Croydonians	9	4	0	5	74	148	8
O Johnians	9	1	1	7	82	224	3
Surrey Police	9	1	0	8	89	211	2

Surrey 5

	P	W	D	L	F	A	Pts
Kew Occasionals	9	9	0	0	456	38	18
London Media	9	7	0	2	166	98	14
Surrey U	8	6	0	2	258	69	12
Haslemere	8	6	0	2	167	94	12
Lightwater	9	3	1	5	74	173	7
Oxted	9	3	0	6	107	179	6
O Epsomians	8	3	0	5	82	165	6
Egham	9	3	0	6	86	247	6
Racal-Decca	9	1	1	7	68	168	3
Economicals	8	1	0	7	72	305	2

Sussex 1

	P	W	D	L	F	A	Pts
Brighton	10	10	0	0	267	59	20
East Grinstead	10	7	0	3	231	89	14
Uckfield	10	6	0	4	160	96	12
Haywards Heath	10	6	0	4	134	140	12
Heathfield & W	10	5	0	5	207	162	10
Burgess Hill	10	5	0	5	150	140	10
O Brightonians	10	5	0	5	125	147	10
Bognor	10	4	0	6	111	152	8
Eastbourne	10	4	0	6	103	140	5
St Francis	10	2	0	8	59	310	4
Hellingly	10	1	0	9	96	248	2

Sussex 2

	P	W	D	L	F	A	Pts
Seaford	8	8	0	0	270	48	16
Crowborough	8	5	1	2	161	93	11
BA Wingspan	8	5	1	2	104	85	11

Pulborough	8	5	0	3	105	83	9
Sussex Police	8	4	0	4	81	120	8
Ditchling	8	4	0	4	127	97	7
Newick	8	2	0	6	59	128	4
Brighton Poly	8	1	0	7	61	184	2
Midhurst	8	1	0	7	49	179	0

Sussex 3

	P	W	D	L	F	A	Pts
Sunallon	4	4	0	0	113	7	8
Plumpton	4	2	0	2	75	22	4
Sussex U	0	0	0	0	0	0	0
Arun	4	0	0	4	0	159	0

MIDLANDS DIVISION

Midlands 1

	P	W	D	L	F	A	Pts
Stoke on T	10	9	0	1	252	74	18
Syston	10	7	1	2	204	91	15
Derby	10	7	0	3	133	134	14
Leamington	10	5	2	3	142	142	12
Newark	10	5	1	4	125	148	11
Westleigh	10	5	0	5	92	109	10
Leighton Buzz	10	4	0	6	85	159	8
Barker's Butts	10	3	1	6	154	161	7
B'ham & S'hull	10	3	1	6	126	151	7
Mansfield	10	2	1	7	77	141	5
Camp Hill	10	0	3	7	76	156	3

Midlands 2 East

	P	W	D	L	F	A	Pts
Vipers	10	8	0	2	174	80	16
Paviors	10	6	1	3	164	116	13
Moderns	10	6	0	4	147	117	12
Stockwood Pk	10	6	0	4	109	91	12
Biggleswade	10	5	0	5	118	100	10
Matlock	10	5	0	5	117	116	10
Peterborough	10	5	0	5	132	156	10
Bedford Ath	10	4	0	6	168	150	8
Amber Valley	10	4	0	6	66	114	8
Scunthorpe	10	3	1	6	113	134	7
Stewarts & L	10	2	0	8	74	208	4

Midlands 2 West

	P	W	D	L	F	A	Pts
Bedworth	10	8	0	2	161	89	16
Wolverhampton	10	7	1	2	151	87	15
Worcester	10	7	0	3	175	131	14
Stafford	10	6	1	3	99	118	13
Burton	10	6	0	4	144	118	12
Whitchurch	10	4	1	5	132	139	9
Keresley	10	4	0	6	98	104	8
Broad Street	10	3	1	6	95	116	7
Newbold	10	3	1	6	107	137	7
Sutton Cold	10	2	1	7	67	131	5
Bromsgrove	10	2	0	8	102	161	4

East Midlands/Leics

	P	W	D	L	F	A	Pts
Hinckley	10	8	1	1	208	62	17
Stoneygate	10	8	0	2	210	68	16
Belgrave	10	8	0	2	172	58	16
Luton	10	6	0	4	115	105	12
Ampthill	10	6	0	4	156	147	12
Coalville	10	5	1	4	87	125	11
Kettering	10	4	0	6	117	134	8
Wellingborough	10	4	0	6	97	117	8
Northampton BB	10	4	0	6	82	182	8
Lutterworth	10	1	0	9	67	182	2
Aylestone St J	10	0	0	10	68	199	0

East Midlands 1

	P	W	D	L	F	A	Pts
Long Buckby	10	10	0	0	285	77	20
St Neots	10	8	0	2	171	66	16
Brackley	10	7	0	3	171	125	14
Northampton MO	10	5	0	5	192	150	10
Northampton OS	10	5	0	5	134	118	10
Huntingdon	10	4	0	6	120	131	8
St Ives	10	4	0	6	60	206	8
Queens	10	3	0	7	102	141	6
N'pton Casuals	10	3	0	7	96	135	6
N'pton Trinity	10	3	0	7	95	153	6
Well'boro OG	10	3	0	7	54	178	6

East Midlands 2

	P	W	D	L	F	A	Pts
Rushden & High	10	8	1	1	205	92	17
Daventry	10	6	2	2	192	59	14
Dunstablians	10	7	0	3	192	85	14
Northamptonians	10	6	1	3	207	63	13
Bedford Swifts	10	6	0	4	139	118	12
Bugbrooke	10	5	0	5	166	154	10
Deepings	10	5	0	5	130	168	10
Colworth House	10	4	0	6	60	162	8
Oundle	10	3	0	7	66	144	6
O Wellingburians	10	3	0	7	77	219	6
Corby	10	0	0	10	43	213	0

East Midlands 3

	P	W	D	L	F	A	Pts
Westwood	7	7	0	0	134	24	14
Kempston	7	6	0	1	192	58	12
Vauxhall Mots	7	4	0	3	115	79	8
Northampton H	7	4	0	3	82	87	8
RAE Bedford	7	3	0	4	47	136	6
Thorney	7	2	0	5	86	76	4
Littlehey	7	1	0	6	57	108	2
Potton	7	1	0	6	21	166	2

Leicestershire 1

	P	W	D	L	F	A	Pts
South Leicester	10	9	0	1	229	50	18

	P	W	D	L	F	A	Pts
Kibworth	10	8	2	0	225	47	18
Market Bosworth	10	7	1	2	167	81	15
O Bosworthians	10	7	0	3	189	110	14
Oadby Wyggs	10	6	0	4	134	81	12
Loughborough	10	5	0	5	131	131	10
Melton Mowbray	10	4	0	6	157	142	8
Wigston	10	1	2	7	67	135	4
Aylestonians	10	2	0	8	79	207	4
New Parks OB	10	2	0	8	51	292	4
O Ashbeians	10	1	1	8	72	225	3

Leicestershire 2

	P	W	D	L	F	A	Pts
Oakham	6	6	0	0	205	22	12
Birstall	6	5	0	1	116	58	10
O Newtonians	6	4	0	2	82	74	8
Anstey	6	2	0	4	61	64	4
Shepshed	6	2	0	4	75	154	4
West Leicester	6	1	0	5	73	147	2
Burbage	6	1	0	5	47	140	2

North Midlands 1

	P	W	D	L	F	A	Pts
O Yardleians	10	8	0	2	142	81	16
Dudley	10	6	2	2	115	68	14
O Halesonians	10	7	0	3	120	109	14
Kings Norton	10	6	0	4	101	89	12
Ludlow	10	5	0	5	109	70	10
Dixonians	10	5	0	5	116	123	10
Woodrush	10	4	2	4	84	96	10
W Midlands Pol	10	5	0	5	86	131	10
Shrewsbury	10	4	0	6	106	93	8
Ashton Old Eds	10	1	2	7	104	137	4
Luctonians	10	1	0	9	71	157	2

North Midlands 2

	P	W	D	L	F	A	Pts
Selly Oak	10	8	0	2	160	63	16
O Griffinians	10	8	0	2	170	106	16
Warley	10	7	1	2	194	114	15
Telford	10	5	2	3	134	86	12
Evesham	10	6	0	4	96	103	12
Newport	10	5	0	5	110	104	10
Pershore	10	4	1	5	134	130	9
Ross-on-Wye	10	4	1	5	105	108	9
Veseyans	10	3	1	6	132	170	7
Redditch	10	1	0	9	87	205	2
Bridgnorth	10	1	0	9	78	211	2

North Midlands 3

	P	W	D	L	F	A	Pts
Five Ways OE	10	8	1	1	158	61	17
O Centrals	10	8	0	2	178	103	16
Kidderminster	10	7	0	3	194	68	14
Birmingham CO	10	6	0	4	130	77	12
Droitwich	10	5	1	4	142	111	11

	P	W	D	L	F	A	Pts
Malvern	10	5	1	4	160	130	11
Edwardians	10	5	0	5	146	131	10
Erdington	10	4	0	6	108	153	8
O Moseleians	10	3	0	7	78	204	6
Tenbury	10	2	1	7	99	170	5
Kynoch	10	0	0	10	68	253	0

North Midlands 4

	P	W	D	L	F	A	Pts
Bournville	13	10	1	2	193	131	21
Birchfield	13	9	0	4	245	119	18
Market Drayton	13	9	0	4	221	101	18
Bromyard	13	9	0	4	191	93	18
Upton-on-Sev	13	9	0	4	200	112	18
Witton	13	8	1	4	268	94	17
Birmingham CS	13	8	0	5	151	149	16
O Saltleians	13	6	2	5	157	96	14
Birmingham Wel	13	6	0	7	213	151	12
Bewdley	13	6	0	7	110	204	12
Ledbury	13	4	0	9	158	214	8
Oswestry	13	2	0	11	67	295	4
Yardley & Dist	13	3	0	10	88	216	2
Thimblemill	13	0	0	13	50	350	0

Notts, Lincs & Derbys 1

	P	W	D	L	F	A	Pts
Chesterfield	10	8	0	2	182	68	16
Spalding	10	7	1	2	278	103	15
West Bridgford	10	7	1	2	144	98	15
Mellish	10	6	1	3	162	114	13
Dronfield	10	5	1	4	102	111	11
Glossop	10	5	1	4	173	199	11
Southwell	10	4	0	6	140	195	8
Stamford	10	3	1	6	105	155	7
Kesteven	10	2	2	6	99	142	6
Lincoln	10	2	0	8	101	196	4
Sleaford	10	2	0	8	69	174	4

Notts, Lincs & Derbys 2

	P	W	D	L	F	A	Pts
Worksop	10	9	1	0	208	46	19
Market Ras & L	10	9	0	1	233	70	18
Ilkeston	10	7	1	2	186	58	15
Nottingham Cas	10	7	0	3	163	110	14
Ashbourne	10	6	1	3	192	109	13
Long Eaton	10	4	1	5	101	132	9
Nottinghamians	10	2	3	5	108	128	7
Keyworth	10	3	0	7	76	179	6
All Spartans	10	3	0	7	52	223	6
East Retford	10	1	1	8	61	177	3
Notts Cons	10	0	0	10	71	219	0

Notts, Lincs & Derbys 3

	P	W	D	L	F	A	Pts
Bakewell Manns	10	9	0	1	192	97	18
Grimsby	10	8	0	2	146	70	16

	P	W	D	L	F	A	Pts
East Leake	10	7	1	2	147	55	15
Belper	10	7	0	3	141	88	14
Ashfield Swans	10	6	0	4	110	108	12
Melbourne	10	4	1	5	116	106	9
Rolls Royce	10	4	0	6	177	128	8
North Kesteven	10	4	0	6	101	151	8
Boots Athletic	10	3	0	7	94	150	6
Cleethorpes	10	1	0	9	97	198	2
Tupton	10	1	0	9	73	243	2

Notts, Lincs & Derbys 4

	P	W	D	L	F	A	Pts
Leesbrook	10	9	0	1	322	60	18
Meden Vale	10	9	0	1	204	67	18
Boston	10	8	0	2	183	66	16
Buxton	10	7	0	3	253	72	14
Barton & Dist	10	7	0	3	134	79	14
Bourne	9	4	0	5	131	127	8
Derby College	10	3	0	7	106	154	6
Bingham	9	2	1	6	103	141	5
Ollerton & Bev	9	2	1	6	82	219	5
Harworth Coll	9	1	1	7	32	264	3
Skegness	9	0	0	9	33	334	0

Notts, Lincs & Derbys 5

	P	W	D	L	F	A	Pts
Stamford Coll	9	9	0	0	376	35	18
Hope Valley	8	6	1	1	129	56	13
Bolsover	7	5	0	2	104	109	10
Yarborough Bs	6	3	1	2	111	77	9
Gainsborough	8	4	0	4	106	103	8
Rainworth	8	3	1	4	65	61	8
Sutton Bonn	6	3	0	3	60	128	6
Whitwell	9	2	0	7	98	128	4
Horncastle	8	1	0	7	89	170	2
Monsons	7	0	0	7	31	302	0

Staffs/Warwicks

	P	W	D	L	F	A	Pts
Old Longtonians	10	9	0	1	211	52	18
Newcastle	10	8	0	2	193	59	16
Willenhall	10	6	1	3	153	122	13
Leek	10	6	0	4	153	139	12
Leamingtonians	10	5	1	4	157	130	11
Nuneaton O Ed	10	4	2	4	125	123	10
Kenilworth	10	4	1	5	121	132	9
Tamworth	10	4	0	6	95	124	8
Stratford	10	3	0	7	152	202	6
Coventry Welsh	10	2	1	7	79	156	5
Eccleshall	10	1	0	9	74	264	2

Staffordshire 1

	P	W	D	L	F	A	Pts
Handsworth	14	12	0	2	325	52	24
Trentham	14	12	0	2	334	107	24
Wednesbury	14	8	0	6	175	127	16
GEC St Leonards	14	7	0	7	187	152	14
Linley	14	7	0	7	196	265	14
Uttoxeter	14	5	1	8	160	208	11
Rubery Owen	14	3	1	10	115	216	7
Cannock	14	1	0	13	97	462	2

Staffordshire 2

	P	W	D	L	F	A	Pts
Rugeley	14	13	1	0	453	94	27
Old Oaks	14	11	1	2	209	133	23
Wheaton Aston	14	8	2	4	255	171	18
Sankey Vending	14	8	1	5	193	223	17
Wulfrun	14	5	0	9	120	211	10
Michelin	14	3	1	10	120	202	7
Burntwood	14	3	0	11	141	213	6
Cheadle	14	2	0	12	84	328	4

Warwickshire 1

	P	W	D	L	F	A	Pts
O Laurentians	10	9	0	1	173	85	18
Trinity Guild	10	7	1	2	159	105	15
O Wheatleyans	10	7	0	3	108	85	14
O Coventrians	10	6	0	4	131	103	12
Manor Park	10	6	0	4	120	94	12
Coventry Sars	10	5	0	5	153	115	10
GEC Coventry	10	4	1	5	152	139	9
Dunlop	10	3	1	6	80	107	7
Spartans	10	3	0	7	137	152	6
Stoke OB	10	2	1	7	69	137	5
Silhillians	10	1	0	9	100	260	2

Warwickshire 2

	P	W	D	L	F	A	Pts
Southam	10	8	0	2	196	54	16
Coventrians	10	7	1	2	128	56	15
Berswell & B	10	7	0	3	133	48	14
Pinley	10	6	1	3	137	81	13
Earlsdon	10	6	0	4	139	111	12
Rugby St A	10	6	0	4	122	109	12
O Warwickians	10	6	0	4	128	138	12
Atherton	10	5	0	5	115	95	10
Shipston-on-S	10	1	1	8	30	158	3
Claverdon	10	1	0	9	70	208	2
Harbury	10	0	1	9	50	190	1

Warwickshire 3

	P	W	D	L	F	A	Pts
Alcester	8	8	0	0	228	26	16
Warwick	8	7	0	1	160	39	14
Standard	8	6	0	2	135	55	12
Coventry Tech	8	5	0	3	114	76	10
Shottery	8	4	0	4	96	86	8
Coventry PO	8	3	0	5	57	127	6
Jaguar (Cov)	8	2	0	6	38	131	4
Ford	8	1	0	7	32	145	2
Rugby Welsh	8	0	0	8	24	199	0

LANCASHIRE'S SHADOW GLORY

ADT COUNTY CHAMPIONSHIP 1991-92
Michael Austin

18 April, Twickenham
Cornwall 6 (2PG) **Lancashire 9** (1G 1PG)

Once again, Cornwall proved that their presence is essential in bringing fervour and crowd appeal to the County Championship final, which attracted 50,000 spectators, almost all from the Duchy. Cornwall lost a disappointing match to what amounted to a Lancashire second team, shorn of 11 first-choice Orrell players, but finished the game hammering away at the opposing line in a thrilling climax. Lancashire equalled Gloucestershire's record of winning the title outright 15 times.

The rearrangement of Orrell's important League match against Harlequins revived the age-old club or county dilemma, which also afflicted Dawe, the Cornwall captain, before the semi-finals. He opted to play for Bath and sportingly told the selectors it would be unfair on the winning team for him to be considered for the final.

Cornwall appeared at Twickenham for the third time in four years but found pluck, passion and perseverance an inadequate substitute for skill. The match had little bearing on the long-term deliberations of the England selectors, and the low standard of play provided a powerful argument for restricting the competition to junior clubs. The few players of genuine class included Laity, the Neath and Cornwall centre, and Lancashire's Jackson and Grayson. They shared the points for Lancashire, who fielded five newcomers. Grayson's goal-kicking was a vital factor, especially as, curiously, Cornwall declined to take several kickable penalties when they were 9-3 adrift in the second half.

Cornwall were handicapped by the loss of Peters, their fly-half, with a head wound sustained after five minutes when Lancashire's pack drove over him with little regard as to where they put their feet. Lancashire's shortcomings stemmed partly from a team of near-strangers being put together at short notice. Their possession was channelled slowly, kicks were charged down and passes fumbled. Kenrick, Bibby and Ireland worked assiduously in Lancashire's back row and Jackson, the full-back, showed an opportunist touch for the game's only try after 25 minutes. Thomas had kicked a penalty goal two minutes earlier, but Jackson's contribution was more precious as Lancashire were playing against the wind. He sprinted down the left wing, kicked high and infield and caught a kind bounce, one-handed, touching down in the same movement. Grayson kicked the conversion and landed a penalty goal when Cornwall collapsed a scrum. Thomas responded by squeezing a penalty attempt from in front of the posts just inside the left upright. The final 23 minutes were scoreless.

Wilkinson of Lancashire has won the ball and Swarbrick, the Lancashire scrum-half, prepares to move it onwards during the County final at Twickenham.

Hampshire, making their first semi-final appearance for 28 years, had been eliminated 29-9 by Lancashire, whose England wing, Heslop, scored three tries at Blundellsands. The match was uneventful, but to reach such an advanced stage Hampshire had thrived on two resurgent clubs, Havant and Basingstoke, and their major achievement was a 30-0 win over Middlesex, a side they had not beaten for 25 years. These unexpected events helped Cornwall to qualify for their fourth consecutive home semi-final, against Yorkshire, in front of a capacity crowd of 13,700 at Redruth. In a repeat of the previous season's final, Yorkshire were beaten 22-3, but this time they played very poorly.

Warwickshire, a time-honoured bastion of the game, were relegated from League 1, leaving no Midlands county in the top division for 1992-93. Northumberland joined Lancashire, Yorkshire and Cumbria while Hertfordshire were replaced in League 1 South by Surrey.

TEAMS IN THE FINAL

Cornwall: K Thomas (Redruth); A Mead (Redruth), C Laity (Neath), M Brain (Clifton), D Weeks (Camborne); W Peters (Bath), R Nancekivell (Northampton); J May (Redruth), B Andrew (Redruth), R Keast (Redruth), A Reed (Bath), A Cook (Redruth), G Williams (Redruth) (*capt*), J Atkinson (St Ives), A Bick (Penzance-Newlyn)
Replacement S Whitworth (Redruth) for Peters
Scorer *Penalty Goals:* Thomas (2)
Lancashire: M Jackson (Fylde); G Meredith (Waterloo), I Wynn (Orrell), B Wellens (Orrell), A Parker (Fylde); P Grayson (Preston Grasshoppers), S Swarbrick (Vale of Lune); J Russell (Broughton Park), A Yates (Broughton Park), M Ridehalgh (Fylde), N Wilkinson (Waterloo), N Allott (Waterloo), M Kenrick (Sale) (*capt*), S Bibby (Orrell), A Ireland (Fylde)
Scorers *Try:* Jackson   *Conversion:* Grayson   *Penalty Goal:* Grayson
Referee E Morrison (Bristol Society)

TEAMS IN THE SEMI-FINALS

21 March, Redruth RFC
Cornwall 22 (1G 4PG 1T)   **Yorkshire 3** (1PG)

Cornwall: K Thomas (Redruth); A Mead (Redruth), C Laity (Neath), M Brain (Clifton), D Weeks (Camborne); W Peters (Bath), R Nancekivell (Northampton); J May (Redruth), B Andrew (Redruth), R Keast (Redruth), A Reed (Bath), A Cook (Redruth), G Williams (Redruth) (*capt*), J Atkinson (St Ives), A Bick (Penzance-Newlyn)
Scorers *Tries:* Mead, Weeks   *Conversion:* Thomas   *Penalty Goals:* Thomas (4)
Yorkshire: P Rutledge (Bradford & Bingley); M Harrison (Wakefield) (*capt*), J Georgiou (Morley), S Burnhill (Sale), E Atkins (Harrogate); S Townend (Wakefield), G Easterby (Harrogate); M Vincent (Bradford & Bingley), N Lineham (Roundhay), S Rice (Otley), S Croft (Harrogate), C Raducanu (Sale), S Tipping (Otley), S Bainbridge (Roundhay), P Buckton (Waterloo) *Replacement* A Scott (Otley) for Atkins
Scorer *Penalty Goal:* Rutledge
Referee C J Harrison (East Midlands Society)

21 March, Waterloo RFC
Lancashire 29 (3G 1PG 2T)   **Hampshire 9** (1G 1PG)

Lancashire (*Orrell unless stated*):S Taberner; N Heslop, S Langford, M Jackson (Fylde), P Halsall; P Grayson (Preston Grasshoppers), D Morris; M Hynes, N Hitchen,

D Southern (*capt*), S Bibby, N Allott (Waterloo), D Cleary, M Kenrick (Sale), P Manley
Replacements B Sandford for Hynes; A Parker (Fylde) for Heslop
Scorers *Tries:* Heslop (3), Cleary, Kenrick   *Conversions:* Grayson (3)
Penalty Goal: Grayson
Hampshire: R Rowledge (Basingstoke); A Wilson (Havant), S Boydell (Havant),
D Guyatt (Basingstoke) (*capt*), J Bates (Havant); C Short (Harlequins), B Short
(Harlequins); D Rees (Havant), I Lillington (Basingstoke), J Garrett (Havant), S Morgan
(Havant), B Rouse (Havant), P Hawkins (Basingstoke), A Hill (Basingstoke), N Roach
(Havant)
Scorers *Try:* Bates   *Conversion:* Rowledge   *Penalty Goal:* Rowledge
Referee M J Bayliss (Gloucester Society)

DIVISIONAL ROUNDS

Area North

League One

Cumbria	17	Lancashire	24
Yorkshire	31	Warwickshire	21
Warwickshire	21	Lancashire	21
Yorkshire	27	Cumbria	6
Cumbria	13	Warwickshire	10
Lancashire	19	Yorkshire	9

	P	W	D	L	F	A	Pts
Lancashire	3	2	1	0	64	47	3
Yorkshire	3	2	0	1	67	46	4
Cumbria	3	1	0	2	36	61	2
Warwickshire	3	0	1	2	52	65	1

League Two

Northumberland	9	North Midlands	4
Leicestershire	10	Notts, Lincs & Derbys	9
Leicestershire	9	Northumberland	17
Notts, Lincs & Derbys	18	North Midlands	27
North Midlands	27	Leicestershire	6
Northumberland	35	Notts, Lincs & Derbys	6

	P	W	D	L	F	A	Pts
Northumberland	3	3	0	0	61	19	6
North Midlands	3	2	0	1	58	33	4
Leicestershire	3	1	0	2	25	53	2
Notts, Lincs & Derbys	3	0	0	3	33	72	0

League Three

Staffordshire	38	East Midlands	13
Durham	30	Cheshire	0
East Midlands	13	Cheshire	34
Staffordshire	10	Durham	20
Cheshire	29	Staffordshire	10
Durham	48	East Midlands	0

	P	W	D	L	F	A	Pts
Durham	3	3	0	0	98	10	6
Cheshire	3	2	0	1	63	53	4
Staffordshire	3	1	0	2	58	62	2
East Midlands	3	0	0	3	26	120	0

Area South
League One

Cornwall	18	Hampshire	9
Middlesex	33	Hertfordshire	8
Hertfordshire	10	Hampshire	21
Middlesex	17	Cornwall	16
Cornwall	37	Hertfordshire	6
Hampshire	30	Middlesex	0

	P	W	D	L	F	A	Pts
Cornwall	3	2	0	1	71	32	4
Hampshire	3	2	0	1	60	28	4
Middlesex	3	2	0	1	50	54	4
Hertfordshire	3	0	0	3	24	91	0

League Two

Kent	13	Berkshire	9
Surrey	28	Devon	13
Berkshire	3	Devon	21
Kent	14	Surrey	22
Devon	12	Kent	23
Surrey	34	Berkshire	19

	P	W	D	L	F	A	Pts
Surrey	3	3	0	0	84	46	6
Kent	3	2	0	1	50	43	4
Devon	3	1	0	2	46	54	2
Berkshire	3	0	0	3	31	68	0

League Three

Gloucestershire	19	Somerset	16
Sussex	17	Dorset & Wilts	10
Gloucestershire	16	Sussex	15
Somerset	21	Dorset & Wilts	19
Dorset & Wilts	15	Gloucestershire	16
Sussex	14	Somerset	6

	P	W	D	L	F	A	Pts
Gloucestershire	3	3	0	0	51	46	6
Sussex	3	1	0	2	38	32	2
Dorset & Wilts	3	1	0	2	44	46	2
Somerset	3	1	0	2	43	52	2

League Four

Oxfordshire	15	Buckinghamshire	17

| | | | | Eastern Counties | 17 | Oxfordshire | 21 |
| | | | | Buckinghamshire | 16 | Eastern Counties | 16 |

	P	W	D	L	F	A	Pts
Buckinghamshire	2	1	1	0	33	31	3
Oxfordshire	2	1	0	1	36	34	2
Eastern Counties	2	0	1	1	33	37	1

ENGLISH COUNTY CHAMPIONS 1889-1992

FIRST SYSTEM

1889	**Yorkshire,** undefeated, declared champions by RU (scored 18G 17T to 1G 3T)	1890	**Yorkshire,** undefeated, declared champions (scored 10G 16T to 2G 4T)

SECOND SYSTEM

1891	**Lancashire** champions.	Group Winners — Yorkshire, Surrey, Gloucestershire.
1892	**Yorkshire** champions.	Group Winners — Lancashire, Kent, Midlands.
1893	**Yorkshire** champions.	Group Winners — Cumberland, Devon, Middlesex.
1894	**Yorkshire** champions.	Group Winners — Lancashire, Gloucestershire, Midlands.
1895	**Yorkshire** champions.	Group Winners — Cumberland, Devon, Midlands.

THIRD SYSTEM

	Champions	*Runners-up*	*Played at*
1896	**Yorkshire**	Surrey	Richmond
1897	**Kent**	Cumberland	Carlisle
1898	**Northumberland**	Midlands	Coventry
1899	**Devon**	Northumberland	Newcastle
1900	**Durham**	Devon	Exeter
1901	**Devon**	Durham	W Hartlepool
1902	**Durham**	Gloucestershire	Gloucester
1903	**Durham**	Kent	W Hartlepool
1904	**Kent**	Durham	Blackheath (2nd meeting)
1905	**Durham**	Middlesex	W Hartlepool
1906	**Devon**	Durham	Exeter
1907	**Devon** and **Durham** joint champions after drawn games at W Hartlepool and Exeter		
1908	**Cornwall**	Durham	Redruth
1909	**Durham**	Cornwall	W Hartlepool
1910	**Gloucestershire**	Yorkshire	Gloucester
1911	**Devon**	Yorkshire	Headingley
1912	**Devon**	Northumberland	Devonport
1913	**Gloucestershire**	Cumberland	Carlisle
1914	**Midlands**	Durham	Leicester
1920	**Gloucestershire**	Yorkshire	Bradford

FOURTH SYSTEM

	Champions	*Runners-up*	*Played at*
1921	**Gloucestershire (31)**	Leicestershire (4)	Gloucester
1922	**Gloucestershire (19)**	N Midlands (0)	Birmingham
1923	**Somerset (8)**	Leicester (6)	Bridgwater
1924	**Cumberland (14)**	Kent (3)	Carlisle
1925	**Leicestershire (14)**	Gloucestershire (6)	Bristol
1926	**Yorkshire (15)**	Hampshire (14)	Bradford
1927	**Kent (22)**	Leicestershire (12)	Blackheath
1928	**Yorkshire (12)**	Cornwall (8)	Bradford
1929	***Middlesex (9)**	Lancashire (8)	Blundellsands
1930	**Gloucestershire (13)**	Lancashire (7)	Blundellsands
1931	**Gloucestershire (10)**	Warwickshire (9)	Gloucester
1932	**Gloucestershire (9)**	Durham (3)	Blaydon
1933	**Hampshire (18)**	Lancashire (7)	Boscombe

1934	**E Midlands (10)**	Gloucestershire (0)	Northampton
1935	**Lancashire (14)**	Somerset (0)	Bath
1936	**Hampshire (13)**	Northumberland (6)	Gosforth
1937	**Gloucestershire (5)**	E Midlands (0)	Bristol
1938	**Lancashire (24)**	Surrey (12)	Blundellsands
1939	**Warwickshire (8)**	Somerset (3)	Weston
1947	†**Lancashire (14)**	Gloucestershire (3)	Gloucester
1948	**Lancashire (5)**	E Counties (0)	Cambridge
1949	**Lancashire (9)**	Gloucestershire (3)	Blundellsands
1950	**Cheshire (5)**	E Midlands (0)	Birkenhead Park
1951	**E Midlands (10)**	Middlesex (0)	Northampton
1952	**Middlesex (9)**	Lancashire (6)	Twickenham
1953	**Yorkshire (11)**	E Midlands (3)	Bradford
1954	**Middlesex (24)**	Lancashire (6)	Blundellsands
1955	**Lancashire (14)**	Middlesex (8)	Twickenham
1956	**Middlesex (13)**	Devon (9)	Twickenham
1957	**Devon (12)**	Yorkshire (3)	Plymouth
1958	**Warwickshire (16)**	Cornwall (8)	Coventry
1959	**Warwickshire (14)**	Gloucestershire (9)	Bristol
1960	**Warwickshire (9)**	Surrey (6)	Coventry
1961	o**Cheshire (5)**	Devon (3)	Birkenhead Park
1962	**Warwickshire (11)**	Hampshire (6)	Twickenham
1963	**Warwickshire (13)**	Yorkshire (10)	Coventry
1964	**Warwickshire (8)**	Lancashire (6)	Coventry
1965	**Warwickshire (15)**	Durham (9)	Hartlepool
1966	**Middlesex (6)**	Lancashire (0)	Blundellsands
1967	****Surrey and Durham**		
1968	**Middlesex (9)**	Warwickshire (6)	Twickenham
1969	**Lancashire (11)**	Cornwall (9)	Redruth
1970	**Staffordshire (11)**	Gloucestershire (9)	Burton-on-Trent
1971	**Surrey (14)**	Gloucestershire (3)	Gloucester
1972	**Gloucestershire (11)**	Warwickshire (6)	Coventry
1973	**Lancashire (17)**	Gloucestershire (12)	Bristol
1974	**Gloucestershire (22)**	Lancashire (12)	Blundellsands
1975	**Gloucestershire (13)**	E Counties (9)	Gloucester
1976	**Gloucester (24)**	Middlesex (9)	Richmond
1977	**Lancashire (17)**	Middlesex (6)	Blundellsands
1978	**N Midlands (10)**	Gloucestershire (7)	Moseley
1979	**Middlesex (19)**	Northumberland (6)	Twickenham
1980	**Lancashire (21)**	Gloucestershire (15)	Vale of Lune
1981	**Northumberland (15)**	Gloucestershire (6)	Gloucester
1982	**Lancashire (7)**	North Midlands (3)	Moseley

FIFTH SYSTEM

	Champions	*Runners-up*	*Played at*
1983	**Gloucestershire (19)**	Yorkshire (7)	Bristol
1984	**Gloucestershire (36)**	Somerset (18)	Twickenham
1985	**Middlesex (12)**	Notts, Lincs and Derbys (9)	Twickenham

SIXTH SYSTEM

1986	**Warwickshire (16)**	Kent (6)	Twickenham
1987	**Yorkshire (22)**	Middlesex (11)	Twickenham
1988	**Lancashire (23)**	Warwickshire (18)	Twickenham
1989	**Durham (13)**	Cornwall (9)	Twickenham
1990	**Lancashire (32)**	Middlesex (9)	Twickenham
1991	**Cornwall (29)**	Yorkshire (20) *(aet)*	Twickenham
1992	**Lancashire (9)**	Cornwall (6)	Twickenham

**After a draw at Twickenham.   †After a draw, 8-8, at Blundellsands.   oAfter a draw 0-0, at Plymouth.
**Surrey and Durham drew 14 each at Twickenham and no score at Hartlepool and thus became joint champions. Gloucestershire and Lancashire have won the title 15 times each, Yorkshire 12, Warwickshire 9, Middlesex 8, Durham 8 (twice jointly), Devon 7 (once jointly), Kent 3 times, Hampshire, East Midlands, Cheshire, Northumberland and Cornwall twice each, Surrey twice (once jointly), and Midlands (3rd System), Somerset, Cumberland, Leicestershire, Staffordshire and North Midlands once each.*

ADAPTING SUCCESSFULLY TO A CHANGING RUGBY WORLD

THE BARBARIANS 1991-92
Geoff Windsor-Lewis

Visits to Ireland, Russia and Hong Kong, and a special match against Scotland, were the highlights of a crowded season in which the Baa-Baas played ten matches, winning seven and drawing one. They were defeated twice, but both games were lost only in the last minute, and the fact that they were the final matches of tours may show that the pace begins to tell after eight days.

The season started with a visit to Murrayfield to play Scotland in their last match before the World Cup. On a perfect afternoon in front of a full house, which included the Princess Royal, whose continued great loyalty to rugby is so much appreciated, the Baa-Baas mounted many attacks but an effective Scottish defence kept them out to enable Scotland to come back at the end of the game to level the scores. The visitors included eight players from different countries and, in a team that was possibly more individual than cohesive, Joubert, Bartmann, Pierce and Rush were in superb form.

The Barbarians then went to Ireland for two matches, against Cork Constitution and Old Wesley, who were celebrating their own centenaries. Both matches were notable for their open, flowing rugby which thrilled capacity crowds in Cork and Dublin. Having easily defeated Cork, the Baa-Baas had an exciting game against Old Wesley. The visitors came from behind to score a try with three minutes remaining, and a conversion from Colin Stephens put them ahead. From the kick-off Old Wesley won the ruck and the fly-half dropped a goal for a famous victory in the last seconds of the match.

At Newport the Barbarians weathered a half-hour storm before racing away to establish a 23-point lead. A typical midfield charge from Fran Clough lifted a defensive siege and took the Baa-Baas deep into the Newport half. Some neat footwork from Pears, who was outstanding, then created space for Ruari Maclean to mark his first appearance for the Barbarians with a try against the Welsh club. Two more tries came before half-time. The Newport midfield was under severe pressure throughout the second half in the face of some determined running from Clough, Maclean and Ian Hunter. The Barbarians continued to dominate, and with an ample supply of ball Richard Moon excelled in setting up the threequarters, especially Hunter, who showed his strength and pace in scoring two more tries.

The annual Leicester visit produced another sparkling match in which the Barbarians, having scored five tries and leading by 29-9, relaxed in the final period and allowed Leicester back into the game for an exciting finish. Sella, Blanco and the Lafond brothers, aided by Guscott and Colin Stephens, produced sweeping attacks from all parts of the field. The style of play was typified by Sella, who used his devastating change of pace to sprint 50 yards down the touchline and score in the corner from what seemed an impossible position. Maybe the best try of the afternoon came when Sella surged into space, lengthening his stride through the tackle, and dummied through the Leicester defence. Only five yards out he was tackled by Hackney, but Blanco was alongside to score a memorable try. A superb individual effort by Colin Stephens produced a side-stepping try, and John Jeffrey, captain for the afternoon, scored after a tremendous effort to end his Barbarian career in the best of ways.

David Sole and Jeff Probyn played together for the first time in the front row against East Midlands, and by all accounts thoroughly enjoyed themselves. Sole led the team effectively, and the Barbarians easily overcame a spirited East Midlands team. Wallace, the Irish wing, showed tremendous potential and both Barry and Bradley had useful games. It was also good to see Goodey and Huish, the Pontypool stalwarts, playing their first game for the Barbarians.

In a cliff-hanging match at Cardiff the Baa-Baas won the first game of the Easter tour, defeating Cardiff by just one point. The club was delighted to introduce Hayashi – the first Japanese player to represent the club – Ennis of Canada and Swords of the USA. During the season, the Barbarians fielded 17 players from different countries. Ian Smith had a superb game on the openside and Greg Oliver played marvellously at scrum-half, showing how lucky Scotland have been to have had him on the bench for so long. The scoring swung round until the departure of Mike Hall of Cardiff, who had been in excellent form. The Barbarians clung on with tries from Oliver and Ennis, and in the second half Woodland reduced their deficit only for Rayer to reply with a try for Cardiff. But then Barley scored two tries for the Barbarians to ensure a narrow victory.

The Barbarians romped to a record victory at Swansea, scoring 11 tries against a below-strength home team who were between vital League and Cup games. The pack, in which Mark Linnett, Swords and Glen Ennis were ably supported by Neil Back and Ian Smith, produced a flowing supply of ball and the Barbarian threequarters enjoyed a profitable afternoon. Bates and Shiel, as playmakers, brought the best out of an eager threequarter line, and the match resulted in a handsome win for the visitors.

After their visit to Hong Kong for the Cathay Pacific-Hong Kong Bank Sevens, in which they reached the quarter-finals, the Barbarians broke new ground with an eight-day tour to Russia, full details of which will appear in the next Yearbook.

The tour was a huge success both on and off the field. After a cultural 48 hours in St Petersburg, the team flew to Krasnayarsk in Siberia, to play the Russian club champions. Krasnayarsk was a closed city until 1990, and so the team enjoyed their dinner in the clubhouse of the Krasny-Yar Rugby Club, which proved that rugby knows no bounds in friendship and generous hospitality.

The Baa-Baas came from behind to win the match after an early lead, to which Jean-Marc Lafond contributed two scintillating tries. The elder Lafond, Jean-Baptiste, then dropped a goal to secure a victory which was hard fought and showed that Russian enthusiasm at club level is of the highest standard.

The team then flew to Moscow to play CIS. In a tense finish the visitors just lost an exciting match in which the Russian forward strength and ability to move the ball throughout the team was of a higher standard than anticipated. Ruari Maclean and Andy Robinson captained the teams on the tour and were ably supported by all their players.

Another memorable season brought down the curtain on further centenary celebrations, the memories of which will be relished for many years to come.

RESULTS 1991-92

Played 8   Won 6   Lost 1   Drawn 1   Points for 292   (54T 4PG 32C)
Points against 229   (24T 8PG 3DG 15C)
1991

7 Sept	**Drew with Scotland** at Murrayfield 16 (2G 1T) to 16 (1G 2PG 1T)
10 Sept	**Beat Cork Constitution** at Templehill 39 (4G 1PG 3T) to 9 (1G 1PG)
12 Sept	**Lost to Old Wesley** at Donnybrook, Dublin 36 (4G 3T) to 37 (4G 1PG 2DG 1T)
6 Nov	**Beat Newport** at Rodney Parade 39 (4G 1PG 3T) to 10 (1G 1T)
27 Dec	**Beat Leicester** at Welford Road 29 (3G 1PG 2T) to 21 (2G 3PG)
1992	
11 Mar	**Beat East Midlands** at Franklins Gardens, Northampton 52 (8G 1T) to 29 (3G 1DG 2T)
18 Apr	**Beat Cardiff** at Cardiff Arms Park 26 (3G 2T) to 25 (1G 1PG 4T)
20 Apr	**Beat Swansea** at St Helens 55 (4G 1PG 7T) to 12 (2G)
4-5 Apr	**Cathay Pacific-Hong Kong Bank Sevens** Government Stadium, Hong Kong **Pool E:** Barbarians 36, Kwang-Hua Taipei 0; Barbarians 22, Romania 0 **Quarter-finals** Barbarians 10 Korea 16

PLAYERS 1991-92

Abbreviations: *S* – Scotland; *CC* – Cork Constitution; *OW* – Old Wesley; *N* – Newport; *L* – Leicester; *EM* – East Midlands; *SW1* – Cardiff; *SW2* – Swansea; *HK* – Hong Kong Sevens; (R) – Replacement; * – New Barbarian

Full-backs: *A J Joubert (Old Greys & South Africa) [*S, CC, HK*]; *E Blanc (Racing Club de France & France) [*S in centre*, *OW*]; I Hunter (Northampton) [*N, CC & OW on wing, HK*]; S Blanco (Biarritz & France) [*L*]; *D Pears (Harlequins & England) [*N at fly-half, EM*]

Threequarters: A T Harriman (Harlequins & England) [*S, CC*]; *S Pierce (North Shore) [*S, CC, OW*]; T Underwood (Cambridge University) [*S, OW*]; *Q E Daniels (Cape Town Police & WP) [*S*(R), *OW*]; *J Eagle (Harlequins) [*N*]; F Clough (Wasps) [*N*]; W L Renwick (London Scottish) [*N*]; *J- M Lafond (Racing Club de France) [*L*]; *P Sella (Agen & France) [*L*]; J C Guscott (Bath & England) [*L*]; J-B Lafond (Racing Club de France and France) [*L*]; *R Wallace (Garryowen & Ireland) [*EM*]; C Laity (Neath) [*EM*]; *R R W Maclean (Moseley) [*N, EM, SW1 at full-back, SW2*]; M H Titley (Swansea & Wales) [*EM*]; I Tukalo (Selkirk & Scotland) [*HK*]; A G Hastings (Watsonians & Scotland) [*HK*]; *S Davies (Swansea) [*HK*]; *A G Stanger (Hawick & Scotland) [*SW1, SW2*]; *H S Thorneycroft (Northampton) [*HK, SW1, SW2*]; *B Barley (Wakefield) [*SW1, SW2 at full-back*]; *H Woodland (Maesteg) [*SW1, SW2*]; S Thomas (Coventry) [*N*(R)]

Half-backs: S Barnes (Bath & England) [*S*]; *P Berbizier (Agen & France) [*S, OW*]; *C J Stephens (Llanelli) [*S*(R), *CC, OW, L*]; Rupert Moon (Llanelli) [*CC, L*]; Richard Moon (Rosslyn Park) [*N*]; *N Barry (Garryowen) [*EM*]; *M T Bradley (Cork Constitution & Ireland) [*EM*]; *A Nicol (Dundee HSFP & Scotland) [*HK*]; *A G Shiel (Melrose & Scotland) [*SW1, SW2*]; *G H Oliver (Hawick & Scotland) [*SW1, SW2*(R)]; S M Bates (Wasps) [*SW2*]

Forwards: *G R Kebble (Durban Collegians) [*S*]; *T A Lawton (Durban HSOB & Australia [*S*]; *E E Rodriguez (Warringah, Argentina & Australia) [*S, CC, OW*]; *A E D Macdonald (Heriot's FP) [*S, CC, OW, N*]; *A H Copsey (Llanelli) [*S, CC, OW*]; *W J Bartmann (Durban Harlequins & South Africa) [*S, CC*]; *K M Tapper (Enkopping & Sweden) [*S, CC*(R), *OW*]; E J Rush (Otahuhu) [*S, CC, OW*]; R G R Dawe (Bath & England) [*CC, OW, N*]; M R Lee (Bath) [*CC, OW, N*]; N A Back (Leicester) [*CC, SW2*]; *B Spillane (Bohemians) [*OW*]; M Linnett (Moseley & England) [*N, L, SW1, SW2*]; S Dear (Rosslyn Park) [*N, L, EM*]; *M Egan (London Irish) [*N*]; *P N Shillingford (Moseley) [*N*]; I Jones (Llanelli & Wales) [*N*]; *J Allan (Edinburgh Acads & Scotland) [*L*]; J A Probyn (Wasps & England) [*L, EM*]; P J Ackford (Harlequins & England) [*L*]; J Jeffrey (Kelso & Scotland) [*L*]; E M Lewis (Llanelli & Wales) [*L*]; R A Robinson (Bath & England) [*L*]; D M B Sole (Edinburgh Acads & Scotland) [*EM*];*A Lamerton (Llanelli) [*EM*]; *R Goodey (Pontypool) [*EM*]; R I Wainwright (Edinburgh Acads & Scotland) [*EM, HK*]; *A W Brooks (Rosslyn Park) [*EM*]; *C Huish (Pontypool) [*EM*]; *N Meek (Pontypool) [*SW1, SW2*(R)]; *T Hayashi (Oxford U & Japan) [*SW1, SW2*]; * M Bayfield (Northampton & England) [*SW1*]; *K Swords (Beacon Hill, Boston & USA) [*SW1, SW2*]; *J P Cassell (Saracens) [*HK, SW1*]; *G Ennis (Vancouver Kats & Canada) [*SW1, SW2*]; *I R Smith (Gloucester & Scotland) [*SW1, SW2*]; C J Hillman (South Wales Police) [*SW2*]; *M Johnson (Leicester) [*SW2*]

ENTERPRISE INITIATIVE FOR THE PERSEVERING LIGHT BLUES

THE VARSITY MATCH 1991
(for the Bowring Bowl)

10 December, Twickenham
Oxford University 11 (1DG 2T)
Cambridge University 17 (2PG 1DG 2T)

It was appropriate that a fiercely-contested match should not be settled until injury-time, since the most thrilling phase of the game was the final quarter – three tries came in the last seven minutes. Cambridge well deserved their success as they were the more enterprising team behind the scrum, but it took them a long time to prosper. On the hour, Oxford still led, thanks largely to the tremendous efforts of their front five, but the Light Blues eventually came out on top in the line-out to offset the scrummage pressure against them.

The first half produced only two scores, but it was nonetheless compelling rugby. Adrian Davies, the Cambridge captain whose kicking was generally superior to that of his opposite number, received quick ball from an early scrum and had time to drop a neat goal, but Oxford were soon in front, courtesy of confusion at the back of a scrum on the Cambridge line. Sheasby failed to control the ball, de Maid lost sight of it and the superb Fanie Du Toit touched down untroubled. Tapper missed the conversion, two awkward penalties and a snap shot at a dropped goal. It was not his afternoon.

Oxford pressed energetically at the start of the second half, but their only reward was a dropped goal by Nick Fitzwater, who collected a loose clearance by Adrian Davies and, with his left foot, sent a scruffy-looking kick to the target.

Cambridge regained control and kept it for the remainder of the match. Oxford started to fall offside and were punished by two Adrian Davies penalties, and Parton of Cambridge twice went close to the line but was foiled by superb tackles. Just when it seemed that kicks might win it for the Light Blues, Tony Underwood's dangerous running paid off when Sheasby's line-out catch and a dummy run by Parton left him with a chance to set his head back and outpace the defence to score in the corner.

Back came the Dark Blues for one final effort, and Du Toit sent Barclay in for a try in the corner, which the scrum-half failed to convert, leaving the last word to Cambridge and Adrian Davies. He feinted to drop at goal but sent Kevin Price through a tired defence to settle matters. Davies' missed conversion was irrelevant.

Once again, a capacity crowd had full value. Oxford did not have any dressing-room distractions this time, but must have rued the decision of full-back Audley Lumsden to play in a spurious sevens tournament during the term – he came back with a broken ankle. Without Lumsden, there was no one to spark the Oxford backs into any form of enterprising play, and nine-man rugby is seldom successful.

Andy Parton of Cambridge beats a path between Barclay and Fitzwater of Oxford during the Varsity Match, in which he could easily have scored two tries.

Oxford University: N Fitzwater (Skinners, Tunbridge Wells & Keble); C Henderson (Sherborne & St Catherine's), R Jones (Chepstow CS & Keble), K Street (King Henry VIII, Coventry & Christ Church), S Barclay (Olchfa CS, Swansea & St Catherine's); A Tapper (Abingdon & Exeter), F Du Toit (Paul Roos Gymnasium, South Africa & Christ Church); S Whiteside (Bridlington & Queen's), M Patton (Campbell College, Belfast & St Catherine's), A Everett (Michaelhouse, South Africa & University) *(capt)*, D Evans (Bro Myrddin CS, Carmarthen & St Anne's), P Thresher (Judd, Tonbridge & Worcester), R Pask (Blackwood & Keble), L Jones (RGS, Guildford & St Edmund Hall), A Milward (Purley HS & Templeton)
Scorers *Tries:* Du Toit, Barclay   *Dropped Goal:* Fitzwater
Cambridge University: A Parton (King Henry VII, Coventry & St Edmund's); R Given (Rugby & Jesus), L Davies (Pencoed CS & St Edmund's), K Price (Aberdare & St Edmund's), T Underwood (Barnard Castle & St Edmund's); A Davies (Pencoed CS & Robinson) *(capt)*, M de Maid (Lady Mary HS, Cardiff & Hughes Hall); B Davies (Brisbane Grammar, Australia & St Edmund's), B Gegg (Wimbledon College & Hughes Hall), M Chapple (Eastbourne & Trinity), M Duthie (Backwell & Queens'), D Dix (Shore, Sydney, Australia & Hughes Hall), E Peters (Brentwood & Hughes Hall), C Bates (Reigate GS & Magdalene), C Sheasby (Radley & Hughes Hall)
Scorers *Tries:* Underwood, Price   *Penalty Goals:* A Davies (2)   *Dropped goal:* A Davies
Referee J Fleming (Scotland)

10 December, Stoop Memorial Ground
Oxford University Under-21s 16 (2G 1T)   **Cambridge University Under-21s 19** (1G 3PG 1T)

Oxford University Under-21s: M Hutchings (St Hugh's); L Archard (New College), M Woodfine (St Edmund Hall), T Watson (St Edmund Hall), J Davies (St Catherine's); E Rayner (Oriel), J Leroy (Oriel); D Thompson (Oriel), A Solomon (Exeter), B Thurston (Brasenose), T Sykes (Christ Church), T Blower (St Peter's), T Leman (St Edmund Hall) *(capt)*, P Blackman (St Peter's), R Bhagobati (University)
Scorers *Tries:* Leroy, Davies, Watson   *Conversions:* Rayner (2)
Cambridge University Under-21s: R Davidson (Sidney Sussex); N Thompson (Emmanuel), C Thompson (Magdalene), M Allan (St John's), N Murphy (Emmanuel); A Boyd (Jesus), J Davies (Downing) *(capt)*; R Brown (Pembroke), T Keith-Roach (Jesus), P Callow (Fitzwilliam), T Dower (St John's), L Longstaff (Downing), A McCracken (Downing), H Jones (Caius), R Midgeley (Magdalene)
Scorers *Tries:* Jones, Midgeley   *Conversion:* Allen   *Penalty Goals:* Allen (3)
Referee A Spreadbury (Somerset)

4 December, Grange Road, Cambridge
Cambridge University LX Club 23 (2G 1PG 2T)   **Oxford University Greyhounds 0**

Cambridge University LX Club: D Macrae (St Catharine's); S Burns (Magdalene), D O'Leary (Caius), S Johnson (Magdalene), S Brammar (Emmanuel); A Boyd (Jesus), C Pring (Queens'); D Meirion-Jones (Magdalene), L Mair (Caius), R Wareham (Hughes Hall), M Duthie (Queens'), C Thomas (Hughes Hall) *(capt)*, R Jenkins (Downing), C Bates (Magdalene), P Davies (Churchill) *Replacements* L Medlock (Robinson) for Brammar (75 mins); J Davies (Downing) for Pring (80 mins)
Scorers *Tries:* Jenkins (2), Duthie, Thomas   *Conversions:* Johnson (2)   *Penalty Goal:* Johnson
Oxford University Greyhounds: A Butler (University) *(capt)*; J Watson (St John's), A Enthoven (St Peter's), I Richards (Wadham), R Sennitt (St Edmund Hall); E Egan (Jesus), G Fell (Hertford); S Whiteside (Queen's), M Humphreys (Brasenose), B Thurston (Brasenose), O Davies (Pembroke), I Jackson (St Anne's), M Merrick (Christchurch), L Jones (St Edmund Hall), P Siddell (Wycliffe Hall) *Replacements* A Solomon (Exeter) for Humphreys (64 mins); C Jones (University) for Fell (80 mins)
Referee E Houston (Hertfordshire)

6 November, Iffley Road, Oxford
Oxford University 36   Major Stanley's XV 14

27 November, Grange Road, Cambridge
Cambridge University 20   M R Steele-Bodger's XV 23

6 December, Grange Road, Cambridge
Cambridge University LX IIs 10   Oxford University Whippets 22

VARSITY MATCH RESULTS

110 Matches played   Oxford 47 wins   Cambridge 50 wins   13 Draws

*Match played at Oxford 1871-72; Cambridge 1872-73; The Oval 1873-74 to 1879-80; Blackheath 1880-81 to 1886-87; Queen's Club 1887-88 to 1920-21; then Twickenham. *At this date no match could be won unless a goal was scored.*

1871-72	**Oxford**	1G 1T to 0	1935-36	Drawn	No score
1872-73	**Cambridge**	1G 2T to 0	1936-37	**Cambridge**	2T (6) to 1G (5)
1873-74	Drawn	1T each	1937-38	**Oxford**	1G 4T (17) to 1DG (4)
1874-75*	Drawn	Oxford 2T to 0	1938-39	**Cambridge**	1G 1PG (8) to 2PG (6)
1875-76	**Oxford**	1T to 0	1939-45	*War-time series*	
1876-77	**Cambridge**	1G 2T to 0	1945-46	**Cambridge**	1G 2T (11) to 1G 1PG (8)
1877-78	**Oxford**	2T to 0	1946-47	**Oxford**	1G 1DG 2T (15) to 1G (5)
1878-79	Drawn	No score	1947-48	**Cambridge**	2PG (6) to 0
1879-80	**Cambridge**	1G 1DG to 1DG	1948-49	**Oxford**	1G 1DG 2T (14) to 1G 1PG (8)
1880-81	Drawn	1T each	1949-50	**Oxford**	1T (3) to 0
1881-82	**Oxford**	2G 1T to 1G	1950-51	**Oxford**	1G 1PG (8) to 0
1882-83	**Oxford**	1T to 0	1951-52	**Oxford**	2G 1T (13) to 0
1883-84	**Oxford**	3G 4T to 1G	1952-53	**Cambridge**	1PG 1T (6) to 1G (5)
1884-85	**Oxford**	3G 1T to 1T	1953-54	Drawn	Oxford 1PG 1T (6)
1885-86	**Cambridge**	2T to 0			Cambridge 2PG (6)
1886-87	**Cambridge**	3T to 0	1954-55	**Cambridge**	1PG(3) to 0
1887-88	**Cambridge**	1DG 2T to 0	1955-56	**Oxford**	1PG 2T (9) to 1G (5)
1888-89	**Cambridge**	1G 2T to 0	1956-57	**Cambridge**	1G 1PG 1DG 1T (14) to
1889-90	**Oxford**	1G 1T to 0			2PG 1T (9)
1890-91	Drawn	1G each	1957-58	**Oxford**	1T (3) to 0
1891-92	**Cambridge**	2T to 0	1958-59	**Cambridge**	1G 1PG 3T (17) to 1PG 1T (6)
1892-93	Drawn	No score	1959-60	**Oxford**	3PG (9) to 1PG (3)
1893-94	**Oxford**	1T to 0	1960-61	**Cambridge**	2G 1T (13) to 0
1894-95	Drawn	1G each	1961-62	**Cambridge**	1DG 2T (9) to 1DG (3)
1895-96	**Cambridge**	1G to 0	1962-63	**Cambridge**	1G 1PG 1DG 1T (14) to 0
1896-97	**Oxford**	1G 1DG to 1G 1T	1963-64	**Cambridge**	2G 1PG 2T (19) to
1897-98	**Oxford**	2T to 0			1G 1PG 1DG (11)
1898-99	**Cambridge**	1G 2T to 0	1964-65	**Oxford**	2G 1PG 2T (19) to 1PG 1GM (6)
1899-1900	**Cambridge**	2G 4T to 0	1965-66	Drawn	1G (5) each
1900-01	**Oxford**	2G to 1G 1T	1966-67	**Oxford**	1G 1T (8) to 1DG 1T (6)
1901-02	**Oxford**	1G 1T to 0	1967-68	**Cambridge**	1T 1PG (6) to 0
1902-03	Drawn	1G 1T each	1968-69	**Cambridge**	1T 1PG 1DG (9) to 2T (6)
1903-04	**Oxford**	3G 1T to 2G 1T	1969-70	**Oxford**	3PG (9) to 2PG (6)
1904-05	**Cambridge**	3G to 2G	1970-71	**Oxford**	1G 1DG 2T (14) to 1PG (3)
1905-06	**Cambridge**	3G (15) to 2G 1T (13)	1971-72	**Oxford**	3PG 3T (21) to 1PG (3)
1906-07	**Oxford**	4T (12) to 1G 1T (8)	1972-73	**Cambridge**	1G 1PG 1DG 1T (16) to
1907-08	**Oxford**	1G 4T (17) to 0			2PG (6)
1908-09	Drawn	1G (5) each	1973-74	**Cambridge**	1PG 1DG 2T (14) to
1909-10	**Oxford**	4G 5T (35) to 1T (3)			1G 2PG (12)
1910-11	**Oxford**	4G 1T (23) to 3G 1T (18)	1974-75	**Cambridge**	1G 2PG 1T (16) to 5PG (15)
1911-12	**Oxford**	2G 3T (19) to 0	1975-76	**Cambridge**	2G 5PG 1DG 1T (34) to
1912-13	**Cambridge**	2G (10) to 1T (3)			3PG 1DG (12)
1913-14	**Cambridge**	1DG 3T (13) to 1T (3)	1976-77	**Cambridge**	1G 3PG (15) to 0
1914-18	*No matches*		1977-78	**Oxford**	4PG 1T (16) to 2PG 1T (10)
1919-20	**Cambridge**	1PG 1DG (7) to 1G (5)	1978-79	**Cambridge**	2G 3PG 1T (25) to
1920-21	**Oxford**	1G 4T (17) to 1G 3T (14)			1PG 1T (7)
1921-22	**Oxford**	1G 2T (11) to 1G (5)	1979-80	**Oxford**	2PG 1DG (9) to 1PG (3)
1922-23	**Cambridge**	3G 2T (21) to 1G 1T (8)	1980-81	**Cambridge**	3PG 1T (13) to 3PG (9)
1923-24	**Cambridge**	3G 2T (21) to 1G 1PG 2T (14)	1981-82	**Cambridge**	3PG (9) to 2PG (6)
1924-25	**Oxford**	1G 2T (11) to 2T (6)	1982-83	**Cambridge**	3PG 1DG 2T (20) to
1925-26	**Cambridge**	3G 6T (33) to 1T (3)			1G 1PG 1T (13)
1926-27	**Cambridge**	3G 5T (30) to 1G (5)	1983-84	**Cambridge**	4PG 2T (20) to 3PG (9)
1927-28	**Cambridge**	2G 2PG 2T (22) to 1G 3T (14)	1984-85	**Cambridge**	4G 2T (32) to 2PG (6)
1928-29	**Cambridge**	1G 3T (14) to	1985-86	**Oxford**	1PG 1T (7) to 2PG (6)
		1PG 1DG 1T (10)	1986-87	**Oxford**	3PG 2DG (15) to 1PG 1DG 1T (10)
1929-30	**Oxford**	1G 1DG (9) to 0	1987-88	**Cambridge**	1DG 3T (15) to 2PG 1T (10)
1930-31	Drawn	Oxford 1PG (3)	1988-89	**Oxford**	2G 1DG 3T (27) to 1DG 1T (7)
		Cambridge 1T (3)	1989-90	**Cambridge**	2G 2PG 1T (22) to
1931-32	**Oxford**	1DG 2T (10) to 1T (3)			1G 1PG 1T (13)
1932-33	**Oxford**	1G 1T (8) to 1T (3)	1990-91	**Oxford**	2G 2PG 1DG (21) to 1G 2PG (12)
1933-34	**Oxford**	1G (5) to 1T (3)	1991-92	**Cambridge**	2PG 1DG 2T (17) to
1934-35	**Cambridge**	2G 1PG 1DG 4T (29) to			1DG 2T (11)
		1DG (4)			

THE WAR-TIME MATCHES

1939-40	**Oxford**	1G 1DG 2T (15) to			1G 1T (8) (at Oxford)
		1T (3) (at Cambridge)	1942-43	**Cambridge**	1G 1DG (9) to 0 (at Oxford)
	Cambridge	1G 3T (14) to		**Cambridge**	2G 2T (16) to
		2G 1T (13) (at Oxford)			1T (3) (at Cambridge)
1940-41	**Cambridge**	1G 2T (11) to	1943-44	**Cambridge**	2G 1T (13) to
		1G 1DG (9) (at Oxford)			1DG (4) (at Cambridge)
	Cambridge	2G 1T (13) to 0		**Oxford**	2T (6) to 1G (5)
		(at Cambridge)			(at Oxford)
1941-42	**Cambridge**	1PG 2T (9) to	1944-45	Drawn	1T (3) each (at Oxford)
		1PG 1T (6) (at Cambridge)		**Cambridge**	2G 2T (16) to
	Cambridge	1G 2PG 2T (17) to			1DG (4) (at Cambridge)

OXFORD and CAMBRIDGE BLUES 1872-1991

(Each year indicates a separate appearance, and refers to the first half of the season. Thus 1879 refers to the match played in the 1879-80 season.) (R) indicates an appearance as a Replacement.

OXFORD

Kennedy, W D	1904	MacLachlan, L P	1953	Owen-Smith, H G O	1932-33
Kent, C P	1972-73-74-75	Maclachlan, N	1879-80		
Kent, P C	1970	Macmillan, M	1876	Page, H V	1884-85
Kershaw, F	1898-99-1900-01	McNeill, A	1884	Painter, P A	1967
Key, K J	1885-86	MacNeill, H P	1982-83-84	Palmer, M S	1960
Kindersley, R S	1882-83	McPartlin, J J	1960-61-62	Parker, L	1905
King, B B H	1963	Macpherson, G P S	1922-23-24	Parker, T	1888
King, P E	1975	Macpherson, N M S	1928	Parkin, W H	1890
King, T W	1929	McQuaid, A S J	1983	Pask, R A	1991
Kininmonth, P W	1947-48	McShane, J M S	1933-35	Paterson, A M	1889-90
Kirk, D E	1987-88	Maddock, W P	1972	Paterson, L R	1886-87
Kitson, J A	1895	Mallalieu, J P W	1927	Patterson, A R	1879-80-81
Kittermaster, H J	1922-24	Mallett, N V H	1979	Patton, M B	1991
Kitto, R C M	1884-85-86-87	Marshall, H P	1921	Payne, C M	1960
Knight, R L	1879	Marshall, R M	1936-37-38	Peacock, M B	1880
Knott, F H	1910-11-12-13	Martin, H	1907-08-09	Peacock, M F	1932-33
Koe, A P	1886	Marvin, T G R	1984-85	Peacock, N C	1987
Kyrke, G V	1902-03	Mather, E G S	1933	Peake, H W	1871
Kyrke-Smith, P St L		Maxwell-Hyslop, J E	1920-21-22	Pearce, J K	1945
	1973-74-75(R)	Mayhew, P K	1937	Pearson, S B	1983-84-85
		Mead, B D	1972-73	Pearson, T S	1871
Lagden, R O	1909-10-11	Meadows, H J	1948	Peat, W H	1898
Laidlaw, C R	1968-69	Merivale, G M	1874	Peck, A Q	1981
Lamb, R H	1962-63-64	Merriam, L P B	1913	Pennington, H H	1937-38
Lamport, N K	1930-31-32	Michell, A T	1871-72-73-74	Percival, L J	1889-91
Landale, D F	1925-26	Millerchip, C J	1981-82	Percy, H R G	1936-38
Lane, R O B	1887-88-89	Mills, D J	1983-84	Pether, S	1938
Langley, P J	1949	Milton, N W	1905-06-07	Phillips, C	1876-77-78-79
Latham, H E	1907	Milward, A W	1991	Phillips, E L	1933
Latter, A	1892	Minns, P C	1930-31-32	Phillips, L R L	1984
Law, A F	1875	Mitchell, M D	1977	Phillips, M S	1956-57-58-59
Lawrence, W S	1954-56	Moberly, W O	1871-72-73	Phillips, P C	1938
Lawrie, A A	1903-05	Moir, M J P	1977	Phillips, R H	1966-67-68
Lawton, T	1921-22-23	Molohan, M J B	1928	Pienaar, J H	1933-34-35
Lee, F H	1874-75-76-77	Moloney, R J	1990	Pitman, I J	1921
Lee, J W	1973-74	Monteath, J G	1912	Plant, W I	1958
Lee, R J	1972	Montgomery, J R	1958	Pleydell-Bouverie, Hon B	1923
Legge, D	1897	Moorcroft, E K	1966	Plumbridge, R A	1954-55-56
Lennox-Cook, J M	1945	Moore, A P	1990	Podmore, G	1872
Leslie, C F H	1880-81	Moore, E J	1882-83	Pollard, D	1952
Leslie, R E	1954	Moore, H B	1912-13	Poole, F O	1891-92-93-94
Leslie-Jones, F A	1894-95-96	Moore, H R	1956	Poulton, R W	1909-10-11
Lewin, A J A	1962-63	Moore, P B C	1945-46	Prescott, A E C	1928
Lewis, A K	1888	Moresby-White, J M	1913-19	Prescott, R E	1932
Lewis, D J	1950	Morgan, A K	1963-64	Preston, B W	1925
Lewis, S M	1973	Morgan, D J	1979	Price, H L	1920-21
Light, B	1977	Morgan, F	1888	Price, V R	1919-20-21
Lindsay, G C	1882-83-84-85	Morgan, R de R	1983	Pritchard, N S M	1985(R)
Littlechild, E J F	1972	Morris, E G	1904	Prodger, J A	1955
Littlewood, R B	1893	Morrison, W E A	1979-80		
Lloyd, E A	1964-65-66	Mortimer, L	1892	Quinnen, P N	1974-75
Lloyd, J E	1872-74	Moubray, J J	1876-77-78	Quist-Arcton, E A K	1978-79
Lloyd, R	1908	Muller, H	1938		
Lombard, L T	1956-57-58	Mullin, B J	1986-87	Rahmatallah, F J	1976
Longdon, J S	1889	Mullins, R C	1894	Ramsay, A W	1952-53
Lorraine, H D B	1932-33-34	Mulvey, R S	1968	Ramsden, J E	1945
Loudoun-Shand, E G	1913-19	Munro, P	1903-04-05	Raphael, J E	1901-02-03-04
Love, R D	1972	Murray, G C	1959	Rashleigh, W	1887-88
Low, R C S	1933			Ravenscroft, J	1877-78
Luce, F M	1899-1900	Nash, E H	1874-75	Raymond, R L	1924
Luddington, R S	1980-81-82	Nelson, T A	1897-98	Rayner-Wood, A C	1895-96
Lusty, W	1927	Nesbitt, J V	1904-05	Read, R F	1965
Luyt, R E	1938	Neser, V H	1919-20	Reed, D K	1984
Lyle, A M P	1902-04-05	Neville, T B	1971-72	Reeler, I L	1955-56
		Newman, A P	1973	Rees, H	1930
McBain, N S	1986-87	Newman, S C	1946-47	Rees, H J V	1913
McCanlis, M A	1926-27	Newton, H F	1895-96-97	Rees, P S	1974-75-78
McClure, R N	1973	Newton, P A	1879-80	Rees-Jones, G R	1933-34-35
Macdonald, C P	1985-86	Newton-Thompson, J O	1945-46	Reid, C J	1896
Macdonald, D A	1975-76	Nicholas, P L	1897-98-99	Reid, G A	1935-36
Macdonald, D S M	1974-75-76	Nicholson, E S	1931-32-33-34	Reid, N	1912-13
Macdonald, G E	1922	North, E G H	1888-89-90	Renwick, W N	1936-37
Macdonald, N L	1926	Norwitz, E R	1988-89-90	Rice-Evans, W	1890
Macdonald, N W	1984-85	Novis, A L	1932	Richards, C A L	1932
MacEwen, G L	1895	Nunn, J A	1925-26	Richards, S B	1962
McFarland, P R E	1967			Richardson, J V	1925
MacGibbon, R R	1930-31	Obolensky, A	1935-37	Richardson, W R	1881
McGlashan, J R C	1945	O'Brien, T S	1983-84	Rigby, J P	1955-56
McGrath, N F	1934-35-36	O'Connor, A	1958	Rimmer, L I	1958
MacGregor, A	1871	Odgers, W B	1901-02	Risman, J M	1984-85-86
Mackenzie, A O M	1880-81	Orpen, L J J	1898	Rittson-Thomas, G C	1949-50
Mackenzie, D W	1974	Osborn, E C	1969	Robbins, P G D	1954-55-56-57
Mackenzie, F J C	1882-83	Osborne, S H	1900-01-02	Roberts, D G	1990
Mackintosh, C E W C	1925	Osler, S G	1931	Roberts, G D	1907-08

CAMBRIDGE

Aarvold, C D	1925-26-27-28	Boggon, R P	1956	Coghlan, G B	1926-27-28
Ackford, P J	1979	Bole, E	1945-46-47	Cohen, A S	1922
Adams, G C A	1929	Bonham-Carter, J	1873	Colbourne, G L	1883
Adams, H F S	1884-85	Booth, A H	1989-90	Coley, M	1964
Agnew, C M	1875-76	Bordass, J H	1923-24	Collett, G F	1898
Agnew, G W	1871-72-73	Borthwick, T J L	1985	Collier, R B	1960-61
Agnew, W L	1876-77-78	Boughton-Leigh, C E W	1878	Collin, T	1871
Albright, G S	1877	Boulding, P V	1975-76	Collins, W O H	1931
Alderson, F H R	1887-88	Bowcott, H M	1927-28	Collis, W R F	1919-20
Alexander, E P	1884-85-86	Bowcott, J E	1933	Collison, L H	1930
Alexander, J W	1905-06	Bowen, R W	1968	Combe, P H	1984-85
Allan, C J	1962	Bowhill, J W	1888-89	Considine, W C D	1919
Allan, J L F	1956	Bowman, J H	1933-34	Conway, G S	1919-20-21
Allchurch, T J	1980-81	Boyd, C W	1909	Cook, D D B	1920-21
Allen, A D	1925-26-27	Boyd-Moss, R J	1980-81-82	Cook, S	1920-21
Allen, D B	1975	Brandram, R A	1896	Cooke, S J	1981
Allen, J	1875-76	Brash, J C	1959-60-61	Cooper, H S	1881
Anderson, W T	1931-32	Brathwaite, G A	1934	Cooper, P T	1927-28
Andrew, C R	1982-83-84	Breakey, J N F	1974-75(R)-77	Cope, W	1891
Anthony, A J	1967	Bree-Frink, F C	1888-89-90	Corry, T M	1966
Archer, G M D	1950-51	Briggs, P D	1962	Cosh, N J	1966
Arthur, T G	1962	Bromet, E	1887-88	Covell, G A B	1949
Ashcroft, A H	1908-09	Brook, P W P	1928-29-30-31	Cove-Smith, R	1919-20-21
Ashford, C L	1929	Brookstein, R	1969	Cox, F L	1879
Ashworth, J	1988-89	Brooman, R J	1977-78	Craig, H J	1891
Askew, J G	1929-30-31	Browell, H H	1877-78	Craigmile, H W C	1920
Asquith, J P K	1953	Brown, A C	1920-21	Crichton-Miller, D	1928
Aston, R L	1889-90	Brown, S L	1975-76	Crothers, G	1977(R)
Atkinson, M L	1908-09	Browning, O C	1934	Crow, W A M	1961-62
Attfield, S J W	1982-84	Bruce Lockhart, J H	1910	Cullen, J C	1980-81-82
		Bruce Lockhart, L	1945-46	Cumberlege, B S	1910-11-12-13
Back, F F	1871-72	Bruce Lockhart, R B	1937-38	Cumberlege, R F	1897
Bailey, G H	1931	Brutton, E B	1883-85-86	Cumming, D C	1922-23-24
Bailey, M D	1982-83-84-85	Bryant, S S	1988	Currie, W C	1905
Bailey, R C	1982-83	Bryce, R D H	1965	Cushing, A	1986
Balding, I A	1961	Bull, H A	1874-75		
Balfour, A	1896-97	Bunting, W L	1894-95	Dalgleish, K J	1951-52-53
Bance, J F	1945	Burt-Marshall, J	1905	Dalton, E R	1872-73-74
Bannerman, C M	1990	Burton, B C	1882-83	Dalton, W L T	1875-76
Barker, R E	1966	Bush, J D	1983	Daniell, J	1898-99-1900
Barlow, C S	1923-24-25-26	Bussey, W M	1960-61-62	Darby, A J L	1896-97-98
Barlow, R M M	1925	Butler, E T	1976-77-78	Darch, W J	1875
Barrow, C	1950	Buzza, A J	1988-89	David, P W	1983
Barter, A F	1954-55-56			Davies, A	1988-89-90-91
Bartlett, R M	1951	Cake, J J	1988	Davies, B P	1991
Bateman-Champain, P J C	1937	Campbell, D A	1936	Davies, G	1988-89
Bates, C S	1991	Campbell, H H	1946	Davies, G	1948-49-50
Batten, J M	1871-72-73-74	Campbell, J A	1897-98-99	Davies, G H	1980-81
Batty, P A	1919-20	Campbell, J D	1927	Davies, H J	1958
Baxter, R	1871-72-73	Campbell, J W	1973-74	Davies, J C	1949
Baxter, W H B	1912-13	Campbell, R C C	1907	Davies, J S	1977
Bealey, R J	1874	Candler, P L	1934	Davies, L	1991
Beard, P L	1987	Cangley, B T G	1946	Davies, P M	1952-53-54
Bearne, K R F	1957-58-59	Carey, G V	1907-08	Davies, T G R	1968-69-70
Beazley, T A G	1971	Carpmael, W P	1885	Davies, W G	1946-47
Bedell-Sivright, D R		Carris, H E	1929	Deakin, J E	1871
	1899-1900-01-02	Carter, C P	1965	Delafield, G E	1932
Bedell-Sivright, JV		Cave, J W	1887-88	De Maid, M W	1991
	1900-01-02-03	Cave, W T C	1902-03-04	De Nobriga, A P	1948
Beer, I D S	1952-53-54	Chadwick, W O	1936-37-38	De Villiers, D I	1913
Bell, D S	1989	Chalmers, P S	1979	Devitt, Sir T G	1923-24-25
Bell, R W	1897-98-99	Chambers, E L	1904	Dewhurst, J H	1885-86
Bell, S P	1894-95-96	Chapman, C E	1881-84	Dick, R C S	1933
Bennett, G M	1897-98	Chapman, E S	1879-80	Dickins, J P	1972-73
Bennett, N J	1981	Chapman, G M	1907-08-09	Dickson, J W	1881
Benthall, E C	1912	Chapman, J M	1873	Dinwiddy, H P	1934-35
Beringer, F R	1951-52	Chapple, M A	1991	Dix, D P A	1991
Beringer, G G	1975-76	Chilcott, E W	1883	Dixon, A M	1928
Berman, J V	1966	Child, H H	1875-76	Dixon, C	1894
Berry, S P	1971	Clarke, B D F	1978	Dods, M	1938
Bevan, G A J	1951	Clarke, S J S	1962-63	Doherty, H D	1950
Bevan, J A	1877-80	Clayton, H R	1876-77-78	Doherty, W D	1913
Bevan, W	1887	Clayton, J R W	1971	Don Wauchope, A R	1880-81
Biddell, C W	1980-81	Clements, J W	1953-54-55	Dorward, A F	1947-48-49
Biggar, M A	1971	Clifford, P H	1876-77-78	Douglas, E A	1882-83-84
Bird, D R J	1958-59	Clough, F J	1984-85-86-87	Douglas, R N	1891
Birdwood, C R B	1932	Coates, C H	1877-78-79	Douty, P S	1924
Bishop, C C	1925	Coates, V H M	1907	Dovey, B A	1960
Black, M A	1897-98	Cobby, W	1900	Downes, K D	1936-37-38
Blair, P C B	1910-11-12-13	Cock, T A	1899	Downey, W J	1954-55-56-57
Blake, W H	1875	Cocks, F W	1935	Doyle, M G	1965

Lewthwaithe, W	1872-73
Lillington, P M	1981-82
Lindsay, P A R	1937-38
Linnecar, R J D	1970
Lintott, T M R	1974
Lister, R C	1969
Lloyd-Davies, R H	1947
Lord, J R C	1933-34-35
Lord, M	1960
Lord, T M	1986
Loveday, B R	1956-57
Low, J D	1935-36-37
Lowden, G S	1945
Lowe, C N	1911-12-13
Lowry, R H W	1923
Loxdale, J W	1874
Lucas, P M	1882
Luscombe, R P	1871-72-73-74
Lushington, A J	1872
Luxmoore, A F C C	1896-97
Lyon, C E	1871
Lyon, D W	1967-68
McAfee, L A	1910
McClung, T	1954
McCosh, E	1910
McCosh, R	1905-06-07
MacDonald, A	1871
Macdonald, A	1989
MacDonald, J A	1936-37
MacDonnell, J C	1889
MacEwen, D L	1887
MacEwen, R K G	1953-54
McGahey, A M J	1979-80-81
McGown, T M W	1896
MacGregor, G	1889-90
McIlwaine, G A	1926-27-28
Mackenzie, W G B	1922
McKenzie, M R	1968
Mackie, O G	1895-96-97
Macklin, A J	1979-80-82
Maclay, J P	1920
MacLeod, K G	1905-06-07-08
MacLeod, L M	1903-04-05
Macleod, W M	1880-82
McMorris, L	1963
MacMyn, D J	1921-22-23-24
McNeill, A H	1902-03
McRoberts, T S	1946-47-48
MacSweeney, D A	1957-58-59
Mainprice, H	1902-03-04-05
Makin, R L	1959
Malik, N A	1975
Mann, F T	1910
Marburg, C L H	1909-10
Margerison, R	1871-72-73
Marques, R W D	1954-55-56-57
Marr, D M	1929-30-31-32
Marr, T C K	1945
Marriott, C J B	1881-82-83
Marsden, E W	1950
Marshall, T R	1950
Martin, A W	1983-84
Martin, N O	1965-66-67
Martin, S A	1961-62-63
Massey, D G	1952-53
Massey, M J O	1951-52-53
Maxwell, D M W	1922
Mayfield, E	1891
Maynard, A F	1912-13
Mayne, W N	1888
Mellor, J E	1906
Melluish, R K	1922
Metcalfe, I R	1978-79
Methuen, C J	1886-87-88
Michaelson, R C B	1960-61-62
Michell, W G	1873-75-76
Middlemas, P	1912
Miliffe, M J	1964
Millard, D E S	1956
Miller, J L H	1920
Mills, D C	1958
Mills, H H	1947-48
Mills, P R	1958-59
Milne, C J B	1882-83-84
Mitchell, F	1893-94-95
Mitchell, W G	1886
Monahan, J D	1967-68
Monro, A H	1973
Monteith, H G	1903-04-05
Montgomery, R	1891
Moon, R H Q B	1984
Moore, A W	1874
Moore, P J de A	1947-48
Morel, T E	1920-22
Morgan, H P	1952-53
Morgan, W G	1926-27-28-29
Moriarty, S P	1980
Morpeth, G	1925
Morrison, B J	1965
Morrison, I R	1983-84
Morrison, P H	1887-88-89-90
Morse, E St J	1871
Mortimer, W	1895-96
Morton, H J S	1908
Moyes, J L	1974-75
Mulligan, A A	1955-56-57
Murray, R A	1982
Murray, R O	1933-34
Napier, Hon M F	1871
Neild, W C	1911-12
Neilson, H	1884
Neilson, W	1891-92-93
Nelson, W E	1892
Newbold, C J	1902-03
Newman, C H	1882
Newton-Thompson, C L	1937-38
Nicholl, C B	1890-91-92-93
Nixon, P J L	1976
O'Brien, T S	1981-82
O'Callaghan, C	1978
O'Callaghan, J J	1989-90
O'Callaghan, M W	1974-75-76-77
O'Leary, S T	1984-85
Odgers, F W	1901
Ogilvy, F J L	1887
Onyett, P S	1966-67
Orr, J C S	1891
Orr-Ewing, D	1919
Oswald, G B R	1945
Oti, C	1986-87
Oulton, E V	1901
Ovens, A B	1910-11
Owen, A V	1945
Owen, J E	1961
Page, J J	1968-69-70
Page, R S	1972-73
Palmer, H R	1899
Parker, G W	1932-33-34-35
Parr, M F	1978
Parry, T R	1936-37-38
Parsons, J	1938
Parton, A R	1990-91
Pater, S	1880-81
Paterson-Brown, T	1983
Patterson, H W T	1890
Patterson, W M	1956
Pattisson, R M	1881-82
Payne, J H	1879
Payne, O V	1900
Pearce, D	1873-74
Pearson, T C	1952-53
Peck, I G	1979
Pender, A R	1963
Penny, W M	1906
Perry, D G	1958
Perry, S V	1946-47
Peters, E W	1991
Phillips, G P	1971-72
Phillips, J H L	1930-32
Phillips, R J	1964
Pienaar, L L	1911
Pierce, D J	1985(R)
Pilkington, L E	1893-94
Pilkington, W N	1896-97
Pinkham, C	1910
Pitt, T G	1905-06
Plews, W J	1884
Pool-Jones, R J	1989-90
Pope, E B	1932
Powell, P	1900
Pratt, S R G	1973-74
Price, K L	1991
Price, P R	1967
Pringle, A S	1897-98
Pringle, J S	1902
Prosser-Harries, A	1957
Pumphrey, C E	1902
Purves, W D C L	1907-08-09
Pyman, F C	1907-08
Rae, A J	1901
Raffle, N C G	1954-55
Raikes, W A	1872-74
Raine, J B	1947
Rainforth, J J	1958-59
Ramsay, A R	1930
Ransome, H F	1882-83-84
Rawlence, J R	1935-36
Raybould, W H	1966
Redmond, G F	1969-70-71
Reed, E D E	1937
Reed, P N	1989-90
Rees, A M	1933-34
Rees, B I	1963-64-65-66
Rees, G	1972-73
Rees, J I	1931-32
Reeve, P B	1950-51
Reid, J L P	1932
Rendall, H D	1892-93
Reynolds, E P	1909
Rice, E	1880-81
Richards, T B	1955
Richardson, W P	1883
Rigby, J C A	1889-90
Riley, H	1871-72-73
Risman, M A	1987(R)
Ritchie, W T	1903-04
Robbie, J C	1977-78
Roberts, A F	1901-02
Roberts, A J R	1901-02
Roberts, J	1952-53-54
Roberts, J	1927-28
Roberts, S N J	1983
Robertson, A J	1990
Robertson, D D	1892
Robertson, I	1967
Robinson, A	1886-87
Robinson, B F	1891-92-93
Robinson, J J	1892
Robinson, N J	1990
Robinson, P J	1962
Rocyn-Jones, D N	1923
Roden, W H	1936-37
Rodgers, A K	1968-69-70
Roffey, D B	1874-75
Rose, H	1872
Rose, W M H	1979-80-81
Rosser, D W A	1962-63-64
Rosser, M F	1972-73
Ross-Skinner, W M	1924
Rotherham, A	1890-91
Rottenburg, H	1898
Rowell, W I	1890
Ryan, C J	1966
Ryan, P H	1952-53
Ryder, D C D	1921-23
Sagar, J W	1899-1900
Salmon, W B	1883
Sample, C H	1882-83-84
Sample, H W	1884
Sanderson, A B	1901
Saunders-Jacobs, S M	1929
Saville, C D	1967-68-69-70
Sawyer, B T C	1910
Saxon, K R J	1919-21
Scholfield, J A	1909-10
Schwarz, R O	1893

Name	Date	Name	Date	Name	Date
Scotland, K J F	1958-59-60	Symington, A W	1911-12-13	Walker, R M	1963
Scott, A W	1945-48	Synge, J S	1927	Walkey, J R	1902
Scott, C T	1899			Wallace, W M	1912-13
Scott, J M	1927	Tait, J G	1880-82	Waller, G S	1932
Scott, M T	1885-86-87	Talbot, S C	1900	Wallis, H T	1895-96
Scott, R R F	1957	Tallent, J A	1929-30-31	Ward, R O C	1903
Scott, W B	1923-24	Tanner, C C	1930	Ware, C H	1882
Scott, W M	1888	Tarrant, J M	1990	Warfield, P J	1974
Scoular, J G	1905-06	Tarsh, D N	1955	Warlow, S	1972-74
Seddon, E R H	1921	Taylor, A S	1879-80-81	Waters, F H	1927-28-29
Shackleton, I R	1968-69-70	Warlow, S	1972-74	Waters, J B	1902-03-04
Shaw, P A V	1977	Taylor, D G	1982	Watherston, J G	1931
Sheasby, C M A	1990-91	Taylor, H B J	1894-96	Watson, C F K	1919-20
Shepherd, J K	1950	Taylor, W J	1926	Watt, J R	1970
Sherrard, P	1938	Templer, J L	1881-82	Webb, G K M	1964-65
Shipsides, J	1970	Thomas, B E	1960-61-62	Webster, A P	1971
Shirer, J A	1885	Thomas, D R	1972-73-74	Wells, C M	1891-92
Silk, D R W	1953-54	Thomas, H W	1912	Wells, T U	1951
Sim, R G	1966-67	Thomas, J	1945	Weston, M T	1958-59-60
Simms, K G	1983-84-85	Thomas, M D C	1986-87	Wheeler, P J F	1951-52-53
Simms, N J	1989	Thomas, N B	1966	White, J B	1922
Simpson, C P	1890	Thomas, R C C	1949	White, W N	1947
Simpson, F W	1930-31	Thomas, T J	1895-96	Whiteway, S E A	1893
Sisson, J P	1871	Thomas, W H	1886-87	Wiggins, C E M	1928
Skinner, R C O	1970-71	Thompson, M J M	1950	Wiggins, C M	1964
Slater, K J P	1964	Thompson, R	1890	Wilby, J B	1989
Smallwood, A M	1919	Thompson, R V	1948-49	Wilkinson, R M	1971-72-73
Smeddle, R W	1928-29-30-31	Thorman, W H	1890	Will, J G	1911-12-13
Smith, A F	1873-74	Thorne, C	1911	Williams, A G	1926-27
Smith, A R	1954-55-56-57	Thornton, J F	1976-78-79	Williams, C C U	1950
Smith, H K P	1920	Threlfall, R	1881-83	Williams, C H	1930
Smith, H Y L	1878-79-80-81	Timmons, F J	1983	Williams, C R	1971-72-73
Smith, J	1889	Todd, A F	1893-94-95	Williams, D B	1973
Smith, J J E	1926	Todd, T	1888	Williams, E J H	1946
Smith, J M	1972	Topping, N P	1986-87	Williams, H A	1876
Smith, J V	1948-49-50	Touzel, C J C	1874-75-76	Williams, J M	1949
Smith, K P	1919	Tredwell, J R	1968	Williams, L T	1874-75
Smith, M A	1966-67	Trethewy, A	1888	Williams, N E	1950
Smith, P K	1970	Trubshaw, A R	1919	Williams, P T	1888-89
Smith, S R	1958-59	Tucker, W E	1892-93-94	Williamson, I S	1972
Smith, S T	1982-83	Tucker, W E	1922-23-24-25	Williamson, P R	1984
Sobey, W H	1925-26	Tudsbery, F C T	1907-08	Willis, H	1949-50-51
Spencer, J S	1967-68-69	Tunningley, A J	1988(R)	Wilson, A H	1911-12-13
Spicer, N	1901-02	Turnbull, B R	1924-25	Wilson, C P	1877-78-79-80
Spray, K A N	1946-47	Turner, J A	1956	Wilton, C W	1936
Sprot, A	1871	Turner, J M P C	1985	Winthrop, W Y	1871
Stauton, H	1891	Turner, M F	1946	Wintle, T C	1960-61
Stead, R J	1977	Tyler, R H	1978-79-80	Withyman, T A	1985-86
Steeds, J H	1938			Wood, G E	1974-75-76
Steel, D Q	1877	Umbers, R H	1954	Wood, G E C	1919
Steele, H K	1970	Underwood, T	1990-91	Woodall, B J C	1951
Steele, J T	1879-80	Ure, C McG	1911	Woodroffe, O P	1952
Steele-Bodger, M R	1945-46			Woods, S M J	1888-89-90
Stevenson, H J	1977(R)-79	Valentine, G E	1930	Wooller, W	1933-34-35
Stevenson, L E	1884-85	Van Schalkwijk, J	1906	Wordley, S A	1988-89
Steward, R	1875-76	Vaughan, G P	1949	Wordsworth, A J	1973-75
Stewart, A A	1975-76	Vaux, J G	1957	Wotherspoon, W	1888-89
Stewart, J R	1935	Vickerstaff, M	1988	Wrench, D F B	1960
Stileman, W M C	1985	Vincent, C A	1913	Wright, C C G	1907-08
Stokes, R R	1921	Vivian, J M	1976	Wrigley, P T	1877-78-79-80
Stone, R J	1901	Vyvyan, C B	1987-88	Wyles, K T	1985-86
Storey, E	1878-79-80	Wace, H	1873-74	Wynne, E H	1887
Storey, L H T	1909	Waddell, G H	1958-60-61		
Storey, T W P	1889-90-91-92	Wade, M R	1958-59-60-61	Yetts, R M	1879-80-81
Stothard, N A	1979	Wainwright, J F	1956	Young, A B S	1919-20
Style, H B	1921	Wainwright, M A	1980	Young, A T	1922-23-24
Surtees, A A	1886	Wainwright, R I	1986-87-88	Young, J S	1935
Sutherland, J F	1908	Wakefield, W W	1921-22	Young, J V	1906
Sutton, A J	1987-88	Walker, A W	1929-30	Young, P D	1949
Swanson, J C	1938	Walker, D R	1980-81	Young, S K	1974
Swayne, F G	1884-85-86	Walker, E E	1899-1900	Young, W B	1935-36-37

VARSITY MATCH REFEREES

(From 1881, when referees first officiated at the match. Prior to this date, the match was controlled by a pair of umpires elected by the Universities.) Each year indicates a separate appearance, and refers to the first half of the season. Thus 1881 refers to the match played in the 1881-82 season.

Allan, M A	1933-34	Freethy, A E	1923-25-27-29-31-32	Norling, C	1977-78-81-88-89
Ashmore, H L	1891-92-93-95-96	Gadney, C H	1935-36-37-38-45-47	Pattinson, K A	1974
Bean, A S	1948-49	Gillespie, J I	1905	Potter-Irwin, F C	1909-11-13-19
Bolton, W N	1882	Harnett, G H		Prideaux, L	1984
Boundy, L M	1958		1897-98-99-1900-01-02	Quittenton, R C	1985-87
Burnett, D I H	1980-82	Hill, G R	1883-84-86-87-88-89-90	Sanson, N R	1976
Burrell, R P	1963	Hosie, A M	1979	Sturrock, J C	1921
Clark, K H	1973	Howard, F A	1986	Taylor, H H	1881
Cooper, Dr P F	1951-53	Jeffares, R W	1930	Titcombe, M H	1969
Crawford, S H	1920	John, K S	1956-67	Trigg, J A F	1983
Currey, F I	1885	Johnson, R F	1972	Vile, T H	1922-24-26-28
Dallas, J D	1910-12	Jones, T	1950	Walters, D G	
D'Arcy, D P	1968	Lamb, Air Cdre G C	1970		1957-60-61-62-64-65-66
David, I	1954-55	Lambert, N H	1946	Welsby, A	1975
Doyle, O E	1990	Lawrence, Capt H D	1894	Williams, R C	1959
Evans, G	1907	Lewis, R	1971	Williams, T	1903
Findlay, J C	1904-08	Marsh, F W	1906		
Fleming, J M	1991	Murdoch, W C W	1952		

MAJOR STRUCTURAL CHANGES

RUGBY IN THE STUDENT SECTOR 1991-92
Harry Townsend

The new Further and Higher Education Act, which took effect in May, will have repercussions in student rugby which at the moment are little understood or appreciated. At present it is all surmise and conjecture, but in essence, Polytechnics, Colleges and Institutes of Higher Education can now opt for University status, which would make them eligible to take part in UAU competitions.

Early in May, only Charing Cross/Westminster Hospital and two Polytechnics had definitely applied for UAU membership, although West London Institute (formerly Borough Road College) also seemed likely members.

However, a mass increase of membership could cause vast rescheduling problems in the UAU competition. The combining of the three current student sport bodies (UAU, BPSA and Colleges) would diminish opportunities for representative rugby as each currently has its own team from which players progress to the national Students team. The unification of all Institutes of Higher Education, which would make regional and Divisional teams a far less tasty carrot on the way to the national Students team, could become an unwieldy organisation.

It is even more likely that, faced with the better organised set-up in most current universities, many smaller IHEs would go to the wall as far as rugby is concerned, and the already rocky Student Leagues might be pressurised out of existence in the light of the new 'improved' UAU competition (will it still be sponsored by Commercial Union, who have pumped £450,000 sponsorship into UAU sport over the past three years?).

The BPSA and Colleges organisations will continue to exist for a further 12 months with only minimal membership change while negotiations take place, but after that, who knows? It will certainly mean hard work for the Development Officer recently appointed to the Students Division, an 'enabling' rather than a coaching appointment, intended initially as a three-year assignment and probably as secondment from Higher Education.

This would certainly see the new student body through its teething stages, sort out the competitive aspects of student rugby and advise on the organisation necessary within the enormous number of member IHEs where lack of continuity has been responsible for the often low esteem in which many are held by non-student clubs.

Money from the Wavell Wakefield Trust, made available this year for the Student League which ground to a stuttering anti-climax through bad weather, rearranged representative fixtures and a resultant fixture build-up, will, one hopes, provide a little help with this.

Student League finalists Crewe and Alsager, winners of Division 1

North, had beaten Division 1 South runners-up Southampton University in one semi-final, but South winners West London Institute were precluded by prior calls from taking the field in the other against North runners-up Liverpool University. Ironically, West London Institute were themselves innocent victims of the unprecedented postponement of the Colleges Cup final until 7 October 1992 because late calls from Wales Under-21s deprived their opponents, Cardiff Institute, of seven players.

Representative matches: Newfoundland President's XV 15, England Students 20; Ontario 12, England Students 10; Rugby Canada 13, England Students 6; Saskatchewan 6, England Students 49; Alberta 13, England Students 28; British Columbia President's XV 10, England Students 24 (all played on Canada tour, August 1991); England Students 0, England XV 35 (Cambridge U); Oxford U 13, Scotland Students 19 (Iffley Road); Scotland U-21s 28, Scotland Students 23 (Murrayfield); Scotland Students 9, England Students 32 (Myreside, Edinburgh); France Students 22, England Students 9 (Ramonville); England Students 25, Wales Students 16 (Newbury); England Students 28, Ireland Students 19 (Blundellsands); Scotland Students 9, France Students 22 (Meggetland); Wales Students 14, Scotland Students 9 (Llanelli); Wales Students 6, France Students 26 (Swansea); Ireland Students 23, Scotland Students 22 (Dublin); England Students U-21s 16, Scotland U-21s 19 (Newcastle); England Students U-21s 27, Combined Students U-21s 4 (Twickenham); England Students U-21s 9, Anglo-Irish U-21s 20 (London Irish); Cork Constitution 23, Irish Universities 9 (Cork); Irish Universities 43, Welsh Universities 6 (Trinity, Dublin); English Universities 26, Irish Universities 11 (London Welsh); French Universities 43, Irish Universities 9 (Nancy); Scottish Universities 7, English Universities 15 (Peffermill, Edinburgh); English Universities 30, Welsh Universities 13 (Bristol); Welsh Universities 13, Scottish Universities 14 (Llanrumney); British Polytechnics (BPSA) 4, Public School Wanderers 54 (London Welsh); British Colleges 13, BPSA 9 (Stourbridge); BPSA 16, UAU 16 (Morley)

COMMERCIAL UNION UAU CHAMPIONSHIP 1991-92

18 March, Twickenham
Loughborough University 34 (3G 4T)
Durham University 10 (1G 1T)

The final brought together the two teams which, for the past ten seasons, have set the standards for university rugby. Durham have won the title three times and Loughborough six in this period, interrupted only last year by University College Cardiff, who were dismissed this season by Durham, 12-10, in the play-off round. Even the swirling Twickenham wind and persistent drizzle could not upset an imperious Loughborough. Bigger, stronger and more adept than gallant Durham, they dominated the set scrums and line-outs, where Welsh Under-21s lock Derwyn Jones and Tony Diprose (London and South-East Under-21s) provided a rock solid platform for Miles and Irish Under-21s fly-half Malone, the general of the final.

Loughborough ground efficiently to a 14-0 half-time lead before threatening to cut loose in the second half of what could have become a one-sided final but for the sheer dogged persistence of Durham. Possession under pressure never allowed Durham to dictate at any time, and the Loughborough back row nipped their every attack in the bud. Loughborough also found time to snap up the first five tries through Middleton (2), Nigel Richardson (2) and Murchison as this predatory trio hunted voraciously over the Twickenham turf.

Happily, Durham were rewarded for their gritty defence, particularly that of No 8 Ben Richardson and their tireless centre and captain, Nick Canning, with two tries in two minutes to cut back a 28-0 deficit five minutes from time. First, Lancashire Under-21s fly-half Greenwood sent replacement hooker Steiger over in the corner; then a drastically misplaced restart allowed wing Parks to sprint 60 metres, to rapturous applause, for a try converted by Greenwood.

But Loughborough did not even allow them the luxury of the last word. Wing Nicholson put Durham in their place with a last-minute try converted by Malone, who had glided through for the previous try.

Loughborough University: C Dosset (*capt*); M Nicholson, M Dawson, T Sanderson, M Wiseheart; N Malone, P Miles; D Lockyer, A Read, N Lowton, A Diprose, D Jones, K Middleton, N Richardson, E Murchison
Scorers *Tries:* Middleton (2), Richardson (2), Murchison, Malone, Nicholson
Conversions: Malone (3)
Durham University: R Walters; J Yeldham, M Yeabsley, N Canning (*capt*), W Parks; W Greenwood, N Coulter; B Fennell, J Hamilton-Smith, C Stamford, D Sibson, D Horsley, A Kane, N Keller, B Richardson *Replacements* C Steiger for Hamilton-Smith; D Pullen for Sibson
Scorers *Tries:* Steiger, Parks   *Conversion:* Greenwood
Referee E F Morrison (Bristol)

Loughborough have won the title 24 times, Durham 8, Liverpool and Swansea 7, Bristol 5, Cardiff and Manchester 4, Bangor and UWIST 2, Aberystwyth, Birmingham, Leeds and Newcastle once each.

Second XV final: Loughborough 10, Durham 6
Third XV final: Loughborough 15, Nottingham 7

1992 was so nearly the year of the underdog, Southampton going down 12-3 only in the quarter-finals to Loughborough as their first Commercial Union UAU semi-final beckoned. Imperial, who had overwhelmed Reading (themselves 10-9 conquerors of strongly-favoured Exeter) by 32-0, defeated Surrey 20-3 with two penalty tries from attempted push-overs and a push-over try in their quarter-final. They then lost to Durham 12-7 in their first-ever semi-final after a try by wing Fleming had given them a 4-0 interval lead. Durham had beaten current champions Cardiff 12-10 in the play-off round before overcoming neighbours Newcastle by 26-13.

Bristol clung on to the vestiges of their 15-0 half-time lead to beat Swansea, finalists for the previous four seasons, 15-13 in their quarter-final. They then gave Loughborough anxious moments in the other semi-final, despite the absence of England Students scrum-half Bracken. Their small pack, led by No 8 Seecharan, gained a wind-assisted 10-9 half-time lead which was overturned 21-13 through lack of set-piece possession and the precision kicking of Loughborough's Malone.

DIVISIONAL RESULTS
The top four teams of each Group go forward to the Play-off Round

Southern Division

SOUTH-WEST GROUP

	P	W	D	L	F	A	Pts
Bristol	4	4	0	0	126	45	8
Bath	4	3	0	1	72	20	6
Exeter	4	2	0	2	54	53	4
Southampton	4	1	0	3	45	56	2
Cranfield	4	0	0	4	27	150	0

SOUTH CENTRAL GROUP

	P	W	D	L	F	A	Pts
Imperial	4	3	0	1	109	23	6
Reading	4	3	0	1	86	32	6
RHBNC	4	2	0	2	36	43	4
Brunel	4	1	0	3	50	98	2
Kings	4	1	0	3	27	112	2

SOUTH-EAST NORTH

	P	W	D	L	F	A	Pts
UCL	3	3	0	0	45	16	6
Essex	3	2	0	1	50	22	4
East Anglia	3	1	0	2	32	61	2
OMWC	3	0	0	3	30	58	0

SOUTH-EAST SOUTH

	P	W	D	L	F	A	Pts
Surrey	4	4	0	0	109	40	8
Kent	4	3	0	1	86	28	6
City	4	2	0	2	81	28	4
LSE	4	1	0	3	39	108	2
Sussex	4	0	0	4	33	96	0

Northern Division

NORTH-EAST GROUP

	P	W	D	L	F	A	Pts
Newcastle	4	3	0	1	113	53	6
Durham	4	3	0	1	91	33	6
Sheffield	4	3	0	1	91	63	6
Hull	4	1	0	3	49	104	2
Leeds	4	0	0	4	39	130	0

NORTH-WEST GROUP

	P	W	D	L	F	A	Pts
Liverpool	6	5	0	1	137	34	10
Keele	6	5	0	1	117	58	10
Manchester	6	4	0	2	105	50	8
Bradford	6	4	0	2	110	71	8
Salford	6	2	0	4	57	135	4
Lancaster	6	1	0	5	44	120	2
UMIST	6	0	0	6	47	149	0

Welsh Division

	P	W	D	L	F	A	Pts
UC Swansea	4	4	0	0	119	32	8
UWCM	4	3	0	1	79	42	6
UWCC	4	2	0	2	63	41	4
UC Aberyst	4	1	0	3	52	121	2
UCNW	4	0	0	4	22	94	0

Midlands Division

	P	W	D	L	F	A	Pts
Loughboro'	4	4	0	0	183	40	8
Nottingham	4	3	0	1	87	59	6
Birmingham	4	2	0	2	68	100	4
Warwick	4	1	0	3	70	108	2
Leicester	4	0	0	4	43	144	0

Play-off Round: Newcastle 50, Aberystwyth 9; UWCM 9, Birmingham 21; Surrey 48, QMWC 0; Kent 12, RHBNC 3; Liverpool 41, Hull 0; Durham 12, UWCC 10; Imperial 78, LSE 9; Reading 10, Exeter 9; UCL 0, Southampton 9; Nottingham 6, Manchester 3; Loughborough 66, Brunel 12; Keele 4, Sheffield 20; UC Swansea 44, Bradford 0; Essex 14, City 6; Bristol 60, Warwick 0; Bath 52, UEA 3

Challenge Round: Newcastle 26, Birmingham 19; Surrey 7, Kent 0; Liverpool 7, Durham 19; Imperial 32, Reading 0; Southampton 26, Nottingham 3; Loughborough w/o Sheffield; UC Swansea 38, Essex 14; Bristol 26, Bath 10

Quarter-finals: Southampton 3, Loughborough 12; Imperial 20, Surrey 3; UC Swansea 13, Bristol 15; Newcastle 13, Durham 26

Semi-finals: Loughborough 21, Bristol 13 (Worcester); Imperial 7, Durham 12 (Nottingham)

COMMERCIAL UNION UAU Seven-a-side Tournament
8 March 1992, Southampton University
Quarter-finals: Kent 12, UCL 20; York 4, Liverpool 16; UWCC (Cardiff) 4, Exeter 24, Bath 6, Bristol 16
Semi-finals: UCL 14, Liverpool 0; Exeter 6, Bristol 32
Final: Bristol 34, UCL 6
Plate final: Leeds 14, Manchester 0

COMMERCIAL UNION UAU INTER-DIVISIONAL CHAMPIONSHIPS
6 January 1992, Nottingham RUFC
Semi-finals: South 22, North 8; Midlands 40, Wales 0
Third place: North 39, Wales 0
Final: South 10, Midlands 0

BRITISH POLYTECHNICS CUP 1992

11 March 1992, Nottingham RFC
Sheffield Polytechnic 16 (3PG 1DG 1T)
Newcastle Polytechnic 6 (1G)

England Students half-backs Gregory (Sheffield) and Douglas (Newcastle and England B) were conspicuous by their absence as both Polytechnics laudably stuck by their regular teams for what could be the last BPSA Cup competition for the Denis Binns Memorial Challenge Trophy – many Institutes of Higher Education will consider opting for University status next season. Newcastle had dismissed nine-times winner Polytechnic of Wales 25-16 in one semi-final, while Sheffield, materially assisted by 21 points from wing Gallagher, had beaten Plymouth-based Polytechnic of the South-West, from the same small group as Wales, 28-4.

The strong Newcastle pack threatened to dominate in the early stages, and shortly before half-time they scored a push-over try touched down by Scotland Students scrum-half Burnett and converted by Medhurst. But BPSA fly-half Hill kept Sheffield in the game with a 45-yard penalty goal shortly after the restart, and replacement wing Andy Vanstone, who earlier that afternoon had collected a Second XV Cup-winner's medal, showed that fairy tales do come true when he touched down the vital try after 54 minutes to give Sheffield a lead that they never looked like surrendering. Hill used the strong breeze to maximum advantage, adding two further penalties and a dropped goal to clinch the title for Sheffield for the second time in three years as Newcastle finished a well-beaten team.

Sheffield Polytechnic: S Judds; M Gallagher, J Baxendale, S Slater, M Leppard (*capt*); D Hill, A Hanson; J McKechnie, B Ludlam, R Moss, G Davies, R Doran, M Winfield, A Morris, M Pinder *Replacement* A Vanstone for Gallagher
Scorers *Try:* Vanstone *Penalty Goals:* Hill (3) *Dropped Goal:* Hill
Newcastle Polytechnic: R Smith; R Allen, R Wharton, P Nicholls, T Penn; B Medhurst, K Burnett; S Bowen, T Gregory, R Morley, P Smith, S Gibbs (*capt*), J Ayton, D Blyth, S Owen
Scorers *Try:* Burnett *Conversion:* Medhurst
Referee E F Morrison (Bristol)

First round proper: Newcastle 7, Leeds 0; Liverpool w/o Leicester; Wales w/o Hatfield; Brighton 15, Thames 7; Central 23, South Bank 7; Oxford 15, South-West 21; Coventry 3, Manchester 25; Sheffield 19, Humberside 6

Quarter-finals: Sheffield 14, Manchester 6; Newcastle 34, Liverpool 6; Wales 13, Brighton 6; South-West 29, Central 4

Semi-finals: Sheffield 28, South-West 4 (Stafford RFC); Newcastle 25, Wales 16 (Keele University)

Second XV final: Sheffield 11, Newcastle 7 (Nottingham RFC)
Third XV final: Sheffield 13, Staffordshire 10 (Nottingham RFC)

BRITISH COLLEGES TOURNAMENT
20-26 April 1992, Isle of Man
Welsh Colleges 41, English Colleges 9; Irish Colleges 37, International Selection 19; English Colleges 15, International Selection 0; Welsh Colleges 17, Irish Colleges 3; Welsh Colleges 40, International Selection 0; Irish Colleges 20, English Colleges 8; British Colleges 10, Isle of Man 4 (Douglas)

HOSPITALS' CHALLENGE CUP

Victor Swain *Daily Telegraph*

4 March, Old Deer Park
St Mary's Hospital 49 (5G 1PG 4T)   UCH/Middlesex 0

Invincible St Mary's produced their finest form, combining forward power play and scintillating attacking skills, and swept aside first-time finalists University College Hospital/Middlesex in the 105th final of the Cup. They equalled and created records in the process. St Mary's' 31st victory overtook Guy's' long-standing record of 30 wins. Their sixth successive victory became the longest winning sequence of the competition and their points total matched their own highest in a final. Richard Wintle, who with Philip Mitchell has appeared in all six finals, took his try-scoring total to 18 in 19 Cup matches.

Middlesex had no answer to St Mary's' all-round strength, speed and Cup-contesting experience. The most they were able to do was to battle grimly in the set-pieces and cover and tackle, which at least cut off a handful of try-scoring moves. They were handicapped by the loss of full-back Davis early on and prop Hayes soon after the interval.

St Mary's made their intentions clear from the start. Tries from one of Walters' frequent sorties into the line and from a powerful thrust by Morgan, plus a penalty and a conversion by fly-half Butland, put them 13 points up in as many minutes. Often running the ball from their own 22, St Mary's added tries through Hunt, Mitchell and Wintle, and two further conversions from Butland established a 29-0 half-time lead. More tries came from Torkington, Mitchell, Kelly and Boos, the latter, a brilliant effort from their own goal-line in which backs and forwards handled at speed, being the best of the game. The huge touch-finding and steady place-kicking of Butland, who collected 13 points, has been an invaluable asset to St Mary's.

St Mary's: J Walters; C Boos, A Morgan, A Field, R Wintle; R Butland, C Wright; N Hunt, L O'Hara, D Vaughan, P Mitchell, P Tooze-Hobson, J Torkington, C Langrish (*capt*), S Kelly
Scorers *Tries:* Mitchell (2), Walters, Morgan, Wintle, Hunt, Torkington, Boos, Kelly
Conversions: Butland (5)   *Penalty Goal:* Butland
UCH/Middlesex: C Davis; A Farquharson (*capt*), S Brownleader, N Cullen, C Mallucci; N Giles, D Penny; D Hayes, P Whitlock, R Russell, J Hyde, C Bevan, D Cheetham, R Griffiths, M Motamed *Replacements* F Haddad for Davis (15 mins); R Steeds for Hayes (55 mins)
Referee R C Quittenton (London Society)

First Round: King's 3, Charing Cross/Westminster 30; St Bartholomew's 21, St Thomas's 7
Second Round: Charing Cross/Westminster 9, St Mary's 25; Royal Free 13, UCH/Middlesex 21; St George's 0, Guy's 31; St Bartholomew's 4, The London 13
Semi-finals: St Mary's 47, Guy's 4; UCH/Middlesex 10, The London 7
St Mary's have won the cup 31 times, Guy's 30, St Thomas's 17, The London 11, St Bartholomew's 9, St George's and Westminster 3 times each and Middlesex once.

ARMY'S CHANCE SLIPS AWAY
THE SERVICES 1991-92
John Mace *Daily Telegraph*

Inter-Services Tournament

The Inter-Services tournament ended in the ninth triple tie of the competition, the first since 1984. Having lost to the Army in the opening match, the Royal Navy made four changes in their team to play the reigning champions, the RAF. The side responded by registering their first tournament victory since 1987. In the final match the Army, needing only a draw to win the competition outright, were well beaten by the RAF, who showed they had learned from their mistakes against the Navy.

21 March, Twickenham
Royal Navy 9 (1G 1PG)   **Army 16** (2G 1T)
for the Willis/Corroon Trophy

The Army belied the indifferent form they had shown in their warm-up matches and produced a spirited and enterprising display to record an unexpected victory over a more favoured Royal Navy side. They deserved to win because their forwards absorbed a sustained onslaught from a strong Navy pack and their backs were more fluent and inventive.

With line-outs and scrums even, the Navy had to rely on the rucks and mauls for possession. However, although their forwards had the better of these, they often retained the ball too long and denied their backs the space and time. The Army worked hard to create overlaps and scored good tries through Bartliff, Fenn and Wood.

Royal Navy: POMEA K Bethwaite (HMS Neptune); AB(S) S Sibson (HMS Cumberland), Lt C Alcock (HMS Ark Royal) (*capt*), Mne G O'Loughlin (RM Poole), LS L Oman (HMS Illustrious); Sub Lt R Perkins (BRNC), L Cpl P Livingstone (RM Plymouth); Capt M Dunham (CTCRM), POPT M Clay (HMS Cornwall), POAEA E Cowie (RNAS Yeovilton), AEM M Leatherland (HMS Osprey), Cpl S French (CTCRM), LPT I Russell (SNONI), POPT S Jones (BRNC), L Cpl R Armstrong (Cdo Log)
Replacement LPT I Torpey (HMS Temeraire) for Livingstone
Scorers *Try:* Sibson   *Conversion:* Bethwaite   *Penalty Goal:* Bethwaite
Army: Capt M Walker (RAMC); Cpl S Bartliff (R Signals), 2 Lt H Graham (RA), Lt W Bramble (RA), Lt J Fenn (RCT); Lt A Deans (RAEC), Lt S Pinder (DWR); Sgt D Coghlan (RHA), Bdr C Woods (RHA), L Bdr J Fowers (RHA), Lt D Orr Ewing (BW), Lt C Buss (DWR), 2 Lt T Rodber (Green Howards), Capt G Richardson (RS) (*capt*), L Sgt S Berryman (Coldm Gds) *Replacement* Lt S Butt (RRW) for Richardson
Scorers *Tries:* Bartliff, Fenn, Wood   *Conversions:* Walker (2)
Referee E Morrison (Gloucestershire Society)

28 March, Twickenham
Royal Navy 22 (3G 1T)   **Royal Air Force 13** (1G 1PG 1T)
for the Windsor Life Challenge Trophy

An excellent team performance, orchestrated by their captain, Chris Alcock, and founded on a vintage contribution from their forwards, carried the Navy to a well-deserved victory over the RAF. The Navy back row, in which Armstrong was outstanding, were influential throughout the game, and although the RAF won parity in the tight and line-outs they were annihilated in the loose and unable to win any quality ball for their dangerous backs. Furthermore, the airmen handicapped their cause by lapses of concentration and an inability to retain possession.

Three of the Navy's tries came from all-consuming forward surges and were scored by Trench (two) and Dunham. Perkins added the other following a long individual run.

Royal Navy: POMEA K Bethwaite (HMS Neptune); Sub Lt A Kellett (RNEC Manadon), Lt S Phillips (DNR Manchester), Lt C Alcock (HMS Ark Royal) (*capt*), LS L Oman (HMS Illustrious); Sub Lt R Perkins (BRNC), Sub Lt C Read (RAF Linton on Ouse); Capt M Dunham (CTCRM), POPT M Clay (HMS Cornwall), POAEA E Cowie (RNAS Yeovilton), Cpl S Trench (CTCRM), LPT I Russell (SNONI), Sgt M Hewitt (CTCRM), POPT S Jones (BRNC), L Cpl R Armstrong (Cdo Log)

Scorers *Tries:* Dunham, Perkins, Trench (2) *Conversions:* Bethwaite (3)

Royal Air Force: Cpl S Lazenby (Brize Norton); SAC S Crossland (Locking), SAC G Sharp (Benson), Cpl S Roke (St Athan), Flt Lt R Underwood (Wyton); Cpl P Hull (Locking), Sgt S Worrall (Cottesmore) (*capt*); Sgt D Robson (Odiham), Sgt S Collins (Innsworth), Cpl A Billett (St Athan), Sgt B Richardson (Rudloe Manor), Cpl A Nisbet (High Wycombe), Cpl C Morgan (Wildenrath), Fg Off D Williams (Brize Norton), Cpl D Parsonage (Wildenrath) *Replacement* Jnr Tech B Williams (Brize Norton) for Billett

Scorers *Tries:* Parsonage, Underwood *Conversion:* Hull *Penalty Goal:* Hull

Referee C J Higham (Manchester Society)

11 April, Twickenham
Army 6 (2PG)   Royal Air Force 18 (1G 4PG)
for the Windsor Life Challenge Cup

The RAF's greater discipline, plus the efficiency of their back row and the all-round kicking ability of fly-half Paul Hull, laid the foundations of their victory in the crucial final match. The Army's ball retention was poor and they were never able to develop a rhythm and so they missed a wonderful chance of taking the tournament outright. They also committed too many infringements, and Hull capitalised on this failing with some long pressure-relieving kicks and four penalty goals from six attempts for the RAF.

The RAF pack denied the Army forwards quick possession and their flankers, Morgan and Williams, made life very difficult for the Army half-backs. Worrall provided a smooth link with his backs, but Underwood and his colleagues were unable to pierce a determined Army defence. The game's only try came when loose-head prop Robson forced his way over from close range for Hull to convert. On several occasions the Army forwards exposed a certain frailty in the RAF's defence around the fringes and their backs also created some chances, but too often the soldiers dropped a critical pass or took a wrong option.

Despite all their efforts they managed only to score two long-range penalty goals, both kicked by Walker.

Army: Capt M Walker (RAMC); Cpl S Bartliff (R Signals), 2 Lt H Graham (RA), Lt W Bramble (RA), Lt J Fenn (RCT); Lt A Deans (RAEC), Lt S Pinder (DWR); Sgt D Coghlan (RHA), Bdr C Woods (RHA), L Bdr J Fowers (RHA), Lt D Orr Ewing (BW), Capt R Castleton (ACC), Capt R Wainwright (RAMC), Capt G Richardson (RS) (*capt*), L Sgt S Berryman (Coldm Gds) *Replacement* Cpl D Williams (RRW) for Pinder
Scorer *Penalty Goals:* Walker (2)

Royal Air Force: Cpl S Lazenby (Brize Norton); SAC S Crossland (Locking), SAC G Sharp (Benson), Cpl M Cooke (Laarbruch), Flt Lt R Underwood (Wyton); Cpl P Hull (Locking), Sgt S Worrall (Cottesmore) (*capt*); Sgt D Robson (Odiham), Sgt S Collins (Innsworth), Cpl A Billett (St Athan), Sgt B Richardson (Rudloe Manor), Cpl A Nisbet (High Wycombe), Cpl C Morgan (Wildenrath), Fg Off D Williams (Brize Norton), Cpl D Parsonage (Wildenrath)
Scorers *Try:* Robson *Conversion:* Hull *Penalty Goals:* Hull (4)
Referee L Prideaux (Cornwall Society)

Inter-Services Tournament Champions

The Army have won the Tournament outright 28 times, the Royal Navy 16 times and the Royal Air Force 12 times. The Army and the Royal Air Force have shared it on 2 occasions and there have been 9 triple ties.

1920 **RN**	1949 **Army and RAF**	1972 **Army**
1921 **RN**	1950 **Army**	1973 **RN**
1922 **RN**	1951 **RN**	1974 **RN**
1923 **RAF**	1952 **Army**	1975 Triple Tie
1924 Triple Tie	1953 **Army**	1976 **Army**
1925 **Army and RAF**	1954 Triple Tie	1977 **RN**
1926 **Army**	1955 **RAF**	1978 Triple Tie
1927 **RN**	1956 Triple Tie	1979 **RAF**
1928 **Army**	1957 **Army**	1980 **Army**
1929 **Army**	1958 **RAF**	1981 RN
1930 **Army**	1959 **RAF**	1982 **RAF**
1931 **RN**	1960 **Army**	1983 **Army**
1932 **Army**	1961 **RN**	1984 Triple Tie
1933 **Army**	1962 **RAF**	1985 **RAF**
1934 **Army**	1963 **Army**	1986 **RAF**
1935 Triple Tie	1964 **Army**	1987 **RN**
1936 **Army**	1965 **Army**	1988 **Army**
1937 **Army**	1966 **RN**	1989 **Army**
1938 **RN**	1967 **Army**	1990 **Army**
1939 **RN**	1968 **Army**	1991 **RAF**
1946 **Army**	1969 **Army**	1992 Triple Tie
1947 **RAF**	1970 **RN**	
1948 Triple Tie	1971 **RAF**	

Royal Navy v Army The Royal Navy have won 31, the Army 41, and 3 matches have been drawn (including matches before 1920) **Royal Navy v Royal Air Force** The Royal Navy have won 37, the Royal Air Force 26, and 4 matches have been drawn **Army v Royal Air Force** The Army have won 38, the Royal Air Force 21, and 8 matches have been drawn

Other Competitions

The Inter-Services Under-21 tournament finished in a triple tie while the Army won the Colts (Under-19) competition. In their only match of the season the Combined Services wrested the Securicor Trophy from the British Police.

The Royal Marines ruffled a few khaki feathers by winning Division 1 of the newly-instituted Army Inter-Corps Merit Table, having been invited to participate because of their long-standing fixtures with some of the senior corps.

HMS Nelson, the Portsmouth shore establishment, beat their Rosyth counterparts, HMS Cochrane, in the final of the Royal Navy Cup. The 7th Parachute Regiment Royal Horse Artillery won the Army Senior Units Cup for the third consecutive time and sixth in eight seasons; they also lifted the Army Sevens title. RAF Odiham won the Royal Air Force Inter-Station Cup for the first time and RAF Lyneham emerged as winners of the coveted Binbrook Bomb from a record entry of 70 teams in the Royal Air Force Sevens tournament.

Inter-Services Under-21 Tournament
Army 10, Royal Air Force 3; Royal Navy 15, Royal Air Force 19; Royal Navy 20, Army 3 **Result:** Triple tie

Inter-Services Colts (Under-19) Tournament
Royal Navy 4, Army 19; Royal Navy 8, Royal Air Force 21; Army 17, Royal Air Force 13 **Winners:** Army

Combined Services Matches
Senior: Combined Services 22, British Police 15 (*for the Securicor Trophy*)
Under-21: Combined Services 9, Anglo Scots 3; Combined Services 12, Harlequins 14; Combined Services 4, England Students 29; Combined Services 22, Rosendaal 0; Combined Services 0, Netherlands B 21
Colts (Under-19): Combined Services 10, Cardiff and District 10; Combined Services 6, Bridgend and District 21

Individual Service Competitions
ROYAL NAVY
Inter-Command Match: Royal Marines 23, Naval Air Command 10
Inter-Unit Cup: HMS Cochrane 9, HMS Nelson 13
ARMY
Inter Corps Merit Table: Division 1 Winners: Royal Marines **Division 2 Winners:** Royal Army Ordnance Corps **Division 3 Winners:** Army Corps of Physical Training
Major Units Cup: 1st Battalion Royal Welch Fusiliers 6, 7th Parachute Regiment Royal Horse Artillery 20
Minor Units Cup: Junior Leaders Regiment Royal Artillery 13, British Military Hospital Rinteln 0
Inter-Unit Sevens: Cup: 7th Parachute Regiment Royal Horse Artillery 18, 21 Signals Regiment 10 **Plate:** 1st Battalion Royal Welch Fusiliers 32, 2nd Battalion The Queen's Regiment 0
RAF
Inter-Command Matches: Strike Command 33, Support Command 7; Strike Command 20, RAF Germany 21; Support Command 16, RAF Germany 10; RAF Germany 0, BAOR 7
Inter-Station Cup: RAF Odiham
Inter-Station Shield: RAF Henlow
Inter-Station Sevens: Binbrook Bomb: RAF Lyneham **Plate:** RAF Rudloe Manor

ENGLAND TAKE THE FINAL STRIDE

SCHOOLS RUGBY 1991-92
Michael Stevenson

In the previous season England's capable 18 Group team had come unbeaten to Colwyn Bay for a match which would have earned them a Junior Grand Slam and Triple Crown. But they faltered against Wales after building a significant half-time lead, and Wales triumphed. There was no similar fallibility at Doncaster in April 1992. The sides met under similar circumstances, England unbeaten and Wales having lost narrowly to France, but England's superior power and organisation proved crucial, and they won 18-3. A reputation such as that of Neil Ryan, the England fly-half, can be hard to live up to. It is a real pleasure to record the excellence of his performance at Doncaster: he looked a class player in all he did.

Wales were certainly no pushover and, with wind advantage, they controlled most of the first half. Nevertheless, they trailed 3-6 at half-time. England's long-striding Greenstock had made a try for Ryan and tackled magnificently as well, and with the wind on their backs in the second half, England were soon in business, showing all the fanatical dedication that the donning of an English jersey seems to bring to its players these days. Robert Leach was the pick of a fine pack and the selection of a man of the match from Ryan, Greenstock and Leach would have been a ticklish problem. For Wales, Steffan Jones at full-back, Chris Loader and Ceri Thomas were outstanding, underlining the presence of some excellent players in the Welsh side.

The only game that England won really comfortably was against Scotland and, just before the final decider at Doncaster, they had really struggled to defeat a resilient, combative Irish side at Bedford. They made more errors in this contest than they could afford, but the lack of real scoring chances that Ireland created through their vigorous but perfectly fair style of play meant that the result, 15-9, was distinctly flattering to the losers.

England's victory over France at Billancourt, in an ill-tempered match, was a triumph of character. They won by four penalties by Jon Ufton to three for France from Richard Dourthé. The fact that Wales had lost at home to France suggested that comparative form, so often fickle, would forecast an England win in the final match.

Three defeats sustained by Scotland at 18 Group level were offset to some degree by a highly creditable win at Murrayfield against France (10-6), which was their first victory in this fixture since its inception. Generally Wales relied rather too heavily on the attacking flair of their talented half-back, Jason Hewlett. England tackled him out of the game and one was left wondering whether his mercurial talents might not flourish more successfully at fly-half than at scrum-half, where he played every game for Wales. In their four matches, Wales scored 39 points, of which Hewlett's contribution was 27.

Whatever the merits of their seniors, arguably the best rugby played by an England side during the past year was provided by the 16 Group in their record defeat of Italy at Luton. During the first half, which was played in appalling conditions of wind and driving rain, the standard of their handling was breathtaking on a day made for use of the boot rather than the hand. England have often had problems with Italy at this level, and their 32-4 win was based on a first half in which wonderful support play and accurate passing bewildered the visitors. The second half came as something of an anti-climax, but Matthew Knowles at full-back, Robert Ashworth at fly-half and Jeffrey Roberts, a mobile flanker, exuded talent and confidence.

England did not fare so well at Pontypridd, where they met Wales' 16 Group in an inaugural fixture, which will now be played annually. Wales eventually won 22-0 after an evenly-contested first half. Tries on the stroke of the interval by Gethin Watts and Robert Saddler, converted by Darren Morris, and second-half tries by replacement Nick Walne and Nathan Thomas saw Wales to victory. Wales also prospered at Under-15 level and recorded a good win (28-15) in Edinburgh against Scotland Under-15s. Youthful precocity was taken to remarkable limits by the Welsh fly-half, Lee Jarvis, who contributed 16 points from a dropped goal, three penalties and two conversions.

Solihull's wonderful run of success continued with their second successive unbeaten season (P17, W17) in which they scored 514 points to 84 conceded. They won well in the early matches against Warwick (12-4), King Edward's, Birmingham (28-6) and Nottingham HS (24-12), but one of their best wins and hardest games was against Loughborough GS, when they came back from an eight-point deficit to win 23-8. Solihull were without their captain, the Midlands centre Richard Chapman, for much of the season, but his Midlands colleague, Alex Brown, a flanker, did well in leading his young side.

There were some outstanding performances from the one-term schools and it would be hard to find a better record than that of Durham, who won all their 15 matches, scoring 495 points and conceding only 52 in the process. They scored 100 tries and had only five scored against them. For a relatively small school their strength in depth is especially commendable: their second team was also unbeaten. The First XV beat Ampleforth, Sedbergh and Rossall but probably played their best rugby in their 28-6 victory over RGS Newcastle.

Bedford won all 16 matches with a points tally of 372 scored to 80 conceded. They play on a very demanding circuit and must have been specially gratified by their 28-6 win against Haileybury and a 15-31 away victory over St Paul's. Andy Gomarsall, their captain, who also captained England 18 Group, No 8 Ben Wyer-Roberts and their solid prop, Alex Penn, were outstanding. Bedford were relieved to survive a tough contest against Uppingham, which they won 4-3. Clifton also have a tough fixture list and did splendidly to win all 11 matches, although they too were extended by their 'bogey' team, Taunton, whom they defeated 6-4. The best wins were against Blundell's (19-0), Downside (32-3), Sherborne (18-15), and Marlborough (19-4). Their captain and scrum-half, Richard Moffatt, played well and contributed significantly in what was essentially a team effort. In their Cup run, Bradford scored 296 points while conceding 29 and, at their best, as in a superb northern final against St Anselm's, showed themselves to be a well-organised and thoroughly formidable outfit. Their fast wing, Nick Miller, who represented England last season in the 16 Group, was unlucky not to force his way into contention for the 18 Group.

The final of the Under-15 Daily Mail Cup was a triumph for Skinner's School and the State Sector. They had beaten Rossall, whom many regarded as favourites, 14-8 in the semi-final and defeated London Oratory 19-6. The Bank of Scotland Cup final, held at Ayr's Millbrae ground, was a desperately close affair, Marr College snatching victory with two minutes to go through a try by Ian MacEwan. Earlier John Riddle had scored Marr's first try, although they still trailed 4-6 going into the closing stages, Richard Craig having kicked two penalties for St Aloysius.

In Wales, Neath College romped home in the final of the Sunday Express Under-19 Cup. They met Ysgol-y-Strade in a one-sided match, scoring eight tries in their 38-0 win. Strade never gave up and tackled superbly, but they were run off their feet, having trailed 26-0 at the interval. Neath's try-scorers included Appleyard (2), Nicky Stubbs, Darren Morris, Chris Loader and Steve Martin, who played so well for Wales 18 Group last season but failed to earn a place in the season just ended.

Probably the most prestigious Schools' Cup in the United Kingdom is the Ulster Bank Cup, contested this spring by Coleraine Academical Institute and Methodist College, Belfast, winners for the previous three years. Some scintillating rugby led to a 31-3 half-time lead for Coleraine, through a 25-minute period of total ascendancy which brought five tries, often created by their talented fly-half and captain, Darryl Callaghan. Full-back Jonathan Bell was, however, the outstanding player. A wonderful second-half rally saw Methodist pull back significantly, but the result was 35-21. It was Coleraine's ninth Schools' Cup success, but only their first since 1939. Remarkably, the final was watched by a crowd of 12,000.

Kelly College from the South-West enjoyed an excellent season: they won all 13 matches with a points record of 473 for to only 59 against. They were particularly pleased with their 12-3 victory over Plymouth College. Prop Guy Smart and fly-half Jonas Hurst excelled.

North of the Border, no school could match the excellence of Dollar Academy (P16, W16), who scored 666 points to 104 conceded. They concluded their season with an 18-12 victory over George Watson's, in which nerves and awareness of their remarkable record played a part. It was their first unbeaten season since records began in the 1870s. It is a measure of Dollar's pedigree that they should have defeated Merchiston Castle (14-21) away and Loretto (18-43). Merchiston had a distinctly good season (P18, W15, L3), scoring 558 points and conceding 154. Merchiston's captain and fly-half, Duncan Hodges, retained his place in the Scottish 18 Group side, as did his vice-captain, Craig Joiner, in the centre. Neil Dickson, their hooker, was on the bench. Loretto's record was similar, with 13 wins from 16 matches and a points tally of 304 scored to 147 conceded. Loretto especially enjoyed their hat-trick of wins against English schools Haileybury, Sedbergh and Millfield.

St Joseph's, Ipswich, met London Oratory in their final match, winning 29-0 and earning the enviable record of 18 wins from 18 matches with a points tally of 481 scored to 57 conceded. Perhaps their best wins were against Campion (9-6) and an astonishing 15-8 success against Essex 18 Group after St Joseph's had been asked to represent Suffolk 18 Group en bloc!

One school which may well have been a strong contender for the title of champion was Bradford GS. They lost just one match, 9-7 to QEGS Wakefield, in the absence of five first-choice backs. They scored 883 points to 113 against, won their own festival and those held at St Joseph's, Ipswich, and Headingley and crowned a marvellous season with a 30-12 victory over Mount St Mary's in the final of the Daily Mail Under-18 Cup.

Some might say that, like television quizzes, sevens tournaments have proliferated beyond the bounds of sense and logic, but the view would not find much sympathy in the Principality. Welsh schools have been amazingly dominant in the past season, which culminated in the Open Tournament at Rosslyn Park, where the final was contested by Llandovery College and Ysgol Glantaf from Cardiff. Previously, Monmouth had won the Stonyhurst Sevens, beating Silcoates in an entertaining final. Llandovery and Christ's College, Brecon were the losing semi-finalists. Christ's, Brecon won the Marches Sevens at Hereford, beating Millfield 10-4 in the final. Glantaf were successful in the Brecon tournament, registering a decisive win against Wellington College (Berks) in the final. Ysgol-y-Strade from Llanelli beat RGS Guildford decisively (36-12) in the final of the prestigious Oxford Sevens, having already won the Herefordshire Open Tournament. Ysgol Llanhari won the International Milk Sevens at Stradey Park, beating Radyr 18-6 in an excellent final.

And so to Rosslyn Park. The Festival Tournament, for one-term rugby schools, was won for the second time in succession by Wellington College, for whom Piers Michell was consistently excellent. Once again a Welsh side was to the fore: Christ's, Brecon were beaten 10-6 in a controversial final. Christ's had been 6-0 up through a try and conversion by their lively scrum-half, Lawicki. Immediately, Wellington's Cooksley kicked ahead around 40 metres out and was badly body-checked; the penalty try, which Michell converted, appeared to have been awarded before the kick by Cooksley went into touch. A late try by Macfarlane saw Wellington home.

Several teams managed to establish themselves as possible winners during the early stages of the Open Competition and, frankly, Llandovery were not all that high on most people's lists. But they kept getting better and better and thoroughly deserved their triumph in the end. In the semi-finals, Glantaf beat Mount St Mary's 12-8 and Llandovery saw off Bradford GS more convincingly (20-10). The final provided rugby of a high quality. Craig Quinnell helped to make the first Llandovery try, the first of two scored by Jeremy Griffiths. Pryce cut the lead with a try for Glantaf on the stroke of half-time. Second-half tries for the winners by Davies and Daniels followed, although Glantaf maintained the spirit to hit back with a second try by Pryce which Hewlett converted for a final score of 18-10.

A wonderful Prep Schools' final saw Sherborne recover from a 4-12 deficit to beat Oratory 16-12, their captain, Ralph Dorey, scoring the winning try. Sherborne have previously won at Rosslyn Park in 1959, 1964 and 1967, and on all four occasions they have been coached by their Headmaster, Robin Lindsay. The Junior Tournament was won by Dwr-y-Felin, who registered a narrow win (10-6) over St Benedict's in the final, having put out London Oratory in the semi-final; St Benedict's comfortably defeated Stamford by 24-6 in the other.

Durham, who had a wonderful season in the 15-a-side game, were equally successful in their sevens campaign, winning the Durham County Sevens, the A M Bain Memorial Sevens and the Keswick Tournament. Merchiston also had a run in sevens rugby, winning every tournament that they entered at Under-16 and Under-18 level. In the Heriot's Tournament they beat Glasgow Academy 32-4 in the Junior final and Dundee HS 38-6 in the Under-18 section. In the George Watson's Sevens they beat the home school 24-12 in the final and defeated Strathallan 32-6 in the final of their own tournament.

The following players took part in the 18 Group International matches. Countries played against are shown in square brackets. Abbreviations: *E* – England, *F* – France, *I* – Ireland, *S* – Scotland, *W* – Wales, (R) – Replacement

ENGLAND
Full-back: J D G Ufton (Whitgift) [*F, I, S, W*]
Threequarters: J U Abadom (Mayfield) [*F, I, S, W*]; J A Shepherd (Silcoates) [*I, S*]; M C Allen (St Dunstan's) [*F, I, S, W*]; T R G Stimpson (Silcoates) [*I, S*]; M Denney (Bedford Modern) [*F, I*(R), *W*]; N J J Greenstock (Sherborne) [*F, W*]
Half-backs: N Ryan (Mount St Mary's) [*F, I, S, W*]; A C T Gomarsall (Bedford) [*F, I, S, W*]
Forwards: N A J Tempest (King's, Taunton) [*F, I, S, W*]; S Perkin (Penwith VI FC) [*F, I, S, W*]; A R Poole (Epsom) [*F, I, S, W*]; M E Corry (Tunbridge Wells GS)

225

[*F, I, S, W*]; G S Archer (Durham) [*F, I, S, W*]; R J Leach (KCS Wimbledon) [*F, I, S, W*]; K C Yates (Airedale & Wharfedale College) [*F, I, S, W*]; P R Scrivener (Coopers Co & Cobern) [*F, S, W*]; B Wyer-Roberts (Bedford) [*I*]
Gomarsall was captain in all four matches

IRELAND
Full-back: J Bell (Coleraine Academical Institute) [*E, S, W*];
Threequarters: B Begley (Crescent College Comprehensive) [*E, W*]; C de Gascun (Terenure College) [*E, S, W*]; D Blewitt (Regent House) [*E, S, W*]; J O'Carroll (Cistercian College, Roscrea) [*E, S, W*]; G Davis (Belfast Royal Academy) [*S*]
Half-backs: G Gamble (Belfast Royal Academy) [*S, W*]; J Philpott (Belvedere College) [*E*]; C McGuinness (St Mary's College) [*E, S, W*]
Forwards: I Cummins (PBC Cork) [*E, W*]; W O'Kelly (St Paul's College) [*S*]; J Blaney (Terenure College) [*E, S, W*]; C Boyd (Royal Belfast Academical Institute) [*E, S, W*]; D Moore (Blackrock College) [*E, S, W*]; J McGovern (Terenure College) [*S, W*]; J Davidson (Methodist College Belfast) [*E*]; A Foley (St Munchins College) [*E, S, W*]; C Davis (Belfast Royal Academy) [*E, S, W*]; R Coveney (Clongowes Wood College) [*E, S, W*]
Blaney was captain in all three matches

SCOTLAND
Full-back: C A Murray (Knox Academy) [*F, W*]; I S Leighton (Earlston HS) [*E, I*];
Threequarters: C G MacRobert (Strathaven Academy) [*F, W*]; H R Gilmour (Heriot's) [*E, I*]; C A Joiner (Merchiston) [*E, F, I, W*]; S G Carnochan (Dollar Academy) [*F, W*]; C A Murray (Knox) [*E, I*]; R A Macfarlane (Dundee HS) [*E, F, I, W*]
Half-backs: D W Hodge (Merchiston) [*E, F, I, W*]; I A Brydie (Dollar Academy) [*E, F, I, W*]
Forwards: A D G Binnie (Heriot's) [*E, F, I, W*]; J W C Taylor (Dollar Academy) [*E, F, I, W*]; E M Johnstone (Galashiels Academy) [*F, W*]; A T Bruce (Stewart's-Melville) [*E, I*]; C R W Baird (Jordanhill) [*E, F, I, W*]; P T Jennings (James Gillespie's) [*F, W*]; B J P Brown (Edinburgh Academy) [*I*(R)]; J P Healy (St Aloysius College) [*E, I*]; D R Thompson (Hutchesons' GS) [*E, F, I, W*]; D T Weir (Stewart's-Melville) [*E, F, I, W*]; D McLeish (Kelso HS) [*E, I*]; I G Melville (Dollar Academy) [*F, W*]
Thompson was captain in all four matches

WALES
Full-backs: E Griffiths (Llanhari CS)[*S*]; S Jones (Strade) [*E, F, I*]
Threequarters: C Moir (Milford) [*E, F, I, S*]; S John (Radyr) [*E, F, I, S*]; W Griffiths (Neath College) [*E, F, I*]; S Lewis (Maes-Yr-Yrfa) [*E, F*(R), *S*]; D Drew (Bryncelynnog CS) [*I, F, S*]
Half-backs: J Thomas (QE Maridunum) [*E, F, I*]; J Hewlett (Glantaf) [*E, F, I, S*]
Forwards: C Loader (Neath College) [*E, F, I, S*]; M Thomas (Morriston) [*E, F, I, S*]; S John (Neath College) [*E, F, I, S*]; D Caswell (Pontypool College) [*E*(R)]; S Ford (Neath College) [*E, F*(R)]; S Mellalieu (Olchfa) [*F, I, S*]; N Thomas (Maesteg) [*E, F, I, S*]; J Savastano (Bishop of Llandaff) [*E, F*(R), *I*]; C Thomas (Llandovery) [*E, F, I, S*]; A Moore (Yale) [*E, F, I, S*]; N Stubbs (Neath) [*F, S*]
Loader was captain in all four matches

MATCH DETAILS 1991-92 (18 Group)

21 December 1991, Murrayfield

SCOTLAND 10 (2PG 1T)   **FRANCE 6** (2PG)
SCOTLAND *Try:* Jennings   *Penalty Goals:* Hodge (2)
FRANCE *Penalty Goals:* Dourthé (2)
Referee A H Watson (Ireland)

4 January 1992, The Gnoll, Neath

WALES 24 (1G 2PG 3T)   **SCOTLAND 15** (2G 1PG)
WALES *Tries:* Drew, C Thomas, Hewlett, penalty try   *Conversion:* Lewis
Penalty Goals: Hewlett (2)
SCOTLAND *Tries:* Weir, Hodge   *Conversions:* Hodge (2)   *Penalty Goal:* Hodge
Referee J Cole (Ireland)

4 April 1992, Galway

IRELAND 17 (1G 1PG 2T)   **SCOTLAND 6** (2PG)
IRELAND *Tries:* Gamble, Bell, Coveney   *Conversion:* Gamble   *Penalty Goal:* Gamble
SCOTLAND *Penalty Goals:* Hodge (2)
Referee B Wallis (Wales)

11 April 1992, Balgray, Glasgow

SCOTLAND 0   ENGLAND 28 (1G 1PG 1DG 4T)
ENGLAND *Tries:* Stimpson (2), Ufton, Gomarsall, Leach   *Conversion:* Stimpson
Penalty Goal: Ufton   *Dropped Goal:* Ufton
Referee R G Davies (Wales)

11 April 1992, Cork

IRELAND 7 (1PG 1T)   **WALES 9** (1G 1PG)
IRELAND *Try:* O'Carroll   *Penalty Goal:* Begley
WALES *Try:* Hewlett   *Conversion:* Hewlett   *Penalty Goal:* Hewlett
Referee S W Piercy (England)

15 April 1992, Bedford

ENGLAND 15 (2G 1PG)   **IRELAND 9** (2PG 1DG)
ENGLAND *Tries:* Gomarsall, Ryan   *Conversions:* Ufton (2)   *Penalty Goal:* Ufton
IRELAND *Penalty Goals:* Begley (2)   *Dropped Goal:* Philpott
Referee P Thomas (France)

18 April 1992, Billancourt, Paris

FRANCE 9 (3PG)   **ENGLAND 12** (4PG)
FRANCE *Penalty Goals:* Dourthé (3)
ENGLAND *Penalty Goals:* Ufton (4)
Referee Dr A Condorelli (Italy)

22 April 1992, Maesteg

WALES 3 (1PG)   **FRANCE 7** (1PG 1T)
WALES *Penalty Goal:* Hewlett
FRANCE *Try:* Carayon   *Penalty Goal:* Dourthé
Referee K McCartney (Scotland)

25 April 1992, Doncaster

ENGLAND 18 (2G 1PG 1DG)   **WALES 3** (1PG)
ENGLAND *Tries:* Ryan, Corry   *Conversions:* Ufton (2)   *Penalty Goal:* Ufton
Dropped Goal: Ryan
WALES *Penalty Goal:* Hewlett
Referee P Gray (Ireland)

ENGLAND RULE AND CELEBRATE
COLTS AND YOUTH RUGBY 1991-92

Michael Stevenson

One vivid memory of the 1991-92 season is of the England Colts team and their trainer performing a lap of honour after their match against Wales at Brecon. They chanted the words to the theme from 'An Officer and a Gentleman' with primitive abandon, but the only words I could make out were 'England boys are best today'. They had already drawn with Italy Youth at Padua and subsequently beat Scotland at Gosforth, but the highest and most demanding fence still lay ahead, and a narrow defeat by France at Bournemouth ended what was still a very encouraging season on a disappointing note.

The pre-season preparation sessions proved conclusively that the England backs were potentially something rather special, and the aim under their coaches, Graham Smith and Jim Robinson, was to develop an expansive game. This enabled their excellent wings. Darren O'Leary and Nick Smith, to be unleashed readily to provide some heady and enterprising play. In the pack, Richard Hill at No 8 was outstanding, closely followed by Andrew Spry and Craig Yandell, and apart from in the later stages of the French match, a plentiful supply of ball was forthcoming for the backs. This was apparent at Brecon, which was the high point of the season. The mature judgement and technique evinced by Diccon Edwards and Jason Keyter in the centre were most impressive, but England's man of the match against Wales, had there been such an award, would definitely have been Hill. Their 29-18 win was the more satisfying as Wales had been superb the previous year and had thoroughly outclassed England. Wales' outstanding player in this game was their powerful and forthright No 8, Adrian Wainwright, who scored two bustling tries and always threatened with the ball in his hands.

The French game represented a considerable anti-climax. A bright opening was followed by a period of French ascendancy, during which first phase possession was regularly won by their giant pack, which sucked England into a mauling game where France's extra poundage was bound to tell. England defended bravely, but in the end France were worthy winners.

Welsh Youth opened their campaign with a convincing 25-7 victory over Welsh Schools 18 Group at Ystradgynlais. Stuart Prendiville had a great game in the centre for the winners. Welsh Youth led by only 8-0 at half-time, but a final try-count of 5-1 indicated their superiority. A good win at the Memorial Ground, Ely, Cardiff followed, where Wales beat off spirited resistance by Italy to win 29-22. Next Wales visited Dax, where French Juniors came on strongly in the second half to win 23-9. Wales led 6-3 at half-time but France brought on a new fly-half and prop, and the loss of the Welsh fly-half, Chris John, whose place was taken by Matthew Allnut, selected as a wing, badly disrupted Wales' rhythm.

Barry Williams, the hooker, had a fine season and will still be eligible next winter, his third year in the side. Full-back Ian Jones, who was capped for the Wales Under-15 soccer side and is on Norwich City's books, and Matthew Allnut also impressed. Brian Nicholas, who has coached Welsh Youth for several seasons, is retiring and his place will be taken by Martyn Davies.

Wales also field an Under-19 side which toured Canada in August and September, winning all seven matches including a Test match against Canada (36-19). Their most spectacular victory, in which they achieved the coveted century, was a 103-3 win against British Columbia – they recovered after trailing 0-3!

Colts rugby, which started in the mid-1980s, is still in its infancy in Ireland and their Under-18 match, against Scotland, was lost 0-4 at Galway. A number of inter-provincial matches are now played, including a fixture between the Under-18 side and Irish Schools B, in its third year in 1991-92. The immediate aim of the organisers is to encourage more clubs to run Under-18 sections and to run them more efficiently.

Scotland's only victory was the game at Galway. They play at Under-19 as well as Under-18 level and were lucky not to register another win when they entertained Spain at Milngavie, Glasgow, where they were narrowly defeated (12-13). The Under-19 side lost to Romania in Bucharest (27-3), to England at Gosforth and to Wales at Stirling (12-16).

In the England Colts set-up, Mike Glogg, who had done a great job, was moved sideways to take charge of the Under-21s. It was felt that his exceptional skill as an organiser would help to stimulate the group which crucially bridges the considerable gap between the Colts and the Under-23s. The man chosen to succeed him as honorary team manager of the Colts is a Midlands policeman, Ian Darnell, formerly of Coventry and Warwickshire. He says: 'It was very pleasing to note that the RFU were going to run an Under-20 Development Squad at Trent during the summer. This would go a long way to making up the shortfall which currently exists between the Under-21 set-up and the Colts'. He is generally happy about the new regime over the Divisions, in which joint divisional teams met England in the trial stage: 'The Divisions have co-operated well in producing joint teams, which have provided stronger opposition for England. This can only be to the benefit of the game'. Graham Smith, the Colts' long-serving coach, retired at the end of the season.

London retained the Divisional Championship with a 24-17 victory at Castlecroft, and an England squad of 27 was chosen in preparation for the internationals. A resounding 46-0 win over the North and Midlands augured well for England's prospects, but a degree of frustration was inevitable with the lengthy postponement of the County final, which was initially scheduled for 14 December but could not, for various reasons, be fitted in until late March. Unbeaten Middlesex, having scored 180 points while conceding only 63, were favourites, but the Cup-holders, Lancashire, were not overawed by statistics and ran out worthy but narrow winners by 19-15. Their captain, Tony Handley, kicked five penalties and the scrum-half, Tim Butterworth, scored their only try. For Middlesex, fly-half Roland Davies kicked three penalties and converted their try, which was scored, close to the final whistle, by James Cook.

Last year's National Colts Sevens champions, Barker's Butts, lost in the semi-finals this year to Northampton by 12-6, and Leicester beat Bristol 22-8 in the other semi-final. In the final, Northampton led 10-8 at half-time but a strong second-half performance snatched the title for Leicester, who won 16-14.

Kelso Harlequins were the outstanding Colts team in Scotland and achieved an unbeaten season. Both Maesteg and Blackheath were heading for similar distinction until they faltered in the closing stages. Maesteg were comfortably defeated by Cardiff in the final of the Esso Youth Cup (34-9, with a devastating 7-0 try count) and Blackheath, who beat Cordoba Athletica from Argentina by 16-0, lost just once during the season, to Newport. A run of 22 matches without defeat had preceded this one blemish.

The following players took part in the Colts/Youth International matches. Countries played against are shown in square brackets. Abbreviations: *E* – England, *F* – France, *I* – Ireland, *It* – Italy, *R* – Romania, *S* – Scotland, *Sp* – Spain, *W* – Wales, (R) – Replacement

ENGLAND
Full-back: A F Handley (De la Salle) [*F, It, S, W*]
Threequarters: N D Smith (Northampton) [*F, It, S, W*]; D S O'Leary (West London Institute & Saracens) [*F, It, S, W*]; J Keyter (Harlequins) [*F, It, S, W*]; D Edwards (Loughborough Students) [*F, It, S, W*]
Half-backs: P A Burke (Loughborough Students) [*F, It, S, W*]; G Becconsall (Bristol) [*F, It, S, W*]
Forwards: A J Spry (Sidcup) [*F, It, S, W*]; N McCarthy (Bath) [*It*]; P Donbavand (Sedgley Park) [*F, It*(R), *S, W*]; C Johnson (Leicester) [*F, It, S, W*]; S Drury (Nottingham) [*S*(R)]; G Webster (Northampton) [*F, It, S, W*]; C A Yandell (Bath) [*F, It, S, W*]; A Jackson (Orrell) [*S*(R)]; J Wright (Northampton) [*F, It, S, W*]; I K McNerlin (Bristol) [*F, It, S, W*]; R Hill (Salisbury)[*F, It, S, W*]
Paul Burke was captain in all four matches

IRELAND
Ireland Under-18 (*against Scotland Under-18*)
Full-back: R Larkin (Curragh)
Threequarters: D Carolan (Dundalk), P Koschinly (Ballynahinch), G Nolan (Tuam), S Kennedy (Carrickfergus)
Half-backs: W Middleton (Curragh), D Daly (Kilkenny)
Forwards: R Faith (Limavady), D Ryan (Highfield), J Hickey (Thomond), M King

(Ballymena), T Brennan (Barnhall), B Turley (Corinthians), M Hill (Omagh),
R Heaslip (Curragh)
Ryan was captain

SCOTLAND
Under-19
Full-backs: M M Thomson (Stewart's-Melville FP) [*R*]; A J Bell (Gala) [*E, W*];
P W B Flockhart (Stewart's-Melville FP) [*W*(R)]
Threequarters: P S McIntyre (Kilmarnock) [*W*(R)]; S S Littlewood (Boroughmuir) [*R*];
J R Jardine (Howe of Fife) [*E, W*]; K R Milligan (Stewart's-Melville FP) [*R*];
D R Hamilton (Dunfermline) [*R*]; J Smith (Kirkcaldy) [*E, W*]; C Smith (Preston
Lodge FP) [*E*]; C A Joiner (Merchiston Castle School) [*W*]; K M Logan (Stirling County)
[*R*]; N C Renton (Edinburgh Acads) [*E, W*]
Half-backs: G P J Townsend (Gala) [*R*]; G M Lawrie (Musselburgh) [*E, W*]; G G Burns
(Stewart's-Melville FP) [*R*]; A R Baines (Edinburgh U) [*E*]; J H Kayne (Northampton)
[*W*]
Forwards: R B McNulty (Stewart's-Melville FP) [*R*]; F A Wiseman (West London
Institute) [*E, W*]; D C M McGavin (Bedford) [*R*]; S A R Crawford (Kilmarnock) [*E*];
W P Haslett (Edinburgh Acads) [*W*]; K B Scott (Hawick) [*E, R, W*]; S J Campbell
(Dundee HSFP) [*R*]; M B Rudkin (Watsonians) [*E, W*]; D G Burns (Biggar) [*E, R, W*];
G W Paxton (Gala) [*W*]; D R M Hathway (Watsonians) [*R*]; M Waite (Gordonians) [*R*];
N J Penny (Stewart's-Melville FP) [*R*]; G N Flockhart (Stirling County [*R*(R)];
M G Browne (Wigtownshire) [*E, W*]; M McNiell (Ross High) [*E*]; M B Gifford
(Watsonians) [*E*]; S A Logan (Livingston) [*W*]
Burns was captain against Romania, Lawrie in the other two games

Under-18
Full-back: P W B Flockhart (Stewart's-Melville FP) [*I, Sp*]
Threequarters: R A Wilson (Coleraine Institute) [*I, Sp*]; C J Murray (Haddington) [*I, Sp*];
R N C Brown (Melrose) [*I, Sp*]; C G Muir (West of Scotland) [*I, Sp*];
Half-backs: B R Easson (Howe of Fife) [*I, Sp*]; M Dungait (Morpeth) [*I, Sp*]
Forwards: M H McCluskie (Musselburgh) [*I, Sp*]; D G Cunningham (Haddington) [*I, Sp*];
L J A Graham (Dunbar) [*I, Sp*]; R Anderson (North Berwick) [*I, Sp*]; S I Forsyth
(Kelso Harlequins) [*I, Sp*]; M Brennan (Kelso Harlequins) [*Sp*]; F Thomson (Perth-
shire) [*I, Sp*]; D Clark (Boroughmuir) [*I*]; S A Logan (Livingston) [*I, Sp*]
Logan was captain in both matches

WALES
Welsh Youth
Full-backs: J Salisbury (Ruthin) [*It*]; I Jones (Camarthen Quins) [*E, F*]
Threequarters: M Allnut (Llandovery) [*E, F, It*]; L Davies (Senghenydd) [*E, F, It*];
S Prendiville (Llangennech) [*E, F, It*]; W Leech (Llandybie) [*E, F, It*]; A Bucknall
(British Steel Co) [*F*(R)]
Half-backs: C Ryan (Trimsaran) [*E, It*]; C John (Cardiff) [*F*]; J Churcher (St Peters)
[*E, F, It*]; H Davies (Lampeter) [*E*(R)]
Forwards: A Lewis (Cardiff) [*E, It*]; M Griffiths (Senghenydd) [*F, It*]; R Colella
(Fishguard) [*F*]; R Young (Trefil) [*E, It*(R)]; B Williams (Llandovery) [*E, F, It*]; L Jones
(Porthcawl) [*E, F, It*]; C Williams (Ystrad Rhondda) [*F, It*]; C Wyatt (Newport) [*E*];
G Howells (Ebbw Vale) [*E, F, It*]; H Edwards (Cwmavon) [*E, F, It*]; A Wainwright
(Llandaff) [*E, F*]; S Griffiths (Swansea) [*It*]; M Tossell (Cefn Cribbwr) [*It*(R)]
Lloyd Davies was captain in all three matches

Wales Under-19 (*against Scotland Under-19*)
Full-back: W Grimstead (Newbridge)
Threequarters: J Reynolds (Neath), P Wintle (Cardiff), L Davies (Senghenydd),

J Payne (Cardiff HSOB)
Half-backs: J Strange (Ebbw Vale), H Harries (Cardiff)
Forwards: A Lewis (Cardiff), B Williams (Llandovery), R Colella (Fishguard),
A McPherson (Tumble), S Martin (Neath Tertiary), R Appleyard (Neath Tertiary),
P Young (Llandybie), A Wainwright (Llandaff)
Huw Harries was captain

MATCH DETAILS 1991-92

31 August 1991, Steaua Stadium, Bucharest

Romania 27   Scotland Under-19 3 (1PG)
Scotland Under-19   *Penalty Goal:* Townsend
Referee J Dume (France)

29 February 1992, Memorial Ground, Ely, Cardiff

Welsh Youth 29 (1G 1PG 5T)   **Italy Youth 22** (3G 1T)
Welsh Youth *Tries:* Salisbury, Allnut (2), Prendiville (2), Churcher   *Conversion:* Ryan
Penalty Goal: Ryan
Italy Youth *Tries:* Plantania, Troncon, Caione, Bortolato   *Conversions:* Babbo (3)
Referee F A Howard (England)

14 March 1992, Padua

Italy Youth 15 (5PG)   **England Colts 15** (2G 1PG)
Italy Youth *Penalty Goals:* Babbo (5)
England Colts *Tries:* O'Leary, Edwards   *Conversions:* Burke (2)   *Penalty Goal:* Burke
Referee J Cole (Ireland)

14 March 1992, Dax

French Juniors 23 (2G 1PG 2T)   **Welsh Youth 9** (3PG)
French Juniors *Tries:* Peiffer, Palatan, Gouchard, Loubsen   *Conversions:* Tessier (2)
Penalty Goal: Tessier
Welsh Youth *Penalty Goals:* I Jones (3)
Referee F Burger (South Africa)

4 April 1992, Brecon

Welsh Youth 18 (2PG 3T)   **England Colts 29** (3G 1PG 2T)
Welsh Youth *Tries:* Wainwright (2), Allnut   *Penalty Goals:* I Jones (2)
England Colts *Tries:* O'Leary, Smith, Keyter, McNerlin, Webster
Conversions: Burke (3)   *Penalty Goal:* Burke
Referee D Leslie (Scotland)

4 April 1992, Burnbrae, Milngavie, Glasgow

Scotland Under-18 12 (1G 2PG)   **Spain Under-18 13**
Scotland Under-18 *Try:* Murray   *Conversion:* Easson   *Penalty Goals:* Easson (2)
Referee J Dume (France)

11 April 1992, Kingston Park, Gosforth

England Colts 20 (2G 2T)   **Scotland Under-19 9** (3PG)
England Colts *Tries:* O'Leary, Becconsall, Smith, Hill   *Conversions:* Burke (2)
Scotland Under-19 *Penalty Goals:* Lawrie (3)
Referee D R Davies (Wales)

11 April 1992, Galway

Ireland Under-18 0   Scotland Under-18 4 (1T)
Scotland Under-18 *Try:* Muir
Referee J Pearson (England)

18 April 1992, Bridgehaugh, Stirling

Scotland Under-19 12 (3T)   **Wales Under-19 16** (2G 1T)
Scotland Under-19 *Tries:* Jardine (2), Bell
Wales Under-19 *Tries:* Payne, Reynolds, Williams   *Conversions:* Strange (2)
Referee D Templeton (Ireland)

25 April 1992, Bournemouth

England Colts 18 (2G 2PG)   **French Juniors 23** (1G 1PG 2DG 2T)
England Colts *Tries:* Becconsall, penalty try   *Conversions:* Burke (2)
Penalty Goals: Burke (2)
French Juniors *Tries:* Loustau (2), Lefevre   *Conversion:* Magne   *Penalty Goal:* Magne
Dropped Goals: Magne (2)
Referee G Black (Ireland)

UNEVEN SCOTS BATTLE ON

THE 1991-92 SEASON IN SCOTLAND
Bill McMurtrie *Glasgow Herald*

Scotland aspired for the top in their 11 internationals in the 1991-92 season, but they fell short. They were not drastically far off the pace, but it was still less than had been hoped for, especially when five of their six World Cup matches were in front of their inspiring home support at Murrayfield. Twice they played England at Murrayfield, first in the World Cup semi-final and then in the opening match of the Five Nations' Championship, but on neither occasion could the Scots raise themselves to the heights of the countries' previous encounter there. England had heeded the warning of the 1990 Grand Slam decider.

Twice, though, the Scots reached minor Murrayfield peaks which promised higher points elsewhere. The first was their 24-15 victory over Ireland in the World Cup, when they recovered from a 9-15 deficit and from the loss of Craig Chalmers through injury. Later, a 10-6 win over France in the Championship was deserved reward for a team whose middle five had had to be severely recast for England's visit to Murrayfield. Not only had John Jeffrey and Finlay Calder retired after the World Cup but Gary Armstrong, Graham Marshall and Chris Gray had succumbed to injury.

Marshall was to have been Calder's successor as openside flanker. Instead Ian Smith, Gloucester's captain, was blooded against England. So were David McIvor as blindside flanker, following in Jeffrey's footsteps, Neil Edwards at lock in place of Gray and the 20-year-old Andy Nicol for Armstrong at scrum-half. With such a changed XV Scotland were unfortunate to have to open the Championship against the best team in the competition, but all four newcomers, especially Nicol, the Dundee High School FP youngster, blended in so well that, despite the 25-7 defeat by England, the team stayed on throughout the Championship (with the exception of the home match against France, which Smith missed through injury).

As part of their World Cup build-up, Scotland's international season began in Bucharest on 31 August. It gave the opportunity for experiment, and Jeffrey and Scott Hastings were omitted. Derek Turnbull was recalled as blindside flanker and Douglas Wyllie was paired with Sean Lineen at centre. Scotland, however, did not click, and Romania won by 18-12. A month later Scotland, disguised as the SRU President's XV, lost to Edinburgh Borderers' invitation team, but even if the dress rehearsals had gone wrong, the World Cup's opening acts went well. Scotland ran in seven tries in beating Japan by 47-9, and eight in their 51-12 win over Zimbabwe. Iwan Tukalo had three of the Scots' tries in the second of those games, and victory followed against Ireland with

The Scotland team which played Wales at Cardiff Arms Park. L-R, back row: P M Jones (replacement), J Allan (replacement), R I Wainwright (replacement), D J McIvor, A G Stanger, G W Weir, N G B Edwards, A P Burnell, K S Milne, S R P Lineen, A G Shiel (replacement), G H Oliver (replacement), D A Stark (replacement); front row: C M Chalmers, I Tukalo, S Hastings, D M B Sole (capt), D B White, I R Smith, A G Hastings, A D Nicol.

tries by Armstrong and Graham Shiel, replacement for his Melrose colleague, Chalmers.

A week later Western Samoa, the World Cup's surprise package, were the Murrayfield visitors for the quarter-final, and Scotland paid the Pacific islanders the backhanded compliment of running the game at them at close quarters. The Samoans had won respect for their aggressive, physical rugby in their pool matches in Wales, and from the start, Scotland launched Gavin Hastings at full throttle against the visitors. The pattern was set, and Scotland went on to a 28-6 victory. Jeffrey scored two of the Scots' three tries, raising his tally to 11 and overtaking Derek White as the Scottish forward with most tries in international rugby.

For the next week, Scots remembered 1990 and dreamed dreams, but a place in the final was not to be. England kept the screws turned down, although Gavin Hastings stirred hopes with two penalty goals before Rob Andrew struck his dropped goal for a 9-6 win, ending Scotland's run of 13 successive Murrayfield victories. All that was left for Scotland was the third-place play-off in Cardiff and a 13-6 defeat by the All Blacks.

Only ten weeks later the international round resumed, and for the second time in successive Murrayfield internationals Scotland had to accept defeat by England. White's try took him level with Jeffrey's record for a Scottish forward and, incredibly, it was scored in a push-over against the much-vaunted English pack. Even so, England went on to win by 25-7, their biggest margin in any of their 12 victories in 33 visits to Murrayfield. Scotland, unchanged despite their defeat, picked themselves up with an 18-10 victory in Dublin, which included tries by Tony Stanger and Andy Nicol. It was not a classic performance, but it satisfied Ian McGeechan, Scotland's coach, and his fellow selectors that their team had again found the way to win away from home.

Nor could the 10-6 win against France at Murrayfield be counted as a highlight. Neil Edwards scored the only try, plundering the ball at the front of a goal-line line-out, and thereafter Scotland were inspired in their defence, exemplified by Derek White's retreating tackle to haul down Franck Mesnel. White, the oldest of Scotland's XV at 34, still had young legs in his final Murrayfield match, but his international swansong was not marked in style in Cardiff. The Scots could not raise their game above the tempo set by the band's ponderous rendering of 'Flower of Scotland'.

Punctuating the season, Scotland played two B internationals, winning neither. Ireland B won 29-19 at Murrayfield on 28 December, the hosts giving as much away as if they were late deputies for Santa Claus, and France B beat the Scots 27-18 in Albi. As a by-product of those games, Nicol, McIvor, Smith, Edwards, Rob Wainwright and Peter Jones went on to full caps before the season was out. Scotland's Albi match was to be their last B international with teams confined to uncapped personnel. In future they will play A teams including capped players as well as those who have yet to reach the heights.

In age-group internationals Scotland had only two successes. They defeated Ireland 4-0 in the Under-18 match in Galway, and the Schools beat the French for the first time, winning 10-6 at Murrayfield. The Under-21 team lost to Wales by 19-28, the Under-19 side fell to England by 9-20 and Wales 12-16, the Under-18 international against Spain was agonisingly close at 12-13, and the Schools could not follow up their excellent result against France, slipping to Wales by 15-24, Ireland 6-17 and England 0-28.

Because of the World Cup the Inter-district Championship was not contested. Instead, a shortened series of six district games was played as preparation for the World Cup, and the annual Inter-city match was held over until late in the season, with Glasgow winning 16-12 at Hughenden, their first victory over Edinburgh since 1983. Glasgow also won the Under-21 District Championship, and Edinburgh were Under-18 champions.

Melrose took the top prizes in club rugby, winning the McEwan's National League for the second time in three years and retaining the Bank of Scotland Border League title for the third successive season. Kelso, as Second Division champions, returned to the top flight after one season out, and they were joined in promotion by Dundee High School FP.

Dundee, coached by David Leslie, Scotland's former captain, not only reached Division 1 for the first time but retained the Tennents Midlands Cup, scored more than 1,000 points in all matches and celebrated two individual achievements within the club. Nicol was only the third player to be capped out of the Dundee club, joining his grandfather, George Ritchie, and his club coach, Leslie, and Jon Newton broke the record for the most points in a season by a Scot. His tally of 527 – 414 for Dundee, 113 in other matches – was 20 more than Colin Flannigan scored with Kelso in 1982-83.

Bay of Plenty, the North Island provincial team from New Zealand, won the prestigious Melrose Sevens, but the other trophies in the Border spring series stayed in Scotland. Hawick won at Gala, Stewart's-Melville FP at Hawick and Jedforest took their own trophy for the first time since 1975. Melrose completed the circuit by winning at Langholm. The autumn sevens trophies went south of the border – to Northampton at Selkirk, and to London Scottish at Kelso.

TITLE GOES HOME TO THE BORDERS

McEWAN'S NATIONAL LEAGUE REVIEW

Border domination of the McEwan's National League was restored as Melrose won the title for the second time in three years. Only Heriot's in 1979 and Boroughmuir in 1991 have denied the Borders a total monopoly as Hawick, Kelso, Gala and Melrose have all taken turns as champions. Melrose were never behind in the race for the title. At times, they held a three-point lead, but they were not confirmed as champions until they finished their League season by beating Glasgow High/Kelvinside 27-16 in front of their home support at the Greenyards.

For Melrose to regain the title was yet another feather in the cap of Jim Telfer, the club's illustrious coach. He has been involved in Scotland's two recent Grand Slams, as coach in 1984 and as assistant to Ian McGeechan in 1990, and he has now steered Melrose to two Championships. Moreover, he has done it with a young team. Although the team included three caps, Craig Chalmers, Graham Shiel and Doddie Weir, the ability of the two flankers, Andrew Kerr and Andrew Redpath, both unsung heroes, was just as crucial as the abounding experience of Craig Chalmers at fly-half and the prodigious line-out and loose talent of Doddie Weir at lock or second row. Robbie Brown, a quiet man off the field, was a capable captain, and Gary Parker proved his value as goal-kicker and utility back, whether playing on the wing or standing in at scrum-half. In his 12 games Parker scored 88 points, including eight tries, and he had a run of six games in which he failed only once to cross the opposing goal-line.

Only a draw with Edinburgh Academicals at the Greenyards and a 23-11 loss to Boroughmuir at Meggetland interrupted Melrose's sequence of League wins. That defeat of the champions-elect left Edinburgh Academicals with a glimmer of hope, but Melrose made sure of their success by beating Stirling County 31-0 and then Glasgow High/Kelvinside, even if their deciding win was a little nervous at times.

Edinburgh Academicals, led by John Allan, Scotland's World Cup hooker, had left themselves too much to do after defeats by Heriot's and Hawick in their first six matches. Although they dropped five points, they finished second, six ahead of third-placed Heriot's.

Boroughmuir soon lost their hold on the title with defeats by Edinburgh Academicals, Watsonians, Jedforest and Stewart's-Melville in their first six matches. Their recovery, however, was exemplary, and they finished fourth.

At the other end of the First Division a tense contest raged before Stewart's-Melville and West of Scotland were relegated. Even Gala and Hawick, both former champions, were threatened. Gala, finishing with a 30-18 win over Boroughmuir, eased up into a group of six clubs who shared fifth place, but Hawick, only two points behind, like Glasgow High/Kelvinside, escaped only by having a better points difference than Stewart's-Melville.

Kelso, relegated in 1991, made a prompt return, winning all 13 of their matches, and they were joined by Dundee High School FP, newcomers to the First Division, who owed much to the off-field guidance of David Leslie, who was as committed as club coach as he had been as captain of Scotland. Peebles, promoted as Third Division champions in 1991, finished creditably in third place.

Andy Nicol, Dundee's new international scrum-half, was top try-scorer in the first two divisions with 17. Ally Donaldson, captain of Currie, topped the points list with 123, four more than David Barrett, from relegated West.

Only Berwick, champions of the Seventh Division in their first season in the National League, matched Kelso in the whole League by winning all 13 games, and Clydebank, winners of the Sixth Division title, were the one other club not to lose a League match.

McEWAN'S NATIONAL LEAGUE 1991-92

Division 1	P	W	D	L	F	A	Pts
Melrose	13	11	1	1	263	142	23
Edinburgh Acs	13	10	1	2	266	130	21
Heriot's FP	13	7	1	5	198	218	15
Boroughmuir	12	6	1	5	210	179	13
Gala	13	6	0	7	237	202	12
Selkirk	12	6	0	6	228	210	12
Watsonians	13	5	2	6	202	185	12
Currie	13	6	0	7	231	227	12
Jedforest	13	6	0	7	174	173	12
Stirling County	13	6	0	7	145	207	12
Hawick	13	4	2	7	176	193	10
Glasgow H/K	13	4	2	7	206	245	10
Stewart's-Mel	13	5	0	8	164	261	10
W of Scotland	13	3	0	10	163	291	6

Previous champions: Hawick 10 times, 1973-74 to 1977-78, 1981-82, 1983-84 to 1986-87; Gala 3 times, 1979-80, 1980-81, 1982-83; Kelso twice, 1987-88, 1988-89; Heriot's FP 1979-80; Melrose 1989-90; Boroughmuir 1990-91

Division 2	P	W	D	L	F	A	Pts
Kelso	13	13	0	0	342	116	26
Dundee HSFP	11	10	0	1	377	86	20
Peebles	13	8	1	4	172	142	17
Ayr	13	8	0	5	225	170	16
Preston Lodge	13	8	0	5	185	216	16
Musselburgh	13	7	0	6	227	192	14
Wigtownshire	13	6	1	6	173	170	13
Glasgow Acs	13	5	0	8	190	212	10
Edinburgh W	13	5	0	8	162	225	10
Dunfermline	13	4	1	8	141	230	9
Kilmarnock	12	4	0	8	103	190	8
Kirkcaldy	12	3	1	8	155	207	7
Royal High	13	3	0	10	133	227	6
Corstorphine	13	3	0	10	102	304	6

Division 3	P	W	D	L	F	A	Pts
Grangemouth	13	11	1	1	255	130	23
Clarkston	13	10	2	1	235	99	22
Haddington	13	9	0	4	201	155	18
Howe of Fife	13	8	0	5	186	206	16
Hillhead/J	13	7	1	5	165	143	15
Langholm	13	6	1	6	177	123	13
Dumfries	13	5	2	6	184	174	12
Biggar	13	5	2	6	164	161	12
Hutchesons'/Al	13	5	1	7	176	175	11
Gordonians	13	5	0	8	126	249	10
Portobello FP	13	4	0	9	152	174	8
Perthshire	13	3	2	8	161	206	8
Trinity Acs	13	4	0	9	147	224	8
Highland	13	2	2	9	123	233	6

Division 4	P	W	D	L	F	A	Pts
Morgan FP	13	11	0	2	260	144	22
St Boswells	13	10	0	3	223	111	20
Alloa	13	10	0	3	191	124	20
Cambuslang	12	8	0	4	170	113	16
Leith Acs	13	7	1	5	171	149	15
Cartha QP	13	7	1	5	163	183	15
Linlithgow	13	6	0	7	193	180	12
Dalziel HSFP	12	5	2	5	161	148	12
East Kilbride	13	5	0	8	140	172	10
Edinburgh U	13	5	0	8	143	183	10
Aberdeen GSFP	13	3	3	7	174	208	9
Lismore	13	4	0	9	153	226	8
Penicuik	13	3	1	9	161	244	7
Madras FP	13	2	0	11	121	239	4

Division 5	P	W	D	L	F	A	Pts
Stewartry	13	12	0	1	302	81	24
Livingston	13	10	1	2	196	79	21
Lenzie	13	9	0	4	231	89	18
Hillfoots	12	7	1	4	143	111	15
Paisley	12	7	0	5	184	140	14
Glenrothes	13	7	0	6	171	131	14
Ardrossan Acs	13	7	0	6	160	146	14
Moray	11	6	1	4	142	142	13
North Berwick	13	6	0	7	178	169	12
Falkirk	13	5	0	8	166	183	10
Waysiders	13	4	0	9	81	257	8

Aberdeenshire	12	3	1	8	101	232	7
Greenock W	11	1	0	10	81	212	2
Dunbar	12	1	0	11	97	261	2

Division 6	P	W	D	L	F	A	Pts
Clydebank	13	12	1	0	354	96	25
Irvine	13	9	1	3	252	77	19
Marr	13	8	1	4	204	122	17
Broughton FP	13	7	1	5	213	102	15
Earlston	12	6	3	3	109	101	15
St Andrews U	12	6	0	6	235	130	12
Harris FP	13	5	2	6	147	96	12
Lasswade	12	5	2	5	182	170	12
Murrayfield	13	5	1	7	142	175	11
Drumpellier	13	5	1	7	166	204	11
Cumbernauld	13	5	0	8	126	174	10
Forrester FP	13	5	0	8	166	215	10
Walkerburn	13	3	1	9	128	242	7
Carnoustie FP	12	1	0	11	58	578	2

Division 7	P	W	D	L	F	A	Pts
Berwick	13	13	0	0	279	56	26
Duns	12	11	0	1	419	62	22
Ross High	13	9	0	4	180	131	18
Allan Glen's	11	7	0	4	202	98	14
Panmure	13	7	0	6	161	186	14

Stirling U	11	6	0	5	118	218	12
Garnock	13	5	1	7	171	186	11
RAF Kinloss	12	5	0	7	185	167	10
Montrose	13	5	0	8	122	202	10
Whitecraigs	12	5	0	7	127	211	10
Strathmore	13	4	1	8	95	235	9
Aberdeen U	13	4	0	9	146	207	8
Rosyth & Dist	13	3	0	10	102	233	6
Cumnock	12	2	0	10	116	231	4

District League Champions (*promoted to Division 7*):
East: Holy Cross
North/Midlands: Waid Academy FP
West: Hyndland FP

BANK OF SCOTLAND BORDER LEAGUE

	P	W	D	L	F	A	Pts
Melrose	11	9	0	2	180	148	18
Kelso	11	7	1	3	254	156	15
Gala	12	7	0	5	281	167	14
Jedforest	12	6	1	5	180	135	13
Selkirk	12	5	0	7	217	191	10
Hawick	11	5	0	6	172	163	10
Langholm	11	0	0	11	71	395	0

DISTRICT MATCHES
(*Limited unofficial tournament due to World Cup*)

14 September, Inverleith, Edinburgh
Edinburgh 18 (1G 3T)   **Anglo-Scots 12** (1G 2PG)

Edinburgh: A G Hastings (Watsonians); A Moore (Edinburgh Acads), S Hastings (Watsonians), S R P Lineen (Boroughmuir), I C Glasgow (Heriot's FP); D S Wyllie (Stewart's-Melville FP), M D Hall (Boroughmuir); D M B Sole (Edinburgh Acads) (*capt*), K S Milne (Heriot's FP), S W Paul (Heriot's FP), J F Richardson (Edinburgh Acads), I A Burnside (Stewart's-Melville FP), G J Drummond (Boroughmuir), F Calder (Stewart's-Melville FP), S J Reid (Boroughmuir)
Scorers *Tries:* Glasgow, Hall, A G Hastings, Moore   *Conversion:* A G Hastings
Anglo-Scots: M Appleson (London Scottish); N J Grecian (London Scottish), F J Harrold (London Scottish), R R W Maclean (Moseley), W L Renwick (London Scottish); R I Cramb (London Scottish), D B Millard (London Scottish); G B Smith (Wolverhampton), B W Gilchrist (London Scottish), A P Burnell (London Scottish), A Cruickshank (London Scottish), D F Cronin (Bath) (*capt*), C I M Dixon (London Scottish), I R Morrison (London Scottish), D B White (London Scottish)
Scorers *Try:* Millard   *Conversion:* Grecian   *Penalty Goals:* Grecian (2)
Referee E F Morrison (England)

14 September, McKane Park, Dunfermline
North and Midlands 12 (1G 2PG)   **SRU President's XV 7** (1PG 1T)

North and Midlands: S A D Burns (Edinburgh Acads); D J McLaughlin (Boroughmuir), P R Rouse (Dundee HSFP), B Edwards (Alloa), C J Macartney (Selkirk); R J S Shepherd (Edinburgh Acads), A D Nicol (Dundee HSFP); I J Michie (Dunfermline), M W Scott (Dunfermline), D Herrington (Dundee HSFP), B M Bell (Highland) (*capt*), J M Thomson (Edinburgh Wands), D J McIvor (Edinburgh Acads), D H Mitchell (Dunfermline), R I Wainwright (Edinburgh Acads) *Replacement* D Timms (Dunfermline) for Michie
Scorers *Try:* Edwards   *Conversion:* Shepherd   *Penalty Goals:* Shepherd (2)
SRU President's XV: S B Douglas (Boroughmuir); M Dods (Gala), D R W Adam (Edinburgh Acads), S R Maclean (Boroughmuir), K M Logan (Stirling County); G P J Townsend (Gala), B W Redpath (Melrose); D F Milne (Heriot's FP), J Allan (Edinburgh Acads) (*capt*), P H Wright (Boroughmuir), A Snow (Heriot's FP), E M Simpson (Melrose), G T Mackay (Glasgow Acads), J P Amos (Gala), C D Hogg (Melrose)
Scorers *Try:* Townsend   *Penalty Goal:* Dods
Referee I C Henderson (Kelso)

14 September, Philiphaugh, Selkirk
South 31 (4G 1PG 1T)   **Glasgow 4** (1T)

South: P W Dods (Gala); A G Stanger (Hawick), R L Pow (Selkirk), A G Shiel (Melrose), M Moncrieff (Gala); C M Chalmers (Melrose), G Armstrong (Jedforest); G R Isaac (Gala), J A Hay (Hawick), S W Ferguson (Peebles), G W Weir (Melrose), J Laing (Gala), D J Turnbull (Hawick), J Jeffrey (Kelso) (capt), A G Roxburgh (Kelso)
Scorers *Tries:* Armstrong, Jeffrey, Moncrieff, Pow (2)   *Conversions:* Dods (4)   *Penalty Goal:* Dods
Glasgow: D N Barrett (West of Scotland); A S M Turner (Stirling County), S R McKee (West of Scotland), I C Jardine (Stirling County), S T G Porter (Malone); G M Breckenridge (Glasgow High/Kelvinside), S M Simmers (Glasgow Acads); G Graham (Stirling County), K D McKenzie (Stirling County), G B Robertson (Stirling County), M Norval (Stirling County), J S Hamilton (Stirling County), D A McVey (Ayr), B Ireland (Stirling County), F D Wallace (Glasgow High/Kelvinside) (capt) *Replacement* W H Malcolm (Glasgow High/Kelvinside) for Hamilton
Scorer *Try:* Turner
Referee J B Anderson (Currie)

21 September, Murrayfield
SRU President's XV 32 (2G 5T)   **Anglo-Scots 4** (1T)

SRU President's XV: A G Hastings (Watsonians); M Moncrieff (Gala), S Hastings (Watsonians), D S Wyllie (Stewart's-Melville FP), I Tukalo (Selkirk); C M Chalmers (Melrose), G Armstrong (Jedforest); D M B Sole (Edinburgh Acads) (capt), J Allan (Edinburgh Acads), A P Burnell (London Scottish), C A Gray (Nottingham), G W Weir (Melrose), J Jeffrey (Kelso), F Calder (Stewart's-Melville FP), D B White (London Scottish)
Scorers *Tries:* Armstrong, Jeffrey, Moncrieff, Sole, Tukalo (2), White   *Conversions:* Chalmers (2)
Anglo-Scots: M Appleson (London Scottish); N J Grecian (London Scottish), F J Harrold (London Scottish), R R W Maclean (Moseley), W L Renwick (London Scottish); R I Cramb (London Scottish), D B Millard (London Scottish); G B Smith (Wolverhampton), B W Gilchrist (London Scottish), A G J Watt (Glasgow High/Kelvinside), A E D Macdonald (Heriot's FP), N G B Edwards (Harlequins), C I M Dixon (London Scottish), I R Morrison (London Scottish), S J Reid (Boroughmuir)
Scorer *Try:* Renwick
Referee R J Megson (Edinburgh Wanderers)

21 September, Bridgehaugh, Stirling
Glasgow 16 (1G 2PG 1T)   **North and Midlands 3** (1PG)

Glasgow: D N Barrett (West of Scotland); A S M Turner (Stirling County), D R McKee (West of Scotland), I C Jardine (Stirling County), K M Logan (Stirling County); G M Breckenridge (Glasgow High/Kelvinside), S M Simmers (Glasgow Acads); G Graham (Stirling County), K D McKenzie (Stirling County), G B Robertson (Stirling County), M Norval (Stirling County), J Ramage (Ayr), D A McVey (Ayr), B Ireland (Stirling County), F D Wallace (Glasgow High/Kelvinside) (capt)
Scorers *Tries:* Jardine, Turner   *Conversion:* Barrett   *Penalty Goals:* Barrett (2)
North and Midlands: S A D Burns (Edinburgh Acads); D J McLaughlin (Boroughmuir), P R Rouse (Dundee HSFP), B Edwards (Alloa), C J Macartney (Selkirk); R J S Shepherd (Edinburgh Acads), M J de G Allingham (Heriot's FP); J J Manson (Dundee HSFP), M W Scott (Dunfermline), D Herrington (Dundee HSFP), B M Bell (Highland) (capt), J M Thomson (Edinburgh Wands), D J McIvor (Edinburgh Acads), R I Wainwright (Edinburgh Acads), A C Murray (Watsonians) *Replacement* A M Fraser (Highland) for Rouse
Scorer *Penalty Goal:* Shepherd
Referee J M Fleming (Boroughmuir)

21 September, Netherdale, Galashiels
South 22 (3G 1T)   **Edinburgh 3** (1PG)

South: P W Dods (Gala); D W Hunter (Selkirk), A J Douglas (Jedforest), S A Nichol (Dundee HSFP), M Dods (Gala); R L Pow (Selkirk), G H Oliver (Hawick); R A Nichol (Hawick), J A Hay (Hawick), S W Ferguson (Peebles), R R Brown (Melrose), J Laing (Gala), D J Turnbull (Hawick), G R Marshall (Selkirk), C D Hogg (Melrose)
Scorers *Tries:* Brown, Hogg, Hunter, Turnbull   *Conversions:* P W Dods (3)
Edinburgh: S B Douglas (Boroughmuir); A Moore (Edinburgh Acads), D R W Adam (Edinburgh Acads), S R Maclean (Boroughmuir), G Stirling (Stewart's-Melville FP); I C Glasgow (Heriot's FP), M D Hall (Boroughmuir); G D Wilson (Boroughmuir), K S Milne (Heriot's FP) (capt), P H Wright (Boroughmuir), J F Richardson (Edinburgh Acads), I A Burnside (Stewart's-Melville FP), K J M Wilson (Boroughmuir), G J Drummond (Boroughmuir), G A R Simpson (Stewart's-Melville FP)
Scorer *Penalty Goal:* Glasgow
Referee D Leslie (Manchester)

SCOTRAIL INTER-CITY MATCH

1 April, Hughenden, Glasgow
Glasgow 16 (1G 2PG 1T)   **Edinburgh 12** (4PG)

Glasgow: K M Logan (Stirling County); G S Agnew (Glasgow High/Kelvinside), S McIntosh (West of Scotland), I C Jardine (Stirling County), G F Hawkes (Glasgow High/Kelvinside); D N Barrett (West of Scotland), F H Stott (West of Scotland); J T Gibson (Stirling County), K D McKenzie (Stirling County), G B Robertson (Stirling County), A G J Watt (Glasgow High/Kelvinside), J F Richardson (Glasgow High/Kelvinside), M I Wallace (Glasgow High/Kelvinside), B Ireland (Stirling County), F D Wallace (Glasgow High/Kelvinside) (capt)
Scorers *Tries:* Logan, Agnew   *Conversion:* Barrett   *Penalty Goals:* Barrett (2)
Edinburgh: I C Glasgow (Heriot's FP); D Macrae (Boroughmuir), D R W Adam (Edinburgh Acads), D S Wyllie (Stewart's-Melville FP), A Moore (Edinburgh Acads); A Donaldson (Currie), D Patterson (Edinburgh Acads); S W Paul (Heriot's FP), D G Ellis (Stewart's-Melville FP), P H Wright (Boroughmuir), S A Aitken (Watsonians), A E D Macdonald (Heriot's FP), B Ward (Currie), G J Drummond (Boroughmuir), D T H Jackson (Edinburgh Acads)
Scorer *Penalty Goals:* Donaldson (4)
Referee K W McCartney (Hawick)

SCOTTISH INTERNATIONAL PLAYERS
(up to 31 March 1992)

ABBREVIATIONS

A – Australia; *Arg* – Argentina; *E* – England; *F* – France; *Fj* – Fiji; *I* – Ireland; *J* – Japan; *NZ* – New Zealand; *R* – Romania; *SA* – South Africa; *W* – Wales; *WS* – Western Samoa; *Z* – Zimbabwe; (C) – Centenary match v England at Murrayfield, 1971 (non-championship); P – Scotland v President's Overseas XV at Murrayfield in SRU's Centenary season, 1972-73; (R) Replacement. Entries in square brackets [ ] indicate appearances in the World Cup.

Note: Years given for Five Nations' matches are for second half of season; eg 1972 means season 1971-72. Years for all other matches refer to the actual year of the match. When a series has taken place, figures have been used to denote the particular matches in which players have featured. Thus 1981 *NZ* 1,2 indicates that a player appeared in the first and second Tests of the series. The abandoned game with Ireland at Belfast in 1885 is now included as a cap-match.

Abercrombie, C H (United Services) 1910 *I*, *E*, 1911 *F*, *W*, 1913 *F*, *W*

Abercrombie, J G (Edinburgh U) 1949 *F*, *W*, *I*, 1950 *F*, *W*, *I*, *E*

Agnew, W C C (Stewart's Coll FP) 1930 *W*, *I*

Ainslie, R (Edinburgh Inst FP) 1879 *I*, *E*, 1880 *I*, *E*, 1881 *E*, 1882 *I*, *E*

Ainslie, T (Edinburgh Inst FP) 1881 *E*, 1882 *I*, *E*, 1883 *W*, *I*, *E*, 1884 *W*, *I*, *E*, 1885 *W*, *I*1,2

Aitchison, G R (Edinburgh Wands) 1883 *I*

Aitchison, T G (Gala) 1929 *W*, *I*, *E*

Aitken, A I (Edinburgh Inst FP) 1889 *I*

Aitken, G G (Oxford U) 1924 *W*, *I*, *E*, 1925 *F*, *W*, *I*, *E*, 1929 *F*

Aitken, J (Gala) 1977 *E*, *I*, *F*, 1981 *F*, *W*, *E*, *I*, *NZ*1,2, *R*, *A*, 1982 *E*, *I*, *F*, *W*, 1983 *F*, *W*, *E*, *NZ*, 1984 *W*, *E*, *I*, *F*, *R*

Aitken, R (London Scottish) 1947 *W*

Allan, B (Glasgow Acads) 1881 *I*

Allan, J (Edinburgh Acads) 1990 *NZ*1, 1991 *W*, *I*, *R*, [*J*, *I*, *WS*, *E*, *NZ*]

Allan, J L (Melrose) 1952 *F*, *W*, *I*, 1953 *W*

Allan, J L F (Cambridge U) 1957 *I*, *E*

Allan, J W (Melrose) 1927 *F*, 1928 *I*, 1929 *F*, *W*, *I*, *E*, 1930 *F*, *E*, 1931 *F*, *W*, *I*, *E*, 1932 *SA*, *W*, *I*, 1934 *I*, *E*

Allan, R C (Hutchesons' GSFP) 1969 *I*

Allardice, W D (Aberdeen GSFP) 1948 *A*, *F*, *W*, *I*, 1949 *F*, *W*, *I*, *E*

Allen, H W (Glasgow Acads) 1873 *E*

Anderson, A H (Glasgow Acads) 1894 *I*

Anderson, D G (London Scottish) 1889 *I*, 1890 *W*, *I*, *E*, 1891 *W*, *E*, 1892 *W*, *E*

Anderson, E (Stewart's Coll FP) 1947 *I*, *E*

Anderson, J W (W of Scotland) 1872 *E*

Anderson, T (Merchiston) 1882 *I*

Angus, A W (Watsonians) 1909 *W*, 1910 *F*, *W*, *E*, 1911 *W*, *I*, 1912 *F*, *W*, *I*, *E*, *SA*, 1913 *F*, *W*, 1914 *E*, 1920 *F*, *W*, *I*, *E*

Anton, P A (St Andrew's U) 1873 *E*

Armstrong, G (Jedforest) 1988 *A*, 1989 *W*, *E*, *I*, *F*, *Fj*, *R*, 1990 *I*, *F*, *W*, *E*, *NZ* 1,2, *Arg*, 1991 *F*, *W*, *E*, *I*, *R*, [*J*, *I*, *WS*, *E*, *NZ*]

Arneil, R J (Edinburgh Acads, Leicester and Northampton) 1968 *I*, *E*, *A*, 1969 *F*, *W*, *I*, *E*, *SA*, 1970 *F*, *W*, *I*, *E*, *A*, 1971 *F*, *W*, *I*, *E*(2[1C]), 1972 *F*, *W*, *E*, *NZ*

Arthur, A (Glasgow Acads) 1875 *E*, 1876 *E*

Arthur, J W (Glasgow Acads) 1871 *E*, 1872 *E*

Asher, A G G (Oxford U) 1882 *I*, 1884 *W*, *I*, *E*, 1885 *W*, 1886 *I*, *E*

Auld, W (W of Scotland) 1889 *W*, 1890 *W*

Auldjo, L J (Abertay) 1878 *E*

Bain, D McL (Oxford U) 1911 *E*, 1912 *F*, *W*, *E*, *SA*, 1913 *F*, *W*, *I*, *E*, 1914 *W*, *I*

Baird, G R T (Kelso) 1981 *A*, 1982 *E*, *I*, *F*, *W*, *A* 1,2, 1983 *I*, *F*, *W*, *E*, *NZ*, 1984 *W*, *E*, *I*, *F*, *A*, 1985 *I*, *W*, *E*, 1986 *F*, *W*, *E*, *I*, *R*, 1987 *E*, 1988 *I*

Balfour, A (Watsonians) 1896 *W*, *I*, *E*, 1897 *E*

Balfour, L M (Edinburgh Acads) 1872 *E*

Bannerman, E M (Edinburgh Acads) 1872 *E*, 1873 *E*

Bannerman, J M (Glasgow HSFP) 1921 *F*, *W*, *I*, *E*, 1922 *F*, *W*, *I*, *E*, 1923 *F*, *W*, *I*, *E*, 1924 *F*, *W*, *I*, *E*, 1925 *F*, *W*, *I*, *E*, 1926 *F*, *W*, *I*, *E*, 1927 *F*, *W*, *I*, *E*, *A*, 1928 *F*, *W*, *I*, *E*, 1929 *F*, *W*, *I*, *E*

Barnes, I A (Hawick) 1972 *W*, 1974 *F* (R), 1975 *E* (R), *NZ*, 1977 *I*, *F*, *W*

Barrie, R W (Hawick) 1936 *E*

Bearne, K R F (Cambridge U, London Scottish) 1960 *F*, *W*

Beattie, J A (Hawick) 1929 *F*, *W*, 1930 *W*, 1931 *F*, *W*, *I*, *E*, 1932 *SA*, *W*, *I*, *E*, 1933 *W*, *E*, *I*, 1934 *I*, *E*, 1935 *W*, *I*, *E*, *NZ*, 1936 *W*, *I*, *E*

Beattie, J R (Glasgow Acads) 1980 *I*, *F*, *W*, *E*, 1981 *F*, *W*, *E*, *I*, 1983 *F*, *W*, *E*, *NZ*, 1984 *E* (R), *R*, *A*, 1985 *I*, 1986 *F*, *W*, *E*, *I*, *R*, 1987 *I*, *F*, *W*, *E*

Bedell-Sivright, D R (Cambridge U, Edinburgh U) 1900 *W*, 1901 *W*, *I*, *E*, 1902 *W*, *I*, *E*, 1903 *W*, *I*, 1904 *W*, *I*, *E*, 1905 *NZ*, 1906 *W*, *I*, *E*, *SA*, 1907 *W*, *I*, *E*, 1908 *W*, *I*

Bedell-Sivright, J V (Cambridge U) 1902 *W*

Begbie, T A (Edinburgh Wands) 1881 *I*, *E*

Bell, D L (Watsonians) 1975 *I*, *F*, *W*, *E*

Bell, J A (Clydesdale) 1901 *W*, *I*, *E*, 1902 *W*, *I*, *E*

Bell, L H I (Edinburgh Acads) 1900 *E*, 1904 *W*, *I*

Berkeley, W V (Oxford U) 1926 *F*, 1929 *F*, *W*, *I*

Berry, C W (Fettesian-Lorettonians) 1884 *I*, *E*, 1885 *W*, *I* 1, 1887 *I*, *W*, *E*, 1888 *W*, *I*

Bertram, D M (Watsonians) 1922 *F*, *W*, *I*, *E*, 1923 *F*, *W*, *I*, *E*, 1924 *W*, *I*, *E*

Biggar, A G (London Scottish) 1969 *SA*, 1970 *F*, *I*, *E*, *A*, 1971 *F*, *W*, *I*, *E* (2[1C]), 1972 *F*, *W*

Biggar, M A (London Scottish) 1975 *I*, *F*, *W*, *E*, 1976 *W*, *E*, *I*, 1977 *I*, *F*, *W*, 1978 *I*, *F*, *W*, *E*, *NZ*, 1979 *W*, *E*, *I*, *F*, *NZ*, 1980 *I*, *F*, *W*, *E*

Birkett, G A (Harlequins, London Scottish) 1975 *NZ*

Bishop, J M (Glasgow Acads) 1893 *I*

Bisset, A A (RIE Coll) 1904 *W*

Black, A W (Edinburgh U) 1947 *F*, *W*, 1948 *E*, 1950 *W*, *I*, *E*

Black, W P (Glasgow HSFP) 1948 *F*, *W*, *I*, *E*, 1951 *E*

Blackadder, W F (W of Scotland) 1938 *E*

Blaikie, C F (Heriot's FP) 1963 *I*, *E*, 1966 *E*, 1968 *A*, 1969 *F*, *W*, *I*, *E*

Blair, P C B (Cambridge U) 1912 *SA*, 1913 *F*, *W*, *I*, *E*

Bolton, W H (W of Scotland) 1876 *E*

Borthwick, J B (Stewart's Coll FP) 1938 *W*, *I*

Bos, F H ten (Oxford U, London Scottish) 1959 *E*, 1960 *F*, *W*, *SA*, 1961 *F*, *SA*, *W*, *I*, *E*, 1962 *F*, *W*, *I*, *E*, 1963 *F*, *W*, *I*, *E*

Boswell, J D (W of Scotland) 1889 *W*, *I*, 1890 *W*, *I*, *E*, 1891 *W*, *I*, *E*, 1892 *W*, *I*, *E*, 1893 *I*, *E*, 1894 *I*, *E*

Bowie, T C (Watsonians) 1913 *I*, *E*, 1914 *I*, *E*

Boyd, G M (Glasgow HSFP) 1926 *E*

Boyd, J L (United Services) 1912 *E*, *SA*

Boyle, A C W (London Scottish) 1963 *F*, *W*, *I*

Boyle, A H W (St Thomas's Hospital, London Scottish) 1966 *A*, 1967 *F*, *NZ*, 1968 *F*, *W*, *I*

Brash, J C (Cambridge U) 1961 *E*

Breakey, R W (Gosforth) 1978 *E*

Brewis, N T (Edinburgh Inst FP) 1876 *E*, 1878 *E*, 1879 *I*, *E*, 1880 *I*, *E*

Brewster, A K (Stewart's-Melville FP) 1977 *E*, 1980 *I*, *F*, 1986 *E*, *I*, *R*

Brown, A H (Heriot's FP) 1928 *E*, 1929 *F*, *W*

Brown, A R (Gala) 1971 *E* (2[1C]), 1972 *F*, *W*, *E*

Brown, C H C (Dunfermline) 1929 *E*

Brown, D I (Cambridge U) 1933 *W, E, I*

Brown, G L (W of Scotland) 1969 *SA*, 1970 *F, W* (R), *I, E, A*, 1971 *F, W, I, E* (2[1C]), 1972 *F, W, E, NZ*, 1973 *E* (R), *P*, 1974 *W, E, I, F*, 1975 *I, F, W, E, A*, 1976 *F, W, E, I*

Brown, J A (Glasgow Acads) 1908 *W, I*

Brown, J B (Glasgow Acads) 1879 *I, E*, 1880 *I, E*, 1881 *I, E*, 1882 *I, E*, 1883 *W, I, E*, 1884 *W, I, E*, 1885 *I* 1,2, 1886 *W, I, E*

Brown, P C (W of Scotland, Gala) 1964 *F, NZ, W, I, E*, 1965 *I, E, SA*, 1966 *A*, 1969 *I, E*, 1970 *W, E*, 1971 *F, W, I, E* (2[1C]), 1972 *F, W, E, NZ*, 1973 *F, W, I, E, P*

Brown, T G (Heriot's FP) 1929 *W*

Brown, W D (Glasgow Acads) 1871 *E*, 1872 *E*, 1873 *E*, 1874 *E*, 1875 *E*

Brown, W S (Edinburgh Inst FP) 1880 *I, E*, 1882 *I, E*, 1883 *W, E*

Browning, A (Glasgow HSFP) 1920 *I*, 1922 *F, W, I*, 1923 *W, I, E*

Bruce, C R (Glasgow Acads) 1947 *F, W, I, E*, 1949 *F, W, I, E*

Bruce, N S (Blackheath, Army and London Scottish) 1958 *F, A, I, E*, 1959 *F, W, I, E*, 1960 *F, W, I, E, SA*, 1961 *F, SA, W, I, E*, 1962 *F, W, I, E*, 1963 *F, W, I, E*, 1964 *F, NZ, W, I, E*

Bruce, R M (Gordonians) 1947 *A*, 1948 *F, W, I*

Bruce-Lockhart, J H (London Scottish) 1913 *W*, 1920 *E*

Bruce-Lockhart, L (London Scottish) 1948 *E*, 1950 *F, W*, 1953 *I, E*

Bruce-Lockhart, R B (Cambridge U and London Scottish) 1937 *I*, 1939 *I, E*

Bryce, C C (Glasgow Acads) 1873 *E*, 1874 *E*

Bryce, R D H (W of Scotland) 1973 *I* (R)

Bryce, W E (Selkirk) 1922 *W, I, E*, 1923 *F, W, I, E*, 1924 *F, W, I, E*

Brydon, W R C (Heriot's FP) 1939 *W*

Buchanan, A (Royal HSFP) 1871 *E*

Buchanan, F G (Kelvinside Acads and Oxford U) 1910 *E*, 1911 *F, W*

Buchanan, J C R (Stewart's Coll FP) 1921 *W, I, E*, 1922 *W, I, E*, 1923 *F, W, I, E*, 1924 *F, W, I, E*, 1925 *F, I*

Buchanan-Smith, G A E (London Scottish, Heriot's FP) 1989 *Fj* (R), 1990 *Arg*

Bucher, A M (Edinburgh Acads) 1897 *E*

Budge, G M (Edinburgh Wands) 1950 *F, W, I, E*

Bullmore, H H (Edinburgh U) 1902 *I*

Burnell, A P (London Scottish) 1989 *E, I, F, Fj, R*, 1990 *I, F, W, E, Arg*, 1991 *F, W, E, I, R, [J, Z, I, WS, E, NZ]*, 1992 *E, I, F, W*

Burnet, P J (London Scottish and Edinburgh Acads) 1960 *SA*

Burnet, W (Hawick) 1912 *E*

Burnet, W A (W of Scotland) 1934 *W*, 1935 *W, I, E, NZ*, 1936 *W, I, E*

Burnett, J N (Heriot's FP) 1980 *I, F, W, E*

Burrell, G (Gala) 1950 *F, W, I*, 1951 *SA*

Cairns, A G (Watsonians) 1903 *W, I, E*, 1904 *W, I, E*, 1905 *W, I, E*, 1906 *W, I, E*

Calder, F (Stewart's-Melville FP) 1986 *F, W, E, I, R*, 1987 *I, F, W, E, [F, Z, R, NZ]*, 1988 *I, F, W, E*, 1989 *W, E, I, F, R*, 1990 *I, F, W, E, NZ* 1,2, 1991 *R, [J, I, WS, E, NZ]*

Calder, J H (Stewart's-Melville FP) 1981 *F, W, E, I, NZ* 1,2, *R, A*, 1982 *E, I, F, W, A* 1,2, 1983 *I, F, W, E, NZ*, 1984 *W, E, I, F, A*, 1985 *I, F, W*

Callander, G J (Kelso) 1984 *R*, 1988 *I, F, W, E, A*

Cameron, A (Glasgow HSFP) 1948 *W*, 1950 *I, E*, 1951 *F, W, I, E, SA*, 1953 *I, E*, 1955 *F, W, I, E*, 1956 *F, W, I*

Cameron, A D (Hillhead HSFP) 1951 *F*, 1954 *F, W*

Cameron, A W (Watsonians) 1887 *W*, 1893 *W*, 1894 *I*

Cameron, D (Glasgow HSFP) 1953 *I, E*, 1954 *F, NZ, I, E*

Cameron, N W (Glasgow U) 1952 *E*, 1953 *F, W*

Campbell, A J (Hawick) 1984 *I, F, R*, 1985 *I, F, W, E*, 1986 *F, W, E, I, R*, 1988 *F, W, A*

Campbell, G T (London Scottish) 1892 *W, I, E*, 1893 *I, E*, 1894 *W, I, E*, 1895 *W, I, E*, 1896 *W, I, E*, 1897 *I*, 1899 *I*, 1900 *E*

Campbell, H H (Cambridge U, London Scottish) 1947 *I, E*, 1948 *I, E*

Campbell, J A (W of Scotland) 1878 *E*, 1879 *I, E*, 1881 *I, E*

Campbell, J A (Cambridge U) 1900 *I*

Campbell, N M (London Scottish) 1956 *F, W*

Campbell-Lamerton, J R E (London Scottish) 1986 *F*, 1987 *[Z, R(R)]*

Campbell-Lamerton, M J (Halifax, Army, London Scottish) 1961 *F, SA, W, I*, 1962 *F, W, I, E*, 1963 *F, W, I, E*, 1964 *I, E*, 1965 *F, W, I, E, SA*, 1966 *F, W, I, E*

Carmichael, A B (W of Scotland) 1967 *I, NZ*, 1968 *F, W, I, E, A*, 1969 *F, W, I, E, SA*, 1970 *F, W, I, E, A*, 1971 *F, W, I, E*(2[1C]), 1972 *F, W, E, NZ*, 1973 *F, W, I, E, P*, 1974 *W, E, I, F*, 1975 *I, F, W, E, NZ, A*, 1976 *F, W, E, I*, 1977 *E, I*(R), *F, W*, 1978 *I*

Carmichael, J H (Watsonians) 1921 *F, W, I*

Carrick, J S (Glasgow Acads) 1876 *E*, 1877 *E*

Cassels, D Y (W of Scotland) 1880 *E*, 1881 *I*, 1882 *I, E*, 1883 *W, I, E*

Cathcart, C W (Edinburgh U) 1872 *E*, 1873 *E*, 1876 *E*

Cawkwell, G L (Oxford U) 1947 *F*

Chalmers, C M (Melrose) 1989 *W, E, I, F, Fj*, 1990 *I, F, W, E, NZ* 1,2, *Arg*, 1991 *F, W, E, I, R, [J, Z(R)], I, WS, E, NZ]*, 1992 *E, I, F, W*

Chalmers, T (Glasgow Acads) 1871 *E*, 1872 *E*, 1873 *E*, 1874 *E*, 1875 *E*, 1876 *E*

Chambers, H F T (Edinburgh U) 1888 *W, I*, 1889 *W, I*

Charters, R G (Hawick) 1955 *W, I, E*

Chisholm, D M (Melrose) 1964 *I, E*, 1965 *E, SA*, 1966 *F, I, E, A*, 1967 *F, W, NZ*, 1968 *F, W, I*

Chisholm, R W T (Melrose) 1955 *I, E*, 1956 *F, W, I, E*, 1958 *F, W, A, I*, 1960 *SA*

Church, W C (Glasgow Acads) 1906 *W*

Clark, R L (Edinburgh Wands, Royal Navy) 1972 *F, W, E, NZ*, 1973 *F, W, I, E, P*

Clauss, P R A (Oxford U) 1891 *W, I, E*, 1892 *W, E*, 1895 *I*

Clay, A T (Edinburgh Acads) 1886 *W, I, E*, 1887 *I, W, E*, 1888 *W*

Clunies-Ross, A (St Andrews U) 1871 *E*

Coltman, S (Hawick) 1948 *I*, 1949 *F, W, I, E*

Colville, A G (Merchistonians, Blackheath) 1871 *E*, 1872 *E*

Connell, G C (Trinity Acads and London Scottish) 1968 *E, A*, 1969 *F, E*, 1970 *F*

Cooper, M McG (Oxford U) 1936 *W, I*

Cordial, I F (Edinburgh Wands) 1952 *F, W, I, E*

Cotter, J L (Hillhead HSFP) 1934 *I, E*

Cottington, G S (Kelso) 1934 *I, E*, 1935 *W, I*, 1936 *E*

Coughtrie, S (Edinburgh Acads) 1959 *F, W, I, E*, 1962 *W, I, E*, 1963 *F, W, I, E*

Couper, J H (W of Scotland) 1896 *W, I*, 1899 *I*

Coutts, F H (Melrose, Army) 1947 *W, I, E*

Coutts, I D F (Old Alleynians) 1951 *F*, 1952 *E*

Cowan, R C (Selkirk) 1961 *F*, 1962 *F, W, I, E*

Cowie, W L K (Edinburgh Wands) 1953 *E*

Cownie, W B (Watsonians) 1893 *W, I, E*, 1894 *W, I, E*, 1895 *W, I, E*

Crabbie, G E (Edinburgh Acads) 1904 *W*

Crabbie, J E (Edinburgh Acads, Oxford U) 1900 *W*, 1902 *I*, 1903 *W, I*, 1904 *E*, 1905 *W*

Craig, J B (Heriot's FP) 1939 *W*

Cramb, R I (Harlequins) 1987 *[R(R)]*, 1988 *I, F, A*

Cranston, A G (Hawick) 1976 *W, E, I*, 1977 *E, W*, 1978 *F* (R), *W, E, NZ*, 1981 *NZ* 1,2

Crawford, J A (Army, London Scottish) 1934 *I*

Crawford, W H (United Services, RN) 1938 *W, I, E*, 1939 *W, E*

Crichton-Miller, D (Gloucester) 1931 *W, I, E*

Crole, G B (Oxford U) 1920 *F, W, I, E*

Cronin, D F (Bath) 1988 *I, F, W, E, A*, 1989 *W, E, I, F, Fj, R*, 1990 *I, F, W, E, NZ* 1,2, 1991 *F, W, E, I, R, [Z]*

Cross, M (Merchistonians) 1875 *E*, 1876 *E*, 1877 *I, E*, 1878 *E*, 1879 *I, E*, 1880 *I, E*

Cross, W (Merchistonians) 1871 *E*, 1872 *E*

Cumming, R S (Aberdeen U) 1921 *F, W*

Cunningham, G (Oxford U) 1908 *W, I*, 1909 *W, E*, 1910 *F, I, E*, 1911 *E*

Cunningham, R F (Gala) 1978 *NZ*, 1979 *W, E*

Currie, L R (Dunfermline) 1947 *A*, 1948 *F, W, I*, 1949 *F, W, I, E*

Cuthbertson, W (Kilmarnock, Harlequins) 1980 *I*, 1981 *W, E, I, NZ* 1,2, *R, A*, 1982 *E, I, F, W, A* 1,2, 1983 *I, F, W, NZ*, 1984 *W, E, A*

Irvine, T W (Edinburgh Acads) 1885 *I* 1,2, 1886 *W, I, E*, 1887 *I, W, E*, 1888 *W, I*, 1889 *I*

Jackson, K L T (Oxford U) 1933 *W, E, I*, 1934 *W*
Jackson, T G H (Army) 1947 *F, W, E, A*, 1948 *F, W, I, E*, 1949 *F, W, I, E*
Jackson, W D (Hawick) 1964 *I*, 1965 *E, SA*, 1968 *A*, 1969 *F, W, I, E*
Jamieson, J (W of Scotland) 1883 *W, I, E*, 1884 *W, I, E*, 1885 *W, I* 1,2
Jeffrey, J (Kelso) 1984 *A*, 1985 *I, E*, 1986 *F, W, E, I, R*, 1987 *I, F, W, E, [F, Z, R]*, 1988 *I, W, A*, 1989 *W, E, I, F, Fj, R*, 1990 *I, F, W, E, NZ* 1,2, *Arg*, 1991 *F, W, E, I, [J, I, WS, E, NZ]*
Johnston, D I (Watsonians) 1979 *NZ*, 1980 *I, F, W, E*, 1981 *R, A*, 1982 *E, I, F, W, A* 1,2, 1983 *I, F, W, NZ*, 1984 *W, E, I, F, R*, 1986 *F, W, E, I, R*
Johnston, H H (Edinburgh Collegian FP) 1877 *I, E*
Johnston, J (Melrose) 1951 *SA*, 1952 *F, W, I, E*
Johnston, W C (Glasgow HSFP) 1922 *F*
Johnston, W G S (Cambridge U) 1935 *W, I*, 1937 *W, I, E*
Jones, P M (Gloucester) 1992 *W*(R)
Junor, J E (Glasgow Acads) 1876 *E*, 1877 *I, E*, 1878 *E*, 1879 *I*, 1881 *I*

Keddie, R R (Watsonians) 1967 *NZ*
Keith, G J (Wasps) 1968 *F, W*
Keller, D H (London Scottish) 1949 *F, W, I, E*, 1950 *F, W, I*
Kelly, R F (Watsonians) 1927 *A*, 1928 *F, W, E*
Kemp, J W Y (Glasgow HSFP) 1954 *W*, 1955 *F, W, I, E*, 1956 *F, W, I, E*, 1957 *F, W, I, E*, 1958 *F, W, A, I, E*, 1959 *F, W, I, E*, 1960 *F, W, I, E, SA*
Kennedy, A E (Watsonians) 1983 *NZ*, 1984 *W, E, A*
Kennedy, F (Stewart's Coll FP) 1920 *F, W, I, E*, 1921 *E*
Kennedy, N (W of Scotland) 1903 *W, I, E*
Ker, A B M (Kelso) 1988 *W, E*
Ker, H T (Glasgow Acads) 1887 *I, W, E*, 1888 *I*, 1889 *W*, 1890 *I, E*
Kerr, D S (Heriot's FP) 1923 *F, W*, 1924 *F*, 1926 *I, E*, 1927 *W, I, E*, 1928 *I, E*
Kerr, G C (Old Dunelmians, Edinburgh Wands) 1898 *I, E*, 1899 *I, W, E*, 1900 *W, I, E*
Kerr, J M (Heriot's FP) 1935 *NZ*, 1936 *I, E*, 1937 *W, I*
Kerr, W (London Scottish) 1953 *E*
Kidston, D W (Glasgow Acads) 1883 *W, E*
Kidston, W H (W of Scotland) 1874 *E*
Kilgour, I J (RMC Sandhurst) 1921 *F*
King, J H F (Selkirk) 1953 *F, W, E*, 1954 *E*
Kininmonth, P W (Oxford U, Richmond) 1949 *F, W, I, E*, 1950 *F, W, I, E*, 1951 *F, W, I, E, SA*, 1952 *F, W, I*, 1954 *F, NZ, I, E, W*
Kinnear, R M (Heriot's FP) 1926 *F, W, I*
Knox, J (Kelvinside Acads) 1903 *W, I, E*
Kyle, W E (Hawick) 1902 *W, I, E*, 1903 *W, I, E*, 1904 *W, I, E*, 1905 *W, I, E, NZ*, 1906 *W, I, E*, 1908 *E*, 1909 *W, I, E*, 1910 *W*

Laidlaw, A S (Hawick) 1897 *I*
Laidlaw, F A L (Melrose) 1965 *F, W, I, E, SA*, 1966 *F, W, I, E, A*, 1967 *F, W, I, E, NZ*, 1968 *F, W, I, A*, 1969 *F, W, I, E, SA*, 1970 *F, W, I, E, A*, 1971 *F, W, I*
Laidlaw, R J (Jedforest) 1980 *I, F, W, E*, 1981 *F, W, E, I, NZ* 1,2, *R, A*, 1982 *E, I, F, W, A* 1,2, 1983 *I, F, W, E, NZ*, 1984 *W, E, I, F, R, A*, 1985 *I, F, W, E, I, R*, 1987 *I, F, W, E, [F, R, NZ]*, 1988 *I, F, W, E*
Laing, A D (Royal HSFP) 1914 *W, I, E*, 1920 *F, W, I*, 1921 *F*
Lambie, I K (Watsonians) 1978 *NZ* (R), 1979 *W, E, NZ*
Lambie, L B (Glasgow HSFP) 1934 *W, I, E*, 1935 *W, I, E, NZ*
Lamond, G A W (Kelvinside Acads) 1899 *W, E*, 1905 *E*
Lang, D (Paisley) 1876 *E*, 1877 *I*
Langrish, R W (London Scottish) 1930 *F*, 1931 *F, W, I*
Lauder, W (Neath) 1969 *I, E, SA*, 1970 *F, W, I, A*, 1973 *F*, 1974 *W, E, I, F*, 1975 *I, F, NZ, A*, 1976 *I*, 1977 *E*
Laughland, I H P (London Scottish) 1959 *F*, 1960 *F, W, I, E*, 1961 *SA, W, I, E*, 1962 *F, W, I, E*, 1963 *F, W, I*, 1964 *F, NZ, W, I, E*, 1965 *F, W, I, E, SA*, 1966 *F, W, I, E*, 1967 *E*

Lawrie, J R (Melrose) 1922 *F, W, I, E*, 1923 *F, W, I, E*, 1924 *W, I, E*
Lawrie, K G (Gala) 1980 *F* (R), *W, E*
Lawson, A J M (Edinburgh Wands, London Scottish) 1972 *F* (R), *E*, 1973 *F*, 1974 *W, E*, 1976 *E, I*, 1977 *E*, 1978 *NZ*, 1979 *W, E, I, F, NZ*, 1980 *W* (R)
Lawther, T H B (Old Millhillians) 1932 *SA, W*
Ledingham, G A (Aberdeen GSFP) 1913 *F*
Lees, J B (Gala) 1947 *I, A*, 1948 *F, W, E*
Leggatt, H T O (Watsonians) 1891 *W, I, E*, 1892 *W, I*, 1893 *W, E*, 1894 *I, E*
Lely, W G (Cambridge U, London Scottish) 1909 *I*
Leslie, D G (Dundee HSFP, W of Scotland, Gala) 1975 *I, F, W, E, NZ, A*, 1976 *F, W, E, I*, 1978 *NZ*, 1980 *E*, 1981 *W, E, I, NZ* 1,2, *R, A*, 1982 *E*, 1983 *I, F, W, E*, 1984 *W, E, I, F, R*, 1985 *F, W, E*
Liddell, E H (Edinburgh U) 1922 *F, W, I*, 1923 *F, W, I, E*
Lind, H (Dunfermline) 1928 *I*, 1931 *F, W, I, E*, 1932 *SA, W, E*, 1933 *W, E, I*, 1934 *W, I, E*, 1935 *I*, 1936 *E*
Lindsay, A B (London Hospital) 1910 *I*, 1911 *I*
Lindsay, G C (London Scottish) 1884 *W*, 1885 *I* 1, 1887 *W, E*
Lindsay-Watson, R H (Hawick) 1909 *I*
Lineen, S R P (Boroughmuir) 1989 *W, E, I, F, Fj, R*, 1990 *I, F, W, E, NZ* 1,2, *Arg*, 1991 *F, W, E, I, R, [J, Z, I, E, NZ]*, 1992 *E, I, F, W*
Little, A W (Hawick) 1905 *W*
Logan, W R (Edinburgh U, Edinburgh Wands) 1931 *E*, 1932 *SA, W, I*, 1933 *W, E, I*, 1934 *W, I, E*, 1935 *W, I, E, NZ*, 1936 *W, I, E*, 1937 *W, I, E*
Lorraine, H D B (Oxford U) 1933 *W, E, I*
Loudoun-Shand, E G (Oxford U) 1913 *E*
Lowe, J D (Heriot's FP) 1934 *W*
Lumsden, I J M (Bath, Watsonians) 1947 *F, W, A*, 1949 *F, W, I, E*
Lyall, G G (Gala) 1947 *A*, 1948 *F, W, I, E*
Lyall, W J C (Edinburgh Acads) 1871 *E*

Macarthur, J P (Waterloo) 1932 *E*
MacCallum, J C (Watsonians) 1905 *E, NZ*, 1906 *W, I, E, SA*, 1907 *W, I, E*, 1908 *W, I, E*, 1909 *W, I, E*, 1910 *F, W, I, E*, 1911 *F, I, E*, 1912 *F, W, I, E*
McClung, T (Edinburgh Acads) 1956 *I, E*, 1957 *W, I, E*, 1959 *F, W, I*, 1960 *W*
McClure, G B (W of Scotland) 1873 *E*
McClure, J H (W of Scotland) 1872 *E*
McCowan, D (W of Scotland) 1880 *I, E*, 1881 *I, E*, 1882 *I, E*, 1883 *I, E*, 1884 *I, E*
McCowat, R H (Glasgow Acads) 1905 *I*
McCrae, I G (Gordonians) 1967 *E*, 1968 *I*, 1969 *F* (R), *W*, 1972 *F, NZ*
McCrow, J W S (Edinburgh Acads) 1921 *I*
McDonald, C (Jedforest) 1947 *A*
Macdonald, D C (Edinburgh U) 1953 *F, W*, 1958 *I, E*
Macdonald, D S M (Oxford U, London Scottish, W of Scotland) 1977 *E, I, F, W*, 1978 *I, W, E*
Macdonald, J D (London Scottish, Army) 1966 *F, W, I, E*, 1967 *W, I, E*
Macdonald, J M (Edinburgh Wands) 1911 *W*
Macdonald, J S (Edinburgh U) 1903 *E*, 1904 *W, I, E*, 1905 *W*
Macdonald, K R (Stewart's Coll FP) 1956 *F, W, I*, 1957 *W, I, E*
Macdonald, R (Edinburgh U) 1950 *F, W, I, E*
McDonald, W A (Glasgow U) 1889 *W*, 1892 *I, E*
Macdonald, W G (London Scottish) 1969 *I* (R)
Macdougall, J B (Greenock Wands, Wakefield) 1913 *F*, 1914 *I*, 1921 *F, I, E*
McEwan, M C (Edinburgh Acads) 1886 *E*, 1887 *I, W, E*, 1888 *W, I*, 1889 *W, I, E*, 1890 *W, I, E*, 1891 *W, I, E*, 1892 *E*
MacEwan, N A (Gala, Highland) 1971 *F, W, I, E* (2[1C]), 1972 *F, W, E, NZ*, 1973 *F, W, I, E, P*, 1974 *W, E, I, F*, 1975 *W, E*
McEwan, W M C (Edinburgh Acads) 1894 *W, E*, 1895 *W, E*, 1896 *W, I, E*, 1897 *I, E*, 1898 *I, E*, 1899 *I, W, E*, 1900 *W, E*
MacEwen, R K G (Cambridge U, London Scottish) 1954 *F, NZ, I, W*, 1956 *F, W, I, E*, 1957 *F, W, I, E*, 1958 *W*
Macfarlan, D J (London Scottish) 1883 *W*, 1884 *W, I, E*, 1886 *W, I*, 1887 *I*, 1888 *I*

McFarlane, J L H (Edinburgh U) 1871 *E*, 1872 *E*, 1873 *E*

McGaughey, S K (Hawick) 1984 *R*

McGeechan, I R (Headingley) 1972 *NZ*, 1973 *F, W, I, E, P*, 1974 *W, E, I, F*, 1975 *I, F, W, E, NZ, A*, 1976 *F, W, E, I*, 1977 *E, I, F, W*, 1978 *I, F, W, NZ*, 1979 *W, E, I, F*

McGlashan, T P L (Royal HSFP) 1947 *F, I, E*, 1954 *F, NZ, I, E, W*

MacGregor, D G (Watsonians, Pontypridd) 1907 *W, I, E*

MacGregor, G (Cambridge U) 1890 *W, I, E*, 1891 *W, I, E*, 1893 *W, I, E*, 1894 *W, I, E*, 1896 *E*

MacGregor, I A A (Hillhead HSFP, Llanelli) 1955 *I, E*, 1956 *F, W, I, E*, 1957 *F, W, I*

MacGregor, J R (Edinburgh U) 1909 *I*

McGuinness, G M (W of Scotland) 1982 *A* 1,2, 1983 *I*, 1985 *I, F, W, E*

McHarg, A F (W of Scotland, London Scottish) 1968 *I, E, A*, 1969 *F, W, I, E*, 1971 *F, W, I, E* (2[1C]), 1972 *F, E, NZ*, 1973 *F, W, I, E, P*, 1974 *W, E, I, F*, 1975 *I, F, W, E, NZ, A*, 1976 *F, W, E, I*, 1977 *E, I, F, W*, 1978 *I, F, W, NZ*, 1979 *W, E*

McIndoe, F (Glasgow Acads) 1886 *W, I*

MacIntyre, I (Edinburgh Wands) 1890 *W, I, E*, 1891 *W, I, E*

McIvor, D J (Edinburgh Acads) 1992 *E, I, F, W*

Mackay, E B (Glasgow Acads) 1920 *W*, 1922 *E*

McKeating, E (Heriot's FP) 1957 *F, W*, 1961 *SA, W, I, E*

McKendrick, J G (W of Scotland) 1889 *I*

Mackenzie, A D G (Selkirk) 1984 *A*

Mackenzie, C J G (United Services) 1921 *E*

Mackenzie, D D (Edinburgh U) 1947 *W, I, E*, 1948 *F, W, I*

Mackenzie, D K A (Edinburgh Wands) 1939 *I, E*

Mackenzie, J M (Edinburgh U) 1905 *NZ*, 1909 *W, I, E*, 1910 *W, I, E*, 1911 *W, I*

Mackenzie, R C (Glasgow Acads) 1877 *I, E*, 1881 *I, E*

Mackie, G Y (Highland) 1975 *A*, 1976 *F, W*, 1978 *F*

MacKinnon, A (London Scottish) 1898 *I, E*, 1899 *I, W, E*, 1900 *E*

Mackintosh, C E W C (London Scottish) 1924 *F*

Mackintosh, H S (Glasgow U, W of Scotland) 1929 *F, W, I, E*, 1930 *F, W, I, E*, 1931 *F, W, I, E*, 1932 *SA, W, I, E*

MacLachlan, L P (Oxford U, London Scottish) 1954 *NZ, I, E, W*

Maclagan, W E (Edinburgh Acads) 1878 *E*, 1879 *I, E*, 1880 *I, E*, 1881 *I, E*, 1882 *I, E*, 1883 *W, I, E*, 1884 *W, I, E*, 1885 *W, I* 1,2, 1887 *I, W, E*, 1888 *W, I*, 1890 *W, I, E*

McLaren, A (Durham County) 1931 *F*

McLaren, E (London Scottish, Royal HSFP) 1923 *F, W, I, E*, 1924 *F*

McLauchlan, J (Jordanhill) 1969 *E, SA*, 1970 *F, W*, 1971 *F, W, I, E* (2[1C]), 1972 *F, W, E, NZ*, 1973 *F, W, I, E, P*, 1974 *W, E, I, F*, 1975 *I, F, W, E, NZ, A*, 1976 *F, W, E, I*, 1977 *W*, 1978 *I, F, W, E, NZ*, 1979 *W, E, I, F, NZ*

McLean, D I (Royal HSFP) 1947 *I, E*

Maclennan, W D (Watsonians) 1947 *F, I*

MacLeod, D A (Glasgow U) 1886 *I, E*

MacLeod, G (Edinburgh Acads) 1878 *E*, 1882 *I*

McLeod, H F (Hawick) 1954 *F, NZ, I, E, W*, 1955 *F, W, I, E*, 1956 *F, W, I, E*, 1957 *F, W, I, E*, 1958 *F, W, A, I, E*, 1959 *F, W, I, E*, 1960 *F, W, I, E, SA*, 1961 *F, SA, W, I, E*, 1962 *F, W, I, E*

MacLeod, K G (Cambridge U) 1905 *NZ*, 1906 *W, I, E, SA*, 1907 *W, I, E*, 1908 *I, E*

MacLeod, L M (Cambridge U) 1904 *W, I, E*, 1905 *W, I, NZ*

Macleod, W M (Fettesian-Lorettonians, Edinburgh Wands) 1886 *W, I*

McMillan, K H D (Sale) 1953 *F, W, I, E*

MacMillan, R G (London Scottish) 1887 *W, I, E*, 1890 *W, I, E*, 1891 *W, E*, 1892 *W, I, E*, 1893 *W, E*, 1894 *W, I, E*, 1895 *W, I, E*, 1897 *I, E*

MacMyn, D J (Cambridge U, London Scottish) 1925 *F, W, I, E*, 1926 *F, W, I, E*, 1927 *E, A*, 1928 *F*

McNeil, A S B (Watsonians) 1935 *I*

McPartlin, J J (Harlequins, Oxford U) 1960 *F, W*, 1962 *F, W, I, E*

Macphail, J A R (Edinburgh Acads) 1949 *E*, 1951 *SA*

Macpherson, D G (London Hospital) 1910 *I, E*

Macpherson, G P S (Oxford U, Edinburgh Acads) 1922 *F, W, I, E*, 1924 *W, E*, 1925 *F, W, E*, 1927 *F, W, I, E*, 1928 *F, W, E*, 1929 *I, E*, 1930 *F, W, I, E*, 1931 *W, E*, 1932 *SA, E*

Macpherson, N C (Newport, Mon) 1920 *W, I, E*, 1921 *F, E*, 1923 *I, E*

McQueen, S B (Waterloo) 1923 *F, W, I, E*

Macrae, D J (St Andrews U) 1937 *W, I, E*, 1938 *W, I, E*, 1939 *W, I, E*

Mabon, J T (Jedforest) 1898 *I, E*, 1899 *I*, 1900 *I*

Madsen, D F (Gosforth) 1974 *W, E, I, F*, 1975 *I, F, W, E*, 1976 *F*, 1977 *E, I, F, W*, 1978 *I*

Mair, N G R (Edinburgh U) 1951 *F, W, I, E*

Maitland, G (Edinburgh Inst FP) 1885 *W, I* 2

Maitland, R (Edinburgh Inst FP) 1881 *E*, 1882 *I, E*, 1884 *W*, 1885 *W*

Maitland, R P (Royal Artillery) 1872 *E*

Malcolm, A G (Glasgow U) 1888 *I*

Marsh, J (Edinburgh Inst FP) 1889 *W, I*

Marshall, A (Edinburgh Acads) 1875 *E*

Marshall, G R (Selkirk) 1988 *A* (R), 1989 *Fj*, 1990 *Arg*, 1991 [*Z*]

Marshall, J C (London Scottish) 1954 *F, NZ, I, E, W*

Marshall, K W (Edinburgh Acads) 1934 *W, I, E*, 1935 *W, I, E*, 1936 *W*, 1937 *E*

Marshall, T R (Edinburgh Acads) 1871 *E*, 1872 *E*, 1873 *E*, 1874 *E*

Marshall, W (Edinburgh Acads) 1872 *E*

Martin, H (Edinburgh Acads, Oxford U) 1908 *W, I, E*, 1909 *W, E*

Masters, W H (Edinburgh Inst FP) 1879 *I*, 1880 *I, E*

Maxwell, F T (Royal Engineers) 1872 *E*

Maxwell, G H H P (Edinburgh Acads, RAF, London Scottish) 1913 *I, E*, 1914 *W, I, E*, 1920 *W, E*, 1921 *F, W, I, E*, 1922 *F, E*

Maxwell, J M (Langholm) 1957 *I*

Mein, J (Edinburgh Acads) 1871 *E*, 1872 *E*, 1873 *E*, 1874 *E*, 1875 *E*

Melville, C L (Army) 1937 *W, I, E*

Menzies, H F (W of Scotland) 1893 *W, I*, 1894 *W, E*

Methuen, A (London Scottish) 1889 *W, I*

Michie, E J S (Aberdeen U, Aberdeen GSFP) 1954 *F, NZ, I, E*, 1955 *W, I, E*, 1956 *F, W, I, E*, 1957 *F, W, I, E*

Millar, J N (W of Scotland) 1892 *W, I, E*, 1893 *W*, 1895 *I, E*

Millar, R K (London Scottish) 1924 *I*

Millican, J G (Edinburgh U) 1973 *W, I, E*

Milne, C J B (Fettesian-Lorettonians, W of Scotland) 1886 *W, I, E*

Milne, D F (Heriot's FP) 1991 [*J*(R)]

Milne, I G (Heriot's FP, Harlequins) 1979 *I, F, NZ*, 1980 *I, F*, 1981 *NZ* 1,2, *R, A*, 1982 *E, I, F, W, A* 1,2, 1983 *I, F, W, E, NZ*, 1984 *W, E, I, F, A*, 1985 *F, W, E*, 1986 *F, W, E, I, R*, 1987 *I, F, W, E*, [*F, Z, NZ*], 1988 *A*, 1989 *W*, 1990 *NZ* 1,2

Milne, K S (Heriot's FP) 1989 *W, E, I, F, Fj, R*, 1990 *I, F, W, E*, 1990 *NZ* 2 *Arg*, 1991 *F, W*(R), *E*, [*Z*], 1992 *E, I, F, W*

Milne, W M (Glasgow Acads) 1904 *I, E*, 1905 *W, I*

Milroy, E (Watsonians) 1910 *W*, 1911 *E*, 1912 *W, I, E, SA*, 1913 *F, W, I, E*, 1914 *I, E*

Mitchell, G W E (Edinburgh Wands) 1967 *NZ*, 1968 *F, W*

Mitchell, J G (W of Scotland) 1885 *W, I* 1,2

Moncreiff, F J (Edinburgh Acads) 1871 *E*, 1872 *E*, 1873 *E*

Monteith, H G (Cambridge U, London Scottish) 1905 *E*, 1906 *W, I, E, SA*, 1907 *W, I*, 1908 *E*

Monypenny, D B (London Scottish) 1899 *I, W, E*

Moodie, A R (St Andrew's U) 1909 *E*, 1910 *F*, 1911 *F*

Moore, A (Edinburgh Acads) 1990 *NZ* 2, *Arg*, 1991 *F, W, E*

Morgan, D W (Stewart's-Melville FP) 1973 *W, I, E, P*, 1974 *I, F*, 1975 *I, F, W, E, NZ, A*, 1976 *F, W*, 1977 *I, F, W*, 1978 *I, F, W, E*

Morrison, M C (Royal HSFP) 1896 *W, I, E*, 1897 *I, E*, 1898 *I, E*, 1899 *I, W, E*, 1900 *W, E*, 1901 *W, I, E*, 1902 *W, I, E*, 1903 *W, I*, 1904 *W, I, E*

Morrison, R H (Edinburgh U) 1886 *W, I, E*

Morrison, W H (Edinburgh Acads) 1900 *W*

Morton, D S (W of Scotland) 1887 *I, W, E*, 1888 *W, I*, 1889 *W, I*, 1890 *I, E*

Mowat, J G (Glasgow Acads) 1883 *W, E*
Muir, D E (Heriot's FP) 1950 *F, W, I, E*, 1952 *W, I, E*
Munnoch, N M (Watsonians) 1952 *F, W, I*
Munro, P (Oxford, London Scottish) 1905 *W, I, E,
NZ*, 1906 *W, I, E, SA*, 1907 *I, E*, 1911 *F, W, I*
Munro, R (St Andrews U) 1871 *E*
Munro, S (Ayr, W of Scotland) 1980 *I, F*, 1981 *F, W,
E, I, NZ* 1,2, *R*, 1984 *W*
Munro, W H (Glasgow HSFP) 1947 *I, E*
Murdoch, W C W (Hillhead HSFP) 1935 *E, NZ*, 1936
W, I, 1939 *E*, 1948 *F, W, I, E*
Murray, G M (Glasgow Acads) 1921 *I*, 1926 *W*
Murray, H M (Glasgow U) 1936 *W, I*
Murray, K T (Hawick) 1985 *I, F, W*
Murray, R O (Cambridge U) 1935 *W, E*
Murray, W A K (London Scottish) 1920 *F, I*, 1921 *F*

Napier, H M (W of Scotland) 1877 *I, E*, 1878 *E*, 1879
I, E
Neill, J B (Edinburgh Acads) 1963 *E*, 1964 *F, NZ, W,
I, E*, 1965 *F*
Neill, R M (Edinburgh Acads) 1901 *E*, 1902 *I*
Neilson, G T (W of Scotland) 1891 *W, I, E*, 1892 *W, E*,
1893 *W*, 1894 *W, I*, 1895 *W, I, E*, 1896 *W, I, E*
Neilson, J A (Glasgow Acads) 1878 *E*, 1879 *E*
Neilson, R T (W of Scotland) 1898 *I, E*, 1899 *I, W*,
1900 *I, E*
Neilson, T (W of Scotland) 1874 *E*
Neilson, W (Merchiston, Cambridge U, London Scottish) 1891 *W, E*, 1892 *W, I, E*, 1893 *I, E*, 1894 *E*, 1895
W, I, E, 1896 *I*, 1897 *I, E*
Neilson, W G (Merchistonians) 1894 *E*
Nelson, J B (Glasgow Acads) 1925 *F, W, I, E*, 1926 *F,
W, I, E*, 1927 *F, W, I, E*, 1928 *I, E*, 1929 *F, W, I, E*,
1930 *F, W, I, E*, 1931 *F, W, I*
Nelson, T A (Oxford U) 1898 *E*
Nicol, A D (Dundee HSFP) 1992 *E, I, F, W*
Nichol, J A (Royal HSFP) 1955 *W, I, E*
Nimmo, C S (Watsonians) 1920 *E*

Ogilvy, C (Hawick) 1911 *I, E*, 1912 *I*
Oliver, G H (Hawick) 1987 [Z], 1990 *NZ* 2 (R), 1991
[Z]
Oliver, G K (Gala) 1970 *A*
Orr, C E (W of Scotland) 1887 *I, E, W*, 1888 *W, I*, 1889
W, I, 1890 *W, I, E*, 1891 *W, I, E*, 1892 *W, I, E*
Orr, H J (London Scottish) 1903 *W, I, E*, 1904 *W, I*
Orr, J E (W of Scotland) 1889 *I*, 1890 *W, I, E*, 1891 *W,
I, E*, 1892 *W, I, E*, 1893 *I, E*
Orr, J H (Edinburgh City Police) 1947 *F, W*
Osler, F L (Edinburgh U) 1911 *F, W*

Park, J (Royal HSFP) 1934 *W*
Paterson, D S (Gala) 1969 *SA*, 1970 *I, E, A*, 1971 *F, W,
I, E* (2[1C]), 1972 *W*
Paterson, G Q (Edinburgh Acads) 1876 *E*
Paterson, J R (Birkenhead Park) 1924 *F, W, I, E*, 1926
F, W, I, E, 1927 *F, W, I, E, A*, 1928 *F, W, I, E*, 1929
F, W, I, E
Patterson, D (Hawick) 1896 *W*
Pattullo, G L (Panmure) 1920 *F, W, I, E*
Paxton, I A M (Selkirk) 1981 *NZ* 1,2, *R, A*, 1982 *E, I,
F, W, A* 1,2, 1983 *I, E, NZ*, 1984 *W, E, I, F*, 1985 *I* (R),
F, W, E, 1986 *W, E, I, R*, 1987 *I, F, W, E*, [*F, Z, R,
NZ*], 1988 *I, E, A*
Paxton, R E (Kelso) 1982 *I, A* 2 (R)
Pearson, J (Watsonians) 1909 *I, E*, 1910 *F, W, I, E*,
1911 *F*, 1912 *F, W, SA*, 1913 *I, E*
Pender, I M (London Scottish) 1914 *E*
Pender, N E K (Hawick) 1977 *I*, 1978 *F, W, E*
Penman, W M (RAF) 1939 *I*
Peterkin, W A (Edinburgh U) 1881 *E*, 1883 *I*, 1884 *W,
I, E*, 1885 *W, I* 1,2
Petrie, A G (Royal HSFP) 1873 *E*, 1874 *E*, 1875 *E*,
1876 *E*, 1877 *I, E*, 1878 *E*, 1879 *I, E*, 1880 *I, E*
Philp, A (Edinburgh Inst FP) 1882 *E*
Pocock, E I (Edinburgh Wands) 1877 *I, E*
Pollock, J A (Gosforth) 1982 *W*, 1983 *E, NZ*, 1984 *E*
(R), *I, F, R*, 1985 *F*
Polson, A H (Gala) 1930 *E*
Purdie, W (Jedforest) 1939 *W, I, E*
Purves, A B H L (London Scottish) 1906 *W, I, E, SA*,
1907 *W, I, E*, 1908 *W, I, E*
Purves, W D C L (London Scottish) 1912 *F, W, I, SA*,
1913 *I, E*

Rea, C W W (W of Scotland, Headingley) 1968 *A*, 1969
F, W, I, SA, 1970 *F, W, I, A*, 1971 *F, W, E* (2[1C])
Reid, C (Edinburgh Acads) 1881 *I, E*, 1882 *I, E*, 1883
W, I, E, 1884 *W, I, E*, 1885 *W, I* 1,2, 1886 *W, I, E*, 1887
I, W, E, 1888 *W, I*
Reid, J (Edinburgh Wands) 1874 *E*, 1875 *E*, 1876 *E*,
1877 *I, E*
Reid, J M (Edinburgh Acads) 1898 *I, E*, 1899 *I*
Reid, M F (Loretto) 1883 *I, E*
Reid-Kerr, J (Greenock Wand) 1909 *E*
Relph, W K L (Stewart's Coll FP) 1955 *F, W, I, E*
Renny-Tailyour, H W (Royal Engineers) 1872 *E*
Renwick, J M (Hawick) 1972 *F, W, E, NZ*, 1973 *F*,
1974 *W, E, I, F*, 1975 *I, F, W, E, NZ, A*, 1976 *F, W,
E*(R), 1977 *I, F, W*, 1978 *I, F, W, E, NZ*, 1979 *W, E,
I, F, NZ*, 1980 *I, F, W, E*, 1981 *F, W, E, I, NZ* 1,2, *R,
A*, 1982 *E, I, F, W*, 1983 *I, F, W, E*, 1984 *R*
Renwick, W L (London Scottish) 1989 *R*
Renwick, W N (London Scottish, Edinburgh Wands)
1938 *E*, 1939 *W*
Ritchie, G (Merchistonians) 1871 *E*
Ritchie, G F (Dundee HSFP) 1932 *E*
Ritchie, J M (Watsonians) 1933 *W, E, I*, 1934 *W; I, E*
Ritchie, W T (Cambridge U) 1905 *I, E*
Robb, G H (Glasgow U) 1881 *I*, 1885 *W*
Roberts, G (Watsonians) 1938 *W, I, E*, 1939 *W, E*
Robertson, A H (W of Scotland) 1871 *E*
Robertson, A W (Edinburgh Acads) 1897 *E*
Robertson, D (Edinburgh Acads) 1875 *E*
Robertson, D D (Cambridge U) 1893 *W*
Robertson, I (London Scottish, Watsonians) 1968 *E*,
1969 *E, SA*, 1970 *F, W, I, E, A*
Robertson, I P M (Watsonians) 1910 *F*
Robertson, J (Clydesdale) 1908 *E*
Robertson, K W (Melrose) 1978 *NZ*, 1979 *W, E, I, F,
NZ*, 1980 *W, E*, 1981 *F, W, E, I, R, A*, 1982 *E, I, F,
A* 1,2, 1983 *I, F, W, E*, 1984 *E, I, F, R, A*, 1985 *I, F,
W, E*, 1986 *I, F*, 1987 *F* (R), *W, E*, [*F, Z, NZ*], 1988 *E, A*,
1989 *E, I, F*
Robertson, L (London Scottish, United Services) 1908
E, 1911 *W, I, E, SA*, 1913 *W, I, F*
Robertson, M A (Gala) 1958 *F*
Robertson, R D (London Scottish) 1912 *F*
Robson, A (Hawick) 1954 *F*, 1955 *F, W, I, E*, 1956 *F,
W, I, E*, 1957 *F, W, I, E*, 1958 *W, A, I, E*, 1959 *F, W,
I, E*, 1960 *F*
Rodd, J A T (United Services, RN, London Scottish)
1958 *F, W, A, I, E*, 1960 *F, W*, 1962 *F*, 1964 *F, NZ, W*,
1965 *F, W, I*
Rogerson, J (Kelvinside Acads) 1894 *W*
Roland, E T (Edinburgh Acads) 1884 *I, E*
Rollo, D M D (Howe of Fife) 1959 *E*, 1960 *F, W, I, E,
SA*, 1961 *F, SA, W, I, E*, 1962 *F, W, E*, 1963 *F, W, I,
E*, 1964 *F, NZ, W, I, E*, 1965 *F, W, I, E, SA*, 1966 *F,
W, I, E, A*, 1967 *F, W, E, NZ*, 1968 *F, W, I*
Rose, D M (Jedforest) 1951 *F, W, I, E, SA*, 1953 *F, W*
Ross, A (Kilmarnock) 1924 *F, W*
Ross, A (Royal HSFP) 1905 *W, I, E*, 1909 *W, I*
Ross, A R (Edinburgh U) 1911 *W, I, E*, 1914 *W, I, E*
Ross, E J (London Scottish) 1904 *W*
Ross, G T (Watsonians) 1954 *NZ, I, E, W*
Ross, I A (Hillhead HSFP) 1951 *F, W, I, E*
Ross, J (London Scottish) 1901 *W, I, E*, 1902 *W*, 1903
E
Ross, K I (Boroughmuir FP) 1961 *SA, W, I, E*, 1962 *F,
W, I, E*, 1963 *F, W, E*
Ross, W A (Hillhead HSFP) 1937 *W, E*
Rottenburg, H (Cambridge U, London Scottish) 1899
W, E, 1900 *W, I, E*
Roughead, W N (Edinburgh Acads, London Scottish)
1927 *A*, 1928 *F, W, I, E*, 1930 *I, E*, 1931 *F, W, I, E*,
1932 *W*
Rowan, N A (Boroughmuir) 1980 *W, E*, 1981 *F, W, E,
I*, 1984 *R*, 1985 *I*, 1987 [R], 1988 *I, F, W, E*
Rowand, R (Glasgow HSFP) 1930 *F, W*, 1932 *E*, 1933
W, E, I, 1934 *W*
Roy, A (Waterloo) 1938 *W, I, E*, 1939 *W, I, E*
Russell, W L (Glasgow Acads) 1905 *NZ*, 1906 *W, I, E*
Rutherford, J Y (Selkirk) 1979 *W, E, I, F, NZ*, 1980 *I,
F, E*, 1981 *F, W, E, I, NZ* 1,2, *A*, 1982 *E, I, F, W*, *A*
1,2, 1983 *E, NZ*, 1984 *W, E, I, F, R*, 1985 *I, F, W, E*,
1986 *F, W, E, I, R*, 1987 *I, F, W, E*, [*F*]

Sampson, R W F (London Scottish) 1939 *W*, 1947 *W*

Sanderson, G A (Royal HSFP) 1907 *W, I, E*, 1908 *I*
Sanderson, J L P (Edinburgh Acads) 1873 *E*
Schulze, D G (London Scottish) 1905 *E*, 1907 *I, E*, 1908 *W, I, E*, 1909 *W, I, E*, 1910 *W, I, E*, 1911 *W*
Scobie, R M (Royal Military Coll) 1914 *W, I, E*
Scotland, K J F (Heriot's FP, Cambridge U, Leicester) 1957 *F, W, I, E*, 1958 *E*, 1959 *F, W, I, E*, 1960 *F, W, I, E*, 1961 *F, SA, W, I, E*, 1962 *F, W, I, E*, 1963 *F, W, I, E*, 1965 *F*
Scott, D M (Langholm, Watsonians) 1950 *I, E*, 1951 *W, I, E, SA*, 1952 *F, W, I*, 1953 *F*
Scott, J M B (Edinburgh Acads) 1907 *E*, 1908 *W, I, E*, 1909 *W, I, E*, 1910 *F, W, I, E*, 1911 *F, W, I*, 1912 *W, I, E, SA*, 1913 *W, I, E*
Scott, J S (St Andrews U) 1950 *E*
Scott, J W (Stewart's Coll FP) 1925 *F, W, I, E*, 1926 *F, W, I, E*, 1927 *F, W, I, E, A*, 1928 *F, W, E*, 1929 *E*, 1930 *F*
Scott, R (Hawick) 1898 *I*, 1900 *I, E*
Scott, T (Langholm, Hawick) 1896 *W*, 1897 *I, E*, 1898 *I, E*, 1899 *I, W, E*, 1900 *W, I, E*
Scott, T M (Hawick) 1893 *E*, 1895 *W, I, E*, 1896 *W, E*, 1897 *I, E*, 1898 *I, E*, 1900 *W, I*
Scott, W P (W of Scotland) 1900 *I, E*, 1902 *I, E*, 1903 *W, I, E*, 1904 *W, I, E*, 1905 *W, I, E, NZ*, 1906 *W, I, E, SA*, 1907 *W, I, E*
Scoular, J G (Cambridge U) 1905 *NZ*, 1906 *W, I, E, SA*
Selby, J A R (Watsonians) 1920 *W, I*
Shackleton, J A P (London Scottish) 1959 *E*, 1963 *F, W*, 1964 *NZ, W*, 1965 *I, SA*
Sharp, G (Stewart's FP, Army) 1960 *F*, 1964 *F, NZ, W*, 1939 *I*
Shaw, G D (Sale) 1935 *NZ*, 1936 *W*, 1937 *W, I, E*, 1939 *I*
Shaw, I (Glasgow HSFP) 1937 *I*
Shaw, J N (Edinburgh Acads) 1921 *W, I*
Shaw, R W (Glasgow HSFP) 1934 *W, I, E*, 1935 *W, I, E, NZ*, 1936 *W, I, E*, 1937 *W, I, E*, 1938 *W, I, E*, 1939 *W, I, E*
Shedden, D (W of Scotland) 1972 *NZ*, 1973 *F, W, I, E, P*, 1976 *W, E, I*, 1977 *I, F, W*, 1978 *I, F, W*
Shiel, A G (Melrose) 1991 *[I(R), WS]*
Shillinglaw, R B (Gala, Army) 1960 *I, E, SA*, 1961 *F, SA*
Simmers, B M (Glasgow Acads) 1965 *F, W*, 1966 *A*, 1967 *F, W, I*, 1971 *F* (R)
Simmers, W M (Glasgow Acads) 1926 *W, I, E*, 1927 *F, W, I, E, A*, 1928 *F, W, I, E*, 1929 *F, W, I, E*, 1930 *F, W, I, E*, 1931 *F, W, I, E*, 1932 *SA, W, I, E*
Simpson, J W (Royal HSFP) 1893 *I, E*, 1894 *W, I, E*, 1895 *W, I, E*, 1896 *W, I*, 1897 *E*, 1899 *W, E*
Simpson, R S (Glasgow Acads) 1923 *I*
Simson, E D (Edinburgh U, London Scottish) 1902 *E*, 1903 *W, I, E*, 1904 *W, I, E*, 1905 *W, I, E, NZ*, 1906 *W, I, E*, 1907 *W, I, E*
Simson, J T (Watsonians) 1905 *NZ*, 1909 *W, I, E*, 1910 *F, W*, 1911 *I*
Simson, R F (London Scottish) 1911 *E*
Sloan, A T (Edinburgh Acads) 1914 *W*, 1920 *F, W, I, E*, 1921 *F, W, I, E*
Sloan, D A (Edinburgh Acads, London Scottish) 1950 *F, W, E*, 1951 *W, I, E*, 1953 *F*
Sloan, T (Glasgow Acads, Oxford U) 1905 *NZ*, 1906 *W, SA*, 1907 *W, E*, 1908 *W*, 1909 *I*
Smeaton, P W (Edinburgh Acads) 1881 *I*, 1883 *I, E*
Smith, A R (Oxford U) 1895 *W, I, E*, 1896 *W, I*, 1897 *I, E*, 1898 *I, E*, 1900 *I, E*
Smith, A R (Cambridge U, Gosforth, Ebbw Vale, Edinburgh Wands) 1955 *W, I, E*, 1956 *F, W, I, E*, 1957 *F, W, I, E*, 1958 *F, W, A, I*, 1959 *F, W, I, E*, 1960 *F, W, I, E, SA*, 1961 *F, SA, W, I, E*, 1962 *F, W, I, E*
Smith, D W C (London Scottish) 1949 *F, W, I, E*, 1950 *F, W, I*, 1953 *I*
Smith, E R (Edinburgh Acads) 1879 *I*
Smith, G K (Kelso) 1957 *I, E*, 1958 *F, W, A*, 1959 *F, W, I, E*, 1960 *F, W, I, E*, 1961 *F, SA, W, I, E*
Smith, H O (Watsonians) 1895 *W*, 1896 *W, I, E*, 1898 *I, E*, 1899 *W, I, E*, 1900 *E*, 1902 *E*
Smith, I R (Gloucester) 1992 *E, I, W*
Smith, I S (Oxford U, Edinburgh U) 1924 *W, I, E*, 1925 *F, W, I, E*, 1926 *F, W, I, E*, 1927 *F, I, E*, 1929 *F, W, I, E*, 1930 *F, W, I*, 1931 *F, W, I, E*, 1932 *SA, W, I, E*, 1933 *W, E, I*
Smith, I S G (London Scottish) 1969 *SA*, 1970 *F, W, I,*

E, 1971 *F, W, I*
Smith, M A (London Scottish) 1970 *W, I, E, A*
Smith, R T (Kelso) 1929 *F, W, I, E*, 1930 *F, W, I*
Smith, S H (Glasgow Acads) 1877 *I*, 1878 *E*
Smith, T J (Gala) 1983 *E, NZ*, 1985 *I, F*
Sole, D M B (Bath, Edinburgh Acads) 1986 *F, W*, 1987 *I, F, W, E, [F, Z, R, NZ]*, 1988 *I, F, W, E, A*, 1989 *W, E, I, F, Fj, R*, 1990 *I, F, W, E, NZ* 1,2, *Arg*, 1991 *F, W, E, I, R, [J, I, WS, E, NZ]*, 1992 *E, I, F, W*
Somerville, D (Edinburgh Inst FP) 1879 *I*, 1882 *I*, 1883 *W, I, E*, 1884 *W*
Speirs, L M (Watsonians) 1906 *SA*, 1907 *W, I, E*, 1908 *W, I, E*, 1910 *F, W, E*
Spence, K M (Oxford U) 1953 *I*
Spencer, E (Clydesdale) 1898 *I*
Stagg, P K (Sale) 1965 *F, W, E, SA*, 1966 *F, W, I, E, A*, 1967 *F, W, I, E, NZ*, 1968 *F, W, I, E, A*, 1969 *F, W, I* (R), *SA*, 1970 *F, W, I, E, A*
Stanger, A G (Hawick) 1989 *Fj, R*, 1990 *I, F, W, E, NZ* 1,2, *Arg*, 1991 *F, W, E, I, R, [J, Z, I, WS, E, NZ]*, 1992 *E, I, F, W*
Steele, W C C (Langholm, Bedford, RAF, London Scottish) 1969 *E*, 1971 *F, W, I, E* (2[1C]), 1972 *F, W, E, NZ*, 1973 *F, W, I, E*, 1975 *I, F, W, E, NZ* (R), 1976 *W, E, I*, 1977 *E*
Stephen, A E (W of Scotland) 1885 *W*, 1886 *I*
Steven, P D (Heriot's FP) 1984 *A*, 1985 *F, W, E*
Steven, R (Edinburgh Wands) 1962 *I*
Stevenson, A K (Glasgow Acads) 1922 *F*, 1923 *F, W, E*
Stevenson, A M (Glasgow U) 1911 *F*
Stevenson, G D (Hawick) 1956 *E*, 1957 *F*, 1958 *F, W, A, I, E*, 1959 *W, I, E*, 1960 *W, I, E, SA*, 1961 *F, SA, W, I, E*, 1963 *F, W, I*, 1964 *E*, 1965 *F*
Stevenson, H J (Edinburgh Acads) 1888 *W, I*, 1889 *W, I*, 1890 *W, I, E*, 1891 *W, I, E*, 1892 *W, I, E*, 1893 *I, E*
Stevenson, L E (Edinburgh U) 1888 *W*
Stevenson, R C (London Scottish) 1897 *I, E*, 1898 *E*, 1899 *I, W, E*
Stevenson, R C (St Andrews U) 1910 *F, I, E*, 1911 *F, W, I*
Stevenson, W H (Glasgow Acads) 1925 *F*
Stewart, A K (Edinburgh U) 1874 *E*, 1876 *E*
Stewart, A M (Edinburgh Acads) 1914 *W*
Stewart, C A R (W of Scotland) 1880 *I, E*
Stewart, C E B (Kelso) 1960 *W*, 1961 *F*
Stewart, J (Glasgow HSFP) 1930 *F*
Stewart, J L (Edinburgh Acads) 1921 *I*
Stewart, M S (Stewart's Coll FP) 1932 *SA, W, I*, 1933 *W, E, I*, 1934 *W, I, E*
Stewart, W A (London Hospital) 1913 *F, W, I*, 1914 *W*
Steyn, S S L (Oxford U) 1911 *E*, 1912 *I*
Strachan, G M (Jordanhill) 1971 *E* (C) (R), 1973 *W, I, E, P*
Stronach, R S (Glasgow Acads) 1901 *W, E*, 1905 *W, I, E*
Stuart, C D (W of Scotland) 1909 *I*, 1910 *F, W, I, E*, 1911 *I, E*
Stuart, L M (Glasgow HSFP) 1923 *F, W, I, E*, 1924 *F*, 1928 *E*, 1930 *I, E*
Suddon, N (Hawick) 1965 *W, I, E, SA*, 1966 *A*, 1968 *E, A*, 1969 *F, W, I*, 1970 *I, E, A*
Sutherland, W R (Hawick) 1910 *W, E*, 1911 *F, E*, 1912 *F, W, E, SA*, 1913 *F, W, I, E*, 1914 *W*
Swan, J S (Army, London Scottish, Leicester) 1953 *E*, 1954 *F, NZ, I, E, W*, 1955 *F, W, I, E*, 1956 *F, W, I, E*, 1957 *F, W*, 1958 *F*
Swan, M W (Oxford U, London Scottish) 1958 *F, W, A, I, E*, 1959 *F, W, I*
Sweet, J B (Glasgow HSFP) 1913 *E*, 1914 *I*
Symington, A W (Cambridge U) 1914 *W, E*

Tait, A V (Kelso) 1987 *[F(R), Z, R, NZ]*, 1988 *I, F, W, E*
Tait, J G (Edinburgh Acads) 1880 *I*, 1885 *I* 2
Tait, P W (Royal HSFP) 1935 *E*
Taylor, E G (Oxford U) 1927 *W, A*
Taylor, R C (Kelvinside-West) 1951 *W, I, E, SA*
Telfer, C M (Hawick) 1968 *A*, 1969 *F, W, I, E*, 1972 *F, W, E*, 1973 *W, I, E, P*, 1974 *W, E, I*, 1975 *A*, 1976 *F*
Telfer, J W (Melrose) 1964 *F, NZ, W, I, E*, 1965 *F, W, I*, 1966 *F, W, I, E*, 1967 *W, I, E*, 1968 *E, A*, 1969 *F, W, I, E, SA*, 1970 *F, W, I*
Tennent, J M (W of Scotland) 1909 *W, I, E*, 1910 *F, W, E*

SCOTTISH INTERNATIONAL RECORDS

Both team and individual records are for official Scotland international matches, up to 31 March 1992.

TEAM RECORDS

Highest score
60 v Zimbabwe (60-21) 1987 Wellington

v individual countries
46 v Argentina (49-3) 1990 Murrayfield
24 v Australia (24-15) 1981 Murrayfield
33 v England (33-6) 1986 Murrayfield
38 v Fiji (38-17) 1989 Murrayfield
31 v France (31-3) 1912 Inverleith
37 v Ireland (37-21) 1989 Murrayfield
47 v Japan (47-9) 1991 Murrayfield
25 v N Zealand (25-25) 1983 Murrayfield
55 v Romania (55-28) 1987 Dunedin
10 v S Africa (10-18) 1960 Port Elizabeth
35 v Wales (35-10) 1924 Inverleith
28 v W Samoa (28-6) 1991 Murrayfield
60 v Zimbabwe (60-21) 1987 Wellington

Biggest winning points margin
46 v Argentina (49-3) 1990 Murrayfield

v individual countries
46 v Argentina (49-3) 1990 Murrayfield
 9 v Australia (24-15) 1981 Murrayfield
27 v England (33-6) 1986 Murrayfield
21 v Fiji (38-17) 1989 Murrayfield
28 v France (31-3) 1912 Inverleith
23 v Ireland (32-9) 1984 Dublin
38 v Japan (47-9) 1991 Murrayfield
No win v N Zealand
32 v Romania (32-0) 1989 Murrayfield
 6 v S Africa (6-0) 1906 Glasgow
25 v Wales (35-10) 1924 Inverleith
22 v W Samoa (28-6) 1991 Murrayfield
39 v Zimbabwe $\begin{cases} \text{(60-21) 1987 Wellington} \\ \text{(51-12) 1991 Murrayfield} \end{cases}$

Highest score by opposing team
44 S Africa (0-44) 1951 Murrayfield

by individual countries
 3 Argentina (49-3) 1990 Murrayfield
37 Australia (12-37) 1984 Murrayfield
30 England (18-30) 1980 Murrayfield
17 Fiji (38-17) 1989 Murrayfield
28 France (22-28) 1987 Parc de Princes
26 Ireland (8-26) 1953 Murrayfield
 9 Japan (47-9) 1991 Murrayfield
40 N Zealand (15-40) 1981 Auckland

28 Romania $\begin{cases} \text{(22-28) 1984 Bucharest} \\ \text{(55-28) 1987 Dunedin} \end{cases}$
44 S Africa (0-44) 1951 Murrayfield
35 Wales (12-35) 1972 Cardiff
 6 W Samoa (28-6) 1991 Murrayfield
21 Zimbabwe (60-21) 1987 Wellington

Biggest losing points margin
44 v S Africa (0-44) 1951 Murrayfield

v individual countries
25 v Australia (12-37) 1984 Murrayfield
20 v England (6-26) 1977 Twickenham
20 v France (3-23) 1977 Parc des Princes
21 v Ireland (0-21) 1950 Dublin
27 v N Zealand (3-30) 1987 Christchurch
 6 v Romania $\begin{cases} \text{(22-28) 1984 Bucharest} \\ \text{(12-18) 1991 Bucharest} \end{cases}$
44 v S Africa (0-44) 1951 Murrayfield
23 v Wales (12-35) 1972 Cardiff
No defeat v Argentina, Fiji, Japan, Western Samoa or Zimbabwe

Most tries by Scotland in an international
12 v Wales 1887 Raeburn Place (Edinburgh)

Most tries against Scotland in an international
9 by S Africa (0-44) 1951 Murrayfield

Most points by Scotland in International Championship in a season – 86
in season 1983-84

Most tries by Scotland in International Championship in a season – 17
in season 1924-25

INDIVIDUAL RECORDS

Most capped player
J M Renwick 52 1972-84
C T Deans 52 1978-87

in individual positions
Full-back
A R Irvine 47(51)[1] 1972-82
Wing
I Tukalo 35 1985-92
Centre
J M Renwick 51(52)[2] 1972-84
Fly-half
J Y Rutherford 42 1979-87
Scrum-half
R J Laidlaw 47 1980-88
Prop
A B Carmichael 50 1967-78
Hooker
C T Deans 52 1978-87
Lock
A J Tomes 48 1976-87
Flanker
J Jeffrey 40 1984-91
No 8
D B White 29(41)[3] 1982-92
[1]*Irvine played 4 matches as a wing*
[2]*Renwick played once, as a replacement, on the wing*
[3]*White won 5 caps as a flanker and 7 as a lock*

Longest international career
W C W Murdoch 14 seasons 1935-48

Most consecutive Tests – 49
A B Carmichael 1967-78

Most internationals as captain
D M B Sole 23 1989-92

Most points in internationals – 384
A G Hastings (40 matches) 1986-92

**Most points in International
Championship in a season – 52**
A G Hastings (4 matches) 1985-86

Most points in an international – 27
A G Hastings v Romania 1987
    Dunedin

Most tries in internationals – 24
I S Smith (32 matches) 1924-33

**Most tries in International
Championship in a season – 8**
I S Smith (4 matches) 1924-25

Most tries in an international – 5
G C Lindsay v Wales 1887 Raeburn Place
(Edinburgh)

Most conversions in internationals – 58
A G Hastings (40 matches) 1986-92

**Most conversions in International
Championship in a season – 8**
P W Dods (4 matches) 1983-84

Most conversions in an international – 8
A G Hastings v Zimbabwe 1987 Wellington
A G Hastings v Romania 1987 Dunedin

**Most dropped goals in internationals –
12**
J Y Rutherford (42 matches) 1972-82

Most penalty goals in internationals – 76
A G Hastings (40 matches) 1986-92

**Most penalty goals in International
Championship in a season – 14**
A G Hastings (4 matches) 1985-86

Most points on major tour – 58
P W Dods (4 matches) N Zealand 1990
*C D R Mair scored 100 points in the Far East in 1977, but
this was not on a major tour*

Most points in a tour match – 24
D W Morgan v Wellington 1975
    Wellington, NZ
A R Irvine v King Country 1981
    Taumarunui, NZ
A R Irvine v Wairarapa-Bush 1981
    Masterton, NZ
*P W Dods scored 43 points v Alberta in 1985, but this was
not on a major tour*

Most tries in a tour match – 3
A R Smith v Eastern Transvaal 1960
    Springs, SA
*K R F Bearne scored 5 tries v Ontario U in 1964, A J W
Hinshelwood scored 5 v Quebec in 1964, and D E W Leckie
scored 5 v Goshawks (Zimbabwe) in 1988, but these were
not on a major tour*

A SEASON OF DOOM AND DISASTER

THE 1991-92 SEASON IN IRELAND
Sean Diffley *Irish Independent*

The season 1991-92 was one in Irish rugby in which, in accordance with Murphy's Law, anything that could do wrong most certainly would. Of course, the elevation of Noel Murphy to the post of Irish manager was coincidental, an administrative change towards the end of the season because of the wish of Ken Reid to retire from the position. It was a change that came in time for Murphy to take over as the manager for the eight-game tour of New Zealand in May and June, in cahoots with coach Ciaran Fitzgerald and the new assistant coach, also a Murphy – but no relation – Gerry, formerly of Trinity College and Wanderers. Gerry replaced John Moloney, whose departure as assistant to Fitzgerald was clouded in a certain amount of acrimony.

So, what happened to Irish rugby? The display of the young newcomers the previous season may not have been covered in any glory, but the promise seemed to suggest some progress to come. It didn't happen. In fact, matters worsened. The two Test defeats in Namibia in July were followed by a doleful series of World Cup 'warm-up' games in September, including a clear defeat by Gloucester at Kingsholm. The squad looked tired and dispirited rather than a unit champing at the bit, anxious to get stuck into the World Cup.

That World Cup yielded one astonishing instance of flashing steel: the splendid quarter-final against Australia, who came within minutes of being defeated at Lansdowne Road. It is ironic to note now that when the Irish, captain Phil Matthews, coach Fitzgerald and manager Reid came to the press centre for the conference after the game, they received from the international press a spontaneous round of sincere applause.

That was the height of the season's acclaim. Less than four months later, again at Lansdowne Road during the match with Scotland, came the utter depths: a section of the Irish support booing their team. That conduct, however despicable, indicated the country's frustration with a squad that seemed incapable of rising to the traditional elements of the Irish game, spirit and commitment. It was clear that the Irish lacked enough players of international class, but what supporters could not accept was the tepid attitude of the team, particularly in the home games against Wales and Scotland. The paradox of the season was that at Twickenham against England, the vastly superior side of the Five Nations Championship, the Irish played their best football. They were, of course, well outplayed, but at least they gave it their best endeavour, something conspicuous by its absence when Wales and Scotland came to Dublin.

Injuries and illness played their part in Ireland's afflictions. Phil Matthews, never easy in the role of captain, was ill and injured towards

The Ireland team which lost narrowly to Wales at Lansdowne Road. L-R, back row: R C Rees (touch-judge), D C Fitzgerald, J E Staples, B F Robinson, N P J Francis, D G Lenihan, M J Fitzgibbon, S J Smith, N J Popplewell, F A Howard (referee), A J Spreadbury (touch-judge); front row: D M Curtis, R M Wallace, B J Mullin, P M Matthews (capt), A D Browne (president, IRFU), R P Keyes, R Saunders, K D Crossan.

the end of the season, and after his dramatic try against Australia, Gordon Hamilton was unable to play in the Five Nations tournament because of a back injury sustained in the Inter-provincial Championship. His ambition, then, was to regain fitness for the tour to New Zealand. He failed. After he returned to club football in April and was picked for New Zealand, the medical judgements were that he would be unwise to subject himself to a tough tour. And Brian Rigney, injured in Namibia, missed the World Cup and came back into the reckoning only late in the season. Then, just before the final match of the season, against France in Paris, Brendan Mullin, Ireland's most prolific try-scorer of all time, decided to retire.

But at Irish club level the story was much happier. In the previous season the All Ireland League, the first national club competition, had been introduced. It was a great success, providing good and keen competition, enthusiastic support and a remarkable upsurge in spectator attendance. But would lightning strike twice? Would the second AIL live up to the standards set in the inaugural year? Well, it did. One AIL tie at Thomond Park in Limerick in late January, between Garryowen and Shannon, attracted a crowd of just over 15,000, an Irish record for a club match.

Garryowen won the First Division title, underlining again the impact of Munster clubs. Much of the credit went to captain Philip Danaher, and to their New Zealand coach, Murray Kidd, who will remain for a third season in Limerick. Not only did Garryowen win the AIL but they did so in style, with a nice, rounded style of 15-man rugby. The Irish selectors, with a neat sense of good timing, made Danaher captain of Ireland for the last international of the season, against France, and then for the tour of New Zealand. It was, strangely enough, the first time in rugby history that a Garryowen player had been picked as captain of Ireland.

WINNERS OF PROVINCIAL TOURNAMENTS

LEINSTER
Senior Cup: Blackrock College **Senior League:** Clontarf **Schools Senior Cup:** Terenure College **Schools Junior Cup:** St Mary's College

ULSTER
Senior Cup: Malone **Senior League:** NIFC **Schools Senior Cup:** Coleraine AI **Schools Medallion:** RBAI

MUNSTER
Senior Cup: Shannon **Senior League:** Old Crescent **Schools Senior Cup:** PBC **Schools Junior Cup:** PBC

CONNACHT
Senior Cup: Ballinasloe **Senior League:** Galwegians **Schools Senior Cup:** Garbally **Schools Junior Cup:** Garbally

INTER-PROVINCIAL TOURNAMENT 1991

7 December, Sportsground, Galway

Connacht 9 (3PG)   **Munster 15** (2G 1PG)
Connacht: A White (St Mary's Coll); N Furlong (UC Galway), M Cosgrave (Wanderers), S Tormey (Galwegians),
G Curley (Athlone); R Cullen (Bective Rangers), K Lawless (Clontarf); P Leahy (Galwegians), J O'Riordan
(Sunday's Well), D Henshaw (Garryowen), S Jameson (St Mary's Coll), T Coughlin (Old Belvedere), N McCarthy
(St Mary's Coll), N Mannion (Lansdowne), M Fitzgibbon (Shannon) *Replacement* P McGrath (Galwegians) for Leahy
Scorer *Penalty Goals:* White (3)
Munster: D Larkin (Garryowen); R Wallace (Garryowen), P P Danaher (Garryowen), J Clarke (Dolphin), B Walsh
(Cork Const); R Keyes (Cork Const), O Kiely (Shannon); J Fitzgerald (Young Munster), T Kingston (Dolphin),
P McCarthy (Cork Const), P O'Grady (Shannon), T Keogh (Dolphin), K Maher (Shannon), P Hogan (Garryowen),
M O'Donoghue (Garryowen)
Scorers *Tries:* Kiely, Wallace   *Conversions:* Keyes(2)   *Penalty Goal:* Keyes
Referee G Black

7 December, Donnybrook, Dublin

Leinster 21 (2G 2PG 1DG)   **Ulster 22** (1G 4PG 1T)
Leinster: C Clarke (Terenure); D Beggy (Currie), V Cunningham (St Mary's Coll), M Ridge (Blackrock), N Woods
(Blackrock); P Hennebry (Terenure), A Rolland (Blackrock); N O'Donoghue (Terenure), J Murphy (Greystones),
D Dowling (St Mary's Coll), K Potts (St Mary's Coll), R Boyd (Greystones), K Leahy (Wanderers), P Lawlor (Bective),
K Devlin (Old Belvedere) *Replacement* M Wyse (Wanderers) for Hennebry
Scorers *Tries:* Woods, Clarke   *Conversions:* Woods (2)   *Penalty Goals:* Woods (2)   *Dropped Goal:* Ridge
Ulster: C Wilkinson (Malone); R Carey (Dungannon), M McCall (Bangor), M Field (Malone), D Smyth (Ballymena);
D McAleese (Ballymena), A Matchett (Ballymena); D Elliott (Bangor), S Smith (Ballymena), G Bell (Instonians),
G Longwell (Queen's U), C Morrison (Malone), P Johns (Dungannon), B Robinson (Ballymena), G Hamilton
(Ballymena) *Replacement* T McMaster (Bangor) for Smyth
Scorers *Tries:* Smyth, Robinson   *Conversion:* McAleese   *Penalty Goals:* McAleese (4)
Referee B Smith

14 December, Donnybrook

Leinster 24 (1G 2PG 3T)   **Connacht 9** (1G 1PG)
Leinster: C Clarke (Terenure); D Beggy (Currie), B Glennon (Lansdowne), M Ridge (Blackrock), N Woods
(Blackrock); V Cunningham (St Mary's Coll), A Rolland (Blackrock); R Ward (Blackrock), J Murphy (Greystones),
D Dowling (St Mary's Coll), K Potts (St Mary's Coll), G Fulcher (UC Dublin), K Leahy (Wanderers), P Lawlor
(Bective), K Devlin (Old Belvedere) *Replacement* M McArdle (Old Wesley) for Clarke
Scorers *Tries:* Rolland (2), Lawlor, Clarke   *Conversion:* Woods   *Penalty Goals:* Woods (2)
Connacht: A White (St Mary's Coll); M Furlong (UC Galway), S Tormey (Galwegians), M Cosgrave (Wanderers),
G Curley (Athlone); R Cullen (Bective), K Lawless (Clontarf); P Leahy (Galwegians), J O'Riordan (Sunday's Well),
D Henshaw (Athlone), S Jameson (St Mary's Coll), T Coughlin (Old Belvedere), N McCarthy (St Mary's Coll),
N Mannion (Lansdowne), M Fitzgibbon (Shannon)
Scorers *Try:* Lawless   *Conversion:* White   *Penalty Goal:* White
Referee D Henderson

14 December, Ravenhill, Belfast

Ulster 37 (3G 5PG 1T)   **Munster 22** (2G 2PG 1T)
Ulster: C Wilkinson (Malone); R Carey (Dungannon), M McCall (Bangor), M Field (Malone), D Smyth (Ballymena);
D McAleese (Ballymena), A Blair (Dungannon); D Elliott (Bangor), S Smith (Ballymena), P Millar (Ballymena),
G Longwell (Queen's U), C Morrison (Malone), D McCartney (Ballymena), B Robinson (Ballymena), G Hamilton
(Ballymena)
Scorers *Tries:* Carey (2), McCartney, Wilkinson   *Conversions:* McAleese (3)   *Penalty Goals:* McAleese (5)
Munster: D Larkin (Garryowen); R Wallace (Garryowen), P Danaher (Garryowen), J Clarke (Dolphin), B Walsh
(Cork Const); R Keyes (Cork Const), O Kiely (Shannon); P Soden (Cork Const), T Kingston (Dolphin), P McCarthy
(Cork Const), T Keogh (Dolphin), P O'Grady (Shannon), K Maher (Shannon), P Hogan (Garryowen), M O'Donoghue
(Garryowen)
Scorers *Tries:* Wallace (2), Danaher   *Conversions:* Keyes (2)   *Penalty Goals:* Keyes (2)
Referee D Lamont

21 December, Sportsground, Galway

Connacht 10 (2PG 1T)   **Ulster 10** (2PG 1T)
Connacht: A White (St Mary's Coll); N Furlong (UC Galway), M Cosgrave (Wanderers), S Tormey (Galwegians),
G Curley (Athlone); E Elwood (Lansdowne), K Lawless (Clontarf); P McGrath (Galwegians), W Mulcahy (Skerries),
D Henshaw (Garryowen), S Jameson (St Mary's Coll), T Coughlin (Old Belvedere), S Moran (Blackrock), N Mannion
(Lansdowne), M Fitzgibbon (Shannon) *Replacements* M Moylett (Shannon) for Jameson; R Cullen (Bective) for Elwood
Scorers *Try:* Lawless   *Penalty Goals:* White (2)
Ulster: C Wilkinson (Malone); R Carey (Dungannon), M McCall (Bangor), M Field (Malone), D Smyth (Ballymena);
D McAleese (Ballymena), A Blair (Dungannon); D Elliott (Bangor), S Smith (Ballymena), P Millar (Ballymena),
G Longwell (Queen's U), C Morrison (Bangor), D McCartney (Ballymena), B Robinson (Ballymena), D McBride (Malone)
Scorers *Try:* Carey   *Penalty Goals:* McAleese (2)
Referee R McDowell

21 December, Thomond Park, Limerick

Munster 20 (2G 2T) **Leinster 3** (1PG)

Munster: D Larkin (Garryowen); R Wallace (Garryowen), C Murphy (Cork Const), P Murray (Shannon), B Walsh (Cork Const); N Barry (Garryowen), O Kiely (Shannon); J Fitzgerald (Young Munster), T Kingston (Dolphin), P McCarthy (Cork Const), P O'Grady (Shannon), R Costello (Garryowen), G Clohessy (Young Munster), B O'Mahony (UC Cork), G Earls (Young Munster)

Scorers *Tries:* Wallace (2), O'Grady, penalty try *Conversions:* Barry (2)

Leinster: D Beggy (Currie); M McArdle (Old Wesley), B Glennon (Lansdowne), M Ridge (Blackrock), N Woods (Blackrock); V Cunningham (St Mary's Coll), A Rolland (Blackrock); R Ward (Blackrock), J Murphy (Greystones), D Dowling (St Mary's Coll), K Potts (St Mary's Coll), G Fulcher (UC Dublin), K Leahy (Wanderers), P Lawlor (Bective), K Devlin (Old Belvedere)

Scorer *Penalty Goal:* Woods

Referee B Stirling

ALL IRELAND LEAGUE

Division 1

	P	W	D	L	F	A	Pts
Garryowen	8	7	0	1	162	91	14
Shannon	8	5	1	2	101	88	11
Ballymena	8	5	1	2	101	96	11
Old Wesley	8	4	0	4	83	91	8
Young Munster	8	3	1	4	71	72	7
St Mary's Coll	8	3	0	5	78	78	6
Cork Const	8	3	0	5	100	112	6
Lansdowne	8	2	1	5	93	92	5
Instonians	8	2	0	6	68	137	4

Division 2

	P	W	D	L	F	A	Pts
Dungannon	9	8	0	1	141	84	16
Greystones	9	6	0	3	184	84	12
Bangor	9	6	0	3	120	129	12
Blackrock Coll	9	5	0	4	189	111	10
Dolphin	9	5	0	4	149	115	10
Terenure Coll	9	5	0	4	142	111	10
Wanderers	9	5	0	4	132	142	10
Malone	9	4	0	5	151	117	8
Sunday's Well	9	1	0	8	103	157	2
CIYMS	9	0	0	9	73	334	0

After a play-off between the club champions of Ulster, Munster, Connacht and Leinster, Old Crescent (Munster), Clontarf (Leinster) and Galwegians (Connacht) are promoted to Division 2 for next season. NIFC, the Ulster champions, remain in the Ulster Senior League.

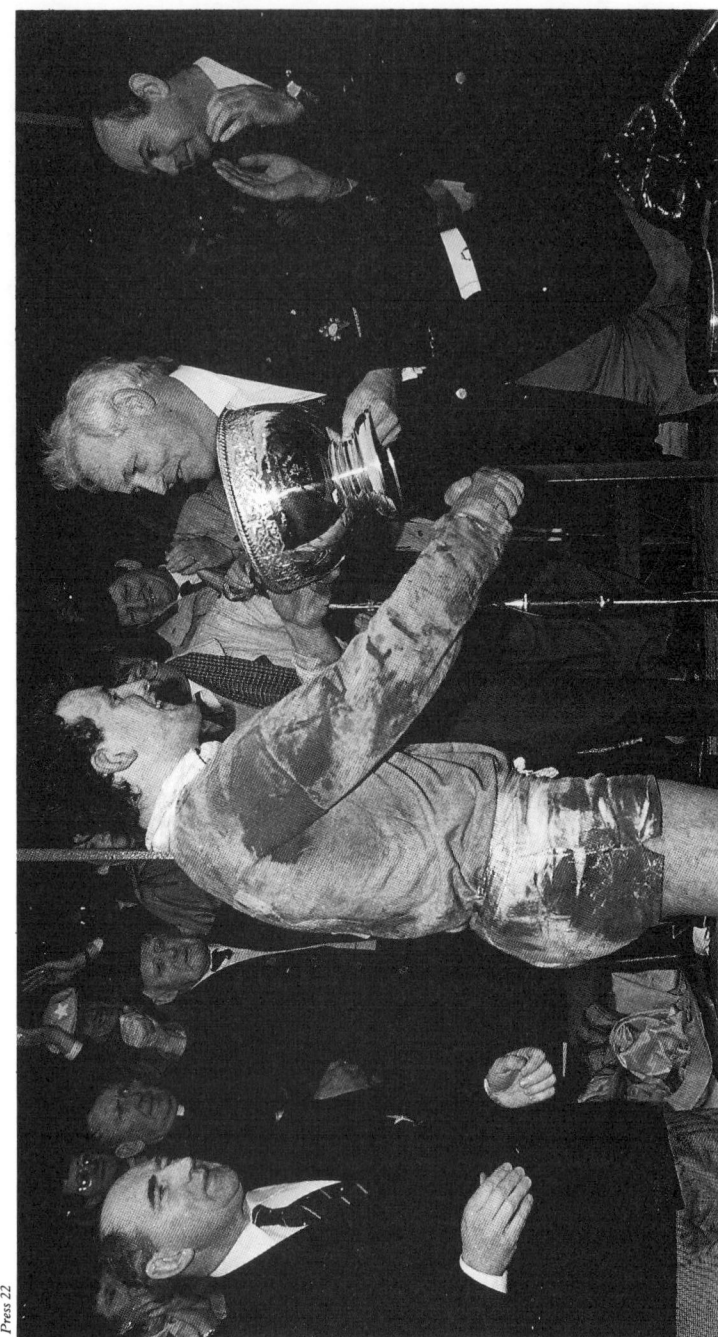

Press 22

Garryowen captain Phil Danaher collects the Insurance Corporation All Ireland League trophy. Danaher went on to captain Ireland in the Five Nations match against France and for their tour to New Zealand.

IRISH INTERNATIONAL PLAYERS
(up to 31 March 1992)

ABBREVIATIONS

A – Australia; *Arg* – Argentina; *C* – Canada; *E* – England; *F* – France; *It* – Italy; *J* – Japan; *M* – Maoris; *Nm* – Namibia; *NZ* – New Zealand; *R* – Romania; *S* – Scotland; *SA* – South Africa; *Tg* – Tonga; *W* – Wales; *WS* – Western Samoa; *Z* – Zimbabwe; *P* – Ireland v IRFU President's XV at Lansdowne Road in IRFU centenary season, 1974-75; (R) – Replacement. Entries in square brackets [ ] indicate appearances in the World Cup. NIFC – North of Ireland Football Club; CIYMS – Church of Ireland Young Men's Society; KCH – King's College Hospital

Note: Years given for Five Nations' matches are for second half of season; eg 1972 means season 1971-72. Years for all other matches refer to the actual year of the match. When a series has taken place, figures have been used to denote the particular matches in which players have featured. Thus 1981 *SA* 2 indicates that a player appeared in the second Test of the series. The abandoned game with Scotland at Belfast in 1885 is now included as a cap match.

NB – The second of Ireland's two matches against France in 1972 was a non-championship match.

Abraham, M (Bective Rangers) 1912 *E, S, W, SA*, 1914 *W*
Adams, C (Old Wesley) 1908 *E*, 1909 *E, F*, 1910 *F*, 1911 *E, S, W, F*, 1912 *S, W, SA*, 1913 *W, F*, 1914 *F, E, S*
Agar, R D (Malone) 1947 *F, E, S, W*, 1948 *F*, 1949 *S, W*, 1950 *F, E , W*
Agnew, P J (CIYMS) 1974 *W* (R), 1976 *A*
Ahearne, T (Queen's Coll, Cork) 1899 *E*
Aherne, L F P (Dolphin, Lansdowne) 1988 *E* 2, *WS, It*, 1989 *F, W, E, S, NZ*, 1990 *E, S, F, W* (R), 1992 *E, S, F*
Alexander, R (NIFC, Police Union) 1936 *E, S, W*, 1937 *E, S, W*, 1938 *E, S*, 1939 *E, S, W*
Allen, C E (Derry, Liverpool) 1900 *E, S, W*, 1901 *E, S, W*, 1903 *S, W*, 1904 *E, S, W*, 1905 *E, S, W, NZ*, 1906 *E, S, W, SA*, 1907 *S, W*
Allen, G G (Derry, Liverpool) 1896 *E, S, W*, 1897 *E, S*, 1898 *E, S*, 1899 *E, W*
Allen, T C (NIFC) 1885 *E, S* 1
Allen, W S (Wanderers) 1875 *E*
Allison, J B (Edinburgh U) 1899 *E, S*, 1900 *E, S, W*, 1901 *E, S, W*, 1902 *E, S, W*, 1903 *S*
Anderson, F E (Queen's U, Belfast, NIFC) 1953 *F, E, S, W*, 1954 *NZ, F, E, S, W*, 1955 *F, E, S, W*
Anderson, H J (Old Wesley) 1903 *E, S*, 1906 *E, S*
Anderson, W A (Dungannon) 1984 *A*, 1985 *S, F, W, E*, 1986 *F, S, R*, 1987 *E, S, F, W*, [*W, C, Tg, A*], 1988 *S, F, W, E* 1,2, 1989 *F, W, E, NZ*, 1990 *E, S*
Andrews, G (NIFC) 1875 *E*, 1876 *E*
Andrews, H W (NIFC) 1888 *M*, 1889 *S, W*
Archer, A M (Dublin U, NIFC) 1879 *S*
Arigho, J E (Lansdowne) 1928 *F, E, W*, 1929 *F, E, S, W*, 1930 *F, E, S, W*, 1931 *F, E, S, W, SA*
Armstrong, W K (NIFC) 1960 *SA*, 1961 *E*
Arnott, D T (Lansdowne) 1876 *E*
Ash, W H (NIFC) 1875 *E*, 1876 *E*, 1877 *S*
Aston, H R (Dublin U) 1908 *E, W*
Atkins, A P (Bective Rangers) 1924 *F*
Atkinson, J M (NIFC) 1927 *F, A*
Atkinson, J R (Dublin U) 1882 *W, S*

Bagot, J C (Dublin U, Lansdowne) 1879 *S, E*, 1880 *E, S*, 1881 *S*
Bailey, A H (UC Dublin, Lansdowne) 1934 *W*, 1935 *E, S, W, NZ*, 1936 *E, S, W*, 1937 *E, S, W*, 1938 *E, S*
Bailey, N (Northampton) 1952 *E*
Bardon, M E (Bohemians) 1934 *E*
Barlow, M (Wanderers) 1875 *E*
Barnes, R J (Dublin U, Armagh) 1933 *W*
Barr, A (Methodist Coll, Belfast) 1898 *W*, 1899 *S*, 1901 *E, S*
Barry, N J (Garryowen) 1991 *Nm*2(R)
Beamish, C E St J (RAF, Leicester) 1933 *W, S*, 1934 *S, W*, 1935 *E, S, W, NZ*, 1936 *E, S, W*, 1938 *W*
Beamish, G R (RAF, Leicester) 1925 *E, S, W*, 1928 *F, E, S, W*, 1929 *F, E, S, W*, 1930 *F, E, S, W*, 1931 *F, E, S, W, SA*, 1932 *E, S, W*, 1933 *W, S*
Beatty, W J (NIFC, Richmond) 1910 *F*, 1912 *F, W*
Becker, V A (Lansdowne) 1974 *F, W*
Beckett, G G P (Dublin U) 1908 *E, S, W*

Bell, R J (NIFC) 1875 *E*, 1876 *E*
Bell, W E (Belfast Collegians) 1953 *F, E, S, W*
Bennett, F (Belfast Collegians) 1913 *S*
Bent, G C (Dublin U) 1882 *W, E*
Berkery, P J (Lansdowne) 1954 *W*, 1955 *W*, 1956 *S, W*, 1957 *F, E, S, W*, 1958 *A, E, S*
Bermingham, J J C (Blackrock Coll) 1921 *E, S, W, F*
Blackham, J C (Queen's U, Cork) 1909 *S, W, F*, 1910 *E, S, W*
Blake-Knox, S E F (NIFC) 1976 *E, S*, 1977 *F* (R)
Blayney, J J (Wanderers) 1950 *S*
Bond, A T W (Derry) 1894 *S, W*
Bornemann, W W (Wanderers) 1960 *E, S, W, SA*
Bowen, D St J (Cork Const) 1977 *W, E, S*
Boyd, C A (Dublin U) 1900 *S*, 1901 *S, W*
Boyle, C V (Dublin U) 1935 *NZ*, 1936 *E, S, W*, 1937 *E, S, W*, 1938 *W*, 1939 *W*
Brabazon, H M (Dublin U) 1884 *E*, 1885 *S* 1, 1886 *E*
Bradley, M J (Dolphin) 1920 *W, F*, 1922 *E, S, W, F*, 1923 *E, S, W, F*, 1925 *F, S, W*, 1926 *F, E, S, W*, 1927 *F, W*
Bradley, M T (Cork Constitution) 1984 *A*, 1985 *S, F, W, E*, 1986 *F, W, E, S, R*, 1987 *E, S, F, W*, [*W, C, Tg, A*], 1988 *S, F, W, E* 1, 1990 *W*
Bradshaw, G (Belfast Collegians) 1903 *W*
Bradshaw, R M (Wanderers) 1885 *E, S* 1,2
Brady, A M (UC Dublin, Malone) 1966 *S*, 1968 *E, S, W*
Brady, J A (Wanderers) 1976 *E, S*
Brady, J R (CIYMS) 1951 *S, W*, 1953 *F, E, S, W*, 1954 *W*, 1956 *W*, 1957 *F, E, S, W*
Bramwell, T (NIFC) 1928 *F*
Brand, T N (NIFC) 1924 *NZ*
Brennan, J J (CIYMS) 1957 *S, W*
Bresnihan, F P K (UC Dublin, Lansdowne, London Irish) 1966 *E, W*, 1967 *A* 1, *E, S, W, F*, 1968 *F, E, S, W, A*, 1969 *F, E, S, W*, 1970 *SA, F, E, S, W*, 1971 *F, E, S, W*
Brett, J T (Monkstown) 1914 *W*
Bristow, J R (NIFC) 1879 *E*
Brophy, N H (Blackrock Coll, UC Dublin, London Irish) 1957 *F, E*, 1959 *E, S, W, F*, 1960 *F, SA*, 1961 *S, W*, 1962 *E, S, W*, 1963 *E, W*, 1967 *E, S, W, F, A* 2
Brown, E L (Instonians) 1958 *F*
Brown, G S (Monkstown, United Services) 1912 *S, W, SA*
Brown, H (Windsor) 1877 *E*
Brown, T (Windsor) 1877 *E, S*
Brown, W H (Dublin U) 1899 *E*
Brown, W J (Malone) 1970 *SA, F, S, W*
Brown, W S (Dublin U) 1893 *S, W*, 1894 *E, S, W*
Browne, A W (Dublin U) 1951 *SA*
Browne, D (Blackrock Coll) 1920 *F*
Browne, H C (United Services and RN) 1929 *E, S, W*
Browne, W F (United Services and Army) 1925 *E, S, W*, 1926 *S, W*, 1927 *F, E, S, W, A*, 1928 *E, S*
Browning, D R (Wanderers) 1881 *E, S*
Bruce, S A M (NIFC) 1883 *E, S*, 1884 *E*
Brunker, A A (Lansdowne) 1895 *E, W*
Bryant, C H (Cardiff) 1920 *E, S*
Buchanan, A McM (Dublin U) 1926 *E, S, W*, 1927 *S, W, A*

Buchanan, J W B (Dublin U) 1882 *S*, 1884 *E*, *S*
Buckley, J H (Sunday's Well) 1973 *E*, *S*
Bulger, L Q (Lansdowne) 1896 *E*, *S*, *W*, 1897 *E*, *S*, 1898 *E*, *S*, *W*
Bulger, M J (Dublin U) 1888 *M*
Burges, J H (Rosslyn Park) 1950 *F*, *E*
Burgess, R B (Dublin U) 1912 *SA*
Burkitt, J C S (Queen's Coll, Cork) 1881 *E*
Burns, I J (Wanderers) 1980 *E* (R)
Butler, L G (Blackrock Coll) 1960 *W*
Butler, N (Bective Rangers) 1920 *E*
Byers, R M (NIFC) 1928 *S*, *W*, 1929 *E*, *S*, *W*
Byrne, E M J (Blackrock Coll) 1977 *S*, *F*, 1978 *F*, *W*, *E*, *NZ*
Byrne, N F (UC Dublin) 1962 *F*
Byrne, S J (UC Dublin, Lansdowne) 1953 *S*, *W*, 1955 *F*
Byron, W G (NIFC) 1896 *E*, *S*, *W*, 1897 *E*, *S*, 1898 *E*, *S*, *W*, 1899 *E*, *S*, *W*

Caddell, E D (Dublin U, Wanderers) 1904 *S*, 1905 *E*, *S*, *W*, *NZ*, 1906 *E*, *S*, *W*, *SA*, 1907 *E*, *S*, 1908 *S*, *W*
Cagney, S J (London Irish) 1925 *W*, 1926 *F*, *E*, *S*, *W*, 1927 *F*, 1928 *E*, *S*, *W*, 1929 *F*, *E*, *S*, *W*
Callan, C P (Lansdowne) 1947 *F*, *E*, *S*, *W*, 1948 *F*, *E*, *S*, *W*, 1949 *F*, *E*
Cameron, E D (Bective Rangers) 1891 *S*, *W*
Campbell, C E (Old Wesley) 1970 *SA*
Campbell, E F (Monkstown) 1899 *S*, *W*, 1900 *E*, *W*
Campbell, S B B (Derry) 1911 *E*, *S*, *W*, *F*, 1912 *F*, *E*, *S*, *W*, *SA*, 1913 *E*, *S*, *F*
Campbell, S O (Old Belvedere) 1976 *A*, 1979 *A* 1,2, 1980 *E*, *S*, *F*, *W*, 1981 *F*, *W*, *E*, *S*, *SA* 1, 1982 *W*, *E*, *S*, *F*, 1983 *S*, *F*, *W*, *E*, 1984 *F*, *W*
Canniffe, D M (Lansdowne) 1976 *W*, *E*
Cantrell, J L (UC Dublin, Blackrock Coll) 1976 *A*, *F*, *W*, *E*, *S*, 1981 *S*, *SA* 1,2, *A*
Carpendale, M J (Monkstown) 1886 *S*, 1887 *W*, 1888 *W*, *S*
Carr, N J (Ards) 1985 *S*, *F*, *W*, *E*, 1986 *W*, *E*, *S*, *R*, 1987 *E*, *S*, *W*
Carroll, C (Bective Rangers) 1930 *F*
Carroll, R (Lansdowne) 1947 *F*, 1950 *S*, *W*
Casement, B N (Dublin U) 1875 *E*, 1876 *E*, 1879 *E*
Casement, F (Dublin U) 1906 *E*, *S*, *W*
Casey, J C (Young Munster) 1930 *S*, 1932 *E*
Casey, P J (UC Dublin, Lansdowne) 1963 *F*, *E*, *S*, *W*, *NZ*, 1964 *E*, *S*, *W*, *F*, 1965 *F*, *E*, *S*
Chambers, J (Dublin U) 1886 *E*, *S*, 1887 *E*, *S*, *W*
Chambers, R R (Instonians) 1951 *F*, *E*, *S*, *W*, 1952 *F*, *W*
Clancy, T P J (Lansdowne) 1988 *W*, *E* 1,2, *WS*, *It*, 1989 *F*, *W*, *E*, *S*
Clarke, D J (Dolphin) 1991 *W*, *Nm* 1,2, [*J*, *A*]
Clarke, J A B (Bective Rangers) 1922 *S*, *W*, *F*, 1923 *F*, 1924 *E*, *S*, *W*
Clegg, R J (Bangor) 1973 *F*, 1975 *E*, *S*, *F*, *W*
Clifford, J T (Young Munster) 1949 *F*, *E*, *S*, *W*, 1950 *F*, *E*, *S*, *W*, 1951 *F*, *E*, *S*, *SA*, 1952 *F*, *S*, *W*
Clinch, A D (Dublin U, Wanderers) 1892 *S*, 1893 *W*, 1895 *E*, *S*, *W*, 1896 *E*, *S*, *W*, 1897 *E*, *S*
Clinch, J D (Wanderers, Dublin U) 1923 *W*, 1924 *F*, *E*, *S*, *W*, *NZ*, 1925 *F*, *E*, *S*, 1926 *E*, *S*, *W*, 1927 *F*, 1928 *F*, *E*, *S*, *W*, 1929 *F*, *E*, *S*, *W*, 1930 *F*, *E*, *S*, *W*, 1931 *F*, *E*, *S*, *W*, *SA*
Clune, J J (Blackrock Coll) 1912 *SA*, 1913 *W*, *F*, 1914 *F*, *E*, *W*
Coffey, J J (Lansdowne) 1900 *E*, 1901 *W*, 1902 *E*, *S*, *W*, 1903 *E*, *S*, *W*, 1905 *E*, *S*, *W*, *NZ*, 1906 *E*, *S*, *W*, *SA*, 1907 *E*, 1908 *W*, 1910 *F*
Cogan, W St J (Queen's Coll, Cork) 1907 *E*, *S*
Collier, S R (Queen's Coll, Belfast) 1883 *S*
Collins, P C (Lansdowne, London Irish) 1987 [*C*], 1990 *S* (R)
Collis, W R F (KCH, Harlequins) 1924 *F*, *W*, *NZ*, 1925 *F*, *E*, *S*, 1926 *F*
Collis, W S (Wanderers) 1884 *W*
Collopy, G (Bective Rangers) 1891 *S*, 1892 *S*
Collopy, R (Bective Rangers) 1923 *E*, *S*, *W*, *F*, 1924 *F*, *E*, *S*, *W*, *NZ*, 1925 *F*, *E*, *S*, *W*
Collopy, W P (Bective Rangers) 1914 *F*, *E*, *S*, *W*, 1921 *E*, *S*, *W*, *F*, 1922 *E*, *S*, *W*, *F*, 1923 *S*, *W*, *F*, 1924 *F*, *E*, *S*, *W*
Combe, A (NIFC) 1875 *E*
Condon, H C (London Irish) 1984 *S* (R)
Cook, H G (Lansdowne) 1884 *W*

Coote, P B (RAF, Leicester) 1933 *S*
Corcoran, J C (London Irish) 1947 *A*, 1948 *F*
Corken, T S (Belfast Collegians) 1937 *E*, *S*, *W*
Corley, H H (Dublin U, Wanderers) 1902 *E*, *S*, *W*, 1903 *E*, *S*, *W*, 1904 *E*, *S*
Cormac, H S T (Clontarf) 1921 *E*, *S*, *W*
Costello, P (Bective Rangers) 1960 *F*
Cotton, J (Wanderers) 1889 *W*
Coulter, H H (Queen's U, Belfast) 1920 *E*, *S*, *W*
Courtney, A W (UC Dublin) 1920 *S*, *W*, *F*, 1921 *E*, *S*, *W*, *F*
Cox, H L (Dublin U) 1875 *E*, 1876 *E*, 1877 *E*, *S*
Craig, R G (Queen's U, Belfast) 1938 *S*, *W*
Crawford, E C (Dublin U) 1885 *E*, *S* 1
Crawford, W E (Lansdowne) 1920 *E*, *S*, *W*, *F*, 1921 *E*, *S*, *W*, *F*, 1922 *E*, *S*, 1923 *E*, *S*, *W*, *F*, 1924 *F*, *E*, *W*, *NZ*, 1925 *F*, *E*, *S*, *W*, 1926 *F*, *E*, *S*, *W*, 1927 *F*, *E*, *S*, *W*
Crean, T J (Wanderers) 1894 *E*, *S*, *W*, 1895 *E*, *S*, *W*, 1896 *E*, *S*, *W*
Crichton, R Y (Dublin U) 1920 *E*, *S*, *W*, *F*, 1921 *F*, 1922 *E*, 1923 *W*, *F*, 1924 *F*, *E*, *S*, *W*, *NZ*, 1925 *E*, *S*
Croker, E W D (Limerick) 1878 *E*
Cromey, G E (Queen's U, Belfast) 1937 *E*, *S*, *W*, 1938 *E*, *S*, *W*, 1939 *E*, *S*, *W*
Cronyn, A P (Dublin U, Lansdowne) 1875 *E*, 1876 *E*, 1880 *S*
Crossan, K D (Instonians) 1982 *S*, 1984 *F*, *W*, *E*, *S*, 1985 *S*, *F*, *W*, *E*, 1986 *E*, *S*, *R*, 1987 *E*, *S*, *F*, *W*, [*W*, *C*, *Tg*, *A*], 1988 *S*, *F*, *W*, *E* 1, *WS*, *It*, 1989 *W*, *S*, *F*, *NZ*, 1990 *E*, *S*, *F*, *W*, *Arg*, 1991 *E*, *S*, *Nm* 2, [*Z*, *J*, *S*], 1992 *W*
Crowe, J F (UC Dublin) 1974 *NZ*
Crowe, L (Old Belvedere) 1950 *E*, *S*, *W*
Crowe, M P (Lansdowne) 1929 *W*, 1930 *E*, *S*, *W*, 1931 *F*, *S*, *W*, *SA*, 1932 *S*, *W*, 1933 *W*, *S*, 1934 *E*
Crowe, P M (Blackrock Coll) 1935 *E*, 1938 *E*
Cullen, T J (UC Dublin) 1949 *F*
Cullen, W J (Monkstown and Manchester) 1920 *E*
Culliton, M G (Wanderers) 1959 *E*, *S*, *W*, *F*, 1960 *E*, *S*, *W*, *F*, *SA*, 1961 *E*, *S*, *W*, *F*, 1962 *S*, *F*, 1964 *E*, *S*, *W*, *F*
Cummins, W E A (Queen's Coll, Cork) 1879 *S*, 1881 *E*, 1882 *E*
Cunningham, D McC (NIFC) 1923 *E*, *S*, *W*, 1925 *F*, *E*, *W*
Cunningham, M J (UC Cork) 1955 *F*, *E*, *S*, *W*, 1956 *F*, *S*, *W*
Cunningham, V J G (St Mary's Coll) 1988 *E* 2, *It* 1990 *Arg* (R), 1991 *Nm* 1,2, [*Z*, *J*(R)]
Cunningham, W A (Lansdowne) 1920 *W*, 1921 *E*, *S*, *W*, *F*, 1922 *E*, *S*, 1923 *S*, *W*
Cuppaidge, J L (Dublin U) 1879 *E*, 1880 *E*, *S*
Currell, J (NIFC) 1877 *S*
Curtis, A B (Oxford U) 1950 *F*, *E*, *S*
Curtis, D M (London Irish) 1991 *W*, *E*, *S*, *Nm* 1,2, [*Z*, *J*, *S*, *A*], 1992 *W*, *E*, *S*(R), *F*
Cuscaden, W A (Dublin U, Bray) 1876 *E*
Cussen, D J (Dublin U) 1921 *E*, *S*, *W*, *F*, 1922 *E*, 1923 *E*, *S*, *W*, *F*, 1926 *F*, *E*, *S*, *W*, 1927 *F*, *E*

Daly, J C (London Irish) 1947 *F*, *E*, *S*, *W*, 1948 *E*, *S*, *W*
Daly, M J (Harlequins) 1938 *E*
Danaher, P P A (Lansdowne, Garryowen) 1988 *S*, *F*, *W*, *WS*, *It*, 1989 *F*, *NZ* (R), 1990 *F*, 1992 *S*, *F*
Dargan, M J (Old Belvedere) 1952 *S*, *W*
Davidson, C T (NIFC) 1921 *F*
Davidson, I G (NIFC) 1899 *W*, 1900 *S*, *W*, 1901 *E*, *S*, *W*, 1902 *E*, *S*, *W*
Davidson, J C (Dungannon) 1969 *F*, *E*, *S*, *W*, 1973 *NZ*, 1976 *NZ*
Davies, F E (Lansdowne) 1892 *S*, *W*, 1893 *E*, *S*, *W*
Davis, J L (Monkstown) 1898 *E*, *S*
Davis, W J N (Edinburgh U, Bessbrook) 1890 *S*, *W*, *E*, 1891 *E*, *S*, *W*, 1892 *E*, *S*, 1895 *S*
Davison, W (Belfast Academy) 1887 *W*
Davy, E O'D (UC Dublin, Lansdowne) 1925 *W*, 1926 *F*, *E*, *S*, *W*, 1927 *F*, *E*, *S*, *W*, *A*, 1928 *F*, *E*, *S*, *W*, 1929 *F*, *E*, *S*, *W*, 1930 *F*, *E*, *S*, *W*, 1931 *F*, *E*, *S*, *W*, *SA*, 1932 *E*, *S*, *W*, 1933 *E*, *W*, *S*, 1934 *E*
Dawson, A R (Wanderers) 1958 *A*, *E*, *S*, *W*, *F*, 1959 *E*, *S*, *W*, *F*, 1960 *F*, *SA*, 1961 *E*, *S*, *W*, *F*, *SA*, 1962 *S*, *F*, *W*, 1963 *F*, *E*, *S*, *W*, *NZ*, 1964 *E*, *S*, *F*
Dean, P M (St Mary's Coll) 1981 *SA* 1,2, *A*, 1982 *W*, *E*, *S*, *F*, 1984 *A*, 1985 *S*, *F*, *W*, *E*, 1986 *F*, *W*, *R*, 1987 *E*,

S, F, W, [W, A], 1988 *S, F, W, E* 1,2, *WS, It*, 1989 *F, W, E, S*
Deane, E C (Monkstown) 1909 *E*
Deering, M J (Bective Rangers) 1929 *W*
Deering, S J (Bective Rangers) 1935 *E, S, W, NZ*, 1936 *E, S, W*, 1937 *E, S*
Deering, S M (Garryowen, St Mary's Coll) 1974 *W*, 1976 *F, W, E, S*, 1977 *W, E*, 1978 *NZ*
de Lacy, H (Harlequins) 1948 *E, S*
Delaney, M G (Bective Rangers) 1895 *W*
Dennison, S P (Garryowen) 1973 *F*, 1975 *E, S*
Dick, C J (Ballymena) 1961 *W, F, SA*, 1962 *W*, 1963 *F, E, S, W*
Dick, J S (Queen's U, Belfast) 1962 *E*
Dick, J S (Queen's U, Cork) 1887 *E, S, W*
Dickson, J A N (Dublin U) 1920 *E, W, F*
Doherty, A E (Old Wesley) 1974 *P* (R)
Doherty, W D (Guy's Hospital) 1920 *E, S, W*, 1921 *E, S, W, F*
Donaldson, J A (Belfast Collegians) 1958 *A, E, S, W*
Donovan, T M (Queen's Coll, Cork) 1889 *S*
Dooley, J F (Galwegians) 1959 *E, S, W*
Doran, B R W (Lansdowne) 1900 *S, W*, 1901 *E, S, W*, 1902 *E, S, W*
Doran, E F (Lansdowne) 1890 *S, W*
Doran, G P (Lansdowne) 1899 *S, W*, 1900 *E, S*, 1902 *S, W*, 1903 *W*, 1904 *E*
Douglas, A C (Instonians) 1923 *F*, 1924 *E, S*, 1927 *A*, 1928 *S*
Downing, A J (Dublin U) 1882 *W*
Dowse, J C A (Monkstown) 1914 *F, S, W*
Doyle, J A P (Greystones) 1984 *E, S*
Doyle, J T (Bective Rangers) 1935 *W*
Doyle, M G (Blackrock Coll, UC Dublin, Cambridge U, Edinburgh Wands) 1965 *F, E, S, W, SA*, 1966 *F, E, S, W*, 1967 *A* 1, *E, S, W, F, A* 2, 1968 *F, E, S, W, A*
Doyle, T J (Wanderers) 1968 *E, S, W*
Duggan, A T A (Lansdowne) 1963 *NZ*, 1964 *F*, 1966 *W*, 1967 *A* 1, *S, W, A* 2, 1968 *F, E, S, W*, 1969 *F, E, S, W*, 1970 *SA, F, E, S, W*, 1971 *F, E, S, W*, 1972 *F* 2
Duggan, W (UC Cork) 1920 *S, W*
Duggan, W P (Blackrock Coll) 1975 *E, S, F, W*, 1976 *A, F, W, S, NZ*, 1977 *W, E, S, F*, 1978 *S, F, W, E, NZ*, 1979 *E, S, A* 1,2, 1980 *E, S, F, W*, 1981 *F, W, E, S, SA* 1,2, *A*, 1982 *W, F, S, E*, 1983 *S, F, W, E*, 1984 *F, W, E, S*
Duncan, W R (Malone) 1984 *W, E*
Dunlea, F J (Lansdowne) 1989 *W, E, S*
Dunlop, R (Dublin U) 1889 *E, W, S*, 1890 *S, W, E*, 1891 *E, S, W*, 1892 *E, S*, 1893 *W*, 1894 *W*
Dunn, P E F (Bective Rangers) 1923 *S*
Dunn, T B (NIFC) 1935 *NZ*
Dunne, M J (Lansdowne) 1929 *F, E, S*, 1930 *F, E, S, W*, 1932 *E, S, W*, 1933 *E, S, W*, 1934 *E, S, W*
Dwyer, P J (UC Dublin) 1962 *W*, 1963 *F, NZ*, 1964 *S, W*

Edwards, H G (Dublin U) 1877 *E*, 1878 *E*
Edwards, R W (Malone) 1904 *W*
Edwards, T (Lansdowne) 1888 *M*, 1890 *S, W, E*, 1892 *W*, 1893 *E*
Edwards, W V (Malone) 1912 *F, E*
Egan, J D (Bective Rangers) 1922 *S*
Egan, J T (Cork Constitution) 1931 *F, E, SA*
Egan, M S (Garryowen) 1893 *E*, 1895 *S*
Ekin, W (Queen's Coll, Belfast) 1888 *W, S*
Elliott, W R J (Bangor) 1979 *S*
English, M A F (Lansdowne, Limerick Bohemians) 1958 *W, F*, 1959 *E, S, F*, 1960 *E, S*, 1961 *S, W, F*, 1962 *F, W*, 1963 *E, S, W, NZ*
Ennis, F N G (Wanderers) 1979 *A* 1 (R)
Ensor, A H (Wanderers) 1973 *W, F*, 1974 *F, W, E, S, P, NZ*, 1975 *E, S, F, W*, 1976 *A, F, W, E, NZ*, 1977 *E*, 1978 *S, F, W, E*
Entrican, J C (Queen's U, Belfast) 1931 *S*

Fagan, G L (Kingstown School) 1878 *E*
Fagan, W B C (Wanderers) 1956 *F, E, S*
Farrell, J L (Bective Rangers) 1926 *F, E, S, W*, 1927 *F, E, S, W, A*, 1928 *F, E, S, W*, 1929 *F, E, S, W*, 1930 *F, E, S, W*, 1931 *F, E, S, W, SA*, 1932 *E, S, W*
Feddis, N (Lansdowne) 1956 *E*
Feighery, C F P (Lansdowne) 1972 *F* 1, *E, F* 2
Feighery, T A O (St Mary's Coll) 1977 *W, E*
Ferris, H H (Queen's Coll, Belfast) 1901 *W*

Ferris, J H (Queen's Coll, Belfast) 1900 *E, S, W*
Finlay, J E (Queen's Coll, Belfast) 1913 *E, S, W*, 1920 *E, S, W*
Finlay, W (NIFC) 1876 *E*, 1877 *E, S*, 1878 *E*, 1879 *S, E*, 1880 *S*, 1882 *S*
Finn, M C (UC Cork, Cork Constitution) 1979 *E*, 1982 *W, E, S, F*, 1983 *S, F, W, E*, 1984 *E, S, A*, 1986 *F, W*
Finn, R G A (UC Dublin) 1977 *F*
Fitzgerald, C C (Glasgow U, Dungannon) 1902 *E*, 1903 *E, S*
Fitzgerald, C F (St Mary's Coll) 1979 *A* 1,2, 1980 *E, S, F, W*, 1982 *W, E, S, F*, 1983 *S, F, W, E*, 1984 *F, W, A*, 1985 *S, F, W, E*, 1986 *F, W, E, S*
Fitzgerald, D C (Lansdowne, De La Salle Palmerston) 1984 *E, S*, 1986 *W, E, S, R*, 1987 *E, S, F, W*, [*W, C, A*], 1988 *S, F, W, E* 1, 1989 *NZ* (R), 1990 *E, S, F, W, Arg*, 1991 *F, W, E, S, Nm* 1,2, [*Z, S, A*], 1992 *W, S*(R)
Fitzgerald, J (Wanderers) 1884 *W*
Fitzgerald, J J (Young Munster) 1988 *S, F*, 1990 *S, F, W*, 1991 *F, W, E, S*, [*J*]
Fitzgibbon, M J J (Shannon) 1992 *W, E, S, F*
Fitzpatrick, M P (Wanderers) 1978 *S*, 1980 *S, F, W*, 1981 *F, E, S, A*, 1985 *F* (R)
Fletcher, W W (Kingstown) 1882 *W, S*, 1883 *E*
Flood, R S (Dublin U) 1925 *W*
Flynn, M K (Wanderers) 1959 *F*, 1960 *F*, 1962 *E, S, F, W*, 1964 *E, S, W, F*, 1965 *F, E, S, W, SA*, 1966 *F, E, S*, 1972 *F* 1, *E, F* 2, 1973 *NZ*
Fogarty, T (Garryowen) 1891 *W*
Foley, B O (Shannon) 1976 *F, E*, 1977 *W* (R), 1980 *F, W*, 1981 *F, E, S, A*, 1,2, *A*
Forbes, R E (Malone) 1907 *E*
Forrest, A J (Wanderers) 1880 *E, S*, 1881 *E, S*, 1882 *W, E*, 1883 *E*, 1885 *S* 2
Forrest, E G (Wanderers) 1888 *M*, 1889 *S, W*, 1890 *S, E*, 1891 *E*, 1893 *S*, 1894 *E, S, W*, 1895 *W*, 1897 *E, S*
Forrest, H (Wanderers) 1893 *S, W*
Fortune, J J (Clontarf) 1963 *NZ*, 1964 *E*
Foster, A R (Derry) 1910 *E, S, F*, 1911 *E, S, W, F*, 1912 *F, E, S, W*, 1914 *E, S, W, F*, 1921 *E, S, W*, 1912 *F, E, S, W*, 1914 *E, S, W, F*, 1921 *E, S, W*
Francis, N P J (Blackrock Coll, London Irish) 1987 [*Tg, A*], 1988 *WS, It*, 1989 *S*, 1990 *E, F, W*, 1991 *E, S, Nm* 1,2, [*Z, J, S, A*], 1992 *W, E, S*
Franks, J G (Dublin U) 1898 *E, S, W*
Frazer, E F (Bective Rangers) 1891 *S*, 1892 *S*
Freer, A E (Lansdowne) 1901 *E, S, W*
Fulton, J (NIFC) 1895 *S, W*, 1896 *E*, 1897 *E*, 1898 *W*, 1899 *E*, 1900 *W*, 1901 *E*, 1902 *E, S, W*, 1903 *E, S, W*, 1904 *E, S*

Gaffikin, W (Windsor) 1875 *E*
Gage, J H (Queen's U, Belfast) 1926 *S, W*, 1927 *S, W*
Galbraith, E (Dublin U) 1875 *E*
Galbraith, H T (Belfast Acad) 1890 *W*
Galbraith, R (Dublin U) 1875 *E*, 1876 *E*, 1877 *E*
Galwey, M J (Shannon) 1991 *F, W, Nm* 2(R), [*J*], 1992 *E, S, F*
Ganly, J B (Monkstown) 1927 *F, E, S, W, A*, 1928 *F, E, S, W*, 1929 *F, S*, 1930 *F*
Gardiner, F (NIFC) 1900 *E, S*, 1901 *E, W*, 1902 *E, S, W*, 1903 *E, W*, 1904 *E, S, W*, 1906 *E, S, W*, 1907 *S, W*, 1908 *S, W*, 1909 *E, S, F*
Gardiner, J B (NIFC) 1923 *E, S, W, F*, 1924 *F, E, S, W, NZ*, 1925 *F, E, S, W*
Gardiner, S (Belfast Albion) 1893 *E, S*
Gardiner, W (NIFC) 1892 *E, S*, 1893 *E, S, W*, 1894 *E, S, W*, 1895 *E, S, W*, 1896 *E, S, W*, 1897 *E, S*, 1898 *W*, 1899 *E, S, W*
Garry, M G (Bective Rangers) 1909 *E, S, W, F*, 1911 *E, S, W*
Gaston, J T (Dublin U) 1954 *NZ, F, E, S, W*, 1955 *W*, 1956 *F, E*
Gavin, T J (Moseley, London Irish) 1949 *F, E*
Geoghegan, S P (London Irish) 1991 *F, W, E, S, Nm* 1, [*Z, S, A*], 1992 *E, S, F*
Gibson, C M H (Cambridge U, NIFC) 1964 *E, S, W, F*, 1965 *F, S, W, SA*, 1966 *F, S, W*, 1967 *A* 1, *E, S, W, F, A* 2, 1968 *E, S, W, A*, 1969 *E, S, W*, 1970 *SA, F, E, S, W*, 1971 *F, E, S, W*, 1972 *F* 1, *E, F* 2, 1973 *NZ, E, S, W, F*, 1974 *F, W, E, S, P*, 1975 *E, S, F, W*, 1976 *A, F, E, S, W, NZ*, 1977 *W, E, S, F*, 1978 *F, W, E, NZ*, 1979 *S, A* 1,2
Gibson, M E (Lansdowne, London Irish) 1979 *F, W, E, S*, 1981 *W* (R), 1986 *R*, 1988 *S, F, W, E* 2
Gifford, H P (Wanderers) 1890 *S*

Gillespie, J C (Dublin U) 1922 *W, F*
Gilpin, F G (Queen's U, Belfast) 1962 *E, S, F*
Glass, D C (Belfast Collegians) 1958 *F*, 1960 *W*, 1961
W, SA
Glennon, J J (Skerries) 1980 *E, S*, 1987 *E, S, F, [W(R)]*
Godfrey, R P (UC Dublin) 1954 *S, W*
Goodall, K G (City of Derry, Newcastle U) 1967 *A* 1,
E, S, W, F, A 2, 1968 *F, E, S, W, A*, 1969 *F, E, S*, 1970
SA, F, E, S, W
Gordon, A (Dublin U) 1884 *S*
Gordon, T G (NIFC) 1877 *E, S*, 1878 *E*
Gotto, R P C (NIFC) 1906 *SA*
Goulding, W J (Cork) 1879 *S*
Grace, T O (UC Dublin, St Mary's Coll) 1972 *F* 1, *E*,
1973 *NZ, E, S, W*, 1974 *E, S, P, NZ*, 1975 *E, S, F, W*,
1976 *A, F, W, E, S, NZ*, 1977 *W, E, S, F*, 1978 *S*
Graham, R I (Dublin U) 1911 *F*
Grant, E L (CIYMS) 1971 *F, E, S, W*
Grant, P J (Bective Rangers) 1894 *S, W*
Graves, C R A (Wanderers) 1934 *E, S, W*, 1935 *E, S,
W, NZ*, 1936 *E, S, W*, 1937 *E, S*, 1938 *E, S, W*
Gray, R D (Old Wesley) 1923 *E, S*, 1925 *F*, 1926 *F*
Greene, E H (Dublin U, Kingstown) 1882 *W*, 1884 *W*,
1885 *E, S* 2, 1886 *E*
Greer, R (Kingstown) 1876 *E*
Greeves, T J (NIFC) 1907 *E, S, W*, 1909 *W, F*
Gregg, R J (Queen's U, Belfast) 1953 *F, E, S, W*, 1954
F, E, S
Griffin, C S (London Irish) 1951 *F, E*
Griffin, J L (Wanderers) 1949 *S, W*
Griffiths, W (Limerick) 1878 *E*
Grimshaw, C (Queen's U, Belfast) 1969 *E* (R)
Guerin, B N (Galwegians) 1956 *S*
Gwynn, A P (Dublin U) 1895 *W*
Gwynn, L H (Dublin U) 1893 *S*, 1894 *E, S, W*, 1897 *S*,
1898 *E, S*

Hakin, R F (CIYMS) 1976 *W, S, NZ*, 1977 *W, E, F*
Hall, R O N (Dublin U) 1884 *W*
Hall, W H (Instonians) 1923 *E, S, W, F*, 1924 *F, S*
Hallaran, C F G T (Royal Navy) 1921 *E, S, W*, 1922 *E,
S, W*, 1923 *E, F*, 1924 *F, E, S, W*, 1925 *F*, 1926 *F, E*
Halpin, G F (Wanderers, London Irish) 1990 *E*, 1991
[*J*], 1992 *E, S, F*
Halpin, T (Garryowen) 1909 *S, W, F*, 1910 *E, S, W*,
1911 *E, S, W, F*, 1912 *F, E, S*
Hamilton, A J (Lansdowne) 1884 *W*
Hamilton, G F (NIFC) 1991 *F, W, E, S, Nm* 2, [*Z, J,
S, A*]
Hamilton, R L (NIFC) 1926 *F*
Hamilton, R W (Wanderers) 1893 *W*
Hamilton, W J (Dublin U) 1877 *E*
Hamlet, G T (Old Wesley) 1902 *E, S, W*, 1903 *E, S, W*,
1904 *S, W*, 1905 *E, S, W, NZ*, 1906 *SA*, 1907 *E, S, W*,
1908 *E, S, W*, 1909 *E, S, W, F*, 1910 *E, S, F*, 1911 *E,
S, W, F*
Hanrahan, C J (Dolphin) 1926 *S, W*, 1927 *E, S, W, A*,
1928 *F, E, S*, 1929 *F, E, S, W*, 1930 *F, E, S, W*, 1931
F, 1932 *S, W*
Harbison, H T (Bective Rangers) 1984 *W* (R), *E, S*,
1986 *R*, 1987 *E, S, F, W*
Hardy, G G (Bective Rangers) 1962 *S*
Harman, G R A (Dublin U) 1899 *E, W*
Harper, J (Instonians) 1947 *F, E, S*
Harpur, T G (Dublin U) 1908 *E, S, W*
Harrison, T (Cork) 1879 *S*, 1880 *S*, 1881 *E*
Harvey, F M W (Wanderers) 1907 *W*, 1911 *F*
Harvey, G A D (Wanderers) 1903 *E, S*, 1904 *W*, 1905
E, S
Harvey, T A (Dublin U) 1900 *W*, 1901 *S, W*, 1902 *E,
S, W*, 1903 *E, W*
Haycock, P P (Terenure Coll) 1989 *E*
Headon, T A (UC Dublin) 1939 *S, W*
Healey, P (Limerick) 1901 *E, S, W*, 1902 *E, S, W*, 1903
E, S, W, 1904 *S*
Heffernan, M R (Cork Constitution) 1911 *E, S, W, F*
Hemphill, R (Dublin U) 1912 *F, E, S, W*
Henderson, N J (Queen's U, Belfast, NIFC) 1949 *S,
W*, 1950 *F*, 1951 *F, E, S, W, SA*, 1952 *F, S, W, E*, 1953
F, E, S, W, 1954 *NZ, F, E, S, W*, 1955 *F, E, S, W*,
1956 *S, W*, 1957 *F, E, S, W*, 1958 *A, E, S, W, F*, 1959
E, S, W, F
Henebrey, G J (Garryowen) 1906 *E, S, W, SA*, 1909
W, F

Heron, A G (Queen's Coll, Belfast) 1901 *E*
Heron, J (NIFC) 1877 *S*, 1879 *E*
Heron, W T (NIFC) 1880 *E, S*
Herrick, R W (Dublin U) 1886 *S*
Heuston, F S (Kingstown) 1882 *W*, 1883 *E, S*
Hewitt, D (Queen's U, Belfast, Instonians) 1958 *A, E,
S, F*, 1959 *S, W, F*, 1960 *E, S, W, F*, 1961 *E, S, W, F*,
1962 *S, F*, 1965 *W*
Hewitt, F S (Instonians) 1924 *W, NZ*, 1925 *F, E, S*,
1926 *E*, 1927 *E, S, W*
Hewitt, J A (NIFC) 1981 *SA* 1 (R), 2 (R)
Hewitt, T R (Queen's U, Belfast) 1924 *W, NZ*, 1925 *F,
E, S*, 1926 *F, E, S, W*
Hewitt, V A (Instonians) 1935 *S, W, NZ*, 1936 *E, S, W*
Hewitt, W J (Instonians) 1954 *E*, 1956 *S*, 1959 *W*, 1961
SA
Hewson, F T (Wanderers) 1875 *E*
Hickie, D J (St Mary's Coll) 1971 *F, E, S, W*, 1972
F 1, *E*
Higgins, J A D (Civil Service) 1947 *S, W, A*, 1948 *F, S, W*
Higgins, W W (NIFC) 1884 *E, S*
Hillary, M F (UC Dublin) 1952 *E*
Hingerty, D J (UC Dublin) 1947 *F, E, S, W*
Hinton, W P (Old Wesley) 1907 *W*, 1908 *E, S, W*, 1909
E, S, 1910 *E, S, W, F*, 1911 *E, S, W*, 1912 *F, E, W*
Hipwell, M L (Terenure Coll) 1962 *E, S*, 1968 *F, A*,
1969 *F* (R), *S* (R), *W*, 1971 *F, E, S, W*, 1972 *F* 2
Hobbs, T H M (Dublin U) 1884 *S*, 1885 *E*
Hobson, E W (Dublin U) 1876 *E*
Hogan, P (Garryowen) 1992 *F*
Hogg, W (Dublin U) 1885 *S* 2
Holland, J J (Wanderers) 1981 *SA* 1,2, 1986 *W*
Holmes, G W (Dublin U) 1912 *SA*, 1913 *E, S*
Holmes, L J (Lisburn) 1889 *S, W*
Hooks, K J (Queen's U, Belfast, Ards, Bangor) 1981 *S*,
1989 *NZ*, 1990 *F, W, Arg*, 1991 *F*
Horan, A K (Blackheath) 1920 *E, W*
Houston, K J (Oxford U, London Irish) 1961 *SA*, 1964
S, W, 1965 *F, E, SA*
Hughes, R W (NIFC) 1878 *E*, 1880 *E, S*, 1881 *S*, 1882
E, S, 1883 *E, S*, 1884 *E, S*, 1885 *E*, 1886 *E*
Hunt, E W F de Vere (Army, Rosslyn Park) 1930 *F*,
1932 *E, S, W*, 1933 *E*
Hunter, D V (Dublin U) 1885 *S* 2
Hunter, L (Civil Service) 1968 *W, A*
Hunter, W R (CIYMS) 1962 *E, S, W, F*, 1963 *F, E, S*,
1966 *F, E, S*
Hutton, S A (Malone) 1967 *S, W, F, A* 2

Ireland, J (Windsor) 1876 *E*, 1877 *E*
Irvine, H A S (Collegians) 1901 *S*
Irwin, D G (Queen's U, Belfast, Instonians) 1980 *F, W*,
1981 *F, W, E, S, SA* 1,2, *A*, 1982 *W*, 1983 *S, F, W, E*,
1984 *F, W*, 1987 [*Tg, A*(R)], 1989 *F, W, E, S, NZ*, 1990
E, S
Irwin, J W S (NIFC) 1938 *E, S*, 1939 *E, S, W*
Irwin, S T (Queen's Coll, Belfast) 1900 *E, S, W*, 1901
E, W, 1902 *E, S, W*, 1903 *S*

Jack, H W (UC Cork) 1914 *S, W*, 1921 *W*
Jackson, A R V (Wanderers) 1911 *E, S, W, F*, 1913 *W,
F*, 1914 *F, E, S*
Jackson, F (NIFC) 1923 *E*
Jackson, H W (Dublin U) 1877 *E*
Jameson, J S (Lansdowne) 1888 *M*, 1889 *S, W*, 1891
W, 1892 *E, W*, 1893 *S*
Jeffares, E W (Wanderers) 1913 *E, S*
Johns, P S C (Dublin U) 1990 *Arg*
Johnston, J (Belfast Acad) 1881 *S*, 1882 *S*, 1884 *S*, 1885
S 1,2, 1886 *E*, 1887 *E, S, W*
Johnston, M (Dublin U) 1880 *E, S*, 1881 *E, S*, 1882 *E*,
1884 *E, S*, 1886 *E*
Johnston, R (Wanderers) 1893 *E, W*
Johnston, R W (Dublin U) 1890 *S, W, E*
Johnston, T J (Queen's Coll, Belfast) 1892 *E, S, W*,
1893 *E, S*, 1895 *E*
Johnstone, W E (Dublin U) 1884 *W*
Johnstone-Smyth, T R (Lansdowne) 1882 *E*

Kavanagh, J R (UC Dublin, Wanderers) 1953 *F, E, S,
W*, 1954 *NZ, S, W*, 1955 *F, E*, 1956 *E, S, W*, 1957 *F,
E, S, W*, 1958 *A, E, S, W*, 1959 *E, S, W, F*, 1960 *E, S,
W, F, SA*, 1961 *E, S, W, F, SA*, 1962 *F*
Kavanagh, P J (UC Dublin, Wanderers) 1952 *E*, 1955 *W*

Keane, M I (Lansdowne) 1974 *F, W, E, S, P, NZ,* 1975 *E, S, F, W,* 1976 *A, F, W, E, S, NZ,* 1977 *W, E, S, F,* 1978 *S, F, W, E, NZ,* 1979 *F, W, E, S, A* 1,2, 1980 *E, S, F, W,* 1981 *F, W, E, S,* 1982 *W, E, S, F,* 1983 *S, F, W, E,* 1984 *F, W, E, S*
Kearney, R K (Wanderers) 1982 *F,* 1984 *A,* 1986 *F, W*
Keeffe, E (Sunday's Well) 1947 *F, E, S, W, A,* 1948 *F*
Kelly, H C (NIFC) 1877 *E, S,* 1878 *E,* 1879 *S,* 1880 *E, S*
Kelly, J C (UC Dublin) 1962 *F, W,* 1963 *F, E, S, W, NZ,* 1964 *E, S, W, F*
Kelly, S (Lansdowne) 1954 *S, W,* 1955 *S,* 1960 *W, F*
Kelly, W (Wanderers) 1884 *S*
Kennedy, A G (Belfast Collegians) 1956 *F*
Kennedy, A P (London Irish) 1986 *W, E*
Kennedy, F (Wanderers) 1880 *E,* 1881 *E,* 1882 *W*
Kennedy, F A (Wanderers) 1904 *E, W*
Kennedy, H (Bradford) 1938 *S, W*
Kennedy, J M (Wanderers) 1882 *W,* 1884 *W*
Kennedy, K W (Queen's U, Belfast, London Irish) 1965 *F, E, S, W, SA,* 1966 *F, E, W,* 1967 *A* 1, *E, S, W, F, A* 2, 1968 *F, A,* 1969 *F, E, S, W,* 1970 *SA, F, E, S, W,* 1971 *F, E, S, W,* 1972 *F* 1, *E, F* 2, 1973 *NZ, E, S, W, F,* 1974 *F, W, E, S, P, NZ,* 1975 *F, W*
Kennedy, T J (St Mary's Coll) 1978 *NZ,* 1979 *F, W, E* (R), *A* 1,2, 1980 *E, S, F, W,* 1981 *SA* 1,2, *A*
Keogh, F S (Bective Rangers) 1964 *W, F*
Keon, J J (Limerick) 1879 *E*
Keyes, R P (Cork Constitution) 1986 *E,* 1991 [*Z, J, S, A*], 1992 *W, E, S*
Kidd, F W (Dublin U, Lansdowne) 1877 *E, S,* 1878 *E*
Kiely, M D (Lansdowne) 1962 *W,* 1963 *F, E, S, W*
Kiernan, M J (Dolphin, Lansdowne) 1982 *W*(R), *E, S, F,* 1983 *S, F, W, E,* 1984 *E, S, A,* 1985 *S, F, W, E,* 1986 *F, W, E, S, R,* 1987 *E, S, F, W,* [*W, C, A*], 1988 *S, F, W, E* 1,2, *WS,* 1989 *F, W, E, S,* 1990 *E, S, F, W, Arg,* 1991 *F*
Kiernan, T J (UC Cork, Cork Const) 1960 *E, S, W, F, SA,* 1961 *E, S, W, F, SA,* 1962 *E, W,* 1963 *F, S, W, NZ,* 1964 *E, S,* 1965 *F, E, S, W, SA,* 1966 *F, E, S, W,* 1967 *A* 1, *E, S, W, F, A* 2, 1968 *F, E, S, W, A,* 1969 *F, E, S, W,* 1970 *SA, F, E, S,* 1971 *F, E,* 1972 *F* 1, *E, F* 2, 1973 *NZ, E, S*
Killeen, G V (Garryowen) 1912 *E, S, W,* 1913 *E, S, W, F,* 1914 *E, S, W*
King, H (Dublin U) 1883 *E, S*
Kingston, T J (Dolphin) 1987 [*W, Tg, A*], 1988 *S, F, W, E* 1, 1990 *F, W,* 1991 [*J*]
Knox, J H (Dublin U, Lansdowne) 1904 *W,* 1905 *E, S, W, NZ,* 1906 *E, S, W,* 1907 *W,* 1908 *S*
Kyle, J W (Queen's U, Belfast, NIFC) 1947 *F, E, S, W, A,* 1948 *F, E, S, W,* 1949 *F, E, S, W,* 1950 *F, E, S, W,* 1951 *F, E, S, W, SA,* 1952 *F, S, W, E,* 1953 *F, E, S, W,* 1954 *NZ, F,* 1955 *F, E, S, W,* 1956 *F, E, S, W,* 1957 *F, E, S, W,* 1958 *A, E, S*

Lambert, N H (Lansdowne) 1934 *S, W*
Lamont, R A (Instonians) 1965 *F, E, SA,* 1966 *F, E, S, W,* 1970 *SA, F, E, S, W*
Landers, M F (Cork Const) 1904 *W,* 1905 *E, S, W, NZ*
Lane, D (UC Cork) 1934 *S, W,* 1935 *E, S*
Lane, M F (UC Cork) 1947 *W,* 1949 *F, E, S, W,* 1950 *F, E, S, W,* 1951 *F, S, W, SA,* 1952 *F, S,* 1953 *F, E*
Lane, P (Old Crescent) 1964 *W*
Langan, D J (Clontarf) 1934 *W*
Langbroek, J A (Blackrock Coll) 1987 [*Tg*]
Lavery, P (London Irish) 1974 *W,* 1976 *W*
Lawler, P J (Clontarf) 1951 *S, SA,* 1952 *F, S, W, E,* 1953 *F,* 1954 *NZ, E, S,* 1956 *F, E*
Lawlor, P J (Bective Rangers) 1935 *E, S, W,* 1937 *E, S, W*
Lawlor, P J (Bective Rangers) 1990 *Arg*
Leahy, M W (UC Cork) 1964 *W*
Lee, S (NIFC) 1891 *E, S, W,* 1892 *E, S, W,* 1893 *E, S, W,* 1894 *E, S, W,* 1895 *E, W,* 1896 *E, S, W,* 1897 *E,* 1898 *E*
Le Fanu, V C (Cambridge U, Lansdowne) 1886 *E, S,* 1887 *E, W,* 1888 *S,* 1889 *W,* 1890 *E,* 1891 *E,* 1892 *E, S, W*
Lenihan, D G (UC Cork, Cork Const) 1981 *A,* 1982 *W, E, S, F,* 1983 *S, F, W, E,* 1984 *F, W, E, S, A,* 1985 *S, F, W, E,* 1986 *F, W, E, S, R,* 1987 *S, F, W,* [*W, C, Tg, A*], 1988 *S, F, W, E* 1,2, *WS, It,* 1989 *F, W, E, S, NZ,* 1990 *S, F, W, Arg,* 1991 *Nm* 2, [*Z, S, A*], 1992 *W*
L'Estrange, L P F (Dublin U) 1962 *E*

Levis, F H (Wanderers) 1884 *E*
Lightfoot, E J (Lansdowne) 1931 *F, E, S, W, SA,* 1932 *E, S, W,* 1933 *E, W, S*
Lindsay, H (Dublin U, Armagh) 1893 *E, S, W,* 1894 *E, S, W,* 1895 *E,* 1896 *E, S, W,* 1898 *E, S, W*
Little, T J (Bective Rangers) 1898 *W,* 1899 *S, W,* 1900 *S, W,* 1901 *E, S*
Lloyd, R A (Dublin U, Liverpool) 1910 *E, S,* 1911 *E, S, W, F,* 1912 *F, E, S, W, SA,* 1913 *E, S, W, F,* 1914 *F, E,* 1920 *E, F*
Lydon, C T J (Galwegians) 1956 *S*
Lyle, R K (Dublin U) 1910 *W, F*
Lyle, T R (Dublin U) 1885 *E, S* 1,2, 1886 *E,* 1887 *E, S*
Lynch, J F (St Mary's Coll) 1971 *F, E, S, W,* 1972 *F* 1, *E, F* 2, 1973 *NZ, E, S, W,* 1974 *F, W, E, S, P, NZ*
Lynch, L (Lansdowne) 1956 *S*
Lytle, J H (NIFC) 1894 *E, S, W,* 1895 *W,* 1896 *E, S, W,* 1897 *E, S,* 1898 *E, S,* 1899 *S*
Lytle, J N (NIFC) 1888 *M,* 1889 *W,* 1890 *E,* 1891 *E, S,* 1894 *E, S, W*
Lyttle, V J (Collegians, Bedford) 1938 *E,* 1939 *E, S*

McAleese, D R (Ballymena) 1992 *F*
McAllan, G H (Dungannon) 1896 *S, W*
Macaulay, J (Limerick) 1887 *E, S*
McBride, W D (Malone) 1988 *W, E* 1, *WS, It,* 1989 *S,* 1990 *F, W, Arg*
McBride, W J (Ballymena) 1962 *E, S, F, W,* 1963 *F, E, S, W, NZ,* 1964 *E, S, F,* 1965 *F, E, S, W, SA,* 1966 *F, E, S, W,* 1967 *A* 1, *E, S, W, F, A* 2, 1968 *F, E, S, W, A,* 1969 *F, E, S, W,* 1970 *SA, F, E, S, W,* 1971 *F, E, S, W,* 1972 *F* 1, *E, F* 2, 1973 *NZ, E, S, W, F,* 1974 *F, W, E, S, P, NZ,* 1975 *E, S, F, W*
McCall, B W (London Irish) 1985 *F* (R), 1986 *E, S*
McCallan, B (Ballymena) 1960 *E, S*
McCarten, R J (London Irish) 1961 *E, W, F*
McCarthy, E A (Kingstown) 1882 *W*
McCarthy, J S (Dolphin) 1948 *F, E, S, W,* 1949 *F, E, S, W,* 1950 *W,* 1951 *F, E, S, W, SA,* 1952 *F, S, W, E,* 1953 *F, E, S,* 1954 *NZ, F, E, S, W,* 1955 *F, E*
MacCarthy, St G (Dublin U) 1882 *W*
McCarthy, T (Cork) 1898 *W*
McClelland, T A (Queen's U, Belfast) 1921 *E, S, W, F,* 1922 *F, W, F,* 1923 *E, S, W, F,* 1924 *F, E, S, W, NZ*
McClenahan, R O (Instonians) 1923 *E, S, W*
McClinton, A N (NIFC) 1910 *W, F*
McCombe, W McM (Dublin U, Bangor) 1968 *F,* 1975 *E, S, F, W*
McConnell, A A (Collegians) 1947 *A,* 1948 *F, E, S, W,* 1949 *F, E*
McConnell, G (Derry, Edinburgh U) 1912 *F, E,* 1913 *W, F*
McConnell, J W (Lansdowne) 1913 *S*
McCormac, F M (Wanderers) 1909 *W,* 1910 *W, F*
McCormick, W J (Wanderers) 1930 *E*
McCoull, H C (Belfast Albion) 1895 *E, S, W,* 1899 *E*
McCourt, D (Queen's U, Belfast) 1947 *A*
McCoy, J J (Dungannon, Bangor, Ballymena) 1984 *W, A,* 1985 *S, F, W, E,* 1986 *F,* 1987 [*Tg*], 1988 *E* 2, *WS, It,* 1989 *F, W, E, S, NZ*
McCracken, H (NIFC) 1954 *W*
McDermott, S J (London Irish) 1955 *S, W*
Macdonald, J A (Methodist Coll, Belfast) 1875 *E,* 1876 *E,* 1877 *S,* 1878 *E,* 1879 *S,* 1880 *E,* 1881 *S,* 1882 *E, S,* 1883 *E, S,* 1884 *E, S*
McDonald, J P (Malone) 1987 [*C*], 1990 *E* (R), *S, Arg*
McDonnell, A C (Dublin U) 1889 *W,* 1890 *S, W,* 1891 *E*
McDowell, J C (Instonians) 1924 *F, NZ*
McFarland, B A T (Derry) 1920 *S, W, F,* 1922 *W*
McGann, B J (Lansdowne) 1969 *F, E, S, W,* 1970 *SA, F, E, S, W,* 1971 *F, E, S, W,* 1972 *F* 1, *E, F* 2, 1973 *NZ, E, S, W,* 1976 *F, W, E, S, NZ*
McGown, T M W (NIFC) 1899 *E, S,* 1901 *S*
McGrath, D G (UC Dublin, Cork Const) 1984 *S,* 1987 [*W, C, Tg, A*]
McGrath, N F (Oxford U, London Irish) 1934 *W*
McGrath, P J (UC Cork) 1965 *E, S, W, SA,* 1966 *F, E, S, W,* 1967 *A* 1, *A* 2
McGrath, R J M (Wanderers) 1977 *W, E, F* (R), 1981 *SA* 1,2, *A,* 1982 *W, E, S, F,* 1983 *S, F, W, E,* 1984 *F, W*
McGrath, T (Garryowen) 1956 *W,* 1958 *F,* 1960 *E, S,* 1961 *SA*
McGuire, E P (UC Galway) 1963 *E, S, W, NZ,* 1964 *E, S, W, F*

F, E, S, W, 1949 *F, E, S, W*, 1950 *F, E, S, W*, 1951 *F, E, S, W, SA*, 1952 *F, S, W*
Mulligan, A A (Wanderers) 1956 *F, E*, 1957 *F, E, S, W*, 1958 *A, E, S, F*, 1959 *E, S, W, F*, 1960 *E, S, W, F, SA*, 1961 *W, F, SA*
Mullin, B J (Dublin U, Oxford U, Blackrock Coll, London Irish) 1984 *A*, 1985 *S, W, E*, 1986 *F, W, E, S, R*, 1987 *E, S, F, W*, [*W, C, Tg, A*], 1988 *S, F, W, E* 1,2, *WS, It*, 1989 *F, W, E, S, NZ*, 1990 *E, S, W, Arg*, 1991 *F, W, E, S, Nm* 1,2, [*J, S, A*], 1992 *W, E, S*
Murphy, C J (Lansdowne) 1939 *E, S, W*, 1947 *F, E*
Murphy, J G M W (London Irish) 1951 *SA*, 1952 *S, W, E*, 1954 *NZ*, 1958 *W*
Murphy, J J (Greystones) 1981 *SA* 1, 1982 *W* (R), 1984 *S*
Murphy, K J (Cork Constitution) 1990 *E, S, F, W, Arg*, 1991 *F, W*(R), *S*(R), 1992 *S, F*
Murphy, N A A (Cork Constitution) 1958 *A, E, S, W, F*, 1959 *A, S, W, F*, 1960 *E, S, W, F, SA*, 1961 *E, S, W*, 1962 *E*, 1963 *NZ*, 1964 *E, S, W, F*, 1965 *F, E, S, W, SA*, 1966 *F, E, S, W*, 1967 *A* 1, *E, S, W, F*, 1969 *F, E, S, W*
Murphy, N F (Cork Constitution) 1930 *E, W*, 1931 *F, E, S, W, SA*, 1932 *E, S, W*, 1933 *E*
Murphy-O'Connor, J (Bective Rangers) 1954 *E*
Murray, H W (Dublin) 1877 *S*, 1878 *E*, 1879 *E*
Murray, J B (UC Dublin) 1963 *F*
Murray, P F (Wanderers) 1927 *F*, 1929 *F, E, S*, 1930 *F, E, S, W*, 1931 *F, E, S, W, SA*, 1932 *E, S, W*, 1933 *E, W, S*
Murtagh, C W (Portadown) 1977 *S*
Myles, J (Dublin U) 1875 *E*

Nash, L C (Queen's Coll, Cork) 1889 *S*, 1890 *W, E*, 1891 *E, S, W*
Neely, M R (Collegians) 1947 *F, E, S, W*
Neill, H J (NIFC) 1885 *E, S* 1,2, 1886 *S*, 1887 *E, S, W*, 1888 *W, S*
Neill, J McF (Instonians) 1926 *F*
Nelson, J E (Malone) 1947 *A*, 1948 *E, S, W*, 1949 *F, E, S, W*, 1950 *F, E, S, W*, 1951 *F, E, W*, 1954 *F*
Nelson, R (Queen's Coll, Belfast) 1882 *E, S*, 1883 *S*, 1886 *S*
Nesdale, T J (Garryowen) 1961 *F*
Neville, W C (Dublin U) 1879 *S, E*
Nicholson, P C (Dublin U) 1900 *E, S, W*
Norton, G W (Bective Rangers) 1949 *F, E, S, W*, 1950 *F, E, S, W*, 1951 *F, E, S*
Notley, J R (Wanderers) 1952 *F, S*

O'Brien, B (Derry) 1893 *S, W*
O'Brien, B A P (Shannon) 1968 *F, E, S*
O'Brien, D J (London Irish, Cardiff, Old Belvedere) 1948 *E, S, W*, 1949 *F, E, S, W*, 1950 *F, E, S, W*, 1951 *F, E, S, W, SA*, 1952 *F, S, W, E*
O'Brien, K A (Broughton Park) 1980 *E*, 1981 *SA* 1 (R), 2
O'Brien-Bulter, P E (Monkstown) 1897 *S*, 1898 *E, S*, 1899 *S, W*, 1900 *E*
O'Callaghan, C T (Carlow) 1910 *W, F*, 1911 *E, S, W, F*, 1912 *F*
O'Callaghan, M P (Sunday's Well) 1962 *W*, 1964 *E, F*
O'Callaghan, P (Dolphin) 1967 *A* 1, *E, A* 2, 1968 *F, E, S, W*, 1969 *F, E, S, W*, 1970 *SA, F, W, E, S, NZ*
O'Connell, P (Bective Rangers) 1913 *W, F*, 1914 *F, E, S, W*
O'Connell, W J (Lansdowne) 1955 *F*
O'Connor, H S (Dublin U) 1957 *F, E, S, W*
O'Connor, J (Garryowen) 1895 *S*
O'Connor, J H (Bective Rangers) 1888 *M*, 1890 *S, W, E*, 1891 *E, S*, 1892 *E, W*, 1893 *E, S*, 1894 *E, S, W*, 1895 *E*, 1896 *E, S, W*
O'Connor, J J (Garryowen) 1909 *F*
O'Connor, J J (UC Cork) 1933 *S*, 1934 *E, S, W*, 1935 *E, S, W, NZ*, 1936 *E, S, W*, 1938 *S*
O'Connor, P J (Lansdowne) 1887 *W*
Odbert, R V M (RAF) 1928 *F*
O'Donnell, R C (St Mary's Coll) 1979 *A* 1,2, 1980 *S, F, W*
O'Donoghue, P J (Bective Rangers) 1955 *F, E, S, W*, 1956 *W*, 1957 *F, E*, 1958 *A, E, S, W*
O'Driscoll, B J (Manchester) 1971 *F* (R), *E, S, W*
O'Driscoll, J B (London Irish, Manchester) 1978 *S*, 1979 *A* 1,2, 1980 *E, S, F, W*, 1981 *F, W, E, S, SA* 1,2, *A*, 1982 *W, E, S, F*, 1983 *S, F, W, E*, 1984 *F, W, E, S*

O'Flanagan, K P (London Irish) 1947 *A*
O'Flanagan, M (Lansdowne) 1948 *S*
O'Hanlon, B (Dolphin) 1947 *E, S, W*, 1948 *F, E, S, W*, 1949 *F, E, S, W*, 1950 *F*
O'Hara, P T J (Sunday's Well) 1988 *WS* (R), 1989 *F, W, E, NZ*, 1990 *E, S, F, W*, 1991 *Nm* 1, [*J*]
O'Leary, A (Cork Constitution) 1952 *S, W, E*
O'Loughlin, D B (UC Cork) 1938 *E, S, W*, 1939 *E, S, W*
O'Meara, J A (UC Cork, Dolphin) 1951 *F, E, S, W, SA*, 1952 *F, S, W, E*, 1953 *F, E, S, W*, 1954 *NZ, F, E, S*, 1955 *F, E*, 1956 *S, W*, 1958 *W*
O'Neill, H O'H (Queen's U, Belfast, UC Cork) 1930 *E, S, W*, 1933 *E, S, W*
O'Neill, J B (Queen's U, Belfast) 1920 *S*
O'Neill, W A (UC Dublin, Wanderers) 1952 *E*, 1953 *F, E, S, W*, 1954 *NZ*
O'Reilly, A J F (Old Belvedere, Leicester) 1955 *F, E, S, W*, 1956 *F, E, S, W*, 1957 *F, E, S, W*, 1958 *A, E, S, W, F*, 1959 *E, S, W, F*, 1960 *E, F, SA*, 1961 *E, F, SA*, 1963 *F, S, W*, 1970 *E*
Orr, P A (Old Wesley) 1976 *F, W, E, S, NZ*, 1977 *W, E, S, F*, 1978 *S, F, W, E, NZ*, 1979 *F, W, E, S, A* 1,2, 1980 *E, S, F, W*, 1981 *F, W, E, S, SA* 1,2, *A*, 1982 *W, E, S, F*, 1983 *S, F, W, E*, 1984 *F, W, E, S, A*, 1985 *S, F, W, E*, 1986 *F, S, R*, 1987 *E, S, F, W*, [*W, C, A*]
O'Sullivan, A C (Dublin U) 1882 *S*
O'Sullivan, J M (Limerick) 1884 *S*, 1887 *S*
O'Sullivan, P J A (Galwegians) 1957 *F, E, S, W*, 1959 *E, S, W, F*, 1960 *SA*, 1961 *E, S*, 1962 *F, W*, 1963 *F, NZ*
O'Sullivan, W (Queen's Coll, Cork) 1895 *S*
Owens, R H (Dublin U) 1922 *E, S*

Parfrey, P (UC Cork) 1974 *NZ*
Parke, J C (Monkstown) 1903 *W*, 1904 *E, S, W*, 1905 *W, NZ*, 1906 *E, S, W, SA*, 1907 *E, S, W*, 1908 *E, S, W*, 1909 *E, S, W*
Parr, J S (Wanderers) 1914 *F, E, S, W*
Patterson, C S (Instonians) 1978 *NZ*, 1979 *F, W, E, S, A* 1,2, 1980 *E, S, F, W*
Patterson, R d'A (Wanderers) 1912 *F, S, W, SA*, 1913 *E, S, W, F*
Payne, C T (NIFC) 1926 *E*, 1927 *F, E, S, A*, 1928 *F, E, S, W*, 1929 *F, E, W*, 1930 *F, E, S, W*
Pedlow, A C (CIYMS) 1953 *W*, 1954 *NZ, F, E*, 1955 *F, E, S, W*, 1956 *F, E, S, W*, 1957 *F, E, S, W*, 1958 *A, E, S, W, F*, 1959 *E, S, W, F*, 1960 *E, S, W, F, SA*, 1961 *S*, 1962 *W*, 1963 *F*
Pedlow, J (Bessbrook) 1882 *S*, 1884 *W*
Pedlow, R (Bessbrook) 1891 *W*
Pedlow, T B (Queen's Coll, Belfast) 1889 *S, W*
Peel, T (Limerick) 1892 *E, S, W*
Peirce, W (Cork) 1881 *E*
Phipps, G C (Army) 1950 *E, W*, 1952 *F, W, E*
Pike, T O (Lansdowne) 1927 *E, S, W, A*, 1928 *F, E, S, W*
Pike, V J (Lansdowne) 1931 *E, S, W, SA*, 1932 *E, S, W*, 1933 *E, W, S*, 1934 *E, S, W*
Pike, W W (Kingstown) 1879 *E*, 1881 *E, S*, 1882 *E*, 1883 *S*
Pinion, G (Belfast Collegians) 1909 *E, S, W, F*
Piper, O J S (Cork Constitution) 1909 *E, S, W, F*, 1910 *E, S, W, F*
Polden, S E (Clontarf) 1913 *W, F*, 1914 *F*, 1920 *F*
Popham, I (Cork Constitution) 1922 *S, W, F*, 1923 *F*
Popplewell, N J (Greystones) 1989 *NZ*, 1990 *Arg*, 1991 *Nm* 1,2, [*Z, S, A*], 1992 *W, E, S, F*
Potterton, H N (Wanderers) 1920 *W*
Pratt, R H (Dublin U) 1933 *E, W, S*, 1934 *E, S*
Price, A H (Dublin U) 1920 *S, F*
Pringle, J C (NIFC) 1902 *S, W*
Purcell, N M (Lansdowne) 1921 *E, S, W, F*
Purdon, H (NIFC) 1879 *S, E*, 1880 *E*, 1881 *E, S*
Purdon, W B (Queen's Coll, Belfast) 1906 *E, S, W*
Purser, F C (Dublin U) 1898 *E, S, W*

Quinlan, S V J (Blackrock Coll) 1956 *F, E, W*, 1958 *W*
Quinn, B T (Old Belvedere) 1947 *F*
Quinn, F P (Old Belvedere) 1981 *F, W, E*
Quinn, J P (Dublin U) 1910 *E, S*, 1911 *E, S, W, F*, 1912 *E, S, W*, 1913 *E, W, F*, 1914 *F, E, S*
Quinn, K (Old Belvedere) 1947 *F, A*, 1953 *F, E, S*

265

Quinn, M A M (Lansdowne) 1973 F, 1974 F, W, E, S, P, NZ, 1977 S, F, 1981 SA 2
Quirke, J M T (Blackrock Coll) 1962 E, S, 1968 S

Rainey, P I (Ballymena) 1989 NZ
Rambaut, D F (Dublin U) 1887 E, S, W, 1888 W
Rea, H H (Edinburgh U) 1967 A 1, 1969 F
Read, H M (Dublin U) 1910 E, S, 1911 E, S, W, F, 1912 F, E, S, W, SA, 1913 E, S
Rearden, J V (Cork Constitution) 1934 E, S
Reid, C (NIFC) 1899 S, W, 1900 E, 1903 W
Reid, J L (Richmond) 1934 S, W
Reid, P J (Garryowen) 1947 A, 1948 F, E, W
Reid, T E (Garryowen) 1953 E, S, W, 1954 NZ, F, 1955 E, S, 1956 F, E, 1957 F, E, S, W
Reidy, C J (London Irish) 1937 W
Reidy, G F (Dolphin, Lansdowne) 1953 W, 1954 F, E, S, W
Richey, H A (Dublin U) 1889 W, 1890 S
Ridgeway, E C (Wanderers) 1932 S, W, 1935 E, S, W
Rigney, B J (Greystones) 1991 F, W, E, S, Nm 1, 1992 F
Ringland, T M (Queen's U, Belfast, Ballymena) 1981 A, 1982 W, E, F, 1983 S, F, W, E, 1984 F, W, E, S, A, 1985 S, F, W, E, 1986 F, W, E, S, R, 1987 E, S, F, W, [W, C, Tg, A], 1988 S, F, W, E 1
Riordan, W F (Cork Constitution) 1910 E
Ritchie, J S (London Irish) 1956 F, E
Robb, C G (Queen's Coll, Belfast) 1904 E, S, W, 1905 NZ, 1906 S
Robbie, J C (Dublin U, Greystones) 1976 A, F, NZ, 1977 S, F, 1981 F, W, E, S
Robinson, B F (Ballymena) 1991 F, W, E, S, Nm 1,2, [Z, S, A], 1992 W, E, S, F
Robinson, T T H (Wanderers) 1904 E, S, 1905 E, S, W, NZ, 1906 SA, 1907 E, S, W
Roche, J (Wanderers) 1890 S, W, E, 1891 E, S, W, 1892 W
Roche, R E (UC Galway) 1955 E, S, 1957 S, W
Roche, W J (UC Cork) 1920 E, S, F
Roddy, P J (Bective Rangers) 1920 S, F
Roe, R (Lansdowne) 1952 E, 1953 F, E, S, W, 1954 F, E, S, W, 1955 F, E, S, W, 1956 F, E, S, W, 1957 F, E, S, W
Rolland, A C (Blackrock Coll) 1990 Arg
Rooke, C V (Dublin U) 1891 E, W, 1892 E, S, W, 1893 E, S, W, 1894 E, S, W, 1895 E, S, W, 1896 E, S, W, 1897 E, S
Ross, D J (Belfast Academy) 1884 E, 1885 S 1,2, 1886 E, S
Ross, G R P (CIYMS) 1955 W
Ross, J F (NIFC) 1886 S
Ross, J P (Lansdowne) 1885 E, S 1,2, 1886 E, S
Ross, N G (Malone) 1927 F, E
Ross, W McC (Queen's U, Belfast) 1932 E, S, W, 1933 E, W, S, 1934 E, S, 1935 NZ
Russell, J (UC Cork) 1931 F, E, S, W, SA, 1933 E, W, S, 1934 E, S, W, 1935 E, S, W, 1936 E, S, W, 1937 E, S
Russell, P (Instonians) 1990 E
Rutherford, W G (Tipperary) 1884 E, S, 1885 E, S 1, 1886 E, 1888 W
Ryan, E (Dolphin) 1937 W, 1938 E, S
Ryan, J (Rockwell Coll) 1897 E, 1898 E, S, W, 1899 E, S, W, 1900 S, W, 1901 E, S, W, 1902 E, 1904 E
Ryan, J G (UC Dublin) 1939 E, S, W
Ryan, M (Rockwell Coll) 1897 E, S, 1898 E, S, W, 1899 E, S, W, 1900 E, S, W, 1901 E, S, W, 1903 E, 1904 E, S

Saunders, R (London Irish) 1991 F, W, E, S, Nm 1,2, [Z, J, S, A], 1992 W, E
Sayers, H J M (Lansdowne) 1935 E, S, W, 1936 E, S, W, 1938 W, 1939 E, S, W
Schute, F (Wanderers) 1878 E, 1879 E
Schute, F G (Dublin U) 1912 SA, 1913 E, S
Scott, D (Malone) 1961 F, SA, 1962 S
Scott, R D (Queen's U, Belfast) 1967 E, F, 1968 F, E, S
Scovell, R H (Kingstown) 1883 E, 1884 E
Scriven, G (Dublin U) 1879 S, E, 1880 E, S, 1881 E, 1882 S, 1883 E, S
Sealy, J (Dublin U) 1896 E, S, W, 1897 S, 1899 E, S, W, 1900 E, S
Sexton, J F (Dublin U, Lansdowne) 1988 E 2, WS, It, 1989 F
Sexton, W J (Garryowen) 1984 A, 1988 S, E 2

Shanahan, T (Lansdowne) 1885 E, S 1,2, 1886 E, 1888 S, W
Shaw, G M (Windsor) 1877 S
Sheehan, M D (London Irish) 1932 E
Sherry, B F (Terenure Coll) 1967 A 1, E, S, A 2, 1968 F, E
Sherry, M J A (Lansdowne) 1975 F, W
Siggins, J A E (Belfast Collegians) 1931 F, E, S, W, SA, 1932 E, S, W, 1933 E, W, S, 1934 E, S, W, 1935 E, S, W, NZ, 1936 E, S, W, 1937 E, S, W
Slattery, J F (UC Dublin, Blackrock Coll) 1970 SA, F, E, S, W, 1971 F, E, S, W, 1972 F 1, E, F 2, 1973 NZ, E, S, W, F, 1974 F, W, E, S, P, NZ, 1975 E, S, F, W, 1976 A, 1977 S, F, 1978 S, F, W, E, NZ, 1979 F, W, E, S, A 1,2, 1980 E, S, F, W, 1981 F, W, E, S, SA 1,2, A, 1982 W, E, S, F, 1983 F, W, E, 1984 F
Smartt, F N B (Dublin U) 1908 E, S, 1909 E
Smith, B A (Oxford U, Leicester) 1989 NZ, 1990 S, F, W, Arg, 1991 F, W, E, S
Smith, J H (London Irish) 1951 F, E, S, W, SA, 1952 F, S, W, E, 1954 NZ, W, F
Smith, R E (Lansdowne) 1892 E
Smith, S J (Ballymena) 1988 E 2, WS, It, 1989 F, W, E, S, NZ, 1990 E, 1991 F, W, E, S, Nm 1,2, [Z, S, A], 1992 W, E, S, F
Smithwick, F F S (Monkstown) 1898 S, W
Smyth, J T (Queen's U, Belfast) 1920 F
Smyth, P J (Belfast Collegians) 1911 E, S, F
Smyth, R S (Dublin U) 1903 E, S, 1904 E
Smyth, T (Malone, Newport) 1908 E, S, W, 1909 E, S, W, 1910 E, S, W, F, 1911 E, S, W, 1912 E
Smyth, W S (Belfast Collegians) 1910 W, F, 1920 E
Solomons, B A H (Dublin U) 1908 E, S, W, 1909 E, S, W, F, 1910 E, S, W
Spain, A W (UC Dublin) 1924 NZ
Sparrow, W (Dublin U) 1893 W, 1894 E
Spillane, B J (Bohemians) 1985 S, F, W, E, 1986 F, W, E, 1987 F, W, [W, C, A(R)], 1989 E (R)
Spring, D E (Dublin U) 1978 S, NZ, 1979 S, 1980 S, F, W, 1981 W
Spring, R M (Lansdowne) 1979 F, W, E
Spunner, H F (Wanderers) 1881 E, S, 1884 W
Stack, C R R (Dublin U) 1889 S
Stack, G H (Dublin U) 1875 E
Staples, J E (London Irish) 1991 W, E, S, Nm 1,2, [Z, J, S, A], 1992 W, E
Steele, H W (Ballymena) 1976 E, 1977 F, 1978 F, W, E, 1979 F, W, E, A 1,2
Stephenson, G V (Queen's U, Belfast, London Hosp) 1920 F, 1921 E, S, W, F, 1922 E, S, W, F, 1923 E, S, W, F, 1924 F, E, S, W, NZ, 1925 F, E, S, W, 1926 F, E, S, W, 1927 F, E, S, W, A, 1928 F, E, S, W, 1929 F, E, W, 1930 F, E, S, W
Stephenson, H W V (United Services) 1922 S, W, F, 1924 F, E, S, W, NZ, 1925 F, E, S, W, 1927 A, 1928 E
Stevenson, J (Dungannon) 1888 M, 1889 S
Stevenson, J B (Instonians) 1958 A, E, S, W, F
Stevenson, R (Dungannon) 1887 E, S, W, 1888 M, 1889 S, W, 1890 S, W, E, 1891 W, 1892 W, 1893 E, S, W
Stevenson, T H (Belfast Acad) 1895 E, W, 1896 E, S, W, 1897 E, S
Stewart, A L (NIFC) 1913 W, F, 1914 F
Stewart, W J (Queen's U, Belfast, NIFC) 1922 F, 1924 S, 1928 F, E, S, W, 1929 F, E, S, W
Stoker, E W (Wanderers) 1888 W, S
Stoker, F O (Wanderers) 1886 S, 1888 W, M, 1889 S, 1891 W
Stokes, O S (Cork Bankers) 1882 E, 1884 E
Stokes, P (Garryowen) 1913 E, S, 1914 F, 1920 E, S, W, F, 1921 E, S, F, 1922 W, F
Stokes, R D (Queen's Coll, Cork) 1891 S, W
Strathdee, E (Queen's U, Belfast) 1947 E, S, W, A, 1948 W, F, 1949 E, S, W
Stuart, C P (Clontarf) 1912 SA
Stuart, I M B (Dublin U) 1924 E, S
Sugars, H S (Dublin U) 1905 NZ, 1906 SA, 1907 S
Sugden, M (Wanderers) 1925 F, E, S, W, 1926 F, E, S, W, 1927 E, S, W, A, 1928 F, E, S, W, 1929 F, E, S, W, 1930 F, E, S, W, 1931 F, E, S, W
Sullivan, D B (UC Dublin) 1922 E, S, W, F
Sweeney, J A (Blackrock Coll) 1907 E, S, W
Symes, G R (Monkstown) 1895 E
Synge, J S (Lansdowne) 1929 S

Taggart, T (Dublin U) 1887 *W*
Taylor, A S (Queen's Coll, Belfast) 1910 *E, S, W*, 1912 *F*
Taylor, D R (Queen's Coll, Belfast) 1903 *E*
Taylor, J (Belfast Collegians) 1914 *E, S, W*
Taylor, J W (NIFC) 1879 *S*, 1880 *E, S*, 1881 *S*, 1882 *E, S*, 1883 *E, S*
Tector, W R (Wanderers) 1955 *F, E, S*
Tedford, A (Malone) 1902 *E, S, W*, 1903 *E, S, W*, 1904 *E, S, W*, 1905 *E, S, W, NZ*, 1906 *E, S, W, SA*, 1907 *E, S, W*, 1908 *E, S, W*
Teehan, C (UC Cork) 1939 *E, S, W*
Thompson, C (Belfast Collegians) 1907 *E, S*, 1908 *E, S, W*, 1909 *E, S, W, F*, 1910 *E, S, W, F*
Thompson, J A (Queen's Coll, Belfast) 1885 *S* 1,2
Thompson, J K S (Dublin U) 1921 *W*, 1922 *E, S, F*, 1923 *E, S, W, F*
Thompson, R G (Lansdowne) 1882 *W*
Thompson, R H (Instonians) 1951 *SA*, 1952 *F*, 1954 *NZ, F, E, S, W*, 1955 *F, S, W*, 1956 *W*
Thornhill, T (Wanderers) 1892 *E, S, W*, 1893 *E*
Thrift, H (Dublin U) 1904 *W*, 1905 *E, S, W, NZ*, 1906 *E, W, SA*, 1907 *E, S, W*, 1908 *E, S, W*, 1909 *E, S, W, F*
Tierney, D (UC Cork) 1938 *S, W*, 1939 *E*
Tillie, C R (Dublin U) 1887 *E, S*, 1888 *W, S*
Todd, A W P (Dublin U) 1913 *W, F*, 1914 *F*
Torrens, J D (Bohemians) 1938 *W*, 1939 *E, S, W*
Tucker, C C (Shannon) 1979 *F, W*, 1980 *F* (R)
Tuke, B B (Bective Rangers) 1890 *E*, 1891 *E, S*, 1892 *E*, 1894 *E, S, W*, 1895 *E, S*
Turley, N (Blackrock Coll) 1962 *E*
Tydings, J J (Young Munster) 1968 *A*
Tyrrell, W (Queen's U, Belfast) 1910 *F*, 1913 *E, S, W, F*, 1914 *F, E, S, W*

Uprichard, R J H (Harlequins, RAF) 1950 *S, W*

Waide, S L (Oxford U, NIFC) 1932 *E, S, W*, 1933 *E, W*
Waites, J (Bective Rangers) 1886 *S*, 1888 *M*, 1889 *W*, 1890 *S, W, E*, 1891 *E*
Waldron, O C (Oxford U, London Irish) 1966 *S, W*, 1968 *A*
Walker, S (Instonians) 1934 *E, S*, 1935 *E, S, W, NZ*, 1936 *E, S, W*, 1937 *E, S, W*, 1938 *E, S, W*
Walkington, D B (NIFC) 1887 *E, W*, 1888 *W*, 1890 *W, E*, 1891 *E, S, W*
Walkington, R B (NIFC) 1875 *E*, 1876 *E*, 1877 *E, S*, 1878 *E*, 1879 *S*, 1880 *E, S*, 1882 *E, S*
Wall, H (Dolphin) 1965 *S, W*
Wallace, Jas (Wanderers) 1904 *E, S*
Wallace, Jos (Wanderers) 1903 *S, W*, 1904 *E, S, W*, 1905 *E, S, W, NZ*, 1906 *W*
Wallace R M (Garryowen) 1991 *Nm* 1(R), 1992 *W, E, S, F*
Wallace, T H (Cardiff) 1920 *E, S, W*
Wallis, A K (Wanderers) 1892 *E, S, W*, 1893 *E, W*
Wallis, C O'N (Old Cranleighans, Wanderers) 1935 *NZ*

Wallis, T G (Wanderers) 1921 *F*, 1922 *E, S, W, F*
Wallis, W A (Wanderers) 1880 *S*, 1881 *E, S*, 1882 *W*, 1883 *S*
Walmsley, G (Bective Rangers) 1894 *E*
Walpole, A (Dublin U) 1888 *S, M*
Walsh, E J (Lansdowne) 1887 *E, S, W*, 1892 *E, S, W*, 1893 *E*
Walsh, H D (Dublin U) 1875 *E*, 1876 *E*
Walsh, J C (UC Cork, Sunday's Well) 1960 *S, SA*, 1961 *E, S, F, SA*, 1963 *E, S, W, NZ*, 1964 *E, S, W, F*, 1965 *F, S, W, SA*, 1966 *F, S, W*, 1967 *E, S, W, F, A* 2
Ward, A J P (Garryowen, St Mary's Coll, Greystones) 1978 *S, F, W, E, NZ*, 1979 *F, W, E, S*, 1981 *W, E, S, A*, 1983 *E* (R), 1984 *E, S*, 1986 *S*, 1987 [C, *Tg*]
Warren, J P (Kingstown) 1883 *E*
Warren, R G (Lansdowne) 1884 *W*, 1885 *E, S* 1,2, 1886 *E*, 1887 *E, S, W*, 1888 *W, S, M*, 1889 *S, W*, 1890 *S, W, E*
Watson, R (Wanderers) 1912 *SA*
Wells, H G (Bective Rangers) 1891 *S, W*, 1894 *E, S*
Westby, A J (Dublin U) 1876 *E*
Wheeler, G H (Queen's Coll, Belfast) 1884 *S*, 1885 *E*
Wheeler, J R (Queen's U, Belfast) 1922 *E, S, W, F*, 1924 *E*
Whelan, P C (Garryowen) 1975 *E, S*, 1976 *NZ*, 1977 *W, E, S, F*, 1978 *S, F, W, E, NZ*, 1979 *F, W, E, S*, 1981 *F, W, E, S*
White, M (Queen's Coll, Cork) 1906 *E, S, W, SA*, 1907 *E, W*
Whitestone, A M (Dublin U) 1877 *E*, 1879 *S, E*, 1880 *E*, 1883 *S*
Whittle, D (Bangor) 1988 *F*
Wilkinson, R W (Wanderers) 1947 *A*
Williamson, F W (Dolphin) 1930 *E, S, W*
Willis, W J (Lansdowne) 1879 *E*
Wilson, F (CIYMS) 1977 *W, E, S*
Wilson, H G (Glasgow U, Malone) 1905 *E, S, W, NZ*, 1906 *E, S, W, SA*, 1907 *E, S, W*, 1908 *E, S, W*, 1909 *E, S, W*, 1910 *W*
Wilson, W H (Bray) 1877 *E, S*
Withers, H H C (Army, Blackheath) 1931 *F, E, S, W, SA*
Wolfe, E J (Armagh) 1882 *E*
Wood, G H (Dublin U) 1913 *W*, 1914 *F*
Wood, B G M (Garryowen) 1954 *E, S*, 1956 *F, E, S, W*, 1957 *F, E, S, W*, 1958 *A, E, S, W, F*, 1959 *E, S, W, F*, 1960 *E, S, W, F, SA*, 1961 *E, S, W, F, SA*
Woods, D C (Bessbrook) 1888 *M*, 1889 *S*
Wright, R A (Monkstown) 1912 *S*

Yeates, R A (Dublin U) 1889 *S, W*
Young, G (UC Cork) 1913 *E*
Young, R M (Collegians) 1965 *F, E, S, W, SA*, 1966 *F, E, S, W*, 1967 *W, F*, 1968 *W, A*, 1969 *F, E, S, W*, 1970 *SA, F, E, S, W*, 1971 *F, E, S, W*

IRISH INTERNATIONAL RECORDS

Both team and individual records are for official Ireland international matches up to 31 March 1992.

TEAM RECORDS

Highest score
60 v Romania (60-0) 1986 Dublin
v individual countries
20 v Argentina (20-18) 1990 Dublin
27 v Australia (27-12) 1979 Brisbane
46 v Canada (46-19) 1987 Dunedin
26 v England (26-21) 1974 Twickenham

25 v France { (25-5) 1911 Cork
              (25-6) 1975 Dublin
31 v Italy (31-15) 1988 Dublin
32 v Japan (32-16) 1991 Dublin
15 v Namibia (15-26) 1991 Windhoek
10 v N Zealand (10-10) 1973 Dublin

60 v Romania (60-0) 1986 Dublin
15 v S Africa (15-23) 1981 Cape Town
26 v Scotland (26-8) 1953 Murrayfield
32 v Tonga (32-9) 1987 Brisbane

21 v Wales
 (21-24) 1979 Cardiff
 (21-7) 1980 Dublin
 (21-9) 1985 Cardiff
 (21-21) 1991 Cardiff

49 v W Samoa (49-22) 1988 Dublin
55 v Zimbabwe (55-11) 1991 Dublin

Biggest winning points margin
60 v Romania (60-0) 1986 Dublin
v individual countries
 2 v Argentina (20-18) 1990 Dublin
15 v Australia (27-12) 1979 Brisbane
27 v Canada (46-19) 1987 Dunedin
22 v England (22-0) 1947 Dublin
24 v France (24-0) 1913 Cork
16 v Italy (31-15) 1988 Dublin
16 v Japan (32-16) 1991 Dublin
No win v Namibia
No win v N Zealand
60 v Romania (60-0) 1986 Dublin
 3 v S Africa (9-6) 1965 Dublin
21 v Scotland (21-0) 1950 Dublin
23 v Tonga (32-9) 1987 Brisbane
16 v Wales (19-3) 1925 Belfast
27 v W Samoa (49-22) 1988 Dublin
44 v Zimbabwe (55-11) 1991 Dublin

Highest score by opposing team
44 France (12-44) 1992 Paris
by individual countries
18 Argentina (20-18) 1990 Dublin
33 Australia (15-33) 1987 Sydney
19 Canada (46-19) 1987 Dunedin
38 England (9-38) 1992 Twickenham
44 France (12-44) 1992 Paris
15 Italy (31-15) 1988 Dublin
16 Japan (32-16) 1991 Dublin
26 Namibia (15-26) 1991 Windhoek
23 N Zealand (6-23) 1989 Dublin
 0 Romania (60-0) 1986 Dublin
38 S Africa (0-38) 1912 Dublin
37 Scotland (21-37) 1989 Murrayfield
 9 Tonga (32-9) 1987 Brisbane
34 Wales (9-34) 1976 Dublin
22 W Samoa (49-22) 1988 Dublin
11 Zimbabwe (55-11) 1991 Dublin

Biggest losing points margin
38 v S Africa (0-38) 1912 Dublin

v individual countries
18 v Australia (15-33) 1987 Sydney
32 v England (3-35) 1988 Twickenham
32 v France (12-44) 1992 Paris
11 v Namibia (15-26) 1991 Windhoek
17 v N Zealand (6-23) 1989 Dublin
38 v S Africa (0-38) 1912 Dublin
23 v Scotland (9-32) 1984 Dublin
29 v Wales (0-29) 1907 Cardiff
No defeats v Argentina, Canada, Italy, Japan, Romania, Tonga, W Samoa or Zimbabwe

Most tries by Ireland in an international
10 v Romania (60-0) 1986 Dublin

Most tries against Ireland in an international
10 by S Africa (0-38) 1912 Dublin

Most points by Ireland in International Championship in a season – 71
in season 1982-83

Most tries by Ireland in International Championship in a season – 12
in seasons 1927-28 and 1952-53

INDIVIDUAL RECORDS

Most capped player
C M H Gibson   69   1964-79
in individual positions
Full-back
T J Kiernan   54   1960-73
Wing
K D Crossan   41   1982-92
Centre
B J Mullin   45[1]   1984-92
Fly-half
J W Kyle   46   1947-58
Scrum-half
M Sugden   28   1925-31
Prop
P A Orr   58   1976-87
Hooker
K W Kennedy   45   1965-75
Lock
W J McBride   63   1962-75
Flanker
J F Slattery   61   1970-84

No 8
W P Duggan   39(41)[2]   1975-84
[1]*C M H Gibson won 40 caps as a centre, 25 at fly-half and 4 as a wing*
[2]*Duggan won 39 caps at No 8 and 2 as a flanker*

Longest international career
A J F O'Reilly 16 seasons 1955-70
C M H Gibson 16 seasons 1964-79
Gibson's career ended during a Southern Hemisphere season

Most consecutive Tests – 52
W J McBride 1964-75

Most internationals as captain
T J Kiernan   24   1963-73

Most points in internationals – 308
M J Kiernan (43 matches) 1982-91

Most points in International Championship in a season – 52
S O Campbell (4 matches) 1982-83

Most points in an international – 23
R P Keyes v Zimbabwe 1991 Dublin

Most tries in internationals – 15
B J Mullin (45 matches) 1984-92

Most tries in International Championship in a season – 5
J E Arigho (3 matches) 1927-28

Most tries in an international – 4
B F Robinson v Zimbabwe 1991 Dublin

Most conversions in internationals – 40
M J Kiernan (43 matches) 1982-91

Most conversions in International Championship in a season – 7
R A Lloyd (4 matches) 1912-13

Most conversions in an international – 7
M J Kiernan v Romania 1986 Dublin

Most dropped goals in internationals – 7
R A Lloyd (19 matches) 1910-20
S O Campbell (22 matches) 1976-84

Most penalty goals in internationals – 62
M J Kiernan (43 matches) 1982-91

Most penalty goals in International Championship in a season – 14
S O Campbell (4 matches) 1982-83

Most points for Ireland on overseas tour – 60
S O Campbell (5 appearances) 1979 Australia
M J Kiernan scored 65 points in Japan 1985, but this was not on a major tour

Most points in any match on tour – 19
A J P Ward v Australian Capital Territory 1979 Canberra
S O Campbell v Australia 1979 Brisbane
M J Kiernan scored 25 points in the second match against Japan 1985, but this was not on a major tour

Most tries in any match on tour – 3
A T A Duggan v Victoria 1967 Melbourne
J F Slattery v SA President's XV 1981 East London
M J Kiernan v Gold Cup XV 1981 Oudtshoorn, SA
T M Ringland scored 3 tries v Japan at Osaka 1985, but this was not on a major tour

SEARCH FOR EXCELLENCE BEGINS

THE 1991-92 SEASON IN WALES
John Billot *Western Mail*

It seemed a dismal documentary on the decline of standards when some found solace in the improved Welsh defensive display at Twickenham where, for the first time in 22 years, Wales failed to score a point. Bleakly, we remembered the 24-0 result. Ah, we said, clutching at the proverbial straw – and, indeed, with some justification – it could have been 50 points but for that tenacious refusal to submit. More realistically, like Mr Lamont's 'green shoots of recovery', fresh confidence took shape during the victory over Scotland which ended the season. There emerged a long overdue purposeful scrummage and aggressive drive from a forceful back row.

While stressing the importance of quality performance, Alan Davies, the new national coach, detected a glimmer of hope for better things to come. There had been undoubted commitment in Dublin to win a game that had looked lost at half-time, and there was a revival of fortunes in the line-out against France. Steadfast tackling restricted England amid the inevitability of defeat before optimism soared at the success against a rebuilding Scottish side at the Arms Park.

Yet, for all these meaningful advances, there was precious little to encourage us in the shape of a resurgence of creative and penetrative back play. The predictable box-kick appeared to be the limit of tactical vision and too much scarce possession was kicked fruitlessly away. There is no disguising the fact that Wales scored just two tries during the Five Nations tournament, and those through back row forwards: in Dublin from sustained pressure and against Scotland in an audacious moment of opportunism and down-to-earth dash. Two victories from a season in which most expected only one, at best, was an achievement of sorts. Nevertheless, the realism of the situation had to be faced and coach Davies, who had taken over from Ron Waldron, observed candidly, 'Now we have to strive for excellence, but we must have a vision of how to do it. We believe that changes in the way we do things still have to be made, not only to achieve success, but to sustain it'.

Ieuan Evans, the new Welsh team captain who succeeded Paul Thorburn, admitted, 'We still have a very long way to go'. Wing is not the ideal position from which to lead a struggling team, but as one of the most experienced players he was prepared to shoulder the responsibility. His team did not fall apart as they had done in Australia during the horrendous defeats of the summer of 1991. Everyone agreed that Welsh rugby 'died of shame' Down Under, and that never had there been such a black chapter in the history of our game. This was followed by the 1991 World Cup and further disaster, when Wales lost 16-13 to Western Samoa at the Arms Park. It was a selection gamble to include Mark

The Welsh team which beat Scotland at Cardiff Arms Park. L–R, back row: M S Morris (replacement), S Roy (replacement), M Griffiths, R E Webster, E W Lewis, A H Copsey, G O Llewellyn, S Davies, N R Jenkins, H Williams-Jones, D C Fox (replacement), D Joseph (replacement); front row: R H Stf B Moon (replacement), R N Jones, M R Hall, I S Gibbs, I C Evans (capt), G R Jenkins, A Clement, R A Bidgood, M A Rayer (replacement).

Ring, nowhere near match-fit, at fly-half. Ring was seen as a source of inspiration, if not a match-winner, but sadly he could not perform. Failing to qualify from their pool with Australia was the crowning indignity for Wales.

The WRU reappointed Robert Norster as manager and Alan Davies as coach to prepare the national team for the 1995 World Cup and to set up a national development player committee to plan, direct, monitor and evaluate senior squads. This committee comprised WRU secretary Denis Evans, technical director Jeff Young, John Maclean and former national coaches John Ryan and Ron Waldron. A four-tier national squad system was formed by the senior team, Under-21 and B team, which will play four matches each season, and a development squad from the over-21 age group. All squads have their own managers, coaches and selectors. Almost £1 million is to be allocated for this purpose, and Mr Young explained, 'We have spent a long time putting this plan together and, although it is now in place, this is where the hard work starts. It will take a great deal of time, money and effort, but I think we will see the benefits within a year or so'.

The traditional Welsh running game must be restored. It has been in cold storage for too long. We need panache as well as passion to reconstruct winning attitudes. It is inevitable that kicking will always have a significant part to play, but the Welsh way once was firmly embedded in running with all its breathtaking embellishment, and this must be rediscovered.

SNELLING SEVENS 1991-92
24 August 1990, Rodney Parade, Newport

Preliminary round: Pontypool 14, Maesteg 6; Bridgend 22, Tredegar 4
First round: Bridgend 30, Pontypool 10; Pontypridd 18, Neath 4; Llanelli 34, Cross Keys 8; South Wales Police 16, Newport 12; Aberavon 20, Glamorgan Wanderers 10; Ebbw Vale 20, Newbridge 18; Swansea 30, Abertillery 0; Cardiff 22, Penarth 10
Second round: Bridgend 24, Pontypridd 6; Llanelli 16, South Wales Police 12; Ebbw Vale 18, Aberavon 12; Swansea 16, Cardiff 4
Semi-finals: Bridgend 16, Llanelli 4; Swansea 16, Ebbw Vale 4
Final: Swansea 26, Bridgend 18
Teams in the Final
Swansea: S Davies, P Williams, M Titley, A Williams; I Davies (*capt*), L Isaac, A Reynolds *Replacements* M Davies for A Williams; M Morgan for Isaac
Bridgend: G Webbe, C Bradshaw, A Williams (*capt*), R Howley; J Apsee, P Yardley, O Williams
Referee G Simmonds (Cardiff)

MOON LIGHTS UP STRADEY

SCHWEPPES CHALLENGE CUP 1991-92
John Billot *Western Mail*

16 May, Cardiff Arms Park
Llanelli 16 (1G 1PG 1DG 1T)   Swansea 7 (1PG 1T)

If ever a golden halo should be awarded it must be ordered for cheerful Rupert Henry St John Barker Moon, chosen by a record margin of 51 votes to 1 by the Welsh Rugby Writers' Association as the Man of the Match after significantly shaping Llanelli's eighth victory in ten Cup finals. He launched the first try, scored the second with an elastic dive for the corner after smart interpassing with Proctor on the wing, and crowned it all with a dramatic and, indeed, majestic, dropped goal. In between those moments of impressive theatre, he worked his heart out, tackling Swansea forwards in the critical plan to cut them down before they could cross the gain-line.

There have been many influential contributions in the 21 Cup finals, but few more decisive. So Moon, the key figure in his side's victory in the final the previous season, retained the Man of the Match title and enhanced his claim to a Welsh cap. 'Choosing to play in Wales is the best thing I could ever have done', he confided, and everyone connected with the Stradey Park club will endorse that view. As English as Nelson's Column, Moon has won the hearts of all Welshmen, with the possible exception of Swansea supporters.

Swansea's hopes of achieving a distinguished double success as Heineken League and Schweppes Cup champions broke down at the inevitable Scarlet barrier. Llanelli are always the team for the big occasion: put your shirt on them every time they reach the final. They talk of Divine right at Stradey, and with Moon on their side who can dispute it?

Aled Williams sniped through for a lovely Swansea try, but kicked just one penalty goal from six attempts. Ieuan Evans' opening try for Llanelli also was a memorable moment. But the rest of the magic was Moon's.

Llanelli: I Jones; I C Evans, N G Davies, S Davies, W Proctor; C J Stephens, R H St J B Moon; R Evans, D C Fox, L Delaney, P T Davies (*capt*), A H Copsey, E W Lewis, S Quinnell, L Jones
Scorers *Tries:* I C Evans, Moon   *Conversion:* Stephens   *Penalty Goal:* Stephens *Dropped Goal:* Moon
Swansea: A Clement; M H Titley, K Hopkins (*capt*), I S Gibbs, S Davies; A Williams, R N Jones; I Buckett, G R Jenkins, K Colclough, P Arnold, R D Moriarty, A Reynolds, S Davies, R E Webster
Scorer *Try:* Williams   *Penalty Goal:* Williams
Referee L J Peard (Castleton)

The moment of ecstasy. Phil Davies brandishes the newly-won Schweppes Cup after Llanelli's hard-fought win at Cardiff Arms Park.

The 'dream ticket' final was set up by the anticipated success of the favourites, the top two teams in the Heineken League, in a double-header semi-finals programme at the National Ground on Spring Bank Holiday Monday, when 24,126 spectators watched events. Llanelli, playing first, had no problems disposing of Pontypridd 27-6, but a defiant Newport almost complicated matters by taking Swansea to extra time before falling 23-9.

Sensationally, Neil Jenkins, the Pontypridd fly-half, was sent off immediately before half-time. The touch-judge saw the incident, in which Jenkins put his knee into a Llanelli player on the ground. Derek Bevan ordered Jenkins from the field and Colin Stephens kicked the penalty goal to increase Llanelli's lead to 14-0. As so often happens in adversity, 14 men resisted stubbornly, but their only points came from two penalty goals by Jon Mason. Llanelli collected four tries through Simon Davies (2), Ian Jones and Ieuan Evans.

Had Paul Turner kicked for goal with his customary accuracy Newport could have stolen their way into the final, but he missed a couple of relatively easy penalty shots and Swansea hung on to force the game into extra time at 9-9. There was an inspiring display by Glen George, the Newport captain, who decided shortly before kick-off to take the field despite a painful injury. A number of other Newport players carried injuries or were not fully match-tuned. It was a fighting performance indeed from the gallant underdogs, but Swansea swooped for three tries during extra time.

In the quarter-final stage, Llanelli maintained their unbroken dominance against Pontypool, knocking them out for the eighth time. Swansea accounted for battling Dunvant and Newport won a tense tussle 9-4 against Bridgend. Pontypridd ruthlessly turned on their forward power to crush Cardiff Harlequins, Jenkins supplying 19 points.

Neath were the subject of criticism in the sixth round as they went out 28-9 at Stradey. Kevin Fox was on the field for only four minutes as a replacement before being sent off for a late tackle on Colin Stephens. Emyr Lewis, the Llanelli flank forward, condemned Neath after being stamped and kicked on the head. Glen Ball, the Neath team manager, replied: 'It is a physical game, but there was nothing malicious'.

The surprise in this round was the 17-0 home defeat of Abertillery by Cardiff Harlequins. Tondu, noted giant-killers, fought tenaciously before losing 12-10 at Pontypridd. Jonathan Westwood's two tries paved the way for Newport's 12-4 success at Cardiff, while Bridgend overturned an amazing 25-0 home League reverse by Newbridge to put the visitors out 18-13.

A fifth-round sensation was Glamorgan Wanderers' feat of holding Newport to 10-10 at Rodney Parade, the home side progressing by scoring two tries to one. Veteran prop Graham Price came out of retirement to help Pontypool defeat Pontarddulais, while Newbridge were forced into extra time before winning 15-12 at Maesteg, where they had won 50-9 in a League fixture. Dunvant knocked out Ebbw Vale in the fourth round.

RESULTS

Third Round

Abercynon 3, Tondu 19; Abergavenny 14, Bridgend Athletic 10; Beddau 3, Pyle 13; Bedwas 3, Pontypool United 9; Bethesda 15, Colwyn Bay 9; Blackwood 38, Llangennech 9; Blaina 21, Llandovery 3; Bonymaen 17, Newcastle Emlyn 19; Caerphilly 15, Mountain Ash 22; Cardiff Harlequins 20, Bridgend Sports 10; Chepstow 7, Tenby United 27; Felinfoel 16, Aberavon Quins 6; Gilfach Goch 9, Cilfyndd 12; Gowerton 13, Trebanos 6; Haverfordwest 18, Ruthin 9; Kidwelly 3, New Dock Stars 0; Llandaff 10, Hendy 9; Llandeilo 3, Fleur de Lys 12; Llanhilleth 0, St Peter's 8; Llantwit Fardre 16, Narberth 15; Merthyr 19, Kenfig Hill 11; Morriston 21, Bryncoch 6; Oakdale 27, Old Illtydians 0; Pencoed 7, Croesyceiliog 6; Pontarddulais 28, Newport Saracens 3; Pontyates 9, Abercarn 20; Rhiwbina 10, Garndiffaith 21; Rumney 20, Ystalyfera 12; RTB Ebbw Vale 9, Usk 3; Taibach 20, Ammanford 28; Talywain 7, Wrexham 3; Treorchy 40, Bynea 0; Vardre 4, Tumble 17; Ystradgynlais 7, Ynysybwl 0

Fourth Round

Aberavon 32, Garndiffaith 7; Abertillery 36, Haverfordwest 0; Ammanford 12, South Wales Police 32; Bethesda 9, Fleur de Lys 10; Cilfyndd 7, Blaina 21; Ebbw Vale 10, Dunvant 12; Felinfoel 3, Blackwood 31; Glamorgan Wanderers 18, Penarth 0; Gowerton 15, Abergavenny 10; Llanharan 9, Cross Keys 23; Llantwit Fardre 8, Talywain 9; Merthyr 21, Kidwelly 10; Mountain Ash 17, Newcastle Emlyn 8; Oakdale 17, Abercarn 7; Pencoed 21, Morriston 9; Pontypool United 24, Tredegar 7; Pyle 27, Ystradgynlais 0; RTB Ebbw Vale 7, Cardiff Harlequins 37; Rumney 9, Llandaff 0; St Peter's 16, Tenby United 26; Tondu 22, Tumble 3; Treorchy 3, Pontarddulais 24

Fifth Round

Abertillery 9, Blaina 6; Bridgend 38, Blackwood 7; Dunvant 27, Gowerton 3; Maesteg 12, Newbridge 15 (*aet*);

Mountain Ash 13, Llanelli 26; Neath 35, Fleur de Lys 7; *Newport 10, Glamorgan Wanderers 10; Oakdale 0, Swansea 25; Pencoed 10, Cardiff 58; Pontypool 28, Pontarddulais 4; Pontypridd 50, Pontypool United 6; Pyle 9, Cardiff Harlequins 10; Rumney 0, Cross Keys 30; South Wales Police 19, Aberavon 10; Talywain 10, Merthyr 3; Tondu 11, Tenby United 7

Sixth Round

Abertillery 0, Cardiff Harlequins 17; Bridgend 18, Newbridge 13; Cardiff 4, Newport 12; Cross Keys 6, Pontypool 19; Dunvant 22, Talywain 0; Llanelli 28, Neath 9; Pontypridd 12, Tondu 10; South Wales Police 13, Swansea 30

Seventh Round

Dunvant 6, Swansea 14; Newport 9, Bridgend 4; Pontypool 3, Llanelli 27; Pontypridd 35, Cardiff Harlequins 15

Semi-finals

Llanelli 27 Pontypridd 6
(*at Cardiff Arms Park*)
Swansea 23 Newport 9
(*at Cardiff Arms Park*)
FINAL (*at Cardiff Arms Park*)
Llanelli 16 Swansea 7

Previous finals

(*all at Cardiff Arms Park*)

1972	Neath 15 Llanelli 9
1973	Llanelli 30 Cardiff 7
1974	Llanelli 12 Aberavon 10
1975	Llanelli 15 Aberavon 6
1976	Llanelli 15 Swansea 4
1977	Newport 16 Cardiff 15
1978	Swansea 13 Newport 9
1979	Bridgend 18 Pontypridd 12
1980	Bridgend 15 Swansea 9
1981	Cardiff 14 Bridgend 6
1982*	Cardiff 12 Bridgend 12
1983	Pontypool 18 Swansea 6
1984	Cardiff 24 Neath 19
1985	Llanelli 15 Cardiff 14
1986	Cardiff 28 Newport 21
1987	Cardiff 16 Swansea 15
1988	Llanelli 28 Neath 13
1989	Neath 14 Llanelli 13
1990	Neath 16 Bridgend 10
1991	Llanelli 24 Pontypool 9

Winners on 'most tries' rule

SUCCESS AT LAST FOR SWANSEA
HEINEKEN LEAGUES 1991-92

So often Swansea have been the lame ducks of Welsh rugby. This season, at last, they became the proud peacocks of the Heineken League. Old inconsistencies had been cast aside and they fulfilled their destiny to the acclaim of all for the exciting rhythm they brought to their style of play. They were irrefutably worthy champions, and the richer by £24,000 as First Division title winners. Their aggregate of 60 tries in 18 matches was three more than Llanelli, runners-up for the second season, and no team in the rest of the League exceeded their total.

Mike Ruddock, the new Swansea coach, was always positive and realistic, and he admitted that the team had achieved more than he anticipated. 'The side has grown up as the season has progressed', he said. 'We started to show more discipline up front, which was vitally important because our backs have always been a match for anybody.'

Pontypridd registered just one victory from their first six games, but recruited Dennis John as coach and he transformed them so successfully that they finished in third place, defeated only twice in their last 12 fixtures. Amazingly, Neil Jenkins scored 173 of their 289 points. Neath recovered after a gloomy sequence of one victory in ten games. Maesteg finished bottom of the table with just one victory, in their penultimate game, 18-15 over Bridgend. Had there been relegation, Cardiff would have dropped to the Second Division, but the increase from ten to 12 teams in each division for the 1992-93 season rescued them from this indignity. In April they appointed Australian Alec Evans as their first full-time paid coaching supremo, to improve matters.

Bridgend, who lost their outstanding fly-half Aled Williams to Swansea, tailed away after a run of seven successes in eight games, yet became the only side to inflict two League defeats in a season on Llanelli. Pontypool also faded disappointingly with just one success in their last ten games, but in their final fixture they forced a 23-23 draw at St Helen's after Swansea, already champions with a game to spare, led 20-0.

South Wales Police took the Second Division title, and £14,200 prize-money, by one point from Aberavon, clinching the top spot in their final game, in which they crushed bottom team Penarth, whose only win was at Ebbw Vale by 13-12. Ebbw recovered from that humiliation with nine victories in a row, only to falter in the final run-in by drawing at Llanharan and losing to Cross Keys. Abertillery defeated the Police twice and toppled Aberavon. Tredegar had two points deducted for failing to fulfil their September fixture against Ebbw Vale.

Tenby United collected £11,450 as Third Division champions and, together with runners-up Llandovery, gained promotion for the second season. Blaina and Narberth also go up to the Second Division with the expansion of numbers. Tumble received £6,750 as Fourth Division title-winners and promoted with them were Kenfig Hill, Abercynon, St Peter's, Blackwood and Pontypool United.

League records were the aggregate of 196 points by Aberavon fly-half Dave Love and 15 tries by South Wales Police No 8 Sean Legge.

HEINEKEN LEAGUES
Division 1

	P	W	D	L	F	A	Pts
Swansea	18	13	1	4	393	205	27
Llanelli	18	11	1	6	381	233	23
Pontypridd	18	11	0	7	289	245	22
Neath	18	9	2	7	309	236	20
Newbridge	18	10	0	8	259	271	20
Bridgend	18	10	0	8	246	270	20
Pontypool	18	7	4	7	282	275	18
Newport	18	7	2	9	240	237	16
Cardiff	18	5	1	12	240	306	11
Maesteg	18	1	1	16	169	530	3

Division 2

	P	W	D	L	F	A	Pts
SW Police	18	12	2	4	337	258	26
Aberavon	18	11	3	4	390	191	25
Cross Keys	18	10	3	5	282	212	23
Ebbw Vale	18	11	1	6	291	254	23
Dunvant	18	10	0	8	280	237	20
Llanharan	18	9	1	8	256	179	19
Abertillery	18	8	1	9	251	234	17
Glam Wands	18	8	1	9	259	269	17
★Tredegar	18	4	0	14	202	351	6
Penarth	18	1	0	17	143	506	2

*Two points deducted

Division 3

	P	W	D	L	F	A	Pts
Tenby Utd	18	15	0	3	348	165	30
Llandovery	18	13	0	5	261	164	26
Blaina	18	12	0	6	290	135	24
Narberth	18	12	0	6	259	174	24
Treorchy	18	9	3	6	231	189	21
Mountain Ash	18	7	0	11	203	227	14
Rumney	18	6	2	10	186	221	14
Wrexham	18	4	2	12	203	339	10
Bonymaen	18	4	1	13	233	358	9
Aberavon Q	18	4	0	14	144	386	8

Division 4

	P	W	D	L	F	A	Pts
Tumble	18	15	0	3	346	176	30
Kenfig Hill	18	11	1	6	259	244	23
Abercynon	18	10	2	6	248	168	22
St Peter's	18	10	2	6	271	198	22
Blackwood	18	9	1	8	257	221	19
Pontypool U	18	8	1	9	253	213	17

Ystradgynlais	18	8	1	9	193	267	17
Kidwelly	18	7	0	11	186	309	14
Cilfynydd	18	5	2	11	228	264	12
Ruthin	18	2	0	16	177	358	4

FEEDER LEAGUES
EAST DISTRICT
(sponsored by S A Brain)

Division 1	P	W	D	L	Pts
Cardiff HSOB	12	10	1	1	21
Pencoed	12	10	0	2	20
Taff's Well	12	6	1	5	13
Cardiff Inst	12	6	0	6	12
Pentyrch	12	4	0	8	8
Hoel-y-Cyw	12	3	0	9	6
Iltydians	12	2	0	10	4

Division 2 finishing order: Old Penarthians, Llandaff, Rhiwbina, Llandaff North, Cowbridge, St Joseph's, Cardiff U **Division 3 finishing order:** Dinas Powis, Barry, Llantwit Major, Llanishen, Pontyclun, Cardiff Medicals

PEMBROKESHIRE CHAMPIONSHIP
(sponsored by Jewsons)

	P	W	D	L	Pts
Cardigan	20	16	3	1	35
Haverfordwest	20	14	1	5	29
Whitland	20	13	1	6	27
Pembroke DQ	20	11	2	7	24
Pembroke	20	11	1	8	23
Milford Haven	20	10	3	7	23
Aberystwyth	20	10	0	10	20
Neyland	20	9	1	10	19
Llangwm	20	6	0	14	12
Fishguard	20	3	0	17	6
St David's	20	1	0	19	2

NORTH WALES LEAGUE
(sponsored by David McLean)

	P	W	D	L	Pts
Colwyn Bay	14	13	0	1	26
Rhyl & Dist	14	12	0	2	24
Mold	14	9	0	5	18
★Pwllheli	14	9	0	5	16
Dolgellau	14	5	0	9	10
Llandudno	14	5	0	9	10

UCNW, Bangor	14	3	0	11	6
Bangor	14	0	0	14	0

Two points deducted

Bangor Normal Coll, Caernarfon, Welshpool and Denbigh join the League for 1992-93.

MONMOUTHSHIRE LEAGUE
(sponsored by Allbright Bitter)

Premier Division	P	W	D	L	Pts
Garndiffaith	12	10	0	2	20
Abergavenny	12	8	0	4	16
Rhymney	12	7	1	4	15
*Croesyceiliog	11	5	0	6	10
*Blaenau Gwent	11	4	2	5	10
Tredegar Iron	12	3	1	8	7
Cwmbran	12	2	0	10	4

One match not played

Division 1 finishing order: Bedwas, Oakdale, Pill Harriers, Newport Saracens, Machen, Caldicot, Trinant **Division 2 finishing order:** Talywain, Abercarn, Llanhilleth, Nelson, Brynmawr, Risca, Chepstow **Division 3 finishing order:** Fleur-de-Lys, Monmouth, RTB Ebbw Vale, Ynysddu, Crumlin, Usk, Blaenavon

MID-DISTRICT CHAMPIONSHIP
(sponsored by Tennents Pilsner)

Division 1	P	W	D	L	Pts
Builth Wells	12	10	0	2	20
Beddau	12	9	0	3	18
Caerphilly	12	7	1	4	15
*Senghenydd	12	8	1	3	15
Llantrisant	12	5	0	7	10
Tonyrefail	12	2	0	10	4
Llantwit Fardre	12	0	0	12	0

Two points deducted

Division 2 finishing order: Nelson, Merthyr, Gilfach Goch, Aberaman, Tylorstown, Cefn Coed **Division 3 finishing order:** Hirwaun, Ynysybwl, Treherbert, Bargoed, Brecon, Penygraig, Rhydyfelin

CENTRAL GLAMORGAN LEAGUE
(sponsored by Wistech)

Division 1	P	W	D	L	Pts
Tondu	18	17	0	1	34
Pyle	18	16	0	2	32
Neath Ath	18	12	0	6	24
Bridgend Ath	18	10	0	8	20
Nantyffyllon	18	10	0	8	20
Bridgend Sports	18	8	0	10	16
Porthcawl	18	8	0	10	16
Maesteg Celt	18	3	0	15	6
Cefn Cribbwr	18	3	0	15	6
Maesteg Quins	18	3	0	15	6

Division 2 finishing order: British Steel, Pontycymmer, Blaengarw, Nantymoel, Taibach, Tonmawr, Cwmavon, Aberavon Green Stars, Ogmore Vale, Briton Ferry

WEST WALES CHAMPIONSHIP
(sponsored by Welsh Brewers)

Premier Division	P	W	D	L	Pts
Carmarthen Quins	18	13	1	4	27
Vardre	18	13	1	4	27
Felinfoel	18	12	2	4	26
Pontyberem	18	12	2	4	26
Pontarddulais	18	11	0	7	22
Seven Sisters	18	8	0	10	16
Waunarlwydd	18	6	1	11	13
Bryncoch	18	6	1	11	13
Ammanford	18	4	0	14	8
*Loughor	18	1	0	17	0

* *Two points deducted*

Winners of Groups A, B, C & D enter the Premier Division next season in place of Carmarthen Quins and Vardre (promoted to National 4) and Ammanford and Loughor (relegated to Groups)

Group A finishing order: Carmarthen Ath, Gowerton, Hendy, Brynamman, Newcastle Emlyn, Cwmgorse, Trebanos, Mumbles, Burry Port, BP Llandarcy **Group B finishing order:** Glynneath, Morriston, Furnace, Penclawdd, Abercrave, Penygroes, Crynant, Ystalyfera, Pontyates, Llanelli Wanderers **Group C finishing order:** Trimsaran, Bynea, New Dock Stars, Llandeilo, Llangennech, Skewen, Swansea Uplands, Tonna, Pontardawe, Cefneithin **Group D finishing order:** Amman United, Llandybie, Cwmgwrach, Gorseinon, Laugharne, Resolven, Alltwen, Cwmllynfell, Glais, Lampeter Town

Qualifiers for National Divisions for 1992-93: Colwyn Bay, Garndiffaith, Cardiff HSOB (to be known as Cardiff Harlequins), Tondu, Carmarthen Quins, Vardre, Cardigan, Builth Wells

279

WELSH INTERNATIONAL PLAYERS
(up to 31 March 1992)

ABBREVIATIONS

A – Australia; *Arg* – Argentina; *Bb* – Barbarians; *C* – Canada; *E* – England; *F* – France; *Fj* – Fiji; *I* – Ireland; *M* – Maoris; *Nm* – Namibia; *NZ* – New Zealand; *NZA* – New Zealand Army; *R* – Romania; *S* – Scotland; *SA* – South Africa; *Tg* – Tonga; *US* – United States; *WS* – Western Samoa; (R) – Replacement. Entries in square brackets [ ] indicate appearances in the World Cup.

Note: Years given for Five Nations' matches are for second half of season; eg 1972 means season 1971-72. Years for all other matches refer to the actual year of the match. When a series has taken place, figures have been used to denote the particular matches in which players have featured. Thus 1969 *NZ* 2 indicates that a player appeared in the second Test of the series.

Ackerman, R A (Newport, London Welsh) 1980 *NZ*, 1981 *E, S, A*, 1982 *I, F, E, S*, 1983 *S, I, F, R*, 1984 *S, I, F, E, A*, 1985 *S, I, F, E, Fj*
Alexander, E P (Llandovery Coll, Cambridge U) 1885 *S*, 1886 *E, S*, 1887 *E, I*
Alexander, W H (Llwynypia) 1898 *I, E*, 1899 *E, S, I*, 1901 *S, I*
Allen, A G (Newbridge) 1990 *F, E, I*
Allen, C P (Oxford U, Beaumaris) 1884 *E, S*
Andrews, F (Pontypool) 1912 *SA*, 1913 *E, S, I*
Andrews, F G (Swansea) 1884 *E, S*
Andrews, G E (Newport) 1926 *E, S*, 1927 *E, F, I*
Anthony, L (Neath) 1948 *E, S, F*
Arnold, P (Swansea) 1990 *Nm* 1,2, *Bb*, 1991 *E, S, I, F*1, *A*, [*Arg, A*]
Arnold, W R (Swansea) 1903 *S*
Arthur, C S (Cardiff) 1888 *I, M*, 1891 *E*
Arthur, T (Neath) 1927 *S, F, I*, 1929 *E, S, F, I*, 1930 *E, S, I, F*, 1931 *E, S, F, I, SA*, 1933 *E, S*
Ashton, C (Aberavon) 1959 *E, S, I*, 1960 *E, S, I*, 1962 *I*
Attewell, S L (Newport) 1921 *E, S, F*

Badger, O (Llanelli) 1895 *E, S, I*, 1896 *E*
Baker, A (Neath) 1921 *I*, 1923 *E, S, F, I*
Baker, A M (Newport) 1909 *S, F*, 1910 *S*
Bancroft, J (Swansea) 1909 *E, S, F, I*, 1910 *F, E, S, I*, 1911 *E, F, I*, 1912 *E, S, I*, 1913 *I*, 1914 *E, S, F*
Bancroft, W J (Swansea) 1890 *S, E, I*, 1891 *E, S, I*, 1892 *E, S, I*, 1893 *E, S, I*, 1894 *E, S, I*, 1895 *E, S, I*, 1896 *E, S, I*, 1897 *E*, 1898 *I, E*, 1899 *E, S, I*, 1900 *E, S, I*, 1901 *E, S, I*
Barlow, T M (Cardiff) 1884 *I*
Barrell, R J (Cardiff) 1929 *S, F, I*, 1933 *I*
Bartlett, J D (Llanelli) 1927 *S*, 1928 *E, S*
Bassett, A (Cardiff) 1934 *I*, 1935 *E, S, I*, 1938 *E, S*
Bassett, J A (Penarth) 1929 *E, S, F, I*, 1930 *E, S, I*, 1931 *E, S, F, I, SA*, 1932 *E, S, I*
Bateman, A G (Neath) 1990 *S, I, Nm* 1,2
Bayliss, G (Pontypool) 1933 *S*
Bebb, D I E (Carmarthen TC, Swansea) 1959 *E, S, I, F*, 1960 *E, S, I, F, SA*, 1961 *E, S, I, F*, 1962 *E, S, F, I*, 1963 *E, F, NZ*, 1964 *E, S, F, SA*, 1965 *E, S, I, F*, 1966 *F, A*, 1967 *S, I, F, E*
Beckingham, G (Cardiff) 1953 *E, S*, 1958 *F*
Bennett, I (Aberavon) 1937 *I*
Bennett, P (Cardiff Harlequins) 1891 *E, S*, 1892 *S, I*
Bennett, P (Llanelli) 1969 *F* (R), 1970 *SA, S, F*, 1972 *S* (R), *NZ*, 1973 *E, S, I, F, A*, 1974 *S, I, F, E*, 1975 *S* (R), *I*, 1976 *E, S, I, F*, 1977 *I, F, E, S*, 1978 *E, S, I, F*
Bergiers, R T E (Cardiff Coll of Ed, Llanelli) 1972 *E, S, F, NZ*, 1973 *E, S, I, F, A*, 1974 *F*, 1975 *I*
Bevan, G W (Llanelli) 1947 *E*
Bevan, J A (Cambridge U) 1881 *E*
Bevan, J C (Cardiff, Cardiff Coll of Ed) 1971 *E, S, I, F*, 1972 *E, S, F, NZ*, 1973 *E, S*
Bevan, J D (Aberavon) 1975 *F, E, S, A*
Bevan, S (Swansea) 1904 *I*
Beynon, B (Swansea) 1920 *E, S*
Beynon, G E (Swansea) 1925 *F, I*
Bidgood, R A (Newport) 1992 *S*
Biggs, N W (Cardiff) 1888 *M*, 1889 *I*, 1892 *I*, 1893 *E, S, I*, 1894 *E, I*
Biggs, S H (Cardiff) 1895 *E, S*, 1896 *S*, 1897 *E*, 1898 *I, E*, 1899 *S, I*, 1900 *I*

Birch, J (Neath) 1911 *S, F*
Birt, F W (Newport) 1911 *E, S*, 1912 *E, S, I, SA*, 1913 *E*
Bishop, D J (Pontypool) 1984 *A*
Bishop, E H (Swansea) 1889 *S*
Blackmore, J H (Abertillery) 1909 *E*
Blackmore, S W (Cardiff) 1987 *I*, [*Tg* (R), *C, A*]
Blake, J (Cardiff) 1899 *E, S, I*, 1900 *E, S, I*, 1901 *E, S, I*
Blakemore, R E (Newport) 1947 *E*
Bland, A F (Cardiff) 1887 *E, S, I*, 1888 *S, I, M*, 1890 *S, E, I*
Blyth, L (Swansea) 1951 *SA*, 1952 *E, S*
Blyth, W R (Swansea) 1974 *E*, 1975 *S* (R), 1980 *F, E, S, I*
Boon, R W (Cardiff) 1930 *S, F*, 1931 *E, S, F, I, SA*, 1932 *E, S, I*, 1933 *E, I*
Booth, J (Pontymister) 1898 *I*
Boots, J G (Newport) 1898 *I, E*, 1899 *I*, 1900 *E, S, I*, 1901 *E, S, I*, 1902 *E, S, I*, 1903 *E, S, I*, 1904 *E*
Boucher, A W (Newport) 1892 *E, S, I*, 1893 *E, S, I*, 1894 *E*, 1895 *E, S, I*, 1896 *E, I*, 1897 *E*
Bowcott, H M (Cardiff, Cambridge U) 1929 *S, F, I*, 1930 *E*, 1931 *E, S*, 1933 *E, I*
Bowdler, F A (Cross Keys) 1927 *A*, 1928 *E, S, I, F*, 1929 *E, S, F, I*, 1930 *E*, 1931 *SA*, 1932 *E, S, I*, 1933 *I*
Bowen, B (S Wales Police, Swansea) 1983 *R*, 1984 *S, I, F, E*, 1985 *Fj*, 1986 *E, S, I, F, Fj, Tg, WS*, 1987 [*C, E, NZ*], *US*, 1988 *E, S, I, F, WS*, 1989 *S, I*
Bowen, C A (Llanelli) 1896 *E, S, I*, 1897 *E*
Bowen, D H (Llanelli) 1883 *E*, 1886 *E, S*, 1887 *E*
Bowen, G E (Swansea) 1887 *S, I*, 1888 *S, I*
Bowen, W (Swansea) 1921 *S, F*, 1922 *E, S, I, F*
Bowen, Wm A (Swansea) 1886 *E, S*, 1887 *E, S, I*, 1888 *M*, 1889 *S, I*, 1890 *S, E, I*, 1891 *S*
Brace, D O (Llanelli, Oxford U) 1956 *E, S, I, F*, 1957 *E*, 1960 *S, I, F*, 1961 *I*
Braddock, K J (Newbridge) 1966 *A*, 1967 *S, I*
Bradshaw, K (Bridgend) 1964 *E, S, I, F, SA*, 1966 *E, S, I, F*
Brewer, T J (Newport) 1950 *E*, 1955 *E, S*
Brice, A B (Aberavon) 1899 *E, S, I*, 1900 *E, S, I*, 1901 *E, S, I*, 1902 *E, S, I*, 1903 *E, S, I*, 1904 *E, S, I*
Bridges, C J (Neath) 1990 *Nm* 1,2, *Bb*, 1991 *E* (R), *I*, *F*1, *A*
Bridie, R H (Newport) 1882 *I*
Britton, G R (Newport) 1961 *S*
Broughton, A S (Treorchy) 1927 *A*, 1929 *S*
Brown, A (Newport) 1921 *I*
Brown, J (Cardiff) 1925 *I*
Brown, J A (Cardiff) 1907 *E, S, I*, 1908 *E, S, F*, 1909 *E*
Brown, M (Pontypool) 1983 *R*, 1986 *E, S,Fj* (R), *Tg, WS*
Bryant, D J (Bridgend) 1988 *NZ* 1,2, *WS, R*, 1989 *S, I, F, E*
Buchanan, A (Llanelli) 1987 [*Tg, E, NZ, A*], 1988 *I*
Burcher, D H (Newport) 1977 *I, F, E, S*
Burgess, R C (Ebbw Vale) 1977 *I, F, E, S*, 1981 *I, F*, 1982 *F, E, S*
Burnett, R (Newport) 1953 *E*
Burns, J (Cardiff) 1927 *F, I*
Bush, P F (Cardiff) 1905 *NZ*, 1906 *E, SA*, 1907 *I*, 1908 *E, S*, 1910 *S, I, F*
Butler, E T (Pontypool) 1980 *F, E, S, I, NZ* (R), 1982 *S*, 1983 *E, S, I, F, R*, 1984 *S, I, F, E, A*

Cale, W R (Newbridge, Pontypool) 1949 *E, S, I*, 1950 *E, S, I, F*
Carter, A J (Newport) 1991 *E, S*
Cattell, A (Llanelli) 1883 *E, S*
Challinor, C (Neath) 1939 *E*
Clapp, T J S (Newport) 1882 *I*, 1883 *E, S*, 1884 *E, S, I*, 1885 *E, S*, 1886 *S*, 1887 *E, S, I*, 1888 *S, I*
Clare, J (Cardiff) 1883 *E*
Clark, S S (Neath) 1882 *I*, 1887 I
Cleaver, W B (Cardiff) 1947 *E, S, F, I, A*, 1948 *E, S, F, I*, 1949 *I*, 1950 *E, S, I, F*
Clegg, B G (Swansea) 1979 *F*
Clement, A (Swansea) 1987 *US* (R), 1988 *E, NZ* 1, *WS* (R), *R*, 1989 *NZ*, 1990 *S* (R), *I* (R), *Nm* 1,2, 1991 *S*(R), *A*(R), *F*2, [*WS, A*], 1992 *I, F, E, S*
Clement, W H (Llanelli) 1937 *E, S, I*, 1938 *E, S, I*
Cobner, T J (Pontypool) 1974 *S, I, F, E*, 1975 *F, E, S, I, A*, 1976 *E, S*, 1977 *F, E, S*, 1978 *E, S, I, F, A* 1
Coldrick, A P (Newport) 1911 *E, S, I*, 1912 *E, S, F*
Coleman, E (Newport) 1949 *E, S, I*
Coles, F C (Pontypool) 1960 *S, I, F*
Collins, J (Aberavon) 1958 *A, E, S, F*, 1959 *E, S, I, F*, 1960 *E*, 1961 *F*
Collins, R G (S Wales Police, Cardiff) 1987 *E* (R), *I*, [*I, E, NZ*], *US*, 1988 *E, S, I, F, R*, 1990 *E, S, I*, 1991 *A, F*2, [*WS*]
Collins, T (Mountain Ash) 1923 *I*
Conway-Rees, J (Llanelli) 1892 *S*, 1893 *E*, 1894 *E*
Cook, T (Cardiff) 1949 *S, I*
Cope, W (Cardiff, Blackheath) 1896 *S*
Copsey, A H (Llanelli) 1992 *I, F, E, S*
Cornish, F H (Cardiff) 1897 *E*, 1898 *I, E*, 1899 *I*
Cornish, R A (Cardiff) 1923 *E, S*, 1924 *E*, 1925 *E, S, F*, 1926 *E, S, I, F*
Coslett, K (Aberavon) 1962 *E, S, F*
Cowey, B T V (Welch Regt, Newport) 1934 *E, S, I*, 1935 *E*
Cresswell, B (Newport) 1960 *E, S, I, F*
Cummins, W (Treorchy) 1922 *E, S, I, F*
Cunningham, L J (Aberavon) 1960 *E, S, I, F*, 1962 *E, S, F, I*, 1963 *NZ*, 1964 *E, S, I, F, SA*

Dacey, M (Swansea) 1983 *E, S, I, F, R*, 1984 *S, I, F, E, A*, 1986 *Fj, Tg, WS*, 1987 *F* (R), [*Tg*]
Daniel, D J (Llanelli) 1891 *S*, 1894 *E, S, I*, 1898 *I, E*, 1899 *E, I*
Daniel, L T D (Newport) 1970 *S*
Daniels, P C T (Cardiff) 1981 *A*, 1982 *I*
Darbishire, G (Bangor) 1881 *E*
Dauncey, F H (Newport) 1896 *E, S, I*
Davey, C (Swansea) 1930 *F*, 1931 *E, S, F, I, SA*, 1932 *E, S, I*, 1933 *E, S*, 1934 *E, S, I*, 1935 *E, S, I, NZ*, 1936 *S*, 1937 *E, I*, 1938 *E, I*
David, R J (Cardiff) 1907 *I*
David, T P (Llanelli, Pontypridd) 1973 *F, A*, 1976 *I, F*
Davidge, G D (Newport) 1959 *F*, 1960 *S, I, F, SA*, 1961 *E, S, I*, 1962 *F*
Davies, A (Cambridge U, Neath) 1990 *Bb*(R), 1991 *A*
Davies, A C (London Welsh) 1889 *I*
Davies, A E (Llanelli) 1984 *A*
Davies, B (Llanelli) 1895 *E*, 1896 *E*
Davies, C (Cardiff) 1947 *S, F, I, A*, 1948 *E, S, F, I*, 1949 *F*, 1950 *E, S, I, F*, 1951 *E, S, I*
Davies, C (Llanelli) 1988 *WS*, 1989 *S, I* (R), *F*
Davies, C H A (Llanelli, Cardiff) 1957 *I*, 1958 *A, E, S, I*, 1960 *SA*, 1961 *E*
Davies, C L (Cardiff) 1956 *E, S, I*
Davies, C R (Bedford, RAF) 1934 *E*
Davies, D (Bridgend) 1921 *I*, 1925 *I*
Davies, D B (Llanelli) 1907 *E*
Davies, D B (Llanelli) 1962 *I*, 1963 *E, S*
Davies, D G (Cardiff) 1923 *E, S*
Davies, D H (Neath) 1904 *S*
Davies, D H (Aberavon) 1924 *E*
Davies, D I (Swansea) 1939 *E*
Davies, D J (Neath) 1962 *I*
Davies, D M (Somerset Police) 1950 *E, S, I, F*, 1951 *E, S, I, F, SA*, 1952 *E, S, I, F*, 1953 *I, F, NZ*, 1954 *E*
Davies, E (Aberavon) 1947 *A*, 1948 *I*
Davies, E (Maesteg) 1919 *NZA*
Davies, E G (Cardiff) 1912 *E, F*
Davies, E G (Cardiff) 1928 *F*, 1929 *E*, 1930 *S*
Davies, G (Swansea) 1900 *E, S, I*, 1901 *E, S, I*, 1905 *E, S, I*

Davies, G (Cambridge U, Pontypridd) 1947 *S, A*, 1948 *E, S, F, I*, 1949 *E, S, F*, 1951 *E, S*
Davies, G (Llanelli) 1921 *F, I*, 1925 *F*
Davies, H (Swansea) 1898 *I, E*, 1901 *S, I*
Davies, H (Swansea, Llanelli) 1939 *S, I*, 1947 *E, S, F, I*
Davies, H (Neath) 1912 *E, S*
Davies, H (Bridgend) 1984 *S, I, F, E*
Davies, H J (Cambridge U, Aberavon) 1959 *E, S*
Davies, H J (Newport) 1924 *S*
Davies, I T (Llanelli) 1914 *S, F, I*
Davies, J (Neath, Llanelli) 1985 *E, Fj*, 1986 *E, S, I, F, Fj, Tg, WS*, 1987 *F, E, S, I*, [*I, Tg* (R), *C, E, NZ, A*], 1988 *E, S, I, F, NZ* 1,2, *WS, R*
Davies, Rev J A (Swansea) 1913 *S, F, I*, 1914 *E, S, F, I*
Davies, J D (Neath) 1991 *I, F*1
Davies, J H (Aberavon) 1923 *I*
Davies, L (Swansea) 1939 *S, I*
Davies, L (Bridgend) 1966 *E, S, I*
Davies, L M (Llanelli) 1954 *F, S*, 1955 *I*
Davies, M (Swansea) 1981 *A*, 1982 *I*, 1985 *Fj*
Davies, M J (Blackheath) 1939 *S, I*
Davies, N G (London Welsh) 1955 *E*
Davies, N G (Llanelli) 1988 *NZ* 2, *WS*, 1989 *S, I*
Davies, P T (Llanelli) 1985 *E, Fj*, 1986 *E, S, I, F, Fj, Tg, WS*, 1987 *F, E, I*, [*Tg, C, NZ*], 1988 *WS, R*, 1989 *S, I, F, E, NZ*, 1990 *F, E, S*, 1991 *I, F*1, *A, F*2, [*WS, Arg, A*]
Davies, R H (Oxford U, London Welsh) 1957 *S, I, F*, 1958 *A*, 1962 *E, S*
Davies, S (Treherbert) 1923 *I*
Davies, S (Swansea) 1992 *I, F, E, S*
Davies, T G R (Cardiff, London Welsh) 1966 *A*, 1967 *S, I, F, E*, 1968 *E, S*, 1969 *S, I, F, NZ* 1,2, *A*, 1971 *E, S, I, F*, 1972 *E, S, F, NZ*, 1973 *E, S, I, F, A*, 1974 *S, F, E*, 1975 *F, E, S, I*, 1976 *E, S, I, F*, 1977 *I, F, E, S*, 1978 *E, S, I, A* 1,2
Davies, T J (Devonport Services, Swansea, Llanelli) 1953 *E, S, I, F*, 1957 *E, S, I, F*, 1958 *A, E, S, F*, 1959 *E, S, I, F*, 1960 *E, SA*, 1961 *E, S, F*
Davies, T M (London Welsh, Swansea) 1969 *S, I, F, E, NZ* 1,2, *A*, 1970 *SA, S, E, I, F*, 1971 *E, S, I, F*, 1972 *E, S, F, NZ*, 1973 *E, S, I, F, A*, 1974 *S, I, F, E*, 1975 *F, E, S, I, A*, 1976 *E, S, I, F*
Davies, W (Cardiff) 1896 *S*
Davies, W (Swansea) 1931 *SA*, 1932 *E, S, I*
Davies, W A (Aberavon) 1912 *S, I*
Davies, W G (Cardiff) 1978 *A* 1,2, *NZ*, 1979 *S, I, F, E*, 1980 *F, E, S, NZ*, 1981 *E, S, A*, 1982 *I, F, E, S*, 1985 *S, I, F*
Davies, W T H (Swansea) 1936 *I*, 1937 *E, I*, 1939 *E, S, I*
Davis, C E (Newbridge) 1978 *A* 2, 1981 *E, S*
Davis, M (Newport) 1991 *A*
Davis, W E N (Cardiff) 1939 *E, S, I*
Dawes, S J (London Welsh) 1964 *I, F, SA*, 1965 *E, S, I, F*, 1966 *A*, 1968 *I, F*, 1969 *E, NZ* 2, *A*, 1970 *SA, S, E, I, F*, 1971 *E, S, I, F*
Day, H C (Newport) 1930 *S, I, F*, 1931 *E, S*
Day, H T (Newport) 1892 *I*, 1893 *E, S*, 1894 *S, I*
Day, T B (Swansea) 1931 *E, S, F, I, SA*, 1932 *E, S, I*, 1934 *S, I*, 1935 *E, S, I*
Deacon, J T (Swansea) 1891 *I*, 1892 *E, S, I*
Delahay, W J (Bridgend) 1922 *E, S, I, F*, 1923 *E, S, F, I*, 1924 *NZ*, 1925 *E, S, F, I*, 1926 *E, S, I, F*, 1927 *S*
Delaney, L (Llanelli) 1989 *I, F, E*, 1990 *E*, 1991 *F*2, [*WS, Arg, A*], 1992 *I, F, E*
Devereux, D (Neath) 1958 *A, E, S*
Devereux, J A (S Glamorgan Inst, Bridgend) 1986 *E, S, I, F, Fj, Tg, WS*, 1987 *F, E, S, I*, [*I, C, E, NZ, A*], 1988 *NZ* 1,2, *R*, 1989 *S, I*
Diplock, R (Bridgend) 1988 *R*
Dobson, G (Cardiff) 1900 *S*
Dobson, T (Cardiff) 1898 *I, E*, 1899 *E, S*
Donovan, A J (Swansea) 1978 *A* 2, 1981 *I* (R), *A*, 1982 *E, S*
Donovan, R (S Wales Police) 1983 *F* (R)
Douglas, M H J (Llanelli) 1984 *S, I, F*
Douglas, W M (Cardiff) 1886 *E, S*, 1887 *E, S*
Dowell, W H (Newport) 1907 *E, S, I*, 1908 *E, S, F, I*
Dyke, J C M (Penarth) 1906 *SA*
Dyke, L M (Penarth, Cardiff) 1910 *I*, 1911 *S, F, I*

Edmunds, D A (Neath) 1990 *I* (R), *Bb*
Edwards, A B (London Welsh, Army) 1955 *E, S*

Edwards, B O (Newport) 1951 *I*
Edwards, D (Glynneath) 1921 *E*
Edwards, G O (Cardiff, Cardiff Coll of Ed) 1967 *F, E, NZ*, 1968 *E, S, I, F*, 1969 *S, I, F, E, NZ* 1,2, *A*, 1970 *SA, S, E, I, F*, 1971 *E, S, I, F*, 1972 *E, S, F, NZ*, 1973 *E, S, I, F, A*, 1974 *S, I, F, E*, 1975 *F, E, S, I, A*, 1976 *E, S, I, F*, 1977 *I, F, E, S*, 1978 *E, S, I, F*
Eidman, I H (Cardiff) 1983 *S, R*, 1984 *I, F, E, A*, 1985 *S, I, Fj*, 1986 *E, S, I, F*
Elliott, J E (Cardiff) 1894 *I*, 1898 *I, E*
Elsey, W J (Cardiff) 1895 *E*
Emyr, Arthur (Swansea) 1989 *E, NZ*, 1990 *F, E, S, I, Nm* 1,2, 1991 *F* 1,2, [*WS, Arg, A*]
Evans, A C (Pontypool) 1924 *E, I, F*
Evans, B (Swansea) 1933 *S*
Evans, B (Llanelli) 1933 *E, S*, 1936 *E, S, I*, 1937 *E*
Evans, B S (Llanelli) 1920 *E*, 1922 *E, S, I, F*
Evans, C (Pontypool) 1960 *E*
Evans, D (Penygraig) 1896 *S, I*, 1897 *E*, 1898 *E*
Evans, D B (Swansea) 1926 *E*
Evans, D D (Cheshire, Cardiff U) 1934 *E*
Evans, D P (Llanelli) 1960 *SA*
Evans, D W (Cardiff) 1889 *S, I*, 1890 *E, I*, 1891 *E*
Evans, D W (Oxford U, Cardiff) 1989 *F, E, NZ*, 1990 *F, E, S, I, Bb*, 1991 *A*(R), *F2*(R), [*A*(R)]
Evans, E (Llanelli) 1937 *E*, 1939 *S, I*
Evans, F (Llanelli) 1921 *S*
Evans, G (Cardiff) 1947 *E, S, F, I, A*, 1948 *E, S, F, I*, 1949 *E, S, I*
Evans, G (Maesteg) 1981 *S* (R), *I, F, A*, 1982 *I, F, E, S*, 1983 *F, R*
Evans, G L (Newport) 1977 *F* (R), 1978 *F, A* 2 (R)
Evans, I (London Welsh) 1934 *S, I*
Evans, I (Swansea) 1922 *E, S, I, F*
Evans, I C (Llanelli) 1987 *F, E, S, I, [I, C, E, NZ, A],* 1988 *E, S, I, F, NZ* 1,2, 1989 *I, F, E*, 1991 *E, S, I, F1, A, F2, [WS, Arg, A],* 1992 *I, F, E, S*
Evans, I L (Llanelli) 1991 *F2*(R)
Evans, J (Llanelli) 1896 *S, I*, 1897 *E*
Evans, J (Blaina) 1904 *E*
Evans, J (Pontypool) 1907 *E, S, I*
Evans, J D (Cardiff) 1958 *I, F*
Evans, J E (Llanelli) 1962 *S*
Evans, J R (Newport) 1934 *E*
Evans, O J (Cardiff) 1887 *E, S*, 1888 *S, I*
Evans, P D (Llanelli) 1951 *E, F*
Evans, R (Cardiff) 1889 *S*
Evans, R (Bridgend) 1963 *S, I, F*
Evans, R T (Newport) 1947 *F, I*, 1950 *E, S, I, F*, 1951 *E, S, I, F*
Evans, S (Swansea, Neath) 1985 *F, E*, 1986 *Fj, Tg, WS*, 1987 *F, E, [I, Tg]*
Evans, T (Swansea) 1924 *I*
Evans, T G (London Welsh) 1970 *SA, S, E, I*, 1972 *E, S, F*
Evans, T H (Llanelli) 1906 *I*, 1907 *E, S, I*, 1908 *I, A,* 1909 *E, S, F, I*, 1910 *F, E, S, I*, 1911 *E, S, F, I*
Evans, T P (Swansea) 1975 *F, E, S, I, A*, 1976 *E, S, I, F*, 1977 *I*
Evans, V (Neath) 1954 *I, F, S*
Evans, W (Llanelli) 1958 *A*
Evans, W F (Rhymney) 1882 *I*, 1883 *S*
Evans, W G (Brynmawr) 1911 *I*
Evans, W H (Llwynypia) 1914 *E, S, F, I*
Evans, W J (Pontypool) 1947 *S*
Evans, W R (Bridgend) 1958 *A, E, S, I, F*, 1960 *SA,* 1961 *E, S, I, F*, 1962 *E, S, I*
Everson, W A (Newport) 1926 *S*

Faulkner, A G (Pontypool) 1975 *F, E, S, I, A*, 1976 *E, S, I, F*, 1978 *E, S, I, F, A* 1,2, *NZ*, 1979 *S, I, F*
Faull, J (Swansea) 1957 *I, F*, 1958 *A, E, S, I, F*, 1959 *E, S, I*, 1960 *E, F*
Fauvel, T J (Aberavon) 1988 *NZ* 1 (R)
Fear, A G (Newport) 1934 *S, I*, 1935 *S, I*
Fender, N H (Cardiff) 1930 *I, F*, 1931 *E, S, F, I*
Fenwick, S P (Bridgend) 1975 *F, E, S, A*, 1976 *E, S, I, F*, 1977 *I, F, E, S*, 1978 *E, S, I, F, A* 1,2, *NZ*, 1979 *S, I, F, E*, 1980 *F, E, S, I, NZ*, 1981 *E, S*
Finch, E (Llanelli) 1924 *F, NZ*, 1925 *F, I*, 1926 *F*, 1927 *A*, 1928 *I*
Finlayson, A A J (Cardiff) 1974 *I, F, E*
Fitzgerald, D (Cardiff) 1894 *S, I*
Ford, F J V (Welch Regt, Newport) 1939 *E*

Ford, I (Newport) 1959 *E, S*
Ford, S P (Cardiff) 1990 *I, Nm* 1,2, *Bb*, 1991 *E, S, I, A*
Forward, A (Pontypool, Mon Police) 1951 *S, SA*, 1952 *E, S, I, F*
Fowler, I J (Llanelli) 1919 *NZA*
Francis, D G (Llanelli) 1919 *NZA*, 1924 *S*
Francis, P (Maesteg) 1987 *S*

Gabe, R T (Cardiff, Llanelli) 1901 *I*, 1902 *E, S, I*, 1903 *E, S, I*, 1904 *E, S, I*, 1905 *E, S, I, NZ*, 1906 *E, I, SA,* 1907 *E, S, I*, 1908 *E, S, F, I*
Gale, N R (Swansea, Llanelli) 1960 *I*, 1963 *E, S, I, NZ,* 1964 *E, S, I, F, SA*, 1965 *E, S, I, F*, 1966 *E, S, I, F,* *A*, 1967 *E, NZ*, 1968 *E*, 1969 *NZ* 1 (R), 2, *A*
Gallacher, I S (Llanelli) 1970 *F*
Garrett, R M (Penarth) 1888 *M*, 1889 *S*, 1890 *S, E, I,* 1891 *S, I*, 1892 *E*
Geen, W P (Oxford U, Newport) 1912 *SA*, 1913 *E, I*
George, E E (Pontypridd, Cardiff) 1895 *S, I*, 1896 *E*
George, G M (Newport) 1991 *E, S*
Gething, G I (Neath) 1913 *F*
Gibbs, I S (Neath, Swansea) 1991 *E, S, I, F1, A, F2, [WS, Arg, A],* 1992 *I, F, E, S*
Gibbs, R A (Cardiff) 1906 *S, I*, 1907 *E, S*, 1908 *E, S, F, I*, 1910 *F, E, S, I*, 1911 *E, S, F, I*
Giles, R (Aberavon) 1983 *R*, 1985 *Fj* (R), 1987 [*C*]
Girling, B E (Cardiff) 1881 *E*
Goldsworthy, S J (Swansea) 1884 *I*, 1885 *E, S*
Gore, J H (Blaina) 1924 *I, F, NZ*, 1925 *E*
Gore, W (Newbridge) 1947 *S, F, I*
Gould, A J (Newport) 1885 *E, S*, 1886 *E, S*, 1887 *E, S, I*, 1888 *S*, 1889 *I*, 1890 *S, E, I*, 1892 *E, S, I*, 1893 *E, S,* 1894 *E, S*, 1895 *E, S, I*, 1896 *E, S, I*, 1897 *E*
Gould, G H (Newport) 1892 *I*, 1893 *S, I*
Gould, R (Newport) 1882 *I*, 1883 *E, S*, 1884 *E, S, I,* 1885 *E, S*, 1886 *E*, 1887 *E, S*
Graham, T C (Newport) 1890 *I*, 1891 *S, I*, 1892 *E, S,* 1893 *E, S, I*, 1894 *E, S*, 1895 *E, S*
Gravell, R W R (Llanelli) 1975 *F, E, S, I, A*, 1976 *E, S, I, F*, 1978 *E, S, I, F, A* 1,2, *NZ*, 1979 *S, I*, 1981 *I, F*, 1982 *F, E, S*
Gray, A J (London Welsh) 1968 *E, S*
Greenslade, D (Newport) 1962 *S*
Greville, H G (Llanelli) 1947 *A*
Griffin, Dr J (Edinburgh U) 1883 *S*
Griffiths, C (Llanelli) 1979 *E* (R)
Griffiths, D (Llanelli) 1888 *M*, 1889 *I*
Griffiths, G (Llanelli) 1889 *I*
Griffiths, G M (Cardiff) 1953 *E, S, I, F, NZ*, 1954 *I, F, S*, 1955 *I, F*, 1957 *E, S*
Griffiths, J L (Llanelli) 1988 *NZ* 2, 1989 *S*
Griffiths, M (Bridgend, Cardiff) 1988 *WS, R*, 1989 *S, I, F, E, NZ*, 1990 *F, E, Nm* 1,2, *Bb*, 1991 *I, F1,2, [WS, Arg, A],* 1992 *I, F, E, S*
Griffiths, V M (Newport) 1924 *S, I, F*
Gronow, B (Bridgend) 1910 *F, E, S, I*
Gwilliam, J A (Cambridge U, Newport) 1947 *A*, 1948 *I,* 1949 *E, S, I, F*, 1950 *E, S, I, F*, 1951 *E, S, I, SA*, 1952 *E, S, I, F*, 1953 *E, S, I, F, NZ*, 1954 *E*
Gwynn, D (Swansea) 1883 *E*, 1887 *S*, 1890 *E, I*, 1891 *E, S*
Gwynn, W H (Swansea) 1884 *E, S, I*, 1885 *E, S*

Hadley, A M (Cardiff) 1983 *R*, 1984 *S, I, F, E*, 1985 *F,* *E, Fj*, 1986 *E, S, I, F, Fj, Tg*, 1987 *S* (R), *I, [I, Tg, C,* *E, NZ, A], US*, 1988 *E, S, I, F*
Hall, I (Aberavon) 1967 *NZ*, 1970 *SA, S, E*, 1971 *S,* 1974 *S, I, F*
Hall, M R (Cambridge U, Bridgend, Cardiff) 1988 *NZ* 1 (R) 2, *WS, R*, 1989 *S, I, F, E, NZ*, 1990 *F, E, S*, 1991 *A, F2, [WS, Arg, A],* 1992 *I, F, E, S*
Hall, W H (Bridgend) 1988 *WS*
Hancock, F E (Cardiff) 1884 *I*, 1885 *E, S*, 1886 *S*
Hannan, J (Newport) 1888 *M*, 1889 *S, I*, 1890 *S, E, I,* 1891 *E*, 1892 *E, S, I*, 1893 *E, S, I*, 1894 *E, S, I*, 1895 *E, S, I*
Harding, A F (London Welsh) 1902 *E, S, I*, 1903 *E, S,* *I*, 1904 *E, S, I*, 1905 *E, S, I, NZ*, 1906 *E, S, I, SA,* 1907 *I*, 1908 *E, S*
Harding, G F (Newport) 1881 *E*, 1882 *I*, 1883 *E, S*
Harding, R (Swansea, Cambridge U) 1923 *E, S, F, I,* 1924 *I, F, NZ*, 1925 *F, I*, 1926 *E, I, F*, 1927 *E, S, F,* *I*, 1928 *E*
Harding, T (Newport) 1888 *M*, 1889 *S, I*

Harris, D J E (Pontypridd, Cardiff) 1959 *I, F*, 1960 *S, I, F, SA*, 1961 *E, S*
Harris, T (Aberavon) 1927 *A*
Hathway, G F (Newport) 1924 *I, F*
Havard, Rev W T (Llanelli) 1919 *NZA*
Hawkins, F (Pontypridd) 1912 *I, F*
Hayward, D (Newbridge) 1949 *E, F*, 1950 *E, S, I, F*, 1951 *E, S, I, F, SA*, 1952 *E, S, I, F*
Hayward, D J (Cardiff) 1963 *E, NZ*, 1964 *S, I, F, SA*
Hayward, G (Swansea) 1908 *S, F, I, A*, 1909 *E*
Hellings, R (Llwynypia) 1897 *E, F*, 1898 *I, E*, 1899 *S, I*, 1900 *E, I*, 1901 *E, S*
Herrerá, R C (Cross Keys) 1925 *S, F, I*, 1926 *E, S, I, F*, 1927 *E*
Hiams, H (Swansea) 1912 *I, F*
Hickman, A (Neath) 1930 *E*, 1933 *S*
Hiddlestone, D D (Neath) 1922 *E, S, I, F*, 1924 *NZ*
Hill, A F (Cardiff) 1885 *S*, 1886 *E, S*, 1888 *S, I, M*, 1889 *S*, 1890 *S, I*, 1893 *E, S, I*, 1894 *E, S, I*
Hinam, S (Cardiff) 1925 *I*, 1926 *E, S, I, F*
Hinton, J T (Cardiff) 1884 *I*
Hirst, G L (Newport) 1912 *S*, 1913 *S*, 1914 *E, S, F, I*
Hodder, W (Pontypool) 1921 *E, S, F*
Hodges, J J (Newport) 1899 *E, S, I*, 1900 *E, S, I*, 1901 *E, S*, 1902 *E, S, I*, 1903 *E, S, I*, 1904 *E, S*, 1905 *E, S, I, NZ*, 1906 *E, S, I*
Hodgson, G T R (Neath) 1962 *I*, 1963 *E, S, I, F, NZ*, 1964 *E, S, I, F, SA*, 1966 *S, I, F*, 1967 *I*
Hollingdale, H (Swansea) 1912 *SA*, 1913 *E*
Hollingdale, T H (Neath) 1927 *A*, 1928 *E, S, I, F*, 1930 *E*
Holmes, T D (Cardiff) 1978 *A* 2, *NZ*, 1979 *S, I, F, E*, 1980 *F, E, S, I, NZ*, 1981 *A*, 1982 *I, F, E*, 1983 *E, S, I, F*, 1984 *E*, 1985 *S, I, F, E, Fj*
Hopkin, W H (Newport) 1937 *S*
Hopkins, K (Cardiff, Swansea) 1985 *E*, 1987 *F, E, S, [Tg, C(R)], US*
Hopkins, P L (Swansea) 1908 *A*, 1909 *E, I*, 1910 *E*
Hopkins, R (Maesteg) 1970 *E* (R)
Hopkins, T (Swansea) 1926 *E, S, I, F*
Hopkins, W J (Aberavon) 1925 *E, S*
Howells, B (Llanelli) 1934 *E*
Howells, W G (Llanelli) 1957 *E, S, I, F*
Howells, W H (Swansea) 1888 *S, I*
Hughes, D (Newbridge) 1967 *NZ*, 1969 *NZ* 2, 1970 *SA, S, E, I*
Hughes, G (Penarth) 1934 *E, S, I*
Hughes, H (Cardiff) 1887 *S*, 1889 *S*
Hughes, K (Cambridge U, London Welsh) 1970 *I*, 1973 *A*, 1974 *S*
Hullin, W (Cardiff) 1967 *S*
Hurrell, J (Newport) 1959 *F*
Hutchinson, F (Neath) 1894 *I*, 1896 *S, I*
Huxtable, R (Swansea) 1920 *F, I*
Huzzey, H V P (Cardiff) 1898 *I, E*, 1899 *E, S, I*
Hybart, A J (Cardiff) 1887 *E*

Ingledew, H M (Cardiff) 1890 *I*, 1891 *E, S*
Isaacs, I (Cardiff) 1933 *E, S*

Jackson, T H (Swansea) 1895 *E*
James, B (Bridgend) 1968 *E*
James, C R (Llanelli) 1958 *A, F*
James, D (Swansea) 1891 *I*, 1892 *S, I*, 1899 *E*
James, D R (Treorchy) 1931 *F, I*
James, E (Swansea) 1890 *S*, 1891 *I*, 1892 *S, I*, 1899 *E*
James, M (Cardiff) 1947 *A*, 1948 *E, S, F, I*
James, T O (Aberavon) 1935 *I*, 1937 *S*
James, W J (Aberavon) 1983 *E, S, I, F, R*, 1984 *S*, 1985 *S, I, F, E, Fj*, 1986 *E, S, I, F, Fj, Tg, WS*, 1987 *E, S, I*
James, W P (Aberavon) 1925 *E, S*
Jarman, H (Newport) 1910 *E, S, I*, 1911 *E*
Jarrett, K S (Newport) 1967 *E*, 1968 *E, S*, 1969 *S, I, F, E, NZ* 1,2, *A*
Jeffery, J J (Cardiff Coll of Ed, Newport) 1967 *NZ*
Jenkin, A M (Swansea) 1895 *I*, 1896 *E*
Jenkins, A (Llanelli) 1920 *E, S, F, I*, 1921 *S, F*, 1922 *F*, 1923 *E, S, F, I*, 1924 *NZ*, 1928 *S, I*
Jenkins, D M (Treorchy) 1926 *E, S, I, F*
Jenkins, D R (Swansea) 1927 *A*, 1929 *E*
Jenkins, E (Newport) 1910 *S, I*
Jenkins, E M (Aberavon) 1927 *S, F, I, A*, 1928 *E, S, I, F*, 1929 *I*, 1930 *E, S, I, F*, 1931 *E, S, F, I, SA*, 1932

E, S, I
Jenkins, G R (Pontypool, Swansea) 1991 *F2*, [*WS*(R)], *Arg, A*], 1992 *I, F, E, S*
Jenkins, J C (London Welsh) 1906 *SA*
Jenkins, J L (Aberavon) 1923 *S, F*
Jenkins, L H (Mon TC, Newport) 1954 *I*, 1956 *E, S, I, F*
Jenkins, N R (Pontypridd) 1991 *E, S, I, F1*, 1992 *I, F, E, S*
Jenkins, V G J (Oxford U, Bridgend, London Welsh) 1933 *E, I*, 1934 *S, I*, 1935 *E, S, NZ*, 1936 *E, S, I*, 1937 *E*, 1938 *E, S*, 1939 *E*
Jenkins, W (Cardiff) 1912 *I, F*, 1913 *S, I*
John, B (Llanelli, Cardiff) 1966 *A*, 1967 *S, NZ*, 1968 *E, S, I, F*, 1969 *S, I, F, E, NZ* 1,2, *A*, 1970 *SA, S, E, I*, 1971 *E, S, I, F*, 1972 *E, S, F*
John, D A (Llanelli) 1925 *I*, 1928 *E, S, I*
John, D E (Llanelli) 1923 *F, I*, 1928 *E, S, I*
John, E R (Neath) 1950 *E, S, I, F*, 1951 *E, S, I, F, SA*, 1952 *E, S, I, F*, 1953 *E, S, I, F, NZ*, 1954 *E*
John, G (St Luke's Coll, Exeter) 1954 *E, F*
John, J H (Swansea) 1926 *E, S, I, F*, 1927 *E, S, F, I*
Johnson, T A (Cardiff) 1921 *E, F, I*, 1923 *E, S, F*, 1924 *E, S, NZ*, 1925 *E, S, F*
Johnson, W D (Swansea) 1953 *E*
Jones, A H (Cardiff) 1933 *E, S*
Jones, B (Abertillery) 1914 *E, S, F, I*
Jones, Bert (Llanelli) 1934 *S, I*
Jones, Bob (Llwynypia) 1901 *I*
Jones, B J (Newport) 1960 *I, F*
Jones, B Lewis (Devonport Services, Llanelli) 1950 *E, S, I, F*, 1951 *E, S, SA*, 1952 *E, I, F*
Jones, C W (Cambridge U, Cardiff) 1934 *E, S, I*, 1935 *E, S, I, NZ*, 1936 *E, S, I*, 1938 *E, S, I*
Jones, C W (Bridgend) 1920 *E, S, F*
Jones, D (Neath) 1927 *A*
Jones, D (Aberavon) 1897 *E*
Jones, D (Swansea) 1947 *E, F, I*, 1949 *E, S, I, F*
Jones, D (Treherbert) 1902 *E, S, I*, 1903 *E, S, I*, 1905 *E, S, I, NZ*, 1906 *E, S, SA*
Jones, D (Newport) 1926 *E, S, I, F*, 1927 *E*
Jones, D (Llanelli) 1948 *E*
Jones, D K (Llanelli, Cardiff) 1962 *E, S, F, I*, 1963 *E, F, NZ*, 1964 *E, S, SA*, 1966 *E, S, I, F*
Jones, D P (Pontypool) 1907 *I*
Jones, E H (Neath) 1929 *E, S*
Jones, E L (Llanelli) 1930 *F*, 1933 *E, S, I*, 1935 *E*
Jones, Elvet L (Llanelli) 1939 *S*
Jones, G (Ebbw Vale) 1963 *S, I, F*
Jones, G (Llanelli) 1988 *NZ* 2, 1989 *F, E, NZ*, 1990 *F*
Jones, G G (Cardiff) 1930 *S*, 1933 *I*
Jones, H (Penygraig) 1902 *S, I*
Jones, H (Neath) 1904 *I*
Jones, H (Swansea) 1930 *I, F*
Jones, Iorwerth (Llanelli) 1927 *A*, 1928 *E, S, I, F*
Jones, I C (London Welsh) 1968 *I*
Jones, Ivor E (Llanelli) 1924 *E, S*, 1927 *S, F, I, A*, 1928 *E, S, I, F*, 1929 *E, S, F, I*, 1930 *E, S*
Jones, J (Aberavon) 1901 *E*
Jones, J (Swansea) 1924 *F*
Jones, Jim (Aberavon) 1919 *NZA*, 1920 *E,S*, 1921 *S, F, I*
Jones, J A (Cardiff) 1883 *S*
Jones, J P (Tuan) (Pontypool) 1913 *S*
Jones, J P (Pontypool) 1908 *A*, 1909 *E, S, F, I*, 1910 *F, E*, 1912 *E, F*, 1913 *F, I*, 1920 *F, I*, 1921 *E*
Jones, K D (Cardiff) 1960 *SA*, 1961 *E, S, I*, 1962 *E, F*, 1963 *E, S, I, NZ*
Jones, K J (Newport) 1947 *E, S, F, I, A*, 1948 *E, S, F, I*, 1949 *E, S, I, F*, 1950 *E, S, I, F*, 1951 *E, S, I, F, SA*, 1952 *E, S, I, F*, 1953 *E, S, I, F, NZ*, 1954 *E, I, F, S*, 1955 *E, S, I, F*, 1956 *E, S, I, F*, 1957 *S*
Jones, K W J (Oxford U, London Welsh) 1934 *E*
Jones, M A (Neath) 1987 *S*, 1988 *NZ* 2 (R), 1989 *S, I, F, E, NZ*, 1990 *F, E, S, I, Nm* 1,2, *Bb*
Jones, P (Newport) 1912 *SA*, 1913 *E, S, F*, 1914 *E, S, F, I*
Jones, P B (Newport) 1921 *S*
Jones, R (Swansea) 1901 *I*, 1902 *E*, 1904 *E, S, I*, 1905 *E*, 1908 *F, I, A*, 1909 *E, S, F, I*, 1910 *F, E*
Jones, R (London Welsh) 1929 *E*
Jones, R (Northampton) 1926 *E, S, F*
Jones, R (Swansea) 1927 *A*, 1928 *F*
Jones, R B (Cambridge U) 1933 *E, S*

Jones, R E (Coventry) 1967 *F, E,* 1968 *S, I, F*
Jones, R N (Swansea) 1986 *E, S, I, F, Fj, Tg, WS,* 1987 *F, E, S, I, [I, Tg, E, NZ, A], US,* 1988 *E, S, I, F, NZ* 1, *WS, R,* 1989 *I, F, E, NZ,* 1990 *F, E, S, I,* 1991 *E, S, F2, [WS, Arg, A],* 1992 *I, F, E, S*
Jones, S T (Pontypool) 1983 *S, I, F, R,* 1984*S,* 1988 *E, S, F, NZ* 1,2
Jones, Tom (Newport) 1922 *E, S, I, F,* 1924 *E, S*
Jones, T B (Newport) 1882 *I,* 1883 *E, S,* 1884 *S,* 1885 *E, S*
Jones, W (Cardiff) 1898 *I, E*
Jones, W (Mountain Ash) 1905 *I*
Jones, W I (Llanelli, Cambridge U) 1925 *E, S, F, I*
Jones, W J (Llanelli) 1924 *I*
Jones, W K (Cardiff) 1967 *NZ,* 1968 *E, S, I, F*
Jones-Davies, T E (London Welsh) 1930 *E, I,* 1931 *E, S*
Jordan, H M (Newport) 1885 *E, S,* 1889 *S*
Joseph, W (Swansea) 1902 *E, S, I,* 1903 *E, S, I,* 1904 *E, S,* 1905 *E, S, I, NZ,* 1906 *E, S, I, SA*
Jowett, W F (Swansea) 1903 *E*
Judd, S (Cardiff) 1953 *E, S, I, F, NZ,* 1954 *E, F, S,* 1955 *E, S*
Judson, J H (Llanelli) 1883 *E, S*

Kedzlie, Q D (Cardiff) 1888 *S, I*
Keen, L (Aberavon) 1980 *F, E, S, I*
Knight, P (Pontypridd) 1990 *Nm* 1,2, *Bb*(R), 1991 *E, S*
Knill, F M D (Cardiff) 1976 *F* (R)

Lane, S M (Cardiff) 1978 *A* 1 (R), 2, 1979 *I* (R), 1980 *S, I*
Lang, J (Llanelli) 1931 *F, I,* 1934 *S, I,* 1935 *E, S, I, NZ,* 1936 *E, S, I,* 1937 *E*
Lawrence, S (Bridgend) 1925 *S, I,* 1926 *S, I, F,* 1927 *E*
Law, V J (Newport) 1939 *I*
Legge, W S G (Newport) 1937 *I,* 1938 *I*
Leleu, J (London Welsh, Swansea) 1959 *E, S,* 1960 *F, SA*
Lemon, A (Neath) 1929 *I,* 1930 *S, I, F,* 1931 *E, S, F, I, SA,* 1932 *E, S, I,* 1933 *I*
Lewis, A J L (Ebbw Vale) 1970 *F,* 1971 *E, I, F,* 1972 *E, S, F,* 1973 *E, S, I, F*
Lewis, A R (Abertillery) 1966 *E, S, I, F, A,* 1967 *I*
Lewis, B R (Swansea, Cambridge U) 1912 *I,* 1913 *I*
Lewis, C P (Llandovery Coll) 1882 *I,* 1883 *E, S,* 1884 *E, S*
Lewis, D H (Cardiff) 1886 *E, S*
Lewis, E J (Llandovery) 1881 *E*
Lewis, E W (Llanelli) 1991 *I, F1, A, F2, [WS, Arg, A],* 1992 *I, F, S*
Lewis, G W (Richmond) 1960 *E, S*
Lewis, H (Swansea) 1913 *S, F, I,* 1914 *E*
Lewis, J G (Llanelli) 1887 *I*
Lewis, J M C (Cardiff, Cambridge U) 1912 *E,* 1913 *S, F, I,* 1914 *E, S, F, I,* 1921 *I,* 1923 *E, S*
Lewis, J R (S Glam Inst, Cardiff) 1981 *E, S, I, F,* 1982 *F, E, S*
Lewis, M (Treorchy) 1913 *F*
Lewis, P I (Llanelli) 1984 *A,* 1985 *S, I, F, E,* 1986 *E, S, I*
Lewis, T W (Cardiff) 1926 *E,* 1927 *E, S*
Lewis, W (Llanelli) 1925 *F*
Lewis, W H (London Welsh, Cambridge U) 1926 *I,* 1927 *E, F, I, A,* 1928 *F*
Llewellyn, D B (Newport, Llanelli) 1970 *SA, S, E, I, F,* 1971 *E, S, I, F,* 1972 *E, S, F, NZ*
Llewellyn, G D (Neath) 1990 *Nm* 1,2, *Bb,* 1991 *E, S, I, F1, A, F2*
Llewellyn, G O (Neath) 1989 *NZ,* 1990 *E, S, I,* 1991 *E, S, A*(R), 1992 *I, F, E, S*
Llewellyn, P D (Swansea) 1973 *I, F, A,* 1974 *S, E*
Llewellyn, W (Llwynypia) 1899 *E, S, I,* 1900 *E, S, I,* 1901 *E, S, I,* 1902 *E, S, I,* 1903 *I,* 1904 *E, S, I,* 1905 *E, S, I, NZ*
Lloyd, D J (Bridgend) 1966 *E, S, I, F, A,* 1967 *S, I, F, E,* 1968 *S, I, F,* 1969 *S, I, F, E, NZ* 1, *A,* 1970 *F,* 1972 *E, S, F,* 1973 *E, S*
Lloyd, E (Llanelli) 1895 *S*
Lloyd, G L (Newport) 1896 *I,* 1899 *S, I,* 1900 *E, S,* 1901 *E, S,* 1902 *S, I,* 1903 *E, S, I*
Lloyd, P (Llanelli) 1890 *S, E,* 1891 *E, I*
Lloyd, R A (Pontypool) 1913 *S, F, I,* 1914 *E, S, F, I*
Lloyd, T (Maesteg) 1953 *I, F*

Lloyd, T C (Neath) 1909 *F,* 1913 *F, I,* 1914 *E, S, F, I*
Lockwood, T W (Newport) 1887 *E, S, I*
Long, E C (Swansea) 1936 *E, S, I,* 1937 *E, S,* 1939 *S, I*
Lyne, H S (Newport) 1883 *S,* 1884 *E, S, I,* 1885 *E*

McCall, B E W (Welch Regt, Newport) 1936 *E, S, I*
McCarley, A (Neath) 1938 *E, S, I*
McCutcheon, W M (Swansea) 1891 *S,* 1892 *E, S,* 1893 *E, S, I,* 1894 *E*
Maddock, H T (London Welsh) 1906 *E, S, I,* 1907 *E, S,* 1910 *F*
Maddocks, K (Neath) 1957 *E*
Main, D R (London Welsh) 1959 *E, S, I, F*
Mainwaring, H J (Swansea) 1961 *F*
Mainwaring, W T (Aberavon) 1967 *S, I, F, E, NZ,* 1968 *E*
Major, W C (Maesteg) 1949 *F,* 1950 *S*
Male, B O (Cardiff) 1921 *F,* 1923 *S,* 1924 *S, I,* 1927 *E, S, F, I,* 1928 *S, I, F*
Manfield, L (Mountain Ash, Cardiff) 1939 *S, I,* 1947 *A,* 1948 *E, S, F, I*
Mann, B B (Cardiff) 1881 *E*
Mantle, J T (Loughborough Colls, Newport) 1964 *E, SA*
Margrave, F L (Llanelli) 1884 *E, S*
Marsden-Jones, D (Cardiff) 1921 *E,* 1924 *NZ*
Martin, A J (Aberavon) 1973 *A,* 1974 *S, I,* 1975 *F, E, S, I, A,* 1976 *E, S, I, F,* 1977 *I, F, E, S,* 1978 *E, S, I, F, A* 1,2, *NZ,* 1979 *S, I, F, E,* 1980 *F, E, S, I, NZ,* 1981 *I, F*
Martin, W J (Newport) 1912 *I, F,* 1919 *NZA*
Mason, J (Pontypridd) 1988 *NZ* 2 (R)
Mathews, Rev A A (Lampeter) 1886 *S*
Mathias, R (Llanelli) 1970 *F*
Matthews, C (Bridgend) 1939 *I*
Matthews, J (Cardiff) 1947 *E, A,* 1948 *E, S, F,* 1949 *E, S, I, F,* 1950 *E, S, I, F,* 1951 *E, S, I, F*
May, P S (Llanelli) 1988 *E, S, I, F, NZ* 1,2, 1991 *[WS]*
Meredith, A (Devonport Services) 1949 *E, S, I*
Meredith, B V (St Luke's Coll, London Welsh, Newport) 1954 *I, F, S,* 1955 *E, S, I, F,* 1956 *E, S, I, F,* 1957 *E, S, I, F,* 1958 *A, E, S, I,* 1959 *E, S, I, F,* 1960 *E, S, F, SA,* 1961 *E, S, I,* 1962 *E, S, F, I*
Meredith, C C (Neath) 1953 *S, NZ,* 1954 *E, I, F, S,* 1955 *E, S, I, F,* 1956 *E, I,* 1957 *E, S*
Meredith, J (Swansea) 1888 *S, I,* 1890 *S, E*
Merry, A E (Pill Harriers) 1912 *I, F*
Michael, G (Swansea) 1923 *E, S, F*
Michaelson, R C B (Aberavon, Cambridge U) 1963 *E*
Miller, F (Mountain Ash) 1896 *I,* 1900 *E, S, I,* 1901 *E, S, I*
Mills, F M (Swansea, Cardiff) 1892 *E, S, I,* 1893 *E, S, I,* 1894 *E, S, I,* 1895 *E, S, I,* 1896 *E*
Moore, W J (Bridgend) 1933 *I*
Morgan, C H (Llanelli) 1957 *I, F*
Morgan, C I (Cardiff) 1951 *I, F, SA,* 1952 *E, S, I,* 1953 *S, I, F, NZ,* 1954 *E, I, S,* 1955 *E, S, I, F,* 1956 *E, S, I, F,* 1957 *E, S, I, F,* 1958 *E, S, I, F*
Morgan, D (Swansea) 1885 *S,* 1886 *E, S,* 1887 *E, S, I,* 1889 *I*
Morgan, D (Llanelli) 1895 *I,* 1896 *E*
Morgan, D R R (Llanelli) 1962 *E, S, F, I,* 1963 *E, S, I, F, NZ*
Morgan, E (Llanelli) 1920 *I,* 1921 *E, S, F*
Morgan, Edgar (Swansea) 1914 *E, S, F, I*
Morgan, E T (London Welsh) 1902 *E, S, I,* 1903 *I,* 1904 *E, S, I,* 1905 *E, S, I, NZ,* 1906 *E, S, I, SA,* 1908 *F*
Morgan, F L (Llanelli) 1938 *E, S, I,* 1939 *E*
Morgan, H J (Abertillery) 1958 *E, S, I, F,* 1959 *I, F,* 1960 *E,* 1961 *E, S, I, F,* 1962 *E, S, F, I,* 1963 *S, I, F,* 1965 *E, S, I, F,* 1966 *E, S, I, F, A*
Morgan, H P (Newport) 1956 *E, S, I, F*
Morgan, I (Swansea) 1908 *A,* 1909 *E, S, F, I,* 1910 *F, E, S, I,* 1911 *E, F, I,* 1912 *S*
Morgan, J L (Llanelli) 1912 *SA,* 1913 *E*
Morgan, M E (Swansea) 1938 *E, S, I,* 1939 *E*
Morgan, N (Newport) 1960 *S, I, F*
Morgan, P E J (Aberavon) 1961 *E, S, F*
Morgan, P J (Llanelli) 1980 *S* (R), *I, NZ* (R), 1981 *I*
Morgan, R (Newport) 1984 *S*
Morgan, T (Llanelli) 1889 *I*
Morgan, W G (Cambridge U) 1927 *F, I,* 1929 *E, S, F, I,* 1930 *I, F*
Morgan, W L (Cardiff) 1910 *S*

Moriarty, R D (Swansea) 1981 *A*, 1982 *I, F, E, S*, 1983 *E*, 1984 *S, I, F, E*, 1985 *S, I, F*, 1986 *Fj, Tg, WS*, 1987 [*I, Tg, C*(R)], *E, NZ, A*]
Moriarty, W P (Swansea) 1986 *I, F, Fj, Tg, WS*, 1987 *F, E, S, I*, [*I, Tg, C, E, NZ, A*], *US*, 1988 *E, S, I, F, NZ* 1
Morley, J C (Newport) 1929 *E, S, F, I*, 1930 *E, I*, 1931 *E, S, F, I, SA*, 1932 *E, S, I*
Morris, G L (Swansea) 1882 *I*, 1883 *E, S*, 1884 *E, S*
Morris, H T (Cardiff) 1951 *F*, 1955 *I, F*
Morris, J I T (Swansea) 1924 *E, S*
Morris, M S (S Wales Police, Neath) 1985 *S, I, F*, 1990 *I, Nm* 1,2, *Bb*, 1991 *I, F*1, [*WS*(R)], 1992 *E*
Morris, R R (Swansea, Bristol) 1933 *S*, 1937 *S*
Morris, S (Cross Keys) 1920 *E, S, F, I*, 1922 *E, S, I, F*, 1923 *E, S, F, I*, 1924 *E, S, F, NZ*, 1925 *E, S, F*
Morris, W (Abertillery) 1919 *NZA*, 1920 *F*, 1921 *I*
Morris, W (Llanelli) 1896 *S, I*, 1897 *E*
Morris, W D (Neath) 1967 *F, E*, 1968 *E, S, I, F*, 1969 *S, I, F, E, NZ* 1,2, *A*, 1970 *SA, S, E, I, F*, 1971 *E, S, I, F*, 1972 *E, S, F, NZ*, 1973 *E, S, I, A*, 1974 *S, I, F, E*
Morris, W J (Newport) 1965 *S*, 1966 *F*
Morris, W J (Pontypool) 1963 *S, I*
Moseley, K (Pontypool, Newport) 1988 *NZ* 2, *R*, 1989 *S, I*, 1990 *F*, 1991 *F*2, [*WS, Arg, A*]
Murphy, C D (Cross Keys) 1935 *E, S, I*

Nash, D (Ebbw Vale) 1960 *SA*, 1961 *E, S, I, F*, 1962 *F*
Newman, C H (Newport) 1881 *E*, 1882 *I*, 1883 *E, S*, 1884 *E, S*, 1885 *E, S*, 1886 *E*, 1887 *E*
Nicholas, D L (Llanelli) 1981 *E, S, I, F*
Nicholas, T J (Cardiff) 1919 *NZA*
Nicholl, C B (Cambridge U, Llanelli) 1891 *I*, 1892 *E, S, I*, 1893 *E, S, I*, 1894 *E, S*, 1895 *E, S, I*, 1896 *E, S, I*
Nicholl, D W (Llanelli) 1894 *I*
Nicholls, E G (Cardiff) 1896 *S, I*, 1897 *E*, 1898 *I, E*, 1899 *E, S, I*, 1900 *S, I*, 1901 *E, S, I*, 1902 *E, S, I*, 1903 *I*, 1904 *E*, 1905 *I, NZ*, 1906 *E, S, I, SA*
Nicholls, F E (Cardiff Harlequins) 1892 *I*
Nicholls, H (Cardiff) 1958 *I*
Nicholls, S H (Cardiff) 1888 *M*, 1889 *S, I*, 1891 *S*
Norris, C H (Cardiff) 1963 *F*, 1966 *F*
Norster, R L (Cardiff) 1982 *S*, 1983 *E, S, I, F*, 1984 *S, I, F, E, A*, 1985 *S, I, F, E, Fj*, 1986 *Fj, Tg, WS*, 1987 *F, E, S, I*, [*I, C, E*], *US*, 1988 *E, S, I, F, NZ* 1, *WS*, 1989 *F, E*
Norton, W B (Cardiff) 1882 *I*, 1883 *E, S*, 1884 *E, S, I*

O'Connor, A (Aberavon) 1960 *SA*, 1961 *E, S*, 1962 *F, I*
O'Connor, R (Aberavon) 1957 *E*
O'Neill, W (Cardiff) 1904 *S, I*, 1905 *E, S, I*, 1907 *E, I*, 1908 *E, S, F, I*
O'Shea, J P (Cardiff) 1967 *S, I*, 1968 *S, I, F*
Oliver, G (Pontypool) 1920 *E, S, F, I*
Osborne, W T (Mountain Ash) 1902 *E, S*, 1903 *E, S, I*
Ould, W J (Cardiff) 1924 *E, S*
Owen, A (Swansea) 1924 *E*
Owen, G D (Newport) 1955 *I, F*, 1956 *E, S, I, F*
Owen, R M (Swansea) 1901 *I*, 1902 *E, S, I*, 1903 *E, S, I*, 1904 *E, S, I*, 1905 *E, S, I, NZ*, 1906 *E, S, I, SA*, 1907 *E, S*, 1908 *F, I, A*, 1909 *E, S, F, I*, 1910 *F, E*, 1911 *E, S, F, I*, 1912 *E, S*

Packer, H (Newport) 1891 *E*, 1895 *S, I*, 1896 *E, S, I*, 1897 *E*
Palmer, F (Swansea) 1922 *E, S, I*
Parfitt, F C (Newport) 1893 *E, S, I*, 1894 *E, S, I*, 1895 *S*, 1896 *S, I*
Parfitt, S A (Swansea) 1990 *Nm* 1(R), *Bb*
Parker, D S (Swansea) 1924 *I, F, NZ*, 1925 *E, S, F, I*, 1929 *F, I*, 1930 *E*
Parker, T (Swansea) 1919 *NZA*, 1920 *E, S, I*, 1921 *E, S, F, I*, 1922 *E, S, I, F*, 1923 *E, S, F*
Parker, W (Swansea) 1899 *E, S*
Parsons, G W (Newport) 1947 *E*
Pascoe, D (Bridgend) 1923 *F, I*
Pask, A E I (Abertillery) 1961 *F*, 1962 *E, S, F, I*, 1963 *E, S, I, F, NZ*, 1964 *E, S, I, F, SA*, 1965 *E, S, I, F*, 1966 *E, S, I, F, A*, 1967 *S, I*
Payne, G W (Army, Pontypridd) 1960 *E, S, I*
Payne, H (Swansea) 1935 *NZ*
Peacock, H (Newport) 1929 *S, F, I*, 1930 *S, I, F*
Peake, E (Chepstow) 1881 *E*

Pearce, G P (Bridgend) 1981 *I, F*, 1982 *I* (R)
Pearson, T W (Cardiff, Newport) 1891 *E, I*, 1892 *E, S*, 1894 *S, I*, 1895 *E, S, I*, 1897 *E*, 1898 *I, E*, 1903 *E*
Pegge, E V (Neath) 1891 *E*
Perego, M A (Llanelli) 1990 *S*
Perkins, S J (Pontypool) 1983 *S, I, F, R*, 1984 *S, I, F, E, A*, 1985 *S, I, F, E, Fj*, 1986 *E, S, I, F*
Perrett, F L (Neath) 1912 *SA*, 1913 *E, S, F, I*
Perrins, V C (Newport) 1970 *SA, S*
Perry, W (Neath) 1911 *E*
Phillips, A J (Cardiff) 1979 *E*, 1980 *F, E, S, I, NZ*, 1981 *E, S, I, F, A*, 1982 *I, F, E, S*, 1987 [*C, E, A*]
Phillips, B (Aberavon) 1925 *E, S, F, I*, 1926 *E*
Phillips, D H (Swansea) 1952 *F*
Phillips, H P (Newport) 1892 *E*, 1893 *E, S, I*, 1894 *E, S*
Phillips, H T (Newport) 1927 *E, S, F, I, A*, 1928 *E, S, I, F*
Phillips, K H (Neath) 1987 *F*, [*I, Tg, NZ*], *US*, 1988 *E, NZ* 1, 1989 *NZ*, 1990 *F, E, S, I, Nm* 1,2, *Bb*, 1991 *E, S, I, F*1, *A*
Phillips, L A (Newport) 1900 *E, S, I*, 1901 *S*
Phillips, R (Neath) 1987 *US*, 1988 *E, S, I, F, NZ* 1,2, *WS*, 1989 *S, I*
Phillips, W D (Cardiff) 1881 *E*, 1882 *I*, 1884 *E, S, I*
Pickering, D F (Llanelli) 1983 *E, S, I, F, R*, 1984 *S, I, F, E, A*, 1985 *S, I, F, E, Fj*, 1986 *E, S, I, F, Fj*, 1987 *F, E, S*
Plummer, R C S (Newport) 1912 *S, I, F, SA*, 1913 *E*
Pook, T (Newport) 1895 *S*
Powell, G (Ebbw Vale) 1957 *I, F*
Powell, J (Cardiff) 1906 *I*
Powell, J (Cardiff) 1923 *I*
Powell, R W (Newport) 1888 *S, I*
Powell, W C (London Welsh) 1926 *S, I, F*, 1927 *E, F, I*, 1928 *S, I, F*, 1929 *E, S, F, I*, 1930 *S, I, F*, 1931 *E, S, F, I, SA*, 1932 *E, S, I*, 1935 *E, S, I*
Powell, W J (Cardiff) 1920 *E, S, F, I*
Price, B (Newport) 1961 *I, F*, 1962 *E, S*, 1963 *E, S, F, NZ*, 1964 *E, S, I, F, SA*, 1965 *E, S, I, F*, 1966 *E, S, I, F, A*, 1967 *S, I*, 1968 *E, S, I, F, NZ* 1,2, *A*
Price, G (Pontypool) 1975 *F, E, S, I, A*, 1976 *E, S, I, F*, 1977 *I, F, E, S*, 1978 *E, S, I, F, A* 1,2, *NZ*, 1979 *S, I, F, E*, 1980 *F, E, S, I, NZ*, 1981 *E, S, I, F, A*, 1982 *I, F, E, S*, 1983 *E, I, F*
Price, M J (Pontypool, RAF) 1959 *E, S, I, F*, 1960 *E, S, I, F*, 1962 *E*
Price, R E (Weston) 1939 *S, I*
Price, T G (Llanelli) 1965 *E, S, I, F*, 1966 *E, S, A*, 1967 *S, F*
Priday, A J (Cardiff) 1958 *I*, 1961 *I*
Pritchard, C (Pontypool) 1928 *E, S, I, F*, 1929 *E, S, F, I*
Pritchard, C C (Newport, Pontypool) 1904 *S, I*, 1905 *NZ*, 1906 *E, S*
Pritchard, C M (Newport) 1904 *I*, 1905 *E, S, NZ*, 1906 *E, S, I, SA*, 1907 *E, S, I*, 1908 *E*, 1910 *F, E*
Prosser, D R (Neath) 1934 *S, I*
Prosser, G (Neath) 1934 *E, S, I*, 1935 *NZ*
Prosser, J (Cardiff) 1921 *I*
Prosser, T R (Pontypool) 1956 *S, F*, 1957 *E, S, I, F*, 1958 *A, E, S, I, F*, 1959 *E, S, I, F*, 1960 *E, S, I, F, SA*, 1961 *I, F*
Prothero, G J (Bridgend) 1964 *S, I, F*, 1965 *E, S, I, F*, 1966 *E, S, I, F*
Pryce-Jenkins, T J (London Welsh) 1888 *S, I*
Pugh, C (Maesteg) 1924 *E, S, I, F, NZ*, 1925 *E, S*
Pugh, J D (Neath) 1987 *US*, 1988 *S* (R), 1990 *S*
Pugh, P (Neath) 1989 *NZ*
Pugsley, J (Cardiff) 1910 *E, S, I*, 1911 *E, S, F, I*
Pullman, J J (Neath) 1910 *F*
Purdon, F T (Newport) 1881 *E*, 1882 *I*, 1883 *E, S*

Quinnell, D L (Llanelli) 1972 *F* (R), *NZ*, 1973 *E, S, A*, 1974 *S, F*, 1975 *E* (R), 1977 *I* (R), *F, E, S*, 1978 *E, S, I, F, A* 1, *NZ*, 1979 *S, I, F, E*, 1980 *NZ*

Radford, W J (Newport) 1923 *I*
Ralph, A R (Newport) 1931 *F, I, SA*, 1932 *E, S, I*
Ramsey, S H (Treorchy) 1896 *E*, 1904 *E*
Randell, R (Aberavon) 1924 *I, F*
Raybould, W H (London Welsh, Cambridge U, Newport) 1967 *S, I, F, E, NZ*, 1968 *I, F*, 1970 *SA, E, I, F* (R)

Rayer, M A (Cardiff) 1991 [*WS*(R), *Arg*, *A*(R)], 1992 *E*(R)
Rees, Aaron (Maesteg) 1919 *NZA*
Rees, Alan (Maesteg) 1962 *E, S, F*
Rees, A M (London Welsh) 1934 *E*, 1935 *E, S, I, NZ*, 1936 *E, S, I*, 1937 *E, S, I*, 1938 *E, S*
Rees, B I (London Welsh) 1967 *S, I, F*
Rees, C F W (London Welsh) 1974 *I*, 1975 *A*, 1978 *NZ*, 1981 *F, A*, 1982 *I, F, E, S*, 1983 *E, S, I, F*
Rees, D (Swansea) 1968 *S, I, F*
Rees, Dan (Swansea) 1900 *E*, 1903 *E, S*, 1905 *E, S*
Rees, E B (Swansea) 1919 *NZA*
Rees, H (Cardiff) 1937 *S, I*, 1938 *E, S, I*
Rees, H E (Neath) 1979 *S, I, F, E*, 1980 *F, E, S, I, NZ*, 1983 *E, S, I, F*
Rees, J (Swansea) 1920 *E, S, F, I*, 1921 *E, S, I*, 1922 *E*, 1923 *E, F, I*, 1924 *E*
Rees, J I (Swansea) 1934 *E, S, I*, 1935 *S, NZ*, 1936 *E, S, I*, 1937 *E, S, I*, 1938 *E, S, I*
Rees, L M (Cardiff) 1933 *I*
Rees, P (Llanelli) 1947 *F, I*
Rees, P M (Newport) 1961 *E, S, I*, 1964 *I*
Rees, T (Newport) 1935 *S, I, NZ*, 1936 *E, S, I*, 1937 *E, S*
Rees, T A (Llandovery) 1881 *E*
Rees, T E (London Welsh) 1926 *I, F*, 1927 *A*, 1928 *E*
Rees-Jones, G R (Oxford U, London Welsh) 1934 *E, S*, 1935 *I, NZ*, 1936 *E*
Reeves, F (Cross Keys) 1920 *F, I*, 1921 *E*
Reynolds, A (Swansea) 1990 *Nm* 1,2(R)
Rhapps, J (Penygraig) 1897 *E*
Rice-Evans, W (Swansea) 1890 *S*, 1891 *E, S*
Richards, B (Swansea) 1960 *F*
Richards, C (Pontypool) 1922 *E, S, I, F*, 1924 *I*
Richards, D S (Swansea) 1979 *F, E*, 1980 *F, E, S, I, NZ*, 1981 *E, S, I, F*, 1982 *I, F*, 1983 *E, S, I, R* (R)
Richards, E G (Cardiff) 1927 *S*
Richards, E S (Swansea) 1885 *E*, 1887 *S*
Richards, H D (Neath) 1986 *Tg* (R), 1987 [*Tg, E* (R), *NZ*]
Richards, I (Cardiff) 1925 *E, S, F*
Richards, K H L (Bridgend) 1960 *SA*, 1961 *E, S, I, F*
Richards, M C R (Cardiff) 1968 *I, F*, 1969 *S, I, F, E, NZ* 1,2, *A*
Richards, R (Aberavon) 1913 *S, F, I*
Richards, R (Cross Keys) 1956 *F*
Richards, T L (Maesteg) 1923 *I*
Richardson, S J (Aberavon) 1978 *A* 2 (R), 1979 *E*
Rickards, A R (Cardiff) 1924 *F*
Ring, J (Aberavon) 1921 *E*
Ring, M G (Cardiff, Pontypool) 1983 *E*, 1984 *A*, 1985 *S, I, F*, 1987 *I*, [*I, Tg, A*], *US*, 1988 *E, S, I, F, NZ* 1,2, 1989 *NZ*, 1990 *F, E, S, I, Nm* 1,2, *Bb*, 1991 *E, S, I, F*1,2, [*WS, Arg, A*]
Ringer, P (Ebbw Vale, Llanelli) 1978 *NZ*, 1979 *S, I, F, E*, 1980 *F, E, NZ*
Roberts, C (Neath) 1958 *I, F*
Roberts, D E A (London Welsh) 1930 *E*
Roberts, E (Llanelli) 1886 *E*, 1887 *I*
Roberts, E J (Llanelli) 1888 *S, I*, 1889 *I*
Roberts, G J (Cardiff) 1985 *F* (R), *E*, 1987 [*I, Tg, C, E, A*]
Roberts, H M (Cardiff) 1960 *SA*, 1961 *E, S, I, F*, 1962 *S, F*, 1963 *I*
Roberts, J (Cardiff) 1927 *E, S, F, I, A*, 1928 *E, S, I, F*, 1929 *E, S, F, I*
Roberts, M G (London Welsh) 1971 *E, S, I, F*, 1973 *I, F*, 1975 *S*, 1979 *E*
Roberts, T (Newport, Risca) 1921 *S, F, I*, 1922 *E, S, I, F*, 1923 *E, S*
Roberts, W (Cardiff) 1929 *E*
Robins, J D (Birkenhead Park) 1950 *E, S, I, F*, 1951 *E, S, I, F*, 1953 *E, I, F*
Robins, R J (Pontypridd) 1953 *S*, 1954 *F, S*, 1955 *E, S, I, F*, 1956 *E, F*, 1957 *E, S, I, F*
Robinson, I R (Cardiff) 1974 *F, E*
Rocyn-Jones, D N (Cambridge U) 1925 *I*
Roderick, W B (Llanelli) 1884 *I*
Rosser, M A (Penarth) 1924 *S, F*
Rowland, E M (Lampeter) 1885 *E*
Rowlands, C F (Aberavon) 1926 *I*
Rowlands, D C T (Pontypool) 1963 *E, S, I, F, NZ*, 1964 *E, S, I, F, SA*, 1965 *E, S, I, F*
Rowlands, G (RAF, Cardiff) 1953 *NZ*, 1954 *E, F*,

1956 *F*
Rowlands, K A (Cardiff) 1962 *F, I*, 1963 *I*, 1965 *I, F*
Rowles, G R (Penarth) 1892 *E*
Russell, S (London Welsh) 1987 *US*

Samuel, D (Swansea) 1891 *I*, 1893 *I*
Samuel, F (Mountain Ash) 1922 *S, I, F*
Samuel, J (Swansea) 1891 *I*
Scourfield, T (Torquay) 1930 *F*
Scrine, G F (Swansea) 1899 *E, S*, 1901 *I*
Shanklin, J L (London Welsh) 1970 *F*, 1972 *NZ*, 1973 *I, F*
Shaw, G (Neath) 1972 *NZ*, 1973 *E, S, I, F, A*, 1974 *S, I, F, E*, 1977 *I, F*
Shaw, T W (Newbridge) 1983 *R*
Shea, J (Newport) 1919 *NZA*, 1920 *E, S*, 1921 *E*
Shell, R C (Aberavon) 1973 *A* (R)
Simpson, H J (Cardiff) 1884 *E, S, I*
Skrimshire, R T (Newport) 1899 *E, S, I*
Skym, A (Llanelli) 1928 *E, S, I, F*, 1930 *E, S, I, F*, 1931 *E, S, F, I, SA*, 1932 *E, S, I*, 1933 *E, S, I*, 1935 *E*
Smith, J S (Cardiff) 1884 *E, I*, 1885 *E*
Sparks, B (Neath) 1954 *I*, 1955 *E, F*, 1956 *E, S, I*, 1957 *S*
Spiller, W J (Cardiff) 1910 *S, I*, 1911 *E, S, F, I*, 1912 *E, F, SA*, 1913 *E*
Squire, J (Newport, Pontypool) 1977 *I, F*, 1978 *E, S, I, F, A* 1, *NZ*, 1979 *S, I, F, E*, 1980 *F, E, S, I, NZ*, 1981 *E, S, I, F, A*, 1982 *I, F, E*, 1983 *E, S, I, F*
Stadden, W J W (Cardiff) 1884 *I*, 1886 *E, S*, 1887 *I*, 1888 *S, M*, 1890 *S, E*
Stephens, C J (Llanelli) 1992 *I, F, E*
Stephens, G (Neath) 1912 *E, S, I, F, SA*, 1913 *E, S, F, I*, 1919 *NZA*
Stephens, I (Bridgend) 1981 *E, S, I, F, A*, 1982 *I, F, E, S*, 1984 *I, F, E, A*
Stephens, Rev J G (Llanelli) 1922 *E, S, I, F*
Stephens, J R G (Neath) 1947 *E, S, F, I*, 1948 *I*, 1949 *S, I, F*, 1951 *F, SA*, 1952 *E, S, I, F*, 1953 *E, S, I, F*, *NZ*, 1954 *E, I*, 1955 *E, S, I, F*, 1956 *S, I, F*, 1957 *E, S, I, F*
Stock, A (Newport) 1924 *F, NZ*, 1926 *E, S*
Stone, P (Llanelli) 1949 *F*
Strand-Jones, J (Llanelli) 1902 *E, S, I*, 1903 *E, S*
Summers, R H B (Haverfordwest) 1881 *E*
Sutton, S (Pontypool, S Wales Police) 1982 *F, E*, 1987 *F, E, S, I*, [*C, NZ* (R), *A*]
Sweet-Escott, R B (Cardiff) 1891 *S*, 1894 *I*, 1895 *I*

Tamplin, W E (Cardiff) 1947 *S, F, I, A*, 1948 *E, S, F*
Tanner, H (Swansea, Cardiff) 1935 *NZ*, 1936 *E, S, I*, 1937 *E, S, I*, 1938 *E, S, I*, 1939 *E, S, I*, 1947 *E, S, F, I*, 1948 *E, S, F, I*, 1949 *E, S, I, F*
Tarr, D J (Swansea, Royal Navy) 1935 *NZ*
Taylor, A R (Cross Keys) 1937 *I*, 1938 *I*, 1939 *E*
Taylor, C G (Ruabon) 1884 *E, S, I*, 1885 *E, S*, 1886 *E, S*, 1887 *E, I*
Taylor, J (London Welsh) 1967 *S, I, F, E, NZ*, 1968 *I, F*, 1969 *S, I, F, E, NZ* 1, *A*, 1970 *F*, 1971 *E, S, I, F*, 1972 *E, S, F, NZ*, 1973 *E, S, I, F*
Thomas, A (Newport) 1963 *NZ*, 1964 *E*
Thomas, A G (Swansea, Cardiff) 1952 *E, S, I, F*, 1953 *S, I, F*, 1954 *E, I, F*, 1955 *S, I, F*
Thomas, Bob (Swansea) 1900 *E, S, I*, 1901 *E*
Thomas, Brian E (Neath, Cambridge U) 1963 *E, S, I, F, NZ*, 1964 *E, S, I, F, SA*, 1965 *E*, 1966 *E, S, I*, 1967 *NZ*, 1969 *S, I, F, E, NZ* 1,2
Thomas, C (Bridgend) 1925 *E, S*
Thomas, C J (Newport) 1888 *I, M*, 1889 *S, I*, 1890 *S, E, I*, 1891 *E, I*
Thomas, D (Aberavon) 1961 *I*
Thomas, D (Llanelli) 1954 *I*
Thomas, Dick (Mountain Ash) 1906 *SA*, 1908 *F, I*, 1909 *S*
Thomas, D J (Swansea) 1904 *E*, 1908 *A*, 1910 *E, S, I*, 1911 *E, S, F, I*, 1912 *E*
Thomas, D J (Swansea) 1930 *S, I*, 1932 *E, S, I*, 1933 *E, S*, 1934 *S*, 1935 *E, S, I*
Thomas, D L (Neath) 1937 *E*
Thomas, E (Newport) 1904 *S, I*, 1909 *S, F, I*, 1910 *F*
Thomas, G (Llanelli) 1923 *E, S, F, I*
Thomas, G (Newport) 1888 *M*, 1890 *I*, 1891 *S*
Thomas, H (Llanelli) 1912 *F*
Thomas, H (Neath) 1936 *E, S, I*, 1937 *E, S, I*
Thomas, H W (Swansea) 1912 *SA*, 1913 *E*

Thomas, I (Bryncethin) 1924 *E*
Thomas, L C (Cardiff) 1885 *E, S*
Thomas, M C (Newport, Devonport Services) 1949 *F*, 1950 *E, S, I, F*, 1951 *E, S, I, F, SA*, 1952 *E, S, I, F*, 1953 *E*, 1956 *E, S, I, F*, 1957 *E, S*, 1958 *E, S, I, F*, 1959 *I, F*
Thomas, M G (St Bart's Hospital) 1919 *NZA*, 1921 *S, F, I*, 1923 *F*, 1924 *E*
Thomas, R (Pontypool) 1909 *F, I*, 1911 *S, F*, 1912 *E, S, SA*, 1913 *E*
Thomas, R C C (Swansea) 1949 *F*, 1952 *I, F*, 1953 *S, I, F, NZ*, 1954 *E, I, F, S*, 1955 *S, I*, 1956 *E, S, I*, 1957 *E*, 1958 *A, E, S, I, F*, 1959 *E, S, I, F*
Thomas, R L (London Welsh) 1889 *S, I*, 1890 *I*, 1891 *E, S, I*, 1892 *E*
Thomas, S (Llanelli) 1890 *S, E*, 1891 *I*
Thomas, W D (Llanelli) 1966 *A*, 1968 *S, I, F*, 1969 *E, NZ 2, A*, 1970 *SA, S, E, I, F*, 1971 *E, S, I, F*, 1972 *E, S, F, NZ*, 1973 *E, S, I, F*, 1974 *E*
Thomas, W G (Llanelli, Waterloo, Swansea) 1927 *E, S, F, I*, 1929 *E*, 1931 *E, S, SA*, 1932 *E, S, I*, 1933 *E, S, I*
Thomas, W H (Llandovery Coll, Cambridge U) 1885 *S*, 1886 *E, S*, 1887 *E, S*, 1888 *S, I*, 1890 *E, I*, 1891 *S, I*
Thomas, W J (Cardiff) 1961 *F*, 1963 *F*
Thomas, W L (Newport) 1894 *S*, 1895 *E, I*
Thomas, W T (Abertillery) 1930 *E*
Thompson, J F (Cross Keys) 1923 *E*
Thorburn, P H (Neath) 1985 *F, E, Fj*, 1986 *E, S, I, F*, 1987 *F, [I, Tg, C, E, NZ, A]*, US, 1988 *S, I, F, WS, R* (R), 1989 *S, I, F, E, NZ*, 1990 *F, E, S, I, Nm* 1,2, *Bb*, 1991 *E, S, I, F1, A*
Titley, M H (Bridgend, Swansea) 1983 *R*, 1984 *S, I, F, E, A*, 1985 *S, I, Fj*, 1986 *F, Fj, Tg, WS*, 1990 *F, E*
Towers, W H (Swansea) 1887 *I*, 1888 *M*
Travers, G (Pill Harriers) 1903 *E, S, I*, 1905 *E, S, I, NZ*, 1906 *E, S, I, SA*, 1907 *E, S, I*, 1908 *E, S, F, I, A*, 1909 *E, S, I*, 1911 *S, F, I*
Travers, W H (Newport) 1937 *S, I*, 1938 *E, S, I*, 1939 *E, S, I*, 1949 *E, S, I, F*
Treharne, E (Pontypridd) 1881 *E*, 1883 *E*
Trew, W J (Swansea) 1900 *E, S, I*, 1901 *E, S*, 1903 *S*, 1905 *S*, 1906 *S*, 1907 *E, S*, 1908 *E, S, F, I, A*, 1909 *E, S, F, I*, 1910 *F, E, S*, 1911 *E, S, F, I*, 1912 *S*, 1913 *S, F*
Trott, R F (Cardiff) 1948 *E, S, F, I*, 1949 *E, S, I, F*
Truman, W H (Llanelli) 1934 *E*, 1935 *E*
Trump, L C (Newport) 1912 *E, S, I, F*
Turnbull, B R (Cardiff) 1925 *I*, 1927 *E, S*, 1928 *E, F*, 1930 *S*
Turnbull, M J L (Cardiff) 1933 *E, I*
Turner, P (Newbridge) 1989 *I* (R), *F, E*

Uzzell, H (Newport) 1912 *E, S, I, F*, 1913 *S, F, I*, 1914 *E, S, F, I*, 1920 *E, S, F, I*
Uzzell, J R (Newport) 1963 *NZ*, 1965 *E, S, I, F*

Vickery, W E (Aberavon) 1938 *E, S, I*, 1939 *E*
Vile, T H (Newport) 1908 *E, S*, 1910 *I*, 1912 *I, F, SA*, 1913 *E*, 1921 *S*
Vincent, H C (Bangor) 1882 *I*

Wakeford, J D M (S Wales Police) 1988 *WS, R*
Waldron, R (Neath) 1965 *E, S, I, F*
Waller, P D (Newport) 1908 *A*, 1909 *E, S, F, I*, 1910 *F*
Walters, N (Llanelli) 1902 *E*
Wanbon, R (Aberavon) 1968 *E*
Ward, W S (Cross Keys) 1934 *S, I*
Warlow, J (Llanelli) 1962 *I*
Waters, D R (Newport) 1986 *E, S, I, F*
Waters, K (Newbridge) 1991 *[WS]*
Watkins, D (Newport) 1963 *E, S, I, F, NZ*, 1964 *E, S, I, F, SA*, 1965 *E, S, I, F*, 1966 *E, S, I, F*, 1967 *I, F, E*
Watkins, E (Neath) 1924 *E, S, I, F*
Watkins, E (Blaina) 1926 *S, I, F*
Watkins, E (Cardiff) 1935 *NZ*, 1937 *S, I*, 1938 *E, S, I*, 1939 *E, S*
Watkins, H (Llanelli) 1904 *S, I*, 1905 *E, S, I*, 1906 *E*
Watkins, I J (Ebbw Vale) 1988 *E* (R), *S, I, F, NZ* 2, *R*, 1989 *S, I, F, E*
Watkins, L (Oxford U, Llandaff) 1881 *E*
Watkins, M J (Newport) 1984 *I, F, E, A*
Watkins, S J (Newport, Cardiff) 1964 *S, I, F*, 1965 *E, S, I, F*, 1966 *E, S, I, F, A*, 1967 *S, I, F, E, NZ*, 1968 *E, S*, 1969 *S, I, F, E, NZ* 1, 1970 *E, I*

Watkins, W R (Newport) 1959 *F*
Watts, D (Maesteg) 1914 *E, S, F, I*
Watts, J (Llanelli) 1907 *E, S, I*, 1908 *E, S, F, I, A*, 1909 *S, F, I*
Watts, W (Llanelli) 1914 *E*
Watts, W H (Newport) 1892 *E, S, I*, 1893 *E, S, I*, 1894 *E, S, I*, 1895 *E, I*, 1896 *E*
Weaver, D (Swansea) 1964 *E*
Webb, J (Abertillery) 1907 *S*, 1908 *E, S, F, I, A*, 1909 *E, S, F, I*, 1910 *F, E, S, I*, 1911 *E, S, F, I*, 1912 *E, S*
Webb, J E (Newport) 1888 *M*, 1889 *S*
Webbe, G M C (Bridgend) 1986 *Tg* (R), 1987 *F, E, S, [Tg]*, US, 1988 *F* (R), *NZ* 1, *R*
Webster, R E (Swansea) 1987 *[A]*, 1990 *Bb*, 1991 *[Arg, A]*, 1992 *I, F, E, S*
Wells, G T (Cardiff) 1955 *E, S*, 1957 *I, F*, 1958 *A, E, S*
Westacott, D (Cardiff) 1906 *I*
Wetter, H (Newport) 1912 *SA*, 1913 *E*
Wetter, J J (Newport) 1914 *S, F, I*, 1920 *E, S, F, I*, 1921 *E*, 1924 *I, NZ*
Wheel, G A D (Swansea) 1974 *I, E* (R), 1975 *F, E, I, A*, 1976 *E, S, I, F*, 1977 *I, E, S*, 1978 *E, S, I, F, A* 1,2, *NZ*, 1979 *S, I*, 1980 *F, E, S, I*, 1981 *E, S, I, F, A*, 1982 *I*
Wheeler, P J (Aberavon) 1967 *NZ*, 1968 *E*
Whitefoot, J (Cardiff) 1984 *A* (R), 1985 *S, I, F, E, Fj*, 1986 *E, S, I, F, Fj, Tg, WS*, 1987 *F, E, S, I, [I, C]*
Whitfield, J (Newport) 1919 *NZA*, 1920 *E, S, F, I*, 1921 *E*, 1922 *E, S, I, F*, 1924 *S, I*
Whitson, G K (Newport) 1956 *F*, 1960 *S, I*
Williams, A (Bridgend) 1990 *Nm* 2(R)
Williams, B (Llanelli) 1920 *S, F, I*
Williams, B L (Cardiff) 1947 *E, S, I, F, A*, 1948 *E, S, F, I*, 1949 *E, S, I*, 1951 *I, SA*, 1952 *S*, 1953 *E, S, I, F, NZ*, 1954 *S*, 1955 *E*
Williams, B R (Neath) 1990 *S, I, Bb*, 1991 *E, S*
Williams, C (Llanelli) 1924 *NZ*, 1925 *E*
Williams, C (Aberavon, Swansea) 1977 *E, S*, 1980 *F, E, S, I, NZ*, 1983 *E*
Williams, C D (Cardiff, Neath) 1955 *F*, 1956 *F*
Williams, D (Ebbw Vale) 1963 *S, I, F*, 1964 *E, S, I, F, SA*, 1965 *E, S, I, F*, 1966 *E, S, I, A*, 1967 *F, E, NZ*, 1968 *E*, 1969 *S, I, F, E, NZ* 1,2, *A*, 1970 *SA, S, E, I*, 1971 *E, S, I, F*
Williams, D B (Newport, Swansea) 1978 *A* 1, 1981 *E, S*
Williams, E (Neath) 1924 *NZ*, 1925 *F*
Williams, E (Aberavon) 1925 *E, S*
Williams, F L (Cardiff) 1929 *S, F, I*, 1930 *E, S, I, F*, 1931 *F, I, SA*, 1932 *E, S, I*, 1933 *I*
Williams, G (Aberavon) 1936 *E, S, I*
Williams, G (London Welsh) 1950 *I, F*, 1951 *E, S, I, F, SA*, 1952 *E, S, I, F*, 1953 *NZ*, 1954 *E*
Williams, G (Bridgend) 1981 *I, F*, 1982 *E* (R), *S*
Williams, G P (Bridgend) 1980 *NZ*, 1981 *E, S, A*, 1982 *I*
Williams, J (Blaina) 1920 *E, S, F, I*, 1921 *S, F, I*
Williams, J F (London Welsh) 1905 *I, NZ*, 1906 *S, SA*
Williams, J J (Llanelli) 1973 *F* (R), *A*, 1974 *S, I, F, E*, 1975 *F, E, S, I, A*, 1976 *E, S, I, F*, 1977 *I, F, E, S*, 1978 *E, S, I, F, A* 1,2, *NZ*, 1979 *S, I, F, E*
Williams, J L (Cardiff) 1906 *SA*, 1907 *E, S, I*, 1908 *E, S, I, A*, 1909 *E, S, F, I*, 1910 *I*, 1911 *E, S, F, I*
Williams, J P R (London Welsh, Bridgend) 1969 *S, I, F, E, NZ* 1,2, *A*, 1970 *SA, S, E, I, F*, 1971 *E, S, I, F*, 1972 *E, S, F, NZ*, 1973 *E, S, I, F, A*, 1974 *S, I, F*, 1975 *F, E, S, I, A*, 1976 *E, S, I, F*, 1977 *I, F, E, S*, 1978 *E, S, I, F, A* 1,2, *NZ*, 1979 *S, I, F, E*, 1980 *NZ*, 1981 *E, S*
Williams, L (Llanelli, Cardiff) 1947 *E, S, F, I, A*, 1948 *I*, 1949 *E*
Williams, L H (Cardiff) 1957 *S, I, F*, 1958 *E, S, I, F*, 1959 *E, S, I*, 1961 *F*, 1962 *E, S*
Williams, M (Newport) 1923 *F*
Williams, O (Bridgend) 1990 *Nm* 2
Williams, O (Llanelli) 1947 *E, S, A*, 1948 *E, S, F, I*
Williams, R (Llanelli) 1954 *S*, 1957 *F*, 1958 *A*
Williams, R D G (Newport) 1881 *E*
Williams, R F (Cardiff) 1912 *SA*, 1913 *E, S*, 1914 *I*
Williams, R H (Llanelli) 1954 *I, F, S*, 1955 *S, I, F*, 1956 *E, S, I*, 1957 *E, S, I, F*, 1958 *A, E, S, I, F*, 1959 *E, S, I, F*, 1960 *E*
Williams, S (Llanelli) 1947 *E, S, F, I*, 1948 *S, F*
Williams, S A (Aberavon) 1939 *E, S, I*
Williams, T (Pontypridd) 1882 *I*
Williams, T (Swansea) 1888 *S, I*

Williams, T (Swansea) 1912 *I*, 1913 *F*, 1914 *E*, *S*, *F*, *I*
Williams, Tudor (Swansea) 1921 *F*
Williams, T G (Cross Keys) 1935 *S*, *I*, *NZ*, 1936 *E*, *S*, *I*, 1937 *S*, *I*
Williams, W A (Crumlin) 1927 *E*, *S*, *F*, *I*
Williams, W A (Newport) 1952 *I*, *F*, 1953 *E*
Williams, W E O (Cardiff) 1887 *S*, *I*, 1889 *S*, 1890 *S*, *E*
Williams, W H (Pontymister) 1900 *E*, *S*, *I*, 1901 *E*
Williams, W O G (Swansea, Devonport Services) 1951 *F*, *SA*, 1952 *E*, *S*, *I*, *F*, 1953 *E*, *S*, *I*, *F*, *NZ*, 1954 *E*, *I*, *F*, *S*, 1955 *E*, *S*, *I*, *F*, 1956 *E*, *S*, *I*
Williams, W P J (Neath) 1974 *I*, *F*
Williams-Jones, H (S Wales Police) 1989 *S*(R), 1990 *F*(R), *I*, 1991 *A*, 1992 *S*
Willis, W R (Cardiff) 1950 *E*, *S*, *I*, *F*, 1951 *E*, *S*, *I*, *F*, *SA*, 1952 *E*, *S*, 1953 *S*, *NZ*, 1954 *E*, *I*, *F*, *S*, 1955 *E*, *S*, *I*, *F*
Wiltshire, M L (Aberavon) 1967 *NZ*, 1968 *E*, *S*, *F*
Windsor, R W (Pontypool) 1973 *A*, 1974 *S*, *I*, *F*, *E*,

1975 *F*, *E*, *S*, *I*, *A*, 1976 *E*, *S*, *I*, *F*, 1977 *I*, *F*, *E*, *S*, 1978 *E*, *S*, *I*, *F*, *A* 1,2, *NZ*, 1979 *S*, *I*, *F*
Winfield, H B (Cardiff) 1903 *I*, 1904 *E*, *S*, *I*, 1905 *NZ*, 1906 *E*, *S*, *I*, 1907 *S*, *I*, 1908 *E*, *S*, *F*, *I*, *A*
Winmill, S (Cross Keys) 1921 *E*, *S*, *F*, *I*
Wintle, R V (London Welsh) 1988 *WS*(R)
Wooller, W (Sale, Cambridge U, Cardiff) 1933 *E*, *S*, *I*, 1935 *E*, *S*, *I*, *NZ*, 1936 *E*, *S*, *I*, 1937 *E*, *S*, *I*, 1938 *S*, *I*, 1939 *E*, *S*, *I*
Wyatt, M A (Swansea) 1983 *E*, *S*, *I*, *F*, 1984 *A*, 1985 *S*, *I*, 1987 *E*, *S*, *I*

Young, D (Swansea, Cardiff) 1987 [*E*, *NZ*], *US*, 1988 *E*, *S*, *I*, *F*, *NZ* 1,2, *WS*, *R*, 1989 *S*, *NZ*, 1990 *F*
Young, G A (Cardiff) 1886 *E*, *S*
Young, J (Harrogate, RAF, London Welsh) 1968 *S*, *I*, *F*, 1969 *S*, *I*, *F*, *E*, *NZ* 1, 1970 *E*, *I*, *F*, 1971 *E*, *S*, *I*, *F*, 1972 *E*, *S*, *F*, *NZ*, 1973 *E*, *S*, *I*, *F*

WELSH INTERNATIONAL RECORDS

Both team and individual records are for official Welsh international matches up to 31 March 1992.

TEAM RECORDS

Highest score
49 v France (49-14) 1910 Swansea
v individual countries
16 v Argentina (16-7) 1991 Cardiff
28 v Australia (28-3) 1975 Cardiff
40 v Canada (40-9) 1987 Invercargill
34 v England (34-21) 1967 Cardiff
49 v France (49-14) 1910 Swansea
40 v Fiji (40-3) 1985 Cardiff
34 v Ireland (34-9) 1976 Dublin
34 v Namibia (34-30) 1990 Windhoek
16 v N Zealand (16-19) 1972 Cardiff
9 v Romania (9-15) 1988 Cardiff
35 v Scotland (35-12) 1972 Cardiff
6 v S Africa (6-6) 1970 Cardiff
29 v Tonga (29-16) 1987 Palmerston North
46 v United States (46-0) 1987 Cardiff
32 v W Samoa (32-14) 1986 Apia

Biggest winning points margin
46 v United States (46-0) 1987 Cardiff
v individual countries
9 v Argentina (16-7) 1991 Cardiff
25 v Australia (28-3) 1975 Cardiff
31 v Canada (40-9) 1987 Invercargill
25 v England (25-0) 1905 Cardiff
42 v France (47-5) 1909 Colombes
37 v Fiji (40-3) 1985 Cardiff
29 v Ireland (29-0) 1907 Cardiff
9 v Namibia (18-9) 1990 Windhoek
5 v N Zealand (13-8) 1953 Cardiff
23 v Scotland (35-12) 1972 Cardiff

13 v Tonga (29-16) 1987 Palmerston North
46 v United States (46-0) 1987 Cardiff
22 v W Samoa (28-6) 1988 Cardiff
No wins v Romania or South Africa

Highest score by opposing team
63 Australia (6-63) 1991 Brisbane
v individual countries
7 Argentina (16-7) 1991 Cardiff
63 Australia (6-63) 1991 Brisbane
9 Canada (40-9) 1987 Invercargill
34 England (6-34) 1990 Twickenham
36 France (3-36) 1991 Paris
15 Fiji (22-15) 1986 Suva
21 Ireland { (24-21) 1979 Cardiff
(7-21) 1980 Dublin
(9-21) 1985 Cardiff
(21-21) 1991 Cardiff }
30 Namibia (34-30) 1990 Windhoek
54 N Zealand (9-54) 1988 Auckland
24 Romania (6-24) 1983 Bucharest
35 Scotland (10-35) 1924 Inverleith
24 S Africa (3-24) 1964 Durban
16 Tonga (29-16) 1987 Palmerston North
0 United States (46-0) 1987 Cardiff
16 W Samoa (13-16) 1991 Cardiff

Biggest losing points margin
49 v N Zealand (3-52) 1988 Christchurch

v individual countries
19 v Australia (9-28) 1984 Cardiff
28 v England (6-34) 1990 Twickenham
33 v France (3-36) 1991 Paris
16 v Ireland (3-19) 1925 Belfast
49 v N Zealand (3-52) 1988 Christchurch
18 v Romania (6-24) 1983 Bucharest
25 v Scotland (10-35) 1924 Inverleith
21 v S Africa (3-24) 1964 Durban
 3 v W Samoa (13-16) 1991 Cardiff
No defeats v Argentina, Canada, Fiji, Namibia, Tonga or United States

Most tries by Wales in an international
11 v France (47-5) 1909 Colombes

Most tries against Wales in an international
13 by England 1881 Blackheath

Most points by Wales in International Championship in a season – 102
in season 1975-76

Most tries by Wales in International Championship in a season – 21
in season 1909-10

INDIVIDUAL RECORDS

Most capped player
J P R Williams 55 1969-81
in individual positions
Full-back
J P R Williams 54(55)[1] 1969-81
Wing
K J Jones 44[2] 1947-57
Centre
S P Fenwick 30[3] 1975-81
Fly-half
C I Morgan 29[3] 1951-58
Scrum-half
G O Edwards 53 1967-78
Prop
G Price 41 1975-83
Hooker
B V Meredith 34 1954-62

Lock
A J Martin 34 1973-81
R L Norster 34 1982-89
Flanker
W D Morris 32(34)[4] 1967-74
No 8
T M Davies 38 1969-76
[1]*Williams won one cap as a flanker*
[2]*T G R Davies, 46 caps, won 35 as a wing, 11 as a centre*
[3]*M G Ring, 32 caps, won 27 at centre, 4 at fly-half and 1 as a full-back. P Bennett, 29 caps, played 25 times as a fly-half*
[4]*Morris won his first two caps as a No 8*

Longest international career
W J Trew
14 seasons 1899-1900 to 1912-13
T H Vile
14 seasons 1907-08   to 1920-21
H Tanner
14 seasons 1935-36   to 1948-49

Most consecutive Tests – 53★
G O Edwards 1967-78
★*entire career*

Most internationals as captain
A J Gould 18 1889-97

Most points in internationals – 304
P H Thorburn (37 matches) 1985-91

Most points in International Championship in a season – 52
P H Thorburn (4 matches) 1985-86

Most points in an international – 21
P H Thorburn v Barbarians 1990 Cardiff

Most tries in internationals – 20
G O Edwards (53 matches) 1967-78
T G R Davies (46 matches) 1966-78

Most tries in International Championship in a season – 6
R A Gibbs (4 matches) 1907-08
M C R Richards (4 matches) 1968-69

Most tries in an international – 4
W M Llewellyn* v England 1899 Swansea
R A Gibbs v France 1908 Cardiff
M C R Richards v England 1969 Cardiff
I C Evans v Canada 1987 Invercargill
*on first appearance

Most conversions in internationals – 43
P H Thorburn (37 matches) 1985-91

Most conversions in International Championship in a season – 11
J Bancroft (4 matches) 1908-09

Most conversions in an international – 8
J Bancroft v France 1910 Swansea

Most dropped goals in internationals – 13
J Davies (27 matches) 1985-88

Most penalty goals in internationals – 70
P H Thorburn (37 matches) 1985-91

Most penalty goals in International Championship in a season – 16
P H Thorburn (4 matches) 1985-86

Most points on major overseas tour – 64
M Rayer (3 matches) Namibia 1990

Most points in a tour match – 28
M Rayer v N Region 1990 Namibia
P Bennett scored 34 points v Japan in Tokyo in 1975, but this was not on a major tour

Most tries in a tour match – 3
M C R Richards v Otago 1969 Dunedin, NZ
S Fealey v Welwitschia 1990 Swakopmund, Namibia
Several others have scored 3 in matches on non-major tours

FRANCE – ODDLY OPTIMISTIC, ROUGH AND YET PROMISING

THE 1991-92 SEASON IN FRANCE
Bob Donahue *International Herald Tribune*

The French were good in 1987, and it is hard indeed to assure the succession of a good team. So the 1991 team was ordinary, as wilful England proved in the World Cup quarter-final in Paris. By February, when England came again, a much-changed French side was so fragile that it fell apart when the going got rough. England well deserved both of those wins: no serious Frenchman doubts that for an instant.

There was something odd about the optimism of the French going into the February clash. No fewer than eight of the starting side were appearing in their first Championship; two more came on as replacements, taking the green contingent to the extraordinary total of ten. And at the fateful scrum that resulted in a penalty try for England (a harsh decision, it seemed), two French back row forwards stood and left the shoving to the other six. The lack of realism was not all, of course; there was also a familiar lack of discipline. In September, the international referee Patrick Robin had warned the World Cup squad that French sides, unlike others, often concede penalties while going forward. In October, with a score of 10-10 and France advancing from a tapped penalty, Pascal Ondarts fell offside and gave Jonathan Webb the opportunity to kick England into the lead.

The sending-off offence committed by Grégoire Lascubé, a boot to the face, was the same offence that earned Kevin Moseley an early shower when France visited Cardiff in 1990. Stephen Hilditch was right to send Lascubé off. One was reminded of a prophetic warning given the previous July by assistant coach Jean Trillo, when violence marred France's matches in the United States and even one of the training sessions: 'This is the French disease, and one of these days it's going to cost us dear'.

All the same, the two England matches left some genuine bitterness in France. Time alone is unlikely to heal it; officialdom on both sides of the Channel will need to help. On the positive side, when referee Hilditch was invited back to France in April to handle a club championship match, all went well and the players of Nîmes and Montauban clapped him off. But the quote of the season belonged to Bernard Lapasset, the new president of the Federation, who declared at the dinner after the expulsions of Lascubé and Vincent Moscato: 'Somehow I feel a bit as if I had been sent off with them'.

The senior side played 13 Tests in the space of 12 months, from June 1991 to May 1992, of which ten were won. The French scored 44 tries and conceded 11. Forty-three players were capped, 17 of them for the first time. Scrum-half Fabien Galthié was one of six new caps in June

The French team which beat Wales at Cardiff Arms Park. L-R, back row: P Gimbert, V Moscato, G Lascubé, J-F Tordo, L Cabannes, M Cecillon, J-M Cadieu, C Mougeot; front row: P Saint-André, J-B Lafond, A Penaud, P Sella (capt), F Galthié, F Mesnel, S Viars.

against Romania, and flanker Jean-François Tordo made his debut in Colorado in July. Captain Serge Blanco (93 caps, 38 tries) and tight head Ondarts retired after the World Cup. So did Trillo and coach Daniel Dubroca, whose disgraceful treatment of the New Zealand referee David Bishop after the World Cup quarter-final against England was amazingly out of character.

Pierre Berbizier and Christophe Mombet were the new coaches, and Philippe Sella the new captain. The Championship introduced fly-half Alain Penaud, left wing Sébastien Viars (whose 24 points against Ireland set up a new record for the Championship), lock Christophe Mougeot, the South African-born No 8 Dries van Heerden and hooker Jean-Pierre Genet. Sella finished the Championship with 83 caps.

On 28 May, Sella was rested and Marc Cecillon assumed the captaincy. Romania were again the opponents, and the venue was interesting: Le Havre, where rugby arrived in France in 1872. Much was made of the 120-year span, as if to remind all and sundry that French rugby, despite its difficulties of the moment, is no young upstart. Tours to Argentina and Zimbabwe were to come next, before a keenly-awaited visit by South Africa in the autumn. Meanwhile, France Youth and France Universities had enjoyed unbeaten seasons, which was good news for the future.

The knock-out phase of the club championship produced many surprises. Reigning champions Bègles were the first to fall, eliminated by modest Chalon. In the second of the five knock-out rounds, Laurent Rodriguez led Dax in an upset of Toulouse. A poll of club coaches had tipped Toulouse and Agen as likely finalists, but Agen, too, disappeared: the executioners were Tarbes, coached by Philippe Dintrans. Racing Club lost to Grenoble, a brawny side who suddenly looked like future champions. Little Colomiers (with Galthié and Jean-Luc Sadourny) got past Perpignan. Chalon were no match for Castres.

In the quarter-finals Grenoble beat Dax, Biarritz defeated Bayonne, and Tarbes and Colomiers lost to Toulon and Castres respectively. Biarritz then knocked out Grenoble, which meant that Blanco would end his career at the Parc des Princes. Blanco had said before the World Cup that he dreamed of leading his one and only club to its first final since 1939, and now he had realised his dream. Toulon, with André Herrero as recently installed president, provided the opposition.

It was also the championship's centenary. In 1992, surviving captains and referees of finals across the years were flown to Paris for a gala occasion attended by President Mitterand. And what a fête it was! Toulon won a gem of a match by 19-14. Alain Ceccon, refereeing for the last time, gave a textbook lesson in the French style of sympathy mixed with rigour, aided by two sides whose only concern was to play the game at top speed. Three of Toulon's men were aged only 19. Blanco and his team-mates gave their all and then saluted Hueber and company as worthy champions, ending the season on a high note.

FRENCH INTERNATIONAL PLAYERS
(up to 31 March 1992)

ABBREVIATIONS

A – Australia; *Arg* – Argentina; *B* – British Forces and Home Union Teams; *C* – Canada; *Cz* – Czechoslovakia; *E* – England; *Fj* – Fiji; *G* – Germany; *I* – Ireland; *It* – Italy; *J* – Japan; *K* – New Zealand Services; *M* – Maoris; *NZ* – New Zealand; *R* – Romania; *S* – Scotland; *SA* – South Africa; *US* – United States of America; *W* – Wales; *Z* – Zimbabwe; (R) – Replacement. Entries in square brackets [ ] indicate appearances in the World Cup.

Club Abbreviations: ASF – Association Sportive Française; BEC – Bordeaux Etudiants Club; CASG – Club Athlétique des Sports Généraux; PUC – Paris Université Club; RCF – Racing Club de France; SB – Stade Bordelais; SBUC – Stade Bordelais Université Club; SCUF – Sporting Club Universitaire de France; SF – Stade Français; SOE – Stade Olympien des Etudiants; TOEC – Toulouse Olympique Employés Club.

Note: Years given for Five Nations' matches refer to second half of season, eg 1972 refers to season 1971-72. Years for all other matches refer to the actual year of the match. When a series has taken place, or more than one match has been played against a country in the same year, figures have been used to denote the particular matches in which players have featured. Thus 1967 *SA* 2,4 indicates that a player appeared in the second and fourth Tests of the 1967 series against South Africa. This list includes only those players who have appeared in FFR International Matches '*donnant droit au titre d'international*'.

Abadie, A (Pau) 1964 *I*
Abadie, A (Graulhet) 1965 *R*, 1967 *SA* 1,3,4, *NZ*, 1968 *S*, *I*
Abadie, L (Tarbes) 1963 *R*
Aguerre, R (Biarritz O) 1979 *S*
Aguilar, D (Pau) 1937 *G*
Aguirre, J-M (Bagnères) 1971 *A* 2, 1972 *S*, 1973 *W*, *I*, *J*, *R*, 1974 *I*, *W*, *Arg* 2, *R*, *SA* 1, 1976 *W* (R), *E*, *US*, *A* 2, *R*, 1977 *W*, *E*, *S*, *I*, *Arg* 1,2, *NZ* 1,2, *R*, 1978 *E*, *S*, *I*, *W*, *R*, 1979 *I*, *W*, *E*, *S*, *NZ* 1,2, *R*, 1980 *W*, *I*
Ainciart, E (Bayonne) 1933 *G*, 1934 *G*, 1935 *G*, 1937 *G*, *It*, 1938 *G* 1
Albaladejo, P (Dax) 1954 *E*, *It*, 1960 *W*, *I*, *It*, *R*, 1961 *S*, *SA*, *E*, *W*, *I*, *NZ* 1,2, *A*, 1962 *S*, *E*, *W*, *I*, 1963 *S*, *I*, *E*, *W*, *It*, 1964 *S*, *NZ*, *W*, *It*, *I*, *SA*, *Fj*
Alvarez, A-J (Tyrosse) 1945 *B* 2, 1946 *B*, *I*, *K*, *W*, 1947 *S*, *I*, *W*, *E*, 1948 *I*, *A*, *S*, *W*, *E*, 1949 *I*, *E*, 1951 *S*, *E*, *W*
Amand, H (SF) 1906 *NZ*
Ambert, A (Toulouse) 1930 *S*, *I*, *E*, *G*, *W*
Amestoy, J-B (Mont-de-Marsan) 1964 *NZ*, *E*
André, G (RCF) 1913 *SA*, *E*, *W*, *I*, 1914 *I*, *W*, *E*
Andrieu, M (Nîmes) 1986 *Arg* 2, *NZ* 1, *R* 2, *NZ* 2, 1987 [*R*, *Z*], *R*, 1988 *E*, *S*, *I*, *W*, *Arg* 1,2,3,4, *R*, 1989 *I*, *W*, *E*, *S*, *NZ* 2, *B*, *A* 2, 1990 *W*, *E*, *I*(R)
Anduran, J (SCUF) 1910 *W*
Araou, R (Narbonne) 1924 *R*
Arcalis, R (Brive) 1950 *S*, *I*, 1951 *I*, *E*, *W*
Arino, M (Agen) 1962 *R*
Aristouy, P (Pau) 1948 *S*, 1949 *Arg* 2, 1950 *S*, *I*, *E*, *W*
Armary, L (Lourdes) 1987 [*R*], *R*, 1988 *S*, *I*, *W*, *Arg* 3,4, *R*, 1989 *W*, *S*, *A* 1,2, 1990 *W*, *E*, *S*, *I*, *A* 1,2,3, *NZ* 1, 1991 *W2*, 1992 *S*, *I*
Arnal, J-M (RCF) 1914 *I*, *W*
Arnaudet, M (Lourdes) 1964 *I*, 1967 *It*, *W*
Arotca, R (Bayonne) 1938 *R*
Arrieta, J (SF) 1953 *E*, *W*
Arthapignet, P (see Harislur-Arthapignet)
Astre, R (Béziers) 1971 *R*, 1972 *I* 1, 1973 *E* (R), 1975 *E*, *S*, *I*, *SA* 1,2, *Arg* 2, 1976 *A* 2, *R*
Augé, J (Dax) 1929 *S*, *W*
Augras-Fabre, L (Agen) 1931 *I*, *S*, *W*
Averous, J-L (La Voulte) 1975 *S*, *I*, *SA* 1,2, 1976 *I*, *W*, *E*, *US*, *A* 2, 1977 *W*, *E*, *S*, *I*, *Arg* 1, *R*, 1978 *E*, *S*, *I*, 1979 *NZ* 1,2, 1980 *E*, *S*, 1981 *A* 2
Azarete, J-L (Dax, St Jean-de-Luz) 1969 *W*, *R*, 1970 *S*, *I*, *W*, *R*, 1971 *S*, *I*, *E*, *SA* 1,2, *A* 1, 1972 *E*, *W*, *I* 2, *A* 1, *R*, 1973 *NZ*, *W*, *I*, *R*, 1974 *I*, *R*, *SA* 1,2, 1975 *W*

Bader, E (Primevères) 1926 *M*, 1927 *I*, *S*
Badin, C (Chalon) 1973 *W*, *I*, 1975 *Arg* 1
Baillette, M (Perpignan) 1925 *I*, *NZ*, *S*, 1926 *W*, *M*, 1927 *I*, *W*, *G* 2, 1929 *G*, 1930 *S*, *I*, *E*, *G*, 1931 *I*, *S*, *E*, 1932 *G*
Baladié, G (Agen) 1945 *B* 1,2, *W*, 1946 *B*, *I*, *K*
Ballarin, J (Tarbes) 1924 *E*, 1925 *NZ*, *S*
Baquey, J (Toulouse) 1921 *I*
Barbazanges, A (Roanne) 1932 *G*, 1933 *G*

Barrau, M (Beaumont, Toulouse) 1971 *S*, *E*, *W*, 1972 *E*, *W*, *A* 1,2, 1973 *S*, *NZ*, *E*, *I*, *J*, *R*, 1974 *I*, *S*
Barrère, P (Toulon) 1929 *G*, 1931 *W*
Barrière, R (Béziers) 1960 *R*
Barthe, E (SBUC) 1925 *W*, *E*
Barthe, J (Lourdes) 1954 *Arg* 1,2, 1955 *S*, 1956 *I*, *W*, *It*, *E*, *Cz*, 1957 *S*, *I*, *E*, *W*, *R* 1,2, 1958 *S*, *E*, *A*, *W*, *It*, *I*, *SA* 1,2, 1959 *S*, *E*, *It*, *W*
Basauri, R (Albi) 1954 *Arg* 1
Bascou, P (Bayonne) 1914 *E*
Basquet, G (Agen) 1945 *W*, 1946 *B*, *I*, *K*, *W*, 1947 *S*, *I*, *W*, *E*, 1948 *I*, *A*, *S*, *W*, *E*, 1949 *S*, *I*, *E*, *W*, *Arg* 1, 1950 *S*, *I*, *E*, *W*, 1951 *S*, *I*, *E*, *W*, 1952 *S*, *I*, *SA*, *W*, *E*, *It*
Bastiat, J-P (Dax) 1969 *R*, 1970 *S*, *I*, *W*, 1971 *SA* 2, 1972 *S*, *A* 1, 1973 *E*, 1974 *Arg* 1,2, *SA* 2, 1975 *W*, *Arg* 1,2, *R*, 1976 *S*, *I*, *W*, *E*, *A* 1,2, *R*, 1977 *W*, *E*, *S*, *I*, 1978 *E*, *S*, *I*, *W*
Baudry, N (Montferrand) 1949 *S*, *I*, *W*, *Arg* 1,2
Baulon, R (Vienne, Bayonne) 1954 *S*, *NZ*, *E*, *It*, 1955 *I*, *E*, *W*, *It*, 1956 *S*, *I*, *W*, *It*, *E*, *Cz*, 1957 *S*, *I*, *It*
Baux, J-P (Lannemezan) 1968 *NZ* 1,2, *SA* 1,2
Bavozet, J (Lyon) 1911 *S*, *E*, *W*
Bayard, J (Toulouse) 1923 *S*, *W*, *E*, 1924 *W*, *R*, *US*
Bayardon, J (Chalon) 1964 *S*, *NZ*, *E*
Beaurin-Gressier, C (SF) 1907 *E*, 1908 *E*
Bégu, J (Dax) 1982 *Arg* 2 (R), 1984 *E*, *S*
Béguerie, C (Agen) 1979 *NZ* 1
Beguet, L (RCF) 1922 *I*, 1923 *S*, *W*, *E*, *I*, 1924 *S*, *I*, *E*, *R*, *US*
Behoteguy, A (Bayonne, Cognac) 1923 *E*, 1924 *S*, *I*, *E*, *W*, *R*, *US*, 1926 *E*, 1927 *E*, *G* 1,2, 1928 *A*, *I*, *E*, *G*, *W*, 1929 *S*, *W*, *E*
Behoteguy, H (RCF, Cognac) 1923 *W*, 1928 *A*, *I*, *E*, *G*, *W*
Belascain, C (Bayonne) 1977 *R*, 1978 *E*, *S*, *I*, *W*, 1979 *I*, *W*, *E*, *S*, 1982 *W*, *E*, *S*, *I*, 1983 *E*, *S*, *I*, *W*
Belletante, G (Nantes) 1951 *I*, *E*, *W*
Benazzi, A (Agen) 1990 *A* 1,2,3, *NZ* 1,2, 1991 *E*, *US1*(R),2, [*R*, *Fj*, *C*]
Bénésis, R (Narbonne) 1969 *W*, *R*, 1970 *S*, *I*, *W*, *E*, *R*, 1971 *S*, *I*, *E*, *W*, *A* 2, *R*, 1972 *S*, *I* 1, *E*, *W*, *I* 2, *A* 1, *R*, 1973 *NZ*, *E*, *W*, *I*, *J*, *R*, 1974 *I*, *W*, *E*, *S*
Benetière, J (Roanne) 1954 *It*, *Arg* 1
Benetton, P (Agen) 1989 *B*, 1990 *NZ* 2, 1991 *US2*
Berbizier, P (Lourdes, Agen) 1981 *S*, *I*, *W*, *E*, *NZ* 1,2, 1982 *I*, *R*, 1983 *S*, *I*, 1984 *S* (R), *NZ* 1,2, 1985 *Arg* 1,2, 1986 *S*, *I*, *W*, *E*, *R* 1, *Arg* 1, *A*, *NZ* 1, *R* 2, *NZ* 2,3, 1987 *W*, *E*, *S*, *I*, [*S*, *R*, *Fj*, *A*, *NZ*], *R*, 1988 *E*, *S*, *I*, *W*, *Arg* 1,2, 1989 *I*, *W*, *E*, *S*, *NZ* 1,2, *B*, *A* 1, 1990 *W*, *E*, 1991 *S*, *I*, *W1*, *E*
Berejnoi, J-C (Tulle) 1963 *R*, 1964 *S*, *W*, *It*, *I*, *SA*, *Fj*, *R*, 1965 *S*, *I*, *E*, *W*, *It*, *R*, 1966 *S*, *I*, *E*, *W*, *It*, 1967 *S*, *A*, *E*, *It*, *W*, *I*, *R*
Berges, B (Toulouse) 1926 *I*
Berges-Cau, R (Lourdes) 1976 *E* (R)
Bergese, F (Bayonne) 1936 *G* 2, 1937 *G*, *It*, 1938 *G* 1, *R*, *G* 2
Bergougnan, Y (Toulouse) 1945 *B* 1, *W*, 1946 *B*, *I*, *K*,

W, 1947 *S*, *I*, *W*, *E*, 1948 *S*, *W*, *E*, 1949 *S*, *E*, *Arg* 1,2
Bernard, R (Bergerac) 1951 *S*, *I*, *E*, *W*
Bernon, J (Lourdes) 1922 *I*, 1923 *S*
Bérot, J-L (Toulouse) 1968 *NZ* 3, *A*, 1969 *S*, *I*, 1970 *E*, *R*, 1971 *S*, *I*, *E*, *W*, *SA* 1,2, *A* 1,2, *R*, 1972 *S*, *I* 1, *E*, *W*, *A* 1, 1974 *I*
Bérot, P (Agen) 1986 *R* 2, *NZ* 2,3, 1987 *W*, *E*, *S*, *I*, *R*, 1988 *E*, *S*, *I*, *Arg* 1,2,3,4, *R*, 1989 *S*, *NZ* 1,2
Bertrand, P (Bourg) 1951 *I*, *E*, *W*, 1953 *S*, *I*, *E*, *W*, *It*
Bertranne, R (Bagnères) 1971 *E*, *W*, *SA* 2, *A* 1,2, 1972 *S*, *I* 1, 1973 *NZ*, *E*, *J*, *R*, 1974 *I*, *W*, *E*, *S*, *Arg* 1,2, *R*, *SA* 1,2, 1975 *W*, *E*, *S*, *I*, *SA* 1,2, *Arg* 1,2, *R*, 1976 *S*, *I*, *W*, *E*, *US*, *A* 1,2, 1977 *W*, *E*, *S*, *I*, *Arg* 1,2, *NZ* 1,2, *R*, 1978 *E*, *S*, *I*, *W*, *R*, 1979 *I*, *W*, *E*, *S*, *R*, 1980 *W*, *E*, *S*, *I*, *SA*, *R*, 1981 *S*, *I*, *W*, *E*, *R*, *NZ* 1,2
Berty, D (Toulouse) 1990 *NZ* 2
Besset, E (Grenoble) 1924 *S*
Besset, L (SCUF) 1914 *W*, *E*
Besson, M (CASG) 1924 *I*, 1925 *I*, *E*, 1926 *S*, *W*, 1927 *I*
Besson, P (Brive) 1963 *S*, *I*, *E*, 1965 *R*, 1968 *SA* 1
Bianchi, J (Toulon) 1986 *Arg* 1
Bichindaritz, J (Biarritz O) 1954 *It*, *Arg* 1,2
Bidart, L (La Rochelle) 1953 *W*
Biemouret, P (Agen) 1969 *E*, *W*, 1970 *I*, *W*, *E*, 1971 *W*, *SA* 1,2, *A* 1, 1972 *E*, *W*, *I* 2, *A* 2, *R*, 1973 *S*, *NZ*, *E*, *W*, *I*
Biénès, R (Cognac) 1950 *S*, *I*, *E*, *W*, 1951 *S*, *I*, *E*, *W*, 1952 *S*, *I*, *SA*, *W*, *E*, *It*, 1953 *S*, *I*, *E*, 1954 *S*, *I*, *NZ*, *W*, *E*, *Arg* 1,2, 1956 *S*, *I*, *W*, *It*, *E*
Bigot, C (Quillan) 1930 *S*, *E*, 1931 *I*, *S*
Bilbao, L (St Jean de Luz) 1978 *I*, 1979 *I*
Billac, E (Bayonne) 1920 *S*, *E*, *W*, *I*, *US*, 1921 *S*, *W*, 1922 *W*, 1923 *E*
Billière, M (Toulouse) 1968 *NZ* 3
Bioussa, A (Toulouse) 1924 *W*, *US*, 1925 *I*, *NZ*, *S*, *E*, 1926 *S*, *I*, *E*, 1928 *E*, *G*, *W*, 1929 *I*, *S*, *W*, *E*, 1930 *S*, *I*, *E*, *G*, *W*
Bioussa, C (Toulouse) 1913 *W*, *I*, 1914 *I*
Biraben, M (Dax) 1920 *W*, *I*, *US*, 1921 *S*, *W*, *E*, *I*, 1922 *S*, *E*, *I*
Blain, A (Carcassonne) 1934 *G*
Blanco, S (Biarritz O) 1980 *SA*, *R*, 1981 *S*, *W*, *E*, *A* 1, 2, *R*, *NZ* 1,2, 1982 *W*, *E*, *S*, *I*, *R*, *Arg* 1,2, 1983 *E*, *S*, *I*, *W*, 1984 *I*, *W*, *E*, *S*, *NZ* 1,2, *R*, 1985 *E*, *S*, *I*, *W*, *Arg* 1,2, 1986 *S*, *I*, *W*, *E*, *R* 1, *Arg* 2, *A*, *NZ* 1, *R* 2, *NZ* 2,3, 1987 *W*, *E*, *S*, *I*, [*S*, *R*, *Fj*, *A*, *NZ*], *R*, 1988 *E*, *S*, *I*, *W*, *Arg* 1,2,3,4, *R*, 1989 *I*, *W*, *E*, *S*, *NZ* 1,2, *B*, *A* 1, 1990 *E*, *S*, *I*, *R*, *A* 1,2,3, *NZ* 1,2, 1991 *S*, *I*, *W*1, *E*, *R*, *US*1,2, *W*2, [*R*, *Fj*, *C*, *E*]
Blond, J (SF) 1935 *G*, 1936 *G* 2, 1937 *G*, 1938 *G* 1, *R*, *G* 2
Blond, X (RCF) 1990 *A* 3, 1991 *S*, *I*, *W*1, *E*
Boffelli, V (Aurillac) 1971 *A* 2, *R*, 1972 *S*, *I* 1, 1973 *J*, *R*, 1974 *I*, *W*, *E*, *S*, *Arg* 1,2, *R*, *SA* 1,2, 1975 *W*, *S*, *I*
Bonal, J-M (Toulouse) 1968 *E*, *W*, *Cz*, *NZ* 2,3, *SA* 1, 2, *R*, 1969 *S*, *I*, *E*, *R*, 1970 *W*, *E*
Bonamy, R (SB) 1928 *A*, *I*
Boniface, A (Mont-de-Marsan) 1954 *I*, *NZ*, *W*, *E*, *It*, *Arg* 1,2, 1955 *S*, *I*, 1956 *S*, *I*, *W*, *It*, *Cz*, 1957 *S*, *I*, *W*, *R* 2, 1958 *S*, *E*, 1959 *E*, 1961 *NZ* 1,3, *A*, *R*, 1962 *E*, *W*, *I*, *It*, *R*, 1963 *S*, *I*, *E*, *W*, *It*, *R*, 1964 *S*, *NZ*, *E*, *W*, *It*, 1965 *W*, *It*, *R*, 1966 *S*, *I*, *E*, *W*
Boniface, G (Mont-de-Marsan) 1960 *W*, *I*, *It*, *R*, *Arg* 1, 2,3, 1961 *S*, *SA*, *E*, *W*, *It*, *I*, *NZ* 1,2,3, *R*, 1962 *R*, 1963 *S*, *I*, *E*, *W*, *It*, *R*, 1964 *S*, 1965 *S*, *I*, *E*, *W*, *It*, *R*, 1966 *S*, *I*, *E*, *W*
Bonnes, E (Narbonne) 1924 *W*, *R*, *US*
Bonneval, E (Toulouse) 1984 *NZ* 2 (R), 1985 *W*, *Arg* 1, 1986 *W*, *E*, *R* 1, *Arg* 1,2, *A*, *R* 2, *NZ* 2,3, 1987 *W*, *E*, *S*, *I*, [*Z*], 1988 *E*
Bonnus, F (Toulon) 1950 *S*, *I*, *E*, *W*
Bonnus, M (Toulon) 1937 *It*, 1938 *G* 1, *R*, *G* 2, 1940 *B*
Bontemps, D (La Rochelle) 1968 *SA* 2
Borchard, G (RCF) 1908 *E*, 1909 *E*, *W*, *I*, 1911 *I*
Borde, F (RCF) 1920 *I*, *US*, 1921 *S*, *W*, *E*, 1922 *S*, *W*, 1923 *S*, *I*, 1924 *E*, 1925 *I*, 1926 *E*
Bordenave, L (Toulon) 1948 *A*, *S*, *W*, *E*, 1949 *S*
Boubée, J (Tarbes) 1921 *S*, *E*, *I*, 1922 *E*, *W*, 1923 *E*, *I*, 1925 *NZ*, *S*
Boudreaux, R (SCUF) 1910 *W*, *S*
Bouet, D (Dax) 1989 *NZ* 1,2, *B*, *A* 2, 1990 *A* 3
Bouguyon, G (Grenoble) 1961 *SA*, *E*, *W*, *It*, *I*, *NZ* 1,2, 3, *A*
Boujet, C (Grenoble) 1968 *NZ* 2, *A* (R), *SA* 1

Bouquet, J (Bourgoin, Vienne) 1954 *S*, 1955 *E*, 1956 *S*, *I*, *W*, *It*, *E*, *Cz*, 1957 *S*, *E*, *W*, *R* 2, 1958 *S*, *E*, 1959 *S*, *It*, *W*, *I*, 1960 *S*, *E*, *W*, *I*, *R*, 1961 *S*, *SA*, *E*, *W*, *It*, *I*, *R*, 1962 *S*, *E*, *W*, *I*
Bourdeu, J R (Lourdes) 1952 *S*, *I*, *SA*, *W*, *E*, *It*, 1953 *S*, *I*, *E*
Bourgarel, R (Toulouse) 1969 *R*, 1970 *S*, *I*, *E*, *R*, 1971 *W*, *SA* 1,2, 1973 *S*
Bourguignon, G (Narbonne) 1988 *Arg* 3, 1989 *I*, *E*, *B*, *A* 1, 1990 *R*
Bousquet, A (Béziers) 1921 *E*, *I*, 1924 *R*
Bousquet, R (Albi) 1926 *M*, 1927 *I*, *S*, *W*, *E*, *G* 1, 1929 *W*, *E*, 1930 *W*
Boyau, M (SBUC) 1912 *I*, *S*, *W*, *E*, 1913 *W*, *I*
Boyer, P (Toulon) 1935 *G*
Branca, G (SF) 1928 *S*, 1929 *I*, *S*
Branlat, A (RCF) 1906 *NZ*, *E*, 1908 *W*
Brejassou, R (Tarbes) 1952 *S*, *I*, *SA*, *W*, *E*, 1953 *W*, *E*, 1954 *S*, *I*, *NZ*, 1955 *S*, *I*, *E*, *W*, *It*
Brethes, R (St Sever) 1960 *Arg* 2
Bringeon, A (Biarritz O) 1925 *W*
Brun, G (Vienne) 1950 *E*, *W*, 1951 *S*, *E*, *W*, 1952 *S*, *I*, *SA*, *W*, *E*, *It*, 1953 *E*, *W*, *It*
Bruneau, M (SBUC) 1910 *W*, *E*, 1913 *SA*, *E*
Brunet, Y (Perpignan) 1975 *SA* 1, 1977 *Arg* 1
Buchet, E (Nice) 1980 *R*, 1982 *E*, *R* (R), *Arg* 1,2
Buisson, H (see Empereur-Buisson)
Buonomo, Y (Béziers) 1971 *A* 2, *R*, 1972 *I* 1
Burgun, M (RCF) 1909 *I*, 1910 *W*, *S*, *I*, 1911 *S*, *E*, 1912 *I*, *S*, 1913 *S*, *E*, 1914 *E*
Bustaffa, D (Carcassonne) 1977 *Arg* 1,2, *NZ* 1,2, 1978 *W*, *R*, 1980 *W*, *E*, *S*, *SA*, *R*
Buzy, C-E (Lourdes) 1946 *K*, *W*, 1947 *S*, *I*, *W*, *E*, 1948 *I*, *A*, *S*, *W*, *E*, 1949 *S*, *I*, *E*, *W*, *Arg* 1,2

Cabanier, J-M (Montauban) 1963 *R*, 1964 *S*, *Fj*, 1965 *S*, *I*, *W*, *It*, *R*, 1966 *S*, *I*, *E*, *W*, *It*, *R*, 1967 *S*, *A*, *E*, *It*, *W*, *I*, *SA* 1,3, *NZ*, *R*, 1968 *S*, *I*
Cabannes, L (RCF) 1990 *NZ* 2(R), 1991 *S*, *I*, *W*1, *E*, *US*2, *W*2, [*R*, *Fj*, *C*, *E*], 1992 *W*, *E*, *S*, *I*
Cabrol, H (Béziers) 1972 *A* 1 (R), *A* 2, 1973 *J*, 1974 *SA* 2
Cadenat, J (SCUF) 1910 *S*, *E*, 1911 *W*, *I*, 1912 *W*, *E*, 1913 *I*
Cadieu, J-M (Toulouse) 1991 *R*, *US*1, [*R*, *Fj*, *C*, *E*], 1992 *W*, *I*
Cahuc, F (St Girons) 1922 *S*
Cals, R (RCF) 1938 *G* 1
Calvo, G (Lourdes) 1961 *NZ* 1,3
Camberabero, D (La Voulte, Béziers) 1982 *R*, *Arg* 1,2, 1983 *E*, 1987 [*R*(R), *Z*, *Fj*(R), *A*, *NZ*], 1988 *I*, 1989 *B*, *A* 1, 1990 *W*, *S*, *I*, *R*, *A* 1,2,3, *NZ* 1,2, 1991 *S*, *I*, *W*1, *E*, *R*, *US*1,2, *W*2, [*R*, *Fj*, *C*]
Camberabero, G (La Voulte) 1961 *NZ* 3, 1962 *R*, 1964 *R*, 1967 *A*, *E*, *It*, *W*, *I*, *SA* 1,3,4, 1968 *S*, *E*, *W*
Camberabero, L (La Voulte) 1964 *R*, 1965 *S*, *I*, 1966 *E*, *W*, 1967 *A*, *E*, *It*, *W*, *I*, 1968 *S*, *E*, *W*
Cambré, T (Oloron) 1920 *E*, *W*, *I*, *US*
Camel, A (Toulouse) 1928 *S*, *A*, *I*, *E*, *G*, *W*, 1929 *W*, *E*, *G*, 1930 *S*, *I*, *E*, *G*, *W*, 1935 *G*
Camel, M (Toulouse) 1929 *S*, *W*, *E*
Camicas, F (Tarbes) 1927 *G* 2, 1928 *S*, *I*, *E*, *G*, *W*, 1929 *I*, *S*, *W*, *E*
Camo, E (Villeneuve) 1931 *I*, *S*, *W*, *E*, *G*, 1932 *G*
Campaes, A (Lourdes) 1965 *W*, 1967 *NZ*, 1968 *S*, *I*, *E*, *W*, *Cz*, *NZ* 1,2, *A*, 1969 *S*, *W*, 1972 *R*, 1973 *NZ*
Cantoni, J (Béziers) 1970 *W*, *R*, 1971 *S*, *I*, *E*, *W*, *SA* 1, 2, *A* 1, *R*, 1972 *S*, *I* 1, 1973 *S*, *NZ*, *W*, *I*, 1975 *W* (R)
Capdouze, J (Pau) 1964 *SA*, *Fj*, *R*, 1965 *S*, *I*, *E*
Capendeguy, J-M (Begles) 1967 *NZ*, *R*
Capitani, P (Toulon) 1954 *Arg* 1,2
Capmau, J-L (Toulouse) 1914 *E*
Carabignac, G (Agen) 1951 *S*, *I*, 1952 *SA*, *W*, *E*, 1953 *S*, *I*
Carbonne, J (Perpignan) 1927 *W*
Carminati, A (Béziers) 1986 *R* 2, *NZ* 2, 1987 [*R*, *Z*], 1988 *I*, *W*, *Arg* 1,2, 1989 *I*, *W*, *S*, *NZ* 1(R),2, *A* 2, 1990 *S*
Caron, L (Lyon O, Castres) 1947 *E*, 1948 *I*, *A*, *W*, *E*, 1949 *S*, *I*, *E*, *W*, *Arg* 1
Carpentier, M (Lourdes) 1980 *E*, *SA*, *R*, 1981 *S*, *I*, *A* 1, 1982 *E*, *S*
Carrère, C (Toulon) 1966 *R*, 1967 *S*, *A*, *E*, *W*, *I*, *SA* 1, 3,4, *NZ*, *R*, 1968 *S*, *I*, *E*, *W*, *Cz*, *NZ* 3, *A*, *R*, 1969 *S*, *I*, 1970 *S*, *I*, *W*, *E*, 1971 *E*, *W*

Carrère, J (Vichy, Toulon) 1956 *S*, 1957 *E*, *W*, *R* 2, 1958 *S*, *SA* 1,2, 1959 *I*
Carrère, R (Mont-de-Marsan) 1953 *E*, *It*
Casaux, L (Tarbes) 1959 *I*, *It*, 1962 *S*
Cassagne, P (Pau) 1957 *It*
Cassayet-Armagnac, A (Tarbes, Narbonne) 1920 *S*, *E*, *W*, *US*, 1921 *W*, *E*, *I*, 1922 *S*, *E*, *W*, 1923 *S*, *W*, *E*, *I*, 1924 *S*, *E*, *W*, *R*, *US*, 1925 *I*, *NZ*, *S*, *W*, 1926 *S*, *I*, *E*, *W*, *M*, 1927 *I*, *S*, *W*
Cassiède, M (Dax) 1961 *NZ* 3, *A*, *R*
Castets, J (Toulon) 1923 *W*, *E*, *I*
Caujolle, J (Tarbes) 1909 *E*, 1913 *SA*, *E*, 1914 *W*, *E*
Caunègre, R (SB) 1938 *R*, *G* 2
Caussade, A (Lourdes) 1978 *R*, 1979 *I*, *W*, *E*, *NZ* 1,2, *R*, 1980 *W*, *E*, *S*, 1981 *S* (R), *I*
Caussarieu, G (Pau) 1929 *I*
Cayrefourcq, E (Tarbes) 1921 *E*
Cazals, P (Mont-de-Marsan) 1961 *NZ* 1, *A*, *R*
Cazenave, A (Pau) 1927 *E*, *G* 1, 1928 *S*, *A*, *G*
Cazenave, F (RCF) 1950 *E*, 1952 *S*, 1954 *I*, *NZ*, *W*, *E*
Cecillon, M (Bourgoin) 1988 *I*, *W*, *Arg* 2,3,4, *R*, 1989 *I*, *E*, *NZ* 1,2, *A* 1, 1991 *S*, *I*, *E* (R), *R*, *US*1, *W*2, [*E*], 1992 *W*, *E*, *S*, *I*
Celaya, M (Biarritz O, SBUC) 1953 *E*, *W*, *It*, 1954 *I*, *E*, *It*, *Arg* 1,2, 1955 *S*, *I*, *E*, *W*, *It*, 1956 *S*, *I*, *W*, *It*, *E*, *Cz*, 1957 *S*, *I*, *E*, *W*, *R* 2, 1958 *S*, *E*, *A*, *W*, *It*, 1959 *S*, *E*, 1960 *S*, *E*, *W*, *I*, *R*, *Arg* 1,2,3, 1961 *S*, *SA*, *E*, *W*, *It*, *I*, *NZ* 1,2,3, *A*, *R*
Celhay, M (Bayonne) 1935 *G*, 1936 *G* 1, 1937 *G*, *It*, 1938 *G* 1, 1940 *B*
Cessieux, N (Lyon) 1906 *NZ*
Cester, E (TOEC, Valence) 1966 *S*, *I*, *E*, 1967 *W*, 1968 *S*, *I*, *E*, *W*, *Cz*, *NZ* 1,3, *A*, *SA* 1,2, *R*, 1969 *S*, *I*, *E*, *W*, 1970 *S*, *I*, *W*, *E*, 1971 *A* 1, 1972 *R*, 1973 *S*, *NZ*, *W*, *I*, *J*, *R*, 1974 *I*, *W*, *E*, *S*
Chaban-Delmas, J (CASG) 1945 *B* 2
Chabowski, H (Nice, Bourgoin) 1985 *Arg* 2, 1986 *R* 2, *NZ* 2, 1989 *B*(R)
Chadebech, P (Brive) 1982 *R*, *Arg* 1,2, 1986 *S*, *I*
Champ, E (Toulon) 1985 *Arg* 1,2, 1986 *I*, *W*, *E*, *R* 1, *Arg* 1,2, *A*, *NZ* 1, *R* 2, *NZ* 2,3, 1987 *W*, *E*, *S*, *I*, [*S*, *R*, *Fj*, *A*, *NZ*], *R*, 1988 *E*, *S*, *Arg* 1,3,4, *R*, 1989 *W*, *S*, *A* 1,2, 1990 *W*, *E*, *NZ* 1, 1991 *R*, *US*1, [*R*, *Fj*, *C*, *E*]
Chapuy, L (SF) 1926 *S*
Charpentier, G (SF) 1911 *E*, 1912 *W*, *E*
Charton, P (Montferrand) 1940 *B*
Charvet, D (Toulouse) 1986 *W*, *E*, *R* 1, *Arg* 1, *A*, *NZ* 1,3, 1987 *W*, *E*, *S*, *I*, [*S*, *R*, *Z*, *Fj*, *A*, *NZ*], 1989 *E*(R), 1990 *W*, *E*, 1991 *S*, *I*
Chassagne, J (Montferrand) 1938 *G* 1
Chatau, A (Bayonne) 1913 *SA*
Chaud, E (Toulon) 1932 *G*, 1934 *G*, 1935 *G*
Chenevay, C (Grenoble) 1968 *SA* 1
Chevallier, B (Montferrand) 1952 *S*, *I*, *SA*, *W*, *E*, *It*, 1953 *E*, *W*, *It*, 1954 *S*, *I*, *NZ*, *W*, *Arg* 1, 1955 *S*, *I*, *E*, *W*, *It*, 1956 *S*, *I*, *W*, *It*, *E*, *Cz*, 1957 *S*
Chiberry, J (Chambéry) 1955 *It*
Chilo, A (RCF) 1920 *S*, *W*, 1925 *I*, *NZ*
Cholley, G (Castres) 1975 *E*, *S*, *I*, *SA* 1,2, *Arg* 1,2, *R*, 1976 *S*, *I*, *W*, *E*, *A* 1,2, *R*, 1977 *W*, *E*, *S*, *I*, *Arg* 1,2, *NZ* 1,2, *R*, 1978 *E*, *S*, *I*, *W*, *R*, 1979 *I*, *S*
Choy, J (Narbonne) 1930 *S*, *I*, *E*, *G*, *W*, 1931 *I*, 1933 *G*, 1934 *G*, 1935 *G*, 1936 *G* 2
Cimarosti, J (Castres) 1976 *US* (R)
Clady, A (Lezignan) 1929 *G*, 1931 *I*, *S*, *E*, *G*
Clarac, H (St Girons) 1938 *G* 1
Claudel, R (Lyon) 1932 *G*, 1934 *G*
Clauzel, F (Béziers) 1924 *E*, *W*, 1925 *W*
Clavé, J (Agen) 1936 *G* 2, 1938 *R*, *G* 2
Claverie, H (Lourdes) 1954 *NZ*, *W*
Clément, G (RCF) 1931 *W*
Clément, J (RCF) 1921 *S*, *W*, *E*, 1922 *S*, *E*, *W*, *I*, 1923 *S*, *W*, *I*
Clemente, M (Oloron) 1978 *R*, 1980 *S*, *I*
Cluchague, L (Biarritz O) 1924 *S*, 1925 *E*
Coderc, J (Chalon) 1932 *G*, 1933 *G*, 1934 *G*, 1935 *G*, 1936 *G* 1
Codorniou, D (Narbonne) 1979 *NZ* 1,2, *R*, 1980 *W*, *E*, *S*, *I*, 1981 *S*, *W*, *E*, *A* 2, 1983 *E*, *S*, *I*, *W*, *A* 1,2, *R*, 1984 *I*, *W*, *E*, *S*, *NZ* 1,2, *R*, 1985 *E*, *S*, *I*, *W*, *Arg* 1,2
Cognet, L (Montferrand) 1932 *G*, 1936 *G* 1,2, 1937 *G*, *It*
Colombier, J (St Junien) 1952 *SA*, *W*, *E*
Colomine, G (Narbonne) 1979 *NZ* 1

Combe, J (SF) 1910 *S*, *E*, *I*, 1911 *S*
Combes, G (Fumel) 1945 *B* 2
Communeau, M (SF) 1906 *NZ*, *E*, 1907 *E*, 1908 *E*, *W*, 1909 *E*, *W*, *I*, 1910 *S*, *E*, *I*, 1911 *S*, *E*, *I*, 1912 *I*, *S*, *W*, *E*, 1913 *SA*, *E*, *W*
Condom, J (Boucau, Biarritz O) 1982 *R*, 1983 *E*, *S*, *I*, *W*, *A* 1,2, *R*, 1984 *I*, *W*, *E*, *S*, *NZ* 1,2, *R*, 1985 *E*, *S*, *I*, *W*, *Arg* 1,2, 1986 *S*, *I*, *W*, *E*, *R* 1, *Arg* 1, 2, *NZ* 1, *R* 2, *NZ* 2,3, 1987 *W*, *E*, *S*, *I*, [*S*, *R*, *Z*, *A*, *NZ*], *R*, 1988 *E*, *S*, *W*, *Arg* 1,2,3,4, *R*, 1989 *I*, *W*, *E*, *S*, *NZ* 1,2, *A* 1, 1990 *I*, *R*, *A* 2,3(R)
Conilh de Beyssac, J-J (SBUC) 1912 *I*, *S*, 1914 *I*, *W*, *E*
Constant, G (Perpignan) 1920 *W*
Coscolla, G (Béziers) 1921 *S*, *W*
Costantino, J (Montferrand) 1973 *R*
Costes, F (Montferrand) 1979 *E*, *S*, *NZ* 1,2, *R*, 1980 *W*, *I*
Coulon, E (Grenoble) 1928 *S*
Courtiols, M (Bègles) 1991 *R*, *US*1, *W*2
Crabos, R (RCF) 1920 *S*, *E*, *W*, *I*, *US*, 1921 *S*, *W*, *E*, *I*, 1922 *S*, *E*, *W*, *I*, 1923 *S*, *I*, 1924 *S*, *I*
Crampagne, J (Begles) 1967 *SA* 4
Crancee, R (Lourdes) 1960 *Arg* 3, 1961 *S*
Crauste, M (RCF, Lourdes) 1957 *R* 1,2, 1958 *S*, *E*, *A*, *W*, *It*, *I*, 1959 *E*, *It*, *W*, *I*, 1960 *S*, *E*, *W*, *I*, *It*, *R*, *Arg* 1, 3, 1961 *S*, *SA*, *E*, *W*, *It*, *I*, *NZ* 1,2,3, *A*, *R*, 1962 *S*, *E*, *W*, *I*, *It*, *R*, 1963 *S*, *I*, *E*, *W*, *It*, *R*, 1964 *S*, *NZ*, *E*, *W*, *It*, *I*, *SA*, *Fj*, *R*, 1965 *S*, *I*, *E*, *W*, *It*, *R*, 1966 *S*, *I*, *E*, *W*, *It*
Cremaschi, M (Lourdes) 1980 *R*, 1981 *R*, *NZ* 1,2, 1982 *W*, *S*, 1983 *A* 1,2, *R*, 1984 *I*, *W*
Crichton, W H (Le Havre) 1906 *NZ*, *E*
Cristina, J (Montferrand) 1979 *R*
Cussac, P (Biarritz O) 1934 *G*
Cutzach, A (Quillan) 1929 *G*

Daguerre, F (Biarritz O) 1936 *G* 1
Daguerre, J (CASG) 1933 *G*
Dal Maso, M (Mont-de Marsan) 1988 *R*(R), 1990 *NZ* 2
Danion, J (Toulon) 1924 *I*
Danos, P (Toulon, Béziers) 1954 *Arg* 1,2, 1957 *R* 2, 1958 *S*, *E*, *W*, *It*, *I*, *SA* 1,2, 1959 *S*, *E*, *It*, *W*, *I*, 1960 *S*, *E*
Darbos, P (Dax) 1969 *R*
Darracq, R (Dax) 1957 *It*
Darrieussecq, A (Biarritz O) 1973 *E*
Darrieussecq, J (Mont-de-Marsan) 1953 *It*
Darrouy, C (Mont-de-Marsan) 1957 *I*, *E*, *W*, *It*, *R* 1, 1959 *E*, 1961 *R*, 1963 *S*, *I*, *E*, *W*, *It*, 1964 *NZ*, *E*, *W*, *It*, *I*, *SA*, *Fj*, *R*, 1965 *S*, *I*, *E*, *W*, *It*, 1966 *S*, *I*, *E*, *W*, *It*, *R*, 1967 *S*, *A*, *E*, *It*, *W*, *I*, *SA* 1,2,4
Daudignon, G (SF) 1928 *S*
Dauga, B (Mont-de-Marsan) 1964 *S*, *NZ*, *E*, *W*, *It*, *I*, *SA*, *Fj*, *R*, 1965 *S*, *I*, *E*, *W*, *It*, *R*, 1966 *S*, *I*, *E*, *W*, *It*, *R*, 1967 *S*, *A*, *E*, *It*, *W*, *I*, *SA* 1,2,3,4, *NZ*, *R*, 1968 *S*, *I*, *NZ* 1,2,3, *A*, *SA* 1,2, *R*, 1969 *S*, *I*, *E*, *R*, 1970 *S*, *I*, *W*, *E*, *R*, 1971 *S*, *I*, *E*, *W*, *A* 1,2, *R*, 1972 *S*, *I* 1, *W*
Dauger, J (Bayonne) 1945 *B* 1,2, 1953 *S*
Daulouede, P (Tyrosse) 1937 *G*, *It*, 1938 *G* 1, 1940 *B*
Decamps, P (RCF) 1911 *S*
Dedet, J (SF) 1910 *S*, *E*, *I*, 1911 *W*, *I*, 1912 *S*, 1913 *E*, *I*
Dedeyn, P (RCF) 1906 *NZ*
Dedieu, P (Béziers) 1963 *E*, *It*, 1964 *W*, *It*, *I*, *SA*, *Fj*, *R*, 1965 *S*, *I*, *E*, *W*
De Gregorio, J (Grenoble) 1960 *S*, *E*, *W*, *I*, *It*, *R*, *Arg* 1,2, 1961 *S*, *SA*, *E*, *W*, *It*, *I*, 1962 *S*, *E*, *W*, 1963 *S*, *W*, *It*, 1964 *NZ*, *E*
Dehez, J-L (Agen) 1967 *SA* 2, 1969 *R*
de Jouvencel, E (SF) 1909 *W*, *I*
de Laborderie, M (RCF) 1921 *I*, 1922 *I*, 1925 *W*, *E*
Delage, C (Agen) 1983 *S*, *I*
de Malherbe, H (CASG) 1932 *G*, 1933 *G*
de Malmann, R (RCF) 1908 *E*, *W*, 1909 *E*, *W*, *I*, 1910 *E*, *I*
de Muizon, J J (SF) 1910 *I*
Delaigue, G (Toulon) 1973 *J*, *R*
Delque, A (Toulouse) 1937 *It*, 1938 *G* 1, *R*, *G* 2
Descamps, P (SB) 1927 *G* 2
Desclaux, F (RCF) 1949 *Arg* 1,2, 1953 *It*
Desclaux, J (Perpignan) 1934 *G*, 1935 *G*, 1936 *G* 1,2, 1937 *G*, *It*, 1938 *G* 1, *R*, *G* 2, 1945 *B* 1
Deslandes, C (RCF) 1990 *A* 1, *NZ* 2, 1991 *W*1
Desnoyer, L (Brive) 1974 *R*

Destarac, L (Tarbes) 1926 *S, I, E, W, M*, 1927 *W, E, G* 1,2
Desvouges, R (SF) 1914 *W*
Detrez, P-E (Nîmes) 1983 *A* 2 (R), 1986 *Arg* 1(R),2, *A* (R), *NZ* 1
Devergie, T (Nîmes) 1988 *R*, 1989 *NZ* 1,2, *B, A* 2, 1990 *W, E, S, I, R, A* 1,2,3, 1991 *US*2, *W*2
Deygas, M (Vienne) 1937 *It*
Dintrans, P (Tarbes) 1979 *NZ* 1,2, *R*, 1980 *E, S, I, SA, R*, 1981 *S, I, W, E, A* 1,2, *R, NZ* 1,2, 1982 *W, E, S, I, R, Arg* 1,2, 1983 *E, W, A* 1,2, *R*, 1984 *I, W, E, S, NZ* 1,2, *R*, 1985 *E, S, I, W, Arg* 1,2, 1987 [*R*], 1988 *Arg* 1,2,3, 1989 *W, E, S*, 1990 *R*
Dizabo, P (Tyrosse) 1948 *A, S, E*, 1949 *S, I, E, W, Arg* 2, 1950 *S, I*, 1960 *Arg* 1,2,3
Domec, A (Carcassonne) 1929 *W*
Domec, H (Lourdes) 1953 *W, It*, 1954 *S, I, NZ, W, E, It*, 1955 *S, I, E, W*, 1956 *I, W, It*, 1958 *E, A, W, It, I* 1,2, 1958 *S, E, It*, 1959 *It*, 1960 *S, E, W, I, It, R, Arg* 1,2,3, 1961 *S, SA, E, W, It, I, NZ* 1,2,3, *A, R*, 1962 *S, E, W, I, It, R*, 1963 *W, It*
Domecq, J (Bayonne) 1912 *I, S*
Dorot, J (RCF) 1935 *G*
Dospital, P (Bayonne) 1977 *R*, 1980 *I*, 1981 *S, I, W, E*, 1982 *I, R, Arg* 1,2, 1983 *E, S, I, W*, 1984 *E, S, NZ* 1,2, *R*, 1985 *E, S, I, W, Arg* 1
Dourthe, C (Dax) 1966 *R*, 1967 *S, A, E, W, I, SA* 1,2, 3, *NZ*, 1968 *W, NZ* 3, *SA* 1,2, 1969 *W*, 1971 *SA* 2 (R), *R*, 1972 *I* 1,2, *A* 1,2, *R*, 1973 *S, NZ, E*, 1974 *I, Arg* 1,2, *SA* 1,2, 1975 *W, E, S*
Doussau, E (Angoulême) 1938 *R*
Droitecourt, M (Montferrand) 1972 *R*, 1973 *NZ* (R), *E*, 1974 *E, S, Arg* 1, *SA* 2, 1975 *SA* 1,2, *Arg* 1,2, *R*, 1976 *S, I, W, A* 1, 1977 *Arg* 2
Dubertrand, A (Montferrand) 1971 *A* 2, *R*, 1972 *I* 2, 1974 *I, W, E, SA* 2, 1975 *Arg* 1,2, *R*, 1976 *S, US*
Dubois, D (Bègles) 1971 *S*
Dubroca, D (Agen) 1979 *NZ* 2, 1980 *NZ* 2 (R), 1982 *E, S*, 1984 *W, E, S*, 1985 *Arg* 2, 1986 *S, I, W, E, R* 1, *Arg* 2, *A, NZ* 1, *R* 2, *NZ* 2,3, 1987 *W, E, S, I*, [*S, Z, Fj, A, NZ*], *R*, 1988 *E, S, I, W*
Duché, A (Limoges) 1929 *G*
Duclos, A (Lourdes) 1931 *S*
Ducousso, J (Tarbes) 1925 *S, W, E*
Dufau, G (RCF) 1948 *I, A*, 1949 *I, W*, 1950 *S, E, W*, 1951 *S, I, E, W*, 1952 *SA, W*, 1953 *S, I, E, W*, 1954 *S, I, NZ, W, E, It*, 1955 *S, I, E, W, It*, 1956 *S, I, W, It*, 1957 *S, I, E, W, It, R* 1
Dufau, J (Biarritz) 1912 *I, S, W, E*
Duffaut, Y (Agen) 1954 *Arg* 1,2
Duffour, R (Tarbes) 1911 *W*
Dufourcq, J (SBUC) 1906 *NZ, E*, 1907 *E*, 1908 *W*
Duhard, Y (Bagnères) 1980 *E*
Duhau, J (SF) 1928 *I*, 1930 *I, G*, 1931 *I, S, W*, 1933 *G*
Dulaurens, C (Toulouse) 1926 *I*, 1928 *S*, 1929 *W*
Duluc, A (Béziers) 1934 *G*
Du Manoir, Y LeP (RCF) 1925 *I, NZ, S, W, E*, 1926 *S*, 1927 *I, S*
Dupont, C (Lourdes) 1923 *S, W, I*, 1924 *S, I, W, R, US*, 1925 *S*, 1927 *E, G* 1,2, 1928 *A, G, W*, 1929 *I*
Dupont, J-L (Agen) 1983 *S*
Dupont, L (RCF) 1934 *G*, 1935 *G*, 1936 *G* 1,2, 1938 *R, G* 2
Dupouy, A (SB) 1924 *W, R*
Duprat, B (Bayonne) 1966 *E, W, It, R*, 1967 *S, A, E, SA* 2,3, 1968 *S, I*, 1972 *E, W, I* 2, *A* 1
Dupré, P (RCF) 1909 *W*
Dupuy, J (Tarbes) 1956 *S, I, W, It, E, Cz*, 1957 *S, I, E, W, It, R* 2, 1958 *S, E, SA* 1,2, 1959 *S, E, It, W, I*, 1960 *W, I, It, Arg* 1,3, 1961 *S, SA, E, NZ* 2, *R*, 1962 *S, E, W, I, It*, 1963 *W, It, R*, 1964 *S*
Du Souich, C J (see Judas du Souich)
Dutin, B (Mont-de-Marsan) 1968 *NZ* 2, *A, SA* 2, *R*
Dutour, F X (Toulouse) 1911 *E, I*, 1912 *S, W, E*, 1913 *S*
Dutrain, H (Toulouse) 1945 *W*, 1946 *B, I*, 1947 *E*, 1949 *I, E, W, Arg* 1
Dutrey, J (Lourdes) 1940 *B*
Duval, R (SF) 1908 *E, W*, 1909 *E*, 1911 *E, W, I*

Echavé, L (Agen) 1961 *S*
Elissalde, E (Bayonne) 1936 *G* 2, 1940 *B*

Elissalde, J-P (La Rochelle) 1980 *SA, R*, 1981 *A* 1,2, *R*
Empereur-Buisson, H (Béziers) 1931 *E, G*
Erbani, D (Agen) 1981 *A* 1,2, *NZ* 1,2, 1982 *Arg* 1,2, 1983 *S* (R), *I, W, A* 1,2, *R*, 1984 *W, E, R*, 1985 *E, W*(R), *Arg* 2, 1986 *S, I, W, E, R* 1, *Arg* 2, *NZ* 1,2(R), 3, 1987 *W, E, S, I*, [*S, R, Fj, A, NZ*], 1988 *E, S*, 1989 *I*(R), *W, E, S, NZ* 1, *A* 2, 1990 *W, E*
Escaffre, P (Narbonne) 1933 *G*, 1934 *G*
Escommier, M (Montelimar) 1955 *It*
Esponda, J-M (RCF) 1967 *SA* 1,2, *R*, 1968 *NZ* 1,2, *SA* 2, *R*, 1969 *S, I*(R), *E*
Estève, A (Béziers) 1971 *SA* 1, 1972 *I* 1, *E, W, I* 2, *A* 2, *R*, 1973 *S, NZ, E, I*, 1974 *I, W, E, S, R, SA* 1,2, 1975 *W, E*
Estève, P (Narbonne, Lavelanet) 1982 *R, Arg* 1,2, 1983 *E, S, I, W, A* 1,2, *R*, 1984 *I, W, E, S, NZ* 1,2, *R*, 1985 *E, S, I, W*, 1986 *S, I*, 1987 [*S, Z*]
Etcheberry, J (Rochefort, Cognac) 1923 *W, I*, 1924 *S, I, E, W, R, US*, 1926 *S, I, E, M*, 1927 *I, S, W, G* 2
Etchenique, J-M (Biarritz O) 1974 *R, SA* 1, 1975 *E, Arg* 2
Etchepare, A (Bayonne) 1922 *I*
Etcheverry, M (Pau) 1971 *S, I*
Eutrope, A (SCUF) 1913 *I*

Fabre, E (Toulouse) 1937 *It*, 1938 *G* 1,2
Fabre, J (Toulouse) 1963 *S, I, E, W, It*, 1964 *S, NZ, E*
Fabre, L (Lezignan) 1930 *G*
Fabre, M (Béziers) 1981 *A* 1, *R, NZ* 1,2, 1982 *I, R*
Failliot, P (RCF) 1911 *S, W, I*, 1912 *I, S, E*, 1913 *E, W*
Fargues, G (Dax) 1923 *I*
Fauré, F (Tarbes) 1914 *I, W, E*
Fauvel, J-P (Tulle) 1980 *R*
Favre, M (Lyon) 1913 *E, W*
Ferrand, L (Chalon) 1940 *B*
Ferrien, R (Tarbes) 1950 *S, I, E, W*
Finat, R (CASG) 1932 *G*, 1933 *G*
Fite, R (Brive) 1963 *W, It*
Forestier, J (SCUF) 1912 *W*
Forgues, F (Bayonne) 1911 *S, E, W*, 1912 *I, W, E*, 1913 *S, SA, W*, 1914 *I, E*
Fort, J (Agen) 1967 *It, W, I, SA* 1,2,3,4
Fourcade, G (BEC) 1909 *E, W*
Foures, H (Toulouse) 1951 *S, I, E, W*
Fournet, F (Montferrand) 1950 *W*
Fouroux, J (La Voulte) 1972 *I* 2, *R*, 1974 *W, E, Arg* 1,2, *R, SA* 1,2, 1975 *W, Arg* 1, *R*, 1976 *S, I, W, E, US, A* 1, 1977 *W, E, S, I, Arg* 1,2, *NZ* 1,2, *R*
Francquenelle, A (Vaugirard) 1911 *S*, 1913 *W, I*
Furcade, R (Perpignan) 1952 *S*

Gabernet, S (Toulouse) 1980 *E, S*, 1981 *S, I, W, E, A* 1,2, *R, NZ* 1,2, 1982 *I*, 1983 *A* 2, *R*
Gachassin, J (Lourdes) 1961 *S, I*, 1963 *R*, 1964 *S, NZ, E, W, It, I, SA, Fj, R*, 1965 *S, I, E, W, It, R*, 1966 *S, I, E, W*, 1967 *S, A, It, W, I, NZ*, 1968 *I, S, R*, 1969 *S, I*
Galau, H (Toulouse) 1924 *S, I, E, W, US*
Galia, J (Quillan) 1927 *E, G* 1,2, 1928 *S, A, I, E, W*, 1929 *I, E, G*, 1930 *S, I, E, G, W*, 1931 *S, W, E, G*
Gallart, P (Béziers) 1990 *R, A* 1,2(R),3, 1992 *S, I*
Gallion, J (Toulon) 1978 *E, S, I, W*, 1979 *I, W, E, S, NZ* 2, *R*, 1980 *W, E, S, I*, 1983 *A* 1,2, *R*, 1984 *I, W, E, S, R*, 1985 *E, S, I, W*, 1986 *Arg* 2
Galthié, P (Colomiers) 1991 *R, US*1, [*R, Fj, C, E*], 1992 *W, E, S*
Galy, J (Perpignan) 1953 *W*
Garuet-Lempirou, J-P (Lourdes) 1983 *A* 1,2, *R*, 1984 *I, NZ* 1,2, *R*, 1985 *E, S, I, W, Arg* 1, 1986 *S, I, W, E, R* 1, *Arg* 1, *NZ* 1, *R* 2, *NZ* 2,3, 1987 *W, E, S, I*, [*S, R, Fj, A, NZ*], 1988 *E, S, Arg* 1,2, *R*, 1989 *E*(R), *S, NZ* 1,2, 1990 *W, E*
Gasc, J (Graulhet) 1977 *NZ* 2
Gasparotto, G (Montferrand) 1976 *A* 2, *R*
Gauby, G (Perpignan) 1956 *Cz*
Gaudermen, P (RCF) 1906 *E*
Gayraud, W (Toulouse) 1920 *I*
Geneste, R (BEC) 1945 *B* 1, 1949 *Arg* 2
Genet, J-P (RCF) 1992 *S, I*
Gensane, R (Béziers) 1962 *S, E, W, I, It, R*, 1963 *S*
Gerald, G (RCF) 1927 *E, G* 2, 1928 *S*, 1929 *I, S, W, E, G*, 1930 *S, I, E, G, W*, 1931 *I, S, E, G*
Gerintes, G (CASG) 1924 *R*, 1925 *I*, 1926 *W*
Geschwind, P (RCF) 1936 *G* 1,2
Giacardy, M (SBUC) 1907 *E*

1924 *S, I, R, US*
Lasserre, J-C (Dax) 1963 *It*, 1964 *S, NZ, E, W, It, I, Fj*, 1965 *W, I, R*, 1966 *R*, 1967 *S*
Lasserre, M (Agen) 1967 *SA* 2,3, 1968 *E, W, Cz, NZ* 3, *A, SA* 1,2, 1969 *S, I, E*, 1970 *E*, 1971 *E, W*
Laterrade, G (Tarbes) 1910 *E, I*, 1911 *S, E, I*
Laudouar, J (Soustons, SBUC) 1961 *NZ* 1,2, *R*, 1962 *I, R*
Lauga, P (Vichy) 1950 *S, I, E, W*
Laurent, A (Biarritz O) 1925 *NZ, S, W, E*, 1926 *W*
Laurent, J (Bayonne) 1920 *S, E, W*
Laurent, M (Auch) 1932 *G*, 1933 *G*, 1934 *G*, 1935 *G*, 1936 *G* 1
Lavail, G (Perpignan) 1937 *G*, 1940 *B*
Lavaud, R (Carcassonne) 1914 *I, W*
Lavergne, P (Limoges) 1950 *S*
Lavigne, B (Agen) 1984 *R*, 1985 *E*
Lavigne, J (Dax) 1920 *E, W*
Lazies, H (Auch) 1954 *Arg* 2, 1955 *It*, 1956 *E*, 1957 *S*
Le Bourhis, R (La Rochelle) 1961 *R*
Lecointre, M (Nantes) 1952 *It*
Le Droff, J (Auch) 1963 *It, R*, 1964 *S, NZ, E*, 1970 *E, R*, 1971 *S, I*
Lefevre, R (Brive) 1961 *NZ* 2
Lefort, J-B (Biarritz O) 1938 *G* 1
Le Goff, R (Métro) 1938 *R, G* 2
Legrain, M (SF) 1909 *I*, 1910 *I*, 1911 *S, E, W, I*, 1913 *S, SA, E, I*, 1914 *I, W*
Lenient, J-J (Vichy) 1967 *R*
Lepatey, J (Mazamet) 1954 *It*, 1955 *S, I, E, W*
Lepatey, L (Mazamet) 1924 *S, I, E*
Lescarboura, J-P (Dax) 1982 *W, E, S, I*, 1983 *A* 1,2, *R*, 1984 *I, W, E, S, NZ* 1,2, *R*, 1985 *E, S, I, W, Arg* 1, 2, 1986 *Arg* 2, *A, NZ* 1, *R* 2, *NZ* 2, 1988 *S, W*, 1990 *R*
Lesieur, É (SF) 1906 *E*, 1908 *E, W*, 1909 *E, W, I*, 1910 *S, E, I*, 1911 *E, I*, 1912 *W*
Leuvielle, M (SBUC) 1908 *W*, 1913 *S, SA, E, W*, 1914 *W, E*
Levasseur, R (SF) 1925 *W, E*
Levée, H (RCF) 1906 *NZ*
Lewis, E W (Le Havre) 1906 *E*
Lhermet, J-M (Montferrand) 1990 *S, I*
Libaros, G (Tarbes) 1936 *G* 1, 1940 *B*
Lira, M (La Voulte) 1962 *R*, 1963 *I, E, W, It, A*, 1964 *W, It, I, SA*, 1965 *S, I, R*
Llari, (Carcassonne) 1926 *S*
Lobies, J (RCF) 1921 *S, W, E*
Lombard, F (Narbonne) 1934 *G*, 1937 *It*
Lombarteix, R (Montferrand) 1938 *R, G* 2
Londios, J (Montauban) 1967 *SA* 3
Lorieux, A (Grenoble, Aix) 1981 *A* 1, *R, NZ* 1,2, 1982 *W*, 1983 *A* 2, *R*, 1984 *I, W, E*, 1985 *Arg* 1,2(*R*), 1986 *R* 2, *NZ* 2,3, 1987 *W, E,* [*S, Z, Fj, A, NZ*], 1988 *S, I, W, Arg* 1,2,4, 1989 *W, A* 2
Loury, A (RCF) 1927 *E, G* 1,2, 1928 *S, A, I*
Loustau, M (Dax) 1923 *E*
Lubin-Lebrère, M-F (Toulouse) 1914 *I, W, E*, 1920 *S, E, W, I, US*, 1921 *S, E, W*, 1924 *W, US*, 1925 *I*
Lubrano, A (Béziers) 1972 *A* 2, 1973 *S*
Lux, J-P (Tyrosse, Dax) 1967 *E, It, W, I, SA* 1,2,4, *R*, 1968 *I, E, Cz, NZ* 3, *A, SA* 1,2, 1969 *S, I, E*, 1970 *S, I, W, E, R*, 1971 *S, I, E, W, A* 1,2, 1972 *S, I* 1, *E, R*, 1973 *S, NZ, E*, 1974 *I, W, E, S, Arg* 1,2, 1975 *W*

Maclos, P (SF) 1906 *E*, 1907 *E*
Magnanou, C (RCF) 1923 *E*, 1925 *W, E*, 1926 *S*, 1929 *S, W*, 1930 *S, I, E, W*
Magnol, L (Toulouse) 1928 *S*, 1929 *S, W, E*
Magois, H (La Rochelle) 1968 *SA* 1,2, *R*
Majerus, R (SF) 1928 *W*, 1929 *I, S*, 1930 *S, I, E, G, W*
Malbet, J-C (Agen) 1967 *SA* 2,4
Maleig, A (Oloron) 1979 *W, E, NZ* 2, 1980 *W, E, SA, R*
Malquier, Y (Narbonne) 1979 *S*
Manterola, T (Lourdes) 1955 *It*, 1957 *R* 1
Mantoulan, C (Pau) 1959 *I*
Marcet, J (Albi) 1925 *I, NZ, S, W, E*, 1926 *I, E*
Marchal, J-F (Lourdes) 1979 *S, R*, 1980 *W, S, I*
Marchand, R (Poitiers) 1920 *S, W*
Marocco, P (Montferrand) 1986 *S, I, E, R* 1, *Arg* 1,2, *A*, 1988 *Arg* 4, 1989 *I*, 1990 *E*(*R*), *NZ* 1(*R*), 1991 *S, I, W1, E, US2*, [*R, Fj, C, E*]

Marot, A (Brive) 1969 *R*, 1970 *S, I, W*, 1971 *SA* 1, 1972 *I* 2, 1976 *A* 1
Marquesuzaa, A (RCF) 1958 *It, SA* 1,2, 1959 *S, E, It, W*, 1960 *S, E, Arg* 1
Marracq, H (Pau) 1961 *R*
Martin, C (Lyon) 1909 *I*, 1910 *W, S*
Martin, H (SBUC) 1907 *E*, 1908 *W*
Martin, J-L (Béziers) 1971 *A* 2, *R*, 1972 *S, I* 1
Martin, L (Pau) 1948 *I, A, S, W, E*, 1950 *S*
Martine, R (Lourdes) 1952 *S, I, It*, 1953 *It*, 1954 *S, I, NZ, W, E, It, Arg* 2, 1955 *S, I, W*, 1958 *A, W, It, I, SA* 1,2, 1960 *S, E, Arg* 3, 1961 *S, It*
Martinez, G (Toulouse) 1982 *W, E, S, Arg* 1,2, 1983 *E, W*
Mas, F (Béziers) 1962 *R*, 1963 *S, I, E, W*
Maso, J (Perpignan, Narbonne) 1966 *It, R*, 1967 *S, R*, 1968 *S, W, Cz, NZ* 1,2,3, *A, R*, 1969 *S, I, W*, 1971 *SA* 1,2, *R*, 1972 *E, W, A* 2, 1973 *W, I, J, R*
Massare, J (PUC) 1945 *B* 1,2, *W*, 1946 *B, I, W*
Massé, A (SBUC) 1908 *W*, 1909 *E, W*, 1910 *W, S, E, I*
Masse, H (Grenoble) 1937 *G*
Matheu-Cambas, J (Agen) 1945 *W*, 1946 *B, I, K, W*, 1947 *S, I, W, E*, 1948 *I, A, S, W, E*, 1949 *S, I, E, W, Arg* 1,2, 1950 *E, W*, 1951 *S, I*
Mauduy, G (Périgueux) 1957 *It, R* 1,2, 1958 *S, E*, 1961 *W, It*
Mauran, J (Castres) 1952 *SA, W, E, It*, 1953 *I, E*
Mauriat, P (Lyon) 1907 *E*, 1908 *E, W*, 1909 *W, I*, 1910 *W, S, E, I*, 1911 *S, E, W, I*, 1912 *I, S*, 1913 *S, SA, W, I*
Maurin, G (ASF) 1906 *E*
Maury, A (Toulouse) 1925 *I, NZ, S, W, E*, 1926 *S, I, E*
Mayssonnié, A (Toulouse) 1908 *E, W*, 1910 *W*
Melville, E (Toulon) 1990 *I*(*R*), *A* 1,2,3, *NZ* 1, 1991 *US2*
Menrath, R (SCUF) 1910 *W*
Menthiller, Y (Romans) 1964 *W, It, SA, R*, 1965 *E*
Meret, F (Tarbes) 1940 *B*
Mericq, S (Agen) 1959 *I*, 1960 *S, E, W*, 1961 *I*
Merquey, J (Toulon) 1950 *S, I, E, W*
Mesnel, F (RCF) 1986 *NZ* 2(*R*),3, 1987 *W, E, S, I,* [*S, Z, Fj, A, NZ*], *R*, 1988 *E, Arg* 1,2,3,4, *R*, 1989 *I, W, E, S, NZ* 1, *A* 1,2, 1990 *E, S, I, A* 2,3, *NZ* 1,2, 1991 *S, I, W1, E, R, US*1,2, *W*2, [*R, Fj, C, E*], 1992 *W, E, S, I*
Mesny, P (RCF, Grenoble) 1979 *NZ* 1,2, 1980 *SA, R*, 1981 *I, W*(*R*), *A* 1,2, *R, NZ* 1,2, 1982 *I, Arg* 1,2
Meyer, G-S (Périgueux) 1960 *S, E, It, R, Arg* 2
Meynard, J (Cognac) 1954 *Arg* 1, 1956 *Cz*
Mias, L (Mazamet) 1951 *S, I, E, W*, 1952 *I, SA, W, E, It*, 1953 *S, I, W, It*, 1954 *S, I, NZ, W*, 1957 *R* 2, 1958 *S, E, A, W, I, SA* 1,2, 1959 *S, It, W, I*
Milliand, P (Grenoble) 1936 *G* 2, 1937 *G, It*
Minjat, R (Lyon) 1945 *B* 1
Mir, J-H (Lourdes) 1967 *R*, 1968 *I*
Mir, J-P (Lourdes) 1967 *A*
Modin, R (Brive) 1987 [*Z*]
Moga, A-M-A (Begles) 1945 *B* 1,2, *W*, 1946 *B, I, K, W*, 1947 *S, I, W, E*, 1948 *I, A, S, W, E*, 1949 *S, I, E, W, Arg* 1,2
Mommejat, B (Cahors, Albi) 1958 *It, I, SA* 1,2, 1959 *S, E, It, W, I*, 1960 *S, E, I, R*, 1962 *S, E, W, I, It, R*, 1963 *S, I, W*
Moncla, F (RCF, Pau) 1956 *Cz*, 1957 *I, E, W, It, R* 1, 1958 *SA* 1,2, 1959 *S, E, It, W, I*, 1960 *S, E, W, I, It, R, Arg* 1,2,3, 1961 *S, SA, E, W, It, I, NZ* 1,2,3
Monié, R (Perpignan) 1956 *Cz*, 1957 *E*
Monier, R (SBUC) 1911 *I*, 1912 *S*
Monniot, M (RCF) 1912 *W, E*
Montade, A (Perpignan) 1925 *I, NZ, S, W*, 1926 *W*
Montlaur, P (Agen) 1992 *E*(*R*)
Moraitis, B (Toulon) 1969 *E, W*
Morel, A (Grenoble) 1954 *Arg* 2
Morere, J (Toulouse) 1927 *E, G* 1, 1928 *S, A*
Moscato, V (Bègles) 1991 *R, US*1, 1992 *W, E*
Mougeot, C (Bègles) 1992 *W, E*
Mouniq, P (Toulouse) 1911 *S, E, W, I*, 1912 *I, E*, 1913 *S, SA, E*
Moure, H (SCUF) 1908 *E*
Moureu, B (Béziers) 1920 *I, US*, 1921 *W, E, I*, 1922 *S, W, I*, 1923 *S, W, E, I*, 1924 *S, I, E, W*, 1925 *E*
Mournet, A (Bagnères) 1981 *A* 1 (*R*)
Mouronval, F (SF) 1909 *I*
Muhr, A H (RCF) 1906 *NZ, E*, 1907 *E*
Murillo, G (Dijon) 1954 *It, Arg* 1

FRENCH INTERNATIONAL RECORDS

Both team and individual records are for official French international matches, up to 31 March 1992.

TEAM RECORDS

Highest score
70 v Zimbabwe (70-12) 1987 Auckland

v individual countries
37 v Argentina (37-3) 1960 Buenos Aires
34 v Australia (34-6) 1976 Parc des Princes
19 v Canada (19-13) 1991 Agen
28 v Czechoslovakia (28-3) 1956 Toulouse
37 v England (37-12) 1972 Colombes
33 v Fiji (33-9) 1991 Grenoble
38 v Germany (38-17) 1933 Parc des Princes
44 v Ireland (44-12) 1992 Parc des Princes
60 v Italy (60-13) 1967 Toulon
30 v Japan (30-18) 1973 Bordeaux
24 v N Zealand (24-19) 1979 Auckland
59 v Romania (59-3) 1924 Colombes
28 v Scotland (28-22) 1987 Parc des Princes
25 v S Africa (25-38) 1975 Bloemfontein
41 v United States (41-9) 1991 Denver
36 v Wales (36-3) 1991 Parc des Princes
70 v Zimbabwe (70-12) 1987 Auckland

Biggest winning points margin
58 v Zimbabwe (70-12) 1987 Auckland

v individual countries
34 v Argentina (37-3) 1960 Buenos Aires
28 v Australia (34-6) 1976 Parc des Princes
6 v Canada (19-13) 1991 Agen
25 v Czechoslovakia (28-3) 1956 Toulouse
25 v England (37-12) 1972 Colombes
24 v Fiji (33-9) 1991 Grenoble
34 v Germany (34-0) 1931 Colombes
32 v Ireland (44-12) 1992 Parc des Princes
47 v Italy (60-13) 1967 Toulon
12 v Japan (30-18) 1973 Bordeaux
13 v N Zealand (16-3) 1986 Nantes
56 v Romania (59-3) 1924 Colombes
20 v Scotland (23-3) 1977 Parc des Princes
5 v S Africa (19-14) 1967 Johannesburg
32 v United States (41-9) 1991 Denver
33 v Wales (36-3) 1991 Parc des Princes
58 v Zimbabwe (70-12) 1987 Auckland

Highest score by opposing team
49 Wales (14-49) 1910 Swansea

S Africa beat 'France' 55-6 at Parc des Princes on 3 January 1907, but it is not regarded as an official international match

by individual countries
27 Argentina (31-27) 1974 Buenos Aires
48 Australia (31-48) 1990 Brisbane
13 Canada (19-13) 1991 Agen
6 Czechoslovakia (19-6) 1968 Prague
41 England (13-41) 1907 Richmond
16 Fiji (31-16) 1987 Auckland
17 Germany { (16-17) 1927 Frankfurt
             (38-17) 1933 Parc des Princes
25 Ireland { (5-25) 1911 Cork
             (6-25) 1975 Dublin
13 Italy (60-13) 1967 Toulon
18 Japan (30-18) 1973 Bordeaux
38 N Zealand (8-38) 1906 Parc des Princes
21 Romania (33-21) 1991 Bucharest
31 Scotland (3-31) 1912 Inverleith
38 S Africa { (5-38) 1913 Bordeaux
             (25-38) 1975 Bloemfontein
17 United States (3-17) 1924 Colombes
49 Wales (14-49) 1910 Swansea
12 Zimbabwe (70-12) 1987 Auckland

Biggest losing points margin
42 v Wales (5-47) 1909 Colombes
The 6-55 defeat by S Africa in Paris in 1907 is regarded as unofficial

v individual countries
12 v Argentina (6-18) 1988 Buenos Aires
17 v Australia { (15-32) 1989 Strasbourg
                (31-48) 1990 Brisbane
37 v England (0-37) 1911 Twickenham
3 v Germany (0-3) 1938 Frankfurt
24 v Ireland (0-24) 1913 Cork
30 v N Zealand (8-38) 1906 Parc des Princes
15 v Romania (0-15) 1980 Bucharest
28 v Scotland (3-31) 1912 Inverleith
33 v S Africa (5-38) 1913 Bordeaux
14 v United States (3-17) 1924 Colombes
42 v Wales (5-47) 1909 Colombes
No defeats v Canada, Czechoslovakia, Fiji, Italy, Japan or Zimbabwe

Most tries by France in an international
13 v Romania (59-3) 1924 Paris

Most tries against France in an international
11 by Wales (5-47) 1909 Colombes

Most points by France in International Championship in a season – 98
in season 1985-86

Most tries by France in International Championship in a season – 13
in seasons 1975-76 and 1985-86

INDIVIDUAL RECORDS

Most capped player
S Blanco 93 1980-91
in individual positions
Full-back
S Blanco 81(93)[1] 1980-91
Wing
P Lagisquet 46 1983-91
Centre
P Sella 76(83)[2] 1982-92
Fly-half
J-P Romeu 33(34)[3] 1972-77
Scrum-half
P Berbizier 56 1981-91
Prop
R Paparemborde 55 1975-83
Hooker
P Dintrans 50 1979-90
Lock
J Condom 61[4] 1982-90
Flanker
J-P Rives 59[4] 1975-84
No 8
G Basquet 33[4] 1945-52

[1]*S Blanco won 12 caps as a wing*
[2]*Sella has won 6 caps as a wing and one as a full-back*
[3]*Romeu was capped once as a replacement full-back. F Mesnel, 48 caps, won 26 as a centre and 22 at fly-half. D Camberabero, 33 caps, has won 27 at fly-half, 3 on the wing and 3 at full-back*
[4]*B Dauga and M Crauste, 63 caps each, are France's most-capped forwards. Dauga was capped as a lock and No 8; Crauste as a flanker and No 8*

Longest international career
F Haget 14 seasons 1974-87

Most consecutive Tests – 46
R Bertranne 1973-79

Most internationals as captain
J-P Rives 34 1978-84

Most points in internationals – 332
D Camberabero (33 matches) 1982-91

Most points in International Championship in a season – 54
J-P Lescarboura (4 matches) 1983-84

Most points in an international – 30
D Camberabero v Zimbabwe 1987
　　Auckland

Most tries in internationals – 38
S Blanco (93 matches) 1980-91

Most tries in International Championship in a season – 5
P Estève (4 matches) 1982-83
E Bonneval (4 matches) 1986-87

Most tries in an international – 4
A Jauréguy v Romania 1924 Colombes
M Celhay v Italy 1937 Parc des Princes

Most conversions in internationals – 46
D Camberabero (33 matches) 1982-91

Most conversions in International Championship in a season – 7
P Villepreux (4 matches) 1971-72

Most conversions in an international – 9
G Camberabero v Italy 1967 Toulon
D Camberabero v Zimbabwe 1987
　　Auckland
Father and son

Most dropped goals in internationals – 15
J-P Lescarboura (28 matches) 1982-90

Most penalty goals in internationals – 56
J-P Romeu (34 matches) 1972-77

Most penalty goals in International Championship in a season – 10
J-P Lescarboura (4 matches) 1983-84

Most points on major tour – 84
P Bérot (6 matches) 1988 South America

Most points in any match on tour – 28
P Lagisquet v Paraguayan XV 1988 Ascunción
P Estève scored 32 points against East Japan in 1984, but this was not on a major tour

Most tries in a tour match – 7
P Lagisquet v Paraguayan XV 1988 Ascunción
P Estève scored 8 tries v East Japan in 1984, but this was not on a major tour

HOPE IN AMALGAMATION

THE 1991 SEASON IN SOUTH AFRICA
John Robbie *Radio 702*

It was another interesting year for South African rugby. Progress along the path to unity was made and, as cricket showed what can be achieved, rugby and other sports faced the future with a degree of optimism. The SARB and the SARU, the two working bodies of old, are dead – long live the SARFU, the new multi-racial body in charge. The news that the 1995 World Cup would take place in South Africa was the icing on the cake.

Many challenges still lie ahead, both on and off the field, but at least movement towards a political settlement has opened the way for more sporting dialogue, co-operation and, it is to be hoped, a full programme of international rugby competition. One detects a new enthusiasm among players here, particularly within the ranks of a talented crop of youngsters.

The format for the Currie Cup competition was changed in 1991, the two weaker unions, Western Transvaal and Northern Free State, dropping out of the top flight. This led to an even more competitive league system than usual with six sides playing each other at home and away. There really was no such thing as an easy game and one wonders if a harder provincial competition exists anywhere. The weaker unions enjoyed regular cross-section matches against the A sides in a contrived side competition, although often the minnows suffered heavy losses.

Transvaal, so often the bridesmaid of Currie Cup rugby, made the early running. Former scrum-half and captain Harry Viljoen took over as coach at the tender age of 31, and his side played enterprising rugby, young wings James Small and Pieter Hendriks scoring many spectacular tries. Hardened observers questioned the heavy pre-season training and suggested that the side might not last the pace – prophetic words.

Eastern Province, who won the Yardley night series at the start of the season, were once again an unhappy side as club factions appeared to chip away at morale. Northern Transvaal started slowly, but with Naas Botha and Robert Du Preez at half-back, they always looked likely to be in at the kill. Western Province, traditionally runners of the ball, looked strangely pedestrian behind the scrum and Natal, the defending champions, were never really able to recapture the magic of the preceding season. Perhaps the most exciting side was Orange Free State, whose young back line contained many who seem destined to wear the South African colours with distinction.

Amazingly, both the Currie Cup and the knock-out Lion Cup ended in victory for the Blue Bulls of Northern Transvaal: in both competitions Divine intervention (or a huge slice of luck) went their way. Quite what Max Boyce would have made of the incidents in question can only be guessed at, but they were extraordinary. In the Lion Cup quarter-final Free State wing Lourens Prinsloo lost the ball as he dived for what would have been a last-minute winning try, and the final minutes of the Western Province versus Free State Currie Cup game in Bloemfontein were even more bizarre. A win for Province would have eliminated Northerns. With minutes to go, giant Province lock F C Smit drove for the Free State line and suddenly a streaker, wearing only a pair of socks, ran from the sideline and tackled Smit. From the scrum, Free State lofted a garryowen which was misfielded by the Province full-back, and wing Izaak Beneke hacked on and scored a wonderful runaway try.

Thus Northerns made a play-off against Free State and won with reserve kicker Gerbrand Grobler kicking six out of six. Northerns went on to beat Transvaal in the final. The record books show a rare double but it could, and perhaps should, have been different.

There was also a great tragedy on Currie Cup final day. Giant Northerns prop Jan Lock, who played in the curtain-raiser, collapsed afterwards in the dressing-room and died on the way to hospital. Rumours of steroid abuse circulated, but a post-mortem revealed that no drugs were involved. Jan, who was selected, but never played, for the 'Boks against the FNB international side in 1989, was one of the strongest men in world rugby. He was an awesome scrummager but, perhaps out of frustration at the lack of international games, he had let his fitness slide and was out of favour. News of a Springbok versus Junior Springbok end-of-season game had encouraged him to attempt a serious comeback. The rugby community was stunned at the death of this popular man at the age of just 28.

South African rugby is just as tough and competitive as ever. The top players are big and fast, and as the game is virtually semi-professional they spend a lot of time working at it. Undoubtedly, some techniques have fallen behind the standards of the rest of the world, but these will develop and catch up. Handling among forwards and retaining possession are problem areas, and line-outs were a shambles when the international interpretations were adopted. It is to be hoped that the world will consider, soon, allowing early binding, which results in cleaner catching and the involvement of props in the lift, rather than in spoiling the opponents' catch. By general consensus, the player of the year was Uli Schmidt, the son of Louis Schmidt who played on the flank for the 'Boks. We hope that the rest of the world will get a chance to see Uli at his best. He is a hooker *par excellence*.

Currie Cup winners: Northern Transvaal
Lion Cup winners: Northern Transvaal
Yardley Gold Cup winners: Eastern Province
Toyota Club champions: Old Greys, Bloemfontein

SOUTH AFRICAN INTERNATIONAL PLAYERS *(up to 31 March 1992)*

ABBREVIATIONS

A – Australia; *BI* – British Isles teams; *Cv* – New Zealand Cavaliers; *E* – England; *F* – France; *I* – Ireland; *NZ* – New Zealand; *S* – Scotland; *S Am* – South America; *US* – United States of America; *W* – Wales; *Wld* – World Invitation XV; (R) – Replacement

PROVINCIAL ABBREVIATIONS

Bor – Border; Bol – Boland; EP – Eastern Province; GW – Griqualand West; N – Natal; NT – Northern Transvaal; OFS – Orange Free State; R – Rhodesia; SET – South East Transvaal; SWA – South West Africa; SWD – South West Districts; Tvl – Transvaal; WP – Western Province; WT – Western Transvaal; Z-R – Zimbabwe-Rhodesia

Note: When a series has taken place, figures denote the particular matches in which players featured. Thus 1968 *BI* 1,2,4 indicates that a player appeared in the first, second and fourth Tests of the 1968 series against the British Isles.

Ackermann, D S P (WP) 1955 *BI* 2,3,4, 1956 *A* 1,2, *NZ* 1,3, 1958 *F* 2
Albertyn, P K (SWD) 1924 *BI* 1,2,3,4
Alexander, E (GW) 1891 *BI* 1,2
Allen, P B (EP) 1960 *S*
Allport, P (WP) 1910 *BI* 2,3
Anderson, J A (WP) 1903 *BI* 3
Anderson, J H (WP) 1896 *BI* 1,3,4
Andrew, J B (Tvl) 1896 *BI* 2
Antelme, M J G (Tvl) 1960 *NZ* 1,2,3,4, 1960-61 *F*
Apsey, J T (WP) 1933 *A* 4,5, 1938 *BI* 2
Ashley, S (WP) 1903 *BI* 2
Aston, F T D (Tvl) 1896 *BI* 1,2,3,4
Aucamp, J (WT) 1924 *BI* 1,2

Baard, A P (WP) 1960-61 *I*
Babrow, L (WP) 1937 *A* 1,2, *NZ* 1,2,3
Barnard, A S (EP) 1984 *S Am* 1,2, 1986 *Cv* 1,2
Barnard, J H (Tvl) 1965 *S, A* 1,2, *NZ* 3,4
Barnard, R W (Tvl) 1970 *NZ* 2(R)
Barnard, W H M (NT) 1949 *NZ* 4, 1951-52 *W*
Barry, J (WP) 1903 *BI* 1,2,3
Bartmann, W J (Tvl) 1986 *Cv* 1,2,3,4
Bastard, W E (N) 1937 *A* 1, *NZ* 1,2,3, 1938 *BI* 1,3
Bates, A J (WT) 1969-70 *E*, 1970 *NZ* 1,2, 1972 *E*
Bayvel, P C R (Tvl) 1974 *BI* 2,4, *F* 1,2, 1975 *F* 1,2, 1976 *NZ* 1,2,3,4
Beck, J J (WP) 1981 *NZ* 2(R), 3 (R), *US*
Bedford, T P (N) 1963 *A* 1,2,3,4, 1964 *W, F*, 1965 *I, A* 1,2, 1968 *BI* 1,2,3,4, *F* 1,2, 1969 *A* 1,2,3,4, 1969-70 *S, E, I, W*, 1971 *F* 1,2
Bekker, H J (WP) 1981 *NZ* 1,3
Bekker, H P J (NT) 1951-52 *E, F*, 1953 *A* 1,2,3,4, 1955 *BI* 2,3,4, 1956 *A* 1,2, *NZ* 1,2,3,4
Bekker, M J (NT) 1960 *S*
Bekker, R P (NT) 1953 *A* 3,4
Bergh, W F (SWD) 1931-32 *W, I, E, S*, 1933 *A* 1,2,3,4,5, 1937 *A* 1,2, *NZ* 1,2,3, 1938 *BI* 1,2,3
Bestbier, A (OFS) 1974 *F* 2(R)
Bester, J J N (WP) 1924 *BI* 2,4
Bester, J L A (WP) 1938 *BI* 2,3
Beswick, A M (Bor) 1896 *BI* 2,3,4
Bezuidenhout, C E (NT) 1962 *BI* 2,3,4
Bezuidenhout, N S E (NT) 1972 *E*, 1974 *BI* 2,3,4, *F* 1,2, 1975 *F* 1,2, 1977 *Wld*
Bierman, J N (Tvl) 1931-32 *I*
Bisset, W M (WP) 1891 *BI* 1,3
Blair, R (WP) 1977 *Wld*
Bosch, G R (Tvl) 1974 *BI* 2, *F* 1,2, 1975 *F* 1,2, 1976 *NZ* 1,2,3,4
Bosman, N J S (Tvl) 1980 *BI* 2,3,4
Botha, D S (NT) 1981 *NZ* 1
Botha, H E (NT) 1980 *S Am* 1,2, *BI* 1,2,3,4, *S Am* 3,4, *F*, 1981 *I* 1,2, *NZ* 1,2,3, *US*, 1982 *S Am* 1,2, 1986 *Cv* 1,2,3,4, 1989 *Wld* 1,2
Botha, J (Tvl) 1903 *BI* 2
Botha, J P F (NT) 1962 *BI* 2,3,4
Botha, P H (Tvl) 1965 *A* 1,2
Boyes, H C (GW) 1891 *BI* 1,2
Brand, G H (WP) 1928 *NZ* 2,3, 1931-32 *W, I, E, S*, 1933 *A* 1,2,3,4,5, 1937 *A* 1,2, *NZ* 2,3, 1938 *BI* 1

Bredenkamp, M (GW) 1896 *BI* 1,3
Breedt, J C (Tvl) 1986 *Cv* 1,2,3,4, 1989 *Wld* 1,2
Brewis, J D (NT) 1949 *NZ* 1,2,3,4, 1951-52 *S, I, W, E, F*, 1953 *A* 1
Briers, T P D (WP) 1955 *BI* 1,2,3,4, 1956 *NZ* 2,3,4
Brink, D J (WP) 1906 *S, W, E*
Brooks, D (Bor) 1906 *S*
Brown, C (WP) 1903 *BI* 1,2,3
Brynard, G S (WP) 1965 *A* 1, *NZ* 1,2,3,4, 1968 *BI* 3,4
Buchler, J U (Tvl) 1951-52 *S, I, W, E, F*, 1953 *A* 1,2,3,4, 1956 *A* 2
Burdett, A F (WP) 1906 *S, I*
Burger, J M (WP) 1989 *Wld* 1,2
Burger, M B (NT) 1980 *BI* 2(R), *S Am* 3, 1981 *US* (R)
Burger, S W P (WP) 1984 *E* 1,2, 1986 *Cv* 1,2,3,4
Burger, W A G (Bor) 1906 *S, I, W*, 1910 *BI* 2

Carelse, G (EP) 1964 *W, F*, 1965 *I, S*, 1967 *F* 1,2,3, 1968 *F* 1,2, 1969 *A* 1,2,3,4, 1969-70 *S*
Carlson, R A (WP) 1972 *E*
Carolin, H W (WP) 1903 *BI* 3, 1906 *S, I*
Castens, H H (WP) 1891 *BI* 1
Chignell, T W (WP) 1891 *BI* 3
Cilliers, G D (OFS) 1963 *A* 1,3,4
Claassen, J T (WT) 1955 *BI* 1,2,3,4, 1956 *A* 1,2, *NZ* 1,2,3,4, 1958 *F* 1,2, 1960 *S, NZ* 1,2,3, 1960-61 *W, I, E, S, F*, 1961 *I, A* 1,2, 1962 *BI* 1,2,3,4
Claassen, W (N) 1981 *I* 1,2, *NZ* 2,3, *US*, 1982 *S Am* 1,2
Clarke, W H (Tvl) 1933 *A* 3
Clarkson, W A (N) 1921 *NZ* 1,2, 1924 *BI* 1
Cloete, H A (WP) 1896 *BI* 4
Cockrell, C H (WP) 1969-70 *S, I, W*
Cockrell, R J (WP) 1974 *F* 1,2, 1975 *F* 1,2, 1976 *NZ* 1,2, 1977 *Wld*, 1981 *NZ* 1,2(R),3, *US*
Coetzee, J H H (WP) 1974 *BI* 1, 1975 *F* 2(R), 1976 *NZ* 1,2,3,4
Cope, D (Tvl) 1896 *BI* 2
Cotty, W (GW) 1896 *BI* 3
Crampton, G (GW) 1903 *BI* 2
Craven, D H (WP) 1931-32 *W, I, S*, 1933 *A* 1,2,3,4,5, 1937 *A* 1,2, *NZ* 1,2,3, 1938 *BI* 1,2,3
Cronje, P A (Tvl) 1971 *F* 1,2, *A* 1,2,3, 1974 *BI* 3,4
Crosby, J H (Tvl) 1896 *BI* 2
Crosby, N J (Tvl) 1910 *BI* 1,3
Currie, C (GW) 1903 *BI* 2

D'Alton, G (WP) 1933 *A* 1
Daneel, G M (WP) 1928 *NZ* 1,2,3,4, 1931-32 *W, I, E, S*
Daneel, H J (WP) 1906 *S, I, W, E*
Davidson, M (EP) 1910 *BI* 1
De Bruyn, J (OFS) 1974 *BI* 3
De Jongh, H P K (WP) 1928 *NZ* 3
De Klerk, I J (Tvl) 1969-70 *E, I, W*
De Klerk, K B H (Tvl) 1974 *BI* 1,2,3(R), 1975 *F* 1,2, 1976 *NZ* 2(R),3,4, 1980 *S Am* 1,2, *BI* 2, 1981 *I* 1,2
De Kock, A (GW) 1891 *BI* 2
De Kock, J S (WP) 1921 *NZ* 3, 1924 *BI* 3
Delport, W H (EP) 1951-52 *S, I, W, E, F*, 1953 *A* 1,2,3,4

307

De Melker, S C (GW) 1903 *BI* 2, 1906 *E*
Devenish, C (GW) 1896 *BI* 2
Devenish, G St L (Tvl) 1896 *BI* 2
Devenish, M (Tvl) 1891 *BI* 1
De Villiers, D I (Tvl) 1910 *BI* 1,2,3
De Villiers, D J (WP, Bol) 1962 *BI* 2,3, 1965 *I, NZ* 1,3,4, 1967 *F* 1,2,3,4, 1968 *BI* 1,2,3,4, *F* 1,2, 1969 *A* 1,4, 1969-70 *E, I, W*, 1970 *NZ* 1,2,3,4
De Villiers, H A (WP) 1906 *S, W, E*
De Villiers, H O (WP) 1967 *F* 1,2,3,4, 1968 *F* 1,2, 1969 *A* 1,2,3,4, 1969-70 *S, E, I, W*
De Villiers, P du P (WP) 1928 *NZ* 1,3,4, 1931-32 *E*, 1933 *A* 4, 1937 *A* 1,2, *NZ* 1
Devine, D (Tvl) 1924 *BI* 3, 1928 *NZ* 2
De Vos, D J J (WP) 1965 *S,* 1969 *A* 3, 1969-70 *S*
De Waal, A N (WP) 1967 *F* 1,2,3,4
De Waal, P (WP) 1896 *BI* 4
De Wet, A E (WP) 1969 *A* 3,4, 1969-70 *E*
De Wet, P (WP) 1938 *BI* 1,2,3
Dinkelmann, E E (NT) 1951-52 *S, I, E, F*, 1953 *A* 1,2
Dirksen, C W (NT) 1963 *A* 4, 1964 *W*, 1965 *I,S*, 1967 *F* 1,2,3,4, 1968 *BI* 1,2
Dobbin, F J (GW) 1903 *BI* 1,2, 1906 *S, W, E*, 1910 *BI* 1, 1912-13 *S, I, W*
Dobie, J A R (Tvl) 1928 *NZ* 2
Dormehl, P J (WP) 1896 *BI* 3,4
Douglass, F W (EP) 1896 *BI* 1
Dryburgh, R G (WP) 1955 *BI* 2,3,4, 1956 *A* 2, *NZ* 1,4, 1960 *NZ* 1,2
Duff, B (WP) 1891 *BI* 1,2,3
Duffy, B A (Bor) 1928 *NZ* 1
Du Plessis, C J (WP) 1982 *S Am* 1,2, 1984 *E* 1,2, *S Am* 1,2, 1986 *Cv* 1,2,3,4, 1989 *Wld* 1,2
Du Plessis, D C (NT) 1977 *Wld*, 1980 *S Am* 2
Du Plessis, F (Tvl) 1949 *NZ* 1,2,3
Du Plessis, M (WP) 1971 *A* 1,2,3, 1974 *BI* 1,2, *F* 1,2, 1975 *F* 1,2, 1976 *NZ* 1,2,3,4, 1977 *Wld*, 1980 *S Am* 1,2, *BI* 1,2,3,4, *S Am* 4, *F*
Du Plessis, M J (WP) 1984 *S Am* 1,2, 1986 *Cv* 1,2,3,4, 1989 *Wld* 1,2
Du Plessis, N J (WT) 1921 *NZ* 2,3, 1924 *BI* 1,2,3
Du Plessis, P G (NT) 1972 *E*
Du Plessis, T D (NT) 1980 *S Am* 1,2
Du Plessis, W (WP) 1980 *S Am* 1,2, *BI* 1,2,3,4, *S Am* 3,4, *F*, 1981 *NZ* 1,2,3, 1982 *S Am* 1,2
Du Plooy, A J J (EP) 1955 *BI* 1
Du Preez, F C H (NT) 1960-61 *E, S*, 1961 *A* 1,2, 1962 *BI* 1,2,3,4, 1963 *A* 1, 1964 *W, F*, 1965 *A* 1,2, *NZ* 1,2,3,4, 1967 *F* 4, 1968 *BI* 1,2,3,4, *F* 1,2, 1969 *A* 1,2, 1969-70 *S, I, W*, 1970 *NZ* 1,2,3,4, 1971 *F* 1,2, *A* 1,2,3
Du Preez, J G H (WP) 1956 *NZ* 1
Du Rand, J A (R, NT) 1949 *NZ* 2,3, 1951-52 *S, I, W, E, F*, 1953 *A* 1,2,3,4, 1955 *BI* 1,2,3,4, 1956 *A* 1,2, *NZ* 1,2,3,4
Du Toit, A F (WP) 1928 *NZ* 3,4
Du Toit, B A (Tvl) 1938 *BI* 1,2,3
Du Toit, P A (NT) 1949 *NZ* 2,3,4, 1951-52 *S, I, W, E, F*
Du Toit, P G (WP) 1981 *NZ* 1, 1982 *S Am* 1,2, 1984 *E* 1,2
Du Toit, P S (WP) 1958 *F* 1,2, 1960 *NZ* 1,2,3,4, 1960-61 *W, I, E, S, F*, 1961 *I, A* 1,2
Duvenhage, F P (GW) 1949 *NZ* 1,3

Edwards, P (NT) 1980 *S Am* 1,2
Ellis, J H (SWA) 1965 *NZ* 1,2,3,4, 1967 *F* 1,2,3,4, 1968 *BI* 1,2,3,4, *F* 1,2, 1969 *A* 1,2,3,4, 1969-70 *S, I, W*, 1970 *NZ* 1,2,3,4, 1971 *F* 1,2, *A* 1,2,3, 1972 *E*, 1974 *BI* 1,2,3,4, *F* 1,2, 1976 *NZ* 1
Ellis, M (Tvl) 1921 *NZ* 2,3, 1924 *BI* 1,2,3,4
Engelbrecht, J P (WP) 1960 *S*, 1960-61 *W, I, E, S, F*, 1961 *A* 1,2, 1962 *BI* 2,3,4, 1963 *A* 2,3, 1964 *W, F*, 1965 *I, S, A* 1,2, *NZ* 1,2,3,4, 1967 *F* 1,2,3,4, 1968 *BI* 1,2, *F* 1,2, 1969 *A* 1,2
Erasmus, F S (NT, EP) 1986 *Cv* 3,4, 1989 *Wld* 2
Etlinger, T E (WP) 1896 *BI* 4

Ferreira, C (OFS) 1986 *Cv* 1,2
Ferreira, P S (WP) 1984 *S Am* 1,2
Ferris, H H (Tvl) 1903 *BI* 3
Forbes, H H (Tvl) 1896 *BI* 2
Fourie, C (EP) 1974 *F* 1,2, 1975 *F* 1,2
Fourie, T T (SET) 1974 *BI* 3
Fourie, W L (SWA) 1958 *F* 1,2

Francis, J A J (Tvl) 1912-13 *S, I, W, E, F*
Frederickson, C A (Tvl) 1974 *BI* 2, 1980 *S Am* 1,2
Frew, A (Tvl) 1903 *BI* 1
Froneman, D C (OFS) 1977 *Wld*
Froneman, I L (Bor) 1933 *A* 1
Fry, S P (WP) 1951-52 *S, I, W, E, F*, 1953 *A* 1,2,3,4, 1955 *BI* 1,2,3,4

Gage, J H (OFS) 1933 *A* 1
Gainsford, J L (WP) 1960 *S, NZ* 1,2,3,4, 1960-61 *W, I, E, S, F*, 1961 *A* 1,2, 1962 *BI* 1,2,3,4, 1963 *A* 1,2,3,4, 1964 *W, F*, 1965 *I, S, A* 1,2, *NZ* 1,2,3,4, 1967 *F* 1,2,3
Geel, P J (OFS) 1949 *NZ* 3
Geere, V (Tvl) 1933 *A* 1,2,3,4,5
Geffin, A O (Tvl) 1949 *NZ* 1,2,3,4, 1951-52 *S, I, W*
Geldenhuys, S B (NT) 1981 *NZ* 2,3, *US*, 1982 *S Am* 1,2, 1989 *Wld* 1,2
Gentles, T A (WP) 1955 *BI* 1,2,4, 1956 *NZ* 2,3, 1958 *F* 2
Geraghty, E M (Bor) 1949 *NZ* 4
Gerber, D M (EP) 1980 *S Am* 3,4, *F*, 1981 *I* 1,2, *NZ* 1,2,3, *US*, 1982 *S Am* 1,2, 1984 *E* 1,2, *S Am* 1,2, 1986 *Cv* 1,2,3,4
Gerber, M C (EP) 1958 *F* 1,2, 1960 *S*
Gericke, F W (Tvl) 1960 *S*
Germishuys, J S (OFS, Tvl) 1974 *BI* 2, 1976 *NZ* 1,2,3,4, 1977 *Wld*, 1980 *S Am* 1,2, *BI* 1,2,3,4, *S Am* 3,4, *F*, 1981 *I* 1,2, *NZ* 1,2,3, *US*
Gibbs, B (GW) 1903 *BI* 2
Goosen, C P (OFS) 1965 *NZ* 2
Gorton, H C (Tvl) 1896 *BI* 1
Gould, R L (N) 1968 *BI* 1,2,3,4
Gray, B G (Tvl) 1931-32 *W, E, S*, 1933 *A* 5
Greenwood, C M (WP) 1961 *I*
Greyling, P J F (OFS) 1967 *F* 1,2,3,4, 1968 *BI* 1, *F* 1,2, 1969 *A* 1,2,3,4, 1969-70 *S, E, I, W*, 1970 *NZ* 1,2,3,4, 1971 *F* 1,2, *A* 1,2,3, 1972 *E*
Grobler, C J (OFS) 1974 *BI* 4, 1975 *F* 1,2
Guthrie, F H (WP) 1891 *BI* 1,3, 1896 *BI* 1

Hahn, C H L (Tvl) 1910 *BI* 1,2,3
Hamilton, F (EP) 1891 *BI* 1
Harris, T A (Tvl) 1937 *NZ* 2,3, 1938 *BI* 1,2,3
Hartley, A J (WP) 1891 *BI* 3
Hattingh, L B (OFS) 1933 *A* 2
Heatlie, B H (WP) 1891 *BI* 2,3, 1896 *BI* 1,4, 1903 *BI* 1,3
Hepburn, T (WP) 1896 *BI* 4
Heunis, J W (NT) 1981 *NZ* 3(R), *US*, 1982 *S Am* 1,2, 1984 *E* 1,2, *S Am* 1,2, 1986 *Cv* 1,2,3,4, 1989 *Wld* 1,2
Hill, R A (R) 1960-61 *W, I*, 1961 *I, A* 1,2, 1962 *BI* 4, 1963 *A* 3
Hirsch, J G (EP) 1906 *I*, 1910 *BI* 1
Hobson, T E C (WP) 1903 *BI* 3
Hoffman, R S (Bol) 1953 *A* 3
Holton, D N (EP) 1960 *S*
Hopwood, D J (WP) 1960 *S, NZ* 3,4, 1960-61 *W, E, S, F*, 1961 *I, A* 1,2, 1962 *BI* 1,2,3,4, 1963 *A* 1,2,4, 1964 *W, F*, 1965 *NZ* 3,4
Howe, B F (Bor) 1956 *NZ* 1,4
Howe-Browne, N R F G (WP) 1910 *BI* 1,2,3
Hugo, D P (WP) 1989 *Wld* 1,2

Immelman, J H (WP) 1912-13 *F*

Jackson, D C (WP) 1906 *I, W, E*
Jackson, J S (WP) 1903 *BI* 2
Jansen, E (OFS) 1981 *NZ* 1
Jansen, J S (OFS) 1970 *NZ* 1,2,3,4, 1971 *F* 1,2, *A* 1,2,3, 1972 *E*
Jennings, C B (Bor) 1937 *NZ* 1
Johnstone, P G A (WP) 1951-52 *S, I, W, E, F*, 1956 *A* 1, *NZ* 1,2,4
Jones, C H (Tvl) 1903 *BI* 1,2
Jones, P S T (WP) 1896 *BI* 1,3,4
Jordaan, R P (NT) 1949 *NZ* 1,2,3,4
Joubert, A J (OFS) 1989 *Wld* 1 (R)
Joubert, S J (WP) 1906 *I, W, E*

Kahts, W J H (NT) 1980 *BI* 1,2,3, *S Am* 3,4, *F*, 1981 *I* 1,2, *NZ* 2, 1982 *S Am* 1,2
Kaminer, J (Tvl) 1958 *F* 2
Kelly, E W (GW) 1896 *BI* 3
Kenyon, B J (Bor) 1949 *NZ* 4

Kipling, H G (GW) 1931-32 *W, I, E, S*, 1933 *A* 1,2,3,4,5
Kirkpatrick, A I (GW) 1953 *A* 2, 1956 *NZ* 2, 1958 *F* 1, 1960 *S, NZ* 1,2,3,4, 1960-61 *W, I, E, S, F*
Knight, A S (Tvl) 1912-13 *S, I, W, E, F*
Knoetze, F (WP) 1989 *Wld* 1,2
Koch, A C (Bol) 1949 *NZ* 2,3,4, 1951-52 *S, I, W, E, F*, 1953 *A* 1,2,4, 1955 *BI* 1,2,3,4, 1956 *A* 1, *NZ* 2,3, 1958 *F* 1,2, 1960 *NZ* 1,2
Koch, H V (WP) 1949 *NZ* 1,2,3,4
Kotze, G J M (WP) 1967 *F* 1,2,3,4
Krantz, E F W (OFS) 1976 *NZ* 1, 1981 *I* 1
Krige, J D (WP) 1903 *BI* 1,3, 1906 *S, I, W*
Kritzinger, J L (Tvl) 1974 *BI* 3,4, *F* 1,2, 1975 *F* 1,2, 1976 *NZ* 4
Kroon, C M (EP) 1955 *BI* 1
Kruger, P E (Tvl) 1986 *Cv* 3,4
Kruger, T L (Tvl) 1921 *NZ* 1,2, 1924 *BI* 1,2,3,4, 1928 *NZ* 1,2
Kuhn, S P (Tvl) 1960 *NZ* 3,4 1960-61 *W, I, E, S, F*, 1961 *I, A* 1,2, 1962 *BI* 1,2,3,4, 1963 *A* 1,2,3, 1965 *I, S*

La Grange, J B (WP) 1924 *BI* 3,4
Larard, A (Tvl) 1896 *BI* 2,4
Lategan, M T (WP) 1949 *NZ* 1,2,3,4, 1951-52 *S, I, W, E, F*, 1953 *A* 1,2
Lawless, M J (WP) 1964 *F*, 1969-70 *E* (R), *I, W*
Ledger, S H (GW) 1912-13 *S, I, E, F*
Le Roux, M (OFS) 1980 *BI* 1,2,3,4, *S Am* 3,4, *F*, 1981 *I* 1
Le Roux, P A (WP) 1906 *I, W, E*
Little, E M M (WP) 1891 *BI* 1,3
Lochner, G P (WP) 1955 *BI* 3, 1956 *A* 1,2, *NZ* 1,2,3,4, 1958 *F* 1,2
Lochner, G P (EP) 1937 *NZ* 3, 1938 *BI* 1,2
Lockyear, R J (GW) 1960 *NZ* 1,2,3,4, 1960-61 *I, F*
Lombard, A C (EP) 1910 *BI* 2
Lotz, J W (Tvl) 1937 *A* 1,2, *NZ* 1,2,3, 1938 *BI* 1,2,3
Loubser, J A (WP) 1903 *BI* 3, 1906 *S, I, W, E*, 1910 *BI* 1,3
Lourens, M J (NT) 1968 *BI* 2,3,4
Louw, J S (Tvl) 1891 *BI* 1,2,3
Louw, M J (Tvl) 1971 *A* 2,3
Louw, M M (WP) 1928 *NZ* 3,4, 1931-32 *W, I, E, S*, 1933 *A* 1,2,3,4,5, 1937 *A* 1,2, *NZ* 2,3, 1938 *BI* 1,2,3
Louw, R J (WP) 1980 *S Am* 1,2, *BI* 1,2,3,4, *S Am* 3,4, *F*, 1981 *I* 1,2, *NZ* 1,3, 1982 *S Am* 1,2, 1984 *E* 1,2, *S Am* 1,2
Louw, S C (WP) 1933 *A* 1,2,3,4,5, 1937 *A* 1, *NZ* 1,2,3, 1938 *BI* 1,2,3
Luyt, F P (WP) 1910 *BI* 1,2,3, 1912-13 *S, I, W, E*
Luyt, J D (EP) 1912-13 *S, W, E, F*
Luyt, R R (WP) 1910 *BI* 2,3, 1912-13 *S, I, W, E, F*
Lyons, D (EP) 1896 *BI* 1
Lyster, P J (N) 1933 *A* 2,5, 1937 *NZ* 1

McCallum, I D (WP) 1970 *NZ* 1,2,3,4, 1971 *F* 1,2, *A* 1,2,3, 1974 *BI* 1,2
McCallum, R J (WP) 1974 *BI* 1
McCulloch, J D (GW) 1912-13 *E, F*
MacDonald, A W (R) 1965 *A* 1, *NZ* 1,2,3,4
Macdonald, D A (WP) 1974 *BI* 2
McDonald, J A J (WP) 1931-32 *W, I, E, S*
McEwan, W M C (Tvl) 1903 *BI* 1,3
McHardy, E E (OFS) 1912-13 *S, I, W, E, F*
McKendrick, J A (WP) 1891 *BI* 3
Malan, A S (Tvl) 1960 *NZ* 1,2,3,4, 1960-61 *W, I, E, S, F*, 1962 *BI* 1, 1963 *A* 1,2,3, 1964 *W*, 1965 *I, S*
Malan, A W (NT) 1989 *Wld* 1,2
Malan, E (NT) 1980 *BI* 3(R),4
Malan, G F (WP) 1958 *F* 2, 1960 *NZ* 1,3,4, 1960-61 *E, S, F*, 1962 *BI* 1,2,3, 1963 *A* 1,2,4, 1964 *W*, 1965 *A* 1,2, *NZ* 1,2
Malan, P (Tvl) 1949 *NZ* 4
Mallett, N V H (WP) 1984 *S Am* 1,2
Mans, W J (WP) 1965 *I, S*
Marais, F P (Bol) 1949 *NZ* 1,2, 1951-52 *S*, 1953 *A* 1,2
Marais, J F K (WP) 1963 *A* 3, 1964 *W, F*, 1965 *I, S, A* 2, 1968 *BI* 1,2,3,4, *F* 1,2, 1969 *A* 1,2,3,4, 1969-70 *S, E, I, W*, 1970 *NZ* 1,2,3,4, 1971 *F* 1,2, *A* 1,2,3, 1974 *BI* 1,2,3,4, *F* 1,2
Maré, D S (Tvl) 1906 *S*
Marsberg, A F W (GW) 1906 *S, W, E*
Marsberg, P A (GW) 1910 *BI* 1
Martheze, W C (GW) 1903 *BI* 2, 1906 *I, W*

Martin, H J (Tvl) 1937 *A* 2
Mellett, T (GW) 1896 *BI* 2
Mellish, F W (WP) 1921 *NZ* 1,3, 1924 *BI* 1,2,3,4
Merry, J (EP) 1891 *BI* 1
Metcalf, H D (Bor) 1903 *BI* 2
Meyer, C du P (WP) 1921 *NZ* 1,2,3
Meyer, P J (GW) 1896 *BI* 1
Michau, J M (Tvl) 1921 *NZ* 1
Michau, J P (WP) 1921 *NZ* 1,2,3
Millar, W A (WP) 1906 *E*, 1910 *BI* 2,3, 1912-13 *I, W, F*
Mills, W J (WP) 1910 *BI* 2
Moll, T (Tvl) 1910 *BI* 2
Montini, P E (WP) 1956 *A* 1,2
Moolman, L C (NT) 1977 *Wld*, 1980 *S Am* 1,2, *BI* 1,2,3,4, *S Am* 3,4, *F*, 1981 *I* 1,2, *NZ* 1,2,3, *US*, 1982 *S Am* 1,2, 1984 *S Am* 1,2, 1986 *Cv* 1,2,3,4
Mordt, R H (Z-R, NT) 1980 *S Am* 1,2, *BI* 1,2,3,4, *S Am* 3,4, *F*, 1981 *I* 2, *NZ* 1,2,3, *US*, 1982 *S Am* 1,2, 1984 *S Am* 1,2
Morkel, A O (Tvl) 1903 *BI* 1
Morkel, D F T (Tvl) 1906 *I, E*, 1910 *BI* 1,3, 1912-13 *S, I, W, E, F*
Morkel, H J (WP) 1921 *NZ* 1
Morkel, H W (WP) 1921 *NZ* 1,2
Morkel, J A (WP) 1921 *NZ* 2,3
Morkel, J W H (WP) 1912-13 *S, I, W, E, F*
Morkel, P G (WP) 1912-13 *S, I, W, E, F*, 1921 *NZ* 1,2,3
Morkel, P K (WP) 1928 *NZ* 4
Morkel, W H (WP) 1910 *BI* 3, 1912-13 *S, I, W, E, F*, 1921 *NZ* 1,2,3
Morkel, W S (Tvl) 1906 *S, I, W, E*
Moss, C (N) 1949 *NZ* 1,2,3,4
Mostert, P J (WP) 1921 *NZ* 1,2,3, 1924 *BI* 1,2,4, 1928 *NZ* 1,2,3,4, 1931-32 *W, I, E, S*
Muller, G H (WP) 1969 *A* 3,4, 1969-70 *S, W*, 1970 *NZ* 1,2,3,4, 1971 *F* 1,2, 1972 *E*, 1974 *BI* 1,3,4
Muller, H L (OFS) 1986 *Cv* 4 (R), 1989 *Wld* 1(R)
Muller, H S V (Tvl) 1949 *NZ* 1,2,3,4, 1951-52 *S, I, W, E, F*, 1953 *A* 1,2,3,4
Myburgh, F R (EP) 1896 *BI* 1
Myburgh, J L (NT) 1962 *BI* 1, 1963 *A* 4, 1964 *W, F*, 1968 *BI* 1,2,3, *F* 1,2, 1969 *A* 1,2,3,4, 1969-70 *E, I, W*, 1970 *NZ* 3,4
Myburgh, W H (WT) 1924 *BI* 1

Naude, J P (WP) 1963 *A* 4, 1965 *A* 1,2, *NZ* 1,3,4, 1967 *F* 1,2,3,4, 1968 *BI* 1,2,3,4
Neethling, J B (WP) 1967 *F* 1,2,3,4, 1968 *BI* 4, 1969-70 *S*, 1970 *NZ* 1,2
Nel, J A (Tvl) 1960 *NZ* 1,2, 1963 *A* 1,2, 1965 *A* 2, *NZ* 1,2,3,4, 1970 *NZ* 3,4
Nel, J J (WP) 1956 *A* 1,2, *NZ* 1,2,3,4, 1958 *F* 1,2
Nel, P A R O (Tvl) 1903 *BI* 1,2,3
Nel, P J (N) 1928 *NZ* 1,2,3,4, 1931-32 *W, I, E, S*, 1933 *A* 1,3,4,5, 1937 *A* 1,2, *NZ* 2,3
Nimb, C F (WP) 1961 *I*
Nomis, S H (Tvl) 1967 *F* 4, 1968 *BI* 1,2,3,4, *F* 1,2, 1969 *A* 1,2,3,4, 1969-70 *S, E, I, W*, 1970 *NZ* 1,2,3,4, 1971 *F* 1,2, *A* 1,2,3, 1972 *E*
Nykamp, J L (Tvl) 1933 *A* 2

Ochse, J K (WP) 1951-52 *I, W, E, F*, 1953 *A* 1,2,4
Oelofse, J S A (Tvl) 1953 *A* 1,2,3,4
Oliver, J F (Tvl) 1928 *NZ* 3,4
Olivier, E (WP) 1967 *F* 1,2,3,4, 1968 *BI* 1,2,3,4, *F* 1,2, 1969 *A* 1,2,3,4, 1969-70 *S, E*
Olver, E (EP) 1896 *BI* 1
Oosthuizen, J J (WP) 1974 *BI* 1, *F* 1,2, 1975 *F* 1,2, 1976 *NZ* 1,2,3,4
Oosthuizen, O W (NT, Tvl) 1981 *I* 1(R),2, *NZ* 2,3, *US*, 1982 *S Am* 1,2, 1984 *E* 1,2
Osler, B L (WP) 1924 *BI* 1,2,3,4, 1928 *NZ* 1,2,3,4, 1931-32 *W, I, E, S*, 1933 *A* 1,2,3,4,5
Osler, S G (WP) 1928 *NZ* 1
Oxlee, K (N) 1960 *NZ* 1,2,3,4, 1960-61 *W, I, S*, 1961 *A* 1,2, 1962 *BI* 1,2,3, 1963 *A* 1,2,4, 1964 *W*, 1965 *NZ* 1,2

Parker, W H (EP) 1965 *A* 1,2
Partridge, J E C (Tvl) 1903 *BI* 1
Payn, C (N) 1924 *BI* 1,2
Pelser, H J M (Tvl) 1958 *F* 1, 1960 *NZ* 1,2,3,4, 1960-61

W, I, F, 1961 *I, A* 1,2
Pfaff, B D (WP) 1956 *A* 1
Pickard, J A J (WP) 1953 *A* 3,4, 1956 *NZ* 2, 1958 *F* 2
Pienaar, Z M J (OFS) 1980 *S Am* 2(R), *BI* 1,2,3,4, *S Am* 3,4, *F*, 1981 *I* 1,2, *NZ* 1,2,3
Pitzer, G (NT) 1967 *F* 1,2,3,4, 1968 *BI* 1,2,3,4, *F* 1,2, 1969 *A* 3,4
Pope, C F (WP) 1974 *BI* 1,2,3,4, 1975 *F* 1,2, 1976 *NZ* 2,3,4
Potgieter, H J (OFS) 1928 *NZ* 1,2
Potgieter, H L (OFS) 1977 *Wld*
Powell, A W (GW) 1896 *BI* 3
Powell, J M (GW) 1891 *BI* 2, 1896 *BI* 3, 1903 *BI* 1,2
Prentis, R B (Tvl) 1980 *S Am* 1,2, *BI* 1,2,3,4, *S Am* 3,4, *F*, 1981 *I* 1,2
Pretorius, N F (Tvl) 1928 *NZ* 1,2,3,4
Prinsloo, J (Tvl) 1958 *F* 1,2
Prinsloo, J (NT) 1963 *A* 3
Prinsloo, J P (Tvl) 1928 *NZ* 1
Putter, D J (WT) 1963 *A* 1,2,4

Raaff, J W E (GW) 1903 *BI* 1,2, 1906 *S, W, E*, 1910 *BI* 1
Ras, W J de Wet (OFS) 1976 *NZ* 1(R), 1980 *S Am* 2(R)
Reid, A (WP) 1903 *BI* 3
Reid, B C (Bor) 1933 *A* 4
Reinach, J (OFS) 1986 *Cv* 1,2,3,4
Rens, I J (Tvl) 1953 *A* 3,4
Retief, D F (NT) 1955 *BI* 1,2,4, 1956 *A* 1,2, *NZ* 1,2,3,4
Reynecke, H J (WP) 1910 *BI* 3
Richards, A R (WP) 1891 *BI* 1,2,3
Riley, N M (ET) 1963 *A* 3
Riordan, C E (Tvl) 1910 *BI* 1,2
Robertson, I W (R) 1974 *F* 1,2, 1976 *NZ* 1,2,4
Rodgers, P H (NT) 1989 *Wld* 1,2
Rogers, C D (Tvl) 1984 *E* 1,2, *S Am* 1,2
Roos, G D (WP) 1910 *BI* 2,3
Roos, P J (WP) 1903 *BI* 3, 1906 *I, W, E*
Rosenberg, W (Tvl) 1955 *BI* 2,3,4, 1956 *NZ* 3, 1958 *F* 1
Rossouw, D H (WP) 1953 *A* 3,4
Roux, F du T (WP) 1960-61 *W*, 1961 *A* 1,2, 1962 *BI* 1,2,3,4, 1963 *A* 2, 1965 *A* 1,2, *NZ* 1,2,3,4, 1968 *BI* 3,4, *F* 1,2, 1969 *A* 1,2,3,4, 1969-70 *I*, 1970 *NZ* 1,2,3,4
Roux, O A (NT) 1969-70 *S, E, I, W*, 1972 *E*, 1974 *BI* 3,4

Samuels, T A (GW) 1896 *BI* 2,3,4
Sauermann, J T (Tvl) 1971 *F* 1,2, *A* 1, 1972 *E*, 1974 *BI* 1
Schlebusch, J J J (OFS) 1974 *BI* 3,4, 1975 *F* 2
Schmidt, L U (NT) 1958 *F* 2, 1962 *BI* 2
Schmidt, U L (NT) 1986 *Cv* 1,2,3,4, 1989 *Wld* 1,2
Schoeman, J (WP) 1963 *A* 3,4, 1965 *I, S, A* 1, *NZ* 1,2
Scholtz, H H (WP) 1921 *NZ* 1,2
Scott, P (Tvl) 1896 *BI* 1,2,3,4
Sendin, W D (GW) 1921 *NZ* 2
Serfontein, D J (WP) 1980 *BI* 1,2,3,4, *S Am* 3,4, *F*, 1981 *I* 1,2, *NZ* 1,2,3, *US*, 1982 *S Am* 1,2, 1984 *S Am* 1,2
Shand, R (GW) 1891 *BI* 2,3
Sheriff, A R (Tvl) 1938 *BI* 1,2,3
Shum, E H (Tvl) 1912-13 *E*
Sinclair, D J (Tvl) 1955 *BI* 1,2,3,4
Sinclair, J H (Tvl) 1903 *BI* 1
Skene, A L (WP) 1958 *F* 2
Slater, J T (EP) 1924 *BI* 3,4, 1928 *NZ* 1
Smal, G P (WP) 1986 *Cv* 1,2,3,4, 1989 *Wld* 1,2
Smith, C M (OFS) 1963 *A* 3,4, 1964 *W, F*, 1965 *A* 1,2, *NZ* 2
Smith, C W (GW) 1891 *BI* 2, 1896 *BI* 2,3
Smith, D (GW) 1891 *BI* 2
Smith, D J (Z-R) 1980 *BI* 1,2,3,4
Smith, G A C (EP) 1938 *BI* 2
Smollan, F C (Tvl) 1933 *A* 3,4,5
Snedden, R C (GW) 1891 *BI* 2
Snyman, D S L (WP) 1972 *E*, 1974 *BI* 1,2(R), *F* 1,2, 1975 *F* 1,2, 1976 *NZ* 2,3, 1977 *Wld*
Snyman, J C P (OFS) 1974 *BI* 2,3,4
Sonnekus, G H H (OFS) 1974 *BI* 3, 1984 *E* 1,2
Spies, J J (NT) 1970 *NZ* 1,2,3,4
Stander, J C J (OFS) 1974 *BI* 4(R), 1976 *NZ* 1,2,3,4
Stapelberg, W P (NT) 1974 *F* 1,2

Starke, J J (WP) 1956 *NZ* 4
Starke, K T (WP) 1924 *BI* 1,2,3,4
Steenekamp, J G A (Tvl) 1958 *F* 1
Stegmann, A C (WP) 1906 *S, I*
Stegmann, J A (Tvl) 1912-13 *S, I, W, E, F*
Stewart, D A (WP) 1960 *S*, 1960-61 *E, S, F*, 1961 *I*, 1963 *A* 1,3,4, 1964 *W, F*, 1965 *I*
Stofberg, M T S (OFS, NT, WP) 1976 *NZ* 2,3, 1977 *Wld*, 1980 *S Am* 1,2, *BI* 1,2,3,4, *S Am* 3,4, *F*, 1981 *I* 1,2, *NZ* 1,2, *US*, 1982 *S Am* 1,2, 1984 *E* 1,2
Strachan, L C (Tvl) 1931-32 *E, S*, 1937 *A* 1,2, *NZ* 1,2,3, 1938 *BI* 1,2,3
Strauss, J A (WP) 1984 *S Am* 1,2
Strauss, J H P (Tvl) 1976 *NZ* 3,4, 1980 *S Am* 1
Strauss, S S F (GW) 1921 *NZ* 3
Strydom, C F (OFS) 1955 *BI* 3, 1956 *A* 1,2, *NZ* 1,4, 1958 *F* 1
Strydom, L J (NT) 1949 *NZ* 1,2
Suter, M R (N) 1965 *I, S*
Swart, J J N (SWA) 1955 *BI* 1

Taberer, W S (GW) 1896 *BI* 2
Taylor, O B (N) 1962 *BI* 1
Theunissen, D J (GW) 1896 *BI* 3
Thompson, G (WP) 1912-13 *S, I, W*
Tindall, J C (WP) 1924 *BI* 1, 1928 *NZ* 1,2,3,4
Tobias, E G (SARF, Bol) 1981 *I* 1,2, 1984 *E* 1,2, *S Am* 1,2
Tod, N S (N) 1928 *NZ* 2
Townsend, W H (N) 1921 *NZ* 1
Trenery, W (GW) 1891 *BI* 2
Truter, D R (WP) 1924 *BI* 2,4
Truter, J T (N) 1963 *A* 1, 1964 *F*, 1965 *A* 2
Turner, F G (EP) 1933 *A* 1,2,3, 1937 *A* 1,2, *NZ* 1,2,3, 1938 *BI* 1,2,3
Twigge, R J (NT) 1960 *S*

Ulyate, C A (Tvl) 1955 *BI* 1,2,3,4, 1956 *NZ* 1,2,3
Uys, P de W (NT) 1960-61 *W, E, S*, 1961 *I, A* 1,2, 1962 *BI* 1,4, 1963 *A* 1,2, 1969 *A* 1(R),2

Van Aswegen, H J (WP) 1981 *NZ* 1
Van Broekhuizen, H D (WP) 1896 *BI* 4
Van Buuren, M C (Tvl) 1891 *BI* 1
Van De Vyver, D F (WP) 1937 *A* 2
Van Den Berg, D S (N) 1975 *F* 1,2 1976 *NZ* 1,2
Van Den Berg, M A (WP) 1937 *A* 1, *NZ* 1,2,3
Van Der Merwe, A J (Bol) 1955 *BI* 2,3,4, 1956 *A* 1,2, *NZ* 1,2,3,4, 1958 *F* 1, 1960 *S, NZ* 2
Van Der Merwe, A V (WP) 1931-32 *W*
Van Der Merwe, B S (NT) 1949 *NZ* 1
Van Der Merwe, H S (NT) 1960 *NZ* 4, 1963 *A* 2,3,4, 1964 *F*
Van Der Merwe, J P (WP) 1969-70 *W*
Van Der Merwe, P R (SWD, WT, GW) 1981 *NZ* 2,3, *US*, 1986 *Cv* 1,2, 1989 *Wld* 1
Vanderplank, B E (N) 1924 *BI* 3,4
Van Der Schyff, J H (GW) 1949 *NZ* 1,2,3,4, 1955 *BI* 1
Van Der Watt, A E (WP) 1969-70 *S* (R), *E, I*
Van Der Westhuizen, J C (WP) 1928 *NZ* 2,3,4, 1931-32 *I*
Van Der Westhuizen, J H (WP) 1931-32 *I, E, S*
Van Druten, N J V (Tvl) 1924 *BI* 1,2,3,4, 1928 *NZ* 1,2,3,4
Van Heerden, A J (Tvl) 1921 *NZ* 1,3
Van Heerden, J L (NT) 1974 *BI* 3,4, *F* 1,2, 1975 *F* 1,2, 1976 *NZ* 1,2,3,4, 1977 *Wld*, 1980 *BI* 1,3,4, *S Am* 3,4, *F*
Van Jaarsveld, C J (Tvl) 1949 *NZ* 1
Van Jaarsveldt, D C (R) 1960 *S*
Van Niekerk, J A (WP) 1928 *NZ* 4
Van Reenen, G L (WP) 1937 *A* 2, *NZ* 1
Van Renen, C G (WP) 1891 *BI* 3, 1896 *BI* 1,4
Van Renen, W (WP) 1903 *BI* 1,3
Van Rooyen, G W (Tvl) 1921 *NZ* 2,3
Van Ryneveld, R C B (WP) 1910 *BI* 2,3
Van Schoor, R A M (R) 1949 *NZ* 2,3,4, 1951-52 *S, I, W, E, F*, 1953 *A* 1,2,3,4
Van Vollenhoven, K T (NT) 1955 *BI* 1,2,3,4, 1956 *A* 1,2, *NZ* 3
Van Vuuren, T F (EP) 1912-13 *S, I, W, E, F*
Van Wyk, C J (Tvl) 1951-52 *S, I, W, E, F*, 1953 *A* 1,2,3,4, 1955 *BI* 1
Van Wyk, J F B (NT) 1970 *NZ* 1,2,3,4, 1971 *F* 1,2, *A*

1,2,3, 1972 *E*, 1974 *BI* 1,3,4, 1976 *NZ* 3,4
Van Wyk, S P (WP) 1928 *NZ* 1,2
Van Zyl, B P (WP) 1961 *I*
Van Zyl, C G P (OFS) 1965 *NZ* 1,2,3,4
Van Zyl, G H (WP) 1958 *F* 1, 1960 *S*, *NZ* 1,2,3,4, 1960-61 *W*, *I*, *E*, *S*, *F*, 1961 *I*, *A* 1,2, 1962 *BI* 1,3,4
Van Zyl, H J (Tvl) 1960 *NZ* 1,2,3,4, 1960-61 *I*, *E*, *S*, 1961 *I*, *A* 1,2
Van Zyl, P J (Bol) 1961 *I*
Veldsman, P E (WP) 1977 *Wld*
Venter, F D (Tvl) 1931-32 *W*, *S*, 1933 *A* 3
Versfeld, C (WP) 1891 *BI* 3
Versfeld, M (WP) 1891 *BI* 1,2,3
Vigne, J T (Tvl) 1891 *BI* 1,2,3
Viljoen, J F (GW) 1971 *F* 1,2, *A* 1,2,3, 1972 *E*
Viljoen, J T (N) 1971 *A* 1,2,3
Villet, J V (WP) 1984 *E* 1,2
Visagie, P J (GW) 1967 *F* 1,2,3,4, 1968 *BI* 1,2,3,4, *F* 1,2, 1969 *A* 1,2,3,4, 1969-70 *S*, *E*, 1970 *NZ* 1,2,3,4, 1971 *F* 1,2, *A* 1,2,3
Visagie, R G (OFS) 1984 *E* 1,2, *S Am* 1,2
Visser, J de V (WP) 1981 *NZ* 2, *US*
Visser, P J (Tvl) 1933 *A* 2
Viviers, S S (OFS) 1956 *A* 1,2, *NZ* 2,3,4
Vogel, M L (OFS) 1974 *BI* 2(R)

Wagenaar, C (NT) 1977 *Wld*

Wahl, J J (WP) 1949 *NZ* 1
Walker, A P (N) 1921 *NZ* 1,3, 1924 *BI* 1,2,3,4
Walker, H N (OFS) 1953 *A* 3, 1956 *A* 2, *NZ* 1,4
Walker, H W (Tvl) 1910 *BI* 1,2,3
Walton, D C (N) 1964 *F*, 1965 *I*, *S*, *NZ* 3,4, 1969 *A* 1,2, 1969-70 *E*
Waring, F W (WP) 1931-32 *I*, *E*, 1933 *A* 1,2,3,4,5
Wessels, J J (WP) 1896 *BI* 1,2,3
Whipp, P J M (WP) 1974 *BI* 1,2, 1975 *F* 1, 1976 *NZ* 1,3,4, 1980 *S Am* 1,2
White, J (Bor) 1931-32 *W*, 1933 *A* 1,2,3,4,5, 1937 *A* 1,2, *NZ* 1,2
Williams, A E (GW) 1910 *BI* 1
Williams, A P (WP) 1984 *E* 1,2
Williams, D O (WP) 1937 *A* 1,2 *NZ* 1,2,3, 1938 *BI* 1,2,3
Williams, J G (NT) 1971 *F* 1,2, *A* 1,2,3, 1972 *E*, 1974 *BI* 1,2,4, *F* 1,2, 1976 *NZ* 1,2
Wilson, L G (WP) 1960 *NZ* 3,4, 1960-61 *W*, *I*, *E*, *F*, 1961 *I*, *A* 1,2, 1962 *BI* 1,2,3,4, 1963 *A* 1,2,3,4, 1964 *W*, *F*, 1965 *I*, *S*, *A* 1,2, *NZ* 1,2,3,4
Wolmarans, B J (OFS) 1977 *Wld*
Wright, G D (EP, Tvl) 1986 *Cv* 3,4, 1989 *Wld* 1,2
Wyness, M R K (WP) 1962 *BI* 1,2,3,4, 1963 *A* 2

Zeller, W C (N) 1921 *NZ* 2,3
Zimerman, M (WP) 1931-32 *W*, *I*, *E*, *S*

SOUTH AFRICAN INTERNATIONAL RECORDS

Both team and individual records are for official South African international matches, up to 31 March 1992.

TEAM RECORDS

Highest score
50 v S America (50-18) 1982 Pretoria
v individual countries
30 v Australia (30-11) 1969 Johannesburg
34 v B Isles (34-14) 1962 Bloemfontein
35 v England (35-9) 1984 Johannesburg
38 v France $\begin{cases} \text{(38-5) 1913 Bordeaux} \\ \text{(38-25) 1975 Bloemfontein} \end{cases}$
38 v Ireland (38-0) 1912 Dublin
24 v N Zealand (24-12) 1981 Wellington
33 v NZ Cavaliers (33-18) 1986 Pretoria
50 v S America (50-18) 1982 Pretoria
44 v Scotland (44-0) 1951 Murrayfield
38 v United States (38-7) 1981 New York
24 v Wales (24-3) 1964 Durban

Biggest winning points margin
44 v Scotland (44-0) 1951 Murrayfield
v individual countries
25 v Australia (28-3) 1961 Johannesburg
20 v B Isles (34-14) 1962 Bloemfontein
26 v England (35-9) 1984 Johannesburg
33 v France (38-5) 1913 Bordeaux

38 v Ireland (38-0) 1912 Dublin
17 v N Zealand (17-0) 1928 Durban
15 v NZ Cavaliers (33-18) 1986 Pretoria
32 v S America (50-18) 1982 Pretoria
44 v Scotland (44-0) 1951 Murrayfield
31 v United States (38-7) 1981 New York
21 v Wales (24-3) 1964 Durban

Highest score by opposing team
28 B Isles (9-28) 1974 Pretoria
by individual countries
21 Australia (6-21) 1933 Durban
28 B Isles (9-28) 1974 Pretoria
18 England (9-18) 1972 Johannesburg
25 France (38-25) 1975 Bloemfontein
15 Ireland (23-15) 1981 Cape Town
25 N Zealand (22-25) 1981 Auckland
19 NZ Cavaliers (18-19) 1986 Durban
21 S America (12-21) 1982 Bloemfontein
10 Scotland (18−10) 1960 Port Elizabeth
 7 United States (38-7) 1981 New York
 6 Wales (6-6) 1970 Cardiff

Biggest losing points margin
19 v B Isles (9-28) 1974 Pretoria
v individual countries
15 v Australia (6-21) 1933 Durban
19 v B Isles (9-28) 1974 Pretoria
9 v England (9-18) 1972 Johannesburg
5 v France (14-19) 1967 Johannesburg
3 v Ireland (6-9) 1965 Dublin
17 v N Zealand (3-20) 1965 Auckland
1 v NZ Cavaliers (18-19) 1986 Durban
9 v S America (12-21) 1982 Bloemfontein
6 v Scotland (0-6) 1906 Glasgow
No defeats v United States or Wales

Most tries by South Africa in an international
10 v Ireland (38-0) 1912 Dublin

Most tries against South Africa in an international
5 ⎰ by B Isles (22-23) 1955 Johannesburg
⎨ by N Zealand (3-20) 1965 Auckland
⎱ by B Isles (9-28) 1974 Pretoria

Most points on overseas tour (all matches)
753 in Australia/N Zealand (26 matches) 1937

Most tries on overseas tour (all matches)
161 in Australia/N Zealand (26 matches) 1937

INDIVIDUAL RECORDS

Most capped player
F C H du Preez ⎱ 38 ⎰ 1960-71
J H Ellis   ⎰   ⎱ 1965-76
in individual positions
Full-back
L G Wilson   27   1960-65
Wing
J P Engelbrecht   33   1960-69
Centre
J L Gainsford   33   1960-67
Fly-half
P J Visagie   25   1967-71
Scrum-half
D J de Villiers   25   1962-70

Prop
J F K Marais   35   1963-74
Hooker
G F Malan   18   1958-65
Lock
F C H du Preez   31(38)[1]   1960-71
Flanker
J H Ellis   38   1965-76
No 8
D J Hopwood   22[2]   1960-65
[1] *du Preez won 7 caps as a flanker*
[2] *T P Bedford, 25 caps, won 19 at No 8 and 6 as a flanker*

Longest international career
J M Powell 13 seasons 1891-1903
B H Heatlie 13 seasons 1891-1903

Most consecutive internationals – 25
S H Nomis 1967-72

Most internationals as captain
D J de Villiers 22 1965-70

Most points in internationals – 268
H E Botha (23 matches) 1980-89

Most points in an international – 22
G R Bosch v France 1975 Pretoria

Most tries in internationals – 15
D M Gerber (19 matches) 1980-86

Most tries in an international – 3
E E McHardy v Ireland 1912 Dublin
J A Stegmann v Ireland 1912 Dublin
K T van Vollenhoven v B Isles
 1955 Cape Town
H J van Zyl v Australia 1961 Johannesburg
R H Mordt v New Zealand 1981 Auckland
R H Mordt v United States
 1981 New York
D M Gerber v S America 1982 Pretoria
D M Gerber v England 1984 Johannesburg

Most conversions in internationals – 43
H E Botha (23 matches) 1980-89

Most conversions in an international – 7
A Geffin v Scotland 1951 Murrayfield

Most dropped goals in internationals – 15
H E Botha (23 matches) 1980-89

Most penalty goals in internationals – 43
H E Botha (23 matches) 1980-89

Most points in international series – 69
H E Botha (4 appearances) v
  NZ Cavaliers 1986

**Most points in international series
on tour – 35**
H E Botha (3 appearances)
  1981 N Zealand

**Most tries in international series
on tour – 6**
E E McHardy (5 appearances) 1912-13
  B Isles/France

Most points on overseas tour – 190
G H Brand (20 appearances) 1937
  Australia/N Zealand

Most tries on overseas tour – 22
J A Loubser (20 appearances) 1906-07
  B Isles/France

Most points in a tour match – 35
W J de Wet Ras v British Schools OB
  1980 Montevideo

Most tries in a tour match – 6
R G Dryburgh v Queensland 1956
  Brisbane

CRACKS BECOME DIVISIONS

THE 1991 SEASON IN NEW ZEALAND
Donald Cameron *New Zealand Herald*

In the previous annual I described how, in 1990, cracks began to appear in the structure of New Zealand rugby which had, in the years since the winning of the first World Cup in 1987, been building toward new heights of efficiency and playing success. In 1991, those cracks became yawning divisions which placed the administration of the sport in question, and which led through bickering and bungling at playing level to the point where the All Blacks' bid to retain the Webb Ellis Trophy did not founder in the glory of the final, but disappeared without trace as early as the semi-final against the wondrous Wallabies.

New Zealand rugby suffered these blows to its public image at a time when it was under white ant attack from another source – the heavy marketing on New Zealand television of the major Rugby League competitions in Australia. There is a warning for the future here, too; for if one or two New Zealand sides are taken into the Australian competition in the next year or so, rugby will find an even stronger competitor in the television/sponsorship/promotions marketplace.

But the most serious blows came on the field, and in the curious relationship that evolved between the coaching and management of the All Blacks, and the overall direction of Eddie Tonks, the New Zealand Rugby Football Union council chairman, whose style seemed to require that he should be frequently engaged in debate, if not dispute, with two All Black selectors, Alex Wyllie, the chairman of selectors, and Lane Penn, a junior selector. Wyllie himself had his own problems. They began with a modestly-efficient tour of Argentina, when the loss through injury of Mike Brewer meant that Wyllie had to rely again on the on-field direction of the captain, Gary Whetton. This tour was followed by a face-saving but narrow goal-kicking win at Eden Park.

About this time, Tonks indicated that Penn would not be required as assistant coach for the World Cup expedition because Penn had already indicated that he would be stepping down as a selector. But in World Cup terms Penn was pushed, he did not fall. This air of dissatisfaction between the running and the administering of the All Blacks heightened when Tonks and his senior officials directed that Wyllie take on John Hart (they were the chalk and cheese of international rugby coaching) as assistant, and then as co-coach for the World Cup tournament.

With some papering over of cracks, the co-coaching of Wyllie and Hart gave the public impression of being amicable, if not amiable. But just below the surface the fact that neither had much personal regard for the other provided just another obstacle in the All Black progress,

314

which stammered through the early rounds of the World Cup and then stuttered to a halt in Dublin.

There was further blood on the NZRFU council carpet when Wyllie, in the course of promoting his book, railed at Tonks and the NZRFU for the severity of the medical testing which had ruled Brewer out of the World Cup. This tiff at least allowed Wyllie to withdraw, in an apparent huff, his nomination for the 1993 All Black panel – his mission had little prospect of success, but Wyllie was able to withdraw as if in high dudgeon. The subsequent vote, against the wishes of a special NZRFU council screening committee, also removed Hart from the All Black panel and left a new committee comprising Laurie Mains, Peter Thorburn and Earle Kirton, the latter being recycled after a one-year term in the late 1980s.

The new panel is being regarded as the signal for the start of a new era in All Black rugby. This theory might be accurate on the point that we may never have another golden phase like the one of 1987-90. At the time of writing the NZRFU, in their quest for more and more promotion and gate-takings, were putting that hope under strain by committing the All Blacks to nine Tests in six months – three against a World XV, two against Ireland on tour, three away against Australia and one in South Africa. Time will tell whether the brave new world of New Zealand rugby is strong enough to take such early stress.

NATIONAL CHAMPIONSHIP
First Division

	P	W	L	D	F	A	Pts
Otago	10	9	1	0	298	119	37
Auckland	10	9	1	0	318	130	36
North Harbour	10	7	3	0	256	168	28
Canterbury	10	6	3	1	252	241	26
Waikato	10	5	5	0	244	248	20
Wellington	10	4	6	0	183	184	18
North Auckland	10	4	6	0	211	228	18
Hawke's Bay	10	3	6	1	170	254	15
Bay of Plenty	10	3	7	0	183	256	14
Taranaki	10	3	7	0	152	249	13
Counties	10	1	9	0	112	302	4

Second Division

	P	W	L	D	F	A	Pts
King Country	7	6	1	0	255	49	25
Southland	7	6	1	0	192	113	24
Manawatu	7	5	2	0	253	113	21
Thames Valley	7	4	3	0	123	141	17
Wairarapa-Bush	7	2	5	0	117	125	12
Poverty Bay	7	2	5	0	117	265	9
Marlborough	7	2	5	0	100	201	8
Wanganui	7	1	6	0	83	214	4

Third Division

	P	W	L	D	F	A	Pts
Sth Canterbury	7	7	0	0	254	110	28
Mid-Canterbury	7	5	1	1	177	74	22
Nelson Bays	7	4	2	1	151	89	19
Horowhenua	7	4	3	0	204	122	16
Buller	7	4	3	0	113	122	16
East Coast	7	2	5	0	109	196	9
North Otago	7	1	6	0	100	255	4
West Coast	7	0	7	0	70	210	0

RANFURLY SHIELD CHALLENGES
Auckland 76, Nelson Bays 0; Auckland 27, Counties 0; Auckland 55, Taranaki 9; Auckland 31, Wellington 21; Auckland 29, Bay of Plenty 18; Auckland 52, Manawatu 4; Auckland 40, Waikato 12; Auckland 32, South Canterbury 6

NEW ZEALAND INTERNATIONAL PLAYERS (*up to 31 March 1992*)

ABBREVIATIONS

A – Australia; *Arg* – Argentina; *AW* – Anglo-Welsh; *BI* – British Isles teams; *C* – Canada; *E* – England; *F* – France; *Fj* – Fiji; *I* – Ireland; *It* – Italy; *R* – Romania; *S* – Scotland; *SA* – South Africa; *US* – United States; *W* – Wales; (R) – Replacement. Entries in square brackets [ ] indicate appearances in the Rugby World Cup.

Note: When a series has taken place, figures denote the particular matches in which players featured. Thus 1959 *BI* 2,4 indicates that a player appeared in the second and fourth Tests of the 1959 series against the British Isles.

Abbott, H L (Taranaki) 1906 *F*
Aitken, G G (Wellington) 1921 *SA* 1,2
Allen, F R (Auckland) 1946 *A* 1,2 1947 *A* 1,2, 1949 *SA* 1,2
Allen, N H (Counties) 1980 *A* 3, *W*
Alley, G T (Canterbury) 1928 *SA* 1,2,3
Anderson, A (Canterbury) 1983 *S, E*, 1984 *A* 1,2,3, 1987 [*Fj*]
Anderson, B L (Wairarapa-Bush) 1986 *A* 1
Archer, W R (Otago, Southland) 1955 *A* 1,2, 1956 *SA* 1,3
Argus, W G (Canterbury) 1946 *A* 1,2, 1947 *A* 1,2
Arnold, D A (Canterbury) 1963 *I*, *W*, 1964 *E*, *F*
Arnold, K D (Waikato) 1947 *A* 1,2
Ashby, D L (Southland) 1958 *A* 2
Asher, A A (Auckland) 1903 *A*
Ashworth, B G (Auckland) 1978 *A* 1,2
Ashworth, J C (Canterbury, Hawke's Bay) 1978 *A* 1,2,3, 1980 *A* 1,2,3, 1981 *SA* 1,2,3, 1982 *A* 1,2, 1983 *BI* 1,2,3,4, *A*, 1984 *F* 1,2 *A* 1,2,3, 1985 *E* 1,2, *A*
Atkinson, H (West Coast) 1913 *A* 1
Avery, H E (Wellington) 1910 *A* 1,2,3

Bachop, G T M (Canterbury) 1989 *W, I*, 1990 *S* 1,2, *A* 1,2,3, *F* 1,2, 1991 *Arg* 1,2, *A* 1,2, [*E, US, C, A, S*]
Badeley, C E O (Auckland) 1921 *SA* 1,2
Baird, J A S (Otago) 1913 *A* 2
Ball, N (Wellington) 1931 *A*, 1932 *A* 2,3, 1935 *W*, 1936 *E*
Barrett, J (Auckland) 1913 *A* 2,3
Barry, E F (Wellington) 1934 *A* 2
Batty, G B (Wellington, Bay of Plenty) 1972 *W, S*, 1973 *E* 1, *I, F, E* 2, 1974 *A* 1,3, *I*, 1975 *S*, 1976 *SA* 1,2,3,4, 1977 *BI* 1
Batty, W (Auckland) 1930 *BI* 1,3,4, 1931 *A*
Beatty, G E (Taranaki) 1950 *BI* 1
Bell, R H (Otago) 1951 *A* 3, 1952 *A* 1,2
Bellis, E A (Wanganui) 1921 *SA* 1,2,3
Bennet, R (Otago) 1905 *A*
Berghan, T (Otago) 1938 *A* 1,2,3
Berry, M J (Wairarapa-Bush) 1986 *A* 3 (R)
Bevan, V D (Wellington) 1949 *A* 1,2, 1950 *BI* 1,2,3,4
Birtwistle, W M (Canterbury) 1965 *SA* 1,2,3,4, 1967 *E, W, S*
Black, J E (Canterbury) 1977 *F* 1, 1979 *A*, 1980 *A* 3
Black, N W (Auckland) 1949 *SA* 3
Black, R S (Otago) 1914 *A* 1
Blake, A W (Wairarapa) 1949 *A* 1
Boggs, E G (Auckland) 1946 *A* 2, 1949 *SA* 1
Bond, J G (Canterbury) 1949 *A* 2
Booth, E E (Otago) 1906 *F*, 1907 *A* 1,3
Boroevich, K G (Wellington) 1986 *F* 1, *A* 1, *F* 3 (R)
Botica, F M (North Harbour) 1986 *F* 1, *A* 1,2,3, *F* 2,3, 1989 *Arg* 1 (R)
Bowden, N J G (Taranaki) 1952 *A* 2
Bowers, R G (Wellington) 1954 *I, F*
Bowman, A W (Hawke's Bay) 1938 *A* 1,2,3
Braid, G J (Bay of Plenty) 1983 *S, E*
Bremner, S G (Auckland, Canterbury) 1952 *A* 2, 1956 *SA* 2
Brewer, M R (Otago) 1986 *F* 1, *A* 1,2,3, *F* 2,3, 1988 *A* 1, 1989 *A, W, I*, 1990 *S* 1,2, *A* 1,2,3, *F* 1,2
Briscoe, K C (Taranaki) 1959 *BI* 2, 1960 *SA* 1,2,3,4, 1963 *I, W*, 1964 *E, S*
Brooke, Z V (Auckland) 1987 [*Arg*], 1989 *Arg* 2 (R), 1990 *A* 1,2,3, *F* 1 (R), 1991 *Arg* 2, *A* 1,2, [*E, It, C, A, S*]
Brooke-Cowden, M (Auckland) 1986 *F* 1, *A* 1, 1987 [*W*]
Brown, C (Taranaki) 1913 *A* 2,3

Brown, R H (Taranaki) 1955 *A* 3, 1956 *SA* 1,2,3,4, 1957 *A* 1,2 1958 *A* 1,2,3, 1959 *BI* 1,3, 1961 *F* 1,2,3, 1962 *A* 1
Brownlie, C J (Hawke's Bay) 1924 *W*, 1925 *E, F*
Brownlie, M J (Hawke's Bay) 1924 *I*, *W*, 1925 *E, F*, 1928 *SA* 1,2,3,4
Bruce, J A (Auckland) 1914 *A* 1,2
Bruce, O D (Canterbury) 1976 *SA* 1,2,4, 1977 *BI* 2,3,4, *F* 1,2, 1978 *A* 1,2, *I*, *W, E, S*
Bryers, R F (King Country) 1949 *A* 1
Budd, T A (Southland) 1946 *A* 2, 1949 *A* 2
Bullock-Douglas, G A H (Wanganui) 1932 *A* 1,2,3, 1934 *A* 1,2
Burgess, G A J (Auckland) 1981 *SA* 2
Burgess, G F (Southland) 1905 *A*
Burgess, R E (Manawatu) 1971 *BI* 1,2,3, 1972 *A* 3, *W*, 1973 *I, F*
Burke, P S (Taranaki) 1955 *A* 1, 1957 *A* 1,2
Burns, P J (Canterbury) 1908 *AW* 2, 1910 *A* 1,2,3, 1913 *A* 3
Bush, R G (Otago) 1931 *A*
Bush, W K (Canterbury) 1974 *A* 1,2, 1975 *S*, 1976 *I, SA* 2,4, 1977 *BI* 2,3,4(R), 1978 *I, W*, 1979 *A*
Buxton, J B (Canterbury) 1955 *A* 3, 1956 *SA* 1

Cain, M J (Taranaki) 1913 *US*, 1914 *A* 1,2,3
Callesen, J A (Manawatu) 1974 *A* 1,2,3, 1975 *S*
Cameron, D (Taranaki) 1908 *AW* 1,2,3
Cameron, L M (Manawatu) 1980 *A* 3, 1981 *SA* 1(R),2,3, *R*
Carleton, S R (Canterbury) 1928 *SA* 1,2,3, 1929 *A* 1,2,3
Carrington, K R (Auckland) 1971 *BI* 1,3,4
Carter, M P (Auckland) 1991 *A* 2, [*It, A*]
Casey, S T (Otago) 1905 *S, I, E, W*, 1907 *A* 1,2,3, 1908 *AW* 1
Catley, E H (Waikato) 1946 *A* 1, 1947 *A* 1,2, 1949 *SA* 1,2,3,4
Caughey, T H C (Auckland) 1932 *A* 1,3, 1934 *A* 1,2, 1935 *S, I*, 1936 *E, A* 1, 1937 *SA* 3
Caulton, R W (Wellington) 1959 *BI* 2,3,4, 1960 *SA* 1,4 1961 *F* 2, 1963 *E* 1,2, *I*, *W*, 1964 *E, S, F*, *A* 1,2,3
Cherrington, N P (North Auckland) 1950 *BI* 1
Christian, D L (Auckland) 1949 *SA* 4
Clamp, M (Wellington) 1984 *A* 2,3
Clark, D W (Otago) 1964 *A* 1,2
Clark, W H (Wellington) 1953 *W*, 1954 *I, E, S*, 1955 *A* 1,2, 1956 *SA* 2,3,4
Clarke, A H (Auckland) 1958 *A* 3, 1959 *BI* 4, 1960 *SA* 1
Clarke, D B (Waikato) 1956 *SA* 3,4, 1957 *A* 1,2, 1958 *A* 1,3, 1959 *BI* 1,2,3,4, 1960 *SA* 1,2,3,4, 1961 *F* 1,2,3, 1962 *A* 1,2,3,4,5, 1963 *E* 1,2, *I, W*, 1964 *E, S, F, A* 2,3
Clarke, I J (Waikato) 1953 *W*, 1955 *A* 1,2,3, 1956 *SA* 1,2,3,4, 1957 *A* 1,2 1958 *A* 1,3, 1959 *BI* 1,2, 1960 *SA* 2,4, 1961 *F* 1,2,3, 1962 *A* 1,2,3, 1963 *E* 1,2
Clarke, R L (Taranaki) 1932 *A* 2,3
Cobden, D G (Canterbury) 1937 *SA* 1
Cockerill, M S (Taranaki) 1951 *A* 1,2,3
Cockroft, E A P (South Canterbury) 1913 *A* 3, 1914 *A* 2,3
Codlin, B W (Counties) 1980 *A* 1,2,3
Collins, A H (Taranaki) 1932 *A* 2,3, 1934 *A* 1
Collins, J L (Poverty Bay) 1964 *A* 1, 1965 *SA* 1,4
Colman, J T H (Taranaki) 1907 *A* 1,2, 1908 *AW* 1,3
Connor, D M (Auckland) 1961 *F* 1,2,3, 1962 *A* 1,2,3, 4,5, 1963 *E* 1,2, 1964 *A* 2,3
Conway, R J (Otago, Bay of Plenty) 1959 *BI* 2,3,4, 1960 *SA* 1,3,4, 1965 *SA* 1,2,3,4

1,2,3, 1989 *F* 1,2, *Arg* 1,2, *A*, *W*, *I*, 1990 *S* 1,2, *A* 1,2,3, *F* 1,2, 1991 *Arg* 1,2, *A* 1,2, [*E*, *It*, *C*, *A*, *S*]
Long, A J (Auckland) 1903 *A*
Loveridge, D S (Taranaki) 1978 *W*, 1979 *S*, *E*, 1980 *A* 1,2,3, *W*, 1981 *S* 1,2, *SA* 1,2,3, *R*, *F* 1,2, 1982 *A* 1,2,3, 1983 *BI* 1,2,3,4, *A*, 1985 *Arg* 2
Lucas, F W (Auckland) 1924 *I*, 1925 *F*, 1928 *SA* 4, 1930 *BI* 1,2,3,4
Lunn, W A (Otago) 1949 *A* 1,2
Lynch, T W (South Canterbury) 1913 *A* 1, 1914 *A* 1,2,3
Lynch, T W (Canterbury) 1951 *A* 1,2,3

McAtamney, F S (Otago) 1956 *SA* 2
McCahill, B J (Auckland) 1987 [*Arg*, *S*(R), *W*(R)], 1989 *Arg* 1(R), 2(R), 1991 *A* 2, [*E*, *US*, *C*, *A*]
McCaw, W A (Southland) 1951 *A* 1,2,3, 1953 *W*, 1954 *F*
McCool, M J (Wairarapa-Bush) 1979 *A*
McCormick, W F (Canterbury) 1965 *SA* 4, 1967 *E*, *W*, *F*, *S*, 1968 *A* 1,2, *F* 1,2,3, 1969 *W* 1,2, 1970 *SA* 1,2,3, 1971 *BI* 1
McCullough, J F (Taranaki) 1959 *BI* 2,3,4
McDonald, A (Otago) 1905 *S*, *I*, *E*, *W*, 1907 *A* 1, 1908 *AW* 1, 1913 *A* 1, *US*
Macdonald, H H (Canterbury, North Auckland) 1972 *W*, *S*, 1973 *E* 1, *I*, *F*, *E* 2, 1974 *I*, 1975 *S*, 1976 *I*, *SA* 1,2,3
McDowell, S C (Auckland, Bay of Plenty) 1985 *Arg* 1,2, 1986 *A* 2,3, *F* 2,3, 1987 [*It*, *Fj*, *S*, *W*, *F*], *A*, 1988 *W* 1,2, *A* 1,2,3, 1989 *F* 1,2, *Arg* 1,2, *A*, *W*, *I*, 1990 *S* 1,2, *A* 1,2,3, *F* 1,2, 1991 *Arg* 1,2, *A* 1,2, [*E*, *US*, *It*, *C*, *A*, *S*]
McEldowney, J T (Taranaki) 1977 *BI* 3,4
MacEwan, I N (Wellington) 1956 *SA* 2, 1957 *A* 1,2, 1958 *A* 1,2,3, 1959 *BI* 1,2,3, 1960 *SA* 1,2,3,4, 1961 *F* 1,2,3, 1962 *A* 1,2,3,4
McGrattan, B (Wellington) 1983 *S*, *E*, 1985 *Arg* 1,2, 1986 *F* 1, *A* 1
McGregor, A J (Auckland) 1913 *A* 1, *US*
McGregor, D (Canterbury, Southland) 1903 *A*, 1904 *BI*, 1905 *E*, *W*
McGregor, N P (Canterbury) 1924 *W*, 1925 *E*
McGregor, R W (Auckland) 1903 *A*, 1904 *BI*
McHugh, M J (Auckland) 1946 *A* 1,2, 1949 *SA* 3
McIntosh, D N (Wellington) 1956 *SA* 1,2, 1957 *A* 1,2
McKay, D W (Auckland) 1961 *F* 1,2,3, 1963 *E* 1,2
McKechnie, B J (Southland) 1977 *F* 1,2, 1978 *A* 2(R),3, *W*(R), *E*, *S*, 1979 *A*, 1981 *SA* 1(R), *F* 1
McKellar, G F (Wellington) 1910 *A* 1,2,3
McKenzie, R J (Wellington) 1913 *A* 1, *US*, 1914 *A* 2,3
McKenzie, R McC (Manawatu) 1934 *A* 1, 1935 *S*, 1936 *A* 1, 1937 *SA* 1,2,3, 1938 *A* 1,2,3
McLachlan, J S (Auckland) 1974 *A* 2
McLaren, H C (Waikato) 1952 *A* 1
McLean, A L (Bay of Plenty) 1921 *SA* 2,3
McLean, H F (Wellington, Auckland) 1930 *BI* 3,4, 1932 *A* 1,2,3, 1934 *A* 1, 1935 *I*, *W*, 1936 *E*
McLean, J K (King Country, Auckland) 1947 *A* 1, 1949 *A* 2
McLeod, B E (Counties) 1964 *A* 1,2,3, 1965 *SA* 1,2,3,4, 1966 *BI* 1,2,3,4, 1967 *E*, *W*, *F*, *S*, 1968 *A* 1,2, *F* 1,2,3, 1969 *W* 1,2, 1970 *SA* 1,2
McMinn, A F (Wairarapa, Manawatu) 1903 *A*, 1905 *A*
McMinn, F A (Manawatu) 1904 *BI*
McMullen, R F (Auckland) 1957 *A* 1,2, 1958 *A* 1,2,3, 1959 *BI* 1,2,3, 1960 *SA* 2,3,4
McNab, J R (Otago) 1949 *SA* 1,2,3, 1950 *BI* 1,2,3
McNaughton, A M (Bay of Plenty) 1971 *BI* 1,2,3
McNeece, J (Southland) 1913 *A* 2,3, 1914 *A* 1,2,3
McPhail, B E (Canterbury) 1959 *BI* 1,4
Macpherson, D G (Otago) 1905 *A*
MacPherson, G L (Otago) 1986 *F* 1
MacRae, I R (Hawke's Bay) 1966 *BI* 1,2,3,4, 1967 *A*, *E*, *W*, *F*, *S*, 1968 *F* 1,2, 1969 *W* 1,2, 1970 *SA* 1,2,3,4
McRae, J A (Southland) 1946 *A* 1(R),2
McWilliams, R G (Auckland) 1928 *SA* 2,3,4, 1929 *A* 1,2,3, 1930 *BI* 1,2,3,4
Mackrell, W H C (Auckland) 1906 *F*
Macky, J V (Auckland) 1913 *A* 2
Maguire, J R (Auckland) 1910 *A* 1,2,3
Mahoney, A (Bush) 1935 *S*, *I*, *W*, 1936 *E*
Mains, L W (Otago) 1971 *BI* 2,3,4, 1976 *I*
Major, J (Taranaki) 1967 *A*
Manchester, J E (Canterbury) 1932 *A* 1,2,3, 1934 *A* 1,2, 1935 *S*, *I*, *W*, 1936 *E*

Mason, D F (Wellington) 1947 *A* 2(R)
Masters, R R (Canterbury) 1924 *I*, *W*, 1925 *E*, *F*
Mataira, H K (Hawke's Bay) 1934 *A* 2
Matheson, J D (Otago) 1972 *A* 1,2,3, *W*, *S*
Max, D S (Nelson) 1931 *A*, 1934 *A* 1,2
Meads, C E (King Country) 1957 *A* 1,2, 1958 *A* 1,2,3, 1959 *BI* 2,3,4, 1960 *SA* 1,2,3,4, 1961 *F* 1,2,3, 1962 *A* 1,2,3,5, 1963 *E* 1,2, *I*, *W*, 1964 *E*, *S*, *F*, *A* 1,2,3, 1965 *SA* 1,2,3,4 1966 *BI* 1,2,3,4, 1967 *A*, *E*, *W*, *F*, *S*, 1968 *A* 1,2, *F* 1,2,3, 1969 *W* 1,2, 1970 *SA* 3,4, 1971 *BI* 1,2,3,4
Meads, S T (King Country) 1961 *F* 1,1962 *A* 4,5, 1963 *I*, 1964 *A* 1,2,3, 1965 *SA* 1,2,3,4, 1966 *BI* 1,2,3,4
Meates, K F (Canterbury) 1952 *A* 1,2
Meates, W A (Otago) 1949 *SA* 2,3,4, 1950 *BI* 1,2,3,4
Metcalfe, T C (Southland) 1931 *A*, 1932 *A* 1
Mexted, G (Wellington) 1950 *BI* 4
Mexted, M G (Wellington) 1979 *S*, *E*, 1980 *A* 1,2,3, *W*, 1981 *S* 1,2, *SA* 1,2,3, *R*, *F* 1,2, 1982 *A* 1,2,3, 1983 *BI* 1,2,3,4, *A*, *S*, *E*, 1984 *F* 1,2, *A* 1,2,3, 1985 *E* 1,2, *A*, *Arg* 1,2
Mill, J J (Hawke's Bay, Wairarapa) 1924 *W*, 1925 *E*, *F*, 1930 *BI* 1
Milliken, H M (Canterbury) 1938 *A* 1,2,3
Milner, H P (Wanganui) 1970 *SA* 3
Mitchell, N A (Southland, Otago) 1935 *S*, *I*, *W*, 1936 *E*, *A* 2, 1937 *SA* 3, 1938 *A* 1,2
Mitchell, T W (Canterbury) 1976 *SA* 4(R)
Mitchell, W J (Canterbury) 1910 *A* 2,3
Mitchinson, F E (Wellington) 1907 *A* 1,2,3, 1908 *AW* 1,2,3, 1910 *A* 1,2,3, 1913 *A* 1(R), *US*
Moffitt, J E (Wellington)1921 *SA* 1,2,3
Moore, G J T (Otago) 1949 *A* 1
Moreton, R C (Canterbury) 1962 *A* 3,4, 1964 *A* 1,2,3, 1965 *SA* 2,3
Morgan, J E (North Auckland) 1974 *A* 3, *I*, 1976 *SA* 2,3,4
Morris, T J (Nelson Bays) 1972 *A* 1,2,3
Morrison, T C (South Canterbury) 1938 *A* 1,2,3
Morrison, T G (Otago) 1973 *E* 2(R)
Morrissey, P J (Canterbury) 1962 *A* 3,4,5
Mourie, G N K (Taranaki) 1977 *BI* 3,4, *F* 1,2, 1978 *I*, *W*, *E*, *S*, 1979 *F* 1,2, *A*, *S*, *E*, 1980 *W*, 1981 *S* 1,2, *F* 1,2, 1982 *A* 1,2,3
Muller, B L (Taranaki) 1967 *A*, *E*, *W*, *F*, 1968 *A* 1, *F* 1, 1969 *W* 1, 1970 *SA* 1,2,4, 1971 *BI* 1,2,3,4
Mumm, W J (Buller) 1949 *A* 1
Murdoch, K (Otago) 1970 *SA* 4, 1972 *A* 3, *W*
Murdoch, P H (Auckland) 1964 *A* 2,3, 1965 *SA* 1,2,3
Murray, H V (Canterbury) 1913 *A* 1, *US*, 1914 *A* 2,3
Murray, P C (Wanganui) 1908 *AW* 2
Myers, R G (Waikato) 1978 *A* 3
Mynott, H J (Taranaki) 1905 *I*, *W*, 1906 *F*, 1907 *A* 1,2,3, 1910 *A* 1,3

Nathan, W J (Auckland) 1962 *A* 1,2,3,4,5, 1963 *E* 1,2, *W*, 1964 *F*, 1966 *BI* 1,2,3,4, 1967 *A*
Nelson, K A (Otago) 1962 *A* 4,5
Nepia, G (Hawke's Bay, East Coast) 1924 *I*, *W*, 1925 *E*, *F*, 1929 *A* 1, 1930 *BI* 1,2,3,4
Nesbit, S R (Auckland) 1960 *SA* 2,3
Newton, F (Canterbury) 1905 *E*, *W*, 1906 *F*
Nicholls, H E (Wellington) 1921 *SA* 1
Nicholls, M F (Wellington) 1921 *SA* 1,2,3, 1924 *I*, *W*, 1925 *E*, *F*, 1928 *SA* 4, 1930 *BI* 2,3
Nicholson, G W (Auckland) 1903 *A*, 1904 *BI*, 1907 *A* 2,3
Norton, R W (Canterbury) 1971 *BI* 1,2,3,4, 1972 *A* 1,2,3, *W*, *S*, 1973 *E* 1, *I*, *F*, *E* 2, 1974 *A* 1,2,3, *I*, 1975 *S*, 1976 *I*, *SA* 1,2,3,4, 1977 *BI* 1,2,3,4

O'Brien, J G (Auckland) 1914 *A* 1
O'Callaghan, M W (Manawatu) 1968 *F* 1,2,3
O'Callaghan, T R (Wellington) 1949 *A* 2
O'Donnell, D H (Wellington) 1949 *A* 2
Old, G H (Manawatu) 1981 *SA* 3, *R*(R), 1982 *A* 1(R)
O'Leary, M J (Auckland) 1910 *A* 1,3, 1913 *A* 2,3
Oliver, C J (Canterbury) 1929 *A* 1,2, 1934 *A* 1, 1935 *S*, *I*, *W*, 1936 *E*
Oliver, D J (Wellington) 1930 *BI* 1,2
Oliver, D O (Otago) 1954 *I*, *F*
Oliver, F J (Southland, Otago, Manawatu) 1976 *SA* 4, 1977 *BI* 1,2,3,4, *F* 1,2, 1978 *A* 1,2,3, *I*, *W*, *E*, *S*, 1979 *F* 1,2, 1981 *SA* 2

Orr, R W (Otago) 1949 *A* 1
Osborne, W M (Wanganui) 1975 *S*, 1976 *SA* 2(R), 4(R), 1977 *BI* 1,2,3,4, *F* 1(R),2, 1978 *I*, *W*, *E*, *S*, 1980 *W*, 1982 *A* 1,3
O'Sullivan, J M (Taranaki) 1905 *S*, *I*, *E*, *W*, 1907 *A* 3
O'Sullivan, T P A (Taranaki) 1960 *SA* 1, 1961 *F* 1, 1962 *A* 1,2

Page, J R (Wellington)1931 *A*, 1932 *A* 1,2,3, 1934 *A* 1,2
Palmer, B P (Auckland) 1929 *A* 2, 1932 *A* 2,3
Parker, J H (Canterbury) 1924 *I*, *W*, 1925 *E*
Parkhill, A A (Otago) 1937 *SA* 1,2,3, 1938 *A* 1,2,3
Parkinson, R M (Poverty Bay) 1972 *A* 1,2,3, *W*, *S*, 1973 *E* 1,2
Paterson, A M (Otago) 1908 *AW* 2,3, 1910 *A* 1,2,3
Paton, H (Otago) 1910 *A* 1,3
Phillips, W J (King Country) 1937 *SA* 2, 1938 *A* 1,2
Philpott, S (Canterbury) 1991 [*It*(R), *S*(R)]
Pickering, E A R (Waikato) 1958 *A* 2, 1959 *BI* 1,4
Pierce, M J (Wellington) 1985 *E* 1,2, *A*, *Arg* 1, 1986 *A* 2,3, *F* 2,3, 1987 [*It*, *Arg*, *S*, *W*, *F*], *A*, 1988 *W* 1,2, *A* 1,2,3, 1989 *F* 1,2, *Arg* 1,2, *A*, *W*, *I*
Pokere, S T (Southland, Auckland) 1981 *SA* 3, 1982 *A* 1,2,3, 1983 *BI* 1,2,3,4, *A*, *S*, *E*, 1984 *F* 1,2, *A* 2,3, 1985 *E* 1,2, *A*
Pollock, H R (Wellington) 1932 *A* 1,2,3, 1936 *A* 1,2
Porter, C G (Wellington) 1925 *F*, 1929 *A* 2,3, 1930 *BI* 1,2,3,4
Preston, J P (Canterbury) 1991 [*US*, *S*]
Procter, A C (Otago) 1932 *A* 1
Purdue, C A (Southland) 1905 *A*
Purdue, E (Southland) 1905 *A*
Purdue, G B (Southland) 1931 *A*, 1932 *A* 1,2,3
Purvis, G H (Waikato) 1991 [*US*]
Purvis, N A (Otago) 1976 *I*

Quaid, C E (Otago) 1938 *A* 1,2

Rangi, R E (Auckland) 1964 *A* 2,3, 1965 *SA* 1,2,3,4, 1966 *BI* 1,2,3,4
Rankin, J G (Canterbury) 1936 *A* 1,2, 1937 *SA* 2
Reedy, W J (Wellington) 1908 *AW* 2,3
Reid, A R (Waikato) 1952 *A* 1, 1956 *SA* 3,4, 1957 *A* 1,2
Reid, H R (Bay of Plenty) 1980 *A* 1,2, *W*, 1983 *S*, *E*, 1985 *Arg* 1,2, 1986 *A* 2,3
Reid, K H (Wairarapa) 1929 *A* 1,3
Reid, S T (Hawke's Bay) 1935 *S*, *I*, *W*, 1936 *E*, *A* 1,2, 1937 *SA* 1,2,3
Reside, W B (Wairarapa) 1929 *A* 1
Rhind, P K (Canterbury) 1946 *A* 1,2
Richardson, J (Otago, Southland) 1921 *SA* 1,2,3, 1924 *I*, *W*, 1925 *E*, *F*
Rickit, H (Waikato) 1981 *S* 1,2
Ridland, A J (Southland) 1910 *A* 1,2,3
Roberts, E J (Wellington) 1914 *A* 1,2,3, 1921 *SA* 2,3
Roberts, F (Wellington) 1905 *S*, *I*, *E*, *W*, 1907 *A* 1,2,3, 1908 *AW* 1,3, 1910 *A* 1,2,3
Roberts, R W (Taranaki) 1913 *A* 1, *US*, 1914 *A* 1,2,3
Robertson, B J (Counties) 1972 *A* 1,3, *S*, 1973 *E* 1, *I*, *F*, 1974 *A* 1,2,3, *I*, 1976 *I*, *SA* 1,2,3,4, 1977 *BI* 1,3,4, *F* 1,2, 1978 *A* 1,2,3, *W*, *E*, *S*, 1979 *F* 1,2, *A*, 1980 *A* 2,3, *W*, 1981 *S* 1,2
Robertson, D J (Otago) 1974 *A* 1,2,3, *I*, 1975 *S*, 1976 *I*, *SA* 1,3,4, 1977 *BI* 1
Robilliard, A C C (Canterbury) 1928 *SA* 1,2,3,4
Robinson, C E (Southland) 1951 *A* 1,2,3, 1952 *A* 1,2
Rollerson, D L (Manawatu) 1980 *W*, 1981 *S* 2, *SA* 1,2,3, *R*, *F* 1(R), 2
Roper, R A (Taranaki) 1949 *A* 2, 1950 *BI* 1,2,3,4
Rowley, H C B (Wanganui) 1949 *A* 2
Rutledge, L M (Southland) 1978 *A* 1,2,3, *I*, *W*, *E*, *S*, 1979 *F* 1,2, *A*, 1980 *A* 1,2,3
Ryan, J (Wellington) 1910 *A* 2, 1914 *A* 1,2,3

Sadler, B S (Wellington) 1935 *S*, *I*, *W*, 1936 *A* 1,2, **Salmon, J L B** (Wellington) 1981 *R*, *F* 1,2(R)
Savage, L T (Canterbury) 1949 *SA* 1,2,4
Saxton, C K (South Canterbury) 1938 *A* 1,2,3
Schuler, K J (Manawatu) 1990 *A* 2(R)
Schuster, N J (Wellington) 1988 *A* 1,2,3, 1989 *F* 1,2, *Arg* 1,2, *A*, *W*, *I*
Scott, R W H (Auckland) 1946 *A* 1,2, 1947 *A* 1,2, 1949 *SA* 1,2,3,4, 1950 *BI* 1,2,3,4, 1953 *W*, 1954 *I*, *E*, *S*, *F*

Scown, A I (Taranaki) 1972 *A* 1,2,3, *W*(R), *S*
Scrimshaw, G (Canterbury) 1928 *SA* 1
Seear, G A (Otago) 1977 *F* 1,2, 1978 *A* 1,2,3, *I*, *W*, *E*, *S*, 1979 *F* 1,2, *A*
Seeling, C E (Auckland) 1904 *BI*, 1905 *S*, *I*, *E*, *W*, 1906 *F*, 1907 *A* 1,2, 1908 *AW* 1,2,3
Sellars, G M V (Auckland) 1913 *A* 1, *US*
Shaw, M W (Manawatu, Hawke's Bay) 1980 *A* 1,2,3(R), *W*, 1981 *S* 1,2, *SA* 1,2, *R*, *F* 1,2, 1982 *A* 1,2,3, 1983 *BI* 1,2,3,4, *A*, *S*, *E*, 1984 *F* 1,2, *A* 1, 1985 *E* 1,2, *A*, *Arg* 1,2, 1986 *A* 3
Shelford, F N K (Bay of Plenty) 1981 *SA* 3, *R*, 1984 *A* 2,3
Shelford, W T (North Harbour) 1986 *F* 2,3, 1987 [*It*, *Fj*, *S*, *W*, *F*], *A*, 1988 *W* 1,2, *A* 1,2,3, 1989 *F* 1,2, *Arg* 1,2, *A*, *W*, *I*, 1990 *S* 1,2,
Siddells, S K (Wellington) 1921 *SA* 3
Simon, H J (Otago) 1937 *SA* 1,2,3
Simpson, J G (Auckland) 1947 *A* 1,2, 1949 *SA* 1,2,3,4, 1950 *BI* 1,2,3
Simpson, V L J (Canterbury) 1985 *Arg* 1,2
Sims, G S (Otago) 1972 *A* 2
Skeen, J R (Auckland) 1952 *A* 2
Skinner, K L (Otago, Counties) 1949 *SA* 1,2,3,4, 1950 *BI* 1,2,3,4, 1951 *A* 1,2,3, 1952 *A* 1,2, 1953 *W*, 1954 *I*, *E*, *S*, *F*, 1956 *SA* 3,4
Skudder, G R (Waikato) 1969 *W* 2
Sloane, P H (North Auckland) 1979 *E*
Smith, A E (Taranaki) 1969 *W* 1,2, 1970 *SA* 1
Smith, B W (Waikato) 1984 *F* 1,2, *A* 1
Smith, G W (Auckland) 1905 *S*, *I*
Smith, I S T (Otago, North Otago) 1964 *A* 1,2,3, 1965 *SA* 1,2,4, 1966 *BI* 1,2,3
Smith, J B (North Auckland) 1946 *A* 1, 1947 *A* 2, 1949 *A* 1,2
Smith, R M (Canterbury) 1955 *A* 1
Smith, W E (Nelson) 1905 *A*
Smith, W R (Canterbury) 1980 *A* 1, 1982 *A* 1,2,3, 1983 *BI* 2,3, *S*, *E*, 1984 *F* 1,2, *A* 1,2,3, 1985 *E* 1,2, *A*, *Arg* 2
Snow, E M (Nelson) 1929 *A* 1,2,3
Solomon, F (Auckland) 1931 *A*, 1932 *A* 2,3
Sonntag, W T C (Otago) 1929 *A* 1,2,3
Speight, M W (Waikato) 1986 *A* 1
Spencer, J C (Wellington) 1905 *A*, 1907 *A* 1(R)
Spiers, J E (Counties) 1979 *S*, *E*, 1981 *R*, *F* 1,2
Spillane, A P (South Canterbury) 1913 *A* 2,3,
Stanley, J T (Auckland) 1986 *F* 1, *A* 1,2,3, *F* 2,3, 1987 [*It*, *Fj*, *Arg*, *S*, *W*, *F*], *A*, 1988 *W* 1,2, *A* 1,2,3, 1989 *F* 1,2, *Arg* 1,2, *A*, *W*, *I*, 1990 *S* 1,2
Stead, J W (Southland) 1904 *BI*, 1905 *S*, *I*, *E*, 1906 *F*, 1908 *AW* 1,3
Steel, A G (Canterbury) 1966 *BI* 1,2,3,4, 1967 *A*, *F*, *S*, 1968 *A* 1,2
Steel, J (West Coast) 1921 *SA* 1,2,3, 1924 *W*, 1925 *E*, *F*
Steele, L B (Wellington) 1951 *A* 1,2,3
Steere, E R G (Hawke's Bay) 1930 *BI* 1,2,3,4, 1931 *A*, 1932 *A* 1
Stephens, O G (Wellington) 1968 *F* 3
Stevens, I N (Wellington) 1972 *S*, 1973 *E* 1, 1974 *A* 3
Stewart, A J (Canterbury, South Canterbury) 1963 *E* 1,2, *I*, *W*, 1964 *E*, *S*, *F*, *A* 3
Stewart, J D (Auckland) 1913 *A* 2,3
Stewart, K W (Southland) 1973 *E* 2, 1974 *A* 1,2,3, *I*, 1975 *S*, 1976 *I*, *SA* 1,3, 1979 *S*, *E*, 1981 *SA* 1,2
Stewart, R T (South Canterbury, Canterbury) 1928 *SA* 1,2,3,4, 1930 *BI* 2
Stohr, L B (Taranaki) 1910 *A* 1,2,3
Stone, A M (Waikato, Bay of Plenty) 1981 *F* 1,2, 1983 *BI* 3(R), 1984 *A* 3, 1986 *F* 1, *A* 1,3, *F* 2,3
Storey, P W (South Canterbury) 1921 *SA* 1,2
Strahan, S C (Manawatu) 1967 *A*, *E*, *W*, *F*, *S*, 1968 *A* 1,2, *F* 1,2,3, 1970 *SA* 1,2,3, 1972 *A* 1,2,3, 1973 *E* 2
Strang, W A (South Canterbury) 1928 *SA* 1,2, 1930 *BI* 3,4, 1931 *A*
Stringfellow, J C (Wairarapa) 1929 *A* 1(R),3
Stuart, K C (Canterbury) 1955 *A* 1
Stuart, R C (Canterbury) 1949 *A* 1,2, 1953 *W*, 1954 *I*, *E*, *S*, *F*
Stuart, R L (Hawke's Bay) 1977 *F* 1(R)
Sullivan, J L (Taranaki) 1937 *SA* 1,2,3, 1938 *A* 1,2,3
Sutherland, A R (Marlborough) 1970 *SA* 2,4, 1971 *BI* 1, 1972 *A* 1,2,3, *W*, 1973 *E* 1, *I*, *F*
Svenson, K S (Wellington) 1924 *I*, *W*, 1925 *E*, *F*
Swain, J P (Hawke's Bay) 1928 *SA* 1,2,3,4

Tanner, J M (Auckland) 1950 *BI* 4, 1951 *A* 1,2,3, 1953 *W*
Tanner, K J (Canterbury) 1974 *A* 1,2,3, *I*, 1975 *S*, 1976 *I*, *SA* 1
Taylor, H M (Canterbury) 1913 *A* 1, *US*, 1914 *A* 1,2,3
Taylor, J M (Otago) 1937 *SA* 1,2,3, 1938 *A* 1,2,3
Taylor, M B (Waikato) 1979 *F* 1,2, *A*, *S*, *E*, 1980 *A* 1,2
Taylor, N M (Bay of Plenty, Hawke's Bay) 1977 *BI* 2, 4(R), *F* 1,2, 1978 *A* 1,2,3, *I*, 1982 *A* 2
Taylor, R (Taranaki) 1913 *A* 2,3
Taylor, W T (Canterbury) 1983 *BI* 1,2,3,4, *A*, *S*, 1984 *F* 1,2, *A* 1,2, 1985 *E* 1,2, *A*, *Arg* 1,2, 1986 *A* 2, 1987 [*It*, *Fj*, *S*, *W*, *F*], *A*, 1988 *W* 1,2
Tetzlaff, P L (Auckland) 1947 *A* 1,2
Thimbleby, N W (Hawke's Bay) 1970 *SA* 3
Thomas, B T (Auckland, Wellington) 1962 *A* 5, 1964 *A* 1,2,3
Thomson, H D (Wellington) 1908 *AW* 1
Thorne, G S (Auckland) 1968 *A* 1,2, *F* 1,2,3, 1969 *W* 1, 1970 *SA* 1,2,3,4
Thornton, N H (Auckland) 1947 *A* 1,2, 1949 *SA* 1
Tilyard, J T (Wellington) 1913 *A* 3
Timu, J K R (Otago) 1991 *Arg* 1, *A* 1,2, [*E*, *US*, *C*, *A*]
Tindill, E W T (Wellington) 1936 *E*
Townsend, L J (Otago) 1955 *A* 1,3
Tremain, K R (Canterbury, Hawke's Bay) 1959 *BI* 2,3,4, 1960 *SA* 1,2,3,4, 1961 *F* 2,3, 1962 *A* 1,2,3, 1963 *E* 1,2, *I*, *W*, 1964 *E*, *S*, *F*, *A* 1,2,3, 1965 *SA* 1,2,3,4, 1966 *BI* 1,2,3,4, 1967 *A*, *E*, *W*, *S*, 1968 *A* 1, *F* 1,2,3
Trevathan, D (Otago) 1937 *SA* 1,2,3
Tuck, J M (Waikato) 1929 *A* 1,2,3
Tuigamala, V L (Auckland) 1991 [*US*, *It*, *C*, *S*]
Turtill, H S (Canterbury) 1905 *A*
Twigden, T M (Auckland) 1980 *A* 2,3
Tyler, G A (Auckland) 1903 *A* 1, 1904 *BI*, 1905 *S*, *I*, *E*, *W*, 1906 *F*

Udy, D K (Wairarapa) 1903 *A*
Urbahn, R J (Taranaki) 1959 *BI* 1,3,4
Urlich, R A (Auckland) 1970 *SA* 3,4
Uttley, I N (Wellington) 1963 *E* 1,2

Vincent, P B (Canterbury) 1956 *SA* 1,2
Vodanovich, I M H (Wellington) 1955 *A* 1,2,3

Wallace, W J (Wellington) 1903 *A*, 1904 *BI*, 1905 *S*, *I*, *E*, *W*, 1906 *F*, 1907 *A* 1,2,3, 1908 *AW* 2
Walsh, P T (Counties) 1955 *A* 1,2,3, 1956 *SA* 1,2,4, 1957 *A* 1,2, 1958 *A* 1,2,3, 1959 *BI* 1, 1963 *E* 2
Ward, R H (Southland) 1936 *A* 2, 1937 *SA* 1,3
Waterman, A C (North Auckland) 1929 *A* 1,2
Watkins, E L (Wellington) 1905 *A*
Watt, B A (Canterbury) 1962 *A* 1,4, 1963 *E* 1,2, *W*, 1964 *E*, *S*, *A* 1
Watt, J M (Otago) 1936 *A* 1,2
Watt, J R (Wellington) 1958 *A* 2, 1960 *SA* 1,2,3,4, 1961 *F* 1,3, 1962 *A* 1,2
Watts, M G (Taranaki) 1979 *F* 1,2, 1980 *A* 1,2,3(R)
Webb, D S (North Auckland) 1959 *BI* 2
Wells, J (Wellington) 1936 *A* 1,2
West, A H (Taranaki) 1921 *SA* 2,3
Whetton, A J (Auckland) 1984 *A* 1(R),3(R), 1985 *A*(R),

Arg 1(R), 1986 *A* 2, 1987 [*It*, *Fj*, *Arg*, *S*, *W*, *F*], *A*, 1988 *W* 1,2, *A* 1,2,3, 1989 *F* 1,2, *Arg* 1,2, *A*, 1990 *S* 1,2, *A* 1,2,3, *F* 1,2, 1991 *Arg* 1, [*E*, *US*, *It*, *C*, *A*]
Whetton, G W (Auckland) 1981 *SA* 3, *R*, *F* 1,2, 1982 *A* 3, 1983 *BI* 1,2,3,4, 1984 *F* 1,2, *A* 1,2,3, 1985 *E* 1,2, *A*, *Arg* 2, 1986 *A* 2,3, *F* 2,3, 1987 [*It*, *Fj*, *Arg*, *S*, *W*, *F*], *A*, 1988 *W* 1,2, *A* 1,2,3, 1989 *F* 1,2, *Arg* 1,2, *A*, *W*, *I*, 1990 *S* 1,2, *A* 1,2,3, *F* 1,2, 1991 *Arg* 1,2, *A* 1,2, [*E*, *US*, *It*, *C*, *A*, *S*]
Whineray, W J (Canterbury, Waikato, Auckland) 1957 *A* 1,2, 1958 *A* 1,2,3, 1959 *BI* 1,2,3,4, 1960 *SA* 1,2,3,4, 1961 *F* 1,2,3, 1962 *A* 1,2,3,4,5, 1963 *E* 1,2, *I*, *W*, 1964 *E*, *S*, *F*, 1965 *SA* 1,2,3,4
White, A (Southland) 1921 *SA* 1, 1924 *I*, 1925 *E*, *F*
White, H L (Auckland) 1954 *I*, *E*, *F*, 1955 *A* 3
White, R A (Poverty Bay) 1949 *A* 1,2, 1950 *BI* 1,2,3,4, 1951 *A* 1,2,3, 1952 *A* 1,2, 1953 *W*, 1954 *I*, *E*, *S*, *F*, 1955 *A* 1,2,3, 1956 *SA* 1,2,3,4
White, R M (Wellington) 1946 *A* 1,2, 1947 *A* 1,2
Whiting, G J (King Country) 1972 *A* 1,2, *S*, 1973 *E* 1, *I*, *F*
Whiting, P J (Auckland) 1971 *BI* 1,2,4, 1972 *A* 1,2,3, *W*, *S*, 1973 *E* 1, *I*, *F*, 1974 *A* 1,2,3, *I*, 1976 *I*, *SA* 1,2,3,4
Williams, B G (Auckland) 1970 *SA* 1,2,3,4, 1971 *BI* 1,2,4, 1972 *A* 1,2,3, *W*, *S*, 1973 *E* 1, *I*, *F*, *E* 2, 1974 *A* 1,2,3, *I*, 1975 *S*, 1976 *I*, *SA* 1,2,3,4, 1977 *BI* 1,2,3,4, *F* 1, 1978 *A* 1,2,3, *I* (R), *W*, *E*, *S*
Williams, G C (Wellington) 1967 *E*, *W*, *F*, *S*, 1968 *A* 2
Williams, P (Otago) 1913 *A* 1
Williment, M (Wellington) 1964 *A* 1, 1965 *SA* 1,2,3, 1966 *BI* 1,2,3,4, 1967 *A*
Willocks, C (Otago) 1946 *A* 1,2, 1949 *SA* 1,3,4
Wilson, B W (Otago) 1977 *BI* 3,4, 1978 *A* 1,2,3, 1979 *F* 1,2, *A*
Wilson, D D (Canterbury) 1954 *E*, *S*
Wilson, H W (Otago) 1949 *A* 1, 1950 *BI* 4, 1951 *A* 1,2,3
Wilson, N A (Wellington) 1908 *AW* 1,2, 1910 *A* 1,2,3, 1913 *A* 2,3, 1914 *A* 1,2,3
Wilson, N L (Otago) 1951 *A* 1,2,3
Wilson, R G (Canterbury) 1979 *S*, *E*
Wilson, S S (Wellington) 1977 *F* 1,2, 1978 *A* 1,2,3, *I*, *W*, *E*, *S*, 1979 *F* 1,2, *A*, *S*, *E*, 1980 *A* 1, *W*, 1981 *S* 1,2, *SA* 1,2,3, *R*, *F* 1,2, 1982 *A* 1,2,3, 1983 *BI* 1,2,3,4, *A*, *S*, *E*
Wolfe, T N (Wellington, Taranaki) 1961 *F* 1,2,3, 1962 *A* 2,3, 1963 *E* 1
Wood, M E (Canterbury, Auckland) 1903 *A*, 1904 *BI*
Woodman, F A (North Auckland) 1981 *SA* 1,2, *F* 2
Wrigley, E (Wairarapa) 1905 *A*
Wright, T J (Auckland) 1986 *F* 1, *A* 1, 1987 [*Arg*], 1988 *W* 1,2, *A* 1,2,3, 1989 *F* 1,2, *Arg* 1,2, *A*, *W*, *I*, 1990 *S* 1,2, *A* 1,2,3, *F* 1,2, 1991 *Arg* 1,2, *A* 1,2, [*E*, *US*, *It*, *S*]
Wylie, J T (Auckland) 1913 *A* 1, *US*
Wyllie, A J (Canterbury) 1970 *SA* 2,3, 1971 *BI* 2,3,4, 1972 *W*, *S*, 1973 *E* 1, *I*, *F*, *E* 2

Yates, V M (North Auckland) 1961 *F* 1,2,3
Young, D (Canterbury) 1956 *SA* 2, 1958 *A* 1,2,3, 1960 *SA* 1,2,3,4, 1961 *F* 1,2,3, 1962 *A* 1,2,3,5, 1963 *E* 1,2, *I*, *W*, 1964 *E*, *S*, *F*

NEW ZEALAND INTERNATIONAL RECORDS

Both team and individual records are for official New Zealand international matches, up to 31 March 1992.

TEAM RECORDS
Highest score
74 v Fiji (74-13) 1987 Christchurch

v individual countries
60 v Argentina (60-9) 1989 Dunedin

38 v Australia { (38-13) 1936 Dunedin
{ (38-3) 1972 Auckland

38 v B Isles (38-6) 1983 Auckland

29 v Canada (29-13) 1991 Lille
42 v England (42-15) 1985 Wellington
74 v Fiji (74-13) 1987 Christchurch
38 v France (38-8) 1906 Paris
23 v Ireland (23-6) 1989 Dublin
70 v Italy (70-6) 1987 Auckland
14 v Romania (14-6) 1981 Bucharest
25 v S Africa (25-22) 1981 Auckland
40 v Scotland (40-15) 1981 Auckland
51 v United States (51-3) 1913 Berkeley
54 v Wales (54-9) 1988 Auckland

Biggest winning points margin
64 v Italy (70-6) 1987 Auckland
v individual countries
51 v Argentina (60-9) 1989 Dublin
35 v Australia (38-3) 1972 Auckland
32 v B Isles (38-6) 1983 Auckland
16 v Canada (29-13) 1991 Lille
27 v England (42-15) 1985 Wellington
61 v Fiji (74-13) 1987 Christchurch
30 v France (38-8) 1906 Paris
17 v Ireland (23-6) 1989 Dublin
64 v Italy (70-6) 1987 Auckland
 8 v Romania (14-6) 1981 Bucharest
17 v S Africa (20-3) 1965 Auckland
27 v Scotland (30-3) 1987 Christchurch
48 v United States (51-3) 1913 Berkeley
49 v Wales (52-3) 1988 Christchurch

Highest score by opposing team
30 Australia (16-30) 1978 Auckland
by individual countries
21 Argentina (21-21) 1985 Buenos Aires
30 Australia (16-30) 1978 Auckland
17 B Isles (18-17) 1959 Dunedin
13 Canada (29-13) 1991 Lille
16 England (10-16) 1973 Auckland
13 Fiji (74-13) 1987 Christchurch
24 France (19-24) 1979 Auckland
10 Ireland (10-10) 1973 Dublin
21 Italy (31-21) 1991 Leicester
 6 Romania (14-6) 1981 Bucharest
24 S Africa (12-24) 1981 Wellington
25 Scotland (25-25) 1983 Edinburgh
 6 United States (46-6) 1991 Gloucester
16 Wales (19-16) 1972 Cardiff

Biggest losing points margin
17 v S Africa (0-17) 1928 Durban
v individual countries
16 v Australia (10-26) 1980 Sydney

10 v B Isles (3-13) 1971 Wellington
13 v England (0-13) 1936 Twickenham
13 v France (3-16) 1986 Nantes
17 v S Africa (0-17) 1928 Durban
 5 v Wales (8-13) 1953 Cardiff
No defeats v Argentina, Canada, Fiji, Ireland, Italy, Romania, Scotland or United States

Most tries by New Zealand in an international
13 v United States (51-3) Berkeley

Most tries against New Zealand in an international
5 by { S Africa (6-17) 1937 Auckland
        { Australia (16-30) 1978 Auckland

Most points on overseas tour (all matches)
868 in B Isles/France (33 matches) 1905-06

Most tries on overseas tour
215 in B Isles/France (33 matches) 1905-06

INDIVIDUAL RECORDS
Most capped player
G W Whetton   58   1981-91
in individual positions
Full-back
D B Clarke   31   1956-64
Wing
J J Kirwan   45   1984-91
Centre (includes 2nd five-eighth)
B J Robertson   34   1972-81
1st five-eighth
G J Fox   35   1985-91
Scrum-half
S M Going   29   1967-77
Prop
S C McDowell   41   1985-91
Hooker
S B T Fitzpatrick   40   1986-91
Lock
G W Whetton   58   1981-91
Flanker
K R Tremain   36(38)[1]   1959-68
I A Kirkpatrick   36(39)[2]   1967-77
No 8
M G Mexted   34   1979-85
[1]*Tremain won 2 caps as a No 8*
[2]*Kirkpatrick won 3 caps as a No 8*

Longest international career

E Hughes	15 seasons	1907-21
C E Meads	15 seasons	1957-71

Most consecutive internationals – 40
G W Whetton 1986-91

Most internationals as captain
W J Whineray   30   1958-65

Most points in internationals – 525
G J Fox (35 matches) 1985-91

Most points in an international – 26
A R Hewson v Australia 1982 Auckland
G J Fox v Fiji 1987 Christchurch

Most tries in internationals – 30
J J Kirwan (45 matches) 1984-91

Most tries in an international – 4
D McGregor v England 1905 Crystal Palace
C I Green v Fiji 1987 Christchurch

J A Gallagher v Fiji 1987 Christchurch
J J Kirwan v Wales 1988 Christchurch

Most conversions in internationals – 103
G J Fox (35 matches) 1985-91

Most conversions in an international – 10
G J Fox v Fiji 1987 Christchurch

Most dropped goals in internationals – 6
G J Fox (35 matches) 1985-91

Most penalty goals in internationals – 99
G J Fox (35 matches) 1985-91

Most points in international series – 46
A R Hewson (4 appearances) v B Isles 1983

Most points in international series on tour – 38
G J Fox (2 appearances) 1990 France

Most tries in international series on tour – 5
K Svenson (4 appearances) 1924-25
  B Isles/France
Svenson scored in each match of the international series

Most points on tour – 230
W J Wallace (25 appearances) 1905-06
  B Isles/France

Most tries on tour – 42
J Hunter (23 appearances) 1905-06
  B Isles/France

Most points in a tour match – 43
R M Deans v South Australia 1984
  Adelaide

Most tries in a tour match – 8
T R Heeps v Northern NSW 1962
  Quirindi

323

EVERY MOUNTAIN CLIMBED

THE 1991 SEASON IN AUSTRALIA
Greg Campbell

Last year's Australian report was headlined 'Wallabies Gathering Strength'. It was a statement of their potential to seriously challenge for international rugby's greatest prize – the Webb Ellis Cup. History now records the Wallabies as thoroughly deserving world champions who risked failure to achieve victory. Along the way they warmed the hearts of all who saw them play, both in Australia and throughout the World Cup tournament, with their enterprising attacking style and their near-faultless defence, which remained strong even when under the blow-torch of the most testing attack.

The final Test match record for the year – nine wins from ten Test matches, the single loss being a heart-stopping 6-3 defeat inflicted by the All Blacks – reflected the overwhelming view that the Wallabies were the team of 1991. The World Cup success also mirrored the careful planning and preparation of the Australian Rugby Football Union administrators right through to the extensive support staff who assisted the Wallabies during their World Cup journey. Along the road, four new players, namely John Eales, Marty Roebuck, Rob Egerton and David Nucifora won their first Test caps.

The early signs of the success that lay ahead were revealed in Australia prior to the World Cup when the Wallabies inflicted a record 63-6 win upon Wales and followed up soon after with another record victory, 40-15 over England. The All Blacks were then beaten 21-12 before a ground record for any code at the Sydney Football Stadium. The natural euphoria of these fine victories was then sobered by the 6-3 loss to the All Blacks in Auckland. But regardless of these results, the focus was always centred on the World Cup.

The Wallabies had the advantage of playing in a strong pool and reached the finals with victories over Argentina (32-19), and Western Samoa (9-3), and a record home defeat of Wales (38-3). A last-minute try by Michael Lynagh gave the Wallabies a nail-biting 19-18 win over Ireland in their quarter-final before they disposed of the All Blacks 16-6 in the semi-final. This set up a place in the final against England, and the Webb Ellis Cup was secured with a gripping 12-6 win, Tony Daly's converted try separating the two teams. The Wallabies' success dominated sports news.

The surge of interest in rugby began with the victories at home and climbed to unprecedented heights during the World Cup. There were record television ratings, thousands of good luck faxes to the team hotel and afterwards over 100,000 Sydney workers lined the streets for a ticker-tape parade, never before witnessed for any Australian sporting team. Various awards were heaped on the Wallabies collectively and individually. In addition to many team records, Nick Farr-Jones and Michael Lynagh broke the world half-back combination record previously held by Scotland's Ray Laidlaw and John Rutherford, while David Campese played his 100th game for Australia in the World Cup final.

The post-World Cup celebrations were tempered at the end of the year when popular referee Kerry Fitzgerald died suddenly after suffering a heart attack. He was 43 years old. Fitzgerald, who refereed the inaugural 1987 World Cup final, was in outstanding form during this World Cup and reached semi-final selection. Australia's participation in the final ruled out the possibility of back-to-back World Cup final appointments.

The year was not without areas of controversy, but fortunately they were few and were not disruptive to the team. Michael Lynagh's involvement with a beer company which was in opposition to the ARFU's official major sponsor threatened his invitation to play for Australia. Happily, the matter was resolved and Lynagh continued to play a crucial role in Australia's on-field success. After the World Cup, the ARFU terminated its long-standing association with its host broadcaster, the Australian Broadcasting Corporation, and opted to sign a new deal with the commercial Network Ten television station. While the ARFU's decision was made for commercial reasons, there was strong opposition from rugby traditionalists.

Australia were again bundled out in the quarter-finals of the Cathay Pacific-Hong Kong Bank Invitation Sevens, a defeat which led to changes in the domestic sevens programme to include a provincial sevens championship. On the domestic front, New South Wales emerged as the dominant state. The Blues were unbeaten in all of their ten matches and won their inter-state series over Queensland. NSW also inflicted a devastating 71-8 win upon Wales. Randwick continued to reign supreme at club level, winning the NSW premiership with a convincing 28-9 victory against Eastern Suburbs. Southern Districts won the Brisbane grand final 22-15 against Western Districts. The Australian club championship final was marred by the unavailability of World Cup team members. Randwick nevertheless reclaimed the title, beating Southern Districts 35-12 without six of their World Cup team members.

MAJOR PROVINCIAL MATCHES
Sydney Origin 39, NSW Country Origin 12; NSW 24, Queensland 18;
NSW 21, Queensland 12; NSW B 40, Queensland B 11; Queensland 52, ACT 12;
NSW 18, ACT 16
SYDNEY GRAND FINAL
Randwick 28, Eastern Suburbs 9
BRISBANE GRAND FINAL
Southern Districts 22, Western Districts 15
AUSTRALIAN CLUB CHAMPIONSHIP FINAL
Randwick 35, Southern Districts 12

AUSTRALIAN INTERNATIONAL PLAYERS *(up to 31 March 1992)*

ABBREVIATIONS

Arg – Argentina; *BI* – British Isles teams; *C* – Canada; *E* – England; *F* – France; *Fj* – Fiji; *I* – Ireland; *It* – Italy; *J* – Japan; *M* – Maoris; *NZ* – New Zealand; *S* – Scotland; *SA* – South Africa; *SK* – South Korea; *Tg* – Tonga; *US* – United States of America; *W* – Wales; *WS* – Western Samoa; (R) – Replacement. Entries in square brackets [ ] indicate appearances in the Rugby World Cup

STATE ABBREVIATIONS

ACT – Australian Capital Territory; NSW – New South Wales; Q – Queensland; V – Victoria; WA – Western Australia

N.B. In the summer of 1986, the ARU retrospectively granted full Australian Test status to the five international matches played by the 1927-28 touring team to Europe. In 1988 Test status was extended to all those who played overseas in the 1920s.

Note: When a series has taken place, figures denote the particular matches in which players featured. Thus 1963 *SA* 2,4 indicates that a player appeared in the second and fourth Tests of the 1963 series against South Africa.

Abrahams, A M F (NSW) 1967 *NZ*, 1968 *NZ* 1, 1969 *W*

Adams, N J (NSW) 1955 *NZ* 1

Adamson, R W (NSW) 1912 *US*

Allan, T (NSW) 1946 *NZ* 1, *M*, *NZ* 2, 1947 *NZ* 2, *S*, *I*, *W*, 1948 *E*, *F*, 1949 *M* 1,2,3, *NZ* 1,2

Anlezark, E A (NSW) 1905 *NZ*

Armstrong, A R (NSW) 1923 *NZ* 1,2

Austin, L R (NSW) 1963 *E*

Baker, R L (NSW) 1904 *BI* 1,2

Baker, W H (NSW) 1914 *NZ* 1,2,3

Ballesty, J P (NSW) 1968 *NZ* 1,2, *F*, *I*, *S*, 1969 *W*, *SA* 2,3,4

Bannon, D P (NSW) 1946 *M*

Bardsley, E J (NSW) 1928 *NZ* 1,3, *M* (R)

Barker, H S (NSW) 1952 *Fj* 1,2, *NZ* 1,2, 1953 *SA* 4, 1954 *Fj* 1,2

Barnett, J T (NSW) 1907 *NZ* 1,2,3, 1908 *W*, 1909 *E*

Barry, M J (Q) 1971 *SA* 3

Barton, R F D (NSW) 1899 *BI* 3

Batch, P G (Q) 1975 *S*, *W*, 1976 *E*, *Fj* 1,2,3, *F* 1,2, 1978 *W* 1,2, *NZ* 1,2,3, 1979 *Arg* 2

Batterham, R P (NSW) 1967 *NZ*, 1970 *S*

Battishall, B R (NSW) 1973 *E*

Baxter, A J (NSW) 1949 *M* 1,2,3, *NZ* 1,2, 1951 *NZ* 1,2, 1952 *NZ* 1,2

Baxter, T J (Q) 1958 *NZ* 3

Beith, B McN (NSW) 1914 *NZ* 3

Bell, K R (Q) 1968 *S*

Bennett, W G (Q) 1931 *M*, 1933 *SA* 1,2,3

Bermingham, J V (Q) 1934 *NZ* 1,2, 1937 *SA* 1

Berne, J E (NSW) 1975 *S*

Besomo, K S (NSW) 1979 *I* 2

Betts, T N (Q) 1951 *NZ* 2,3, 1954 *Fj* 2

Biilmann, R R (NSW) 1933 *SA* 1,2,3,4

Birt, R (Q) 1914 *NZ* 2

Black, J W (NSW) 1985 *C* 1,2, *NZ*, *Fj* 1

Blackwood, J G (NSW) 1923 *NZ* 1,2,3, 1925 *NZ*, 1927 *I*, *W*, *S*, 1928 *E*, *F*

Blair, M R (NSW) 1928 *F*, 1931 *M*, *NZ*

Bland, G V (NSW) 1928 *NZ* 3, *M*, 1932 *NZ* 1,2,3, 1933 *SA* 1,2,4,5

Blomley, J (NSW) 1949 *M* 1,2,3, *NZ* 1,2, 1950 *BI* 1,2

Boland, S B (Q) 1899 *BI* 3,4, 1903 *NZ*

Bond, J H (NSW) 1921 *NZ*

Bonis, E T (Q) 1929 *NZ* 1,2,3, 1930 *BI*, 1931 *M*, *NZ*, 1932 *NZ* 1,2,3, 1933 *SA* 1,2,3,4,5, 1934 *NZ* 1,2, 1936 *NZ* 1,2, *M*, 1937 *SA* 1, 1938 *NZ* 1

Bosler, J M (NSW) 1953 *SA* 1

Bouffler, R G (NSW) 1899 *BI* 3

Bourke, T K (Q) 1947 *NZ* 2

Bowers, A J A (NSW) 1923 *NZ* 3, 1925 *NZ*, 1927 *I*

Boyce, E S (NSW) 1962 *NZ* 1,2, 1964 *NZ* 1,2,3, 1965 *SA* 1,2, 1966 *W*, *S*, 1967 *E*, *I* 1, *F*, *I* 2

Boyce, J S (NSW) 1962 *NZ* 3,4,5, 1963 *E*, *SA* 1,2,3,4, 1964 *NZ* 1,3, 1965 *SA* 1,2

Boyd, A (NSW) 1899 *BI* 3

Boyd, A F McC (Q) 1958 *M* 1

Brass, J E (NSW) 1966 *BI* 2, *W*, *S*, 1967 *E*, *I* 1, *F*, *I* 2, *NZ*, 1968 *NZ* 1, *F*, *I*, *S*

Breckenridge, J W (NSW) 1927 *I*, *W*, *S*, 1928 *E*, *F*, 1929 *NZ* 1,2,3, 1930 *BI*

Bridle, O L (V) 1931 *M*, 1932 *NZ* 1,2,3, 1933 *SA* 3,4,5, 1934 *NZ* 1,2, 1936 *NZ* 1,2, *M*

Broad, E G (Q) 1949 *M* 1

Brockhoff, J D (NSW) 1949 *M* 2,3, *NZ* 1,2, 1950 *BI* 1,2, 1951 *NZ* 2,3

Brown, B R (Q) 1972 *NZ* 1,3

Brown, J V (NSW) 1956 *NZ* 1,2, 1957 *NZ* 1,2, 1958 *W*, *I*, *E*, *S*, *F*

Brown, R C (NSW) 1975 *E* 1,2

Brown, S W (NSW) 1953 *SA* 2,3,4

Bryant, H (NSW) 1925 *NZ*

Buchan, A J (NSW) 1946 *NZ* 1,2, 1947 *NZ* 1,2, *S*, *I*, *W*, 1948 *E*, *F*, 1949 *M* 3

Bull, D (NSW) 1928 *M*

Buntine, H (NSW) 1923 *NZ* 1(R)

Burdon, A (NSW) 1903 *NZ*, 1904 *BI* 1,2, 1905 *NZ*

Burge, A B (NSW) 1907 *NZ* 3, 1908 *W*

Burge, P H (NSW) 1907 *NZ* 1,2

Burge, R (NSW) 1928 *NZ* 1,2,3(R), *M* (R)

Burke, B T (NSW) 1988 *S* (R)

Burke, C T (NSW) 1946 *NZ* 2, 1947 *NZ* 1,2, *S*, *I*, *W*, 1948 *E*, *F*, 1949 *M* 2,3, *NZ* 1,2, 1950 *BI* 1,2, 1951 *NZ* 1,2,3, 1953 *SA* 2,3,4, 1954 *Fj* 1, 1955 *NZ* 1,2,3, 1956 *SA* 1,2

Burke, M P (NSW) 1984 *E*, *I*, 1985 *C* 1,2, *NZ*, *Fj* 1,2, 1986 *It* (R), *F*, *Arg* 1,2, *NZ* 1,2,3, 1987 *SK*, [*US*, *J*, *I*, *F*, *W*], *NZ*, *Arg* 1,2

Burnet, D R (NSW) 1972 *F* 1,2, *NZ* 1,2,3, *Fj*

Butler, O F (NSW) 1969 *SA* 1,2, 1970 *S*, 1971 *SA* 2,3, *F* 1,2

Calcraft, W J (NSW) 1985 *C* 1, 1986 *It*, *Arg* 2

Caldwell, B C (NSW) 1928 *NZ* 3

Cameron, A S (NSW) 1951 *NZ* 1,2,3, 1952 *Fj* 1,2, *NZ* 1,2, 1953 *SA* 1,2,3,4, 1954 *Fj* 1,2, 1955 *NZ* 1,2,3, 1956 *SA* 1,2, 1957 *NZ* 1, 1958 *I*

Campbell, J D (NSW) 1910 *NZ* 1,2,3

Campbell, W A (Q) 1984 *Fj*, 1986 *It*, *F*, *Arg* 1,2, *NZ* 1,2,3, 1987 *SK*, [*E*, *US*, *J*(R), *I*, *F*], *NZ*, 1988 *E*, 1989 *BI* 1,2,3, *NZ*, 1990 *NZ* 2,3

Campese, D I (ACT, NSW) 1982 *NZ* 1,2,3, 1983 *US*, *Arg* 1,2, *NZ*, *It*, *F* 1,2, 1984 *Fj*, *NZ* 1,2,3, *E*, *I*, *W*, *S*, 1985 *Fj* 1,2, 1986 *It*, *F*, *Arg* 1,2, *NZ* 1,2,3, 1987 [*E*, *US*, *J*, *I*, *F*, *W*], *NZ*, 1988 *E* 1,2, *NZ* 1,2,3, *E*, *S*, *It*, 1989 *BI* 1,2,3, *NZ*, *F* 1,2, 1990 *F* 2,3, *US*, *NZ* 1,2,3, 1991 *W*, *E*, *NZ* 1,2, [*Arg*, *WS*, *W*, *I*, *NZ*, *E*]

Canniffe, P J (Q) 1907 *NZ* 2

Carberry, C M (NSW, Q) 1973 *Tg* 2, *E*, 1976 *I*, *US*, *Fj* 1,2,3, 1981 *F* 1,2, *I*, *W*, *S*, 1982 *E*

Cardy, A M (NSW) 1966 *BI* 1,2, *W*, *S*, 1967 *E*, *I* 1, *F*, 1968 *NZ* 1,2

Carew, P J (Q) 1899 *BI* 1,2,3,4

Carmichael, P (Q) 1904 *BI* 2, 1907 *NZ* 1, 1908 *W*, 1909 *E*
Carozza, P V (Q) 1990 *F* 1,2,3, *NZ* 2,3
Carpenter, M G (V) 1938 *NZ* 1,2
Carr, E T A (NSW) 1913 *NZ* 1,2,3, 1914 *NZ* 1,2,3
Carr, E W (NSW) 1921 *NZ* 1 (R)
Carroll, D B (NSW) 1908 *W*, 1912 *US*
Carroll, J C (NSW) 1953 *SA* 1
Carroll, J H (NSW) 1958 *M* 2,3, *NZ* 1,2,3, 1959 *BI* 1,2
Carson, J (NSW) 1899 *BI* 1
Carson, P J (NSW) 1979 *NZ*, 1980 *NZ* 3
Carter, D G (NSW) 1988 *E* 1,2, *NZ* 1, 1989 *F* 1,2
Casey, T V (NSW) 1963 *SA* 2,3,4, 1964 *NZ* 1,2,3
Catchpole, K W (NSW) 1961 *Fj* 1,2,3, *SA* 1,2, *F*, 1962 *NZ* 1,2,4, 1963 *SA* 2,3,4, 1964 *NZ* 1,2,3, 1965 *SA* 1,2, 1966 *BI* 1,2, *W*, *S*, 1967 *E*, *I* 1, *F*, *I* 2, *NZ*, 1968 *NZ* 1
Cawsey, R M (NSW) 1949 *M* 1, *NZ* 1,2
Cerutti, W H (NSW) 1928 *NZ* 1,2,3, *M*, 1929 *NZ* 1,2,3, 1930 *BI*, 1931 *M*, *NZ*, 1932 *NZ* 1,2,3, 1933 *SA* 1,2,3,4,5, 1936 *M*, 1937 *SA* 1,2
Challoner, R L (NSW) 1899 *BI* 2
Chapman, G A (NSW) 1962 *NZ* 3,4,5
Clark, J G (Q) 1931 *M*, *NZ*, 1932 *NZ* 1,2, 1933 *SA* 1
Clarken, J C (NSW) 1905 *NZ*, 1910 *NZ* 1,2,3
Cleary, M A (NSW) 1961 *Fj* 1,2,3, *SA* 1,2, *F*
Clements, P (NSW) 1982 *NZ* 3
Clifford, M (NSW) 1938 *NZ* 3
Cobb, W G (NSW) 1899 *BI* 3,4
Cocks, M R (NSW, Q) 1972 *F* 1,2, *NZ* 2,3, *Fj*, 1973 *Tg* 1,2, *W*, *E*, 1975 *J* 1
Codey, D (NSW Country, Q) 1983 *Arg* 1, 1984 *E*, *W*, *S*, 1985 *C* 2, *NZ*, 1986 *F*, *Arg* 1, 1987 [*US*, *J*, *F*(R), *W*], *NZ*
Cody, E W (NSW) 1913 *NZ* 1,2,3
Coker, T (Q) 1987 [*E*, *US*, *F*, *W*], 1991 *NZ* 2, [*Arg*, *WS*, *NZ*, *E*]
Colbert, R (NSW) 1952 *Fj* 2, *NZ* 1,2, 1953 *SA* 2,3,4
Cole, J W (NSW) 1968 *NZ* 1,2, *F*, *I*, *S*, 1969 *W*, *SA* 1,2,3,4, 1970 *S*, 1971 *SA* 1,2,3, *F* 1,2, 1972 *NZ* 1,2,3, 1973 *Tg* 1,2, 1974 *NZ* 1,2,3
Collins, P K (NSW) 1937 *SA* 2, 1938 *NZ* 2,3
Colton, A J (Q) 1899 *BI* 1,3
Colton, T (Q) 1904 *BI* 1,2
Comrie-Thomson, I R (NSW) 1928 *NZ* 1,2,3, *M*
Connor, D M (Q) 1958 *W*, *I*, *E*, *S*, *F*, *M* 2,3, *NZ* 1,2,3, 1959 *BI* 1,2
Cook, M T (Q) 1986 *F*, 1987 *SK*, [*J*], 1988 *E* 1,2, *NZ* 1,2,3, *E*, *S*, *It*
Cooke, B P (NSW) 1979 *I* 1
Cooke, G M (Q) 1932 *NZ* 1,2,3, 1933 *SA* 1,2,3, 1946 *NZ* 2, 1947 *NZ* 2, *S*, *I*, *W*, 1948 *E*, *F*
Coolican, J E (NSW) 1982 *NZ* 1, 1983 *It*, *F* 1,2
Corfe, A C (Q) 1899 *BI* 2
Cornelsen, G (NSW) 1974 *NZ* 2,3, 1975 *J* 2, *S*, *W*, 1976 *E*, *F* 1,2, 1978 *W* 1,2, *NZ* 1,2,3, 1979 *I* 1,2, *NZ*, *Arg* 1,2, 1980 *NZ* 1,2,3, 1981 *I*, *W*, *S*, 1982 *E*
Cornes, J R (Q) 1972 *Fj*
Cornforth, R G W (NSW) 1947 *NZ* 1, 1950 *BI* 2
Cornish, P (ACT) 1990 *F* 2,3, *NZ* 1
Costello, P P S (Q) 1950 *BI* 2
Cottrell, N V (Q) 1949 *M* 1,2,3, *NZ* 1,2, 1950 *BI* 1,2, 1951 *NZ* 1,2,3, 1952 *Fj* 1,2, *NZ* 1,2
Cowper, D L (V) 1931 *NZ*, 1932 *NZ* 1,2,3, 1933 *SA* 1,2,3,4,5
Cox, B P (NSW) 1952 *Fj* 1,2, *NZ* 1,2, 1954 *Fj* 2, 1955 *NZ* 1, 1956 *SA* 2, 1957 *NZ* 1,2
Cox, M H (NSW) 1981 *W*, *S*
Cox, P A (NSW) 1979 *Arg* 1,2, 1980 *Fj*, *NZ* 1,2, 1981 *W* (R), *S*, 1982 *S* 1,2, *NZ* 1,2,3, 1984 *Fj*, *NZ* 1,2,3
Craig, R R (NSW) 1908 *W*
Crakanthorp, J S (NSW) 1923 *NZ* 3
Cremin, J F (NSW) 1946 *NZ* 1,2, 1947 *NZ* 1
Crittle, C P (NSW) 1962 *NZ* 4,5, 1963 *SA* 2,3,4, 1964 *NZ* 1,2,3, 1965 *SA* 1,2, 1966 *BI* 1,2, *S*, 1967 *E*, *I*
Croft, B H D (NSW) 1928 *M*
Cross, J R (NSW) 1955 *NZ* 1,2,3
Cross, K A (NSW) 1949 *M* 1, *NZ* 1,2, 1950 *BI* 1,2, 1951 *NZ* 2,3, 1952 *NZ* 1, 1953 *SA* 1,2,3,4, 1954 *Fj* 1,2, 1955 *NZ* 3, 1956 *SA* 1,2, 1957 *NZ* 1,2
Crossman, O C (NSW) 1925 *NZ*, 1929 *NZ* 2, 1930 *BI*
Crowe, P J (NSW) 1976 *F* 2, 1978 *W* 1,2, 1979 *I* 2, *NZ*, *Arg* 1
Crowley, D (Q) 1989 *BI* 1,2,3, 1991 [*WS*]
Curley, T J P (NSW) 1957 *NZ* 1,2, 1958 *W*, *I*, *E*, *S*, *F*,

M 1, *NZ* 1,2,3
Curran, D J (NSW) 1980 *NZ* 3, 1981 *F* 1,2, *W*, 1983 *Arg* 1
Currie, E W (Q) 1899 *BI* 2
Cutler, S A G (NSW) 1982 *NZ* 2(R), 1984 *NZ* 1,2,3, *E*, *I*, *W*, *S*, 1985 *C* 1,2, *NZ*, *Fj* 1,2, 1986 *It*, *F*, *NZ* 1,2,3, 1987 *SK*, [*E*, *J*, *I*, *F*, *W*], *NZ*, *Arg* 1,2, 1988 *E* 1,2, *NZ* 1,2,3, *E*, *S*, *It*, 1989 *BI* 1,2,3, *NZ*, 1991 [*WS*]
Daly, A J (NSW) 1989 *NZ*, *F* 1,2, 1990 *F* 1,2,3, *US*, *NZ* 1,2,3, 1991 *W*, *E*, *NZ* 1,2, [*Arg*, *W*, *I*, *NZ*, *E*]
D'Arcy, A M (Q) 1980 *Fj*, *NZ* 3, 1981 *F* 1,2, *I*, *W*, *S*, 1982 *E*, *S* 1,2
Darveniza, P (NSW) 1969 *W*, *SA* 2,3,4
Davidson, R A L (NSW) 1952 *Fj* 1,2, *NZ* 1,2, 1953 *SA* 1, 1957 *NZ* 1,2, 1958 *W*, *I*, *E*, *S*, *F*, *M* 1
Davis, C C (NSW) 1949 *NZ* 1, 1951 *NZ* 1,2,3
Davis, E H (V) 1947 *S*, *W*, 1949 *M* 1,2
Davis, G V (NSW) 1963 *E*, *SA* 1,2,3,4, 1964 *NZ* 1,2,3, 1965 *SA* 1, 1966 *BI* 1,2, *W*, *S*, 1967 *E*, *I* 1, *F*, *I* 2, *NZ*, 1968 *NZ* 1,2, *F*, *I*, *S*, 1969 *W*, *SA* 1,2,3,4, 1970 *S*, 1971 *SA* 1,2,3, *F* 1,2, 1972 *F* 1,2, *NZ* 1,2,3
Davis, G W G (NSW) 1955 *NZ* 2,3
Davis, R A (NSW) 1974 *NZ* 1,2,3
Davis, T S R (NSW) 1921 *NZ*, 1923 *NZ* 1,2,3
Davis, W (NSW) 1899 *BI* 1,3,4
Dawson, W L (NSW) 1946 *NZ* 1,2
Diett, L J (NSW) 1959 *BI* 1,2
Dix, W (NSW) 1907 *NZ* 1,2,3, 1909 *E*
Dixon, E J (Q) 1904 *BI* 3
Donald, K J (Q) 1957 *NZ* 1, 1958 *W*, *I*, *E*, *S*, *M* 2,3, 1959 *BI* 1,2
Dore, E (Q) 1904 *BI* 1
Dore, M J (Q) 1905 *NZ*
Dorr, R W (V) 1936 *M*, 1937 *SA* 1
Douglas, J A (V) 1962 *NZ* 3,4,5
Dowse, J H (NSW) 1961 *Fj* 1,2, *SA* 1,2
Dunbar, A R (NSW) 1910 *NZ* 1,2,3, 1912 *US*
Dunlop, E E (V) 1932 *NZ* 3, 1934 *NZ* 1
Dunn, P K (NSW) 1958 *NZ* 1,2,3, 1959 *BI* 1,2
Dunn, V A (NSW) 1921 *NZ*
Dunworth, D A (Q) 1971 *F* 1,2, 1972 *F* 1,2, 1976 *Fj* 2
Dwyer, L J (NSW) 1910 *NZ* 1,2,3, 1912 *US*, 1913 *NZ* 3, 1914 *NZ* 1,2,3

Eales, J A (Queensland) 1991 *W*, *E*, *NZ* 1,2, [*Arg*, *WS*, *W*, *I*, *NZ*, *E*]
Eastes, C C (NSW) 1946 *NZ* 1,2, 1947 *NZ* 1,2, 1949 *M* 1,2
Egerton, R H (NSW) 1991 *W*, *E*, *NZ* 1,2, [*Arg*, *W*, *I*, *NZ*, *E*]
Ella, G A (NSW) 1982 *NZ* 1,2, 1983 *F* 1,2, 1988 *E* 2, *NZ* 1
Ella, G J (NSW) 1982 *S* 1, 1983 *It*, 1985 *C* 2 (R), *Fj* 2
Ella, M G (NSW) 1980 *NZ* 1,2,3, 1981 *F* 2, *S*, 1982 *E*, *S* 1, *NZ* 1,2,3, 1983 *US*, *Arg* 1,2, *NZ*, *It*, *F* 1,2, 1984 *Fj*, *NZ* 1,2,3, *E*, *I*, *W*, *S*
Ellem, M A (NSW) 1976 *Fj* 3(R)
Elliott, F M (NSW) 1957 *NZ* 1
Elliott, R E (NSW) 1921 *NZ*, 1923 *NZ* 1,2,3
Ellis, C S (NSW) 1899 *BI* 1,2,3,4
Ellis, K J (NSW) 1958 *NZ* 1,2,3, 1959 *BI* 1,2
Ellwood, B J (NSW) 1958 *NZ* 1,2,3, 1960 *Fj* 2,3, *SA* 1, *F*, 1962 *NZ* 1,2,3,4,5, 1963 *SA* 1,2,3,4, 1964 *NZ* 3, 1965 *SA* 1,2, 1966 *BI* 1
Emanuel, D M (NSW) 1957 *NZ* 2, 1958 *W*, *I*, *E*, *S*, *F*, *M* 1,2,3
Emery, N A (NSW) 1947 *NZ* 2, *S*, *I*, *W*, 1948 *E*, *F*, 1949 *M* 2,3, *NZ* 1,2
Erasmus, D J (NSW) 1923 *NZ* 1,2
Erby, A B (NSW) 1923 *NZ* 2,3
Evans, L J (Q) 1903 *NZ*, 1904 *BI* 1,3
Evans, W T (Q) 1899 *BI* 1,2

Fahey, E J (NSW) 1912 *US*, 1913 *NZ* 1,2, 1914 *NZ* 3
Fairfax, R L (NSW) 1971 *F* 1,2, 1972 *F* 1,2, *NZ* 1, *Fj*, 1973 *W*, *E*
Farmer, E H (Q) 1910 *NZ* 1
Farr-Jones, N C (NSW) 1984 *E*, *I*, *W*, *S*, 1985 *C* 1,2, *NZ*, *Fj* 1,2, 1986 *It*, *F*, *Arg* 1,2, *NZ* 1,2,3, 1987 *SK*, [*E*, *I*, *F*, *W*(R)], *NZ*, *Arg* 2, 1988 *E* 1,2, *NZ* 1,2,3, *E*, *S*, *It*, 1989 *BI* 1,2,3, *NZ*, *F* 1,2, 1990 *F* 1,2,3, *US*, *NZ* 1,2,3, 1991 *W*, *E*, *NZ* 1,2, [*Arg*, *WS*, *I*, *NZ*, *E*]
Fay, G (NSW) 1971 *SA* 2, 1972 *NZ* 1,2,3, 1973 *Tg* 1,2,

F, I 2, *NZ*, 1968 *NZ* 1,2, *F, I, S*, 1970 *S*, 1971 *SA* 1,2, *F* 1,2

Jones, G G (Q) 1952 *Fj* 1,2, 1953 *SA* 1,2,3,4, 1954 *Fj* 1,2, 1955 *NZ* 1,2,3, 1956 *SA* 1
Jones, H (NSW) 1913 *NZ* 1,2,3
Jones, P A (NSW) 1963 *E, SA* 1
Joyce, J E (NSW) 1903 *NZ*
Judd, H A (NSW) 1903 *NZ*, 1904 *BI* 1,2,3, 1905 *NZ*
Judd, P B (NSW) 1925 *NZ*, 1927 *I, W, S*, 1928 *E*, 1931 *M, NZ*
Junee, D K (NSW) 1989 *F* 1(R), 2 (R)

Kassulke, N (Q) 1985 *C* 1,2
Kay, A R (V) 1958 *NZ* 2, 1959 *BI* 2
Kay, P (NSW) 1988 *E* 2
Kearney, K H (NSW) 1947 *NZ* 1,2, *S, I, W*, 1948 *E, F*
Kearns, P N (NSW) 1989 *NZ*, *F* 1,2, 1990 *F* 1,2,3, *US, NZ* 1,2,3, 1991, *W, E, NZ* 1,2, [*Arg, WS, W, I, NZ, E*]
Kelaher, J D (NSW) 1933 *SA* 1,2,3,4,5, 1934 *NZ* 1,2, 1936 *NZ* 1,2, *M*, 1937 *SA* 1,2, 1938 *NZ* 3
Kelleher, R J (Q) 1969 *SA* 2,3
Keller, D H (NSW) 1947 *NZ* 1, *S, I, W*, 1948 *E, F*
Kelly, A J (NSW) 1899 *BI* 1
Kelly, R L F (NSW) 1936 *NZ* 1,2, *M*, 1937 *SA* 1,2, 1938 *NZ* 1,2
Kent, A (Q) 1912 *US*
Kerr, F R (V) 1938 *NZ* 1
King, S C (NSW) 1927 *W, S*, 1928 *E, F*, 1929 *NZ* 1,2,3, 1930 *BI*, 1932 *NZ* 1,2
Knight, M (NSW) 1978 *W* 1,2, *NZ* 1
Knight, S O (NSW) 1969 *SA* 2,4, 1970 *S*, 1971 *SA* 1,2,3
Knox, D J (NSW) 1985 *Fj* 1,2, 1990 *US* (R)
Kraefft, D F (NSW) 1947 *NZ* 2, *S, I, W*, 1948 *E, F*
Kreutzer, S D (Q) 1914 *NZ* 2

Lamb, J S (NSW) 1928 *NZ* 1,2, *M*
Lambie, J K (NSW) 1974 *NZ* 1,2,3, 1975 *W*
Lane, T A (Q) 1985 *C* 1,2, *NZ*
Lang, C W P (V) 1938 *NZ* 2,3
Larkin, E R (NSW) 1903 *NZ*
Larkin, K K (Q) 1958 *M* 2,3
Latimer, N B (NSW) 1957 *NZ* 2
Lawton, R (Q) 1988 *E* 1, *NZ* 2 (R), 3, *S*
Lawton, T (NSW, Q) 1925 *NZ*, 1927 *I, W, S*, 1928 *E, F*, 1929 *NZ* 1,2,3, 1930 *BI*, 1932 *NZ* 1,2
Lawton, T A (Q) 1983 *F* 1 (R), 2, 1984 *Fj, NZ* 1,2,3, *E, I, W, S*, 1985 *C* 1,2, *NZ, Fj* 1, 1986 *It, F, Arg* 1,2, *NZ* 1,2,3, 1987 *SK*, [*E, US, I, F, W*], *NZ, Arg* 1,2, 1988 *E* 1,2, *NZ* 1,2,3, *E, S, It*, 1989 *BI* 1,2,3
Laycock, W M B (NSW) 1925 *NZ*
Leeds, A J (NSW) 1986 *NZ* 3, 1987 [*US, W*], *NZ, Arg* 1,2, 1988 *E* 1,2, *NZ* 1,2,3, *E, S, It*
Lenehan, J K (NSW) 1958 *W, E, S, F, M* 1,2,3, 1959 *BI* 1,2, 1961 *SA* 1,2, *F*, 1962 *NZ* 2,3,4,5, 1965 *SA* 1,2, 1966 *W, S*, 1967 *E, I* 1, *F, I* 2
L'Estrange, R D (Q) 1971 *F* 1,2, 1972 *NZ* 1,2,3, 1973 *Tg* 1,2, *W, E*, 1974 *NZ* 1,2,3, 1975 *S, W*, 1976 *I, US*
Lewis, L S (Q) 1934 *NZ* 1,2, 1936 *NZ* 2, 1938 *NZ* 1
Lidbury, S (NSW) 1987 *Arg* 1, 1988 *E* 2
Lillicrap, C P (Q) 1985 *Fj* 2, 1987 [*US, I, F, W*], 1989 *BI* 1, 1991 [*WS*]
Lindsay, R T G (Q) 1932 *NZ* 3
Lisle, R J (NSW) 1961 *Fj* 1,2,3, *SA* 1
Little, J S (Q) 1989 *F* 1,2, 1990 *F* 1,2,3, *US*, 1991 *W, E, NZ* 1,2, [*Arg, W, I, NZ, E*]
Livermore, A E (Q) 1946 *NZ* 1, *M*
Loane, M E (Q) 1973 *Tg* 1,2, 1974 *NZ* 1, 1975 *E* 1,2, *Fj* 1, 1976 *E, I, Fj* 1,2,3, *F* 1,2, 1978 *W* 1,2, 1979 *I* 1,2, *NZ, Arg* 1,2, 1981 *F* 1,2, *I, W, S*, 1982 *E, S* 1,2
Logan, D L (NSW) 1958 *M* 1
Loudon, D B (NSW) 1921 *NZ*
Loudon, R B (NSW) 1923 *NZ* 1 (R), 2,3, 1928 *NZ* 1,2,3, *M*, 1929 *NZ* 2, 1933 *SA* 2,3,4,5, 1934 *NZ* 2
Love, E W (NSW) 1932 *NZ* 1,2,3
Lowth, D R (NSW) 1958 *NZ* 1
Lucas, B C (Q) 1905 *NZ*
Lucas, P W (NSW) 1982 *NZ* 1,2,3
Lutge, D (NSW) 1903 *NZ*, 1904 *BI* 1,2,3
Lynagh, M P (Q) 1984 *Fj, E, I, W, S*, 1985 *C* 1,2, *NZ*, 1986 *It, F, Arg* 1,2, *NZ* 1,2,3, 1987 [*E, US, J, I, F, W*], *Arg* 1,2, 1988 *E* 1,2, *NZ* 1,3 (R), *E, S, It*, 1989 *BI* 1,2,3, *NZ, F* 1,2, 1990 *F* 1,2,3, *US, NZ* 1,2,3, 1991 *W, E, NZ* 1,2, [*Arg, WS, W, I, NZ, E*]

McArthur, M (NSW) 1909 *E*
McBain, M I (Q) 1983 *It, F* 1, 1985 *Fj* 2, 1986 *It* (R), 1987 [*J*], 1988 *E* 2 (R), 1989 *BI* 1 (R)
MacBride, J W T (NSW) 1946 *NZ* 1, *M, NZ* 2, 1947 *NZ* 1,2, *S, I, W*, 1948 *E, F*
McCabe, A J M (NSW) 1909 *E*
McCall, R J (Q) 1989 *F* 1,2, 1990 *F* 1,2,3, *US, NZ* 1,2,3, 1991 *W, E, NZ* 1,2, [*Arg, W, I, NZ, E*]
McCarthy, F J C (Q) 1950 *BI* 1
McCowan, R H (Q) 1899 *BI* 1,2,4
McCue, P A (NSW) 1907 *NZ* 1,3, 1908 *W*, 1909 *E*
McDermott, L C (Q) 1962 *NZ* 1,2
McDonald, B S (NSW) 1969 *SA* 4, 1970 *S*
McDonald, J C (Q) 1938 *NZ* 2,3
Macdougall, D G (NSW) 1961 *Fj* 1, *SA* 1
Macdougall, S G (NSW, ACT) 1971 *SA* 3, 1973 *E*, 1974 *NZ* 1,2,3, 1975 *E* 1,2, 1976 *E*
McGhie, G H (Q) 1929 *NZ* 2,3, 1930 *BI*
McGill, A N (NSW) 1968 *NZ* 1,2, *F*, 1969 *W, SA* 1,2,3,4, 1970 *S*, 1971 *SA* 1,2,3, *F* 1,2, 1972 *F* 1,2, *NZ* 1,2,3, 1973 *Tg* 1,2
McIntyre, A J (Q) 1982 *NZ* 1,2,3, 1983 *F* 1,2, 1984 *Fj, NZ* 1,2,3, *E, I, W, S*, 1985 *C* 1,2, *NZ, Fj* 1,2, 1986 *It, F, Arg* 1,2, 1987 [*E, US, I, F, W*], *NZ, Arg* 2, 1988 *E* 1,2, *NZ* 1,2,3, *E, S, It*, 1989 *NZ*
McKenzie, E J A (NSW) 1990 *F* 1,2,3, *US, NZ* 1,2,3, 1991 *W, E, NZ* 1,2, [*Arg, W, I, NZ, E*]
McKid, W A (NSW) 1976 *E, Fj* 1, 1978 *NZ* 2,3, 1979 *I* 1,2
McKinnon, A (Q) 1904 *BI* 2
McKivat, C H (NSW) 1907 *NZ* 1,3, 1908 *W*, 1909 *E*
McLaughlin, R E M (NSW) 1936 *NZ* 1,2
McLean, A D (Q) 1933 *SA* 1,2,3,4,5, 1934 *NZ* 1,2, 1936 *NZ* 1,2, *M*
McLean, J D (Q) 1904 *BI* 2,3, 1905 *NZ*
McLean, J J (Q) 1971 *SA* 2,3, *F* 1,2, 1972 *F* 1,2, *NZ* 1,2,3, *Fj*, 1973 *W, E*, 1974 *NZ* 1
McLean, P E (Q) 1974 *NZ* 1,2,3, 1975 *J* 1,2, *S, W*, 1976 *E, I, Fj* 1,2,3, *F* 1,2, 1978 *W* 1,2, *NZ* 2, 1979 *I* 1,2, *NZ, Arg* 1,2, 1980 *Fj*, 1981 *F* 1,2, *I, W, S*, 1982 *E, S* 2
McLean, P W (Q) 1978 *NZ* 1,2,3, 1979 *I* 1,2, *NZ, Arg* 1,2, 1980 *Fj* (R), *NZ* 3, 1981 *I, W, S*, 1982 *E, S* 1,2
McLean, R A (NSW) 1971 *SA* 1,2,3, *F* 1,2
McLean, W M (Q) 1946 *NZ* 1, *M, NZ* 2, 1947 *NZ* 1,2
McMahon, M J (Q) 1913 *NZ* 1
McMaster, R E (Q) 1946 *NZ* 1, *M, NZ* 2, 1947 *NZ* 1,2, *I, W*
MacMillan, D I (Q) 1950 *BI* 1,2
McMullen, K V (NSW) 1962 *NZ* 3,5, 1963 *E, SA* 1
McShane, J M S (NSW) 1937 *SA* 1,2
Mackney, W A R (NSW) 1933 *SA* 1,5, 1934 *NZ* 1,2
Magrath, E (NSW) 1961 *Fj* 1, *SA* 2, *F*
Maguire, D J (Q) 1989 *BI* 1,2,3
Malcolm, S J (NSW) 1927 *S*, 1928 *E, F, NZ* 1,2, *M*, 1929 *NZ* 1,2,3, 1930 *BI*, 1931 *NZ*, 1932 *NZ* 1,2,3, 1933 *SA* 4,5, 1934 *NZ* 1,2
Malone, J H (NSW) 1936 *NZ* 1,2, *M*, 1937 *SA* 2
Malouf, B P (NSW) 1982 *NZ* 1
Mandible, E F (NSW) 1907 *NZ* 2,3, 1908 *W*
Manning, J (NSW) 1904 *BI* 2
Manning, R C S (Q) 1967 *NZ*
Mansfield, B W (NSW) 1975 *J* 2
Marks, H (NSW) 1899 *BI* 1,2
Marks, R J P (Q) 1962 *NZ* 4,5, 1963 *E, SA* 2,3,4, 1964 *NZ* 1,2,3, 1965 *SA* 1,2, 1966 *W, S*, 1967 *E, I* 1, *F, I* 2
Marrott, W J (NSW) 1923 *NZ* 1,2
Marshall, J S (NSW) 1949 *M* 1
Martin, G J (Q) 1989 *BI* 1,2,3, *NZ, F* 1,2, 1990 *F* 1,3 (R), *NZ* 1
Martin, M C (NSW) 1980 *Fj, NZ* 1,2, 1981 *F* 1,2, *W* (R)
Massey-Westropp, M (NSW) 1914 *NZ* 3
Mathers, M J (NSW) 1980 *Fj, NZ* 2 (R)
Maund, J W (NSW) 1903 *NZ*
Meadows, J E C (V, Q) 1974 *NZ* 1, 1975 *S, W*, 1976 *I, US, Fj* 1,3, *F* 1,2, 1978 *NZ* 1,2,3, 1979 *I* 1,2, 1981 *I, S*, 1982 *E, NZ* 2,3, 1983 *US, Arg* 2, *NZ*
Meadows, R W (NSW) 1958 *M* 1,2,3, *NZ* 1,2,3
Meagher, F W (NSW) 1923 *NZ* 3, 1925 *NZ*, 1927 *I, W*
Meibusch, J H (Q) 1904 *BI* 3
Meibusch, L S (Q) 1912 *US*
Melrose, T C (NSW) 1978 *NZ* 3, 1979 *I* 1,2, *NZ, Arg* 1,2
Messenger, H H (NSW) 1907 *NZ* 2,3

329

Sayle, J L (NSW) 1967 *NZ*
Schulte, B G (Q) 1946 *NZ* 1, *M*
Scott, P R I (NSW) 1962 *NZ* 1,2
Scott-Young, S J (Q) 1990 *F* 2,3 (R), *US, NZ* 3
Shambrook, G G (Q) 1976 *Fj* 2,3
Shaw, A A (Q) 1973 *W, E*, 1975 *E* 1,2, *J* 2, *S, W*, 1976 *E, I, US, Fj* 1,2,3, *F* 1,2, 1978 *W* 1,2, *NZ* 1,2,3, 1979 *I* 1,2, *NZ, Arg* 1,2, 1980 *Fj, NZ* 1,2,3, 1981 *F* 1,2, *I, W, S*, 1982 *S* 1,2
Shaw, C (NSW) 1925 *NZ* (R)
Shaw, G A (NSW) 1969 *W, SA* 1 (R), 1970 *S*, 1971 *SA* 1,2,3, *F* 1,2, 1973 *W, E*, 1974 *NZ* 1,2,3, 1975 *E* 1,2, *J* 1,2, *W*, 1976 *E, I, US, Fj* 1,2,3, *F* 1,2, 1979 *NZ*
Sheehan, W B J (NSW) 1923 *NZ* 1,2,3, 1927 *W, S*
Shehadie, N M (NSW) 1947 *NZ* 2, 1948 *E, F*, 1949 *M* 1,2,3, *NZ* 1,2, 1950 *BI* 1,2, 1951 *NZ* 1,2,3, 1952 *Fj* 1,2, *NZ* 2, 1953 *SA* 1,2,3,4, 1954 *Fj* 1,2, 1955 *NZ* 1,2,3, 1956 *SA* 1,2, 1957 *NZ* 2, 1958 *W, I*
Sheil, A G R (Q) 1956 *SA* 1
Shepherd, D J (V) 1964 *NZ* 3, 1965 *SA* 1,2, 1966 *BI* 1,2
Simpson, R J (NSW) 1913 *NZ* 2
Skinner, A J (NSW) 1969 *W, SA* 4, 1970 *S*
Slack, A G (Q) 1978 *W* 1,2, *NZ* 1,2, 1979 *NZ, Arg* 1,2, 1980 *Fj*, 1981 *I, W, S*, 1982 *E, S* 1, *NZ* 3, 1983 *US, Arg* 1,2, *NZ, It*, 1984 *Fj, NZ* 1,2,3, *E, I, W, S*, 1986 *It, F, NZ* 1,2,3, 1987 *SK*, [*E, US, J, I, F, W*]
Slater, S H (NSW) 1910 *NZ* 3
Slattery, P J (Q) 1990 *US* (R), 1991 *W*(R), *E*(R), [*WS*(R), *W, I*(R)]
Smairl, A M (NSW) 1928 *NZ* 1,2,3
Smith, B A (NSW) 1987 *SK*, [*US, J, I* (R), *W*], *Arg* 1
Smith, F B (NSW) 1905 *NZ*, 1907 *NZ* 1,2,3
Smith, L M (NSW) 1905 *NZ*
Smith, N C (NSW) 1923 *NZ* 1
Smith, P V (NSW) 1967 *NZ*, 1968 *NZ* 1,2, *F, I, S*, 1969 *W, SA* 1
Smith, R A (NSW) 1971 *SA* 1,2, 1972 *F* 1,2, *NZ* 1,2 (R), 3, *Fj*, 1975 *E* 1,2, *J* 1,2, *S, W*, 1976 *E, I, US, Fj* 1,2,3, *F* 1,2
Smith, T S (NSW) 1921 *NZ*, 1925 *NZ*
Snell, H W (NSW) 1928 *NZ* 3
Solomon, H J (NSW) 1949 *M* 3, *NZ* 2, 1950 *BI* 1,2, 1951 *NZ* 1,2, 1952 *Fj* 1,2, *NZ* 1,2, 1953 *SA* 1,2,3, 1955 *NZ* 1
Spragg, S A (NSW) 1899 *BI* 1,2,3,4,
Stanley, R G (NSW) 1921 *NZ*, 1923 *NZ* 1,2,3
Stapleton, E T (NSW) 1951 *NZ* 1,2,3, 1952 *Fj* 1,2, *NZ* 1,2, 1953 *SA* 1,2,3,4, 1954 *Fj* 1, 1955 *NZ* 1,2,3, 1958 *NZ* 1
Steggall, J C (Q) 1931 *M, NZ*, 1932 *NZ* 1,2,3, 1933 *SA* 1,2,3,4,5
Stegman, T R (NSW) 1973 *Tg* 1,2
Stephens, O G (NSW) 1973 *Tg* 1,2, *W*, 1974 *NZ* 2,3
Stewart, A A (NSW) 1979 *NZ, Arg* 1,2
Stone, A H (NSW) 1937 *SA* 2, 1938 *NZ* 2,3
Stone, C G (NSW) 1938 *NZ* 1
Stone, J M (NSW) 1946 *M, NZ* 2
Storey, G P (NSW) 1927 *I, W, S*, 1928 *E, F*, 1929 *NZ* 3 (R), 1930 *BI*
Storey, K P (NSW) 1936 *NZ* 2
Storey, N J D (NSW) 1962 *NZ* 1
Strachan, D J (NSW) 1955 *NZ* 2,3
Street, N O (NSW) 1899 *BI* 2
Streeter, S F (NSW) 1978 *NZ* 1
Stuart, R (NSW) 1910 *NZ* 2,3
Stumbles, B D (NSW) 1972 *NZ* 1 (R), 2,3, *Fj*
Sturtridge, G S (V) 1929 *NZ* 2, 1932 *NZ* 1,2,3, 1933 *SA* 1,2,3,4,5
Sullivan, P D (NSW) 1971 *SA* 1,2,3, *F* 1,2, 1972 *F* 1,2, *NZ* 1,2, *Fj*, 1973 *Tg* 1,2, *W*
Summons, A J (NSW) 1958 *W, I, E, S, M* 2, *NZ* 1,2,3, 1959 *BI* 1,2
Suttor, D C (NSW) 1913 *NZ* 1,2,3
Swannell, B I (NSW) 1905 *NZ*
Sweeney, T L (Q) 1953 *SA* 1

Taafe, B S (NSW) 1969 *SA* 1, 1972 *F* 1,2
Tancred, A J (NSW) 1927 *I, W, S*
Tancred, J L (NSW) 1928 *F*
Tanner, W H (Q) 1899 *BI* 1,2
Tasker, W G (NSW) 1913 *NZ* 1,2,3, 1914 *NZ* 1,2,3
Tate, M J (NSW) 1951 *NZ* 3, 1952 *Fj* 1,2, *NZ* 1,2, 1953 *SA* 1, 1954 *Fj* 1,2
Taylor, D A (Q) 1968 *NZ* 1,2, *F, I, S*

Taylor, H C (NSW) 1923 *NZ* 1,2,3
Taylor, J I (NSW) 1971 *SA* 1, 1972 *F* 1,2, *Fj*
Teitzel, R G (Q) 1966 *W, S*, 1967 *E, I* 1, *F, I* 2, *NZ*
Thompson, C E (NSW) 1923 *NZ* 1
Thompson, E G (Q) 1929 *NZ* 1,2,3, 1930 *BI*
Thompson, F (NSW) 1913 *NZ* 1,2,3, 1914 *NZ* 1,2,3
Thompson, J (Q) 1914 *NZ* 1
Thompson, P D (Q) 1950 *BI* 1
Thompson, R J (WA) 1971 *SA* 3, *F* 2 (R), 1972 *Fj*
Thorn, A M (NSW) 1921 *NZ*
Thorn, E J (NSW) 1923 *NZ* 1,2,3
Thornett, J E (NSW) 1955 *NZ* 1,2,3, 1956 *SA* 1,2, 1958 *W, I, S, F, M* 2,3, *NZ* 2,3, 1959 *BI* 1,2, 1961 *Fj* 2,3, *SA* 1,2, *F*, 1962 *NZ* 2,3,4,5, 1963 *E, SA* 1,2,3,4, 1964 *NZ* 1,2,3, 1965 *SA* 1,2, 1966 *BI* 1,2, 1967 *F*
Thornett, R N (NSW) 1961 *Fj* 1,2,3, *SA* 1,2, *F*, 1962 *NZ* 1,2,3,4,5
Thorpe, A C (NSW) 1929 *NZ* 1 (R)
Timbury, F R V (Q) 1910 *NZ* 1,2
Tindall, E N (NSW) 1973 *Tg* 2
Toby, A E (NSW) 1925 *NZ*
Tolhurst, H A (NSW) 1931 *M, NZ*
Tonkin, A E J (NSW) 1947 *S, I, W*, 1948 *E, F*, 1950 *BI* 2
Tooth, R M (NSW) 1951 *NZ* 1,2,3, 1954 *Fj* 1,2, 1955 *NZ* 1,2,3, 1957 *NZ* 1,2
Towers, C H T (NSW) 1927 *I*, 1928 *E, F, NZ* 1,2,3, *M*, 1929 *NZ* 1,3, 1930 *BI*, 1931 *M, NZ*, 1934 *NZ* 1,2, 1937 *SA* 1,2
Trivett, R K (Q) 1966 *BI* 1,2
Turnbull, A (V) 1961 *Fj* 3
Turnbull, R V (NSW) 1968 *I*
Tuynman, S N (NSW) 1983 *F* 1,2, 1984 *E, I, W, S*, 1985 *C* 1,2, *NZ, Fj* 1,2, 1986 *It, F, Arg* 1,2, *NZ* 1,2,3, 1987 *SK*, [*E, US, J, I, W*], *NZ, Arg* 1 (R), 2, 1988 *E, It*, 1989 *BI* 1,2,3, *NZ*, 1990 *NZ* 1
Tweedale, E (NSW) 1946 *NZ* 1,2, 1947 *NZ* 2, *S, I*, 1948 *E, F*, 1949 *M* 1,2,3

Vaughan, D (NSW) 1983 *US, Arg* 1, *It, F* 1,2
Vaughan, G N (V) 1958 *E, S, F, M* 1,2,3
Verge, A (NSW) 1904 *BI* 1,2

Walden, R J (NSW) 1934 *NZ* 2, 1936 *NZ* 1,2, *M*
Walker, A K (NSW) 1947 *NZ* 1, 1948 *E, F*, 1950 *BI* 1,2
Walker, A S B (NSW) 1912 *US*, 1921 *NZ*
Walker, L F (NSW) 1988 *NZ* 2,3, *S, It*, 1989 *BI* 1,2,3, *NZ*
Walker, L R (NSW) 1982 *NZ* 2,3
Wallace, A C (NSW) 1921 *NZ*, 1927 *I, W, S*, 1928 *E, F*
Wallach, C (NSW) 1913 *NZ* 1,3, 1914 *NZ* 1,2,3
Walsh, J J (NSW) 1953 *SA* 1,2,3,4
Walsh, P B (NSW) 1904 *BI* 1,2,3
Walsham, K P (NSW) 1962 *NZ* 3, 1963 *E*
Ward, P G (NSW) 1899 *BI* 1,2,3,4
Ward, T (Q) 1899 *BI* 2
Watson, G W (Q) 1907 *NZ* 1
Watson, W T (NSW) 1912 *US*, 1913 *NZ* 1,2,3, 1914 *NZ* 1
Weatherstone, L J (ACT) 1975 *E* 1,2, *J* 1,2, *S* (R), 1976 *E, I*
Webb, W (NSW) 1899 *BI* 3,4
Wells, B G (NSW) 1958 *M* 1
Westfield, R E (NSW) 1928 *NZ* 1,2,3, *M*, 1929 *NZ* 2,3
White, C J B (NSW) 1899 *BI* 1, 1903 *NZ*, 1904 *BI* 1
White, J M (NSW) 1904 *BI* 3
White, J P L (NSW) 1958 *NZ* 1,2,3, 1961 *Fj* 1,2,3, *SA* 1,2, *F*, 1962 *NZ* 1,2,3,4,5, 1963 *E, SA* 1,2,3,4, 1964 *NZ* 1,2,3, 1965 *SA* 1,2
White, M C (Q) 1931 *M, NZ*, 1932 *NZ* 1,2, 1933 *SA* 1,2,3,4,5
White, S W (NSW) 1956 *SA* 1,2, 1958 *I, E, S, M* 2,3
White, W G S (Q) 1933 *SA* 1,2,3,4,5, 1934 *NZ* 1,2, 1936 *NZ* 1,2, *M*
White, W J (NSW) 1928 *NZ* 1,2, *M*, 1932 *NZ* 1
Wickham, S M (NSW) 1903 *NZ*, 1904 *BI* 1,2,3, 1905 *NZ*
Williams, D (Q) 1913 *NZ* 3, 1914 *NZ* 1,2,3
Williams, I M (NSW) 1987 *Arg* 1,2, 1988 *E* 1,2, *NZ* 1,2,3, 1989 *BI* 2,3, *NZ, F* 1,2, 1990 *F* 1,2,3, *US, NZ* 1
Williams, J L (NSW) 1963 *SA* 1,3,4
Williams, S A (NSW) 1980 *Fj, NZ* 1,2, 1981 *F* 1,2, 1982 *E, NZ* 1,2,3, 1983 *US, Arg* 1 (R), 2, *NZ, It, F* 1,2, 1984 *NZ* 1,2,3, *E, I, W, S*, 1985 *C* 1,2, *NZ, Fj* 1,2

331

Wilson, B J (NSW) 1949 *NZ* 1,2
Wilson, C R (Q) 1957 *NZ* 1, 1958 *NZ* 1,2,3
Wilson, V W (Q) 1937 *SA* 1,2, 1938 *NZ* 1,2,3
Windon, C J (NSW) 1946 *NZ* 1,2, 1947 *NZ* 1, *S, I, W,*
1948 *E, F,* 1949 *M* 1,2,3, *NZ* 1,2, 1951 *NZ* 1,2,3, 1952
Fj 1,2, *NZ* 1,2
Windon, K S (NSW) 1937 *SA* 1,2, 1946 *M*
Windsor, J C (Q) 1947 *NZ* 2
Winning, K C (Q) 1951 *NZ* 1
Wogan, L W (NSW) 1913 *NZ* 1,2,3, 1914 *NZ* 1,2,3,
1921 *NZ*

Wood, F (NSW) 1907 *NZ* 1,2,3, 1910 *NZ* 1,2,3, 1913
NZ 1,2,3, 1914 *NZ* 1,2,3
Wood, R N (Q) 1972 *Fj*
Woods, H F (NSW) 1925 *NZ,* 1927 *I, W, S,* 1928 *E*
Wright, K J (NSW) 1975 *E* 1,2, *J* 1, 1976 *US, F* 1,2,
1978 *NZ* 1,2,3

Yanz, K (NSW) 1958 *F*

AUSTRALIAN INTERNATIONAL RECORDS

Both team and individual records are for official Australian international matches, up to 31 March 1992.

TEAM RECORDS

Highest score
67 v United States (67-9) 1990 Brisbane
v individual countries
39 v Argentina (39-19) 1986 Brisbane
30 v British Isles (30-12) 1989 Sydney
59 v Canada (59-3) 1985 Sydney
40 v England (40-15) 1991 Sydney
52 v Fiji (52-28) 1985 Brisbane
48 v France (48-31) 1990 Brisbane
33 v Ireland (33-15) 1987 Sydney
55 v Italy (55-6) 1988 Rome
50 v Japan (50-25) 1975 Brisbane
30 v N Zealand (30-16) 1978 Auckland
37 v Scotland (37-12) 1984 Murrayfield
21 v South Africa (21-6) 1933 Durban
65 v South Korea (65-18) 1987 Brisbane
30 v Tonga (30-12) 1973 Sydney
67 v United States (67-9) 1990 Brisbane
63 v Wales (63-6) 1991 Brisbane
9 v Western Samoa (9-3) 1991 Pontypool

Biggest winning points margin
58 v United States (67-9) 1990 Brisbane
v individual countries
26 v Argentina (26-0) 1986 Sydney
18 v British Isles (30-12) 1989 Sydney
56 v Canada (59-3) 1985 Sydney
25 v England (40-15) 1991 Sydney
24 v Fiji (52-28) 1985 Brisbane
17 v France { (32-15) 1989 Strasbourg
{ (48-31) 1990 Brisbane
18 v Ireland (33-15) 1987 Sydney
49 v Italy (55-6) 1988 Rome
30 v Japan (37-7) 1975 Sydney
16 v N Zealand (26-10) 1980 Sydney
25 v Scotland (37-12) 1984 Murrayfield

15 v South Africa (21-6) 1933 Durban
47 v South Korea (65-18) 1987 Brisbane
18 v Tonga (30-12) 1973 Sydney
58 v United States (67-9) 1990 Brisbane
57 v Wales (63-6) 1991 Brisbane
6 v Western Samoa (9-3) 1991 Pontypool

Highest score by opposing team
38 { N Zealand (13-38) 1936 Dunedin
{ N Zealand (3-38) 1972 Auckland
by individual countries
27 Argentina (19-27) 1987 Buenos Aires
31 British Isles (0-31) 1966 Brisbane
15 Canada (43-15) 1985 Brisbane
28 England (19-28) 1988 Twickenham
28 Fiji (52-28) 1985 Brisbane
34 France (6-34) 1976 Paris
27 Ireland (12-27) 1979 Brisbane
18 Italy (39-18) 1986 Brisbane
25 Japan (50-25) 1975 Brisbane
38 { N Zealand (13-38) 1936 Dunedin
{ N Zealand (3-38) 1972 Auckland
24 Scotland (15-24) 1981 Murrayfield
30 South Africa (11-30) 1969 Johannesburg
18 South Korea (65-18) 1987 Brisbane
16 Tonga (11-16) 1973 Brisbane
12 United States (47-12) 1987 Brisbane
28 Wales (3-28) 1975 Cardiff
3 Western Samoa (9-3) 1991 Pontypool

Biggest losing points margin
35 v N Zealand (3-38) 1972 Auckland
v individual countries
15 v Argentina (3-18) 1983 Brisbane

31 v British Isles (0-31) 1966 Brisbane

17 v England $\left\{ \begin{array}{l} (3\text{-}20)\ 1973\ \text{Twickenham} \\ (6\text{-}23)\ 1976\ \text{Twickenham} \end{array} \right.$

2 v Fiji $\left\{ \begin{array}{l} (15\text{-}17)\ 1952\ \text{Sydney} \\ (16\text{-}18)\ 1954\ \text{Sydney} \end{array} \right.$

28 v France (6-34) 1976 Paris

15 v Ireland (12-27) 1979 Brisbane

35 v New Zealand (3-38) 1972 Auckland

9 v Scotland (15-24) 1981 Murrayfield

25 v South Africa (3-28) 1961 Johannesburg

5 v Tonga (11-16) 1973 Brisbane

25 v Wales (3-28) 1975 Cardiff

No defeats v Canada, Italy, Japan, South Korea, United States or Western Samoa.

Most tries by Australia in an international

13 v South Korea (65-18) 1987 Brisbane

Most tries against Australia in an international

9 by N Zealand (13-38) 1936 Dunedin

Most points on overseas tour (all matches)

500 in B Isles/France (35 matches) 1947-48

Most tries on overseas tour (all matches)

115 in B Isles/France (35 matches) 1947-48

INDIVIDUAL RECORDS

Most capped player

D I Campese   64   1982-91

in individual positions

Full-back

R G Gould   25   1980-87

Wing

D I Campese   48(64)[1]   1982-91

Centre

A G Slack   39   1978-87

Fly-half

M P Lynagh   45(53)[2]   1984-91

Scrum-half

N C Farr-Jones   52(53)[3]   1984-91

Prop

A J McIntyre   38   1982-89

Hooker

P G Johnson   42   1959-71

Lock

S A G Cutler   40   1982-91

Flanker

S P Poidevin   59   1980-91

No 8

S N Tuynman   28(34)[4]   1983-90

[1] *Campese has played 16 times as a full-back*

[2] *Lynagh has played 7 times as a centre and once as a replacement full-back*

[3] *Farr-Jones was capped once as a replacement wing*

[4] *Tuynman played 6 times as a flanker*

Longest international career

G M Cooke 16 seasons 1932-1947/8

A R Miller 16 seasons 1952-1967

Cooke's career ended during a Northern hemisphere season

Most consecutive internationals – 37

P G Johnson 1959-68

Most internationals as captain

N C Farr-Jones   30   1988-91

Most points in internationals – 689

M P Lynagh (53 matches) 1984-91

Most points in an international – 24

M P Lynagh v France 1990 Brisbane

M P Lynagh v United States 1990 Brisbane

Most tries in internationals – 46

D I Campese (64 matches) 1982-91

Most tries in an international – 4

G Cornelsen v N Zealand 1978 Auckland

D I Campese v United States 1983 Sydney

Most conversions in internationals – 120

M P Lynagh (53 matches) 1984-91

Most conversions in an international – 8

M P Lynagh v Italy 1988 Rome

M P Lynagh v United States 1990 Brisbane

Most dropped goals in internationals – 9

P F Hawthorne (21 matches) 1962-67

M P Lynagh (53 matches) 1984-91

Most penalty goals in internationals – 126
M P Lynagh (53 matches) 1984-91

Most points in international series on tour – 42
M P Lynagh (4 appearances) 1984
   B Isles

Most tries in international series on tour – 4
G Cornelsen (3 appearances) 1978
   N Zealand
M G Ella (4 appearances) 1984
   B Isles
Ella scored in each match of the international series

Most points on overseas tour – 154
P E McLean (18 appearances) B Isles
   1975-76

Most tries on overseas tour – 23
C J Russell B Isles 1908-09

Most points in a tour match – 26
A J Leeds v Buller 1986 Westport

Most tries in a tour match – 6
J S Boyce v Wairarapa (NZ) 1962
   Masterton

INTERNATIONAL MATCH APPEARANCES FOR BRITISH ISLES TEAMS (*up to 31 March 1992*)

From 1910 onwards, when British Isles teams first became officially representative of the four Home Unions. (★Uncapped when first selected to play in a Test match for the British Isles.)

ABBREVIATIONS

A – Australia; *NZ* – New Zealand; *SA* –South Africa; (R) – Replacement.

CLUB ABBREVIATIONS

NIFC – North of Ireland Football Club; CIYMS – Church of Ireland Young Men's Society

Note: When a series has taken place, figures have been used to denote the particular matches in which players have featured. Thus 1962 *SA* 1,4 indicates that a player appeared in the first and fourth Tests of a series.

Aarvold, C D (Cambridge U, Blackheath and England) 1930 *NZ* 1,2,3,4, *A*
Ackerman, R A (London Welsh and Wales) 1983 *NZ* 1,4(R)
Ackford, P J (Harlequins and England) 1989 *A* 1,2,3
Alexander, R (NIFC and Ireland) 1938 *SA* 1,2,3
Andrew, C R (Wasps and England) 1989 *A* 2,3
Arneil, R J (Edinburgh Acads and Scotland) 1968 *SA* 1,2,3,4
Ashcroft, A (Waterloo and England) 1959 *A* 1, *NZ* 2

Bainbridge, S J (Gosforth and England) 1983 *NZ* 3,4
Baird, G R T (Kelso and Scotland) 1983 *NZ* 1,2,3,4
Baker, A M (Newport and Wales) 1910 *SA* 3
Baker, D G S (Old Merchant Taylors' and England) 1955 *SA* 3,4
Bassett, J (Penarth and Wales) 1930 *NZ* 1,2,3,4, *A*
Beamish, G R (Leicester, RAF and Ireland) 1930 *NZ* 1,2,3,4, *A*
Beattie, J R (Glasgow Acads and Scotland) 1983 *NZ* 2(R)
Beaumont, W B (Fylde and England) 1977 *NZ* 2,3,4, 1980 *SA* 1,2,3,4
Bebb, D I E (Swansea and Wales) 1962 *SA* 2,3, 1966 *A* 1,2, *NZ* 1,2,3,4
Bennett, P (Llanelli and Wales) 1974 *SA* 1,2,3,4, 1977 *NZ* 1,2,3,4
Bevan, J C (Cardiff Coll of Ed, Cardiff and Wales) 1971 *NZ* 1
Black, A W (Edinburgh U and Scotland) 1950 *NZ* 1,2
Black, B H (Oxford U, Blackheath and England) 1930 *NZ* 1,2,3,4, *A*
Blakiston, A F (Northampton and England) 1924 *SA* 1,2,3,4
Bowcott, H M (Cambridge U, Cardiff and Wales) 1930 *NZ* 1,2,3,4, *A*
Boyle, C V (Dublin U and Ireland) 1938 *SA* 2,3
Brand, T N (NIFC and ★Ireland) 1924 *SA* 1,2
Bresnihan, F P K (UC Dublin and Ireland) 1968 *SA* 1,2,4
Brophy, N H (UC Dublin and Ireland) 1962 *SA* 1,4
Brown, G L (W of Scotland and Scotland) 1971 *NZ* 3,4, 1974 *SA* 1,2,3, 1977 *NZ* 2,3,4
Budge, G M (Edinburgh Wands and Scotland) 1950 *NZ* 4
Burcher, D H (Newport and Wales) 1977 *NZ* 3
Butterfield, J (Northampton and England) 1955 *SA* 1,2,3,4

Calder, F (Stewart's-Melville FP and Scotland) 1989 *A* 1,2,3
Calder, J H (Stewart's-Melville FP and Scotland) 1983 *NZ* 3
Cameron, A (Glasgow HSFP and Scotland) 1955 *SA* 1,2
Campbell, S O (Old Belvedere and Ireland) 1980 *SA* 2(R), 3,4, 1983 *NZ* 1,2,3,4
Campbell-Lamerton, M J (Halifax, Army and Scotland) 1962 *SA* 1,2,3,4, 1966 *A* 1,2, *NZ* 1,3

Carleton, J (Orrell and England) 1980 *SA* 1,2,4, 1983 *NZ* 2,3,4
Chalmers, C M (Melrose and Scotland) 1989 *A* 1
Cleaver, W B (Cardiff and Wales) 1950 *NZ* 1,2,3
Clifford, T (Young Munster and Ireland) 1950 *NZ* 1,2,3,4 1,2
Cobner, T J (Pontypool and Wales) 1977 *NZ* 1,2,3
Colclough, M J (Angoulême and England) 1980 *SA* 1,2,3,4, 1983 *NZ* 1,2,3,4
Connell, G C (Trinity Acads and Scotland) 1968 *SA* 4
Cotton, F E (Loughborough Colls, Coventry and England) 1974 *SA* 1,2,3,4, 1977 *NZ* 2,3,4
Coulman, M J (Moseley and England) 1968 *SA* 3
Cove-Smith, R (Old Merchant Taylors' and England) 1924 *SA* 1,2,3,4
Cowan, R C (Selkirk and Scotland) 1962 *SA* 4
Cromey, G E (Queen's U, Belfast and Ireland) 1938 *SA* 3
Cunningham, W A (Lansdowne and Ireland) 1924 *SA* 3

Dancer, G T (Bedford) 1938 *SA* 1,2,3
Davies, C (Cardiff and Wales) 1950 *NZ* 4
Davies, D M (Somerset Police and Wales) 1950 *NZ* 3,4, *A* 1
Davies, D S (Hawick and Scotland) 1924 *SA* 1,2,3,4
Davies, H J (Newport and Wales) 1924 *SA* 2
Davies, T G R (Cardiff, London Welsh and Wales) 1968 *SA* 3, 1971 *NZ* 1,2,3,4
Davies, T J (Llanelli and Wales) 1959 *NZ* 2,4
Davies, T M (London Welsh, Swansea and Wales) 1971 *NZ* 1,2,3,4, 1974 *SA* 1,2,3,4
Davies, W G (Cardiff and Wales) 1980 *SA* 2
Davies, W P C (Harlequins and England) 1955 *SA* 1,2,3
Dawes, S J (London Welsh and Wales) 1971 *NZ* 1,2,3,4
Dawson, A R (Wanderers and Ireland) 1959 *A* 1,2, *NZ* 1,2,3,4
Dixon, P J (Harlequins and England) 1971 *NZ* 1,2,4
Dodge, P W (Leicester and England) 1980 *SA* 3,4
Dooley, W A (Preston Grasshoppers and England) 1989 *A* 2,3
Doyle, M G (Blackrock Coll and Ireland) 1968 *SA* 1
Drysdale, D (Heriot's FP and Scotland) 1924 *SA* 1,2,3,4
Duckham, D J (Coventry and England) 1971 *NZ* 2,3,4
Duggan, W P (Blackrock Coll and Ireland) 1977 *NZ* 1,2,3,4
Duff, P L (Glasgow Acads and Scotland) 1938 *SA* 2,3

Edwards, G O (Cardiff and Wales) 1968 *SA* 1,2, 1971 *NZ* 1,2,3,4, 1974 *SA* 1,2,3,4
Evans, G (Maesteg and Wales) 1983 *NZ* 3,4
Evans, G L (Newport and Wales) 1977 *NZ* 2,3,4
Evans, I C (Llanelli and Wales) 1989 *A* 1,2,3
Evans, R T (Newport and Wales) 1950 *NZ* 1,2,3,4, *A* 1,2
Evans, T P (Swansea and Wales) 1977 *NZ* 1
Evans, W R (Cardiff and Wales) 1959 *A* 2, *NZ* 1,2,3

Williams, W O G (Swansea and Wales) 1955 *SA* 1,2,3,4
Willis, W R (Cardiff and Wales) 1950 *NZ* 4, *A* 1,2
Wilson, S (London Scottish and Scotland) 1966 *A* 2, *NZ* 1,2,3,4
Windsor, R W (Pontypool and Wales) 1974 *SA* 1,2,3,4, 1977 *NZ* 1
Winterbottom, P J (Headingley and England) 1983 *NZ* 1,2,3,4
Wood, B G M (Garryowen and Ireland) 1959 *NZ* 1,3
Wood, K B (Leicester) 1910 *SA* 1,3

Woodward, C R (Leicester and England) 1980 *SA* 2,3

Young, A T (Cambridge U, Blackheath and England) 1924 *SA* 2
Young, D (Cardiff and Wales) 1989 *A* 1,2,3
Young, J (Harrogate, RAF and Wales) 1968 *SA* 1
Young, J R C (Oxford U, Harlequins and England) 1959 *NZ* 2
Young, R M (Queen's U, Belfast, Collegians and Ireland) 1966 *A* 1,2, *NZ* 1, 1968 *SA* 3

Mike Teague, of Gloucester and England, who played for the Lions in Australia in 1989.

RESULTS OF BRITISH ISLES MATCHES
(*up to 31 March 1992*)

From 1910 onwards – the tour to South Africa in that year was the first fully representative one in which the four Home Unions co-operated.

v SOUTH AFRICA
Played 30   British Isles won 8, South Africa won 18, Drawn 4

1910 *1* Johannesburg
South Africa 1G 3T (14) to 1DG 2T (10)

2 Port Elizabeth
British Isles 1G 1T (8) to 1T (3)

3 Cape Town
South Africa 3G 1PG 1T (21) to 1G (5)
South Africa won series 2-1

1924 *1* Durban
South Africa 1DG 1T (7) to 1T(3)

2 Johannesburg
South Africa 1G 1PG 3T (17) to 0

3 Port Elizabeth
Drawn 1T (3) each

4 Cape Town
South Africa 1DG 4T (16) to 1PG 2T (9)
South Africa won series 3-0, with 1 draw

1938 *1* Johannesburg
South Africa 4G 2PG (26) to 4PG (12)

2 Port Elizabeth
South Africa 2G 2PG 1T (19) to 1T (3)

3 Cape Town
British Isles 1G 1PG 1DG 3T (21)
to 2G 1PG 1T (16)
South Africa won series 2-1

1955 *1* Johannesburg
British Isles 4G 1T (23) to 2G 2PG 2T (22)

2 Cape Town
South Africa 2G 5T (25) to 1PG 2T (9)

3 Pretoria
British Isles 1PG 1DG 1T (9)
to 2PG (6)

4 Port Elizabeth
South Africa 2G 1DG 3T (22)
to 1G 1T (8)
Series drawn 2-2

1962 *1* Johannesburg
Drawn 1T (3) each

2 Durban
South Africa 1PG (3) to 0

3 Cape Town
South Africa 1G 1PG (8) to 1DG (3)

4 Bloemfontein
South Africa 5G 2PG 1T (34)
to 1G 1PG 2T (14)
South Africa won series 3-0, with 1 draw

1968 *1* Pretoria
South Africa 2G 4PG 1T (25)
to 1G 5PG (20)

2 Port Elizabeth
Drawn 2PG (6) each

3 Cape Town
South Africa 1G 2PG (11) to 2PG (6)

4 Johannesburg
South Africa 2G 1DG 2T (19) to 2PG (6)
South Africa won series 3-0, with 1 draw

1974 *1* Cape Town
British Isles 3PG 1DG (12) to 1DG (3)

2 Pretoria
British Isles 1G 1PG 1DG 4T (28)
to 2PG 1DG (9)

3 Port Elizabeth
British Isles 1G 2PG 2DG 2T (26)
to 3PG (9)

4 Johannesburg
Drawn British Isles 1G 1PG 1T (13)
South Africa 3PG 1T (13)
British Isles won series 3-0, with 1 draw

1980 *1* Cape Town
South Africa 3G 2T (26)
to 5PG 1DG 1T (22)

2 Bloemfontein
South Africa 2G 2PG 2T (26)
to 1G 3PG 1T (19)

3 Port Elizabeth
South Africa 1G 1PG 1DG (12)
to 2PG 1T (10)

4 Pretoria
British Isles 1G 1PG 2T (17)
to 3PG 1T (13)
South Africa won series 3-1

v NEW ZEALAND
Played 28   British Isles won 5, New Zealand won 21, Drawn 2

1930 *1* Dunedin
British Isles 2T (6) to 1T (3)

2 Christchurch
New Zealand 2G 1GM (13) to 2G (10)

3 Auckland
New Zealand 1G 1DG 2T (15)
to 2G (10)

4 Wellington
New Zealand 2G 4T (22) to 1G 1PG (8)
New Zealand won series 3-1

1950 *1* Dunedin
Drawn 1PG 2T (9) each

2 Christchurch
New Zealand 1G 1T (8) to 0

3 Wellington
New Zealand 1PG 1T (6) to 1PG (3)

4 Auckland
New Zealand 1G 1DG 1T (11)
to 1G 1PG (8)
New Zealand won series 3-0, with 1 draw

1959 *1* Dunedin
New Zealand 6PG (18)
to 1G 1PG 3T (17)

2 Wellington
New Zealand 1G 2T (11) to 1G 1PG (8)

3 Christchurch
New Zealand 2G 1PG 1DG 2T (22)
to 1G 1PG (8)

4 Auckland
British Isles 3T (9) to 2PG (6)
New Zealand won series 3-1

1966 *1* Dunedin
New Zealand 1G 2PG 1DG 2T (20)
to 1PG (3)

2 Wellington
New Zealand 2G 1PG 1T (16)
to 3PG 1DG (12)

3 Christchurch
New Zealand 2G 2PG 1T (19) to 2T (6)

4 Auckland
New Zealand 3G 1PG 1DG 1T (24)
to 1G 1PG 1T (11)
New Zealand won series 4-0

1971 *1* Dunedin
British Isles 2PG 1T (9) to 1PG (3)

2 Christchurch
New Zealand 2G 1PG 3T (22)
to 1PG 1DG 2T (12)

3 Wellington
British Isles 2G 1DG (13) to 1T (3)

4 Auckland
Drawn British Isles 1G 2PG 1DG (14)
New Zealand 1G 2PG 1T (14)
British Isles won series 2-1, with 1 draw

1977 *1* Wellington
New Zealand 2G 1T (16) to 4PG (12)

2 Christchurch
British Isles 3PG 1T (13) to 3PG (9)

3 Dunedin
New Zealand 1G 2PG 1DG 1T (19)
to 1PG 1T (7)

4 Auckland
New Zealand 2PG 1T (10) to 1G 1PG (9)
New Zealand won series 3-1

1983 *1* Christchurch
New Zealand 3PG 1DG 1T (16)
to 3PG 1DG (12)

2 Wellington
New Zealand 1G 1PG (9) to 0

3 Dunedin
New Zealand 1G 3PG (15) to 2T (8)

4 Auckland
New Zealand 4G 2PG 2T (38) to 2PG (6)
New Zealand won series 4-0

v AUSTRALIA

Played 10   British Isles won 8, Australia won 2, Drawn 0

1930 *1* Sydney
Australia 2T (6) to 1G (5)

1950 *1* Brisbane
British Isles 2G 2PG 1DG (19)
to 2PG (6)

2 Sydney
British Isles 3G 1PG 2T (24) to 1T (3)
British Isles won series 2-0

1959 *1* Brisbane
British Isles 1G 2PG 1DG 1T (17)
to 2PG (6)

2 Sydney
British Isles 3G 1PG 2T (24) to 1PG (3)
British Isles won series 2-0

1966 *1* Sydney
British Isles 1G 1PG 1T (11)
to 1G 1PG (8)

2 Brisbane
British Isles 5G 1PG 1DG (31) to 0
British Isles won series 2-0

1989 *1* Sydney
Australia 4G 1PG 1DG (30)
to 3PG 1DG (12)

2 Brisbane
British Isles 1G 2PG 1DG 1T (19)
to 1G 2PG (12)

3 Sydney
British Isles 5PG 1T (19) to 1G 4PG (18)
British Isles won series 2-1

BRITISH ISLES RECORDS
(*up to 31 March 1992*)

From 1910 onwards – the tour to South Africa in that year was the first fully representative one in which the four Home Unions co-operated.

TEAM RECORDS

Highest score
31 v Australia (31-0) 1966 Brisbane
v individual countries
28 v S Africa (28-9) 1974 Pretoria
17 v New Zealand (17-18) 1959 Dunedin
31 v Australia (31-0) 1966 Brisbane

Biggest winning points margin
31 v Australia (31-0) 1966 Brisbane
v individual countries
19 v S Africa (28-9) 1974 Pretoria
10 v New Zealand (13-3) 1971 Wellington
31 v Australia (31-0) 1966 Brisbane

Highest score by opposing team
38 New Zealand (6-38) 1983 Auckland
by individual countries
34 S Africa (14-34) 1962 Bloemfontein
38 New Zealand (6-38) 1983 Auckland
30 Australia (12-30) 1989 Sydney

Biggest losing points margin
32 v New Zealand (6-38) 1983 Auckland
v individual countries
20 v S Africa (14-34) 1962 Bloemfontein
32 v New Zealand (6-38) 1983 Auckland
18 v Australia (12-30) 1989 Sydney

Most tries by B Isles in an international

5 ⎰ v Australia (24-3) 1950 Sydney
⎱ v S Africa (23-22) 1955 Johannesburg
  v Australia (24-3) 1959 Sydney
  v Australia (31-0) 1966 Brisbane
  v S Africa (28-9) 1974 Pretoria

Most tries against B Isles in an international
7 by South Africa (9-25) 1955 Cape Town

Most points on overseas tour (all matches)
842 in Australia, New Zealand and
    Canada (33 matches) 1959
(includes 582 points in 25 matches in New Zealand)

Most tries on overseas tour (all matches)
165 in Australia, New Zealand and
    Canada (33 matches) 1959
(includes 113 tries in 25 matches in New Zealand)

INDIVIDUAL RECORDS

Most capped player
W J McBride 17 1962-74

in individual positions
Full-back
J P R Williams   8[1]   1971-74
Wing
A J F O'Reilly   9(10)[2]   1955-59
Centre
C M H Gibson   8(12)[3]   1966-71
Fly-half
P Bennett   8   1974-77
Scrum-half
R E G Jeeps   13   1955-62
Prop
G Price   12   1977-83
Hooker
B V Meredith   8   1955-62
Lock
W J McBride   17   1962-74
Flanker
N A A Murphy   8   1959-66
No 8
T M Davies   8[4]   1971-74

[1] *A R Irvine, 9 Tests, played 7 times at full-back and twice as a wing*
[2] *O'Reilly played once as a centre*
[3] *Gibson played 4 times as a fly-half. I R McGeechan, 8 Tests, played 7 times as a centre and once, as a replacement, on the wing*
[4] *Both A E I Pask and J W Telfer (8 Tests each), played 4 Tests at No 8 and 4 Tests at flanker*

Longest international career
W J McBride   13 seasons   1962-74

Most internationals as captain – 6
A R Dawson 1959

Most points in internationals – 44
P Bennett (8 appearances) 1974-77

Most points in an international – 18
A J P Ward v S Africa 1980 Cape Town

Most tries in internationals – 6
A J F O'Reilly (10 appearances) 1955-59

Most tries in an international – 2
C D Aarvold v New Zealand 1930
  Christchurch
J E Nelson v Australia 1950 Sydney
M J Price v Australia 1959 Sydney
M J Price v New Zealand 1959 Dunedin
D K Jones v Australia 1966 Brisbane
T G R Davies v New Zealand 1971
  Christchurch
J J Williams v S Africa 1974 Pretoria
J J Williams v S Africa 1974 Port Elizabeth

Most conversions in internationals – 6
S Wilson (5 matches) 1966

Most conversions in an international – 5
S Wilson v Australia 1966 Brisbane

Most dropped goals in internationals – 2
D Watkins (6 matches) 1966
B John (5 matches) 1968-71
P Bennett (8 matches) 1974-77
*(P F Bush also dropped 2 goals in Tests played by British
teams prior to 1910)*

Most penalty goals in internationals – 11
T J Kiernan (5 matches) 1962-68

**Most points for B Isles on overseas tour
– 188**
B John (17 appearances) 1971 Australia/
  N Zealand
(including 180 points in 16 appearances in
  N Zealand)

**Most tries for B Isles on overseas tour
– 22★**
A J F O'Reilly (23 appearances) 1959
  Australia/N Zealand/Canada
(includes 17★ tries in 17 appearances in
  N Zealand)
★Includes one penalty try

**Most points for B Isles in international
series – 35**
T J Kiernan (4 appearances) 1968 S Africa

**Most tries for B Isles in international
series – 4**
J J Williams (4 appearances) 1974 S Africa

**Most points for B Isles in any match on
tour – 37**
A G B Old v South Western Districts
  1974 Mossel Bay, S Africa

**Most tries for B Isles in any match on
tour – 6**
D J Duckham v West Coast-Buller 1971
  Greymouth, N Zealand
J J Williams v South Western Districts
  1974 Mossel Bay, S Africa
(A R Irvine scored 5 tries from full-back
  v King Country-Wanganui 1977
  Taumarunui, N Zealand)

LEADING CAP-WINNERS
(up to 31 March 1992)

ENGLAND

R Underwood	55
P J Winterbottom	52
W A Dooley	50
C R Andrew	48
A Neary	43
J V Pullin	42
P J Wheeler	41
B C Moore	40
D J Duckham	36
W D C Carling	36
G S Pearce	36
D P Rogers	34
W B Beaumont	34
J P Scott	34
J A Probyn	33
D Richards	33
P W Dodge	32
W W Wakefield	31
F E Cotton	31
M A C Slemen	31
E Evans	30
R Cove-Smith	29
C R Jacobs	29
M P Weston	29
P J Squires	29
R J Hill	29
J Butterfield	28
S J Smith	28
P A G Rendall	28
A T Voyce	27
J S Tucker	27
J M Webb	27
J Carleton	26
C N Lowe	25
J D Currie	25
M S Phillips	25
C B Stevens	25
W H Hare	25
M J Colclough	25

SCOTLAND

J M Renwick	52
C T Deans	52
A R Irvine	51
A B Carmichael	50
A J Tomes	48
R J Laidlaw	47
A F McHarg	44
K W Robertson	44
I G Milne	44
J McLauchlan	43
J Y Rutherford	42
D M B Sole	42
D B White	41
J Jeffrey	40
A G Hastings	40
S Hastings	40
H F McLeod	40
D M D Rollo	40
J MacD Bannerman	37
I A M Paxton	36
I Tukalo	35
F Calder	34
A R Smith	33
I S Smith	32
F A L Laidlaw	32
I R McGeechan	32
D G Leslie	32
N S Bruce	31
I H P Laughland	31
G L Brown	30
W I D Elliot	29
W M Simmers	28
P K Stagg	28
J W Y Kemp	27
K J F Scotland	27
P C Brown	27
J H Calder	27
D I Johnston	27
G R T Baird	27
C M Chalmers	27
S R P Lineen	27
W E Maclagan	26
D Drysdale	26
J C McCallum	26
G P S Macpherson	26
J B Nelson	25
J P Fisher	25
J R Beattie	25
J W Telfer	25
A P Burnell	25

IRELAND

C M H Gibson	69
W J McBride	63
J F Slattery	61
P A Orr	58
T J Kiernan	54
D G Lenihan	52
M I Keane	51
J W Kyle	46
K W Kennedy	45
B J Mullin	45
M J Kiernan	43
G V Stephenson	42
N A A Murphy	41
W P Duggan	41
K D Crossan	41
N J Henderson	40
R J McLoughlin	40
P M Matthews	38
S Millar	37
H P MacNeill	37
J R Kavanagh	35
W A Mulcahy	35
E O'D Davy	34
T M Ringland	34
D C Fitzgerald	34
P M Dean	32
A C Pedlow	30
G T Hamlet	30
W E Crawford	30
J D Clinch	30
J L Farrell	29
B G M Wood	29
A J F O'Reilly	29
M Sugden	28
J S McCarthy	28
A M Magee	27
A R Dawson	27
M G Molloy	27
J J Moloney	27
W A Anderson	27
J C Walsh	26
R M Young	26
J B O'Driscoll	26
G R Beamish	25
K D Mullen	25
F P K Bresnihan	25
A T A Duggan	25
B J McGann	25
T O Grace	25
S A McKinney	25
C F Fitzgerald	25
D G Irwin	25

WALES

J P R Williams	55
G O Edwards	53
T G R Davies	46
K J Jones	44
R N Jones	42
G Price	41
T M Davies	38
P H Thorburn	37
D Williams	36
R M Owen	35
B V Meredith	34
D I E Bebb	34
W D Morris	34
A J Martin	34
R L Norster	34
W J Bancroft	33
B Price	32
J R G Stephens	32
G A D Wheel	32
M G Ring	32
P T Davies	32
I C Evans	31
J J Williams	30
S P Fenwick	30
W J Trew	29
C I Morgan	29

P Bennett	29	D Camberabero	33	J J Kirwan	45
J Squire	29	J Gachassin	32	A M Haden	41
R W Windsor	28	J-P Bastiat	32	S C McDowell	41
A J Gould	27	A Cassayet	31	S B T Fitzpatrick	40
W C Powell	27	A Jauréguy	31	I A Kirkpatrick	39
M C Thomas	27	M Prat	31	K R Tremain	38
H J Morgan	27	F Moncla	31	B G Williams	38
A M Hadley	27	G Cholley	31	G A Knight	36
J Davies	27	D Codorniou	31	A G Dalton	35
R C C Thomas	26	J-B Lafond	31	G J Fox	35
A E I Pask	26	P Albaladéjo	30	A J Whetton	35
S J Watkins	26	A Roques	30	B J Robertson	34
J Taylor	26	R Bénésis	30	S S Wilson	34
G Travers	25	A Lorieux	30	M G Mexted	34
H Tanner	25	R Biénès	29	W J Whineray	32
B John	25	L Mias	29	D B Clarke	31
N R Gale	25	J Trillo	28	M W Shaw	30
W D Thomas	25	J-P Lescarboura	28	R W Loe	30
T D Holmes	25	H Rancoule	27	T J Wright	30
		P Lacroix	27	S M Going	29
FRANCE		J-C Berejnoi	27	R W Norton	27
		C Carrère	27	J T Stanley	27
S Blanco	93	J Fouroux	27	M J Pierce	26
P Sella	83	J Gallion	27	B J Lochore	25
R Bertranne	69	O Roumat	27	B E McLeod	24
M Crauste	63	B Chevallier	26	K F Gray	24
B Dauga	63	J Barthe	26	I J Clarke	24
J Condom	61	J-M Cabanier	26	J C Ashworth	24
J-P Rives	59	A Gruarin	26	D S Loveridge	24
P Berbizier	56	J-L Azarète	26	W T Taylor	24
L Rodriguez	56	A Vaquerin	26	R A White	23
R Paparemborde	55	M Andrieu	26	B G Fraser	23
A Domenech	52	R Martine	25	D J Graham	22
J Prat	51	J Maso	25	D Young	22
W Spanghéro	51	J-L Averous	25	M N Jones	22
J-L Joinel	51	P Estève	25	W T Shelford	22
M Celaya	50			G N K Mourie	21
P Dintrans	50			M J B Hobbs	21
A Boniface	48	**SOUTH AFRICA**		K L Skinner	20
F Mesnel	48			C R Laidlaw	20
J-P Lux	47	F C H Du Preez	38	I N MacEwan	20
J-C Skréla	46	J H Ellis	38	P J Whiting	20
D Erbani	46	J F K Marais	35	C I Green	20
P Lagisquet	46	J P Engelbrecht	33		
M Vannier	43	J L Gainsford	33		
J-P Garuet	42	J T Claassen	28	**AUSTRALIA**	
E Champ	42	F du T Roux	27		
P Ondarts	42	L G Wilson	27	D I Campese	64
J Dupuy	40	T P Bedford	25	S P Poidevin	59
C Darrouy	40	D J de Villiers	25	N C Farr-Jones	53
F Haget	40	P J F Greyling	25	M P Lynagh	53
J-M Aguirre	39	S H Nomis	25	P G Johnson	42
G Dufau	38	P J Visagie	25	A R Miller	41
G Boniface	35	L C Moolman	24	T A Lawton	41
E Cester	35	H E Botha	23	S A G Cutler	40
A Paco	35	D J Hopwood	22	G V Davis	39
E Ribère	34	A C Koch	22	A G Slack	39
J Bouquet	34	M Du Plessis	22	A J McIntyre	38
P Villepreux	34	J A du Rand	21	J E Thornett	37
J Iraçabal	34	M T S Stofberg	21	J N B Hipwell	36
J-P Romeu	34	J S Germishuys	20	A A Shaw	36
G Basquet	33			B J Moon	35
C Lacaze	33			S N Tuynman	34
C Dourthe	33	**NEW ZEALAND**		N M Shehadie	30
D Dubroca	33	G W Whetton	58	P E McLean	30
		C E Meads	55	M E Loane	28

S A Williams	28	P C Grigg	25	W A Campbell	22
K W Catchpole	27	M J Hawker	25	E T Bonis	21
G A Shaw	27	J K Lenehan	24	P F Hawthorne	21
C T Burke	26	J P L White	24	R J Heming	21
E E Rodriguez	26	J W Cole	24	A N McGill	21
J S Miller	26	G Fay	24	W H Cerutti	21
R B Prosser	25	R Phelps	23	A S Cameron	20
G Cornelsen	25	M P Burke	23	B J Ellwood	20
M G Ella	25	R A Smith	22	C J Windon	20
R G Gould	25	J E C Meadows	22	P N Kearns	20

WORLD'S LEADING CAP-WINNERS
(*up to 31 March 1992*)

For purposes of comparison, the following list includes appearances for individual countries in major international matches.

S Blanco	France	93	R Underwood	England	55
P Sella	France	83	T J Kiernan	Ireland	54
C M H Gibson	Ireland	69	G O Edwards	Wales	53
R Bertranne	France	69	N C Farr-Jones	Australia	53
D I Campese	Australia	64	M P Lynagh	Australia	53
M Crauste	France	63	A Domenech	France	52
W J McBride	Ireland	63	J M Renwick	Scotland	52
B Dauga	France	63	C T Deans	Scotland	52
J Condom	France	61	P J Winterbottom	England	52
J F Slattery	Ireland	61	J Prat	France	51
J-P Rives	France	59	W Spanghéro	France	51
S P Poidevin	Australia	59	A R Irvine	Scotland	51
P A Orr	Ireland	58	M I Keane	Ireland	51
G W Whetton	New Zealand	58	J-L Joinel	France	51
L Rodriguez	France	56	M Celaya	France	50
P Berbizier	France	56	A B Carmichael	Scotland	50
C E Meads	New Zealand	55	P Dintrans	France	50
J P R Williams	Wales	55	W A Dooley	England	50
R Paparemborde	France	55			

The following list incorporates appearances by home countries' players for British Isles teams (the Lions) in International matches against New Zealand, Australia and South Africa (up to 31 March 1992). The number of Lions' appearances is shown in brackets.

S Blanco	France	93		P J Winterbottom	England	56	(4)
P Sella	France	83		C E Meads	New Zealand	55	
C M H Gibson	Ireland	81	(12)	R Paparemborde	France	55	
W J McBride	Ireland	80	(17)	J M Renwick	Scotland	53	(1)
R Bertranne	France	69		G Price	Wales	53	(12)
J F Slattery	Ireland	65	(4)	N C Farr-Jones	Australia	53	
D I Campese	Australia	64		M P Lynagh	Australia	53	
G O Edwards	Wales	63	(10)	A Domenech	France	52	
J P R Williams	Wales	63	(8)	C T Deans	Scotland	52	
M Crauste	France	63		J W Kyle	Ireland	52	(6)
B Dauga	France	63		M I Keane	Ireland	52	(1)
J Condom	France	61		W A Dooley	England	52	(2)
A R Irvine	Scotland	60	(9)	J Prat	France	51	
T J Kiernan	Ireland	59	(5)	W Spanghéro	France	51	
J-P Rives	France	59		T G R Davies	Wales	51	(5)
P A Orr	Ireland	59	(1)	J McLauchlan	Scotland	51	(8)
S P Poidevin	Australia	59		J-L Joinel	France	51	
G W Whetton	New Zealand	58		M Celaya	France	50	
R Underwood	England	58	(3)	A B Carmichael	Scotland	50	
L Rodriguez	France	56		P Dintrans	France	50	
P Berbizier	France	56					

Most appearances for the Lions are by W J McBride 17, R E G Jeeps (England) 13, C M H Gibson 12, G Price 12, and A J F O'Reilly (Ireland), R H Williams (Wales), and G O Edwards 10 each, up to 31 March 1992.

INTERNATIONAL REFEREES 1991-92

Leading Referees

Up to 31 March 1992, in major international matches. These include all matches for which senior members of the International Board have awarded caps, and also all matches played in the World Cup final stages.

12 or more internationals

C Norling	Wales	25	D I H Burnett	Ireland	15
K D Kelleher	Ireland	23	C H Gadney	England	15
D G Walters	Wales	23	W D Bevan	Wales	15
M Joseph	Wales	22	D J Bishop	New Zealand	15
R C Williams	Ireland	21	I David	Wales	14
K V J Fitzgerald	Australia	21	Dr I R Vanderfield	Australia	14
F A Howard	England	20	J M Fleming	Scotland	14
A M Hosie	Scotland	19	R G Byres	Australia	13
Capt M J Dowling	Ireland	18	J P Murphy	New Zealand	13
A E Freethy	Wales	18	N R Sanson	Scotland	13
R C Quittenton	England	18	O E Doyle	Ireland	13
J R West	Ireland	18	K H Lawrence	New Zealand	13
J B Anderson	Scotland	18	R F Johnson	England	12
R Hourquet	France	18	T D Schofield	Wales	12
D P D'Arcy	Ireland	17	T H Vile	Wales	12
F Palmade	France	17	W Williams	England	12
B S Cumberlege	England	16	S R Hilditch	Ireland	12

Major international match appearances 1991-92

Matches controlled between 30 April 1991 and 31 March 1992.

1991

R v F	E Morrison (England)
Arg v NZ(2)	B W Stirling (Ireland)
US v F(2)	*A Adams (South Africa)
Fj v E	B Kinsey (Australia)
Nm v I(2)	C Norling (Wales)
A v W	F A Howard (England)
A v E	K H Lawrence (New Zealand)
A v NZ	R J Megson (Scotland)
NZ v A	K W McCartney (Scotland)
R v S	A Ceccon (France)
W v F	J M Fleming (Scotland)
E v NZ	J M Fleming (Scotland)
A v Arg	D J Bishop (New Zealand)
F v R	L J Peard (Wales)
It v US	O E Doyle (Ireland)
S v J	E Morrison (England)
Fj v C	K V J Fitzgerald (Australia)
W v WS	P Robin (France)
I v Z	K H Lawrence (New Zealand)
NZ v US	*E Sklar (Argentina)
E v It	J B Anderson (Scotland)
F v Fj	W D Bevan (Wales)
A v WS	E Morrison (England)
S v Z	*D Reordan (United States)
I v J	*L Colati (Fiji)

C v R	A R MacNeill (Australia)
W v Arg	R Hourquet (France)
E v US	L J Peard (Wales)
S v I	F A Howard (England)
W v A	K H Lawrence (New Zealand)
Fj v R	O E Doyle (Ireland)
Arg v WS	J B Anderson (Scotland)
	rep by J M Fleming (Scotland)
NZ v It	K V J Fitzgerald (Australia)
F v C	S R Hilditch (Ireland)
Z v J	R Hourquet (France)
S v WS	W D Bevan (Wales)
F v E	D J Bishop (New Zealand)
I v A	J M Fleming (Scotland)
NZ v C	F A Howard (England)
S v E	K V J Fitzgerald (Australia)
NZ v A	J M Fleming (Scotland)
S v NZ	S R Hilditch (Ireland)
E v A	W D Bevan (Wales)

1992

S v E	W D Bevan (Wales)
I v W	F A Howard (England)
E v I	W D Bevan (Wales)
W v F	O E Doyle (Ireland)

F v E	**S R Hilditch** (Ireland)	S v F	**F Burger** (South Africa)
I v S	**A Spreadbury** (England)	W v S	***M Desclaux** (France)
E v W	**R J Megson** (Scotland)	F v I	**F Burger** (South Africa)

*Denotes debut in a major international

Referees dismissing players in a major international

A E Freethy	E v NZ	1925	**B W Stirling** (two)	E v Fj	1989
K D Kelleher	S v NZ	1967	**F A Howard**	W v F	1990
R T Burnett	A v E	1975	**F A Howard**	S v F	1990
W M Cooney	A v Fj	1976	**F A Howard**	Nm v W	1990
N R Sanson (two)	W v I	1977	**A Spreadbury**	A v F	1990
D I H Burnett	E v W	1980	**C Norling**	A v F	1990
C Norling	F v I	1984	**C J Hawke**	E v Arg	1990
K V J Fitzgerald	NZ v W	1987*	**E Morrison**	R v F	1991
F A Howard	A v W	1987*	**J M Fleming** (two)	Arg v WS	1991*
K V J Fitzgerald	Fj v E	1988	**S R Hilditch** (two)	F v E	1992
O E Doyle	Arg v F	1988			

* World Cup matches

INTERNATIONAL REFEREES

The list which follows shows referees who have controlled major internationals (i.e. games for which a senior member country of the IB has awarded caps, or the final stages of the official World Cup) since 1876, when referees were first appointed, up to 31 March, 1992.

ABBREVIATIONS

A – Australia; *Arg* – Argentina; *AW* – Anglo-Welsh; *B* – British Forces' and Home Union Teams; *Bb* – Barbarians; *BI* – British Isles; *C* – Canada; *Cv* – New Zealand Cavaliers; *Cz* – Czechoslovakia; *E* – England; *F* – France; *Fj* – Fiji; *GB* – Great Britain; *G* – Germany; *I* – Ireland; *It* – Italy; *J* – Japan; *K* – New Zealand Kiwis; *M* – New Zealand Maoris; *Nm* – Namibia; *NZ* – New Zealand; *NZA* – New Zealand Army; *P* – President's XV; *R* – Romania; *S* – Scotland; *SA* – South Africa; *SAm* – South America; *SK* – South Korea; *Tg* – Tonga; *US* – United States of America; *W* – Wales; *Wld* – World XV; *WS* – Western Samoa; *Z* – Zimbabwe; (C) – Special Centenary Match; (R) – Replacement. Entries in square brackets [ ] indicate matches in the World Cup final stages.

N.B. The Australian Rugby Union now recognises the internationals played by the New South Wales touring teams of the 1920s as cap matches.

Ackermann, C J (South Africa) 1953 *SA v A* (2), 1955 *SA v BI*, 1958 *SA v F*
Acton, W H (Ireland) 1926 *W v E, E v S*
Adams, A (South Africa) 1991 *US v F* (2)
Alderson, F H R (England) 1903 *S v I*
Allan, M A (Scotland) 1931 *I v W, I v SA*, 1933 *E v I, I v W*, 1934 *I v E*, 1935 *E v I, I v W*, 1936 *I v E*, 1937 *I v W*, 1947 *I v E*, 1948 *I v W*
Allen, J W (Ireland) 1906 *W v S, S v E*
Anderson, C (Scotland) 1928 *I v F*
Anderson, J B (Scotland) 1981 *W v E, I v A*, 1982 *R v F*, 1983 *I v E, A v NZ*, 1984 *E v W*, 1986 *W v F, NZ v A*, 1987 *[A v US, A v I, F v A]*, 1988 *A v NZ*(2), 1989 *I v F, R v E, F v B*, 1991 *[E v It, Arg v WS]*
Anderson, J H (South Africa) 1903 *SA v GB*
Angus, A W (Scotland) 1924 *W v E*, 1927 *I v A*
Ashmore, H L (England) 1890 *S v I*, 1891 *S v W*, 1892 *S v I*, 1894 *I v S*, 1895 *S v I*
Austin, A W C (Scotland) 1952 *W v F*, 1953 *I v E*, 1954 *I v W*
Austry, R (France) 1972 *E v I*

Badger, Dr (England) 1900 *I v S*
Baise, M (South Africa) 1967 *SA v F* (2), 1968 *SA v BI* (2), 1969 *SA v A*, 1974 *SA v BI* (2)

Baise, S (South Africa) 1969 *SA v A*
Barnes, P (Australia) 1938 *A v NZ*
Baxter, J (England) 1913 *F v S, S v I*, 1914 *I v S*, 1920 *S v I*, 1921 *W v S, I v S*, 1923 *W v S*, 1925 *W v S, I v W*
Bean, A S (England) 1939 *W v S*, 1945 *W v F*, 1946 *F v W*, 1947 *F v W, W v A*, 1948 *S v F, W v F*, 1949 *S v I*
Beattie, R A (Scotland) 1937 *E v W*, 1938 *W v E*, 1945 *B v F*, 1947 *W v E, I v A*, 1948 *E v W*, 1949 *I v E*, 1950 *E v I, I v W*
Beattie, W H (Australia) 1899 *A v GB*, 1904 *A v GB*
Bell, T (Ireland) 1932 *S v W*, 1933 *E v W*
Bevan, W D (Wales) 1985 *E v R*, 1986 *F v E, NZ v A* (2), 1987 *[NZ v Fj, F v Z], A v NZ*, 1988 *I v WS*, 1990 *NZ v S*, 1991 *I v F, [F v Fj, S v WS, E v A]*, 1992 *S v E, E v I*
Beves, G (South Africa) 1896 *SA v GB*
Bezuidenhout, G P (South Africa) 1976 *SA v NZ* (3)
Bishop, D J (New Zealand) 1986 *Fj v W, R v F, I v R*, 1987 *[W v Tg, W v C]*, 1988 *A v E* (2), *E v A, S v A*, 1990 *S v E, I v W*, 1991 *S v W, W v I, [A v Arg, F v E]*
Bissett, W M (South Africa) 1896 *SA v GB*
Bonnet, J-P (France) 1979 *W v E*, 1980 *S v E, SA v BI* (2), 1981 *I v E, Arg v E* (2), 1982 *W v S*
Bott, J G (Scotland) 1931 *W v S*, 1933 *W v S*
Boundy, L M (England) 1955 *S v I*, 1956 *W v S*, 1957 *F*

v S, I v F, S v I, R v F, 1958 *S v F*, 1959 *S v I*, 1961 *S v SA*
Bowden, G (Scotland) 1910 *F v E*
Bowen, D H (Wales) 1905 *E v S*
Bradburn, T J (England) 1928 *F v A*, 1929 *F v G*
Bressy, Y (France) 1988 *W v S*
Brook, P G (England) 1963 *F v W*, 1964 *W v S*, 1965 *W v I, I v SA*, 1966 *F v I, I t v F, R v F*
Brown, A (Australia) 1907 *A v NZ*
Brown, D A (England) 1960 *I v W, I t v F*
Brunton, J (England) 1924 *W v NZ*
Buchanan, A (Scotland) 1877 *I v S*, 1880 *S v I*
Bullerwell, I M (England) 1988 *W v R*, 1990 *F v R*
Burger F (South Africa) 1989 *F v A* (2), 1990 *S v Arg*, 1992 *S v F, F v I*
Burmeister, R D (South Africa) 1949 *SA v NZ* (2), 1953 *SA v A*, 1955 *SA v BI* (2), 1960 *SA v NZ* (2), 1961 *SA v A*
Burnand, F W (England) 1890 *I v W*
Burnet, W (Scotland) 1932 *I v E*, 1934 *W v I*
Burnett, D I H (Ireland) 1977 *W v E*, 1979 *F v W*, 1980 *E v W*, 1981 *S v W, E v S*, 1982 *W v F, F v Arg*, 1983 *E v F*, 1984 *S v E, A v NZ*, 1985 *E v F, NZ v A*, 1986 *S v F*, 1987 *[S v Z, NZ v S]*
Burnett, R T (Australia) 1973 *A v Tg*, 1974 *A v NZ*, 1975 *A v E, A v J*, 1978 *A v W*
Burrell, G (Scotland) 1958 *E v I*, 1959 *W v I*
Burrell, R P (Scotland) 1966 *I v W*, 1967 *I v F, F v NZ*, 1969 *I v E, F v W*
Butt, C C (Australia) 1914 *A v NZ*
Byres, R G (Australia) 1976 *A v Fj*, 1978 *A v W*, 1979 *A v I* (2), *A v NZ*, 1980 *A v NZ*, 1981 *NZ v S*, 1982 *A v S* (2), 1983 *NZ v BI* (2), 1984 *I v W, W v F*

Calitz, M (South Africa) 1961 *SA v I*
Calmet, R (France) 1970 *E v W*
Calver, E W (England) 1914 *F v I*
Camardon, J (Argentina) 1960 *Arg v F*
Campbell, A (New Zealand) 1908 *NZ v AW* (2)
Carlson, K R V (South Africa) 1962 *SA v BI*
Cartwright, V H (England) 1906 *I v S*, 1909 *S v I*, 1910 *I v S, F v I*, 1911 *S v I*
Castens, H H (South Africa) 1891 *SA v GB*
Ceccon, A (France) 1991 *I v E, R v S*
Chambers, J (Ireland) 1888 *W v S, I v M*, 1890 *S v E*, 1891 *E v S*
Chapman, W S (Australia) 1938 *A v NZ* (2)
Charman, R (England) 1919 *W v NZA*
Chevrier, G (France) 1980 *I v S*
Chiene, Dr J (Scotland) 1879 *I v S*
Clark, K H (Ireland) 1973 *E v F*, 1974 *S v F*, 1976 *F v E*
Cochrane, C B (Australia) 1907 *A v NZ*
Coffey, J J (Ireland) 1912 *S v F*
Colati, L (Fiji) 1991 *[I v J]*
Coles, P (England) 1903 *W v I*, 1905 *S v I*
Collett C K (Australia) 1981 *NZ v S*
Combe, A (Ireland) 1876 *I v E*
Cook, H G (Ireland) 1886 *S v E*
Cooney, R C (Australia) 1929 *A v NZ*, 1930 *A v BI*, 1932 *A v NZ*, 1934 *A v NZ*
Cooney, W M (Australia) 1972 *A v F*, 1975 *A v E, A v J*, 1976 *A v Fj*
Cooper, Dr P F (England) 1952 *I v W*, 1953 *S v W, W v I, F v It, W v NZ*, 1954 *I v NZ, W v S, It v F*, 1956 *F v I, W v F, It v F*, 1957 *F v W*
Corley, H H (Ireland) 1906 *S v SA*, 1908 *S v E*
Corr, W S (Australia) 1899 *A v GB* (2)
Costello, J (Fiji) 1972 *F j v A*
Craven, W S D (England) 1920 *F v W*
Crawford, S H (Ireland) 1913 *W v E, S v W*, 1920 *S v W*, 1921 *S v E*
Cross, W (Scotland) 1877 *S v E*
Crowe, K J (Australia) 1965 *A v SA*, 1966 *A v BI*, 1968 *A v NZ*, 1976 *A v Fj*
Cumberlege, B S (England) 1926 *S v I, W v I*, 1927 *S v F, I v S, I v W*, 1928 *S v I*, 1929 *F v I, S v F, I v S*, 1930 *I v F, S v I*, 1931 *I v S*, 1932 *S v SA, S v I*, 1933 *I v S*, 1934 *S v I*
Cunningham, J G (Scotland) 1913 *W v I*, 1921 *F v I*
Cuny, Dr A (France) 1976 *W v S*
Curnow, J (Canada) 1976 *US v F*
Currey, F I (England) 1887 *S v W*

Dallas, J D (Scotland) 1905 *W v NZ*, 1908 *I v W*, 1909

W v E, I v E, 1910 *E v W, I v W*, 1911 *I v E*, 1912 *I v W*
D'Arcy, D P (Ireland) 1967 *E v F, E v S, F v W, F v R*, 1968 *E v W, S v E, F v SA*, 1969 *E v F, W v E*, 1970 *W v S*, 1971 *W v E*, 1973 *F v NZ, F v W, F v R*, 1975 *E v S, F v Arg, W v S*
David, I (Wales) 1938 *E v S*, 1939 *S v E*, 1947 *E v S*, 1952 *S v F, I v S, E v I*, 1953 *S v I*, 1954 *S v F, E v NZ, S v NZ, F v NZ, F v E*, 1955 *I v F*, 1956 *F v E*
Davidson, I G (Ireland) 1911 *S v W*
Day, H L V (England) 1934 *S v W*
Day, P W (South Africa) 1903 *SA v GB*
Dedet, L (France) 1906 *F v NZ, F v E*
De Bruyn, C J (South Africa) 1969 *SA v A*, 1974 *SA v BI* (2)
Delany, M G (Ireland) 1899 *S v W*, 1900 *S v E*
Desclaux, M (France) 1992 *W v S*
Dickie, A I (Scotland) 1954 *F v I, E v I, W v F*, 1955 *I v E, W v I*, 1956 *E v I, I v W*, 1957 *W v E, I v E*, 1958 *W v A, W v F*
Dodds, J (Ireland) 1898 *S v E*
Domercq, G (France) 1972 *S v NZ*, 1973 *W v E*, 1976 *E v W*, 1977 *S v W*, 1978 *I v W*
Donaldson, S (Ireland) 1937 *S v E*
Donaldson, W P (Scotland) 1903 *SA v GB*
Don Wauchope, A R (Scotland) 1889 *W v I*, 1890 *E v I*, 1893 *I v E*
Doocey, T F (New Zealand) 1976 *NZ v I*, 1983 *E v S, F v W*
Douglas, W M (Wales) 1891 *I v E*, 1894 *E v I*, 1896 *S v E*, 1903 *E v S*
Doulcet, J-C (France) 1989 *S v W*
Dowling, M J (Ireland) 1947 *S v W*, 1950 *W v S, S v E, W v F*, 1951 *W v E, S v W, F v W, E v S, S v SA*, 1952 *W v S, F v SA, S v E*, 1953 *W v E, E v S*, 1954 *E v W*, 1955 *S v W*, 1956 *S v F, S v E*
Downes, A D (New Zealand) 1913 *NZ v A*
Doyle, O E (Ireland) 1984 *W v S, R v S, W v A*, 1987 *E v S*, 1988 *F v E, Arg v F* (2), *W v WS*, 1989 *F v S*, 1990 *F v E*, 1991 *[I t v US, F j v R]*, 1992 *W v F*
Drennan, V (Ireland) 1914 *W v S*
Duffy, B (New Zealand) 1977 *NZ v BI*
Duncan, J (New Zealand) 1908 *NZ v AW*
Durand, C (France) 1969 *E v S*, 1970 *I v S*, 1971 *E v S*

Eckhold, A E (New Zealand) 1923 *NZ v A*
Elliott, H B (England) 1955 *F v S, F v It*, 1956 *I v S*
Engelbrecht, Dr G K (South Africa) 1964 *SA v W*
Evans, F T (New Zealand) 1904 *NZ v GB*
Evans, G (England) 1905 *E v NZ*, 1908 *W v A*
Evans, W J (Wales) 1958 *I v A, F v E*

Farquhar, A B (New Zealand) 1961 *NZ v F* (3), 1962 *NZ v A* (2), 1964 *NZ v A*
Faull, J W (Wales) 1936 *E v NZ, S v I*, 1937 *E v I*
Ferguson, C F (Australia) 1963 *A v E*, 1965 *A v SA*, 1968 *A v F*, 1969 *A v W*, 1971 *A v SA* (2)
Ferguson, P (Australia) 1914 *A v NZ*
Findlay, D G (Scotland) 1895 *I v E*, 1896 *E v W, E v I*, 1897 *I v E*, 1898 *E v I*, 1899 *I v E*, 1900 *E v I*
Findlay, J C (Scotland) 1902 *I v W*, 1903 *I v E*, 1904 *E v W, I v W*, 1905 *I v NZ*, 1911 *I v F*
Finlay, A K (Australia) 1961 *A v Fj*, 1962 *A v NZ*
Fitzgerald, K V J (Australia) 1985 *I v F, W v I, NZ v E* (2), *Arg v NZ* (2), 1987 *[I v W, E v US, NZ v W, NZ v F]*, 1988 *F j v E*, 1989 *S v I, W v E, SA v Wld* (2), 1990 *A v US*, 1991 *F v W, S v I, [F j v C, NZ v It, S v E]*
Fleming, G R (Scotland) 1879 *S v E*
Fleming, J M (Scotland) 1985 *I v E*, 1986 *A v Arg* (2), 1987 *E v F, [A v J, F j v Arg]*, *F v R*, 1989 *F v W*, 1990 *NZ v A*, 1991 *W v F, [E v NZ, Arg v WS* (R), *I v A, NZ v A]*
Fleury, A L (New Zealand) 1959 *NZ v BI*
Fong, A S (New Zealand) 1946 *NZ v A*, 1950 *NZ v BI*
Fordham, R J (Australia) 1986 *E v W, F v I, Arg v F* (2), 1987 *[NZ v It, F v R]*
Fornès, E (Argentina) 1954 *Arg v F* (2)
Forsyth, R A (New Zealand) 1958 *NZ v A*
Frames, P R (South Africa) 1891 *SA v GB*
Francis, R C (New Zealand) 1984 *E v A, I v A*, 1985 *Arg v F* (2), 1986 *W v S, S v E, WS v W*
Freeman, W L (Ireland) 1932 *E v SA*
Freethy, A E (Wales) 1923 *F v E*, 1924 *E v F, I v NZ, F v US*, 1925 *E v NZ, I v S, S v E, E v S*, 1926 *E v F*, 1927 *F v E*, 1928 *I v E, E v F*, 1929 *E v I, F v E*, 1930

I v E, *E v F*, 1931 *E v I*, *F v E*
Fright, W H (New Zealand) 1956 *NZ v SA* (2)
Frood, J (New Zealand) 1952 *NZ v A*
Fry, H A (England) 1945 *F v B*
Furness, D C (Australia) 1952 *A v Fj* (2), 1954 *A v Fj*

Gadney, C H (England) 1935 *S v NZ*, *W v NZ*, 1936 *S v W*, *W v I*, 1937 *W v S*, *I v S*, 1938 *S v W*, *S v I*, 1939 *I v S*, 1940 *F v B*, 1946 *F v B*, 1947 *F v S*, *S v I*, 1948 *F v A*, *I v S*
Games, J (Wales) 1909 *E v A*, 1913 *E v F*, 1914 *F v E*
Gardiner, F (Ireland) 1912 *S v E*
Gardner, J A (Scotland) 1884 *E v W*, 1887 *W v I*
Garling, A F (Australia) 1981 *A v NZ* (2)
Garrard, W G (New Zealand) 1899 *A v GB*
Gilchrist, N R (New Zealand) 1936 *M v A*
Gillespie, J I (Scotland) 1907 *W v E*, 1911 *W v E*
Gilliard, P (England) 1902 *W v S*
Gillies, C R (New Zealand) 1958 *NZ v A* (2), 1959 *NZ v BI* (2)
Gilliland, R W (Ireland) 1964 *It v F*, 1965 *S v W*, *E v F*, *F v W*, *F v R*, 1966 *E v W*, 1967 *F v A*
Gillmore, W N (England) 1956 *F v Cz*, 1958 *I v S*, *It v F*
Glasgow, O B (Ireland) 1953 *F v S*, *F v W*, 1954 *S v E*, 1955 *W v E*, *F v W*
Goulding, W J (Ireland) 1882 *I v W*
Gourlay, I W (South Africa) 1976 *SA v NZ*
Gouws, Dr J (South Africa) 1977 *SA v Wld*
Greenlees, Dr J R C (Scotland) 1913 *I v E*, 1914 *E v W*
Grierson, T F E (Scotland) 1970 *I v SA*, 1971 *F v R*, 1972 *F v E* , 1973 *W v I*, 1975 *E v F*
Griffin, Dr (South Africa) 1891 *SA v GB*
Griffiths, A A (New Zealand) 1946 *M v A*, 1952 *NZ v A*
Guillemard, A G (England) 1877 *E v I*, 1878 *E v S*, 1879 *E v I*, 1880 *E v S*, 1881 *E v I*, *E v W*
Gurdon, E T (England) 1898 *I v S*, 1899 *S v I*

Hamilton, F M (Ireland) 1902 *S v E*
Harland, R W (Ireland) 1922 *F v W*, 1925 *W v F*, 1926 *F v W*, 1928 *W v E*, *S v W*, *F v W*, 1929 *E v W*, 1931 *W v F*
Harnett, G H (England) 1896 *W v S*, 1901 *S v I*, *W v I*
Harris, G A (Ireland) 1910 *S v F*
Harrison, G L (New Zealand) 1980 *Fj v A*, 1981 *A v F*, 1983 *A v US*, *F v A* (2), 1984 *Fj v A*
Harrison, H C (England) 1922 *F v S*
Hartley, A (England) 1900 *W v S*
Haslett, F W (Ireland) 1934 *W v E*, *E v S*, 1935 *E v W*, *W v S*, 1936 *W v E*
Hawke, C J (New Zealand) 1990 *I v Arg*, *E v Arg*
Haydon, N V (Australia) 1957 *A v NZ*
Helliwell, D (England) 1926 *S v W*, 1927 *W v A*, 1929 *W v S*, 1930 *F v S*, *W v I*, *G v F*, *F v W*
Herbert, D (Wales) 1883 *W v E*
Herck, M (Romania) 1938 *F v G*
High, C J (England) 1987 *F v W*, *W v US*, 1990 *NZ v S*
Hilditch, S R (Ireland) 1984 *S v A*, 1985 *W v Fj*, 1987 *[R v Z*, *S v R]*, 1988 *E v W*, 1989 *E v F*, *NZ v A*, *S v R*, 1991 *E v S*, *[F v C*, *S v NZ]*, 1992 *F v E*
Hill, A (England) 1902 *I v S*
Hill, E D (New Zealand) 1949 *NZ v A*
Hill, G R (England) 1883 *S v W*, 1884 *S v I*, *W v I*, 1885 *S v W*, 1886 *S v I*, 1887 *W v E*, *I v S*, 1888 *I v W*, 1889 *E v M*, 1891 *I v S*, 1893 *I v S*
Hill, W W (Australia) 1913 *US v NZ*
Hinton, W P (Ireland) 1921 *S v F*
Hodgson, J (England) 1892 *W v S*
Hofmeyr, E W (South Africa) 1949 *SA v NZ* (2), 1961 *SA v A*, 1963 *SA v A*
Hollander, S (New Zealand) 1930 *NZ v BI* (3), 1931 *NZ v A*
Hollis, M (England) 1931 *F v G*
Holmes, E (England) 1931 *W v SA*, 1932 *W v I*
Holmes, E B (England) 1892 *I v W*, 1894 *W v S*, 1895 *S v W*, *W v I*, 1896 *I v S*, *I v W*, 1897 *S v I*
Horak, A T (South Africa) 1938 *SA v BI*
Hosie, A M (Scotland) 1973 *I v E*, 1974 *F v I*, 1975 *W v E*, 1976 *E v I*, *F v A*, 1977 *F v W*, *I v F* , 1979 *W v I*, *I v E*, 1980 *W v F*, *F v I*, 1981 *E v F*, *R v NZ*, 1982 *E v I*, *NZ v A* (2), 1983 *I v F*, *E v W*, 1984 *F v E*
Hourquet, R (France) 1983 *S v NZ*, 1984 *E v I*, *SA v E* (2), *SA v SAm* (2), 1985 *S v W*, 1987 *I v E*, *[E v J*, *W v*

E], 1988 *I v E*, 1989 *A v BI* (2), 1990 *W v S*, *NZ v A* (2), 1991 *[W v Arg*, *Z v J]*
Howard, F A (England) 1984 *I v S*, 1986 *I v W*, *A v F*, *NZ v F*, 1987 *[F v S*, *I v C*, *A v W]*, 1988 *W v F*, *A v NZ*, 1989 *NZ v F*(2), 1990 *W v F*, *S v F*, *Nm v W*(2), *W v Bb*, 1991 *A v W*, *[S v I*, *NZ v C]*, 1992 *I v W*
Hughes, D M (Wales) 1965 *F v It*, 1966 *S v F*, *I v S*, 1967 *I v E*, *S v I*
Hughes, J (England) 1935 *I v S*
Hughes, P E (England) 1977 *F v R*, 1978 *I v S*
Humphreys, W H (England) 1893 *S v W*, *W v I*

Ireland, J C H (Scotland) 1938 *I v E*, *W v I*, 1939 *E v W*, *E v I*, *I v W*
Irving, A L C (Australia) 1934 *A v NZ*, 1937 *A v SA*

Jackson, W H (England) 1926 *F v M*, 1927 *W v S*, *W v F*, *F v G*, *G v F*
Jamison, G A (Ireland) 1972 *W v S*
Jardine, A (Scotland) 1906 *E v W*
Jeffares, R W (Ireland) 1930 *W v E*, *E v S*, 1931 *S v F*, 1935 *S v E*, *I v NZ*
Jeffares, R W (Sen) (Ireland) 1901 *S v W*, *E v S*, 1902 *E v W*, 1909 *S v W*
Jeffreys, M (England) 1920 *F v US*
Johns, E A (Wales) 1911 *E v F*
Johnson, R F (England) 1969 *F v R*, 1970 *F v I*, *E v W* (R), 1971 *W v I*, 1972 *I v F*, *W v NZ*, 1973 *I v F*, 1974 *W v S*, *I v NZ*, *F v SA*, 1975 *S v I*, *S v A*
Jones, A O (England) 1906 *W v SA*, 1907 *S v I*, 1911 *F v S*, 1912 *F v I*, *W v F*
Jones, T (Wales) 1947 *E v F*, 1948 *E v I*, *F v E*, 1949 *E v F*, 1950 *S v F*, 1951 *I v E*
Jones, W (Wales) 1984 *S v F*, *NZ v F* (2), 1988 *S v E*
Jones, W K M (Wales) 1968 *I v A*, 1970 *F v E*, 1971 *S v I*
Joseph, M (Wales) 1966 *S v A*, 1967 *I v A*, 1968 *I v S*, *E v I*, *E v F*, 1969 *S v I*, *S v SA*, 1970 *S v E*, 1971 *I v E*, *S v E*(C), 1972 *S v F*, *S v E*, 1973 *I v NZ*, *S v P*(C), *F v J*, 1974 *E v I*, 1975 *F v Arg*, 1976 *E v A*, *F v A*, 1977 *E v S*, *S v I*, *F v S*
Joynson, D C (Wales) 1955 *E v S*

Keenan, H (England) 1962 *It v F*, 1963 *I v NZ*
Kelleher, J C (Wales) 1973 *E v S*, 1974 *F v E*, 1976 *R v F*, 1977 *E v F*
Kelleher, K D (Ireland) 1960 *W v S*, 1961 *W v E*, *E v S*, 1962 *S v E*, *W v F*, 1963 *W v E*, *F v It*, 1964 *E v W*, *R v F*, 1965 *F v S*, *W v E*, 1966 *S v E*, *W v F*, *W v A*, 1967 *E v A*, *F v S*, *S v W*, *S v NZ*, 1968 *S v F*, 1969 *S v W*, *E v SA*, 1970 *W v F*, 1971 *F v S*
Kelly, H C (Ireland) 1881 *I v S*, 1883 *I v S*, *S v E*, 1885 *S v I*
Kemsley, H B (South Africa) 1896 *SA v GB*
Kennedy, G H B (Ireland) 1905 *S v W*, 1910 *W v S*, *S v E*
Kennedy, W (Ireland) 1905 *S v NZ*
Kilner, W F B (Australia) 1937 *A v SA*
King, J S (New Zealand) 1937 *NZ v SA* (2)
King, M H R (England) 1961 *S v I*
Kinsey, B (Australia) 1986 *Tg v W*, 1990 *Arg v E* (2), 1991 *Fj v E*
Knox, J (Argentina) 1949 *Arg v F*
Krembs, M (Germany) 1938 *G v F*

Lacroix, M (Belgium) 1962 *R v F*
Laidlaw, H B (Scotland) 1963 *I v E*, 1964 *W v F*, 1965 *I v E*, 1968 *F v E*, *W v F*
Lamb, G C (England) 1968 *F v I*, *W v S*, *F v SA*, 1969 *F v S*, *I v F*, 1970 *S v F*, *W v SA*, *I v W*, *R v F*, 1971 *I v F*, *F v A*
Lambert, N H (Ireland) 1947 *S v A*, 1948 *E v A*, *S v E*, 1949 *W v E*, *S v W*, *E v S*, *F v W*, 1950 *E v W*, *F v E*, 1951 *W v SA*, 1952 *E v W*
Lang, J S (Scotland) 1884 *I v E*
Larkin, F A (Australia) 1932 *A v NZ*
Lathwell, H G (England) 1946 *I v F*
Lawrence, K H (New Zealand) 1985 *A v C* (2), 1986 *A v It*, 1987 *F v S*, *S v W*, *[Fj v It*, *A v E]*, *Arg v A* (2), 1989 *A v BI*, 1991 *A v E*, *[I v Z*, *W v A]*
Lawrie, A A (Scotland) 1924 *I v F*, 1925 *E v W*, 1926 *I v F*
Lee, S (Ireland) 1904 *S v E*
Lefevre, C (Ireland) 1905 *W v E*, 1907 *S v W*

Rowsell, A (England) 1891 *W v I*
Royds, P M R (England) 1921 *W v F*, 1923 *F v I*
Rutherford, C F (Scotland) 1908 *F v E*
Rutter, A (England) 1876 *E v S*

St Guilhem, J (France) 1974 *S v E*, 1975 *W v I*
Sanson, N R (Scotland) 1974 *W v F*, *F v SA*, 1975 *I v P* (C), *SA v F* (2), *F v R*, 1976 *I v A*, *I v W*, 1977 *W v I*, 1978 *F v E*, *E v W*, *E v NZ*, 1979 *E v NZ*
Schoeman, J P J (South Africa) 1968 *SA v BI*
Schofield, T D (Wales) 1907 *E v S*, 1908 *E v I*, 1910 *E v I*, 1911 *E v S*, 1912 *E v I*, *F v E*, 1913 *E v S*, 1914 *E v I*, *S v E*, 1920 *E v S*, 1921 *E v I*, 1922 *S v I*
Schwoenberg, M (Germany) 1938 *R v F*
Scott, J M B (Scotland) 1923 *E v W*
Scott, R L (Scotland) 1927 *F v I*, *E v W*
Scriven, G (Ireland) 1884 *E v S*
Short, J A (Scotland) 1979 *F v R*, 1982 *I v W*
Simpson, J W (Scotland) 1906 *I v W*
Simpson, R L (New Zealand) 1913 *NZ v A*, 1921 *NZ v A*, 1923 *NZ v A*
Sklar, E (Argentina) 1991 [*NZ v US*]
Slabber, M J (South Africa) 1955 *SA v BI*, 1960 *SA v NZ*
Smith, J A (Scotland) 1892 *E v I*, 1894 *E v W*, 1895 *W v E*
Spreadbury, A (England) 1990 *A v F*, 1992 *I v S*
Stanton, R W (South Africa) 1910 *SA v GB* (3)
Steyn, M (Germany) 1932 *G v F*
Stirling, B W (Ireland) 1989 *E v Fj*, 1991 *Arg v NZ* (2)
Strasheim, Dr E A (South Africa) 1958 *SA v F*, 1960 *SA v S*, *SA v NZ*, 1962 *SA v BI* (2), 1964 *SA v F*, 1967 *SA v F*, 1968 *SA v BI*
Strasheim, Dr J J (South Africa) 1938 *SA v BI*
Strydom, S (South Africa) 1977 *Arg v A* (2), 1982 *SA v SAm*, 1985 *S v I*, *F v W*, 1986 *F v NZ* (2)
Sturrock, J C (Scotland) 1921 *E v W*, *F v E*, 1922 *W v I*
Sullivan, G (New Zealand) 1950 *NZ v BI*
Sutherland, F E (New Zealand) 1925 *NZ v A*, 1928 *NZ v A* (2), 1930 *NZ v BI*
Swainston, E (England) 1878 *I v E*

Tagnini, S (Italy) 1968 *Cz v F*
Taylor, A R (New Zealand) 1965 *NZ v SA* (R), 1972 *NZ v A*
Taylor, J A S (Scotland) 1957 *W v I*, 1960 *E v W*, *F v E*, *W v SA*, 1961 *F v It*, 1962 *E v W*, *F v I*, *I v W*
Tennent, J M (Scotland) 1920 *I v F*, 1921 *I v W*, 1922 *W v E*, *E v F*, *I v F*, *I v E*, 1923 *I v W*
Thomas, C (Wales) 1979 *S v I*, 1980 *E v I*
Thomas, C G P (Wales) 1977 *F v NZ*, 1978 *S v F*, *F v I*
Tierney, A T (Australia) 1957 *A v NZ*, 1958 *A v M*, 1959 *A v BI*
Tindill, E W T (New Zealand) 1950 *NZ v BI* (2), 1955 *NZ v A*
Titcomb, M H (England) 1966 *W v S*, 1967 *W v I*, *W v NZ*, 1968 *I v W*, *S v A*, 1971 *S v W*, *E v P* (C), 1972 *W v F*
Tolhurst, H A (Australia) 1951 *A v NZ* (2)
Tomalin, L C (Australia) 1947 *A v NZ*, 1949 *A v M* (2) 1950 *A v BI*
Treharne, G J (Wales) 1960 *I v SA*, 1961 *E v SA*, *I v E*, *I v F*, 1963 *S v I*

Trigg, J A F (England) 1981 *F v R*, 1982 *S v F*, 1983 *W v I*
Tulloch, J T (Scotland) 1906 *I v SA*, *E v SA*, 1907 *I v E*, 1908 *E v W*, 1912 *E v W*, 1913 *E v SA*, 1914 *I v W*, 1920 *W v E*, 1924 *W v I*
Turnbull, A (Scotland) 1898 *I v W*, 1899 *W v E*, *W v I*, 1900 *E v W*, *I v W*, 1901 *W v E*, *I v E*

Vanderfield, Dr I R (Australia) 1956 *A v SA*, 1958 *A v M*, 1961 *A v Fj* (2), *A v F*, 1962 *A v NZ*, 1966 *A v BI*, 1967 *A v I*, 1968 *A v NZ*, 1970 *A v S*, 1971 *A v SA*, 1973 *A v Tg*, 1974 *A v NZ* (2)
Van der Horst, A W (South Africa) 1933 *SA v A*
Van der Merwe, A (South Africa) 1936 *G v F*
Vile, T H (Wales) 1923 *S v F*, *E v I*, *I v S*, *S v E*, 1924 *I v E*, *S v I*, *E v S*, 1925 *E v I*, 1927 *E v I*, 1928 *E v A*, *E v S*, 1931 *F v I*

Waldron, C A (Australia) 1986 *F v R*, 1987 *A v SK*
Waldron, H (England) 1957 *F v It*
Walsh, L (New Zealand) 1949 *NZ v A*
Walters, D G (Wales) 1959 *F v S*, *I v E*, *E v S*, *I v F*, 1960 *S v F*, *E v I*, *I v S*, *F v I*, 1961 *F v SA*, *E v F*, 1962 *E v I*, *F v E*, 1963 *E v S*, *F v R*, 1964 *E v I*, *F v E*, *F v I*, *F v Fj*, 1965 *I v F*, *S v I*, *E v S*, *S v SA*, 1966 *F v E*
Warden, G (Ireland) 1946 *F v K*
Warren, R G (Ireland) 1892 *S v E*
Warren, T H H (Scotland) 1928 *W v I*
Watson, D H (Scotland) 1881 *S v E*
Waugh, Dr R (Australia) 1903 *A v NZ*
Welsby, A (England) 1976 *F v I*, 1978 *W v F*, 1981 *F v W*, 1982 *F v I*
Welsh, R (Scotland) 1902 *E v I*, 1903 *W v E*, 1905 *I v E*
West, J R (Ireland) 1974 *E v W*, 1975 *S v W*, 1976 *W v F*, 1977 *F v NZ*, 1978 *W v S*, *S v E*, *S v NZ*, 1979 *E v F*, *NZ v F* (2), 1980 *S v F*, *SA v F*, *W v NZ*, 1981 *F v NZ*, *W v A*, 1982 *F v Arg*, 1983 *W v E*, 1984 *R v F*
Wheeler, Dr E de C (Ireland) 1925 *S v F*
Wheeler, Dr J R (Ireland) 1929 *S v E*, 1930 *S v W*, 1931 *E v W*, *S v E*, 1932 *E v S*, 1933 *S v E*
Whittaker, J B G (England) 1947 *I v F*, *W v I*
Wiesse, M (Germany) 1936 *G v F*
Wilkins, H E B (England) 1925 *F v NZ*, 1928 *G v F*, 1929 *W v F*
Wilkins, W H (Wales) 1893 *E v S*, 1894 *S v E*, 1895 *E v S*
Williams, J (New Zealand) 1905 *NZ v A*
Williams, R C (Ireland) 1957 *S v W*, *E v F*, 1958 *E v W*, *E v A*, *S v A*, *S v E*, 1959 *W v E*, *S v W*, *E v F*, 1960 *S v E*, 1961 *F v S*, *S v W*, *F v R*, 1962 *S v F*, 1963 *F v S*, *S v W*, *W v NZ*, 1964 *S v F*, *S v NZ*, *F v NZ*, *S v E*
Williams, T (Wales) 1904 *E v I*
Williams, W (England) 1904 *I v S*, 1905 *W v I*, 1907 *E v F*, 1908 *W v S*, *I v S*, *W v F*, 1909 *E v F*, *F v W*, *I v F*, 1910 *W v F*, 1911 *F v W*, 1913 *F v SA*
Wolstenholme, B H (New Zealand) 1955 *NZ v A*
Woolley, A (South Africa) 1970 *SA v NZ*
Wyllie, W D (Australia) 1949 *A v M*

Yché, J-C (France) 1983 *S v I*, *R v W*, *It v A*, 1985 *A v Fj* (2)
Young, J (Scotland) 1971 *F v W*, 1972 *E v W*, *R v F*, 1973 *E v NZ*

WORLD INTERNATIONAL RECORDS

Both team and individual records are for official cap matches played by senior members of the International Board, up to 31 March 1992.

TEAM RECORDS

Highest score – 74
New Zealand (74-13) v Fiji 1987
  Christchurch

Biggest winning margin – 64
New Zealand (70-6) v Italy 1987 Auckland

Most tries in an international – 13
England v Wales 1881 Blackheath
New Zealand v United States 1913 Berkeley
France v Romania 1924 Paris
France v Zimbabwe 1987 Auckland

Most conversions in an international – 10
New Zealand v Fiji 1987 Christchurch

Most penalty goals in an international – 7
South Africa v France 1975 Pretoria
England v Wales 1991 Cardiff

**Most consecutive international
  victories – 17**
New Zealand between 1965 and 1969

**Most consecutive internationals
  undefeated – 23**
New Zealand between 1987 and 1990

**Most points in an international
  series – 109**
New Zealand v Argentina (2 matches)
  1989 in New Zealand

Most tries in an international series – 18
New Zealand v Wales (2 matches) 1988
  in New Zealand

**Most points in Five Nations
Championship in a season – 118**
England 1991-92

**Most tries in Five Nations
Championship in a season – 21**
Wales 1909-10

**Most points on an overseas tour
(all matches) – 868**
New Zealand to B Isles/France
  (33 matches) 1905-06

**Most tries on an overseas tour
(all matches) – 215**
New Zealand to B Isles/France
  (33 matches) 1905-06

**Biggest win on a major tour
(all matches)**
117-6 New Zealand v S Australia 1974
  Adelaide

INDIVIDUAL RECORDS

*including appearances for British Isles,
shown in brackets*

Most capped player
S Blanco (France) 93 1980-91
in individual positions
Full-back
S Blanco (France) 81[1] 1980-91
Wing
R Underwood (England) 58(3)[2] 1984-92
Centre (includes 2nd five-eighth)
P Sella (France) 76[3] 1982-92
Fly-half (includes 1st five-eighth)
J W Kyle (Ireland) 52(6)[4] 1947-58

Scrum-half
G O Edwards (Wales) 63(10) 1967-78
Prop
P A Orr (Ireland) 59(1) 1976-87
Hooker
C T Deans (Scotland) 52 1978-87
Lock
W J McBride (Ireland) 80(17) 1962-75
Flanker
J F Slattery (Ireland) 65(4) 1970-84
No 8
T M Davies (Wales) 46(8)[5] 1969-76

[1] *Blanco also played 12 times as a wing*
[2] *D I Campese (Australia), 64 caps, has won 48 as a wing*
[3] *Sella has also played 6 times on the wing and once at full-back*
[4] *M P Lynagh (Australia), 53 caps in all, has played 45 times at fly-half, 7 at centre and once at full-back*
[5] *Several French utility forwards have won more caps than Davies, but none has played as frequently at No 8*

Most consecutive internationals for a country – 53
G O Edwards (Wales) 1967-78

Most internationals as captain – 34
J-P Rives (France) 1979-84

Most points in internationals – 689
M P Lynagh (Australia) (53 matches) 1984-91

Most points in an international – 30
D Camberabero (France) v Zimbabwe 1987 Auckland

Most tries in internationals – 46
D I Campese (Australia) (64 matches) 1982-91

Most tries in an international – 5
G C Lindsay (Scotland) v Wales 1887 Edinburgh
D Lambert (England) v France 1907 Richmond
R Underwood (England) v Fiji 1989 Twickenham

Most conversions in internationals – 120
M P Lynagh (Australia) (53 matches) 1984-91

Most conversions in an international – 10
G J Fox (New Zealand) v Fiji 1987 Christchurch

Most dropped goals in internationals – 15
J-P Lescarboura (France) (28 matches) 1982-90
H E Botha (South Africa) (23 matches) 1980-89
C R Andrew (England) (50[2] matches) 1985-92
One of Andrew's goals was dropped in one of his two Test appearances for the British Lions

Most dropped goals in an international – 3
P Albaladejo (France) v Ireland 1960 Paris
P F Hawthorne (Australia) v England 1967 Twickenham
H E Botha (South Africa) v S America 1980 Durban
H E Botha (South Africa) v Ireland 1981 Durban
J-P Lescarboura (France) v England 1985 Twickenham
J-P Lescarboura (France) v New Zealand 1986 Christchurch
D Camberabero (France) v Australia 1990 Sydney

Most penalty goals in internationals – 126
M P Lynagh (Australia) (53 matches) 1984-91

Most penalty goals in an international – 7
S D Hodgkinson (England) v Wales 1991 Cardiff

Fastest player to 100 points in internationals
G J Fox (New Zealand) in his 6th match

**Fastest player to 200 points in
internationals**
G J Fox (New Zealand) in his 13th match

**Fastest player to 300 points in
internationals**
G J Fox (New Zealand) in his 18th match

**Fastest player to 400 points in
internationals**
G J Fox (New Zealand) in his 26th match

**Most points in a Five Nations
match – 24**
S Viars (France) v Ireland 1992

**Most points in Five Nations
Championship in a season – 67**
J M Webb (England) (4 matches)
1991-92

**Most tries in Five Nations
Championship in a season – 8**
C N Lowe (England) (4 appearances)
1913-14
I S Smith (Scotland) (4 appearances)
1924-25

**Tries in each match of a Five Nations
Championship**
H C Catcheside (England) 1923-24
A C Wallace (Scotland) 1924-25
P Estève (France) 1982-83
P Sella (France) 1985-86

**Most penalty goals in Five Nations
Championship in a season – 18**
S D Hodgkinson (England) (4 matches)
1990-91

**Most conversions in Five Nations
Championship in a season – 11**
J Bancroft (Wales) (4 appearances)
1908-09
J M Webb (England) (4 matches)
1991-92

**Most dropped goals in Five Nations
Championship in a season – 5**
G Camberabero (France) (3 appearances)
1966-67
*J-P Lescarboura (France) dropped a goal in each Cham-
pionship match 1983-84, a feat never performed before*

Most points on an overseas tour – 230
W J Wallace (NZ) (25 appearances) in
B Isles/France 1905-06

Most tries on an overseas tour – 42
J Hunter (NZ) (23 appearances) in
B Isles/France 1905-06

Most points in any match on tour – 43
R M Deans (NZ) v South Australia 1984
Adelaide

Most tries in any match on tour – 8
T R Heeps (NZ) v Northern NSW 1962
*P Estève scored 8 for France v East Japan in 1984, but this
was not on a major tour*

PARTNERSHIP RECORDS
Centre threequarters
S Hastings and S R P Lineen
(Scotland) 26
Half-backs
M P Lynagh and N C Farr-Jones
(Australia) 41
Front row
S C McDowell, S B T Fitzpatrick and
R W Loe (New Zealand) 29
Second row
A J Martin and G A D Wheel (Wales) 27
Back row
J Matheu, G Basquet and J Prat (France) 22

OTHER INTERNATIONAL MATCH RECORDS

Up to 31 March 1992. These are included for comparison and cover performances since 1971 by teams and players in Test matches for nations which are not *senior members of the International Board.*

Most points in a match
By a team
111 Zimbabwe v Nigeria 1987 Nairobi
By a player
31 M Grobler Zimbabwe v Nigeria 1987
29 S Bettarello Italy v Canada 1983

Most tries in a match
By a team
20 Zimbabwe v Nigeria 1987 Nairobi
By a player
5 R Tsimba Zimbabwe v Nigeria 1987
5 M Neill Zimbabwe v Nigeria 1987

Most conversions in a match
By a team
14 Zimbabwe v Nigeria Nairobi 1987
By a player
14 M Grobler Zimbabwe v Nigeria 1987

Most penalty goals in a match
By a team
8 Canada v Scotland 1991 St John
By a player
8 M A Wyatt Canada v Scotland 1991 St John

Most dropped goals in a match
By a team
3 Argentina v SA Gazelles 1971 Pretoria
3 Argentina v Australia 1979 Buenos Aires
3 Argentina v New Zealand 1985 Buenos Aires
By a player
3 T A Harris-Smith Argentina v SA Gazelles 1971
3 H Porta Argentina v Australia 1979
3 H Porta Argentina v New Zealand 1985

Most points in matches
530 H Porta Argentina/South America
483 S Bettarello Italy

Most tries in matches
21 M Marchetto Italy

Most conversions in matches
54 H Porta Argentina/South America
46 S Bettarello Italy

Most penalties in matches
109 H Porta Argentina/South America
104 S Bettarello Italy

Most dropped goals in matches
25 H Porta Argentina/South America
17 S Bettarello Italy

Most matches as captain
43 H Porta Argentina/South America

TOP SCORERS 1991-92

Peter Jackson *Daily Mail*

Last season Jonathan Newton achieved a feat that no British or Irish player had accomplished for the best part of 20 years – he topped 500 points, and in the process he achieved rather more than merely out-scoring everyone else during a most unforgettable season. In accumulating a total of 527 for his club and Scotland's Under-21 team, the prodigious Dundee High School former pupil eclipsed the figure set by Robin Williams, the Pontypool full-back who had raised goal-kicking to an art form. Williams' total of 517 had stood the test of time since the early 1970s, surviving all kinds of assaults until Newton came up with the startling proof in support of his theory that what goes up, keeps going up.

David Johnson matched the young Scot's tally of 190 goals, enough for Newcastle Gosforth's venerable fly-half to consolidate his status as a prolific scorer, second only to Dusty Hare in the all-time list of English kickers. It was quite a season, too, for another Dundee High School old boy – and not just because of the injury which forced Gary Armstrong to miss the Five Nations Championship after an outstanding World Cup. Andy Nicol, deservedly acclaimed as the Young Player of the Year, was one of only five players to score 30 or more tries. The vast majority of his haul helped his club clinch promotion to the Scottish First Division.

Only three players finished above him, one from Wales, David Manley, and two from England, one from the First Division, the other from the Third. Tony Underwood's 34 tries included one good enough to bring Twickenham to its feet in World Cup year, for Cambridge University in the Varsity Match.

Doug Woodman topped the lot, and even if his collection of tries couldn't quite lift Clifton into the Second Division, it was more than enough to keep him ahead of a very competitive field.

POINTS

527 – Jonathan Newton (Dundee HSFP); **450** – David Johnson (Newcastle Gosforth); **425** – John Steele (Northampton); **394** – Alistair Donaldson (Currie); **356** – John Liley (Leicester); **353** – Paul Grayson (Preston Grasshoppers); **349** – Aled Williams (Swansea, including 183 for Bridgend); **331** – Andy Finnie (Bedford); **327** – Byron Hayward (Newbridge); **319** – Neil Jenkins (Pontypridd); **318** – David Love (Aberavon); **314** – John Stabler (West Hartlepool); **292** – Simon Hogg (Clifton); **289** – Kevin Thomas (Redruth); **286** – Colin Stephens (Llanelli); **280** – Mark Mapletoft (Rugby), Graham Aitchison (Kelso); **278** – Peter Russell (Havant); **276** – Martin Livesey (Richmond); **271** – Nick Grecian (London Scottish); **263** – Calum McDonald (Stirling County); **262** – Martin Jones (Pontypool); **259** – Michael Kiernan (Dolphin); **252** – Dave Barrett (West of Scotland); **248** – John Watkins (Hereford); **242** – Jonathan Webb (Bath); **240** – Ralph Keyes (Cork Constitution), Derek McAleese (Ballymena); **236** – Richard Mills (Walsall); **235** – Chris Thompson (Sheffield); **234** – John Graves (Rosslyn Park); **232** – David

Breakwell (Roundhay); **230** – Steve Pilgrim (Wasps); **224** – Richard Rowledge (Basingstoke); **223** – Darren Chapman (Camborne); **220** – Kenny Smith (Garryowen); **218** – Graham Breckenridge (Glasgow High/Kelvinside); **217** – David Changleng (Heriot's FP); **213** – Ben Rudling (Saracens); **212** – Stuart Barnes (Bath); **211** – Mark Slade (Plymouth Albion); **210** – Gavin Hastings (Watsonians), Andy Dwyer (Bohemians); **206** – Tim Smith (Gloucester), Ian Aitchison (Waterloo); **205** – David Pears (Harlequins); **204** – Rodney Pow (Selkirk); **200** – Alun Harries (Newport); **190** – Paul Thorburn (Neath), Martin Strett (Orrell); **188** – Vasile Ion (Nuneaton); **187** – Brian Bolderson (Glamorgan Wanderers); **181** – Chris Howells (Penarth)

TRIES

37 – Doug Woodman (Clifton); **34** – Tony Underwood (Cambridge U & Leicester), David Manley (Newbridge); **31** – Andy Nicol (Dundee HSFP); **30** – Frank Packman (Northampton); **25** – Peter Walton (Newcastle Gosforth), Jonathan Wrigley (West Hartlepool); **24** – Richard Wallace (Garryowen), Scott Forrester (Currie); **23** – Rory Underwood (Leicester), Peter Holdstock (Newcastle Gosforth), Ian Hunter (Northampton), Steve Titcombe (Sudbury); **22** – Nick Grecian (London Scottish), Derek Stark (Ayr), Anthony Dragone (Aberavon), Gerry Hawkes (Glasgow High/ Kelvinside); **21** – Jim Fallon (Bath), Mike Harrison (Wakefield), Alan Drysdale (Wigtownshire), Aled Williams (Swansea, including 11 for Bridgend), Graham Agnew (Glasgow High/Kelvinside); **20** – Graham Clark (Newcastle Gosforth), Harvey Thorneycroft (Northampton), Steve Douglas (Newcastle Gosforth); **19** – Charlie Larkin (Weston-super-Mare), John Jeffrey (Kelso), Kenny Logan (Stirling County), Jim Miller (Aspatria); **17** – Michael Jaffray (Selkirk), Tony Stanger (Hawick), Martin Kelly (Broughton Park), Jonathan Sleightholme (Wakefield); **16** – Eddie Saunders (Rugby), Glen Webbe (Bridgend), Alun Edmunds (Glamorgan Wanderers), Stuart Jardine (Pontypool), Iwan Tukalo (Selkirk), Simon Davies (Swansea), Jonathan Newton (Dundee HSFP), John Mitchell (Kirkcaldy); **15** – Sean Legge (South Wales Police), Lesley Smitham (Camborne), Keith Suddon (Hawick), Andy McLeod (Musselburgh), Graham Burns (Stewart's-Melville FP), Steve Ford (Cardiff), Paul Rouse (Dundee HSFP), Graham Waddle (Gala); **14** – Tony Swift (Bath), Alan Taffetsauffer (Llanelli), Nigel Heslop (Orrell), Phil Halsall (Orrell), Ieuan Evans (Llanelli), Mike Wedderburn (Harlequins), Paul John (Pontypridd), Jamie Graham (Askeans), Grant Nolan (Currie), Steve Pilgrim (Wasps), Alex Moore (Edinburgh Academicals), Alan Linton (Selkirk)

Figures include all first-class fixtures, Cup ties, County, Barbarian, representative and international matches

EXPANSION BRINGS SUCCESS AND ALSO FINANCIAL PROBLEMS

WOMEN'S RUGBY 1991-92
Alice Cooper

In the wake of the two 1991 World Cups, the female version of the game continued its Topsy-like expansion with a further 37 new clubs last season. This takes the total to 157 clubs in the four home nations, including eight sides 'discovered' in Ireland who are now affiliated. Everyone in women's rugby agreed that the Women's World Cup in April 1991 had been unqualified success, especially as the RFU generously made up the £7,000 shortfall in running costs. The recent international conference in Spain agreed that the next World Cup will be held in Holland in 1994.

England, the losing World Cup finalists, made few changes to the established squad of recent years, although injury and retirements allowed some new faces to appear. Of these, Annie Cole (wing), Mickey Cave (centre), Maxine Edwards (flanker), Sarah Escott (prop) and Val Blackett (wing) were notable additions.

Wales, by contrast, had an enormous change-round after a disappointing World Cup. So a new broom swept in new selectors and coaches, Jonathan Moore and Jeff Brothers, and as a result many new caps. Of particular note was the new fly-half, Sam Porter of Cardiff, who had not played rugby until the beginning of the season and already held Welsh caps for football and athletics.

The annual meeting of Wales and England had particular significance this year as it was staged for the first time at Cardiff Arms Park national ground. In previous years England have won convincingly, but this was a closer, more exciting match which England won 14-10, only clinching it in the dying minutes of the game.

A B international was also played between England and Wales, in freezing, swirling winds at Wasps, and was won 15-4 by England. In a surprise move, Wales' dynamic flanker, Carol Thomas, was switched to scrum-half for this match and even took the goal-kicks. For the first time, a student international took place between England and Wales at Oxford, which England won 14-3.

Scotland made their debut on the international scene, fielding a select XV from players resident in Scotland. They are some way behind Wales and England, but what they lack in skill they make up for in sheer determination. In November they played a Richmond touring side, losing 50-0, and met a full-strength England side in March in an exhibition match, losing 74-0. Next year, it is hoped that full international trials will be held to bring a few 'old heads' into the Scottish squad from English clubs.

Another development has been the establishment of youth sides for girls aged 11 to 16. An increasing number of girls playing mini-rugby found a big void when they reached 11, and instinctive skills and enthusiasm were being lost because the girls couldn't play again until they reached 16. Now youth sides are springing up everywhere, and rugby is increasingly being taught to girls in schools. New Image rugby has been an ideal starting point for new players, many of whom then move on to the full contact game. Bedfordshire were the first county to progress, running an Under-12 and an Under-13 tournament in March.

However, the expansion of the sport has created a problem: it is putting increasing strain on the WRFU's miniscule resources and voluntary administrators. In May, the WRFU held its AGM, where it was decided to make evolutionary changes to the Union's constitution, increasing the number of administrators and altering some Union playing policies. But the fact remains that while it is neither possible nor desirable to stop the expansion in the number of clubs, the Union and the sport could suffer in the long term unless major financial support is forthcoming in the short term.

INTERNATIONAL RESULTS
5 February: English Students 14, Welsh Students 3 (Iffley Road, Oxford);
9 February: Wales 10, England 14 (Cardiff Arms Park); **20 March:** England B 15, Wales 4 (Wasps); **29 March:** England 74, Scottish Select XV 0 (Blackheath); **11 April:** England 23, Holland 3 (London Welsh); **11 April:** Wales 18, Catalonia 4 (Llandybie)

WRFU NATIONAL LEAGUE

Division 1

	P	W	D	L	F	A	Pts
Wasps	12	12	0	0	320	20	24
Saracens	12	9	0	3	304	77	18
Richmond	12	9	0	3	244	88	18
*Waterloo	11	5	0	6	137	159	10
Clifton	12	3	0	9	52	268	6
*Blackheath	11	2	0	9	52	231	4
Headingley	12	1	0	11	45	283	2

Division 2

	P	W	D	L	F	A	Pts
Richmond II	10	8	1	1	211	40	16
Lampeter	10	8	1	1	166	26	16
Medway	10	6	0	4	84	48	12
Sale	10	5	0	5	64	92	10
Bedford	10	2	0	8	38	274	4
Oxford OB	10	0	0	10	18	101	0

Division 3 Wales

	P	W	D	L	F	A	Pts
Pontypool	8	8	0	0	147	12	24
Cardiff	8	7	0	1	135	4	22
Swansea Uplds	8	5	0	3	131	51	18
Blaenau Gwent	8	5	0	3	96	66	18
Llandovery	8	4	0	4	47	62	15
Neath	8	2	0	6	39	123	12
[2]Aber U	6	2	0	4	18	88	10
[2]N'castle E	6	1	0	5	22	103	8
[2]Weston H	6	0	0	6	12	138	6

Division 3 London

	P	W	D	L	F	A	Pts
Eton Manor	8	8	0	0	219	14	24
St Albans	8	6	1	1	170	25	21
Exeter	8	6	0	2	154	42	20
[1]Saracens II	7	5	0	2	39	8	17
Wasps II	8	4	1	3	190	30	16
Swindon S	8	2	1	5	48	213	13
Southend	8	2	0	5	38	132	11

[1]Abbotstons	7	1	1	5	92	156	10
[2]Camberley	6	0	0	6	0	374	6

Division 3 North

	P	W	D	L	F	A	Pts
York	6	6	0	0	164	4	18
Bury	6	5	0	1	239	12	16
Waterloo II	6	3	1	2	64	104	13
Newcastle	6	2	0	4	0	36	10
[1]Edinburgh	5	2	0	3	100	75	9
Headingley II	5	1	1	3	4	168	8
[4]Northern	3	0	0	3	0	124	3

Division 3 Midlands

	P	W	D	L	F	A	Pts
N'pton L	8	8	0	0	164	25	24
N'pton OS	8	6	0	2	197	22	18
O Leamingtns	8	6	1	3	159	47	18
Sutton Coldfd	8	4	1	3	60	82	17
[1]Witham Ams	7	4	1	2	112	66	16
Oxford U	8	3	0	5	58	100	14
Bury St Eds	8	3	0	7	74	162	14
Shipston-on-S	8	1	0	7	10	290	10
[4]Shelford	4	0	0	4	22	112	4

Division 3 South

	P	W	D	L	F	A	Pts
Teddington A	8	8	0	0	146	32	24
Crawley	8	7	0	1	151	25	22
Wimbledon	8	5	0	3	42	100	18
[1]Richmond III	7	5	0	2	92	49	17
Staines	8	4	0	4	59	40	16
P'mth Nomads	8	2	1	5	43	118	13
[1]Hove	7	2	1	4	32	102	12
[1]London Welsh	7	1	0	6	22	146	9
[3]Blackheath II	5	1	0	4	17	56	7

Division 3 Scotland

	P	W	D	L	F	A	Pts
Edinburgh	9	8	0	1	332	15	25
Edinburgh U	9	8	0	1	301	16	25
Stirling U	9	6	1	2	128	50	22
St Andrews	9	6	0	3	165	70	21
Biggar	9	5	1	3	90	72	20
★Dundee U	9	4	0	5	66	172	16
RDVC	9	3	1	5	42	170	16
Heriot W U	9	2	0	7	12	261	12
★Aberdeen U	9	1	1	7	33	100	11
Glasgow U	9	0	0	9	0	243	9

[1]*Defaulted once*
[2]*Defaulted twice*
[3]*Defaulted three times*
[4]*Defaulted four times*
★ *Match void*

Division 3 play-offs: The top 16 sides in the Third Division went into the play-offs for the title and promotion. The semi-finalists – Northampton Old Scouts, Bury, Cardiff and Eton Manor – were all promoted to National League Division 2. Cardiff went on to defeat Bury 34-3 in the final to take the title.

National Cup Richmond 16, Saracens 11 **Student Cup:** Birmingham University 24, Sheffield University 6 **Student League Winners:** Birmingham University **BPSA Winners:** Brighton Polytechnic

National Sevens Cup final: Wasps 18, Saracens 4 **Rugby Travel Plate final:** St Albans II 18, W Sussex Inst of HE 4

Warwickshire Sevens
Sun Alliance Trophy final (Under-15s): Blue Coat School 8, De Aston School 0
Quaif & Lilley Challenge Trophy final: Birmingham University 12, Northampton Old Scouts 8 **Rugby Tackle Plate final:** Portsmouth Polytechnic 20, Shipston-on-Stour 0

CLUBS SECTION
Records of most-capped players are complete up to 30 April 1992

ENGLAND

Bath

Year of formation 1865
Grounds Recreation Ground, London Road, Bath   Tel: Bath (0225) 425192
Colours Blue, white and black
Most capped player D M B Sole (Scotland) 42 caps
Captain 1991-92 R A Robinson
Courage League Div 1 *Winners* **Pilkington Cup** *Winners* Beat Harlequins 15-12 *(aet)* (final)

League Record 1991-92

Date	Venue	Opponents	Result	Scorers
16 Nov	A	London Irish	26-21	*T:* Heatherley, Swift, Fallon *C:* Barnes *PG:* Barnes (4)
7 Dec	H	Northampton	15-6	*PG:* Webb (5)
14 Dec	A	Orrell	9-10	*T:* Swift *C:* Webb *DG:* Barnes
21 Dec	H	Bristol	9-4	*PG:* Webb (2) *DG:* Guscott
4 Jan	A	Harlequins	18-18	*T:* pen try, de Glanville *C:* Webb (2) *PG:* Webb (2)
11 Jan	H	Leicester	37-6	*T:* Swift (3), Fallon (2), Mallett, Lewis *C:* Webb (3) *PG:* Webb
29 Jan	H	Gloucester	29-9	*T:* Swift, Barnes, de Glanville, Guscott *C:* Barnes (2) *PG:* Barnes (3)
14 Mar	A	Wasps	24-12	*T:* Hill, Fallon, Clarke, Swift *C:* Barnes *PG:* Barnes (2)
21 Mar	A	Rugby	32-0	*T:* de Glanville, Redman, Swift, Fallon, Robinson *C:* Barnes (3) *PG:* Webb (2)
28 Mar	H	Nottingham	25-15	*T:* Hill, Egerton, Robinson *C:* Barnes (2) *PG:* Barnes (3)
11 Apr	A	Rosslyn Park	21-13	*T:* Fallon *C:* Barnes *PG:* Barnes (4) *DG:* Barnes
25 Apr	H	Saracens	32-12	*T:* Barnes (2), Clarke, Fallon *C:* Webb (2) *PG:* Barnes (2), Webb (2)

Bedford

Year of formation 1886
Ground Goldington Road, Bedford   Tel: Bedford (0234) 354619 or 359160
Colours Hoops in Oxford and Cambridge blue
Most capped player D P Rogers (England) 34 caps
Captain 1991-92 M Howe
Courage League Div 2 10th **Pilkington Cup** Lost 3-33 to Harlequins (3rd round)

League Record 1990-91

Date	Venue	Opponents	Result	Scorers
16 Nov	H	Wakefield	6-25	*PG:* Finnie *DG:* Finnie
23 Nov	A	Liverpool SH	22-6	*T:* Rennell, Binnington, Williams *C:* Finnie (2) *PG:* Finnie (2)

A delighted Bath team, League and Cup winners in 1991-92, celebrate their Courage League title. L-R, back row: Dawe, Barnes, Ojomoh, de Glanville, Chilcott, Clarke, Fallon, Ubogu, Redman, Haag, Webb; front row: Hill, Robinson, Lewis, Swift.

14 Dec	A	Plymouth Alb	9-24	T: Rennell C: Finnie PG: Finnie
7 Dec	H	W Hartlepool	6-39	T: Rennell C: Finnie
4 Jan	H	Moseley	8-9	T: Finnie, Rennell
11 Jan	A	Sale	6-16	T: Clift C: Finnie
29 Feb	A	London Scottish	0-38	
14 Mar	H	Blackheath	52-0	T: Turner (2), Taylor (2), Gabriel (2), Pascall (2), Rees C: Finnie (5) PG: Finnie (2)
28 Mar	A	Coventry	13-19	T: Rennell PG: Finnie (2) DG: Finnie
4 Apr	H	Waterloo	25-4	T: Gabriel (2) C: Finnie PG: Finnie (5)
11 Apr	H	Newcastle Gos	9-4	PG: Finnie (2) DG: Finnie
25 Apr	A	Morley	12-19	PG: Finnie (4)

Blackheath

Year of formation 1858
Ground Rectory Field, Blackheath, London SE3   Tel: 081-858 1578 or 858 3677
Colours Red and black hoops
Most capped player C N Lowe (England) 25 caps
Captain 1991-92 J Swain
Courage League Div 2 11th **Pilkington Cup** Lost 12-22 to Richmond (2nd round)

League Record 1991-92

Date	Venue	Opponents	Result	Scorers
16 Nov	A	London Scottish	16-36	T: Aldridge PG: Munn (4)
7 Dec	H	Coventry	21-13	T: Aris C: Munn PG: Munn (5)
21 Dec	H	Morley	3-9	PG: Munn
14 Dec	H	Newcastle Gos	0-39	
4 Jan	A	Wakefield	6-20	T: P Jones C: Munn
11 Jan	H	Liverpool SH	9-6	PG: Munn (3)
15 Feb	A	W Hartlepool	8-21	T: Clark, Mercer
29 Feb	H	Plymouth Alb	16-20	T: Turner PG: Munn (3) DG: Munn
14 Mar	A	Bedford	10-52	T: R Smith PG: Munn (2)
28 Mar	H	Moseley	31-6	T: P Jones, Griffiths C: Eagle PG: Eagle (6) DG: King
11 Apr	A	Sale	14-10	T: Begley, Slack PG: Eagle DG: King
25 Apr	H	Waterloo	6-34	T: Mercer C: Eagle

Bristol

Year of formation 1888
Ground Memorial Ground, Filton Ave, Horsfield Bristol   Tel: Bristol (0272) 514448
Colours Navy blue and white
Most capped player J V Pullin (England) 42 caps
Captain 1991-92 D J Eves
Courage League Div 1 10th **Pilkington Cup** Lost 6-15 to Bath (quarter-final)

League Record 1991-92

Date	Venue	Opponents	Result	Scorers
16 Nov	A	Nottingham	32-0	T: Davis, Hull, Barrow, Kitchen, Knibbs C: Painter (3) PG: Painter (2)

23 Nov	H	Bristol	22-4	T: Duggan (2), Collings C: Painter, Hull
				PG: Hull DG: Knibbs
7 Dec	A	Saracens	4-13	T: Stiff
21 Dec	A	Bath	4-9	T: Eves
4 Jan	H	Northampton	9-15	PG: Hull (3)
11 Jan	A	Orrell	9-23	T: Hull C: Hull DG: Painter
29 Feb	H	Harlequins	16-0	T: Stiff (2), Davis C: Tainton (2)
14 Mar	A	Leicester	9-25	T: Eves C: Tainton DG: Tainton
28 Mar	H	Rugby	48-4	T: Lloyd (3), Stiff (2), Collings (2). Wring, Duggan,
				Davis C: Tainton (3), Redrup
4 Apr	A	Gloucester	15-29	T: Davis C: Tainton PG: Tainton (3)
18 Apr	H	London Irish	14-19	T: Eves, Wring PG: Tainton, Hull
25 Apr	H	Wasps	10-33	T: Redrup PG: Wring (2)

Coventry

Year of formation 1874
Ground Coundon Road, Coventry   Tel: Coventry (0203) 591274 or 593399
Colours Navy and white
Most capped player D J Duckham (England) 36 caps
Captain 1991-92 J Hyde
Courage League Div 2 6th **Pilkington Cup** Lost 7-31 to Northampton (3rd round)

League Record 1991-92

Date	Venue	Opponents	Result	Scorers
16 Nov	A	Waterloo	6-10	PG: Angell, S Thomas
23 Nov	H	London Scottish	15-32	T: Minshull C: Fairn PG: Angell (3)
7 Dec	A	Blackheath	13-21	T: Angell, Bennett C: Angell PG: S Thomas
21 Dec	H	Newcastle Gos	6-30	PG: Angell (2)
4 Jan	A	Morley	16-12	T: Minshull PG: S Thomas (3) DG: Lakey
11 Jan	H	Wakefield	21-10	T: Ferdinand, Hickey C: S Thomas (2)
				PG: S Thomas (2) DG: Angell
8 Feb	A	Liverpool SH	19-0	T: Turner, Hickey, Minshull C: Angell (2)
				PG: Angell
29 Feb	H	W Hartlepool	18-24	T: Minshull C: S Thomas PG: S Thomas (4)
14 Mar	A	Plymouth Alb	13-10	T: Hickey PG: S Thomas (3)
28 Mar	H	Bedford	19-13	T: Angell, Ferdinand C: S Thomas
				PG: S Thomas (3)
11 Apr	A	Moseley	22-12	T: Street, Medford, Hickey C: Angell (2)
				PG: Fairn (2)
25 Apr	H	Sale	19-12	T: Street, S Thomas C: S Thomas
				PG: S Thomas (3)

Gloucester

Year of formation 1873
Ground Kingsholm, Kingsholm Road, Gloucester   Tel: Gloucester (0452) 520901
Colours Cherry and white
Most capped player A T Voyce (England) 27 caps
Captain 1991-92 I R Smith
Courage League Div 1 4th **Pilkington Cup** Lost 18-27 (aet) to Bath (semi-final)

League Record 1991-92

Date	Venue	Opponents	Result	Scorers
16 Nov	H	Leicester	21-3	*T:* Caskie, Phillips *C:* T Smith (2) *PG:* T Smith (3)
23 Nov	A	Rugby	19-16	*T:* Morris, Miles *C:* T Smith *PG:* T Smith (3)
21 Dec	A	Nottingham	14-3	*T:* Morris, Masters *PG:* T Smith (2)
4 Jan	H	Rosslyn Park	12-9	*T:* Ashmead, T Smith *C:* T Smith (2)
11 Jan	A	Saracens	12-12	*PG:* T Smith (4)
29 Feb	A	Bath	9-29	*T:* Hannaford *C:* T Smith *DG:* Matthews
14 Mar	H	Northampton	10-17	*T:* Hawker *PG:* T Smith (2)
25 Mar	H	London Irish	22-15	*T:* Morris, Perrins, Ashmead *C:* Marment (2) *PG:* Marment *DG:* Hamlin
28 Mar	A	Orrell	12-18	*PG:* Hamlin (4)
4 Apr	H	Bristol	29-15	*T:* Morris (2), Scrivens, Masters, Sims *C:* T Smith (3) *PG:* T Smith
18 Apr	H	Wasps	15-10	*T:* Gardiner *C:* Roberts *PG:* Roberts (3)
25 Apr	A	Harlequins	18-21	*T:* Masters *C:* T Smith *PG:* T Smith (4)

Harlequins

Year of formation 1866
Ground Stoop Memorial Ground, Craneford Way, Twickenham, Middlesex
Tel: 081-892 0822
Colours Light blue, magenta, chocolate, French grey, black and light green
Most capped player P J Winterbottom (England) 52 caps
Captain 1991-92 P J Winterbottom
Courage League Div 1 8th **Pilkington Cup** Lost 12-15 (*aet*) to Bath (final)

League Record 1991-92

Date	Venue	Opponents	Result	Scorers
16 Nov	A	Wasps	6-20	*T:* Molyneux *C:* Pears
23 Nov	H	Nottingham	23-6	*T:* Pears, Bray, Killick *C:* Pears *PG:* Pears (3)
7 Dec	A	Rosslyn Park	24-12	*PG:* Pears (7) *DG:* Bray
21 Dec	A	London Irish	39-3	*T:* Wedderburn, Edwards, Pears, Thompson, Russell, Glenister, Challinor *C:* Pears (4) *PG:* Pears
4 Jan	H	Bath	18-18	*T:* Carling, pen try *C:* Pears (2) *PG:* Pears (2)
11 Jan	A	Northampton	14-25	*T:* Wedderburn, Shortland *PG:* S Thresher *DG:* Challinor
29 Feb	A	Bristol	0-16	
21 Mar	H	Saracens	21-37	*T:* Wedderburn, Fox, Glenister *C:* Pears (3) *PG:* Pears
28 Mar	H	Leicester	20-13	*T:* Sheasby, Pears, Thompson *C:* Pears *PG:* Pears (2)
11 Apr	A	Rugby	20-29	*T:* Carling, Thompson, Pears *C:* Pears *PG:* Pears (2)
20 Apr	H	Orrell	7-10	*T:* Halliday *PG:* S Thresher
25 Apr	H	Gloucester	21-18	*T:* Challinor, Carling *C:* Pears (2) *PG:* Pears (3)

Leicester

Year of formation 1880
Ground Welford Road, Leicester   Tel: Leicester (0533) 540276 or 541607
Colours Scarlet, green and white
Most capped player P J Wheeler (England) 41 caps
Captain 1991-92 J Wells
Courage League Div 1 6th **Pilkington Cup** Lost 9-15 to Harlequins (semi-final)

League Record 1991-92

Date	Venue	Opponents	Result	Scorers
16 Nov	A	Gloucester	3-21	*PG:* Liley
23 Nov	H	Wasps	31-12	*T:* R Underwood, Wells *C:* Liley *PG:* Liley (4) *DG:* Harris (3)
7 Dec	A	Nottingham	27-14	*T:* R Underwood (2) *C:* Liley (2) *PG:* Liley (4) *DG:* Harris
21 Dec	A	Saracens	20-9	*T:* Back, Wells, Hackney *C:* Liley *PG:* Liley (2)
4 Jan	H	London Irish	36-13	*T:* Hackney (3), R Underwood (2), Liley, Richards *C:* Liley (4)
11 Jan	A	Bath	6-37	*PG:* Liley (2)
29 Feb	A	Orrell	9-21	*PG:* Liley (3)
14 Mar	H	Bristol	25-9	*T:* T Underwood, Garforth, Ainscough, Boyle *PG:* Liley (3)
21 Mar	H	Rosslyn Park	51-16	*T:* R Underwood (3), Liley (2), Ainscough, Kardooni *C:* Liley (7) *PG:* Liley (3)
28 Mar	A	Harlequins	13-20	*T:* Wills, Povoas *C:* Wills *PG:* Wills
7 Apr	H	Northampton	19-22	*T:* Harris, Grewcock *C:* Liley *PG:* Liley (3)
25 Apr	H	Rugby	22-22	*T:* T Underwood (2), R Underwood, Bates *C:* Liley (3)

Liverpool St Helens

Year of formation 1986 (on amalgamation of Liverpool – founded 1857 – with St Helens)
Ground Moss Lane, Windle, St Helens, Merseyside   Tel: St Helens (0744) 25708
Colours Red, blue and black
Most capped player M A C Slemen (England) 31 caps
Captain 1991-92 M Hale
Courage League Div 2 13th *relegated* **Pilkington Cup** Lost 10-21 to Waterloo (2nd round)

League Record 1991-92

Date	Venue	Opponents	Result	Scorers
16 Nov	A	Plymouth Alb	10-25	*T:* Sephton *PG:* Ramsden (2)
23 Nov	H	Bedford	6-22	*PG:* Ramsden, Elliott
7 Dec	A	Moseley	3-33	*PG:* Ramsden
14 Dec	H	Sale	11-38	*T:* Gill, Elliott *PG:* Ramsden
21 Dec	A	Waterloo	12-40	*T:* Elliott, Wales, Sephton
4 Jan	H	London Scottish	4-41	*T:* Lloyd
11 Jan	A	Blackheath	6-9	*T:* Sephton *C:* Elliott

Mark Egan gets the ball away for London Irish in their League match against Northampton, which was drawn 12-12.

8 Feb	H	Coventry	0-19	
29 Feb	A	Newcastle Gos	4-76	*T:* Bromley
14 Mar	H	Morley	6-49	*T:* Lloyd *C:* Ramsden
28 Mar	A	Wakefield	25-35	*T:* Elliott (2), Lloyd, Moss *C:* Ramsden (3)
				PG: Ramsden
25 Apr	H	W Hartlepool	0-32	

London Irish

Year of formation 1898
Ground The Avenue, Sunbury-on-Thames, Middlesex   Tel: Sunbury (0932) 783034
Colours Emerald green
Most capped player K W Kennedy (Ireland) 45 caps
Captain 1991-92 J Staples
Courage League Div 1 9th **Pilkington Cup** Lost 10-16 to Thurrock (3rd round)

League Record 1991-92

Date	Venue	Opponents	Result	Scorers
16 Nov	H	Bath	21-26	*T:* Curtis *C:* Mullen *PG:* Mullen (4) *DG:* Mullen
23 Nov	A	Northampton	12-12	*T:* Hennessey, Mullen *C:* Mullen (2)
7 Dec	H	Orrell	7-21	*T:* Staples *PG:* Mullen
21 Dec	H	Harlequins	3-39	*PG:* Mullen
4 Jan	A	Leicester	13-36	*T:* Hennessey *PG:* Mullen (2) *DG:* Mullen
11 Jan	H	Rugby	6-6	*PG:* Mullen (2)
29 Feb	H	Wasps	18-13	*PG:* Corcoran (4) *DG:* Curtis, Moloney
14 Mar	A	Nottingham	12-9	*T:* Corcoran *C:* Corcoran *PG:* Corcoran (2)
25 Mar	A	Gloucester	15-22	*T:* Corcoran, Moloney *C:* Corcoran (2) *PG:* Corcoran
28 Mar	H	Rosslyn Park	12-12	*PG:* Graves (4)
11 Apr	A	Saracens	9-27	*PG:* Corcoran (3)
18 Apr	A	Bristol	19-14	*T:* Corcoran (2), Staples *C:* Corcoran (2) *PG:* Corcoran

London Scottish

Year of formation 1878
Ground Richmond Athletic Ground, Richmond, Surrey   Tel: 081-940 0397
Colours Blue jersey with red lion crest
Most capped player A F McHarg (Scotland) 44 caps
Captain 1991-92 R Cramb
Courage League Div 2 *Winners* **Pilkington Cup** Lost 7-20 to Gloucester (4th round)

League Record 1991-92

Date	Venue	Opponents	Result	Scorers
16 Nov	H	Blackheath	36-16	*T:* Wainwright, Beazley, Grecian, Dixon *C:* Grecian (4) *PG:* Grecian (4)
23 Nov	A	Coventry	32-15	*T:* Grecian, Harrold, Millard, Beazley, Morrison *C:* Grecian (2), Appleson *PG:* Grecian (2)

7 Dec	H	Newcastle Gos	16-11	*T:* Appleson, Grecian *C:* Grecian
				PG: Grecian *DG:* Cramb
14 Dec	A	Morley	13-12	*T:* Wainwright, Grecian *C:* Grecian
				PG: Grecian
21 Dec	H	Wakefield	31-4	*T:* Grecian (2), White (2), Renwick *C:* Grecian
				PG: Grecian (3)
4 Jan	A	Liverpool SH	41-4	*T:* Troup, Sly, Appleson, Grecian, McBain, Dixon,
				pen try *C:* Appleson (2) *PG:* Appleson, Grecian
				DG: Appleson
11 Jan	H	W Hartlepool	7-6	*T:* White *PG:* Grecian
29 Feb	H	Bedford	38-0	*T:* Grecian (2), Renwick (2), White (2)
				C: Grecian (3), Appleson *PG:* Grecian, Appleson
14 Mar	A	Moseley	25-18	*T:* Millard (2), Morrison, White *PG:* Grecian (2),
				Russell
28 Mar	H	Sale	40-13	*T:* Grecian, Signorini, Cramb, Beazley, Scott
				C: Appleson (2), Grecian, Morrison
				PG: Appleson (3), Grecian
11 Apr	A	Waterloo	15-22	*T:* Morrison, Brown *C:* Appleson (2)
				PG: Appleson
18 Apr	A	Plymouth Alb	10-9	*T:* Grecian, Cronin *C:* Appleson

Morley

Year of formation 1878
Ground Scatard Lane, Morley, Leeds   Tel: Leeds (0532) 533487
Colours Maroon
Most capped player J Orwin (England) 14 caps
Captain 1991-92 J Orwin
Courage League Div 2 9th **Pilkington Cup** Lost 9-10 to Newcastle Gosforth
(2nd round)

League Record 1991-92

Date	*Venue*	*Opponents*	*Result*	*Scorers*
16 Nov	A	Moseley	3-19	*PG:* Grayshon
23 Nov	H	Sale	12-13	*T:* Collins *C:* Hall *PG:* Hall *DG:* White
7 Dec	A	Waterloo	9-16	*PG:* Hall, Collins *DG:* White
14 Dec	H	London Scottish	12-12	*T:* Thomas *C:* Hall *PG:* Hall (2)
21 Dec	A	Blackheath	9-3	*PG:* Hall (3)
4 Jan	H	Coventry	12-16	*T:* Collins *C:* Grayshon *PG:* Grayshon (2)
11 Jan	A	Newcastle Gos	12-60	*T:* Higgins, Hill, Georgiou
29 Feb	H	Wakefield	9-13	*PG:* Grayshon (3)
14 Mar	A	Liverpool SH	49-6	*T:* Faulkner (2), Clark (2), Collins (2), Cayzer,
				White, McGowan *C:* Grayshon (5)
				PG: Grayshon
11 Apr	A	Plymouth Alb	12-10	*T:* Georgiou *C:* Grayshon *PG:* Grayshon (2)
25 Apr	H	Bedford	19-12	*T:* White, Clark *C:* Grayshon
				PG: Grayshon (2) *DG:* Grayshon
27 Apr	H	W Hartlepool	13-21	*T:* Clark, White *C:* Grayshon *PG:* Grayshon

Moseley

Year of formation 1873
Ground The Reddings, Reddings Road, Moseley, Birmingham   Tel: 021-499 2149

Colours Red and black
Most capped player N E Horton (England) 20 caps
Captain 1991-92 P Shillingford
Courage League Div 2 7th **Pilkington Cup** Lost 12-18 to Sale (2nd round)

League Record 1991-92

Date	Venue	Opponents	Result	Scorers
16 Nov	H	Morley	19-3	T: Purdy PG: Pennington (5)
23 Nov	A	Wakefield	9-13	T: Shillingford C: Pennington PG: Pennington
7 Dec	H	Liverpool SH	33-3	T: Shillingford (2), James, Martin, Barr C: Kerr (2) PG: Kerr (3)
14 Dec	A	W Hartlepool	4-27	T: Milner
21 Dec	H	Plymouth Alb	15-10	PG: Pennington (3) DG: Kerr (2)
4 Jan	A	Bedford	9-8	T: Linnett C: Kerr PG: Kerr
29 Feb	A	Waterloo	17-18	T: Maclean, Martin, Spiller C: Kerr PG: Kerr
14 Mar	H	London Scottish	18-25	T: Spiller, Fenley, Harknett, Martin C: Kerr
28 Mar	A	Blackheath	6-31	PG: Kerr (2)
4 Apr	H	Sale	47-15	T: Spiller (3), Morris (2), Purdy, Sherriffe, Harknett, Hardcastle C: Kerr (4) PG: Kerr
11 Apr	H	Coventry	12-22	T: Purdy, Spiller C: Kerr (2)
25 Apr	A	Newcastle Gos	26-20	T: Martin (2), Morris, Purdy C: Kerr (2) PG: Kerr (2)

Newcastle Gosforth

Year of formation 1877
Ground New Ground, Great North Road, Gosforth, Newcastle
Tel: Newcastle (0632) 856915
Colours Green and white
Most capped player R J McLoughlin (Ireland) 40 caps
Captain 1991-92 J Curry
Courage League Div 2 4th **Pilkington Cup** Lost 0-10 to Leicester (quarter-final)

League Record 1991-92

Date	Venue	Opponents	Result	Scorers
16 Nov	A	Sale	15-19	PG: Johnson (5)
23 Nov	H	Waterloo	37-6	T: Clark (2), Wilkinson (2), Walton, Holdstock C: Johnson (5) PG: Johnson
7 Dec	A	London Scottish	11-16	T: White (2) PG: Johnson
14 Dec	H	Blackheath	39-0	T: Walton (3), Holdstock, Campbell, Curry, Chick C: Johnson (4) PG: Johnson
21 Dec	A	Coventry	30-6	T: Walton (2), Arnold C: Johnson (3) Johnson (4)
11 Jan	H	Morley	60-12	T: Walton (2), Douglas (2), Wilkinson, Holdstock, Chick, Frankland C: Johnson (5) PG: Johnson (6)
15 Feb	A	Wakefield	18-8	T: Holdstock, Wilkinson, Arnold, Walker C: Johnson

29 Feb	H	Liverpool SH	76-4	*T:* Clark (3), Walton, Bennett, Arnold (3), White, Holdstock, Johnson, Meadows, pen try *C:* Johnson (9) *PG:* Johnson (2)
14 Mar	A	W Hartlepool	7-13	*T:* White *PG:* Johnson
28 Mar	H	Plymouth Alb	54-21	*T:* White (2), Curry (2), Clark (2), Holdstock, Walton, Frankland *C:* Johnson (3) *PG:* Johnson (3) *DG:* Johnson
11 Apr	A	Bedford	4-9	*T:* Bainbridge
25 Apr	H	Moseley	20-26	*T:* Williams, Douglas, Arnold *C:* Johnson *PG:* Johnson (2)

Northampton

Year of formation 1888
Ground Franklins Gardens, Weedon Road, Northampton
Tel: Northampton (0604) 751543
Colours Black, green and gold
Most capped player G S Pearce (England) 31 caps
Captain 1991-92 J Olver
Courage League Div 1 3rd **Pilkington Cup** Lost 9-13 to Bath (*aet*) (4th round)

League Record 1991-92

Date	*Venue*	*Opponents*	*Result*	*Scorers*
16 Nov	A	Saracens	14-9	*T:* Thorneycroft, McNaughton *PG:* Steele (2)
23 Nov	H	London Irish	12-12	*PG:* Steele (4)
7 Dec	A	Bath	6-15	*PG:* Steele *DG:* Steele
21 Dec	H	Orrell	12-3	*PG:* Steele (4)
4 Jan	A	Bristol	15-9	*T:* Thame *C:* Steele *PG:* Steele (3)
11 Jan	H	Harlequins	25-14	*T:* Hunter, Thorneycroft, Bayfield *C:* Steele (2) *PG:* Steele *DG:* Steele, Hunter
29 Feb	H	Rugby	29-0	*T:* Thorneycroft, Rodber, Hunter *C:* Steele *PG:* Steele (5)
14 Mar	A	Gloucester	17-10	*T:* Hunter, Thorneycroft, Packman *C:* Steele *PG:* Steele
28 Mar	H	Wasps	28-15	*T:* Hunter, Packman, McNaughton, Dawson *C:* Steele (3) *PG:* Steele (2)
7 Apr	A	Leicester	22-19	*T:* Olver, Baldwin *C:* Steele *PG:* Steele (4)
11 Apr	A	Nottingham	9-18	*T:* Shelford *C:* Steele *PG:* Steele
25 Apr	H	Rosslyn Park	20-12	*T:* Griffiths, Thorneycroft, Shelford *C:* Dawson *PG:* Dawson (2)

Nottingham

Year of formation 1877
Ground Ireland Avenue, Beeston, Nottingham   Tel: Nottingham (0602) 254238
Colours White and green
Most capped player B C Moore (England) 40 caps
Captain 1991-92 C Gray
Courage League Div 1 12th *relegated* **Pilkington Cup** Lost 0-52 to Bath (3rd round)

League Record 1991-92

Date	Venue	Opponents	Result	Scorers
16 Nov	H	Bristol	0-32	
23 Nov	A	Harlequins	6-23	PG: Hodgkinson (2)
7 Dec	H	Leicester	14-27	T: Byrom, Pepper PG: Kilford (2)
21 Dec	H	Gloucester	3-14	PG: Kilford
4 Jan	A	Wasps	7-11	T: Walker PG: Gregory
22 Feb	A	Rugby	9-9	PG: Hodgkinson (3)
29 Jan	A	Saracens	12-13	T: Potter C: Hodgkinson PG: Hodgkinson (2)
14 Mar	H	London Irish	9-12	PG: Hodgkinson (3)
28 Mar	A	Bath	15-25	PG: Gregory (5)
4 Apr	H	Rosslyn Park	34-9	T: Pepper (3), Byrom C: Gregory (3) PG: Gregory (2) DG: Gregory (2)
11 Apr	H	Northampton	18-9	T: Potter, Hughes C: Gregory (2) PG: Gregory DG: Gregory
25 Apr	A	Orrell	6-20	T: Wilby C: Gregory

Orrell

Year of formation 1927
Ground Edge Hill Road, Orrell, Nr Wigan, Lancashire
Tel: Up Holland (0695) 623193
Colours Black and amber
Most capped player J Carleton (England) 25 caps
Captain 1991-92 D V Southern
Courage League Div 1 2nd **Pilkington Cup** Lost 16-25 to Gloucester (quarter-final)

League Record 1991-92

Date	Venue	Opponents	Result	Scorers
16 Nov	A	Rosslyn Park	22-4	T: Ashurst, Heslop, Morris C: Strett (2) PG: Strett (2)
23 Nov	H	Saracens	23-0	T: Taberner, Hynes, Kimmins C: Strett PG: Strett (3)
7 Dec	A	London Irish	21-7	T: Morris (2), Heslop, Fielden C: Strett PG: Strett
14 Dec	H	Bath	10-9	T: Heslop PG: Strett DG: Strett
21 Dec	A	Northampton	3-12	PG: Strett
11 Jan	H	Bristol	23-9	T: Halsall, Morris, Manley C: Strett PG: Strett (2) DG: Strett
29 Jan	H	Leicester	21-9	T: Heslop (2), Halsall PG: Strett (3)
14 Mar	A	Rugby	21-7	T: Morris, Heslop, Halsall PG: Strett (3)
28 Mar	H	Gloucester	18-12	PG: Strett (6)
11 Apr	A	Wasps	12-13	T: Morris C: Strett PG: Strett (2)
20 Apr	A	Harlequins	10-7	T: Taberner PG: Strett (2)
25 Apr	H	Nottingham	20-6	T: Strett, Kimmins, Morris, pen try C: Strett (2)

Plymouth Albion

Year of formation 1876
Ground Beacon Park, Plymouth   Tel: Plymouth (0752) 772924

The Gloucester forwards impede Orrell's Bob Kimmins in the Pilkington Cup quarter-final.

Colours Cherry, white and green
Most capped player E Stanbury (England) 16 caps
Captain 1991-92 I Gregory
Courage League Div 2 12th **Pilkington Cup** Lost 0-21 to Clifton (2nd round)

League Record 1991-92

Date	Venue	Opponents	Result	Scorers
16 Nov	H	Liverpool SH	25-10	*T:* Slade, Oman, Kench *C:* Slade (2) *PG:* Slade (3)
23 Nov	A	W Hartlepool	4-21	*T:* Greenland
14 Dec	H	Bedford	24-9	*T:* Courtenay *C:* Slade *PG:* Slade (6)
21 Dec	A	Moseley	10-15	*T:* Vallance, Russell *C:* Slade
4 Jan	H	Sale	10-15	*T:* Russell *PG:* Mayne (2)
11 Jan	A	Waterloo	3-12	*PG:* Slade
29 Feb	A	Blackheath	20-16	*T:* Verner, Armstrong, Gregory *C:* Slade *PG:* Slade (2)
14 Mar	H	Coventry	10-13	*T:* Courtenay, Oman *C:* Slade
28 Mar	A	Newcastle Gos	21-54	*T:* Slade *C:* Rawlings *PG:* Rawlings (3), Slade (2)
11 Apr	H	Morley	10-12	*T:* Verner *PG:* Rawlings (2)
18 Apr	H	London Scottish	9-10	*PG:* Rawlings (3)
25 Apr	A	Wakefield	7-22	*T:* Mayne *PG:* Rawlings

Rosslyn Park

Year of formation 1879
Ground Priory Lane, Roehampton, London SW15   Tel: 081-876 1879
Colours Red and white
Most capped player A G Ripley (England) 24 caps
Captain 1991-92 R H Q B Moon
Courage League Div 1 13th *relegated* **Pilkington Cup** Lost 12-34 to Harlequins (quarter-final)

League Record 1991-92

Date	Venue	Opponents	Result	Scorers
16 Nov	H	Orrell	4-22	*T:* Hunter
23 Nov	A	Bristol	4-22	*T:* Thomas
7 Dec	H	Harlequins	12-24	*T:* Barnett, Roblin, Thomas
21 Dec	H	Rugby	7-15	*T:* McGauley *PG:* Graves
4 Jan	A	Gloucester	9-12	*PG:* Graves *DG:* Roblin (2)
11 Jan	H	Wasps	7-15	*T:* Wyles *PG:* Graves
14 Mar	H	Saracens	6-10	*PG:* Graves (2)
21 Mar	A	Leicester	16-51	*T:* Whiting, Wyles, Moon *C:* Holder (2)
28 Mar	A	London Irish	12-12	*PG:* Graves (4)
4 Apr	A	Nottingham	9-34	*PG:* Graves (3)
11 Apr	H	Bath	13-21	*T:* Griffiths, Mantel *C:* Graves *PG:* Graves
25 Apr	A	Northampton	12-20	*PG:* Graves (4)

Rugby

Year of formation 1873
Ground Webb Ellis Road (off Bilton Road), Rugby   Tel: Rugby (0788) 542252
Colours Orange, black and white
Most capped player S Brain (England) 13 caps
Captain 1991-92 S Brain
Courage League Div 1 11th **Pilkington Cup** Lost 3-23 to Gloucester (3rd round)

League Record 1991-92

Date	Venue	Opponents	Result	Scorers
16 Nov	H	Gloucester	16-19	*T:* Saunders, Bowman *C:* Mapletoft *PG:* Pell (2)
7 Dec	A	Wasps	10-17	*T:* Bishop *PG:* Mapletoft (2)
21 Dec	A	Rosslyn Park	15-7	*T:* Cox *C:* Mapletoft *PG:* Mapletoft (3)
4 Jan	H	Saracens	6-22	*PG:* Mapletoft (2)
11 Jan	A	London Irish	6-6	*PG:* Mapletoft (2)
22 Feb	H	Nottingham	9-9	*PG:* Mapletoft (3)
29 Feb	A	Northampton	0-29	
14 Mar	H	Orrell	7-21	*T:* Ellis *PG:* Mapletoft
21 Mar	H	Bath	0-32	
28 Mar	A	Bristol	4-48	*T:* Bishop
11 Apr	H	Harlequins	29-20	*T:* Mapletoft, Saunders, Charles, pen try *C:* Mapletoft (2) *PG:* Mapletoft (2) *DG:* Mapletoft
25 Apr	A	Leicester	22-22	*T:* Quantrill *PG:* Hensley (6)

Sale

Year of formation 1861
Ground Heywood Road, Brooklands, Sale, Cheshire   Tel: Manchester (061) 973 6348
Colours Blue and white
Most capped player F E Cotton (England) 31 caps
Captain 1991-92 G Parker
Courage League Div 2 8th **Pilkington Cup** Lost 0-36 to Orrell (4th round)

League Record 1991-92

Date	Venue	Opponents	Result	Scorers
16 Nov	H	Newcastle Gos	19-15	*T:* Young, Taylor *C:* Booth *PG:* Booth (2) *DG:* Jee
23 Nov	A	Morley	13-12	*T:* Young *PG:* Booth (3)
7 Dec	H	Wakefield	37-3	*T:* Mallinder (2), Alexander, Williams, Macfarlane, Kenrick *C:* Alexander (5) *DG:* Alexander
14 Dec	A	Liverpool SH	38-11	*T:* Burnhill (2), Mallinder (2), Powell (2), Young, Whitcombe *C:* Alexander (3)
21 Dec	H	W Hartlepool	13-15	*T:* Alexander *PG:* Alexander (3)
4 Jan	A	Plymouth Alb	15-10	*T:* Burnhill *C:* Alexander *PG:* Alexander (3)
11 Jan	H	Bedford	16-6	*T:* Mallinder, Burnhill *C:* Alexander *PG:* Alexander, Booth

Saracens' Fijian forward, Sam Domoni, on the receiving end of a Nigel Redman tackle in their last League match of the season at Bath.

14 Mar	H	Waterloo	3-17	*PG:* Alexander
28 Mar	A	London Scottish	13-43	*T:* Raducanu *PG:* Alexander (3)
4 Apr	A	Moseley	15-47	*PG:* Alexander (5)
11 Apr	H	Blackheath	10-14	*T:* Harper *PG:* Harrison (2)
25 Apr	A	Coventry	12-19	*PG:* Jee (4)

Saracens

Year of formation 1876
Ground Bramley Sports Ground, Green Road, Southgate, London N14
Tel: 081-449 3770
Colours Black with red star and crescent
Most capped player V S Harding (England) 6 caps
Captain 1991-92 J Buckton
Courage League Div 1 5th **Pilkington Cup** Lost 6-13 to Bristol (4th round)

League Record 1991-92

Date	Venue	Opponents	Result	Scorers
16 Nov	H	Northampton	9-14	*T:* Crawley *C:* Tunningley *PG:* Tunningley
23 Nov	A	Orrell	0-23	
7 Dec	H	Bristol	13-4	*T:* Tarbuck *PG:* Rudling (2) *DG:* Rudling
21 Dec	H	Leicester	9-20	*T:* Davies *C:* Rudling *PG:* Rudling
4 Jan	A	Rugby	22-6	*T:* Butler (2) *C:* Rudling *PG:* Rudling (4)
11 Jan	H	Gloucester	12-12	*T:* Gregory *C:* Rudling *PG:* Rudling (2)
22 Feb	A	Wasps	12-6	*PG:* Lee (2) *DG:* Lee (2)
29 Feb	H	Nottingham	13-12	*T:* Gregory *PG:* Rudling (3)
14 Mar	A	Rosslyn Park	10-6	*T:* Reed *PG:* Rudling *DG:* Rudling
21 Mar	A	Harlequins	37-21	*T:* Crawley, Gregory, Buckton, Cassell, Rudling *C:* Rudling (4) *PG:* Rudling (3)
11 Apr	H	London Irish	27-9	*T:* Davies (2), Gregory, Choules *C:* Rudling *PG:* Rudling *DG:* Rudling (2)
25 Apr	A	Bath	12-32	*T:* Buckton *C:* Rudling *PG:* Rudling (2)

Wakefield

Year of formation 1901
Ground Pinderfields Road, College Grove, Wakefield   Tel: Wakefield (0924) 372038
Colours Black and gold hoops
Most capped player M Harrison (England) 15 caps
Captain 1991-92 M Harrison
Courage League Div 2 5th **Pilkington Cup** Lost 20-21 to Tynedale (2nd round)

League Record 1991-92

Date	Venue	Opponents	Result	Scorers
16 Nov	A	Bedford	25-6	*T:* Harrison, Scully, Stewart *C:* Rawnsley (2) *PG:* Rawnsley (3)

377

23 Nov	H	Moseley	14-9	T: Maynard, Sleightholme, Scully C: Rawnsley
7 Dec	A	Sale	3-37	PG: Rawnsley
14 Dec	H	Waterloo	24-18	T: Sleightholme (2), Harrison, Scully, Wood C: Rawnsley (2)
21 Dec	A	London Scottish	4-31	T: Harrison
4 Jan	H	Blackheath	20-6	T: Sleightholme (3) C: Atkinson PG: Atkinson (2)
11 Jan	A	Coventry	20-21	T: Harrison (2), Sleightholme, Atkinson C: Atkinson (2)
29 Feb	A	Morley	13-9	T: Barley, Rawnsley C: Rawnsley PG: Rawnsley
28 Mar	H	Liverpool SH	34-35	T: Liley, Harrison, Maynard, Cruise C: Liley (3) PG: Liley (4)
11 Apr	A	W Hartlepool	0-7	
25 Apr	H	Plymouth Alb	22-7	T: Sleightholme, Townend, Griffiths C: Liley (2) PG: Liley (2)

Wasps

Year of formation 1867
Ground Repton Avenue (off Rugby Road), Sudbury, Middlesex   Tel: 081-902 4220
Colours Black with gold wasp on left breast
Most capped player C R Andrew (England) 48 caps
Captain 1991-92 M Rigby
Courage League Div 1 7th **Pilkington Cup** Lost 9-20 to Harlequins (4th round)

League Record 1991-92

Date	Venue	Opponents	Result	Scorers
16 Nov	H	Harlequins	20-6	T: Davies, Pilgrim, Dunstan, Kennell C: Pilgrim (2)
23 Nov	A	Leicester	12-31	PG: Pilgrim (4)
7 Dec	H	Rugby	17-10	T: Rigby, Harris, Pilgrim C: Pilgrim PG: Pilgrim
4 Jan	H	Nottingham	11-7	T: Allan, Clough PG: Pilgrim
11 Jan	A	Rosslyn Park	15-7	PG: Pilgrim (5)
22 Feb	H	Saracens	6-12	PG: Davies (2)
29 Feb	A	London Irish	13-18	T: D Hopley PG: Pilgrim (3)
14 Mar	H	Bath	12-24	T: Childs C: Pilgrim PG: Pilgrim (2)
21 Mar	A	Northampton	15-28	T: D Hopley C: Pilgrim PG: Pilgrim (2) DG: Davies
11 Apr	H	Orrell	13-12	T: Oti PG: Pilgrim (2) DG: Davies
18 Apr	A	Gloucester	10-15	T: Oti PG: Pilgrim (2)
25 Apr	A	Bristol	33-10	T: Oti (3), Ryan C: Pilgrim PG: Pilgrim (5)

Waterloo

Year of formation 1882
Ground St Anthony's Road, Blundellsands, Liverpool   Tel: Liverpool (051) 924 4552
Colours Green, red and white

Damian Hopley scores a try for Wasps at Franklins Gardens in spite of the efforts of Northampton's Tebbutt and McNaughton.

Most capped player H G Periton (England) 21 caps
Captain 1991-92 N Allott
Courage League Div 2 3rd **Pilkington Cup** Lost 12-20 to Leicester (4th round)

League Record 1991-92

Date	Venue	Opponents	Result	Scorers
16 Nov	H	Coventry	10-6	*T:* Meredith *PG:* Cropper (2)
23 Nov	A	Newcastle Gos	6-37	*PG:* Ashcroft, Cropper
7 Dec	H	Morley	16-9	*T:* Bracegirdle, Meredith *C:* Cropper *PG:* Cropper (2)
14 Dec	A	Wakefield	18-24	*T:* Northey, Peters *C:* Cropper (2) *PG:* Cropper (2)
21 Dec	H	Liverpool SH	40-12	*T:* Bracegirdle (2), Beckett, Saverimutto, Jenkins *C:* Aitchison (4) *PG:* Aitchison (4)
4 Jan	A	W Hartlepool	9-27	*T:* Jenkins *C:* Aitchison *PG:* Aitchison
11 Jan	H	Plymouth Alb	12-3	*T:* Walmsley *C:* Aitchison *PG:* Aitchison (2)
29 Feb	H	Moseley	18-17	*T:* pen try *C:* Aitchison *PG:* Aitchison (4)
14 Mar	A	Sale	17-3	*T:* Jenkins, Meredith *PG:* Aitchison (3)
4 Apr	A	Bedford	4-25	*T:* Saverimutto
11 Apr	H	London Scottish	22-15	*T:* Meredith, Ashcroft *C:* Aitchison *PG:* Aitchison (3) *DG:* Aitchison
25 Apr	A	Blackheath	34-6	*T:* Buckton, Jenkins, Hackett *C:* Aitchison (2) *PG:* Aitchison (6)

West Hartlepool

Year of formation 1881
Ground Brierton Lane, Hartlepool   Tel: Hartlepool (0429) 272640
Colours Red, green and white hoops
Most capped player C D Aarvold (England) 16 caps
Captain 1991-92 J Stabler
Courage League Div 2 2nd *promoted* **Pilkington Cup** Lost 16-18 to Waterloo (3rd round)

League Record 1991-92

Date	Venue	Opponents	Result	Scorers
23 Nov	H	Plymouth Alb	21-4	*T:* Lee, Wrigley *C:* Stabler (2) *PG:* Stabler (3)
7 Dec	A	Bedford	30-6	*T:* Brown (2), Hodder, Pook *C:* Stabler (4) *PG:* Stabler (2)
14 Dec	H	Moseley	27-4	*T:* Wrigley (3), Brown, S Mitchell *C:* Stabler (2) *PG:* Stabler
21 Dec	A	Sale	15-13	*PG:* Stabler (5)
4 Jan	H	Waterloo	27-9	*T:* Cooke (2), Evans (2), pen try *C:* Stabler (2) *PG:* Stabler
11 Jan	A	London Scottish	6-7	*PG:* Stabler (2)
8 Feb	H	Blackheath	21-8	*T:* Oliphant, Evans, Pook, Whitelock *C:* Lee *PG:* Stabler
29 Feb	A	Coventry	24-18	*T:* A Mitchell, Brown *C:* Stabler (2) *PG:* Stabler (4)

14 Mar	H	Newcastle Gos	13-7	*T:* Hodder *PG:* Stabler (3)
11 Apr	H	Wakefield	7-0	*T:* Mitchell *PG:* Stabler
25 Apr	A	Liverpool SH	32-0	*T:* Wrigley (2), Brown, pen try, Stabler *C:* Stabler (3) *PG:* Stabler (2)
27 Apr	A	Morley	21-13	*T:* Stabler, Dixon, Evans, Wrigley *C:* Stabler *PG:* Stabler

SCOTLAND

Ayr

Year of formation 1897
Ground Millbrae, Alloway, Ayr   Tel: Alloway (0292) 41944
Colours Pink and black
Most capped player S Munro (Scotland) 10 caps
Captain 1991-92 A D Brown
1st XV 1991-92 P31 W16 D1 L14 F538 A531
McEwan's/SRU Div 2 joint 4th

League Record 1991-92

Date	Venue	Opponents	Result	Scorers
9 Nov	H	Preston Lodge	27-12	*T:* Gilmour, Stark (4) *C:* Courtney (2) *PG:* Courtney
16 Nov	A	Kilmarnock	4-13	*T:* Gilmour
23 Nov	A	Corstorphine	33-6	*T:* D W Brown (3), Fairgrieve, McCallum, Stark *C:* Courtney (3) *PG:* Courtney
30 Nov	H	Musselburgh	29-4	*T:* Edgar, Gilmour, Gordon McMillan, Ramage, Stark *C:* Courtney (3) *PG:* Courtney
7 Dec	A	Royal High	15-12	*T:* George McMillan, Stark (2) *PG:* Courtney
14 Dec	H	Glasgow Acads	37-24	*T:* D W Brown, Gilmour (2), Gordon McMillan (2), Stark *C:* Courtney (2) *PG:* Courtney (2) *DG:* Courtney
21 Dec	H	Wigtownshire	12-6	*T:* Gilmour, McHarg, Manning
11 Jan	A	Dundee HSFP	9-25	*T:* Stark *C:* George McMillan *PG:* George McMillan
25 Jan	H	Peebles	19-3	*T:* Gordon McMillan, Stark (2) *C:* A D Brown, Courtney *PG:* Courtney
8 Feb	A	Dunfermline	10-22	*T:* Gray *PG:* Bottomley (2)
29 Feb	H	Kirkcaldy	9-4	*T:* Gilmour *C:* Courtney *PG:* Courtney
14 Mar	A	Edinburgh Wands	6-16	*PG:* Courtney (2)
28 Mar	H	Kelso	15-23	*T:* D W Brown, Gilmour *C:* Hay (2) *PG:* Hay

Boroughmuir

Year of formation 1919 (Boroughmuir FP until 1974)
Ground Meggetland, Colinton Road, Edinburgh EH14 1AS   Tel: 031-443 7571
Colours Navy blue and emerald green
Most capped player B H Hay (Scotland) 23 caps
Captain 1991-92 J D Price
1st XV 1991-92 P31 W23 D2 L6 F745 A380
McEwan's/SRU Div 1 4th

League Record 1991-92

Date	Venue	Opponents	Result	Scorers
9 Nov	H	Edinburgh Acads	15-21	*T:* Lineen (2) *C:* Walker (2) *PG:* Walker
16 Nov	A	Watsonians	12-23	*PG:* Walker (4)

23 Nov	H	Currie	27-19	*T:* Reid (3), Drummond, penalty try *C:* Walker (2) *PG:* Walker
30 Nov	A	West of Scotland	22-3	*T:* Hall, Maclean, Reid, Walker *PG:* Maclean (2)
14 Dec	H	Jedforest	10-21	*T:* Reid *PG:* Walker (2)
11 Jan	A	Stewart's-Melville FP	10-12	*T:* Macrae, Reid *C:* Maclean
25 Jan	H	Hawick	15-15	*T:* Hall, Reid *C:* Walker (2) *PG:* Walker
8 Feb	A	Stirling County	20-9	*T:* Macrae, Price, Reid, Walker *C:* Walker (2)
22 Feb	H	Melrose	23-10	*T:* Drummond, Elliot, Seagar, Smith, Walker *PG:* Walker
29 Feb	H	Glasgow H/K'side	21-10	*T:* Hall, Smith, Walker *PG:* Walker (3)
14 Mar	A	Heriot's FP	17-6	*T:* Dryburgh, Hall, Smith *C:* Walker *PG:* Walker
7 Apr	H	Gala	18-30	*T:* Hall, Reid, Smith *PG:* Walker (2)

Corstorphine

Year of formation Reformed in 1950
Ground Union Park, Carrick Knowe Parkway, Corstorphine, Edinburgh
Tel: 031-334 8063
Colours Navy blue and scarlet quarters
Captain 1991-92 G Donaldson
1st XV 1991-92 P28 W12 D0 L16 F393 A593
McEwan's/SRU Div 2 joint 13th *relegated*

League Record 1991-92

Date	Venue	Opponents	Result	Scorers
9 Nov	H	Glasgow Acads	16-9	*T:* Hutton, Inglis, Reece *C:* Liddle (2)
16 Nov	A	Dunfermline	12-21	*T:* Johnston, Inglis *C:* Ferguson (2)
23 Nov	A	Ayr	6-33	*T:* Mitchell *C:* Inglis
30 Nov	A	Dundee HSFP	7-54	*T:* Swanson *DG:* Oliver
7 Dec	H	Wigtownshire	4-25	*T:* S I Pilkington
14 Dec	A	Musselburgh	3-49	*PG:* Ferguson
21 Dec	A	Royal High	10-6	*T:* Oliver *PG:* Ferguson (2)
25 Jan	A	Preston Lodge	4-14	*T:* Inglis
1 Feb	H	Kilmarnock	16-6	*T:* Inglis, Oliver *C:* Liddle *PG:* Liddle (2)
8 Feb	H	Edinburgh Wands	3-25	*PG:* Liddle
22 Feb	A	Kirkcaldy	4-24	*T:* Maclean
29 Feb	H	Kelso	4-21	*T:* Inglis
14 Mar	A	Peebles	10-17	*T:* Swanson *PG:* Gillespie (2)

Currie

Year of formation 1970
Ground Malleny Park, Balerno, Edinburgh Tel: 031-449 2492
Colours Amber and black
Captain 1991-92 A Donaldson
1st XV 1991-92 P30 W22 D0 L8 F829 A431
McEwan's/SRU Div 1 joint 5th

League Record 1991-92

Date	Venue	Opponents	Result	Scorers
9 Nov	A	Stirling County	6-12	PG: Donaldson DG: Donaldson
16 Nov	H	West of Scotland	42-18	T: Forrester (3), Beggy (2), Laugerson C: Donaldson (6) PG: Donaldson (2)
23 Nov	A	Boroughmuir	19-27	T: Beggy, Nolan C: Donaldson PG: Donaldson (3)
30 Nov	H	Glasgow H/K'side	25-23	T: Forrester, Nolan C: Donaldson PG: Donaldson (3) DG: Donaldson (2)
7 Dec	A	Heriot's FP	14-16	T: Nolan, Tonkin PG: Donaldson DG: Donaldson
14 Dec	A	Melrose	7-16	T: Nolan DG: Donaldson
11 Jan	A	Jedforest	7-18	T: Forrester PG: Donaldson
25 Jan	H	Gala	28-25	T: Beggy, Farrer, Nolan, Scott C: Donaldson (3) PG: Donaldson (2)
8 Feb	A	Stewart's-Melville FP	35-18	T: Dickson, Forrester, Nolan (2) C: Donaldson (2) PG: Donaldson (5)
22 Feb	H	Hawick	18-6	T: Donaldson, Farrer C: Donaldson (2) PG: Donaldson (2)
29 Feb	H	Edinburgh Acads	0-18	
14 Mar	A	Watsonians	4-30	T: Beggy
28 Mar	H	Selkirk	30-3	T: Beggy, Farrer (2), Forrester C: Donaldson (4) PG: Donaldson (2)

Dundee High School FP

Year of formation 1880
Ground Mayfield, Arbroath Road, Dundee   Tel: Dundee (0382) 453517 (ground) and 451045 (clubhouse)
Colours Blue and red
Most capped player D G Leslie (Scotland) 32 caps
Captain 1991-92 A Keys
1st XV 1991-92 P31 W23 D1 L7 F1029 A352
McEwan's/SRU Div 2 2nd *promoted*

League Record 1991-92

Date	Venue	Opponents	Result	Scorers
9 Nov	H	Kelso	9-18	PG: J R Newton (3)
16 Nov	A	Wigtownshire	25-4	T: Nicol (2), C R H Newton C: J R Newton (2) PG: J R Newton (3)
23 Nov	H	Dunfermline	56-3	T: Nicol (2), Batchelor, Cairney, Milne, C R H Newton, J R Newton, Rouse C: J R Newton (6) PG: J R Newton (3), Rouse
30 Nov	H	Corstorphine	54-7	T: Cousin, Keys, Milne, C R H Newton, J R Newton, Nicol (2), Rouse (2), Turnbull C: J R Newton (7)
14 Dec	H	Edinburgh Wands	41-19	T: Batchelor, Milne, J R Newton, Nicol (4), Tully C: J R Newton (2), Rouse PG: J R Newton
11 Jan	H	Ayr	25-9	T: Cousin, J R Newton, Nicol C: J R Newton (2) PG: J R Newton (2) DG: J R Newton
25 Jan	A	Musselburgh	23-10	T: Nicol (2), Turnbull C: J R Newton DG: J R Newton (3)

8 Feb	H	Royal High	56-12	*T:* Astley-Jones (2), Batchelor, Cousin, Milne (2), C R H Newton (2), J R Newton, Nicol *C:* J R Newton (5) *PG:* J R Newton (2)
29 Feb	H	Preston Lodge	56-0	*T:* Batchelor, Cousin, Hamilton, C R H Newton (2), J R Newton, Nicol (2), Rouse *C:* J R Newton (7) *PG:* J R Newton (2)
14 Mar	A	Glasgow Acads	17-0	*T:* Cousin, Herrington, Nicol *C:* J R Newton *DG:* J R Newton
28 Mar	A	Peebles	15-4	*T:* Milne *C:* J R Newton *PG:* J R Newton (3)

Dunfermline

Year of formation 1904
Ground McKane Park, Dunfermline, Fife   Tel: Dunfermline (0383) 721279
Colours Royal blue and white
Most capped player J T Greenwood (Scotland) 20 caps
Captain 1991-92 M W Scott
1st XV 1991-92 P28 W7 D1 L20 F333 A571
McEwan's/SRU Div 2 10th

League Record 1991-92

Date	*Venue*	*Opponents*	*Result*	*Scorers*
9 Nov	A	Wigtownshire	16-36	*T:* Drummond, Hannah *C:* Cross *PG:* Cross (2)
16 Nov	H	Corstorphine	21-12	*T:* McGrath, Cross *C:* Cross (2) *PG:* Cross (3)
23 Nov	A	Dundee HSFP	3-56	*PG:* Cross
30 Nov	H	Kelso	9-13	*T:* Smith *C:* Cross *PG:* Cross
7 Dec	A	Glasgow Acads	7-20	*T:* Mormon *PG:* Cross
14 Dec	H	Kilmarnock	10-12	*T:* Cross, Watson *C:* Dalton
21 Dec	A	Preston Lodge	12-23	*T:* McDonald *C:* Dalton *PG:* Dalton (2)
11 Jan	H	Edinburgh Wands	9-7	*PG:* Dalton (3)
25 Jan	A	Kirkcaldy	6-6	*PG:* Dalton (2)
8 Feb	H	Ayr	22-10	*T:* Mormon, Watson *C:* Dalton *PG:* Dalton (3) *DG:* Dalton
22 Feb	A	Musselburgh	13-23	*T:* Bryce, Timms *C:* Dalton *PG:* Dalton
29 Feb	H	Peebles	3-10	*PG:* Dalton
14 Mar	H	Royal High	10-3	*T:* McDonald *PG:* Dalton (2)

Edinburgh Academicals

Year of formation 1857
Ground Raeburn Place, Edinburgh   Tel: 031-332 1070
Colours Blue and white stripes
Most capped player W I D Elliot (Scotland) 29 caps
Captain 1991-92 J Allan
1st XV 1991-92 P31 W19 D1 L11 F690 A517
McEwan's/SRU Div 1 2nd

League Record 1991-92

Date	Venue	Opponents	Result	Scorers
9 Nov	A	Boroughmuir	21-15	*T:* Hay-Smith, Moore, Ross *PG:* Hay-Smith (2) *DG:* Shepherd
16 Nov	H	Glasgow H/K'side	21-6	*T:* Allan, Burns *C:* Burns, Shepherd *PG:* Shepherd (2) *DG:* Shepherd
23 Nov	A	Heriot's FP	13-18	*T:* McLean *PG:* Shepherd (2) *DG:* Shepherd
30 Nov	A	Stewart's-Melville FP	43-10	*T:* Burns, Jackson (2), McIvor, Patterson (2), Sole *C:* Hay-Smith (3) *PG:* Hay-Smith (2) *DG:* Hay-Smith
7 Dec	H	Watsonians	33-7	*T:* Allan, Hay-Smith, Moore, Patterson (2), Porter, *C:* Hay-Smith (3) *PG:* Hay-Smith
14 Dec	A	Hawick	7-9	*T:* Porter *PG:* Hay-Smith
21 Dec	H	Stirling County	18-3	*T:* Moore, Patterson, Wainwright *PG:* Hay-Smith (2)
11 Jan	A	Melrose	15-15	*T:* Moore *C:* Shepherd *PG:* Shepherd (2) *DG:* Shepherd
25 Jan	H	Selkirk	16-13	*T:* McIvor, Moore *C:* Burns *PG:* Hay-Smith *DG:* Hay-Smith
8 Feb	A	Jedforest	22-16	*T:* Adam, Burns, Wainwright *C:* Shepherd (2) *PG:* Shepherd (2)
22 Feb	H	Gala	12-9	*T:* Sole *C:* Shepherd *PG:* Shepherd (2)
29 Feb	A	Currie	18-0	*T:* Patterson, Wainwright *C:* Shepherd (2) *PG:* Shepherd (2)
14 Mar	H	West of Scotland	27-9	*T:* Patterson (2) *C:* Shepherd (2) *PG:* Shepherd (5)

Edinburgh Wanderers

Year of formation 1868
Ground Murrayfield, Edinburgh   Tel: 031-337 2196
Colours Red and black
Most capped player A R Smith (Scotland) 33 caps
Captain 1991-92 J M Thomson
1st XV 1991-92   P27   W11   D0   L16   F367   A597
McEwan's/SRU Div 2 joint 8th

League Record 1991-92

Date	Venue	Opponents	Result	Scorers
9 Nov	A	Musselburgh	0-32	
16 Nov	H	Royal High	27-3	*T:* K J W Hamilton, Reid *C:* Pulfrey (2) *PG:* Pulfrey (3) *DG:* B A Craig (2)
23 Nov	A	Kirkcaldy	15-12	*T:* K R Gillies, Pulfrey, Reid *PG:* Pulfrey
30 Nov	A	Wigtownshire	3-17	*PG:* Pulfrey
7 Dec	H	Preston Lodge	15-18	*PG:* Pulfrey (3) *DG:* B A Craig (2)
14 Dec	A	Dundee HSFP	19-41	*T:* Brown (2) *C:* B A Craig *PG:* B A Craig (3)
21 Dec	H	Peebles	3-26	*PG:* Reid
11 Jan	A	Dunfermline	7-9	*T:* M D Smith *PG:* B A Craig
25 Jan	H	Kelso	14-47	*T:* K J W Hamilton, Rowley (2) *C:* B A Craig
8 Feb	A	Corstorphine	25-3	*T:* E S Gillies, G W M Hamilton, M W M Horne *C:* Pulfrey (2) *PG:* B A Craig (3)
22 Feb	H	Glasgow Acads	12-0	*T:* E S Gillies, K R Gillies (2)
29 Feb	A	Kilmarnock	6-21	*PG:* Pulfrey (2)
14 Mar	H	Ayr	16-6	*T:* B A Craig, Granger, K J W Hamilton *C:* B A Craig (2)

Gala

Year of formation 1875
Ground Netherdale, Galashiels   Tel: Galashiels (0896) 3811
Colours Maroon
Most capped player P C Brown (Scotland) 27 caps
Captain 1991-92 I Corcoran
1st XV 1991-92   P31   W19   D0   L12   F763   A469
McEwan's/SRU Div 1 joint 5th

League Record 1991-92

Date	Venue	Opponents	Result	Scorers
9 Nov	A	Jedforest	18-10	*T:* Amos, Liddle *C:* M Dods, P W Dods *PG:* M Dods, P W Dods
16 Nov	H	Heriot's FP	27-8	*T:* Isaac, Liddle, penalty try *C:* P W Dods (3) *PG:* P W Dods (3)
23 Nov	A	Selkirk	12-11	*T:* Swan *C:* P W Dods *PG:* P W Dods (2)
30 Nov	H	Stirling County	31-9	*T:* Boland, Isaac, Maitland (2) *C:* P W Dods (3) *PG:* P W Dods (3)
7 Dec	H	Melrose	16-28	*T:* P W Dods, Townsend *C:* P W Dods *PG:* P W Dods (2)
14 Dec	A	West of Scotland	17-18	*T:* M Dods, Gray, Liddle *C:* P W Dods *PG:* P W Dods
11 Jan	H	Glasgow H/K'side	20-23	*T:* M Dods, Learmouth, Moncreiff *C:* P W Dods *PG:* P W Dods (2)
25 Jan	A	Currie	25-28	*T:* Amos, Boland, M Dods, Maitland *C:* P W Dods (3) *PG:* P W Dods
8 Feb	H	Watsonians	16-20	*T:* P W Dods *PG:* P W Dods (3) *DG:* Townsend
22 Feb	A	Edinburgh Acads	9-12	*T:* Turnbull *C:* P W Dods *PG:* P W Dods
29 Feb	A	Stewart's-Melville FP	13-8	*T:* P W Dods, Moncrieff *C:* P W Dods *PG:* P W Dods
14 Mar	H	Hawick	3-9	*PG:* M Dods
7 Apr	A	Boroughmuir	30-18	*T:* Laing, Moncrieff, Temple, Turnbull, Waddell *C:* M Dods (5)

Glasgow Academicals

Year of formation 1867
Ground New Anniesland, Helensburgh Drive, Glasgow   Tel: 041-959 1323
Colours Navy blue and white
Most capped player W M Simmers (Scotland) 28 caps
Captain 1991-92 A G Ker
1st XV 1991-92   P29   W12   D0   L17   F460   A570
McEwan's/SRU Div 2 joint 8th

League Record 1991-92

Date	Venue	Opponents	Result	Scorers
9 Nov	A	Corstorphine	9-16	*DG:* C G MacGregor (3)
16 Nov	H	Kirkcaldy	31-6	*T:* J F Mason, G T MacGregor, Mackay, Peoples *C:* C G MacGregor (3) *DG:* C G MacGregor (3)

23 Nov	A	Kelso	9-22	*T:* Richmond *C:* Simmers *DG:* G T MacGregor
30 Nov	H	Peebles	14-21	*T:* Bremner, J F Mason *PG:* Simmers (2)
7 Dec	H	Dunfermline	20-7	*T:* A G Ker, J F Mason, Smith *C:* C G MacGregor *PG:* C G MacGregor (2)
14 Dec	A	Ayr	24-37	*T:* Mackay (2), J F Mason, Peoples *C:* C G MacGregor *PG:* C G MacGregor *DG:* C G MacGregor
11 Jan	H	Royal High	15-6	*T:* A G Ker, Thomson *C:* C G MacGregor (2) *PG:* C G MacGregor
25 Jan	A	Kilmarnock	22-11	*T:* Mackay (2), J F Mason *C:* C G MacGregor (2) *PG:* C G MacGregor (2)
1 Feb	A	Musselburgh	24-20	*T:* Lightbody (2), J F Mason *C:* C G MacGregor (3) *PG:* C G MacGregor (2)
8 Feb	H	Preston Lodge	13-17	*T:* Mackay *PG:* C G MacGregor (2) *DG:* C G MacGregor
22 Feb	A	Edinburgh Wands	0-12	
29 Feb	A	Wigtownshire	9-20	*T:* Afuakwah *C:* A G Ker *PG:* Smith
14 Mar	H	Dundee HSFP	0-17	

Glasgow High/Kelvinside

Year of formation 1982 (on amalgamation of Glasgow High RFC and Kelvinside Academicals)
Ground Old Anniesland, 637 Crow Road, Glasgow   Tel: 041-959 1154
Colours Chocolate and gold
Most capped player None (before amalgamation J M Bannerman (Glasgow HSFP) was capped 37 times and D M White (Kelvinside Academicals) 4 times – both for Scotland)
Captain 1991-92 F D Wallace
1st XV 1991-92 P35 W18 D4 L12 Ab1 F819 A542
McEwan's/SRU Div 1 joint 11th

League Record 1991-92

Date	*Venue*	*Opponents*	*Result*	*Scorers*
9 Nov	H	Heriot's FP	19-19	*T:* M I Wallace *PG:* Breckenridge (4) *DG:* Breckenridge
16 Nov	A	Edinburgh Acads	6-21	*PG:* Breckenridge (2)
23 Nov	H	Watsonians	6-6	*PG:* Little (2)
30 Nov	A	Currie	23-25	*T:* Agnew (3) *C:* Breckenridge *PG:* Breckenridge (3)
7 Dec	H	West of Scotland	32-19	*T:* Agnew (2), Bassi, Hawkes *C:* Breckenridge (2) *PG:* Breckenridge (3) *DG:* Breckenridge
14 Dec	A	Selkirk	10-34	*T:* Breckenridge, Murphy *C:* Breckenridge
21 Dec	H	Jedforest	10-16	*T:* Agnew *PG:* Breckenridge (2)
11 Jan	A	Gala	23-20	*T:* McClymont, Ritchie *PG:* Breckenridge (4) *DG:* Breckenridge
25 Jan	H	Stewart's-Melville FP	18-7	*T:* Agnew, Umaga *C:* Breckenridge (2) *PG:* Breckenridge *DG:* Breckenridge
8 Feb	A	Hawick	20-15	*T:* Michie (2) *PG:* Breckenridge (2) *DG:* Breckenridge (2)
29 Feb	A	Boroughmuir	10-21	*T:* Agnew *PG:* Agnew (2)
14 Mar	A	Melrose	16-27	*T:* Agnew, Hawkes, Little *C:* Breckenridge (2)
28 Mar	H	Stirling County	13-15	*T:* McClymont *PG:* Breckenridge (3)

Hawick

Year of formation 1873
Ground Mansfield Park, Mansfield Road, Hawick, Roxburghshire
Tel: Hawick (0450) 74291
Colours Green
Most capped player J M Renwick (Scotland) 52 caps
Captain 1991-92 G H Oliver
1st XV 1991-92 P34 W15 D2 L17 F694 A628
McEwan's/SRU Div 1 joint 11th

League Record 1991-92

Date	Venue	Opponents	Result	Scorers
9 Nov	H	Selkirk	20-33	*T:* Armstrong, G Renwick, Willison *C:* N A C Bannerman *PG:* D Scott (2)
16 Nov	A	Stewart's-Melville FP	21-4	*T:* Hay, N A C Bannerman, Oliver, Suddon *C:* Oliver *PG:* Oliver
23 Nov	H	Melrose	9-11	*T:* N Scott *C:* G Renwick *PG:* G Renwick
30 Nov	H	Jedforest	13-15	*T:* N A C Bannerman *PG:* Oliver (3)
7 Dec	A	Stirling County	3-14	*PG:* D Scott
14 Dec	H	Edinburgh Acads	9-7	*PG:* D Gray (3)
21 Dec	A	Heriot's FP	14-31	*T:* Hay, Suddon *PG:* D Gray (2)
11 Jan	H	West of Scotland	33-13	*T:* Hay, Tait, Welsh, Willison *C:* Welsh (4) *PG:* Welsh (3)
25 Jan	A	Boroughmuir	15-15	*T:* Turnbull *C:* Welsh *PG:* Welsh (2) *DG:* Welsh
8 Feb	H	Glasgow H/K'side	15-20	*T:* A G Stanger *C:* Welsh *PG:* Welsh (3)
22 Feb	A	Currie	6-18	*PG:* Welsh (2)
29 Feb	H	Watsonians	9-9	*PG:* D Gray *DG:* D Gray, Welsh
14 Mar	A	Gala	9-3	*T:* Tomes *C:* Welsh *PG:* Welsh

Heriot's FP

Year of formation 1890
Ground Goldenacre, Bangholm Terrace, Edinburgh EH3 5QN   Tel: 031-552 5925
Colours Blue and white horizontal stripes
Most capped player A R Irvine (Scotland) 51 caps
Captain 1991-92 I C Glasgow
1st XV 1991-92 P26 W15 D2 L9 F533 A423
McEwan's/SRU Div 1 3rd

League Record 1991-92

Date	Venue	Opponents	Result	Scorers
9 Nov	A	Glasgow H/K'side	19-19	*T:* Glasgow, Hewitt, Stoddart (2) *PG:* Changleng
16 Nov	A	Gala	8-27	*T:* Glasgow, McRobbie
23 Nov	H	Edinburgh Acads	18-13	*T:* McLean *C:* Changleng *PG:* Changleng (3) *DG:* Changleng
30 Nov	A	Watsonians	19-15	*T:* Buchanan-Smith, Stoddart *C:* Changleng *PG:* Changleng (2) *DG:* Glasgow

7 Dec	H	Currie	16-14	*T:* D F Milne, Robertson *C:* Changleng
				PG: Changleng (2)
14 Dec	A	Stewart's-Melville FP	35-10	*T:* Allingham, Buchanan-Smith, Macaulay,
				McRobbie, Robertson, Whitaker *C:* Changleng (4)
				PG: Changleng
21 Dec	H	Hawick	31-14	*T:* Allingham (2), Kenhard, Robertson
				C: Changleng (3) *PG:* Changleng (3)
11 Jan	A	Stirling County	21-12	*T:* Allingham *C:* Changleng *PG:* Changleng (5)
25 Jan	H	Melrose	6-32	*PG:* Changleng (2)
8 Feb	A	Selkirk	9-36	*PG:* Changleng (3)
22 Feb	H	Jedforest	7-3	*T:* Watt *PG:* Changleng
29 Feb	A	West of Scotland	3-6	*PG:* Changleng
14 Mar	H	Boroughmuir	6-17	*PG:* Glasgow (2)

Jedforest

Year of formation 1885
Ground Riverside Park, Jedburgh   Tel: Jedburgh (0835) 62232 and 62855
Colours Royal blue
Most capped player R J Laidlaw (Scotland) 47 caps
Captain 1991-92 G Armstrong
1st XV 1991-92 P30   W15   D1   L14   F553   A433
McEwan's/SRU Div 1 joint 5th

League Record 1991-92

Date	Venue	Opponents	Result	Scorers
9 Nov	H	Gala	10-18	*T:* G Armstrong *PG:* McKechnie (2)
16 Nov	A	Melrose	9-15	*T:* Brian Hughes *C:* McKechnie *DG:* Shiel
23 Nov	H	West of Scotland	6-18	*T:* K Armstrong *C:* McKechnie
30 Nov	A	Hawick	15-13	*T:* G Armstrong *C:* Miller *PG:* Miller (3)
14 Dec	A	Boroughmuir	21-10	*T:* A J Douglas, Hogg, Brian Hughes, Miller
				C: Miller *PG:* Miller
21 Dec	A	Glasgow H/K'side	16-10	*T:* G Armstrong, A J Douglas *C:* Miller
				PG: Miller (2)
11 Jan	H	Currie	18-7	*T:* G Armstrong, Brian Hughes
				C: McKechnie (2) *PG:* McKechnie (2)
25 Jan	A	Watsonians	23-6	*T:* Docherty, J P Douglas, Elder, Hogg,
				C: Hogg (2) *PG:* Hogg
8 Feb	H	Edinburgh Acads	16-22	*T:* Barrie, Yule *C:* Hogg *PG:* Hogg (2)
22 Feb	A	Heriot's FP	3-7	*PG:* Hogg
29 Feb	H	Selkirk	16-10	*T:* Brian Hughes *PG:* Hogg (4)
14 Mar	A	Stirling County	7-15	*T:* Brian Hughes *PG:* Hogg
28 Mar	H	Stewart's-Melville FP	14-22	*T:* Amos, K Armstrong, J P Douglas *C:* Amos

Kelso

Year of formation 1876
Ground Poynder Park, Kelso, Roxburghshire   Tel: Kelso (0573) 224300 and 223773
Colours Black and white
Most capped player J Jeffrey (Scotland) 40 caps
Captain 1991-92 C Millar
1st XV 1991-92 P29   W21   D1   L7   F666   A395
McEwan's/SRU Winners Div 2 *promoted*

League Record 1991-92

Date	Venue	Opponents	Result	Scorers
9 Nov	A	Dundee HSFP	18-9	*PG:* Aitchison (6)
16 Nov	H	Peebles	23-3	*T:* A T Jeffrey, P S Dunkley, Walker *C:* Aitchison *PG:* Aitchison (3)
23 Nov	H	Glasgow Acads	22-9	*T:* Walker (3), K B Dunkley, J Jeffrey *C:* Aitchison
30 Nov	A	Dunfermline	13-9	*T:* Little *PG:* Aitchison *DG:* Wichary (2)
14 Dec	H	Royal High	33-3	*T:* Cassie, J Jeffrey (3), Millar *C:* Aitchison (2) *PG:* Aitchison (3)
21 Dec	A	Kilmarnock	8-4	*T:* J Jeffery, Wichary
28 Dec	H	Musselburgh	34-9	*T:* Aitchison, J Jeffrey, McArthur, Roxburgh (3), penalty try *C:* Aitchison (3)
11 Jan	H	Preston Lodge	32-9	*T:* Bennet, Heseltine (2), Millar, Standish *C:* Aitchison (3) *PG:* Aitchison (2)
25 Jan	A	Edinburgh Wands	47-14	*T:* Bennet (2), Carss, J Jeffrey, Roxburgh (2), J Thomson, penalty try *C:* Aitchison (3) *PG:* Aitchison (3)
8 Feb	H	Kirkcaldy	44-12	*T:* K B Dunkley, P S Dunkley, J Jeffery (2), Roxburgh (2), J Thomson, Wichary *C:* Aitchison (3) *PG:* Aitchison, Heseltine
29 Feb	A	Corstorphine	21-4	*T:* P S Dunkley, J Jeffery, Millar *PG:* Aitchison (3)
14 Mar	H	Wigtownshire	24-16	*T:* Aitchison, Bennet, J Jeffery *PG:* Aitchison (4)
28 Mar	A	Ayr	23-15	*T:* J Jeffrey (2), K Thomson, Walker *C:* Aitchison (2) *PG:* Aitchison

Kilmarnock

Year of formation 1868
Ground Bellsland, Queens Drive, Kilmarnock, Ayrshire   Tel: Kilmarnock (0563) 22314
Colours White with red hoop surmounted by a white Maltese cross
Most capped player W Cuthbertson (Scotland) 22 caps
Captain 1991-92 R S Carswell
1st XV 1991-92   P26   W8   D0   L18   F289   A558
McEwan's/SRU Div 2 11th

League Record 1991-92

Date	Venue	Opponents	Result	Scorers
9 Nov	A	Peebles	3-23	*DG:* A McCall
16 Nov	H	Ayr	13-4	*T:* J Adams, penalty try *C:* A McCall *PG:* A McCall
23 Nov	A	Musselburgh	10-35	*T:* Bark, Carswell *C:* J McCall
30 Nov	H	Royal High	0-12	
7 Dec	A	Kirkcaldy	6-25	*PG:* J McCall (2)
14 Dec	A	Dunfermline	12-10	*T:* Hinshelwood, Muirhead, Pattie
21 Dec	H	Kelso	4-8	*T:* Hinshelwood
25 Jan	H	Glasgow Acads	11-22	*T:* Barrie, Muirhead *PG:* J McCall
1 Feb	A	Corstorphine	6-16	*T:* J W R Adams *C:* J McCall
8 Feb	A	Wigtownshire	6-16	*PG:* A McCall (2)
29 Feb	H	Edinburgh Wands	21-6	*T:* J W R Adams, Barrie, Carswell, W Smith *C:* A McCall *PG:* A McCall
14 Mar	A	Preston Lodge	11-10	*T:* Brown, Milloy *PG:* A McCall

Kirkcaldy

Year of formation 1873
Ground Beveridge Park, Balwearie Road, Kirkcaldy   Tel: Kirkcaldy (0592) 263470
Colours Royal blue
Most capped player D D Howie and R Howie (both Scotland) 9 caps each
Captain 1991-92 A K Carruthers
1st XV 1991-92   P31   W13   D1   L17   F533   A571
McEwan's/SRU Div 2 12th

League Record 1991-92

Date	Venue	Opponents	Result	Scorers
9 Nov	A	Royal High	3-25	*PG:* Robertson
16 Nov	A	Glasgow Acads	6-31	*PG:* Robertson (2)
23 Nov	H	Edinburgh Wands	12-15	*T:* Cuthbert, Mitchell *C:* Mitchell (2)
30 Nov	A	Preston Lodge	9-18	*T:* D Stewart *C:* Kent *PG:* Mitchell
7 Dec	H	Kilmarnock	25-6	*T:* Flett, Kent, Mitchell *C:* Mitchell (2) *PG:* Mitchell (2) *DG:* Carruthers
14 Dec	A	Wigtownshire	12-19	*PG:* Carruthers (4)
11 Jan	A	Peebles	17-18	*T:* Ferguson, Mitchell (2) *C:* Mitchell *PG:* Mitchell
25 Jan	H	Dunfermline	6-6	*T:* Carruthers *C:* Mitchell
8 Feb	A	Kelso	12-44	*PG:* Brett (4)
22 Feb	H	Corstorphine	24-4	*T:* Carruthers, Ferguson (2), Thomson (2) *C:* Carruthers (2)
29 Feb	A	Ayr	4-9	*T:* Ferguson
14 Mar	H	Musselburgh	25-12	*T:* Ferguson, Henderson, Mitchell *C:* Mitchell (2) *PG:* Mitchell (3)

Melrose

Year of formation 1877
Ground The Greenyards, Melrose, Roxburghshire TD6 9SA
Tel: Melrose (089 682) 2993 (office) and 2559 (clubrooms)
Colours Yellow and black
Most capped player K W Robertson (Scotland) 40 caps
Captain 1991-92 R R Brown
1st XV 1991-92   P32   W23   D1   L8   F616   A416
McEwan's/SRU Div 1 *Winners*

League Record 1991-92

Date	Venue	Opponents	Result	Scorers
8 Nov	A	Stewart's-Melville FP	18-7	*T:* Sudlow *C:* Chalmers *PG:* Chalmers (4)
16 Nov	H	Jedforest	15-9	*T:* B W Redpath *C:* Chalmers *PG:* Chalmers (3)
23 Nov	A	Hawick	11-9	*T:* A Redpath, Parker *PG:* Chalmers
30 Nov	H	Selkirk	16-10	*T:* Purves *PG:* Chalmers (3) *DG:* Chalmers
7 Dec	A	Gala	28-16	*T:* Parker, A Redpath, Scott, Sudlow *C:* Chalmers (3) *PG:* Chalmers (2)
14 Dec	H	Currie	16-7	*T:* McCreath, Parker *C:* Parker *PG:* Parker (2)
21 Dec	A	Watsonians	12-6	*T:* A Redpath, R R Brown, Parker

Fotosport

Melrose captain Robbie Brown with the McEwan's National League trophy.

11 Jan	H	Edinburgh Acads	15-15	T: R R Brown C: Parker PG: Parker (2) DG: Parker
25 Jan	A	Heriot's FP	32-6	T: Bain, R R Brown, Chalmers, Parker, Shiel C: Parker (3) PG: Parker DG: Chalmers
8 Feb	H	West of Scotland	32-18	T: Chalmers, Parker, Purves (2), B W Redpath, Weir C: Parker (4)
22 Feb	A	Boroughmuir	10-23	T: Bain, Purves C: Parker
29 Feb	H	Stirling County	31-0	T: Chalmers (2), Purves, B W Redpath, Weir C: Parker PG: Parker (3)
14 Mar	H	Glasgow H/K'side	27-16	T: Parker, Purves (2), Shiel C: Parker PG: Parker (3)

Musselburgh

Year of formation 1921
Ground Stoneyhill, Stoneyhill Farm Road, Musselburgh   Tel: 031-665 3435
Colours Navy blue with narrow white hoops
Captain 1991-92 A McCall
1st XV 1991-92 P29 W16 D0 L13 F502 A463
McEwan's/SRU Div 2 6th

League Record 1991-92

Date	Venue	Opponents	Result	Scorers
8 Nov	H	Edinburgh Wands	22-0	T: Horsburgh, Macdonald, Weatherhead C: C Livingstone (2) PG: C Livingstone (2)
16 Nov	A	Preston Lodge	10-18	T: McLeod, Ramsay C: Macdonald
23 Nov	H	Kilmarnock	35-10	T: McColl (2), Macdonald, McLeod, Robertson C: C Livingstone (3) PG: C Livingstone (3)
30 Nov	A	Ayr	4-29	T: C Livingstone
14 Dec	H	Corstorphine	49-3	T: C Livingstone, McLeod, McMillan, Pow, Ramsay (2), Stewart (2), Weatherhead (2) C: C Livingstone (3) PG: C Livingstone
28 Dec	A	Kelso	9-34	T: McLeod C: C Livingstone PG: C Livingstone
11 Jan	A	Wigtownshire	12-0	T: penalty try C: C Livingstone PG: C Livingstone (2)
25 Jan	H	Dundee HSFP	10-23	T: C Livingstone, N Smith C: C Livingstone
1 Feb	H	Glasgow Acads	20-24	T: McLeod (2), McMillan, Patterson C: C Livingstone (2)
8 Feb	A	Peebles	6-0	PG: C Livingstone (2)
22 Feb	H	Dunfermline	23-13	T: McLeod (3), McMillan C: Lockhart (2) PG: Lockhart
29 Feb	H	Royal High	15-13	T: McLeod, McMillan, Stewart PG: Lockhart
14 Mar	A	Kirkcaldy	12-25	PG: C Livingstone (4)

Peebles

Year of formation 1923
Ground Hay Lodge Park, Neidpath Road, Peebles EH45 8NN; 10 Eastgate, Peebles EH45 8AD (clubhouse)
Tel: Peebles (0721) 21600 (ground); 20494 (clubhouse)

Colours Red with white hoops
Captain 1991-92 S W Ferguson
1st XV 1991-92 P30 W20 D1 L9 F627 A378
McEwan's/SRU Div 2 3rd

League Record 1991-92

Date	*Venue*	*Opponents*	*Result*	*Scorers*
9 Nov	H	Kilmarnock	23-3	*T:* Anderson, Kilner (2), penalty try
				C: Mutch (2) *PG:* Mutch
16 Nov	A	Kelso	3-23	*PG:* Mutch
23 Nov	H	Wigtownshire	9-9	*PG:* Mutch (3)
30 Nov	A	Glasgow Acads	21-14	*T:* Kilner (2) *C:* Mutch (2) *PG:* Mutch (3)
14 Dec	H	Preston Lodge	18-10	*T:* Kilner (2), McDonald, penalty try *C:* McBride
21 Dec	A	Edinburgh Wands	26-3	*T:* McDonald (3), McIvor, Wills, Wilson
				C: McIvor
11 Jan	H	Kirkcaldy	18-17	*T:* McDonald, Nisbet, G Wilson (2) *C:* R Wilson
25 Jan	A	Ayr	3-19	*PG:* Kilner
8 Feb	H	Musselburgh	0-6	
22 Feb	A	Royal High	20-10	*T:* Ferguson, McDonald (2), O'Rourke
				C: Mutch (2)
29 Feb	A	Dunfermline	10-3	*T:* Gray *PG:* Mutch (2)
14 Mar	H	Corstorphine	17-10	*T:* Gray, Kilner, Nisbet *C:* Mutch *PG:* Mutch
28 Mar	H	Dundee HSFP	4-15	*T:* Kilner

Preston Lodge

Year of formation 1929
Ground Pennypit Park, Prestonpans, East Lothian   Tel: 031-661 4554
Colours Black with maroon and white hoops
Most capped player R F Cunningham (Scotland) 3 caps
Captain 1991-92 R Allan
1st XV 1991-92 P31 W18 D0 L13 F574 A515
McEwan's/SRU Div 2 joint 4th

League Record 1991-92

Date	*Venue*	*Opponents*	*Result*	*Scorers*
9 Nov	A	Ayr	12-27	*T:* McMillan *C:* Palmer *PG:* Palmer (2)
16 Nov	H	Musselburgh	18-10	*T:* Redpath, penalty try *C:* Palmer (2)
				PG: Palmer (2)
23 Nov	A	Royal High	17-9	*T:* McMillan, Redpath, Stewart *C:* Watters
				PG: Watters
30 Nov	H	Kirkcaldy	18-9	*T:* Palmer *C:* Watters *PG:* Watters (4)
7 Dec	A	Edinburgh Wands	18-15	*T:* M Henderson, Redpath, penalty try
				C: Watters (3)
14 Dec	A	Peebles	10-18	*T:* Clyde *PG:* Watters (2)
21 Dec	H	Dunfermline	23-23	*T:* R Allan, Lees, Love *C:* Watters
				PG: Watters (3)
11 Jan	A	Kelso	9-32	*T:* G Henderson *C:* Watters *PG:* Watters
25 Jan	H	Corstorphine	14-4	*T:* R Allan, G Henderson, Payne *C:* Watters
8 Feb	A	Glasgow Acads	17-13	*T:* Hood, Redpath, Smith *C:* Robertson
				PG: Robertson

22 Feb	H	Wigtownshire	19-0	*T:* M Henderson, Watters, penalty try
				C: Robertson (2) *PG:* Robertson
29 Feb	A	Dundee HSFP	0-56	
14 Mar	H	Kilmarnock	10-11	*T:* R Allan, penalty try *C:* Robertson

Royal High

Year of formation 1867
Ground Barnton, East Barnton Avenue, Edinburgh EH4 6JP   Tel: 031-312 6033
Colours Black and white hoops
Most capped player J P Fisher (Scotland) 25 caps
Captain 1991-92 N L Stewart
1st XV 1991-92   P31   W12   D1   L18   F475   A608
McEwan's/SRU Div 2 joint 13th

League Record 1991-92

Date	*Venue*	*Opponents*	*Result*	*Scorers*
9 Nov	H	Kirkcaldy	25-3	*T:* Armstrong, Conlin, McKenzie *C:* Lynch (2)
				PG: Lynch (3)
16 Nov	A	Edinburgh Wands	3-27	*PG:* Lynch
23 Nov	H	Preston Lodge	9-17	*PG:* Lynch (3)
30 Nov	A	Kilmarnock	12-0	*T:* A Scott *C:* Lynch *PG:* Lynch (2)
7 Dec	H	Ayr	12-15	*T:* Baker *C:* Lynch *PG:* Lynch (2)
14 Dec	A	Kelso	3-33	*PG:* Lynch
21 Dec	H	Corstorphine	6-10	*PG:* Lynch (2)
11 Jan	A	Glasgow Acads	6-15	*T:* Wardrop *C:* Lynch
25 Jan	H	Wigtownshire	19-6	*T:* Baker *PG:* Lynch (5)
8 Feb	A	Dundee HSFP	12-56	*T:* Baker *C:* Wardrop *PG:* Wardrop (2)
22 Feb	H	Peebles	10-20	*T:* Godfrey, Lynch *C:* Lynch
29 Feb	A	Musselburgh	13-15	*T:* Conlin, Lynch *C:* Lynch *PG:* Lynch
14 Mar	A	Dunfermline	3-10	*PG:* Mather

Selkirk

Year of formation 1907
Ground Philiphaugh, Selkirk   Tel: Selkirk (0750) 20403
Colours Navy blue
Most capped player J Y Rutherford (Scotland) 42 caps
Captain 1991-92 G R Marshall
1st XV 1991-92   P27   W17   D0   L10   F604   A373
McEwan's/SRU Div 1 joint 5th

League Record 1991-92

Date	*Venue*	*Opponents*	*Result*	*Scorers*
9 Nov	A	Hawick	33-20	*T:* Marshall, Nichol, Tukalo (2) *C:* Pow (4)
				PG: Pow (3)

16 Nov	H	Stirling County	26-15	*T:* Jaffray (2), McConnell, Pow *C:* Pow (2)
				PG: Pow (2)
23 Nov	H	Gala	11-12	*T:* Jaffray, Nichol *PG:* Pow
30 Nov	A	Melrose	10-16	*T:* Johnstone *PG:* Pow (2)
14 Dec	H	Glasgow H/K'side	34-10	*T:* Jaffray (3), Paxton, Stewart (2), Tukalo
				PG: Hunter, Pow
11 Jan	H	Watsonians	17-15	*T:* Marshall, Minto, Nichol *C:* Hunter
				PG: Hunter
25 Jan	A	Edinburgh Acads	13-16	*T:* Johnstone *PG:* Pow (2) *DG:* Pow
8 Feb	H	Heriot's FP	36-9	*T:* Buckley, Hunter, Tukalo (4) *C:* Pow (3)
				PG: Pow (2)
29 Feb	A	Jedforest	10-12	*T:* Johnston *PG:* Pow (2)
14 Mar	H	Stewart's-Melville FP	18-35	*T:* Jaffray, Johnstone, Tukalo *PG:* Pow (2)
28 Mar	A	Currie	3-30	*PG:* Hunter
14 Apr	A	West of Scotland	17-16	*T:* Jaffray, Johnston, Paxton *C:* Pow
				PG: Pow

Stewart's-Melville FP

Year of formation 1973 (on amalgamation of Daniel Stewart's College FP and Melville College FP)
Ground Inverleith, Ferry Road, Edinburgh EH5 2DW   Tel: 031-552 1515
Colours Scarlet with black and gold bands
Most capped player F Calder (Scotland) 34 caps
Captain 1991-92 D S Wyllie
1st XV 1991-92 P30 W11 D1 L18 F471 A701
McEwan's/SRU Div 1 joint 11th *relegated*

League Record 1991-92

Date	*Venue*	*Opponents*	*Result*	*Scorers*
9 Nov	H	Melrose	7-18	*T:* MacKenzie *PG:* Stirling
16 Nov	H	Hawick	4-21	*T:* Wilson
23 Nov	A	Stirling County	16-14	*T:* Lauder, MacKenzie *C:* Wyllie
				PG: Stirling (2)
30 Nov	H	Edinburgh Acads	10-43	*T:* Lockie *PG:* Stirling (2)
14 Dec	H	Heriot's FP	10-35	*T:* MacKenzie, Wilson *C:* Stirling
21 Dec	A	West of Scotland	14-9	*T:* MacKenzie, Wyllie *PG:* Stirling (2)
11 Jan	H	Boroughmuir	12-10	*T:* Wilson *C:* Stirling *PG:* Stirling (2)
25 Jan	A	Glasgow H/K'Side	7-18	*T:* Milligan *PG:* Stirling
8 Feb	H	Currie	18-35	*T:* D Thomson *C:* Stirling *PG:* Stirling (4)
22 Feb	A	Watsonians	4-17	*T:* Milligan
29 Feb	H	Gala	8-13	*T:* Burns, Wilson
14 Mar	A	Selkirk	35-18	*T:* Burns (2), Maclean, Milligan, Wyllie (2)
				C: Stirling (4) *PG:* Stirling
28 Mar	A	Jedforest	22-14	*T:* Burns, MacKenzie, Wilson
				C: M M Thomson (2) *PG:* M M Thomson (2)

Stirling County

Year of formation 1904
Ground Bridgehaugh Park, Stirling   Tel: Stirling (0786) 74827
Colours Red, white and black

Most capped player Dr W Welsh (Scotland) 8 caps
Captain 1991-92 G B Robertson
1st XV 1991-92 P33 W23 D0 L10 F779 A432
McEwan's/SRU Div 1 joint 5th

League Record 1991-92

Date	Venue	Opponents	Result	Scorers
9 Nov	H	Currie	12-6	*T:* Elliot *C:* MacDonald *PG:* MacDonald *DG:* M McKenzie
16 Nov	A	Selkirk	15-26	*T:* Harper, Turner *C:* MacDonald (2) *PG:* MacDonald
23 Nov	H	Stewart's-Melville FP	12-15	*T:* Brough, James McLaren *PG:* MacDonald (2)
30 Nov	A	Gala	9-31	*T:* Turner *C:* MacDonald *PG:* MacDonald
7 Dec	H	Hawick	14-3	*T:* Brough, Ireland, Jardine *C:* MacDonald
14 Dec	H	Watsonians	20-9	*T:* Ireland, Logan, MacDonald *C:* MacDonald *PG:* MacDonald, Stewart
21 Dec	A	Edinburgh Acads	3-18	*PG:* MacDonald
11 Jan	A	Heriot's FP	12-21	*PG:* MacDonald (4)
25 Jan	A	West of Scotland	7-6	*T:* Brough *PG:* MacDonald
8 Feb	H	Boroughmuir	9-20	*T:* Brough *C:* MacDonald *PG:* MacDonald
29 Feb	A	Melrose	0-31	
14 Mar	H	Jedforest	15-7	*T:* Brough, Jardine, Stewart *PG:* MacDonald
28 Mar	A	Glasgow H/K'side	15-13	*T:* MacDonald, penalty try *C:* MacDonald (2) *PG:* MacDonald

Watsonians

Year of formation 1875
Ground Myreside, Edinburgh   Tel: 031-447 1395
Colours Maroon
Most capped player A G Hastings and S Hastings (both Scotland) 40 caps each
Captain 1991-92 I H Smith
1st XV 1991-92 P34 W14 D3 L17 F736 A618
McEwan's/SRU Div 1 joint 5th

League Record 1991-92

Date	Venue	Opponents	Result	Scorers
9 Nov	A	West of Scotland	39-10	*T:* Campbell, A G Hastings, F M Henderson, Munro, Murray *C:* A G Hastings (5) *PG:* A G Hastings (3)
16 Nov	H	Boroughmuir	23-12	*T:* Kelly (2), Baird *C:* A G Hastings *PG:* A G Hastings (3)
23 Nov	A	Glasgow H/K'side	6-6	*PG:* A G Hastings (2)
30 Nov	H	Heriot's FP	15-19	*T:* Johnston *C:* A G Hastings *PG:* A G Hastings (3)
7 Dec	A	Edinburgh Acads	7-33	*T:* S Hastings *PG:* A G Hastings
14 Dec	A	Stirling County	9-20	*T:* Garry *C:* A G Hastings *DG:* Lee
21 Dec	H	Melrose	6-12	*PG:* A G Hastings *DG:* Lee
11 Jan	A	Selkirk	15-17	*T:* A G Hastings *C:* A G Hastings *PG:* A G Hastings (3)
25 Jan	H	Jedforest	6-23	*PG:* A G Hastings (2)
8 Feb	A	Gala	20-16	*T:* Hathway, F M Henderson, Ker *C:* A G Hastings *PG:* A G Hastings (2)

22 Feb	H	Stewart's-Melville FP	17-4	*T:* Aitken, Baird, A G Hastings *C:* A G Hastings *PG:* A G Hastings
29 Feb	A	Hawick	9-9	*T:* Baird *C:* A G Hastings *DG:* Ker
14 Mar	H	Currie	30-4	*T:* Garry, S Hastings, F M Henderson (3), MacDonald *C:* A G Hastings (3)

West of Scotland

Year of formation 1865
Ground Burnbrae, Glasgow Road, Milngavie, Glasgow G62 6HX
Tel: 041-956 2891 and 956 1960
Colours Red and yellow hoops
Most capped player A B Carmichael (Scotland) 50 caps
Captain 1991-92 S Blair
1st XV 1991-92 P33   W12   D1   L20   F590   A642
McEwan's/SRU Div 1 14th *relegated*

League Record 1991-92

Date	*Venue*	*Opponents*	*Result*	*Scorers*
9 Nov	H	Watsonians	10-39	*T:* Barrett, Williamson *C:* Barrett
16 Nov	A	Currie	18-42	*T:* McKee *C:* Barrett *PG:* Barrett (4)
23 Nov	A	Jedforest	18-6	*T:* Stott *C:* Barrett *PG:* Barrett (3) *DG:* Barrett
30 Nov	H	Boroughmuir	3-22	*PG:* Barrett
7 Dec	A	Glasgow H/K'side	19-32	*T:* Stott, Tasker *C:* Barrett *PG:* Barrett (3)
14 Dec	H	Gala	18-17	*T:* Stott *C:* Barrett *PG:* Barrett *DG:* Barrett (3)
21 Dec	H	Stewart's-Melville FP	9-14	*PG:* Barrett (3)
11 Jan	A	Hawick	13-33	*T:* Barrett, Munro *C:* Barrett *PG:* Barrett
25 Jan	H	Stirling County	6-7	*PG:* Barrett (2)
8 Feb	A	Melrose	18-32	*T:* Robertson (2) *C:* Barrett (2) *PG:* Barrett (2)
29 Feb	H	Heriot's FP	6-3	*PG:* Barrett (2)
14 Mar	A	Edinburgh Acads	9-27	*PG:* Barrett (3)
14 Apr	H	Selkirk	16-17	*T:* Robertson (2) *C:* Barrett *PG:* Barrett (2)

Wigtownshire

Year of formation 1922
Ground London Road Playing Fields, Stranraer; Ladies Walk, Stranraer (clubhouse)
Tel: Stranraer (0776) 4133 (clubhouse)
Colours Royal blue
Captain 1991-92 H M Parker
1st XV 1991-92 P30   W19   D2   L9   F550   A376
McEwan's/SRU Div 1 7th

League Record 1991-92

Date	*Venue*	*Opponents*	*Result*	*Scorers*
9 Nov	H	Dunfermline	36-16	*T:* A Drysdale (4), David Drysdale, H M Parker *C:* Kelly (3) *PG:* Kelly (2)

16 Nov	H	Dundee HSFP	4-25	*T:* Dougie Drysdale
23 Nov	A	Peebles	9-9	*PG:* M Hose (2), Mackay
30 Nov	H	Edinburgh Wands	17-3	*T:* A Drysdale, Gemmell, Paxton *C:* Stewart *PG:* Stewart
7 Dec	A	Corstorphine	25-4	*T:* A Drysdale, Andrew Hose, Jessop *C:* David Drysdale (2) *PG:* David Drysdale, Stewart *DG:* Stewart
14 Dec	H	Kirkcaldy	19-12	*T:* Kilkerr, H M Parker (2) *C:* David Drysdale (2) *PG:* Mackay
21 Dec	A	Ayr	6-12	*PG:* Mackay
11 Jan	H	Musselburgh	0-12	
25 Jan	A	Royal High	6-19	*PG:* M Hose *DG:* Gemmell
8 Feb	H	Kilmarnock	16-6	*T:* A Drysdale (2), Kilkerr *C:* David Drysdale, M Hose
22 Feb	A	Preston Lodge	0-19	
29 Feb	H	Glasgow Acads	20-9	*T:* A Drysdale, R Drysdale, Kilkerr, McTurk *C:* M Hose (2)
14 Mar	A	Kelso	16-24	*T:* A Drysdale, Alister Hose *C:* M Hose *PG:* M Hose (2)

WALES

Aberavon

Year of formation 1876
Ground Talbot Athletic Ground, Manor Street, Port Talbot, West Glamorgan
Tel: Port Talbot (0639) 882427
Colours Red and black hoops
Most capped player A J Martin (Wales) 34 caps
Captain 1991-92 M Woodward, succeeded by L Lewis
1st XV 1991-92 P53 W28 D6 L19 F1151 A775
Heineken League Div 2 2nd **WRU/Schweppes Cup** Lost 10-19 to South Wales Police
(5th round)

League Record 1991-92

Date	Venue	Opponents	Result	Scorers
28 Sept	A	Dunvant	9-23	*PG:* Love (3)
9 Nov	H	Ebbw Vale	20-6	*T:* Graham, Spender *PG:* Love (4)
16 Nov	A	Llanharan	18-10	*T:* Edwards *C:* Love *PG:* Love (4)
23 Nov	H	Abertillery	13-3	*T:* Graham *PG:* Love (3)
30 Nov	A	Tredegar	34-9	*T:* Dragone (2), Love (2), D Griffiths, D Edwards *C:* Love (2) *PG:* Love (2)
7 Dec	A	Cross Keys	7-7	*T:* Dragone *PG:* Love
14 Dec	H	Penarth	53-12	*T:* Graham (3), D Edwards (2), Dragone (2), Wilkins, Alan Williams, Hamley *C:* Love (5) *DG:* Love
4 Jan	A	S W Police	15-15	*T:* D Edwards *C:* Love *PG:* Love (3)
8 Feb	H	Dunvant	6-0	*T:* D Edwards *C:* Love
15 Feb	A	Ebbw Vale	15-19	*T:* M Evans *C:* Love *PG:* Love (3)
29 Feb	H	Llanharan	10-16	*T:* G Evans *PG:* I Morgan (2)
14 Mar	A	Abertillery	15-19	*PG:* Love (5)
28 Mar	H	Tredegar	43-6	*T:* Dragone (2), G Evans, Love, Diplock, D Griffiths, Jardine *C:* Love (6) *PG:* Love
1 Apr	H	Glam Wands	32-0	*T:* Dragone (2), Love, Hamley, Diplock, D Griffiths, G Evans *C:* Love (2)
11 Apr	H	Cross Keys	31-15	*T:* Dragone (2), Diplock *C:* Love (2) *PG:* Love (4) *DG:* Love
18 Apr	A	Penarth	35-10	*T:* G Evans (2), R Williams, Love, Dragone, Diplock *C:* Love (4) *PG:* Love
25 Apr	H	S W Police	15-15	*T:* Roach *C:* Love *PG:* Love (3)
9 May	A	Glam Wands	19-6	*T:* Lewis (2), M Evans *C:* Love (2) *PG:* Love

Abertillery

Year of formation 1884
Ground The Park, Abertillery, Gwent   Tel: Abertillery (0495) 212555
Colours Green and white hoops
Most capped player H J Morgan (Wales) 27 caps
Captain 1991-92 M Picton
1st XV 1991-92 P41 W18 D1 L22 F566 A705
Heineken League Div 2 7th **WRU/Schweppes Cup** Lost 0-17 to Cardiff Harlequins
(6th round)

League Record 1991-92

Date	Venue	Opponents	Result	Scorers
28 Sept	A	Llanharan	0-20	
9 Nov	H	Cross Keys	6-13	*PG:* J Williams (2)
16 Nov	H	Tredegar	26-0	*T:* Thompson, E Williams, M Davies, Picton, Atkins *C:* Crane (3)
23 Nov	A	Aberavon	3-13	*PG:* J Williams
30 Nov	H	Penarth	32-0	*T:* S Davies (2), Preece (2), Atkins, Crane *C:* Crane (4)
7 Dec	A	S W Police	16-15	*T:* Thompson *PG:* Crane (3) *DG:* Crane
4 Jan	A	Dunvant	10-23	*T:* Richards *PG:* Crane (2)
8 Feb	H	Llanharan	13-6	*T:* Picton (2) *C:* M Williams *PG:* Crane
15 Feb	A	Cross Keys	15-15	*T:* Crane *C:* Crane *PG:* Crane (2), M Williams
29 Feb	A	Tredegar	6-21	*T:* Preece *C:* J Williams
8 Mar	H	Glam Wands	4-12	*T:* Cross
14 Mar	H	Aberavon	19-15	*T:* Jervis, pen try *C:* J Williams *PG:* J Williams (3)
24 Mar	A	Ebbw Vale	6-10	*T:* Atkins *C:* J Williams
28 Mar	A	Penarth	27-9	*T:* Atkins, Rees, A Richards, McCluney *C:* J Williams (4) *PG:* J Williams
11 Apr	H	S W Police	28-16	*T:* Picton, McCluney, Graham *C:* J Williams (2) *PG:* J Williams (4)
18 Apr	A	Glam Wands	16-30	*T:* Preece, M Williams, Picton *C:* Chapman (2)
25 Apr	H	Dunvant	21-3	*T:* J Williams, M Williams, Richards *C:* J Williams (3) *PG:* J Williams
9 May	H	Ebbw Vale	3-13	*PG:* J Williams

Bridgend

Year of formation 1878
Ground Brewery Field, Tondu Road, Bridgend, Mid-Glamorgan
Tel: Bridgend (0656) 659032
Colours Blue and white hoops
Most capped player J P R Williams (Wales) 55 caps
Captain 1991-92 J Apsee
1st XV 1991-92 P47 W33 D1 L13 F1084 A674
Heineken League Div 1 6th **WRU/Schweppes Cup** Lost 4-9 to Newport
(7th round)

League Record 1991-92

Date	Venue	Opponents	Result	Scorers
9 Nov	H	Newport	12-7	*T:* Webbe *C:* A Williams *PG:* A Williams (2)
16 Nov	A	Pontypool	9-16	*T:* Apsee *C:* A Williams *PG:* A Williams
23 Nov	H	Cardiff	28-9	*T:* Flood (2), A Williams *C:* A Williams (2) *PG:* A Williams (4)
30 Nov	A	Swansea	6-30	*T:* Webbe *C:* A Williams
7 Dec	H	Newbridge	0-25	
21 Dec	A	Pontypridd	11-4	*T:* Prosser, Webbe *PG:* Barber
4 Jan	H	Maesteg	24-7	*T:* H Lewis, Apsee, D Bryant, G Davies *C:* Brown *PG:* Brown, Barber
11 Jan	A	Llanelli	17-12	*T:* H Lewis, Bradshaw *PG:* G Thomas (3)
3 Feb	H	Neath	8-0	*T:* G Thomas, G Davies
8 Feb	A	Newport	7-14	*T:* H Lewis *PG:* L Evans

15 Feb	H	Pontypool	22-15	*T:* L Evans, Webbe *C:* L Evans *PG:* L Evans (4)
29 Feb	A	Cardiff	18-14	*T:* L Evans, Prosser *C:* L Evans (2) *PG:* L Evans (2)
14 Mar	H	Swansea	22-15	*T:* G Davies, Webbe *C:* L Evans *PG:* L Evans (4)
28 Mar	A	Newbridge	16-22	*T:* L Evans, S Bryant *C:* L Evans *PG:* L Evans (2)
11 Apr	A	Neath	6-34	*T:* Bradshaw *C:* Howley
18 Apr	H	Pontypridd	10-14	*T:* D Thomas, H Lewis *C:* D Thomas
25 Apr	A	Maesteg	15-18	*T:* Webbe, H Lewis *C:* L Evans (2) *PG:* L Evans
9 May	H	Llanelli	15-14	*T:* ap Dafydd, Prosser *C:* L Evans (2) *PG:* L Evans

Cardiff

Year of formation 1876
Ground Cardiff Arms Park, Westgate Street, Cardiff   Tel: Cardiff (0222) 383546
Colours Cambridge blue and black
Most capped player G O Edwards (Wales) 53 caps
Captain 1991-92 D W Evans
1st XV 1991-92 P39 W16 D2 L21 F690 A600
Heineken League Div 1 9th **WRU/Schweppes Cup** Lost 4-12 to Newport
(6th round)

League Record 1991-92

Date	Venue	Opponents	Result	Scorers
9 Nov	A	Swansea	9-23	*PG:* D Evans (3)
16 Nov	H	Newbridge	3-6	*PG:* D Evans
23 Nov	A	Bridgend	9-28	*T:* Ford *C:* Rayer *PG:* Rayer
30 Nov	H	Pontypridd	19-12	*T:* Jeffreys, Emyr, Miller *C:* Rayer (2) *DG:* Miller
7 Dec	A	Maesteg	32-6	*T:* Rayer, Booth, Ford, Emyr, Roy *C:* Rayer (3) *PG:* Rayer (2)
14 Dec	H	Llanelli	22-28	*T:* Ford, Miller, Booth *C:* Rayer (2) *PG:* Rayer (2)
21 Dec	A	Newport	6-12	*PG:* Rayer (2)
4 Jan	H	Pontypool	10-24	*T:* M Thomas *PG:* Miller (2)
11 Jan	A	Neath	3-3	*PG:* D Evans
5 Feb	H	Swansea	14-36	*T:* Hall (2) *PG:* Rayer (2)
15 Feb	A	Newbridge	6-16	*PG:* Rayer (2)
29 Feb	H	Bridgend	14-18	*T:* Kawulok, Hall *PG:* Ring (2)
14 Mar	A	Pontypridd	12-17	*T:* Ford *C:* Booth *PG:* Booth (2)
28 Mar	H	Maesteg	22-9	*T:* Ford, Hall, Watkins *C:* M Thomas (2) *PG:* M Thomas (2)
11 Apr	A	Llanelli	6-22	*T:* Jeffreys *C:* Rayer
21 Apr	H	Newport	18-13	*T:* P Thomas *C:* Rayer *PG:* Rayer (3) *DG:* Miller
25 Apr	A	Pontypool	23-10	*T:* Kawulok, Hall, Ford *C:* Rayer PG: Rayer (3)
9 May	H	Neath	12-23	*T:* Ford, Moore *C:* Rayer (2)

Cross Keys

Year of formation 1885
Ground Pandy Park, Cross Keys, Gwent   Tel: Cross Keys (0495) 270289
Colours Black and white
Most capped player S Morris (Wales) 19 caps
Captain 1991-92 N Parkes
1st XV 1991-92 P47   W28   D4   L15   F828   A694
Heineken League Div 2 3rd **WRU/Schweppes Cup** Lost 6-19 to Pontypool
(6th round)

League Record 1991-92

Date	Venue	Opponents	Result	Scorers
28 Sept	H	S W Police	6-12	*PG:* Taylor (2)
9 Nov	A	Abertillery	13-6	*T:* N Griffiths *PG:* Withers (2) *DG:* Withers
16 Nov	A	Glam Wands	23-15	*T:* Nicholls (2), Withers, N Griffiths *C:* N Davies (2) *PG:* N Davies
23 Nov	H	Tredegar	11-6	*T:* N Davies, Marshall *PG:* Withers
30 Nov	A	Dunvant	21-10	*T:* Parkes (2), A Thomas, Withers *C:* Taylor *PG:* Taylor
7 Dec	H	Aberavon	7-7	*T:* Withers *PG:* Taylor
4 Jan	H	Penarth	30-9	*T:* T Williams, Withers, Peebles, Anthony, Hopkin, Nicholls *C:* Withers (2), Taylor
11 Jan	A	Llanharan	3-11	*PG:* Withers
8 Feb	A	S W Police	27-13	*T:* Nicholls (2), Taylor, Derrick *C:* Withers *PG:* Withers *DG:* Withers (2)
15 Feb	H	Abertillery	15-15	*T:* T Williams, Rossiter, Withers *DG:* N Davies
29 Feb	H	Glam Wands	12-12	*T:* P Jones *C:* N Davies *PG:* N Davies (2)
14 Mar	A	Tredegar	9-10	*T:* T Williams *C:* N Davies *PG:* N Davies
28 Mar	H	Dunvant	25-15	*T:* Scrivens (2) *C:* N Davies *PG:* N Davies (4) *DG:* Pople
11 Apr	A	Aberavon	15-31	*T:* P Jones *C:* N Davies *PG:* N Davies (2) *DG:* Taylor
18 Apr	H	Ebbw Vale	14-24	*T:* N Davies, Nicholls *PG:* N Davies (2)
25 Apr	A	Penarth	17-0	*T:* A Williams, Rossiter, Andrew Thomas *C:* Withers *PG:* Withers
29 Apr	A	Ebbw Vale	16-7	*T:* Withers (2) *C:* Withers *PG:* Withers, N Davies
9 May	H	Llanharan	18-9	*T:* Withers *C:* Withers *PG:* Withers (4)

Dunvant

Year of formation 1888
Ground Broadacre, Killay, Swansea   Tel: Swansea (0792) 207291
Colours Red and green hoops
Captain 1991-92 R Llewellyn
1st XV 1991-92 P32   W17   D0   L15   F474   A397
Heineken League Div 2 5th **WRU/Schweppes Cup** Lost 6-14 to Swansea
(7th round)

League Record 1991-92

Date	Venue	Opponents	Result	Scorers
28 Sept	H	Aberavon	23-9	*T:* N Davies, R Bolton, pen try *C:* Snell *PG:* Snell (2), D Evans

9 Nov	A	Penarth	17-6	*T:* Jeffreys, Niblo, pen try *C:* Snell *PG:* D Evans
16 Nov	H	S W Police	7-20	*T:* N Bolton *PG:* Snell
23 Nov	A	Glam Wands	12-16	*T:* N Davies *C:* Snell *PG:* Snell *DG:* Snell
30 Nov	H	Cross Keys	10-21	*T:* Farnworth *PG:* Snell (2)
7 Dec	H	Ebbw Vale	31-3	*T:* Niblo, P Morris, P John, Crane *C:* Harris (3) *PG:* Harris (2) *DG:* Harris
4 Jan	H	Abertillery	23-10	*T:* N Bolton (2), Greenwood *C:* Harris *PG:* Harris (3)
8 Feb	A	Aberavon	0-6	
15 Feb	H	Penarth	33-6	*T:* M Jones (2), P John, G Price, D Thomas, A Jeffries *C:* Harris (3) *PG:* Harris
29 Feb	A	S W Police	15-19	*T:* P Morris *C:* M Thomas *PG:* M Thomas (2), Harris
14 Mar	H	Glam Wands	16-9	*T:* M Jones, P Morris *C:* M Thomas *PG:* M Thomas (2)
20 Mar	A	Tredegar	15-7	*T:* N Bolton *C:* M Thomas *PG:* M Thomas (3)
28 Mar	A	Cross Keys	15-25	*T:* W Lloyd *C:* M Thomas *PG:* M Thomas (3)
11 Apr	A	Ebbw Vale	20-28	*T:* C Hutchings, Farnworth *PG:* M Thomas (4)
18 Apr	H	Llanharan	16-13	*T:* Farnworth, M Thomas *C:* M Thomas *PG:* M Thomas *DG:* W Lloyd
25 Apr	A	Abertillery	3-21	*PG:* M Thomas
2 May	A	Llanharan	10-6	*T:* Jeffreys *PG:* M Thomas (2)
9 May	H	Tredegar	14-12	*T:* W Lloyd, Niblo *PG:* M Thomas (2)

Ebbw Vale

Year of formation 1880
Ground Eugene Cross Park, Ebbw Vale, Gwent   Tel: Ebbw Vale (0495) 302955
Colours Red, white and green
Most capped player D Williams (Wales) 36 caps
Captain 1991-92 D Parry, succeeded by P Booth
1st XV 1991-92 P40 W16 D1 L23 F616 A754
Heineken League Div 2 4th **WRU/Schweppes Cup** Lost 10-12 to Dunvant
(4th round)

League Record 1991-92

Date	*Venue*	*Opponents*	*Result*	*Scorers*
9 Nov	A	Aberavon	6-20	*T:* Parry *C:* Cheshire
16 Nov	H	Penarth	12-13	*T:* Booth (2) *C:* Cheshire (2)
23 Nov	A	S W Police	7-19	*T:* G Thomas *PG:* Cheshire
30 Nov	H	Glam Wands	24-15	*T:* Cheshire, D Harris *C:* Cheshire (2) *PG:* Cheshire (3) *DG:* Cheshire
7 Dec	A	Dunvant	3-31	*PG:* Cheshire
4 Jan	H	Llanharan	0-16	
8 Feb	A	Tredegar	35-12	*T:* Booth (2), Hodges, Price, Jewitt, Knill *C:* Cheshire *PG:* Cheshire (3)
15 Feb	H	Aberavon	19-15	*T:* Jewitt, R Williams *C:* Strange *PG:* Strange (2) *DG:* Strange
29 Feb	A	Penarth	31-15	*T:* Booth, Burt, Jewitt, Price *C:* Strange (3) *PG:* Strange (2) *DG:* Strange
6 Mar	H	Tredegar	16-9	*T:* Booth, G Thomas *C:* McKie *PG:* McKie (2)
14 Mar	H	S W Police	29-6	*T:* G Thomas (2), Stephens, Price *C:* Strange (2) *PG:* Strange (2) *DG:* Strange
24 Mar	A	Abertillery	10-6	*T:* Bowden *PG:* Strange *DG:* Strange

28 Mar	A	Glam Wands	15-12	*T:* G Thomas *C:* Strange *PG:* Strange (3)
11 Apr	H	Dunvant	28-20	*T:* Bowden (2), Price *C:* Strange (2) *PG:* Strange (4)
18 Apr	A	Cross Keys	24-14	*T:* Hardacre, Burt, Jewitt *C:* McKie (2), Hardacre *PG:* McKie (2)
25 Apr	A	Llanharan	12-12	*T:* Bowden, Puddy, R Williams
29 Apr	H	Cross Keys	7-16	*T:* R Williams *DG:* Strange
9 May	A	Abertillery	13-3	*T:* G Thomas, Price *C:* Strange *PG:* Strange

Glamorgan Wanderers

Year of formation 1893
Ground The Memorial Ground, Stirling Road, Ely, Cardiff   Tel: Cardiff (0222) 591039
Colours Cambridge blue, black and white
Captain 1991-92 P Goodfellow
1st XV 1991-92 P42 W18 D2 L22 F756 A865
Heineken League Div 2 8th **WRU/Schweppes Cup** Lost to Newport on try count in
10-10 draw (5th round)

League Record 1991-92

Date	*Venue*	*Opponents*	*Result*	*Scorers*
28 Sept	H	Penarth	28-10	*T:* Edmunds, Simmons, Baston *C:* Bolderson (2) *PG:* Bolderson (3), Goodfellow
9 Nov	A	S W Police	9-30	*T:* Richards *C:* Bolderson *PG:* Bolderson
16 Nov	H	Cross Keys	15-23	*T:* A Morgan *C:* Bolderson *PG:* Bolderson (3)
23 Nov	H	Dunvant	16-12	*T:* Clarke, A Morgan, Dunleavy *C:* Bolderson (2)
30 Nov	A	Ebbw Vale	15-24	*T:* Richards *C:* Bolderson *PG:* Bolderson (3)
7 Dec	H	Llanharan	7-12	*T:* W Evans *PG:* Bolderson
4 Jan	H	Tredegar	20-6	*T:* Bebb (2), W Evans *C:* Bolderson *PG:* Bolderson (2)
8 Feb	A	Penarth	18-8	*T:* Duly (2), S Williams, Bolderson *C:* Bolderson
15 Feb	H	S W Police	13-21	*T:* Edmunds, St John *C:* S Williams *PG:* S Williams
29 Feb	A	Cross Keys	12-12	*T:* Duly *C:* S Williams *PG:* S Williams (2)
8 Mar	A	Abertillery	12-4	*T:* N Davies *C:* Bolderson *PG:* Bebb (2)
14 Mar	A	Dunvant	9-16	*PG:* Bolderson (2), Bebb
28 Mar	H	Ebbw Vale	12-15	*PG:* Bebb (4)
1 Apr	A	Aberavon	0-32	
11 Apr	A	Llanharan	15-6	*T:* pen try *C:* Bolderson *PG:* Bolderson (2), Goodfellow
18 Apr	H	Abertillery	30-16	*T:* Collins, Edmunds *C:* Bolderson, Goodfellow *PG:* Bolderson (3) *DG:* Bolderson (2), Goodfellow
25 Apr	A	Tredegar	22-3	*T:* Duly, S Williams, Edmunds *C:* Goodfellow (2) *PG:* Goodfellow (2)
9 May	H	Aberavon	6-19	*PG:* Bolderson *DG:* Bolderson

Llanelli

Year of formation 1872
Ground Stradey Park, Llanelli, Dyfed   Tel: Llanelli (0554) 774060

Emyr Lewis and Tony Copsey protect Phil Davies as he feeds the ball to his scrum-half in Llanelli's 16-7 victory over Swansea in the Schweppes Cup final.

Colours Scarlet
Most capped player P T Davies (Wales) 32 caps
Captain 1991-92 P T Davies
1st XV 1991-92 P42 W30 D2 L10 F1000 A604
Heineken League Div 1 2nd **WRU/Schweppes Cup** *Winners* Beat Swansea 16-7 (final)

League Record 1991-92

Date	Venue	Opponents	Result	Scorers
9 Nov	A	Pontypridd	22-16	*T:* Taffetsauffer, Perego *C:* Stephens *PG:* Stephens *DG:* Stephens (3)
16 Nov	H	Maesteg	34-15	*T:* H Williams, I Evans, L Jones *C:* Stephens (2) *PG:* Stephens (6)
23 Nov	A	Neath	23-13	*T:* A Morgan (2), S Davies, Stephens *C:* Stephens (2) *PG:* Stephens
30 Nov	A	Newport	9-19	*PG:* Stephens (3)
7 Dec	H	Pontypool	21-21	*T:* Proctor *C:* Stephens *PG:* Stephens (5)
14 Dec	A	Cardiff	28-22	*T:* H Williams, Copsey, Gale, E Lewis, I Evans *C:* H Williams (4)
21 Dec	H	Swansea	11-6	*T:* I Jones, Proctor *DG:* Moon
4 Jan	A	Newbridge	9-13	*PG:* Stephens (3)
11 Jan	H	Bridgend	12-17	*T:* S Davies, S Quinnell *C:* Boobyer, H Williams
8 Feb	H	Pontypridd	11-18	*T:* N Davies, Proctor *PG:* Stephens
15 Feb	A	Maesteg	32-3	*T:* I Evans (2), Stephens (2), Moon, Proctor *C:* Stephens (4)
29 Feb	H	Neath	31-10	*T:* I Evans (2), I Jones, S Quinnell, Stephens *C:* Stephens (4) *PG:* Stephens
14 Mar	H	Newport	16-12	*T:* E Lewis, I Evans, G Jones, Stephens
28 Mar	A	Pontypool	36-15	*T:* G Jones (2), I Evans, P Davies, Moon, S Quinnell *C:* Stephens (3) *PG:* Stephens (2)
11 Apr	H	Cardiff	22-6	*T:* E Lewis, N Davies, Boobyer, I Evans *C:* Stephens (3)
18 Apr	A	Swansea	3-9	*PG:* Stephens
25 Apr	H	Newbridge	47-3	*T:* I Evans (2), R Evans, S Davies (2), N Davies, Proctor (2), S Quinnell *C:* Stephens (4) *PG:* Stephens
9 May	A	Bridgend	14-15	*T:* Boobyer, Proctor *PG:* Stephens (2)

Llanharan

Year of formation 1891
Ground Bridgend Rd, Llanharan, Mid-Glamorgan Tel: Llanharan (0443) 222209
Colours White with black and blue hoops
Captain 1991-92 J Pick
1st XV 1991-92 P18 W9 D1 L8 F256 A179
Heineken League Div 2 6th **WRU/Schweppes Cup** Lost 9-23 to Cross Keys
(4th round)

League Record 1991-92

Date	Venue	Opponents	Result	Scorers
28 Sept	H	Abertillery	20-0	*T:* Pritchard (2), G Evans, Brown *C:* Morris (2)
9 Nov	A	Tredegar	30-9	*T:* Morris, Taylor, Brain, pen try *C:* Morris *PG:* Morris (4)

16 Nov	H	Aberavon	10-18	*T:* Reynolds *PG:* Morris (2)
23 Nov	A	Penarth	29-0	*T:* G Evans, Martin, Reynolds, pen try *C:* Morris (2) *PG:* Morris (3)
30 Nov	H	S W Police	15-19	*T:* Merry *C:* Morris *PG:* Morris (3)
7 Dec	A	Glam Wands	12-7	*PG:* Morris (4)
4 Jan	A	Ebbw Vale	16-0	*T:* M Jones, Reffell *C:* Morris *PG:* Morris *DG:* Morris
11 Jan	H	Cross Keys	11-3	*T:* Dodd, B Lewis *PG:* Morris
8 Feb	A	Abertillery	6-13	*PG:* Morris (2)
15 Feb	H	Tredegar	20-12	*T:* Morris, Langdon *PG:* Morris (3) *DG:* Morris
29 Feb	A	Aberavon	16-10	*T:* Lewis *PG:* Morris (3) *DG:* R Williams
14 Mar	H	Penarth	12-6	*T:* Pritchard *C:* Morris *PG:* Morris (2)
28 Mar	A	S W Police	13-14	*T:* D Thompson (2) *C:* Morris *PG:* Morris
11 Apr	H	Glam Wands	6-15	*PG:* Morris (2)
18 Apr	A	Dunvant	13-16	*T:* D Thompson, Morris *C:* Morris *PG:* Morris
25 Apr	H	Ebbw Vale	12-12	*PG:* Morris (4)
2 May	H	Dunvant	6-10	*PG:* Morris (2)
9 May	A	Cross Keys	9-18	*PG:* Morris (3)

Maesteg

Year of formation 1882
Ground Old Parish Ground, Llynvi Road, Maesteg, Mid-Glamorgan
Tel: Maesteg (0656) 732283
Colours Black and amber hoops
Most capped player G Evans (Wales) 10 caps
Captain 1991-92 A Henson
1st XV 1991-92 P45 W13 D2 L30 F659 A893
Heineken League Div 1 10th **WRU/Schweppes Cup** Lost 12-15 to Newbridge
(5th round)

League Record 1991-92

Date	Venue	Opponents	Result	Scorers
9 Nov	H	Neath	10-31	*T:* Brown *PG:* D Williams (2)
16 Nov	A	Llanelli	15-34	*T:* N Lewis *C:* D Williams *PG:* D Williams (2) *DG:* D Williams
23 Nov	H	Newport	6-21	*PG:* D Edwards (2)
30 Nov	A	Pontypool	0-28	
7 Dec	H	Cardiff	6-32	*PG:* D Edwards (2)
14 Dec	A	Swansea	6-47	*PG:* D Edwards (2)
21 Dec	H	Newbridge	9-50	*T:* P Thomas *C:* D Edwards *PG:* D Edwards
4 Jan	A	Bridgend	7-24	*T:* Wilcox *DG:* D Williams
8 Feb	A	Neath	20-20	*T:* Doble, A Williams, Woodland *C:* D Edwards *PG:* D Edwards (2)
15 Feb	H	Llanelli	3-32	*PG:* D Edwards
29 Feb	A	Newport	6-48	*PG:* D Edwards *DG:* D Williams
14 Mar	H	Pontypool	18-27	*T:* Harvey, Dodd *C:* D Edwards (2) *PG:* D Edwards (2)
24 Mar	H	Pontypridd	12-42	*T:* Thornton *C:* Holley *PG:* D Edwards, Holley
28 Mar	A	Cardiff	9-22	*T:* Dodd *C:* D Edwards *PG:* Edwards
11 Apr	H	Swansea	4-23	*T:* A Henson
18 Apr	A	Newbridge	17-22	*T:* Holley, Dodd, C Evans *C:* Holley *PG:* Holley

| 25 Apr | H | Bridgend | 18-15 | *T:* Woodland *C:* D Williams *PG:* D Williams (4) |
| 9 May | A | Pontypridd | 3-12 | *PG:* Thornton |

Neath

Year of formation 1871
Ground The Gnoll, Gnoll Park Road, Neath, West Glamorgan   Tel: Neath (0639) 636547
Colours Black with white Maltese cross
Most capped player W D Morris (Wales) 34 caps
Captain 1991-92 P H Thorburn
1st XV 1991-92 P41 W26 D2 L13 F909 A558
Heineken League Div 1 4th **WRU/Schweppes Cup** Lost 12-15 to Newbridge
(5th round)

League Record 1991-92

Date	Venue	Opponents	Result	Scorers
9 Nov	A	Maesteg	31-10	*T:* Reynolds (2), Bowling (2), R Jones *C:* Thorburn *PG:* Thorburn (3)
16 Nov	H	Swansea	22-6	*T:* Ball (2) *C:* Bird *PG:* Bird (2), Thorburn *DG:* Bird
23 Nov	H	Llanelli	13-23	*T:* Gareth Llewellyn, Gibbs *C:* Thorburn *PG:* Thorburn
30 Nov	A	Newbridge	3-9	*PG:* McCarthy
7 Dec	H	Newport	18-7	*T:* Ball *C:* Thorburn *PG:* Thorburn (4)
21 Dec	H	Pontypool	10-13	*T:* S Williams *PG:* Thorburn (2)
4 Jan	A	Pontypridd	6-18	*T:* Thorburn *C:* Thorburn
11 Jan	H	Cardiff	3-3	*PG:* Thorburn
3 Feb	A	Bridgend	0-8	
8 Feb	H	Maesteg	20-20	*T:* Reynolds (3) *C:* Thorburn *PG:* Thorburn (2)
15 Feb	A	Swansea	13-24	*T:* Morris, Thorburn *C:* Thorburn *PG:* Thorburn
29 Feb	A	Llanelli	10-31	*T:* Phillips, Ball *C:* Ball
14 Mar	H	Newbridge	20-4	*T:* Reynolds, P Jones, Thorburn, Young *C:* Ball (2)
28 Mar	A	Newport	34-16	*T:* Thorburn (3), Ball *C:* Ball (3) *PG:* Ball (3), Thorburn
11 Apr	H	Bridgend	34-6	*T:* A Thomas (2), Ball, Barclay, J Davies, Morris *C:* Ball (2) *PG:* Ball (2)
18 apr	A	Pontypool	26-13	*T:* Fox, Young, Bridges, J Davies *C:* Bird (2) *PG:* Bird (2)
25 Apr	H	Pontypridd	23-13	*T:* S Williams (2), K Phillips, J Davies *C:* Ball (2) *PG:* Ball
9 May	A	Cardiff	23-12	*T:* Reynolds (2), Bridges, pen try *C:* Ball (2) *PG:* Ball

Newbridge

Year of formation 1888
Ground Welfare Ground, Bridge Street, Newbridge, Gwent
Tel: Newbridge (0495) 243247

Colours Blue and black hoops
Most capped player D Hayward (Wales) 15 caps
Captain 1991-92 D Rees
1st XV 1991-92 P51 W38 D1 L12 F1265 A700
Heineken League Div 1 5th **WRU/Schweppes Cup** Lost 13-18 to Bridgend
(6th round)

League Record 1991-92

Date	Venue	Opponents	Result	Scorers
9 Nov	H	Pontypool	9-21	*T:* Hill *C:* Hayward *PG:* Hayward
16 Nov	A	Cardiff	6-3	*PG:* Hayward (2)
23 Nov	H	Swansea	9-22	*T:* Green *C:* Hayward *PG:* Hayward
30 Nov	H	Neath	9-3	*T:* Jenkins *C:* Hayward *DG:* P Williams
7 Dec	A	Bridgend	25-0	*T:* Hayward, Fealey, Crane, D Roberts *PG:* Hayward (3)
21 Dec	A	Maesteg	50-9	*T:* D Manley (2), P Williams, Sutton, Taylor, Glasson, Crandon, Rees, Hayward, D Roberts *C:* Hayward (5)
4 Jan	H	Llanelli	13-9	*T:* Crane *PG:* Hayward (2) *DG:* Rees
11 Jan	A	Newport	4-20	*T:* D Manley
8 Feb	A	Pontypool	25-6	*T:* D Manley (2), Gibbs, Fealey, Glasson *C:* Hayward *PG:* Hayward
15 Feb	H	Cardiff	16-6	*T:* Hayward *PG:* Hayward (4)
29 Feb	A	Swansea	9-20	*PG:* Hayward (3)
10 Mar	H	Pontypridd	6-24	*T:* Brown *C:* Hayward
14 Mar	A	Neath	4-20	*T:* D Roberts
28 Mar	H	Bridgend	22-16	*T:* P Crane (2), Fealey *C:* Hayward (2) *PG:* Hayward (2)
11 Apr	A	Pontypridd	6-25	*PG:* Hayward (2)
15 Apr	H	Newport	21-3	*T:* Perry (2), Fealey *PG:* Hayward (3)
18 Apr	H	Maesteg	22-17	*T:* Hill, Taylor, E John *C:* Hayward (2) *PG:* Hayward (2)
25 Apr	A	Llanelli	3-47	*PG:* Hayward

Newport

Year of formation 1874
Ground Rodney Parade, Rodney Road, Newport, Gwent
Tel: Newport (0633) 258193 or 267410
Colours Black and amber hoops
Most capped player K J Jones (Wales) 44 caps
Captain 1991-92 G M George
1st XV 1991-92 P43 W22 D5 L16 F798 A593
Heineken League Div 1 8th **WRU/Schweppes Cup** Lost 9-23 *(aet)* to Swansea
(semi-final)

League Record 1991-92

Date	Venue	Opponents	Result	Scorers
9 Nov	A	Bridgend	7-12	*T:* Harries *PG:* Harries
16 Nov	H	Pontypridd	13-6	*T:* Sagoe, George *C:* McCracken *PG:* McCracken

23 Nov	A	Maesteg	21-6	*T:* Lee (2), Bidgood, Hale *C:* Harries
				PG: Harries
30 Nov	H	Llanelli	19-9	*T:* Orrell (2), Pill *C:* Turner (2) *PG:* Turner
7 Dec	A	Neath	7-18	*T:* Bidgood *DG:* Turner
21 Dec	H	Cardiff	12-6	*PG:* Turner (4)
4 Jan	A	Swansea	0-14	
11 Jan	H	Newbridge	20-4	*T:* Bidgood (2), I Jones *C:* Harries
				PG: Turner (2)
21 Jan	A	Pontypool	7-7	*T:* Harries *PG:* Harries
8 Feb	H	Bridgend	14-7	*T:* Westwood (2) *PG:* Harries (2)
15 Feb	A	Pontypridd	12-25	*T:* Yendle *C:* Harries *PG:* Harries (2)
29 Feb	H	Maesteg	48-6	*T:* Harries (3), Bidgood (2), Pugh (2), Llewellyn (2), Orrell *C:* Turner (2), R Jones (2)
14 Mar	A	Llanelli	12-16	*T:* McGauchie *C:* Turner *PG:* Turner (2)
28 Mar	H	Neath	16-34	*T:* Yendle, pen try *C:* Harries *PG:* Harries (2)
11 Apr	H	Pontypool	10-10	*T:* Westwood, George *C:* R Jones
15 Apr	A	Newbridge	3-21	*PG:* Harries
21 Apr	A	Cardiff	13-18	*T:* Orrell, R Jones *C:* Turner *PG:* Turner
25 Apr	H	Swansea	6-18	*T:* Westwood *C:* Turner

Penarth

Year of formation 1880
Ground Athletic Field, Lavernock Road, Penarth, South Glamorgan
Tel: Penarth (0222) 708402
Colours Royal blue with white chevron
Most capped player J Bassett (Wales) 15 caps
Captain 1991-92 C Lakin
1st XV 1991-92 P43 W8 D1 L34 F540 A996
Heineken League Div 2 10th **WRU/Schweppes Cup** Lost 0-18 to Glamorgan
Wanderers (4th round)

League Record 1991-92

Date	Venue	Opponents	Result	Scorers
28 Sept	A	Glam Wands	10-23	*T:* Payne *PG:* Howells (2)
9 Nov	H	Dunvant	6-17	*T:* Howells *C:* Howells
16 Nov	A	Ebbw Vale	13-12	*T:* Morgan, G Lewis *C:* G Evans
				PG: Howells
23 Nov	H	Llanharan	0-29	
30 Nov	A	Abertillery	0-32	
7 Dec	H	Tredegar	10-19	*T:* Howells, Roberts *C:* Howells
14 Dec	A	Aberavon	12-53	*T:* Morgan, Ball *C:* Howells (2)
4 Jan	A	Cross Keys	9-30	*T:* Clark *C:* Howells *PG:* Howells
11 Jan	H	S W Police	10-25	*T:* Goult *PG:* Howells (2)
8 Feb	H	Glam Wands	8-18	*T:* Gwyn Lewis, D Williams
15 Feb	A	Dunvant	6-33	*PG:* Howells (2)
29 Feb	H	Ebbw Vale	15-31	*T:* Goult *C:* Howells *PG:* Howells (3)
14 Mar	A	Llanharan	6-12	*PG:* Howells (2)
28 Mar	H	Abertillery	9-27	*T:* D Roberts *C:* Howells *PG:* Howells
11 Apr	A	Tredegar	7-43	*T:* Gwyn Lewis *PG:* Howells
18 Apr	H	Aberavon	10-35	*T:* Graham Lewis, Goult *C:* Howells
25 Apr	H	Cross Keys	0-17	
9 May	A	S W Police	12-45	*T:* Riddlestone-Holmes, Ritchie, Weekes

Pontypool

Year of formation 1901
Ground The Park, Pontypool, Gwent   Tel: Pontypool (0495) 763492 or 762524
Colours Black, white and red hoops
Most capped player G Price (Wales) 41 caps
Captain 1991-92 C Huish
1st XV 1991-92 P52   W35   D5   L12   F1485   A681
Heineken League Div 1 7th **WRU/Schweppes Cup** Lost 3-27 to Llanelli
(7th round)

League Record 1991-92

Date	Venue	Opponents	Result	Scorers
9 Nov	A	Newbridge	21-9	T: Oswald, Jardine C: Parry (2) PG: Parry DG: Phillips (2)
16 Nov	H	Bridgend	16-9	T: White, Oswald C: Parry PG: Parry DG: Phillips
23 Nov	A	Pontypridd	3-16	PG: Parry
30 Nov	H	Maesteg	28-0	T: S Davies, Goodey, Oswald, Jardine C: Parry (3) PG: Parry DG: Phillips
7 Dec	A	Llanelli	21-21	T: Oswald, Jonathan, Phillips C: Parry (2), M Jones PG: M Jones
21 Dec	A	Neath	13-10	T: Parry, Phillips C: Parry PG: Parry
4 Jan	A	Cardiff	24-10	T: Meek, Huish, Parry, Mruk, N Jones C: Phillips (2)
11 Jan	H	Swansea	27-4	T: Pawson, Goodey, Lintern, Parry C: M Jones (4) PG: M Jones
21 Jan	H	Newport	7-7	T: Oswald PG: Parry
8 Feb	H	Newbridge	6-25	PG: M Jones (2)
15 Feb	A	Bridgend	15-22	T: Phillips C: M Jones PG: M Jones (3)
29 Feb	H	Pontypridd	3-6	PG: Parry
14 Mar	A	Maesteg	27-18	T: Huish, Spiller, Goodey, White, D Phillips C: M Jones (2) PG: M Jones
28 Mar	H	Llanelli	15-36	T: Huish, D Phillips C: M Jones (2) PG: M Jones
11 Apr	A	Newport	10-10	T: M Jones PG: M Jones (2)
18 Apr	H	Neath	13-26	T: Jardine, Hanson C: Dyke PG: Dyke
25 Apr	H	Cardiff	10-23	T: pen try PG: Dyke DG: Dyke
9 May	A	Swansea	23-23	T: White (2), Jardine, S Jackson C: D Phillips (2) PG: D Phillips

Pontypridd

Year of formation 1876
Ground Sardis Road Ground, Pwllgwaun, Pontypridd   Tel: Pontypridd (0433) 405006
Colours Black and white hoops
Most capped player R J Robins (Wales) 13 caps
Captain 1991-92 S Lewis
1st XV 1991-92 P47   W35   D0   L12   F1029   A530
Heineken League Div 1 3rd **WRU/Schweppes Cup** Lost 6-27 to Llanelli (semi-final)

League Record 1991-92

Date	Venue	Opponents	Result	Scorers
9 Nov	H	Llanelli	16-22	T: Paul John (2) C: Jenkins PG: Jenkins (2)
16 Nov	A	Newport	6-13	PG: Jenkins (2)
23 Nov	H	Pontypool	16-3	T: Hughes, Rowley C: Jenkins PG: Jenkins (2)
30 Nov	A	Cardiff	12-19	PG: Jenkins (4)
7 Dec	H	Swansea	9-27	PG: Jenkins (3)
21 Dec	H	Bridgend	4-11	T: Mason
4 Jan	H	Neath	18-6	T: Jenkins C: Jenkins PG: Jenkins (3) DG: Jenkins
8 Feb	A	Llanelli	18-11	T: Mason C: Jenkins PG: Jenkins (4)
15 Feb	H	Newport	25-12	T: Jenkins, Paul John C: Jenkins PG: Jenkins (5)
29 Feb	A	Pontypool	6-3	PG: Jenkins (2)
10 Mar	A	Newbridge	24-6	T: McIntosh (2), J Lewis C: Jenkins (3) PG: Jenkins (2)
14 Mar	H	Cardiff	17-12	T: Jackson, Hughes PG: Jenkins (3)
24 Mar	A	Maesteg	42-12	T: Harries (2), Hughes, Dicks, Bezani, Jenkins, Paul John C: Jenkins (4) PG: Jenkins (2)
28 Mar	A	Swansea	12-46	T: Bezani C: Jenkins PG: Jenkins (2)
11 Apr	H	Newbridge	25-6	T: Sheppeard, G Jones, Hughes, Mason C: Jenkins (3) PG: Jenkins
18 Apr	A	Bridgend	14-10	T: Jenkins (2), G Jones C: Jenkins
25 Apr	A	Neath	13-23	T: Harries, Mason C: Jenkins PG: Jenkins
9 May	H	Maesteg	12-3	T: McIntosh, Paul John, Richards

South Wales Police

Year of formation 1969
Ground Waterton Cross, Bridgend, Mid-Glamorgan
Tel: Bridgend (0656) 655555 ext 218
Colours Red, white and blue
Most capped player Bleddyn Bowen (Wales) 22 caps
Captain 1991-92 C Hillman
1st XV 1991-92 P39 W21 D2 L16 F737 A716
Heineken League Div 2 *Winners* **WRU/Schweppes Cup** Lost 13-30 to Swansea (6th round)

League Record 1991-92

Date	Venue	Opponents	Result	Scorers
28 Sept	A	Cross Keys	12-6	T: Donovan C: Phillips PG: Parfitt (2)
9 Nov	H	Glam Wands	30-9	T: J Williams, Hemburrow, Price, Parfitt, Hughes, pen try C: Price (3)
16 Nov	A	Dunvant	20-7	T: J Williams, Wakeford, Price, Parfitt C: Hughes (2)
23 Nov	H	Ebbw Vale	19-7	T: Hughes (2), Legge C: Hughes, Phillips PG: Phillips
30 Nov	A	Llanharan	19-15	T: Hillman, pen try C: Phillips PG: Hughes (3)
7 Dec	H	Abertillery	15-16	T: Legge (2) C: Hughes (2) PG: Hughes
4 Jan	H	Aberavon	15-15	T: Legge (2) C: Hughes (2) PG: Hughes
11 Jan	A	Penarth	25-10	T: Legge (3), J Williams, Donovan C: Hughes PG: Hughes

8 Feb	H	Cross Keys	13-27	*T:* Legge, M Trigg *C:* Price *PG:* Price
15 Feb	A	Glam Wands	21-13	*T:* Donovan, Phillips *C:* Hughes (2)
				PG: Hughes (3)
29 Feb	H	Dunvant	19-15	*T:* Hughes, P Phillips *C:* Hughes
				PG: Hughes (3)
14 Mar	A	Ebbw Vale	6-29	*PG:* P Phillips *DG:* Parfitt
24 Mar	A	Tredegar	16-9	*T:* N Davies (2), Legge *C:* P Phillips (2)
28 Mar	H	Llanharan	14-13	*T:* Legge, Hillman, pen try *C:* P Phillips
11 Apr	A	Abertillery	16-28	*T:* J Williams *PG:* Price (3) *DG:* Price
18 Apr	H	Tredegar	17-12	*T:* Legge (2), Donovan *C:* P Phillips
				PG: P Phillips
25 Apr	A	Aberavon	15-15	*T:* Parfitt *C:* Price *PG:* Price (2) *DG:* Price
9 May	H	Penarth	45-12	*T:* Legge (2), Price (2), Sutton, P Phillips, D Rees,
				Hughes *C:* Price (5) *PG:* Price

Swansea

Year of formation 1873
Ground St Helen's, Swansea, West Glamorgan   Tel: Swansea (0792) 464918
Colours All white
Most capped player R N Jones (Wales) 42 caps
Captain 1991-92 K Hopkins
1st XV 1991-92   P44   W31   D1   L12   F928   A582
Heineken League Div 1 *Winners* **WRU/Schweppes Cup** Lost 7-16 to Llanelli (final)

League Record 1991-92

Date	*Venue*	*Opponents*	*Result*	*Scorers*
9 Nov	H	Cardiff	23-9	*T:* Hopkins, Titley, Taylor, Stuart Davies, Webster
				PG: S Jones
16 Nov	A	Neath	6-22	*PG:* R Jones (2)
23 Nov	A	Newbridge	22-9	*T:* Clement, Simon Davies *C:* S Jones
				PG: S Jones (2), R Jones (2)
30 Nov	H	Bridgend	30-6	*T:* Titley (2), Simon Davies (2), Clement
				C: S Jones, R Jones *PG:* S Jones (2)
7 Dec	A	Pontypridd	27-9	*T:* Taylor, Reynolds, Clement *C:* S Jones (2),
				R Jones *PG:* S Jones (2) *DG:* S Jones
14 Dec	H	Maesteg	47-6	*T:* Ian Davies (4), Reynolds (2), Titley, Taylor,
				Hopkins *C:* S Jones (3), R Jones *PG:* R Jones
21 Dec	A	Llanelli	6-11	*PG:* S Jones (2)
4 Jan	H	Newport	14-0	*T:* Titley, Stuart Davies *PG:* Aled Williams (2)
11 Jan	A	Pontypool	4-27	*T:* Ian Davies
5 Feb	A	Cardiff	36-14	*T:* Gibbs (3), Simon Davies, Titley, Webster
				C: Aled Williams (3) *PG:* Aled Williams (2)
15 Feb	H	Neath	24-13	*T:* Aled Williams, Stuart Davies, Gibbs
				C: Aled Williams (3) *PG:* Aled Williams (2)
29 Feb	H	Newbridge	20-9	*T:* Webster, Simon Davies, Hopkins
				C: Aled Williams *PG:* Aled Williams (2)
14 Mar	A	Bridgend	15-22	*T:* Aled Williams *C:* Aled Williams
				PG: Aled Williams (2) *DG:* Aled Williams
28 Mar	H	Pontypridd	46-12	*T:* Clement (3), Simon Davies (2), Hopkins,
				R Jones *C:* Aled Williams (3)
				PG: Aled Williams (3) *DG:* Aled Williams
11 Apr	A	Maesteg	23-4	*T:* Stuart Davies (2), Titley, Simon Davies
				C: Aled Williams (2) *PG:* Aled Williams
18 Apr	H	Llanelli	9-3	*T:* Aled Williams *C:* Aled Williams
				PG: Aled Williams

25 Apr	A	Newport	18-6	*T:* Aled Williams, Simon Davies, Gibbs, Robert Jones *C:* Aled Williams
9 May	H	Pontypool	23-23	*T:* Clement, S Jones, Taylor, Titley *C:* S Jones (2) *PG:* S Jones

Tredegar

Year of formation 1893
Ground Recreation Ground, Parc Hill, Tredegar, Gwent   Tel: Tredegar (0495) 252879
Colours Red, black and white
Captain 1991-92 C Lake
1st XV 1991-92 P40 W11 D0 L29 F462 A831
Heineken League Div 2 9th **WRU/Schweppes Cup** Lost 7-24 to Pontypool United (4th round)

League Record 1991-92

Date	Venue	Opponents	Result	Scorers
9 Nov	H	Llanharan	6-30	*T:* Burridge *C:* K Smith
16 Nov	A	Abertillery	0-26	
23 Nov	A	Cross Keys	6-11	*T:* Moyle *C:* K Smith
30 Nov	H	Aberavon	9-34	*T:* Burridge *C:* K Smith *PG:* K Smith
7 Dec	A	Penarth	19-10	*T:* Powell (2), Green *C:* Green (2) *PG:* Green
4 Jan	A	Glam Wands	6-20	*T:* Powell *C:* Green
8 Feb	H	Ebbw Vale	12-35	*T:* Burridge *C:* K Smith *PG:* K Smith (2)
15 Feb	A	Llanharan	12-20	*T:* Green, I Morgan *C:* Green (2)
29 Feb	H	Abertillery	21-6	*T:* Ford (2), Burridge *C:* Green (3) *PG:* Green
6 Mar	A	Ebbw Vale	9-16	*T:* Green *C:* Green *PG:* Green
14 Mar	H	Cross Keys	10-9	*T:* I Morgan *PG:* Green (2)
20 Mar	H	Dunvant	7-15	*T:* Green *PG:* Green
24 Mar	H	S W Police	9-16	*T:* J Williams *C:* Green *PG:* Green
28 Mar	A	Aberavon	6-43	*T:* Moyle *C:* Green
11 Apr	H	Penarth	43-7	*T:* Burridge (2), Powell, J Williams, Jenkins, Green, Harris, Hunt *C:* Green (4) *PG:* Green
18 Apr	A	S W Police	12-17	*T:* Lake (2) *C:* Green (2)
25 Apr	H	Glam Wands	3-22	*PG:* Green
9 May	A	Dunvant	12-14	*T:* J Williams *C:* Green *PG:* Green (2)

OBITUARY 1991-92 (*up to 1 May 1992*)

Stanley John ADKINS (Coventry, England) made his England debut in 1950 and was a lock forward in the team which won the 1953 International Championship. In the final game of that year he scored a try against Scotland, following up a rush by the English forwards. A retired publican, 'Akker' Adkins died in Coventry on 2 January 1992. He was 69.

Albert William BOWMAN (Hawke's Bay, New Zealand), who died aged 76 on 20 January 1992 at Waipukurau, was a flanker who toured Australia with the 1938 New Zealand team. 'Snow' Bowman played on the winning side in all three Tests of the series, scoring tries in the second and third internationals.

Norman Scott BRUCE (Blackheath, London Scottish, Scotland) died of cancer in Oswestry on 28 March 1992, aged 59. One of the fittest hookers of his day, Bruce won 31 caps between 1958 and 1964, forming with Hugh McLeod and David Rollo a formidable Scottish front row which appeared together in 14 internationals. A product of the Borders, he followed a service career in the Royal Army Ordnance Corps before retiring to become a schoolmaster at a prep school in Shropshire.

Brigadier James Thomas BURROWS (Canterbury, New Zealand), the distinguished New Zealand soldier and former All Black, died in Christchurch on 10 June 1991, aged 86. He was selected for the All Blacks' visit to South Africa in 1928, but he sustained a rib injury early in the tour which prevented him from challenging for a Test place. A fine all-round sportsman, he was a schoolmaster by profession.

Angus CAMERON (Glasgow HSFP, Scotland), winner of 17 Scottish caps between 1948 and 1956, was a versatile back and a shrewd tactical kicker who captained his country nine times and was vice-captain of the 1955 Lions in South Africa. He died on 1 April 1991, aged 61.

Dr Peter Laurence CANDLER (St Bart's Hospital, England) died on 27 November 1991 in Natal after a long illness. He was 77. Educated at Sherborne School and Cambridge, where he won a rugby Blue in 1934, Dr Candler was capped ten times for England between 1935 and 1938. Equally at home as a centre or outside half, he played in the latter position in 1936 when England beat the All Blacks 13-0 at Twickenham, and the following season his rigid defence as a centre was a key element of England's Triple Crown success.

Robin William Taylor CHISHOLM (Melrose, Scotland) who died on 2 November 1991 aged 62, vied with Ken Scotland for the full-back position in the Scottish sides of the late 1950s. Chisholm's sound yet unspectacular style was preferred by the selectors in 1958, when his steadiness in defence was an important factor in Scotland's win against Australia. He won the last of his 11 caps against South Africa in 1960, when Scotland became the first Home Union to make a short tour.

Air Chief Marshal Sir Hugh CONSTANTINE KBE, CB, DSO (Leicester, RAF, Eastern Counties), former Commander-in-Chief of Flying Training Command and the man who taught Douglas Bader to fly, died on 16 April 1992, aged 83. At six feet and weighing more than 14 stone, 'Connie' Constantine was a useful forward in his youth and played for the Probables in the second England trial at Twickenham in 1933.

Mervyn Miles Nelson CORNER (Auckland, New Zealand) was, at only five feet five inches tall and under ten stone, one of the smallest backs to play for New Zealand. He made his Test debut against the 1930 Lions and went on to win six caps as a bustling scrum-half. He retired after touring Britain and Ireland with the 1935-36 All Blacks, and went on to serve as President of the Auckland RFU from 1959 to 1961. He died at the age of 83 on 3 February 1992.

Michael DAUNT OBE (RAF, London Irish), the pilot who test flew the Gloster-Whittle, the pioneer gas turbine aircraft, died in Ipswich on 26 July 1991, aged 81. In the mid-1930s he was a well-known wing threequarter for the RAF and London Irish.

Joseph DUTREY (Lourdes, France), a lock who played for France against the British Army in 1940, died at Tarbes in January 1992, aged 77. He spent most of the 1939-45 war as a prisoner of the Germans, but returned to captain Lourdes when they reached the French Championship final in 1946. He later led Tarbes.

Sir Norman ELLIOTT CBE (Cambridge University, Southend, Eastern Counties), the former chairman of the Electricity Council, died on 23 March 1992, aged 88. Between the wars he was an enthusiastic hooker for Eastern Counties and a keen Sussex referee.

James Huck FERGUSON (Gala, Scotland) died in Edinburgh on 3 April 1992. He was 88. Jimmy Ferguson, who won his only cap for Scotland against Wales in 1928, was Gala's captain when they won the Scottish Championship in 1931-32. Later he became Gala's president, and since 1974 had been a life member of the club.

Kerry Victor Joseph FITZGERALD (Teachers RFC, Brisbane) was the distinguished Australian rugby referee whose predilection for applying the advantage laws invariably produced entertaining, high-scoring matches. The last of his 21 full International Board Tests was the Scotland-England World Cup semi-final in October. Two months later, on 18 December 1991, he died suddenly at work in Brisbane after a heart attack. He was 43.

Arthur GRAY (Otley, England) was England's first full-back after the last war. He won three caps in 1947 before joining Wakefield Trinity Rugby League club. He died aged 73 on 25 August 1991 while on holiday in Scarborough.

Thomas HEWITT (Queen's University, Belfast, Instonians, Ireland) was the senior member of a distinguished Irish rugby family, six of whom were capped by their country. Tom died in July 1991, aged 86. He won nine caps as a threequarter between 1924 and 1926.

Murray Bernard HOFMEYR (Oxford University, England) was a Pretoria-born all-round sportsman who won rugby and cricket Blues at Oxford between 1948 and 1950. Soon after making three appearances at full-back for England in 1950, he returned to his native South Africa and played for Northern Transvaal in the Currie Cup. He died in Johannesburg on 26 June 1990, aged 64.

John Robert HOWE (West Hartlepool) collapsed and died on 28 March 1992 during West Hartlepool's League match against Morley. He was 28. The six feet seven giant entered first-class rugby with Hartlepool Rovers in 1982-83 and in a varied career appeared for Saracens and Sale before contributing to West Hartlepool's recent bid for promotion to Courage League 1. A Barbarian in 1988, John played in the Middlesex (1987) and Durham (1989) teams which reached County Championship finals, and he played for England Under-23 against Spain in 1986.

James LANG (Llanelli, Wales) was the No 8 who ruled the line-out when the All Blacks were beaten 13-12 by Wales at Cardiff in 1935. A steelworker, he won 12 caps between 1931 and 1937, scoring his only try for Wales on his debut against France. Jim Lang died at Morriston Hospital on 22 December 1991, aged 82.

Jan Lodewyk LOCK (Northern Transvaal), a prop who was a Springbok trialist in 1984, collapsed and died from heart failure on 5 October 1991 while playing for Northern Transvaal B in a curtain-raiser to the Currie Cup final in Pretoria. He was 26.

Maurice Alfred McCANLIS (Oxford University, Gloucester, England) was an all-round sportsman who won cricket and rugby Blues for Oxford and was capped twice for England in 1931. A schoolmaster by profession, he died on 27 September 1991, aged 85.

Lt Col Timothy Dennis MORGAN MC, who was the administrative secretary of the RFU between 1970 and 1987, died on 29 April 1992, aged 69. 'Dai' Morgan, who was of Welsh stock, was a former Marine.

Dr Edward Sealy NICHOLSON MBE (Oxford University, Leicester, England), who died aged 79 on 16 March 1992 at Beccles Hospital, was the last survivor of England's winning pack against the 1936 All Blacks. He studied medicine at Oxford, played on the winning side in three of his four Varsity Matches and scored the crucial try in Oxford's 5-3 victory over Cambridge in 1933. His five caps for England were won as a hooker in 1935 and 1936. After the war he was in general practice in Beccles.

Desmond Hillary O'DONNELL (Wellington, New Zealand), who died aged 71 on 18 January 1992, was capped once as a prop for New Zealand against Australia in 1949. He was still playing club rugby for Raetihi as a 43-year-old in 1964.

Thomas William PRICE (Gloucester, Cheltenham, England), the England prop capped six times in 1948 and 1949, died on 11 July 1991. He was 76. Mr Price had captained Gloucester in 1947 before joining Cheltenham, and played for Gloucestershire in the 1947 and 1949 County Championship finals.

John Idwal REES (Swansea, Edinburgh Wanderers, Wales), the former Welsh threequarter and captain, died at Cefn Coed on 31 August 1991, aged 81. He won Cambridge Blues in 1931 and 1932 before entering the Welsh side as one of 13 new caps against England in 1934. Several of his 14 Welsh caps were gained from Edinburgh Wanderers while he was teaching at Fettes College. His appointment as headmaster of Cowbridge Grammar School in 1938 signalled the end of his playing career.

Joseph Patrick Irwin REIDY (London Irish), the distinguished plastic surgeon who died on 10 September 1991, aged 83, was a noted lock forward in the 1930s. He appeared for the Barbarians against the East Midlands in 1934 and played for the London Counties against the 1935 All Blacks. As an undergraduate at Cambridge he was a skilful boxer.

Maurice SAVY (Montferrand, France) was full-back in 1931 in France's last season in the Five Nations Championship for 16 years. The French were then excommunicated by the Home Unions for alleged professionalism. Savy won five caps and later served the FFR as treasurer general. He died on 1 December 1991, aged 85, at Clermont-Ferrand.

Eric SMITH (Orrell), the Orrell president who transformed the Lancashire club into a thriving First Division outfit, died in August 1991, aged 67. His connection with the club began as a player after the last war. Des Seabrook described him as 'Mr Orrell'.

Frank SOLOMON (Auckland, New Zealand) died aged 85 on 21 December 1991 at Auckland Hospital. In 1931 he was the last loose forward to play for New Zealand before the 2-3-2 scrum gave way to the 3-4-1 formation. An American Samoan by birth, he was also a noted oarsman. His brother David toured Britain with the 1935 All Blacks.

Terry TANDY, Gloucester's long-serving secretary, died at his home on 20 February 1992, aged 57. He ran a tight ship at Kingsholm, and during his 25 years' service to Gloucester the club were regularly in the top flight of English rugby.

Alun Gruffydd THOMAS (Llanelli, Swansea, Cardiff, Wales), the Welsh utility back of the 1950s who later reached the top as an administrator, died at Swansea on 8 May 1991, aged 65. After winning 13 Welsh caps, appearing at wing, centre and fly-half, he finished his representative career as a Lion in South Africa in 1955. Nineteen years later he returned to South Africa as manager of the invincible 1974 Lions. As an administrator he was largely responsible for initiating the coaching movement in Wales, and the culmination of his 25 years' unbroken service to the WRU was his presidency in 1985-86.

William Eldon TUCKER CVO, MBE, TD, FRCS (Cambridge University, Blackheath, England), the orthopaedic surgeon with a special interest in sporting injuries, died in Bermuda on 4 August 1991, aged 87. As a youth Bill Tucker won four Blues and captained Cambridge in the 1925 Varsity Match before winning three caps as a forward for England between 1926 and 1930.

Michel VANNIER (Racing Club de France, Chalon, France) overcame serious injuries to win 43 caps between 1953 and 1961 during the spectacular rise of French rugby. One of the small band of French caps born and bred north of Paris, Vannier was an accomplished full-back with a flair for attack, sure defence and a penchant for dropping goals. He died at Chalon-sur-Saône on 28 June 1991, aged 59.

David Alun WILLIAMS OBE, the popular Welsh broadcaster whose duties included countless commentaries on Welsh rugby internationals, died on 30 March 1992 during a working holiday in the Mediterranean. He was 71. Once described by Brian Johnston as 'possibly the most versatile of all modern commentators', Alun Williams covered the 1971 and 1974 Lions tours of New Zealand and South Africa, bringing vivid descriptions of famous British wins to BBC listeners.

Charles WILLOCKS (Otago, New Zealand), a key forward in Otago's successful run of Ranfurly Shield defences in the 1940s, died on 25 August 1991, aged 72. He was chosen as one of New Zealand's five Players of the Year for his outstanding form in 1946, and his citation stated that his value to Otago was inestimable. His 22 appearances for New Zealand included five Tests between 1946 and 1949.

FIXTURES 1992-93

Venues and fixtures are understood to be correct at the time of going to press, but are subject to alteration. We should like to thank all those who have assisted in the compilation of this list, especially those at the various headquarters of the Home Unions. Additional thanks go to Peter Jackson and LeRoy Angel for help with Courage League fixtures.

Saturday, 29 August

Selkirk Sevens

Sunday, 30 August

Glasgow High/Kelvinside Sevens

Tuesday, 1 September

Ulster v Cornwall (Ravenhill)
Askeans v Old Colfeians
Crumlin v Newbridge
Exeter v Newbury
Glasgow Acads v Glasgow High/Kelvinside
Kendal v Orrell
Kirkcaldy v Glenrothes
Langholm v Jedforest
Lydney v Gloucester
Maesteg v Penarth
Manchester v Liverpool St Helens
Munster v Saracens
Northampton v Rugby
Preston Grasshoppers v Sale
Wasps v High Wycombe

Wednesday, 2 September

Fylde v Aspatria
Hinckley v Coventry
Middlesbrough v West Hartlepool
Portadown v Newcastle Gosforth
Stirling County v Corstorphine

Thursday, 3 September

Watsonians v Belmont Shore

Saturday, 5 September

Leicester v England XV (Welford Road)
Glasgow Dist v Leinster
Yorkshire v Ulster
Collegians Tournament

WRU Heineken Leagues
Division 1
Aberavon v Cardiff
Bridgend v South Wales Police
Newport v Maesteg

Pontypool v Llanelli
Pontypridd v Neath
Swansea v Newbridge
Division 2
Abertillery v Tredegar
Cross Keys v Dunvant
Ebbw Vale v Blaina
Glam Wands v Tenby Utd
Llandovery v Penarth
Narberth v Llanharan
Division 3
Blackwood v Bonymaen
Kenfig Hill v Pontypool Utd
Mountain Ash v Wrexham
St Peters v Aberavon Quins
Treorchy v Abercynon
Tumble v Rumney

Askeans v Streatham/Croydon
Aspatria v Glasgow High/Kelvinside
Ballymena v Newcastle Gosforth
Brixham v Lydney
Broughton Park v Widnes
Cork Const v Saracens
Dundee HSFP v Edinburgh Wands
Durham City v Morley
Exeter v Clifton
Gala v Hawick
Glasgow Acads v Currie
Gloucester v Blackheath
Harrogate v Bedford
Hawick YM v Kirkcaldy
Heriot's FP v London Scottish
Highfield v Dungannon
Liverpool St Helens v Northern
Maidenhead v Met Police
Melrose v Kelso
Moseley v Wasps
Northampton v Harlequins
Nottingham v Rugby
Orrell v Sale
Plymouth Albion v Bristol
Redruth v Taunton
Rosslyn Park v Coventry
Vale of Lune v West of Scotland
Wakefield v Boroughmuir
Wanderers v Waterloo
Watsonians v Tynedale

West Hartlepool v Otley
Wigton v Stirling County

Sunday, 6 September

Cumbria v Ulster
Harlequins/Lord's Taverners Sevens
Kelso Sevens
Northern Sevens
Devon v Bristol
Old Wesley v Wanderers

Tuesday, 8 September

Devonport Services v Redruth
Langholm v Gala
Liverpool St Helens v New Brighton
Newbridge v Ebbw Vale
Nottingham v Nuneaton
Selkirk v Hawick
Wasps v Ealing

Wednesday, 9 September

Esher v Met Police
Harlequins v Askeans
Leicester v County XV
Lydney v Abertillery
Newcastle Gosforth v Stockton
Rugby v Coventry
West Hartlepool v Gateshead Fell

Thursday, 10 September

Kilmarnock v Glasgow Acads

Saturday, 12 September

Irish Exiles v Munster
Ireland Under-21 v Wolfhounds
  (Arklow)

WRU Heineken Leagues
Division 1
Cardiff v Pontypridd
Llanelli v Bridgend
Maesteg v Swansea
Neath v Pontypool
Newbridge v Aberavon
South Wales Police v Newport
Division 2
Blaina v Abertillery
Dunvant v Ebbw Vale
Llanharan v Glam Wands
Penarth v Narberth
Tenby Utd v Cross Keys
Tredegar v Llandovery
Division 3
Aberavon Quins v Blackwood

Abercynon v Mountain Ash
Bonymaen v Treorchy
Pontypool Utd v Tumble
Rumney v St Peters
Wrexham v Kenfig Hill

Armagh v CIYMS
Askeans v Nuneaton
Ballymena v Hawick
Bedford v London Welsh
Bristol v Rugby
Broughton Park v Waterloo
City of Derry v Queen's U, Belfast
Collegians v Ards
Coventry v Northampton
Currie v Alnwick
Dungannon v Lansdowne
Edinburgh Acads v Harrogate
Exeter v Stourbridge
Glasgow Acads v Clarkston
Glasgow High/Kelvinside v Instonians
Gloucester v Sale
Kirkcaldy v Edinburgh Wands
Langholm v Melrose
Leicester v Mediolanum (Milan)
London Scottish v Nottingham
Malone v Portadown
Met Police v Vale of Lune
Morley v Birmingham Solihull
Moseley v Orrell
Newcastle Gosforth v Wasps
Plymouth Albion v Harlequins
Redruth v Brixham
Rosslyn Park v London Irish
Saracens v Wakefield
Stirling County v Dundee HSFP
Treviso v Bath
Tynedale v Heriot's FP
Walsall v Lydney
West Hartlepool v Liverpool St Helens

Sunday, 13 September

Cumbria v Anti-Assassins

Monday, 14 September

Cornwall v Crawshay's Welsh
  (Camborne)

Tuesday, 15 September

Glasgow Acads v Allan Glen's
Glasgow High/Kelvinside v Kilmarnock
Hawick v Kelso
Selkirk v Langholm
Wakefield v Hull Ionians

Wednesday, 16 September

Gateshead Fell v Newcastle Gosforth
Pontypool v Ontario
Sale v Lymm

Saturday, 19 September

RFU Courage Leagues

Division 1
Bath v Harlequins
London Irish v Leicester
London Scottish v Gloucester
Northampton v Bristol
Saracens v Rugby
West Hartlepool v Wasps
Division 2
Blackheath v Wakefield
Coventry v Morley
Moseley v Bedford
Nottingham v Richmond
Sale v Fylde
Waterloo v Rosslyn Park

WRU Heineken Leagues

Division 1
Aberavon v Maesteg
Bridgend v Neath
Cardiff v Newbridge
Newport v Llanelli
Pontypool v Pontypridd
Swansea v South Wales Police
Division 2
Abertillery v Dunvant
Cross Keys v Glam Wands
Ebbw Vale v Tenby Utd
Llandovery v Blaina
Llanharan v Penarth
Narberth v Tredegar
Division 3
Blackwood v St Peters
Kenfig Hill v Abercynon
Mountain Ash v Bonymaen
Rumney v Pontypool Utd
Treorchy v Aberavon Quins
Tumble v Wrexham

RFU Pilkington Cup *1st round*
WRU Cup *1st round*

Ards v City of Derry
Armagh v Collegians
Ballina v CIYMS
Dungannon v Old Crescent
Edinburgh Acads v Ayr
Edinburgh Wands v Corstorphine
Galwegians v Ballymena
Glasgow High/Kelvinside v Stirling County

Hawick v Langholm
Howe of Fife v Kirkcaldy
Lansdowne v Heriot's FP
Melrose v Selkirk
Newcastle Gosforth v Kendal
Peebles v Kelso
Portadown v NIFC
Preston Lodge v Currie
Queen's U, Belfast v Malone

Wednesday, 23 September

Cambridge U v Cambridge City

Saturday, 26 September

RFU Courage Leagues

Division 1
Bath v London Irish
Bristol v West Hartlepool
Harlequins v Wasps
Leicester v Gloucester
Northampton v Saracens
Orrell v London Scottish
Division 2
Blackheath v Nottingham
Coventry v Waterloo
Morley v Moseley
Newcastle Gosforth v Sale
Richmond v Fylde
Wakefield v Bedford
Division 3
Askeans v Headingley
Clifton v Sheffield
Exeter v Redruth
Havant v Roundhay
Liverpool St Helens v Broughton Park
Plymouth Albion v Otley
Divison 4 (South)
Berry Hill v Sudbury
Camborne v Basingstoke
High Wycombe v Weston-super-Mare
London Welsh v Thurrock
Lydney v North Walsham
Maidstone v Met Police
Division 4 (North)
Durham City v Hereford
Harrogate v Stoke-on-Trent
Lichfield v Stourbridge
Nuneaton v Kendal
Preston Grasshoppers v Towcestrians
Rotherham v Winnington Park

SRU McEwan's Leagues

Division 1
Dundee HSFP v Heriot's FP
Edinburgh Acads v Currie

Gala v Boroughmuir
Hawick v Selkirk
Kelso v Glasgow High/Kelvinside
Stirling County v Jedforest
Watsonians v Melrose
Division 2
Clarkston v Peebles
Edinburgh Wands v Dunfermline
Glasgow Acads v West of Scotland
Grangemouth v Wigtownshire
Kilmarnock v Preston Lodge
Kirkcaldy v Stewart's-Melville FP
Musselburgh v Ayr

WRU Heineken Leagues
Division 1
Llanelli v Swansea
Maesteg v Cardiff
Neath v Newport
Pontypool v Bridgend
Pontypridd v Newbridge
South Wales Police v Aberavon
Division 2
Blaina v Narberth
Cross Keys v Ebbw Vale
Dunvant v Llandovery
Glam Wands v Penarth
Tenby Utd v Abertillery
Tredegar v Llanharan
Division 3
Aberavon Quins v Mountain Ash
Abercynon v Tumble
Blackwood v Treorchy
Bonymaen v Kenfig Hill
St Peters v Pontypool Utd
Wrexham v Rumney

Blackrock Coll v Dungannon
City of Derry v Armagh
Collegians v CIYMS
Lansdowne v Ballymena
Malone v Ards
NIFC v Queen's U, Belfast
Rosslyn Park v Walsall

Monday, 28 September

Hawick v Glasgow Acads

Wednesday, 30 September

Cambridge U v St Mary's Hosp
Pontypool v Munster

Saturday, 3 October

French Under-21 v South Africans
(Bordeaux)

RFU Courage Leagues
Division 1
Gloucester v Rugby
London Irish v Northampton
London Scottish v Bristol
Saracens v Orrell
Wasps v Leicester
West Hartlepool v Harlequins
Division 2
Bedford v Richmond
Fylde v Rosslyn Park
Moseley v Wakefield
Nottingham v Coventry
Sale v Morley
Waterloo v Newcastle Gosforth
Division 3
Broughton Park v Plymouth Albion
Headingley v Exeter
Otley v Clifton
Redruth v Liverpool St Helens
Roundhay v Aspatria
Sheffield v Havant
Division 4 (South)
Basingstoke v High Wycombe
Met Police v Southend
North Walsham v Berry Hill
Sudbury v London Welsh
Thurrock v Maidstone
Weston-super-Mare v Lydney
Division 4 (North)
Hereford v Lichfield
Kendal v Harrogate
Stoke-on-Trent v Durham City
Stourbridge v Rotherham
Towcestrians v Walsall
Winnington Park v Preston Grasshoppers

SRU McEwan's Leagues
Division 1
Currie v Stirling County
Glasgow High/Kelvinside v Dundee HSFP
Heriot's FP v Boroughmuir
Jedforest v Hawick
Melrose v Edinburgh Acads
Selkirk v Kelso
Watsonians v Gala
Division 2
Ayr v Stewart's-Melville FP
Dunfermline v Kilmarnock
Edinburgh Wands v Kirkcaldy
Peebles v Musselburgh
Preston Lodge v Grangemouth
West of Scotland v Clarkston
Wigtownshire v Glasgow Acads

WRU Heineken Leagues
Division 1
Aberavon v Llanelli
Bridgend v Pontypridd
Cardiff v South Wales Police
Newbridge v Maesteg
Newport v Pontypool
Swansea v Neath
Division 2
Abertillery v Cross Keys
Ebbw Vale v Glam Wands
Llandovery v Tenby Utd
Llanharan v Blaina
Narberth v Dunvant
Penarth v Tredegar
Division 3
Kenfig Hill v Aberavon Quins
Mountain Ash v Blackwood
Pontypool Utd v Wrexham
Rumney v Abercynon
Treorchy v St Peters
Tumble v Bonymaen

Ards v NIFC
Armagh v Malone
Askeans v Loughborough U
Ballymena v Bangor
Bath v Blackheath
CIYMS v City of Derry
Cambridge U v Dublin U
Collegians v Dungannon
Queen's U, Belfast v Portadown

Tuesday, 6 October

Cardiff v Penarth
Ebbw Vale v Newbridge

Wednesday, 7 October

Wales XV v Italy XV (Cardiff)
French Selection v South Africans (Pau)
Lydney v Bristol U

Saturday, 10 October

French Selection v South Africans
   (Toulouse)

RFU Courage Leagues
Division 1
Bristol v Saracens
Harlequins v London Scottish
Leicester v West Hartlepool
Northampton v Bath
Orrell v London Irish
Rugby v Wasps

Division 2
Coventry v Blackheath
Morley v Waterloo
Newcastle Gosforth v Nottingham
Richmond v Moseley
Rosslyn Park v Bedford
Wakefield v Sale
Division 3
Aspatria v Sheffield
Clifton v Broughton Park
Exeter v Askeans
Havant v Otley
Liverpool St Helens v Headingley
Plymouth Albion v Redruth
Division 4 (South)
Berry Hill v Weston-super-Mare
High Wycombe v Camborne
London Welsh v North Walsham
Lydney v Basingstoke
Maidstone v Sudbury
Southend v Thurrock
Division 4 (North)
Durham City v Kendal
Harrogate v Nuneaton
Lichfield v Stoke-on-Trent
Preston Grasshoppers v Stourbridge
Rotherham v Hereford
Walsall v Winnington Park

SRU McEwan's Leagues
Division 1
Boroughmuir v Glasgow High/Kelvinside
Dundee HSFP v Selkirk
Edinburgh Acads v Watsonians
Gala v Heriot's FP
Hawick v Currie
Kelso v Jedforest
Stirling County v Melrose
Division 2
Clarkston v Wigtownshire
Glasgow Acads v Preston Lodge
Grangemouth v Dunfermline
Kilmarnock v Edinburgh Wands
Kirkcaldy v Ayr
Musselburgh v West of Scotland
Stewart's-Melville FP v Peebles

IRU Insurance Corporation Leagues
Division 1
Cork Const v Old Wesley
Garryowen v St Mary's Coll
Greystones v Dungannon
Young Munster v Ballymena
Division 2
Bangor v Wanderers
Dolphin v Blackrock Coll

Galwegians v Instonians
Lansdowne v Clontarf
Terenure Coll v Old Crescent

WRU Heineken Leagues
Division 1
Bridgend v Newport
Llanelli v Cardiff
Neath v Aberavon
Pontypool v Swansea
Pontypridd v Maesteg
South Wales Police v Newbridge
Division 2
Blaina v Penarth
Cross Keys v Llandovery
Dunvant v Llanharan
Ebbw Vale v Abertillery
Glam Wands v Tredegar
Tenby Utd v Narberth
Division 3
Aberavon Quins v Tumble
Abercynon v Pontypool Utd
Blackwood v Kenfig Hill
Bonymaen v Rumney
St Peters v Wrexham
Treorchy v Mountain Ash

City of Derry v Collegians
Malone v CIYMS
NIFC v Armagh
Portadown v Ards
UC Dublin v Cambridge U

Tuesday, 13 October

Durham v Cumbria
Launceston v Exeter
Lydney v Penarth
Northampton v Nuneaton
Nottingham v Loughborough U

Wednesday, 14 October

French Selection v South Africans
(Béziers)
Wales B v North of England (Pontypool)
Royal Navy v Hampshire (Portsmouth)
Sussex v CLOB (Brighton)
West London Inst v Saracens

Saturday, 17 October

ENGLAND v CANADA (Wembley)
FRANCE v SOUTH AFRICA (Lyons)
Leinster v Australians (Dublin)

SRU McEwan's Leagues
Division 1
Currie v Kelso
Edinburgh Acads v Gala
Glasgow High/Kelvinside v Heriot's FP
Jedforest v Dundee HSFP
Melrose v Hawick
Selkirk v Boroughmuir
Watsonians v Stirling County
Division 2
Dunfermline v Glasgow Acads
Edinburgh Wands v Grangemouth
Kilmarnock v Kirkcaldy
Peebles v Ayr
Preston Lodge v Clarkston
West of Scotland v Stewart's-Melville FP
Wigtownshire v Musselburgh

WRU Heineken Leagues
Division 1
Aberavon v Pontypool
Cardiff v Neath
Maesteg v South Wales Police
Newbridge v Llanelli
Newport v Pontypridd
Swansea v Bridgend
Division 2
Abertillery v Glam Wands
Llandovery v Ebbw Vale
Llanharan v Tenby Utd
Narberth v Cross Keys
Penarth v Dunvant
Tredegar v Blaina
Division 3
Kenfig Hill v Treorchy
Mountain Ash v St Peters
Pontypool Utd v Bonymaen
Rumney v Aberavon Quins
Tumble v Blackwood
Wrexham v Abercynon

WRU Cup *2nd round*
Ards v Queen's U, Belfast
Armagh v Portadown
Askeans v Sudbury
Ballymena v City of Derry
Bath v Coventry
Bradford & Bingley v Morley
Broughton Park v Vale of Lune
Cambridge U v Rosslyn Park
CIYMS v NIFC
Collegians v Malone
Durham City v West Hartlepool
Gloucester v Bristol
Harlequins v Bedford
Headingley v Newcastle Gosforth

Hereford v Lydney
Instonians v Dungannon
Launceston v Redruth
Loughborough U v Blackheath
Moseley v Leicester
Nottingham v Northampton
Orrell v Fylde
Oxford U v London Irish
Reading v Met Police
Richmond v London Scottish
Sale v Saracens
Wakefield v Liverpool St Helens
Waterloo v Kendal
Weston-super-Mare v Exeter

Tuesday, 20 October

Berry Hill v Penarth
Exeter v Crediton
Leicester v Oxford U

Wednesday, 21 October

French Selection v South Africans
(Marseilles)
Munster v Australians (Cork)

Friday, 23 October

Dungannon v City of Derry

Saturday, 24 October

FRANCE v SOUTH AFRICA (Paris)
Ulster v Australians (Belfast)

RFU Courage Leagues
Division 1
Bath v Orrell
Gloucester v Wasps
London Irish v Bristol
London Scottish v Leicester
Saracens v Harlequins
West Hartlepool v Rugby
Division 2
Bedford v Fylde
Blackheath v Newcastle Gosforth
Moseley v Rosslyn Park
Nottingham v Morley
Sale v Richmond
Waterloo v Wakefield
Division 3
Askeans v Liverpool St Helens
Broughton Park v Havant
Headingley v Plymouth Albion
Otley v Aspatria
Redruth v Clifton
Sheffield v Roundhay

Division 4 (South)
Basingstoke v Berry Hill
Camborne v Lydney
North Walsham v Maidstone
Sudbury v Southend
Thurrock v Met Police
Weston-super-Mare v London Welsh
Division 4 (North)
Hereford v Preston Grasshoppers
Kendal v Lichfield
Nuneaton v Durham City
Stoke-on-Trent v Rotherham
Stourbridge v Walsall
Winnington Park v Towcestrians

SRU McEwan's Leagues
Division 1
Boroughmuir v Jedforest
Dundee HSFP v Currie
Gala v Glasgow High/Kelvinside
Hawick v Watsonians
Heriot's FP v Selkirk
Kelso v Melrose
Stirling County v Edinburgh Acads
Division 2
Ayr v West of Scotland
Clarkston v Dunfermline
Glasgow Acads v Edinburgh Wands
Grangemouth v Kilmarnock
Kirkcaldy v Peebles
Musselburgh v Preston Lodge
Stewart's-Melville FP v Wigtownshire

WRU Heineken Leagues
Division 1
Bridgend v Aberavon
Llanelli v Maesteg
Neath v Newbridge
Newport v Swansea
Pontypool v Cardiff
Pontypridd v South Wales Police
Division 2
Abertillery v Llandovery
Cross Keys v Llanharan
Dunvant v Tredegar
Ebbw Vale v Narberth
Glam Wands v Blaina
Tenby Utd v Penarth
Division 3
Aberavon Quins v Pontypool Utd
Blackwood v Rumney
Bonymaen v Wrexham
Mountain Ash v Kenfig Hill
St Peters v Abercynon
Treorchy v Tumble

CIYMS v Sligo
Exeter v Exeter U
Coventry v Harrogate
Northampton v Cambridge U

Tuesday, 27 October

Connacht v Australians (Galway)

Wednesday, 28 October

French Universities v South Africans
(Tours)
Ireland Under-21 v Wales Under-21
(Dublin)

Saturday, 31 October

IRELAND v AUSTRALIA (Dublin)
French Barbarians v South Africans
(Lille)

RFU Courage Leagues
Division 1
Bristol v Bath
Gloucester v West Hartlepool
Harlequins v London Irish
Leicester v Saracens
Orrell v Northampton
Rugby v London Scottish
Division 2
Fylde v Moseley
Morley v Blackheath
Newcastle Gosforth v Coventry
Richmond v Waterloo
Rosslyn Park v Sale
Wakefield v Nottingham
Division 3
Aspatria v Broughton Park
Clifton v Headingley
Havant v Redruth
Liverpool St Helens v Exeter
Plymouth Albion v Askeans
Roundhay v Otley
Division 4 (South)
Berry Hill v Camborne
Maidstone v Weston-super-Mare
London Welsh v Basingstoke
Lydney v High Wycombe
Met Police v Sudbury
Southend v North Walsham
Division 4 (North)
Durham City v Harrogate
Lichfield v Nuneaton
Preston Grasshoppers v Stoke-on-Trent
Rotherham v Kendal
Towcestrians v Stourbridge
Walsall v Hereford

SRU McEwan's Leagues
Division 1
Currie v Boroughmuir
Edinburgh Acads v Hawick
Jedforest v Heriot's FP
Melrose v Dundee HSFP
Selkirk v Glasgow High/Kelvinside
Stirling County v Gala
Watsonians v Kelso
Division 2
Dunfermline v Musselburgh
Edinburgh Wands v Clarkston
Grangemouth v Kirkcaldy
Kilmarnock v Glasgow Acads
Preston Lodge v Stewart's-Melville FP
West of Scotland v Peebles
Wigtownshire v Ayr

WRU Heineken Leagues
Division 1
Aberavon v Newport
Cardiff v Bridgend
Maesteg v Neath
Newbridge v Pontypool
Swansea v Pontypridd
South Wales Police v Llanelli
Division 2
Blaina v Dunvant
Llandovery v Glam Wands
Llanharan v Ebbw Vale
Narberth v Abertillery
Penarth v Cross Keys
Tredegar v Tenby Utd
Division 3
Abercynon v Bonymaen
Kenfig Hill v St Peters
Pontypool Utd v Blackwood
Rumney v Treorchy
Tumble v Mountain Ash
Wrexham v Aberavon Quins

Clontarf v CIYMS
Loughborough U v Bedford
Monkstown v Dungannon
Wanderers v Ballymena
Wasps v Cambridge U

Monday, 2 November

Devon v Cornwall (Plymouth)

Tuesday, 3 November

Newport v Barbarians
Glam Wands v Pontypool
Pontypridd v Swansea U

Wednesday, 4 November

Monmouthshire v Australians
(Ebbw Vale)
Midland Division v South Africans
(Leicester)
Sussex v Surrey Clubs (Brighton)
Cambridge U v Leicester
Penarth v Swansea

Thursday, 5 November

French Selection v Argentinians
(Bayonne)

Friday, 6 November

Ebbw Vale v Pontypridd
Llanelli v Bristol

Saturday, 7 November

England B v South Africans (Bristol)
Wales B v Australians (Cardiff)

SRU McEwan's Leagues
Division 1
Boroughmuir v Melrose
Dundee HSFP v Watsonians
Gala v Selkirk
Glasgow High/Kelvinside v Jedforest
Hawick v Stirling County
Heriot's FP v Currie
Kelso v Edinburgh Acads
Division 2
Ayr v Preston Lodge
Clarkston v Kilmarnock
Glasgow Acads v Grangemouth
Kirkcaldy v West of Scotland
Musselburgh v Edinburgh Wands
Peebles v Wigtownshire
Stewart's-Melville FP v Dunfermline

IRU Insurance Corporation Leagues
Division 1
Ballymena v Garryowen
Dungannon v Cork Const
Old Wesley v Young Munster
Shannon v Greystones
Division 2
Blackrock Coll v Clontarf
Galwegians v Bangor
Old Crescent v Lansdowne
Terenure Coll v Dolphin
Wanderers v Instonians

RFU Pilkington Cup *2nd round*
Aberavon v Northampton

Barnstaple v Redruth
Bath v Cardiff
Durham City v Broughton Park
Exeter v Cheltenham
Harlequins v Cambridge U
London Irish v Ealing
Lydney v Mountain Ash
Malone v City of Derry
Newbridge v Glam Wands
Newport v London Scottish
NIFC v Collegians
Northern v West Hartlepool
Orrell v Leicester
Pontypool v Gloucester
Portadown v CIYMS
Queen's U, Belfast v Armagh
Saracens v Maesteg
Swansea v Wasps

Sunday, 8 November

French Selection v Argentinians
(Perpignan)

Tuesday, 10 November

Northern Division v South Africans
(Leeds)
Cambridge U v Crawshay's Welsh
Blaina v Newbridge
Penarth v South Wales Police
Pontypool v Ebbw Vale
Pontypridd v Cardiff Inst
Wasps v Oxford U

Wednesday, 11 November

Neath v Australians
French Selection v Argentinians
(Brive)
Glam Wands v Swansea
Newport v Newport and Dist

Friday, 13 November

Bristol v Wasps
Cambridge U v Bedford

Saturday, 14 November

ENGLAND v SOUTH AFRICA
(Twickenham)
FRANCE v ARGENTINA (Nantes)
Llanelli v Australians

RFU Courage Leagues
Division 3
Askeans v Clifton

Broughton Park v Roundhay
Exeter v Plymouth Albion
Headingley v Havant
Otley v Sheffield
Redruth v Aspatria
Division 4 (South)
Basingstoke v Maidstone
Camborne v London Welsh
High Wycombe v Berry Hill
North Walsham v Met Police
Sudbury v Thurrock
Weston-super-Mare v Southend
Divison 4 (North)
Harrogate v Lichfield
Hereford v Towcestrians
Kendal v Preston Grasshoppers
Nuneaton v Rotherham
Stoke-on-Trent v Walsall
Stourbridge v Winnington Park

SRU McEwan's Leagues
Division 1
Currie v Glasgow High/Kelvinside
Edinburgh Acads v Dundee HSFP
Hawick v Gala
Jedforest v Selkirk
Melrose v Heriot's FP
Stirling County v Kelso
Watsonians v Boroughmuir
Division 2
Dunfermline v Ayr
Edinburgh Wands v Stewart's-Melville FP
Glasgow Acads v Kirkcaldy
Grangemouth v Clarkston
Kilmarnock v Musselburgh
Preston Lodge v Peebles
Wigtownshire v West of Scotland

IRU Insurance Corporation Leagues
Division 1
Cork Const v Shannon
Garryowen v Old Wesley
St Mary's Coll v Ballymena
Young Munster v Dungannon
Division 2
Bangor v Blackrock Coll
Clontarf v Galwegians
Instonians v Dolphin
Lansdowne v Terenure Coll
Old Crescent v Wanderers

WRU Heineken Leagues
Division 3
Aberavon Quins v Abercynon
Blackwood v Wrexham
Kenfig Hill v Tumble

Mountain Ash v Rumney
St Peters v Bonymaen
Treorchy v Pontypool Utd

Armagh v Ards
Bath v Waterloo
Cardiff v Ebbw Vale
City of Derry v NIFC
CIYMS v Queen's U, Belfast
Collegians v Portadown
Coventry v Saracens
Cross Keys v Pontypool
Fylde v Liverpool St Helens
Harlequins v Nottingham
Leicester v Northampton
Morley v Rugby
Newport v Penarth
Orrell v Swansea
Pontypridd v Glam Wands
Richmond v London Irish
Rosslyn Park v London Scottish
Tredegar v Newbridge
West Hartlepool v Wakefield

Monday, 16 November

Scottish Students v Oxford U

Tuesday, 17 November

Welsh Students v Australians (Bridgend)
Cross Keys v Newport
Pontypridd v Abertillery

Wednesday, 18 November

Royal Navy v Civil Service (Portsmouth)
Surrey v British Police (London Irish)

Friday, 20 November

Wales B v Spain (Cardiff)
Abertillery v Pontypool
Glam Wands v Cardiff
Llanelli v Cambridge U
Newbridge v Cross Keys
Penarth v Maesteg
Tredegar v Pontypridd

Saturday, 21 November

WALES v AUSTRALIA (Cardiff)
Edinburgh Dist v Glasgow Dist
  (Edinburgh)
**Scottish North and Midlands v South
  of Scotland**

RFU Courage Leagues
Division 1
Bristol v Orrell
Gloucester v Saracens
Harlequins v Northampton
Leicester v Bath
Rugby v London Irish
Wasps v London Scottish
Division 2
Bedford v Sale
Fylde v Waterloo
Morley v Newcastle Gosforth
Richmond v Blackheath
Rosslyn Park v Nottingham
Wakefield v Coventry
Division 3
Aspatria v Headingley
Clifton v Exeter
Havant v Askeans
Plymouth Albion v Liverpool St Helens
Roundhay v Redruth
Sheffield v Broughton Park
Division 4 (South)
Berry Hill v Lydney
London Welsh v High Wycombe
Maidstone v Camborne
Met Police v Weston-super-Mare
Southend v Basingstoke
Thurrock v North Walsham
Division 4 (North)
Lichfield v Durham City
Preston Grasshoppers v Nuneaton
Rotherham v Harrogate
Towcestrians v Stoke-on-Trent
Walsall v Kendal
Winnington Park v Hereford

IRU Insurance Corporation Leagues
Division 1
Dungannon v Garryowen
Greystones v Cork Const
Old Wesley v St Mary's Coll
Shannon v Young Munster
Division 2
Blackrock Coll v Old Crescent
Dolphin v Bangor
Galwegians v Lansdowne
Instonians v Clontarf
Wanderers v Terenure Coll

Ballymena v Kelso
City of Derry v Portadown
CIYMS v Ards
Collegians v Queen's U, Belfast
Dundee HSFP v Glasgow High/Kelvinside
Edinburgh Wands v Edinburgh U

Gala v Glasgow Acads
Heriot's FP v Edinburgh Acads
Malone v NIFC
Melrose v Langholm
Preston Lodge v Clarkston
Selkirk v Kirkcaldy
Stirling County v Kilmarnock
Watsonians v Stewart's-Melville FP

Tuesday, 24 November

Swansea v Australians
Cumbria v Cheshire

Wednesday, 25 November

Cambridge U v M R Steele-Bodger's XV
Royal Navy v NZ Armed Forces
(Devonport)
Berkshire v Hampshire (Abbey RFC)
Oxfordshire v Sussex
Wasps v Loughborough U

Saturday, 28 November

Barbarians v Australians
(Twickenham)
Glasgow Dist v South of Scotland
Scottish North and Midlands v
Edinburgh Dist
Connacht v Leinster (Galway)
Munster v Ulster (Limerick)

WRU Heineken Leagues
Division 1
Bridgend v Newbridge
Neath v South Wales Police
Newport v Cardiff
Pontypool v Maesteg
Pontypridd v Llanelli
Swansea v Aberavon
Division 2
Abertillery v Llanharan
Cross Keys v Tredegar
Ebbw Vale v Penarth
Glam Wands v Dunvant
Llandovery v Narberth
Tenby Utd v Blaina

RFU Pilkington Cup *3rd round*
WRU Cup *3rd round*
Ards v Collegians
CIYMS v Armagh
Currie v Biggar
Cambridge U v Loughborough U
Corstorphine v Kirkcaldy
Edinburgh Wands v Perthshire

Glasgow High/Kelvinside v Hillhead-
  Jordanhill
Harrogate v Newcastle Gosforth
Hawick v Tynedale
Heriot's FP v Preston Lodge
Kelso v Langholm
Kendal v Morley
Liverpool St Helens v Halifax
Melrose v Ayr
Met Police v Askeans
Queen's U, Belfast v City of Derry
Stirling County v Musselburgh
Vale of Lune v Moseley
Wakefield v Broughton Park
Watsonians v Glasgow Acads

Sunday, 29 November

Cornwall v NZ Armed Forces (Redruth)

Tuesday, 1 December

Edinburgh Wands v Boroughmuir
Newbridge v Pretoria U

Wednesday, 2 December

Anglo-Scots v Glasgow Dist
Dungannon v Ards
London Irish v Army
Met Police v RAF
Sale v Loughborough U

Saturday, 5 December

RFU Divisional Championship
London Division v Midland Division
Northern Division v South &
  South-West Division

Glasgow Dist v Scottish North and
  Midlands
South of Scotland v Anglo-Scots
Leinster v Munster (Dublin)
Ulster v Connacht (Belfast)

RFU County Championship
Division 1 (South)
Cornwall v Middlesex (Redruth)
Hampshire v Surrey (US Portsmouth)
Division 1 (North)
Cumbria v Yorkshire
Lancashire v Northumberland
Division 2 (South)
Devon v Gloucestershire (Barnstaple)
Hertfordshire v Kent (Croxley Green)
Division 2 (North)
North Midlands v Durham

Warwickshire v Leicestershire
Division 3 (South)
Dorset & Wilts v Buckinghamshire
Sussex v Berkshire (Worthing)
Division 3 (North)
Cheshire v East Midlands
Notts, Lincs & Derbys v Staffordshire
Division 4
Oxfordshire v Eastern Counties

WRU Leagues
Division 1
Aberavon v Pontypridd
Cardiff v Swansea
Llanelli v Neath
Maesteg v Bridgend
Newbridge v Newport
South Wales Police v Pontypool
Division 2
Blaina v Cross Keys
Dunvant v Tenby Utd
Llanharan v Llandovery
Narberth v Glam Wands
Penarth v Abertillery
Tredegar v Ebbw Vale
Division 3
Abercynon v Blackwood
Bonymaen v Aberavon Quins
Pontypool Utd v Mountain Ash
Rumney v Kenfig Hill
Tumble v St Peters
Wrexham v Treorchy

Blackheath v Richmond
Broughton Park v Morley
Clifton v Bristol
Coventry v Wanderers
Currie v Ayr
Dungannon v Galwegians
Gateshead v Hawick
Glasgow High/Kelvinside v Boroughmuir
Gloucester v Leicester
Grangemouth v Edinburgh Wands
Jedforest v Langholm
Kilmarnock v Heriot's FP
Kirkcaldy v Alloa
Liverpool St Helens v Orrell
London Irish v Met Police
London Scottish v Moseley
London Welsh v Wasps
Lydney v Torquay Ath
Melrose v Glasgow Acads
Northampton v Bedford
Nottingham v Bath
Sale v Kendal
Saracens v Exeter

Southend v Askeans
Stewart's-Melville FP v Ballymena
Tenerure Coll v CIYMS
Tynedale v Newcastle Gosforth
Vale of Lune v Fylde
Wakefield v Otley
Watsonians v Edinburgh Acads
West Hartlepool v Preston Grasshoppers
Widnes v Waterloo

Sunday, 6 December

Redruth v Launceston

Tuesday, 8 December

Oxford U v Cambridge U (Twickenham)

Wednesday, 9 December

Edinburgh Dist v Anglo-Scots

Saturday, 12 December

RFU Divisional Championship
Northern Division v Midlands Division
South & South-West Division v
  London Division

Anglo-Scots v Scottish North and
  Midlands
South of Scotland v Edinburgh Dist
Irish Exiles v Ulster
Munster v Connacht (Cork)

RFU County Championship
Division 1 (South)
Middlesex v Hampshire (Met Police RFC)
Surrey v Cornwall (London Irish)
Division 1 (North)
Northumberland v Cumbria
Yorkshire v Lancashire
Division 2 (South)
Gloucestershire v Hertfordshire
  (Lydney)
Kent v Devon
Division 2 (North)
Durham v Warwickshire
Leicestershire v North Midlands
Division 3 (South)
Berkshire v Dorset & Wilts
Buckinghamshire v Sussex (Aylesbury)
Division 3 (North)
East Midlands v Notts, Lincs & Derbys
Staffordshire v Cheshire
Division 4
Eastern Counties v Somerset

WRU Heineken Leagues
Division 1
Cardiff v Aberavon
Llanelli v Pontypool
Maesteg v Newport
Neath v Pontypridd
Newbridge v Swansea
South Wales Police v Bridgend
Division 2
Blaina v Ebbw Vale
Dunvant v Cross Keys
Llanharan v Narberth
Penarth v Llandovery
Tenby Utd v Glam Wands
Tredegar v Abertillery
Division 3
Aberavon Quins v St Peters
Abercynon v Treorchy
Bonymaen v Blackwood
Pontypool Utd v Kenfig Hill
Rumney v Tumble
Wrexham v Mountain Ash

Colts County final (Twickenham)
Askeans v Sidcup
Ballymena v Clontarf
Bedford v Wasps
Blackheath v Leicester
Bristol v Moseley
City of Derry v Ards
CIYMS v Bangor
Clarkston v Stirling County
Collegians v Armagh
Dunfermline v Edinburgh Wands
Edinburgh Acads v Glasgow High/
  Kelvinside
Exeter v Gloucester
Glasgow Acads v Stewart's-Melville FP
Fylde v Rugby
Harrogate v Orrell
Hartlepool Rovers v Hawick
Kirkcaldy v Haddington
Langholm v Selkirk
London Welsh v Northampton
Malone v Queen's U, Belfast
Met Police v Newbury
Morley v Preston Grasshoppers
Newcastle Gosforth v Gala
NIFC v Portadown
Otley v Sale
Penryn v Redruth
Plymouth Albion v Coventry
Preston Lodge v Trinity Acads
Richmond v Bath
Royal High v Heriot's FP
Saracens v Rosslyn Park

Stourbridge v Broughton Park
Tynedale v Melrose
Wakefield v Liverpool St Helens
Waterloo v West Hartlepool
Watsonians v London Scottish
West of Scotland v Currie

Sunday, 13 December

London Irish v Esher

Wednesday, 16 December

Bedford v RAF

Saturday, 19 December

Scotland A v Spain

RFU Divisional Championship
London Division v Northern Division
Midlands Division v South & South-
  West Division

Connacht v Irish Exiles (Galway)
Ulster v Leinster (Belfast)

RFU County Championship
Division 1 (South)
Hampshire v Cornwall (Basingstoke)
Surrey v Middlesex (London Irish)
Division 1 (North)
Lancashire v Cumbria
Northumberland v Yorkshire
Division 2 (South)
Devon v Hertfordshire
Gloucestershire v Kent (Bristol)
Division 2 (North)
Durham v Leicestershire
North Midlands v Warwickshire
Division 3 (South)
Buckinghamshire v Berkshire (Aylesbury)
Dorset & Wilts v Sussex
Division 3 (North)
Cheshire v Notts, Lincs & Derbys
East Midlands v Staffordshire
Division 4
Somerset v Oxfordshire
  (Weston-super-Mare)

WRU Cup *4th round*
Ayr v Watsonians
Ballymena v NIFC
Bath v London Welsh
Blackheath v Met Police
CIYMS v UC Dublin
Coventry v Gloucester
Currie v Northern

Edinburgh Acads v Edinburgh Wands
Fylde v Nuneaton
Gala v Langholm
Glasgow High/Kelvinside v Hutchesons
Harrogate v Morley
Hawick v Melrose
Heriot's FP v Glasgow Acads
Kelso v Alnwick
Kendal v West Hartlepool
Kirkcaldy v Dalziel HSFP
Leicester v Bristol
London Irish v Rosslyn Park
London Scottish v Richmond
Lydney v Bridgwater Albion
Middlesbrough v Newcastle Gosforth
Moseley v Northampton
Nottingham v Headingley
Orrell v Broughton Park
Plymouth Albion v Exeter
Redruth v Penzance-Newlyn
Rugby v Bedford
Sale v Sheffield
Stewart's-Melville FP v Preston Lodge
Tynedale v Liverpool St Helens
Wasps v Wakefield
West of Scotland v Stirling County

Tuesday, 22 December

Pontypridd v Penarth

Saturday, 26 December

Ireland A v Scotland A
Armagh v City of Derry
Ballymena v Dungannon
Bath v Clifton
Bedford v Old Paulines
Bristol v Newport
Broughton Park v Sale
Cardiff v Pontypridd
Corstorphine v Currie
Dundee HSFP v Kirkcaldy
Edinburgh Acads v Co-optimists
Fylde v Preston Grasshoppers
Glasgow High/Kelvinside v Glasgow Acads
Gloucester v Lydney
Hartlepool Rovers v West Hartlepool
Langholm v Kelso
Leith Acads v Preston Lodge
London Irish v Old Millhillians
Melrose v Jedforest
Morley v Otley
Moseley v Coventry
Northampton v Stirling County
Northern v Newcastle Gosforth
Orrell v Wigan

433

Penarth v Old Penarthians
Pontypool v Tredegar
Queen's U, Belfast v NIFC
Redruth v Camborne
Swansea v Dunvant
Torquay Ath v Exeter
Trinity Acads v Edinburgh Wands
Waterloo v Birkenhead Park
Watsonians v Heriot's FP

Monday, 28 December

Leicester v Barbarians
Glam Wands v Bristol
Harlequins v Richmond
Hawick v Jedforest
Lydney v Stroud
Melrose v Gala
Musselburgh v Preston Lodge
Newquay Hornets v Redruth
Pontypool v Cross Keys
Preston Grasshoppers v Broughton Park
Rugby v Nottingham
West Hartlepool v Stockton

Tuesday, 29 December

Kirkcaldy v Stirling County

Wednesday, 30 December

Rosslyn Park v Met Police

Friday, 1 January 1993

Carlisle v Langholm
Newcastle Gosforth v Novocastrians

Saturday, 2 January

Scotland Trial (Murrayfield)

WRU Heineken Leagues
Division 1
Aberavon v Newbridge
Bridgend v Llanelli
Newport v South Wales Police
Pontypool v Neath
Pontypridd v Cardiff
Swansea v Maesteg
Division 2
Abertillery v Blaina
Cross Keys v Tenby Utd
Ebbw Vale v Dunvant
Glam Wands v Llanharan
Llandovery v Tredegar
Narberth v Penarth
Division 3
Blackwood v Aberavon Quins

Kenfig Hill v Wrexham
Mountain Ash v Abercynon
St Peters v Rumney
Treorchy v Bonymaen
Tumble v Pontypool Utd

Bangor v Dungannon
Bath v Sale
Bedford v Rosslyn Park
Bristol v Nottingham
City of Derry v CIYMS
Coventry v Orrell
Currie v Grangemouth
Edinburgh Acads v Kelso
Exeter v Barnstaple
Haddington v Preston Lodge
Heriot's FP v Hawick
Hillhead-Jordanhill v Glasgow Acads
Leicester v Headingley
Liverpool St Helens v Kendal
London Irish v Blackheath
London Welsh v London Scottish
Malone v Armagh
Melrose v Glasgow High/Kelvinside
Met Police v Stroud
Morley v Northampton
Newcastle Gosforth v Aspatria
NIFC v Ards
Perthshire v Kirkcaldy
Plymouth Albion v Wasps
Portadown v Queen's U, Belfast
Richmond v Saracens
Rotherham v Broughton Park
Rugby v Harlequins
Stirling County v Watsonians
Sutton/Epsom v Askeans
Vale of Lune v Wakefield
Waterloo v Fylde
West Hartlepool v Sheffield
West of Scotland v Edinburgh Wands

Monday, 4 January

**Scotland Schools v Wales Schools
(18 Group)**

Saturday, 9 January

RFU Courage Leagues
Division 1
Bath v Rugby
London Irish v Gloucester
London Scottish v West Hartlepool
Northampton v Leicester
Orrell v Harlequins
Saracens v Wasps

Division 2
Blackheath v Rosslyn Park
Coventry v Richmond
Newcastle Gosforth v Wakefield
Nottingham v Fylde
Sale v Moseley
Waterloo v Bedford
Division 3
Askeans v Aspatria
Broughton Park v Otley
Exeter v Havant
Headingley v Roundhay
Liverpool St Helens v Clifton
Redruth v Sheffield
Division 4 (South)
Basingstoke v Met Police
Camborne v Southend
High Wycombe v Maidstone
Lydney v London Welsh
North Walsham v Sudbury
Weston-super-Mare v Thurrock
Division 4 (North)
Durham City v Rotherham
Hereford v Stourbridge
Harrogate v Preston Grasshoppers
Kendal v Towcestrians
Nuneaton v Walsall
Stoke-on-Trent v Winnington Park

SRU McEwan's Leagues
Division 1
Boroughmuir v Edinburgh Acads
Dundee HSFP v Stirling County
Gala v Jedforest
Glasgow High/Kelvinside v Melrose
Heriot's FP v Watsonians
Kelso v Hawick
Selkirk v Currie
Division 2
Ayr v Edinburgh Wands
Clarkston v Glasgow Acads
Kirkcaldy v Wigtownshire
Musselburgh v Grangemouth
Peebles v Dunfermline
Stewart's-Melville FP v Kilmarnock
West of Scotland v Preston Lodge

IRU Insurance Corporation Leagues
Division 1
Ballymena v Old Wesley
St Mary's Coll v Dungannon
Young Munster v Greystones
Division 2
Bangor v Instonians
Clontarf v Wanderers
Lansdowne v Blackrock Coll

Old Crescent v Dolphin
Terenure Coll v Galwegians

WRU Heineken Leagues
Division 1
Llanelli v Newport
Maesteg v Aberavon
Neath v Bridgend
Newbridge v Cardiff
Pontypridd v Pontypool
South Wales Police v Swansea
Division 2
Blaina v Llandovery
Dunvant v Abertillery
Glam Wands v Cross Keys
Penarth v Llanharan
Tenby Utd v Ebbw Vale
Tredegar v Narberth
Division 3
Aberavon Quins v Treorchy
Abercynon v Kenfig Hill
Bonymaen v Mountain Ash
Pontypool Utd v Rumney
St Peters v Blackwood
Wrexham v Tumble

Ards v Portadown
Armagh v NIFC
Bristol v Loughborough U
CIYMS v Malone
Collegians v City of Derry

Sunday, 10 January

IRU Insurance Corporation Leagues
Division 1
Garryowen v Shannon

Tuesday, 12 January

Lydney v Berry Hill
Royal Navy v Plymouth Albion

Wednesday, 13 January

Army v Hampshire (Aldershot)

Thursday, 14 January

West of Scotland v Glasgow High/
    Kelvinside

Friday, 15 January

England B v France B
Scotland Under-21 v England Under-21
Scottish Students v Irish Students
Ayr v Glasgow Acads
Bedford v Leicester

435

Bristol v Exeter
Cheltenham v Lydney
Dunfermline v Currie
Gloucester v Northampton
Hawick v Dungannon
Kelso v Old Wesley
Northampton v Harrogate
Stirling County v Portadown

Saturday, 16 January

SCOTLAND v IRELAND (Murrayfield)
ENGLAND v FRANCE (Twickenham)

WRU Heineken Leagues
Division 1
Aberavon v South Wales Police
Bridgend v Pontypool
Cardiff v Maesteg
Newbridge v Pontypridd
Newport v Neath
Swansea v Llanelli
Division 2
Abertillery v Tenby Utd
Ebbw Vale v Cross Keys
Llandovery v Dunvant
Llanharan v Tredegar
Narberth v Blaina
Penarth v Glam Wands
Division 3
Kenfig Hill v Bonymaen
Mountain Ash v Aberavon Quins
Pontypool Utd v St Peters
Rumney v Wrexham
Treorchy v Blackwood
Tumble v Abercynon

Bridgwater Albion v Redruth
Bradford Bingley v Broughton Park
Cambridge U v Durham U
Coventry v Wakefield
De La Salle-Palmerston v CIYMS
Edinburgh Acads v Old Wesley
Harlequins v Saracens
Hawick v Dungannon
Kirkcaldy v City of Derry
London Welsh v Rosslyn Park
Melrose v Ballymena
Met Police v Taunton
Morpeth v Newcastle Gosforth
Moseley v London Irish
Preston Lodge v Howe of Fife
Richmond v Askeans
Rugby v Blackheath
Sale v Orrell
Sheffield v Morley

Vale of Lune v Otley
Waterloo v Liverpool St Helens
Watsonians v Old Belvedere

Sunday, 17 January

Wasps v Racing Club de France

Wednesday, 20 January

**Scotland Schools v NZ Schools
(18 Group)** (Murrayfield)
Cambridge U v RAF
Oxford U v Royal Navy

Saturday, 23 January

RFU Pilkington Cup *4th round*

SRU McEwan's Leagues
Division 1
Currie v Jedforest
Edinburgh Acads v Heriot's FP
Hawick v Dundee HSFP
Kelso v Gala
Melrose v Selkirk
Stirling County v Boroughmuir
Watsonians v Glasgow High/Kelvinside
Division 2
Clarkston v Kirkcaldy
Dunfermline v West of Scotland
Edinburgh Wands v Peebles
Glasgow Acads v Musselburgh
Grangemouth v Stewart's-Melville FP
Kilmarnock v Ayr
Preston Lodge v Wigtownshire

IRU Insurance Corporation Leagues
Division 1
Cork Const v Young Munster
Dungannon v Ballymena
Greystones v Garryowen
Shannon v St Mary's Coll
Division 2
Bangor v Terenure Coll
Dolphin v Clontarf
Galwegians v Blackrock Coll
Instonians v Old Crescent
Wanderers v Lansdowne

WRU Cup *5th round*
Bath v Exeter
Bedford v Bristol
Blackheath v London Scottish
Broughton Park v Northern
Fylde v Harrogate
London Irish v Waterloo

Loughborough U v Coventry
Maidstone v Askeans
Malone v Collegians
Met Police v Streatham/Croydon
Morley v Middlesbrough
NIFC v CIYMS
Nottingham v Plymouth Albion
Portadown v Armagh
Queen's U, Belfast v Ards
Richmond v Northampton
Roundhay v Newcastle Gosforth
St Ives v Redruth
Vale of Lune v West Hartlepool
Wakefield v Headingley
Wasps v Newport

Tuesday, 26 January

Exeter v Bridgwater Albion

Wednesday, 27 January

Bedford v Bedfordshire
Navy XV v CLOB
Royal Navy v Cambridge U

Saturday, 30 January

IRU Insurance Corporation Leagues
Division 1
Ballymena v Shannon
Garryowen v Cork Const
Old Wesley v Dungannon
St Mary's Coll v Greystones
Division 2
Blackrock Coll v Instonians
Galwegians v Wanderers
Lansdowne v Dolphin
Old Crescent v Bangor
Terenure Coll v Clontarf

WRU Heineken Leagues
Division 1
Llanelli v Aberavon
Maesteg v Newbridge
Neath v Swansea
Pontypool v Newport
Pontypridd v Bridgend
South Wales Police v Cardiff
Division 2
Blaina v Llanharan
Cross Keys v Abertillery
Dunvant v Narberth
Glam Wands v Ebbw Vale
Tenby Utd v Llandovery
Tredegar v Penarth
Division 3
Aberavon Quins v Kenfig Hill

Abercynon v Rumney
Blackwood v Mountain Ash
Bonymaen v Tumble
St Peters v Treorchy
Wrexham v Pontypool Utd

Aberdeen GSFP v Kirkcaldy
Armagh v Queen's U, Belfast
Askeans v Bedford
Basingstoke v Exeter
Broughton Park v Loughborough U
City of Derry v Malone
CIYMS v Portadown
Collegians v NIFC
Coventry v Leicester
Currie v Clarkston
Edinburgh Acads v Wakefield
Glasgow Acads v Jedforest
Glasgow High/Kelvinside v Peebles
Harrogate v Melrose
Havant v London Scottish
Langholm v Hawick
London Irish v Harlequins
Newcastle Gosforth v Rugby
Northampton v Moseley
Orrell v Bristol
Otley v Waterloo
Plymouth Albion v Bath
Preston Grasshoppers v Liverpool
  St Helens
Preston Lodge v Stirling County
Redruth v Truro
Richmond v Nottingham
Roundhay v Vale of Lune
Sale v Gloucester
Saracens v London Welsh
Sheffield v Cambridge U
Stewart's-Melville FP v Heriot's FP
US Portsmouth v Met Police
Wasps v Rosslyn Park
Watsonians v Edinburgh Wands
West Hartlepool v Morley

Tuesday, 2 February

Edinburgh Wands v Currie
Glam Wands v Pontypridd
Swansea v Ebbw Vale

Wednesday, 3 February

Cornwall v Royal Navy (St Austell)
Cambridge U v Army
London Irish v RAF

Thursday, 4 February

Ayr v Glasgow High/Kelvinside

437

Friday, 5 February

England B v Italy B
France Under-21 v Scotland Under-21
French Students v Scottish Students
Bristol v Bridgend
Exeter v Tiverton
Gloucester v Newport
Kirkcaldy v Royal High
Penarth v Lydney
Pontypridd v Nottingham
Swansea v Tredegar

Saturday, 6 February

WALES v ENGLAND (Cardiff)
FRANCE v SCOTLAND (Paris)

IRU Insurance Corporation Leagues
Division 1
Cork Const v St Mary's Coll
Greystones v Ballymena
Shannon v Old Wesley
Division 2
Bangor v Lansdowne
Clontarf v Old Crescent
Dolphin v Galwegians
Instonians v Terenure Coll
Wanderers v Blackrock Coll

Ards v Armagh
Blackheath v Harlequins
Broughton Park v Hartlepool Rovers
Cambridge U v Askeans
Cardiff v London Welsh
Dungannon v Malone
Leicester v Rosslyn Park
Liverpool St Helens v Newcastle Gosforth
London Irish v Rosslyn Park
London Scottish v Hawick
Melrose v Alnwick
Middlesbrough v Kelso
NIFC v City of Derry
Orrell v Bedford
Portadown v Collegians
Queen's U, Belfast v CIYMS
Redruth v Stroud
Vale of Lune v Sale
Wakefield v Bradford Bingley
Waterloo v Coventry
West Hartlepool v Fylde
West of Scotland v Heriot's FP

Sunday, 7 February

Holland v Wales B

438

IRU Insurance Corporation Leagues
Division 1
Young Munster v Garryowen

Met Police v Saracens

Saturday, 13 February

RFU Courage Leagues
Division 1
Gloucester v Bath
Harlequins v Bristol
Leicester v Orrell
Rugby v Northampton
Wasps v London Irish
West Hartlepool v Saracens
Division 2
Bedford v Nottingham
Fylde v Blackheath
Moseley v Waterloo
Richmond v Newcastle Gosforth
Rosslyn Park v Coventry
Wakefield v Morley
Division 3
Aspatria v Exeter
Havant v Liverpool St Helens
Otley v Redruth
Plymouth Albion v Clifton
Roundhay v Askeans
Sheffield v Headingley
Division 4 (South)
London Welsh v Berry Hill
Maidstone v Lydney
Met Police v Camborne
Southend v High Wycombe
Sudbury v Weston-super-Mare
Thurrock v Basingstoke
Division 4 (North)
Preston Grasshoppers v Durham City
Rotherham v Lichfield
Stourbridge v Stoke-on-Trent
Towcestrians v Nuneaton
Walsall v Harrogate
Winnington Park v Kendal

SRU McEwan's Leagues
Division 1
Boroughmuir v Hawick
Dundee HSFP v Kelso
Gala v Currie
Glasgow High/Kelvinside v Edinburgh
  Acads
Heriot's FP v Stirling County
Jedforest v Melrose
Selkirk v Watsonians
Division 2
Ayr v Grangemouth

Kirkcaldy v Preston Lodge
Musselburgh v Clarkston
Peebles v Kilmarnock
Stewart's-Melville FP v Glasgow Acads
West of Scotland v Edinburgh Wands
Wigtownshire v Dunfermline

IRU Insurance Corporation Leagues
Division 1
Ballymena v Cork Const
Dungannon v Shannon
Old Wesley v Greystones
St Mary's Coll v Young Munster
Division 2
Blackrock Coll v Terenure Coll
Clontarf v Bangor
Instonians v Lansdowne
Old Crescent v Galwegians
Wanderers v Dolphin

WRU Heineken Leagues
Division 1
Aberavon v Neath
Cardiff v Llanelli
Maesteg v Pontypridd
Newbridge v South Wales Police
Newport v Bridgend
Swansea v Pontypool
Division 2
Abertillery v Ebbw Vale
Llandovery v Cross Keys
Llanharan v Dunvant
Narberth v Tenby Utd
Penarth v Blaina
Tredegar v Glam Wands
Division 3
Kenfig Hill v Blackwood
Mountain Ash v Treorchy
Pontypool Utd v Abercynon
Rumney v Bonymaen
Tumble v Aberavon Quins
Wrexham v St Peters

Ards v CIYMS
NIFC v Malone
Portadown v City of Derry
Sale v London Scottish

Tuesday, 16 February

Pontypool v Glam Wands
Pontypridd v Cross Keys
Swansea v Lansdowne

Wednesday, 17 February

Surrey v Army (London Irish)

Aberavon v Bristol
Abertillery v Newport
Cambridge U v Luddites
Royal Navy v Exeter

Thursday, 18 February

Dungannon v Instonians

Friday, 19 February

Scotland Under-21 v Wales Under-21
**Scottish Universities v Welsh
  Universities**
Ayr v Cardiff
Bath v Swansea
Clarkston v Glasgow High/Kelvinside
Ebbw Vale v Pontypool
Gloucester v Pontypridd
Kelso v Heriot's FP
Kirkcaldy v Currie
Melrose v Peebles

Saturday, 20 February

SCOTLAND v WALES (Murrayfield)
IRELAND v FRANCE (Dublin)
RFU County Championship *semi-finals*
Blackheath v Askeans
Brixham v Exeter
Broughton Park v Walsall
Cambridge U v Vale of Lune
Edinburgh Acads v South Wales Police
Fylde v Northampton
Harlequins v Headingley
London Irish v Richmond
London Scottish v Rugby
Met Police v Cheltenham
Morley v Roundhay
Newcastle Gosforth v Sheffield
Northampton v Coventry
Nottingham v Rosslyn Park
Nuneaton v Leicester
Old Wesley v CIYMS
Orrell v Wakefield
Saracens v Moseley
Stirling County v Bridgend
Torquay Ath v Redruth
Wasps v Sale
Waterloo v Preston Grasshoppers
West Hartlepool v Bedford

Wednesday, 24 February

Askeans v West London Inst
Cambridge U v Penguins
Lydney v RAF
Met Police v Royal Navy

Saturday, 27 February

RFU Pilkington Cup *quarter-finals*

SRU McEwan's Leagues
Division 1
Dundee HSFP v Gala
Edinburgh Acads v Selkirk
Hawick v Heriot's FP
Kelso v Boroughmuir
Melrose v Currie
Stirling County v Glasgow High/
  Kelvinside
Watsonians v Jedforest
Division 2
Clarkston v Stewart's-Melville FP
Dunfermline v Preston Lodge
Edinburgh Wands v Wigtownshire
Glasgow Acads v Ayr
Grangemouth v Peebles
Kilmarnock v West of Scotland
Musselburgh v Kirkcaldy

WRU Cup *6th round*
Ards v Malone
Askeans v Fylde
Ballymena v CIYMS
Bristol v London Irish
Cambridge U v Harrogate
Cardiff v Wasps
Coventry v Newbridge
Dungannon v UC Dublin
Exeter v Blackheath
Gloucester v Swansea
Harlequins v Waterloo
Liverpool St Helens v Winnington Park
London Scottish v Sheffield
London Welsh v Leicester
Middlesbrough v Broughton Park
Morley v Orrell
Moseley v Bath
Newcastle Gosforth v West Hartlepool
Newport v Richmond
Penarth v Pontypridd
Redruth v St Ives
Rosslyn Park v Havant
Rugby v Wakefield
Saracens v Bedford
Tredegar v Lydney

Tuesday, 2 March

Abertillery v Swansea
Bristol v Royal Navy
Cross Keys v Newbridge
Edinburgh Wands v Heriot's FP
Leicester v Loughborough U

Lydney v Cinderford
Newport v Gloucester
Pontypool v Penarth
Pontypridd v Ebbw Vale

Wednesday, 3 March

United Banks v Middlesex
Cambridge U v Anti-Assassins
Met Police v Army

Friday, 5 March

England B v Spain
Wales B v Ireland B (Cardiff)
England Under-21 v Scotland Under-21
England Students v Scotland Students
English Universities v Scottish
  Universities
Abertillery v Lydney
Ayr v Stirling County
Bedford v Selkirk
Bristol v Pontypridd
Cardiff v Bective Rangers
Cheltenham v Pontypool
Exeter v Devon & Cornwall Police
Hawick v Boroughmuir
Kirkcaldy v Madras FP
London Irish v Heriot's FP
Newbridge v Bath
Northampton v Gala
Wasps v Melrose

Saturday, 6 March

ENGLAND v SCOTLAND
  (Twickenham)
WALES v IRELAND (Cardiff)
Broughton Park v Newcastle Gosforth
Cambridge U v Bradford Bingley
CIYMS v Collegians
Coventry v Nottingham
Dungannon v Terenure Coll
Fylde v Headingley
Instonians v Ballymena
Kelso v Northern
Leicester v Moseley
London Scottish v Edinburgh Acads
Morley v Liverpool St Helens
Penzance-Newlyn v Redruth
Rosslyn Park v Orrell
Royal High v Preston Lodge
Sheffield v Vale of Lune
Waterloo v Harrogate
Watsonians v Musselburgh
West Hartlepool v Sale

Sunday, 7 March

Blackheath v Saracens

Wednesday, 10 March

London Irish v Loughborough U

Saturday, 13 March

Royal Navy v Army (Twickenham)

RFU Courage Leagues
Division 1
Bath v Wasps
Bristol v Leicester
London Irish v West Hartlepool
Northampton v Gloucester
Orrell v Rugby
Saracens v London Scottish
Division 2
Blackheath v Bedford
Coventry v Fylde
Morley v Richmond
Newcastle Gosforth v Rosslyn Park
Nottingham v Moseley
Waterloo v Sale
Division 3
Askeans v Sheffield
Exeter v Roundhay
Headingley v Otley
Liverpool St Helens v Aspatria
Plymouth Albion v Havant
Redruth v Broughton Park
Division 4 South
Basingstoke v Sudbury
Berry Hill v Maidstone
Camborne v Thurrock
High Wycombe v Met Police
Lydney v Southend
Weston-super-Mare v North Walsham
Division 4 (North)
Durham City v Walsall
Harrogate v Towcestrians
Kendal v Stourbridge
Lichfield v Preston Grasshoppers
Nuneaton v Winnington Park
Stoke-on-Trent v Hereford

SRU McEwan's Leagues
Division 1
Boroughmuir v Dundee HSFP
Currie v Watsonians
Gala v Melrose
Glasgow High/Kelvinside v Hawick
Heriot's FP v Kelso
Jedforest v Edinburgh Acads
Selkirk v Stirling County

Division 2
Ayr v Clarkston
Kirkcaldy v Dunfermline
Peebles v Glasgow Acads
Preston Lodge v Edinburgh Wands
Stewart's-Melville FP v Musselburgh
West of Scotland v Grangemouth
Wigtownshire v Kilmarnock

WRU Heineken Leagues
Division 1
Bridgend v Swansea
Llanelli v Newbridge
Neath v Cardiff
Pontypool v Aberavon
Pontypridd v Newport
South Wales Police v Maesteg
Division 2
Blaina v Tredegar
Cross Keys v Narberth
Dunvant v Penarth
Ebbw Vale v Llandovery
Glam Wands v Abertillery
Tenby Utd v Llanharan
Division 3
Abercynon v Wrexham
Aberavon Quins v Rumney
Blackwood v Tumble
Bonymaen v Pontypool Utd
St Peters v Mountain Ash
Treorchy v Kenfig Hill

Ballymena v De La Salle Palmerston
CIYMS v Sunday's Well
Clontarf v Dungannon
London Welsh v Cambridge U
Portadown v Malone
Queen's U, Belfast v Collegians
Wakefield v Harlequins

Tuesday, 16 March

Abertillery v Pontypridd
Cardiff v Bristol
Glam Wands v Newbridge
Northampton v RAF
Penarth v Aberavon
Swansea v Cross Keys
Tredegar v Pontypool

Wednesday, 17 March

UAU Final (Twickenham)
Sussex v United Banks (Brighton)
Scotland Schools Cup Final
   (Murrayfield)

Coventry v Nuneaton
Newport v Ebbw Vale

Thursday, 18 March

Dungannon v CIYMS

Friday, 19 March

Ireland B v England B
Bective Rangers v Northampton
Bedford v London Scottish
Gloucester v Cardiff
Nottingham v Leicester
Penarth v Cheltenham
Pontypool v Bath
Swansea v Moseley

Saturday, 20 March

IRELAND v ENGLAND (Dublin)
FRANCE v WALES (Paris)
Scotland A v France A
Clarkston v Kirkcaldy
Currie v Kilmarnock
Durham City v Newcastle Gosforth
Edinburgh Acads v Stirling County
Exeter v Camborne
Haddington v Edinburgh Wands
Harlequins v Coventry
Harrogate v Broughton Park
Hawick v Sale
Headingley v Morley
Heriot's FP v Glasgow High/Kelvinside
Langholm v Blaydon
London Irish v Askeans
Lydney v Birmingham Solihull
Orrell v Saracens
Redruth v Penryn
Rosslyn Park v Blackheath
Stewart's-Melville FP v Melrose
St Mary's Coll v Ballymena
Tynedale v Kelso
Vale of Lune v Liverpool St Helens
Wakefield v Gala
Wanderers v Wasps
Waterloo v Sheffield
West Hartlepool v Boroughmuir

Tuesday, 23 March

Penarth v Pontypool

Wednesday, 24 March

Army v RAF (Twickenham)
London Irish v Royal Navy

Saturday, 27 March

RFU Courage Leagues
Division 1
Gloucester v Orrell
Leicester v Harlequins
London Scottish v London Irish
Rugby v Bristol
Wasps v Northampton
West Hartlepool v Bath
Division 2
Bedford v Coventry
Fylde v Newcastle Gosforth
Moseley v Blackheath
Richmond v Wakefield
Rosslyn Park v Morley
Sale v Nottingham
Division 3
Aspatria v Plymouth Albion
Broughton Park v Headingley
Havant v Clifton
Otley v Askeans
Roundhay v Liverpool St Helens
Sheffield v Exeter
Division 4 (South)
Maidstone v London Welsh
Met Police v Lydney
North Walsham v Basingstoke
Southend v Berry Hill
Sudbury v Camborne
Thurrock v High Wycombe
Division 4 (North)
Hereford v Kendal
Preston Grasshoppers v Rotherham
Stourbridge v Nuneaton
Towcestrians v Durham City
Walsall v Lichfield
Winnington Park v Harrogate

WRU Cup *quarter-finals*
**Scotland Youth v Scotland Schools
  (18 Group)**
Glam Wands v Newport
Heriot's FP v Ayr
Jedforest v Glasgow High/Kelvinside
Kirkcaldy v Hawick
Melrose v Kilmarnock
Musselburgh v Currie
Pontypool v Abertillery
Pontypridd v Tredegar
Preston Lodge v Selkirk
Royal High v Edinburgh Wands
Stewart's-Melville FP v Kelso
Stirling County v Hillhead-Jordanhill
South Wales Police v Penarth
Waterloo v Saracens
Weston-super-Mare v Redruth

Sunday, 28 March

Watsonians v Boroughmuir

Wednesday, 31 March

Royal Navy v RAF (Twickenham)

Saturday, 3 April

RFU Courage Leagues
Division 1
Bath v London Scottish
Bristol v Gloucester
Harlequins v Rugby
London Irish v Saracens
Northampton v West Hartlepool
Orrell v Wasps
Division 2
Blackheath v Sale
Coventry v Moseley
Morley v Fylde
Newcastle Gosforth v Bedford
Nottingham v Waterloo
Wakefield v Rosslyn Park
Division 3
Askeans v Broughton Park
Clifton v Aspatria
Exeter v Otley
Headingley v Redruth
Liverpool St Helens v Sheffield
Plymouth Albion v Roundhay
Division 4 (South)
Basingstoke v Weston-super-Mare
Berry Hill v Met Police
Camborne v North Walsham
High Wycombe v Sudbury
London Welsh v Southend
Lydney v Thurrock
Division 4 (North)
Durham City v Winnington Park
Harrogate v Stourbridge
Kendal v Stoke-on-Trent
Lichfield v Towcestrians
Nuneaton v Hereford
Rotherham v Walsall

WRU Heineken Leagues
Division 1
Aberavon v Bridgend
Cardiff v Pontypool
Maesteg v Llanelli
Newbridge v Neath
Swansea v Newport
South Wales Police v Pontypridd
Division 2
Blaina v Glam Wands

Llandovery v Abertillery
Llanharan v Cross Keys
Narberth v Ebbw Vale
Penarth v Tenby Utd
Tredegar v Dunvant
Division 3
Abercynon v St Peters
Kenfig Hill v Mountain Ash
Pontypool Utd v Aberavon Quins
Rumney v Blackwood
Tumble v Treorchy
Wrexham v Bonymaen

Provincial Insurance final (Twickenham)
Gala Sevens
**Scotland Schools v Ireland Schools
  (18 Group)**
CIYMS v Corinthians
Edinburgh Wands v Ayr

Sunday, 4 April

Currie Sevens

Monday, 5 April

**Wales Schools v Scotland Schools
  (15 Group)**

Tuesday, 6 April

Northampton v Met Police

Wednesday, 7 April

WRU Heineken Leagues
Division 1
Bridgend v Cardiff

**England Schools v Scotland Schools
  (18 Group)**

Friday, 9 April

Redruth v St Mary's Hosp

Saturday, 10 April

RFU Pilkington Cup *semi-finals*

WRU Heineken Leagues
Division 1
Llanelli v South Wales Police
Neath v Maesteg
Newport v Aberavon
Pontypool v Newbridge
Pontypridd v Swansea
Division 2
Abertillery v Narberth

Cross Keys v Penarth
Dunvant v Blaina
Ebbw Vale v Llanharan
Glam Wands v Llandovery
Tenby Utd v Tredegar
Division 3
Aberavon Quins v Wrexham
Blackwood v Pontypool Utd
Bonymaen v Abercynon
Mountain Ash v Tumble
St Peters v Kenfig Hill
Treorchy v Rumney

Cardiff v Barbarians
Melrose Sevens
Scotland Under-19 v England Under-19
Scotland Under-18 v England Under-18
Alnwick v Newcastle Gosforth
Askeans v Basingstoke
Ballymena v Leicester
Bath v Rosslyn Park
Bedford v Northampton
Blackheath v Maidstone
Bridgend v Bristol
Broughton Park v Kendal
Exeter v Torquay Ath
London Welsh v Coventry
Lydney v Hereford
Morley v Wakefield
Moseley v Nottingham
Orrell v Waterloo
Roundhay v West Hartlepool
Rugby v Met Police
Sale v Liverpool St Helens

Monday, 12 April

Swansea v Barbarians
Bristol v Glam Wands
Davenport v Broughton Park
Gloucester v Fylde
Leicester v Wasps
Newbridge v Abertillery
Newport v London Welsh
Okehampton v Exeter
Pontypool v Nuneaton
Redruth v Rugby
Stroud v Lydney
Vale of Lune v Waterloo

Friday, 16 April

IRFB Sevens (Murrayfield)

Saturday, 17 April

IRFB Sevens (Murrayfield)

Italy v Scotland A
RFU County Championship *final*
  (Twickenham)
WRU Cup *semi-final*
Hawick Sevens
Wales Under-19 v Scotland Under-19
Askeans v Lichfield
Bath v Gloucester
Bedford v Sheffield
Broughton Park v West of Scotland
Coventry v Maesteg
Cross Keys v Pontypridd
Leicester v Sale
Liverpool St Helens v Birkenhead Park
London Irish v Morley
London Scottish v Saracens
Met Police v Richmond
Newcastle Gosforth v Vale of Lune
Newport v Bristol
Northampton v Wakefield
Nottingham v Cardiff
Orrell v Moseley
Rosslyn Park v Harlequins
Truro v Redruth
Wasps v Llanelli
Waterloo v Pontypool
West Hartlepool v Harrogate

Sunday, 18 April

IRFB Sevens (Murrayfield)
Redruth v Newquay Hornets

Saturday, 24 April

RFU Courage Leagues
Division 1
Gloucester v Harlequins
London Scottish v Northampton
Rugby v Leicester
Saracens v Bath
Wasps v Bristol
West Hartlepool v Orrell
Division 2
Bedford v Morley
Fylde v Wakefield
Moseley v Newcastle Gosforth
Rosslyn Park v Richmond
Sale v Coventry
Waterloo v Blackheath
Division 3
Aspatria v Havant
Broughton Park v Exeter
Otley v Liverpool St Helens
Roundhay v Clifton
Sheffield v Plymouth Albion
Redruth v Askeans

Division 4 (South)
Met Police v London Welsh
North Walsham v High Wycombe
Southend v Maidstone
Sudbury v Lydney
Thurrock v Berry Hill
Weston-super-Mare v Camborne
Division 4 (North)
Hereford v Harrogate
Stoke-on-Trent v Nuneaton
Stourbridge v Durham City
Towcestrians v Rotherham
Walsall v Preston Grasshoppers
Winnington Park v Lichfield

WRU Heineken Leagues
Division 1
Aberavon v Swansea
Cardiff v Newport
Llanelli v Pontypridd
Maesteg v Pontypool
Newbridge v Bridgend
South Wales Police v Neath
Division 2
Blaina v Tenby Utd
Dunvant v Glam Wands
Llanharan v Abertillery
Narberth v Llandovery
Penarth v Ebbw Vale
Tredegar v Cross Keys
Division 3
Abercynon v Aberavon Quins
Bonymaen v St Peters
Pontypool Utd v Treorchy
Rumney v Mountain Ash
Tumble v Kenfig Hill
Wrexham v Blackwood

Ulster Cup final
Jedforest Sevens

Omagh Sevens
Nottingham v Basingstoke

Wednesday, 28 April
SRU Youth final (Murrayfield)

Saturday, 1 May
RFU Pilkington Cup *final* (Twickenham)

WRU Heineken Leagues
Division 1
Bridgend v Maesteg
Neath v Llanelli
Newport v Newbridge
Pontypool v South Wales Police
Pontypridd v Aberavon
Swansea v Cardiff
Division 2
Abertillery v Penarth
Cross Keys v Blaina
Ebbw Vale v Tredegar
Glam Wands v Narberth
Llandovery v Llanharan
Tenby Utd v Dunvant
Division 3
Aberavon Quins v Bonymaen
Blackwood v Abercynon
Kenfig Hill v Rumney
Mountain Ash v Pontypool Utd
St Peters v Tumble
Treorchy v Wrexham

Langholm Sevens

Saturday, 8 May
WRU Cup *final* (Cardiff)
Middlesex Sevens (Twickenham)

MAJOR TOURS

SOUTH AFRICANS TO FRANCE AND ENGLAND

October

3	**French Under-21** (Bordeaux)
7	**French Selection** (Pau)
10	**French Selection** (Toulouse)
14	**French Selection** (Béziers)
17	**FRANCE** (Lyons)
21	**French Selection** (Marseilles)
24	**FRANCE** (Parc des Princes)
28	**French Universities** (Tours)
31	**French Barbarians** (Lille)

November

4	**Midland Division** (Leicester)
7	**England B** (Bristol)
10	**Northern Division** (Leeds)
14	**ENGLAND** (Twickenham)

ARGENTINIANS TO FRANCE

November

5	**French Selection** (Bayonne)
8	**French Selection** (Perpignan)
11	**French Selection** (Brive)
14	**FRANCE** (Nantes)

AUSTRALIANS TO BRITAIN & IRELAND

October

17	**Leinster** (Dublin)
21	**Munster** (Cork)

24	**Ulster** (Belfast)
27	**Connacht** (Galway)
31	**IRELAND** (Dublin)

November

4	**Monmouthshire** (Ebbw Vale)
7	**Wales B** (Cardiff)
11	**Neath**
14	**Llanelli**
17	**Welsh Students** (Bridgend)
21	**WALES** (Cardiff)
24	**Swansea**
28	**Barbarians** (Twickenham)

BRITISH LIONS TO NEW ZEALAND
(*provisional itinerary*)

May 1993

22	**North Auckland** (Whangarei)
26	**North Harbour** (Auckland)
29	**NZ Maoris** (Wellington)

June

2	**Canterbury** (Christchurch)
5	**Otago** (Dunedin)
8	**Southland** (Invercargill)
12	**NEW ZEALAND** (Christchurch)
16	**Taranaki** (New Plymouth)
19	**Auckland** (Auckland)
22	**Hawke's Bay** (Napier)
26	**NEW ZEALAND** (Wellington)
29	**Waikato** (Hamilton)

July

3	**NEW ZEALAND** (Auckland)

MAJOR FIXTURES IN BRITAIN, IRELAND AND FRANCE 1992-93

October

7   **Wales XV v Italy XV** (Cardiff)
17 **FRANCE v SOUTH AFRICA** (Lyons)
    ENGLAND v CANADA (Wembley)
24 **FRANCE v SOUTH AFRICA** (Paris)
31 **IRELAND v AUSTRALIA** (Dublin)

November

7   **England B v South Africans** (Bristol)
    Wales B v Australians (Cardiff)
14 **ENGLAND v SOUTH AFRICA** (Twickenham)
    FRANCE v ARGENTINA (Nantes)
21 **WALES v AUSTRALIA** (Cardiff)
28 **Barbarians v Australians** (Twickenham)

December

5   **RFU Divisional Championship**
8   **Oxford University v Cambridge University** (Twickenham)
12 **RFU Divisional Championship**
19 **RFU Divisional Championship**

January 1993

16 **SCOTLAND v IRELAND** (Murrayfield)
    ENGLAND v FRANCE (Twickenham)

February

6   **WALES v ENGLAND** (Cardiff)
    FRANCE v SCOTLAND (Paris)
20 **SCOTLAND v WALES** (Murrayfield)
    IRELAND v FRANCE (Dublin)

March

6   **ENGLAND v SCOTLAND** (Twickenham)
    WALES v IRELAND (Cardiff)
13 **Royal Navy v Army** (Twickenham)
17 **UAU final** (Twickenham)
20 **IRELAND v ENGLAND** (Dublin)
    FRANCE v WALES (Paris)
24 **Army v RAF** (Twickenham)
31 **Royal Navy v RAF** (Twickenham)

April

3   **Provincial Insurance final** (Twickenham)
16 **International Board Sevens** (Murrayfield)
17 **International Board Sevens** (Murrayfield)
    RFU County Championship final (Twickenham)
18 **International Board Sevens** (Murrayfield)

May

1   **RFU Pilkington Cup final** (Twickenham)
8   **WRU Cup final** (Cardiff)
    Middlesex Sevens (Twickenham)

ROTHMANS FOOTBALL YEARBOOK 1992-93	Jack Rollin	£14.99
ROTHMANS RUGBY LEAGUE YEARBOOK 1992-93	Howes/Fletcher	£14.99
PLAYFAIR FOOTBALL ANNUAL 1992-93	Jack Rollin	£3.99
PLAYFAIR NON-LEAGUE FOOTBALL ANNUAL 1992-93	Bruce Smith	£3.99
WILLIE CARSON: THE ILLUSTRATED BIOGRAPHY	Michael Seely	£9.99

Headline offers an exciting range of quality titles by both established and new authors available from:

Headline Book Publishing PLC
Cash Sales Department
P.O. Box 11
Falmouth
Cornwall TR10 9EN

Alternatively, you may fax your order to the above address:
Fax No. 0326 376423.

Payments can be made as follows: cheque, postal order (payable to Headline Book Publishing PLC) or by credit cards, Visa/Access. Do not send cash or currency. UK and BFPO customers: please send a cheque or postal order (no currency) and allow £1.00 for postage and packing for the first book plus 50p for each additional book up to a maximum charge of £3.00.

Overseas customers including Ireland, please allow £2.00 for postage and packing for the first book, £1.00 for the second book, and 50p for each additional book.

NAME (Block Letters) ....

ADDRESS ....

....

....

I enclose my remittance for.................................
I wish to pay by Visa/Access card

Number | | | | | | | | | | | | | | | |

Card expiry date................................